TESTS IN PRINT IX

EARLIER PUBLICATIONS IN THIS SERIES

TESTS
IN PRINT IX

AN INDEX TO TESTS, TEST REVIEWS, AND THE LITERATURE ON SPECIFIC TESTS

Edited by

**NANCY ANDERSON
JENNIFER E. SCHLUETER
JANET F. CARLSON
KURT F. GEISINGER**

The Buros Center for Testing
The University of Nebraska-Lincoln
Lincoln, Nebraska

2016
Distributed by The University of Nebraska Press

LC 83-18866
ISBN 978-0-910674-65-2

Manufactured in the United States of America.

The paper used in this publication meets the minimum requirements of American National Standard for Information Sciences—Permanence of Paper for Printed Library Materials, ANSI Z39.48-1984.

Note to Users

The staff of the Buros Center for Testing has made every effort to ensure the accuracy of the test information included in this work. However, the Buros Center for Testing and the Editors of *Tests in Print IX* do not assume, and hereby expressly and absolutely disclaim, any liability to any party for any loss or damage caused by errors or omissions or statements of any kind in *Tests in Print IX*.

All material included in *Tests in Print IX* is intended solely for the use of our readers. None of this material may be used in advertising or for any other commercial purpose.

TABLE OF CONTENTS

INTRODUCTION

The *Tests in Print* (TIP) series consists of descriptive listings of commercially published tests. This volume also serves as a comprehensive index to all editions of the *Mental Measurements Yearbook* series (MMY) published to date.

There are key differences between the *Tests in Print* series and the *Mental Measurements Yearbook* series. In contrast to TIP, the MMY series contains both descriptive entries and critical reviews of commercially published tests available in the English language. Each MMY, of which there are now 19, includes reviews and descriptions of only those tests that are new or substantially revised since the previous MMY. The MMY series is, therefore, sequential and cumulative in nature.

Each TIP, of which there are now nine, is a comprehensive volume describing, to the best of our ability, every test that is currently commercially available (i.e., for sale). *TIP IX*, therefore, supersedes *TIP VIII*. Although it is necessary to have the entire MMY series to be sure of finding a descriptive entry or a review of a particular test, only the latest edition in the TIP series is needed for comprehensive coverage of currently available testing products.

To complement these two publications, Tests Reviews Online (www.buros.org) has been developed to permit users instant access to test descriptions and reviews from the Buros Center for Testing (formerly the Buros Institute of Mental Measurements). Test information and reviews available from Tests Reviews Online appear exactly as in the *The Ninth* through *The Nineteenth Mental Measurements Yearbooks* with regular updates from our current database. A total of more than 3,700 tests are briefly described and, for a small fee, users may download descriptive information and critiques for more than 2,700 tests. In addition, electronic versions of the complete *Mental Measurements Yearbook* series and *Tests in Print* are available to libraries through EBSCO Information Services and Ovid Technologies (Wolters Kluwer).

TIP IX may be best used as a means to locate and learn about commercially available testing products.

Because *TIP IX* indexes all 19 books in the MMY series (for tests still in print), it is an invaluable guide to both descriptive and analytical information. As a directory of commercially available tests, *TIP IX* is not designed to include all known tests. Specifically, the TIP series does not include research or proprietary instruments. Research instruments are often published in journals and serve the limited uses of test authors. Proprietary instruments are frequently designed for specialized audiences (e.g., licensure, certification, admissions) or for highly secured markets (e.g., government, industry) and are not considered "commercially available" tests.

In the Preface of the first *Tests in Print* volume (1961), Oscar Buros noted that this work had been in preparation for more than 20 years. The first two volumes of *The Mental Measurements Yearbook* were published in 1938 and 1940. It became increasingly apparent that a comprehensive bibliography of tests and an index to the contents of the MMY volumes was needed. The initial delay in *Tests in Print* was due to World War II, and then various other financial and production limitations postponed its publication. *Tests in Print II* was published in 1974. After the death of Oscar Buros in 1978, the Buros Institute was established at the University of Nebraska-Lincoln. The first publication from the new Institute was *Tests in Print III* in 1983. *Tests in Print IV* was published in 1994, *Tests in Print V* in 1999, *Tests in Print VI* in 2002, *Tests in Print VII* in 2006, and *Tests in Print VIII* in 2011. *Tests in Print IX* is the first volume in the TIP series to be published under the name Buros Center for Testing, recognizing the integration of the several facets of our Center.

The need for a comprehensive bibliography of tests has never been more essential. Because of the proliferation of commercially available tests, we have adopted a policy of reviewing in *The Mental Measurements Yearbook* series only those tests with at least a minimum of technical and development information. This policy was implemented with tests reviewed in the *14th MMY*. Therefore, not all commercially available tests will be reviewed in the MMY. However, the *Tests in Print* series continues to include descriptive information for all known in-print commercially available tests in the English language. With the more rapid publication of *The Mental Measurements Yearbook* series (approximately every 36 months), it also became necessary to update our listing of commercially available tests on a more frequent basis. Beginning with *Tests in Print VI*, we embarked on a plan to publish a new edition of TIP approximately every 5 years. In addition, we began an initiative in 2010 to publish a similar book of descriptive entries for all known in-print commercially available tests in the Spanish language. The inaugural volume of *Pruebas Publicadas en Español: An Index of Spanish Tests in Print*, was published in 2013 and contains descriptive entries in both Spanish and English for more than 400 tests. This information also is available, along with the MMY and TIP, in a subscription database from EBSCO Information Services (Mental Measurements Yearbook with Tests in Print Internacional).

Our efforts in this massive enterprise have been consistent with those initially proposed by Oscar K. Buros: to improve the science and practice of testing by offering information and evaluative reviews of commercial products to informed consumers. *Tests in Print IX* represents a continuation of our efforts to provide a product for people who develop, evaluate, study, purchase and/or use tests. We hope and expect that informed users will consider the reviews of tests, if available, prior to their purchasing tests for use with clients, especially in high-stakes situations.

TESTS IN PRINT IX

The contents of *Tests in Print IX* include: (a) a comprehensive bibliography of commercially available tests published in print or electronic form as separates for use with English-speaking individuals; (b) a list of contributing reviewers for the entire MMY series; (c) a test title index that includes all in-print tests, tests that have gone out of print since the publication of *TIP VIII*, and alternative or superseded titles for some tests; (d) a listing of the tests that have gone out of print since the publication of *TIP III* (1983); (e) a list of test acronyms; (f) a classified subject index that also describes the population for which each test is intended; (g) a publishers directory and index, including contact information and test listings by publisher; (h) a name index, which includes the names of all authors of tests and of reviews; and (i) a score index listing all scores generated by tests listed in *TIP IX*.

The organization of the volume is encyclopedic in nature, with tests being ordered alphabetically by

TABLE 1

Test Entries in *TIP IX* by Major Classification

Classification	Number of Test Entries
Achievement	50
Behavior Assessment	152
Developmental	119
Education	75
English and Language	127
Fine Arts	10
Foreign Language	8
Intelligence and General Aptitude	177
Mathematics	39
Miscellaneous	212
Neuropsychological	121
Personality	529
Reading	95
Science	20
Sensory-Motor	52
Social Studies	7
Speech and Hearing	56
Vocations	465

title. Thus, if the title of a test is known, the reader can locate the test description immediately without having to consult the Index of Titles. Test classifications appear in the Classified Subject Index.

The page headings reflect the encyclopedic organization. The page heading of the left-hand page cites the number and title of the first test listed on that page, and the page heading of the right-hand page cites the number and title of the last test listed on that page. All numbers presented in the various indexes are test numbers, not page numbers. Page numbers, important only for the Table of Contents, are indicated at the bottom of each page.

TESTS

Tests in Print IX contains 2,314 test entries. The in-print status of these tests was confirmed by direct correspondence with publishers. Table 1 presents the number of test entries included in each major classification of the Classified Subject Index. Any classification system is to some degree dependent on human judgment, but broad comparisons between categories are often useful. It is interesting to note, for example, that the Personality test category continues to include the greatest number of tests of any category in *TIP IX*.

REVIEWS AND EXCERPTS

Tests in Print IX serves as a master index of in-print tests that refers the reader to all the original test reviews and excerpted test reviews that appeared for these tests in all of the *Mental Measurements Yearbooks* to date. In addition, it provides references to TIP entries or reviews in earlier *Yearbooks*—whichever is most recent—for all tests that have gone out of print since *TIP III*. Authors of reviews and excerpts are named following the test entries in cross references to the appropriate MMY. Although *TIP IX* will serve a very useful function by providing a comprehensive bibliography of tests in print, the cross references to the critical reviews are also of great importance if tests are to be used wisely. Thus TIP and the MMYs are inseparable partners in the cause of promoting effective selection and use of tests.

More than 3,000 individuals have contributed reviews to one or more MMYs. Because of their important contributions to the *Mental Measurements Yearbooks*, a complete listing of MMY test reviewers is presented in the index section of *TIP IX*.

REFERENCES

Earlier volumes have included specific test references selected by Buros staff members who searched through hundreds of professional journals. Because of the current availability of online search features that allow users to do independent reference searches, it was our decision to discontinue providing these references in the MMY and TIP series. Cross references for a number of test descriptions will still indicate when references were provided in previous publications (e.g., "See T5:326 [10 references]").

INDEXES

As mentioned earlier, *TIP IX* includes eight indexes invaluable as aids to effective use: (a) Index of MMY Test Reviewers, (b) Index of Titles, (c) Index of Out-of-Print Tests, (d) Index of Acronyms, (e) Classified Subject Index, (f) Publishers Directory and Index, (g) Index of Names, and (h) Score Index. Additional comment on these indexes is provided below.

Index of MMY Test Reviewers. This listing represents all test reviewers who have had their reviews published in *The Mental Measurements Yearbook* series and the volume numbers of their test reviews.

Index of Titles. Because the organization of TIP is comprehensive in nature, with the tests ordered alphabetically by title throughout the volume, the test title index does not have to be consulted to find a test for which the title is known. However, the title index has some features that make it useful beyond its function as a complete title listing. First, it includes cross-reference information useful for tests with superseded or alternative titles or tests commonly (and sometimes inaccurately) known by multiple titles.

Second, it lists the 774 tests that have gone out of print since being listed in *TIP VIII*. To differentiate between in-print and out-of-print tests in the title index, it is important to read carefully the instructions on the use of the index that precede the title listing. One should keep in mind that the numbers in this index, like those for all TIP and MMY indexes, are test numbers and not page numbers.

Index of Out-of-Print Tests. This index is a comprehensive and cumulative listing of all tests that have gone out of print since the publication of *Tests in Print III* (1983). The number following the title indicates the last Buros publication in which the test was listed as an in-print test.

Index of Acronyms. Some tests seem to be better known by their acronyms than by their full titles. The Index of Acronyms can help in these instances; it refers the reader to the full title of the test and to the relevant descriptive information and reviews.

Classified Subject Index. The Classified Subject Index classifies all tests listed in *TIP IX* into 18 major categories: Achievement, Behavior Assessment, Developmental, Education, English and Language, Fine Arts, Foreign Languages, Intelligence and General Aptitude, Mathematics, Miscellaneous, Neuropsychological, Personality, Reading, Science, Sensory-Motor, Social Studies, Speech and Hearing, and Vocations. Each test entry includes test title, population for which the test is intended, and test number. The Classified Subject Index is of great help to readers who seek a listing of tests in given subject areas. The Classified Subject Index represents a starting point for readers who know their area of interest but do not know how to further focus that interest in order to identify the best test(s) for their particular purposes. A descriptive listing of the categories precedes the Classified Subject Index.

Publishers Directory and Index. The Publishers Directory and Index includes the names and addresses of the publishers of all tests included in *TIP IX* plus a listing of test numbers for each individual publisher. This index also includes telephone and FAX numbers and addresses for electronic access (email and web pages). Publishers were given an opportunity to provide this information as they wanted it listed. This index can be particularly useful in obtaining addresses for specimen sets or catalogs after the test descriptions have been read and evaluated. It can also be useful when a reader knows the publisher of a certain test but is uncertain about the test title, or when a reader is interested in the range of tests published by a given publisher. A few publishers are listed as "Status Unknown" because recent correspondence has been returned by the Postal Service, email communication bounced, and/or online searches were unsuccessful.

Index of Names. The Index of Names provides a comprehensive list of names, indicating authorship of a test or a test review.

Score Index. The Score Index is an index to all scores generated by the tests in *TIP IX*. Test titles are sometimes misleading or ambiguous, and test content may be difficult to define with precision. Test scores represent operational definitions of the variables the test author is trying to measure, and as such they often define test purpose and content more adequately than other descriptive information. A search for a particular test is most often a search for a test that measures some specific variables. Test scores and their associated labels often offer the best definitions of the variables of interest. It is, in fact, a detailed subject index based on the most critical operational features of any test–the scores and their associated labels.

HOW TO USE TIP IX

A reference work like *TIP IX* can be of far greater benefit to a reader if a little time is taken to become familiar with what it has to offer and how one might use it most effectively to obtain the information sought. The first step in this process is to read the Introduction to *TIP IX*. The second step is to become familiar with the eight indexes and particularly with the instructions preceding each index listing. The third step is to make actual use of the book by looking up needed information. This third step is simple if one keeps in mind the following possibilities:

1. If you know the title of the test, use the alphabetical page headings to go directly to the test entry.

2. If you do not know, cannot find, or are unsure of the title of a test, consult the Index of Titles for possible variants of the title or consult the appropriate subject area of the Classified Subject Index for other possible leads or for similar or related tests in the same area. (Other uses for both of these indexes were described earlier.)

3. If you know the author of a test but not the title or publisher, consult the Index of Names and look up the author and corresponding test titles until you find the test you want.

4. If you know the test publisher but not the title or author, consult the Publishers Directory and Index and look up the publisher's titles until you find the test you want.

5. If you are looking for a test that yields a particular kind of score, but have no knowledge of which test that might be, look up the score in the Score Index and locate the test or tests that include the score variable of interest.

6. Once you have found the test or tests you are looking for, read the descriptive entries for these tests carefully so that you may take advantage of the information provided. A description of the information available in these test entries is presented later in this section.

7. After you have read the descriptive information, you may want to order a specimen set for a particular test so that you can examine it firsthand. The Publishers Directory and Index includes the information needed to contact the test publisher.

Making Effective Use of the Test Entries. The test entries include extensive information. For each test, descriptive information is presented in the following order:

a) TITLE. Test titles are printed in boldface type. Secondary or series titles are set off from main titles by a colon.

b) PURPOSE. For each test a brief, clear statement is included describing the purpose of the test. Often these statements are quotations from the test manual.

c) POPULATION. This is a description of the groups for which the test is intended. The grade, chronological age, semester range, or employment category is usually given. "Grades 1.5–2.5, 2–3, 4–12, 13–17" means that there are four test booklets: a booklet for the middle of first grade through the middle of the second grade, a booklet for the beginning of the second grade through the end of third grade, a booklet for Grades 4 through 12 inclusive, and a booklet for undergraduate and graduate students in colleges and universities.

d) PUBLICATION DATE. The inclusive range of publication dates for the various forms, accessories, and editions of a test is reported.

e) ACRONYM. When a test publisher refers to a test by an acronym, the acronym is provided in the test entry.

f) SCORES. The number of part scores (e.g., subscores or component scores) is presented along with their titles or descriptions of what they are intended to represent or measure.

g) ADMINISTRATION. Individual or group administration is indicated. A test is considered a group test unless it may be administered only individually.

h) FORMS, PARTS, AND LEVELS. All available forms, parts, and levels are listed.

i) MANUAL. Notation is made if no manual is available. All other manual information is included under Price Data.

j) RESTRICTED DISTRIBUTION. This is noted only for tests that are put on a special market by the test publisher. Educational and psychological restrictions are not noted (unless a special training course is required for use).

k) PRICE DATA. Price information is reported for test packages (usually 20 to 35 tests), answer sheets, all other accessories, and specimen sets. The statement "$17.50 per 35 tests" means that all accessories are included unless otherwise indicated by the reporting of separate prices for accessories. The statement also means 35 tests of one level, one edition, or one part unless stated otherwise. Because test prices can change very quickly, the year that the listed test prices were obtained is also given. Foreign currency is assigned the appropriate symbol. When prices are given in foreign dollars, a qualifying symbol is added (e.g., A$16.50 refers to 16 dollars and 50 cents in Australian currency). Along with cost, the publication date and number of pages on which print occurs is reported for manuals and technical reports (e.g., 1995, 102 pages). Scoring and reporting services provided by publishers are reported along with information on costs. As stated earlier, TIP contains descriptive information about commercially available tests. Sometimes tests that were once commercially available later become available at no charge. In this case, we have noted the test's free status in the Price Data field along with where or from whom the test may be obtained. Descriptions of these tests will not be included in future volumes of *Tests in Print* unless we learn that the test is again for sale.

l) FOREIGN LANGUAGE AND OTHER SPECIAL EDITIONS. This section concerns foreign language editions published by the same publisher who sells the English edition. It also indicates special editions (e.g., Braille, large type) available from the same or a different publisher. Many entries note that test materials are available in Spanish; for information about these and other Spanish-language tests, please consult *Pruebas Publicadas en Español*, mentioned earlier.

m) TIME. The number of minutes of actual working time allowed examinees and the approximate length of time needed for administering a test are reported whenever obtainable. The latter figure is always enclosed in parentheses. Thus, "50(60) minutes" indicates that the examinees are allowed 50 minutes of working time and that a total of 60 minutes is needed to administer the test. A time of "40–50 minutes" indicates an untimed test that takes approximately 45 minutes to administer, or–in a few instances–a test so timed that working time and administration time are very difficult to disentangle. When the time necessary to administer a test is not reported or suggested in the test materials but has been obtained through correspondence with the test publisher or author, the time is enclosed in brackets.

n) COMMENTS. Some entries contain special notations, such as: "for research use only"; "revision of the ABC Test"; and "tests administered monthly at centers throughout the United States." Some of the test entries include additional factual statements that may influence one's perception of the test. For example, when a test title notes a revision of some test materials but not others, a comment such as "manual has been updated, but instrument itself has not changed" may be included. The field also may contain information about ways in which the test can be administered, such as "online version available" or "administered via paper and pencil or online." Finally, to maintain our independent status, it is the policy of the Buros Center for Testing to write test descriptions based on test materials that test publishers provide to us. Therefore, if a test publisher has advised us that a test has been updated (e.g., is available in a newer edition), but we have not yet seen the materials ourselves, we have noted the existence of an update in the Comments field. In these cases, the appropriate descriptive fields will be updated when the new test materials are received. Between publication of books in the *Tests in Print* series, updated descriptive information can be found at Test Reviews Online and in our subscription databases, mentioned earlier.

o) AUTHOR. For most tests, all authors are reported. In the case of tests that appear in a new form each year, typically only authors of the most recent forms are listed. Names are reported exactly as printed on test booklets. Names of editors generally are not reported.

p) PUBLISHER. The name of the publisher or distributor is reported for each test. Foreign publishers are identified by listing the country in brackets immediately following the name of the publisher. The Publishers Directory and Index must be consulted for a publisher's address and other contact information. Unfortunately, despite our many efforts—through email, surface mail, telephone calls, and websites—to reach every publisher for updated information, some could not be reached or would not provide updates. When we could discern from the publisher's website that a test we listed previously is now available in a newer edition, we included this information in brackets.

q) FOREIGN ADAPTATIONS. Revisions and adaptations of tests for foreign use are listed in a separate paragraph following the original edition.

r) SUBLISTINGS. Levels, editions, subtests, or parts of a test available in separate booklets are sometimes presented as sublistings with titles indented and set in small capital letters. Sub-sublistings are indented and titles are set in italic type.

s) CROSS REFERENCES. For tests that have been listed previously in a Buros Center publication, a test entry includes–if relevant–a final paragraph containing a cross reference to the reviews, excerpts, and references for that test in those volumes. For example, in the cross references, "T3:467" refers to test 467 in *Tests in Print III*, "8:1023" refers to test 1023 in *The Eighth Mental Measurements Yearbook*, "T2:144" refers to test 144 in Tests in Print II, "7:637" refers to test 637 in *The Seventh Mental Measurements Yearbook*, "P:262" refers to test 262 in *Personality Tests and Reviews I*, "2:1427" refers to test 1427 in *The 1940 Yearbook*, and "1:1110" refers to test 1110 in *The 1938 Yearbook*. In the case of batteries and programs, the paragraph also includes cross references–from the battery to the separately listed subtests and vice versa–to entries in this volume and to entries and reviews in earlier editions of TIP and the MMY. Reviews that are scheduled to appear in *The Twentieth Mental Measurements Yearbook*—the next volume of the MMY series—also are noted.

ACKNOWLEDGEMENTS

The publication of a volume of this kind is only accomplished with the effort and cooperation of many people. The editors are grateful to all who have given of their time and expertise in the publication process.

Staff members of the Buros Center for Testing have been major contributors and vital to the success of gathering and compiling the information to be included in *TIP IX*. It has truly been a team effort. Gary Anderson, Assistant Editor, worked long and hard in helping to organize, proofread, and present the information included. His careful and conscientious efforts are very important to our final product. Robert Spies has ensured that our subscription database operations, serving hundreds of libraries worldwide, have run smoothly. The administrative support of Zoe McManaman and Rasma Strautkalns has been very important and helpful, as has clerical assistance from student workers Kaley Smith, Kirstie Smith, and Marta Jonson. The professional staff of the Buros Center's Assessment Literacy and Psychometric Consulting initiatives—Jessica Jonson, Katherine (Tzu-Yun) Chin, Carina McCormick, Douglas (Min Sung) Kim, Anja Römhild, and Theresa Glanz—has provided valuable assistance and insights that have made this publication better. Angela Mittan has coordinated our marketing and communication efforts, attending conferences and spreading the word about not only our publications, but also all of the work that occurs at the Buros Center. Thanks also are owed to Linda Murphy, who retired in 2013 after serving as managing editor for 10 yearbooks and as an editor for Volumes IV through VIII in the *Tests in Print* series. Her work over three decades laid the groundwork for this publication, and her influence is apparent in the final product.

The Buros Center is housed at the University of Nebraska-Lincoln, and many people from the university have contributed to this publication. In particular, we want to thank Web Programmer/Developer Michael Fairchild of the Office of University Communications and Brett Bieber of the Office of Information Technology Services. Their database development and management expertise greatly enabled production of this volume. We appreciate the support of Ralph de Ayala, Chair of the Department of Educational Psychology, and Marjorie Kostelnik, Dean of the College of Education and Human Sciences, as well as the many students from the department and the university who have contributed to this work. We thank the following graduate research assistants who helped with the preparation of *TIP IX*: Allen Garcia, Sara Gonzalez, Chelsi Klentz Davis, HyeSun Lee, and Lindsey Sherd.

Appreciation is also extended to our National Advisory Council for their willingness to assist in the operation of the Buros Center. The members of the National Advisory Council during the time of preparation of this volume were Angee Baker, Gregory Cizek, John Fremer, Paula Kaufman, Michael Rodriguez, Jonathan Sandoval, and Neal Schmitt.

Most of the publishers of the tests listed have been extremely cooperative in providing us with their materials and information to make these listings comprehensive and accurate. We appreciate their timely assistance. A small minority of publishers refuses to provide information and materials. We sincerely regret that we were not able to list their products. Some others did not respond to our requests for an accuracy check of information, so we have included the information we have together with their contact information. We have made every effort to stay alert to new tests, publishers, and publisher addresses. We apologize for any oversights and hope that the test authors or publishers will make us aware of omissions and discrepancies so that their entries can be corrected in future editions, which may take the familiar tangible form or an electronic form.

And finally, we thank our friends and families for their patience and encouragement during the publication process.

Nancy Anderson
Jennifer E. Schlueter
Janet F. Carlson
Kurt F. Geisinger

May 2016

Tests in Print

[1]
Abbreviated Torrance Test for Adults.
Purpose: To assess creative thinking ability.
Population: Adults.
Publication Date: 2002.
Acronym: ATTA.
Scores, 23: Norm-Referenced Measures (Fluency, Originality, Elaboration, Flexibility, Total Scaled Score), Criterion-Referenced Creativity Indicators (Richness and Colorfulness of Imagery, Emotions/Feelings, Future Orientation, Humor: Conceptual Incongruity, Provocative Questions, Verbal Responses Total, Openness: Resistance to Premature Closure, Unusual Visualization/Different Perspective, Movement and/or Sound, Richness and/or Colorfulness of Imagery, Abstractness of Titles, Articulateness in Telling Story, Combination/Synthesis of Two or More Figures, Internal Visual Perspective, Expressions of Feelings and Emotions, Fantasy, Figural Responses Total), Creativity Index.
Administration: Group.
Price Data, 2015: $34.80 per starter set including manual and 10 booklets (specify English or Spanish); $22.55 per 10 booklets (specify English or Spanish); $19.50 per manual (specify English or Spanish).
Foreign Language Edition: Spanish edition available.
Time: 15 minutes.
Comments: Based on 1980 Demonstration Form of the Torrance Tests; may be self-administered; norm- and criterion-referenced.
Authors: Kathy Goff and E. Paul Torrance.
Publisher: Scholastic Testing Service, Inc.
Cross References: For reviews by James A. Athanasou and Alan C. Bugbee, Jr., see 17:1.

[2]
Aberrant Behavior Checklist.
Purpose: Constructed to rate "inappropriate and maladaptive behavior of mentally retarded individuals in residential and community settings, and developmental centers."
Population: Mentally retarded adolescents and adults.
Publication Date: 1986.
Acronym: ABC.
Scores, 5: Irritability, Lethargy, Stereotypy, Hyperactivity, Inappropriate Speech.
Administration: Individual.
Price Data, 2015: $107 per Residential complete kit including manual (32 pages) and Community supplemental manual; $122 per Community complete kit including manual, supplementary manual, and 50 Residential/Community forms/score sheets; $61 per 50 Residential/Community forms/score sheets; $58.25 per manual; $26.75 per Community supplemental manual.
Time: (5) minutes.
Comments: Ratings by direct care or professional staff member acquainted with individual.
Authors: Michael G. Aman and Nirbhay N. Singh.
Publisher: Slosson Educational Publications, Inc.
Cross References: See T5:4 (23 references); for reviews by Lena R. Gaddis and by J. Jeffrey Grill, see 12:1 (5 references); see T4:4 (2 references).

[3]
Ability Explorer, Third Edition.
Purpose: "Designed to help middle school/junior high, high school, and postsecondary students, as well as adults, complete a self-exploration of their abilities and relate this information to educational and/or career planning.

Population: Middle school/junior high students to adults.
Publication Dates: 1996-2012.
Scores, 12: Artistic, Clerical, Interpersonal, Language, Leadership/Persuasive, Manual/Technical, Musical/Dramatic, Numerical/Mathematical, Organizational, Scientific, Social, Spatial.
Administration: Individual or group.
Price Data, 2016: $63.95 per package of 25 consumable booklets; volume discounts available. Professional manual (2012, 58 pages) and user's guide (2012, 8 pages) available for download from test publisher's website.
Time: (35-45) minutes.
Authors: Joan C. Harrington, Thomas F. Harrington, and Janet E. Wall.
Publisher: JIST/EMC Publishing.
Cross References: Reviews are scheduled for *The Twentieth Mental Measurements Yearbook*.

[4]

Abortion Scale.

Purpose: To measure attitudes toward abortion.
Population: Older adolescents and adults.
Publication Dates: 1972–1988.
Scores: Total score only.
Manual: No manual.
Price Data, 2015: $2 per scale.
Time: [10] minutes.
Comments: Supplementary article available.
Author: Panos D. Bardis.
Publisher: Donna Bardis.
Cross References: See T4:4 (2 references).

[5]

Abstract Reasoning Test.

Purpose: "Assesses student ability to use non-verbal reasoning skills."
Population: Middle primary through middle secondary school students.
Publication Date: 2008.
Acronym: ART.
Scores: Total score only.
Administration: Group.
Forms, 5: Level A Series 1, Level B Series 1, Level C Series 1, Level D Series 1, Level E Series 1.
Price Data: Available from publisher.
Time: (30) minute time limit per Levels A and B; (40) minute time limit per Levels C, D, and E.
Comments: Administered via paper-and-pencil or online.
Author: Australian Council for Educational Research Ltd.
Publisher: Australian Council for Educational Research Ltd. [Australia].

[6]

Abuse Disability Questionnaire.

Purpose: "Designed to assess both the extent of exposure to partner abuse, as well as its associated consequences."
Population: Women ages 18 years and older.
Publication Date: 2005.
Acronym: ADQ.
Scores, 8: Relationship Disability, Psychological Dysfunction, Substance Abuse, Anxiety, Life Restriction, Health Status Issues, Inadequate Life Control, Concern with Physical Harm.
Administration: Individual or group.
Price Data, 2015: $70 per complete kit including 50 questionnaires/profile forms and manual (27 pages); $45 per 50 questionnaires/profile forms; $30 per manual.
Time: (5-15) minutes.
Comments: Includes a self-report questionnaire/profile form and an information/diagnostics form to be completed via an interview.
Author: John R. McNamara.
Publisher: Stoelting Co.
Cross References: For reviews by Sheri Bauman and by Carl J. Sheperis and Tiffany D. Chandler, see 17:2.

[7]

Abuse Risk Inventory for Women.

Purpose: To identify women who are current victims of abuse or who are at risk for abuse by their intimate partners or ex-partners.
Population: Adult women.
Publication Date: 1989.
Acronym: ARI.
Scores: Total score only.
Administration: Group and individual.
Price Data: Available from publisher.
Time: (10–15) minutes.
Comments: Title on test is Interpersonal Relationship Survey.
Author: Bonnie L. Yegidis.
Publisher: Mind Garden, Inc.
Cross References: For reviews by Cynthia A. Rohrbeck and Janice G. Williams, see 11:1.

[8]

Academic Achievement Battery Comprehensive Form.

Purpose: Designed to assess "an individual's performance in the main areas of achievement defined by the Individuals with Disabilities Education Act."
Population: Ages 4 to 85.
Publication Date: 2014.
Acronym: AAB Comprehensive Form.
Scores, 21: Basic Reading (Reading Foundational Skills, Letter/Word Reading, Reading Fluency), Reading Comprehension (Reading Comprehension: Words and

Sentences, Reading Comprehension: Passages), Listening Comprehension (Listening Comprehension: Words and Sentences, Listening Comprehension: Passages), Expressive Communication (Oral Fluency, Oral Expression, Oral Production), Written Expression (Pre-Writing Skills, Spelling, Written Composition), Mathematical Calculation, Mathematical Reasoning, Academic Achievement Battery Composite.

Administration: Individual (certain subtests may be administered to groups).

Price Data, 2015: $495 per print kit including professional manual with fast guide, 25 item booklets, 25 response booklets, 2 stimulus books, stimulus card, 5 free Screening Form item booklets, 5 free Screening Form response booklets, and 5 free score reports on PARiConnect; $495 per digital kit; $130 per stimulus book (Book 1 or Book 2); $95 per manual (406 pages) including fast guide; $80 per 25 item booklets; $70 per 25 response booklets; $10 per stimulus card.

Time: (30-90) minutes, depending on examinee's age.

Comments: Computer scoring available.

Author: Melissa A. Messer.

Publisher: Psychological Assessment Resources, Inc.

Cross References: Reviews are scheduled for *The Twentieth Mental Measurements Yearbook.*

[9]
Academic Achievement Battery Screening Form.

Purpose: Designed to assess "basic academic skills including reading, spelling, and mathematical calculation" with an optional writing subtest.

Population: Ages 4 to 85.

Publication Date: 2014.

Acronym: AAB Screening Form.

Scores, 5: Letter/Word Reading, Spelling, Written Comprehension (optional), Mathematical Calculation, Screening Academic Achievement Battery Composite.

Administration: Individual (certain subtests may be administered to groups).

Price Data, 2016: $149 per print kit including professional manual with fast guide, 25 item booklets, 25 response booklets, stimulus card, and 5 free score reports on PARiConnect; $80 per manual (200 pages) including fast guide; $30 per 25 item booklets; $30 per 25 response booklets; $10 per stimulus card.

Time: (20-30) minutes for Letter/Word Reading, Spelling, and Mathematical Calculation subtests; (15) minutes for optional Written Composition subtest.

Comments: Computer scoring available. Written Composition subtest administered only to examinees in Grade 3 and above; subtest is optional, but it is required to calculate Screening Academic Achievement Battery Composite score. Content is a subset of content in the Academic Achievement Battery Comprehensive Form.

Author: Melissa A. Messer.

Publisher: Psychological Assessment Resources, Inc.

Cross References: Reviews are scheduled for *The Twentieth Mental Measurements Yearbook.*

[10]
Academic Advising Inventory.

Purpose: "Designed to measure three aspects of academic advising: (1) the nature of advising relationships, seen along a developmental-prescriptive continuum, (2) the frequency of activities taking place during advising sessions, and (3) satisfaction with advising."

Population: Undergraduate students.

Publication Dates: 1984–1986.

Acronym: AAI.

Scores, 3: Developmental-Prescriptive Advising, Advisor-Advisee Activity Scales, Student Satisfaction with Advising.

Administration: Group.

Price Data: Available at no charge from test distributor.

Time: (20) minutes.

Comments: Manual titled Evaluating Academic Advising.

Authors: Roger B. Winston, Jr. and Janet A. Sandor.

Publisher: Student Development Associates, Inc. [Distributed by National Academic Advising Association (NACADA)].

Cross References: See T5:8 (1 reference) and T4:7 (2 references); for a review by Robert D. Brown, see 10:3.

[11]
Academic Competence Evaluation Scales.

Purpose: "Measures academic skills (reading/language arts, mathematics, critical thinking) as well as academic enablers (motivation, study skills, engagement, interpersonal skills)."

Population: Grades K–12, Grades 6–12, 2- or 4-year college.

Publication Date: 2000.

Acronym: ACES.

Scores, 9: Academic Skills (Reading/Language Arts, Mathematics, Critical Thinking, Total), Academic Enablers (Interpersonal Skills, Motivation, Study Skills, Engagement, Total).

Administration: Group.

Forms, 3: Teacher (Grades K–12), Student (Grades 6–12), College (2- or 4-year college).

Price Data, 2015: $181.60 per K–12 basic kit including manual and 25 each of student and teacher record forms; $292.95 per K–12 complete kit including manual, 25 each of student and teacher record forms, and CD-ROM scoring assistant; $247.20 per college complete kit including manual, 25 college record forms, and CD-ROM scoring assistant; $104 per K–12 manual; $101.40 per college manual; $54.10 per 25 record K-12 forms (specify Student, Teacher); $53.85 per 25 College record forms.

Time: (10–15) minutes.
Comments: Standardized; indicates confidence intervals for each subscale; allows ranking of scale and subscale scores into one of three competence levels (developing, competent, advanced); Assistant software (version 2.0) scores, monitors change in scores over time, graphs data, generates descriptive reports.
Authors: James C. DiPerna and Stephen N. Elliott.
Publisher: Pearson.
Cross References: For reviews by Ronald K. Hambleton and by Darrell L. Sabers and Sarah Bonner, see 16:1.

[12]

Academic Intervention Monitoring System.

Purpose: Guidebook and intervention planning questionnaires "designed to provide teachers and other school-based professionals with the resources they need for developing, monitoring, and evaluating classroom-based, empirically supported interventions for academic difficulties."
Population: Grades K–12.
Publication Date: 2001.
Acronym: AIMS.
Scores: Not scored.
Administration: Individual.
Forms, 3: Student, Parent, Teacher.
Price Data, 2015: $233.70 per complete kit including manual (147 pages), 25 each of Student, Parent, and Teacher forms; $28.20 per 25 Student forms; $27.15 per 25 Parent forms; $53.30 per 25 Teacher forms; $142 per manual.
Foreign Language Edition: Parent form available in Spanish.
Time: (10–15) minutes.
Comments: Developed in conjunction with the Academic Competence Evaluation Scales (11).
Authors: James C. DiPerna, Stephen N. Elliott, with Edward Shapiro.
Publisher: Pearson.
Cross References: For reviews by Kathleen M. Johnson and Jeffrey Smith, see 17:4.

[13]

Academic Perceptions Inventory [2000 Revision].

Purpose: "Developed to assess a profile of the academic self in various classrooms and in the learning environment … with perceptions of the self as a person, as a student, and at school."
Population: Grades K–16.
Publication Dates: 1979–2000.
Acronym: API.
Administration: Group.
Price Data, 2002: $20 per packet of 25 scales (specify level); $25 per test manual (specify Primary Level [2000, 83 pages], Intermediate Level [2000, 76 pages], Advanced

Level [2000, 79 pages], or College Level [2000, 73 pages]); $40 per composite test manual (2000, 146 pages); $.40 per answer sheet; $.30 per scale for scoring.
Foreign Language Editions: Available in Spanish, Italian, and French.
Time: (5–20) minutes per test.
Comments: Ratings by self and others; previous edition entitled The Affective Perception Inventory.
Authors: Louise M. Soares and Anthony T. Soares.
Publisher: Soares Institute of Neuroscience and Education.
　　a) PRIMARY LEVEL.
　　Population: Grades K–3.
　　Scores: 9 Scales: Self Concept, Student Self, School, Reading, Social Studies, Science, Arithmetic, Fine Arts, Sports and Games.
　　b) INTERMEDIATE LEVEL.
　　Population: Grades 4–8.
　　Scores: 11 Scales: Self Concept, Student Self, School, Language Arts, Reading, Foreign Languages, History and Geography, Science, Mathematics, Fine Arts, Physical Education.
　　c) ADVANCED LEVEL.
　　Population: Grades 9–12.
　　Scores: 13 Scales: Self Concept, Student Self, School, English, Foreign Languages, American History, Mathematics, Biology, Chemistry, Earth Sciences, Physics, Fine Arts, Sports.
　　d) COLLEGE LEVEL.
　　Population: Grades 13–16.
　　Scores: 15 Scales: Self Concept, Student Self, Campus, English, Foreign Languages, World History, Political Science, Business, Mathematics, Biology, Chemistry, Physics, Humanities, Fine Arts, Sports.
Cross References: For reviews by Carol E. Kessler and Aimin Wang, see 15:1; see T4:130 (3 references); for reviews by Rosa A. Hagin and Gerald R. Smith of The Affective Perception Inventory, see 9:59.

[14]

Access Management Survey.

Purpose: Designed to measure the extent to which a manager provides opportunities and support for employee involvement, and the necessary resources for people to influence work-life issues.
Population: Adults.
Publication Dates: 1989–1995.
Acronym: AMS.
Scores, 5: Access to the Problem, Access to People, Access to Information and Resources, Access to Support, Access to the Solution.
Administration: Group.
Price Data, 2016: $12.95 per instrument.
Time: Untimed.
Comments: Self-assessment survey.
Author: Jay Hall.
Publisher: Teleometrics International, Inc.
Cross References: For reviews by Thomas M. Haladyna and Mary A. Lewis, see 12:2.

[15]

Accountant Staff Selector.

Purpose: Designed "to evaluate the administrative, intellectual and analytical skills necessary for successful performance as an accountant."

Population: Adult applicants for accounting positions.

Publication Dates: 1982–2002.

Scores, 7: Numerical Skills, Attention to Detail, Problem Solving Ability, Reading Comprehension, Spreadsheet Simulation, Verbal Fluency, Bookkeeping Skills.

Administration: Individual or group.

Price Data: Available from publisher.

Foreign Language Edition: Available in French.

Time: (66) minutes.

Author: Walden Personnel Testing and Consulting, Inc.

Publisher: Walden Personnel Testing & Consulting Inc. [Canada].

Cross References: For a review by JoEllen V. Carlson, see 16:2.

[16]

ACCUPLACER.

Purpose: Designed as a suite of tests that assess reading, writing, math, and computer skills for course placement and remediation.

Population: Students in high schools, community colleges, four-year colleges, and technical schools.

Publication Dates: 1985–2016.

Acronym: ACCUPLACER.

Administration: Individual.

Price Data: Available from publisher.

Special Editions: All Companion tests are available in Braille and large print.

Time: Untimed.

Author: The College Board.

Publisher: The College Board.

a) ARITHMETIC.

Purpose: Measures students' ability to perform basic arithmetic operations and to solve problems that involve fundamental arithmetic concepts.

Scores: Total score only.

Comments: Each student is administered 17 items, which are adaptively delivered depending on student responses to prior items. Three content areas are measured on this test: Operations with Whole Numbers and Fractions, Operations with Decimals and Percents, and Applications and Problem Solving.

b) COLLEGE LEVEL MATH.

Purpose: Measures students' ability to solve problems that involve college-level mathematics concepts.

Scores: Total score only.

Comments: Each student is administered 20 items, which are adaptively delivered depending on student responses to prior items. Five content areas are measured on this test: Algebraic Operations, Solutions of Equations and Inequalities, Coordinate Geometry, Applications and Other Topics, Functions and Trigonometry.

c) ELEMENTARY ALGEBRA.

Purpose: Measures a student's ability to perform basic algebraic operations and to solve problems that involve elementary algebraic concepts.

Scores: Total score only.

Comments: Each student is administered 12 items, which are adaptively delivered depending on student responses to prior items. Three content areas are measured with this test: Operations with Integers and Rational Numbers; Operations with Algebraic Expressions; and Solution of Equations, Inequalities, and Word Problems.

d) READING COMPREHENSION.

Purpose: Measures students' ability to understand what they have read.

Scores: Total score only.

Comments: Each student is administered 20 items, which are adaptively delivered depending on student responses to prior items.

e) SENTENCE SKILLS.

Purpose: Measures students' understanding of sentence structure.

Scores: Total score only.

Comments: Each student is 20 items, which are adaptively delivered depending on student responses to prior items.

f) WRITERPLACER (WRITTEN ESSAY).

Purpose: Measures writing skill at the level expected of an entering level college student.

Scores: 1 holistic score and 6 dimension scores: Focus, Organization, Development and Support, Sentence Structure, and Mechanical Conventions.

g) ESL LANGUAGE USE.

Purpose: Measures a student's proficiency in using correct grammar in English sentences.

Scores: Total score only.

Comments: Each student is administered 20 items, which are adaptively delivered depending on student responses to prior items.

h) ESL LISTENING.

Purpose: Measures a student's proficiency in using correct grammar in English sentences.

Scores: Total score only.

Comments: Each student is administered 20 items, which are adaptively delivered depending on student responses to prior items.

i) ESL READING SKILLS.

Purpose: Measures a student's ability to read English.

Scores: Total score only.

Comments: Each student is administered 20 items, which are adaptively delivered depending on student responses to prior items.

j) ESL SENTENCE MEANING.

Purpose: Measures how well students understand the meaning of sentences in English.

Scores: Total score only.

Comments: Each student is administered 20 items, which are adaptively delivered depending on student responses to prior items.

Cross References: For reviews by Martin A. Fischer and Steven V. Owen of an earlier version (1993), see 13:4.

[17]

ACDI-Corrections Version and Corrections Version II.

Purpose: "Designed for troubled youth screening and assessment."

Population: Troubled youth between the ages of 12 and 18 years in juvenile probation, parole, and corrections programs.

Publication Dates: 1988–1995.

Acronym: ACDI.

Administration: Group.

Price Data: Available from publisher.

Foreign Language Edition: Spanish forms are available.

Time: (15–25) minutes.

Author: Risk & Needs Assessment, Inc.

Publisher: Behavior Data Systems, Ltd. [Efforts to obtain updated information from the test publisher were unsuccessful. Version I could not be found on the test publisher's website; its status is unknown.]

a) VERSION I.
Scores, 5: Truthfulness, Alcohol, Drug, Adjustment, Distress.
b) VERSION II.
Scores, 6: Truthfulness, Alcohol, Drug, Adjustment, Distress, Violence.

Cross References: For reviews by Carol Collins and Mark Pope, see 14:2.

[18]

ACER Advanced Test B90: New Zealand Edition.

Purpose: "Designed to measure general intellectual ability."

Population: College students and adults.

Publication Date: 1991.

Scores: Total score only.

Administration: Group.

Price Data: Available from publisher.

Time: 50(55) minutes.

Comments: "Selected items from the ACER Advanced Test B40 and the ACER Test of Cognitive Ability."

Authors: Australian Council for Educational Research Ltd. and manual by Neil Reid and Cedric Croft.

Publisher: New Zealand Council for Educational Research [New Zealand].

Cross References: For a review by John Rust, see 12:4; for a review of ACER Advanced Test B40 by Harriet C. Cobb, see 9:4; see also T2:323 (6 references) and 7:328 (4 references); for a review of ACER Advanced Test B40 by C. Sanders, see 5:296 (3 references).

[19]

ACER Applied Reading Test.

Purpose: Designed to measure ability to read and understand technical material.

Population: Apprentices, trainees, technical and trade personnel.

Publication Dates: 1989–1990.

Scores: Total score only.

Administration: Group.

Forms, 2: A, B.

Price Data, 2005: A$9.95 per test booklet; A$9.95 per 10 answer sheets; A$9.95 per score key; A$34.95 per manual (1990, 24 pages); A$54.95 per specimen set A–Personnel only or B–Personnel or Technical and Further Education Colleges.

Time: 40–45 minutes.

Authors: J. M. van den Berg and I. R. Woff.

Publisher: Australian Council for Educational Research Ltd. [Australia; Efforts to obtain updated information from the test publisher were unsuccessful. An updated edition of this test appears on the test publisher's website.].

Cross References: For reviews by Mark H. Daniel and Michael S. Trevisan, see 12:5.

[20]

ACER Mechanical Reasoning Test [Revised 1997].

Purpose: "Designed to assess a person's aptitude for solving problems requiring the understanding of mechanical ideas."

Population: Ages 15 and over.

Publication Dates: 1951–1997.

Scores: Total score only.

Administration: Group.

Forms, 2: Parallel Forms A and B.

Price Data, 2016: A$19.95 per test booklet; A$18.95 per scoring key; A$24.95 per 10 answer sheets; A$74.95 per manual (1997, 58 pages); A$129.95 per specimen set.

Time: 20(25) minutes.

Comments: Revision of ACER Mechanical Comprehension Test (T7:27).

Author: Australian Council for Educational Research Ltd.

Publisher: Australian Council for Educational Research Ltd. [Australia].

Cross References: For a review by Gerald R. Schneck, see 15:2; see T2:2238 (3 references); for reviews by John R. Jennings and Hayden S. Williams of an earlier edition, see 5:875.

[21]

ACER Short Clerical Test.

Purpose: Designed to measure aptitudes for speed and accuracy in routine clerical work.

Population: Age 15 and over.

Publication Dates: 1953–2001.

Scores, 2: Checking, Arithmetic.

Administration: Group.

Price Data, 2016: A$64.96 per 10 test booklets; A$5.95 per score key; A$39.95 per manual; A$49.95 per specimen set.

Time: 5(10) minutes per test.

Author: Australian Council for Educational Research Ltd.

Publisher: Australian Council for Educational Research Ltd. [Australia].

[22]
ACER Test of Employment Entry Mathematics.

Purpose: "A group test of basic mathematical ability ... used for the selection of apprentices, trainees, and any other technical and trades personnel."

Population: Apprentice, trainee, technical and trade applicants.

Publication Date: 1992.

Acronym: TEEM.

Scores: Total score only.

Administration: Group.

Price Data, 2016: A$19.95 per test booklet; A$18.95 per score key; A$29.95 per 10 answer sheets; A$94.95 per specimen set.

Time: 25(40) minutes.

Comments: Can be hand scored or scored by testing service.

Authors: John Izard, Ian Woff, and Brian Doig.

Publisher: Australian Council for Educational Research Ltd. [Australia].

Cross References: For reviews by Jay R. Stewart and Patricia H. Wheeler, see 15:3.

[23]
ACER Word Knowledge Test.

Purpose: Designed to obtain a quick assessment of verbal or language ability.

Population: Australian years 9–12 and job applicants.

Publication Dates: 1984–1990.

Scores: Total score only.

Administration: Group.

Editions, 2: E, F.

Restricted Distribution: Distribution of Form E restricted to personnel use.

Price Data, 2016: A$19.95 per reusable test booklet; A$14.95 per 10 answer sheets; A$18.95 per score key; A$44.95 per manual (1990, 44 pages); A$69.95 per specimen set (specify Form E or F).

Time: 10(20) minutes.

Comments: Replacement for the ACER Adult Form B.

Author: Marion M. de Lemos.

Publisher: Australian Council for Educational Research Ltd. [Australia].

Cross References: See T5:34 (6 references); for reviews by Douglas Ayers and William R. Merz, Sr., see 11:2.

[24]
Achenbach System of Empirically Based Assessment [2015 Update].

Purpose: "An integrated ... [approach] designed to provide standardized descriptions of ... competencies, adaptive functioning, and problems."

Population: Ages 18 months to 90+ years.

Publication Dates: 1980–2015.

Acronym: ASEBA.

Administration: Individual or group.

Levels, 4: Preschool, School-Age, Adult, Older Adult.

Foreign Language Editions: One or more forms have been translated into 100 languages, check website (www.aseba.org) for availability.

Comments: Revised version of the Child Behavior Checklist; includes both empirically based syndrome scales and DSM-oriented scales for scoring consistent with DSM-5 categories; designed to be usable in diverse contexts, including schools, mental health, medical, child and family service, and other settings; all forms except TOF, DOF, and SCICA are parallel, facilitating comparisons across informants; hand- or computer-scorable; reusable hand-scoring templates available; data processed by ASEBA-PC; cross-informant bar graphs; can be completed using paper forms (hand- or machine-readable), by direct data-entry on computer, or via ASEBA-Web.

Authors: Thomas M. Achenbach (all forms, manuals, and guides), Leslie A. Rescorla (some manuals, forms, and guides for the ASEBA), Stephanie H. McConaughy (SCICA, SCICA manual, and School-Based Practitioners' Guide for the ASEBA), Peter J. Pecora and Kathleen M. Wetherbee (Child and Family Service Workers' Guide for the ASEBA), Thomas M. Ruffle (Medical Practitioners' Guide for the ASEBA), Paul A. Newhouse (older adult forms, manual, and Guide for Adult and Older Adult Forms); Masha Y. Ivanova (Guide to Family Assessment Using the ASEBA).

Publisher: ASEBA Research Center for Children, Youth, and Families.

a) PRESCHOOL FORMS AND PROFILES.

Purpose: To provide "systematic assessment of maladaptive behavior among preschoolers."

Price Data, 2016: $375 per computer-scoring starter kit; $160 per hand-scoring starter kit; $40 per manual (2000, 189 pages); $35 per Multicultural Supplement to the Preschool Manual (2010, 144 pages).

Comments: DSM-Oriented Scales rated as very consistent with the following DSM-5 categories: Depressive Problems consistent with Persistent Depressive Disorder, Major Depressive Disorder; Anxiety Problems consistent with Generalized Anxiety Disorder, Separation Anxiety Disorder, Specific Phobia; Autism Spectrum Disorder; Attention Deficit/Hyperactivity Problems consistent with Hyperactive-Impulsive and Inattentive types of ADHD.

1) *Child Behavior Checklist for Ages 1 1/2-5.*

Population: Ages 18 months to 5 years.

Publication Dates: 1988–2010.

Acronym: CBCL/1 1/2-5.

Scores: 7 Syndrome scales (Emotionally Reactive, Anxious/Depressed, Somatic Complaints, Withdrawn, Sleep Problems, Attention Problems, Aggressive Behavior), plus Internalizing, Externalizing, Total Problems; Language Development Survey (LDS) scored (for children age 18–35 months); 5 DSM-Oriented scales (Depressive Problems, Anxiety Problems, Autism Spectrum Problems, Attention Deficit/Hyperactivity Problems, Oppositional Defiant Problems).
Time: (10) minutes.
Comments: Designed to be completed by parents and others who see children in home-like settings; includes the Language Development Survey (LDS) for evaluating language delays in children under age 3 as well as those over age 3 suspected of having language delays.
2) Caregiver-Teacher Report Form for Ages 1 1/2-5.
Population: Ages 18 months to 5 years.
Publication Dates: 1997–2010.
Acronym: C-TRF.
Scores: 6 Syndrome scales (Emotionally Reactive, Anxious/Depressed, Somatic Complaints, Withdrawn, Attention Problems, Aggressive Behavior), plus 5 DSM-oriented scales, Internalizing, Externalizing, Total Problems.
Time: (10) minutes.
Comments: Designed to be completed by daycare providers and preschool teachers who have known a child in daycare, preschool, or similar settings for at least 2 months.

b) SCHOOL-AGE FORMS AND PROFILES.
Price Data: $475 per computer-scoring starter kit; $40 per manual (2001, 238 pages); $35 per Multicultural Supplement to the School-Age Manual (2007, 116 pages).
Comments: DSM-Oriented Scales rated as very consistent with the following DSM-5 categories: Depressive Problems consistent with Persistent Depressive Disorder, Major Depressive Disorder; Anxiety Problems consistent with Generalized Anxiety Disorder, Separation Anxiety Disorder, Specific Phobia; Attention Deficit/Hyperactivity Problems consistent with Hyperactive-Impulsive and Inattentive types of ADHD; Somatic Problems consistent with Somatization Disorder and Somatoform Disorder.
1) Child Behavior Checklist for Ages 6–18.
Population: Ages 6–18.
Publication Dates: 1981–2001.
Acronym: CBCL/6–18.
Scores: 4 Competence scales (Activities, Social, School, Total Competence); 8 Syndrome scales (Anxious/Depressed, Withdrawn/Depressed, Somatic Complaints, Social Problems, Thought Problems, Attention Problems, Rule-Breaking Behavior, Aggressive Behavior), plus Internalizing, Externalizing, Total Problems; 6 DSM-Oriented scales (Depressive Problems, Anxiety Problems, Somatic Problems, Attention Deficit/Hyperactivity Problems, Oppositional Defiant Problems, Conduct Problems).
Time: (15–20) minutes.
2) Teacher's Report Form for Ages 6–18.
Purpose: "Quickly obtain[s] a picture of children's functioning in school, as seen by teachers and other personnel."

Population: Teachers of children ages 6–18.
Publication Dates: 1981–2001.
Acronym: TRF.
Scores: 6 Adaptive Functioning scales (Academic Performance, Working Hard, Behaving Appropriately, Learning, Happy, Total); same Syndrome and DSM-Oriented scales as CBCL/6–18; yields separate scores for Inattention and Hyperactivity-Impulsivity.
Time: (15–20) minutes.
3) Youth Self-Report for Ages 11–18.
Purpose: To obtain youths' reports of their own problems and competencies in a standardized format.
Population: Ages 11–18.
Publication Dates: 1981–2001.
Acronym: YSR.
Scores: 2 Competence scales (Activities, Social) plus Total Competence; same Syndrome and DSM-Oriented scales as CBCL/6–18.
4) Brief Problem Monitor for Ages 6-18.
Purpose: To assess changes over user-selected intervals of days, weeks or months.
Population: Ages 6-18.
Publication Date: 2011.
Acronym: BPM.
Scores: Scales for Internalizing, Attention Problems, Externalizing, and Total Problems, plus user-supplied strengths and problems.
Forms, 3: Parent, Teacher, Youth.
Price Data: $230 per starter kit.
Time: (1-2) minutes.
5) Direct Observation Form for Ages 6-11.
Purpose: "Used to record and rate behavior in group settings."
Publication Dates: 1983–2009.
Acronym: DOF.
Price Data: $195 per computer-scoring starter kit.
Comments: Used to obtain 10-minute samples of children's behavior in classrooms and other group settings; enables users to compare an observed child with 2 control children for on-task, Internalizing, Externalizing, and Total Problems, averaged for up to 6 observation sessions; 6 syndrome scales available (computer-scored profiles only).
6) Semistructured Clinical Interview for Children and Adolescents.
Purpose: "Used to record and rate children's behavior and self-reports during an interview."
Population: Ages 6–18.
Publication Dates: 1989–2001.
Acronym: SCICA.
Scores: 8 Syndrome scales (Anxious, Anxious/Depressed, Withdrawn/Depressed, Language/Motor Problems, Aggressive/Rule-Breaking Behavior, Attention Problems, Self-Control Problems, Somatic Complaints (ages 12–18 only), plus Internalizing, Externalizing, Total Problems; same DSM-Oriented scales as CBCL/6–18.
Price Data: $320 per computer-scoring starter kit.
Time: (60–90) minutes.
Comments: Designed for use by experienced clinical interviewers; protocol form includes topic questions and activities, such as kinetic family drawing and tasks for screening fine and gross

motor functioning; observation and self-report form for rating what a child does and says during interview.

c) ADULT FORMS AND PROFILES.
Publication Dates: 1997–2015.
Price Data: $345 per computer-scoring starter kit; $230 per hand-scoring starter kit; $40 per manual (2003, 228 pages); $35 per Multicultural Supplement to the Adult Manual (2015, 164 pages); $30 per 50 Adult Behavior Checklists.

1) *Adult Self-Report for Ages 18–59.*
Population: Ages 18–59.
Acronym: ASR.
Scores: 5 Adaptive Functioning scales (Education, Friends, Job, Family, Spouse or Partner), Personal Strengths, 3 Substance Use scales (Tobacco, Alcohol, Drugs) plus Mean Substance Use score, 6 DSM-oriented scales (Depressive Problems, Anxiety Problems, Somatic Problems, Avoidant Personality Problems, Attention Deficit/Hyperactivity Problems, Antisocial Personality Problems), same Syndrome scales as CBCL/6–18, plus Intrusive, Internalizing, Externalizing, Total Problems.
Time: (15–20) minutes.

2) *Adult Behavior Checklist for Ages 18–59.*
Population: Ages 18–59.
Acronym: ABCL.
Scores: 2 Adaptive Functioning scales (Friends, Spouse/Partner), other scales same as ASR.
Time: (10–15) minutes.
Comments: Ratings by parents, surrogates, friends, and spouses of adults.

d) OLDER ADULT FORMS AND PROFILES.
Publication Date: 2004.
Price Data: $245 per computer-scoring starter kit; $210 per hand-scoring starter kit; $40 per manual (2004, 200 pages); $30 per 50 Older Adult Behavior Checklists.

1) *Older Adult Self-Report for Ages 60-90+.*
Population: Ages 60-90+.
Acronym: OASR.
Scores: 3 Adaptive Functioning scales (Friends, Spouse/Partner, Personal Strengths), 7 Syndrome scales (Anxious/Depressed, Worries, Somatic Complaints, Functional Impairment, Memory/Cognition Problems, Thought Problems, Irritable/Disinhibited), 6 DSM-oriented scales (Depressive Problems, Anxiety Problems, Somatic Problems, Dementia Problems, Psychotic Problems, Antisocial Personality Problems), plus Total Problems.
Time: (15-20) minutes.

2) *Older Adult Behavior Checklist for Ages 60-90+.*
Population: Ages 60-90+.
Acronym: OABCL.
Scores: Same scales as OASR.
Time: (15-20) minutes.
Comment: Ratings by people who know the older adult well.

Cross References: Reviews are scheduled for *The Twentieth Mental Measurements Yearbook*. For reviews by Rosemary Flanagan and T. Steuart Watson of an earlier (2004) edition, see 16:3; see also T5:451 (292 references); for reviews by Beth Doll and by Michael J. Furlong

and Michelle Wood of an earlier (1994) edition titled Child Behavior Checklist, see 13:55 (556 references); see also T4:433 (135 references); for reviews by Sandra L. Christenson and by Stephen N. Elliott and R. T. Busse of the Teacher's Report Form and the Youth Self-Report, see 11:64 (216 references); for additional information and reviews by B. J. Freeman and Mary Lou Kelley, see 9:213 (5 references).

[25]
Achievement Identification Measure.

Purpose: Developed to provide a measure of the characteristics that distinguish achieving students from underachievers.
Population: School age children.
Publication Date: 1985.
Acronym: AIM.
Scores, 6: Competition, Responsibility, Control, Achievement, Communication, Respect.
Administration: Individual.
Price Data, 2015: $120 per 30 tests, manual for administration (8 pages), manual for interpretation of scores (7 pages), and computer scoring of 30 tests; $15 per specimen set.
Foreign Language Edition: Spanish edition available.
Time: (20) minutes.
Comments: Parent report inventory.
Author: Sylvia B. Rimm.
Publisher: Educational Assessment Service, Inc.
Cross References: See T5:35 (1 reference); for reviews by Howard M. Knoff and Sharon B. Reynolds, see 10:5.

[26]
Achievement Identification Measure—Teacher Observation.

Purpose: Identify underachievers.
Population: School-age children.
Publication Date: 1988.
Acronym: AIM-TO.
Scores: 5 dimension scores: Competition, Responsibility, Achievement Communication, Independence/Dependence, Respect/Dominance.
Administration: Individual.
Price Data, 2015: $120 per set of 30 test booklets/answer sheets (scoring by publisher included); $15 per specimen set.
Foreign Language Edition: Spanish edition available.
Time: (20) minutes.
Comments: Ratings by teacher.
Author: Sylvia B. Rimm.
Publisher: Educational Assessment Service, Inc.
Cross References: For reviews by William P. Erchul and Geoffrey F. Schultz, see 11:3.

[27]

Achievement Motivation Inventory.

Purpose: Designed to evaluate "all major aspects of job-related achievement motivation."
Population: Adults.
Publication Date: 2004.
Acronym: AMI.
Scores, 17: Compensatory Effort, Competitiveness, Confidence in Success, Dominance, Eagerness to Learn, Engagement, Fearlessness, Flexibility, Flow, Goal Setting, Independence, Internality, Persistence, Preference for Difficult Tasks, Pride in Productivity, Self-Control, Status Orientation.
Administration: Individual or group.
Price Data, 2016: $229 per complete kit including manual (60 pages), question booklet, 20 response sheets, 20 score profiles, and case; $39 per question booklet; $106 per 20 response sheets; $22 per 20 score profiles; $165 per manual.
Time: Administration time not reported.
Authors: Heinz Schuler, George C. Thornton III, Andreas Frintrup, and Rose Mueller-Hanson.
Publisher: Hogrefe Ltd [United Kingdom].
Cross References: For reviews by Jeffrey A. Jenkins and Eleanor E. Sanford-Moore, see 17:4.

[28]

Achievement Motivation Profile.

Purpose: "Designed to be a measure of a student's motivation to achieve" and related personality characteristics.
Population: Ages 10 to 14 for AMP Juniors; 14 years and older in high school, junior college, and college.
Publication Dates: 1995–1996.
Acronym: AMP.
Scores, 18: Response style (Inconsistent Responding, Self-Enhancing, Self-Critical), Motivation for Achievement (Achiever, Motivation, Competitiveness, Goal Orientation), Inner Resources (Relaxed Style, Happiness, Patience, Self-Confidence), Interpersonal Strengths (Assertiveness, Personal Diplomacy, Extroversion, Cooperativeness), Work Habits (Planning and Organization, Initiative, Team Player).
Administration: Group.
Price Data, 2016: $91 per manual (1996, 93 pages); $307 per 25-use scoring and interpretation CD.
Time: (20–30) minutes.
Authors: Jotham G. Friedland, Harvey P. Mandel, and Sander I. Marcus.
Publisher: Multi-Health Systems, Inc.
Cross Reference: For reviews by Steven V. Owen and Jay R. Stewart, see 14:3.

[29]

Achieving Behavioral Competencies.

Purpose: To develop a program of instruction in social/emotional skills.

Population: "Students who are seriously emotionally disturbed, closed head injured, juvenile offenders, learning disabled, or at-risk for school drop-out" and "adults served by voc rehab programs."
Publication Date: 1992.
Acronym: ABC.
Scores, 24: Relating to Others (Building Friendships, Maintaining Friendships, Apologizing, Compromising/Negotiating, Giving/Accepting Praise or Criticism, Total), Personal Responsibility (Goal Setting, Decision Making, Assuming Responsibility, Promptness, Asking for Assistance, Total), Coping with Stress (Handling Frustration, Coping with Anger, Dealing with Stress, Accepting Authority, Resisting Peer Pressure, Total), Personal/Affective Development (Building Self-Esteem, Coping with Depression, Coping with Anxiety, Controlling Impulsivity, Sensitivity to Others, Total).
Administration: Group.
Editions, 2: Individual Student Report, Class Report.
Price Data, 2015: $215 per set including curriculum, 25 rating forms, and computer program (Windows or Macintosh).
Time: Administration time not reported.
Comments: Teacher rating scale; responses entered on computer to generate individual or group profiles.
Authors: Lawrence T. McCarron, Kathleen McConnell Fad, and Melody B. McCarron.
Publisher: McCarron-Dial Systems, Inc.
Cross References: For reviews by Sally Kuhlenschmidt and Robert A. Leark, see 13:6.

[30]

Ackerman-Banks Neuropsychological Rehabilitation Battery.

Purpose: Designed as a comprehensive neuropsychological screening instrument.
Population: Adult clients referred for psychological or neuropsychological assessment and/or cognitive rehabilitation.
Publication Dates: 1991–2006.
Acronym: ABNRB.
Scores, 40: Alertness (Attention/Concentration), Prosody (Receptive Prosody, Expressive Prosody), Memory (Long-Term Memory, Short-Term Interference Memory, Short-Term Input Memory, Short-Term Retrieval Memory), Sensorimotor (Auditory Input, Auditory Discrimination, Tactile Input, Tactile Output, Visual Input, Visual Discrimination, Visual-Spatial Construction, Proprioception, Motor Quality, Motor Writing), Speech (Speech Production, Dysarthria, Dysnomia, Neologisms, Confabulation, Perseveration, Lisping), Academic Abilities (Mathematics, Reading, Writing), Cognitive Problem Solving (Concreteness, Integration, Judgment, Speed), Organic Emotions (Depression, Anxiety, Impulsivity), Asymmetry (Left-Right Confusion, Left-Brain Controlled Balance, Right-Brain

Controlled Balance), Treatment Problems (Peripheral Control, Awareness of Deficits, Socially Appropriate Comments, Frustration Tolerance).
Administration: Individual.
Price Data, 2015: $800 per complete kit including professional manual (2006, 192 pages), stimulus card book, 10 administration protocols, 10 response booklets, 10 scoring forms, and processing fee for web-based, mail-in, or faxed computer score submission; $500 per administration package including 10 administration protocols, 10 response booklets, 10 scoring forms, and processing fee for web-based, mail-in, or faxed computer score submission; $300 per professional manual; student, volume, and research discounts available.
Time: (45–120) minutes.
Authors: Rosalie J. Ackerman and Martha E. Banks.
Publisher: ABackans DCP, Inc.
Cross References: For reviews by Surendra P. Singh and by Wilfred G. Van Gorp and Colleen A. Ewing, see 15:5.

[31]

Ackerman-Schoendorf Scales for Parent Evaluation of Custody.

Purpose: "A clinical tool designed to aid mental health professionals in making child custody recommendations."
Population: Parents of children ages 2 to 18 years.
Publication Date: 1992.
Acronym: ASPECT.
Scores, 3: Scales (Observational, Social, Cognitive-Emotional) yielding 1 score: Parental Custody Index (PCI).
Administration: Individual.
Price Data, 2016: $190.50 per kit including 20 parent questionnaires, 10 AutoScore™ forms, 5 short forms, and manual (77 pages); $50.50 per 20 answer forms; $42 per 20 parent questionnaires; $74 per manual.
Time: Administration time varies.
Comments: For complete set of information to score, need results of each parent's MMPI or MMPI-2, Rorschach, WAIS-R, and WRAT-R or NEAT tests.
Authors: Marc J. Ackerman and Kathleen Schoendorf.
Publisher: Western Psychological Services.
Cross References: See T5:41 (1 reference); for reviews by Joyce A. Arditti and Gary R. Melton, see 12:9.

[32]

ACS Examination in Analytical Chemistry.
Purpose: Designed to measure a student's achievement in analytical chemistry.
Population: 1 year college.
Publication Dates: 1944–2013.
Scores: Total score only.
Administration: Group.
Manual: No specific manual; general directions (no date, 4 pages).

Price Data: Available from publisher.
Time: 90(100) minutes.
Comments: ACS test program is continually updated by retiring an older form of the test upon release of a new form; separate answer sheet must be used; exam carries secure copyright.
Author: ACS DivCHED Examinations Institute.
Publisher: ACS DivCHED Examinations Institute.
Cross References: See 7:836 (1 reference) and 6:907 (1 reference); for an excerpted review by H. E. Wilcox of an earlier form, see 5:735; for reviews by William B. Meldrum and William Rieman III, see 3:563.

[33]

ACS Examination in Biochemistry.
Purpose: Designed to measure a student's achievement in biochemistry.
Population: 1 year college.
Publication Dates: 1947–2012.
Scores: Total score only.
Administration: Group.
Manual: No specific manual; general directions (no date, 4 pages).
Price Data: Available from publisher.
Time: 120(130) minutes.
Comments: ACS test program is continually updated by retiring an older form of the test upon release of a new form; separate answer sheet must be used; exam carries secure copyright.
Author: ACS DivCHED Examinations Institute.
Publisher: ACS DivCHED Examinations Institute.
Cross References: See 7:823 (1 reference); for an excerpted review by Wilhelm R. Frisell of an earlier form, see 6:898 (2 references).

[34]

ACS Examination in General Chemistry.
Purpose: Designed to measure a student's achievement in general chemistry.
Population: 1 year college.
Publication Dates: 1934–2015.
Scores: Total score only.
Administration: Group.
Manual: No specific manual; general directions (no date, 4 pages).
Price Data: Available from publisher.
Time: 110(120) minutes.
Comments: ACS test program is continually updated by retiring an older form of the test upon release of a new form; separate answer sheet must be used; exam carries secure copyright.
Author: ACS DivCHED Examinations Institute.
Publisher: ACS DivCHED Examinations Institute.
Cross References: For a review by Frank J. Fornoff of an earlier edition, see 8:837 (3 references); see also T2:1819 (1 reference) and 7:826 (5 references); for reviews

by J. A. Campbell and William Hered and an excerpted review by S. L. Burson, Jr., see 6:902 (3 references); for reviews by Frank P. Cassaretto and Palmer O. Johnson, see 5:732 (2 references); for a review by Kenneth E. Anderson, see 4:610 (1 reference); for reviews by Sidney J. French and Florence E. Hooper, see 3:557 (3 references); see also 2:1593 (5 references).

[35]

ACS Examination in General Chemistry (Brief Test).

Purpose: Designed to measure a student's achievement in general chemistry.
Population: 1 year college.
Publication Dates: 1981–2014.
Scores: Total score only.
Administration: Group.
Manual: No specific manual; general directions (no date, 4 pages).
Price Data: Available from publisher.
Time: 55(60) minutes.
Comments: ACS test program is continually updated by retiring an older form of the test upon release of a new form; separate answer sheet must be used; exam carries secure copyright.
Author: ACS DivCHED Examinations Institute.
Publisher: ACS DivCHED Examinations Institute.

[36]

ACS Examination in General-Organic-Biological Chemistry.

Purpose: Designed to measure a student's achievement in general, organic, and biological chemistry.
Population: Nursing and other paramedical and home economics students.
Publication Dates: 1979–2014.
Scores, 10: General (Part A, Part B, Total), Organic (Part A, Part B, Total), Biological (Part A, Part B, Total), Part A Total.
Administration: Group.
Manual: No specific manual; general directions (no date, 4 pages).
Price Data: Available from publisher.
Time: 165(180) minutes.
Comments: ACS test program is continually updated by retiring an older form of the test upon release of a new form; separate answer sheet must be used; exam carries secure copyright.
Author: ACS DivCHED Examinations Institute.
Publisher: ACS DivCHED Examinations Institute.

[37]

ACS Examination in High School Chemistry [Advanced Level].

Purpose: To measure achievement in high school chemistry.

Population: Advanced high school chemistry students.
Publication Dates: 1963–2010.
Scores: Total score only.
Administration: Group.
Price Data: Available from publisher.
Time: 110(120) minutes.
Comments: ACS test program is continually updated by retiring an older form of the test upon release of a new form; exam carries secure copyright.
Author: ACS DivCHED Examinations Institute.
Publisher: ACS DivCHED Examinations Institute.
Cross References: See T5:48 (1 reference) and T4:57 (1 reference); for reviews by Peter A. Dahl and John P. Penna of an earlier form, see 8:844 (1 reference); for a review by Irvin J. Lehmann, see 7:838 (3 references); for reviews by Frank J. Fornoff and William Hered, see 6:909.

[38]

ACS Examination in High School Chemistry [Lower Level].

Purpose: To measure achievement in high school chemistry.
Population: High school first year chemistry students.
Publication Dates: 1957–2013.
Scores, 3: Part I, Part II, Total.
Administration: Group.
Price Data: Available from publisher.
Time: 80(90) minutes.
Comments: ACS test program is continually updated by retiring an older form of the test upon release of a new form; exam carries secure copyright.
Author: ACS DivCHED Examinations Institute.
Publisher: ACS DivCHED Examinations Institute.
Cross References: See T5:49 (1 reference), T4:59 (1 reference) and 9:41 (1 reference); for a review by Edward F. DeVillafranca of an earlier form, see 8:845 (11 references); see also T2:1830 (3 references); for reviews by William R. Crawford and Irvin J. Lehmann, see 7:837 (9 references); for reviews by Frank J. Fornoff and William Hered and excerpted reviews by Christine Jansing and Joseph Schmuckler, see 6:908 (5 references); for reviews by Edward G. Rietz and Willard G. Warrington, see 5:729.

[39]

ACS Examination in Inorganic Chemistry.

Purpose: Designed to measure a student's achievement in inorganic chemistry.
Population: 1 year college.
Publication Dates: 1961–2014.
Scores: Total score only.
Administration: Group.
Manual: No specific manual; general directions (no date, 4 pages).
Price Data: Available from publisher.

Time: 120(130) minutes.
Comments: ACS test program is continually updated by retiring an older form of the test upon release of a new form; separate answer sheet must be used; exam carries secure copyright.
Author: ACS DivCHED Examinations Institute.
Publisher: ACS DivCHED Examinations Institute.
Cross References: See T3:64 (1 reference), 8:838 (2 references), T2:1820 (1 reference), and 7:827 (2 references); for a review by Frank J. Fornoff and an excerpted review by George B. Kauffman of an earlier form, see 6:903 (1 reference).

[40]

ACS Examination in Instrumental Analysis.

Purpose: Designed to measure a student's achievement in instrumental determinations.
Population: 1 year college.
Publication Dates: 1966–2001.
Scores: Total score only.
Administration: Group.
Manual: No specific manual; general directions (no date, 4 pages).
Price Data: Available from publisher.
Time: 110(120) minutes.
Comments: ACS test program is continually updated by retiring an older form of the test upon release of a new form; separate answer sheet must be used; exam carries secure copyright.
Author: ACS DivCHED Examinations Institute.
Publisher: ACS DivCHED Examinations Institute.
Cross References: See 7:830 (1 reference).

[41]

ACS Examination in Organic Chemistry.

Purpose: Designed to measure a student's achievement in organic chemistry.
Population: 1 year college.
Publication Dates: 1942–2012.
Scores: Total score only.
Administration: Group.
Manual: No specific manual; general directions (no date, 4 pages)
Price Data: Available from publisher.
Time: 115(125) minutes.
Comments: ACS test program is continually updated by retiring an older form of the test upon release of a new form; separate answer sheet must be used; Exam carries secure copyright.
Author: ACS DivCHED Examinations Institute.
Publisher: ACS DivCHED Examinations Institute.
Cross References: See 8:840 (3 references), 7:831 (3 references), and 6:905 (4 references); for a review by Shailer Peterson of an earlier form, see 3:558.

[42]

ACS Examination in Physical Chemistry.

Purpose: Designed to measure a student's mastery of physical chemistry.
Population: 1 year college.
Publication Dates: 1946–2014.
Administration: Group.
Manual: No specific manual.
Price Data: Available from publisher.
Comments: ACS test program is continually updated by retiring an older form of the test upon release of a new form; subtests may be administered separately or together; separate answer sheet must be used; includes a comprehensive exam and three subject matter exams.
Author: ACS DivCHED Examinations Institute.
Publisher: ACS DivCHED Examinations Institute.
  a) THERMODYNAMICS.
    Scores, 3: Part A, Part B, Total.
    Time: 90(100) minutes.
  b) CHEMICAL DYNAMICS.
    Scores, 3: Part A, Part B, Total.
    Time: 90(100) minutes.
  c) QUANTUM CHEMISTRY.
    Scores, 3: Part A, Part B, Total.
    Time: 100(110) minutes.
Cross References: For a review by Gerald R. Van Hecke of an earlier form, see 8:842 (2 references); see also T2:1826 (2 references), 7:833 (2 references), and 6:904 (1 reference); for a review by Alfred S. Brown, see 3:559.

[43]

ACS Examination in Polymer Chemistry.

Purpose: Designed to measure a student's achievement in polymer chemistry.
Population: 1 year college.
Publication Dates: 1978–1990.
Scores: Total score only.
Administration: Group.
Price Data: Available from publisher.
Time: 75(85) minutes.
Comments: ACS test program is continually updated by retiring an older form of the test upon release of a new form; separate answer sheet must be used; exam carries secure copyright.
Author: ACS DivCHED Examinations Institute.
Publisher: ACS DivCHED Examinations Institute.

[44]

ACS Toledo Chemistry Placement Examination.

Purpose: Designed to measure a student's achievement in general chemistry.
Population: 1 year college.
Publication Dates: 1959–2009.
Scores, 4: General Mathematics, General Chemical Knowledge, Specific Chemical Knowledge, Total.

Administration: Group.
Manual: No specific manual; general directions (no date, 4 pages).
Price Data: Available from publisher.
Time: 55(65) minutes.
Comments: ACS test program is continually updated by retiring an older form of the test upon release of a new form; separate answer sheet must be used; exam carries secure copyright.
Author: ACS DivCHED Examinations Institute.
Publisher: ACS DivCHED Examinations Institute.
Cross References: For a review by Frank J. Fornoff of an earlier form, see 8:853 (3 references); see also T2:1847 (2 references); for reviews by Kenneth E. Anderson and William R. Crawford, see 6:920 (1 reference).

[45]
ACT CAAP.

Purpose: Designed to allow postsecondary institutions to assess selected academic skills typically obtained in a core general education curriculum.
Population: College students.
Publication Dates: 1989–2016.
Acronym: ACT CAAP.
Administration: Group.
Restricted Distribution: Available to institutions.
Price Data: Available from publisher.
Time: 40 minutes per test.
Comments: Institutions can customize their assessment program by choosing from the 6 independent test modules; up to 9 local questions can be added to each test module.
Author: ACT, Inc.
Publisher: ACT, Inc.
  a) WRITING SKILLS.
  Purpose: Designed to measure "students' understanding of the conventions of standard written English."
  Scores, 3: Usage/Mechanics, Rhetorical Skills, Total.
  b) MATHEMATICS.
  Purpose: Designed to measure "students' mathematical reasoning abilities."
  Scores, 3: Basic Algebra, College Algebra, Total.
  c) READING.
  Purpose: Designed to measure "reading comprehension referring and reasoning skills."
  Scores, 3: Arts/Literature, Social Studies/Sciences, Total.
  d) CRITICAL THINKING.
  Purpose: Designed to measure "students' skills in analyzing, evaluating, and extending arguments."
  Score: Total score only.
  e) SCIENCE.
  Purpose: "Designed to measure students' knowledge and skills in science...subjects are drawn from biology, chemistry, physics, and the physical sciences."
  Score: Total score only.
  f) WRITING ESSAY.
  Purpose: "Designed to demonstrate a student's level of proficiency in the writing skills commonly taught in college-level writing courses."

Scores, 3: Composite score plus scores for 2 separate writing prompts.
Cross References: See T5:621 (2 references); for reviews by Steven V. Owen and Jeffrey K. Smith of an earlier version titled Collegiate Assessment of Academic Proficiency, see 13:74 (3 references); see also T4:589 (1 reference).

[46]
The ACT Test.

Purpose: "Contains five curriculum-based tests (four multiple-choice tests and an optional writing test) that measure academic achievement in English/writing, mathematics, reading, and science as well as noncognitive components (high school course/grade information, ACT interest inventory, and the student profile section). Results of the cognitive section are used by high schools and post-secondary institutions to understand what students are likely to know and ready to learn next in preparation for, and the transition to, post-secondary education. Results from the ACT are used in admissions, scholarship determination, academic advising, course placement, and career counseling."
Population: Grades 11–12.
Publication Dates: 1959–2016.
Administration: Group.
Price Data: Available from publisher.
Time: 175 minutes; 215 with the optional writing test.
Comments: Tests administered nationally 6 times per year (February, April, June, September, October, December) at centers established by the publisher; also offered up to 5 times per year at international test centers outside the U.S.; special testing with extended time and alternate test formats are available for students who receive special accommodations in school due to professionally diagnosed and documented disabilities.
Author: ACT, Inc.
Publisher: ACT, Inc.
  a) ACT ENGLISH TEST.
  Purpose: "Measures the student's understanding of the conventions of standard written English."
  Scores, 3: Usage/Mechanics, Rhetorical Skills, Total.
  Time: 45 minutes.
  b) ACT MATHEMATICS TEST.
  Purpose: "Measures reasoning and mathematical skills."
  Scores, 4: Pre-Algebra/Elementary Algebra, Intermediate Algebra/Coordinate Geometry, Plane Geometry/Trigonometry, Total.
  Time: 60 minutes.
  c) ACT READING TEST.
  Purpose: "Measures reading comprehension as a product of skill in referring and reasoning."
  Scores, 3: Social Studies/Sciences, Arts/Literature, Total.
  Time: 35 minutes.
  d) ACT SCIENCE TEST.
  Purpose: "Measures the interpretation, analysis, evaluation, reasoning, and problem-solving skills required in the natural sciences."

Scores: Total score only.
Time: 35 minutes.
e) ACT WRITING TEST (Optional).
Purpose: "Measures writing skills emphasized in high school English classes and in college-level composition courses."
Scores, 5: Ideas and Analysis, Development and Support, Organization/Language Use and Conventions, Writing Test Subject Score.
Time: 40 minutes.
Cross References: See T5:56 (19 references); for reviews by A. Harry Passow and James S. Terwilliger of the Enhanced ACT Assessment, see 12:139 (35 references); see also T4:913 (71 references); for reviews by Lewis R. Aiken and Edward Kifer of the ACT Assessment Program, see 9:43 (27 references); see also T3:76 (76 references); for a review by John R. Hills, see 8:469 (208 references); see also T2:1044 (97 references); for a review by Wimburn L. Wallace of an earlier program, see 7:330 (265 references); for reviews by Max D. Engelhart and Warren G. Findley and an excerpted review by David V. Tiedeman, see 6:1 (14 references).

[47]

Adaptability Test.
Purpose: "Designed to measure mental adaptability or mental alertness."
Population: Job applicants.
Publication Dates: 1942–1994.
Scores: Total score only.
Administration: Individual or group.
Forms, 2: A, B.
Price Data: Available from publisher.
Time: 15 minutes.
Authors: Joseph Tiffin and C. H. Lawshe.
Publisher: General Dynamics Information Technology.
Cross References: See T4:80 (2 references), T3:111 (1 reference), T2:337 (3 references), and 7:333 (6 references); for a review by John M. Willits, see 5:305 (13 references); for reviews by Anne Anastasi and Marion A. Bills, see 3:216 (3 references).

[48]

Adaptive Behavior Assessment System, Third Edition.
Purpose: Designed as a "norm-referenced assessment of adaptive skills needed to effectively and independently care for oneself, respond to others, and meet environmental demands at home, school, work, and in the community."
Population: Birth to 89 years.
Publication Dates: 2002-2015.
Acronym: ABAS-3.
Scores, 15: 11 skill areas, 3 adaptive domains, 1 overall score: Conceptual (Communication, Functional Academics/Pre-Academics, Self Direction, Composite), Social (Leisure, Social, Composite), Practical (Community Use, Home/School Living, Health and Safety, Self-Care,

Work, Composite), Motor, General Adaptive Composite.
Administration: Individual.
Forms, 5: Parent/Primary Caregiver Form (Ages Birth-5); Parent Form (Ages 5-21); Teacher/Daycare Provider Form (Ages 2-5); Teacher Form (Ages 5-21); Adult Form (Ages 16-89).
Price Data, 2016: $310 per comprehensive print kit including 5 of each form (Parent/Primary Caregiver, Teacher/Daycare Provider, Parent, Teacher, and Adult), manual (2015, 289 pages), and intervention planner (2015, 217 pages); $450 per comprehensive software kit including 5 print copies of each form, print manual, unlimited use scoring assistant, and intervention planner software; $450 per comprehensive online kit including 5 online form uses for each form, online manual, and online intervention planner; $175 per manual; $95 per intervention planner; $75 per 25 forms (Parent/Primary Caregiver, Teacher/Daycare Provider, Parent, Teacher, or Adult).
Foreign Language Edition: Spanish forms available.
Time: (20) minutes.
Comments: Online, computer, and paper administration and scoring available.
Authors: Patti L. Harrison and Thomas Oakland.
Publisher: Western Psychological Services.
Cross References: Reviews are scheduled for *The Twentieth Mental Measurements Yearbook*. For reviews by Matthew K. Burns and by Joyce Meikamp and Carolyn H. Suppa of the second edition, see 16:4; for a review by James K. Benish of the original edition, see 15:6.

[49]
Adaptive Behavior Diagnostic Scale.
Purpose: Designed as "a norm-referenced, interview-based rating scale ... to estimate adaptive behavior skills in children and young adults."
Population: Ages 2-21 years.
Publication Date: 2016.
Acronym: ABDS.
Scores, 4: Conceptual Domain, Social Domain, Practical Domain, Adaptive Behavior Composite.
Administration: Individual.
Price Data, 2016: $135 per complete kit including manual (125 pages), Rating Scale Reference Card, and 25 record booklets; $45 per 25 record booklets; $90 per manual.
Time: (25-45) minutes.
Authors: Nils A. Pearson, James R. Patton, and Daniel W. Mruzek.
Publisher: PRO-ED.

[50]
Adaptive Behavior Evaluation Scale, Revised.
Purpose: Designed to assist in "making diagnostic, placement, and programming decisions for mentally retarded and emotionally disturbed/behaviorally disordered children and adolescents."

Population: Ages 5-0 to 18-0.
Publication Dates: 1983–1995.
Acronym: ABES-R.
Scores, 10: Communication, Self-Care, Home Living, Social, Community Use, Self-Direction, Health and Safety, Functional Academics, Leisure, Work.
Administration: Individual.
Forms, 2: Adaptive Behavior Evaluation Scale, School Version; Adaptive Behavior Evaluation Scale, Home Version.
Price Data: Available from publisher.
Time: (15–20) minutes.
Comments: The test publisher has indicated there is a newer edition of this test; description will be updated when complete test materials are received.
Author: Stephen B. McCarney.
Publisher: Hawthorne Educational Services, Inc.
Cross References: For reviews by John H. Kranzler and by Mark D. Shriver and Merilee McCurdy, see 14:4; for reviews by Mary Ross Moran and Harvey N. Switzky of an earlier edition, see 12:14.

[51]

Adaptive Behavior Inventory.

Purpose: Designed to evaluate functional daily living skills.
Population: Mentally retarded students ages 6-0 through 18-11 years and normal students ages 5-0 through 18-11 years
Publication Date: 1986.
Acronym: ABI.
Scores, 6: Self-Care Skills, Communication Skills, Social Skills, Academic Skills, Occupational Skills, Composite Quotient.
Administration: Individual.
Price Data, 2015: $108 per complete kit including 25 profile and response sheets, 25 short form response sheets, and examiner's manual (69 pages); $42 per 25 profile and response sheets; $19 per 25 short form response sheets; $54 per examiner's manual.
Time: (20–25) minutes.
Comments: Inventory is completed by classroom teacher or other professional having regular contact with the student; ABI-Short Form available for research and screening purposes.
Authors: Linda Brown and James E. Leigh.
Publisher: PRO-ED.
Cross References: For a review by Corinne Roth Smith, see 10:9 (2 references).

[52]

Adaptive Behavior: Street Survival Skills Questionnaire.

Purpose: "To assess fundamental community living and prevocational skills of mentally disabled adolescents and adults."

Population: Ages 9.5 and over.
Publication Dates: 1979–1993.
Acronym: SSSQ.
Scores, 10: Basic Concepts, Functional Signs, Tools, Domestics, Health and Safety, Public Services, Time, Monetary, Measurements, Total.
Administration: Individual.
Price Data, 2016: $575 per complete kit including 9 picture volumes (1993, 50 pages each), 50 scoring forms, 50 planning charts, Curriculum Guide (1982, 272 pages), and manual (1993, 95 pages); $57.50 per 50 scoring forms; $37.50 per 50 planning charts; $96 per Curriculum Guide; $78 per manual; $275 per computer software.
Time: [45] minutes.
Authors: Dan Linkenhoker and Lawrence McCarron.
Publisher: McCarron-Dial Systems, Inc.
Cross References: See T4:139 (1 reference); for a review by Thomas G. Haring, see 11:6.

[53]

Addiction Severity Index–Multimedia Version.

Purpose: "An interactive, multimedia administration of the Addiction Severity Index," "a measure of addiction severity."
Population: Adults seeking substance abuse treatment.
Publication Date: 1999.
Acronym: ASI-MV.
Scores, 7: Composite scores and severity ratings provided for 7 domains: Medical Status, Employment/Support Status, Alcohol Use, Drug Use, Legal Status, Family/Social Relationships, Psychiatric Status.
Administration: Individual or group.
Price Data: Available from publisher.
Time: (45) minutes.
Comments: Same clinical interview as Addiction Severity Index (5th edition) adapted for self-report, multimedia format; clients are guided through a series of on-screen offices and meet with virtual interviewers; produces narrative report, severity profile, utilization report; customized reports available.
Author: Innovative Training Systems, Inc.
Publisher: Inflexxion, Inc.

[54]

AD/HD Comprehensive Teacher's Rating Scale, Second Edition [1998 Revision].

Purpose: "Designed to help identify attention disorder, with or without hyperactivity."
Population: Grades K–adult.
Publication Dates: 1986–2000.
Acronym: ACTeRS.
Administration: Individual.
Price Data, 2015: $70 per Teacher and Parent Form examiner's kit including manual (2000, 31 pages) and 50

rating/profile forms; $50 per 50 rating/profile forms; $75 per Self-Report examiner's kit including manual and 50 rating/profile forms; $55 per 50 rating/profile forms; $25 per introductory kit including manual, sample Parent rating/profile Form, sample Teacher rating/profile Form, sample Self-Report Form, and annotated bibliography of research; $25 per manual.

Time: [5–15] minutes.

Comments: Paper and pencil edition; parent forms available in Spanish.

Authors: Rina K. Ullmann, Esther K. Sleator, Robert L. Sprague, and MetriTech staff.

Publisher: MetriTech, Inc.

a) ACTeRS TEACHER FORM.
Population: Grades K–8.
Scores, 4: Attention, Hyperactivity, Social Skills, Oppositional Behavior.
Time: Untimed.

b) ACTeRS PARENT FORM.
Scores, 5: Attention, Hyperactivity, Social Skills, Oppositional Behavior, Early Childhood.
Time: Untimed.

c) ACTeRS SELF-REPORT.
Population: Adolescence through adulthood.
Scores, 3: Attention, Hyperactivity/Impulsivity, Social Adjustment.
Time: Untimed [10–15 minutes].

Cross References: For reviews by Cederick O. Lindskog and Janet V. Smith and by Everett V. Smith, Jr., see 14:5; for reviews by Robert J. Miller and Judy Oehler-Stinnett of an earlier edition, see 12:15 (2 references); see also T4:89 (1 reference); for reviews by Ellen H. Bacon and Ayres G. D'Costa of an earlier edition, see 11:7 (2 references).

[55]
ADHD Rating Scale–IV.

Purpose: Designed to help identify the frequency of ADHD symptoms of a child as reported by a parent or educator.

Population: Ages 5–18 years

Publication Date: 1998.

Scores, 3: Inattention, Hyperactivity-Impulsivity, Total.

Administration: Individual.

Forms, 2: Home, School.

Price Data, 2015: $131.75 per scale including manual (79 pages) and photocopiable scales.

Foreign Language Edition: Spanish questionnaires available.

Time: Administration time not reported.

Comments: Symptom criteria based on the DSM-IV; 18-item rating scale.

Authors: George J. DuPaul, Thomas J. Power, Arthur D. Anastopolous, and Robert Reid.

Publisher: Guilford Publications, Inc.

Cross References: For reviews by Jill Ann Jenkins and Cederick O. Lindskog, see 15:7.

[56]
ADHD Symptom Checklist—4.

Purpose: Designed as "a screening instrument for the behavioral symptoms of attention-deficit/hyperactivity disorder (AD/HD) and oppositional defiant disorder (ODD)."

Population: Ages 3–18.

Publication Dates: 1997-2008.

Acronym: ADHD-SC4.

Scores, 3: Screening Cutoff, Symptom Count, Symptom Severity.

Administration: Individual.

Forms, 1: Same checklist completed by parent and teacher.

Price Data, 2015: $63 per kit including 50 checklists, 50 symptom count score sheets, 50 symptom severity profile score sheets, and manual (2008, 111 pages); $32 per 50 checklists.

Foreign Language Edition: Spanish edition available.

Time: (5) minutes.

Comments: Manual and norms updated in 2008.

Authors: Kenneth D. Gadow and Joyce Sprafkin.

Publisher: Checkmate Plus, Ltd.

Cross References: For reviews by James C. DiPerna and Robert J. Volpe and by Cynthia A. Rohrbeck of the original version (1997), see 15:8.

[57]
ADHD Symptoms Rating Scale.

Purpose: Designed "to assess behaviors symptomatic of Attention Deficit Hyperactivity Disorder in children and adolescents."

Population: Ages 5–18 years.

Publication Date: 2001.

Acronym: ADHD-SRS.

Scores, 4: Hyperactive, Impulsive, Inattentive, Total.

Administration: Individual.

Price Data: Available from publisher.

Foreign Language Edition: Spanish edition available.

Time: (10–15) minutes.

Authors: Melissa Lea Holland, Gretchen A. Gimpel, and Kenneth W. Merrell.

Publisher: Pearson.

Cross References: For reviews by Kevin M. Jones and Ronald A. Madle, see 15:9.

[58]
The Adjective Check List.

Purpose: Designed to identify personal characteristics of individuals.

Population: High school and over.

Publication Dates: 1952-1983.

Acronym: ACL.

Scores: 37 in 5 higher-order standard scales: Modus Operandi (Number of Adjectives Checked, Number of Favorable Adjectives, Number of Unfavorable Adjectives, Communality), Need Scales (Achievement, Dominance, Endurance, Order, Intraception, Nurturance, Affiliation, Heterosexuality, Exhibition, Autonomy, Aggression, Change, Succorance, Abasement, Deference), Topical Scales (Counseling Readiness, Self-Control, Self-Confidence, Personal Adjustment, Ideal Self, Creative Personality, Military Leadership, Masculine Attributes, Feminine Attributes), Transactional Analysis (Critical Parent, Nurturing Parent, Adult, Free Child, Adapted Child), Origence-Intellectence (High Origence-Low Intellectence, High Origence-High Intellectence, Low Origence-Low Intellectence, Low Origence-High Intellectence).

Administration: Individual or group.

Price Data, 2015: $50 per manual, including review-only copy of the ACL form; $50 per multi-rater report; $15 per Individual Report; $15 per Report About Me; $2.40 per online administration license (minimum 50); $2 per Remote Online Survey License (minimum 50); $2 per License to Reproduce (minimum 50).

Time: 10-15 minutes.

Authors: Harrison G. Gough and Alfred B. Heilbrun, Jr. (manual and bibliography).

Publisher: Mind Garden, Inc.

Cross References: See T5:68 (62 references) and T4:93 (92 references); for reviews by Phyllis Anne Teeter and John A. Zarske, see 9:52 (39 references); see also T3:116 (117 references), 8:495 (202 references), and T2:1094 (85 references); for reviews by Leonard G. Rorer and Forrest L. Vance of an earlier (1965) edition, see 7:38 (131 references); see also P:4 (102 references).

[59]
Adjustment Scales for Children and Adolescents.

Purpose: "Designed to assess through teacher observation behavior pathology in youths."

Population: Ages 5–17.

Publication Dates: 1993–1994.

Acronym: ASCA.

Scores, 10: Overactivity, Underactivity, Attention-Deficit Hyperactive, Solitary Aggressive-Provocative, Solitary Aggressive-Impulsive, Oppositional Defiant, Diffident, Avoidant, Delinquent, Lethargic-Hypoactive.

Administration: Individual.

Price Data, 2015: $120 per complete kit including 25 male and 25 female self-scoring forms and profiles and manual (1994, 68 pages); $31.25 per 25 self-scoring forms and profiles (specify male or female); $34.95 per manual.

Time: (10–20) minutes.

Comments: Behavior checklist to be completed by a teacher about a student; scored by a psychologist or assessment specialist.

Authors: Paul A. McDermott, Neville C. Marston, and Denis H. Stott.

Publisher: Ed & Psych Associates.

Cross References: For reviews by Gary L. Canivez and Richard V. Schowengerdt, see 14:6; see also T5:69 (1 reference).

[60]
Administrative Series Modules.

Purpose: Designed to assess skills needed in various administrative positions.

Population: Candidates for administrative positions.

Publication Dates: 1975-1997.

Administration: Individual or group.

Price Data: Available from publisher.

Comments: "Designed in module format so test users can select the modules that best suit their testing needs"; "hand scoring is available for all individual and combined modules"; "machine scoring is available for all modules except I, K, and L"; previous version listed as SCC Clerical Skills Series.

Author: International Public Management Association for Human Resources.

Publisher: International Public Management Association for Human Resources (IPMA-HR).

   a) INDIVIDUAL ADMINISTRATIVE MODULE TESTS.

     1) *Grammar (A).*
     Score: Total score only.
     Time: 15 minutes.
     2) *Punctuation (B).*
     Score: Total score only.
     Time: 11 minutes.
     3) *Vocabulary (C).*
     Score: Total score only.
     Time: 9 minutes.
     4) *Spelling (D).*
     Score: Total score only.
     Time: 6 minutes.
     5) *Basic Filing Skills (E).*
     Score: Total score only.
     Time: 18 minutes.
     6) *Reasoning (F).*
     Score: Total score only.
     Time: 9 minutes.
     7) *Following Oral Instructions (G).*
     Score: Total score only.
     Time: 33 minutes.
     8) *Following Written Instructions (H).*
     Score: Total score only.
     Time: 25 minutes.
     9) *Forms, Completion/Listening (I).*
     Score: Total score only.
     Time: 30 minutes.
     10) *Data Proofing (J).*
     Score: Total score only.
     Time: 13 minutes.
     11) *Document Proofing-Part A (K).*
     Score: Total score only.
     Time: 15 minutes.

12) *Document Proofing–Part B (L).*
Score: Total score only.
Time: 20 minutes.
13) *Mathematical Reasoning (M).*
Score: Total score only.
Time: 35 minutes.
14) *Basic Math Calculations (N).*
Score: Total score only.
Time: 20 minutes.
b) COMBINED ADMINISTRATIVE MODULE TESTS.
1) *CLERICAL SERIES 1-A.*
Acronym: CS1-A.
Scores: 5 modules: Grammar, Punctuation, Vocabulary, Spelling, Basic Filing.
Time: 59 minutes.
2) *CLERICAL SERIES 1-B.*
Acronym: CS1-B.
Scores: 3 modules: Reasoning, Following Written Instructions, Basic Math Calculations.
Time: 54 minutes.
Cross References: For a review by Thomas R. O'Neill, see 18:2; for a review by Lorraine D. Eyde of a previous version, see 9:1074.

[61]

Adolescent/Adult Sensory Profile.

Purpose: Designed "to promote self-evaluation of behavioral responses to everyday sensory experiences."
Population: Ages 11–65+.
Publication Date: 2002.
Scores, 4: Low Registration, Sensation Seeking, Sensory Sensitivity, Sensation Avoiding.
Administration: Individual.
Price Data, 2015: $140.45 per complete kit including user's manual (144 pages) and 25 self-questionnaire/summary reports; $104.55 per user's manual; $52.30 per 25 self-questionnaire/summary reports.
Time: (10–15) minutes.
Comments: Self-report inventory based on the Sensory Profile, a measure developed for children.
Authors: Catana E. Brown and Winnie Dunn.
Publisher: Pearson.
Cross References: For reviews by Corine Fitzpatrick and Janet V. Smith, see 16:5.

[62]

Adolescent American Drug and Alcohol Survey with Prevention Planning Survey.

Purpose: Designed to survey youth about their experiences with alcohol, tobacco and other drugs, and "about various risk and protective factors associated with the Prevention Planning Model."
Population: Grades 6–12.
Publication Dates: 1999-2005.
Acronym: ADAS/PPS.
Scores: Not scored.
Administration: Group.

Price Data: The publisher of this survey dissolved in 2011 and released the copyright on this survey; it may be used at no charge.
Time: (20–30) minutes.
Comments: For information about the Children's ADAS, see T6:147.
Authors: Ruth Edwards, Fred Beauvais, and Eugene R. Oetting.
Publisher: Rocky Mountain Behavioral Science Institute, Inc.
Cross References: For reviews by Jody L. Kulstad and by Nathaniel J. Pallone and James J. Hennessy, see 16:6.

[63]

Adolescent and Child Urgent Threat Evaluation.

Purpose: Designed to "assess the risk of near-future violence (both homicidal and suicidal) among children and adolescents."
Population: Ages 8-18.
Publication Date: 2005.
Acronym: ACUTE.
Scores, 8: Threat Cluster, Precipitating Factors Cluster, Early Precipitating Factors Cluster, Late Precipitating Factors Cluster, Predisposing Factors Cluster, Impulsivity Cluster, Overall Threat Classification, Total Score.
Administration: Individual.
Price Data: Available from publisher.
Time: (20) minutes.
Comments: Some items may require the examiner to "obtain information from additional sources" to gather the most "accurate information regarding a client." The test publisher has advised there is a newer edition of the test manual; description will be updated when complete test materials are received.
Authors: Russell Copelan and David Ashley.
Publisher: eMed International Inc.
Cross References: For reviews by Mary M. Clare and Thomas P. Hogan, see 18:3.

[64]

Adolescent Anger Rating Scale.

Purpose: Developed to "assess the intensity and frequency of anger expression in adolescents."
Population: Ages 11–19.
Publication Date: 2001.
Acronym: AARS.
Scores, 4: Instrumental Anger, Reactive Anger, Anger Control, Total Anger.
Administration: Individual or group.
Price Data, 2015: $188 per introductory kit including professional manual (69 pages) and 50 test booklets.
Time: (5–10) minutes for individuals; (10–20) minutes per group.
Comments: Self-rating scale.

Author: DeAnna McKinnie Burney.
Publisher: Psychological Assessment Resources, Inc.
Cross References: For reviews by Carlen Henington and Hugh Stephenson, see 15:10.

[65]
Adolescent Apperception Cards.

Purpose: "Intended to suggest themes and evoke narratives that include … family, sibling, and peer relationships; abuse and neglect."
Population: Ages 12–19.
Publication Date: 1993.
Acronym: AAC.
Scores: No scores.
Administration: Individual.
Forms, 2: Black, White.
Price Data, 2016: $137 per kit including Adolescent Apperception Cards (Black and White versions included); $80.50 per card version (specify version).
Time: [45–60] minutes.
Comments: Publisher recommends (a) training and experience in projective testing and in working with adolescents, and (b) that the test be used as one component of a comprehensive battery of measures.
Authors: Leigh Silverton; illustrated by Laurie Harden.
Publisher: Western Psychological Services.
Cross References: For reviews by David M. Kaplan and Molly L. Vanduser and by Jody L. Swartz-Kulstad, see 14:7.

[66]
Adolescent Chemical Dependency Inventory.

Purpose: "Designed for assessing troubled youth in school settings, counseling or treatment programs."
Population: Ages 14-17.
Publication Dates: 1988-1998.
Acronym: ACDI.
Scores, 5: Truthfulness, Alcohol, Drugs, Adjustment, Distress.
Administration: Group.
Price Data, 2016: $9.95 per test; volume discounts available.
Foreign Language Edition: Spanish version available.
Time: (15-20) minutes.
Comments: May be administered via paper and pencil, computer, or human voice audio.
Author: Behavior Data Systems, Ltd.
Publisher: Behavior Data Systems, Ltd.

[67]
Adolescent Coping Scale.

Purpose: Assesses 18 possible coping strategies used by adolescents and young adults in dealing with stress.
Population: Ages 12–18.

Publication Dates: 1993–1997.
Acronym: ACS.
Scores, 18: Seek Social Support, Focus on Solving the Problem, Work Hard and Achieve, Worry, Invest in Close Friends, Seek to Belong, Wishful Thinking, Not Coping, Tension Reduction, Social Action, Ignore the Problem, Self-Blame, Keep to Self, Seek Spiritual Support, Focus on the Positive, Seek Professional Help, Seek Relaxing Diversions, Physical Recreation.
Administration: Group.
Price Data, 2005: A$121 per complete kit including manual (48 pages) and all required material in a notebook; A$24.95 per 10 questionnaires (short form); A$24.95 per 10 questionnaires (long form); A$11.55 per 10 scoring sheets; A$11.55 per 10 profile charts; A$51.80 per manual.
Time: 10 minutes for Long Form; 3 minutes for Short Form.
Authors: Erica Frydenberg and Ramon Lewis.
Publisher: Australian Council for Educational Research Ltd. [Australia; Efforts to obtain updated information from the test publisher were unsuccessful. An updated edition of this test appears on the test publisher's website].
Cross References: See T5:72 (3 references); for reviews by Frederick T. L. Leong and Judy J. Oehler-Stinnett, see 13:8.

[68]
Adolescent Diagnostic Interview.

Purpose: Designed to assess "psychoactive substance use disorders" and other health behaviors.
Population: Ages 12–18.
Publication Dates: 1993-2014.
Acronym: ADI.
Scores: 9 sections: Sociodemographic Factors, Psychosocial Stressors, Substance Use/Consumption History, Alcohol Use DSM-5 Symptoms, Cannabis Use DSM-5 Symptoms, Additional Drug Use DSM-5 Symptoms, Level of Functioning Domains, Orientation and Memory Screen, Psychiatric Status Screens (Depression, Mania, Eating Disorder, Delusional Thinking, Hallucinations, Attention Deficit Hyperactivity Disorder, Anxiety Disorder, Conduct Disorder).
Administration: Individual.
Price Data: Available at no charge from first author.
Time: (45–75) minutes.
Comments: Structured interview for use with adolescents aligned with the DSM-5; complements the Personal Experience Inventory (1499).
Authors: Ken C. Winters and George A. Henly.
Publisher: Ken C. Winters.
Cross References: See T5:73 (1 reference); for reviews by Tony Toneatto and by Logan Wright, Donna Ford, and Karyll Kiser of an earlier version aligned with DSM-III-R (1993), see 12:16.

[69]
Adolescent Dissociative Experiences Scale.
Purpose: Designed as a "screening measure for pathological dissociation during adolescence."
Population: Ages 11–17.
Publication Date: 1996.
Acronym: A-DES.
Scores, 5: Dissociative Amnesia, Absorption and Imaginative Involvement, Depersonalization and Derealization, Passive Influence, Total.
Administration: Individual or group.
Price Data, 2016: $12 per PDF download.
Time: (10–15) minutes.
Comments: A 30-item self-report measure, derived from the Dissociative Experiences Scale (original adult version) (670).
Authors: Judith Armstrong, Frank Putnam, and Eve Carlson.
Publisher: The Sidran Institute.
Cross References: For reviews by Rosemary Flanagan and Ramasamy Manikam, see 14:8.

[70]
Adolescent Drinking Index.
Purpose: Constructed to "assess alcohol abuse in adolescents with psychological, emotional, or behavioral problems; identify referred adolescents who need further evaluation or treatment; and define the type of drinking problem the adolescent is experiencing."
Population: Ages 12–17.
Publication Dates: 1985–1989.
Acronym: ADI.
Scores, 3: Self-Medicated Drinking (MED), Aggressive/Rebellious Behavior (REB), Total.
Administration: Group or individual.
Price Data, 2015: $104 per Introductory Kit including manual (1989, 34 pages) and 25 test booklets.
Time: (5) minutes.
Comments: Test booklet title is Drinking & You.
Authors: Adele V. Harrell and Philip W. Wirtz.
Publisher: Psychological Assessment Resources, Inc.
Cross References: See T5:75 (1 reference); for reviews by Thomas F. Donlon and by Kevin J. McCarthy and Penelope W. Dralle, see 12:17.

[71]
Adolescent Language Screening Test.
Purpose: "Developed to screen for deficits in the dimensions of language use, content, and form" in adolescents.
Population: Ages 11–17.
Publication Date: 1984.
Acronym: ALST.
Scores: 7 subtests: Pragmatics, Receptive Vocabulary, Concepts, Expressive Vocabulary, Sentence Formulation, Morphology, Phonology.

Administration: Individual.
Price Data, 2015: $168 per complete kit including 50 test booklets, picture book, and examiner's manual (26 pages); $48 per 25 test booklets; $85 per picture book; $48 per examiner's manual.
Time: (10–15) minutes.
Authors: Denise L. Morgan and Arthur M. Guilford.
Publisher: PRO-ED.
Cross References: For reviews by Linda Crocker and by Robert T. Williams and Amy Finch-Williams, see 10:10.

[72]
Adolescent Psychopathology Scale.
Purpose: Designed to "evaluate symptoms of psychological disorders and distress in adolescents ... measures psychopathology, personality, and social-emotional problems and competencies."
Population: Ages 12–19.
Publication Date: 1998.
Acronym: APS.
Scores: 40 scales in 4 domains: Clinical Disorders Domain (Attention-Deficit/Hyperactivity Disorder, Conduct Disorder, Oppositional-Defiant Disorder, Adjustment Disorder, Substance Abuse Disorder, Anorexia Nervosa, Bulimia Nervosa, Sleep Disorder, Somatization Disorder, Panic Disorder, Obsessive-Compulsive Disorder, Generalized Anxiety Disorder, Social Phobia, Separation Anxiety Disorder, Posttraumatic Stress Disorder, Major Depression, Dysthymic Disorder, Mania, Depersonalization Disorder, Schizophrenia); Personality Disorder Domain (Avoidant, Obsessive-Compulsive, Borderline, Schizotypal, Paranoid); Psychosocial Problem Content Domain (Self-Concept, Psycho-social Substance Use Difficulties, Introversion, Alienation-Boredom, Anger, Aggression, Interpersonal Problems, Emotional Lability, Disorientation, Suicide, Social Adaptation; Response Style Indicators (Lie, Consistency, Infrequency, Critical Item Endorsement); Factor Scales (Internalizing Disorder Factor, Externalizing Disorder Factor, Personality Disorder Factor).
Administration: Individual or group.
Price Data, 2015: $460 per introductory kit including administration and interpretation manual, psychometric and technical manual, and 25 test booklets, and scoring program with on-screen help and quick start guide.
Time: (45–60) minutes.
Comments: A 346-item self-report scale; developed to be consistent with the DSM-IV disorders; test form is entitled Adolescent Mental Health Questionnaire; software for computerized (Windows) scoring program included.
Author: William M. Reynolds.
Publisher: Psychological Assessment Resources, Inc.
Cross References: For reviews by Timothy R. Konold and Wayne C. Piersel, see 14:9.

[73]

Adolescent Psychopathology Scale—Short Form.

Purpose: Constructed as a "multidimensional measure of psychopathology and personality characteristics derived from the APS to evaluate symptoms of psychological disorder and distress consistent with DSM-IV symptom specifications."

Population: Ages 12–19 years.

Publication Dates: 1998–2000.

Acronym: APS-SF.

Scores, 14: Defensiveness, Consistency Response, Conduct Disorder, Oppositional Defiant Disorder, Substance Abuse Disorder, Anger/Violence Proneness, Academic Problems, Generalized Anxiety Disorder, Posttraumatic Stress Disorder, Major Depression, Eating Disturbance, Suicide, Self-Concept, Interpersonal Problems.

Administration: Group or individual.

Price Data, 2015: $295 per Introductory kit including scoring program (CD-ROM) with on-screen help and quick start guide, professional manual, and 25 test booklets.

Time: (15–20) minutes.

Comments: Derived from the Adolescent Psychopathology Scale (APS; 72).

Author: William M. Reynolds.

Publisher: Psychological Assessment Resources, Inc.

Cross References: For reviews by Janet F. Carlson and Steven I. Pfeiffer, see 15:11.

[74]

Adolescent Substance Abuse Subtle Screening Inventory–A2.

Purpose: "Designed to screen for the presence or absence of substance use disorders."

Population: Ages 12 to 18.

Publication Dates: 1990-2013.

Acronym: SASSI-A2.

Scores, 12: Face Valid Alcohol, Face Valid Other Drug, Family-Friends Risk, Attitudes, Symptoms, Obvious Attributes, Subtle Attributes, Defensiveness, Supplemental Addiction Measure, Correctional, Validity Check, Secondary Classification Scale.

Administration: Individual or group.

Price Data, 2015: $135 per small starter kit including manual (2001, 74 pages), user's guide, scoring key, and 25 paper tests and profiles; $235 per large starter kit including manual, user's guide, scoring key, and 100 tests and profiles; $55 per 25 tests; $10 per scoring key; $35 per user's guide; $45 per manual.

Time: (15) minutes.

Comments: May be administered via paper and pencil with hand scoring or optical scanning, computer software for PC, or online; audio CD is available for people with special needs regarding vision or literacy.

Authors: Glenn A. Miller (inventory and user's guide), Franklin G. Miller (manual), and Linda E. Lazowski (manual and user's guide).

Publisher: The SASSI Institute.

Cross References: Reviews are scheduled for *The Twentieth Mental Measurements Yearbook*.

[75]

Adult Attention Deficit Disorders Evaluation Scale.

Purpose: Designed to provide a measure of inattention and hyperactivity-impulsivity in adults.

Population: Adults.

Publication Dates: 1996–1997.

Scores, 3: Inattentive, Hyperactive-Impulsive, Total Percentile Rank.

Administration: Individual.

Price Data, 2015: $226 per complete kit including 50 Self-Report Rating Forms, 50 Home Version Rating Forms, 50 Work Version Rating Forms, Self-Report Technical Manual (1996, 43 pages), Home Version Technical Manual (1996, 41 pages), Work Version Technical Manual (1996, 40 pages), and Adult Attention Deficit Disorders Intervention Manual (1997, 183 pages); $4 per 50 rating forms (specify Self-Report, Home Version, or Work Version); $25 per 50 ADDES/DSM-IV forms; $21 per technical manual (specify Self-Report, Home Version, or Work Version); $25 per Adult Attention Deficit Disorders Intervention manual.

Time: Untimed.

Comments: Behavioral rating system with three forms: Home, Work, and Self-Report; may be completed in one sitting or over a period of days.

Authors: Stephen B. McCarney and Paul D. Anderson.

Publisher: Hawthorne Educational Services, Inc.

    a) HOME VERSION.

    Comments: To be completed by a spouse or other close relative/friend who observes daily behavior in the home; best when used in conjunction with Work and Self-Report versions.

    b) WORK VERSION.

    Comments: To be completed by an employer, supervisor, or fellow employee who can closely observe the subject's work behaviors; best when used in conjunction with Work and Self-Report versions.

Cross References: For reviews by Helen Kitchens and James C. Reed, see 14:10.

[76]

Adult Level of Care Index-2R.

Purpose: "To provide assessment summation and documentation for addictions treatment planning."

Population: Adults.

Publication Date: 2001.

Acronym: LOCI-2R.

Scores: 56 ratings: 5 Acute Intoxication/Withdrawal (Outpatient Detoxification, Ambulatory Detoxification

with Extended On-Site Monitoring, Clinically Managed Residential Detoxification, Medically Monitored Inpatient Detoxification, Medically Managed Intensive Inpatient Detoxification); 8 Biomedical Conditions/ Complications (Outpatient Treatment, Intensive Outpatient Treatment, Partial Hospitalization, Clinically Managed Low-/Medium-/High-Intensity Residential Treatment, Medically Monitored Intensive Inpatient, Medically Managed Inpatient Services); 9 Emotional, Behavioral, or Cognitive Conditions and Complications (Early Intervention, Outpatient Services, Intensive Outpatient, Partial Hospitalization, Clinically Managed Low-/Medium-/High-Intensity Residential Treatment, Medically Monitored Intensive Inpatient Services, Medically Managed Inpatient Services); 9 Readiness to Change (Early Intervention, Outpatient Services, Intensive Outpatient Treatment, Partial Hospitalization, Clinically Managed Low-/Medium-/High-Intensity Residential Treatment, Medically Monitored Inpatient Treatment, Medically Managed Inpatient Treatment); 9 Relapse, Continued Use, or Continued Problem Potential (Early Intervention, Outpatient Treatment, Intensive Outpatient Treatment, Partial Hospitalization, Clinically Managed Low-/Medium-/High-Intensity Residential Treatment, Medically Monitored Intensive Inpatient, Medically Managed Inpatient Treatment); 9 Recovery Environment (Early Intervention, Outpatient Treatment, Intensive Outpatient Treatment, Partial Hospitalization, Clinically Managed Low-/Medium-/High-Intensity Residential Treatment, Medically Monitored Inpatient Treatment, Medically Managed Inpatient Treatment); 6 Opioid Maintenance Therapy (Acute Intoxication/Withdrawal; Biomedical Conditions and Complications; Emotional, Behavioral, or Cognitive Conditions and Complications; Readiness to Change; Relapse, Continued Use, or Continued Problem Potential; Recovery Environment); Level of Care Indicated.
Administration: Individual.
Price Data, 2016: $78.75 per 25 assessments.
Time: Variable.
Comments: Not a psychometric instrument; summary checklist provides an estimate of the likelihood that an individual meets the criteria for substance abuse or dependency on six dimensions in accordance with the criteria of the American Society of Addiction Medicine; also indicates overall level of care needed.
Authors: Norman G. Hoffmann, David Mee-Lee, and Gerald D. Shulman.
Publisher: Change Companies.

[77]

The Adult Manifest Anxiety Scale.

Purpose: Used to evaluate the level of anxiety experienced by individuals across the age spectrum from early adulthood to elderly.

Population: Ages 19–59, college students, ages 60 and over.
Publication Date: 2003.
Administration: Group.
Levels, 3: AMAS-A, AMAS-C, AMAS-E.
Price Data, 2016: $131.50 per kit including 30 AutoScore™ answer forms (10 for each subtest) and manual (44 pages); $46.50 per 20 AutoScore™ answer forms (specify adult, elderly or college); $65.50 per manual.
Time: 10 minutes.
Comments: All three scales together represent an upward extension of the Revised Children's Manifest Anxiety Scale (1720); the original CMAS was a downward extension of the Taylor Manifest Anxiety Scale.
Authors: Cecil R. Reynolds, Bert O. Richmond, and Patricia A. Lowe.
Publisher: Western Psychological Services.
  a) AMAS-A.
  Population: Ages 19–59.
  Acronym: AMAS-A.
  Scores, 5: Worry/Oversensitivity, Physiological Anxiety, Social Concerns/Stress, Lie, Worry.
  b) AMAS-C.
  Population: College students.
  Acronym: AMAS-C.
  Scores, 6: Worry/Oversensitivity, Physiological Anxiety, Social Concerns/Stress, Test Anxiety, Lie, Total.
  c) AMAS-E.
  Population: Ages 60 and over.
  Acronym: AMAS-E.
  Scores, 5: Worry/Oversensitivity, Physiological Anxiety, Fear of Aging, Lie, Total.
Cross References: For a review by Ashraf Kagee, see 16:7.

[78]

Adult Personality Inventory [Revised].

Purpose: Designed to analyze "individual differences in personality, interpersonal style, and career/lifestyle preferences."
Population: Ages 16–adult.
Publication Dates: 1982–1996.
Acronym: API.
Scores: 25: Personality Scores (Extroverted, Adjusted, Tough-Minded, Independent, Disciplined, Creative, Enterprising); Interpersonal Style Scores (Caring, Adapting, Withdrawn, Submissive, Hostile, Rebellious, Sociable, Assertive); Career/Life-style Scores (Practical, Scientific, Aesthetic, Social, Competitive, Structured); Validity Scores (Good Impression, Bad Impression, Infrequency, Uncertainty).
Administration: Group or individual.
Time: (45–60) minutes.
Comments: Self-report; computer scored and interpreted.
Authors: Samuel E. Krug.
Publisher: Institute for Personality and Ability Testing, Inc. (IPAT).

Cross References: For a review by Kevin Lanning, see 14:12; for a review by Rik Carl D'Amato of an earlier edition (1988), see 12:20; see also T4:106 (4 references); for a review by Brian Bolton of an earlier edition (1984), see 9:54.

[79]

The Adult Self Expression Scale.

Purpose: Assesses the assertiveness level of the respondent.
Population: Adults.
Publication Dates: 1974-1975.
Acronym: ASES.
Scores: Total score only.
Administration: Group or individual.
Price Data: Available at no charge from test publisher.
Time: Administration time not reported.
Authors: Melvin L. Gay, James G. Hollandsworth, Jr., and John P. Galassi.
Publisher: Adult Self Expression Scale.
Cross References: See T5:88 (2 references) and T4:107 (1 reference); for reviews by Philip H. Dreyer and Goldine C. Gleser, see 9:55 (15 references).

[80]

Adult Self-Report Inventory-4.

Purpose: Designed to be "a guide for conducting clinical interviews" and be used "as a tool to assist the clinician in making a diagnosis" and to help identify possible psychiatric disorders.
Population: Ages 18-75.
Publication Dates: 2004-2008.
Acronyms: ASRI-4; AI-4.
Scores, 20: Symptom Severity Score (Normative Data Model): Anxiety Disorders, Mood Disorders, Eating Disorders, Somatoform Disorders, Psychotic Disorders, Sleep Disorders, Impulse Control Disorders, Personality Disorders, Child-Onset Disorders, Other Disorders; Symptom Count Cutoff Score (Diagnostic Model): Anxiety Disorders, Mood Disorders, Eating Disorders, Somatoform Disorders, Psychotic Disorders, Sleep Disorders, Impulse Control Disorders, Personality Disorders, Child-Onset Disorders, Other Disorders.
Administration: Individual.
Forms, 2: Adult Self Report Inventory-4, Adult Inventory-4.
Price Data, 2015: $124 per Deluxe Kit including manual (2004, 173 pages), 50 Adult Self-Report Inventories-4, 5 Adult Inventories-4, 50 Symptom Count score sheets, and 50 Symptom Severity Profile score sheets; $63 per 50 copies of Adult Self-Report Inventory-4 Checklist in English or Spanish or 50 copies of Adult Inventory-4 Checklist in English or Spanish; $49 per manual.
Foreign Language Edition: Spanish edition available.
Time: (15-20) minutes.

Comments: The assessments are taken by the patient and by a person who knows the patient well "(e.g., parent, partner, roommate)."
Authors: Kenneth D. Gadow, Joyce Sprafkin, and Margaret D. Weiss.
Publisher: Checkmate Plus, Ltd.
Cross References: For reviews by Tony Cellucci and by Beth Doll and Jonathon Sikorski, see 19:1.

[81]

Adult Suicidal Ideation Questionnaire.

Purpose: "Designed to evaluate the presence and frequency of suicidal thoughts."
Population: Ages 18 and over.
Publication Dates: 1987–1991.
Acronym: ASIQ.
Scores: Total score only.
Administration: Individual or group.
Price Data, 2015: $102 per introductory kit including manual (1991, 62 pages) and 25 respondent forms.
Time: (5–10) minutes.
Author: William M. Reynolds.
Publisher: Psychological Assessment Resources, Inc.
Cross References: See T5:89 (1 reference); for reviews by Debra E. Cole and Isadore Newman, see 12:21.

[82]

Advanced Management Practices.

Purpose: Designed to assess the ability of managers to move toward full strategic responsibility.
Population: Directors and functional managers.
Publication Dates: 1996-2009.
Acronym: AMP.
Scores, 21: Envisioning Opportunities, Establishing Goals, Innovation/Risk-Taking, Market Insight, Business & Financial Acumen, Collaborative Planning, Customer Focus, Clarity of Communications, Cross Team Collaboration/Influence, Empowering Employees, Building a Team Environment, Coaching for Performance, Managing Conflict, Openness to Feedback, Standards of Performance, Persuasiveness, Goal Pressure, Recognizing & Rewarding Others, Trustworthiness/Integrity, Tension Level, Overall Effectiveness.
Administration: Individual.
Price Data: Available from publisher.
Time: 20-30 minutes.
Comments: Publisher suggests allowing 2-3 weeks to collect feedback.
Authors: Paul M. Connolly, Daniel Booth, and Clark L. Wilson.
Publisher: The Clark Wilson Group, Inc. (subsidiary of The Booth Company, Inc.).

[83]

Advanced Measures of Music Audiation.

Purpose: Developed to measure music aptitude.

Population: Junior high school through college.
Publication Date: 1989.
Scores, 3: Tonal, Rhythm, Total.
Administration: Group.
Price Data, 2015: $70 per complete kit including compact disc, 100 answer sheets, and manual (54 pages); $20 per 100 answer sheets; $10 per manual; $20 per set of scoring stencils (scoring stencils not part of complete kit); $25 per compact disc; scoring service available from publisher at $1 per student. Also available on CD-ROM: $49.95 for one computer, volume discounts available.
Time: 16(20) minutes.
Comments: CD player necessary for administration; upward extension of the Intermediate Measures of Music Audiation (996).
Author: Edwin E. Gordon.
Publisher: GIA Publications, Inc.
Cross References: For reviews by Rudolf E. Radocy and James W. Sherbon, see 12:22.

[84]

Advanced Multi-Dimensional Personality Matrix Abridged—Big 5 Personality Test.

Purpose: Designed to "measure five main personality traits ... for personal and professional development."
Population: Under age 17 through adult.
Publication Date: 2011.
Acronym: AMPM-Ab.
Scores, 5: Emotional Stability, Extroversion, Openness, Agreeableness, Conscientiousness.
Administration: Individual.
Price Data: Available from publisher.
Time: (15) minutes.
Comments: Self-administered online assessment. The test publisher provides clients with information about the methods and theoretical basis used in the development of the test as well as benchmarks for relevant industries and racial/ethnic group comparison data.
Author: PsychTests AIM, Inc.
Publisher: PsychTests AIM, Inc. [Canada].
Cross References: For reviews by Sandra M. Harris and Steven V. Rouse, see 19:2.

[85]

Advanced Test Battery.

Purpose: "Designed for use in the selection, development, or guidance of personnel at graduate level or in management positions."
Population: Personnel at graduate level or in management positions.
Publication Dates: 1979–1983.
Acronym: ATB.
Administration: Group.
Levels, 2: Higher order aptitudes, Higher order aptitudes in a work setting.

Restricted Distribution: Restricted to persons who have completed the publisher's training course or members of the Division of Occupational Psychology of the British Psychological Society.
Price Data: Available from publisher.
Comments: Subtests available as separates; separate answer sheets must be used.
Authors: Roger Holdsworth (VA3, NA4, manual); Peter Saville (VA1, NA2, manual), Gill Nyfield (manual), Dave Hawkey (DA5, ST7, DT8), Steve Blinkhorn (VA3), and Alan Iliff (NA4).
Publisher: CEB.
    a) LEVEL 1. 1979–1980; HIGHER ORDER APTITUDES, 3 TESTS.
        1) Verbal Concepts.
        Publication Date: 1980.
        Acronym: VA1.
        Time: 15(20) minutes.
        2) Number Series.
        Publication Date: 1980.
        Acronym: NA2.
        Time: 15(20) minutes.
        3) Diagramming.
        Publication Date: 1980.
        Acronym: DA5.
        Time: 20(25) minutes.
    b) LEVEL 2. 1979–1980; HIGHER ORDER APTITUDES IN A WORK CONTEST; 4 TESTS.
        1) Verbal Critical Reasoning.
        Publication Date: 1983.
        Acronym: VA3.
        Time: 30(35) minutes.
        2) Numerical Critical Reasoning.
        Publication Dates: 1979–1983.
        Acronym: NA4.
        Time: 35(40) minutes.
        3) Spatial Reasoning.
        Publication Dates: 1979–1981.
        Acronym: ST7.
        Time: 20(25) minutes.
        4) Diagrammatic Reasoning.
        Publication Dates: 1979–1981.
        Acronym: DT8.
        Time: 15(20) minutes.

[86]

Advocacy/Inquiry Skill Inventory.

Purpose: Designed to "assess preference for using advocacy and inquiry communication skills."
Population: Employees.
Publication Date: 1997.
Scores, 6: Initiating Communication, Comprehending Others, Being Direct, Respecting Others, Advocacy, Inquiry.
Administration: Individual.
Price Data, 2016: $9.95 per instrument; $32.95 per facilitator's guide and sample instrument.
Time: Administration time not reported.
Authors: Kittie W. Watson and Larry L. Barker.
Publisher: Innolect, Inc.

[87]

Affair–Spouse's Comprehensive Worksheets.

Purpose: Designed to "analyze the spouse's reaction to [an] affair, the impact on the marriage and everyone involved, decisions that need to be made and what needs to be done to solve the problems caused by the affair."
Population: Spouses of persons who had an affair.
Publication Dates: 1996-2010.
Scores: 14 sections: Therapy, Marriage Before the Affair, Pre-Affair, Spouse's Relationship with the Lover, Cheating Opinions, Keeping It Secret, Reaction to the Affair, Others Finding Out, Spouse's Reaction, Effects on the Person, Sex After the Affair, Decisions and Planning, Repairing the Marriage, Other Problems.
Administration: Individual.
Manual: Instructions included with the worksheet.
Price Data: Available from publisher.
Time: [20-60] minutes.
Author: Allan Roe.
Publisher: Diagnostic Specialists, Inc.

[88]

Age Projection Test.

Purpose: Designed as "an imagery test aimed at revealing self-images at various age [and self] levels and their associated structures of imagery functioning useful toward the understanding of a presented problem or a symptom."
Population: Adults.
Publication Date: 1988.
Acronym: APT.
Scores: No scores.
Administration: Individual.
Price Date, 2016: $15 spiral-bound paperback.
Time: [60–120] minutes.
Author: Akhter Ahsen.
Publisher: Brandon House, Inc. [Eidetic Image Psychology, distributor]
Cross References: For reviews by Edward Aronow and Michael D. Botwin, see 12:23.

[89]

Ages & Stages Questionnaires®: A Parent-Completed Child Monitoring System, Third Edition.

Purpose: Designed to "screen young children for developmental delays-that is, to identify those children who are in need of further evaluation and those who appear to be developing typically."
Population: Ages 1 to 66 months.
Publication Dates: 1995-2009.
Acronym: ASQ-3 (tm).
Scores, 5: Communication, Gross Motor, Fine Motor, Problem Solving, Personal-Social.
Administration: Individual.

Levels, 21: 2, 4, 6, 8, 9, 10, 12, 14, 16, 18, 20, 22, 24, 27, 30, 33, 36, 42, 48, 54, and 60 months.
Price Data, 2015: $275 per starter kit including 21 copies of questionnaires and scoring sheets, CD-ROM, user's guide (2009, 256 pages), and quick start guide; $275 per starter kit with Spanish questionnaires; $225 per 21 questionnaires, scoring sheets, and CD-ROM in English or Spanish; $50 per user's guide.
Foreign Language Edition: The questionnaires and Quick-Start Guide are available in Spanish and French.
Time: (10-15) minutes.
Comments: The questionnaire is to be completed by the child's primary caregiver in the home; the authors state, however, that "professionals will need to establish the screening and monitoring system, develop the necessary community interfaces, train individuals who will score the questionnaires, and provide feedback to parents of children who are completing the questionnaires."
Authors: Jane Squires and Diane Bricker (questionnaires and user's guide); Elizabeth Twombly and LaWanda Potter (user's guide only).
Publisher: Paul H. Brookes Publishing Co., Inc.
Cross References: For reviews by Kenneth M. Hanig and by Rachel J. Valleley and Brandy M. Roane, see 18:4; for reviews by B. Ann Boyce and G. Michael Poteat of the second edition, see 16:8; for reviews by Dorothy M. Singleton and Rhonda H. Solomon of the original edition, see 14:14.

[90]

Ages & Stages Questionnaires: Social-Emotional, Second Edition.

Purpose: "Designed to identify infants and young children who need more comprehensive assessment of their social-emotional behavioral repertoire."
Population: Ages 1 to 72 months.
Publication Dates: 2002-2015.
Acronym: ASQ:SE-2.
Scores: Total score only.
Administration: Individual.
Levels, 9: 2, 6, 12, 18, 24, 30, 36, 48, and 60 month questionnaires.
Price Data, 2016: $275 per starter kit including reproducible masters of the questionnaires and scoring sheets, CD-ROM with printable PDF questionnaires, user's guide, and quick start guide; $225 per reproducible master copies on paper and printable PDF master copies on CD-ROM; $50 per user's guide (2015, 315 pages); $24.95 per quick start guide.
Foreign Language Edition: Spanish version available.
Time: (10-15) minutes.
Comments: The ASQ:SE-2 "should be used in conjunction with ASQ-3 [Ages & Stages Questionnaires, Third Edition; 89] or another screening measure that

provides more broad-based information about children's developmental status"; parent-completed questionnaires.

Authors: Jane Squires, Diane Bricker, and Elizabeth Twombly.

Publisher: Paul H. Brookes Publishing Co., Inc.

Cross References: Reviews are scheduled for *The Twentieth Mental Measurements Yearbook*. For a review by John J. Vacca of the original edition, see 16:9.

[91]
Aggression Questionnaire.

Purpose: Designed to aid in evaluating an individual's aggressive responses and ability to channel those responses in a safe and constructive manner.

Population: Ages 9–88.

Publication Date: 2000.

Scores, 7: Physical Aggression, Verbal Aggression, Anger, Hostility, Indirect Aggression, Inconsistent Responding, Total Score.

Administration: Individual or group.

Price Data, 2016: $118 per complete kit including 25 AutoScore™ forms and manual; $52.50 per 25 AutoScore™ answer forms; $280.50 per 25-use administration, scoring and interpretation CD; $20.50 per 100 answer sheets; $74 per manual (2000, 95 pages).

Time: (10) minutes.

Comments: Updated version of the Buss-Durkee Hostility Inventory.

Authors: Arnold H. Buss and W. L. Warren.

Publisher: Western Psychological Services.

Cross References: For reviews by Johnnie A. Brown and Mary Lou Kelley, see 15:13.

[92]
Air Conditioning Specialist (Form SWA-C).

Purpose: For selecting candidates with knowledge of air conditioning.

Population: Applicants and incumbents for jobs requiring air conditioning knowledge and skills.

Publication Dates: 1992–2008.

Scores, 7: Print Reading/Electrical/and Test Equipment, Controls, Welding/Piping and Plumbing, Mechanical Maintenance and Machines & Equipment, Heating & Ventilation and Combustion, Air Conditioning and Refrigeration, Total.

Administration: Group.

Price Data, 2015: $24 per consumable self-scoring test booklet (minimum order of 20); $24.95 per manual (2008, 16 pages); $26 per online test administration.

Foreign Language Edition: Available in Spanish.

Time: (60-70) minutes.

Comments: Online test administration available.

Author: Roland T. Ramsay.

Publisher: Ramsay Corporation.

Cross References: For a review by James A. Penny, see 17:5.

[93]
The Alcadd Test, Revised Edition.

Purpose: "Designed to: a) provide an objective measurement of alcoholic addiction that could identify individuals whose behavior and personality structure indicated that they were alcoholic addicts or had serious alcoholic problems; b) identify specific areas of maladjustment in alcoholics to facilitate therapeutic and rehabilitation activities; and c) obtain better insight into the psychodynamics of alcoholic addiction."

Population: Adults.

Publication Dates: 1949–1988.

Scores, 6: Regularity of Drinking, Preference for Drinking over Other Activities, Lack of Controlled Drinking, Rationalization of Drinking, Excessive Emotionality, Total.

Administration: Individual or group.

Price Data, 2016: $101.50 per complete kit including 25 AutoScore™ test/profile forms (1988, 4 pages) and manual (1988, 24 pages); $52.50 per 25 AutoScore™ test booklets; $62.50 per manual.

Time: (5–15) minutes.

Comments: Self-administered.

Authors: Morse P. Manson, Lisa A. Melchior, and G. J. Huba.

Publisher: Western Psychological Services.

Cross References: For reviews by William L. Curlette and Paul Retzlaff, see 11:12 (1 reference); see also T3:152 (3 references), T2:1098 (1 reference), and P:7 (3 references); for a review by Dugal Campbell, see 6:60 (6 references); for reviews by Charles H. Honzik and Albert L. Hunsicker, see 4:30.

[94]
Alcohol Dependence Scale.

Purpose: "Provides a brief measure of the extent to which the use of alcohol has progressed from psychological involvement to impaired control."

Population: Problem drinkers.

Publication Date: 1984.

Acronym: ADS.

Scores: Total score only.

Administration: Group.

Price Data, 2016: $11 per 25 scales.

Foreign Language Edition: Questionnaire available in French.

Time: (5–10) minutes.

Comments: Test booklet title is Alcohol Use Questionnaire.

Authors: Harvey A. Skinner and John L. Horn.

Publisher: Centre for Addiction and Mental Health [Canada].

Cross References: See T5:134 (41 references) and T4:145 (5 references); for reviews by Robert E. Deysach and Nick J. Piazza, see 10:12 (1 reference).

[95]

Alcohol Use Disorders Identification Test.

Purpose: A screening procedure "to identify persons whose alcohol consumption has become hazardous or harmful to their health."
Population: Adults.
Publication Dates: 1992–1993.
Acronym: AUDIT.
Scores: Total score only.
Administration: Individual or group.
Price Data: Test and manual (88 pages) available at no charge from test publisher.
Foreign Language Editions: Available in Japanese, Spanish, Norwegian, Romanian, Portuguese, German, Indian, French, Swedish, Russian, Catalan, and Italian.
Time: [2] minutes.
Comments: Developed by World Health Organization and validated on primary care patients in six countries.
Authors: Thomas F. Babor, Juan Ramon de la Fuente, John Saunders, O. G. Aasland, and Marcus Grant.
Publisher: World Health Organization [Switzerland].
Cross References: For reviews by Philip Ash and Herbert Bischoff, see 14:15; see T5:135 (6 references).

[96]

Alcohol Use Inventory.

Purpose: To assess patterns of behavior, attitudes, and symptoms associated with alcohol use and abuse.
Population: Individuals 16 years and older.
Publication Date: 1987.
Acronym: AUI.
Scores, 24: Social Improvement, Mental Improvement, Manage Moods, Marital Coping, Gregarious, Compulsive, Sustained, Loss of Control, Role Maladaptation, Delirium, Hangover, Marital Problems, Quantity, Guilt and Worry, Help Before, Receptivity, Awareness, Enhanced, Obsessed, Disruption 1, Disruption 2, Anxious Concern, Receptive Awareness, Alcohol Involvement.
Administration: Group.
Price Data, 2015: $53.50 per manual (1987, 95 pages); $18.15 per 10 reusable test booklets; $34.35 per 50 hand-scoring answer sheets with 50 profile forms; $27.65 per mail-in interpretive report; $16.65 per mail-in profile report.
Time: (35–60) minutes.
Comments: Scoring options are hand scoring, mail-in scoring, or Q Local software; report options are Interpretive or Profile.
Authors: John L. Horn, Kenneth W. Wanberg, and F. Mark Foster.
Publisher: Pearson.
Cross References: See T5:136 (12 references); for reviews by Robert J. Drummond and Sharon McNeely, see 12:25 (3 references); see also T4:146 (6 references).

[97]

Alleman Mentoring Activities Questionnaire.

Purpose: "Measures the amount, quality and impact of mentoring activity."
Population: Mentors, proteges, and bosses.
Publication Dates: 1987–2000.
Acronym: AMAQ.
Scores, 10: Teach the Job, Provide Challenge, Teach Politics, Career Help, Protect, Sponsor, Counsel, Friendship, Demonstrate Trust, Total.
Administration: Group or individual.
Price Data, 2011: $25 per pair for assessment and graph report; student, research, and large sample discounts available from publisher; sample test and manual are available through email for $25.
Time: (10–15) minutes.
Comments: Previously listed as Alleman Mentoring Scales Questionnaire; available in paper-and-pencil or electronic format. The test publisher has indicated there is a newer edition of this test; description will be updated when complete test materials are received.
Authors: Elizabeth Alleman and Diana Clarke.
Publisher: Silverwood Enterprises, LLC
Cross References: See T5:139 (1 reference).

[98]

Alternate Uses.

Purpose: "Designed to represent an expected factor of 'flexibility of thinking' in an investigation of creative thinking."
Population: Individuals with a fifth-grade reading level or higher.
Publication Dates: 1960-1978.
Scores: Total score only.
Administration: Individual or group.
Forms, 2: B, C.
Price Data, 2015: $50 per manual, including a review-only copy of the test form; $2 per Remote Online Survey License (minimum 50); $2 per License to Reproduce (minimum 50).
Time: 8 minutes.
Comments: Also known as Guilford's Alternate Uses.
Authors: J. P. Guilford, Paul R. Christensen, Philip R. Merrifield, and Robert C. Wilson.
Publisher: Mind Garden, Inc.
Cross References: See T5:142 (8 references) and T4:154 (4 references); for a review by Edys S. Quellmalz, see 9:71 (3 references); see also T3:157 (21 references), 8:235 (32 references), T2:542 (94 references), and 6:542 (7 references).

[99]

Am I Musical? Music Audiation Games.

Purpose: Designed to objectively reveal a general estimate of the extent of music potential a child or adult possesses.

Population: Ages 7–12, 13–adult.
Publication Date: 2003.
Score: Total score only.
Administration: Group.
Levels, 2: Youth Game, Adult Game.
Price Data: Available from publisher.
Time: (12) minutes.
Comments: Test administered via CD; self-administered, self-scored.
Author: Edwin E. Gordon.
Publisher: GIA Publications, Inc.
Cross References: For reviews by Christopher M. Johnson and James W. Sherbon, see 16:12.

[100]
The AMA DISC Survey.
Purpose: Personal styles survey that focuses on the ways in which people approach their work and relate to others within their organization.
Population: Adults.
Publication Date: 2000.
Scores: 4 styles of behavior: Directing, Influencing, Supportive, Contemplative.
Administration: Individual or group.
Price Data: Available from publisher.
Time: 20–25 minutes.
Author: Robert A. Cooke.
Publisher: American Management Association [distributed by Human Synergistics International].

[101]
The American Drug and Alcohol Survey.
Purpose: Designed to estimate levels of drug use in youth populations.
Population: Schools and school districts.
Publication Dates: 1989–2005.
Scores: Item scores, High/Moderate/Low Drug Involvement.
Administration: Group.
Levels, 2: Grades 4–6, Grades 6–12.
Price Data: The publisher of this survey dissolved in 2011 and released the copyright; it may be used freely.
Time: (20–30) minutes.
Authors: Eugene R. Oetting, Frederick Beauvais, and Ruth Edwards.
Publisher: Rocky Mountain Behavioral Science Institute, Inc.
Cross References: See T5:143 (1 reference); for reviews by Jeffrey Jenkins and Steven Schinke, see 12:27; see also T4:155 (1 reference).

[102]
American Invitational Mathematics Examination.
Purpose: Designed to provide "challenge and recognition to high school students in the United States and Canada who have exceptional mathematical ability."
Population: U. S. and Canadian high school students.
Publication Dates: 1983–2016.
Acronym: AIME.
Score: Total score only.
Administration: Group.
Manual: No manual.
Price Data: Available from publisher.
Time: 180 minutes.
Comments: Administered annually in March.
Authors: Sponsored jointly by the Mathematical Association of America, Society of Actuaries, Mu Alpha Theta, National Council on Teachers of Mathematics, Casualty Actuarial Society, American Statistical Association, and American Mathematical Association of Two Year Colleges, and others.
Publisher: MAA American Mathematics Competition.
Cross References: For reviews by Robert W. Lissitz and Claudia R. Wright, see 11:14.

[103]
American Mathematics Competitions, Contest 8 (AMC 8).
Purpose: "To increase interest in mathematics and to develop problem solving ability through a friendly competition."
Population: American and Canadian students in grade 8 or below.
Publication Dates: 1985–2016.
Acronym: AMC 8.
Scores: Total score only.
Administration: Group.
Price Data: Available from publisher.
Foreign Language and Special Editions: Spanish, Braille, and large-print editions available.
Time: 40 minutes.
Comments: Test administered annually in November; test previously called American Junior High School Mathematics Examination.
Authors: Sponsored jointly by Mathematical Association of America, Society of Actuaries, Mu Alpha Theta, National Council of Teachers of Mathematics, Casualty Actuarial Society, American Statistical Association, and American Mathematical Association of Two Year Colleges.
Publisher: MAA American Mathematics Competition.
Cross References: For reviews by John M. Enger and Darrell Sabers, see 11:15.

[104]
American Mathematics Competitions, Contest 12 (AMC12).
Purpose: "To identify, through friendly competition, students with an interest and a talent for mathematical problem solving."

Population: High school students competing for individual and school awards.
Publication Dates: 1950–2016.
Acronym: AMC 12.
Scores: Total score only.
Administration: Group.
Price Data: Available from publisher.
Foreign Language and Special Editions: Spanish, French, Braille, and large-print editions available.
Time: (75) minutes.
Comments: Administered annually in February; test previously called American High School Mathematics Examination (AHSME).
Authors: Sponsored jointly by the Mathematical Association of America, Society of Actuaries, Mu Alpha Theta, National Council of Teachers of Mathematics, Casualty Actuarial Society, American Statistical Association, and American Mathematical Association of Two-Year Colleges, and others.
Publisher: MAA American Mathematics Competition.
Cross References: For reviews by Camilla Persson Benbow and Randy W. Kamphaus of the American High School Mathematics Examination, see 11:13; for a review by Thomas P. Hogan, see 8:252 (1 reference); see also T2:598 (3 references).

[105]
American Mathematics Contest 10.

Purpose: Designed to "spur interest in mathematics and to develop talent through the excitement of solving challenging problems."
Population: Grades 10 and below.
Publication Dates: 1999-2016.
Acronym: AMC 10.
Scores: Total score only.
Administration: Group.
Forms: Contest A, Contest B.
Price Data: Available from publisher.
Foreign Language and Special Editions: French, Spanish, Braille, and large-print editions available.
Time: (75) minutes.
Comments: Administered annually in February.
Authors: Sponsored jointly by Mathematical Association of America, Society of Actuaries, Mu Alpha Theta, National Council of Teachers of Mathematics, Casualty Actuarial Society, American Statistical Association, and American Mathematical Association of Two Year Colleges.
Publisher: MAA American Mathematics Competition.
Cross References: For reviews by Camilla Persson Benbow and Randy W. Kamphaus of the American High School Mathematics Examination, see 11:13; for a review by Thomas P. Hogan, see 8:252 (1 reference); see also T2:598 (3 references).

[106]
The American Occupational Therapy Association, Inc. Fieldwork Evaluation for the Occupational Therapist.

Purpose: Constructed to evaluate "student competence at the completion of each Level II fieldwork experience."
Population: Occupational therapy students.
Publication Dates: 1973–1987.
Scores, 3: Performance, Judgment, Attitude.
Administration: Individual.
Price Data: Available from publisher.
Time: Administration time not reported.
Comments: Ratings by supervisor; revision of the Field Work Performance Report (T3:885).
Author: The American Occupational Therapy Association, Inc.
Publisher: The American Occupational Therapy Association, Inc.
Cross References: For reviews by James T. Austin and Brian Bolton, see 12:28; for information on the Field Work Performance Report, see T3:885 (2 references) and 8:1107 (1 reference).

[107]
Amsterdam Short-Term Memory Test.

Purpose: Designed to be used in "neuropsychological evaluation of persons who claim to have memory and/ or concentration problems, but in whom these problems are not clinically obvious, while the possibility exists that they are exaggerating or simulating their problems."
Population: Individuals who claim to have memory and/or concentration problems, but do not have clinical symptoms.
Publication Dates: 1999-2005.
Acronym: ASTM.
Scores: Total score only.
Administration: Individual.
Price Data, 2016: €433 per complete kit including manual (2005, 75 pages), administration software, and record forms; €54 per manual; €38 per 100 test booklets.
Foreign Language Editions: Manual and record forms available in German and Dutch.
Time: (10-30) minutes.
Authors: Ben Schmand and Jaap Lindeboom with collaboration of Thomas Merten and Scott R. Millis.
Publisher: Hogrefe Ltd [United Kingdom].
Cross References: For a review by Daniel C. Miller, see 17:6.

[108]
Analytic Learning Disability Assessment.

Purpose: Designed to match student learning style with instructional strategies.
Population: Ages 8-14.
Publication Date: 1982.

Acronym: ALDA.
Scores: Fail, Weak, or Solid in 77 unit skill subtests.
Administration: Individual.
Price Data, 2015: $253.25 per complete kit; $84.50 per 20 test forms including test score formulation sheet and student worksheets.
Time: (75) minutes.
Authors: Thomas D. Gnagey and Patricia A. Gnagey.
Publisher: Slosson Educational Publications, Inc.
Cross References: For a review by Marcia B. Shaffer, see 9:72.

[109]

Analytical Aptitude Skills Evaluation.

Purpose: To evaluate aptitude and potential for analyzing business problems.
Population: Entry-level and experienced candidates for positions requiring the ability to analyze business problems.
Publication Date: 1993.
Acronym: AASE.
Scores, 4: Total Score, Narrative Evaluation, Rating, Recommendation.
Administration: Group.
Price Data: Available from publisher.
Foreign Language Edition: French version available.
Time: (60) minutes.
Comments: Scored by publisher; must be proctored.
Author: Bruce A. Winrow.
Publisher: Walden Personnel Testing & Consulting Inc. [Canada].
Cross References: For a review by John S. Geisler, see 15:14.

[110]

Analytical Reasoning Skills Battery.

Purpose: Measures high level analytical reasoning skills.
Population: Adults.
Publication Date: 1998.
Acronym: ANAL.
Scores, 4: Total Score, Narrative Evaluation, Ranking, Recommendation.
Administration: Group.
Price Data: Available from publisher.
Time: (68) minutes.
Author: Bruce A. Winrow.
Publisher: Walden Personnel Testing & Consulting Inc. [Canada].

[111]

Analytical Thinking Test.

Purpose: Designed as a self-assessment exercise in analytical thinking.
Population: Adults.
Publication Dates: 1992–1994.

Scores, 2: Situations, Proposals.
Administration: Group.
Manual: No manual.
Price Data, 2016: $195; quantity discounts available.
Time: [30–40] minutes.
Comments: Self-administered, self-scored; now sold as part of the Training House Assessment Kit.
Author: Training House, Inc.
Publisher: HRD Press, Inc.

[112]

Anger Disorders Scale.

Purpose: "Designed to help practitioners identify clinically dysfunctional anger by assessing anger as an independent problem, rather than as a secondary symptom to another issue."
Population: Ages 18 and over.
Publication Date: 2004.
Administration: Individual or group.
Forms, 2: Anger Disorders Scale; Anger Disorders Scale: Short.
Price Data, 2015: $215 per complete kit including manual (2004, 172 pages), 10 reusable item booklets, 25 ADS QuikScore forms, and 25 ADS:S QuikScore forms; $86 per technical manual; $55 per 25 ADS QuikScore forms; $55 per 25 ADS:S Quikscore forms; $32 per 10 reusable item booklets. $189 per Online interpretive report kit including manual and 25 Interpretive Reports; $7 per Online Interpretive Reports (min. purchase of 25); $6 per ADS Online Profile Reports. $239 per V.5 Software kit including manual, V.5 getting started guide, and 25 interpretive Reports; $62 per V.5 software preview version including V.5 getting started guide, and 3 Interpretive Reports; $7 per V.5 Software Interpretive Report (min. purchase of 25); $5 per V.5 Software Profile Report(min. purchase of 50); $38 per 50 ADS Data Entry Sheets; $38 per 50 ADS:S Data Entry Sheets.
Authors: Raymond DiGiuseppe and Raymond Chip Tafrate.
Publisher: Multi-Health Systems, Inc.
  a) ANGER DISORDERS SCALE.
  Acronym: ADS.
  Scores, 22: Reactivity/Expression (Scope of Anger Provocations, Physiological Arousal, Duration of Anger Problems, Rumination, Impulsivity, Coercion, Verbal Expression, Total), Anger-In (Hurt/Social Rejection, Episode Length, Suspiciousness, Resentment, Tension Reduction, Brooding, Total), Vengeance (Revenge, Physical Aggression, Relational Aggression, Passive Aggression, Indirect Aggression, Total), Total.
  Time: (20) minutes.
  b) ANGER DISORDERS SCALE: SHORT.
  Acronym: ADS:S.
  Scores, 4: Reactivity/Expression, Anger-In, Vengeance, Total.
  Time: (5-10) minutes.
Cross References: For reviews by Laura L. B. Barnes and Matthew E. Lambert, see 17:7.

[113]

Anger Regulation and Expression Scale.

Purpose: Designed as "a self-report assessment of the expression and regulation of anger in children and adolescents."

Population: Ages 10-17.

Publication Date: 2011.

Acronym: ARES; ARES(S).

Scores, 25: 3 clusters, 13 scales, 8 subscales, Total Score: Internalizing Anger [Arousal (Physiological Arousal, Cognitive Arousal), Rejection, Anger-In, Bitterness (Resentment, Suspiciousness)], Externalizing Anger [Overt Aggression/Expression (Physical Aggression, Verbal Expression), Covert Aggression, Revenge, Subversion (Relational Aggression, Passive Aggression), Bullying, Impulsivity], Extent of Anger [Scope of Triggers, Problem Duration, Episode Duration].

Administration: Individual or group.

Forms, 2: Full-length, Short.

Price Data, 2015: $229 per online kit including manual (114 pages), 25 online response forms, and 25 short online response forms; $309 per complete scoring software kit including manual, unlimited use scoring software (USB key), 25 response forms, and 25 short response forms; $55 per 25 full or short response forms; $132 per complete scoring software program (USB key); $3 per full or short online response form; $89 per manual.

Time: (15) minutes for ARES; (5) minutes for ARES(S).

Comments: May be administered via paper-and-pencil or online; online scoring or software (USB key) is required for scoring paper-and-pencil assessments.

Authors: Raymond DiGiuseppe and Raymond Chip Tafrate.

Publisher: Multi-Health Systems, Inc.

Cross References: For reviews by Cynthia E. Hazel and Susan McDonald and by Christopher A. Sink and Lauren D. Moore, see 19:3.

[114]

Antisocial Process Screening Device.

Purpose: Designed to assess personality processes related to antisocial behavior in young populations.

Population: Ages 6–13

Publication Date: 2001.

Acronym: APSD.

Scores, 4: Callous/Unemotional, Impulsivity, Narcissism, Total.

Administration: Individual.

Price Data, 2015: $245 per complete kit including manual (84 pages), and 25 Quikscore forms for each of APSD-T, APSD-P, and APSD-C; $81 per technical manual; $59 per 25 QuikScore forms (specify APSD-T, APSD-P, or APSD-C).

Time: 10 minutes per rater for Parent and Teacher forms.

Comments: Individual Parent and Teacher ratings.

Authors: Paul J. Frick and Robert D. Hare.

Publisher: Multi-Health Systems, Inc.

Cross References: For reviews by Arthur S. Ellen and Mary Lou Kelley, see 16:13.

[115]

AP Examinations.

Purpose: Designed to measure college-level achievement of students in various subject areas.

Population: High school students desiring credit for college-level courses and admission to advanced courses.

Publication Dates: 1954–2016.

Acronym: AP®.

Scores: Total score only for 38 tests in 7 subject areas.

Administration: Group.

Price Data: Available from publisher.

Time: 120–200 minutes.

Comments: Available to secondary schools for annual administration on specified days in May; inactive forms and previous essay/free-response sections available; administered by the College Board and Educational Testing Service.

Author: Educational Testing Service.

Publisher: The College Board.

    a) AP CAPSTONE.
        1) *Research.*
        2) *Seminar.*
    b) ARTS.
        1) *Art History.*
        2) *Music Theory.*
        3) *Studio Art: 2-D Design.*
        4) *Studio Art: 3-D Design.*
        5) *Studio Art: Drawing.*
    c) ENGLISH.
        1) *English Language and Composition.*
        2) *English Literature and Composition.*
    d) HISTORY & SOCIAL SCIENCE.
        1) *Comparative Government and Politics.*
        2) *European History.*
        3) *Human Geography.*
        4) *Macroeconomics.*
        5) *Microeconomics.*
        6) *Psychology.*
        7) *United States Government and Politics.*
        8) *United States History.*
        9) *World History.*
    e) MATH & COMPUTER SCIENCE.
        1) *Calculus AB.*
        2) *Calculus BC.*
        3) *Computer Science A.*
        4) *Computer Science Principles.*
        5) *Statistics.*
    f) SCIENCES.
        1) *Biology.*
        2) *Chemistry.*
        3) *Environmental Science.*
        4) *Physics C: Electricity and Magnetism.*
        5) *Physics C: Mechanics.*
        6) *Physics 1: Algebra-Based.*
        7) *Physics 2: Algebra-Based.*
    g) WORLD LANGUAGES & CULTURES.
        1) *Chinese Language and Culture.*
        2) *French Language and Culture.*

3) *German Language and Culture.*
4) *Italian Language and Culture.*
5) *Japanese Language and Culture.*
6) *Latin.*
7) *Spanish Language and Culture.*
8) *Spanish Literature and Culture.*

Cross References: See T5:118 (1 reference) and T3:124 (1 reference); for additional information and reviews by Paul L. Dressel and David A. Frisbie of an earlier edition of the Advanced Placement Examinations, see 8:471 (5 references); see also T2:1045 (4 references); for reviews by Warren G. Findley and Alexander G. Wesman of an earlier program, see 7:662 (3 references); see also 6:761 (5 references). For reviews of earlier editions of individual tests, see 8:112 (1 review) for French Language Level 3, 8:113 (2 reviews) for French Literature Level 3, 8:126 (1 review) for German Literature Level 3, 8:153 (1 review) for Spanish, 8:846 (1 review) for Chemistry, 8:862 (1 review) for Physics, 6:893 (1 review) for Biology, 6:1000 (1 review) for American History, 5:205 (1 review) for English Composition, 5:211 (1 review) for Literature, 5:273 (1 review) for German, 5:419 (1 review) for Mathematics, 5:724 (1 review) for Biology, 5:743 (1 review) for Chemistry, 5:750 (1 review) for Physics, and 5:812 (2 reviews) for American History.

[116]
Aphasia Diagnostic Profiles.

Purpose: "Provides a systematic method of assessing language and communication impairment associated with aphasia."
Population: Adults with acquired brain damage.
Publication Date: 1992.
Acronym: ADP.
Scores: Behavioral Profile Score plus 9 subtests: Personal Information, Writing, Reading, Fluency, Naming, Auditory Comprehension, Repetition, Elicited Gestures, Singing.
Administration: Individual.
Price Data, 2015: $202 per complete kit including 25 record forms, manual (55 pages), stimulus cards/letterboard/pointer, and carrying case; $63 per 25 record forms; $80 per manual; $68 per stimulus cards/letterboard/pointer.
Time: (40–50) minutes.
Author: Nancy Helm-Estabrooks.
Publisher: PRO-ED.
Cross References: See T5:159 (2 references); for reviews by Wilfred G. Van Gorp and Richard G. Whitten, see 13:11.

[117]
Applicant Potential Inventory.

Purpose: Designed as a pre-employment screening assessment to help determine the employability of applicants.

Population: Job applicants.
Publication Date: 1996.
Acronym: API™.
Scores, 11: Candidness, Accuracy, Customer Service, Honesty, Drug Avoidance, Employee Relations, Safety Attitudes, Work Values, Supervision Attitudes, Tenure, Employability.
Administration: Group.
Price Data: Available from publisher.
Time: (15) minutes.
Author: General Dynamics Information Technology.
Publisher: General Dynamics Information Technology.

[118]
Applicant Productivity Profile.

Purpose: Designed "to help screen applicants with limited reading abilities for low-skill positions."
Population: Age 18 and over.
Publication Dates: 1994–1997.
Acronym: APP.
Scores: 3 scores (Validity, Reading Ease, Employability Index), and 7 supplementary scores (Honesty II, Drug Avoidance II, Employee/Customer Relations II, Safety Attitude II, Work Values II, Supervision Attitudes II, Tenure II.
Administration: Individual or group.
Price Data: Available from Publisher.
Foreign Language Editions: Spanish and Mexican Spanish versions available.
Time: (15) minutes.
Comments: Test can be scored online, by fax, optical screening; software is available.
Author: General Dynamics Information Technology.
Publisher: General Dynamics Information Technology.

[119]
Applicant Risk Profiler.

Purpose: "Designed to assist companies in determining which applicants are a potential risk or threat to their supervisors, coworkers and/or themselves."
Population: Job applicants.
Publication Date: 2001.
Acronym: ARP.
Scores, 5: Deception, Integrity, Illegal Drug Use, Workplace Policy Compliance, Workplace Aggression.
Administration: Individual.
Price Data, 2016: $18.99 (sold in quantities of 5; quantity discounts available.)
Time: (30) minutes.
Comments: Online and paper-and-pencil administration available; online version includes interpretive reports and follow-up interview questions.
Author: J. M. Llobet.
Publisher: HRdirect | G. Neil.
Cross References: For reviews by Richard E. Harding and William I. Sauser, Jr., see 17:8.

[120]

Appraise Your World™.

Purpose: Constructed "to measure the complexity and richness of the way individuals develop their personal worlds and make life choices."

Population: Adults.

Publication Dates: 1983-2001.

Acronym: AYW.

Scores: 29 dimensions: Emphasis (Career, Economic, Community, Interpersonal, Recreation, Travel, Nature, Palate, Arts, Practical Arts, Home, Romance, Family, Intellectual, Ideological, Physical, Emotional, Spiritual), World Dynamics (Level of Security, Level of Insecurity, Level of Satisfaction, Level of Dissatisfaction, Internal Focus of World, External Focus of World, Flexibility of Boundaries, Level of Growth, Balance of World, Level of Public Success, Level of Present Support).

Administration: Group.

Price Data: Available from publisher.

Foreign Language Editions: Available in Arabic, British English, Danish, Dutch, French, German, Italian, Swedish, and Spanish.

Time: (45) minutes.

Comments: Purchase and use requires training by publisher.

Authors: James T. Mahoney, Joan W. Chadbourne (test), and Robert I. Kabacoff (manual).

Publisher: Management Research Group.

[121]

Apraxia Battery for Adults, Second Edition.

Purpose: Designed to "verify the presence of apraxia in the adult patient and to estimate the severity of the disorder."

Population: Adults.

Publication Dates: 1979–2000.

Acronym: ABA-2.

Scores: 6 subtests: Diadochokinetic Rate, Increasing Word Length, Limb Apraxia and Oral Apraxia, Latency Time and Utterance Time for Polysyllabic Words, Repeated Trials, Inventory of Articulation Characteristics of Apraxia.

Administration: Individual.

Price Data, 2015: $157 per complete kit including 25 profile/examiner record forms, picture book, and manual (2000, 46 pages); $56 per 25 profile/examiner record forms; $62 per manual; $48 per picture book.

Time: (20) minutes.

Comments: Publisher states that the "vocabulary and conceptual structure of the six subtests allows administration of the battery to adolescents and children down to about age 9"; however, the norming group included only adults.

Author: Barbara L. Dabul.

Publisher: PRO-ED.

Cross References: For reviews by Elaine Clark and by Raymond S. Dean and John J. Brinkman, Jr., see 15:15; see T5:163 (3 references) and T4:179 (4 references); for a review by Norma Cooke of an earlier edition, see 9:77 (1 reference).

[122]

The APT Inventory.

Purpose: Designed to measure an individual's relative strength on each of ten personal traits.

Population: Adults.

Publication Date: 1992.

Scores, 10: Communication, Analytical Thinking, Administrative, Relating to Others, Influencing, Achieving, Empowering, Developing, Leadership, Ethics.

Administration: Individual or group.

Manual: No manual.

Price Data, 2016: $195; quantity discounts available.

Time: (40) minutes.

Comments: Self-administered; self-scored; now sold as part of the Training House Assessment Kit.

Author: Training House, Inc.

Publisher: HRD Press, Inc.

Cross References: For reviews by E. Scott Huebner and Jayne E. Stake, see 13:13.

[123]

Aptitude Assessment Battery: Programming.

Purpose: Designed to measure programming aptitude.

Population: Programmers and trainees.

Publication Date: 1967.

Acronym: AABP.

Scores: Total score only.

Administration: Group.

Restricted Distribution: Restricted to employers of programmers, not available to school personnel.

Price Data: Available from publisher.

Foreign Language and Special Editions: French, Spanish, Braille, and left-handed editions available.

Time: Untimed.

Comments: Percentile and qualitative information provided in detailed report.

Author: Jack M. Wolfe.

Publisher: Rose Wolfe Family Partnership LLP [Canada].

Cross References: See 7:1087 (1 reference).

[124]

Aptitude Profile Test Series.

Purpose: Designed to assess a range of core cognitive abilities relevant to and known to predict success in many occupations and areas of study.

Population: Years 9–11 in Australian school system to adults.

Publication Date: 2000.
Acronym: APTS.
Scores, 4: Abstract Reasoning, Quantitative Reasoning, Spatial-Visual Reasoning, Verbal Reasoning.
Administration: Individual or group.
Price Data, 2016: A$219.95 per APTS specimen set (including one of each component); A$79.95 per APTS manual; A$29.95 per APTS scoring keys; $24.95 per APTS test booklet (Verbal Reasoning Test, Quantitative Reasoning Test, Abstract Reasoning Test or Spatial Reasoning Test); A$24.95 per 10 answer sheets.
Authors: George Morgan, Andrew Stephanou, and Brian Simpson.
Publisher: Australian Council for Educational Research Ltd. [Australia].
    a) APTITUDE PROFILE TEST SERIES—OCCU-PATIONAL.
    Purpose: "Developed for use … with assessing people's abilities in relation to employment and to occupational needs of organisations and industry."
    Population: Adults.
    Acronym: APTS-O.
    b) APTITUDE PROFILE TEST SERIES—EDUCA-TIONAL.
    Purpose: "Developed for … assessing students' abilities in an educational context."
    Population: Years 9–11 in Australian school system.
    Acronym: APTS-E.
Cross References: For a review by Robert M. Thorndike, see 15:16.

[125]

Aptitude Tests for School Beginners.

Purpose: "Obtain a differentiated picture of certain aptitudes of school beginners."
Population: Grade 1 entrants.
Publication Dates: 1974–1994.
Acronym: ASB.
Scores, 8: Perception, Spatial, Reasoning, Numerical, Gestalt, Co-ordination, Memory, Verbal Comprehension.
Administration: Group.
Price Data: Available from publisher.
Time: (390–450) minutes for full battery, (180–240) minutes for abbreviated battery.
Comments: An abbreviated battery (Reasoning, Numerical, and Gestalt subtests) may be administered to obtain total score only; revised 1994 norms include norms for all South-Africans, norms for nonenvironmentally disadvantaged children, and norms for environmentally disadvantaged children.
Authors: D. J. Swart (manuals), T. M. Coetzee (manual), Margaretha Tredoux (manual), and N. M. Oliver (manual).
Publisher: Human Sciences Research Council [South Africa].
Cross References: See T5:169 (1 reference) and T4:186 (1 reference).

[126]

Areas of Worklife Survey.

Purpose: Designed for use "as an element within an organizational survey" to assess six areas of worklife.
Population: Employees.
Publication Dates: 2000-2011.
Acronym: AWS.
Scores, 6: Workload, Control, Reward, Community, Fairness, Values.
Administration: Individual or group.
Price Data, 2016: $50 per electronic copy of Fifth Edition Manual (2011, 32 pages) including review-only copy of the AWS form; $15 per individual report; $250 per group report; $2 per survey (minimum 50); $60 per printed manual.
Time: [15] minutes.
Comments: Short version available "for large projects in which participants have a great amount of questions to respond to for the survey being administered … should not be used for individual assessment"; may be combined with Maslach Burnout Inventory (1209).
Authors: Michael P. Leiter and Christina Maslach.
Publisher: Mind Garden, Inc.

[127]

Arizona Articulation Proficiency Scale, Third Revision.

Purpose: An "assessment measure of articulatory proficiency in children, adolescents, and adults."
Population: Ages 1.5–18 years.
Publication Dates: 1963–2000.
Acronym: Arizona-3.
Scores: Total score only.
Administration: Individual.
Price Data, 2016: $194.50 per kit including 42 picture cards, 25 test booklets, and manual (2000, 60 pages); $93 per picture cards; $38.50 per 25 test booklets; $72 per manual.
Time: (3) minutes.
Comments: Replaces the Arizona Articulation Proficiency Scale, Second Edition (AAPS); has updated picture cards, new gender-specific norms.
Author: Janet Barker Fudala.
Publisher: Western Psychological Services.
Cross References: For reviews by Steven Long and Roger L. Towne, see 16:15; see also T5:175 (12 references) and T4:191 (4 references); for reviews by Penelope K. Hall and Charles Wm. Martin of a previous edition, see 11:17 (12 references); see also T3:200 (8 references); for reviews by Raphael M. Haller and Ronald K. Sommers, and an excerpted review by Barton B. Proger, see 8:954 (6 references); see also T2:2065 (2 references), 7:948 (2 references), and 6:307a (2 references).

[128]

The Arizona Battery for Communication Disorders of Dementia.

Purpose: To measure "the effects and severity of Alzheimer's Disease."
Population: Alzheimer's patients.
Publication Dates: 1991–1993.
Acronym: ABCD.
Scores, 6: Mental Status, Episodic Memory, Linguistic Expression, Linguistic Comprehension, Visuospatial Construction, Total.
Administration: Individual.
Price Data, 2015: $270 per complete kit including manual (77 pages), scoring and interpretation card, 25 response record forms, stimulus book A, stimulus book B, and nail and envelope; $43 per 25 response record forms; $67 per stimulus book A; $79 per stimulus book B; $25 per scoring and interpretation card; $72 per manual.
Time: (45-90) minutes.
Authors: Kathryn A. Bayles and Cheryl K. Tomoeda.
Publisher: PRO-ED.
Cross References: For reviews by Charles J. Long and Kenneth Sakauye, see 12:31.

[129]

Arlin Test of Formal Reasoning.

Purpose: Designed to assess "individual's ability to use the eight specific concepts associated with (Piaget's) stages of formal operations"; profiles individual as "concrete, high concrete, transitional, low formal, or high formal."
Population: Grades 6-12 and adults.
Publication Date: 1984.
Acronym: ATFR.
Scores, 9: Volume, Probability, Correlations, Combinations, Propositions, Momentum, Mechanical Equilibrium, Frames of Reference, Total.
Administration: Group.
Price Data, 2016: $114.75 per complete kit; $63.75 per 35 test question booklets; $23.75 per 35 answer sheets; $10.50 per hand-scoring template; $29 per manual (28 pages).
Time: (45–50) minutes.
Author: Patricia Kennedy Arlin.
Publisher: Slosson Educational Publications, Inc.
Cross References: See T5:178 (1 reference) and T4:194 (3 references); for a review by Toni E. Santmire, see 9:80 (5 references).

[130]

Armed Services Vocational Aptitude Battery.

Purpose: Intended "for use in educational and vocational counseling and to stimulate interest in job and training opportunities in the Armed Forces."
Population: High school, junior college, and young adult applicants to the Armed Forces.
Publication Dates: 1967–2012.
Acronyms: ASVAB.
Scores, 3 composite scores: Science and Technical Skills, Verbal Skills, Math Skills.
Subtests, 8: General Science, Arithmetic Reasoning, Word Knowledge, Paragraph Comprehension, Mathematics Knowledge, Electronics Information, Auto and Shop Information, Mechanical Comprehension.
Administration: Group.
Price Data: Administered free of charge at participating high schools by Department of Defense personnel.
Time: 144(180) minutes.
Comments: A computer-adaptive version (CAT-ASVAB) is also available; in that version, Auto and Shop Information subtests are given separately and an additional subtest (Assembling Objects) is added.
Author: United States Military Entrance Processing Command.
Publisher: United States Military Entrance Processing Command.
Cross References: See T5:180 (37 references) and T4:196 (27 references); for a review by R. A. Weitzman, see 9:81 (3 references); see also T3:202 (8 references); for a review by David J. Weiss, see 8:483 (4 references); see also T2:1067 (1 reference).

[131]

Ashland Interest Assessment.

Purpose: "A career interest inventory for individuals with restricted abilities developed in response to a need for a career measure to accommodate individuals with barriers to employment due to educational, physical, emotional, cognitive, or psychiatric conditions."
Population: Adults and adolescents.
Publication Date: 1997.
Acronym: AIA.
Scores, 12: Arts and Crafts, Sales, Clerical, Protective Service, Food Service, Personal Service, Health Care, General Service, Plant or Animal Care, Construction, Transportation, Mechanical.
Administration: Group or individual.
Price Data, 2015: $97 per examination kit including manual on CD (1997, 94 pages), 5 hand-scorable question and answer booklets, 5 profile sheets, 5 scoring sheets, one set of templates, and one machine-scorable question and answer booklet for a Mail-in Extended Report; $25 per test manual on CD; $65 per 25 hand-scorable question and answer booklets; $73 per 25 response sheets (includes 25 scoring sheets and 25 profile sheets); $38 per set of templates; $76–$86 (depending on volume) per 10 machine-scorable question and answer documents for Mail-in Extended Reports; $155 per software installation package, includes 10 scoring coupons; $8 per online report.
Comments: Scored by self, mail-in scoring, computer scoring, and online scoring at www.SigmaTesting.com.
Authors: Douglas N. Jackson and Connie W. Marshall.

Publisher: SIGMA Assessment Systems, Inc.

Cross References: For reviews by Richard J. Mc-Cowan and Sheila C. McCowan and by Mary Roznowski, see 14:20.

[132]
Asperger Syndrome Diagnostic Scale.

Purpose: "Designed to assess individuals who manifest the characteristics of Asperger syndrome."

Population: Ages 5–18.

Publication Date: 2001.

Acronym: ASDS.

Scores, 6: Language, Social, Maladaptive, Cognitive, Sensorimotor, Total.

Administration: Individual.

Price Data, 2015: $121 per complete kit including 50 summary/response forms, and examiner's manual (39 pages); $62 per 50 summary response forms; $67 per examiner's manual.

Time: (10–15) minutes.

Comments: Ratings by parents, teachers, and professionals at home and school.

Authors: Brenda Smith Myles, Stacey Jones-Bock, and Richard L. Simpson.

Publisher: PRO-ED.

Cross References: For reviews by Kimberly Ann Blair and Pat Mirenda, see 15:17.

[133]
Aspiring to Leadership.

Purpose: Designed to assess employee development and succession planning.

Population: Individual contributors with management potential.

Publication Date: 2006.

Acronym: ATL.

Scores, 13: Commitment to Goals, Assertiveness, Problem Solving/Resourcefulness, Teamwork, Working with Diversity, Openness to Feedback, Attention to Detail, Push/Pressure, Acknowledges Others' Efforts, Approachability, Dependability, Effectiveness/Outcomes, Leadership Promise.

Administration: Individual.

Price Data: Available from publisher.

Time: 20-30 minutes.

Comments: Publisher suggests allowing 2-3 weeks to collect feedback.

Authors: Daniel Booth and Paul M. Connolly.

Publisher: The Clark Wilson Group, Inc. (subsidiary of The Booth Company, Inc.).

[134]
Assess Expert System.

Purpose: A web-based assessment system that provides assessment for selection and development of managers and professionals.

Population: Current employees, potential employees, and candidates for promotion in professional, managerial, and sales positions.

Publication Dates: 1997-2010.

Acronym: ASSESS.

Scores: Updated and shortened versions of the Guilford Zimmerman Temperament Survey (GZTS) and Dynamic Factors Opinion Survey (DFOS) provide normative results on 24 characteristics grouped in the areas of Thinking, Working, and Relating; Intellectual Ability Tests: 7 possible scores: Watson-Glaser Critical Thinking, Raven's Standard Progressive Matrices (Abstract Reasoning), Thurstone Test of Mental Alertness, Employee Aptitude Survey 7 (EAS-7)—Verbal Reasoning, RBH Arithmetic Reasoning Test, Employee Aptitude Survey 2 (EAS-2)—Numerical Ability, Employee Aptitude Survey 1 (EAS-1)—Verbal Comprehension.

Administration: Group or individual.

Parts, 8: Access v2 Personality Survey, Watson-Glaser Critical Thinking, Raven's Standard Progressive Matrices, Thurstone Test of Mental Alertness, Employee Aptitude Survey 7 (EAS-7)—Verbal Reasoning, RBH Arithmetic Reasoning Test, Employee Aptitude Survey 2 (EAS-2)—Numerical Ability, Employee Aptitude Survey 1 (EAS-1)—Verbal Comprehension.

Price Data: Available from publisher.

Foreign Language Editions: Survey available in English, Spanish, Portuguese, French, German, Czech, Hungarian, Dutch, Italian, Polish, Swedish, Slovenian, Bahasa Indonesian, Chinese, Korean, and Arabic; Reporting available in English, Spanish, Portuguese, German, Czech, Hungarian, Dutch, Bahasa Indonesian, Chinese, and Korean.

Time: Administration time varies for each assessment.

Comments: The personality survey is the main component of the assessment. Intellectual ability tests are optional and may be given in any combination. The test publisher has indicated there is a newer edition of this test; description will be updated when complete test materials are received.

Author: Assess Systems.

Publisher: Bigby, Havis & Associates, Inc., d/b/a Assess Systems.

Cross References: For reviews by Laura L. B. Barnes and R. Evan Davis and by Kate Hattrup, see 19:4; for reviews by Peter F. Merenda and Stephen Olejnik of an earlier version titled Assess Expert Assessment System Version 5.X, see 14:21.

[135]
Assessing and Teaching Phonological Knowledge.

Purpose: Designed to assess children's reading readiness and diagnose a child's reading difficulty.

Population: Young children.

Publication Date: 1998.

Scores, 5: Acquiring Implicit Awareness of Sound Patterns in Words, Segmenting Words into Sounds, Sound Blending, Manipulating Sounds Within Words, Phonemic Recoding: Bridging to Written Words.
Administration: Individual.
Forms, 3: Screening Checklist, Parental Referral Form, Profile Sheet.
Price Data, 2016: A$139.95 per starter set including manual (144 pages), record book, checklist, and task sheets; A$73.95 per manual; A$27.95 per package of 10 record books; A$18.95 per package of 10 checklists; A$20.95 per set of task sheets.
Time: Administration time not reported.
Author: John Munro.
Publisher: Australian Council for Educational Research Ltd. [Australia].
Cross References: For reviews by Rebecca McCauley and Steven A. Stahl, see 14:22.

[136]

Assessing Motivation to Communicate, Second Edition.

Purpose: Designed to assess communication apprehension and willingness to communicate.
Population: Postsecondary students.
Publication Dates: 1994-2007.
Acronym: AMTC.
Scores, 5: Group Discussions, Meetings, Interpersonal Conversations, Public Speaking, Total.
Administration: Group.
Price Data: Available at no charge from test publisher.
Time: Administration time not reported.
Comments: Instrument consists of two assessment tools: The Personal Report of Communication Apprehension and The Willingness to Communicate.
Author: Speech Communication Association.
Publisher: National Communication Association.
Cross References: For reviews by Ric Brown and Claudia R. Wright of an earlier edition, see 14:23.

[137]

Assessing Reading: Multiple Measures, 2nd Edition.

Purpose: Designed to "identify why a student is having reading difficulty, determine what the next step in instruction should be to remediate that difficulty, and monitor progress throughout the course of instruction."
Publication Dates: 1999-2008.
Parts, 6: Phonological Awareness, Decoding and Word Attack, Vocabulary, Comprehension, Fluency, Assessments in Spanish.
Price Data, 2015: $45 per book.
Authors: Linda Diamond and B. J. Thorsnes (Editors).
Publisher: Arena Press.

a) CORE PHONEME DELETION TEST.
Population: Grades K-3.
Scores, 4: Initial Sounds, Final Sounds, First Sound/Blend, Embedded Sound/Blend.
Administration: Individual.
Time: (10-15) minutes.
Author: Orna Lenchner.
b) CORE PHONOLOGICAL SEGMENTATION TEST.
Population: Grades K-1.
Scores, 3: Sentences into Words, Words into Syllables, Words into Phonemes.
Administration: Individual.
Time: (5-10) minutes.
Author: Orna Lenchner.
c) CORE PHONEME SEGMENTATION TEST.
Population: Grades 2-12.
Score: Performance Level.
Administration: Individual.
Time: (5-10) minutes.
Author: Orna Lenchner.
d) CORE PHONICS SURVEY.
Population: Grades K-12.
Score: Mastery English.
Administration: Individual.
Time: (10-15) minutes.
Author: Consortium On Reading Excellence.
e) SAN DIEGO QUICK ASSESSMENT OF READING ABILITY.
Population: Grades K-11.
Score: Reading Level.
Administration: Individual.
Time: 10 minutes.
Authors: Margaret La Pray et al.
f) CORE GRADED HIGH-FREQUENCY WORD SURVEY.
Population: Grades K-4, older struggling readers.
Score: Mastery.
Administration: Individual.
Time: (5-7) minutes.
Author: Consortium on Reading Excellence.
g) CORE VOCABULARY SCREENING.
Population: Grades 1-8.
Score: Vocabulary Screening.
Administration: Group.
Time: (10-20) minutes.
Author: Michael Milone.
h) CORE READING MAZE COMPREHENSION TEST.
Population: Grades 2-10.
Score: Correct Replacement.
Administration: Group.
Time: 3 minutes.
Author: Michael Milone.
i) MASI-R ORAL READING FLUENCY MEASURE.
Population: Grades 1-6.
Score: Oral Reading Fluency.
Administration: Individual.
Time: (10-15) minutes.
Authors: Kenneth W. Howell, Michelle K. Hosp, and Mada Kay Morehead.
j) CORE SPANISH PHONEMIC AWARENESS TEST.
Population: Grades K-2.

Scores, 2: Phoneme Oddity, Phoneme Deletion.
Administration: Individual.
Time: (5-10) minutes.
Author: Jacalyn Mahler.
k) CORE Spanish Phonics Survey
Score: Mastery Spanish.
Administration: Individual.
Time: (10-15) minutes.
Author: Consortium On Reading Excellence.
l) CORE SPANISH SPELLING INVENTORY.
Population: Grades K-6.
Score: Performance Score.
Administration: Group.
Time: (10-15) minutes.
Author: Jacalyn Mahler.
m) CRITCHLOW SPANISH VERBAL LANGUAGE SCALES.
Population: Grades K-8.
Score: Grade Level.
Administration: Individual.
Time: 15 minutes.
Author: Donald E. Critchlow.

[138]

Assessment, Evaluation, and Programming System for Infants and Children (AEPS®): Second Edition.

Purpose: Designed "to assist interventionists and caregivers in developing functional and coordinated assessment, goal development, intervention and evaluation activities for young children who have or who are at risk for disabilities."
Population: Birth to 3 years, 3 to 6 years.
Publication Dates: 1993-2002.
Acronym: AEPS(r).
Scores, 7: 6 developmental areas: Fine Motor, Gross Motor, Adaptive, Cognitive, Social-Communication, Social; 1 Total raw score.
Administration: Individual or group.
Levels, 2: Birth to Three Years, Three to Six Years.
Price Data, 2015: $239 per 4-Volume Set, including Volume 1: Administration Guide (2002, 336 pages), Volume 2: Test: Birth to Three Years and Three to Six Years (2002, 304 pages), Volume 3: Curriculum for Birth to Three Years (2002, 512 pages), Volume 4: Curriculum for Three to Six Years (2002, 352 pages); $179 per Administration Guide, Test, and choice of Birth to Three Years Curriculum or Three to Six Years Curriculum; $65 per each Volume 1: Administration Guide, Volume 3: Curriculum for Birth to Three Years, Volume 4: Curriculum for Three to Six Years; $75 per Volume 2: Test: Birth to Three Years and Three to Six Years; $249.95 per Forms on CD-ROM; annual subscription to web-based management system AEPSinteractive (AEPSi) priced at $19.95-$16.95 per child record, depending on the number of children (1-500) for whom data are being managed (the user is directed to contact the publisher if data will be managed for more than 500 children).

Foreign Language Edition: CD-ROM Forms also available in Spanish; CODRF also available in AEPSi in Spanish.
Time: Administration time varies.
Comments: Administration time depends on several factors; recommended to be administered over a 2-week period to permit observation of the child in a variety of activities. AEPS can also be used for children up to age 9 with significant delays. AEPS is a curriculum-based assessment, not a norm-referenced assessment. As such, the Child Observation Data Recording Form (CODRF) is used by the professional to organize and display assessment information gathered in the six developmental areas that are assessed. Observations for up to four test sessions may be recorded on the CODRF. AEPS is a flexible assessment system designed so that professionals may choose the developmental areas and the number of children who are assessed at each testing session. Each developmental area in each level is composed of strands, or behaviors that are developmentally related. An appendix is included in the Administration Guide that links a child's performance on each developmental area with Individualized Family Service Plan or Individualized Education Program goals. The test elicits family participation through the use of the Family Report Form, which encourages family assessment of the child. AEPSinteractive (AEPSi) is a "web-based management system (www.aepsi.com) [that] streamlines AEPS administration, provides new reporting features, and includes sets of activities that allow users to assess multiple children at the same time."
Authors: Diane Bricker, Betty Capt, Kristie Pretti-Frontczak, JoAnn Johnson, Kristine Slentz, Elizabeth Straka, and Misti Waddell.
Publisher: Paul H. Brookes Publishing Co., Inc.
Cross References: For a review by James Van Haneghan, see 18:5.

[139]

Assessment for Persons Profoundly or Severely Impaired.

Purpose: Designed to measure the responsiveness of a preverbal individual's communicative functioning.
Population: Infants through adults who are preverbal and functioning with a mental age between approximately 0 and 8 months.
Publication Dates: 1984–1998.
Acronym: APPSI.
Administration: Individual.
Price Data, 2015: $222 per complete kit including examiner's manual (1998, 31 pages), 25 record booklets, 25 profile/summary forms, set of cards, and other manipulatives; $62 per examiner's manual; $62 per 25 record booklets; $37 per 25 profile/summary forms; $72 per object kit.
Time: Untimed.

Comments: A revision of the Preverbal Assessment—Intervention Profile (T4:2093).
Authors: Patricia Connard and Sharon Bradley-Johnson.
Publisher: PRO-ED.
   a) STAGE I.
   Population: Mental age 0–1 month.
   Scores: 4 domains: Visual Responsiveness, Auditory Responsiveness, Tactile Responsiveness, Interaction with Others.
   b) STAGE II.
   Population: Mental age 1–4 months.
   Scores: Same as *a* above.
   c) STAGE III.
   Population: Mental age 4–8 months.
   Scores: 2 domains: Responsiveness to Objects, Interaction with Others.
Cross References: For reviews by Carolyn Mitchell-Person and Lawrence J. Ryan, see 15:18; for reviews by Karen T. Carey and Joe Olmi of the earlier edition, see 11:301.

[140]

The Assessment of Basic Language and Learning Skills–Revised.

Purpose: Designed to identify "language and other critical skills that are in need of intervention in order for a child to become more capable of learning from his everyday experiences."
Population: Children with autism or other developmental disabilities.
Publication Dates: 2006-2010.
Acronym: ABLLS-R.
Scores, 25: Basic Learner Skills (Cooperation and Reinforcer Effectiveness, Visual Performance, Receptive Language, Imitation, Vocal Imitation, Requests, Labeling, Intraverbals, Spontaneous Vocalizations, Syntax and Grammar, Play and Leisure, Social Interaction, Group Interaction, Follow Classroom Routines, Generalized Responding), Academic Skills (Reading Skills, Math Skills, Writing Skills, Spelling), Self-Help Skills (Dressing Skills, Eating Skills, Grooming, Toileting Skills), Motor Skills (Gross Motor Skills, Fine Motor Skills).
Administration: Individual.
Price Data, 2016: $64.95 per set of ABLLS-R Protocol and ABLLS-R Guide (2010, 153 pages); quantity discounts available.
Foreign Language Editions: Available in Arabic, French, Hebrew, Italian, Norwegian, and Spanish.
Time: Administration time not reported.
Comments: Provides "criterion-referenced information regarding a child's current skills that can serve as a basis for the selection of educational objectives"; also includes curriculum guide for an educational program for children with language delays; web-based version (WebABLLS) available.
Authors: James W. Partington.
Publisher: Behavior Analysts, Inc.

[141]

Assessment of Classroom Communication and Study Skills.

Purpose: Designed to "provide classroom teachers and specialists with a tool that efficiently comments on the quality of a student's school language skills."
Population: Grades 5-12.
Publication Dates: 1998-2000.
Acronym: ACCSS.
Scores, 2: Total Score, Vocabulary Score.
Administration: Group or individual.
Forms, 3: ACCSS-Long Form, ACCSS-Short Form, ACCSS-esl.
Price Data, 2016: $40 per test and manual (1998, 211 pages).
Time: (40-60) minutes.
Comments: Criterion-referenced measure; revised and expanded edition of the Classroom Communication Screening Procedure.
Author: Charlann S. Simon.
Publisher: Communi-Cog Publications.
Cross References: For reviews by Thomas Emerson Hancock and S. Kathleen Krach, see 17:9.

[142]

Assessment of Classroom Environments.

Purpose: "Identifies [teachers'] preferences [and approaches] for establishing classroom environments [by comparing] the Leadership Model, the Guidance Model, and the Integrated Model."
Population: Teachers.
Publication Dates: 2000-2008.
Acronym: ACE.
Scores: 3 models (Leadership, Guidance, Integration) for each of 8 scales: Self-Attributions, Self-Reflections, Ideal Teacher, Peers, Students, Supervisors, General Form, Comparative Form.
Administration: Group.
Forms, 8: Self-Attributions (ratings by teacher), Self-Reflections (ratings by teacher [teacher's perception of how students, peers, and supervisors view teacher]), 4 Observation Checklists (General Form [ratings by "community members, parents, visitors, [or] college students in teacher preparation programs"], Peer Form [ratings by teacher's peers], Student Form [ratings by teacher's students], Supervisor Form [ratings by teacher's supervisors]), Ideal Checklist (ratings by teacher [teacher's perception of the ideal classroom environment]), Comparative Form (ratings by teacher [comparison of the teacher's classroom environment, other professional teachers' classroom environment, and the ideal classroom environment]).
Price Data, 2016: $50 per 25 Self-Attributions forms; $50 per 25 Self-Reflections forms; $50 per 25 Observation Checklist-General forms; $50 per 25

Observation Checklist-Peer forms; $50 per 25 Observation Checklist-Student forms; $50 per 25 Observation Checklist-Supervisor forms; $50 per 25 Ideal Checklist forms; $50 per 25 Comparative forms; $40 per test manual (2008, 34 pages); $.40 per scoring/profiling per scale; $40 per analysis report.

Time: Administration time not reported.

Authors: Louise M. Soares and Anthony T. Soares (test).

Publisher: Soares Institute of Neuroscience and Education.

Cross References: For reviews by Amanda Nolen and Steven W. Schmidt, see 18:6.

[143]

Assessment of Competencies for Instructor Development.

Purpose: To measure six competencies important to being an effective instructor in an industrial setting.

Population: Instructors in industrial settings.

Publication Date: 1986.

Scores, 7: Analyzing the Needs and "Entering Behavior" of the Learner, Specifying Outcomes and "Terminal Behaviors" for a Course, Designing Instructional Sequences and Learning Materials, Instructing in Both the Inductive and Deductive Modes, Maintaining Adult-to-Adult (not "Parent-Child") Relationships in Class, Staying Learner-Centered not Information-Centered, Overall Instructional Competency.

Administration: Individual or group.

Manual: No manual.

Price Data, 2016: $49.75 per 5 assessments.

Time: (45) minutes.

Comments: Self-administered, self-scored.

Author: Training House, Inc.

Publisher: HRD Press, Inc.

Cross References: For a review by Stephen F. Davis, see 11:20.

[144]

Assessment of Comprehension and Expression 6–11.

Purpose: Designed to "assess language development."

Population: Ages 6-0 to 11-11.

Publication Date: 2002.

Acronym: ACE 6–11.

Administration: Individual.

Price Data, 2016: £210 per set including manual, picture book, 25 record forms, and scoring keys; £65 per 25 record forms.

Comments: Subtests may be administered individually although it is recommended that a minimum of three subtests be employed.

Authors: Catherine Adams, Rosanne Cooke, Alison Crutchley, Anne Hesketh, and David Reeves.

Publisher: GL Assessment [England].

a) MAIN TEST.

Scores, 6: Sentence Completion, Inferential Comprehension, Naming, Syntactic Formulation, Semantic Decisions, Total.

Time: (26–32) minutes.

b) EXTENDED TEST.

Scores, 10: Same as above with the addition of Non-Literal Comprehension, Narrative Propositions, Narrative Syntax/Discourse, Total.

Time: (46–59) minutes.

Cross References: For reviews by Cleborne D. Maddux and Sheila Pratt, see 16:16.

[145]

Assessment of Core Goals.

Purpose: Constructed to help a person define core sources of motivation and satisfaction and to identify activities that will lead to satisfaction of these goals.

Population: High school and over.

Publication Date: 1991.

Acronym: ACG.

Scores: No scores. Introspective process guided by workbook instructions and worksheets.

Administration: Group or individual.

Price Data: Available for free from publisher.

Time: 2-4 hours.

Comments: Method and length of administration depends on desired depth of information.

Author: C. W. Nichols.

Publisher: C. W. Nichols.

Cross References: For reviews by Gary J. Dean and Carol Kehr Tittle, see 12:35.

[146]

Assessment of Individual Learning Style: The Perceptual Memory Task.

Purpose: "To provide measures of the individual's perception and memory for spatial relationships; visual and auditory sequential memory; intermediate term memory; and discrimination of detail."

Population: Ages 4 and over.

Publication Dates: 1984–1993.

Acronym: PMT.

Scores: 7 scores, 3 alternate scores: Spatial Relations, Visual Designs Recognition, Visual Designs-Sequencing, Auditory-Visual Colors Recognition, Auditory-Visual Colors Sequencing, Discrimination Recall, Total PMT, Visual-Visual (alternate), Auditory-Auditory (alternate), Visual-Auditory (alternate).

Administration: Individual.

Price Data, 2015: $650 per complete kit including carrying case containing various subtest components, 25 scoring forms, 25 alternate forms, and manual (129 pages); $61.50 per 25 scoring forms; $36 per 25 alternate forms; $92.50 per manual; $375 per PMT computer report.

Time: (30–40) minutes.

Comments: PMT Computer Report (2003) is available for use in profiling PMT scores for ages 14 through adult.
Author: Lawrence McCarron.
Publisher: McCarron-Dial Systems, Inc.
Cross References: For reviews by Steven Ferrara and Arlene Coopersmith Rosenthal, see 11:21 (1 reference).

[147]
Assessment of Intelligibility of Dysarthric Speech.

Purpose: Designed "to provide clinicians and researchers with a means of measuring intelligibility and speaking rate of dysarthric individuals."
Population: Adult and adolescent dysarthric speakers.
Publication Dates: 1981–1984.
Scores, 6: Single Word Intelligibility (Transcription, Multiple Choice), Sentence Intelligibility (Transcription, Speaking Rate, Rate of Intelligible Speech, Communication Efficiency Ratio).
Administration: Individual.
Price Data, 2015: $122 per complete kit including examiner's manual (60 pages) and picture book of stimulus words and sentences.
Time: Administration time not reported.
Authors: Kathryn M. Yorkston, David R. Beukelman, and Charles Traynor.
Publisher: PRO-ED.
Cross References: See T5:209 (5 references) and T4:217 (3 references); for reviews by Katharine G. Butler and C. Dale Carpenter, see 10:19.

[148]
Assessment of Language-Related Functional Activities.

Purpose: Designed to answer the question, "Despite this person's impairment, is he or she able to integrate skills adequately to perform selected functional daily activities?"
Population: People with suspected language or cognitive compromise, aged 16 to 95.
Publication Date: 1999.
Acronym: ALFA.
Scores, 10: Telling Time, Counting Money, Addressing an Envelope, Solving Daily Math Problems, Writing a Check and Balancing a Checkbook, Understanding Medicine Labels, Using a Calendar, Reading Instructions, Using the Telephone, Writing a Phone Message.
Administration: Individual.
Price Data, 2015: $191 per complete kit including 25 profile/examiner record forms, picture book, examiner's manual (39 pages), and an additional materials kit; $40 per materials kit including 10 tokens, clock, medicine chart, and 25 envelopes; $33 per 25 profile/examiner record forms; $68 per picture book; $56 per examiner's manual.
Time: (30–120) minutes.

Authors: Kathleen Anderson Baines, Heidi McMartin Heeringa, and Ann W. Martin.
Publisher: PRO-ED.
Cross References: For reviews by Steven R. Shaw and by T. Steuart Watson and R. Anthony Doggett, see 15:19.

[149]
Assessment of Literacy and Language.

Purpose: Designed to "diagnose children who exhibit language disorders and to identify children who are at risk for later reading disabilities."
Population: Grades PK-1.
Publication Date: 2005.
Acronym: ALL.
Administration: Individual.
Levels, 4: Pre-K (Fall and Spring), K-Fall, K-Spring, 1st Grade (Fall and Spring).
Price Data, 2015: $275.50 per complete kit including manual (2005, 200 pages), stimulus book, 25 parent questionnaires, 25 record forms, and story cards; $31 per 25 questionnaires; $60.50 per 25 record forms; $103 per stimulus book; $126.25 per manual.
Time: (60) minutes.
Authors: Linda J. Lombardino, R. Jane Lieberman, and Jaumeiko J. C. Brown.
Publisher: Pearson.
  a) PRE-K.
  Scores, 16: 6 subtest scores (Letter Knowledge, Rhyme Knowledge, Basic Concepts, Receptive Vocabulary, Parallel Sentence Production, Listening Comprehension); 4 index scores (Emergent Literacy, Language, Phonological, Phonological-Orthographic); 6 criterion-referenced scores (Book Handling, Concept of Word, Matching Symbols, Word Retrieval, Rapid Automatic Naming, Invented Spelling).
  b) K-FALL.
  Scores, 18: Same as for Pre-K plus Elision and Word Relationships subtest scores.
  c) K-SPRING.
  Scores, 21: Same as for K-Fall plus Phonics Knowledge, Sound Categorization, and Sight Word Recognition subtest scores.
  d) 1st GRADE.
  Scores, 21: Same as for K-Spring.
Cross References: For reviews by Abigail Baxter and Mildred Murray-Ward, see 18:7.

[150]
Assessment of Living Skills and Resources.

Purpose: Assesses "daily tasks that require a high level of cognitive function," or Instrumental Activities of Daily Living (IADLs), "in community-dwelling elders."
Population: Community-dwelling elders.
Publication Date: 1991.
Acronym: ALSAR.
Scores: 11 task scores: Telephoning, Reading, Leisure, Medication Management, Transportation, Shopping,

Meal Preparation, Laundering, Housekeeping, Home Maintenance.

Administration: Individual.

Price Data: Instrument available at no charge.

Time: (15–20) minutes.

Comments: Incorporates assessment of Instrumental Activities of Daily Living (IADL); administered by health professionals from any discipline.

Authors: Theresa J. K. Drinka, Jane H. Williams, Martha Schram, Jean Farrell-Holtan, and Reenie Euhardy.

Publisher: Madison Geriatric Research, Education, and Clinical Center, VA Medical Center.

Cross References: For reviews by Cameron J. Camp and Anita M. Hubley, see 13:20.

[151]

Assessment of Multiple Intelligences.

Purpose: Designed to "assess which of Gardner's Eight Intelligence Types a person possesses."

Population: Below age 17 to over age 40.

Publication Date: 2011.

Acronym: AMI.

Scores, 8: Bodily-Kinesthetic, Logical-Mathematical, Linguistic, Visual-Spatial, Musical, Intrapersonal, Interpersonal, Naturalistic.

Administration: Group.

Price Data: Available from publisher.

Time: (20) minutes.

Comments: Self-administered online assessment. The test publisher provides clients with information about the methods and theoretical basis used in the development of the test as well as benchmarks for relevant industries and racial/ethnic group comparison data.

Authors: PsychTests AIM, Inc.

Publisher: PsychTests AIM, Inc. [Canada].

Cross References: For reviews by Gary L. Canivez and Eleanor E. Sanford-Moore, see 19:5.

[152]

Assessment of Parenting Skills: Infant and Preschooler.

Purpose: Designed to "evaluate the parenting skills of parents of children between birth and five years of age."

Population: Parents of children between birth and 5 years of age.

Publication Dates: 1998–2002.

Acronym: APSIP.

Scores, 13: Discipline, Fears (Stranger Anxiety, Mobility Fears, Separation Fears, Nightmares and Night Terrors, Fears of Real Events, Abstract Fears, Doctors and Dentists), Tantrums, Crying, Individual Differences and Temperament, Daily Routine, Parental Strengths and Weaknesses.

Administration: Individual.

Price Data, 2016: $289 per complete kit including 8 booklets, 8 summary sheets, and instruction manual (21 pages); $159 per 10 booklets with summary sheets; $219 per 20 booklets with summary sheets; $289 per 30 booklets with summary sheets; $149 per instruction manual.

Time: [45] minutes.

Author: Gail Elliot.

Publisher: Village Publishing.

Cross References: For a review by T. Steuart Watson, see 14:26.

[153]

The Assessment of Personal Goals.

Purpose: Designed to help people improve their lives by providing a method for identifying the personal goals that are their greatest source of motivation and life meaning based on the Taxonomy of Human Goals.

Population: High school age and older.

Publication Dates: 1988–2007.

Scores, 24: Task Goals (Mastery, Task Creativity, Management, Material Gain, Safety), Self-Assertive Social Relationship Goals (Individuality, Self-Determination, Superiority, Resource Acquisition), Integrative Social Relationship Goals (Belongingness, Social Responsibility, Equity, Resource Provision), Cognitive Goals (Exploration, Understanding, Intellectual Creativity, Positive Self-Evaluations), Affective Goals (Entertainment, Tranquility, Happiness, Bodily Sensations, Physical Well-Being), Subjective Organization Goals (Unity, Transcendence).

Administration: Individual.

Price Data: Available at no charge from test publisher.

Time: 15-40 minutes.

Comments: Web-based administration and reporting of goal profiles.

Authors: Martin E. Ford and Charles W. Nichols.

Publisher: Madison Learning, LLC.

[154]

Assessment of Practices in Early Elementary Classrooms.

Purpose: "Designed to evaluate the use of developmentally appropriate practices in early elementary classrooms … that include children with disabilities."

Population: Kindergarten through Grade 3 classrooms.

Publication Date: 2001.

Acronym: APEEC.

Scores: Total score only.

Administration: Group or individual.

Manual: No manual.

Price Data, 2016: $23.95 per booklet (39 pages).

Time: Administration time not reported.

Comments: Assesses three domains of classroom practices: physical environment, curriculum and instruction, social context.

Authors: Mary Louise Hemmeter, Kelly L. Maxwell, Melinda Jones Ault, and John W. Schuster.

Publisher: Teachers College Press.

Cross References: For reviews by Edward J. Daly III and Michael Persampieri and by Kathleen A. Dolgos, see 15:20.

[155]

Assessment of Qualitative and Structural Dimensions of Object Representations, Revised Edition.

Purpose: Designed to measure aspects of an individual's conceptualization of others.
Population: Adolescents and adults (patients and normals).
Publication Dates: 1981–1992.
Acronym: AQSDOR.
Scores: Ratings in 4 areas: Personal Qualities, Degree of Ambivalence in Description, Length of Description, Conceptual Level.
Administration: Group.
Price Data: Available for free from publisher.
Time: (5) minutes per description.
Comments: Subjects' descriptions of significant figures (e.g., parent) rated by judges; no reading by examinees.
Authors: Sidney J. Blatt, Eve S. Chevron, Donald M. Quinlan, Carrie E. Schaffer, and Steven Wein.
Publisher: Sidney J. Blatt [c/o Dr. John S. Auerbach].
Cross References: For a review by C. H. Swensen, see 9:92.

[156]

Assessment of School Needs for Low-Achieving Students: Staff Survey.

Purpose: Designed to measure "staff perceptions as to whether certain behaviors are occurring in their school."
Population: Teachers and administrators.
Publication Dates: 1988–1989.
Acronym: ASNLAS.
Scores, 9: School Programs and Policies, Classroom Management, Instruction, Teacher Expectations, Principal Leadership, Staff Development, Student Involvement in Learning, School Climate, Parent Involvement.
Administration: Group.
Price Data: Available as free download from test publisher's website.
Time: (45–50) minutes.
Authors: Francine S. Beyer and Ronald L. Houston.
Publisher: Research for Better Schools, Inc.
Cross References: For a review by Dean H. Nafziger and Ann M. Muench, see 11:22.

[157]

Assessment of Spirituality and Religious Sentiments.

Purpose: Designed to measure spirituality constructs "with individuals across a wide range of faith traditions."
Population: Ages 15 and over.
Publication Dates: 1999-2010.
Acronym: ASPIRES.
Scores, 7: Religiosity, Religious Crisis, Prayer Fulfillment, Universality, Connectedness, Total Religious Sentiments, Total Spiritual Transcendence.
Administration: Group or individual.
Forms, 4: Self-Report, Observer Rating, Self-Report Short Form, Observer Rating Short Form.
Price Data, 2016: $.50 per Self-Report Long Form; $.50 per Self-Report Short Form; $.50 per Observer Rating Long Form; $.50 per Observer Rating Short Form; $25 per Scoring and Interpretive Manual; $50 per Scoring Software 2007 Excel; $50 per Scoring Software 2003 Excel.
Foreign Language Editions: Available in Spanish, Tagalog, Czech, Polish, Chinese, Malay, Korean, Hungarian, Portuguese, Arabic, French, Vietnamese, and Russian.
Time: Approximately 10 minutes.
Author: Ralph L. Piedmont.
Publisher: Ralph L. Piedmont [the author].
Cross References: For reviews by Frank M. Bernt and Patricia Schoenrade, see 19:6.

[158]

Athletic Success Profile.

Purpose: Constructed to measure the personality, attitude, and motivation of athletes participating in competitive sports at all levels of competition.
Population: Male and female athletes at the high school, college and professional levels.
Publication Dates: 1969–1995.
Acronym: ASP.
Scores, 14: Drive, Aggressiveness, Determination, Responsibility, Leadership, Self-Confidence, Emotional Control, Mental Toughness, Coachability, Conscientiousness, Trust, Validity Scales (Accuracy, Desirability, Completion Rate).
Administration: Group or individual.
Price Data, 2016: $25 per high-school-level athletes; $49 per college-level athletes; $95 per individual athletes; $150 per professional-level athletes; fee includes free online administration of test (including an administration website for a team), three report versions (coach, athlete, and consultant), team profile, and sub-group profiles.
Foreign Language Editions: French and Spanish editions available.
Time: (30) minutes.
Comments: May be used for individual self-assessment; test formerly titled Athletic Motivation Inventory.
Authors: Thomas A. Tutko, Leland P. Lyon, and Bruce C. Ogilvie; manual by Science Research Associates.
Publisher: Athletic Success Institute.
Cross References: For a review by John W. Shepard under the test's former name, Athletic Motivation Inventory, see 12:37; for a review by Andrew L. Comrey of an earlier edition, see 8:409 (19 references).

[159]

Attention Deficit Disorder Evaluation Scale—Fourth Edition.

Purpose: Designed to "provide a measure of the ADHD characteristics of inattention and hyperactivity-impulsivity identified in the DSM-5."
Population: Ages 4 through 18 years.
Publication Dates: 1989-2013.
Acronym: ADDES-4.
Scores, 3: Inattentive, Hyperactive-Impulsive, Total.
Administration: Individual.
Forms, 2: School Version, Home Version.
Price Data, 2015: $273 per complete kit including 50 pre-referral attention deficit checklists, 50 intervention strategies documentation forms, School Version technical manual (2013, 44 pages), 50 School Version rating forms, Home Version technical manual (2013, 44 pages), 50 Home Version rating forms, Attention Deficit Disorder Intervention Manual including CD with pdf files (1994, 387 pages), and Parent's Guide to Attention Deficit Disorder (1995, 390 pages); $38 per 50 pre-referral attention deficit checklists; $38 per 50 intervention strategies documentation forms; $21 per technical manual (Home Version or School Version); $44 per 50 rating forms (Home Version or School Version); $42 per Attention Deficit Disorder Intervention Manual with CD; $25 per Parent's Guide to Attention Deficit Disorder; $44 per 50 Spanish rating forms (Home Version or School Version).
Foreign Language Edition: Spanish forms available.
Time: (20) minutes.
Comments: Scale is rated by parent/caregiver or educator.
Authors: Stephen B. McCarney and Tamara J. Arthaud.
Publisher: Hawthorne Educational Services, Inc.
Cross References: Reviews are scheduled for *The Twentieth Mental Measurements Yearbook*. For reviews by Timothy J. Makatura and Jamie G. Wood of the third edition, see 17:10; for reviews by Hugh W. Glenn and Beverly M. Klecker of the second edition, see 14:27; for reviews by Deborah Collins and Stephen Olejnik of the original edition, see 12:38 (1 reference).

[160]

Attention-Deficit/Hyperactivity Disorder Test–Second Edition.

Purpose: Designed as a screening instrument for identifying individuals "who present severe behavioral problems that may be indicative of ADHD."
Population: Ages 5 through 17.
Publication Dates: 1995-2015.
Acronym: ADHDT-2.
Scores, 3: Inattention, Hyperactivity/Impulsivity, ADHD Index.
Administration: Individual.

Price Data, 2015: $144 per kit including examiner's manual (2015, 59 pages) and 50 summary/response forms; $81 per manual; $63 per 50 summary/response forms.
Time: [3-5] minutes.
Comments: Ratings completed by teacher, parent, or other caregiver who has had regular sustained contact with the individual for at least two weeks.
Authors: James E. Gilliam.
Publisher: PRO-ED.
Cross References: Reviews are scheduled for *The Twentieth Mental Measurements Yearbook*. For reviews by Robert S. Miller and Anthony W. Paolitto of the original edition, see 14:30.

[161]

Attention-Deficit Scales for Adults.

Purpose: Designed as an objective measure of attention deficit in adults.
Population: Adults.
Publication Date: 1996.
Acronym: ADSA.
Scores, 11: Attention-Focus/Concentration, Interpersonal, Behavior-Disorganized Activity, Coordination, Academic Theme, Emotive, Consistency/Long Term, Childhood, Negative-Social, Internal Consistency, Total.
Administration: Individual.
Price Data, 2016: £49.99 per complete test with manual and 10 scoring sheets; £34.99 per 10 scoring sheets; £36.99 per manual.
Time: Untimed.
Comments: A 54-item, Likert-scale questionnaire to be administered in a clinical setting; self-report.
Authors: Santo James Triolo and Kevin Richard Murphy.
Publisher: Routledge Psychology.
Cross References: For reviews by Joseph G. Law, Jr. and James C. Reed, see 14:29.

[162]

Attention Test Linking Assessment and Services.

Purpose: "To provide a comprehensive assessment system for diagnosing and remediating ADHD."
Population: Ages 8-18.
Publication Dates: 2001-2007.
Acronym: ATLAS.
Administration: Individual.
Forms, 5: Parent Attention Report, Teacher Attention Report, Attention Performance Assessment, Examiner's Observation Report, Mental Health Interview Screener.
Price Data, 2015: $250 per ATLAS kit including examiner's manual (2007, 129 pages) and 25 each of the Parent/Teacher Attention Report forms, Mental Health Interview Screener, Examiner's Observation Report forms, Attention Performance Summary Report forms, Youth

Response booklets, and Client Profile Summary Report forms; $70 per 50 Parent/Teacher Attention Report forms; $40 per 25 Mental Health Interview Screener; $35 per 25 Examiner's Observation Report forms; $35 per 25 Attention Performance Summary Report forms; $40 per 25 Subject Response booklets; $35 per 25 Client Profile Summary Report forms; $65 per examiner's manual.
Time: (50) minutes.
Authors: Gregory R. Anderson and Patricia C. Post.
Publisher: Stoelting Co.
 a) PARENT ATTENTION REPORT.
 Scores, 6: Inattention, Concentration/Sustained Attention, Organization, Impulsivity, Hyperactivity, Divided Attention.
 b) TEACHER ATTENTION REPORT.
 Scores, 6: Inattention, Concentration/Sustained Attention, Organization, Impulsivity, Hyperactivity, Divided Attention.
 c) ATTENTION PERFORMANCE ASSESSMENT.
 Scores, 16: Sustained Attention/Vigilance, Random Letter Response-Vigilance, Trails A (Pathways 1), Complex Figure/Complex Figure for Organization, Memory (Verbal and Spatial), Digit Memory Span Forward, Verbal Memory-Superspan List, Complex Figure/Complex Figure by Memory, Working Memory, Trails B (Pathways 2) Shifting Sets/Attention, Serial Subtraction (7's), Digits Memory Span Reverse, Divided Attention, Divided/Alternating Attention: Cancellation of 4's/Trails A (Pathways 1), Verbal Fluency, Fluency for Names.
 d) EXAMINER'S OBSERVATION.
 Scores, 8: Inattention, Concentration, Impulse Control, Hyperactivity, Organization for Task Completion, Social Skills, Irritability, Motor Difficulties.
 e) MENTAL HEALTH INTERVIEW SCREENER.
 Scores, 8: Oppositional Defiant/Conduct Disorderd, Obsessive-Compulsive Disorder, Depression, Bipolar Disorder, Post-Traumatic Stress Disorder (PTSD), Generalized Anxiety Disorder (GAD), Autistic Spectrum Disorder.
Cross References: For reviews by Mary (Rina) M. Chittooran and by Tawnya J. Meadows and Eric Grady, see 18:8.

[163]

The Attentional and Interpersonal Style Inventory.

Purpose: "Developed to measure the critical concentration and interpersonal determinants of performance."
Population: Adults and adolescents.
Publication Dates: 1993–1996.
Acronym: TAIS.
Scores: 18 scales: Attentional (Broad External Awareness, External Distractibility, Conceptual/Analytical, Internal Distractibility, Narrow/Focused, Reduced Flexibility), Interpersonal (Information Processing, Orientation Toward Rules and Risk/Impulse Control, Need for Control, Self Esteem, Physical Competitiveness, Decision Making Speed, Extroversion, Introversion, Expression of Ideas, Expression of Criticism, Expression of Support, Self Critical).

Administration: Individual or group.
Price Data, 2016: $58 per manual; $92 per online report.
Time: [20–25] minutes.
Author: Robert M. Nideffer.
Publisher: Simpson Associates.
Cross References: For reviews by Phillip L. Ackerman and Eugene V. Aidman, see 14:31; see also T5:226 (2 references).

[164]

Attitudes and Values Questionnaire.

Purpose: Assesses "secondary school students' social, moral and spiritual development."
Population: Current and past (less than 10 years out) secondary school students.
Publication Date: 2008.
Acronym: AVQ.
Scores, 7: Conscience, Compassion, Emotional Growth, Social Growth, Service of Others, Commitment to God, Commitment to Jesus.
Administration: Group.
Forms, 3: Program A (focuses on social dimensions only), Program B (focuses on social dimensions and commitment to God), Program C (focuses on social dimensions, commitment to God, and commitment to Jesus).
Price Data, 2016: A$8.95 per paper-and-pencil questionnaire; A$8.50 per online questionnaire.
Time: (30) minutes.
Comments: Developed "with the support of John XXIII College in Perth"; available online or in paper-and-pencil format; publisher provides scoring and summary report; each form contains item level summaries (109 [Program A], 130 [Program B], 152 [Program C]) and averaged summaries for 5 social dimensions (Conscience, Compassion, Emotional growth, Social Growth, Service of Others) and 2 religious dimensions (Commitment to God [Programs B and C], Commitment to Jesus [Program C]; some items are "check statements [that] show whether respondents are answering the questionnaire thoughtfully" and are not included in report; data are aggregated across like subjects; client school's scores are separated by gender and year level, and are compared "against 'All Schools' results"; summary report does not provide data for individual students.
Author: Australian Council for Educational Research Ltd.
Publisher: Australian Council for Educational Research Ltd. [Australia].

[165]

Attitudes Toward Guns and Violence Questionnaire.

Purpose: Designed to measure "attitudes concerning guns, physical aggression, and interpersonal conflict."

Population: Ages 6–29.
Publication Date: 2000.
Acronym: AGVQ.
Scores, 6: Total (Favorable or Unfavorable to Violence and Guns), Inconsistent Responding, Aggressive Response to Shame, Comfort with Aggression, Excitement, Power/Safety.
Administration: Group.
Price Data, 2016: $118 per kit including 25 autoscore forms, manual, and 50 Aggressive Behavior checklists (25 teacher forms and 25 student forms); $52.50 per 25 answer forms; $65.50 per manual; $35.50 per 100 Aggressive Behavior checklists (teacher or student form); $167 per Windows scoring CD (good for 50 uses); $20.50 per 100 PC answer sheets.
Time: (5–10) minutes.
Author: Jeremy P. Shapiro.
Publisher: Western Psychological Services.
Cross References: For reviews by Stephen E. Trotter and Delores D. Walcott, see 15:22.

[166]

Auditory Phoneme Sequencing Test.

Purpose: Designed to assess "a child's ability to discriminate among and retain sounds of language presented in spoken single-syllable words."
Population: Ages 5 through 9.
Publication Date: 2014.
Acronym: APST.
Score: Total score only.
Administration: Individual.
Price Data, 2015: $110 per kit including manual (58 pages), test plates, 25 record forms, and administration CD; $33 per manual; $30 per 25 record forms; $27 per test plates; $20 per administration CD.
Time: (10-12) minutes.
Comments: Test stimuli are prerecorded on CD.
Authors: Deborah Ross-Swain and James L. Aten.
Publisher: Academic Therapy Publications.
Cross References: Reviews are scheduled for *The Twentieth Mental Measurements Yearbook*.

[167]

Auditory Processing Abilities Test.

Purpose: Designed to assess auditory processing.
Population: Ages 5-0 through 12-11.
Publication Date: 2004.
Acronym: APAT.
Scores, 20: Phonemic Awareness, Word Sequences, Semantic Relationships, Sentence Memory, Cued Recall, Content Memory, Complex Sentences, Sentence Absurdities, Following Directions, Passage Comprehension, Global Index, Auditory Memory Index, Linguistic Processing Index, Auditory Discrimination Index (optional), Auditory Sequencing Index (optional), Auditory Cohesion Index (optional), Immediate Recall Index (optional), Delayed Recall Index (optional), Sequential Recall Index (optional), Cued Recall Index (optional).
Administration: Individual.
Price Data, 2015: $130 per test kit including manual (95 pages), 25 test booklets, and 25 summary sheets; $55 per manual; $50 per 25 test booklets; $25 per 25 summary sheets.
Time: (30–45) minutes.
Authors: Deborah Ross-Swain and Nancy Long.
Publisher: Academic Therapy Publications.
Cross References: For reviews by Jeffery P. Braden and Kelly M. Laugle and by Christopher A. Sink and Rick Eigenbrood, see 16:17.

[168]

Auditory Skills Assessment.

Purpose: Designed for the "early identification of young children who might be at risk for auditory skill deficits and/or early literacy skill difficulties."
Publication Date: 2010.
Acronym: ASA.
Administration: Individual.
Price Data, 2015: $204.75 per complete kit including examiner's manual (53 pages), 25 record forms, stimulus book, and stimulus CD-ROM; $79.45 per 25 record forms; $77.40 per examiner's manual; $75.85 per stimulus book.
Authors: Donna Geffner and Ronald Goldman.
Publisher: Pearson.
a) ASA FOR AGES 3-6 TO 4-11.
Population: Ages 3-6 to 4-11.
Time: 5 minutes.
Scores, 4: Speech Discrimination (Speech Discrimination in Noise, Mimicry, Total), Total ASA.
b) ASA FOR AGES 5-0 TO 6-11.
Population: Ages 5-0 to 6-11.
Time: 15 minutes.
Scores, 10: Speech Discrimination (Speech Discrimination in Noise, Mimicry, Total), Phonological Awareness (Blending, Rhyming, Total), Nonspeech Processing (Tonal Discrimination, Tonal Patterning, Total), Total ASA.
Cross References: For reviews by Kathleen D. Allen and Connie T. England, see 19:7.

[169]

Authentic Leadership Questionnaire.

Purpose: Designed to measure "authenticity in leadership."
Population: Adults.
Publication Date: 2007.
Acronym: ALQ.
Scores, 4: Transparency, Moral/Ethical, Balanced Processing, Self Awareness.
Administration: Individual or group.
Forms, 2: Self, Rater.
Manual: No manual.

Price Data: Available from publisher.
Time: [10-15] minutes.
Authors: Bruce J. Avolio, William L. Gardner, and Fred O. Walumbwa.
Publisher: Mind Garden, Inc.

[170]

Autism Detection in Early Childhood.

Purpose: "Developed to detect Autistic Disorder (AD) in pre-verbal infants … and very young children."
Population: Ages 12-36 months.
Publication Date: 2007.
Acronym: ADEC.
Scores, 17: Response to Name, Imitation, Stereotypical Behaviour, Gaze Switching, Eye Contact in a Game of Peek-a-Boo, Functional Play, Pretend Play, Reciprocity of a Smile, Response to Everyday Sounds, Gaze Monitoring, Responds to a Verbal Command, Demonstrates Use of Words, Anticipatory Posture, Nestling into Caregiver, Use of Gestures, Ability to Switch from Task to Task, Total.
Administration: Individual.
Price Data, 2016: A$519.95 per kit including manual (56 pages), Introduction and Training DVD, 10 score sheets, and set of stimulus materials; A$32.94 per 10 score sheets; A$209.95 per manual and Introduction and Training DVD combination; A$279.95 per set of stimulus materials.
Time: (10) minutes or less.
Comments: Parent/guardian should be present during administration.
Author: Robyn Young.
Publisher: Australian Council for Educational Research Ltd. [Australia].
Cross References: For a review by John J. Vacca, see 18:9.

[171]

Autism Screening Instrument for Educational Planning–Third Edition.

Purpose: Designed to assist with "identification, placement, educational program planning, and analysis of the progress of individuals with autism."
Population: Children ages 2 through 13 who are suspected of having autism.
Publication Dates: 1978-2008.
Acronym: ASIEP-3.
Administration: Individual.
Price Data, 2014: $282 for complete kit including examiner's manual (2008, 100 pages), 25 Autism Behavior Checklist record forms, 25 Sample of Vocal Behavior record forms, 25 Interaction Assessment record forms, 25 Educational Assessment record forms, 25 Prognosis of Learning record forms, audio CD, and toys/manipulatives; $72 per manual; $67 per toys/manipulatives; $29 per 25 forms; $23 per audio CD.

Comments: Contains 5 individual components. The Autism Behavior Checklist is normed for use "during the initial screening process with individuals suspected of being autistic." The other 4 components can be administered to develop an educational plan postdiagnosis.
Authors: David A. Krug, Joel R. Arick, and Patricia J. Almond.
Publisher: PRO-ED.
   a) AUTISM BEHAVIOR CHECKLIST.
   Acronym: ABC.
   Score: Total score only.
   b) EDUCATIONAL ASSESSMENT.
   Scores, 6: In-Seat Behavior, Receptive Language, Expressive Language, Body Concept, Speech Imitation, Total.
   Time: (10-20) minutes.
   c) SAMPLE OF VOCAL BEHAVIOR.
   Scores, 10: Autistic Speech Characteristics (Repetitive, Noncommunicative, Unintelligible, Babbling, Total), Interpreted Language Age (First Use, Communicative, Intelligible, Total), Average Length of Vocalization.
   Time: (30) minutes.
   d) INTERACTION ASSESSMENT.
   Scores, 5: Interaction Score, Constructive Independent Play, No Response, Aggressive Negative, Autistic Interaction Score.
   Time: (12) minutes.
   e) PROGNOSIS OF LEARNING RATE.
   Scores, 5: Hand Shaping, Random Position I, Fixed Position Left, Fixed Position Right, Random Position II.
   Time: (20) minutes.
Cross References: Reviews are scheduled for *The Twentieth Mental Measurements Yearbook.* See T5:234 (3 references); for reviews by D. Joe Olmi and Donald P. Oswald of the second edition, see 13:24 (3 references); see also T4:235 (1 reference); for reviews by Lawrence J. Turton and Richard L. Wikoff of the first edition, see 9:105(1 reference).

[172]

Autism Spectrum Rating Scales.

Purpose: Measures behaviors associated with Autism Spectrum Disorders.
Population: Ages 2-18.
Publication Date: 2010.
Acronym: ASRS.
Scores, 13: 5 ASRS scale scores (Total Score, Social/Communication, Unusual Behaviors, Self-Regulation, Short Form Score) and 8 Treatment scale scores (Peer Socialization, Adult Socialization, Social/Emotional Reciprocity, Atypical Language, Stereotypy, Behavioral Rigidity, Sensory Sensitivity, Attention/Self-Regulation).
Administration: Individual or group.
Levels, 2: 2–5 years, 6–18 years.
Price Data, 2015: $419 per complete hand-scored kit with DSM-5 update including manual (167 pages), 25 ASRS (2-5 years) Parent, Teacher, and Short QuikScore forms, and 25 ASRS (6-18 years) Parent, Teacher, and Short QuikScore forms (forms updated with DSM-5

scoring); $549 per complete scoring software kit including manual, 25 ASRS (2-5 years) Parent, Teacher, and Short Response forms, and 25 ASRS (6-18 years) Parent, Teacher, and Short Response forms; $249 per handscored kit with DSM-5 update (2-5 or 6-18 years) including manual, and 25 Parent, Teacher, and Short QuikScore Forms (forms updated with DSM-5 scoring); $399 per software kit (2-5 or 6-18 years) including the manual, and 25 parent, teacher, and short response forms; $150 per scoring software (unlimited use)- USB key; $89 per manual; $499 per complete online kit including manual, 25 (2-5 years) Parent, Teacher, and Short online forms, and 25 ASRS (6-18 years) Parent, Teacher, and Short online forms; $289 per online kit (2-5 or 6-18 years) including the manual and 25 Parent, Teacher, and Short online forms.

Time: (5-15) minutes.

Comments: All scales include a parent and teacher score form.

Authors: Sam Goldstein and Jack A. Naglieri.

Publisher: Multi-Health Systems, Inc.

Cross References: For reviews by Annette S. Kluck and Steven R. Shaw, see 19:8.

[173]

The Autobiographical Memory Interview.

Purpose: "Provides an assessment of a subject's personal remote (retrograde) memory."

Population: Ages 18–80.

Publication Date: 1990.

Acronym: AMI.

Scores, 8: Personal Semantic (Childhood, Young Adult, Recent, Total), Autobiographical Incidents (Childhood, Young Adult, Recent, Total).

Administration: Individual.

Price Data, 2015: £120 per complete kit including manual (24 pages) and 25 scoring sheets; £67 per 50 scoring sheets.

Time: Untimed.

Comments: Semistructured interview format.

Authors: Michael Kopelman, Barbara Wilson, and Alan Baddeley.

Publisher: Pearson Assessment [England].

Cross References: For reviews by Carolyn M. Callahan and by Michael Furlong and Diane Tanigawa, see 17:11.

[174]

Automated Office Battery.

Purpose: Aptitude tests designed for the selection of staff to work in offices with a high degree of automation.

Population: Student and employed clerical staff.

Publication Dates: 1985–1986.

Acronym: AOB.

Scores: 3 tests: Numerical Estimation, Computer Checking, Coded Instructions.

Administration: Group.

Price Data: Available from publisher.

Time: 40(60) minutes for entire battery.

Comments: "Tests may be used individually or as a complete battery as particular requirements dictate."

Authors: Bill Mabey and Hazel Stevenson.

Publisher: CEB.

   a) NUMERICAL ESTIMATION.
   Purpose: A test to measure the ability to estimate the answer to a calculation.
   Acronym: NE-1.
   Time: 10(15) minutes.
   b) COMPUTER CHECKING.
   Purpose: A test to measure the ability to check machine input information with the corresponding output.
   Acronym: CC-2.
   Time: 12(17) minutes.
   c) CODED INSTRUCTIONS.
   Purpose: A test to measure the ability to comprehend and follow written instructions when a form of coded language is used.
   Time: 18(23) minutes.

Cross References: For a review by Philip Ash, see 11:24.

[175]

The Awareness of Social Inference Test.

Purpose: To test "the ability of the viewer to recognize basic emotions shown by other people" and to test "the ability of the viewer to determine speaker intention, attitude, and meaning."

Population: Ages 14–60.

Publication Date: 2002.

Acronym: TASIT.

Scores: Emotion Evaluation Test (Happy, Surprised, Neutral, Sad, Angry, Anxious, Revolted, Total Positive Emotions, Total Negative Emotions, Total Positive and Negative Emotions), Social Inference [Minimal] Test (Sincere, Sarcasm, Total), Social Inference [Enriched] Test (Lies, Sarcasm, Total).

Administration: Individual.

Forms, 2: A, B.

Price Data, 2015: £305 per complete kit including manual (16 pages), 2 packs of 25 scoring sheets, and 2 DVDs; £91.50 per 2 packs of 25 scoring sheets.

Time: (30–45) minutes.

Authors: Skye McDonald, Sharon Flanagan, and Jennifer Rollins.

Publisher: Pearson Assessment [England].

[176]

Bankson-Bernthal Test of Phonology.

Purpose: "Designed for use by speech-language clinicians to assess the phonology of preschool and school-age children."

Population: Ages 3-9.

Publication Dates: 1989–1990.

Acronym: BBTOP.
Scores, 3: Word Inventory, Consonants Composite, Phonological Processes Composite.
Administration: Individual.
Price Data, 2015: $203 per complete kit; $96 per picture book; $56 per 25 record forms; $62 per manual (1990, 111 pages).
Time: (10-15) minutes.
Authors: Nicholas W. Bankson and John E. Bernthal.
Publisher: PRO-ED.
Cross References: See T5:240 (4 references); for reviews by Lynn S. Bliss and Lawrence J. Turton, see 12:41.

[177]
Bankson Language Test—2.

Purpose: Constructed "to establish the presence of a language disorder and identify areas in need of further, in-depth testing."
Population: Ages 3-0 to 6-11.
Publication Dates: 1977–1990.
Acronym: BLT-2.
Scores, 4: Semantic Knowledge, Morphological and Syntactic Rules, Language Quotient, Pragmatic Knowledge (optional).
Administration: Individual.
Forms, 2: BLT-2; BLT-2 Screen.
Price Data, 2015: $171 per complete kit including 25 profile/examiner's record booklets, 25 screen record forms, picture book, and examiner's manual (1990, 32 pages); $62 per picture book; $43 per 25 profile/examiner's record booklets; $22 per 25 screen record forms; $56 per examiner's manual.
Time: (30) minutes.
Comments: Revision of Bankson Language Screening Test.
Author: Nicholas W. Bankson.
Publisher: PRO-ED.
Cross References: See T5:241 (4 references) and T4:241 (3 references); for reviews by Ronald B. Gillam and Roger L. Towne, see 11:26 (4 references); for a review of an earlier edition by Barry W. Jones, see 9:107 (1 reference).

[178]
Bar-Ilan Picture Test for Children.

Purpose: "A semi-projective device to pinpoint the child's perception of his place in society, in his formal educational setting, and in his home, as well as his perception of his weaker points and of his potential for coping with life."
Population: Ages 4–16.
Publication Dates: 1982–1989.
Scores: Guidelines for analysis in 8 areas: Emotional Makeup, Motivation, Interpersonal Behavior and Areas of Conflict, Attitudes of Teachers-Parents Toward Testee, Attitudes of Peers and Siblings Towards Testee, Degree of Mastery and Feeling of Competence, Quality of Thinking Process, Activity.
Administration: Individual.
Forms, 1: 9 drawings (6 of which have different versions for boys and girls).
Price Data: Available from publisher.
Time: Administration time not reported.
Comments: 1989 edition is identical to 1982 edition except Appendix II was added.
Authors: Rivkah Itskowitz and Helen Strauss.
Publisher: Hogrefe Psykologisk Forlag A/S [Denmark].
Cross References: See T5:242 (1 reference) and T4:242 (1 reference).

[179]
Barkley Adult ADHD Rating Scale-IV.

Purpose: Designed "for clinical purposes to evaluate the range of ADHD symptoms in clinic-referred or high-risk adults ... includes a section of items for assessing ... a subtype of ADHD known as sluggish cognitive tempo."
Population: Ages 18 to 89.
Publication Date: 2011.
Acronym: BAARS-IV.
Price Data, 2015: $136 for manual (160 pages) containing forms and score sheets (includes permission to photocopy).
Author: Russell A. Barkley.
Publisher: Guilford Publications, Inc.
  a) SELF-REPORT: CURRENT SYMPTOMS.
  Scores, 9: Inattention, Hyperactivity, Impulsivity, Sluggish Cognitive Tempo, Total ADHD Score, Symptom Counts (Inattention, Hyperactivity-Impulsivity, Total ADHD, Sluggish Cognitive Tempo).
  Time: (5-7) minutes.
  b) SELF-REPORT: CHILDHOOD SYMPTOMS.
  Scores, 6: Inattention, Hyperactivity-Impulsivity, Total, Symptom Count (Inattention, Hyperactivity-Impulsivity, Total).
  Time: (5-7) minutes.
  c) OTHER-REPORT: CURRENT SYMPTOMS.
  Scores, 10: Inattention, Hyperactivity, Impulsivity, Total, Sluggish Cognitive Tempo, Symptom Counts (Inattention, Hyperactivity, Impulsivity, Total, Sluggish Cognitive Tempo).
  Time: (5-7) minutes.
  d) OTHER-REPORT: CHILDHOOD SYMPTOMS.
  Scores, 6: Inattention, Hyperactivity-Impulsivity, Total, Symptom Counts (Inattention, Hyperactivity-Impulsivity, Total).
  Time: (5-7) minutes.
  e) SELF-REPORT: QUICK SCREEN.
  Scores, 3: Current Symptoms, Childhood Symptoms, Total.
  Time: (3-5) minutes.
  f) OTHER-REPORT: QUICK SCREEN.
  Scores, 2: Current Symptoms, Childhood Symptoms.
  Time: (3-5) minutes.

g) SELF-REPORT: CURRENT SYMPTOMS IN-TERVIEW.

Scores, 5: Symptom Count (Inattention, Hyperactivity, Impulsivity, Total, Sluggish Cognitive Tempo).

Time: (5-7) minutes.

h) SELF-REPORT: CHILDHOOD SYMPTOMS INTERVIEW.

Scores, 3: Symptom Count (Inattention, Hyperactivity-Impulsivity, Total).

Time: (5-7) minutes.

Cross References: For reviews by Nancy L. Crumpton and Carolyn H. Suppa, see 19:9.

[180]
Barkley Deficits in Executive Functioning Scale.

Purpose: Designed "for evaluating dimensions of adult executive functioning in daily life."

Population: Ages 18-81.

Publication Date: 2011.

Acronym: BDEFS.

Scores, 8: Self-Management to Time, Self-Organization/Problem Solving, Self-Restraint, Self-Motivation, Self-Regulation of Emotions, Total EF Summary, ADHD-EF Index, EF Symptom Count.

Administration: Individual.

Forms, 4: Self-Report, Other-Report, Short Form, Long Form.

Price Data, 2015: $136 per manual (184 pages) including all forms and score sheets (includes permission to photocopy).

Time: (15-20) minutes long form; (4-5) minutes short form.

Author: Russell A. Barkley.

Publisher: Guilford Publications, Inc.

Cross References: For reviews by Martin W. Anderson and Gregory Schraw, see 19:10.

[181]
Barkley Deficits in Executive Functioning Scale–Children and Adolescents.

Purpose: Designed to "evaluate the major components of executive functioning in daily life activities of children … for whom there is concern about deficits in EF, such as children with neurological, developmental, or psychiatric disorders or those having psychological difficulties with which deficits in EF may be thought to be associated."

Population: Ages 6-17 years.

Publication Date: 2012.

Acronym: BDEFS-CA.

Scores, 9: Self-Management to Time, Self-Organization/Problem Solving, Self-Restraint, Self-Motivation, Self-Regulation of Emotion, EF Summary Score, EF Symptom Count, EF Summary Score–Short Form, ADHD-EF Index (optional).

Administration: Individual.

Forms, 3: Long Form, Short Form, Interview.

Price Data, 2015: $136 per manual (192 pages), includes permission to reproduce forms and score sheets (found in manual) for repeated use.

Time: (10-15) minutes (Long Form); (3-5) minutes (Short Form).

Comments: "If an individual is unable to complete the BDEFS-CA Long Form or BDEFS-CA Short Form … the examiner may opt to use the BDEFS-CA Interview, which is based on the BDEFS-CA Short Form (20 items)."

Author: Russell A. Barkley.

Publisher: Guilford Publications, Inc.

Cross References: For reviews by Joe W. Dixon and Kathleen Torsney, see 19:11.

[182]
Barkley Functional Impairment Scale.

Purpose: A self-report assessment "intended for clinical purposes—specifically, to be used to evaluate the range of functional impairment in clinic-referred or high-risk adults."

Population: Ages 18-89.

Publication Date: 2011.

Acronym: BFIS.

Scores, 2: Mean Impairment, Percent Domains Impaired; 15 domains: Home-Family, Home-Chores, Work, Social-Strangers, Social-Friends, Community Activities, Education, Marriage/Cohabitation/Dating, Money Management, Driving, Sexual Relations, Daily Responsibilities, Self-Care Routines, Health Maintenance, Childrearing. Administration: Individual.

Forms, 4: Long Form: Self-Report, Quick Screen: Self-Report, Long Form: Other-Report, Quick Screen: Other-Report.

Price Data, 2015: $136 per manual, including all forms and scoresheets (including permission to photocopy).

Time: (5-7) minutes for Long Form; (3-5) minutes for Quick Screen.

Author: Russell A. Barkley.

Publisher: Guilford Publications, Inc.

Cross References: For reviews by Merith Cosden and Robert Wright, see 19:12.

[183]
Barkley Functional Impairment Scale–Children and Adolescents.

Purpose: Designed to "[assess] psychosocial impairments in 15 domains of major life activities."

Population: Parents of children ages 6–17.

Publication Date: 2012.

Acronym: BFIS-CA.

Scores, 18: With Mother, With Father, School Performance, With Siblings, Playing in Neighborhood,

Community Activities, Visiting Others, Playing at School, Managing Money, Self-Care, Doing Chores, School Homework, Following Rules, With Other Adults, Playing Sports, Home–School Mean Impairment Score, Community–Leisure Mean Impairment Score, Number of Impaired Domains.
Administration: Individual.
Forms, 2: Parent Rating Scale, Parent Interview.
Price Data, 2015: $136 per manual (176 pages), includes permission to reproduce forms and score sheets for personal use.
Time: (5–7) minutes.
Author: Russell A. Barkley.
Publisher: Guilford Publications, Inc.
Cross References: For reviews by Justin Low and Cynthia A. Rohrbeck, see 19:13.

[184]
Barriers to Employment Success Inventory, Fourth Edition.

Purpose: Designed to "[help] individuals identify their major barriers to obtaining a job or succeeding in their employment."
Population: Job seekers, those who have been unsuccessful in getting a job, and those who are unable to keep a job.
Publication Dates: 2002-2011.
Acronym: BESI.
Scores, 5: Personal and Financial, Emotional and Physical, Career Decision-Making and Planning, Job-Seeking Knowledge, Training and Education.
Administration: Individual or group.
Price Data, 2016: $63.95 per 25 consumable booklets; volume discount available. Administrator's guide (16 pages) available for download from publisher's website.
Time: (20) minutes.
Author: John J. Liptak.
Publisher: JIST/EMC Publishing.
Cross References: Reviews are scheduled for *The Twentieth Mental Measurements Yearbook*. For reviews by Wayne J. Camara and Kathy E. Green of the second edition, see 16:22.

[185]
Barron-Welsh Art Scale.

Purpose: Designed for use in studies of creativity.
Population: Ages 6 and over.
Publication Dates: 1959-1980.
Acronym: BWAS.
Score: Total score only.
Administration: Individual or group.
Price Data: Available from publisher.
Time: Untimed.
Comments: Included in the Welsh Figure Preference Test (2240).

Authors: George S. Welsh and Frank Barron.
Cross References: For reviews by Leonard Baird and G. Helmstadter, see 7:41; see also T3:243 (15 references).

[186]
Barsch Learning Style Inventory-Revised.

Purpose: Designed to assess an individual's learning style.
Population: 14 through adult.
Publication Dates: 1980–1996.
Scores: 4: Visual Preference, Auditory Preference, Tactile Preference, Kinesthetic Preference.
Administration: Group.
Manual: No manual.
Price Data, 2015: $14 per test kit (10 Inventories and 10 Effective Study Tips).
Time: Administration time not reported.
Comments: Intended as an "informal survey, such as would be used by teachers or education specialists to guide them in setting up an appropriate educational plan."
Author: Jeffrey R. Barsch.
Publisher: Academic Therapy Publications.
Cross References: For reviews by John Biggs and Jayne A. Parker, see 9:111.

[187]
BASC-3 Behavioral and Emotional Screening System.

Purpose: Designed as a set of screening measures "to assess behavioral and emotional strengths and weaknesses in children and adolescents."
Population: Ages 3-18.
Publication Dates: 2007-2015.
Acronym: BASC-3 BESS.
Administration: Individual or group.
Forms, 5: Teacher–Preschool, Teacher–Child/Adolescent, Parent–Preschool, Parent–Child/Adolescent, Student–Child/Adolescent.
Price Data, 2016: $247 per hand scored kit including manual (2015, 95 pages) and 25 of each record form and hand scored worksheet (teacher, parent, student; preschool, child/adolescent); $70 per manual; $32 per 25 forms; $9 per 25 hand scored worksheets.
Foreign Language Edition: Spanish versions of parent and student forms available.
Time: (5-15) minutes.
Comments: Scores linked to interventions in the BASC-3 Behavior Intervention Guide; digital administration, scoring, and reporting available.
Authors: Randy W. Kamphaus and Cecil R. Reynolds.
Publisher: Pearson.
   a) TEACHER FORMS.
     Scores, 5: Behavioral and Emotional Risk, Externalizing Risk, Internalizing Risk, Adaptive Skills Risk, Validity Index.

1. Teacher–Preschool.
Population: Ages 3-5.
2. Teacher–Child/Adolescent.
Population: Grades K-12.
b) PARENT FORMS.
Scores, 5: Behavioral and Emotional Risk, Externalizing Risk, Internalizing Risk, Adaptive Skills Risk, Validity Index.
1. Parent–Preschool.
Population: Ages 3-5.
2. Parent–Child/Adolescent.
Population: Grades K-12
c) STUDENT FORM.
1. Student–Child/Adolescent.
Population: Students in Grades 3-12.
Scores, 5: Behavioral and Emotional Risk, Internalizing Risk, Self-Regulation Risk, Personal Adjustment Risk, Validity Index.
Cross References: Reviews are scheduled for *The Twentieth Mental Measurements Yearbook*. For reviews by Michael J. Furlong and Lindsey O'Brennan and by Kathleen M. Johnson of the original edition, see 18:10.

[188]
BASC-2 Progress Monitor.
Purpose: Designed "to monitor the behavioral and emotional functioning of a child or adolescent who is participating in an intervention or treatment program."
Population: Ages 2 to 21 years.
Publication Dates: 2008-2009.
Acronym: BASC-2 PM.
Administration: Individual.
Price Data, 2015: $227.40 per starter set including manual (2009, 125 pages) and 10 each of all teacher, parent, and student forms; $66.95 per manual; $27.30 per 25 forms; $39 per audio CD.
Foreign Language Edition: Parent and student forms available in Spanish.
Time: (5) minutes per form.
Comments: Forms may be used individually or in any combination; parent and student forms may be administered via audio recordings in English or Spanish to parents or students with reading difficulties; computer scoring available.
Authors: Cecil R. Reynolds and Randy W. Kamphaus.
Publisher: Pearson.
a) PRESCHOOL.
Population: Ages 2 to 5.
Scores, 4: Externalizing and ADHD Problems, Internalizing Problems, Social Withdrawal, Adaptive Skills.
Forms, 2: Teacher, Parent.
b) CHILD AND ADOLESCENT.
Population: Children in Grades K-12.
Scores, 5: Externalizing and ADHD Problems (Parent and Teacher Forms), School and ADHD Problems (Student Form), Internalizing Problems (all forms), Social Withdrawal (Teacher and Parent Forms), Adaptive Skills (Teacher and Parent Forms).
Forms, 3: Teacher, Parent, Student.

Cross References: Reviews are scheduled for *The Twentieth Mental Measurements Yearbook*.

[189]
Basic Achievement Skills Inventory.
Purpose: Designed "to measure reading, written language, and math skills among children and adults."
Population: Grades 3 & 4, 5 & 6, 7 & 8, 9–12, and ages 8 to 80.
Publication Date: 2004.
Acronym: BASI.
Administration: Individual or group.
Tests, 2: Comprehensive, Survey.
Price Data, 2015: $181.50 per Q Local/BASI Starter kit: Comprehensive with adult summary report including manual (382 pages), 1 test booklet for each level (Levels 1–4, Forms A and B), and 12 answer sheets (3 for each level), and 12 Q Local administrations; $195.75 per Q Local/BASI starter kit: Comprehensive with student summary report; $78.90 per Q Local Survey starter kit: Survey with summary report.
Comments: Form A is for August-December testing; Form B is for January-July testing.
Author: Achilles N. Bardos.
Publisher: Pearson.
a) BASI COMPREHENSIVE.
Population: Grades 3 & 4, 5 & 6, 7 & 8, 9–12.
Scores, 9: Reading (Vocabulary, Reading Comprehension, Total), Written Language (Spelling, Language Mechanics, Total), Math (Math Comprehension, Math Application, Total).
Subtests, 6: Vocabulary, Spelling, Language Mechanics, Reading Comprehension, Math Computation, Math Application.
Levels, 4: Grades 3 & 4, Grades 5 & 6, Grades 7 & 8, Grades 9–12.
Forms, 2: A, B at each level.
Time: 115 minutes.
b) BASI SURVEY.
Population: Ages 8 to 80.
Scores, 7: Verbal Skills (Vocabulary, Language Mechanics, Reading Comprehension, Total), Math Skills (Math Computation, Math Application, Total).
Subtests, 2: Verbal Skills, Math Skills.
Price Data: $36.05 per 10 test booklets (Math and Verbal).
Time: 50 minutes.
Comments: Brief version of the Comprehensive Test.
Cross References: For reviews by Elizabeth Kelley Rhoades and Michael S. Trevisan, see 17:13.

[190]
Basic Banking Skills Battery.
Purpose: Designed to "measure skills and abilities for financial services jobs."
Population: Age 18 and over.
Publication Dates: 1987–1995.
Acronym: BBSB.

Scores, 14: Number Comparison, Name Comparison, Arithmetic Computation, Error Recognition, Drive, School Achievement, Interpersonal Skills, Cognitive Skills, Motor Ability, Math Ability, Self Discipline, Leadership, Perceptual Skills, Error Perception.
Administration: Group.
Forms, 2: Timed, Untimed.
Price Data: Available from publisher.
Time: (45) minutes.
Comments: Test can be scored online, by fax, optical screening; software is available.
Author: General Dynamics Information Technology.
Publisher: General Dynamics Information Technology.

[191]

Basic Early Assessment of Reading™.

Purpose: Designed "to assess young students' acquisition of the essential components of reading—phonemic awareness, phonics, vocabulary, comprehension, and oral reading fluency."
Population: Grades K–3.
Publication Date: 2002.
Acronym: BEAR®.
Levels, 4: K, 1, 2, 3.
Price Data, 2015: $368 per complete BEAR (specify: Kindergarten & Grade 1 or Grade 2 & 3) COMBO kit including Teacher's Guide, Level K-3 Oral Reading Fluency Assessment Scoring Guide, 13 Level K-3 Oral Reading Fluency Assessment Passage Cards, Scoring and Reporting Software, and the following components in both Levels: Initial-Skills Analysis Administration and Scoring Guide, 25 Initial-Skills Analysis Test Booklets, Summative Assessment Administration Guide, Summative Assessment Scoring Guide, 25 Summative Assessment Comprehension, 25 Summative Assessment Reading Basics, 25 Summative Assessment Language Arts, Specific-Skill Analysis Administration and Scoring Guide, and 3 Specific-Skill Analysis Black Line Masters;
Comments: Criterion-referenced testing program with modules designed for use in conjunction with classroom activities; computer-scoring and reporting available for PC.
Author: Riverside Publishing.
Publisher: PRO-ED.
　　a) INITIAL-SKILLS ANALYSIS.
　　Purpose: Designed to provide a quick overview of students' skills in Reading Basics, Comprehension, and Language Arts.
　　Scores, 4: Reading Basics, Comprehension, Language Arts, Total.
　　Administration: Individual or group.
　　Time: (45–60) minutes.
　　b) SPECIFIC-SKILL ANALYSIS.
　　Purpose: Designed to provide diagnostic information about students' specific skills in Reading Basics, Comprehension, and Language Arts.
　　Scores, 4: Reading Basics, Comprehension, Language Arts, Total.

　　Administration: Individual or group.
　　Time: (30–40) minutes per content area.
　　c) ORAL READING FLUENCY ASSESSMENT.
　　Purpose: Designed to provide information about students' accuracy, ability to retell what was read, oral reading skills, and reading rate (for Levels 1–3).
　　Scores, 3: Letter Recognition, Informational, Narrative.
　　Administration: Individual.
　　Forms: 6 (8 at Level K).
　　Time: (15–30) minutes per passage or list.
　　d) SUMMATIVE ASSESSMENT.
　　Purpose: Designed to assess early reading and language arts skills for placement and instructional planning.
　　Scores, 4: Reading Basics, Comprehension, Language Arts, Total.
　　Administration: Individual or group.
　　Time: (30–40) minutes per content area.
Cross References: For reviews by Zandra S. Gratz and Annita Marie Ward, see 16:23.

[192]

Basic Economics Test, Third Edition.

Purpose: "An updated economics achievement test for curriculum development, for the assessment of student understanding, and for determining the effectiveness of educational materials and teaching strategies."
Population: Grades 5–6.
Publication Dates: 1980–2010.
Acronym: BET.
Scores: Total score only.
Administration: Group.
Forms, 2: A, B.
Price Data, 2016: This test is now available at no cost from the test publisher.
Time: 30 minutes.
Authors: William B. Walstad, Ken Rebeck, and Roger B. Butters.
Publisher: Council for Economic Education.
Cross References: For reviews by Irvin J. Lehmann and A. Harry Passow of the 1981 edition, see 11:27; for reviews by Mary Friend Adams and James O. Hodges of an earlier edition titled Test of Elementary Economics, Revised Experimental Edition, see 8:901 (1 reference).

[193]

Basic Number Diagnostic Test [2001 Revision].

Purpose: Designed to "show what a child can do (and cannot do) so that teaching objectives for that child can be determined."
Population: Ages 5–7.
Publication Dates: 1980–2001.
Scores, 13: Reciting Numbers, Naming Numerals, Copying Over Numerals, Copying Underneath Numerals, Counting Bricks, Selecting Bricks, Writing Numerals in Sequence, Writing Numerals to Dictation, Addition

with Objects, Addition with Numerals, Subtraction with Objects, Subtraction with Numerals, Total.

Administration: Individual.

Forms, 2: A, B.

Price Data, 2016: £17.50 per set of 10 copies; £28 per manual (2001, 30 pages); £30.50 per specimen set.

Time: (15–25) minutes.

Comments: "Criterion-referenced."

Author: Bill Gillham.

Publisher: Hodder Education [United Kingdom].

Cross References: For reviews by Cleborne D. Maddux and Jeffrey K. Smith, see 15:27; for a review by Mary Montgomery Lindquist of an earlier edition, see 9:117.

[194]

Basic Number Screening Test [2001 Edition].

Purpose: "Quick assessment of a child's understanding of … number concepts and number skills."

Population: Ages 7–12.

Publication Dates: 1976–2001.

Scores: No scores.

Administration: Group.

Forms, 2: A, B.

Price Data: Available from publisher.

Time: (20–35) minutes.

Comments: May be orally administered. The test publisher has indicated there is a newer edition of this test; description will be updated when complete test materials are received.

Authors: Bill Gillham and Kenneth Heese.

Publisher: Hodder Education [United Kingdom].

Cross References: For reviews by Kevin D. Crehan and Thanos Patelis, see 16:24; for reviews by John O. Anderson and Suzanna Lance of the 1996 edition, see 15:28; for reviews by Mary Montgomery Lindquist and Marilyn N. Suydam of an earlier edition, see 9:118.

[195]

Basic Personality Inventory.

Purpose: Constructed to be a "measure of personality and psychopathology."

Population: Adult and adolescent.

Publication Dates: 1988-1997.

Acronym: BPI.

Scores, 12: Hypochondriasis, Depression, Denial, Interpersonal Problems, Alienation, Persecutory Ideas, Anxiety, Thinking Disorder, Impulse Expression, Social Introversion, Self Depreciation, Deviation.

Administration: Individual or group.

Price Data, 2015: $97 per examination kit including 5 reusable test booklets, scoring template, 5 hand-scorable answer sheets, 5 profile sheets, answer sheet and coupon for BPI Basic Report, and manual on CD (1996, 120 pages); $25 per test manual on CD; $65 per 25 test booklets; $55 per 25 hand-scorable answer sheets; $55 per 25 profile sheets (select adult or adolescent); $24 per

scoring template; $76–$86 (depending on volume) per 10 machine-scorable answer sheets and coupons for Basic Reports; $155 per software package including installation package and 10 coupons for computer report; $12-$20 (depending on volume) per online password.

Time: 35 minutes.

Author: Douglas N. Jackson.

Publisher: SIGMA Assessment Systems, Inc.

Cross References: See T5:256 (4 references); for reviews by Susana Urbina and Tamela Yelland, see 12:42 (1 reference); see also T4:254 (16 references).

[196]

Basic Reading Inventory, Eleventh Edition.

Purpose: Designed as an informal measure of students' reading behavior.

Population: Students who are pre-primer through Grade 12.

Publication Dates: 1978-2012.

Acronym: BRI.

Scores, 16: Reading Level Score (Independent, Instructional, Frustration), Word Recognition in Isolation, Word Recognition in Context, Comprehension, Listening Level, Reading Rate, 10 Informal Assessments of Early Literacy (Alphabet Knowledge, Writing, Literacy Knowledge, Wordless Picture Reading, Caption Reading, Auditory Discrimination, Phoneme Awareness, Phoneme Segmentation, Basic Word Knowledge, Pre-Primer Passages).

Administration: Individual.

Forms, 7: A, B, C, D, E, LL, LI.

Price Data, 2016: $70 per eBook (3 year access); $56 per eBook (6 month access); $85 per printed book with CD (contains video clips, performance booklets, summary sheets, observation guide, bibliography).

Time: Administration time not reported.

Author: Jerry L. Johns.

Publisher: Kendall/Hunt Publishing Company.

Cross References: Reviews are scheduled for *The Twentieth Mental Measurements Yearbook*. For reviews by Matthew K. Burns and Zandra S. Gratz of the eighth edition, see 15:29; for reviews by Michael Harwell and Steven A. Stahl of the seventh edition, see 14:34 (6 references); see also T5:257 (4 references); for reviews by Jerrilyn V. Andrews and Robert T. Williams of the fifth edition, see 12:43 (3 references); see also T4:255 (4 references); for a review by Gus Plessas of the second edition, see 9:119.

[197]

Basic School Skills Inventory, Third Edition.

Purpose: Designed to locate children who are at-risk for school failure, who need more in-depth assessment, and who should be referred for additional study.

Population: Ages 4-0 to 8-11.

Publication Dates: 1975–1998.

Acronym: BSSI-3.
Scores, 7: Spoken Language, Reading, Writing, Mathematics, Classroom Behavior, Daily Living Skills, Overall Skill Level.
Administration: Individual.
Price Data, 2015: $126 per complete kit including examiner's manual (1998, 77 pages), and 25 profile/response forms; $72 per examiner's manual; $62 per 25 profile/response forms.
Time: (5–8) minutes.
Comments: Replaces the Basic School Skills Inventory—Diagnostic (T4:256).
Authors: Donald D. Hammill, James E. Leigh, Nils A. Pearson, and Taddy Maddox.
Publisher: PRO-ED.
Cross References: For reviews by R. W. Kamphaus and Leah M. Nellis, see 14:35; see also T5:258 and T4:256 (1 reference); for a review by William J. Webster of the Basic School Skills Inventory Diagnostic, see 9:120; for reviews by Byron R. Egeland and Lawrence M. Kasdon of an earlier edition, see 8:424 (2 references).

[198]

Basic Skills Locater Test.

Purpose: "Designed to assess a person's functional skill levels in math and language."
Population: Ages 15 to adult who are functioning below a 12th grade level.
Publication Date: 1998.
Scores, 2: Language, Math.
Administration: Group or individual.
Price Data, 2016: $195 per Basic Skills Locater Test (software version) including 1 guide, 1 reproducible test master, and software; $195 per Basic Skills Locater Test (print version) including 1 user's guide, 10 reusable test booklets, 100 answer sheets, 1 test key, and a Windows scoring disk; web-based version available.
Time: (30–60) minutes.
Comments: Test results place test-takers into four levels corresponding to GED and grade levels: GED Level 1 (grades 1–3); GED Level 2 (grades 4–6); GED Level 3 (grades 7–8) and GED Level 4 (grades 9–12). Bar graphs representing competency in each level in the two domains of Language and Math yield 8 levels of competency for each test-taker.
Author: Helena Hendrix-Frye.
Publisher: Piney Mountain Press.
Cross References: For a review by Hoi K. Suen, see 15:30.

[199]

BASIS-A Inventory [Basic Adlerian Scales for Interpersonal Success—Adult].

Purpose: Designed "to help understand how an individual's life-style, based on beliefs developed in early childhood, contributes to one's effectiveness in social, work, and intimate relationships."
Population: Adults.
Publication Dates: 1993–1997.
Acronym: BASIS-A.
Scores, 10: BASIS scales (Belonging-Social Interest, Taking Charge, Going Along, Wanting Recognition, Being Cautious); HELPS scales (Harshness, Entitlement, Liked By All, Striving for Perfection, Softness).
Administration: Group or individual.
Price Data, 2015: $109 per introductory package including 10 test booklets, 10 scoring booklets, technical manual (1997, 87 pages), interpretive manual (1997, 61 pages), and 10 copies of interpretive guide; $44 per 25 interpretive guides; $26 per technical manual; $26 per interpretive manual.
Foreign Language Editions: Test items and instructions available in Spanish, German, and Lithuanian.
Time: (10–15) minutes.
Comments: Self-scored.
Authors: Mary S. Wheeler, Roy M. Kern, and William L. Curlette.
Publisher: TRT Associates, Inc.
Cross References: For reviews by James P. Choca and Peggy E. Gallaher, see 13:26.

[200]

Bass Orientation Inventory.

Purpose: Designed to measure the core elements of interpersonal behavior in organizations, including self, interaction, and task behaviors.
Population: College and industry.
Publication Dates: 1962–1977.
Acronym: ORI.
Scores, 3: Self-Orientation, Interaction-Orientation, Task-Orientation.
Administration: Individual and group.
Price Data: Available from publisher.
Time: (20–25) minutes.
Comments: Previously listed as The Orientation Inventory.
Author: Bernard M. Bass.
Publisher: Mind Garden, Inc.
Cross References: See T3:1748 (1 reference); for a review by Thomas J. Bouchard, Jr., see 8:636 (15 references); see also T2:1306 (26 references) and P:187 (13 references); for reviews by Richard S. Barrett and H. Bradley Sagen, see 6:153 (2 references).

[201]

Batería III Woodcock-Muñoz™.

Purpose: Designed to "measure intellectual abilities and academic achievement" in Spanish-speaking individuals.
Population: Ages 2–90+.
Publication Dates: 1982–2007.
Acronym: Batería III.

Price Data, 2015: $2,132.75 per complete Batería III with 2 carrying cases including Cognitive standard and extended test books, examiner's manual (158 pages), examiner training workbook, audio CD, 25 test records and 25 subject response booklets, 5 BIA test records, scoring guides, Achievement standard and extended test books, examiner's manual (180 pages), examiner training workbook, audio CD, 25 test records and subject response booklets, WJ III NU Compuscore® and Profiles Program, NU technical manual, and scoring guides; $1,418.80 per Batería III Cognitive Battery with carrying case including Cognitive standard and extended test books, examiner's manual, examiner training workbook, audio CD, 25 test records and subject response booklets, 5 BIA test records, WJ III NU Compuscore and Profiles Program, NU technical manual, and scoring guides; $621.50 per Diagnostic Supplement including test book, examiner's manual (2005, 151 pages), 25 test records, audio CD, WJ III technical manual, WJ III NU Compuscore and Profiles Program, NU technical manual, and scoring guide; $957.60 per Batería III Achievement Battery with carrying case including Achievement standard and extended test books, examiner's manual, examiner training workbook, audio CD, 25 test records and subject response booklets, WJ III NU Compuscore and Profiles Program, NU technical manual, and scoring guides.

Foreign Language Editions: All of the materials are in Spanish including the examiner's manuals and the technical manual.

Time: (5–10) minutes per test.

Comments: The Batería III Woodcock-Muñoz is the parallel Spanish adaption/translation of the Woodcock-Johnson III (15:281).

Authors: Ana F. Muñoz-Sandoval, Richard W. Woodcock, Kevin S. McGrew, and Nancy Mather (test); Fredrick A. Schrank, Kevin S. McGrew, Mary L. Ruef, Criselda G. Alvarado, Ana F. Muñoz-Sandoval, and Richard W. Woodcock (manual).

Publisher: Houghton Mifflin Harcourt.

   a) PRUEBAS DE HABILIDADES COGNITIVAS (TESTS OF COGNITIVE ABILITIES).

   Acronym: Batería III COG.

   Scores: 20 tests: Standard Battery (Comprensión verbal, Aprendizaje visual-auditivo, Relaciones espaciales, Integración de sonidos, Formación de conceptos, Pareo visual, Inversión de números, Palabras incompletas, Memoria de trabajo auditiva, Memoria diferida—aprendizaje visual-auditivo), Extended Battery (Información general, Fluidez de recuperación, Reconocimiento de dibujos, Atención auditiva, Análisis-síntesis, Rapidez en la decisión, Memoria para palabras, Rapidez en la idenificación de dibujos, Planeamiento, Cancelación de pares).

   1) *Suplemento Diagnóstico (Diagnostic Supplement).*

   Acronym: Bateria III SD.

   Scores: 11 tests: Memoria para nombres, Integración visual, Configuración de sonidos—vocalizada, Series numéricas, Números matrices, Tachar, Memoria para frases, Rotación de bloques, Configuración de sonidos—musical, Memoria diferida—Memoria para nombes, Comprensión verbal bilingüe—español/inglés.

   b) PRUEBAS DE APROVECHAMIENTO (TESTS OF ACHIEVEMENT).

   Acronym: Batería III APROV.

   Scores: 22 tests: Standard Battery (Identificación de letras y palabras, Fluidez en la lectura, Rememoración de cuentos, Comprensión de indicaciones, Cálculo, Fluidez en matemáticas, Ortografiá, Fluidez en la escritura, Comprensión de textos, Problemas aplicados, Muestras de redacción, Memoria diferida—Rememoración de cuentos), Extended Battery (Análisis de palabras, Vocabulario sobre dibujos, Comprensión oral, Corrección de textos, Vocabulario de lectura, Conceptos cuantitativos, Conocimientos academicos, Análisis de sonidos, Discernimiento de sonidos, Puntuación y mayúsculas).

Cross References: For reviews by Beth Doll and Courtney LeClair and by Arturo Olivarez, Jr. and Allison Boroda, see 17:14; for reviews by Robert B. Frary and Maria Prendes Lintel of a previous edition, see 13:27; for reviews by Jack A. Cummings and by Steven W. Lee and Elaine Flory Stefany of the Woodcock-Johnson Psycho-Educational Battery—Revised, see 12:415 (36 references); see also T4:2973 (90 references) and T3:2639 (3 references); for reviews by Jack A. Cummings and Alan S. Kaufman of an earlier edition of the Woodcock-Johnson Psycho-Educational Battery, see 9:1387 (6 references).

[202]

Battelle Developmental Inventory™, 2nd Edition.

Purpose: "Screening, diagnosis, and evaluation of early development."

Population: Birth to 7 years, 11 months.

Publication Dates: 1984–2005.

Acronym: BDI-2™.

Administration: Individual.

Forms, 2: Full Assessment, Screening Test.

Foreign Language Editions: Test items available in Spanish translation/adaptation for use by bilingual examiner or with a Spanish monolingual examiner.

Comments: Screening Test available as separate; hand-scoring, web-based, or standalone computer scoring available; the test publisher advises that a normative update is scheduled for release in 2016.

Author: Jean Newborg.

Publisher: Houghton Mifflin Harcourt.

   a) FULL ASSESSMENT.

   Purpose: Assess and identify "strengths and opportunities for learning of typically developing infants, preschoolers, kindergarteners, and early primary school students, as well as those who are advanced," and "children who have a disability or delay in any area of development."

   Scores, 19: Self-Care, Personal Responsibility, Adaptive Total, Adult Interaction, Peer Interaction, Self-Concept and Social Role, Personal-Social Total, Receptive Communication, Expressive Communication, Communication

Total, Gross Motor, Fine Motor, Perceptual Motor, Motor Total, Attention and Memory, Reasoning and Academic Skills, Perception and Concepts, Cognitive Total, Total. **Domains, 5:** Adaptive, Personal-Social, Communication, Motor, Cognitive.
Administration Methods, 3: Structured Procedure, Observation Procedure, Interview Procedure.
Price Data, 2015: $1,282 per complete kit with manipulatives including 5 Test Item Books, Examiner's Manual, Stimulus Book, Set of Presentation Cards, 15 Complete Record Forms, 15 Workbooks, the Screening Test Item Book with 30 Screening Test Record Forms, Set of Screening Presentation Cards, Screening Stimulus Book, the complete set of BDI-2 manipulatives, and a carrying case; $405.70 per screener kit with manipulatives including Examiner's Manual, the Screening Test Item Book with 30 Screening Test Record Forms, set of Screening Presentation Cards, Screening Stimulus Book, Screening Test Quick Reference Guide, manipulatives needed to administer the Screening Test, and a canvas carrying case).
Time: (60–90) minutes.
b) SCREENING TEST.
Purpose: Provides "method for determining in which areas of development, if any, a comprehensive assessment is needed for a given child."
Scores, 6: Adaptive, Personal-Social, Communication, Motor, Cognitive, Total.
Price Data: $299 per Screener Kit including Screening Test Item Book with 30 Screening Test booklets, set of screening visuals, examiner's manual, Quick Reference Guide, manipulatives needed to administer the Screening Test, and a canvas carrying case; $178.25 per Screener Kit including the screening test item book with 30 screening test booklets, and set of screening visuals (must purchase BDI-2 examiner's manual separately); $70.25 per examiner's manual; $51.50 per 30 screening test booklets.
Time: (10-30) minutes.
Cross References: For reviews by Michelle Athanasiou and by Lauren R. Barton and Donna Spiker, see 17:15; see also T5:265 (15 references) and T4:263 (4 references); for reviews by Judy Oehler-Stinnett and Kathleen D. Paget of an earlier edition, see 10:25 (1 reference); for information about the Screening Test, see T5:266 (4 references) and T4:264 (1 reference); for reviews by David W. Barnett and by Joan Ershler and Stephen N. Elliott of an earlier edition of the Screening Test, see 11:30.

[203]
Battery for Health Improvement 2.

Purpose: A psychomedical assessment designed "to provide relevant information and treatment recommendations to professionals who treat injured patients in a variety of settings."
Population: Ages 18–65, individuals who are being treated for a physical injury.
Publication Dates: 1996–2003.
Acronym: BHI 2.
Scores: 18 scales: Validity (Self-Disclosure, Defensiveness), Physical Symptoms (Somatic Complaints, Pain Complaints, Functional Complaints, Muscular Bracing), Affective Scales (Depression, Anxiety, Hostility), Character Scales (Borderline, Symptom Dependency, Chronic Maladjustment, Substance Abuse, Perseverance), Psychosocial Scales (Family Dysfunction, Survivor of Violence, Doctor Dissatisfaction, Job Dissatisfaction).
Administration: Group or individual.
Price Data, 2015: $120.45 per Q Local scoring starter kit with enhanced interpretive reports including manual (2003, 291 pages), 1 soft-cover test booklet, and answer sheets; $107.90 per Q Local scoring starter kit with basic interpretive reports; $83.80 per Q Local scoring starter kit with profile reports; $125.55 per mail-in starter kit with enhanced interpretive reports including manual, 1 soft-cover test booklet, and answer sheets; $133.25 per mail-in starter kit with basic interpretive reports; $89.20 per mail-in starter kit with profile reports; $54.85 per manual; $11.30 per 5 test booklets (English); $2.55 per test booklet (Spanish); $59.45 per compact disc.
Foreign Language Edition: Spanish forms available.
Time: (30–45) minutes.
Comments: Computer administration and audio CD.
Authors: Daniel Bruns and John Mark Disorbio.
Publisher: Pearson.
Cross References: For reviews by Michael G. Kavan and Romeo Vitelli, see 17:16; for reviews by Gregory J. Boyle and Ephrem Fernandez of an earlier edition, see 14:36.

[204]
Bay Area Functional Performance Evaluation, Second Edition.

Purpose: Developed to assess "general components of functioning that are needed to perform activities of daily living."
Population: Psychiatric patients.
Publication Dates: 1978–1987.
Acronym: BaFPE.
Administration: Individual.
Price Data, 2016: $492 per complete test kit.
Comments: Task-Oriented Assessment and Social Interaction Scale may be used separately.
Authors: Susan Lang Williams and Judith Bloomer.
Publisher: Maddak Inc.
a) TASK-ORIENTED ASSESSMENT.
Acronym: TOA.
Scores, 138: 16 Component scores: Cognitive (Memory for Written/Verbal Instruction, Organization of Time and Materials, Attention Span, Evidence of Thought Disorder, Ability to Abstract, Total), Performance (Task Completion, Errors, Efficiency, Total), Affective (Motivation/Compliance, Frustration Tolerance, Self-Confidence, General Affective Impression, Total), Total for the following 11 Parameters: Sorting Shells, Money/Marketing, Home Drawing, Block Design, Kinetic Person Drawing, Total; also 11 Qualitative Signs and Referral Indicators ratings:

Language, Comprehension, Hemispatial Neglect, Memory, Abstraction, Task-Specific Observations, Total for the above parameters.
Time: (30–45) minutes.
b) SOCIAL INTERACTION SCALE.
Acronym: SIS.
Scores, 13: Parameter scores (Verbal Communication, Psychomotor Behavior, Socially Appropriate Behavior, Response to Authority Figures, Degree of Independence/Dependence, Ability to Work with Others, Participation in Group Activities), Social Situations (One-to-One, Mealtime, Unstructured Group, Structured Task or Activity Group, Structured Verbal Group), Total Interaction.
Time: [50–60] minutes.
Cross References: See T5:268 (1 reference); for reviews by Deborah D. Roman and Orest E. Wasyliw, see 12:44; see also T4:265 (1 reference).

[205]

Bayley Infant Neurodevelopmental Screener.

Purpose: "Designed to identify infants between the ages of 3 and 24 months who are developmentally delayed or have neurological impairments."
Population: Ages 3–24 months.
Publication Dates: 1992–1995.
Acronym: BINS.
Scores: 4 areas: Basic Neurological Functions/Intactness, Auditory and Visual Receptive Functions, Verbal and Motor Expressive Functions, Cognitive Processes; total score for each level.
Administration: Individual.
Levels, 6: 3–4 months, 5–6 months, 7–10 months, 11–15 months, 16–20 months, 21–24 months.
Price Data, 2015: $225.50 per complete kit including 25 record forms, manual (1995, 105 pages), stimulus cards, and manipulables in soft-sided carrying case; $53.30 per 25 record forms; $76.90 per manual; $15.40 per stimulus card.
Time: (10–15) minutes.
Comments: Includes a subset of items from the Bayley Scales of Infant Development—Second Edition (BSID–II), but is not an abbreviated form of the BSID-II.
Author: Glen P. Aylward.
Publisher: Pearson.
Cross References: For reviews by James K. Benish and by Damon Krug and Brandon Davis, see 13:28.

[206]

Bayley Scales of Infant and Toddler Development–Third Edition.

Purpose: Designed to "assess the developmental functioning of infants and young children."
Population: Ages 1–42 months.
Publication Dates: 1969-2006.
Acronym: Bayley-III.
Scores, 19: Cognitive, Language (Receptive Communication, Expressive Communication, Total), Motor (Fine Motor, Gross Motor, Total), Social-Emotional, Adaptive Behavior (Communication, Community Use, Functional Pre-Academics, Home Living, Health and Safety, Leisure, Self-Care, Self-Direction, Social, Motor, Total).
Administration: Individual.
Price Data, 2015: $1,025 per complete kit including administration manual (2006, 266 pages), technical manual (2006, 163 pages), 25 Cognitive, Language, and Motor record forms, stimulus book, picture book, manipulative set, 25 Social-Emotional/Adaptive Behavior Questionnaires, 25 Caregiver Report forms, and rolling case; $122.25 per 25 Cognitive, Language, and Motor record forms; $104.55 per 25 Social-Emotional/Adaptive Behavior Questionnaires; $289.55 per stimulus book; $24.30 per picture book; $187.60 per administration manual; $187 per technical manual.
Time: (30-60) minutes.
Author: Nancy Bayley.
Publisher: Pearson.
Cross References: For reviews by Renee M. Tobin and Kathryn E. Hoff and by John J. Venn, see 17:17; see also T5:270 (48 references); for reviews by Carl J. Dunst and Mark H. Fugate of a previous edition, see 13:29 (130 references); see also T4:266 (58 references); for reviews by Michael J. Roszkowski and Jane A. Rysberg of an earlier edition, see 10:26 (80 references); see also 9:126 (42 references) and T3:270 (101 references); for a review by Fred Damarin, see 8:206 (28 references); see also T2:484 (11 references); for reviews by Roberta R. Collard and Raymond H. Holden, see 7:402 (20 references).

[207]

Bayley Scales of Infant and Toddler Development—Third Edition, Screening Test.

Purpose: Designed to "briefly assess the cognitive, language, and motor functioning of infants and young children."
Population: Ages 1-42 months.
Publication Date: 2006.
Acronym: Bayley-III Screening Test.
Scores, 5: Cognitive, Receptive Communication, Expressive Communication, Fine Motor, Gross Motor.
Administration: Individual.
Price Data, 2015: $230.10 per screening test kit including manual (138 pages), 25 screening record forms, screening stimulus book, picture book, and screening manipulative set; $48.95 per 25 screening record forms; $130.70 per stimulus book; $64.85 per manual.
Time: (15-30) minutes.
Author: Nancy Bayley.
Publisher: Pearson.
Cross References: For reviews by R. Anthony Doggett and Kristin N. Johnson-Gros and by Theresa Graham, see 17:18.

[208]

BDI-FastScreen for Medical Patients.

Purpose: Designed to screen for depression in patients reporting somatic and behavioral symptoms that may be attributable to biological, medical, alcohol, and/or substance abuse problems.

Population: Ages 12–82.

Publication Date: 2000.

Acronym: BDI-FastScreen.

Scores: Total score only.

Administration: Group.

Price Data, 2015: $105 per complete kit including manual and 50 score forms; $81 per manual; $56.40 per 50 record forms; $56.40 per 50 scannable record forms.

Foreign Language Edition: Spanish record forms available.

Time: (5) minutes.

Comments: Formerly called Beck Depression Inventory for Primary Care; based upon Beck Depression Inventory—II (210).

Authors: Aaron T. Beck, Robert A. Steer, and Gregory K. Brown.

Publisher: Pearson.

Cross References: For reviews by James J. Hennessy and Nathaniel J. Pallone and by Susan C. Whiston and Kelly Eder, see 16:25.

[209]

Beck Anxiety Inventory [1993 Edition].

Purpose: "Measures the severity of anxiety in adults and adolescents."

Population: Adults and adolescents ages 17 and over.

Publication Dates: 1987–1993.

Acronym: BAI.

Scores: Total score only.

Administration: Individual or group.

Price Data, 2015: $128 per complete kit including 25 record forms and manual (1993, 23 pages); $56.40 per 25 record forms; $81 per manual.

Foreign Language Edition: Available in Spanish.

Time: (5–10) minutes.

Comments: Computer scoring and interpretation available.

Authors: Aaron T. Beck and Robert A. Steer.

Publisher: Pearson.

Cross References: See T5:271 (18 references); for reviews by E. Thomas Dowd and Niels G. Waller, see 13:30 (73 references); see also T4:267 (2 references).

[210]

Beck Depression Inventory—II.

Purpose: "Developed for the assessment of symptoms corresponding to criteria for diagnosing depressive disorders listed in the ... DSM IV."

Population: Ages 13 and over.

Publication Dates: 1961–1996.

Acronym: BDI-II.

Scores: Total score only.

Administration: Group or individual.

Price Data, 2015: $128 per complete kit including manual (1996, 38 pages) and 25 recording forms; $81 per manual; $56.40 per 25 recording forms.

Foreign Language Edition: Available in Spanish.

Time: (5–10) minutes.

Comments: Hand-scored or computer-based administration, scoring, and interpretation available; "revision of BDI based upon new information about depression."

Authors: Aaron T. Beck, Robert A. Steer, and Gregory K. Brown.

Publisher: Pearson.

Cross References: For reviews by Paul A. Arbisi and Richard F. Farmer, see 14:37; see also T5:272 (384 references); for reviews by Janet F. Carlson and Niels G. Waller of an earlier edition, see 13:31 (1026 references); see also T4:268 (660 references); for reviews by Collie W. Conoley and Norman D. Sundberg of an earlier edition, see 11:31 (286 references).

[211]

Beck Hopelessness Scale [Revised].

Purpose: Measures "the extent of negative attitudes about the future (pessimism) as perceived by adolescents and adults."

Population: Adolescents and adults ages 17 and over.

Publication Dates: 1978–1993.

Acronym: BHS.

Scores: Total score only.

Administration: Individual or group.

Price Data, 2015: $128 per complete kit including 25 record forms and manual (1993, 29 pages); $56.40 per 25 record forms; $81 per manual; $10.25 per scoring key.

Foreign Language Edition: Available in Spanish.

Time: (5–10) minutes.

Comments: Computer scoring and interpretation available.

Authors: Aaron T. Beck and Robert A. Steer.

Publisher: Pearson.

Cross References: See T5:273 (34 references); for a review by Ephrem Fernandez, see 13:32 (83 references); see also T4:269 (37 references); for reviews by E. Thomas Dowd and Steven V. Owen of an earlier edition, see 11:32 (13 references).

[212]

Beck Scale for Suicide Ideation.

Purpose: "To detect and measure the severity of suicidal ideation in adults and adolescents."

Population: Adults and adolescents ages 17 and over.

Publication Dates: 1991–1993.

Acronym: BSS.

Scores: Total score only; item score ranges.

Administration: Group or individual.
Price Data, 2015: $128 per complete kit including 25 record forms and manual (1993, 24 pages); $56.40 per 25 record forms; $81 per manual.
Foreign Language Edition: Spanish forms available.
Time: (5–10) minutes.
Comments: Computer scoring and interpretation available.
Authors: Aaron T. Beck and Robert A. Steer.
Publisher: Pearson.
Cross References: For reviews by Karl R. Hanes and Jay R. Stewart, see 13:33 (14 references).

[213]

BECK Youth Inventories for Children and Adolescents: Second Edition.

Purpose: Designed to "assess a child's experience of depression, anxiety, disruptive behavior, and self-concept."
Population: Ages 7-18.
Publication Dates: 2001-2005.
Acronyms: BYI-II, BDI-Y, BSCI-Y, BAI-Y, BANI-Y, BDBI-Y.
Scores, 5: Depression, Anxiety, Anger, Disruptive Behavior, Self-Concept.
Subtests, 5: Beck Depression Inventory for Youth, Beck Anxiety Inventory for Youth, Beck Anger Inventory for Youth, Beck Disruptive Inventory for Youth, Beck Self-Concept.
Administration: Individual or group.
Price Data, 2015: $315 per starter kit including manual (2005, 85 pages) and 25 combination inventory booklets; $250 per 25 combination inventory booklets; $56.40 per 25 depression inventory booklets; $56.40 per 25 anxiety inventory booklets; $56.40 per 25 anger inventory booklets; $56.40 per 25 disruptive behavior inventory booklets; $56.40 per self-concept inventory booklets; $81 per manual.
Time: (30-60) minutes for combination form.
Comments: Subtests may be administered separately or via combination form; previous edition was titled Beck Youth Inventories of Emotional & Social Impairment.
Authors: Judith S. Beck, Aaron T. Beck, John B. Jolly, and Robert A. Steer.
Publisher: Pearson.
Cross References: For reviews by Rosemary Flanagan and Carlen Henington, see 18:11; for reviews by Mike Bonner and Hugh Stephenson of the earlier edition, see 15:31.

[214]

Becker Work Adjustment Profile: 2.

Purpose: Designed to "assess work habits, attitudes, and skills of people with special needs" and to assess level of supports needed.

Population: Individuals ages 13 and over, who are mentally retarded, physically disabled, emotionally disturbed, learning disabled, and/or economically disadvantaged.
Publication Dates: 1989-2005.
Acronym: BWAP:2.
Scores, 5: Work Habits/Attitudes, Interpersonal Relations, Cognitive Skills, Work Performance Skills, Broad Work Adjustment.
Administration: Individual.
Price Data: Available from publisher.
Time: (15) minutes.
Comments: Ratings by teachers, counselors, or other vocational professionals; 5 levels of work supports are also assessed.
Author: Ralph L. Becker.
Publisher: Elbern Publications.
Cross References: For reviews by James T. Austin and Stephanie D. Tischendorf and by Pam Lindsey, see 17:19; see also T5:275 (1 reference); for reviews by Brian Bolton and Elliot L. Gory of an earlier form, see 11:33.

[215]

Bedside Evaluation of Dysphagia, Revised Edition.

Purpose: Designed to assess swallowing abilities and the factors that may influence those abilities.
Population: Adults neurologically impaired.
Publication Date: 1995.
Acronym: BED.
Scores, 13: Behavioral Characteristics, Cognition and Communication Screening (Cognition, Receptive Language, Expressive Language/Speech Production), Oral Motor Examination (Lips, Tongue, Soft Palate, Cheeks, Mandible, Larynx), Oral-Pharyngeal Dysphagia Symptoms Assessment (Oral State, Pharyngeal State, Additional Observations).
Administration: Individual.
Price Data, 2015: $111 per complete kit including 25 evaluation forms, manual (54 pages), 25 evaluation forms, and 25 screening forms; $49 per 25 standard evaluation forms; $14 per 25 short forms.
Time: (15–45) minutes.
Author: Edward Hardy.
Publisher: PRO-ED.
Cross References: For reviews by Carlos Inchaurralde and Steven B. Leder, see 14:38.

[216]

Bedside Evaluation Screening Test, Second Edition.

Purpose: "Designed to assess and quantify language disorders in adults resulting from aphasia."
Population: Patients with language deficits.

Publication Dates: 1987–1998.

Acronym: BEST-2.

Scores, 8: Conversational Expression, Naming Objects, Describing Objects, Repeating Sentences, Pointing to Objects, Pointing to Parts of a Picture, Reading, Total.

Administration: Individual.

Price Data, 2015: $198 per complete kit including examiner's manual (1998, 49 pages), picture book, 25 record forms, and 25 profile/summary sheets; $56 per examiner's manual; $72 per picture book; $56 per 25 record forms; $25 per 25 profile/summary sheets.

Time: (20–30) minutes.

Comments: Replaces the Bedside Evaluation and Screening Test of Aphasia (T4:272).

Authors: Joyce Fitch West, Elaine S. Sands, and Deborah Ross-Swain.

Publisher: PRO-ED.

Cross References: For reviews by Pamilla Morales and Carolyn Mitchell-Person, see 14:39; for a review by Malcolm R. McNeil of an earlier edition, see 11:34.

[217]

The Beery-Buktenica Developmental Test of Visual-Motor Integration, Sixth Edition (Beery VMI).

Purpose: "Designed to assess the extent to which individuals can integrate their visual and motor abilities (eye-hand coordination)."

Publication Dates: 1967-2010.

Acronym: Beery VMI.

Scores, 3: Beery VMI, Visual Perception (optional), Motor Coordination (optional).

Administration: Individual or group.

Forms, 2: Full, Short.

Price Data, 2015: $141 per starter kit including manual, 10 full forms, 10 short forms, 10 Visual Perception forms, and 10 Motor Coordination forms; $68.70 per manual; $106.60 per 25 full forms; $81.50 per 25 short forms; $18.70 per 25 Visual Perception forms; $18.70 per 25 Motor Coordination forms (bulk discounts available for forms); $174.25 per Teaching Materials starter kit including My Book of Shapes, My Book of Letters and Numbers, Developmental Teaching Activities, Developmental Wall Chart, Parent Checklist, and materials on CD; $43.50 per My Book of Shapes; $46.15 per My Book of Letters and Numbers; $56.40 per Developmental Teaching Activities; $31.75 per Stepping Stones Parent Checklist; $25.65 per Developmental Wall Chart for Visual-Motor Integration.

Comments: Includes updated norms for ages 2 through 18; subtests must be administered in the appropriate sequence.

Authors: Keith A. Beery, Natasha A. Beery, and Norman A. Buktenica (full and short forms).

Publisher: Pearson.

a) BEERY VMI.
 1) *Full form.*
 Population: Ages 2-100.
 Time: (10-15) minutes.
 2) *Short form.*
 Population: Ages 2-7.
 Time: (5-15) minutes.
b) VISUAL PERCEPTION [OPTIONAL].
 Population: Ages 2-100.
 Time: (3-7) minutes.
c) MOTOR COORDINATION [OPTIONAL].
 Population: Ages 2-100.
 Time: (3-7) minutes.

Cross References: For a review by G. Michael Poteat, see 19:14; for reviews by Theresa Graham and by Thomas McKnight and Tiffany Chandler of the fifth edition, see 17:20; for a review by Jan Visser of the fourth edition, revised, see 14:119; see also T5:815 (52 references); for reviews by Darrell L. Sabers and James E. Ysseldyke of the third revision, see 12:111 (25 references); see also T4:768 (42 references), 9:329 (15 references), and T3:701 (57 references; for reviews by Donald A. Leton and James A. Rice of an earlier edition, see 8:870 (24 references); see also T2:1875 (6 references); for a review by Brad S. Chissom of an earlier edition, see 7:867 (5 references).

[218]

Behavior Analysis Forms for Clinical Intervention.

Purpose: To gather client interview data in a structured manner.

Population: Behavior therapy clients.

Publication Dates: 1977–1981.

Scores: Volume 1: 36 plans, questionnaires, scales, forms, schedules, and data forms in areas such as Client History, Motivation for Change, Reinforcement, Social Performance; Volume 2: 59 questionnaires, scales, forms, schedules, and data forms in areas such as Reinforcers for Specific Populations, Survey of Phobic or Relationship Reactions, and Guidelines for Clients.

Administration: Group or individual.

Price Data, 2016: $79.95 for each volume.

Time: Administration times vary.

Author: Joseph R. Cautela.

Publisher: Cambridge Center for Behavioral Studies.

Cross References: For reviews by Mary Lou Kelley and Francis E. Lentz, Jr., see 9:127.

[219]

Behavior Assessment System for Children, Third Edition.

Purpose: Designed as a "multimethod, multidimensional system used to evaluate the behavior and self-perceptions of children and young adults."

Population: Ages 2 through 25 years.

Publication Dates: 1992-2015.

Acronym: BASC-3.

Administration: Individual.

Forms, 12: Teacher Rating Scales–Preschool, Teacher Rating Scales–Child, Teacher Rating Scales–Adolescent, Parent Rating Scales–Preschool, Parent Rating Scales–Child, Parent Rating Scales–Adolescent, Self-Report of Personality–Interview, Self-Report of Personality–Child, Self-Report of Personality–Adolescent, Self-Report of Personality–College, Structured Developmental History, Student Observation System.

Price Data, 2016: $614 per hand-scored starter set including manual (2015, 466 pages), 25 of each record form (TRS, PRS, SRP, SDH, SOS), and 25 of each hand-score worksheet; $582 per starter kit with 1-year Q-global online scoring subscription including manual and 25 of each record form; $102 per manual.

Foreign Language Edition: Spanish version available for the Parent Rating Scales, the Self-Report of Personality, and the Structured Developmental History.

Comments: Digital administration and scoring available; other BASC-3 components include the Behavioral and Emotional Screening System (187), the Parenting Relationship Questionnaire (220), the Behavior Intervention Guide, the Behavioral and Emotional Skill Building Guide, and the Flex Monitor.

Authors: Cecil R. Reynolds and Randy W. Kamphaus.

Publisher: Pearson.

a) TEACHER RATING SCALES.

Price Data: $39 per 25 record forms; $9 per 25 hand-score worksheets.

Time: (10-15) minutes.

   1) *Teacher Rating Scales–Preschool.*

Population: Ages 2 through 5.

Acronym: TRS-P.

Scores, 29: Externalizing Problems (Hyperactivity, Aggression), Internalizing Problems (Anxiety, Depression, Somatization), Behavioral Symptoms Index (Attention Problems, Atypicality, Withdrawal), Adaptive Skills (Adaptability, Social Skills, Functional Communication), 7 Content Scales (Anger Control, Bullying, Developmental Social Disorders, Emotional Self-Control, Executive Functioning, Negative Emotionality, Resiliency), 2 Clinical Indexes (Clinical Probability, Functional Impairment), 4 Executive Functioning Indexes (Attentional Control, Behavioral Control, Emotional Control, Overall Executive Functioning), Validity Index (F).

   2) *Teacher Rating Scales–Child.*

Population: Ages 6 through 11.

Acronym: TRS-C.

Scores, 37: Externalizing Problems (Hyperactivity, Aggression, Conduct Problems), Internalizing Problems (Anxiety, Depression, Somatization), School Problems (Attention Problems, Learning Problems), Behavioral Symptoms Index (Atypicality, Withdrawal), Adaptive Skills (Adaptability, Social Skills, Leadership, Study Skills, Functional Communication), 7 Content Scales (Anger Control, Bullying, Developmental Social Disorders, Emotional Self-Control, Executive Functioning, Negative Emotionality, Resiliency), 4 Clinical Indexes (ADHD Probability, Autism Probability, EBD Probability, Functional Impairment), 5 Executive Functioning Indexes (Attentional Control, Behavioral Control, Emotional Control, Overall Executive Functioning, Problem Solving), Validity Index (F).

   3) *Teacher Rating Scales–Adolescent.*

Population: Ages 12 through 21.

Acronym: TRS-A.

Scores: Same as Teacher Rating Scales–Child.

b) PARENT RATING SCALES.

Price Data: $39 per 25 record forms; $9 per 25 hand-score worksheets.

Time: (10-20) minutes.

   1) *Parent Rating Scales–Preschool.*

Population: Ages 2 through 5.

Acronym: PRS-P.

Scores, 30: Externalizing Problems (Hyperactivity, Aggression), Internalizing Problems (Anxiety, Depression, Somatization), Behavioral Symptoms Index (Attention Problems, Atypicality, Withdrawal), Adaptive Skills (Adaptability, Social Skills, Activities of Daily Living, Functional Communication), 7 Content Scales (Anger Control, Bullying, Developmental Social Disorders, Emotional Self-Control, Executive Functioning, Negative Emotionality, Resiliency), 2 Clinical Indexes (Clinical Probability, Functional Impairment), 4 Executive Functioning Indexes (Attentional Control, Behavioral Control, Emotional Control, Overall Executive Functioning), Validity Index (F).

   2) *Parent Rating Scales–Child.*

Population: Ages 6 through 11.

Acronym: PRS-C.

Scores, 35: Externalizing Problems (Hyperactivity, Aggression, Conduct Problems), Internalizing Problems (Anxiety, Depression, Somatization), Behavioral Symptoms Index (Attention Problems, Atypicality, Withdrawal), Adaptive Skills (Adaptability, Social Skills, Leadership, Activities of Daily Living, Functional Communication), 7 Content Scales (Anger Control, Bullying, Developmental Social Disorders, Emotional Self-Control, Executive Functioning, Negative Emotionality, Resiliency), 4 Clinical Indexes (ADHD Probability, Autism Probability, EBD Probability, Functional Impairment), 5 Executive Functioning Indexes (Attentional Control, Behavioral Control, Emotional Control, Overall Executive Functioning, Problem Solving), Validity Index (F).

   3) *Parent Rating Scales–Adolescent.*

Population: Ages 12 through 21.

Acronym: PRS-A.

Scores: Same as Parent Rating Scales–Child (see above).

c) SELF-REPORT OF PERSONALITY.

Price Data: $39 per 25 record forms; $9 per 25 hand-score worksheets.

Time: (20-30) minutes.

   1) *Self-Report of Personality–Interview.*

Population: Ages 6 through 7.

Acronym: SRP-I.

Score: Total score only.

   2) *Self-Report of Personality–Child.*

Population: Ages 8 through 11.

Acronym: SRP-C.

Scores, 23: School Problems (Attitude to School, Attitude to Teachers), Internalizing Problems (Atypicality, Locus of Control, Social Stress, Anxiety, Depression, Sense of Inadequacy), Inattention/Hyperactivity (Attention Problems, Hyperactivity), Personal Adjustment (Relations with Parents, Interpersonal Relations, Self-Esteem, Self-Reliance), Emotional Symptoms Index, Functional Impairment Index, 3 Validity Indexes (F, V, L).

3) *Self-Report of Personality–Adolescent.*
Population: Ages 12 through 21.
Acronym: SRP-A.
Scores, 29: School Problems (Attitude to School, Attitude to Teachers, Sensation Seeking), Internalizing Problems (Atypicality, Locus of Control, Social Stress, Anxiety, Depression, Sense of Inadequacy, Somatization), Inattention/Hyperactivity (Attention Problems, Hyperactivity), Personal Adjustment (Relations with Parents, Interpersonal Relations, Self-Esteem, Self-Reliance), Emotional Symptoms Index, 4 Content Scales (Anger Control, Ego Strength, Mania, Test Anxiety), Functional Impairment Index, 3 Validity Indexes (F, V, L).

4) *Self-Report of Personality–College.*
Population: Ages 18 through 25.
Acronym: SRP-COL.
Scores, 27: Internalizing Problems (Atypicality, Locus of Control, Social Stress, Anxiety, Depression, Sense of Inadequacy, Somatization), Inattention/Hyperactivity (Attention Problems, Hyperactivity), Personal Adjustment (Relations with Parents, Interpersonal Relations, Self-Esteem, Self-Reliance), Sensation Seeking, Alcohol Abuse, School Maladjustment, Emotional Symptoms Index, 4 Content Scales (Anger Control, Ego Strength, Mania, Test Anxiety), 3 Validity Indexes (F, V, L).

d) STRUCTURED DEVELOPMENTAL HISTORY.
Acronym: SDH.
Price Data: $55 per 25 forms.
Comments: Administered as structured interview or questionnaire.
e) STUDENT OBSERVATION SYSTEM.
Acronym: SOS.
Price Data: $55 per 25 forms.
Time: (15) minutes.
Comments: Designed for observing student behavior in the classroom.

Cross References: For reviews by Stephanie Stein and by T. Steuart Watson and Katherine Wickstrom of the second edition, see 17:21; for reviews by James Clyde DiPerna and by Robert Spies and Christina Finley Jones of the revised version, see 14:40; see also T5:280 (6 references); for reviews by Jonathon Sandoval and by Joseph C. Witt and Kevin M. Jones of the original edition, see 13:34 (6 references).

[220]

Behavior Assessment System for Children, Third Edition, Parenting Relationship Questionnaire.

Purpose: Designed "to capture a parent's perspective of the parent-child relationship"; assesses traditional parent-child dimensions and provides information about parenting style, confidence, stress, and satisfaction with the child's school.
Population: Parents or caregivers of children ages 2 through 18.
Publication Date: 2015.
Acronym: BASC-3 PRQ.
Administration: Individual.
Levels: 2 levels.
Price Data, 2015: $153 per hand-scoring set including manual, 25 Preschool record forms, 25 Child/Adolescent record forms, 25 Preschool hand-scoring worksheets, and 25 Child/Adolescent hand-scoring worksheets; $94 per Q-global starter set including manual and 10 Q-global interpretive summary report usages; $75 per manual (92 pages); $39 per 25 record forms (Preschool or Child/Adolescent); $9 per 25 hand-scoring worksheets (Preschool or Child/Adolescent).
Foreign Language Edition: Spanish version available.
Time: (10-15) minutes.
Authors: Randy W. Kamphaus and Cecil R. Reynolds.
Publisher: Pearson.
  a) PRESCHOOL
  Population: Ages 2-5.
  Acronym: BASC-3 PRQ-P.
  Scores, 9: Attachment, Discipline Practices, Involvement, Parenting Confidence, Relational Frustration, and 4 validity indexes.
  b) CHILD/ADOLESCENT
  Population: Ages 6-18.
  Acronym: BASC-3 PRQ-CA.
  Scores, 11: Attachment, Communication, Discipline Practices, Involvement, Parenting Confidence, Satisfaction with School, Relational Frustration, and 4 validity indexes.
Cross References: Reviews are scheduled for *The Twentieth Mental Measurements Yearbook.*

[221]

Behavior Dimensions Scale.

Purpose: Designed to categorize and document existing behavior patterns into recognized areas of behavior disorders to assist in making diagnostic, placement, and programming decisions.
Population: Ages 3–19.
Publication Date: 1995.
Acronym: BDS.
Scores, 7: Inattentive, Hyperactive-Impulsive, Oppositional Defiant, Conduct, Avoidant Personality, Anxiety, Depression.
Administration: Individual.
Price Data: Available from publisher.
Time: (20–25) minutes.
Comments: The test publisher has indicated there is a newer edition of this test; description will be updated when complete test materials are received.

Author: Stephen B. McCarney.
Publisher: Hawthorne Educational Services, Inc.
Cross References: For reviews by Kevin M. Jones and Beverly M. Klecker, see 14:41.

[222]
Behavior Disorders Identification Scale—Second Edition.

Purpose: "To document the existence of behaviors which meet the criteria for identifying the student as behaviorally disordered."
Population: Ages 4.5-21.
Publication Dates: 1988–2000.
Acronym: BDIS-2 SV (School Version); BDIS-2 HV (Home Version).
Scores, 5: Learning Problems, Interpersonal Relations, Inappropriate Behavior, Unhappiness/Depression, Physical Symptoms/Fears.
Administration: Individual.
Forms, 2: School Version, Home Version.
Price Data: Available from publisher.
Time: [20] minutes for School Version; [15] minutes for Home Version.
Comments: Completed by adult observers; based on federal definitions of serious emotional disturbance (PL 94-142 and IDEA Amendments of 1997); available in paper or computer version. The test publisher has indicated there is a newer edition of this test; description will be updated when complete test materials are received.
Authors: Stephen B. McCarney and Tamara J. Arthaud (Technical Manuals, Home Version and School Version), and Kathy Cummins Wunderlich (Teacher's Guide to Behavioral Interventions).
Publisher: Hawthorne Educational Services, Inc.
Cross References: For reviews by Judy Oehler-Stinnett and by Stephanie Stein and Phil Diaz, see 16:26; for reviews by Doreen Ward Fairbank and Harlan J. Stientjes of an earlier edition, see 12:46.

[223]
Behavior Evaluation Scale—Third Edition.

Purpose: Designed "to contribute to the early identification and service delivery for students with serious emotional disturbance or behavior disorders."
Population: Ages 4-19.
Publication Dates: 1990-2005.
Acronym: BES-3:L, BES-3:S.
Scores, 6: Learning Problems, Interpersonal Difficulties, Inappropriate Behavior, Unhappiness/Depression, Physical Symptoms/Fears, Total Score.
Administration: Individual.
Forms, 4: Long-School Version, Long-Home Version, Short-School Version, Short-Home Version.
Price Data: Available from publisher.

Foreign Language Edition: Long-Home and Short-Home Version Spanish rating forms available.
Time: (20) minutes.
Comments: Includes Home Version and School Version; scale is completed by parent/caregiver or an educator. The test publisher has indicated there is a newer edition of this test; description will be updated when complete test materials are received.
Authors: Stephen B. McCarney and Tamara J. Arthaud.
Publisher: Hawthorne Educational Services, Inc.
Cross References: For reviews by Matthew K. Burns and by Mark E. Swerdlik and W. Joel Schneider, see 17:22; see also T5:284 (1 reference); for reviews by Bert A. Goldman and D. Joe Olmi of a previous edition, see 12:47; for reviews by J. Jeffrey Grill, Lester Mann, and Leonard Kenowitz of an earlier edition, see 9:128.

[224]
Behavior Intervention Monitoring Assessment System.

Purpose: Designed to "monitor children/youth's progress in behavioral and psychosocial intervention."
Population: Ages 5-18.
Publication Date: 2011.
Acronym: BIMAS.
Scores: 5 scales: Conduct, Negative Affect, Cognitive/Attention, Social, Academic Functioning.
Administration: Individual or Group.
Parts, 2: BIMAS Standard, BIMAS Flex.
Forms, 4: Self-Report (ages 12–18), Teacher, Parent, Clinician.
Price Data, 2015: $99 per manual paper; $4 per annual site license (min. purchase of 25 students/clients); $4 per annual site license renewal (min. purchase of 25 students/clients); Volume discounts are available.
Time: (5–10) minutes.
Comments: Following administration of BIMAS Standard form, "assessors can custom-design Flex items ... one- to five-item mini-assessments [used] for frequent progress monitoring." Online and paper-and-pencil administration available.
Authors: James L. McDougal, Achilles N. Bardos, and Scott T. Meier.
Publisher: Multi-Health Systems, Inc.
Cross References: For reviews by Kathy J. Bohan and Felicia Castro-Villarreal, see 19:15.

[225]
Behavior Rating Instrument for Autistic and Other Atypical Children, 2nd Edition.

Purpose: Designed to evaluate the status of autistic, atypical, and other developmentally delayed children by assessing their present levels of functioning and measuring changes in their behavior.
Population: Autistic children.

Publication Dates: 1977–1991.
Acronym: BRIAAC.
Scores, 9: Relationship to an Adult, Communication, Drive for Mastery, Vocalization and Expressive Speech, Sound and Speech Reception, Social Responsiveness, Psychobiological Development, Expressive Gesture and Sign Language, Receptive Gesture and Sign Language.
Administration: Individual.
Price Data, 2015: $130 per complete kit including manual (1991, 140 pages) and report form masters with permission to reproduce the report forms; $50 per manual; $80 per reproducible masters.
Time: Untimed.
Authors: Bertram A. Ruttenberg, Enid G. Wolf-Schein, and Charles Wenar.
Publisher: Stoelting Co.
Cross References: For a review by Doreen Ward Fairbank, see 13:35; see also T4:280 (1 reference); for a review by Edward Workman of an earlier edition, see 9:129; see also T3:272 (1 reference).

[226]
Behavior Rating Inventory of Executive Function—Adult Version.

Purpose: Designed to capture "views of an adult's own executive functions, or self-regulation, in his or her everyday environment."
Population: Ages 18-90.
Publication Dates: 1996-2005.
Acronym: BRIEF-A.
Scores, 12: 9 subscales: Inhibit, Shift, Emotional Control, Self-Monitor, Initiate, Working Memory, Plan/Organize, Task Monitor, Organization of Materials; 3 composite scores: Behavioral Regulation Index, Metacognition Index, Global Executive Composite.
Administration: Individual.
Price Data, 2015: $226 per introductory kit including professional manual (2005, 147 pages), 25 self-report forms, 25 informant report forms, 25 self-report scoring summary/profile forms, and 25 informant report scoring summary/profile forms; $66 per professional manual; $54 per 25 self-report forms; $54 per 25 informant report forms; $36 per 25 self-report scoring summary/profile forms; $36 per 25 informant report scoring summary/profile forms.
Foreign Language Edition: Spanish form available.
Time: (15) minutes.
Comments: It is preferable to administer the informant report form to a knowledgeable informant such as a spouse, adult child, caregiver, or other person who has frequent face-to-face interaction with the individual completing the self-report form.
Authors: Robert M. Roth, Peter K. Isquith, and Gerard A. Gioia.
Publisher: Psychological Assessment Resources, Inc.

Cross References: For reviews by Gary J. Dean and Sandra F. Dean and by Kathy E. Green, see 17:23.

[227]
Behavior Rating Inventory of Executive Function—Preschool Version.

Purpose: Designed to "assess executive function behaviors of preschool aged children in the home and preschool environments using the observations of parents, teachers, and daycare providers."
Population: Ages 2-0 to 5-11.
Publication Dates: 1996–2003.
Acronym: BRIEF-P™.
Scores, 9: Inhibit, Shift, Emotional Control, Working Memory, Plan/Organize, Inhibitory Self-Control Index, Flexibility Index, Emergent Metacognition Index, Global Executive Composite.
Administration: Individual.
Price Data, 2015: $154 per introductory kit including manual (2003, 111 pages), 25 rating forms, and 25 scoring summary/profile forms.
Foreign Language Editions: Spanish rating and scoring forms available.
Time: (10–15) minutes.
Comments: Behavior rating scale is completed by parent or teacher/child care worker who is familiar with the child.
Authors: Gerard A. Gioia, Kimberly Andrews Espy, and Peter K. Isquith.
Publisher: Psychological Assessment Resources, Inc.
Cross References: For reviews by R. Anthony Doggett and Carl J. Sheperis and by Leah M. Nellis, see 16:27.

[228]
Behavior Rating Inventory of Executive Function, Second Edition.

Purpose: Designed to assess "everyday behaviors associated with executive functions in the home and school environments."
Population: Ages 5-18.
Publication Dates: 1996-2015.
Acronym: BRIEF2.
Scores, 14-16: 10 clinical scale scores: Inhibit, Self-Monitor, Shift, Emotional Control, Initiate (Parent and Teacher forms only), Working Memory, Plan/Organize, Task-Monitor (Parent and Teacher forms only), Organization of Materials (Parent and Teacher forms only), Task Completion (Self-Report form only); 4 index scores: Behavior Regulation Index, Emotion Regulation Index, Cognitive Regulation Index, Global Executive Composite; 3 validity scale scores: Inconsistency, Negativity, Infrequency.
Administration: Individual or group.
Forms, 6: Parent, Teacher, Self-Report core forms and screening forms.

Price Data, 2016: $330 per hand-scored kit including professional manual (2015, 341 pages) with fast guide, 25 Parent forms, 25 Teacher forms, 25 Self-Report forms, 25 Parent scoring summary/profile forms, 25 Teacher scoring summary/profile forms, and 25 Self-Report scoring summary profile forms; $95 per manual; $59 per 25 forms (Parent, Teacher, or Self-Report); $25 per 25 scoring summary/profile forms (Parent, Teacher or Self-Report); $45 per 25 screening forms (Parent, Teacher or Self-Report).

Foreign Language Edition: Spanish versions available for the Parent and Self-Report core and screening forms.

Time: (10-15) minutes.

Comments: Completed by parents and teachers of school-age children (5 to 18 years) and by adolescents ages 11 to 18 years. Administered via paper and pencil or computer.

Authors: Gerard A. Gioia, Peter K. Isquith, Steven C. Guy, and Lauren Kenworthy.

Publisher: Psychological Assessment Resources, Inc.

Cross References: For reviews by Corine Fitzpatrick and Gregory Schraw of the original edition (Parent and Teacher forms), see 15:32; for reviews by Stephen L. Benton and Sheryl Benton and by Manuel Martinez-Pons of the original BRIEF–Self-Report Version, see 16:28.

[229]

Behavior Rating Profile, Second Edition.

Purpose: "To evaluate students' behaviors at home, in school, and in interpersonal relationships."

Population: Ages 6-6 to 18-6.

Publication Dates: 1978–1990.

Acronym: BRP-2.

Scores: 5 checklists: Student Rating Scales (Home, School, Peers), Teacher Rating Scale, Parent Rating Scale, plus Sociogram score.

Administration: Individual.

Price Data, 2010: $229 per complete kit; $45 per 50 rating scale booklets (specify student, parent, or teacher form); $45 per 50 profile forms; $55 per examiner's manual (1990, 75 pages).

Time: (15–30) minutes per scale.

Authors: Linda Brown and Donald D. Hammill.

Publisher: PRO-ED.

Cross References: See T5:286 (3 references); for reviews by Sarah J. Allen and Lisa A. Bloom, see 12:48 (1 reference); see also T4:281 (1 reference); for reviews by Thomas R. Kratochwill and Joseph C. Witt of an earlier edition, see 9:130 (1 reference); see also T3:273 (1 reference).

[230]

Behavior Rating Scale.

Purpose: Designed to sample teachers' perceptions about their pupils' behavior in the classroom.

Population: Grades K–8.

Publication Dates: 1970–1975.

Score: Total score only.

Administration: Group.

Forms, 3: Forms differ only in number of rating categories.

Manual: No manual.

Price Data: Available in the Southern Illinois University Archives at the Morris Library at Southern Illinois University.

Time: Administration time not reported.

Comments: Ratings by teachers; research instrument; may be used with or separately from Characteristics Scale (381).

Authors: Patricia B. Elmore and Donald L. Beggs.

Publisher: Patricia B. Elmore.

Cross References: See T5:287 (1 reference) and T4:282 (2 references); for a review by Jayne A. Parker, see 9:131 (2 references).

[231]

Behavioral and Emotional Rating Scale, Second Edition.

Purpose: Designed to "measure the personal strengths and competencies of children."

Population: Ages 5-0 to 18-11.

Publication Dates: 1998–2004.

Acronym: BERS-2.

Scores, 6: 5 subscales: Interpersonal Strength, Family Involvement, Intrapersonal Strength, School Functioning, Affective Strength, plus Strength Index.

Administration: Individual.

Price Data, 2015: $198 per complete kit including examiner's manual (2004, 112 pages), 25 teacher rating scales, 25 parent rating scales, 25 youth rating scales, and 50 summary forms; $69 per examiner's manual; $37 per 25 teacher rating scales; $37 per parent rating scales; $37 per youth rating scales; $37 per 50 summary forms.

Foreign Language Edition: Spanish version available.

Time: (10) minutes.

Comments: Revised edition adds Parent and Youth Rating Scales.

Author: Michael H. Epstein.

Publisher: PRO-ED.

Cross References: For reviews by John D. King and by Mark E. Swerdlik and W. Joel Schneider, see 16:29; for reviews by Beth Doll and D. Joe Olmi of an earlier edition, see 14:42.

[232]

Behavioral and Psychological Assessment of Dementia.

Purpose: Designed to "assess changes in behavior and mood associated with the onset of various dementia syndromes."

Population: Ages 30-90.
Publication Date: 2007.
Acronym: BPAD.
Scores, 24: Total Current, Total Past, Total Change, Perceptual/Delusional Current, Perceptual/Delusional Past, Perceptual/Delusional Change, Positive Mood/Anxiety Current, Positive Mood/Anxiety Past, Positive Mood/Anxiety Change, Negative Mood/Anxiety Current, Negative Mood/Anxiety Past, Negative Mood/Anxiety Change, Aggressive Current, Aggressive Past, Aggressive Change, Perseverative/Rigid Current, Perseverative/Rigid Past, Perseverative/Rigid Change, Disinhibited Current, Disinhibited Past, Disinhibited Change, Biological Rhythms Current, Biological Rhythms Past, Biological Rhythms Change.
Administration: Individual.
Price Data, 2015: $290 per introductory kit including software portfolio with on-screen help and quick start guide, professional manual (67 pages), and 25 response booklets; $70 per 25 response booklets; $72 per professional manual.
Time: (15) minutes.
Comments: "Should be completed by family members, paraprofessionals, or other professionals ages 18-90 who have regular contact with individuals who have suspected or diagnosed dementia."
Authors: Kara S. Schmidt and Jennifer L. Gallo.
Publisher: Psychological Assessment Resources, Inc.
Cross References: For reviews by Shawn K. Acheson and Anita M. Hubley, see 18:12.

[233]

Behavioral Assessment of Pain-2 Questionnaire.

Purpose: An assessment tool to understand "factors which may be working to exacerbate and/or maintain subacute and chronic nonmalignant pain."
Population: Subacute and chronic pain patients.
Publication Dates: 1990-2009.
Acronyms: BAP-2, Post BAP-2.
Scores, 51: 15 scales, 35 subscales, plus Disability Index: Pain Behavior Scale (Affective/Behavioral, Audible/Visible), Pain Descriptor Scale (Pulling, Tight and Dull [PTD], Sore, Aching, and Tender [SAT], Throbbing and Sharp [TS]), Activity Interference Scale (Domestic/Household Activities, Heavy Activities, Social Activities, Personal Care Activities, Personal Hygiene Activities), Avoidance Scale, Spouse/Partner Influence Scale (Reinforcement of Pain, Discouragement/Criticism of Pain, Reinforcement of Wellness, Discouragement/Criticism of Wellness), Physician Influence Scale (Physician Discouragement/Criticism of Pain, Physician Reinforcement of Wellness, Physician Discouragement/Criticism of Wellness, Physician Reinforcement of Pain), Pain Beliefs Scale (Catastrophizing, Fear of Reinjury, Expectation for Cure, Blaming Self, Entitlement, Future Despair, Social

Disbelief, Lack of Medical Comprehensiveness), Perceived Consequences Scale (Social Interference, Physical Harm, Psychological Harm, Pain Exacerbation, Productivity Interference), Mood Scale (Depression, Muscular Discomfort, Anxiety, Change in Weight), 6 validity scales.
Administration: Individual.
Forms, 2: Behavioral Assessment of Pain-2 Questionnaire, Post Behavioral Assessment of Pain-2 Questionnaire.
Price Data, 2012: $21 per computer-generated clinical report from BAPTrax Software (volume discounts available); $25 per prepaid mail-in answer premium full-service reports (volume discounts available).
Foreign Language Editions: Spanish and French editions (unnormed) available.
Time: (30) minutes or less per test.
Comments: Self-report instrument; two options for generating a clinical profile: via BAP-2 software or mail/fax service; Post BAP-2 analyzes the changes over the course of treatment providing outcome data for the pain program.
Authors: Michael J. Lewandowski and Blake H. Tearnan.
Publisher: Pain Assessment Resources.
Cross References: For reviews by Brian F. French and Chad M. Gotch and by Ashraf Kagee, see 19:16; for reviews by Gerald E. DeMauro and Ronald J. Ganellen of an earlier edition, see 12:49.

[234]

Behavioral Characteristics Progression (BCP) Assessment Record.

Purpose: Assesses developmental skills/behaviors.
Population: Children and adults with mental and physical disabilities.
Publication Dates: 1973-1997.
Acronym: BCP.
Scores: Item scores only.
Administration: Individual.
Price Data, 2015: $6.50 per record booklet (1997, 64 pages); $59.95 per BCP Instructional Activities resource book (1997, 400 pages).
Time: Administration time not reported.
Comments: "Criterion-referenced" assessment for developmental ages 1-14 years.
Author: VORT Corporation.
Publisher: VORT Corporation.
Cross References: See T5:292 (1 reference); for reviews by Rosemery O. Nelson-Gray and Harvey N. Switzky of an earlier edition, see 11:38.

[235]

Behavioral Objective Sequence.

Purpose: Designed to "assist special educators and other professionals assess behavioral competencies of students with emotional and behavioral disorders."

Population: Students (grades 1-12) with emotional and behavioral disorders.
Publication Date: 1998.
Acronym: BOS.
Scores, 6: Adaptive Behaviors, Self-Management Behaviors, Communication Behaviors, Interpersonal Behaviors, Task Behaviors, Personal Behaviors.
Administration: Individual.
Price Data, 2015: $44.99 per manual (1998, 104 pages), recording forms, and test.
Time: Administration time not reported.
Comments: "Can be used as a bank of (behavioral) objectives, as a rating scale, or as a structured observational system"; completed by educational/psychological professionals about a student.
Authors: Sheldon Braaten.
Publisher: Research Press.
Cross References: For reviews by M. David Miller and Stephanie Stein, see 15:33.

[236]

Behavioral Summary.

Purpose: Provides "screening of behavioral adjustment problems in children and adolescents."
Population: Grades K-12.
Publication Date: 2009.
Administration: Group.
Price Data, 2016: $69.50 per hand scoring kit including 10 Parent Report AutoScore forms, 10 Teacher Report AutoScore forms, 10 Student Report AutoScore forms, and manual (134 pages); $346 per computer scoring kit including 10 Parent Report AutoScore forms, 10 Teacher Report AutoScore forms, 10 Student Report AutoScore forms, manual, and unlimited-use scoring CD; $21.50 per 25 AutoScore forms; $52.50 per manual; $318.50 per unlimited-use scoring CD.
Comments: Ratings by parents, teachers, and self-report.
Authors: David Lachar and Christian P. Gruber (all forms and manual), Sabine A. Wingenfeld and Rex B. Kline (teacher report form).
Publisher: Western Psychological Services.
   a) PARENT REPORT.
   Population: Grades K-12.
   Scores, 14: 2 Validity scales (Inconsistent Responding, Exaggeration), 8 Adjustment scales (Impulsivity & Distractibility, Defiance, Family Problems, Atypical Behavior, Somatic Concern, Emotional Problems, Social Withdrawal, Social Skill Deficits), 3 Composite scales (Externalization, Internalization, Social Adjustment), Total score.
   Time: (15) minutes.
   b) STUDENT REPORT.
   Population: Same as *a* above.
   Scores: Same as *a* above.
   Time: Same as *a* above.
   c) TEACHER REPORT.
   Population: Grades 4-12.

Scores, 15: 4 Academic Resources scales (Academic Performance, Academic Habits, Social Skills, Parent Participation), 7 Adjustment Problems scales (Health Concerns, Emotional Distress, Unusual Behavior, Social Problems, Verbal Aggression, Physical Aggression, Behavior Problems), 3 Disruptive Behavior scales (Attention-Deficit/Hyperactivity, Oppositional Defiant, Conduct Problems), Total score.
Time: (20) minutes.
Cross References: For reviews by John S. Geisler and Stephanie Stein, see 19:17.

[237]

Behaviors & Attitudes Drinking & Driving Scale.

Purpose: Designed to identify pre-intervention risk of future impaired driving, and changes in DUI-related risky behaviors and attitudes following intervention.
Population: Ages 18 and older.
Publication Date: 2007.
Acronym: BADDS.
Scores, 5: Rationalizations for Drinking and Driving, Lenient Attitudes toward Drinking and Driving, Likelihood of Drinking and Driving, Drinking and Driving Behaviors, Riding Behaviors with a Drinking Driver.
Administration: Individual or group.
Price Data, 2014: $105 per small starter kit including 25 paper tests, 25 pre and posttest profiles, reliability and validity summary, and manual (108 pages); $210 per large starter kit including 100 paper tests, 100 pre and posttest profiles, reliability and validity summary, and manual; $40 per 25 paper tests and 25 pre and posttest profiles; $75 per manual.
Time: (10) minutes.
Authors: Jeremy D. Jewell (inventory; user's guide and manual), Stephen D. A. Hupp (inventory; user's guide and manual), Linda E. Lazowski (user's guide and manual), and Glenn A. Miller (user's guide and manual).
Publisher: The SASSI Institute.
Cross References: Reviews are scheduled for *The Twentieth Mental Measurements Yearbook.*

[238]

Behaviors and Experiences Inventory.

Purpose: "An initial screen for Attention-Deficit/Hyperactivity Disorder (ADHD), Conduct Disorder (CD), and Antisocial Personality Disorder (ASPD)."
Population: Adults.
Publication Dates: 1998–1999.
Acronym: BEI.
Scores, 24: ADHD: Inattention (Difficulty Sustaining Attention, Fails to Finish Assignments, Inattention to Details/Careless, Difficulty Organizing Tasks/Activities, Tendency to Lose Things, Distractible), Hyperactivity, Impulsivity, Conduct Disorder as a Child/Adolescent (Aggression, Destruction of Property, Deceitfulness or

Theft, Serious Violation of Rules, Cruelty to Animals and Fire-Setting), Antisocial Personality Disorder (Failure to Conform to Social Norms, Deceitfulness, Impulsivity, Irritability/Aggressiveness, Reckless Disregard for Safety, Irresponsibility, Lack of Remorse), History of Abuse as a Child/Adolescent (Physical, Sexual, Emotional).
Administration: Individual.
Price Data, 2016: $52.50 per 25 inventories; $15 per manual.
Time: (15–20) minutes.
Comments: Can be administered as paper-and-pencil questionnaire or as a structured interview; screens for DSM-IV diagnostic criteria, providing an estimate of the likelihood that an individual meets the criteria for ADHD, CD, and ASPD; covers current problems only.
Authors: Norman G. Hoffmann, David Mee-Lee, and Gerald D. Shulman.
Publisher: Change Companies.
Cross References: For a review by Mark R. Cooper, see 15:34.

[239]

Behavioural Assessment of the Dysexecutive Syndrome.

Purpose: "A test battery aimed at predicting everyday problems arising from the Dysexecutive Syndrome."
Population: Ages 16–87.
Publication Date: 1996.
Acronym: BADS.
Scores, 7: Rule Shift Card, Action Program, Key Search, Temporal Judgement, Zoo Map, Modified Six Elements, Total.
Administration: Individual.
Price Data: 2015: £444.50 per complete kit including manual, 25 scoring sheets, 5 stimulus books, stimulus cards, three-dimensional plastic materials, timer, 25 self-rater dex questionnaires, and 25 independent rater questionnaires; £36.50 per 2 packs of 25 dex questionnaires (self-rater and independent rater).
Time: 40 minutes.
Comments: Subtest scores "may be used individually, although validation studies have indicated that the overall battery score is the most sensitive predictor of executive problems"; useful with brain-injured and schizophrenic patients for identifying general or specific deficits in executive functions; supplemental information about patients can be gathered using the self-rating and caregiver rating forms included in the test kit.
Authors: Barbara A. Wilson, Nick Alderman, Paul W. Burgess, Hazel Emslie, and Jonathan J. Evans.
Publisher: Pearson Assessment [England].
Cross References: For reviews by Rik Carl D'Amato and Sandra D. Haynes, see 14:43.

[240]

Behavioural Assessment of the Dysexecutive Syndrome for Children.

Purpose: Tests the executive functioning of children and adolescents.
Population: Children and adolescents ages 7 to 16.
Publication Date: 2003.
Acronym: BADS-C.
Scores, 8: Playing Cards Test, Water Test, Key Search Test, Zoo Map Test 1, Zoo Map Test 2, Six Part Test, Dysexecutive Questionnaire for Children, Total Score.
Administration: Individual.
Price Data, 2015: £509.50 per complete kit including manual (41 pages), 25 scoring sheets, stimulus cards, three-dimensional plastic materials, timer, 25 Dysexecutive Questionnaire for Children (DEX-C), independent rater questionnaires, beads, nuts, bolts, and washers; £18 per 25 DEX-C questionnaires; £22 per 25 scoring sheets.
Time: (35–45) minutes.
Comments: Adaptation of Behavioural Assessment of the Dysexecutive Syndrome (239); examinee IQ-score must be available to determine scaled score and percentile rank.
Authors: Hazel Emslie, F. Colin Wilson, Vivian Burden, Ian Nimmo-Smith, and Barbara A. Wilson.
Publisher: Pearson Assessment [England].
Cross References: For reviews by Lorraine Cleeton and Rama K. Mishra, see 17:24.

[241]

Behavioural Inattention Test.

Purpose: Developed to measure unilateral visual neglect.
Population: Ages 19-83.
Publication Date: 1987.
Acronym: BIT.
Scores, 17: Conventional Subtest Scores (Line Crossing, Letter Cancellation, Star Cancellation, Figure and Shape Copying, Line Bisection, Representational Drawing, Total), Behavioural Subtests (Picture Scanning, Telephone Dialling, Menu Reading, Article Reading, Telling and Setting the Time, Coin Sorting, Address and Sentence Copying, Map Navigation, Card Sorting, Total).
Administration: Individual.
Price Data, 2015: £324.50 per complete kit including manual (19 pages), various stimuli, test, playing cards, clock face, and 25 scoring sheets; £41 per manual; £41 per 25 scoring sheets.
Time: (40) minutes.
Authors: Barbara Wilson, Janet Cockburn, and Peter Halligan.
Publisher: Pearson Assessment [England].
Cross References: For reviews by William R. Horstman and Robert M. Thorndike, see 17:25.

[242]

Belbin Team-Roles Self-Perception Inventory.
Purpose: Designed to determine which contributions each team member can make best.
Population: Teams.
Publication Date: 1994.
Scores: 9 Profiles: Plant, Coordinator, Resource Investigator, Monitor Evaluator, Implementer, Team Worker, Completer-Finisher, Specialist, Shaper.
Administration: Group.
Price Data: Available from publisher.
Time: [1 day].
Author: Meredith Belbin.
Publisher: Belbin.
Cross References: For reviews by K. Hattrup and by Kristin O. Prien and Erich P. Prien, see 14:44.

[243]

Bell Object Relations and Reality Testing Inventory.
Purpose: Designed to assess "dimensions of object relations and reality testing ego functioning."
Population: Ages 18 and older
Publication Date: 1995.
Acronym: BORRTI.
Scores, 8: Object Relations (Alienation, Insecure Attachment, Egocentricity, Social Incompetence); Reality Testing (Reality Distortion, Uncertainty of Perception, Hallucinations and Delusions); Inconsistent Responding; plus two validity indexes: FREQ, INFREQ.
Administration: Group.
Price Data, 2016: $113.50 for complete kit, including 20 Full Form AutoScore Forms, and manual; $54 Full Form Autoscore Form (pack of 20); $48 Form O Autoscore Form (pack of 20); $65.50 per manual; $345.50 per 20-use CD-ROM for computer scoring and interpretation (Full Form or Form O), includes interpretive report; $149.50 per 20-use CD-ROM for computer scoring only (Full Form or Form O); $20.50 per Full Form or Form O PC answer sheet for use with the CDs (pads of 100).
Time: (15–20) minutes.
Comments: Form O including only items measuring object relations also available.
Author: Morris D. Bell.
Publisher: Western Psychological Services.
Cross References: For reviews by Glen Fox and Steven I. Pfeiffer, see 14:45; see also T5:297 (2 references).

[244]

Bell Relationship Inventory for Adolescents.
Purpose: Designed for use "in schools and clinical settings for quickly and accurately assessing object relations ego functioning in children and adolescents."
Population: Ages 11-17.

Publication Date: 2005.
Acronym: BRIA.
Scores, 6: Alienation, Insecure Attachment, Egocentricity, Social Incompetence, Positive Attachment, Response Bias.
Administration: Group.
Price Data, 2016: $118 per kit including Autoscore forms, 1 manual for the Bell Object Relations and Reality Testing Inventory (1995, 82 pages), and 1 manual supplement for the BRIA (2005, 27 pages); $44 per 25 Autoscore forms; $65.50 per manual for the Bell Object Relations and Reality Testing Inventory; $25.50 per manual supplement for the BRIA.
Time: (10-15) minutes.
Comments: The BRIA is a version of the Bell Object Relations and Reality Testing Inventory, Form O (243) adapted for use with adolescents aged 11-17; self-report format.
Author: Morris D. Bell.
Publisher: Western Psychological Services.
Cross References: For reviews by Gene N. Berg and Glen E. Ray, see 19:18; for reviews by Glen Fox and Steven I. Pfeiffer of the Bell Object Relations and Reality Testing Inventory, see 14:45; see also T5:297 (2 references).

[245]

Bem Sex-Role Inventory.
Purpose: Provides independent assessments of masculinity and femininity in terms of the respondent's self-reported possession of socially desirable, stereotypically masculine and feminine personality characteristics; can also be used as a measurement of the extent to which respondents spontaneously sort self-relevant information into distinct masculine and feminine categories.
Population: Ages 16 and older.
Publication Dates: 1978-1981.
Acronym: BSRI.
Scores, 3: Femininity, Masculinity, Femininity-minus-Masculinity Differences.
Administration: Individual or group.
Price Data, 2015: $50 for manual, including a review-only copy of the test form; $2.40 per license for Transform Survey Hosting: Original Form, Short Form (minimum 50); $250 Group Report; $2 per Remote Online Survey License (minimum 50); $2 License to Reproduce (minimum 50).
Time: (10-15) minutes.
Comments: Test is titled Bem Inventory; self-administered; short and long form available (short form consists of first 30 items only).
Author: Sandra Lipsitz Bem.
Publisher: Mind Garden, Inc.
Cross References: See T5:298 (167 references) and T4:288 (204 references); for reviews by Richard Lippa and Frank D. Rayne, see 9:137 (121 references).

[246]
Bench Mark Measures.

Purpose: Measures a student's general knowledge of phonics.
Population: Ungraded.
Publication Date: 1977.
Scores: 3 levels in 4 areas: Alphabet and Dictionary Skills, Reading, Handwriting, Spelling.
Administration: Individual in part.
Price Data, 2015: $104.35 per complete kit including administrator's guide (16 pages), test booklet (26 pages), 24 summary sheets (6 pages), graph of concepts and multisensory introductions (16 pages), sheet of block capitals, set of three-dimensional letters, skeleton dictionary (Anna Gillingham and Bessie Stillman, 1956, 79 pages), test cards (56), spirit duplicating master (1 page); $24.30 per 24 summary sheets; $11.15 per graph; $12.20 per skeleton dictionary; quantity discounts available.
Time: (30–60) minutes.
Comments: "Criterion-referenced"; follows the sequence of the Alphabetic Phonics curriculum developed in the Language Research and Training Laboratory of the Texas Scottish Rite Hospital for its remedial language training program.
Author: Aylett R. Cox.
Publisher: Educators Publishing Service, Inc.
Cross References: For a review by David J. Carroll, see 9:138.

[247]
Benchmark of Organizational Emotional Intelligence.

Purpose: "Designed to measure the level of emotional intelligence in an organization as a whole and across departments, teams, or divisions."
Population: Ages 18 and over.
Publication Date: 2005.
Acronym: BOEI
Scores, 24: 7 scale scores (Job Happiness, Compensation, Work/Life Stress Management, Organizational Cohesiveness, Supervisory Leadership, Diversity and Anger Management, Organizational Responsiveness), 14 subscale scores (Pay, Benefits, Stability, Stress Management, Work/Life Balance, Coworker Relationships, Teamwork, Diversity Climate, Gender/Racial Acceptance, Anger Management, Training and Innovation, Optimism and Integrity, Courage and Adaptability, Top Management Leadership), 2 validity scale scores (Positive Impression, Negative Impression), Total Score.
Administration: Group or individual.
Price Data, 2015: $352 per Online Organization Report kit including manual (176 pages), and 1 Organizational Report; $371 per Online Organizational Report; $66 per technical manual; $66 per Group Report (compare up to 5 groups); $18 per Individual Report.
Time: (30) minutes.

Authors: Steven J. Stein and Multi-Health Systems Staff.
Publisher: Multi-Health Systems, Inc.
Cross References: For reviews by Malinda Hendricks Green and Michael J. Zickar, see 17:26.

[248]
Benchmarks for Executives.

Purpose: Designed to assess leadership effectiveness.
Population: Top-level senior executives.
Publication Dates: 2004-2015.
Scores, 16: Sound Judgment, Strategic Planning, Leading Change, Results Orientation, Global Awareness, Business Perspective, Inspiring Commitment, Forging Synergy, Developing and Empowering, Leveraging Differences, Communicating Effectively, Interpersonal Savvy, Courage, Executive Image, Learning from Experience, Credibility.
Administration: Group.
Restricted Distribution: The publisher requires a 2-day certification program for those who wish to give feedback from Benchmarks for Executives in their own organization or as a consultant.
Price Data, 2016: $400 per 1-10 participants including all surveys, online status for administrators and participants, feedback report, Development Planning Guide, and access to online Technical Manual (2015, 33 pages) and other facilitator materials (quantity discounts available); $300 per group profile.
Foreign Language Editions: Available in Dutch, French, German, Latin American Spanish, and Spanish.
Time: (30-40) minutes.
Comments: Previously titled Executive Dimensions; new edition of manual and normative update; assessment content has not changed.
Authors: Center for Creative Leadership, Jean Brittain Leslie (Technical Manual), Phillip W. Braddy (Technical Manual), and Craig Chappelow (Technical Manual).
Publisher: Center for Creative Leadership.
Cross References: For reviews by Ayres D'Costa and Matt Vassar of Executive Dimensions, see 18:50.

[249]
Benchmarks for Learning Agility.

Purpose: A 360-degree assessment designed to measure the learning agility skills most often found in successful leaders and to provide feedback on an individual's willingness to engage in behaviors needed to acquire those skills.
Population: Employed adults.
Publication Dates: 1996-2015.
Scores, 11: Seeks Opportunities to Learn, Seeks and Uses Feedback, Learns from Mistakes, Open to Criticism, Committed to Making a Difference, Insightful: Sees Things From New Angles, Has the Courage to Take Risks, Brings Out the Best in People, Acts with Integrity, Seeks Broad Business Knowledge, Adapts to Cultural Differences.

Administration: Group.

Price Data, 2016: $225 per participant including all surveys, online status for administrators and participants, feedback report, Development Planning Guide (2013, 49 pages), and access to online Technical Manual (2015, 39 pages) and other facilitator materials (quantity discounts available); $300 per group profile.

Time: [10-15] minutes.

Comments: Previously titled Prospector: Discovering the Ability to Learn and to Lead; new edition of manual and normative update; assessment content has not changed.

Authors: Morgan W. McCall, Gretchen M. Spreitzer, Joan Jay Mahoney, Jean Brittain Leslie (Technical Manual, Development Planning Guide), Phillip W. Braddy (Technical Manual), Cynthia D. McCauley (Development Planning Guide).

Publisher: Center for Creative Leadership.

Cross References: For reviews by Theodore L. Hayes and Neil P. Lewis of Prospector: Discovering the Ability to Learn and to Lead, see 14:299.

[250]

Benchmarks® for Managers™.

Purpose: Designed to "assess the caliber and leadership potential as well as career derailment potential among mid- to senior-level executives."

Population: Mid- to senior-level managers and executives with at least 3 years of managerial experience.

Publication Dates: 1990-2015.

Scores: 21 in 4 areas: Leading The Organization (Strategic Perspective, Being a Quick Study, Decisiveness, Change Management), Leading Others (Leading Employees, Confronting Problem Employees, Participative Management, Building Collaborative Relationships, Compassion and Sensitivity, Putting People at Ease, Respect for Differences), Leading Yourself (Taking Initiative, Composure, Balance Between Personal and Work Life, Self-Awareness, Career Management), Problems That Stall a Career (Problems with Interpersonal Relationships, Difficulty Building and Leading a Team, Difficulty Changing or Adapting, Failure to Meet Business Objectives, Too Narrow a Functional Orientation).

Administration: Group.

Restricted Distribution: The publisher requires a 2-day certification program for those who wish to give feedback from Benchmarks for Managers in their own organization or as a consultant.

Price Data, 2016: $330 per participant including all surveys, online status for administrators and participants, feedback report, development planning guide, and access to online technical manual (2015, 140 pages) and other facilitator materials (quantity discounts available).

Foreign Language Editions: Available in Dutch, French, German, Spanish, Simplified Chinese, and Russian.

Time: [30-40] minutes.

Comments: Previously titled Benchmarks; new edition of manual and normative update; assessment content has not changed.

Authors: Michael Lombardo, Cynthia McCauley, Dana McDonald-Mann, Jean Brittain Leslie, and Phillip Braddy (technical manual).

Publisher: Center for Creative Leadership.

   a) BENCHMARKS FOR MANAGERS GROUP PROFILE.

   Purpose: Designed to "provide an aggregate view of the leadership effectiveness and career derailment potential among mid- to senior-level executives."

   Price Data: $300 per group profile.

Cross References: For reviews by Heidi M. Carty and Michael Spangler of an earlier edition titled Benchmarks, see 15:35; for a review by Sheldon Zedeck of a previous edition, see 12:50.

[251]

Bender® Visual-Motor Gestalt Test, Second Edition.

Purpose: Designed to measure visual-motor integration skills in children and adults.

Population: Ages 4–85+.

Publication Dates: 1938–2003.

Acronym: Bender®-Gestalt II.

Scores, 4: Copy Score, Recall Score, Motor Test Score, Perception Test Score.

Administration: Individual.

Price Data, 2015: $228.80 per complete kit including manual (2003, 181 pages), stimulus cards, 25 test records (observation forms), 25 motor test booklets, and 25 perception test booklets; $115.20 per manual; $23.50 per 25 observation forms; $23.50 per 25 motor test booklets; $23.50 per 25 perception test booklets.

Time: Untimed; typically (10-15) minutes.

Comments: Revision of the Visual Motor Gestalt Test [Bender-Gestalt Test].

Authors: Gary G. Brannigan and Scott L. Decker.

Publisher: Houghton Mifflin Harcourt.

Cross References: For reviews by D. Joe Olmi and by Darrell L. Sabers and Sarah Bonner, see 16:30; see also T5:301 (61 references) and T4:291 (34 references); for reviews by Jack A. Naglieri and by John E. Obrzut and Carol A. Boliek of an earlier edition, see 11:40 (92 references) for reviews by Kenneth W. Howell and Jerome M. Sattler, see 9:139 (65 references); see also T3:280 (159 references), 8:506 (253 references), and T2:1447 (144 references); for a review by Phillip M. Kitay, see 7:161 (192 references); see also P:415 (170 references); for a review by C. B. Blakemore and an excerpted review by Fred Y. Billingslea, see 6:203 (99 references); see also 5:172 (118 references); for reviews by Arthur L. Benton and Howard R. White, see 4:144 (34 references); see also 3:108 (8 references).

[252]

Bennett Mechanical Comprehension Test, Second Edition.

Purpose: "Designed to measure the ability to perceive and understand the relationship of physical forces and mechanical elements in practical situations."

Population: Industrial employees and high school and adult applicants for mechanical positions or engineering schools.

Publication Dates: 1940–1994.

Acronym: BMCT.

Scores: Total score only.

Administration: Group.

Forms, 2: S, T (equivalent forms).

Price Data, 2015: $520 per comprehensive kit including 25 form S test booklets, 50 scannable answer documents, key for hand scoring form S, and manual (1994, 89 pages); $314 per 25 test booklets; $268 per 50 scannable answer document S/T; $149 per hand-scoring answer documents; $77 per manual.

Foreign Language Edition: Spanish version available.

Time: (30) minutes.

Comments: Tape recordings of test questions read aloud are available for use with examinees who have limited reading abilities; total assessment score and percentile score provided; available online and via pencil-and-paper.

Author: George K. Bennett.

Publisher: Pearson.

Cross References: For reviews by Joseph C. Ciechalski and Michael Spangler, see 16:31; see also T5:302 (4 references) and T4:292 (2 references); for a review by Hilda Wing of an earlier edition, see 11:41 (3 references); see also T3:282 (7 references) and T2:2239 (9 references); for reviews by Harold P. Bechtoldt and A. Oscar H. Roberts, and an excerpted review by Ronald K. Hambleton of the first edition, see 7:1049 (22 references); see also 6:1094 (15 references) and 5:889 (46 references); for a review by N. W. Morton of earlier forms, see 4:766 (28 references); for reviews by Charles M. Harsh, Lloyd G. Humphreys, and George A. Satter, see 3:683 (19 references).

[253]

Benton Visual Retention Test, Fifth Edition.

Purpose: "To assess visual perception, visual memory, and visuoconstructive abilities."

Population: Age 8–adults.

Publication Dates: 1946–1991.

Acronym: BVRT.

Scores, 9: Omissions, Distortions, Perseverations, Rotations, Misplacements, Size Errors, Total Left, Total Right, Total.

Administration: Individual.

Forms, 3: C, D, E in a single booklet.

Price Data, 2015: $255.25 per complete set including stimulus booklet (all 30 designs), scoring template, 25 response booklets, record form, and manual (1992, 108 pages); $124 per stimulus booklet; $57.40 per 25 response booklets; $20.50 per scoring template; $104.55 per manual.

Time: (15–20) minutes.

Author: Arthur L. Benton.

Publisher: Pearson.

Cross References: See T5:303 (32 references); for reviews by Anita M. Hubley and Cynthia A. Rohrbeck, see 13:36 (66 references); see also T4:293 (62 references), 9:140 (30 references), T3:283 (27 references), 8:236 (32 references), T2:543 (71 references), and 6:543 (22 references); for a review by Nelson G. Hanawalt, see 5:401 (5 references); for reviews by Ivan Norman Mensh, Joseph Newman, and William Schofield of the original edition, see 4:360 (3 references); for an excerpted review, see 3:297.

[254]

The Benziger Thinking Styles Assessment.

Purpose: Designed to "help individuals increase their general effectiveness, collaborative skills and overall well-being through enhanced self-awareness and understanding."

Population: Working adults, aged 18 or older.

Publication Dates: 1988–2004.

Acronym: BTSA, E-BTSA.

Scores, 5: Frontal Left, Basal Left, Basal Right, Frontal Right, Introversion/Extraversion.

Administration: Individual or group.

Restricted Distribution: Administrators must be persons (licensees) who have completed the publisher's training course.

Price Data, 2016: $100 per E-BTSA (electronic version) in U.S.; $125-135 with feedback/coaching with EBTSA; £100 per E-BTSA and feedback in U.K.; price data available from publisher for 6 related books: Thriving in Mind, Thriving in Mind: Workbook, Physiological and Psycho-physiological Bases for Jungian Concepts, Overcoming Depression, Falsification of Type, and BTSA User Manual.

Time: (30–45) minutes.

Comments: Not intended as a psychometric measure; paper and electronic versions available.

Author: Katherine Benziger.

Publisher: KBA, LLC.

Cross References: For reviews by Richard E. Harding and Mark L. Pope, see 16:32.

[255]

BEST Instruments.

Purpose: A series of learning instruments designed to help managers and employees understand their behavior.

Population: Adults.

Publication Dates: 1989–2015.

Acronym: BEST.
Administration: Group.
Price Data: Available from publisher.
Comments: Subtests available as separates.
Author: James H. Brewer.
Publisher: BEST Instruments, LLC.

   a) MY BEST PROFILE.
   Purpose: "To promote positive interpersonal relations."
   Publication Dates: 1989-2006.
   Scores: 4 personality types: Bold, Expressive, Sympathetic, Technical.
   Foreign Language Editions: Available in Chinese (Simplified and Traditional), French, German, Italian, Japanese, Korean, Portuguese, Russian, Spanish and Taiwanese.
   Time: (15–20) minutes.

   b) MY BEST COMMUNICATION STYLE.
   Purpose: "To improve communication skills."
   Publication Dates: 1989–1990.
   Scores: 4 styles: Bold, Expressive, Sympathetic, Technical.
   Foreign Language Editions: Available in Spanish.
   Time: (15–20) minutes.

   c) MY BEST LEADERSHIP STYLE.
   Purpose: "To improve leadership skills."
   Publication Dates: 1989–2003.
   Scores: Same as *a* above.
   Time: (15–20) minutes.

   d) LEADERSHIP/PERSONALITY COMPATIBILITY INVENTORY.
   Purpose: "To promote more productive leadership in organizations."
   Acronym: L/PCI.
   Scores: Same as *a* above plus 4 Leadership Role Characteristics: Active/Competitive, Persuasive/Interactive, Precise/Systematic, Willing/Steady.
   Publication Dates: 1990–2010.
   Time: (15–20) minutes.
   Comments: Includes form with information about four personality types (B, E, S, or T) and Leadership Role Characteristics form.

   e) WORKING WITH MY BOSS.
   Purpose: "To improve the productive relationship between employee and supervisor."
   Publication Dates: 1989-2003.
   Scores: Same as *a* above.
   Time: (15-20) minutes.

   f) PRE-EVALUATION PROFILE.
   Purpose: "To prepare supervisors for performance evaluations of employees without personality type bias."
   Acronym: PEP.
   Publication Date: 1989.
   Scores: Same as *a* above.
   Time: (15–20) minutes.
   Comments: Supervisor completes profile for self and employee.

   g) OUR BEST TEAM.
   Purpose: "To build a more productive team."
   Publication Dates: 1989-2007.
   Scores: Same as *a* above.
   Time: (20–30) minutes.
   Comments: Ratings of all team members are combined for a composite profile. Includes four individual assessment administrations.

   h) MY TIMESTYLE.
   Purpose: "To develop more productive time usage."
   Publication Date: 1990.
   Scores: 4 timestyles: Road Runner, Race Horse, New Pup, Tom Cat.
   Time: (10–15) minutes.

   i) MY BEST PRESENTATION STYLE.
   Purpose: "To assist individuals in making more effective presentations."
   Publication Dates: 1989-2003.
   Scores: Same as *a* above.
   Time: (15–20) minutes.

   j) SALES STYLE.
   Purpose: "To sharpen sales skills."
   Publication Date: 1990.
   Scores: 4 sales styles: Quick-Sell, Persistent-Sell, Talkative-Sell, Precise-Sell.
   Time: (10–15) minutes.

   k) NEGOTIATING STYLE.
   Purpose: "To build productive negotiating skills."
   Publication Date: 1991.
   Scores: Bold, Expressive, Sympathetic, Technical.
   Scores: 4 negotiating styles: Pushy, Stand Pat, Buddy, Check All.
   Time: (10–15) minutes.

   l) TRAINING STYLE.
   Purpose: "To determine an individual's specific training style."
   Publication Date: 2005.
   Scores: 4 training styles: Bold, Expressive, Sympathetic, Technical.
   Time: (15-20) minutes.

   m) BEHAVIORAL INVENTORY.
   Purpose: "To help individuals gain an understanding of how others perceive them."
   Publication Date: 2006
   Scores: 4 personality types: Bold, Expressive, Sympathetic, Technical.
   Time: (15-20) minutes.

   n) QUALITY SERVICE AUDIT FOR EMPLOYEES.
   Purpose: "To evaluate employees' skills in quality customer service."
   Publication Dates: 1992-2015.
   Scores: Attitudes and Beliefs, Knowledge, Personal Commitment, and Performance.
   Time: (15-20) minutes.

Cross References: For reviews by Mary A. Lewis and Frank Schmidt, see 13:37.

[256]

BEST Literacy.

Purpose: Designed to "measure adult English language learners' ability to read and write in English in authentic situations in the United States."
Population: Ages 16 and over.
Publication Date: 2008.
Scores, 3: Reading, Writing, Final Scale Score.
Administration: Group or individual.
Forms, 3: Form B, Form C, Form D.
Price Data, 2016: $36-50 per Form B (including 20 booklets with corresponding scoring sheets); $36-50 per

Form C (including 20 booklets with corresponding scoring sheets); $36-50 per Form D (including 20 booklets with corresponding scoring sheets); $26 per test manual (64 pages); $25 per printed technical report (130 pages) or $10 per PDF of technical report.

Time: (60) minutes.

Comments: May be used as a pretest and posttest using the different forms available.

Author: Center for Applied Linguistics.

Publisher: Center for Applied Linguistics.

Cross References: For reviews by George Engelhard, Jr. and Aminah Perkins and by Yuanzhong Zhang, see 19:19.

[257]

BEST Plus: Oral English Proficiency Assessment.

Purpose: Designed "to assess the oral language proficiency of adult" English language learners enrolled in educational programs "who need to use English to function in day-to-day life in the United States."

Population: Adults.

Publication Dates: 2003–2005.

Acronym: BEST Plus.

Scores: 3 subscales: Listening Comprehension, Language Complexity, Communication; Total scale score.

Administration: Individual.

Levels: Aligned to Student Performance Level descriptors (SPL) for Listening Comprehension and Oral Communication 0-10; National Reporting System (NRS) Educational Functioning Levels (June 2006) – Beginning ESL Literacy, Low Beginning ESL, High Beginning ESL, Low Intermediate ESL, High Intermediate ESL, Advanced ESL.

Versions, 2: Computer-adaptive version, semi-adaptive print-based version (3 parallel forms A, B, and C); the computer-adaptive version is available in two formats: CD-ROM or network version.

Price Data: Available from publisher.

Time: [5-20] minutes, depending on proficiency level of the examinee.

Comments: Training is required for all test administrators and must be conducted by a CAL certified BEST Plus trainer. The test publisher advises that Best Plus 2.0 is scheduled for release in summer 2016.

Author: Center for Applied Linguistics.

Publisher: Center for Applied Linguistics.

Cross References: For reviews by S. Kathleen Krach and Annita Ward, see 17:27.

[258]

Beta III.

Purpose: "Provides a quick ... measure of nonverbal intellectual ability."

Population: Ages 16–89.

Publication Dates: 1934–1999.

Scores, 6: Coding, Picture Completion, Clerical Checking, Picture Absurdities, Matrix Reasoning, IQ Score.

Administration: Group or individual.

Price Data, 2015: $234.75 per complete kit including manual (1999, 58 pages), 25 response booklets, and scoring key; $84 per manual; $146.50 per 25 response booklets; $36.60 per scoring key.

Time: 15(25–30) minutes including 10–15 minutes of instruction and practice.

Comments: Revision of the Revised Beta Examination, Second Edition.

Authors: C. E. Kellogg and N. W. Morton.

Publisher: Pearson.

Cross References: For reviews by C. G. Bellah and Louise M. Soares, see 16:33; for information regarding the previous edition, see T5:2212 (3 references) and T4:2255 (4 references); for reviews by Louis M. Hsu and Mark D. Reckase of the Revised Beta Examination, Second Edition, see 9:1044; see also T2:447 (29 references); for a review by Bert A. Goldman, see 6:494 (13 references); see also 5:375 (14 references); for reviews by Raleigh M. Drake and Walter C. Shipley, see 3:259 (5 references); for reviews by S. D. Porteus and David Wechsler, see 2:1419 (4 references).

[259]

Bilingual Two-Language Assessment Battery of Tests.

Purpose: Designed to reveal "levels of language proficiency" and to determine language skills, acquisition, and loss.

Population: Students, adults, and potential employees with a language proficiency at second grade or higher level.

Publication Dates: 1983-2008.

Scores, 13: First Letter Recognition, Second Letter Recognition, Spelling, Opposites, Similarities, Comparisons, Reading, Listening, Items, Actions, Relationships, Total, Oral Proficiency.

Administration: Individual or group.

Forms, 7: Spanish-English, Portuguese-English, Vietnamese-English, Italian-English, French-English, English-Russian, English-Chinese.

Price Data, 2016: $99 per battery including manual (2005, 104 pages), profile cards, one language test, student's test work pages, and test answers; $792 per complete battery including manual, profile cards, six language tests, student's test work pages, and test answers.

Foreign Language Editions: Spanish, Portuguese, Vietnamese, Italian, French, Russian, and Chinese.

Time: (20-30) minutes per language.

Comments: "Criterion-referenced"; each session consists of a Native language sitting followed by an English language sitting within 2 weeks; the battery is prerecorded and requires access to a CD player; optimal administration frequency is every 6 to 8 months.

Author: Adolph Caso.

Publisher: Branden Publishing Co.

[260]

Bilingual Verbal Ability Tests.

Purpose: "Provides a measure of overall verbal ability, and an unique combination of cognitive/academic language abilities for bilingual individuals."
Population: Ages 5 and older.
Publication Date: 1998.
Acronym: BVAT.
Scores, 5: Bilingual Verbal Ability, English Language Proficiency, Picture Vocabulary, Oral Vocabulary, Verbal Analogies.
Administration: Individual.
Price Data, 2015: $1,306.60 per complete test kit including an Easel Test Book Binder with English Test Pages and 18 Sets of tests (1 of each language), Storage Box, Comprehensive Manual, Test Records, and Normative Update Package; $142.10 per test pages of 1 language; $317.75 per English test kit; $493.60 per Spanish test kit; $68.75 per 25 test records.
Time: (20–30) minutes.
Comments: Yields an aptitude measure that can be used in conjunction with the WJ-R® Tests of Achievement; an optional training video with administration procedures is available.
Authors: Ana F. Muñoz-Sandoval, Jim Cummins, Criselda G. Alvarado, and Mary L. Ruef.
Publisher: Houghton Mifflin Harcourt.
Cross References: For reviews by Alan Garfinkel and Charles W. Stansfield, see 14:46.

[261]

Biofeedback Certification Examination.

Purpose: A certification examination covering "the knowledge needed by providers of biofeedback services at the time they begin practice."
Population: Entry-level biofeedback service providers.
Publication Dates: 1980–1984.
Scores: 11 Blueprint Areas: Introduction to Biofeedback, Preparing for Clinical Intervention, Neuromuscular Intervention: General, Neuromuscular Intervention: Specific, Central Nervous System Interventions: General, Autonomic Nervous System Interventions: General, Autonomic Nervous System Interventions: Specific, Biofeedback and Distress, Instrumentation, Adjunctive Techniques and Cognitive Interventions, Professional Conduct.
Administration: Group.
Manual: No manual.
Price Data: Available from publisher.
Time: (180) minutes.
Comments: Administration schedule available from test publisher.
Author: Biofeedback Certification Institute of America.
Publisher: Biofeedback Certification Institute of America.

[262]

The Birkman Method.

Purpose: "Developed as a self-report questionnaire eliciting responses about perception of self, perception of social context and perception of occupational opportunities."
Population: Ages 25-65.
Publication Dates: 1992-2011.
Scores, 33: Esteem Usual, Esteem Need, Acceptance Usual, Acceptance Need, Structure Usual, Structure Need, Authority Usual, Authority Need, Advantage Usual, Advantage Need, Activity Usual, Activity Need, Challenge Usual, Challenge Need, Empathy Usual, Empathy Need, Change Usual, Change Need, Freedom Usual, Freedom Need, Thought Usual, Thought Need, Persuasive Interest, Social Service Interest, Scientific Interest, Mechanical Interest, Outoor Interest, Numerical Interest, Clerical Interest, Artistic Interest, Literacy Interest, Musical Interest, Stress Behaviors.
Administration: Group.
Price Data: Available from publisher.
Time: [30-45] minutes.
Comments: Publisher advises that 2011 edition is available for ages 15 and up. However, these new materials have not been made available for review.
Author: Roger W. Birkman.
Publisher: Birkman International, Inc.
Cross References: For reviews by David F. Ciampi and Gypsy M. Denzine, see 17:28.

[263]

Birmingham Cognitive Screen: Brain Behavior Analysis.

Purpose: "Designed to provide a cognitive profile, which will indicate whether an examinee has a clinical impairment (related to norms) in five primary domains of cognition."
Population: Stroke survivors and individuals with brain injury or dementia.
Publication Date: 2012.
Acronym: BCoS.
Scores: 38 in 5 domains: Attention (Apple Cancellation [accuracy], Asymmetry [egocentric], Asymmetry [allocentric], Left Visual Unilateral, Right Visual Unilateral, Left Visual Bilateral, Right Visual Bilateral, Left Tactile Unilateral, Right Tactile Unilateral, Left Tactile Bilateral, Right Tactile Bilateral, Auditory Attention Accuracy, Auditory Attention Practice, Auditory Attention Word Recall, Sustained Attention Index, Birmingham Rule Finding Accuracy, Birmingham Rule Finding Rules), Language (Instruction Comprehension, Picture Naming, Sentence Construction, Nonword Reading–Accuracy, Sentence Reading–Accuracy, Word/Nonword Writing), Memory (Personal, Time and Space, Story–Free Recall 1, Story–Recognition 1, Story–Free Recall 2, Story–Rec-

ognition 2, Task–Recognition), Number Skills (Reading, Writing, Calculation), Praxis (Figure Copy, Multi-Step Object Use, Gesture Production, Gesture Recognition, Imitation).

Administration: Individual.

Price Data, 2015: $475 per complete kit including manual (85 pages), test book, auditory attention test stimuli on CD, 15 examiner booklets, 15 examinee booklets, and test objects.

Time: (60) minutes.

Authors: Glyn W. Humphreys, Wai-Ling Bickerton, Dana Samson, and M. Jane Riddoch.

Publisher: Routledge Psychology.

Cross References: Reviews are scheduled for *The Twentieth Mental Measurements Yearbook.*

[264]

Birmingham Object Recognition Battery.

Purpose: Designed to "assess whether the processes of visual recognition and naming are intact following brain damage."

Population: Patients who may be experiencing visual object recognition impairment due to a brain injury.

Publication Date: 1993.

Acronym: BORB.

Scores: 14 tasks: Copying, Length Match, Size Match, Orientation Match, Position of Gap Match, Overlapping Figures, Minimal Feature View, Foreshortened View, Drawing from Memory, Object Decision, Item Match Task, Associative Match, Picture Naming (Short Version), Picture Naming (Long Version).

Administration: Individual.

Price Data, 2016: $54 per paperback; $335 per hardcover.

Time: Administration time not reported.

Comments: Not all tests must be administered; test publisher suggests initial set of screening tests should include Copying, Overlapping Figures Drawing from Memory, Object Decision, Associative Match, and Picture Naming (Short Version).

Authors: M. Jane Riddoch and Glyn W. Humphreys.

Publisher: Routledge Psychology.

[265]

Birth to Three Assessment and Intervention System, Second Edition.

Purpose: Designed to "identify children who are developmentally at risk in the areas of language and learning."

Population: Birth to 3 years.

Publication Dates: 1986–2000.

Acronym: BTAIS-2.

Scores, 5: Language Comprehension, Language Expression, Nonverbal Thinking, Social/Personal Behaviors, Motor Behaviors.

Administration: Individual.

Price Data, 2010: $277 per complete kit including screening test kit, comprehensive test kit, and teaching manual (2000, 163 pages); $76 per teaching manual.

Time: Untimed.

Authors: Jerome J. Ammer and Tina E. Bangs.

Publisher: PRO-ED.

a) SCREENING TEST OF DEVELOPMENTAL ABILITIES.

Purpose: Designed "to identify young children who may have developmental delays."

Price Data: $91 per complete screening test kit including manual (2000, 93 pages) and 25 record forms; $66 per manual; $28 per 25 record forms.

b) COMPREHENSIVE TEST OF DEVELOPMENTAL ABILITIES.

Purpose: Designed "to identify each child's specific strengths and weaknesses and to guide the preparation of instructional plans."

Price Data, 2015: $295 per complete kit including screening test kit, comprehensive test kit, and teaching manual (2000, 163 pages); $82 per manual for teaching.

Cross References: For reviews by Kimberly A. Blair and Leah M. Nellis, see 15:36; see T5:315; for a review by Donna Spiker of an earlier edition, see 11:45; for a review by Bonnie W. Camp of an earlier edition, see 9:152.

[266]

Blox Test.

Purpose: Designed to measure the individual's perceptual ability for spatial relations.

Population: Job applicants with at least 10 years of education.

Publication Dates: 1961–1963.

Scores: Total score only.

Administration: Group.

Manual: No manual.

Price Data: Available from publisher.

Time: 30(35) minutes.

Comments: Test previously known as Perceptual Battery (T3:1777).

Author: National Institute for Personnel Research of the Human Sciences Research Council.

Publisher: Human Sciences Research Council [South Africa]. [Efforts to obtain updated information from the test publisher were unsuccessful. This test could not be found on the test publisher's website; its status is unknown.]

[267]

Bochum Matrices Test–Advanced–Short Version.

Purpose: Designed to "measure general intelligence and intellectual capacity in the upper cognitive ability range."

Population: "Students and graduates of universities and advanced technical colleges and academically educated managers."

Publication Dates: 2001-2015.

Acronym: BOMAT.
Score: Total score only.
Administration: Individual or group.
Forms, 2: A, B.
Price Data, 2016: £35 per online administration and technical report (subscription discounts available).
Foreign Language Edition: Originally published in German.
Time: 45(60) minutes.
Comments: Administered online.
Authors: Rüdiger Hossiep, Daniela Turck, and Michele Hasella.
Publisher: Hogrefe Ltd [United Kingdom].

[268]

Body Insight Scale.

Purpose: Designed to "measure awareness of internal and external bodily sensations that support comfort, health and overall well-being."
Population: Adults.
Publication Date: 2011.
Acronym: BIS.
Scores, 3: Energy Body Awareness, Comfort Body Awareness, Inner Body Awareness.
Administration: Individual or group.
Manual: No manual.
Price Data, 2016: $2.40 per Transform Survey Hosting (minimum purchase of 50); $2 per Remote Online Survey License (minimum purchase of 50); $2 per License to Reproduce (minimum purchase of 50).
Foreign Language Edition: Available in Spanish.
Time: [8-10] minutes.
Author: Rosemarie Anderson.
Publisher: Mind Garden, Inc.

[269]

Boehm Test of Basic Concepts–Third Edition.

Purpose: Designed to "assess … [school] readiness or [to] identify students who may be at risk for learning difficulty."
Population: Grades K–2.
Publication Dates: 1967–2001.
Acronym: Boehm-3.
Scores: Total score only.
Administration: Group or individual.
Forms, 2: E, F.
Price Data, 2015: $88.60 per examination set including examiner's manual (2001, 145 pages), 1 Form E booklet, 1 Form F booklet, 1 Form E class key, 1 Form F class key, and 1 directions for administration (Forms E and F, English and Spanish); $88.60 per testing kit (Form E or F) including directions for administration (English and Spanish), 1 package of 25 booklets, and 1 class key; $82.75 per examiner's manual (Fall and Spring norms manual); $62.25 per 25 booklets (Form E or F); $11.10 per class key (Form

E or F); $28.65 per directions for administration (English and Spanish).
Foreign Language Edition: Directions for administering in Spanish are available for both forms.
Time: 30(45) minutes if administered in one session; 45(60) minutes if administered in two test sessions.
Comments: Revision of the Boehm Test of Basic Concepts—Revised; yields raw scores, percent correct, performance range, and percentiles by grade.
Author: Ann E. Boehm.
Publisher: Pearson.
Cross References: For reviews by Sherry K. Bain and James Hawkins and by Harold R. Keller, see 16:34; for information regarding previous editions, see T5:324 (12 references) and T4:314 (5 references); for reviews by Robert L. Linn and by Colleen Fitzmaurice and Joseph C. Witt, see 10:32 (16 references); see also T3:302 (18 references); for an excerpted review by Theodore A. Dahl, see 8:178 (22 references); se also T2:344 (1 reference); for reviews by Boyd R. McCandless and Charles D. Smock, and excerpted reviews by Frank S. Freeman, George Lawlor, Victor H. Noll, and Barton B. Proger, see 7:335 (1 reference).

[270]

Boehm Test of Basic Concepts–3 Preschool.

Purpose: "Designed to assess young children's understanding of the basic relational concepts" ("quality, spatial, temporal, quantity") "important for language and cognitive development."
Population: Ages 3-0 to 5-11.
Publication Dates: 1986–2001.
Scores: Total score only.
Administration: Individual.
Price Data, 2015: $203.85 per complete kit including examiner's manual (2001, 111 pages), picture manual, and 25 record forms; $71.15 per examiner's manual; $106.60 per stimulus manual; $49.85 per 25 record forms.
Foreign Language Edition: Spanish edition available.
Time: (15–20) minutes.
Comments: Revision of Boehm Test of Basic Concepts–Preschool Version; norms extended upward; provides Parent Report Form, Ongoing Observation and Intervention Planning Form (Spanish versions included); includes directions for Spanish administration and scoring; separate English and Spanish norms available.
Author: Ann E. Boehm.
Publisher: Pearson.
Cross References: For reviews by Theresa Graham and Koressa Kutsick Malcolm, see 16:35; see also T5:323 (1 reference) and T4:313 (1 reference); for reviews by Judy Oehler-Stinnett and Stephanie Stein of an earlier edition, see 11:46 (1 reference).

[271]

The Booklet Category Test, Second Edition.

Purpose: Designed to "distinguish individuals with brain damage from normal individuals by measuring concept formation and abstract reasoning."

Population: Ages 15 and older.

Publication Dates: 1979–1997.

Acronym: BCT.

Scores: Total score only.

Administration: Individual.

Price Data, 2015: $580 per introductory kit including professional manual, 2-volume set of stimulus books, and 50 response forms.

Time: (30–60) minutes.

Authors: Nick A. DeFilippis and Elizabeth Mc-Campbell.

Publisher: Psychological Assessment Resources, Inc.

Cross References: For reviews by Carolyn M. Callahan and David C. S. Richard, see 14:47; see also T5:326 (10 references) and T4:315 (4 references); for reviews by Raymond S. Dean and Thomas A. Hammeke of an earlier edition, see 9:156.

[272]

Borromean Family Index.

Purpose: Developed to measure "attitudes and feelings about one's family."

Population: Adolescents and adults.

Publication Dates: 1975–1988.

Scores, 2: Internal (forces that attract toward family), External (forces that pull away).

Subtests, 2: For Married Persons, For Single Persons.

Administration: Group.

Manual: No manual.

Price Data, 2015: $2 per test.

Time: [10] minutes.

Comments: Supplementary article available.

Author: Panos D. Bardis.

Publisher: Donna Bardis.

Cross References: For additional information, see 8:332 (1 reference).

[273]

Boston Assessment of Severe Aphasia.

Purpose: Developed to identify "preserved abilities that might form the beginning steps of rehabilitation programs for severely aphasic patients."

Population: Aphasic adults.

Publication Date: 1989.

Acronym: BASA.

Scores, 5: Auditory Comprehension, Praxis, Oral-Gestural Expression, Reading Comprehension, Other.

Administration: Individual.

Price Data, 2015: $331 per complete kit; $80 per package of manipulatives; $56 per set of stimulus cards;

$49 per clipboard; $48 per 25 record forms; $68 per manual (96 pages); $73 per DVD.

Time: (30–40) minutes.

Authors: Nancy Helm-Estabrooks, Gail Ramsberger, Alisa R. Morgan, and Marjorie Nicholas.

Publisher: PRO-ED.

Cross References: See T5:328 (1 reference); for reviews by Steven B. Leder and Roger L. Towne, see 12:52 (3 references).

[274]

Boston Diagnostic Aphasia Examination—Third Edition.

Purpose: Designed to help "identify and distinguish among disorders of language function and neurologically recognized aphasic syndromes."

Population: Individuals with aphasia

Publication Dates: 1972-2001.

Acronym: BDAE-3.

Scores, 59: Conversational and Expository Speech (Simple Social Responses, Free Conversation, Picture Description [Discourse Analysis-Segmentation into Utterances], Severity Rating and Profile of Speech Characteristics), Auditory Comprehension (Word Comprehension [Basic Word Discrimination, Supplemental Test], Commands and Complex Ideational Material Test), Oral Expression (Oral Agility [Nonverbal Agility and Verbal Agility], Automatized Sequences, Recitation, Melody, and Rhythm [Recitation, Melody and Rhythm], Repetition [Single Word Repetition and Repetition of Sentences], Naming [Responsive Naming, Boston Naming Test-Visual Confrontation Naming, Screening for Naming of Special Categories]), Reading (Basic Symbol Recognition [Matching Across Cases and Scripts and Number Matching], Word Identification [Picture-Word Match], Phonics [Homophone Matching], Derivational and Inflectional Morphology [Free Grammatical Morphemes], Oral Reading [Basic Oral Word Reading and Oral Reading of Special Word Lists (Mixed Morphological Types and Semantic Paralexia-Prone Words)], Oral Reading of Sentences with Comprehension, Reading Comprehension-Sentences and Paragraphs), Writing (Mechanics of Writing, Basic Encoding Skills [Primer Word Vocabulary, Regular Phonics and Common Irregular Forms], Written Picture Naming and Narrative Writing) and Apraxia Assessment (Natural Gestures, Conventional Gestures, Use of Pretend Objects without an Action Goal, Use of Pretend Objects with an Action Goal and Bucco-Facial Respiratory Movements).

Administration: Individual.

Forms, 3: Short, Standard (Long), Boston Naming Test (Short and Long combined).

Price Data, 2015: $532 per complete kit including manual (2001, 136 pages), long form stimulus cards picture book, 25 long form record booklets, short form stimulus cards picture book, 25 short form record booklets, Naming Test stimulus cards picture book, 25 Naming Test record booklets, and DVD; $109 per manual; $48 per DVD; $121 per Boston Naming Test kit including stimulus cards picture book and 25 Naming Test record booklets; $42 per 25 Naming Test record booklets; $79 per Boston Naming Test stimulus cards picture book.

Time: (35-45) minutes.

Comments: Previously listed as The Assessment of Aphasia and Related Disorders and that is the title of the manual.

Authors: Harold Goodglass with the collaboration of Edith Kaplan and Barbara Barresi.

Publisher: PRO-ED.

    a) SHORT FORM.

    Purpose: Designed "to provide a comprehensive, but brief sampling of the performances necessary for an informed quantitative assessment" of individuals with aphasia.

    Price Data: $90 per short form kit including 27 short form stimulus cards picture book and 25 short form record booklets; $40 per 25 short form record booklets; $67 per short form stimulus cards picture book.

    Time: (30-45) minutes.

    Comments: The short form consists of shortened or omitted sections that are included in the standard form.

    b) STANDARD (LONG) FORM.

    Purpose: Designed to be a "more probing evaluation of particular language functions within each area of testing."

    Scores, 18: Aesop's Fables, Word Comprehension in Categories, Syntactic Processing (Touching A with B, Reversible Possessives, Embedded Sentences), Repetition of Nonsense Words, Naming in Categories, Advanced Phonic Analysis–Pseudo-Homophone Matching, Bound Grammatical Morphemes, Derivational Morphemes, Uncommon Irregularities, Nonsense Words, Oral Spelling, and Cognitive/Grammatical Influences (Part of Speech Effects: Dictated Words, Subtest 2: "Dictated Functor Loaded Sentences").

    Price Data: $214 per long form kit including manual, 147 long form stimulus cards picture book, and 25 long form record booklets; $45 per 25 long form record booklets; $85 per long form stimulus cards picture book.

    Time: Administration time not reported.

    Comments: All scores included in the standard form are also included in the extended form.

    c) BOSTON NAMING TEST, SECOND EDITION.

    Population: Ages 55-59.

    Scores: Total score only.

    Time: Administration time not reported.

    Authors: Edith Kaplan, Harold Goodglass, and Sandra Weintraub.

Cross References: For reviews by Shawn K. Acheson and Anthony T. Dugbartey, see 17:29; see also T5:199 (18 references) and T4:207 (105 references); for reviews by Rita Sloan Berndt and Malcolm R. McNeil of an earlier edition, see 10:15 (3 references); see also 9:86 (2 references) and T3:308 (28 references); for reviews by Daniel R. Boone and Manfred J. Meier of an earlier edition, see 8:955 (1 reference).

[275]

The Boston Qualitative Scoring System for the Rey-Osterrieth Complex Figure.

Purpose: Designed as a quantifiable approach to rating the qualitative features of the ROCF (which was designed to assess visuoconstructional ability and visual memory performance in brain-impaired patients).

Population: Ages 18–94.

Publication Dates: 1994–1999.

Acronym: BQSS.

Scores, 23: Qualitative (Configural Presence, Configural Accuracy, Cluster Presence, Cluster Accuracy, Cluster Placement, Detail Presence, Detail Placement, Fragmentation, Planning, Neatness, Vertical Expansion, Horizontal Expansion, Reduction, Rotation, Perseveration, Confabulation, Asymmetry), Summary (Copy Presence and Accuracy, Immediate Presence and Accuracy, Delayed Presence and Accuracy, Immediate Retention, Delayed Retention, Organization).

Administration: Individual.

Price Data, 2015: $260 per introductory kit including professional manual, 50 scoring booklets, 50 response sheets, stimulus card, reference guide, scoring templates, and metric ruler.

Time: (45) minutes, including a (20–30) minute delay interval.

Authors: Robert A. Stern, Debbie J. Javorsky, Elizabeth A. Singer, Naomi G. Singer Harris, Jessica A. Somerville, Lisa M. Duke, Jodi A. Thompson, and Edith Kaplan.

Publisher: Psychological Assessment Resources, Inc.

Cross References: For reviews by D. Ashley Cohen and Robert A. Leark, see 15:37.

[276]

Bracken Basic Concept Scale: Expressive.

Purpose: Used to measure "a child's ability to verbally label basic concepts."

Population: Ages 3-0 to 6-11.

Publication Date: 2006.

Acronym: BBCS:E.

Scores, 13: 10 subtest scores (Colors, Letters/Sounds, Numbers/Counting, Sizes/Comparisons, Shapes, Direction/Position, Self-/Social Awareness, Texture/Material, Quantity, Time/Sequence); 3 composite scores (School Readiness Composite, Expressive School Readiness Composite, Expressive Total Composite).

Administration: Individual.

Price Data, 2015: $353.65 per complete kit including manual (2006, 205 pages), stimulus manual, and 25 English record forms; $238.30 per stimulus manual; $61 per 25 record forms (specify English or Spanish) $89.95 per manual; $178.25 per scoring assistant CD.

Foreign Language Edition: Criterion-referenced Spanish edition included.

Time: 25(30) minutes.

Comments: For use with the Bracken Basic Concept Scale–Third Edition: Receptive (277).
Author: Bruce A. Bracken.
Publisher: Pearson.
Cross References: For reviews by R. Anthony Doggett and Gregory Snyder, see 18:13.

[277]

Bracken Basic Concept Scale–Third Edition: Receptive.

Purpose: Designed to measure relevant educational concepts and receptive language skills.
Population: Ages 3-0 to 6-11.
Publication Dates: 1984-2006.
Acronym: BBCS-3:R.
Scores, 8: 5 subtest scores (Direction/Position, Self-/Social Awareness, Texture/Material, Quantity, Time/Sequence); 3 composite scores (School Readiness Composite, Receptive School Readiness Composite, Receptive Total Composite).
Administration: Individual.
Price Data, 2015: $353.65 per complete kit including examiner's manual (2006, 208 pages), stimulus manual, and 25 English record forms; $257.75 per stimulus manual; $61 per 25 record forms (specify English or Spanish); $124 per manual; $178.25 per scoring assistant CD.
Foreign Language Edition: Criterion-referenced Spanish edition included.
Time: (30-40) minutes.
Comments: For use with the Bracken Basic Concept Scale: Expressive (276).
Author: Bruce A. Bracken.
Publisher: Pearson.
Cross References: For reviews by Gretchen Owens and Loraine J. Spenciner, see 18:14; for reviews of an earlier edition by Leah M. Nellis and Rhonda H. Solomon, see 14:48; see also T5:331 (6 references) and T4:319 (4 references); for reviews by Timothy L. Turco and James E. Ysseldyke of the original edition, see 10:33.

[278]

Bracken School Readiness Assessment, Third Edition.

Purpose: Designed to "assess a child's readiness for school by evaluating his or her understanding of 85 important foundational academic concepts in the categories of Colors, Numbers/Counting, Sizes/Comparisons, and Shapes."
Population: Ages 3:0 to 6:11.
Publication Dates: 2002-2007.
Acronym: BSRA-3.
Scores, 6: Colors, Letters, Numbers/Counting, Sizes/Comparisons, Shapes, School Readiness Composite.
Administration: Individual.

Price Data, 2015: $179.85 per complete kit including examiner's manual (2007, 163 pages), stimulus manual, 25 record forms and 25 parent/teacher forms; $106 per stimulus manual; $63.80 per examiner's manual; $31.15 per 25 record forms; $31.15 per 25 parent/teacher forms; $106 per scoring assistant CD.
Foreign Language Edition: Spanish edition available.
Time: (10-15) minutes.
Comments: The subtests in this test are the first five subtests of the Bracken Basic Concept Scale–Third Edition: Receptive (277).
Author: Bruce A. Bracken.
Publisher: Pearson.
Cross References: Reviews are scheduled for *The Twentieth Mental Measurements Yearbook*. For reviews by Thomas McKnight and Gene Schwarting of the original edition, see 16:36.

[279]

Brain Injury Rehabilitation Trust Memory and Information Processing Battery.

Purpose: Designed to "assess memory and information processing skills or to detect and/or assess impairments in these skills for either clinical, educational, occupational or research purposes."
Population: Adults.
Publication Date: 2007.
Acronym: BMIPB.
Administration: Individual.
Forms, 4: 1, 2, 3, 4.
Price Data, 2016: £445 per complete battery; £44 per 25 Memory and Learning forms and 25 Speed of Information Processing forms Form 1; £44 per 25 Memory and Learning forms and 25 Speed of Information Processing forms Form 2; £44 per 25 Memory and Learning Forms and 25 Speed of Information Processing forms Form 3; £44 per 25 Memory and Learning forms and 25 Speed of Information Processing forms Form 4.
Time: (45-60) minutes.
Comments: Test authors suggest the assessment be administered by "chartered psychologists with post qualification experience and knowledge of neuropsychology or the psychology of aging."
Authors: Anthony K. Coughlan, Michael Oddy, and John R. Crawford.
Publisher: The Brain Injury Rehabilitation Trust [England].
a) STORY RECALL.
    Scores, 3: Immediate, Delayed, Retained%.
b) FIGURE RECALL.
    Scores, 4: Copy%, Immediate%, Delayed%, Retained%.
c) LIST LEARNING.
    Scores, 4: A1-A5 Total, A6, B, Intrusions.
d) WORD RECOGNITION.
    Scores, 6: A Words, B Words, Total Word Recognition, List A, List B, Total List Recognition.

e) DESIGN LEARNING.
Scores, 4: A1-A5 Total, A6, B, Intrusions.
f) DESIGN RECOGNITION.
Scores, 6: Correct Positive, Correct Negative, Recognition Total, Design A Correct, Design B Correct, Identification Total.
g) SPEED OF INFORMATION PROCESSING.
Scores, 4: Total, Errors%, Speed, Adjusted Total.
Cross References: For reviews by Andrew S. Davis and W. Holmes Finch and by Stephen J. Freeman, see 19:20.

[280]
The BrainMap™.
Purpose: "A tool for determining the world-building (or thinking/information-processing) style of individuals and of groups."
Population: Adults.
Publication Dates: 1981–1986.
Scores, 4: Posterior Brain Scale, Anterior Brain Scale, Left Brain Scale, Right Brain Scale.
Administration: Group.
Price Data, 2016: $19.95 per assessment (volume discounts available).
Time: [30–40] minutes.
Comments: Self-administered, self-scored. The test publisher has indicated there is a newer edition of this test; description will be updated when complete test materials are received.
Author: Dudley Lynch.
Publisher: Brain Technologies Corporation.
Cross References: For a review by Manfred J. Meier, see 11:47.

[281]
Bricklin Perceptual Scales [2010 Revision].
Purpose: Designed to yield information about a child's "perceptions, expressed both verbally and nonverbally, of each parent in the areas of competence, supportiveness, follow-up consistency, and possession of admirable traits" for utility in child-custody decisions.
Population: Ages 6 and older.
Publication Dates: 1984–2010.
Acronym: BPS.
Scores, 10: 5 scores each for mother and father: Perception of Competency, Perception of Supportiveness, Perception of Follow-Up Consistency, Perception of Admirable Character Traits, Total.
Administration: Individual.
Price Data, 2016: $289 per complete kit including 8 sets of response cards, 8 scoring sheets, stylus-pen, placement dots, test box with foam insert, manual (2009, 74 pages), instructions, and Bricklin Updates; $159 per 10 additional sets of response cards with summaries (volume discounts available); $289 per computer scoring profile (CD ROM).
Time: (40) minutes.

Comments: Test publisher advises that with 2010 revision, "The administration and scoring procedures remain the same. However, the research databases in terms of which the scores are interpreted have been significantly revised."
Author: Barry Bricklin.
Publisher: Village Publishing.
Cross References: For reviews by Rosa A. Hagin and Marcia B. Shaffer of an earlier version (1990), see 11:48.

[282]
Brief Battery for Health Improvement 2.
Purpose: Designed for "assessing medical patients who may be experiencing problems with pain, functioning, somatization, depression, anxiety, or other factors relevant to rehabilitation and recovery."
Population: 18–65 years.
Publication Date: 2002.
Acronym: BBHI 2.
Scores, 6: Validity Scale (Defensiveness), Physical Symptom Scales (Somatic Complaints, Pain Complaints, Functional Complaints), Affective Symptom Scales (Depression, Anxiety).
Administration: Individual.
Parts, 4: Part I (Pain Complaints scale), Part II (Somatic Complaints scale), Part III (Functional Complaints scale), Part IV (Depression, Anxiety, and Defensiveness scales).
Price Data, 2015: $147.10 per Q local starter kit 10 including manual (151 pages), 10 answer sheets with test items and 10 Q local administrations; $177.85 per fax-in starter kit 10 including manual (151 pages), pre-paid fax-in answer sheets with test items, scoring and reports. $43.05 per manual; $56 per compact disc; $28 per 25 fax-in answer sheets; $16.10 per pre-paid fax-in answer sheet and report; $28 per 25 Q Local fax-in answer sheets; $12.45 per Q Local standard/extended reports; $15.70 per mail-in Standard/Extended Reports.
Foreign Language Edition: Spanish materials available.
Time: (7–10) minutes.
Comments: Shorter version of the Battery for Health Improvement 2 (BHI 2; 203); mail-in and fax-in scoring available from publisher along with on-site computer (Q Local software) and hand-held electronic device (Patient Assessment Device) scoring; three automated reports available (Standard Report, Extended Report, Progress Report).
Authors: John Mark Disorbio and Daniel Bruns.
Publisher: Pearson.
Cross References: For reviews by Theodore L. Hayes and Wes Sime, see 17:30.

[283]
Brief Cognitive Status Exam.
Purpose: Designed "to determine an individual's general cognitive status" with a focus on level of impairment.

Population: Ages 16 through 90.
Publication Date: 2009.
Acronym: BCSE.
Scores, 8: Orientation, Time Estimation, Mental Control, Clock Drawing, Incidental Recall, Inhibition, Verbal Production, Total.
Administration: Individual.
Price Data, 2015: $142.50 per complete kit including examiner's manual/stimulus book (82 pages) and 25 record forms; $104.55 per administration/stimulus book; $46.15 per 25 record forms.
Time: (10-15) minutes.
Comments: Originally published as a subtest in the Wechsler Memory Scale–Fourth Edition (2233).
Authors: James A. Holdnack and Lisa Whipple Drozdick.
Publisher: Pearson.
Cross References: Reviews are scheduled for *The Twentieth Mental Measurements Yearbook*.

[284]
Brief Neuropsychological Cognitive Examination.

Purpose: Constructed as "an assessment of the severity and nature of cognitive impairment" for psychiatric and neurological patients.
Population: Ages 18 and older.
Publication Date: 1997.
Acronym: BNCE.
Scores, 4: Validity Index, Part I, Part II, Total.
Administration: Individual.
Price Data, 2016: $181 per complete kit including manual (58 pages), stimulus booklet, 20 response booklets, and 20 administration and scoring forms; $56 per 20 response booklets; $40.50 per 20 administration and scoring forms; $50.50 per stimulus booklet; $69.50 per manual.
Time: (30) minutes.
Author: Joseph Tonkonogy.
Publisher: Western Psychological Services.
Cross References: For reviews by Eugene V. Aidman and Sheila Mehta, see 14:50.

[285]
Brief Symptom Inventory.

Purpose: "Designed to reflect the psychological symptom patterns of psychiatric and medical patients as well as non-patients."
Population: Adults and adolescents age 13 or older.
Publication Date: 1975.
Acronym: BSI®.
Scores: 9 primary dimensions: Somatization, Obsessive-Compulsive, Interpersonal Sensitivity, Depression, Anxiety, Hostility, Phobic Anxiety, Paranoid Ideation, Psychoticism; plus 3 global indices: Global Sever-

ity Index, Positive Symptom Distress Index, Positive Symptom Total.
Administration: Group or individual.
Price Data, 2015: $124 per hand-scoring starter kit including manual, 50 answer sheets, 50 profile forms, 2 worksheets, and answer keys (specify Nonpatient Adult, Nonpatient Adolescent, Outpatient Psychiatric, or Inpatient Psychiatric); $65.35 per 50 answer sheets; $30.25 per 50 profile forms and 2 worksheets (specify Nonpatient Adult, Nonpatient Adolescent, Outpatient Psychiatric, or Inpatient Psychiatric); $43.05 per manual.
Foreign Language Edition: Spanish materials available.
Time: (8–10) minutes.
Comments: Essentially the brief form of the Symptom Checklist-90-Revised (2037); self-report; useful in initial evaluation and measurement of patient progress during treatment to monitor change and after treament for assessment of treatment outcome; companion clinician and observer rating forms are also available.
Author: Leonard R. Derogatis.
Publisher: Pearson.
Cross References: See T5:337 (198 references) and T4:324 (59 references); for reviews by Bert P. Cundick and Charles A. Peterson, see 10:35 (7 references); see also 9:160 (1 reference).

[286]
Brief Symptom Inventory 18.

Purpose: Designed to "screen for psychological distress and psychiatric disorders in medical and community populations."
Population: Age 18 and older.
Publication Dates: 2000–2001.
Acronym: BSI 18.
Scores, 4: Somatization, Depression, Anxiety, Total (Global Severity Index).
Administration: Individual or group.
Price Data, 2015: $49.20 per Q Local starter kit with profile reports including manual (2001, 54 pages), 3 answer sheets with test items to conduct and receive 3 Q local administrations; $28 per 25 answer sheets; $3.20 per profile report (quantity discounts available); $120.95 per hand-scoring starter kit including manual, 50 answer sheets with test items, and 50 profile forms (specify Community or Oncology norms); $65.35 per 50 answer sheets; $30.25 per 50 profile forms (specify Community or Oncology norms); $41 per manual; quantity discounts available for the reports.
Foreign Language Edition: Spanish materials available.
Time: (4–5) minutes.
Comments: Abbreviated adaptation of Brief Symptom Inventory (285); self-report; may be administered in paper-and-pencil format or online.
Author: Leonard R. Derogatis.

Publisher: Pearson.

Cross References: For reviews by Roger A. Boothroyd and William E. Hanson, see 15:38; for information on the Brief Symptom Inventory, see T5:337 (198 references); for reviews by Bert P. Cundick and Charles A. Peterson of an earlier edition, see 10:35 (7 references); see also 9:160 (1 reference).

[287]

Brief Test of Attention.

Purpose: Designed "to assess the severity of attentional impairment among nonaphasic hearing adult patients."
Population: Ages 17–82.
Publication Date: 1997.
Acronym: BTA.
Scores: Total score only.
Administration: Individual.
Forms, 2: N (Numbers), L (Letters).
Price Data, 2015: $100 per introductory kit including professional manual (34 pages), stimulus audio CD, and 50 scoring forms.
Time: (10) minutes.
Author: David Schretlen.
Publisher: Psychological Assessment Resources, Inc.
Cross References: For reviews by Elizabeth Kelley Boyles and Steven R. Shaw, see 15:39.

[288]

Brief Test of Head Injury.

Purpose: Designed to provide information about cognitive, linguistic, and communicative abilities of patients with severe head trauma.
Population: Acute and long-term head-injured adults.
Publication Dates: 1989–1991.
Acronym: BTHI.
Scores, 8: Orientation/Attention, Following Commands, Linguistic Organization, Reading Comprehension, Naming, Memory, Visual-Spatial Skills, Total.
Administration: Individual.
Price Data, 2015: $215 per complete kit including 25 record forms, examiner's manual (1991, 85 pages), manipulatives package, stimulus cards and letter board, and carrying case; $63 per 25 record forms; $92 per stimulus cards; $92 per examiner's manual.
Time: (25–30) minutes.
Authors: Nancy Helm-Estabrooks and Gillian Hotz.
Publisher: PRO-ED.
Cross References: For reviews by Deborah D. Roman and Michael Lee Russell, see 13:39.

[289]

Brief Visuospatial Memory Test—Revised.

Purpose: Designed as an equivalent, multiple-test form assessment of visuospatial memory.
Population: Ages 18–79.

Publication Dates: 1988–1997.
Acronym: BVMT-R.
Scores, 12: Trial 1, Trial 2, Trial 3, Total Recall, Learning, Delayed Recall, Percent Retained, Recognition Hits, Recognition False Alarms, Recognition Discrimination Index, Recognition Response Bias, Copy (Optional).
Administration: Individual.
Forms, 6: 1, 2, 3, 4, 5, 6.
Price Data, 2015: $360 per introductory kit including professional manual (1997, 131 pages), recognition stimulus booklet, reusable recall stimulus booklet, 25 response forms, and manual supplement.
Time: (45) minutes including 25-minute delay.
Comments: Can be administered bed-side by appropriately trained personnel.
Author: Ralph H. B. Benedict.
Publisher: Psychological Assessment Resources, Inc.
Cross References: For review by Anita M. Hubley and Terry A. Stinnett, see 15:40.

[290]

BRIGANCE® Comprehensive Inventory of Basic Skills II.

Purpose: Designed to compare "a student's mastery of various skills to those of other students around the country" and can be completed "as part of a battery to determine eligibility for special education services."
Publication Dates: 1976-2010.
Acronym: CIBS-II.
Administration: Individual.
Price Data, 2016: $339 per classroom kit including Reading/ELA and Math Inventory, 20 record books, and 1 canvas tote; $249 per Standardized Inventory including assessments, Standardization and Validation manual (2010, 152 pages), and 20 record books; $49 per Standardization and Validation manual; $39 per 10 record books; $359 per 100 record books.
Authors: Brian F. French and Frances Page Glascoe.
Publisher: Curriculum Associates.
  a) READINESS ASSESSMENTS.
  Population: Ages 5-0 to 6-11.
  Scores, 40: 21 Task Scores (Personal Data Response, Identifies Body Parts, Understands Directional and Positional Concepts, Standing Gross-Motor Skills, Walking Gross-Motor Skills, Prints Uppercase Letters in Sequence, Prints Personal Data, Writes Numerals in Sequence, Readiness for Reading, Knows Common Signs, Oral Expression, Reads Lowercase Letters, Rote Counting, Understands Quantitative Concepts, Counts Objects, Reads Numerals, Articulation-Initial Sounds of Words, Articulation-Final Sounds of Words, Auditory Discrimination, Identifies Initial Consonants in Spoken Words, Sounds of Letters), 13 Supplemental Task Scores (Recognizes Colors, Self-Help Skills, Running and Skipping Gross-Motor Skills, Draws a Person, Visual Motor Skills-Forms, Prints Lowercase Letters in Sequence, Prints Uppercase Letters Dictated, Prints Lowercase Letters Dictated, Reads Lowercase Letters, Visual Discrimination-Forms/Letters/and Words,

Recites Alphabet, Joins Sets, Numeral Comprehension), and 6 Composite Scores (General Knowledge and Language, Gross-Motor Skills, Graphomotor and Writing Skills, Reading, Math, Phonemic Awareness.
Time: (60) minutes.
b) FIRST-GRADE THROUGH SIXTH-GRADE ASSESSMENTS.
Forms, 2: Form A (Pretest), Form B (Post Test).
Population: Ages 7-0 to 12-0.
Scores, 16: 9 Task Scores (Word Recognition Grade-Placement Test, Word Analysis Survey, Reading Vocabulary Comprehension Grade-Placement Test, Comprehends Passages, Computational Skills Grade-Placement Test, Problem Solving Grade-Placement Test, Spelling Grade-Placement Test, Sentence- Writing Grade-Placement Test, Listening Vocabulary Comprehension Grade-Placement Test), 2 Supplemental Task Scores (Warning and Safety Signs, Warning Labels), and 5 Composite Scores (Basic Reading, Reading Comprehension, Math, Written Expression, Listening Comprehension).
Time: (45-60) minutes.
Cross References: For reviews by Jennifer N. Mahdavi and Connie T. England, see 19:21; for reviews by Gregory J. Cizek and Mary J. McLellan of an earlier edition, see 14:51; see also T5:340 (1 reference); for reviews by Craig N. Mills and Mark E. Swerdlik of the original edition, see 9:162.

[291]

BRIGANCE® Diagnostic Assessment of Basic Skills–Revised Spanish Edition.

Purpose: Designed to assess and progress monitor language dominance, oral and written English language proficiency, and basic math skills.
Population: Grades PreK-9.
Publication Dates: 1984-2007.
Acronym: ABS-R.
Scores, 163: Readiness, Speech, Listening, Word Recognition Grade Placement, Oral Reading, Reading Comprehension, Word Analysis, Functional Word Recognition, Spelling, Writing, Reference Skills, Graphs and Maps, Math Grade Placement, Numbers, Number Facts, Computation of Whole Numbers, Fractions and Mixed Numbers, Decimals, Percents, Time, Money, U.S. Customary Measurement and Geometry, Metrics.
Administration: Individual.
Price Data, 2016: $185 per administration binder (2007, 484 pages); $35 per 10 student record books.
Time: Administration time not reported.
Comments: Criterion-referenced testing system.
Author: Albert H. Brigance.
Publisher: Curriculum Associates, Inc.

[292]

BRIGANCE® Inventory of Early Development III.

Purpose: Designed to aid in identifying children's developmental strengths and weaknesses, documenting eligibility for special education services, determining school readiness, informing instructional decisions, tracking developmental progress, and supporting program evaluation.
Publication Dates: 1978-2013.
Administration: Individual.
Editions, 2: BRIGANCE® Inventory of Early Development III Early Childhood Edition; BRIGANCE® Inventory of Early Development III Standardized.
Comments: Assessments in the standardized version are a subset of those found in the criterion-referenced version; based on previous editions by Albert H. Brigance.
Authors: Curriculum Associates, LLC (screens) and Brian F. French (standardization and validation manual).
Publisher: Curriculum Associates, LLC.
a) BRIGANCE® INVENTORY OF EARLY DEVELOPMENT III EARLY CHILDHOOD EDITION.
Population: Developmental ages birth through 7 years.
Acronym: IED III.
Scores: More than 100 assessments in 7 domains (Physical Development, Language Development, Literacy, Mathematics and Science, Daily Living, Social and Emotional Development, Approaches to Learning).
Price Data, 2016: $349 per early childhood classroom kit including inventory, 20 record books, accessories, and canvas tote; $229 per inventory; $39 per 10 record books; $359 per 100 record books; $69 per accessories kit.
Time: Varies by child and number of skills assessed.
Comments: "Criterion-referenced ... to specific educational objectives."
b) BRIGANCE® INVENTORY OF EARLY DEVELOPMENT III STANDARDIZED.
Population: Children from birth through age 7 years.
Acronym: IED III Standardized.
Scores: 55 assessments in 5 domains (Physical Development, Language Development, Academic Skills/Cognitive Development, Adaptive Behavior, Social and Emotional Development), Total Development Score.
Price Data: $349 per kit including inventory, 20 record books, standardization and validation manual (2013, 296 pages), accessories, and tote; $189 per inventory; $56 per standardization and validation manual; $39 per 10 record books; $359 per 100 record books; $69 per accessories kit.
Time: (30-60) minutes.
Cross References: Reviews are scheduled for *The Twentieth Mental Measurements Yearbook*. For reviews by Abigail Baxter and Lisa F. Smith of the Inventory of Early Development II, see 19:22; for reviews by Andrew S. Davis and W. Holmes Finch and by Lauren R. Barton and Donna Spiker of the previous edition titled BRIGANCE Diagnostic Inventory of Early Development–II, see 17:31; for reviews by C. Dale Carpenter and Douglas A. Penfield of the revised edition, see 12:326; see also T4:2256 (3 references); for reviews by Stephen J. Bagnato and Elliot L. Gory of the first edition, see 9:164.

[293]

BRIGANCE® Screens III.

Purpose: Designed to "screen children to identify potential developmental delays and giftedness as well as specific strengths and needs in physical development, language, academic/cognitive, self-help, and social-emotional skills."

Population: Children from birth to 7-6.

Publication Dates: 1982-2013.

Administration: Individual.

Levels: 3 levels.

Price Data, 2016: $65 per Screens III technical manual (2013, 224 pages); $189 per test manual (0-35 Months, 3-5 years, or K&1); $65 per 60 data sheets (Infant, Toddler, Age 2, 3, 4, 5, Kindergarten, or Grade 1); $65 per accessories set (0-35 Months); kit discounts available.

Foreign Language Edition: Spanish directions available.

Time: (10-15) minutes.

Comments: May be conducted by observation or by parent interview; includes optional forms for screening observations, parent-child interactions, teacher feedback, parent feedback, self-help/social-emotional scales, and reading readiness scale; also available as BRIGANCE Early Head Start and Head Start Screens III; assessment content is identical to that contained in forms for 0-35 Months and 3-5 Years; BRIGANCE Early Childhood Screen III 0-35 Months based on previous editions by Albert H. Brigance and Frances Page Glascoe; BRIGANCE Early Childhood Screen III 3-5 Years and K & 1 based on previous editions by Albert H. Brigance.

Authors: Curriculum Associates, LLC (screens) and Brian F. French (technical manual).

Publisher: Curriculum Associates, LLC.

a) BRIGANCE EARLY CHILDHOOD SCREEN III 0-35 MONTHS.

1) *Infant (birth-11 months).*

Scores, 7: Gross Motor Skills, Fine Motor Skills, Receptive Language Skills, Expressive Language Skills, Self-Help Skills, Social and Emotional Skills, Total Score.

2) *Toddler (12-23 months).*

Scores, 12: Receptive Language Skills—General, Receptive Language Skills—Identifies Parts of the Body, Receptive Language Skills—Identifies Pictures, Receptive Language Skills—Knows Sounds Animals Make, Gross Motor Skills, Fine Motor Skills, Expressive Language Skills—General, Expressive Language Skills—Names Objects, Expressive Language Skills—Uses Phrases, Self-Help Skills, Social and Emotional Skills, Total Score.

3) *Two-Year-Old Child.*

Scores, 11 to 16: 10 Core Assessments: Identifies Parts of the Body, Identifies Pictures by Naming, Knows Uses of Objects, Repeats Sentences, Gross Motor Skills, Understands Concepts of Number and Size, Visual Motor Skills, Builds Tower with Blocks, Matches Colors, Verbal Fluency and Articulation, Total Score; 5 Supplemental Assessments: Knows Personal Information, Responds to Picture, Follows Verbal Directions, Gross Motor Skills, Visual Motor Skills.

b) BRIGANCE EARLY CHILDHOOD SCREEN III 3-5 YEARS.

1) *Three-Year-Old Child.*

Scores, 12 to 17: 11 Core Assessments: Knows Personal Information, Identifies Colors, Identifies Pictures by Naming, Knows Uses of Objects, Visual Motor Skills, Understands Number Concepts, Builds Tower with Blocks, Gross Motor Skills, Identifies Parts of the Body, Repeats Sentences, Uses Prepositions and Irregular Plural Nouns, Total Score; 5 Supplemental Assessments: Responds to Picture, Articulates Initial Sounds, Names Colors, Gross Motor Skills, Visual Motor Skills.

2) *Four-Year-Old Child.*

Scores, 12 to 17: 11 Core Assessments: Knows Personal Information, Names Colors, Identifies Pictures by Naming, Visual Discrimination—Forms and Uppercase Letters, Visual Motor Skills, Gross Motor Skills, Names Parts of the Body, Follows Verbal Directions, Counts by Rote, Recognizes Quantities, Verbal Fluency and Articulation, Total Score; 5 Supplemental Assessments: Responds to Picture, Auditory Discrimination, Matches Quantities with Numerals, Gross Motor Skills, Visual Motor Skills.

3) *Five-Year-Old Child.*

Scores, 14 to 19: 13 Core Assessments: Knows Personal Information, Names Parts of the Body, Gross Motor Skills, Visual Motor Skills, Prints Personal Information, Recites Alphabet, Sorts Objects (by Size, Color, Shape), Counts by Rote, Matches Quantities with Numerals, Determines Total of Two Sets, Reads Uppercase Letters, Reads Lowercase Letters (alternate), Experience with Books and Text, Verbal Fluency and Articulation, Total Score; 5 Supplemental Assessments: Auditory Discrimination, Prints Uppercase Letters, Prints Lowercase Letters, Adds and Subtracts, Solves Word Problems.

Comments: Assessment items are identical to Kindergarten screen.

c) BRIGANCE EARLY CHILDHOOD SCREEN III K & 1.

1) *Kindergarten.*

Population: Children ages 5-0 to 5-11.

Scores, 14 to 19: 13 Core Assessments: Knows Personal Information, Names Parts of the Body, Gross Motor Skills, Visual Motor Skills, Prints Personal Information, Recites Alphabet, Sorts Objects (by Size, Color, Shape), Counts by Rote, Matches Quantities with Numerals, Determines Total of Two Sets, Reads Uppercase Letters, Reads Lowercase Letters (alternate), Experience with Books and Text, Verbal Fluency and Articulation, Total Score; 5 Supplemental Assessments: Auditory Discrimination, Prints Uppercase Letters, Prints Lowercase Letters, Adds and Subtracts, Solves Word Problems.

Comments: Assessment items are identical to Five-Year-Old Child screen.

2) *First Grade.*

Population: Children ages 6-0 to 7-6.

Scores, 13 to 18: 12 Core Assessments: Knows Personal Information, Auditory Discrimination, Visual Discrimination—Lowercase Letters and Words, Reads Lowercase Letters, Identifies Initial Letters, Sorts Objects (by Size, Color, Shape), Listening Vocabulary

Comprehension, Word Recognition, Prints Personal Information, Writes Numerals in Sequence, Adds and Subtracts, Solves Word Problems, Total Score; 5 Supplemental Assessments: Word Recognition, Writes Simple Sentences, Writes Following and Preceding Numerals, Adds and Subtracts, Solves Word Problems.

Cross References: Reviews are scheduled for *The Twentieth Mental Measurements Yearbook*. For reviews of the BRIGANCE Infant & Toddler Screen by Theresa Graham and Loraine J. Spenciner, see 15:41. For reviews of the BRIGANCE Early Preschool Screen-II by Michelle Athanasiou and Gene Schwarting, see 17:32; for reviews of an earlier edition by William M. Bart and Joseph M. Ryan, see 11:49. For reviews of the BRIGANCE Preschool Screen-II by Shawn Powell and John J. Vacca, see 17:14; for reviews of an earlier edition by Edith S. Heil and Timothy L. Turco, see 10:36. For reviews of the BRIGANCE K & 1 Screen-II by Koressa Kutsick Malcolm and Theresa Volpe-Johnstone, see 17:33; for reviews of the previous edition by Ronald A. Berk and T. Steuart Watson, see 12:53 (1 reference); see also T4:331 (3 references); for reviews of an earlier edition by Ann E. Boehm and Dan Wright, see 9:166.

[294]
BRIGANCE® Transition Skills Inventory.

Purpose: "Criterion-referenced" assessments designed to "help special educators and transition specialists identify a student's present level of performance, plan appropriate instruction, and monitor progress" in transition to adult life.

Population: Middle and high school students with special needs.

Publication Dates: 1994-2010.

Acronym: TSI.

Scores: 124 assessments in 17 skill areas: Academic [Reading Grade Placement (3 assessments), Listening and Speaking Skills (4 assessments), Functional Writing Skills (2 assessments), Math Skills (20 assessments)]; Post-Secondary [Interests & Choices (4 assessments), Job-Related Writing Skills (7 assessments), Job-Related Knowledge and Skills (14 assessments), Communication and Technology Skills (5 assessments)]; Independent Living [Food (11 assessments), Clothing (2 assessments), Housing (2 assessments), Money and Finance (10 assessments), Health (14 assessments), Travel and Transportation (7 assessments)]; Community Participation [Community Resources (9 assessments), Community Signs (8 assessments), Citizenship (2 assessments)].

Administration: Individual in part.

Price Data, 2016: $259 per kit including Transition Skills Inventory (2010, 537 pages), 20 record books, and tote; $199 per Transition Skills Inventory; $39 per 10 record books.

Time: Administration time varies.

Comments: "Compiled from the BRIGANCE Employability Skills Inventory and the BRIGANCE Life Skills Inventory, both by Albert H. Brigance."

Author: Curriculum Associates, Inc.

Publisher: Curriculum Associates, Inc.

Cross References: For reviews of the BRIGANCE Diagnostic Employability Skills Inventory by JoEllen V. Carlson and William C. Tirre, see 14:52. For reviews of the BRIGANCE Diagnostic Life Skills Inventory by Cleborne D. Maddux and Rhoda Cummings and by James A. Wollack, see 14:53; see also T5:344 (1 reference).

[295]
British Ability Scales: Second Edition.

Purpose: Designed as a battery to assess "cognitive abilities and educational achievement."

Population: Ages 2.6 to 17.11.

Publication Dates: 1977–1997.

Acronym: BAS II.

Scores, 4: Early Years Core Scales (Block Building, Verbal Comprehension, Picture Similarities, Naming Vocabulary, Pattern Construction, Early Number Concepts, Copying), School Age Core Scales (Recall of Designs, Word Definitions, Pattern Construction, Matrices, Verbal Similarities, Quantitative Reasoning), Diagnostic Scales (Speed of Information Processing, Recall of Digits Forward, Recall of Objects—Immediate, Recall of Objects—Delayed, Matching Letter-Like Forms, Recognition of Pictures, Recall of Digits Backward), Achievement Scales (Number Skills, Spelling, Word Reading).

Administration: Individual.

Forms, 2: Early Years, School Age.

Price Data, 2005: £810 per full age range complete set including stimulus books, 10 relevant record forms and consumable booklets; £575 per early years complete set including stimulus books, 10 record forms and consumable booklets; £495 per school age complete set including stimulus books, 10 record forms and consumable booklets; £40.50 per 25 early years record booklets; £52.50 per 25 school age record booklets; £10.90 per 25 achievement scales record forms; £12 per 10 Speed of Information Processing booklets A, B, or C; £12 per 10 Quantitative Reasoning booklets set A; £6 per 100 sheets copying paper; £6 per 100 recall of designs sheets; £17.50 per 25 number skills/spelling worksheets; £8.75 per 25 number skills worksheets; $8.75 per 25 spelling worksheets; £87.25 per administration and scoring manual (1996, 544 pages); £70 per technical manual (1997, 341 pages); £168.80 per BAS II Scoring and Reporting Software.

Time: Administration time varies.

Comments: Considerations for testing special populations detailed in manual.

Authors: Colin D. Elliott with Pauline Smith and Kay McCulloch.

Publisher: GL Assessment [England; Efforts to obtain updated information from the test publisher were unsuccessful. An updated edition of this test appears on the test publisher's website].

Cross References: For reviews by Colin Cooper and Robert W. Hiltonsmith, see 16:37; see also T5:349 (39 references) and T4:336 (25 references); for reviews by Susan Embretson (Whitely), Benjamin D. Wright, and Mark H. Stone of an earlier edition, see 9:172 (5 references); for reviews by Steve Graham and William D. Schafer of an earlier edition of the British Ability Scales: Spelling Scale, see 12:55.

[296]

The British Picture Vocabulary Scale, Second Edition.

Purpose: Designed to serve as a "norm referenced wide-range test of hearing vocabulary for Standard English."
Population: Ages 3.0 to 15.8.
Publication Dates: 1982–1997.
Acronym: BPVS-II.
Scores: Total score only.
Administration: Individual.
Price Data: Available from publisher.
Time: (5–8) minutes.
Comments: Manual is incorporated in the easeled test book.
Authors: Lloyd M. Dunn, Leota M. Dunn, Chris Whetton, and Juliet Burley.
Publisher: GL Assessment [England; Efforts to obtain updated information from the test publisher were unsuccessful. An updated edition of this test appears on the test publisher's website].
Cross References: For reviews by Alfred P. Longo and Dolores Kluppel Vetter, see 16:38; for information regarding the original edition, see T5:350 (53 references) and T4:338 (16 references).

[297]

British Spelling Test Series.

Purpose: Developed to serve as a "comprehensive screening test that delivers detailed information about the spelling ability of groups or individuals."
Population: Ages 5–adult.
Publication Date: 1997.
Acronym: BSTS.
Administration: Individual or group.
Levels, 5: 1, 2, 3, 4, 5.
Forms, 2: X and Y, alternate forms.
Price Data: Available from publisher.
Time: (30–40) minutes.
Authors: Denis Vincent and Mary Crumpler.
Publisher: GL Assessment [England; Efforts to obtain updated information from the test publisher were unsuccessful. An updated edition of this test appears on the test publisher's website].
Cross References: For reviews by Timothy Z. Keith and S. Kathleen Krach, see 16:39.

Brown Attention-Deficit Disorder Scales.

Purpose: Designed to "elicit cognitive and affective indications of Attention-Deficit Disorder."
Publication Dates: 1996–2001.
Acronym: Brown ADD Scales.
Scores, 6: Organizing and Activating to Work, Sustaining Attention and Concentration, Sustaining Energy and Effort, Managing Affective Interference, Utilizing "Working Memory" and Assessing Recall, Total.
Administration: Individual or group.
Price Data, 2015: $267.30 per complete kit for adolescents and adults, including adolescents and adults manual, treatment monitoring worksheet, 50 Ready Score answer documents (25 each for ages 12-18 and 18+), and diagnostic forms (10 each for ages 12-18 and 18+); $195.50 per adolescents and adults manual; $30.35 per 10 diagnostic forms (ages 12-18); $81.20 per 25 Ready Score self-report forms/answer documents (ages 12-18); $30.35 per 10 diagnostic forms (ages 18+); $81.20 per 25 Ready Score self-report forms/answer documents (ages 18+); $267.30 per starter kit for children and adolescents, including manual for children and adolescents, 5 Ready Score parent and teacher forms for ages 3-7, 5 Ready Score parent, teacher and self-report forms for ages 8-12, 5 Ready Score answer documents for ages 12-18, and diagnostic forms (10 each, Children and Adolescents); $170.60 per child and adolescent manual; $30.35 per 10 diagnostic forms (ages 3-12 or 12-18); $81.20 per 25 Ready Score self-report forms/answer documents (ages 8-12 or 12-18); $81.20 per 25 parent forms (ages 3-7 or 8-12); $81.20 per teacher forms (ages 3-7 or 8-12).
Time: (10–20) minutes.
Author: Thomas E. Brown.
Publisher: Pearson.
    a) PRIMARY/PRESCHOOL.
    Population: Ages 3–7.
    b) SCHOOL-AGE.
    Population: Ages 8–12.
    c) ADOLESCENT SCALE.
    Population: Ages 12 to 18.
    d) ADULT SCALE.
    Population: Ages 18 and over.
Cross References: For reviews by Nadeen L. Kaufman and Alan S. Kaufman, by E. Jean Newman, and by Judy Oehler-Stinnett, see 14:54.

[299]

Brown Attention-Deficit Disorder Scales for Children and Adolescents.

Purpose: "Designed to elicit … [information] that may indicate impairment in executive functions related to Attention-Deficit/Hyperactivity Disorders (AD/HD)."
Population: Ages 3–18.
Publication Date: 2001.
Acronym: Brown ADD Scales for Children.

Scores, 7: 6 cluster scores (Organizing/Prioritizing/ and Activating to Work, Focusing/Sustaining/and Shifting Attention to Tasks, Regulating Alertness/Sustaining Effort/and Processing Speed, Managing Frustration and Modulating Emotions, Utilizing Working Memory and Accessing Recall, Monitoring and Self-Regulating Action), Total Score.
Administration: Group or individual.
Price Data, 2015: $267.30 per starter kit for children and adolescents, including manual for children and adolescents, 5 Ready Score parent and teacher forms for ages 3-7, 5 Ready Score parent, teacher and self-report forms for ages 8-12, 5 Ready Score answer documents for ages 12-18, and diagnostic forms (10 each, Children and Adolescents); $170.60 per child and adolescent manual; $30.35 per 10 diagnostic forms (ages 3-12 or 12-18); $81.20 per 25 Ready Score self-report forms/ answer documents (ages 8-12 or 12-18); $81.20 per 25 parent forms (ages 3-7 or 8-12); $81.20 per teacher forms (ages 3-7 or 8-12).
Author: Thomas E. Brown.
Publisher: Pearson.
   a) PRIMARY/PRESCHOOL LEVEL.
   Population: Ages 3–7.
   Forms, 2: Parent Form, Teacher Form.
   Comments: Elicits parent and teacher reports of symptoms.
   b) SCHOOL-AGE LEVEL.
   Population: Ages 8–12.
   Forms, 3: Self-Report Form, Parent Form, Teacher Form.
   Comments: Elicits parent, teacher and self-reports of symptoms.
   c) ADOLESCENT LEVEL.
   Population: Ages 13–18.
   Form, 1: Ready-Score Answer Document.
   Comments: Elicits parent and self-reports of symptoms.
Cross References: For reviews by Karen E. Jennings and William K. Wilkinson, see 15:42.

[300]
Bruininks Motor Ability Test.

Purpose: Designed to assess "an adult's motor abilities related to improvement in physical functioning and/or requirements for activities of daily living … to guide treatment, set treatment goals, and monitor progress toward those goals."
Population: Ages 40 and older.
Publication Date: 2012.
Acronym: BMAT.
Scores, 8: Fine Motor Composite (Fine Motor Integration, Manual Dexterity, Total), Gross Motor Composite (Balance and Mobility, Strength and Flexibility, Total), Coordination, Total Motor Composite.
Subtests, 5: Fine Motor Integration, Manual Dexterity, Coordination, Balance and Mobility, Strength and Flexibility.
Administration: Individual.

Forms, 2: Full, Short.
Price Data, 2015: $580 per complete kit including manual (227 pages), administration easel, comprehensive record form (25), comprehensive form examinee booklet (25), short form (25), short form examinee booklet (25), scoring transparency, blocks with string, penny pad, penny box, plastic pennies (50), elbow pad, tennis ball, stopwatch, red pen, black marker, adult scissors, hand gripper–blue, hand gripper–green, envelope, numbered half cones (4), sewing board with string; $92.25 per manual.
Time: (8–16) minutes per subtest, (60–75) minutes complete battery, (15–25) minutes short form.
Comments: Test is an adult adaptation of the Bruininks-Oseretsky Test of Motor Proficiency, Second Edition. Subtests may be administered individually.
Authors: Brett D. Bruininks and Robert H. Bruininks.
Publisher: Pearson.
Cross References: For reviews by Kenneth M. Hanig and Martin J. Wiese, see 19:23.

[301]
Bruininks-Oseretsky Test of Motor Proficiency, Second Edition.

Purpose: Designed to measure gross and fine motor skills of children.
Population: Ages 4–21.
Publication Dates: 1978–2005.
Acronym: BOT-2.
Scores: 3 scores: Gross Motor Composite, Fine Motor Composite, Battery Composite, for 8 subtests: Fine Motor Precision, Fine Motor Integration, Manual Dexterity, Bilateral Coordination, Balance, Running Speed and Agility, Upper-Limb Coordination, Strength.
Administration: Individual.
Price Data, 2015: $857.95 per kit including manual (2005, 273 pages), administration easel, 25 record forms, 25 examinee booklets, scoring transparency, balance beam, blocks with string, penny box, penny pad, plastic pennies, knee pad, peg board and pegs, 2 red pencils, scissors, target, tennis ball, shape cards, shuttle block, and training video; $50.25 per 25 complete form record forms; $48.20 per 25 examinee booklets.
Time: (45–60) minutes for complete battery; (15–20) minutes for short form.
Comments: Second revised edition of the Oseretsky Tests of Motor Proficiency.
Authors: Robert H. Bruininks and Brett D. Bruininks.
Publisher: Pearson.
Cross References: For reviews by Katharine A. Snyder and Gabrielle Stutman, see 18:15; see T5:353 (22 references) and T4:340 (18 references); for a review by David A. Sabatino of an earlier edition, see 9:174 (7 references); see also T3:324 (3 references) and T2:1898 (15 references); for a review by Anna Espenschade, see 4:650 (10 references); for an excerpted review, see 3:472 (6 references).

[302]

Burks Behavior Rating Scales, Second Edition.

Purpose: Designed to measure child and adolescent behaviors that are relevant to school and community activities.

Population: Ages 4-18.

Publication Dates: 1968-2006.

Acronym: BBRS-2.

Scores, 7: Disruptive Behavior, Attention and Impulse Control Problems, Emotional Problems, Social Withdrawal, Ability Deficits, Physical Deficits, Weak Self-Confidence.

Administration: Individual.

Forms, 2: Teacher, Parent.

Price Data, 2016: $145.50 per complete kit including 25 parent autoscore forms, 25 teacher autoscore forms, and manual (2006, 74 pages); $52.50 per 25 autoscore forms (specify parent or teacher); $59.50 per manual; $374.50 per unlimited use scoring CD-ROM; $21.50 per 100 answer sheets for use with CD.

Time: (10-15) minutes.

Comments: Ratings by teachers or parents.

Authors: Harold F. Burks and Christian P. Gruber.

Publisher: Western Psychological Services.

Cross References: For reviews by Ronald A. Madle and Hoi K. Suen, see 18:16; see T5:355 (1 reference) and T4:342 (5 references); for reviews by Lisa G. Bischoff and by Leland C. Zlomke and Brenda R. Bush of an earlier edition, see 11:50 (7 references); see also T3:328 (1 reference), T2:1115 (1 reference), and 7:46 (2 references).

[303]

Burns Brief Inventory of Communication and Cognition.

Purpose: Designed to "assist in determining which of a client's cognitive or communication skills are impaired as a result of a neurological lesion or other disease process, and to assist in selecting appropriate treatment targets and functional treatment goals."

Population: Adults with neurological impairment.

Publication Date: 1997.

Acronym: Burns Inventory.

Scores: Left Hemisphere Inventory: 16 scores in 5 domains: Auditory Comprehension (Yes/No Questions, Comprehension of Words and Sentences, Comprehension of Paragraphs), Verbal Expression (Automatic Speech, Verbal Repetition, Responsive Naming-Nouns, Responsive Naming-Verbs, Confrontation Naming), Reading (Oral Reading of Words and Sentences, Reading Comprehension of Words and Sentences, Reading Comprehension of Functional Paragraphs), Writing (Writing to Dictation, Functional Writing), Numerical Reasoning (Time, Money, Calculation); Right Hemisphere Inventory: 12 scores in 3 domains: Scanning and Tracking (Functional Scanning and Tracking, Scanning and Tracking of Single Words), Visuo-Spatial Skills (Functional Spatial Distribution of Attention, Spatial Distribution of Attention, Recognition of Familiar Faces, Gestalt Perception, Visuo-Spatial Construction-Clock, Visuo-Spatial Organization for Writing), Prosody and Abstract Language (Spontaneous Expressive Prosody, Receptive Prosody, Inferences, Metaphorical Language); Complex Neuropathology Inventory: 15 scores in 4 domains: Orientation to Factual Memory (Orientation to Person/Place/Time, Factual Current and Remote Memory), Auditory Attention and Memory (Auditory Attention/Vigilance, Immediate Auditory Recall of Digits, Immediate Auditory Recall of Digits with Distractions, Immediate Auditory Recall of Functional Information); Visual Perception (Color Recognition, Picture Matching, Word Matching); Visual Attention and Memory (Functional Short-Term Recognition, Short-Term Recognition of Pictures, Short-Term Recognition of Words, Divided Visual Attention, Delayed Recognition of Pictures, Delayed Recognition of Words).

Administration: Individual.

Forms, 3: Inventories: Left Hemisphere Inventory, Right Hemisphere Inventory, Complex Neuropathology Inventory.

Price Data, 2015: $235.25 per complete kit; $37.40 per 15 Right Hemisphere record forms; $37.40 per 15 Complex Neuropathology record forms; $37.40 per 15 Left Hemisphere record forms; $65.75 per stimulus plates; $65.85 per examiner's manual (116 pages); $22.30 per audio CD.

Time: (30) minutes per inventory.

Comments: For use by speech pathologists; each inventory can be used separately or all three can be used as a battery.

Author: Martha S. Burns.

Publisher: Pearson.

Cross References: For reviews by Joan C. Ballard and Richard I. Frederick, see 14:55.

[304]

Burt Word Reading Test, New Zealand Revision.

Purpose: Designed to provide an estimate of word recognition skills for 110 words.

Population: Ages 6-0 to 12-11 years.

Publication Date: 1981.

Score: Overall performance score only.

Administration: Individual.

Price Data, 2015: NZ$4.20 per 10 record forms; $1.15 per test card; $8.50 per manual (10 pages); $8.95 per specimen set.

Time: [5] minutes.

Comments: Revision and New Zealand standardization of the Burt Word Reading Test; identical to 1974 revision except for word order.

Authors: Alison Gilmore, Cedric Croft, and Neil Reid.
Publisher: New Zealand Council for Educational Research [New Zealand].
Cross References: See T5:358 (13 references) and T4:344 (4 references); for reviews by Mark W. Aulls and John Elkins, see 9:175 (2 references).

[305]

Business Administration Scale for Family Child Care.

Purpose: Designed "for measuring and improving the overall quality of business practices in family child care settings."
Population: Family child care providers and those working to monitor and improve the quality of family child care business practices.
Publication Date: 2009.
Acronym: BAS.
Scores, 12: 10 items: Qualifications and Professional Development, Income and Benefits, Work Environment, Fiscal Management, Recordkeeping, Risk Management, Provider-Parent Communication, Community Resources, Marketing and Public Relations, Provider as Employer, plus Total Score, Average Item Score.
Administration: Individual.
Price Data, 2016: $23.95 per manual with complete scale (2009, 48 pages).
Foreign Language Edition: Spanish version available.
Time: (60) minutes for interview and (60) minutes for document review.
Comments: Designed to complement the Family Child Care Environment Rating Scale–Revised (798).
Authors: Teri N. Talan and Paula Jorde Bloom.
Publisher: Teachers College Press.
Cross References: Reviews are scheduled for *The Twentieth Mental Measurements Yearbook*.

[306]

Business Analyst Skills Evaluation [One-Hour].

Purpose: Measures practical and analytical skills for the position of Business Systems Analyst.
Population: Candidates for Business Analyst positions.
Publication Dates: 1984–1998.
Acronym: BUSAN.
Scores: Total Score, Narrative Evaluation, Ranking, Recommendation.
Administration: Group.
Price Data: Available from publisher.
Foreign Language Edition: Available in French.
Time: (60) minutes.
Comments: Available in booklet and online; scored by publisher; must be proctored.
Author: Bruce A. Winrow.

Publisher: Walden Personnel Testing & Consulting Inc. [Canada].
Cross References: For reviews by Charles K. Parsons and Michael Spangler, see 16:40.

[307]

Business Analyst Skills Evaluation [Two-Hour].

Purpose: "Measures practical and analytical skills required for the position of Business Systems Analyst."
Population: Candidates for business analyst positions.
Publication Date: 1984.
Acronym: PRBUSAN.
Scores, 4: Total Score, Narrative Evaluation, Rating, Recommendation.
Administration: Group.
Price Data: Available from publisher.
Time: (120) minutes.
Comments: Also available with interpersonal skills; graded by publisher; must be proctored.
Author: Bruce A. Winrow.
Publisher: Walden Personnel Testing & Consulting Inc. [Canada].
Cross References: For a review by Lenore W. Harmon, see 10:39.

[308]

The Business Critical Thinking Skills Test.

Purpose: "Developed to assess the critical thinking skills of business professionals and business students."
Population: Adult business professionals and business students.
Publication Dates: 2007-2008.
Acronym: BCTST.
Scores, 6: Analysis, Inference, Evaluation, Deductive, Inductive, Total.
Administration: Group.
Price Data: Available from publisher.
Time: (50) minutes.
Comments: This test can be administered online or via paper and pencil.
Authors: Peter A. Facione, Stephen Blohm, and Noreen C. Facione.
Publisher: Insight Assessment-The California Academic Press LLC.
Cross References: For reviews by Patricia A. Bachelor and Jean P. Kirnan, see 18:17.

[309]

Business-focused Inventory of Personality (UK Edition).

Purpose: Designed as "a work-based personality test" for use in job selection, development, coaching, and career counseling.
Population: Ages 20 older.

Publication Date: 2008.

Acronym: BIP.

Scores, 19: 14 primary scales arranged into 4 domains: Occupational Orientation (Achievement Motivation, Power Motivation, Leadership Motivation), Occupational Behaviour (Conscientiousness, Flexibility, Action Orientation), Social Competencies (Social Sensitivity, Openness to Contact, Sociability, Team Orientation, Assertiveness), Psychological Constitution (Emotional Stability, Working under Pressure, Self-Confidence) plus Impression Management and 4 supplementary indicies: Sense of Control, Competitiveness, Mobility, Time Orientation.

Administration: Individual or group.

Forms, 2: Form S (self-report); Form O (observer-rated).

Price Data, 2015: £148 per starter set including manual (97 pages), 5 self-rated item booklets, 10 observer-rated item booklets, 5 self-rated profile sheets, 10 observer-rated profile sheets, 5 self-rated summary score sheets, 1 self-rated scoring key/acetates, 5 self-rated test taker guides, and 10 observer-rated test taker guides; £48 per manual; £50 per self-rating standard report; £40 per observer-rating standard report; subscription discounts available.

Foreign Language Editions: Available in German, French, Czech, and Danish.

Time: (40) minutes.

Comments: Administered via paper and pencil or computer; observer-rated version "is not normed and is intended only as a support tool"; originally developed in Germany.

Authors: Rüdiger Hossiep and Michael Paschen.

Publisher: Hogrefe Ltd [United Kingdom].

Cross References: Reviews are scheduled for *The Twentieth Mental Measurements Yearbook.*

[310]
Butcher Treatment Planning Inventory.

Purpose: Designed to provide psychotherapists with "relevant personality and symptomatic information early in the treatment process."

Population: Adults in therapy.

Publication Date: 1998.

Acronym: BTPI.

Administration: Individual or group.

Price Data, 2015: $259 per starter kit including manual (236 pages), 10 full form and 10 symptom monitoring item booklets, and 25 full form and 25 symptom monitoring QuikScore forms; $41 per 10 full form item booklets; $38 per 10 symptom monitoring item booklets; $55 per 25 full form QuikScore forms; $55 per 25 symptom monitoring QuikScore forms; $8 per interpretive report (minimum 25 uses); $59 per preview version; $96 per technical manual; $41 per 50 full form data entry sheets; $41 per 50 symptom monitoring data entry sheets.

Comments: Normed on ages 18 and over; hand- or computer-scored; paper-and-pencil or computerized administration; computer-generated interpretive reports available.

Author: James N. Butcher.

Publisher: Multi-Health Systems, Inc.

a) FULL FORM.

Scores, 16: Validity Scales (Inconsistent Responding, Overly Virtuous Self-Views, Exaggerated Problem Presentation, Closed-Mindedness), Treatment Issues Scales (Problems in Relationship Formation, Somatization of Conflict, Low Expectation of Benefit, Self-Oriented/Narcissism, Perceived Lack of Environmental Support), Current Symptom Scales (Depression, Anxiety, Anger-Out, Anger-In, Unusual Thinking), General Pathology Composite, Treatment Difficulty Composite.

Time: [30] minutes.

b) SYMPTOM MONITORING FORM.

Scores: Includes only Current Symptom Scales from *a* above.

Time: [12] minutes.

c) TREATMENT PROCESS/SYMPTOM FORM.

Scores: Includes only Treatment Issues Scales and Current Symptom Scales from *a* above.

Time: Administration time not reported.

d) TREATMENT ISSUES FORM.

Scores: Includes only Validity Scales and Treatment Issues Scales from *a* above.

Time: Administration time not reported.

Cross References: For reviews by Wiliam E. Hanson and Samuel Juni, see 14:57.

[311]
C-BDQ Correctional Officer Background Data Questionnaire.

Purpose: Developed to assess background and personal characteristics.

Population: Candidates for entry-level correctional officer positions.

Publication Date: 1995.

Acronym: C-BDQ.

Scores: 7 biodata subtypes: Unscored Demographic Information, Background, Lifestyle, Interest, Personality, Ability, Opinion-Based.

Administration: Individual or group.

Price Data: Available from publisher.

Time: 60 minutes.

Comments: "It is recommended that this test be given in conjunction with one of IPMA-HR's other entry-level correctional officer tests."

Authors: International Public Management Association for Human Resources & Bruce Davey Associates.

Publisher: International Public Management Association for Human Resources (IPMA-HR).

Cross References: For a review by Susan M. Brookhart, see 18:18.

[312]
Calibrated Ideational Fluency Assessment.

Purpose: Designed "to characterize a respondent's verbal, nonverbal, and overall generativity."

Population: Ages 18 to 92.
Publication Date: 2010.
Acronym: CIFA.
Scores, 11: Acceptable Designs, Unacceptable Designs, Percent Unacceptable Designs, S Words, P Words, Letter Word Fluency, Animals, Supermarket Items, Category Word Fluency, Verbal Fluency Total, Ideational Fluency Composite.
Subtests, 2: Design Fluency, Verbal Fluency.
Administration: Individual.
Price Data, 2015: $210 per introductory kit, including professional manual (108 pages) and 50 record booklets; $66 per 25 record booklets; $96 per professional manual.
Time: (10) minutes.
Authors: David J. Schretlen and Tracy D. Vannorsdall.
Publisher: Psychological Assessment Resources, Inc.
Cross References: For reviews by Marta J. Coleman and Anthony T. Dugbartey, see 19:24.

[313]
Calibrated Neuropsychological Normative System.

Purpose: "Designed to assist clinicians and researchers in their interpretation of the tests that make up the system…by accounting for variation in test performance in demographic background and estimated premorbid IQ."
Population: Ages 18 to 92.
Publication Date: 2010.
Acronym: CNNS.
Scores, 95: 67 measure scores and 6 factor scores (Processing Speed, Attention/Working Memory, Verbal Learning and Memory, Visual Learning and Memory, Ideational Fluency, Executive Functioning) derived from 25 tests; 22 Discrepancy Scores.
Administration: Individual.
Price Data, 2015: $170 per introductory kit, including professional manual (175 pages) and 50 record forms; $650 per CNNS-SP scoring CD-ROM; $56 per 50 record forms; $124 per professional manual.
Time: Administration time not reported.
Comments: The system "consists of widely used neuropsychological measures that are co-normed." Scores are derived from the following tests, which are not included in the price of the system: Hopkins Adult Reading Test, Mini-Mental State Examination, Mental Status Examination-Telephone, Right-Left Orientation, Grooved Pegboard Test, Salthouse Perceptual Comparison Test, Trail Making Test, Digit Span, Brief Test of Attention, Modified Wisconsin Card Sorting Task, Cognitive Estimation Task, Iowa Gambling Task, Calibrated Ideational Fluency Assessment, Boston Naming Test, Benton Facial Recognition Test, Career Abilities Placement Survey, Clock Drawing, Rey Complex Figure Test, Hopkins Verbal Learning Test-Revised, Brief Visuospatial Memory Test-Revised, Wechsler Memory Scale-Revised, Prospective Memory Test, Recency

Discrimination Test, Lawton Activities of Daily Living Questionnaire, Geriatric Depression Scale-15. Professional manual provides age-based norms; CNNS-SP computerized scoring program provides norms based on eight different combinations of demographic and premorbid variables.
Authors: David J. Schretlen, S. Marc Testa, and Godfrey D. Pearlson.
Publisher: Psychological Assessment Resources, Inc.
Cross References: For reviews by Rik Carl D'Amato and Yuan Yuan Wang and by Jennifer M. Strang, see 19:25.

[314]
California Computerized Assessment Package.

Purpose: Designed as a "standardized assessment of reaction time and speed of information processing."
Population: Ages 10–90.
Publication Dates: 1986–2011.
Acronym: CalCAP.
Scores: 7: Simple Reaction Time, Choice Reaction Time for Single Digits, Serial Pattern Matching, Lexical Discrimination, Visual Selective Attention, Response Reversal and Rapid Visual Scanning, Form Discrimination.
Administration: Individual.
Forms, 2: Standard, Abbreviated.
Price Data, 2015: $195 per complete kit including manual (2001, 80 pages), standard battery and abbreviated battery; available only by Internet download.
Foreign Language Editions: Danish, Flemish, French, Norwegian, and Spanish editions available.
Time: (20–25) minutes-Standard battery; (8-10) minutes-Abbreviated battery.
Author: Eric N. Miller.
Publisher: Eric N. Miller.
Cross References: For reviews by Howard A. Lloyd and by Goran Westergren and Ingela Westergren, see 14:58.

[315]
The California Critical Thinking Disposition Inventory [2007 Edition].

Purpose: Designed to measure the dispositional dimension of critical thinking.
Population: Working professionals, high school, and college students.
Publication Dates: 1992-2007.
Acronym: CCTDI.
Scores, 8: Overall score, Truth-Seeking, Open-Mindedness, Analyticity, Systematicity, CT-Confidence, Inquisitiveness, Cognitive Maturity.
Administration: Group.
Price Data: Available from publisher.
Foreign Language Editions: French, Spanish, Chinese, Hebrew, Japanese, and Thai.

Time: Administration time not reported.
Comments: This test can be administered online or via paper and pencil.
Authors: Peter A. Facione and Noreen C. Facione.
Publisher: Insight Assessment.
Cross References: For reviews by Brad M. Merker and John F. Wakefield, see 18:20; for reviews by Carolyn M. Callahan and Salvador Hector Ochoa of an earlier edition, see 12:57.

[316]

The California Critical Thinking Skills Test [Revised].

Purpose: "Specifically designed to measure the skills dimension of critical thinking."
Population: College students and adults.
Publication Dates: 1990-2007.
Acronym: CCTST.
Administration: Group.
Price Data: Available from publisher.
Foreign Language Editions: All forms available in English; Form A is available in Chinese (Beijing and Taiwan), Hebrew, Korean, Spanish (Mexico), and Thai; Form B is available in Portuguese; Form 2000 is available in French (Canadian), Italian, Korean, and Spanish (Spain).
Time: (45) minutes or unlimited.
Comments: This test can be administered online or via paper and pencil.
Authors: Peter A. Facione, Noreen C. Facione, Stephen W. Blohm, and Carol Ann F. Giancarlo.
Publisher: Insight Assessment-The California Academic Press LLC.
a) FORM A.
Scores, 4: Analysis, Inference, Evaluation, Total.
b) FORM B.
Scores, 4: Analysis, Inference, Evaluation, Total.
c) FORM C.
Scores, 6: Analysis, Inference, Evaluation, Deductive Reasoning, Inductive Reasoning, Total.
Cross References: For reviews by Matthew E. Lambert and William E. Martin, Jr., see 18:21; for reviews by Robert F. McMorris and William B. Michael of an earlier edition, see 12:58.

[317]

California Measure of Mental Motivation.

Purpose: Designed to "measure the degree to which an individual is motivated toward thinking."
Population: Grade K through adult.
Publication Dates: 1997-2006.
Acronym: CM3.
Administration: Group.
Levels, 4: IA, IB, II, III.
Price Data: Available from publisher.
Time: (15-20) minutes.

Comments: This test can be administered online or via paper and pencil.
Authors: Carol A. F. Giancarlo and P. A. Facione.
Publisher: Insight Assessment-The California Academic Press LLC.
a) LEVEL IA.
Population: Grades K-2.
Scores, 4: Mental Focus/Self-Regulation, Learning Orientation, Creative Problem Solving, Cognitive Integrity.
b) LEVEL IB.
Population: Grades 3-5.
Scores, 4: Mental Focus/Self-Regulation, Learning Orientation, Creative Problem Solving, Cognitive Integrity.
c) LEVEL II.
Population: Grades 6-12.
Scores, 5: Mental Focus/Self-Regulation, Learning Orientation, Creative Problem Solving, Cognitive Integrity, Scholarly Rigor.
d) LEVEL III.
Population: Adults.
Scores, 4: Mental Focus/Self-Regulation, Learning Orientation, Creative Problem Solving, Cognitive Integrity.
Cross References: For reviews by John J. Brinkman and Amber Carter and by William D. Schafer, see 18:22.

[318]

California Older Adult Stroop Test.

Purpose: A Stroop Test adaptation "designed to minimize errors due to decreased visual acuity or color naming difficulty secondary to confusion or cataracts."
Population: Ages 60 and older.
Publication Date: 2010.
Acronym: COAST.
Scores, 9: Color (Time, Self-Corrected Errors, Total Errors), Word (Time, Self-Corrected Errors, Total Errors), Interference (Time, Self-Corrected Errors, Total Errors).
Administration: Individual.
Price Data, 2016: $50 per PDF manual (17 pages); $60 per paper manual; $10 per License to Reproduce.
Time: (15) minutes.
Authors: Nancy A. Pachana, Bernice A. Marcopulos, Ruth E. Yoash-Gantz, and Larry W. Thompson.
Publisher: Mind Garden, Inc.

[319]

California Psychological Inventory™ 434.

Purpose: Designed to assess personality characteristics and to predict what people will say and do in specified contexts.
Population: Ages 13 and over.
Publication Dates: 1956–1996.
Acronym: CPI 434.
Scores, 36: 20 Folk Scales: Dominance (Do), Capacity for Status (Cs), Sociability (Sy), Social Presence (Sp), Self-Acceptance (Sa), Independence (In), Empathy (Em), Responsibility (Re), Socialization (So), Self-Control (Sc), Good Impression (Gi), Communality (Cm), Well-Being

(Wb), Tolerance (To), Achievement via Conformance (Ac), Achievement via Independence (Ai), Intellectual Efficiency (Ie), Psychological-Mindedness (Py), Flexibility (Fx), Femininity/Masculinity (F/M); 3 Vector Scales: v. 1 (Internality/Externality), v. 2 (Norm Questioning/Norm Favoring), v. 3 (Self-Realization), plus 13 Special Purpose scales: Managerial Potential, Work Orientation, Creative Temperament, Leadership, Amicability, Law Enforcement Orientation, Tough-mindedness, Baucom Scale for Masculinity, Baucom Scale for Femininity, Leventhal Scale for Anxiety, Wink-Gough Scale for Narcissism, Dicken Scale for Social Desirability, Dicken Scale for Aquiescence.
Administration: Individual or group.
Price Data, 2015: $24.95 each for the Profile (online); $49.95 each for the Narrative Report (online); $59.95 each for the Configural Analysis Report (online); $99 per manual; $93.50 per Practical Guide to CPI(TM) Interpretation.
Foreign Language Editions: French, German, Italian, and Spanish editions available in an earlier edition.
Time: (45–60) minutes.
Comments: Previous edition was titled California Psychological Inventory, Third Edition and is still available; 1 form; reports available: Narrative, Configural Analysis, Profile; Scoring Options: Prepaid (mail-in), CPP Software System, skillsone.com.
Authors: Harrison G. Gough and Pamela Bradley (manual).
Publisher: CPP, Inc.
Cross References: For reviews by Mark J. Atkinson and K. Hattrup, see 15:43; see also T5:372 (118 references) and T4:361 (57 references); for reviews by Brian Bolton and George Engelhard, Jr., see 11:54 (108 references); for reviews by Donald H. Baucom and H. J. Eysenck, see 9:182 (61 references); see also T3:354 (195 references); for a review by Malcolm D. Gynther, see 8:514 (452 references); see also T2:1121 (166 references); for reviews by Lewis R. Goldberg and James A. Walsh and an excerpted review by John O. Crites, see 7:49 (370 references); see also P:27 (249 references); for a review by E. Lowell Kelly, see 6:71 (116 references); for reviews by Lee J. Cronbach and Robert L. Thorndike and an excerpted review by Laurance F. Shaffer, see 5:37 (33 references).

[320]
California Q-Sort for Adults (Revised Edition).

Purpose: Designed as "a systematic way of comparing different [intra-individual] personalities with one another."
Population: Adults.
Publication Dates: 1961–1990.
Acronym: CAQAD.

Scores: Ratings in 9 categories ranging from most uncharacteristic to most characteristic.
Administration: Individual.
Price Data, 2015: $50 per manual, including review-only copy of the CAQAD cards; $2 per License to Reproduce (minimum 50).
Time: (30–40) minutes.
Comments: For an adaptation for children, see California Q-Sort for Children (321).
Author: Jack Block.
Publisher: Mind Garden, Inc.
Cross References: For a review by George Domino, see 14:59; see also T5:373 (43 references); T4:362 (20 references), and T3:356 (1 reference); for reviews by Allen L. Edwards and David T. Lykken of an earlier edition and excerpted reviews by Samuel J. Beck and John E. Exner, Jr., see 6:72 (2 references); see also P:28 (1 reference).

[321]
California Q-Sort for Children.

Purpose: "Designed to describe a child's behavior and personality."
Population: Children.
Publication Date: 1980.
Acronym: CAQCH.
Scores: Q-sort rating in 9 categories ranging from extremely uncharacteristic to extremely characteristic.
Administration: Individual.
Price Data, 2015: $50 per manual, including review-only copy of cards; $2 per License to Reproduce (minimum 50).
Time: (35-60) minutes.
Comments: For an upward extension see California Q-Sort for Adults (Revised Edition) (320).
Authors: Jeanne Block and Jack Block.
Publisher: Mind Garden, Inc.
Cross References: See T5:365 (11 references) and T4:354 (6 references); for a review by Alfred B. Heilbrun, Jr., see 9:181; see also T3:348 (2 references).

[322]
California Verbal Learning Test, Children's Version.

Purpose: "Designed to assess multiple components of verbal learning/memory, interference effects on memory and recall strategy/control."
Population: Ages 5–16.
Publication Dates: 1989–1994.
Acronym: CVLT-C.
Scores, 13: List A Trials 1–5 Total, List B Free-Recall Trial, Short Delay Free Recall, Short-Delay Cued Recall, Long-Delay Free Recall, Long-Delay Cued Recall, Semantic Cluster Ratio, Perseverations, Free-Recall

Intrusions, Cued-Recall Intrusions, Recognition Hits, Discriminability, False Positives.
Administration: Individual
Price Data, 2015: $204 per set including manual (1994, 147 pages) and 25 record forms; $87.15 per 25 record forms; $99 per scoring assistant including CD-ROM, user's guide, and keyboard overlay; $153.75 per manual.
Time: (55) minutes with 20 minute interval between short and long delay.
Authors: Dean C. Delis, Joel H. Kramer, Edith Kaplan, and Beth A. Ober; Alan J. Fridlund, and Dean C. Delis (Scoring Assistant User's Guide).
Publisher: Pearson.
Cross References: See T5:375 (8 references); for reviews by Billy T. Ogletree and LeAdelle Phelps, see 13:41 (2 references).

[323]

California Verbal Learning Test, Second Edition, Adult Version.

Purpose: To "assess multiple cognitive components of verbal learning and memory functioning including recall strategy/organization, interference effects, recall accuracy and effort."
Population: 16–89 years.
Publication Dates: 1983–2000.
Acronym: CVLT-II (Standard); CVLT-II SF (Short Form).
Scores, 29: Immediate Recall (Trial 1, Trials 2–5, Trials 1–5 Total), Learning Slope, Semantic Clustering, Serial Clustering, Subjective Clustering, Primacy/Recency Recall, Percentage of Recall Consistency, List B Trial, Proactive Interference, Short-Delay Free Recall, Retroactive Interference, Short-Delay Cued Recall, Long-Delay Free Recall, Long-Delay Free Recall Retention, Long-Delay Cued Recall, Repetition Errors, Synonym/Subordinate Intrusions, Across-List Intrusions, Categorical Intrusions, Non-Categorical Intrusions, Yes/No Recognition Testing, False-Positive Errors, Total Recognition Discriminability, Source Recognition Discriminability, Semantic Recognition Discriminability, Novel Recognition Discriminability, Response Bias, Critical Item Analysis, Forced-Choice Recognition [optional].
Administration: Individual.
Forms, 3: Standard Form, Alternate Form, Short Form.
Price Data, 2015: $511.50 per complete kit including software package (CD-ROM), manual (2000, 287 pages), 25 Standard Record Forms, 1 Alternate Record Form, and 25 Short Record Forms; $87.15 per 25 Standard or Alternate Record Forms; $76.90 per 25 Short Record Forms.
Time: (30) minutes plus 30 minutes of delay for Standard and Alternate Forms; (15) minutes plus 15 minutes of delay for Short Form.

Comments: Comprehensive Scoring System software generates Core Report (generates 27 scores), Expanded Report (generates 66 scores), Research Report (generates over 260 scores).
Authors: Dean C. Delis, Joel H. Kramer, Edith Kaplan, and Beth A. Ober.
Publisher: Pearson.
Cross References: For reviews by Anita M. Hubley and Cederick O. Lindskog, see 16:41; see also T5:376 (35 references); for a review by Ray Fenton of the previous edition, see 13:42 (57 references); see also T4:364 (12 references).

[324]

Caliper Profile.

Purpose: Designed for "consultants to provide clear, objective information on an individual's strengths, limitations and motivations, along with solid suggestions for improving performance."
Population: Potential and existing employees.
Publication Date: 2001.
Scores, 4: Persuasiveness, Interpersonal, Problem Solving/Decision Making, Personal Organization/Time Management.
Administration: Group.
Price Data: Available from publisher.
Foreign Language Editions: Available in Chinese, Czech, Dutch, English, French, German, Italian, Japanese, Korean, Portuguese, Quebecois, Russian, Spanish, Swedish, and Taiwanese.
Manual: No manual.
Time: [120] minutes, untimed.
Comments: Can be administered online or in paper-pencil format.
Authors: Caliper.
Publisher: Caliper Corporation.

[325]

Call Center Skills Test.

Purpose: Measures practical and intellectual skills for call center positions.
Population: Candidates for call center positions.
Publication Date: 2001.
Acronym: CCTR.
Scores, 4: Total Score, Narrative Evaluation, Ranking, Recommendation.
Administration: Group.
Price Data: Available from publisher.
Foreign Language Edition: Available in French.
Time: (60) minutes.
Author: Bruce A. Winrow.
Publisher: Walden Personnel Testing & Consulting Inc. [Canada].
Cross References: For reviews by Theodore L. Hayes and Judith A. Rein, see 16:42.

[326]
The Callier-Azusa Scale: G Edition.

Purpose: A developmental scale "designed to aid in the assessment of deaf-blind and severely and profoundly handicapped children."

Population: Deaf-blind and severely/profoundly handicapped children.

Publication Date: 1978.

Scores: 18 subscales in 5 areas: Motor Development (Postural Control, Locomotion, Fine Motor, Visual Motor), Perceptual Development (Vision, Auditory, Tactile), Daily Living Skills (Dressing, Personal Hygiene, Feeding, Toileting), Cognition, Communication and Language (Cognition, Receptive, Expressive, Speech), Social Development (Adults, Peers, Environment).

Administration: Individual.

Price Data, 2016: $20.

Time: Administration time not reported.

Comments: Criterion-referenced.

Author: Robert Stillman (Editor).

Publisher: Callier Center for Communication Disorders.

Cross References: See T5:377 (1 reference).

[327]
Cambridge Prospective Memory Test.

Purpose: Designed to "assess prospective memory" (remembering to do previously planned actions).

Population: Ages 16 and over.

Publication Date: 2005.

Acronym: CAMPROMPT.

Score: Total score only.

Administration: Individual.

Forms, 2: Parallel Forms A and B.

Price Data, 2015: £244 per complete kit including manual (44 pages), 25 record forms, quiz question cards, puzzle cards, message card, clock, and two timers; £51 per 25 record forms; £66.50 per manual.

Time: 20(25) minutes.

Authors: Barbara A. Wilson, Hazel Emslie, Jennifer Foley, Agnes Shiel, Peter Watson, Kari Hawkins, Yvonne Groot, and Jonathan J. Evans.

Publisher: Pearson Assessment [England].

Cross References: For reviews by Mark A. Albanese and Linda E. Brody, see 17:36.

[328]
The Camden Memory Tests.

Purpose: Designed "to fulfill a clinical need that was not met by existing memory tests."

Population: Available from publisher.

Publication Date: 1996.

Scores: 5 tests: Pictorial Recognition Memory Test, Topographical Recognition Memory Test, Paired Associate Learning Test, Short Recognition Memory Test for Words, Short Recognition Memory Test for Faces.

Administration: Available from publisher.

Price Data, 2016: $220 per Pictorial Recognition Memory Test; $220 per Topographical Recognition Memory Test; $85 per Paired Associate Learning Test; $85 per Short Recognition Memory Test for Words; $85 per Short Recognition Memory Test for Faces; $30 per test manual; $415 per set of all 5 tests including 1 manual and 5 packs of scoring sheets; $20 per 25 scoring sheets.

Time: Administration time not reported.

Author: Elizabeth Warrington.

Publisher: Routledge Psychology.

[329]
Campbell-Hallam Team Development Survey.

Purpose: "Designed to give teams standardized feedback on their strengths and weaknesses."

Population: Members of intact working teams.

Publication Date: 1994.

Acronym: TDS.

Scores, 19: Resources (Time and Staffing, Information, Material Resources, Organizational Support, Skills, Commitment), Efficiency (Mission Clarity, Team Coordination, Team Unity, Individual Goals, Empowerment), Improvement (Team Assessment, Innovation, Feedback, Rewards, Leadership), Success (Satisfaction, Performance, Overall Index).

Administration: Group.

Price Data: Available from publisher.

Time: (20–25) minutes.

Authors: Glenn Hallam and David Campbell.

Publisher: General Dynamics Information Technology.

Cross References: For reviews by Frederick T. L. Leong and Mary A. Lewis, see 14:60; see also T5:379 (1 reference).

[330]
Campbell™ Interest and Skill Survey.

Purpose: "Measures self-reported interests and skills."

Population: Ages 15 years to adult.

Publication Dates: 1988–1992.

Acronym: CISS™.

Scores, 99: 7 Orientation Scales (Influencing, Organizing, Helping, Creating, Analyzing, Producing, Adventuring), 29 Basic Scales (Leadership, Law/Politics, Public Speaking, Sales, Advertising/Marketing, Supervision, Financial Services, Office Practices, Adult Development, Child Development, Counseling, Religious Activities, Medical Practice, Art/Design, Performing Arts, Writing, International Activities, Fashion, Culinary Arts, Mathematics, Science, Mechanical Crafts, Woodworking, Farming/Forestry, Plants/Gardens, Animal Care, Athletics/Physical Fitness, Military/Law Enforcement, Risks/Adventure), 58 Occupational Scales (Attorney, Financial Planner, Hotel Manager, Manufacturer's Representative,

Marketing Director, Realtor, CEO/President, Human Resources Director, School Superintendent, Advertising Account Executive, Media Executive, Public Relations Director, Corporate Trainer, Secretary, Bank Manager, Insurance Agent, Retail Store Manager, Hospital Administrator, Accountant/CPA, Bookkeeper, Child Care Worker, Guidance Counselor, Religious Leader, Teacher K–12, Social Worker, Psychologist, Nursing Administrator, Commercial Artist, Fashion Designer, Liberal Arts Professor, Librarian, Musician, Translator/Interpreter, Writer/Editor, Restaurant Manager, Chef, Physician, Chemist, Medical Researcher, Math/Science Teacher, Computer Programmer, Statistician, Systems Analyst, Carpenter, Electrician, Veterinarian, Airline Mechanic, Agribusiness Manager, Landscape Architect, Architect, Police Officer, Military Officer, Ski Instructor, Test Pilot, Athletic Coach, Athletic Trainer, Emergency Medical Technician, Fitness Instructor), 2 Special Scales (Academic Focus, Extraversion), 3 Procedural Checks (Response Percentage Check, Inconsistency Check, Omitted Items Check).

Administration: Group.

Price Data, 2015: $2.85 per Career Planner; $65.35 per hardcover (ring-binder) manual; $42.30 per softcover manual; $15.70 per 50 interest/skill pattern worksheets; $23.60 per 25 Q Local answer sheets; $10.70 per Q Local report; $75.35 per Q Local starter kit including softcover manual, 3 career planners, interest/skill pattern worksheets, 3 answer sheets with test items, and 3 Q Local administrations; $75.50 per mail-in scoring starter kit including softcover manual, 3 career planners, interest/skill pattern worksheets, 3 answer sheets with test items, and all materials necessary to generate 3 reports using mail-in scoring service; quantity discounts available for the reports; price information for Spanish materials available from publisher.

Time: (35) minutes.

Comments: Each scale contains both an interest and a skill score; combined gender scales allow for broadest interpretation of survey results; workshops available.

Author: David Campbell.

Publisher: Pearson.

Cross References: See T5:380 (1 reference); for reviews by Richard C. Pugh and Michael J. Roszkowski, see 13:43; see also T4:368 (1 reference).

[331]
Campbell Leadership Index.

Purpose: "A multi-rater instrument to help measure personal characteristics that are directly related to the nature and demands of leadership."

Population: Leaders.

Publication Date: 1991.

Acronym: CLI.

Scores, 22: Ambitious, Daring, Dynamic, Enterprising, Experienced, Farsighted, Original, Persuasive, Energy,

Affectionate, Considerate, Empowering, Entertaining, Friendly, Credible, Organized, Productive, Thrifty, Calm, Flexible, Optimistic, Trusting.

Administration: Group or individual.

Price Data: Available from publisher.

Time: (45–60) minutes.

Comments: Self-ratings plus 3–5 observer ratings.

Author: David Campbell.

Publisher: General Dynamics Information Technology.

Cross References: See T5:381 (1 reference); for reviews by George Domino and Charles Houston, see 12:59; see also T4:369 (1 reference).

[332]
Campbell Organizational Survey.

Purpose: Designed to measure attitudes of employees regarding the organization.

Population: Working adults.

Publication Dates: 1988–1990.

Acronym: COS.

Scores, 14: The Work Itself, Working Conditions, Freedom from Stress, Co-Workers, Supervision, Top Leadership, Pay, Benefits, Job Security, Promotional Opportunities, Feedback/Communications, Organizational Planning, Support for Innovation, Overall Satisfaction Index.

Administration: Group.

Price Data: Available from publisher.

Time: (15–25) minutes.

Comments: A component of Campbell Development Surveys (CDS); scoring and reporting discounts for 50, 250, 1,000 or 2,500+ examinees.

Author: David Campbell.

Publisher: General Dynamics Information Technology.

Cross References: For reviews by Ralph O. Mueller and Kevin R. Murphy, see 12:60; see T4:370 (1 reference).

[333]
Canadian Achievement Survey Tests for Adults.

Purpose: "Designed to measure achievement in reading, language, and mathematics … subject areas commonly found in adult basic education curricula."

Population: Adults.

Publication Date: 1994.

Acronym: CAST.

Scores, 6: Reading (Vocabulary, Comprehension), Language (Language Mechanics, Language Expression), Mathematics (Mathematics Computation, Mathematics Concepts and Applications).

Administration: Group.

Levels, 3: Completed up to Grade 6, completed Grades 7 to 9, completed Grades 10 and above.

Price Data, 2015: $67 per 25 test booklets (specify level); $34 per 25 hand-scorable answer sheets; $65 per

50 machine scorable answer sheets; $46 per manual (53 pages); $25 per review kit including brochure, 1 copy each of Levels 1, 2, and 3 test booklets, hand-scorable answer sheet, machine-scorable answer sheet, and directions for administering.

Time: (90) minutes.

Author: Canadian Test Centre.

Publisher: Canadian Test Centre, Educational Assessment Services [Canada].

Cross References: For reviews by John O. Anderson and Mark H. Daniel, see 14:61.

[334]

Canadian Achievement Tests, Fourth Edition.

Purpose: Designed to fit Canadian curricula and measure achievement in reading, writing, and mathematics.

Population: Students in kindergarten through postsecondary school.

Publication Dates: 1981-2010.

Acronym: CAT-4.

Administration: Group.

Levels, 11: 10, 11, 12, 13, 14, 15, 16, 17, 18, 19, 20-22.

Price Data: Available from publisher.

Time: Varies by level and number of subtests.

Comments: Hand or machine scoring options available; yields both norm-referenced and criterion-referenced scores; multiple choice tests can be administered as complete batteries or as independent modules.

Author: Canadian Test Centre.

Publisher: Canadian Test Centre.

a) LEVEL 10.

Population: Students in kindergarten (Spring) through Grade 1 (Fall).

Scores, 6: Reading, Word Analysis, Mathematics, Total Reading, Total Mathematics, Total Battery.

Time: (80) minutes.

b) LEVEL 11.

Population: Students in Grade 1 (Spring) through Grade 2 (Fall).

Scores, 11: 8 multiple choice scores: Reading, Word Analysis, Vocabulary, Mathematics, Computation and Estimation, Total Reading, Total Mathematics, Total Battery; 3 constructed response scores: Response to Text, Writing, Dictation.

Time: (170) minutes for multiple choice; (50) minutes for constructed response.

c) LEVEL 12.

Population: Students in Grade 2 (Spring) through Grade 3 (Fall).

Scores, 13: 10 multiple choice scores: Reading, Word Analysis, Vocabulary, Writing Conventions, Mathematics, Computation and Estimation, Total Reading, Total Writing Conventions, Total Mathematics, Total Battery; 3 constructed response scores: Response to Text, Writing, Dictation.

Time: (205) minutes for multiple choice; (50) minutes for constructed response.

d) LEVEL 13.

Population: Students in Grade 3 (Spring) through Grade 4 (Fall).

Scores, 13: 10 multiple choice scores: Reading, Word Analysis, Vocabulary, Writing Conventions, Mathematics, Computation and Estimation, Total Reading, Total Mathematics, Total Writing Conventions, Total Battery; 3 constructed response scores: Response to Text, Writing, Dictation.

Time: (225) minutes for multiple choice; (50) minutes for constructed response.

e) LEVELS 14–19.

Population: Students in Grade 4 (Spring) and Grade 5 (Fall) through students in Grade 9 (Spring) and Grade 10 (Fall).

Scores, 12: 10 multiple choice scores: Reading, Vocabulary, Writing Conventions, Spelling, Mathematics, Computation and Estimation, Total Reading, Total Writing Conventions, Total Mathematics, Total Battery; 2 constructed response scores: Response to Text, Writing.

Time: (230) minutes for multiple choice; (40) minutes for constructed response.

f) LEVELS 20-22.

Population: Students in Grade 10 (Spring) through postsecondary students.

Scores, 14: 12 multiple choice scores: Informational Reading, Literary Reading, Vocabulary, Writing Conventions, Spelling, Pre-Algebra, Algebra, Computation and Estimation, Total Reading, Total Writing Conventions, Total Mathematics, Total Battery; 2 constructed response scores: Response to Text, Writing.

Time: (310) minutes for multiple choice; (40) minutes for constructed response.

Cross References: Reviews are scheduled for *The Twentieth Mental Measurements Yearbook*. For reviews by John O. Anderson and Louise M. Soares of the third edition, see 16:43; see T5:384; for reviews by John Hattie and Leslie Eastman Lukin of the second edition, see 13:44 (2 references); see also T4:371 (3 references); for a review by L. A. Whyte of an earlier edition, see 9:187.

[335]

Canadian Cognitive Abilities Test, Form K.

Purpose: "Designed to assess the development of cognitive abilities related to verbal, quantitative, and nonverbal reasoning and problem solving."

Population: Grades K–2, 3–12.

Publication Dates: 1970–1997.

Acronym: CCAT.

Scores: 4: Verbal, Quantitative, Nonverbal, Composite.

Administration: Group.

Price Data: Available from publisher.

Time: 90 minutes for Grades 3-12.

Comments: Canadian version of Cognitive Abilities Test, Form 5 (T4:537); statistical information for CCAT is available from publisher.

Authors: Original edition by Robert L. Thorndike and Elizabeth P. Hagen; Canadian version by Edgar N. Wright.

Publisher: Nelson Education Ltd. [Canada].

a) PRIMARY BATTERIES.

Population: Grades K–1, 2–3.

Levels, 2: 1, 2.

b) MULTILEVEL EDITION.
Population: Grades 3–12.
Levels, 8: A, B, C, D, E, F, G, and H.
Cross References: See T5:385 (3 references); for reviews by John O. Anderson and John Hattie of an earlier edition, see 12:61 (3 references); for reviews by Giuseppe Costantino and Jack A. Cummings of an earlier edition, see 10:42 (3 references); see also T3:361 (5 references) and 8:180 (2 references).

[336]
Canadian Dental Aptitude Test.
Purpose: "Designed to measure general academic achievement, comprehension of scientific information, perceptual ability, and manual dexterity."
Population: Canadian dental school applicants.
Publication Dates: 1946-2005.
Scores, 7: Reading Comprehension, Natural Sciences (Biology, General Chemistry, Total), Perceptual Ability Test, Chalk Carving Test, Academic Average.
Administration: Group.
Price Data: Available from publisher.
Time: 235(330) minutes in 2 sessions.
Comments: Based on the Dental Admission Testing program (604).
Authors: Department of Testing Services, American Dental Association.
Publisher: American Dental Association.

[337]
Canadian Test of Cognitive Skills.
Purpose: Designed to assess the academic aptitude important for scholastic success of students in grades 2 through 12.
Population: Grades 2–12.
Publication Dates: 1992–1996.
Acronym: CTCS.
Scores, 4: Sequences, Memory, Analogies, Verbal Reasoning.
Administration: Group.
Levels, 5: Level 1 (Grades 2–3); Level 2 (Grades 4–5); Level 3 (Grades 6–7); Level 4 (Grades 8–9); Level 5 (Grades 10–12+).
Price Data: Available from publisher.
Time: (52) minutes for Level 1; (55) minutes for Level 2–5.
Comments: A Practice Test (15–20 minute administration time) is available and is recommended to be administered at least one day prior to the actual testing session; adapted from Test of Cognitive Skills, Second Edition (T5:2677).
Author: Canadian Test Centre, Educational Services.
Publisher: Canadian Test Centre, Educational Assessment Services [Canada]
Cross References: For reviews by Martine Hébert and Susan J. Maller, see 13:45.

[338]
Canadian Tests of Basic Skills, Forms K and L.
Purpose: Constructed to measure growth in the fundamental skills crucial to day-to-day learning.
Population: Grades K–2, 3–8, and 9–12.
Publication Dates: 1955–1997.
Acronym: CTBS.
Scores, 12: Vocabulary, Reading Comprehension, Spelling, Capitalization, Punctuation, Usage, Reference Materials, Math Concepts & Estimation, Math Problems & Data, Math Computation, Science, Maps & Diagrams.
Administration: Group.
Price Data: Available from publisher.
Time: (280) minutes for Grades 3-8 Form K; (100) for Grades 3-8 Form L.
Comments: Scoring service available from publisher; statistical information available from publisher.
Authors: A. N. Hieronymus, H. D. Hoover, E. F. Lindquist, and others (original Level 5–14 tests); Dale P. Scannell and others (original Level 15–18 tests); Ethel King-Shaw and others (Canadian adaptation).
Publisher: Nelson Education Ltd. [Canada].
    a) PRIMARY BATTERY FORM K.
    Population: Grades K.1–1.5, K.8–1.9, 1.7–2.6, 2.5–3.5.
    Levels, 4: 5, 6, 7, 8.
    b) LEVELS 9–14 FORM K.
    Population: Grades 3–8.
    Levels, 6: 9, 10, 11, 12, 13, 14.
    c) LEVELS 15–18 FORM K.
    Population: Grades 9–12.
    Levels, 3: 15, 16, 17/18.
    d) LEVELS 9–14 FORM L.
    Population: Grades 3–8.
    Levels, 6: 9, 10, 11, 12, 13, 14.
Cross References: See T5:389 (14 references) and T4:375 (5 references); for reviews by John O. Anderson and by Jean-Jacques Bernier and Martine Hébert of an earlier edition, see 11:55 (9 references); see also T3:363 (15 references) and 8:11 (1 reference); for a review by L. B. Birch of an earlier edition, see 7:6.

[339]
The Capute Scales.
Purpose: "Designed to help the clinician determine the presence of atypical development in the two streams of cognitive development: language and visual motor skills."
Population: Ages 1 month to 36 months.
Publication Date: 2005.
Acronyms: CAT; CLAMS.
Scores, 3: Cognitive Adaptive Test Developmental Quotient, Clinical Linguistic & Auditory Milestone Scale Developmental Quotient, Full Scale Developmental Quotient.
Administration: Individual.
Price Data, 2015: $380 per complete test system including manual (115 pages), scoring sheets, and test kit; $30 per 20 scoring sheets; $325 per test kit including

laminated card of images, notepad, crayons, cloth, form board, plexiglass pane, pegboard, dowel, cup, plastic jar, 10 blocks, plastic ring, bell, and tote bag; $55 per manual.
Foreign Language Editions: Spanish and Russian editions available.
Time: (6-20) minutes for both scales.
Comments: Developmental quotients are provided for the Cognitive Adaptive Test and Clinical Linguistic and Auditory Milestone Scale. These are summed to yield a Full Scale Developmental Quotient for the entire scale.
Authors: Pasquale J. Accardo and Arnold J. Capute.
Publisher: Paul H. Brookes Publishing Co., Inc.
Cross References: For reviews by Stefan C. Dombrowski and William Tanguay and by Carlen Henington and Carmen D. Reisener, see 19:26.

[340]

CARE-2 Assessment: Chronic Violent Behavior Risk and Needs Assessment.

Purpose: Designed to identify youth "at risk for violence and aggression and to determine the interventions needed to prevent any future risk of aggression."
Population: Ages 6-19.
Publication Dates: 2003-2007.
Acronym: CARE-2.
Scores, 3: Risk, Resiliency, Total.
Administration: Individual.
Price Data, 2016: $39.95 including manual (2007, 35 pages) and one assessment booklet; $45 per 25 assessment booklets.
Time: (15-30) minutes.
Comments: Clinician obtains information for assessment through interviews with the youth, family, and caregivers; earlier edition entitled Child and Adolescent Risk Evaluation: A Measure of the Risk for Violent Behavior.
Author: Kathryn Seifert.
Publisher: Acanthus Publishing.
Cross References: For reviews by Randy G. Floyd and by Michael J. Furlong and Amy-Jane Griffiths, see 18:23; for reviews by Christopher A. Sink and Beverly J. Wilson and by Jamie G. Wood of the original edition, see 17:40.

[341]

Career Ability Placement Survey.

Purpose: Designed to measure abilities as they relate to careers.
Population: Junior high students through adults.
Publication Dates: 1976–1995.
Acronym: CAPS.
Scores: Scores in 14 COPSystem Career Clusters: Science-Professional, Science-Skilled, Technology-Professional, Technology-Skilled, Consumer Economics, Outdoor, Business-Professional, Business-Skilled, Clerical, Communication, Arts-Professional, Arts-Skilled,

Service-Professional, Service-Skilled; and 8 ability scores: Mechanical Reasoning, Spatial Relations, Verbal Reasoning, Numerical Ability, Language Usage, Word Knowledge, Perceptual Speed and Accuracy, Manual Speed and Dexterity.
Administration: Group.
Price Data, 2016: $111.50 per 25 self-scoring booklets; $24 per 25 self-interpretation profile and guides; $62.50 per 25 machine-scoring booklets; $18.25 per individual test forms; $50.25 per hand-scoring keys; quantity discounts available.
Foreign Language and Special Editions: Available in Spanish and large-print versions.
Time: (5) minutes per test; (50) minutes for entire battery.
Comments: Test publisher indicates materials have been updated; description will be updated when those test materials are received.
Authors: Lila F. Knapp and Robert R. Knapp.
Publisher: EdITS/Educational and Industrial Testing Service.
Cross References: See T5:395 (1 reference) and T4:382 (1 reference).

[342]

Career Anchors Self-Assessment: The Changing Nature of Work and Careers, Fourth Edition.

Purpose: Designed to help test taker think about how his or her motives, competencies, and values relate to career choices.
Population: Adults.
Publication Dates: 1990-2013.
Scores, 8: Technical/Functional Competence, General/Managerial Competence, Autonomy/Independence, Security/Stability, Entrepreneurial Creativity, Service/Dedication to a Cause, Pure Challenge, Lifestyle.
Administration: Individual.
Price Data, 2016: $21 per test booklet (2013, 22 pages) including instructions and scoring information; $76 per facilitator's guide; $36 per participant workbook.
Time: [10-15] minutes.
Authors: Edgar H. Schein and John Van Maanen.
Publisher: John Wiley and Sons, Inc.
Cross References: See T5:396 (1 reference); for reviews by Michael B. Bunch and Gary J. Robertson of an earlier edition, see 13:46.

[343]

Career & Life Explorer, 3rd Edition.

Purpose: Designed to "engage youths in planning their futures ... [and] to think about their career and life options from multiple perspectives."
Population: Middle school and high school students, particularly those in Grades 6-10.

Publication Dates: 2002-2011.
Acronym: CLE.
Scores, 6: Realistic, Investigative, Artistic, Social, Enterprising, Conventional.
Administration: Individual or group.
Price Data, 2016: $52.95 per 25 inventories; administrator's guide (2011, 20 pages) may be downloaded at no charge.
Time: (20-30) minutes.
Comments: Self-administered, self-scored, and self-interpreted.
Authors: Michael Farr.
Publisher: JIST/EMC Publishing.

[344]

Career Assessment Inventory™—The Enhanced Version.

Purpose: A vocational interest assessment tool focusing on careers requiring "various amounts of post-secondary education."
Population: Grade 9 through adult.
Publication Dates: 1975–1994.
Scores, 142: 6 themes (Realistic, Investigative, Artistic, Social, Enterprising, Conventional), 25 basic interest (Mechanical/Fixing, Electronics, Carpentry, Manual/Skilled Trades, Protective Service, Athletics/Sports, Nature/Outdoors, Animal Service, Mathematics, Scientific Research/Development, Medical Science, Writing, Creative Arts, Performing/Entertaining, Educating, Community Service, Medical Service, Religious Activities, Public Speaking, Law/Politics, Management/Supervision, Sales, Office Practices, Clerical/Clerking, Food Service), 111 occupational (Accountant, Advertising Artist/Writer, Advertising Executive, Aircraft Mechanic, Architect, Athletic Trainer, Author/Writer, Auto Mechanic, Bank Manager, Bank Teller, Barber/Hairstylist, Biologist, Bookkeeper, Bus Driver, Buyer/Merchandiser, Cafeteria Worker, Camera Repair Technician, Card/Gift Shop Manager, Carpenter, Caterer, Chef, Chemist, Child Care Assistant, Chiropractor, Computer Programmer, Computer Scientist, Conservation Officer, Cosmetologist, Counselor-Chemical Dependency, Court Reporter, Data Input Operator, Dental Assistant, Dental Hygienist, Dental Lab Technician, Dentist, Dietitian, Drafter, Economist, Elected Public Official, Electrician, Electronic Technician, Elementary School Teacher, Emergency Medical Technician, Engineer, Executive Housekeeper, Farmer/Rancher, Firefighter, Florist, Food Service Manager, Forest Ranger, Guidance Counselor, Hardware Store Manager, Hospital Administrator, Hotel/Motel Manager, Insurance Agent, Interior Designer, Janitor/Janitress, Lawyer, Legal Assistant, Librarian, Machinist, Mail Carrier, Manufacturing Representative, Mathematician, Math-Science Teacher, Medical Assistant, Medical Lab Technician, Military Enlisted, Military Officer, Musical Instrument Repair, Musician, Newspaper Reporter, Nurse Aide, Nurse/LPN,

Nurse/RN, Occupational Therapist, Operating Room Technician, Orthotist/Prosthetist, Painter, Park Ranger, Personnel Manager, Pharmacist, Pharmacy Technician, Photographer, Physical Therapist, Physician, Piano Technician, Pipefitter/Plumber, Police Officer, Printer, Private Investigator, Psychologist, Purchasing Agent, Radio/TV Repair, Radiologic Technician, Real Estate Agent, Religious Leader, Reservation Agent, Respiratory Therapy Technician, Restaurant Manager, Secretary, Security Guard, Sheet Metal Worker, Surveyor, Teacher Aide, Telephone Repair Technician, Tool and Die Maker, Travel Agent, Truck Driver, Veterinarian, Waiter/Waitress.
Administration: Group or individual.
Price Data, 2015: $42.05 per manual; $69.20 to $70.75 per starter kit including manual, 3 answer sheets with test items, and 3 administrations (online-based, software-based, or mail-in scoring).
Time: (35–40) minutes.
Author: Charles B. Johansson.
Publisher: Pearson.
Cross References: See T5:398 (4 references); for a review by James B. Rounds, see 10:43 (2 references); see also T3:367 (1 reference); for reviews by Jack L. Bodden and Paul R. Lohnes of an earlier edition, see 8:993.

[345]

Career Assessment Inventory™—Vocational Version.

Purpose: "A vocational interest assessment tool for individuals planning to enter occupations requiring 0-2 years of post-secondary training."
Population: Grade 9 through adult.
Publication Dates: 1973–1994.
Scores, 125: 2 Administrative Indices (Total Responses, Response Patterning), 4 Nonoccupational (Fine Arts-Mechanical, Occupational Extroversion-Introversion, Educational Orientation, Variability of Interests), 6 General Themes (Realistic, Investigative, Artistic, Social, Enterprising, Conventional), 22 Basic Interest Area Scales (Mechanical/Fixing, Electronics, Carpentry, Manual/Skilled Trades, Agriculture, Nature/Outdoors, Animal Service, Science, Numbers, Writing, Performing/Entertaining, Arts/Crafts, Social Service, Teaching, Child Care, Medical Service, Religious Activities, Business, Sales, Office Practices, Clerical/Clerking, Food Service), 91 Occupational Scales (Aircraft Mechanic, Auto Mechanic, Bus Driver, Camera Repair Technician, Carpenter, Conservation Officer, Dental Laboratory Technician, Drafter, Electrician, Emergency Medical Technician, Farmer/Rancher, Firefighter, Forest Ranger, Hardware Store Manager, Janitor/Janitress, Machinist, Mail Carrier, Musical Instrument Repair, Navy Enlisted, Orthodontist/Prosthetist, Painter, Park Ranger, Pipefitter/Plumber, Police Officer, Printer, Radio/TV Repair, Security Guard, Sheet Metal Worker, Telephone Repair, Tool/Die Maker, Truck Driver, Veterinary Technician,

Chiropractor, Computer Programmer, Dental Hygienist, Electronic Technician, Math-Science Teacher, Medical Laboratory Technician, Radiological Technician, Respiratory Therapeutic Technician, Surveyor, Advertising Artist/Writer, Advertising Executive, Author/Writer, Counselor-Chemical Dependency, Interior Designer, Legal Assistant, Librarian, Musician, Newspaper Reporter, Photographer, Piano Technician, Athletic Trainer, Child Care Assistant, Cosmetologist, Elementary School Teacher, Licensed Practical Nurse, Nurse Aide, Occupational Therapist Assistant, Operating Room Technician, Physical Therapist Assistant, Registered Nurse, Barber/Hairstylist, Buyer/Merchandiser, Card/Gift Shop Manager, Caterer, Florist, Food Service Manager, Hotel/Motel Manager, Insurance Agent, Manufacturing Representative, Personnel Manager, Private Investigator, Purchasing Agent, Real Estate Agent, Reservation Agent, Restaurant Manager, Travel Agent, Accountant, Bank Teller, Bookkeeper, Cafeteria Worker, Court Reporter, Data Entry Operator, Dental Assistant, Executive Housekeeper, Medical Assistant, Pharmacy Technician, Secretary, Teacher Aide, Waiter/Waitress).

Administration: Group.
Price Data, 2015: $42.05 per manual (1984, 152 pages); $70.75 per mail-in starter kit including manual and 3 answer sheets with test items to conduct and receive 3 interpretive reports; $69.20 per Q Local or Q-global starter kit including manual, 3 answer sheets with test items, and 3 administrations; $23.60 per 25 Q Local answer sheets with test items; $12.15 per Q Local or Q-global interpretive report; $7.35 per Q Local or Q-global profile report; $18.25 per mail-in interpretive answer sheets with test items; $13.80 per mail-in profile report; quantity discounts available for reports.
Foreign Language Editions: Spanish and French editions available.
Time: (30–45) minutes.
Author: Charles B. Johansson.
Publisher: Pearson.
Cross References: See T5:399 (5 references) and T4:385 (4 references); for reviews by Jerard F. Kehoe and Nicholas A. Vacc, see 11:59 (1 reference); see also T3:367 (1 reference); for reviews by Jack L. Bodden and Paul R. Lohnes of an earlier edition, see 8:993.

[346]

Career Attitudes and Strategies Inventory: An Inventory for Understanding Adult Careers.

Purpose: "Developed to assess some common attitudes, feelings, experiences, and obstacles that influence the careers of employed and unemployed adults."
Population: Adults seeking vocational counseling.
Publication Dates: 1992–1994.
Acronym: CASI.
Scores, 9: Job Satisfaction, Work Involvement, Skill Development, Dominant Style, Career Worries, Inter-

personal Abuse, Family Commitment, Risk-Taking Style, Geographical Barriers.
Administration: Individual.
Price Data, 2015: $156 per introductory kit including professional manual (1994, 53 pages), 25 inventory booklets, 25 hand-scorable answer sheets, and 25 interpretive summary booklets.
Time: (35) minutes.
Comments: Also includes Career Obstacles Checklist designed to assess "personal problems that may influence an individual's job situation."
Authors: John L. Holland and Gary D. Gottfredson.
Publisher: Psychological Assessment Resources, Inc.
Cross References: For reviews by Michael B. Brown and Richard T. Kinnier, see 13:47.

[347]

Career Beliefs Inventory.

Purpose: Designed to assist people to identify career beliefs that may influence their career goals.
Population: 13 years and above.
Publication Dates: 1991–1998.
Acronym: CBI.
Scores: 25 scores in 5 categories: My Current Career Situation (Employment Status, Career Plans, Acceptance of Uncertainty, Openness), What Seems Necessary for My Happiness (Achievement, College Education, Intrinsic Satisfaction, Peer Equality, Structured Work Environment), Factors That Influence My Decisions (Control, Responsibility, Approval of Others, Self-Other Comparisons, Occupation/College Variation, Career Path Flexibility), Changes I Am Willing to Make (Post-Training Transition, Job Experimentation, Relocation), Effort I Am Willing to Initiate (Improving Self, Persisting While Uncertain, Taking Risks, Learning Job Skills, Negotiating/Searching, Overcoming Obstacles, Working Hard).
Administration: Individual or group.
Price Data, 2015: $50 per manual, including review-only copy of form; $15 per individual Report; $15 per Report About Me; $2.40 per Transform Survey Hosting license (minimum 50); $2 per Remote Online Survey license (minimum 50); $2 per License to Reproduce (minimum 50).
Time: (20–30) minutes.
Author: John D. Krumboltz.
Publisher: Mind Garden, Inc.
Cross References: See T5:401 (3 references); for reviews by David L. Bolton and Robert M. Guion, see 12:64 (9 references).

[348]

Career Decision Scale.

Purpose: Developed to provide "an estimate of career indecision and its antecedents."
Population: Grades 9–12 and college.

Publication Dates: 1976–1987.
Scores: 2: Certainty, Career Indecision.
Administration: Group or individual.
Price Data, 2015: $85 per introductory kit including 50 test booklets and manual (1987, 28 pages).
Time: (10-15) minutes.
Authors: Samuel H. Osipow, Clarke G. Carney (test), Jane Winer (test), Barbara Yanico (test), and Maryanne Koschier (test).
Publisher: Psychological Assessment Resources, Inc.
Cross References: See T5:404 (47 references) and T4:390 (49 references); for reviews by Lenore W. Harmon and David O. Herman, see 9:194 (4 references).

[349]

Career Decision Self-Efficacy Scale.

Purpose: Designed to "measure an individual's degree of belief that he/she can successfully complete tasks necessary to making career decisions."
Population: College students.
Publication Dates: 1983–1994.
Acronym: CDMSE.
Scores, 6: Self-Appraisal, Occupational Information, Goal Selection, Planning, Problem Solving, Total.
Administration: Group.
Price Data: Available from publisher.
Time: Administration time not reported.
Comments: A 25-item short form is also available.
Authors: Nancy E. Betz and Karen M. Taylor.
Publisher: Mind Garden, Inc.
Cross References: For reviews by James K. Benish and Richard W. Johnson, see 14:62; see also T5:403 (1 reference).

[350]

Career Directions Inventory [Second Edition].

Purpose: "Designed to identify areas of greater or lesser interest from among a wide variety of occupations."
Population: Adolescents and adults ages 15 years or older.
Publication Dates: 1986–2003.
Acronym: CDI.
Scores, 49: 15 Basic Interest Scales (Administration, Art, Clerical, Food Service, Industrial Art, Health Service, Outdoors, Personal Service, Sales, Science, Teaching/Social Service, Writing, Assertive, Persuasive, Systematic); 7 General Occupational Themes (Realistic/Practical, Enterprising, Artistic/Communicative, Social/Helping, Investigative/Logical, Conventional, Serving); 27 Job Clusters (Computer and Mathematical Science, Science and Engineering, Electronic Technology, Medical and Health Care, Health Record Technology, Social Science, Banking and Accounting, Funeral Services, Architectural Technology/Drafting and Design, Word Processing and

Administrative Assistant, Public and Protective Services, Art, Social Services, Sales, Administration, Performing Arts, Communication Arts, Food Services, Education, Hospitality and Travel Services, Law Enforcement, Agriculture and Animal Science, Personal Care, Renewable Resource Technology, Marketing and Merchandising, Skilled Trades, Library Science).
Administration: Group and individual.
Price Data, 2015: $32 per examination kit including manual on CD (2003, 116 pages) and question and answer document for the Mail-in Extended Report; $25 per test manual on CD; $97-$107 per 10 Mail-in Extended Reports; $155 per SigmaSoft CDI for Windows Software installation package and 10 coupons; $8 per online password.
Time: 30 minutes.
Foreign Language Edition: French language materials available for mail-in scoring and software scoring.
Comments: Test may be administered through Mail-in Scoring, SigmaSoft for Windows Software, or via the Internet at www.sigmatesting.com.
Author: Douglas N. Jackson.
Publisher: SIGMA Assessment Systems, Inc.
Cross References: For reviews by Bert A. Goldman and Cleborne D. Maddux, see 17:37; for reviews by Darrell L. Sabers and Fredrick A. Schrank of an earlier edition, see 9:44.

[351]

Career Exploration Inventory: A Guide for Exploring Work, Leisure, and Learning, Fifth Edition.

Purpose: Designed to help participants explore and plan three major areas in their lives—work, leisure activities, and education or learning.
Population: Ages 18-73.
Publication Dates: 1992-2015.
Acronym: CEI.
Scores: 16 occupational categories: Agriculture and Natural Resources, Architecture and Construction, Arts and Communication, Business and Administration, Education and Training, Finance and Insurance, Government and Public Administration, Health Science, Hospitality/Tourism/Recreation, Human Service, Information Technology, Law and Public Safety, Manufacturing, Retail and Wholesale Sales and Service, Scientific Research/Engineering/Mathematics, Transportation/Distribution/Logistics.
Administration: Group.
Price Data, 2016: $60.95 per 25 12-panel foldout inventories; manual (2015, 64 pages) available as free download from test publisher's website.
Time: Administration time not reported.
Author: John J. Liptak.
Publisher: JIST/EMC Publishing.

Cross References: For reviews by Bert A. Goldman and Douglas J. McRae of the original (1992) edition, see 13:49.

[352]

Career Exploration Inventory EZ, Second Edition.

Purpose: Designed to "help people explore their career and job alternatives based on their interests."
Population: Working and unemployed adults, students, and youth.
Publication Date: 2011.
Acronym: CEI-EZ.
Scores, 16: Agriculture and Natural Resources, Architecture and Construction, Arts and Communication, Business and Administration, Education and Training, Finance and Insurance, Government and Public Administration, Health Science, Hospitality/Tourism/Recreation, Human Service, Information Technology, Law and Public Safety, Manufacturing, Retail and Wholesale Sales and Service, Scientific Research/Engineering/Mathematics, Transportation/Distribution/Logistics.
Administration: Group.
Price Data, 2016: $55.95 per 25 inventories; administrator's guide (10 pages) can be downloaded from test publisher's website.
Time: [20] minutes.
Comments: "Designed for self-administration and interpretation"; based on the Career Interest Inventory, Fourth Edition.
Author: John J. Liptak.
Publisher: JIST/EMC Publishing.

[353]

Career Matchmaker.

Purpose: An online self-assessment for "people who want to find careers that suit their interests."
Population: Grade 6 to adults.
Publication Date: 2011.
Scores: Results include 40 suggested careers.
Administration: Individual.
Price Data, 2011: $595 per English site license for one year; $795 per Spanish and English site license for one year; $795 per French and English site license for one year; multi-year discounts available.
Foreign Language Editions: Spanish and French versions available.
Time: Administration time not reported.
Comments: "Interface helps users satisfy five…career guidance needs: self-assessment, career exploration, post-secondary education planning, work search, and portfolio development."
Authors: Career Cruising.
Publisher: Career Cruising [Canada].

[354]

Career Motivation Profile.

Purpose: "Designed to determine which components, out of 17 identified motivators, one values as essential to his/her career fulfillment."
Population: Under age 17 through adult.
Publication Date: 2011.
Acronym: CAMOP.
Scores: 17 motivators: Achievement, Balanced Lifestyle, Change and Variety, Creativity, Financial Reward, Identity and Purpose, Improvement, Independence, Inspiration, Learning, Mobility, Power, Recognition and Appreciation, Social Factors, Stability, Status, Fun and Enjoyment.
Administration: Individual.
Price Data: Available from publisher.
Time: (20) minutes.
Comments: Self-administered online assessment. The test publisher provides clients with information about the methods and theoretical basis used in the development of the test as well as benchmarks for relevant industries and racial/ethnic group comparison data.
Author: PsychTests AIM, Inc.
Publisher: PsychTests AIM, Inc. [Canada].
Cross References: For reviews by Caroline M. Adkins and Bruce Biskin, see 19:27.

[355]

Career Occupational Preference System, Interest Inventory, Form R.

Purpose: Designed to measure interests as they relate to careers using simplified language.
Population: Grade 6 through high school.
Publication Dates: 1984–1992.
Acronym: COPS-R.
Scores: Scores in the 14 COPSystem Career Clusters: Science-Professional, Science-Skilled, Technology-Professional, Technology-Skilled, Consumer Economics, Outdoor, Business-Professional, Business-Skilled, Clerical, Communication, Arts-Professional, Arts-Skilled, Service-Professional, Service-Skilled.
Administration: Group.
Price Data, 2016: $39 per 25 self-scoring booklets/interpretation guides; $45.75 per 25 career guides.
Time: (20) minutes.
Authors: Lila F. Knapp and Robert R. Knapp.
Publisher: EdITS/Educational and Industrial Testing Service.
Cross References: See T5:414 (2 references and T4:399 (12 references).

[356]

Career Occupational Preference System, Intermediate Inventory.

Purpose: To measure career interests and provide a rating of interests based on knowledge of school subjects

and activities familiar to elementary and intermediate grade students.
Population: Elementary through high school with 4th grade reading level.
Publication Dates: 1981–1997.
Acronym: COPS-II.
Scores: Scores in 14 COPSystem Career Clusters: Science-Professional, Science-Skilled, Technology-Professional, Technology-Skilled, Consumer Economics, Outdoor, Business-Professional, Business-Skilled, Clerical, Communication, Arts-Professional, Arts-Skilled, Service-Professional, Service-Skilled.
Administration: Group.
Price Data, 2015: $36.25 per 25 combined self-scoring booklet & self-interpretation guides (quantity discounts available); $6 per manual.
Time: (15–20) minutes.
Comments: Test publisher indicates materials have been updated; description will be updated when those test materials are received.
Authors: Robert R. Knapp and Lila F. Knapp.
Publisher: EdITS/Educational and Industrial Testing Service.
Cross References: See T5:415 (1 reference).

[357]

Career Occupational Preference System— Professional Level Interest Inventory.

Purpose: Designed to measure career interest for those wanting to focus on the professional level careers.
Population: College and adult professionals, college-bound senior high school students.
Publication Dates: 1982–1989.
Acronym: COPS-P.
Scores: Scores in the 16 COPSystem Career Clusters: Service-Social, Service-Instructional, Science-Physical, Science-Medical/Life, Technology-Civil, Technology-Electrical, Technology-Mechanical, Outdoor-Agri-business, Outdoor-Nature, Business-Management, Business-Finance, Computation, Communication-Written, Communication-Oral, Arts-Design, Arts-Performing.
Administration: Group.
Price Data, 2016: $24.50 per 25 self-scoring booklets; $24 per 25 self-interpretation profiles and guides; $45.75 per 25 comprehensive career guides; $24.50 per 25 machine-scoring booklet & answer sheet combined; quantity discounts available.
Time: (15–20) minutes.
Comments: Test publisher indicates materials have been updated; description will be updated when those test materials are received.
Authors: Lisa Knapp-Lee, Lila F. Knapp, Robert R. Knapp.
Publisher: EdITS/Educational and Industrial Testing Service.

Cross References: For reviews by Mark A. Albanese and Jeffrey A. Jenkins, see 14:65; see also T5:416 (1 reference).

[358]

Career Orientation Placement and Evaluation Survey.

Purpose: Designed to measure values having a demonstrated effect on vocational motivation.
Population: Grade 7 through high school, college, and adult.
Publication Dates: 1981–1995.
Acronym: COPES.
Scores: Scores in 8 work values dimensions: Investigative v. Accepting, Practical v. Carefree, Independence v. Conformity, Leadership v. Supporting, Orderliness v. Flexibility, Recognition v. Privacy, Aesthetic v. Realistic, Social v. Reserved; and 14 COPSystem Career Clusters: Science-Professional, Science-Skilled, Technology-Professional, Technology-Skilled, Consumer Economics, Outdoor, Business-Professional, Business-Skilled, Clerical, Communication, Arts-Professional, Arts-Skilled, Service-Professional, Service-Skilled.
Administration: Group.
Price Data, 2016: $24.50 per 25 self-scoring booklets; $8.75 per 25 self-interpretation profile and guides; $25 per 25 booklet and answer sheets combined (quantity discounts available).
Time: (15–20) minutes.
Comments: Test publisher indicates materials have been updated; description will be updated when those test materials are received.
Authors: Robert R. Knapp and Lila F. Knapp.
Publisher: EdITS/Educational and Industrial Testing Service.

[359]

Career Profile +.

Purpose: "Predicts an individual's probability of success in an insurance sales career."
Population: Candidates for financial services sales representative positions.
Publication Dates: 1983-2000.
Administration: Individual.
Price Data: Available from publisher.
Foreign Language Editions: English-speaking Canada and French-speaking Canada editions available; U.S. Spanish and Chinese editions of nonstudent version are available.
Time: Untimed.
Comments: Profiles processed by publisher.
Author: LIMRA International.
Publisher: LIMRA International.
a) STUDENT CAREER PROFILE.
Population: High school–college student.
Scores: Career Profile rating.

Comments: Career Profile rating indicates probability of success in financial services sales; versions available for Financial Services Sales, Life and Health Sales, and Multiple-Line & Property-Casualty Sales.

    1) *Personality Assessment.*

    Scores: 4 personality characteristics: Persuasiveness, Energy, Achievement Drive, Initiative & Persistence.

b) NONSTUDENT CAREER PROFILE.

Population: Inexperienced candidates.

Scores: Same as above.

Comments: Versions available for Financial Services Sales, Life and Health Sales, and Multiple-Line & Property-Casualty Sales.

    1) *Personality Assessment.*

    Scores: Same as *a*-1 above.

Cross References: For reviews by Ayres G. D'Costa and Michael S. Trevisan, see 13:52.

[360]
Career Thoughts Inventory.

Purpose: Constructed to " identify an individual who is likely to need career counseling and identify the nature of the individual's career problems."

Population: Adults, college students, and high school students.

Publication Dates: 1994–1996.

Acronym: CTI.

Scores, 4: Decision Making Confusion, Commitment Anxiety, External Conflict, Total.

Administration: Group.

Price Data, 2015: $258 per introductory kit including manual (1996, 99 pages), 25 test booklets, and 10 workbooks (1996, 39 pages).

Time: (7–15) minutes.

Authors: James P. Samson, Jr., Gary W. Peterson, Janet G. Lenz, Robert C. Reardon, and Denise E. Saunders.

Publisher: Psychological Assessment Resources, Inc.

Cross References: For a review by Janet H. Fontaine, see 14:66.

[361]
Career Transitions Inventory.

Purpose: "Designed to assess the resources and barriers" experienced "in making a career transition."

Population: Adults.

Publication Date: 1991.

Acronym: CTI.

Scores, 5: Readiness, Confidence, Personal Control, Support, Independence.

Administration: Group.

Manual: No manual.

Price Data, 2015: $75 per packet of 10 inventories, interpretive booklet, and article describing the CTI's development; volume discounts available.

Time: Administration time not reported.

Author: Mary J. Heppner.

Publisher: Mary J. Heppner (the author).

Cross References: For reviews by Robert J. Drummond and Jean Powell Kirnan, see 15:45.

[362]
Career Values Card Sort.

Purpose: Defines factors that affect career satisfaction, the intensity of feelings about these factors, determines areas of value conflict and congruence, helps make career decisions.

Population: Adults.

Publication Dates: 1977-2005.

Scores: No scores.

Administration: Group or individual.

Price Data, 2016: $12 per one card sort deck and one worksheet; $15 per manual; $24 per pack of 24 worksheets.

Foreign Language Editions: Available in Arabic and Korean.

Time: (20–30) minutes.

Comments: Self-administered; worksheet includes career decision matrix; distributors are available in Canada, Australia, Egypt, and U.S. List of distributor information available online from test publisher.

Authors: Richard L. Knowdell.

Publisher: Career Research & Testing, Inc.

Cross References: For reviews by Esther E. Diamond and Richard T. Kinnier, see 13:53.

[363]
Careers for Me.

Purpose: Designed "to encourage students to think about their interests and the world of work around them."

Population: Grades K-9.

Publication Dates: 2000-2009.

Scores: Not scored.

Administration: Group.

Manual: No manual.

Author: Career Kids.

Publisher: Career Kids.

    a) CAREERS FOR ME JUNIOR.

Purpose: Designed to "start the process of career awareness with young children."

Population: Grades K-3.

Publication Date: 2000.

Price Data, 2010: $33.75 per 25 consumable folders; volume discounts available.

Foreign Language Edition: Spanish translation available.

    b) CAREERS FOR ME II.

Purpose: Designed to "encourage students to think about their interests and the world of work around them."

Population: Grades 3-7.

Publication Date: 2000.

Price Data: $36.25 per 25 consumable booklets (12 pages); volume discounts available.

Foreign Language Edition: Spanish translation available.

c) CAREERS FOR ME PLUS.

Purpose: Designed to "transition student to the next step in their career awareness and education."

Population: Grades 6-9.

Publication Date: 2009.

Price Data: $47.50 per 25 consumable booklets (24 pages); volume discounts available.

Foreign Language Edition: Spanish translation available.

d) CAREERS FOR ME SN.

Purpose: To assist special needs children in thinking about career interests.

Population: Lower functioning special needs students.

Publication Date: 2003.

Price Data: $33.75 per 25 consumable folders; volume discounts available.

[364]
Caregiver-Teacher Report Form.

Purpose: Designed "to assess behavioral/emotional problems and identify syndromes of problems that tend to occur together."

Population: Ages 1.5–5.

Publication Dates: 1997– 2000.

Acronym: C-TRF.

Scores, 10: Emotionally Reactive, Anxious/Depressed, Somatic Complaints, Withdrawn, Attention Problems, Aggressive Behavior; Internalizing, Externalizing, Total; DMS oriented scales: Affective Problems, Anxiety Problems, Attention Deficit/Hyperactivity Problems, Oppositional Defiant Problems, Pervasive Developmental Problems.

Administration: Group.

Price Data: Available from publisher.

Time: [10] minutes.

Comments: Ratings by daycare providers and preschool teachers.

Author: Thomas M. Achenbach.

Publisher: ASEBA Research Center for Children, Youth, and Families

Cross References: For reviews by Karen T. Carey and by Michael Furlong and Renee Pavelski, see 14:67.

[365]
Careprovider Aptitude Personality & Attitude Profile.

Purpose: Designed to examine "whether the personality traits and skills a person possesses match those required to excel in the caregiving field."

Population: Potential caregivers.

Publication Date: 2011.

Acronym: CAPAP.

Scores, 29: Overall Results, Emotional Strength, Fortitude, Impression Management, Interpersonal Skills, Work Abilities, Work Attitudes, Helpfulness, Empathy, Reaction to Stress, Discretion, Social Insight, Communication Skills, Assertive Communication, Diligence, Organization, Dependability, Attention to Detail, Efficiency, Self-Discipline, Comfort with Decision-Making, Physical Hardiness, Patience, Attitude Towards Honesty, Attitude Towards Safety, Attitude Towards Teamwork, Optimism, Social at Work, Acquiescence.

Administration: Individual.

Price Data: Available from publisher.

Time: (30) minutes.

Comments: Self-administered online assessment. The test publisher provides clients with information about the methods and theoretical basis used in the development of the test as well as benchmarks for relevant industries and racial/ethnic group comparison data.

Author: PsychTests AIM, Inc.

Publisher: PsychTests AIM, Inc. [Canada].

Cross Reference: For reviews by Richard Reilly and Keith F. Widaman, see 19:28.

[366]
Carey Temperament Scales.

Purpose: Designed to assess "temperamental characteristics in infants and children."

Population: Ages 1 month to 12 years-11 months.

Publication Dates: 1996–1998.

Acronym: CTS.

Scores: 9 categories of temperament: Activity, Rhythmicity, Approach, Adaptability, Intensity, Mood, Persistence, Distractibility, Threshold.

Administration: Individual.

Price Data: Available from publisher.

Time: [15–20] minutes for administration. 2-3 minutes for software scoring; 10-15 minutes for hand scoring.

Comments: Parent/caregiver ratings of infant and child temperament; also assesses the caregiver's overall general impression of each category of temperament and provides a general manageability score; measures the nine NYLS temperament dimensions; or use in research and in clinical work with parents of preadolescent children; five separate questionnaires are included in the series, based on age levels in early infancy, infancy, toddlerhood, early childhood and middle childhood. The test publisher has indicated there is a newer edition of this test; description will be updated when complete test materials are received.

Authors: William B. Carey, Sean C. McDevitt, Barbara Medoff-Cooper, William Fullard, and Robin L. Hegvik.

Publisher: Behavioral-Developmental Initiatives.

Cross References: For reviews by Aimee Langlois and E. Jean Newman, see 14:68.

[367]
Caring Relationship Inventory.

Purpose: Designed to "measure the ... elements of love or caring in human relationships."

Population: Premarital and marital counselees.

Publication Dates: 1966–1975.

Acronym: CRI.

Scores, 7: Affection, Friendship, Eros, Empathy, Self-Love, Being Loved, Deficiency Love.
Administration: Individual.
Price Data, 2016: $27.25 per 25 booklets (specify male or female); $17.50 per 50 profile sheets; $29.50 per hand-scoring stencils (set of 7); $12 per specimen set including a manual and one copy of all forms; $6.75 per manual.
Time: (40) minutes.
Author: Everett L. Shostrom.
Publisher: EdITS/Educational and Industrial Testing Service.
Cross References: See T4:408 (3 references); for reviews by Donald L. Mosher and Robert F. Stahmann, see 8:333 (5 references); for a review by Albert Ellis, see 7:561; see also P:31 (1 reference).

[368]

Carlson Psychological Survey.

Purpose: Developed to assess and classify offenders quickly and accurately.
Population: Adult and adolescent offenders.
Publication Dates: 1982–1997.
Acronym: CPS.
Scores, 5: Chemical Abuse, Thought Disturbance, Anti-Social Tendencies, Self-Depreciation, Validity.
Administration: Group or individual.
Price Data, 2015: $90 per examination kit including manual on CD (1982, 28 pages), 5 question and answer booklets, 5 scoring sheets, 5 profile sheets, and one machine-scorable question-and-answer document for an Extended Report; $25 per test manual on CD; $65 per 25 question-and-answer booklets; $72 per 25 response sheets (including 25 scoring sheets and 25 profile sheets); $76-$86 (depending on volume) per 10 machine-scorable question-and-answer sheets for Extended Reports; $155 per software package including installation package and 10 coupons for computer reports.
Time: 15 minutes.
Author: Kenneth A. Carlson.
Publisher: SIGMA Assessment Systems, Inc.
Cross References: See T4:409 (2 references); for a review by H. C. Ganguli, see 9:203.

[369]

The Carolina Curriculum.

Purpose: Designed as an assessment and intervention program for use with young children who have mild to severe disabilities.
Population: Birth to age 5.
Publication Date: 2004.
Scores: 5 domains: Cognition, Communication, Social Adaptation, Fine Motor, Gross Motor.
Administration: Individual
Price Data, 2015: $99.95 per 2-book set; $30 per 10 assessment and development progress charts; $150

per printable masters on CD-ROM; $54.95 per special bound book (specify level).
Foreign Language Edition: Spanish version available.
Time: 60-90 minutes (may be split into two sessions).
Comments: A criterion-referenced system that links assessment with intervention.
Authors: Nancy M. Johnson-Martin, Susan M. Attermeier, and Bonnie J. Hacker.
Publisher: Paul H. Brookes Publishing Co., Inc.
    a) THE CAROLINA CURRICULUM FOR INFANTS & TODDLERS WITH SPECIAL NEEDS, THIRD EDITION.
    Population: Birth to 36 months.
    Acronym: CCITSN.
    Price Data: $54.95 per special-bound book (512 pages).
    b) THE CAROLINA CURRICULUM FOR PRESCHOOLERS WITH SPECIAL NEEDS, SECOND EDITION.
    Population: 24–60 months.
    Acronym: CCPSN.
    Price Data: $54.95 per special-bound book (448 pages).

[370]

Carolina Picture Vocabulary Test (for Deaf and Hearing Impaired).

Purpose: "To measure the receptive sign vocabulary in individuals where manual signing [is] the primary mode of communication."
Population: Deaf and hearing-impaired children ages 4–11.5 years.
Publication Date: 1985.
Acronym: CPVT.
Scores: Total score only.
Administration: Individual.
Price Data, 2015: $84 per picture book; $41 per 50 record forms; $53 per manual (38 pages).
Time: (10-15) minutes.
Authors: Thomas L. Layton and David W. Holmes.
Publisher: PRO-ED.
Cross References: For additional information, see 11:62 (1 reference).

[371]

Carroll Depression Scales.

Purpose: Designed as a measure of depression; providing diagnostic as well as level of severity information.
Population: Ages 18 and older.
Publication Date: 1998.
Scores, 6: Major Depression, Dysthymic Disorder, Melancholic Features, Atypical Features, HDRS, Total.
Administration: Individual or Group.
Price Data, 2015: $96 per Technical Manual; $62 per preview version including 3 profile reports, 3 Brief profile reports, and V.5 getting started guide; $6 per profile report; $4 per Brief profile report.

Foreign Language Editions: Arabic, Chinese, Dutch, French, French-Canadian, German, Greek, Italian, Japanese, Russian, Slovakian, and Spanish available upon special request.
Comments: Interpretation by qualified professionals only.
Author: Bernard Carroll.
Publisher: Multi-Health Systems, Inc.
   a) CARROLL DEPRESSION SCALES.
   Acronym: CDS-R.
   Time: (20) minutes.
   Comments: A 52-item self-report measure.
   b) CARROLL DEPRESSION SCALE—REVISED.
   Acronym: CDS-R.
   Time: (10) minutes.
   Comments: A 52-item self-report measure; includes diagnostic index in addition to severity score provided by CDS.
   c) BRIEF CARROLL DEPRESSION INVENTORY.
   Acronym: Brief CDS-R.
   Time: (2) minutes.
   Comments: A 12-item self-report rapid screening measure of depressive symptoms.
Cross References: For a review by Susan M. Swearer, see 14:69.

[372]
CASAS Functional Writing Assessment [Picture Task].

Purpose: Designed to provide "teachers of ESL (English as a second language), ABE (adult basic education), and ASE (adult secondary education) at the adult or high school level with a means of assessing their students' writing skills in a functional, workplace, employability, and life skills context."
Population: Adult learners with beginning to advanced level writing skills.
Publication Dates: 2006-2010.
Acronym: FWA.
Score: Total score only.
Administration: Group.
Forms: 7 equivalent forms: 460, 461, 462, 463, 464, 465, 466.
Price Data, 2015: $360 per starter kit including manual (2006, 41 pages), Forms 460-463 (25 of each), and 100 picture task response and scoring sheets; $79 per manual; $75 per 25 laminated, reusable picture task prompts (Form 460, 461, 462, 463, 464, 465, or 466); $20 per 100 picture task response and scoring sheets.
Time: 30 minutes.
Comments: Forms 460-463 contain "functional life context" writing prompts; forms 464-466 contain "workplace-related prompts." Scorer training and certification required.
Author: CASAS.
Publisher: CASAS.
Cross References: Reviews are scheduled for *The Twentieth Mental Measurements Yearbook*.

[373]
CASAS Life and Work Listening Assessments.

Purpose: Designed "to measure English language learners' listening comprehension skills" for progress monitoring and evaluation.
Population: Adult English language learners.
Publication Date: 2012.
Scores, 3: Appraisal (optional), Pre-Test, Post-Test.
Administration: Group.
Levels, 3: A, B, C.
Forms, 6: 981L, 982L, 983L, 984L, 985L, 986L.
Restricted Distribution: Distribution restricted to agencies completing the CASAS Implementation Training.
Price Data, 2015: $490 per Testing Package with Appraisal, including Form 80 Appraisal Listening Test CD, 25 Form 80 Appraisal Reading Test Booklets, Form 80 Appraisal Test Administration Manual, Level A Form 981 CD, Level A Form 982 CD, Level A Forms 981 and 982 test booklets (25 each), Level B Form 983 CD, Level B Form 984 CD, Level C Form 985 CD, Level C Form 986 CD; $375 per package without Appraisal material; $50 per CD (Appraisal, Form 981, Form 982, Form 983, Form 984, Form 985, or Form 986); $44 per 25 Appraisal Form 80 answer sheets; $90 per 25 Appraisal Form 80 Reading Test Booklets; $90 per Level A CD and 25 Test Booklets (Form 981 or Form 982); $40 per 25 Level A test booklets (Form 981 or Form 982); $25 per Test Administration Manual (41 pages).
Time: (50) minutes.
Comments: May be administered via paper and audio CD or via computer.
Author: CASAS.
Publisher: CASAS.
Cross References: For reviews by Jorge Gonzalez and Heather Davis and by Stephen T. Schroth, see 19:29.

[374]
CASAS Life and Work Reading Assessments.

Purpose: Designed to "measure learning progress of members of the youth and adult education population in the content domain of reading."
Population: Youth and adult learners.
Publication Dates: 2005-2010.
Scores, 3: Appraisal, Pre-Test, Post-Test.
Administration: Group.
Levels, 4: A, B, C, D.
Forms, 12: 81, 82, 81X, 82X, 83, 84, 185, 186, 85, 86, 187, 188.
Restricted Distribution: Distribution restricted to agencies completing the CASAS Implementation Training.

Price Data, 2015: $70 per 25 Level A, Form 81; $75 per 25 Level A, Form 82; $75 per 25 Level A, Form 81X; $70 per 25 Level A, Form 82X; $70 per 25 Level B, Form 83; $70 per 25 Level B, Form 84; $70 per 25 Level C, Form 85; $70 per 25 Level C, Form 86; $70 per 25 Level C, Form 185; $70 per 25 Level C, Form 186; $70 per 25 Level D, Form 187; $70 per 25 Level D, Form 188; $25 per Test Administration Manual (2005, 22 pages); price information for technical manual (2010, 274 pages) available from publisher.

Time: (60) minutes.

Comments: An appraisal test is administered first to identify the appropriate level of pretest. The pretest is administered and the score from the pretest guides the choice of posttest. A chart for guiding pretest/posttest choice is provided in the administration manual. Students move up through the levels of testing as their skills develop. Includes test items based on the application of functional reading skills as found in realistic life-skill or workplace contexts. Available via both paper-and-pencil tests and computer-based delivery.

Author: CASAS.

Publisher: CASAS.

Cross References: For reviews by Zandra S. Gratz and by Darrell L. Sabers and Christine Calderon Vriesema, see 19:30.

[375]

Category Test.

Purpose: "Measures an individual's ability to perform in an ambiguous, problem-solving situation" and is intended to be used "in settings that require the assessment of brain damage and/or problem solving ability."

Population: Ages 9-15 (ICat); [Ages 16-69 (HCT, ACat, RCat)].

Publication Dates: 1989-2008.

Acronym: Cat.

Scores: Information available from publisher.

Administration: Individual.

Forms: 4 computer-adapted versions: Halstead Category Test (HCT), Adaptive Category Test (ACat), Russell Revised Short Form (RCat), Intermediate Category Test (ICat).

Price Data, 2015: $242 per V 7.0 kit including software CD, and software manual (2008, 104 pages).

Time: (30-40) minutes; "up to [95] minutes for impaired clients."

Comments: The Cat is composed of four computer-adapted versions administered depending on respondents' ages. The HCT is the full adult version of the Halstead Category Test; the ACat is a shortened version that uses "a subset of responses on items of [each HCT] subtest… to predict the respondent's final score for that subtest"; the RCat is a shortened version that eliminates one of the HCT subtests and reduces "half the number of items from most [other] subtests"; the ICat "is designed for

children"; software is Windows compatible; instructions available in visual and auditory form; each score is based on "the ability to discover and apply certain" problem-solving rules.

Authors: James Choca, Linda Laatsch, Dan Garside, Rahul Gupta, and James Fenstermacher.

Publisher: Multi-Health Systems, Inc.

Cross References: For reviews by Karen T. Carey and Catherine P. Cook-Cottone, see 18:24; for a review by Robert A. Leark of an earlier form, The Computer Category Test, see 15:62.

[376]

CERAD Behavior Rating Scale for Dementia, Second Edition.

Purpose: Designed to "assess the behavioral problems and psychiatric symptoms of individuals with no history of mental retardation who have or are suspected to have acquired cognitive deficits."

Population: Adults who have, or are suspected to have, acquired cognitive deficits.

Publication Dates: 1991–2001.

Acronym: BRSD.

Scores, 7: Depressive Symptoms, Inertia, Vegetative Symptoms, Irritability/Aggression, Behavioral Dysregulation, Psychotic Symptoms, Total Weighted Score.

Administration: Individual.

Price Data, 2015: $85 per test kit including manual; $75 per training video.

Foreign Language Editions: Available in Arabic, Chinese (Mandarin), French, Japanese, Korean.

Time: [20–40] minutes.

Comments: Informant report interview; short form available; may be administered via telephone.

Authors: James L. Mack and Marion Patterson.

Publisher: CERAD, Duke University Medical Center.

Cross References: For a review by Pamilla Ramsden, see 16:44.

[377]

CERAD (Consortium to Establish a Registry for Alzheimer's Disease) Assessment Battery.

Purpose: "To develop brief, standardized instruments for the assessment of patients with probable Alzheimer's disease."

Population: Patients with mild to moderate dementia.

Publication Dates: 1987-1995.

Acronym: CERAD.

Scores: Information gathered in 19 areas: Demographic, Drug Inventory, Informant History (Clinical, Blessed Dementia Rating Scale), Subject History, Short Blessed Test, Depression and Calculation and Language, Examinations (Physical, Neurological), Laboratory Studies, Diagnostic Impression, Neuropsychological Battery (Neuropsychology Battery Status, Verbal Fluency, Boston

Naming Test, Mini-Mental State Exam, Word List Memory, Constructional Praxis, Word List Recall, Word List Recognition, Constructional Praxis Recall).

Administration: Individual.

Restricted Distribution: Current use only with permission of CERAD.

Price Data: Price information available from publisher.

Foreign Language Editions: Neuropsychology measures available in Arabic, Bulgarian, Chinese (Cantonese, Mandarin), Dutch, French, Finnish, German, Italian, Japanese, Korean, Norwegian, Polish, Portuguese, Russian, and Spanish. Clinical assessment available in Arabic, Bulgarian, Chinese (Cantonese, Mandarin), French, Japanese, Portuguese, and Spanish.

Time: [50–70] minutes; 30-40 minutes for neuropsychology measures only.

Comments: Available in electronic format.

Authors: Consortium to Establish a Registry for Alzheimer's Disease, Albert Heyman (Principal Investigator).

Publisher: CERAD, Duke University Medical Center.

Cross References: For reviews by Frank M. Bernt and Gabrielle Stutman, see 12:66 (1 reference).

[378]

Certified Picture Framer Examination.

Purpose: "To provide professional recognition to competent individuals who are engaged in the business of picture framing."

Population: Individuals actively involved in the business of picture framing for one year.

Publication Dates: 1986–1993.

Acronym: CPF.

Scores: Total score only.

Administration: Group.

Price Data, 2016: $225 for members; $325 for nonmembers.

Time: (210) minutes.

Comments: Test administered on specific dates at centers established by the publisher.

Author: Certification Board of the Professional Picture Framers Association.

Publisher: Professional Picture Framers Association.

[379]

Change Abilitator.

Purpose: Designed to identify six types of concerns people experience when change is introduced into their organization.

Population: Teams.

Publication Date: 1995.

Scores, 6: Information, Personal, Operational, Impact, Collaboration, Transforming.

Administration: Group.

Price Data, 2016: $59.95 per leader's guide and questionnaire; $49.75 per 5 questionnaires.

Time: (15) minutes.

Comments: Revision of the Stages of Concern Questionnaire.

Author: LHE, INC.

Publisher: HRD Press, Inc.

Cross References: For a review by Cynthia A. Larson-Daugherty, see 14:70.

[380]

Chapin Social Insight Test.

Purpose: Designed to "assess the perceptiveness and accuracy with which an individual can appraise others and forecast what they might say and do."

Population: Ages 13 and over.

Publication Dates: 1960–1993.

Acronym: SCLT.

Scores: Total score only.

Administration: Individual or group.

Price Data: Available from publisher.

Time: (20–30) minutes.

Authors: F. Stuart Chapin (test) and Harrison G. Gough (manual).

Publisher: Mind Garden, Inc.

Cross References: For reviews by Frank M. Bernt and by Collie W. Conoley and Linda Castillo, see 16:45; see also T3:384 (5 references); for reviews by Richard I. Lanyon and David B. Orr of an earlier edition, see 7:51; see also P:34 (3 references).

[381]

Characteristics Scale.

Purpose: To determine teachers' views of important pupil characteristics and behaviors.

Population: Grades K-8.

Publication Dates: 1970-1975.

Scores: Total score only.

Administration: Group.

Manual: No manual.

Price Data: Available in the Southern Illinois University Archives at the Morris Library at Southern Illinois University.

Time: Administration time not reported.

Comments: Ratings by teachers; research instrument; may be used with or separately from Behavior Rating Scale (230).

Authors: Patricia B. Elmore and Donald L. Beggs.

Publisher: Patricia B. Elmore.

[382]

Checking Individual Progress in Phonics.

Purpose: Designed to "assess pupils' progress in phonics, identify their learning strategies and improve their skills."

Population: Ages 6 to 7.

Publication Date: 2001.

Acronym: ChIPPs.

Scores: Total words read correctly.
Administration: Individual.
Forms, 2 parallel forms: Version 1 and Version 2.
Price Data, 2016: A$139.95 per complete set teacher's manual (106 pages), test materials, and reproducible Individual, Class, and Pupil record sheets.
Time: Administration time not reported.
Authors: Sue Palmer and Rea Reason.
Publisher: Australian Council for Educational Research Ltd. [Australia].
Cross References: For reviews by Jorge E. Gonzalez and Rebekah Haynes and by William K. Wilkinson, see 17:38.

[383]

Checklist for Autism Spectrum Disorder.

Purpose: Designed as a "means of screening for and diagnosing children with autism across the entire autism spectrum."
Population: Ages 1 through 16.
Publication Date: 2012.
Acronym: CASD.
Score: Total score only.
Administration: Individual.
Price Data, 2015: $125 per kit including manual (33 pages) and 25 record forms; $58 per 25 record forms; $70 per manual; $70 per training DVD.
Time: (15) minutes.
Comments: "If used to diagnose autism, the CASD must be completed by a qualified clinician based on a semi-structured interview with the parent. If used for screening or research, the CASD can be completed independently by the parent."
Author: Susan Dickerson Mayes.
Publisher: Stoelting Co.
Cross References: Reviews are scheduled for *The Twentieth Mental Measurements Yearbook*.

[384]

Checklist for Child Abuse Evaluation.

Purpose: Designed as a "tool for investigating and evaluating children and adolescents who may have been neglected or abused."
Population: Children and adolescents.
Publication Dates: 1988–1990.
Acronym: CCAE.
Scores: 24 sections: Identification and Case Description, The Child's Status, Accuracy of Allegations by the Reporter, Interview with the Child (Physical/Behavioral Observations, Disclosure, Emotional Abuse, Sexual Abuse, Physical Abuse, Neglect), Events Witnessed or Reported by Others (Neglect, Emotional Abuse, Sexual Abuse, Physical Abuse), The Child's Psychological Status, History and Observed/Reported Characteristics of the Accused, Credibility of the Child—Observed/Reported, Competence of the Child—Observed/Reported, Con-

clusions (Consistency of Other Information, Allegation Motives, Substantiation of Allegations, Competence of the Child as a Witness, Level of Stress Experienced by the Child, Protection of the Child), Treatment Recommendations.
Administration: Individual.
Price Data, 2015: $168 per introductory kit including manual (1990, 19 pages) and 25 checklists.
Time: Untimed.
Author: Joseph Petty.
Publisher: Psychological Assessment Resources, Inc.
Cross References: For reviews by Denise M. DeZolt and Janice G. Williams, see 12:68.

[385]

Checklist of Adaptive Living Skills.

Purpose: "A criterion-referenced measure of adaptive living skills and a tool for program planning."
Population: Infants to adults.
Publication Date: 1991.
Acronym: CALS.
Scores, 4 areas: Personal Living Skills, Home Living Skills, Community Living Skills, Employment Skills; and 24 subscales: Socialization, Eating, Grooming, Toileting, Dressing, Health Care, Sexuality, Clothing Care, Meal Planning and Preparation, Home Cleaning and Organization, Home Maintenance, Home Safety, Home Leisure, Social Interaction, Mobility and Travel, Time Management, Money Management and Shopping, Community Safety, Community Leisure, Community Participation, Job Search, Job Performance and Attitudes, Employee Relations, Job Safety.
Administration: Individual.
Price Data, 2015: $166 per complete program including manual (62 pages) and 25 checklists; $100.45 per manual; $115.75 per 25 checklists.
Time: [60] minutes.
Comments: "Designed to be completed by a respondent who has had the opportunity to observe the learner in natural environments for a period of three or more months"; conceptually and statistically linked to two normative measures of adaptive behavior: Scales of Independent Behavior—Revised (SIB-R; 1794) and Inventory for Client and Agency Planning (ICAP; 1005); companion publication is the Adaptive Living Skills Curriculum.
Authors: Lanny E. Morreau and Robert H. Bruininks.
Publisher: Houghton Mifflin Harcourt.
Cross References: See T5:443 (1 reference); for reviews by Patricia A. Bachelor and James P. Van Haneghan, see 12:69.

[386]

ChemTest.

Purpose: Designed for selecting candidates with basic chemical knowledge.

Population: Applicants and incumbents for jobs requiring knowledge of chemical principles.
Publication Dates: 2001-2008.
Scores, 9: Physical Knowledge, Acids/Bases & Salts, Compounds, Elements, Miscellaneous, Chemical Knowledge, Mechanical Principles, Gases & Fluids, Total.
Administration: Group.
Price Data, 2015: $24 per consumable self-scoring test booklet or $26 per online test administration (minimum order of 20); $24.95 per manual (2014, 17 pages).
Time: Untimed; no longer than 60 minutes.
Comments: Self-scoring instrument; available for online test administration; test publisher advises changes in form names indicate minor revisions and updating.
Author: Roland T. Ramsay.
Publisher: Ramsay Corporation.
Cross References: For reviews by Ronald S. Landis and Stephen Stark of Form AR-C (2008), see 19:31; for a review by John Tivendell of an earlier edition, see 17:39.

[387]
Child Abuse/Husband Abuse/Wife Abuse/Girlfriend Abuse.

Purpose: Designed to compile an individual's history of abuse.
Population: Children, husbands, wives, girlfriends.
Publication Dates: 1991-2010.
Administration: Individual or group.
Forms, 4: Child Abuse, Husband Abuse, Wife Abuse, Girlfriend Abuse.
Manual: Instructions included with the worksheet.
Price Data: Available from publisher.
Time: Administration time not reported.
Author: Allan Roe.
Publisher: Diagnostic Specialists, Inc.

[388]
The Child Abuse Potential Inventory, Form VI.

Purpose: "To assist in the screening of suspected physical child abuse cases."
Population: Male and female parents or primary caregivers who are suspected of physical child abuse.
Publication Dates: 1980–1993.
Acronym: CAP Inventory.
Scores: 12 scale scores: Abuse scale (Distress, Rigidity, Unhappiness, Problems With Child and Self, Problems With Family, Problems With Others, Total Physical Child Abuse), Validity scales (Lie Scale, Random Response Scale, Inconsistency Scale), Loneliness, Ego-Strength, and 3 Response Distortion Indexes (Faking-Good, Faking-Bad, Random Response).
Administration: Individual administration recommended.
Price Data: Available from publisher.

Time: (12–20) minutes.
Author: Joel S. Milner.
Publisher: Psytec Inc.
Cross References: See T5:448 (30 references) and T4:429 (10 references); for reviews by Stuart N. Hart and Gary B. Melton, see 10:50 (5 references).

[389]
Child and Adolescent Memory Profile.

Purpose: Designed as "a norm-referenced test of memory and learning" for children, adolescents, and young adults.
Population: Ages 5 through 21.
Publication Date: 2015.
Acronym: ChAMP.
Scores, 16: Lists, Lists Delayed, Lists Recognition, Instructions, Instructions Delayed, Instructions Recognition, Objects, Objects Delayed, Places, Places Delayed, Verbal Memory Index, Visual Memory Index, Immediate Memory Index, Delayed Memory Index, Total Memory Index, Screening Index.
Administration: Individual.
Price Data, 2015: $385 per kit including 25 examiner record forms, stimulus book, and manual (152 pages); $110 per 25 record forms; $200 per stimulus book; $110 per manual.
Time: (35) minutes for full test, (10) minutes for two-subtest Screening Index.
Authors: Elizabeth M. S. Sherman and Brian L. Brooks.
Publisher: Psychological Assessment Resources, Inc.
Cross References: Reviews are scheduled for *The Twentieth Mental Measurements Yearbook.*

[390]
Child & Adolescent Symptom Inventory–5.

Purpose: Designed as "a behavior rating scale for DSM-5-defined emotional and behavioral disorders in youth."
Population: Ages 5–18.
Publication Dates: 1994–2013.
Acronym: CASI-5.
Scores, 22: ADHD, Oppositional Defiant Disorder, Conduct Disorder, Generalized Anxiety Disorder, Separation Anxiety Disorder, Disruptive Mood Dysregulation Disorder, Major Depressive Episode, Manic Episode, Dysthymic Disorder, Schizophrenia, Autistic/Asperger's Disorder, Anorexia, Bulimia, Posttraumatic Stress Disorder, Obsessive-Compulsive Disorder, Specific Phobia, Panic Disorder, Selective Mutism, Trichotillomania, Motor Tics, Vocal Tics, Substance Use.
Administration: Individual.
Forms, 2: Parent Checklist, Teacher Checklist.
Price Data, 2015: $119 per deluxe kit including screening and norms manual (2002, 179 pages), 25 parent checklists, 25 teacher checklists, 50 symptom count score sheets, and 50 symptom severity profile score sheets; $54 per screening and norms manual; $40 per 50 parent

checklists; $73 per 100 parent checklists; $40 per 50 teacher checklists; $40 per 50 Spanish parent checklists; $17 per 50 profiles for parent or teacher checklists.

Foreign Language Edition: Available in Spanish.

Time: [10–15] minutes.

Comments: Includes all of the items from the Child Symptom Inventory–4 and the Adolescent Symptom Inventory–4 in a single measure.

Authors: Kenneth D. Gadow and Joyce Sprafkin.

Publisher: Checkmate Plus Ltd.

Cross References: For a review by Kathryn E. Hoff and W. Joel Schneider of a previous version (2002) of the Child Symptom Inventory–4, see 16:46; for reviews by James C. DiPerna and Robert J. Volpe and by Rosemary Flanagan based on an earlier edition of the CSI-4 manual, see 15:47; for reviews by Stephen N. Axford and Patti L. Harrison of a previous version of the Adolescent Symptom Inventory–4, see 15:12.

[391]
Child Care Inventory.

Purpose: Developed to evaluate child care programs in order to improve program effectiveness or to determine the level of program implementation.

Population: Child care programs.

Publication Date: 1986.

Scores: 11 performance areas: Classroom Arrangement, Safety, Curriculum, Interacting, Scheduling, Child Assessment, Health, Special Needs, Parent Involvement, Outdoor Play, Infant Programs.

Administration: Individual.

Price Data, 2015: $22.95 per complete kit including test booklet and manual (32 pages).

Time: Administration time not reported.

Authors: Martha S. Abbott-Shim and Annette M. Sibley.

Publisher: Green Dragon Publishing.

Cross References: For reviews by Lisa G. Bischoff and Annette M. Iverson, see 12:71.

[392]
Child Development Inventory.

Purpose: "Designed to provide systematic ways of obtaining in depth developmental information from parents."

Population: Ages 1–3 to 6–3.

Publication Dates: 1968–1992.

Acronym: CDI.

Scores, 9: Social, Self Help, Gross Motor, Fine Motor, Expressive Language, Language Comprehension, Letters, Numbers, General Development.

Administration: Individual.

Price Data, 2015: $150 per starter set including 20 reusable test booklets, 75 answer sheets, 75 CDI profiles, and manual (2005, 44 pages) with scoring template; $45 per 20 test booklets; $45 per 75 answer sheets; $45 per 25 CDI profiles; $40 per manual with scoring template.

Foreign Language Edition: The test booklets are available in Spanish.

Time: [30–50] minutes.

Comments: Parent-completed questionnaire; formerly called the Minnesota Child Development Inventory.

Author: Harold Ireton.

Publisher: Child Development Review - Behavior Science Systems, Inc.

Cross References: For reviews by Jean Powell Kirnan and Diana Crespo and by Stephanie Stein, see 13:56; see also T4:436 (14 references); for a review of an earlier edition by Jane A. Rysberg, see 9:712; see also T3:1492 (6 references); for a review by William L. Goodwin, see 8:220 (3 references).

[393]
Child Development Review Parent Questionnaire.

Purpose: A brief screening inventory "designed to help identify children with developmental, behavioral, or health problems."

Population: 18 months to age 5.

Publication Date: 1994.

Acronym: CDR.

Scores, 5: Development (Social, Self-Help, Gross Motor, Fine Motor, Language), Possible Problems, Child Description, Parents' Questions/Concerns, Parents' Functioning.

Administration: Individual.

Price Data, 2015: $45 per 75 parent questionnaire/child development charts; $45 per manual (22 pages).

Foreign Language Edition: The Parent Questionnaire is available in Spanish.

Time: [5–10] minutes.

Comments: Parent-completed questionnaire; scores reflect parents' report of child's present functioning-development; Child Development Chart on back, can be used for observation or for parent report.

Author: Harold Ireton.

Publisher: Child Development Review - Behavior Science Systems, Inc.

Cross References: For reviews by Terry Overton and Gary J. Stainback, see 14:71.

[394]
Child Sexual Behavior Inventory.

Purpose: Designed as a "measure of sexual behavior in children"; used in the identification of sexual abuse.

Population: Ages 2–12.

Publication Dates: 1986–1997.

Acronym: CSBI.

Scores, 3: Developmentally Related Sexual Behaviors, Sexual Abuse Specific Items, Total.

Administration: Individual.

Price Data, 2015: $194 per introductory kit including manual (1997, 61 pages) and 50 test booklets.

Time: [10–15] minutes.

Comments: Completed by a child's primary caregiver.

Author: William N. Friedrich.

Publisher: Psychological Assessment Resources, Inc.

Cross References: For reviews by Frank M. Bernt and Thomas McKnight, see 14:72; see also T5:457 (1 reference).

[395]

Childhood Autism Rating Scale, Second Edition.

Purpose: "For identifying the presence of behavioral symptoms of autism to support the diagnostic process and also for research and classification purposes."

Publication Dates: 1986-2010.

Administration: Group.

Price Data, 2016: $193 per test kit including 25 Standard Version rating booklets, 25 High-Functioning rating booklets, 25 Questionnaires for Parents or Caregivers, and manual (2010, 109 pages); $46.25 per 25 Standard Version rating booklets; $46.25 per 25 High-Functioning rating booklets; $32.50 per 25 Questionnaires for Parents or Caregivers; $88 per manual.

Time: (5-10) minutes.

Comments: Questionnaires for Parents or Caregivers are included to aid in diagnostic decision-making and supplement data-gathering but are not scored.

Authors: Eric Schopler, Mary. E. Van Bourgondien, G. Janette Wellman, and Steven R. Love.

Publisher: Western Psychological Services.

a) CHILDHOOD AUTISM RATING SCALE, SECOND EDITION-STANDARD VERSION.

Acronym: CARS2-ST.

Population: Ages 2 through 5 (or older if estimated IQ below 79).

Scores, 16: Relating to People, Imitation, Emotional Response, Body Use, Object Use, Adaptation to Change, Visual Response, Listening Response, Taste, Smell, and Touch Response and Use, Fear or Nervousness, Verbal Communication, Nonverbal Communication, Activity Level, Level and Consistency of Intellectual Response, General Impressions, Total.

b) CHILDHOOD AUTISM RATING SCALE, SECOND EDITION-HIGH-FUNCTIONING VERSION.

Acronym: CARS2-HF.

Population: Ages 6 and over (with estimated IQ above 80).

Scores, 16: Social-Emotional Understanding, Emotional Expression and Regulation of Emotions, Relating to People, Body Use, Object Use in Play, Adaptation to Change/Restricted Interests, Visual Response, Listening Response, Taste, Smell, and Touch Response and Use, Fear or Anxiety, Verbal Communication, Nonverbal Communication, Thinking/Cognitive Integration Skills, Level and Consistency of Intellectual Response, General Impressions, Total.

Cross References: For reviews by Koressa Kutsick Malcolm and Mary J. McLellan, see 19:32; see T5:459

(40 references) and T4:439 (6 references); for reviews by Barry M. Prizant and J. Steven Welsh of the first edition, see 11:65 (4 references).

[396]

Childhood Trauma Questionnaire.

Purpose: Designed as a self-report inventory for "screening for histories of abuse and neglect."

Population: Ages 12 and up.

Publication Dates: 1997–1998.

Acronym: CTQ.

Scores, 5: Emotional Abuse, Physical Abuse, Sexual Abuse, Emotional and Physical Neglect and Minimization/Denial of Abuse.

Administration: Individual.

Price Data, 2015: $168 per complete kit including 25 READYSCORE answer documents and manual (1998, 76 pages); $67.65 per 25 READYSCORE answer documents; $110.70 per manual.

Time: (5) minutes.

Comments: A 28-item, self-report inventory.

Authors: David P. Bernstein and Laura Fink.

Publisher: Pearson.

Cross References: For reviews by Michael Furlong and Renee Pavelski and by Jonathan Sandoval, see 14:73; see also T5:460 (2 references).

[397]

Children's Academic Intrinsic Motivation Inventory.

Purpose: "To measure academic intrinsic motivation … defined as enjoyment of school learning characterized by an orientation toward mastery, curiosity, persistence, and the learning of challenging, difficult, and novel tasks."

Population: Grades 4–8.

Publication Date: 1986.

Acronym: CAIMI.

Scores: 5 scales: Reading, Math, Social Studies, Science, General.

Administration: Individual or group.

Price Data, 2015: $208 per introductory kit including 50 test booklets, 50 profile forms, and manual (24 pages).

Time: (20–30) minutes for individual administration; (60) minutes for group administration.

Comments: Self-report inventory.

Author: Adele Gottfried.

Publisher: Psychological Assessment Resources, Inc.

Cross References: See T5:464 (5 references); for a review by C. Dale Posey, see 10:54.

[398]

Childrens Adaptive Behavior Scale, Revised.

Purpose: Provides a means to gather information on the relevant knowledge and concepts requisite to adaptive functioning.

Population: Ages 5–11.
Publication Dates: 1980–2002.
Acronym: CABS.
Scores, 6: Language Development, Independent Functioning, Family Role Performance, Economic-Vocational Activity, Socialization, Total.
Administration: Individual.
Price Data, 2016: $34.95 per 25 student booklets; $14.95 per manual (1983, 42 pages); $14.95 per picture book, $59.95 per specimen set including 25 student booklets, picture book, and manual.
Time: (45–50) minutes.
Comments: Other test materials (e.g., coins, blocks, scissors, paper) must be supplied by examiner.
Authors: Richard H. Kicklighter and Bert O. Richmond.
Publisher: Green Dragon Publishing.
Cross References: See T4:442 (1 reference); for reviews by Kenneth A. Kavale and Esther Sinclair, see 10:55 (1 reference); for reviews by Thomas R. Kratochwill and Corinne R. Smith of the original edition, see 9:218; see also T3:395 (1 reference).

[399]
Children's Aggression Scale.
Purpose: Designed to "evaluate the nature, severity, and frequency of aggressive behaviors in children, distinct from those behaviors better characterized as oppositional/defiant or hostile."
Population: Ages 5-18.
Publication Dates: 2002-2008.
Acronym: CAS.
Scores, 11: Scale scores (Verbal Aggression, Aggression Against Objects and Animals, Physical Aggression, Use of Weapons, Total Aggression Index), Cluster scores (Provoked Physical Aggression, Initiated Physical Aggression, Aggression Toward Peers, Aggression Toward Adults, Aggression Against Family Members [Parent form only], Aggression Against Non-Family Members [Parent form only]).
Administration: Group.
Forms, 2: Parent (CAS-P), Teacher (CAS-T).
Price Data, 2015: $268 per introductory kit including professional manual (2008, 473 pages), 25 Parent rating forms, 25 Teacher rating forms, 25 Parent score summary forms/profiles, and 25 Teacher score summary forms/profiles; $60 per 25 Parent rating forms; $60 per 25 Teacher rating forms; $41 per 25 Parent score summary forms/profiles; $41 per 25 Teacher score summary forms/profiles; $90 per professional manual.
Time: (10-15) minutes.
Comments: Ratings by parents and teachers (multiple forms may be completed by multiple parents and teachers); Children's Aggression Scale Scoring Program (CAS-SP) offered separately.
Authors: Jeffrey M. Halperin and Kathleen E. McKay.

Publisher: Psychological Assessment Resources, Inc.
Cross References: For reviews by Jeffrey A. Atlas and David F. Ciampi, see 18:25.

[400]
Children's Apperception Test [2012 Revision].
Purpose: A projective "method of investigating personality by studying the dynamic meaningfulness of the individual differences in perception of standard stimuli."
Population: Ages 3–10.
Publication Dates: 1949–2012.
Acronym: C.A.T.
Scores: No scores.
Administration: Individual.
Editions, 3: Animal, Human, Supplement, plus Short Form.
Price Data, 2015: $142 per C.A.T.–A, C.A.T.–S, C.A.T.–H, manual (1991, 24 pages), 25 recording and analysis blanks (short form), and 10 copies of Haworth's Schedule of Adaptive Mechanisms in C.A.T. Responses; $43 per C.A.T.–A (black and white) or C.A.T.–H; $45 per C.A.T.–A (color) or C.A.T.–S; $24 per 25 recording and analysis blanks (short form); $22.50 per 30 Haworth's Schedules.
Foreign Language Edition: Spanish edition available.
Time: (15–20) minutes.
Authors: Leopold Bellak and Sonya Sorel Bellak.
Publisher: C.P.S. Publishing, LLC
Cross References: See T5:466 (1 reference); for reviews by Howard M. Knoff and Robert C. Reinehr of the 1991 revision, see 13:58 (4 references); see also T4:444 (4 references); for reviews by Clifford V. Hatt and Marcia B. Shaffer of an earlier edition, see 9:219 (1 reference); see also T3:396 (1 reference), T2:1451 (23 references), and P:419 (18 references); for reviews by Bernard L. Murstein and Robert D. Wirt, see 6:206 (19 references); for reviews by Douglas T. Keeny and Albert I. Rabin, see 5:126 (15 references); for reviews by John E. Bell and L. Joseph Stone and excerpted reviews by M. M. Genn, Herbert Herman, Robert R. Holt, Laurance F. Shaffer, and Adolf G. Woltmann, see 4:103 (2 references).

[401]
Children's Auditory Verbal Learning Test-2.
Purpose: Constructed to "measure auditory verbal learning and memory abilities" in children.
Population: Ages 6-6 to 17-11.
Publication Dates: 1988–1993.
Acronym: CAVLT-2.
Scores, 6: Immediate Memory Span, Level of Learning, Immediate Recall, Delayed Recall, Recognition Accuracy, Total Intrusions.

Administration: Individual.
Price Data, 2015: $136 per introductory kit including 25 test booklets and professional manual (1993, 68 pages).
Time: (25–30) minutes.
Comments: Orally administered.
Author: Jack L. Talley.
Publisher: Psychological Assessment Resources, Inc.
Cross References: For reviews by John O. Anderson and Sherwyn Morreale, see 12:76.

[402]

Children's Category Test.

Purpose: "Designed to assess non-verbal concept formation, ability to benefit from verbal feedback to alter problem solving behavior and abstract reasoning."
Population: Ages 5-0 to 16-11.
Publication Date: 1993.
Acronym: CCT.
Scores, 6: Subtest I, Subtest II, Subtest III, Subtest IV, Subtest V, Total.
Administration: Individual.
Levels, 2: Level 1 (Ages 5 to 8), Level 2 (Ages 9 to 16).
Price Data, 2015: $485 per complete kit including manual (72 pages), 25 Level 1 record forms, 25 Level 2 record forms, stimulus booklets, and color response cards (1 for each level); $55 per 25 record forms; $103 per manual; $163 per stimulus book and card (specify 1 or 2).
Time: (15–20) minutes.
Author: Thomas Boll.
Publisher: Pearson.
Cross References: For reviews by Mark D. Shriver and Nicholas A. Vacc, see 13:59.

[403]

Children's Color Trails Test.

Purpose: "Designed to provide an easily administered and objectively scored measure of alternating and sustained visual attention, sequencing, psychomotor speed, cognitive flexibility, and inhibition-disinhibition."
Population: Ages 8–16.
Publication Dates: 1989–2003.
Acronym: CCTT.
Scores, 6: Time Scores, Prompt Scores, Near-Miss Scores, Error Scores (Number Sequence Errors, Color Sequence Errors), Interference Index.
Subtest: 2: CCTT-1, CCTT-2.
Administration: Individual.
Forms, 4: K, X, Y, Z.
Price Data, 2015: $196 per Introductory kit including professional manual (2003, 81 pages), 50 record forms, and 50 copies of CCTT Form K, Parts 1 & 2.
Time: (5–7) minutes.
Comments: Also called Kid's Color Trails, Kiddie Color Trails, K Color Trails; modeled after Color Trails Test.
Authors: Antolin M. Llorente, Jane Williams, Paul Satz, and Louis F. D'Elia.

Publisher: Psychological Assessment Resources, Inc.
Cross References: For reviews by Andrew S. Davis and W. Holmes Finch and by Shawn Powell and Michelle A. Butler, see 16:47.

[404]

Children's Communication Checklist-2: United States Edition.

Purpose: "Designed to assess children's communication skills in the areas of pragmatics, syntax, morphology, semantics, and speech."
Population: Ages 4-16.
Publication Date: 2006.
Acronym: CCC-2.
Scores, 12: 10 communication domains: Speech, Syntax, Semantics, Coherence, Initiation, Scripted Language, Context, Nonverbal Communication, Social Relations, Interests; plus General Communication Composite, Social Interaction Difference Index.
Administration: Individual.
Price Data, 2015: $193.75 per complete kit including manual (2006, 112 pages), 25 caregiver response forms, 25 scoring worksheets, and scoring CD; $73.80 per manual; $46.15 per 25 caregiver response forms; $26.65 per 25 scoring worksheets.
Time: (5-10) minutes.
Comments: Scaled scores, general communication composite, social interaction difference index, confidence intervals, and percentile ranks are provided for each scale score.
Author: D. V. M. Bishop.
Publisher: Pearson.
Cross References: For reviews by Rebecca McCauley and Roger L. Towne, see 18:26.

[405]

Children's Depression Inventory 2nd Edition.

Purpose: Designed to provide "comprehensive multi-rater assessment of depressive symptoms in children."
Population: Ages 7-17.
Publication Dates: 1977-2011.
Acronym: CDI 2.
Scores, 14: Self-Report Full-Length-7: Total Score, Emotional Problems Scale Score, Functional Problems Scale Score, Negative Mood/Physical Symptoms Subscale Score, Negative Self-Esteem Subscale Score, Ineffectiveness Subscale Score, Interpersonal Problems Subscale Score; Self-Report Short-1: Total Score; Parent Report-3: Total Score, Emotional Problems Scale Score, Functional Problems Scale Score; Teacher Report-3: Total Score, Emotional Problems Scale Score, Functional Problems Scale Score.
Administration: Group.

Forms, 4: Self-Report Full-Length, Self-Report Short, Parent Report, Teacher Report.

Price Data, 2015: $399 per complete software kit including manual (2011, 172 pages), Software Scoring Installation, 25 self-report response forms, 25 self-report short response forms, 25 parent response forms, and 25 teacher response forms; $88 per technical manual; $289 per handscored kit including manual, 25 self-report QuikScore forms, 25 self-report short QuikScore forms, 25 parent QuikScore forms, and 25 teacher QuikScore forms.

Foreign Language Edition: Available in Spanish online.

Time: (15) minutes for Self-Report Full-Length; (5) minutes for Self-Report Short; (10) minutes for Parent Report; (5) minutes for Teacher Report.

Comments: This is a multi-rater assessment; available in paper-and-pencil and online administration and scoring.

Authors: Maria Kovacs and MHS Staff.

Publisher: Multi-Health Systems, Inc.

Cross References: For reviews by Jeffrey A. Atlas and Renée M. Tobin, see 19:33; for reviews by Janet F. Carlson and Stephen J. Freeman of the 2003 update, see 17:41; see also T5:472 (235 references) and T4:450 (71 references); for reviews by Michael G. Kavan and Howard M. Knoff of the first edition, see 11:66 (63 references).

[406]

Children's Depression Rating Scale, Revised.

Purpose: Constructed as a "screening instrument, diagnostic tool, and severity measure of depression in children."

Population: Ages 6–12

Publication Date: 1996.

Acronym: CDRS-R.

Scores: Total score only.

Administration: Group.

Price Data, 2016: $118 per complete kit including manual (91 pages) and 25 administration booklets; $52.50 per 25 administration booklets; $72 per manual.

Time: (15–20) minutes.

Comments: Ratings by health care professionals.

Authors: Elva O. Poznanski and Hartmut B. Mokros.

Publisher: Western Psychological Services.

Cross References: For reviews by E. Thomas Dowd and Donald Lee Stovall, see 14:74; see also T5:473 (8 references).

[407]

Children's Interview for Psychiatric Syndromes.

Purpose: Designed to identify "symptoms of 20 common Axis I psychiatric disorders in children and adolescents."

Population: Ages 6–18.

Publication Date: 1999.

Acronym: ChIPS.

Scores, 20: Attention-Deficit/Hyperactivity Disorder, Oppositional Defiant Disorder, Conduct Disorder, Substance Abuse, Specific Phobia, Social Phobia, Separation Anxiety Disorder, Generalized Anxiety Disorder, Obsessive-Compulsive Disorder, Acute Stress Disorder, Posttraumatic Stress Disorder, Anorexia, Bulimia, Depressive Episode, Dysthymic Disorder, Manic Episode, Hypomanic Episode, Enuresis, Encopresis, Schizophrenia/Psychosis.

Administration: Individual.

Price Data, 2016: $62 per administration manual (60 pages); $89 per reusable interview administration booklet (30 pages); $61 per 20 scoring forms; $41.95 per 20 report forms; $236 per starter kit.

Time: Administration time not reported.

Authors: Elizabeth B. Weller, Ronald A. Weller, Mary A. Fristad, and Marijo Teare Rooney.

Publisher: American Psychiatric Publishing, Inc.

Cross References: For reviews by Janet F. Carlson and R. Joel Farrell II, see 15:48.

[408]

Children's Inventory of Anger.

Purpose: Designed "to measure aspects of a youngster's experience of anger."

Population: Ages 6–16.

Publication Date: 2000.

Acronym: ChIA.

Scores, 6: Frustration, Physical Aggression, Peer Relationship, Authority Relations, Total, plus Inconsistent Responding Validity Index.

Administration: Group or individual.

Price Data, 2016: $118 per complete kit including 25 autoscore answer forms, and manual; $52.50 per 25 autoscore answer forms; $72 per manual; $167 per CD-ROM that offers scoring for 25 uses; $20.50 per PC answer sheet pads of 100.

Foreign Language Editions: Available in Italian and Korean.

Time: 10 minutes.

Comments: Self-report inventory.

Authors: W. Michael Nelson III and A. J. Finch, Jr.

Publisher: Western Psychological Services.

Cross References: For reviews by Theresa Volpe-Johnstone and Delores D. Walcott, see 15:49.

[409]

Children's Measure of Obsessive-Compulsive Symptoms.

Purpose: Designed to provide an "objective assessment and quantification of the subjective experience of children and adolescents with both overt and covert behavior problems related to obsessions or compulsions at either a subclinical or clinical level."

Population: Ages 8-19.

Publication Date: 2010.

Acronym: CMOCS.
Scores, 10: Defensiveness, Inconsistent Responding, Fear of Contamination, Rituals, Intrusive Thoughts, Checking, Fear of Mistakes and Harm, Picking/Slowing, Impact, Total.
Administration: Group.
Price Data, 2016: $123.50 per complete kit including 25 AutoScore forms and manual (62 pages); $52.50 per 25 AutoScore forms; $77 per manual.
Time: (10-15) minutes.
Authors: Cecil R. Reynolds and Ronald B. Livingston.
Publisher: Western Psychological Services.
Cross References: For reviews by Annette S. Kluck and Kelly Brey Love, see 19:34.

[410]
Children's Memory Scale.

Purpose: "Comprehensive assessment of visual/verbal learning and memory skills" in children and adolescents.
Population: Ages 5–16.
Publication Dates: 1997–1998.
Acronym: CMS.
Scores, 34: 14 Core Battery Subtest Scores: Dot Locations (Learning, Total Score, Long Delay); Stories (Immediate, Delayed, Delayed Recognition); Faces (Immediate, Delayed); Word Pairs (Learning, Total Score, Long Delay, Delayed Recognition); Numbers (Total Score); Sequences (Total Score); 6 supplemental scores: Dot Locations (Short Delay), Stories (Immediate Thematic, Delayed Thematic), Word Pairs (Immediate), Numbers (Forward, Backward); 6 Supplemental scores from 3 Supplemental Subtests: Word Lists (Learning, Delayed, Delayed Recognition), Picture Locations (Total Score), Family Pictures (Immediate, Delayed); 8 Indexes: Visual Immediate, Visual Delayed, Verbal Immediate, Verbal Delayed, General Memory, Attention/Concentration, Learning, Delayed Recognition.
Administration: Individual.
Levels, 2: 5–8, 9–16.
Price Data, 2015: $476 per complete kit including manual (1997, 288 pages), 25 record forms for both age levels, 2 stimulus booklets, 5 family picture cards, response grid, and 8 chips; $81 per 25 record forms (ages 5-8); $91 per 25 record forms (ages 9-16); $166 per manual; $615 per computer scoring assistant.
Time: (20–50) minutes.
Author: Morris J. Cohen.
Publisher: Pearson.
Cross References: For reviews by Scott A. Napolitano and Margot B. Stein, see 14:75.

[411]
Children's Organizational Skills Scales.

Purpose: Measures "how children organize their time, materials, and actions to accomplish important tasks at home and school."

Population: Ages 8-13.
Publication Date: 2009.
Acronym: COSS.
Scores, 15: 5 scores per form: Task Planning, Organized Actions, Memory and Materials Management, Total, Inconsistency Index (COSS-Parent & COSS-Teacher only), Positive Impression (COSS-Child only).
Administration: Individual or group.
Forms, 3: COSS-Parent, COSS-Teacher, and COSS-Child.
Price Data, 2015: $219 per complete handscored kit including 25 Parent/Teacher/Child QuikScore forms and manual (2009, 153 pages); $329 per complete scoring software kit including 25 Parent/Teacher/Child response forms, manual, and unlimited use scoring software; $279 per online kit including 25 Parent/Teacher/ Child online forms, and manual; $55 per 25 COSS-Parent, COSS-Teacher or COSS-Child QuikScore forms; $55 per 25 COSS-Parent, COSS-Teacher or COSS-Child Response forms; $3 per COSS-Parent, COSS-Teacher, or COSS-Child online form; $69 per manual; $121 per COSS scoring software (unlimited use).
Time: (20) minutes.
Comments: Global assessment of overall organizational difficulty (COSS-Teacher only) and Impairment Questions (COSS-Teacher & COSS-Parent only) are interpreted qualitatively; ratings by teachers, parents, and child (self-rating); available online and in paper-and-pencil format; forms can be scored by hand, using the COSS scoring software, or using the COSS online program. Online subscription option is available.
Authors: Howard Abikoff and Richard Gallagher.
Publisher: Multi-Health Systems, Inc.
Cross References: For reviews by Michael S. Matthews and Rayne A. Sperling, see 18:27.

[412]
Children's Personality Questionnaire.

Purpose: Designed to measure personality traits to predict and evaluate the course of personal, social, and academic development.
Population: Ages 8–12.
Publication Dates: 1959–1985.
Acronym: CPQ.
Scores, 18: 14 Primary Factors: Warmth, Abstract Thinking, Emotional Stability, Excitability, Dominance, Enthusiasm, Conformity, Boldness, Sensitivity, Withdrawal, Shrewdness, Apprehension, Self-Discipline, Tension; 4 Second Order Factors: Extraversion, Anxiety, Tough Poise, Independence.
Administration: Group or individual.
Forms: Parallel forms available.
Price Data: Available from publisher.
Time: (30–60) minutes per form.
Comments: Test booklet is titled "What You Do and What You Think."

Authors: Rutherford B. Porter and Raymond B. Cattell.
Publisher: Institute for Personality and Ability Testing, Inc. (IPAT)
Cross References: For reviews by Rosa A. Hagin and Terry A. Stinnett, see 13:60 (3 references); see also T4:454 (9 references); for reviews by Steven Klee and Howard M. Knoff of an earlier edition, see 9:222 (11 references); for a review by Harrison G. Gough, see 8:520 (46 references); see also T3:1129 (60 references) and P:38 (14 references); for reviews by Anne Anastasi, by Wilbur L. Layton, and by Robert D. Wirt of the 1963 edition, see 6:122 (2 references).

[413]
Children's Problems Checklist.
Purpose: "To identify relevant problems, establish rapport, and provide written documentation of presenting problems consistent with community standards of care."
Population: Ages 5-12.
Publication Date: 1985.
Acronym: CPC.
Scores: 11 areas: Emotions, Self-Concept, Peers and Play, School, Language and Thinking, Concentration and Organization, Activity Level and Motor Control, Behavior, Values, Habits, Health.
Administration: Individual or group.
Manual: No manual.
Price Data, 2015: $62 per package of 50.
Time: (10-20) minutes.
Comments: Ratings by parent or guardian.
Author: John A. Schinka.
Publisher: Psychological Assessment Resources, Inc.
Cross References: For a review by Wayne C. Piersel, see 10:56.

[414]
Children's Psychological Processes Scale.
Purpose: An Internet-based teacher rating scale designed "to facilitate the identification of psychological processing deficits in children referred for a learning disability evaluation."
Population: Ages 5-0 to 12-11.
Publication Date: 2012.
Acronym: CPPS.
Scores, 12: Attention, Auditory Processing, Executive Functions, Fine Motor, Fluid Reasoning, Long-Term Recall, Oral Language, Phonological Processing, Processing Speed, Visual-Spatial Processing, Working Memory, General Processing Ability.
Administration: Individual.
Price Data, 2016: $179 per introductory kit including printed manual (87 pages) and 50 online reports and rating forms; $159 per introductory kit including PDF manual and 50 online reports and rating forms; $62 per 25 online reports and rating forms (volume discounts available); $39 per PDF manual; $59 per printed manual.

Time: (12-15) minutes.
Author: Milton J. Dehn.
Publisher: Schoolhouse Educational Services, LLC.
Cross References: For a review by Ronald A. Madle, see 19:35.

[415]
Children's PTSD Inventory: A Structured Interview for Diagnosing Posttraumatic Stress Disorder.
Purpose: "Designed for the identification and assessment of posttraumatic stress disorder in children and adolescents."
Population: Ages 6–18.
Publication Date: 2004.
Scores, 7: Exposure, Situational Reactivity, Reexperiencing, Avoidance and Numbing, Increased Arousal, Significant Distress, Total.
Administration: Individual.
Price Data, 2015: $164 per complete kit including manual (52 pages) and 25 inventory forms; $71.50 per 25 inventory forms; $99 per manual.
Foreign Language Editions: Inventory form is available in Spanish and Canadian French.
Time: (5–20) minutes.
Comments: Five overall diagnostic categories (PTSD Negative, Acute PTSD, Chronic PTSD, Delayed Onset PTSD, or No Diagnosis) provided.
Author: Philip A. Saigh.
Publisher: Pearson.
Cross References: For reviews by Robert Christopher and by Beth Doll and Allison Osborn, see 17:42.

[416]
The Children's Test of Nonword Repetition.
Purpose: To assess short term memory in children.
Population: Ages 4–8.
Publication Date: 1996.
Acronym: CN REP.
Scores: Total score only.
Administration: Individual.
Price Data, 2015: £105 per complete set including record forms, CD, and manual (29 pages); £42.50 per 25 record forms.
Time: [15] minutes.
Authors: Susan Gathercole and Alan Baddeley.
Publisher: Pearson Assessment [England].
Cross References: For reviews by Patrick Grehan and Manuel Martinez-Pons, see 16:48.

[417]
Children's Version of the Family Environment Scale.
Purpose: "Provides a measure of young children's subjective appraisal of their family environment."

Population: Ages 5–12.
Publication Date: 1984.
Acronym: CV/FES.
Scores, 10: Cohesion, Expressiveness, Conflict, Independence, Achievement Orientation, Intellectual-Cultural Orientation, Active-Recreational Orientation, Moral-Religious Emphasis, Organization, Control.
Administration: Group.
Price Data, 2016: $106 per complete kit; $24.50 per manual (15 pages); $30.50 per 5 (reusable) test answer booklets; $52.50 per 25 profiles; $34 per 25 examiner's worksheets; $34 per 25 individual student answer sheets.
Time: Administration time not reported.
Comments: Downward extension of the Family Environment Scale (800).
Authors: Christopher J. Pino, Nancy Simons, and Mary Jane Slawinowski.
Publisher: Slosson Educational Publications, Inc.
Cross References: For a review by Nancy A. Busch-Rossnagel, see 10:57.

[418]

Choosing Outcomes & Accommodations for Children (COACH): A Guide to Educational Planning for Students with Disabilities, Third Edition.

Purpose: Designed to help teams plan individualized education programs for students with disabilities.
Population: Students ages 3-21 with disabilities who have intensive special educational needs.
Publication Dates: 1998-2011.
Acronym: COACH.
Scores: Item scores only.
Administration: Individual.
Parts, 2: Part A: Determining a Student's Educational Program; Part B: Translating the Family-Identified Priorities into Goals and Objectives.
Price Data, 2016: $46.95 per manual (2011, 223 pages) with CD.
Time: (60-85 minutes) for Step 1 (Family Interview; (45-60) minutes for Step 2 (Additional Learning Outcomes); additional time required for Steps 3-6.
Comments: "Designed to be used with a student's family, special educator, and general educator(s) together."
Authors: Michael F. Giangreco, Chigee J. Cloninger, and Virginia S. Iverson.
Publisher: Paul H. Brookes Publishing Co., Inc.
Cross References: See T5:553 (1 reference); for a review by Jay Kuder and David E. Kapel of a previous edition titled C.O.A.C.H.: Cayuga-Onondaga Assessment for Children with Handicaps, Version 6.0, see 11:73.

[419]

Chronic Pain Battery.

Purpose: Constructed to assess chronic pain by collecting "medical, psychological, behavioral, social, demographic and pain data."
Population: Patients ages 18 and over
Publication Dates: 1983–1986.
Acronym: CPB.
Scores, 10: Demographic and Social History, Past and Present Pain History, Past Treatment, Medications, Medical History, Personality-Pain Coping Style, Patient Expectations and Goals, Behavioral-Learning Factors, Psychosocial Factors, Patient Problem Ratings.
Administration: Group or individual.
Manual: No manual.
Price Data, 2016: $22 per online scoring; quantity discounts available.
Time: (30–60) minutes.
Comments: Comprises the Pain Assessment Questionnaire–Revised and the Symptom Checklist 90–Revised (2037); self-administered by paper-and-pencil with scoring and report generation online on a secure testing website.
Author: Stephen R. Levitt.
Publisher: Pain Resource Center, Inc.

[420]

Chronic Pain Coping Inventory.

Purpose: Designed to "assess the use of coping strategies that are typically targeted for change in multidisciplinary pain treatment programs."
Population: Ages 20-80.
Publication Dates: 1995-2008.
Acronym: CPCI.
Scores, 9: Guarding, Resting, Asking for Assistance, Exercise/Stretch, Relaxation, Task Persistence, Coping Self-Statements, Pacing, Seeking Social Support.
Administration: Individual or group.
Price Data, 2015: $205 per manual (2008, 60 pages), 25 rating forms, 25 score summary/profile sheets, and 25 pain worksheets; computer scoring software price available from publisher.
Time: (15) minutes.
Authors: Mark P. Jensen, Judith A. Turner, Joan M. Romano, and Warren R. Nielson.
Publisher: Psychological Assessment Resources, Inc.
Cross References: For reviews by Tony Cellucci and James P. Donnelly, see 18:28.

[421]

CID Early Childhood Vocabulary Rating Form.

Purpose: Designed as a criterion-referenced assessment to determine present levels of receptive and expressive vocabulary skills, identify future goals and objectives, and track and report progress over time.

Population: Children from birth to age 5 years who are deaf or hard of hearing.
Publication Date: 2013.
Scores: Mastery ratings in 5 sections: Functional Vocabulary, First 100 Words List, Other Basic Vocabulary, Theme-Based Vocabulary Planning Agenda, Preschool-Specific Vocabulary.
Administration: Individual.
Price Data, 2016: $28 per 25 8-page forms with instructions.
Time: Administration time not reported.
Author: Ellie White.
Publisher: CID - Central Institute for the Deaf.

[422]

CID Preschool Developmental Checklists.

Purpose: Designed as rating forms to "track typical development of literacy, cognitive, social, fine motor, and gross motor skills."
Population: Children ages 3 to 5 who are deaf or hard of hearing.
Publication Date: 2014.
Administration: Individual.
Levels, 3: Age 3, Age 4, Age 5.
Price Data, 2016: $20 per 25 forms for each age level with instructions.
Time: Administration time not reported.
Author: Patti Hoffman.
Publisher: CID - Central Institute for the Deaf.
  a) AGE 3.
    Scores: 65 ratings in 5 categories: Cognitive Development, Literacy Development, Fine Motor Development, Gross Motor Development, Social Development.
  b) AGE 4.
    Scores: Same as *a* above.
  c) AGE 5.
    Scores: 62 ratings in 6 categories: Cognitive Development, Technology Development, Literacy Development, Fine Motor Development, Gross Motor Development, Social Development.

[423]

CID Preschool Pragmatic Language Rating Form.

Purpose: Designed as a criterion-referenced assessment to determine present levels of pragmatic language skills, identify goals and objectives, and track and report progress.
Population: Children ages 3 to 5 who are deaf and hard of hearing.
Publication Date: 2013.
Scores: Mastery ratings for 67 pragmatic language skills.
Administration: Individual.
Price Data, 2016: $15 per 25 4-page forms with instructions.
Time: Administration time not reported.
Author: Ellie White.
Publisher: CID - Central Institute for the Deaf.

[424]

CID Preschool Symbolic Play Rating Form.

Purpose: Designed to "track play skills and their related language skills."
Population: Ages 8 months to 5 years.
Publication Date: 2014.
Scores: Mastery ratings in 12 categories: Play Skills (Object Permanence, Means-End/Problem Solving, Object Use, Decontexutalization, Thematic Concepts, Organization, Self/Other Relations), Language Skills (Function, Form and Content), Communication Skills.
Administration: Individual.
Levels, 10: Pre-Symbolic Level 1: 8-12 months, Pre-Symbolic Level II: 12-17 months, Symbolic Level 1: 17-19 months, Symbolic Level II: 19-22 months, Symbolic Level III: 2 years, Symbolic Level IV: 2.5 years, Symbolic Level V: 3 years, Symbolic Level VI: 3-3.5 years, Symbolic Level VII: 3.5-4 years, Symbolic Level VIII: 5 years.
Price Data, 2016: $28 per 25 8-page forms with instructions.
Time: Administration time not reported.
Authors: Carol Westby and Ellie White.
Publisher: CID - Central Institute for the Deaf.

[425]

CID Speech Skills Rating Form.

Purpose: Designed as a criterion-referenced assessment to determine present speech skills, identify speech goals and objectives, and track and report progress over time.
Population: Children who are deaf and hard of hearing.
Publication Dates: 2008-2013.
Scores: Item ratings in 6 categories: Voice, Suprasegmental Aspects of Speech, Vowels, Consonants, Initial Blends and Clusters, Final Blends and Clusters.
Administration: Individual.
Price Data, 2016: $28 per 25 8-page forms with instructions.
Time: Administration time not reported.
Authors: Lauren Dieckmann and Ellie White.
Publisher: CID - Central Institute for the Deaf.

[426]

CID Toddler Developmental Rating Form.

Purpose: Designed as a rating form to "track typical development of self-help, social and emotional, cognitive, fine motor, and gross motor skills."
Population: Toddlers ages 1 to 2 with hearing loss.
Publication Date: 2014.
Administration: Individual.
Levels, 2: Age 1, Age 2.
Price Data, 2016: $20 per 25 forms for each age level with instructions.
Time: Administration time not reported.
Authors: Natalie Lutkewitte and Ellie White.
Publisher: CID - Central Institute for the Deaf.

a) AGE 1.

Scores: 35 ratings in 5 categories: Self-Help Skills Development, Social and Emotional Development, Gross Motor Development, Fine Motor Development, Cognitive Development.

b) AGE 2.

Scores: 38 ratings in 5 categories: Self-Help Skills Development, Social and Emotional Development, Gross Motor Development, Fine Motor Development, Cognitive Development.

[427]

Cigarette Use Questionnaire.

Purpose: Designed for "evaluation, referral, and treatment of individuals who smoke cigarettes and wish to quit or must do so for health reasons."

Population: Ages 18-83.

Publication Date: 2006.

Acronym: CUQ.

Scores, 6: Defensiveness, Environmental Cues, Inconsistent Responding, Nicotine Addiction, Negative Emotional Relief, Readiness for Change.

Administration: Group.

Price Data, 2016: $118 per kit including manual (41 pages) and 25 Autoscore forms; $52.50 per 25 Autoscore forms; $72 per manual.

Time: (10) minutes.

Comments: Self-report.

Author: Ken Winters.

Publisher: Western Psychological Services.

Cross References: For reviews by Mark A. Albanese and Delores D. Walcott, see 18:29.

[428]

The City University Colour Vision Test, Second Edition 1980.

Purpose: To assess defects of color vision.

Population: Adults and children.

Publication Date: 1980.

Scores, 3: Chroma Four, Chroma Two, Overall.

Administration: Individual.

Manual: No manual (introductory notes and instructions included in binder of test plates).

Price Data, 2016: $322 per complete kit including profile sheets, 10 test pages, and instructions.

Time: Administration time not reported.

Author: Robert Fletcher.

Publisher: Keeler Instruments Inc.

Cross References: For a review by Karen T. Carey, see 13:65.

[429]

Clark-Beck Obsessive-Compulsive Inventory.

Purpose: Developed to "provide an efficient, yet comprehensive and precise self-report screening instrument for obsessive and compulsive symptoms."

Population: Adolescents and adults suspected of having Obsessive Compulsive Disorder.

Publication Date: 2002.

Acronym: CBOCI.

Scores, 3: Obsessions, Compulsions, Total.

Administration: Individual.

Price Data, 2015: $128 per complete kit including manual (68 pages) and 25 record forms; $81 per manual; $56.40 per 25 record forms.

Time: (10–30) minutes.

Comments: Requires eighth-grade reading level.

Authors: David A. Clark and Aaron T. Beck.

Publisher: Pearson.

Cross References: For a review by Tony Cellucci, see 16:49.

[430]

Clarke Sex History Questionnaire for Males—Revised.

Purpose: Designed "to evaluate a sex offender's sexual preference profile as well as evaluating their potential for sexually conventional behavior."

Population: Sex offenders.

Publication Dates: 1999-2002.

Acronym: SHQ-R.

Scores: 23 scales: Childhood and Adolescent Sexual Experiences and Sexual Abuse, Sexual Dysfunction, Female Adult Frequency, Female Pubescent Frequency, Female Child Frequency, Male Adult Frequency, Male Pubescent Frequency, Male Child Frequency, Child Identification, Fantasy Activities with Females, Fantasy Activities with Males, Exposure to Pornography, Transvestism, Fetishism, Feminine Gender Identity, Voyeurism, Exhibitionism Frequency, Exhibiting Behavior, Obscene Phone Calls, Toucheurism and Frotteurism, Sexual Aggression, Lie, Infrequency.

Administration: Individual.

Price Data, 2015: $62 per 3 reusable item booklets; $189 per 10 reusable item booklets; $79 per technical manual; $56 per software preview version (V.5) including manual, getting started guide, and 2 comprehensive reports; $21 per comprehensive report.

Time: (60-90) minutes.

Comments: Self-report paper-and-pencil inventory scored electronically by publisher or by software by the user.

Authors: Ron Langevin and Dan Paitich.

Publisher: Multi-Health Systems, Inc.

Cross References: For reviews by Roger A. Boothroyd and Delores D. Walcott, see 16:50.

[431]

Classroom Assessment Scoring System Infant.

Purpose: Designed as an "observation instrument ... to assess effective teacher-child interactions in infant" classrooms and settings.

Population: Settings providing care for children between 6 weeks and 18 months of age.
Publication Date: 2014.
Acronym: CLASS Infant.
Scores, 5: Relational Climate, Teacher Sensitivity, Facilitated Exploration, Early Language Support, Responsive Caregiving.
Administration: Individual settings.
Price Data, 2015: $54.95 per manual (61 pages); $30 per 10 observation forms; $30 per 5 dimensions overview forms; $19.95 per dimensions guide.
Foreign Language Edition: Spanish version available.
Time: (15) minutes per observation cycle; multiple cycles required.
Comments: "The CLASS is a multifaceted observation system that requires in-depth training for appropriate use"; downward extension of the CLASS Pre-K (432) and CLASS Toddler (433) observation assessments.
Authors: Bridget K. Hamre, Karen M. La Paro, Robert C. Pianta, and Jennifer LoCasale-Crouch.
Publisher: Paul H. Brookes Publishing Co., Inc.
Cross References: Reviews are scheduled for *The Twentieth Mental Measurements Yearbook*.

[432]

Classroom Assessment Scoring System, Pre-K and K-3.

Purpose: Designed to "assess classroom quality in preschool through third-grade classrooms."
Population: Preschool through third-grade students.
Publication Dates: 2008-2009.
Acronym: CLASS.
Scores, 13: (10 dimension scores) Positive Climate, Negative Climate, Teacher Sensitivity, Regard for Student Perspectives, Behavior Management, Productivity, Instructional Learning Formats, Concept Development, Quality of Feedback, Language Modeling; (3 composite domain scores) Emotional Support, Classroom Organization, Instructional Support.
Administration: Group.
Price Data, 2015: $54.95 per CLASS Manual Pre-K with Dimensions Overview (2008, 108 pages); $54.95 per CLASS Manual K-3 with Dimensions Overview (2008, 112 pages); $30 per 10 CLASS Pre-K and K-3 forms.
Foreign Language Edition: Spanish version available.
Time: (120-180) minutes.
Comments: The CLASS is a comprehensive observation system; researchers, teachers, principals, school psychologists, educational consultants, or other potential users must receive training to use the test.
Authors: Robert C. Pianta, Karen M. La Paro, and Bridget K. Hamre.
Publisher: Paul H. Brookes Publishing Co., Inc.

Cross References: For reviews by Sarah M. Bonner and Mary (Rina) M. Chittooran, see 19:36.

[433]

Classroom Assessment Scoring System Toddler.

Purpose: Designed for collecting "standardized information on the quality of classroom environments for young children."
Population: Settings providing care for toddlers (approximately 15 to 36 months old).
Publication Date: 2012.
Acronym: CLASS Toddler.
Scores, 10: Positive Climate, Negative Climate, Teacher Sensitivity, Regard for Child Perspectives, Behavior Guidance, Facilitation of Learning and Development, Quality of Feedback, Language Modeling, Emotional and Behavioral Support, Engaged Support for Learning.
Administration: Individual settings.
Price Data, 2016: $54.95 per manual (85 pages); $30 per 10 observation forms; $30 per 5 dimensions overview forms; $19.95 per dimensions guide.
Foreign Language Edition: Spanish version available.
Time: (15-20) minutes per observation cycle; multiple cycles required.
Comments: "Reliable use of the CLASS tool requires training. The level of training required depends on the intended use of the system. It is essential that all individuals interested in using the CLASS to collect standardized data on classrooms or for research, accountability, or evaluation purposes attend official training workshops." Part of the Classroom Assessment Scoring System; Infant, Pre-K, and K-3 versions available.
Authors: Karen M. La Paro, Bridget K. Hamre, and Robert C. Pianta.
Publisher: Paul H. Brookes Publishing Co., Inc.
Cross References: Reviews are scheduled for *The Twentieth Mental Measurements Yearbook*.

[434]

Classroom Environment Scale [Third Edition Manual].

Purpose: Designed to "assess the social climate of junior high and high school classrooms. It focuses on teacher-student and student-student relationships and on the organizational structure of a classroom."
Population: Junior high and senior high classrooms.
Publication Dates: 1974–2002.
Acronym: CES.
Scores, 9: Relationship dimensions (Involvement, Affiliation, Teacher Support), Personal Growth/Goal Orientation dimensions (Task Orientation, Competition), System Maintenance and Change dimensions (Order and Organization, Rule Clarity, Teacher Control, Innovation).

Administration: Group.

Forms, 3: Real Form (Form R), Ideal Form (Form I), Expectations Form (Form E); a shortened version can be given by administering the first 36 items of Form R.

Price Data, 2016: $50 per manual; $2.40 per Transform Survey Hosting: Form R or Form I; $250 per Group Report: Form R; $2 per Remote Online Survey License; $2 per License to Reproduce.

Foreign Language Edition: Form R is available in Spanish and Simplified Mandarin Chinese; all forms also available in Bengali, Estonian, Finnish, French, and Hebrew.

Time: [15–20] minutes.

Comments: One of ten Social Climate Scales (T5:2445).

Authors: Rudolf H. Moos and Edison J. Trickett.

Publisher: Mind Garden, Inc.

Cross References: See T5:495 (16 references) and T4:475 (5 references); for reviews by Richard A. Saudargas and Corinne Roth Smith, see 10:60 (16 references); see also T3:409 (9 references); for reviews by Maurice J. Eash and C. Robert Pace of an earlier edition, see 8:521 (3 references). For a review of the Social Climate Scales, see 8:681.

[435]

Classroom Reading Inventory, Twelfth Edition.

Purpose: Designed to "quickly diagnose a student's present ability to decode words both in isolation and in context, and to answer questions about the meaning."

Population: Elementary grades to adult learners.

Publication Dates: 1965-2012.

Acronym: CRI.

Scores, 5: Word Recognition, Comprehension, Independent Reading Level, Instructional Reading Level, Frustration Reading Level.

Administration: Individual.

Forms: Form A Subskill Format (pretest K-8th), Form A Subskill Format (posttest (K-8th), Form B Reader Response Format (pretest 1st-8th), Form B Reader Response Format (posttest 1st-8th), Form C Subskill Format (pretest high school/adult), Form C Subskill Format (posttest high school/adult).

Price Data, 2016: $160.33 per hardcopy book.

Time: (15) minutes.

Authors: Warren H. Wheelock and Connie J. Campbell.

Publisher: McGraw Hill Higher Education.

Cross References: See T5:496 (4 references) and T4:476 (4 references); for reviews by Ira E. Aaron and Sylvia M. Hutchinson and by Janet A. Norris of the Fourth Edition, see 10:61 (4 references); for a review of an earlier edition by Marjorie S. Johnson, see 8:749; see also T2:1618 (1 reference); for an excerpted review by Donald L. Cleland, see 7:715.

[436]

CLEP (College Level Examination Program).

Purpose: Designed to test "mastery of college-level material acquired in a variety of ways—through general academic instructions, significant independent study or extracurricular work."

Population: Individuals with 1–2 years of college or equivalent.

Publication Dates: 1964–2016.

Acronym: CLEP.

Scores: Total score only for 33 tests in 5 subject areas.

Administration: Group.

Price Data, 2016: $80 per exam.

Time: (90) minutes per test.

Comments: Tests administered at centers throughout the U.S. and internationally; program administered by the College Board and Educational Testing Service.

Author: Educational Testing Service.

Publisher: The College Board.

a) BUSINESS.
1) *Information Systems.*
2) *Principles of Management.*
3) *Financial Accounting.*
4) *Introductory Business Law.*
5) *Principles of Marketing.*

b) COMPOSITION AND LITERATURE.
Comments: Composition and Literature tests have optional essay supplement that is scored by the college.
1) *American Literature.*
2) *Analyzing and Interpreting Literature.*
3) *College Composition.*
4) *English Literature.*
5) *College Composition Modular.*
6) *Humanities.*

c) WORLD LANGUAGES.
1) *French, Levels 1 and 2.*
2) *German, Levels 1 and 2.*
3) *Spanish, Levels 1 and 2.*

d) HISTORY AND SOCIAL SCIENCES.
1) *American Government.*
2) *History of the United States I: Early Colonization to 1877.*
3) *History of the United States II: 1865 to the Present.*
4) *Introduction to Educational Psychology.*
5) *Introductory Psychology.*
6) *Human Growth and Development.*
7) *Principles of Macroeconomics.*
8) *Principles of Microeconomics.*
9) *Introductory Sociology.*
10) *Western Civilization I: Ancient Near East to 1648.*
11) *Western Civilization II: 1648 to the Present.*
12) *Social Sciences and History.*

e) SCIENCE AND MATHEMATICS.
1) *Biology.*
2) *Calculus.*
3) *Chemistry.*
4) *College Algebra.*
5) *College Mathematics.*
6) *Natural Sciences.*
7) *Precalculus.*

Cross References: See 9:245 (1 reference) and T3:506 (7 references); for reviews by Paul L. Dressel, David A. Frisbie, and Wimburn L. Wallace of an earlier program, see 8:473 (15 references); for reviews of the General Examinations, see 8:8 (2 reviews); for reviews of earlier editions of the separate Subject Examinations, see 8:43 (1 review) for College Composition, 8:44 (1 review) for Freshman English Examination, 8:64 (1 review) for American Literature, 8:65 (1 review) for Analysis and Interpretation of Literature, 8:66 (1 review) for English Literature, 8:255 (1 review) for Calculus with Analytic Geometry, 8:256 (1 review) for College Algebra and Trigonometry, 8:297 (1 review) for College Algebra, 8:365 (1 review) for Tests and Measurements, 8:460 (1 review) for General Psychology, 8:832 (1 review) for Biology, 8:847 (1 review) for General Chemistry, 8:911 (1 review) for American History, 8:919 (1 review) for American Government, 8:1119 (1 review) for Medical-Surgical Nursing: North Carolina Nursing Equivalency, and 8:1120 (1 review) for Clinical Experience Record for Nursing Students; see also T2:1050 (4 references); for reviews by Alexander W. Astin, Benjamin S. Bloom, and Warren G. Findley of an earlier edition of the College-Level Examination Program, see 7:664 (7 references).

[437]
Clerical Aptitude Assessment.

Purpose: Designed to "examine how well the test-taker is suited for a career in the clerical field."
Population: Potential clerical workers.
Publication Date: 2011.
Acronym: CLAA.
Scores, 34: Work Habits (Diligence, Organization, Time Management, Dependability, Attention to Detail, Efficiency, Self-Discipline, Concentration, Initiative, Adaptability/Trainability, Tolerance for Routine Work), Interpersonal Skills (Communication Skills, Conflict Resolutions Skills, Willingness to Compromise, Desire for Control, Likeability, Emotional Strength, Helpfulness, Discretion, Reaction to Criticism), Office Skills (Arithmetic, Filing, Reading Comprehension, Graph and Chart Reading, Proofreading Skills, Data Entry Skills, Typing Skills, Short-Term Memory Skills), Impression Management, Acquiescence, Overall Score.
Administration: Individual.
Price Data: Available from publisher.
Time: (40) minutes.
Comments: Self-administered online assessment. The test publisher provides clients with information about the methods and theoretical basis used in the development of the test as well as benchmarks for relevant industries and racial/ethnic group comparison data.
Author: PsychTests AIM, Inc.
Publisher: PsychTests AIM, Inc. [Canada].
Cross References: For reviews by James T. Austin and Sheldon Zedeck, see 19:37.

[438]
Clerical Skills Test.

Purpose: "Designed to assist companies in identifying individuals who have strong reading, mathematical and analytical skills."
Population: Current and prospective employees.
Publication Dates: 1999–2001.
Acronym: CST.
Scores, 7: Writing, Analyzing, Proofreading, Filing, Math, Checking, Total.
Administration: Group.
Price Data, 2016: $15.99 (sold in quantities of 5; quantity discounts available.)
Time: 21(26) minutes.
Comments: Paper-and-pencil and online versions available.
Author: J. M. Llobet.
Publisher: HRdirect | G. Neil.
Cross References: For a review by Eleanor E. Sanford-Moore, see 17:44.

[439]
Clerical Skills Test Series [Scored By Client].

Purpose: Measures 16 different clerical-administrative skills.
Population: Adults.
Publication Date: 1990.
Scores: 16 skills: Alphabetizing—Filing, Attention to Detail With Words & Numbers, Bookkeeping Skills, Coding, Grammar & Punctuation, Manual Dexterity, Mechanical Comprehension, Numerical Skills, Problem Solving, Proofreading Skills, Reading Comprehension, Receptionist Skills, Spatial Perception, Spelling, Verbal Fluency, English Vocabulary, plus Total Score.
Administration: Group.
Price Data: Available from publisher.
Time: (5) minutes per subtest.
Author: Stephen Berke.
Publisher: Walden Personnel Testing & Consulting Inc. [Canada].
Cross References: For reviews by Phillip L. Ackerman and Eleanor E. Sanford, see 16:51.

[440]
Clinical Assessment of Articulation and Phonology.

Purpose: Designed to "assess English articulation and phonology in preschool and school aged children."
Population: Ages 3 to 9 years.
Publication Date: 2002.
Acronym: CAAP.
Administration: Individual.
Price Data: Available from publisher.
Comments: This is a norm-referenced instrument. This test is now available in a second edition; description will be updated when test materials are received.

Authors: Wayne A. Secord and JoAnn S. Donohue.
Publisher: PRO-ED.
   a) ARTICULATION INVENTORY.
   Scores, 2: Consonant Inventory Score, School Age Sentence Score.
   Time: (15-20) minutes.
   b) PHONOLOGICAL PROCESS CHECKLISTS I AND II.
   Scores, 10: Final Consonant Deletion, Cluster Reduction, Syllable Reduction, Gliding, Vocalization, Fronting, Deaffrication, Stopping, Prevocalic Voicing, Postvocalic Devoicing.
   Time: (20) minutes.
Cross References: For reviews by Steven Long and Roger L. Towne, see 17:45.

[441]

Clinical Assessment of Attention Deficit–Adult.

Purpose: Designed to provide a "comprehensive assessment of attention deficit with and without hyperactivity (ADD/ADHD)" in adults.
Population: Ages 19-79.
Publication Dates: 1994-2005.
Acronym: CAT-A.
Scores, 17: Clinical Index, Childhood Memories Clinical Index (Inattention, Impulsivity, Hyperactivity), Childhood Memories Context Clusters (Personal, Academic/Occupational, Social), Childhood Memories Locus Clusters (Internal, External), Current Symptoms Clinical Index (Inattention, Impulsivity, Hyperactivity), Current Symptoms Context Clusters (Personal, Academic/Occupational, Social), Current Symptoms Locus Clusters (Internal, External).
Administration: Group or individual.
Price Data, 2015: $196 per introductory kit including professional manual (2005, 139 pages), 25 rating forms, and 25 score summary/profile forms; $82 per professional manual; $92 per 25 rating forms; $35 per 25 score summary/profile forms; $225 per software (CD-ROM) with on-screen help and quick start guide.
Time: (20-25) minutes.
Comments: Can be computer scored; a child and adolescent form (CAT-C; 442) is also available and shares the same professional manual.
Authors: Bruce A. Bracken and Barbara S. Boatwright.
Publisher: Psychological Assessment Resources, Inc.
Cross References: For reviews by Rama K. Mishra and Sean Reilley, see 17:46.

[442]

Clinical Assessment of Attention Deficit–Child.

Purpose: Designed to provide a "comprehensive assessment of attention deficit with and without hyperactivity (ADD/ADHD)" in children and adolescents.

Population: 8-18 years.
Publication Dates: 1994-2005.
Acronym: CAT-C.
Scores, 12: Clinical (Inattention, Impulsivity, Hyperactivity), Clinical Index, Context (Personal, Academic/Occupational, Social), Locus (Internal, External), Validity (Negative Impression, Infrequency, Positive Impression) .
Administration: Individual.
Parts, 3: Self-Report, Parent Report, Teacher Report.
Price Data, 2015: $340 per introductory kit including CAT-A/CAT-C professional manual, 25 Self-Rating Forms, 25 Parent Rating Forms, 25 Teacher Rating Forms, 25 Self-Rating Score Summary/Profile Forms, 25 Parent Score Summary/Profile Forms, and 25 Teacher Score Summary/Profile Forms; $82 per professional manual; $68 per 25 Self-Rating forms; $68 per 25 Parent Rating Forms; $68 per 25 Teacher Rating Forms; $28 per 25 Parent Score Summary/Profile Forms; $28 per 25 Self-Rating Score Summary/Profile Forms; $28 per 25 Teacher Score Summary/Profile Forms; $225 per CAT-C SP software (CD-ROM) with on-screen help and quick start guide.
Time: (10-20) minutes.
Comments: An adult form (CAT-A; 441) is also available and shares the same professional manual.
Authors: Bruce A. Bracken and Barbara S. Boatwright.
Publisher: Psychological Assessment Resources, Inc.
Cross References: For reviews by George J. Demakis and Rosemary Flanagan, see 17:47.

[443]

Clinical Assessment of Behavior.

Purpose: "Assists in the identification of children and adolescents across a wide age range who are in need of behavioral, educational, or psychiatric treatment or intervention."
Population: Ages 2–18.
Publication Dates: 1996–2004.
Acronym: CAB.
Scores, 21: Internalizing Behaviors, Externalizing Behaviors, Critical Behaviors, Social Skills, Competence, Adaptive Behaviors, CAB Behavioral Index, Anxiety, Depression, Anger, Aggression, Bullying, Conduct Problems, Attention-Deficit/Hyperactivity, Autistic Spectrum Behaviors, Learning Disability, Mental Retardation, Executive Function, Gifted and Talented, Emotional Disturbance, Social Maladjustment.
Administration: Individual.
Forms, 3: Parent Extended Rating Form, Parent Rating Form, Teacher Rating Form.
Price Data, 2015: $274 per introductory kit including CD-ROM-based scoring program with on-screen professional manual, installation guide, and professional manual (2004, 309 pages), 25 Parent Rating Forms, 25 Parent Extended Forms, and 25 Teacher Rating Forms.
Time: (10–30) minutes.

Comments: Informant-completed behavior rating scale.
Authors: Bruce A. Bracken and Lori K. Keith.
Publisher: Psychological Assessment Resources, Inc.
Cross References: For reviews by Mike Bonner and Metta K. Volker-Fry and by John Hattie, see 16:52.

[444]
Clinical Assessment of Depression.

Purpose: "Developed to aid in the clinical assessment and diagnosis of depression."
Population: Ages 8 to 79.
Publication Dates: 1994–2004.
Acronym: CAD.
Scores, 14: Symptom Scale Scores (Depressed Mood, Anxiety/Worry, Diminished Interest, Cognitive and Physical Fatigue, Total), Validity Scale Scores (Inconsistency, Negative Impression, Infrequency), Critical Item Cluster Scores (Hopelessness, Self-Devaluation, Sleep/Fatigue, Failure, Worry, Nervous).
Administration: Group.
Price Data, 2015: $164 per introductory kit including professional manual (2004, 96 pages), 25 rating forms, and 25 score summary/profile forms; $230 per software (CD-ROM) with on-screen help and quick start guide.
Time: 10 minutes.
Authors: Bruce A. Bracken and Karen Howell.
Publisher: Psychological Assessment Resources, Inc.
Cross References: For reviews by Michael G. Kavan and Jody L. Kulstad, see 17:48.

[445]
Clinical Assessment Scales for the Elderly and Clinical Assessment Scales for the Elderly—Short Form.

Purpose: "A comprehensive measure of acute psychopathology in the elderly" and to "screen for acute psychopathology in the elderly."
Population: Ages 55–90.
Publication Dates: 1999–2001.
Scores, 10: Anxiety, Cognitive Competence, Depression, Fear of Aging, Mania, Obsessive-Compulsive, Paranoia, Psychoticism, Somatization, Substance Abuse.
Administration: Individual or group.
Forms, 2: R (caregiver rating), S (self-rating).
Comments: Addresses selected DSM-IV Axis I disorders.
Authors: Cecil R. Reynolds (test and manual) and Erin D. Bigler (test).
Publisher: Psychological Assessment Resources, Inc.
a) CLINICAL ASSESSMENT SCALES FOR THE ELDERLY.
Purpose: "A comprehensive measure of acute psychopathology in the elderly."
Acronym: CASE.

Price Data, 2015: $276 per introductory kit including CASE/CASE-SF professional manual (2001, 140 pages), 25 CASE Form S item booklets, 25 CASE Form R item booklets, 25 CASE Form S hand-scorable answer sheets, 25 CASE Form R answer sheets, and 50 CASE profile forms.
Time: 20–40(30–50) minutes.
b) CLINICAL ASSESSMENT SCALES FOR THE ELDERLY—SHORT FORM.
Purpose: To "screen for acute psychopathology in the elderly."
Acronym: CASE-SF.
Price Data: $212 per Short Form introductory kit including CASE/CASE-SF professional manual, 25 CASE-SF Form S test booklets, 25 CASE-SF Form R test booklets, and 50 CASE profile forms.
Time: 10–20(20–30) minutes.
Cross References: For reviews by Stephen J. DePaola and Iris Phillips, see 15:51.

[446]
Clinical Evaluation of Language Fundamentals–Fifth Edition.

Purpose: Designed as a "clinical tool for the identification, diagnosis, and follow-up evaluation of language and communication disorders."
Population: Ages 5 through 21.
Publication Dates: 1980-2013.
Acronym: CELF-5.
Administration: Individual.
Levels: 3.
Forms, 4: Record Form 1 (Ages 5-8), Record Form 2 (Ages 9-21), Reading and Writing Supplement 1 (Ages 8-10), Reading and Writing Supplement 2 (Ages 11-21).
Price Data, 2015: $699 per complete kit including case, examiner's manual, technical manual, 2 stimulus books, 15 each record forms 1 and 2, 10 each reading and writing supplements 1 and 2, and 50 observational rating scale forms; $99 per examiner's manual (2013, 304 pages); $76.90 per technical manual (2013, 95 pages); $179.40 per stimulus book; $76.90 per 25 record forms (1 or 2); $25 per 25 reading and writing supplements (1 or 2); $50 per 50 observational rating scales.
Comments: Battery includes Observational Rating Scale, which may be completed by parents, teachers, and the student.
Authors: Elisabeth H. Wiig, Eleanor Semel, Wayne A. Secord.
Publisher: Pearson.
a) AGES 5-8.
Scores, 17: Core Language Score (Sentence Comprehension, Word Structure, Formulated Sentences, Recalling Sentences), Receptive Language Index (Sentence Comprehension, Word Classes, Following Directions), Expressive Language Index (Word Structure, Formulated Sentences, Recalling Sentences), Language Content Index (Linguistic Concepts, Word Classes, Following Directions), Language Structure Index (Sentence Comprehension, Word Structure, Formulated Sentences, Recalling Sentences), Understanding Spoken Paragraphs, Pragmatics Profile,

Pragmatics Activities Checklist, Reading Comprehension (Age 8 only), Structured Writing (Age 8 only).
Time: (5-14) minutes per test; (34) minutes for all tests comprising Core Language Score.
b) AGES 9-12.
Scores, 17: Core Language Score (Word Classes, Formulated Sentences, Recalling Sentences, Semantic Relationships), Receptive Language Index (Word Classes, Following Directions, Semantic Relationships), Expressive Language Index (Formulated Sentences, Recalling Sentences, Sentence Assembly), Language Content Index (Word Classes, Understanding Spoken Paragraphs, Word Definitions), Language Memory Index (Following Directions, Formulated Sentences, Recalling Sentences), Pragmatics Profile, Pragmatics Activities Checklist, Reading Comprehension, Structured Writing.
Time: (7-15) minutes per test; (42) minutes for all tests comprising Core Language Score.
c) AGES 13-21.
Scores, 17: Core Language Score (Formulated Sentences, Recalling Sentences, Understanding Spoken Paragraphs, Semantic Relationships), Receptive Language Index (Word Classes, Understanding Spoken Paragraphs, Semantic Relationships), Expressive Language Index (Formulated Sentences, Recalling Sentences, Sentence Assembly), Language Content Index (Word Classes, Understanding Spoken Paragraphs, Sentence Assembly), Language Memory Index (Following Directions, Formulated Sentences, Recalling Sentences), Word Definitions, Pragmatics Profile, Pragmatics Activities Checklist, Reading Comprehension, Structured Writing.
Time: (6-15) minutes per test; (42) minutes for all tests comprising Core Language Score.
Cross References: Reviews are scheduled for *The Twentieth Mental Measurements Yearbook*. For reviews by Aimee Langlois and Vincent J. Samar of the fourth edition, see 16:53; for reviews by Robert R. Haccoun and David P. Hurford of the third edition–observational rating scales, see 14:76; see also T5:540 (26 references); for reviews by Ronald B. Gillam and John MacDonald of the third edition see 13:68 (38 references); see also T4:521 (5 references); for reviews by Linda Crocker and David A. Shapiro of the revised edition, see 11:72; for a review by Dixie D. Sanger of an earlier edition, see 9:233 (2 references); see also T3:474.

[447]

Clinical Evaluation of Language Fundamentals–Fifth Edition Metalinguistics.

Purpose: Designed to identify students "who have not acquired the expected levels of communicative competence and metalinguistic ability for their age."
Population: Ages 9 through 21.
Publication Dates: 1989-2014.
Acronym: CELF-5 Metalinguistics.
Scores, 8: Metalinguistics Profile, Total Metalinguistics Index (Making Inferences, Conversation Skills, Multiple Meanings, Figurative Language), Meta-Pragmatics Index (Making Inferences, Conversation Skills), Meta-Semantics Index (Multiple Meanings, Figurative Language).

Administration: Individual.
Price Data, 2016: $374 per digital flash drive kit for manual scoring including flash drive with examiner's manual, stimulus book and 25 print record forms; $180 per stimulus book; $120 per examiner's manual (228 pages); $77 per technical manual (74 pages); $77 per 25 record forms.
Time: (30-45) minutes.
Comments: A revision of the Test of Language Competence–Expanded Edition; computer scoring available.
Authors: Elizabeth H. Wiig and Wayne A. Secord.
Publisher: Pearson.
Cross References: Reviews are scheduled for *The Twentieth Mental Measurements Yearbook*. See T5:2693 (10 references); for reviews by Dolores Kluppel Vetter and Carol E. Westby of a previous edition titled Test of Language Competence–Expanded Edition, see 11:435 (1 reference).

[448]

Clinical Evaluation of Language Fundamentals-Fifth Edition Screening Test.

Purpose: Designed to "assist in the identification of individuals who may need in-depth assessment of their language abilities."
Population: Ages 5 through 21.
Publication Dates: 1995–2013.
Acronym: CELF-5 Screening Test.
Score: Total score only
Administration: Individual.
Price Data, 2015: $281.90 per complete kit including manual with stimulus pages, administration and scoring information, and technical information (2013; technical manual, 55 pages) plus 25 record forms; $255.25 per manual; $43.05 per 25 record forms.
Time: 15 minutes.
Comments: Contains updated age-based criterion scores and new pragmatic screening section.
Authors: Elisabeth H. Wiig, Eleanor Semel, and Wayne A. Secord.
Publisher: Pearson.
Cross References: Reviews are scheduled for *The Twentieth Mental Measurements Yearbook*. For reviews by Aimee Langlois and Gregory Snyder of the Fourth Edition, see 18:30; see T5:542 (2 references); for reviews by Billy T. Ogletree and Marcel O. Ponton of the Third Edition, see 13:69 (1 reference); for reviews by Linda M. Crocker and Jon F. Miller of an earlier edition, see 9:234.

[449]

Clinical Evaluation of Language Fundamentals Preschool—Second Edition.

Purpose: Designed as a "clinical tool for identifying, diagnosing, and performing follow-up evaluations of language deficits."

Population: Ages 3–6.
Publication Dates: 1992–2004.
Acronym: CELF Preschool-2.
Scores, 16: 11 subtests (Sentence Structure, Word Structure, Expressive Vocabulary, Concepts and Following Directions, Recalling Sentences, Basic Concepts, Word Classes, Recalling Sentences in Context, Phonological Awareness, Pre-Literacy Rating Scale, Descriptive Pragmatics Profile); 5 Composites (Core Language, Receptive Language, Expressive Language, Language Content, Language Structure).
Administration: Individual.
Price Data, 2015: $398.75 per complete kit including examiner's manual, 2 stimulus books, 25 record forms, 25 pragmatics and pre-literacy forms, and 25 stimulus sheets; $106.10 per examiner's manual (2004, 220 pages); $261.40 per Stimulus Book #1; $67.15 per Stimulus Book #2; $80.45 per 25 record forms.
Foreign Language Editions: Spanish edition available.
Time: (15–20) minutes.
Comments: A downward extension of the Clinical Evaluation of Language Fundamentals—Fourth Edition (16:53).
Authors: Elisabeth H. Wiig, Wayne A. Secord, and Eleanor Semel.
Publisher: Pearson.
Cross References: For reviews by Rick Eigenbrood and Gene Schwarting, see 17:49; see also T5:539 (2 references); for reviews by Janet A. Norris and Nora M. Thompson of an earlier edition, see 13:67 (2 references).

[450]

Clinical Evaluation of Language Fundamentals Preschool–Second Edition–Spanish Edition.

Purpose: Designed to provide "comprehensive language evaluation for Spanish-speaking preschool children."
Population: Ages 3-0 to 6-11.
Publication Dates: 2004-2009.
Acronym: CELF Preschool-2 Spanish.
Scores, 15: Basic Concepts, Word Structure, Recalling Sentences, Concepts and Following Directions, Expressive Vocabulary, Sentence Structure, Word Classes, Phonological Awareness, Early Literacy Rating Scale, Descriptive Pragmatics Profile, Core Language Score, Receptive and Expressive Language Index Score, Expressive Language, Language Content, Language Structure Index Score.
Subtests, 10: Basic Concepts, Word Structure, Recalling Sentences, Concepts and Following Directions, Expressive Vocabulary, Sentence Structure, Word Classes, Phonological Awareness, Early Literacy Rating Scale, Descriptive Pragmatics Profile.
Administration: Individual.

Levels, 4: Level 1: Identify whether there is a language disorder; Level 2: Describe the nature of the disorder; Level 3: Evaluate early classroom and literacy fundamentals; Level 4: Evaluate language and communication in context.
Price Data, 2015: $416.15 per kit including manual (2009, 310 pages), 25 record forms, Spanish stimulus manual, and 25 rating scale forms; $117.90 per manual; $360.80 per Spanish stimulus manual.
Time: (15-20) minutes for Level 1; remaining subtest time varies.
Comments: This is a parallel edition to the Clinical Evaluation of Language Fundamentals Preschool-Second Edition (449), not a translation; subtests can be used individually.
Authors: Elisabeth H. Wigg, Wayne A. Secord, and Eleanor Semel.
Publisher: Pearson.
Cross References: For reviews by James Dean Brown and Marta Gonzalez-Lloret and by Gerald Tindal, see 19:38.

[451]

Clinical Rating Scale for Circumplex Model.

Purpose: Designed to type marital and family systems and identify intervention targets related to Circumplex Model.
Population: Couples and families.
Publication Dates: 1980–2004.
Acronym: CRS.
Scores: 3 rating scales (Cohesion, Flexibility, Communication) yielding Family System Type related to Circumplex Model.
Administration: Group (couple or family).
Price Data, 2015: $30 for CRS and manual (includes unlimited copying privileges).
Time: (5-10) minutes.
Comments: Rating of couple or family system based on interview and/or observation.
Author: David H. Olson.
Publisher: Life Innovations, Inc.
Cross References: For reviews by Stuart N. Hart and Steven W. Lee of an earlier edition titled Clinical Rating Scale, see 12:81 (4 references).

[452]

Closed High School Placement Test.

Purpose: Designed as a measure of cognitive and basic skills to assist in placement decisions for entering freshmen.
Population: Eighth grade students.
Publication Dates: 1958-2015.
Acronym: HSPT.
Scores, 8: Cognitive Skills (Verbal, Quantitative, Total), Basic Skills (Reading, Mathematics, Language, Total), Composite.

Administration: Group.
Price Data: Available from publisher.
Time: 150 minutes plus 15–25 minutes per optional test.
Comments: Optional tests include science, mechanical aptitude, and Catholic religion; new form developed yearly.
Author: Scholastic Testing Service, Inc.
Publisher: Scholastic Testing Service, Inc.
Cross References: For reviews by George Engelhard, Jr. and Ernest Kimmel of the 1991 edition, see 14:80; see also T5:547 (1 reference) and T3:2324 (1 reference); for reviews by Leonard S. Cahen and Irvin J. Lehmann of an earlier edition, see 8:26 (1 reference); see also 7:21 (2 references); for reviews by Marion F. Shaycoft and James R. Hayden of an earlier series, see 6:6; for reviews by William C. Cottle and Robert A. Jones of the 1955 "open" test, see 5:15.

[453]
Closure Flexibility (Concealed Figures).

Purpose: "To measure the ability to hold a configuration in mind despite distracting irrelevancies."
Population: Wide range of higher level occupations personnel.
Publication Dates: 1956–1965.
Scores: Total score only.
Administration: Individual or group.
Price Data: Available from publisher.
Time: (10) minutes.
Authors: L. L. Thurstone and T. E. Jeffrey.
Publisher: General Dynamics Information Technology.
Cross References: See T5:548 (1 reference), T3:477 (5 references), T2:547 (9 references), and 7:435 (9 references); for a review by Leona E. Tyler, see 6:545 (4 references).

[454]
Closure Speed (Gestalt Completion).

Purpose: "To measure the ability to see apparently disorganized or unrelated parts as a meaningful whole."
Population: Employees in wide range of occupations.
Publication Date: 1959.
Scores: Total score only.
Administration: Individual or group.
Price Data: Available from publisher.
Time: 3 minutes.
Authors: L. L. Thurstone and T. E. Jeffrey.
Publisher: General Dynamics Information Technology.
Cross References: See T4:530 (2 references), T3:478 (2 references), T2:548 (1 reference), and 7:436 (2 references); for a review by Leona E. Tyler, see 6:546 (3 references).

[455]
Cloze Reading Tests 1-3, Second Edition.

Purpose: Designed to provide a method of testing reading skills.

Population: Ages 8-0 to 10-6, 8-5 to 11-10, 9-5 to 12-6.
Publication Dates: 1982–1992.
Scores: Overall performance score.
Administration: Individual or group.
Levels, 3: Level 1 (Ages 8-0 to 10-6), Level 2 (Ages 8-5 to 11-10), Level 3 (Ages 9-5 to 12-6).
Price Data, 2016: £11.50 per 10 tests (specify Test 1, 2, or 3); £28 per manual (16 pages); £31 per specimen set.
Time: 35(45) minutes.
Author: D. Young.
Publisher: Hodder Education [United Kingdom].
Cross References: See T5:550 (5 references) and T4:531 (3 references); for a review by Esther Geva, see 9:237.

[456]
CNS Vital Signs Computerized Cognitive Battery.

Purpose: A computerized cognitive testing platform designed for assessing an individual's neurocognitive state.
Population: Ages 8 to 80.
Publication Dates: 2003-2015.
Acronym: CNSVS.
Scores, 17: 12 Brief-Core Domains (Neurocognitive Index, Composite Memory, Verbal Memory, Visual Memory, Psychomotor Speed, Reaction Time, Complex Attention, Cognitive Flexibility, Processing Speed, Executive Function, Simple Visual Attention, Motor Speed), 4 Expanded Domains (Social Acuity, Reasoning, Sustained Attention, Working Memory), Severity of Impairment.
Subtests, 10: Verbal Memory, Visual Memory, Finger Tapping, Symbol Digit Coding, Stroop, Shifting Attention, Continuous Performance, Perception of Emotions, Non-Verbal Reasoning, 4-Part Continuous Performance.
Administration: Individual.
Price Data, 2016: $35 per neurocognitive battery (volume discounts available); free retest within 24 hours.
Foreign Language Editions: Available in more than 50 languages.
Time: (10-45) minutes.
Comments: Computer administered and scored; available as a local running application or as a web-based application; battery includes 10 normed neurocognitive tests and multiple patient reported outcome instruments; battery may be customized for test taker.
Author: CNS Vital Signs.
Publisher: CNS Vital Signs.
Cross References: Reviews are scheduled for *The Twentieth Mental Measurements Yearbook*. For reviews by D. Ashley Cohen and Karl R. Hanes of an earlier edition titled CNS Vital Signs Screening Battery, see 16:54.

[457]

Coaching for Commitment: Coaching Skills Inventory Self, Third Edition.

Purpose: Designed "for use by anyone who wants to identify a coaching gap compared to an ideal, the role(s) he or she gravitates toward, and proficiency levels in using certain coaching skills during interactions with others."

Population: Adults.

Publication Dates: 1991-2008.

Acronym: CSI.

Scores, 10: 4 Roles (Coach, Mentor, Instructor, Manager), 5 Coaching Skills (Challenge, Listen, Encourage, Ask, Refine), Coaching Gap.

Administration: Individual.

Price Data, 2016: $21 per test booklet including instructions and scoring (2008, 25 pages).

Time: [20-30] minutes.

Authors: Cindy Coe, Amy Zehnder, and Dennis C. Kinlaw.

Publisher: John Wiley and Sons, Inc.

[458]

Coaching Process Questionnaire.

Purpose: "Provides managers with an assessment of their coaching ability."

Population: Managers and employees.

Publication Date: 1992.

Acronym: CPQ.

Administration: Group or individual.

Foreign Language Editions: Available in Chinese (Simplified), Chinese (Traditional), French (Canada), German, Italian, Japanese, Portuguese (Brazil), Russian, and Spanish (Mexico).

Time: [30–40] minutes.

Comments: Self-scored instrument.

Author: Hay Group.

Publisher: Hay Group.

    a) PARTICIPANT VERSION.

    Population: Managers.

    Scores, 5: Diagnostic Skills, Coaching Techniques, Coaching Qualities, Coaching Model, Overall CPQ score.

    Price Data, 2016: $152 per complete kit including 10 questionnaires and 10 profiles and interpretive notes.

    b) FEEDBACK VERSION.

    Scores, 5: Diagnostic Skills, Coaching Techniques, Coaching Qualities, Coaching Model, Overall Employee score.

    Price Data: $70 per 10 questionnaires.

Cross References: For reviews by Patricia A. Bachelor and Geneva D. Haertel, see 13:70.

[459]

Coddington Life Events Scales.

Purpose: "Designed to assess the influence of life events and change in a young person's life, and help determine how these events affect their personal growth and ability to adjust."

Population: Ages 5 and under, ages 6–10, ages 11–19.

Publication Dates: 1981–1999.

Acronym: CLES.

Scores: Total Life Change Unit score only.

Administration: Individual or Group.

Forms, 3: Preschool (CLES-P), Child (CLES-C), Adolescent (CLES-A).

Price Data, 2015: $225 per complete kit including manual (1999, 48 pages) and 25 Quikscore forms for each of the CLES-P, CLES-C, and CLES-A; $84 per technical manual; $55 per 25 Quikscore forms (specify CLES-P, CLES-C, or CLES-A).

Time: (15) minutes.

Comments: Self-report, assisted self-report.

Author: R. Dean Coddington.

Publisher: Multi-Health Systems, Inc.

Cross References: For reviews by James A. Athanasou and Howard M. Knoff, see 15:52; see T5:557 (7 references) and T4:1453 (3 references).

[460]

Cognistat (The Neurobehavioral Cognitive Status Examination).

Purpose: Designed to assess intellectual functioning.

Population: Adults.

Publication Dates: 1983–1995.

Acronym: Cognistat.

Scores, 11: Level of Consciousness, Orientation, Attention, Language (Comprehension, Repetition, Naming), Constructional Ability, Memory, Calculations, Reasoning (Similarities, Judgment).

Administration: Individual.

Price Data, 2016: $575 per paper-and-pencil starter kit including stimulus book, tokens, 25 test booklets, and manual; $525 per online assessment starter kit including 25 online tests, stimulus booklet and 8 tokens; $35 per stimulus book; $475 per 25 test booklets; $35 per set of 8 tokens; $75 per manual.

Foreign Language Editions: Available in Spanish, French, Japanese, Chinese (Mandarin and Cantonese), Hebrew, Swedish, Norwegian, Finnish, and Czech.

Time: Administration time not reported.

Comments: Administered via paper and pencil or online.

Authors: R. J. Kiernan, J. Mueller, and J. W. Langston.

Publisher: Cognistat, Inc.

Cross References: For reviews by Charles J. Long and Faith Gunning-Dixon and by Steven R. Shaw, see 14:81.

[461]

Cognitive Abilities Scale—Second Edition.

Purpose: Developed to assess the cognitive abilities of infants and young children and to identify children who have delays in cognitive development.

Population: Ages 3-23 months; 24-47 months.
Publication Dates: 1987–2001.
Acronym: CAS-2.
Administration: Individual.
Price Data, 2015: $88 per examiner's manual (2001, 83 pages); $48 per 25 Profile/Examiner Record Booklets (Infant Form); $48 per 25 Profile/Examiner Record Booklets (Preschool Form); $20 per 25 Symbol Reproduction Forms; $49 per 25 Mikey's Favorite Things Book; $37 per Picture Cards; $14 per Ramp; $244 per Manipulatives Kit; $521 per complete kit including examiner's manual, 25 Profile/Examiner Record Booklets (Infant Form), 25 Profile/Examiner Record Booklets (Preschool Form), 25 Symbol Reproduction Forms, 25 copies of "Mikey's Favorite Things," Picture Cards, Ramp, and Manipulatives Kit.
Time: (20–30) minutes.
Authors: Sharon Bradley-Johnson and C. Merle Johnson.
Publisher: PRO-ED.
  a) INFANT FORM.
  Population: Ages 3–23 months.
  Scores, 3: Exploration of Objects, Communication with Others, Initiation and Imitation.
  b) PRESCHOOL FORM.
  Population: Ages 24–47 months.
  Scores, 5: Oral Language, Reading, Math, Writing, Enabling Behaviors.
Cross References: For reviews by Bert A. Goldman and Joyce Meikamp, see 15:53; see T5:559 (1 reference); for reviews by A. Dirk Hightower and Gary J. Robertson of the original edition, see 10:65.

[462]

Cognitive Abilities Test™, Form 7.

Purpose: Designed to measure students' "verbal, quantitative, and nonverbal reasoning abilities" and to help educators determine instructional strategies.
Population: Students in Grades K-12.
Publication Dates: 1954-2012.
Acronym: CogAT.
Scores, 4-7: Verbal Battery, Quantitative Battery, Nonverbal Battery, 3 optional partial composites (Verbal and Quantitative Composite, Quantitative and Nonverbal Composite, Verbal and Nonverbal Composite), Overall Composite.
Administration: Group.
Price Data: Available from publisher.
Foreign Language and Special Editions: Directions for administering are available in Spanish; large-print edition available.
Comments: Online administration available; Screening Form available for "determining eligibility for gifted and talented programs" (includes analogies portion of each battery from the full form).
Author: David F. Lohman.
Publisher: Houghton Mifflin Harcourt.

a) GRADES K-2.
Subtests, 9: Picture Analogies, Sentence Completion, Picture Classification, Number Analogies, Number Puzzles, Number Series, Figure Matrices, Paper Folder, Figure Classification.
Levels, 3: 5/6, 7, 8.
Time: Untimed; (31-45) minutes per battery, plus time for practice items.
b) GRADES 3-12.
Subtests, 9: Verbal Analogies, Sentence Completion, Verbal Classification, Number Analogies, Number Puzzles, Number Series, Figure Matrices, Paper Folder, Figure Classification.
Levels, 7: 9, 10, 11, 12, 13/14, 15/16, 17/18.
Time: Timed; 30 minutes per battery, plus time for practice items.
Cross References: Reviews are scheduled for *The Twentieth Mental Measurements Yearbook*. For reviews by James C. DiPerna and Bruce G. Rogers of Form 6, see 16:55; see also T5:560 (4 references); for reviews by Bert A. Goldman and Stephen H. Ivens of Form 5, see 13:71 (23 references); see also T4:537 (19 references); for reviews by Anne Anastasi and Douglas Fuchs of an earlier edition, see 10:66 (13 references); for a review by Charles J. Ansorge of an earlier edition, see 9:240 (5 references); see also T3:483 (32 references); for reviews by Kenneth D. Hopkins and Robert C. Nichols, see 8:181 (12 references); for reviews by Marcel L. Goldschmid and Carol K. Tittle and an excerpted review by Richard C. Cox of the primary batteries, see 7:343.

[463]

Cognitive Assessment of Young Children.

Purpose: Designed to assess "a broad array of cognitive, perceptual, and early learning processes."
Population: Ages 2 months through 5 years.
Publication Date: 2010.
Acronym: CAYC.
Score: Cognitive Ability Index.
Administration: Individual.
Levels, 6: 2-12 months, 13-24 months, 25-36 months, 37-48 months, 49-62 months, 63-71 months.
Price Data, 2014: $592 per complete kit including examiner's manual, card kit, 25 examiner's record booklets, and object kit; $89 per examiner's manual (77 pages); $82 per 25 examiner's record booklets; $63 per card kit; $365 per object kit.
Time: (15-30) minutes.
Comments: Designed "as a replacement, not a revision," of the Developmental Activities Screening Inventory–II (10:87).
Authors: M. Beth Langley, Rebecca R. Fewell, and Taddy Maddox.
Publisher: PRO-ED.
Cross References: Reviews are scheduled for *The Twentieth Mental Measurements Yearbook*.

[464]

Cognitive Assessment System–Second Edition.

Purpose: "Designed to evaluate neurocognitive abilities ... based on the Planning, Attention, Simultaneous, and Successive (PASS) theory."

Population: Ages 5 through 18 years.

Publication Dates: 1997-2014.

Acronym: CAS2.

Administration: Individual.

Levels, 2: Ages 5-7, ages 8-18.

Price Data, 2015: $999 per complete kit including administration and scoring manual, interpretive and technical manual, stimulus books 1-3, 25 Examiner Record Forms, Student Response Books for ages 5-7 and ages 8-18 (5 each), 10 Figure Memory Response Books, scoring templates, and red pencil in carrying case; $875 per complete kit without carrying case; $99 per administration and scoring manual; $99 per interpretive and technical manual; $45 per 10 Examiner Record Forms; $37 per 10 Figure Memory Response Books; $25 per scoring templates; $23 per 5 Student Response Books (ages 5-7 or ages 8-18).

Comments: Sentence Repetition subtest is administered to ages 5-7 years; Sentence Questions subtest is administered to ages 8-18 years.

Authors: Jack A. Naglieri, J. P. Das, and Sam Goldstein.

Publisher: PRO-ED.

   a) CORE BATTERY.

   Scores, 18: 5 scale scores from 8 subtest scores: Planning (Planned Codes, Planned Connections), Simultaneous (Matrices, Verbal-Spatial Relations), Attention (Expressive Attention, Number Detection), Successive (Word Series, Sentence Repetition/Questions), Full Scale; 5 supplemental scale scores: Executive Function Without Working Memory, Executive Function With Working Memory, Working Memory, Verbal Content, Nonverbal Content.

   Time: [40] minutes.

   b) EXTENDED BATTERY.

   Scores, 22: Same as *a* above plus 4 additional subtest scores: Planned Number Matching, Figure Memory, Receptive Attention, Visual Digit Span.

   Time: [60] minutes.

Cross References: Reviews are scheduled for *The Twentieth Mental Measurements Yearbook*. For reviews by Joyce Meikamp and Donald Thompson of an earlier edition titled Das•Naglieri Cognitive Assessment System, see 14:109; see also T5:763 (5 references).

[465]

Cognitive Assessment System, Second Edition: Brief.

Purpose: Designed to "evaluate four kinds of abilities needed to solve problems and acquire knowledge based on the Planning, Attention, Simultaneous, and Successive (PASS) theory of cognitive processing."

Population: Ages 4 through 18.

Publication Date: 2014.

Acronym: CAS2: Brief.

Scores, 5: Planned Codes, Simultaneous Matrices, Expressive Attention, Successive Digits, Total.

Administration: Individual.

Levels, 2: Ages 4-11, ages 12-18.

Price Data, 2014: $266 per complete kit including examiner's manual (194 pages), stimulus book, 25 examiner record forms, 25 student response books, scoring templates, and red pencil; $100 per stimulus book; $65 per examiner's manual; $41 per 25 student response booklets; $39 per 25 examiner record forms; $21 per scoring templates.

Time: [30-40] minutes.

Authors: Jack A. Naglieri, J.P. Das, and Sam Goldstein.

Publisher: PRO-ED.

Cross References: Reviews are scheduled for *The Twentieth Mental Measurements Yearbook*.

[466]

Cognitive Assessment System, Second Edition: Rating Scale.

Purpose: Designed to measure classroom "behaviors that reflect Planning, Attention, Simultaneous, and Successive (PASS) neurocognitive abilities."

Population: Ages 4 through 18.

Publication Date: 2014.

Acronym: CAS2: Rating Scale.

Scores, 5: Planning, Simultaneous, Attention, Successive, Total Score.

Administration: Individual.

Price Data, 2014: $127 per complete kit including examiner's manual (192 pages) and 25 rating forms; $71 per manual; $56 per 25 rating forms.

Time: [5-10] minutes.

Comments: Ratings should be completed by a teacher with at least 4 weeks of experience with the student.

Authors: Jack A. Naglieri, J. P. Das, and Sam Goldstein.

Publisher: PRO-ED.

Cross References: Reviews are scheduled for *The Twentieth Mental Measurements Yearbook*.

[467]

Cognitive Behavior Rating Scales.

Purpose: Intended to "evaluate the presence and severity of cognitive impairment" using observations of family and/or significant others.

Population: Patients with possible neurological impairment.

Publication Date: 1987.

Acronym: CBRS.

Scores: 9 scales: Language Deficit, Apraxia, Disorientation, Agitation, Need for Routine, Depression, Higher Cognitive Deficits, Memory Disorder, Dementia.

Administration: Individual.

Price Data, 2015: $99 per kit including manual, 25 reusable item booklets, and 25 rating booklets; $59 per 50 rating booklets.
Time: (15-20) minutes.
Comments: Completed by family and/or significant others.
Author: J. Michael Williams.
Publisher: Brainmetric.
Cross References: For reviews by Ron Edwards and David J. Mealor, see 11:74.

[468]
Cognitive Distortion Scales.
Purpose: Designed to measure cognitive/distortions (dysfunctional thinking patterns) that interfere with optimal functioning.
Population: Ages 18 and over.
Publication Date: 2000.
Acronym: CDS.
Scores, 5: Self-Criticism, Self-Blame, Helplessness, Hopelessness, Preoccupation with Danger.
Administration: Individual or group.
Price Data, 2015: $172 per introductory kit including manual (2000, 40 pages), 25 test booklets, and 25 profile forms.
Time: (10–15) minutes.
Author: John Briere.
Publisher: Psychological Assessment Resources, Inc.
Cross References: For reviews by Sandra D. Haynes and Timothy J. Makatura, see 15:54.

[469]
Cognitive Linguistic Quick Test.
Purpose: "To assess the relative status of five cognitive domains in adults with known or suspected neurological dysfunction."
Population: Adults ages 18–89 with known or suspected acquired neurological dysfunction.
Publication Date: 2001.
Acronym: CLQT.
Scores, 7: 5 Cognitive Domain Scores (Attention, Memory, Language, Executive Functions, Visuospatial Skills), Total Composite Severity Rating, Clock Drawing Severity Rating.
Administration: Individual.
Price Data, 2015: $229.60 per complete kit including examiner's manual (146 pages), stimulus manual, 15 record forms, and 15 response forms; $102.50 per examiner's manual; $102.50 per stimulus manual; $78.65 per 25 record response forms.
Foreign Language Editions: Spanish materials available.
Time: (15–30) minutes.
Comments: Test is composed of 10 tasks (Personal Facts, Symbol Cancellation, Confrontation Naming, Clock Drawing, Story Retelling, Symbol Trails, Genera-

tive Naming, Design Memory, Mazes, Design Generation); includes 5 tasks with minimal language demands; hand-scored.
Author: Nancy Helm-Estabrooks.
Publisher: Pearson.
Cross References: For reviews by Tony Cellucci and Thomas McKnight, see 15:55.

[470]
Cognitrax.
Purpose: Designed as a web-based computerized cognitive battery "for primary-care market needs such as the annual wellness visit ... for the baselining and characterization of neurocognitive deficits."
Population: Ages 8-80.
Publication Date: 2013.
Scores, 5: Verbal Memory, Psychomotor Speed, Processing Speed, Simple Visual Attention, Motor Speed.
Administration: Individual.
Price Data, 2016: $25 per battery for 10-24 assessments (volume discounts available).
Foreign Language Edition: Audio available in Spanish.
Time: (20) minutes.
Comments: Battery includes 4 neurocognitive tests (Verbal Memory Test, Finger Tapping Test, Continuous Performance Test, Symbol Digit Coding) and the Patient Health Questionnaire (PHQ-9); cognitive tests in the battery are a subset of CNS Vital Signs (456) tests.
Author: CNS Vital Signs.
Publisher: CNS Vital Signs.
Cross References: Reviews are scheduled for *The Twentieth Mental Measurements Yearbook*.

[471]
CogScreen Aeromedical Edition.
Purpose: "Designed to rapidly assess deficits or changes in" various cognitive abilities associated with flying.
Population: Aviators ages 25–73 with 12 or more years of education.
Publication Date: 1995.
Acronym: CogScreen-AE.
Scores, 65: 19 Speed Measures (Math Speed, Visual Sequence Comparison Speed, Matching-to-Sample Speed, Manikin Speed, Divided Attention Sequence Comparison Speed, Divided Attention Indicator Alone Speed, Divided Attention Indicator Dual Speed, Auditory Sequence Comparison Speed, Pathfinder Number Speed, Pathfinder Letter Speed, Pathfinder Combined Speed, Shifting Attention Arrow Direction Speed, Shifting Attention Arrow Color Speed, Shifting Attention Instruction Speed, Shifting Attention Discovery Speed, Dual Task Previous Number Alone Speed, Dual Task Previous Number Dual Speed, Dual Task Tracking Alone Error, Dual Task Tracking Dual Error), 19 Accuracy Measures

(Backward Digit Span Accuracy, Math Accuracy, Visual Sequence Comparison Accuracy, Symbol Digit Coding Accuracy, Symbol Digit Coding Immediate Recall Accuracy, Symbol Digit Coding Delayed Recall Accuracy, Matching-to-Sample Accuracy, Manikin Accuracy, Divided Attention Sequence Comparison Accuracy, Auditory Sequence Comparison Accuracy, Pathfinder Number Accuracy, Pathfinder Letter Accuracy, Pathfinder Combined Accuracy, Shifting Attention Arrow Direction Accuracy, Shifting Attention Arrow Color Accuracy, Shifting Attention Instruction Accuracy, Shifting Attention Discovery Accuracy, Dual Task Previous Number Alone Accuracy, Dual Task Previous Number Dual Accuracy), 16 Thruput Measures (Math Thruput, Visual Sequence Comparison Thruput, Symbol Digit Coding Thruput, Matching-to-Sample Thruput, Manikin Thruput, Divided Attention Sequence Comparison Thruput, Auditory Sequence Comparison Thruput, Pathfinder Number Thruput, Pathfinder Letter Thruput, Pathfinder Combined Thruput, Shifting Attention Arrow Direction Thruput, Shifting Attention Arrow Color Thruput, Shifting Attention Instruction Thruput, Shifting Attention Discovery Thruput, Dual Task Previous Number Alone Thruput, Dual Task Previous Number Dual Thruput), 11 Process Measures (Divided Attention Indicator Alone Premature Responses, Divided Attention Indicator Dual Premature Responses, Pathfinder Number Coordination, Pathfinder Letter Coordination, Pathfinder Combined Coordination, Shifting Attention Discovery Rule Shifts Completed, Shifting Attention Discovery Failures to Maintain Set, Shifting Attention Discovery Nonconceptual Responses, Shifting Attention Discovery Perseverative Errors, Dual Task Tracking Alone Boundary Hits, Dual Task Tracking Dual Boundary Hits).
Administration: Individual.
Price Data: Available from publisher.
Time: (45–60) minutes.
Author: Gary G. Kay.
Publisher: CogScreen LLC.
Cross References: For reviews by Robert W. Elliott and Hilda Wing, see 14:83.

[472]

Coitometer.
Purpose: Designed to "measure knowledge of the physical aspects of human coitus."
Population: Adults.
Publication Dates: 1974–1988.
Scores: Total score only.
Administration: Group.
Manual: No manual.
Price Data, 2015: $2 per test.
Time: [10] minutes.

Comments: Supplementary article available.
Author: Panos D. Bardis.
Publisher: Donna Bardis.

[473]

College ADHD Response Evaluation.

Purpose: Designed to assess ADHD in postsecondary students.
Population: College students, parents of college students.
Publication Date: 2002.
Acronym: CARE.
Scores, 6: Inattention, Hyperactivity, Impulsivity, Total Score, DSM-IV Inattentive, DSM-IV Hyperactive/Impulsive.
Administration: Individual.
Forms, 2: Student Response Inventory, Parent Response Inventory.
Price Data: Available from publisher.
Time: 10–15 minutes.
Comments: Oral administration permitted.
Authors: Joseph Glutting, David Sheslow, and Wayne Adams.
Publisher: Pearson.
  a) STUDENT RESPONSE INVENTORY.
  Population: College students.
  Scores, 6: Inattention, Hyperactivity, Impulsivity, Total Score, DSM-IV Inattentive, DSM-IV Hyperactive/Impulsive.
  b) PARENT RESPONSE INVENTORY.
  Population: Parents of college students.
  Scores, 5: Inattention, Hyperactivity, Total Score, DSM-IV Inattentive, DSM-IV Hyperactive/Impulsive.
Cross References: For reviews by Mary "Rina" M. Chittooran and William K. Wilkinson, see 16:57.

[474]

College Adjustment Scales.

Purpose: Identifies psychological and adjustment problems experienced by college students.
Population: College and university students.
Publication Date: 1991.
Acronym: CAS.
Scores, 9: Anxiety, Depression, Suicidal Ideation, Substance Abuse, Self-Esteem Problems, Interpersonal Problems, Family Problems, Academic Problems, Career Problems.
Administration: Individual or group.
Price Data, 2015: $160 per introductory kit including professional manual (25 pages), 25 reusable item booklets, and 25 answer sheets.
Time: (15–20) minutes.
Authors: William D. Anton and James R. Reed.
Publisher: Psychological Assessment Resources, Inc.
Cross References: For reviews by William E. Martin, Jr. and Edward R. Starr, see 13:72 (3 references); see also T4:544 (1 reference).

[475]

College Basic Academic Subjects Examination.

Purpose: Designed to assess skills and competencies achieved through the general education component of a college curriculum.

Population: College students having completed the general education component of a college curriculum.

Publication Dates: 1989–2010.

Acronym: College BASE, CBASE.

Scores, 40: Competency (Interpretive Reasoning, Strategic Reasoning, Adaptive Reasoning), Skill (Social Science Procedures, Political/Economic Structures, Geography, Significance of U.S. Events, Significance of World Events, Physical Sciences, Life Sciences, Interpreting Results, Laboratory/Field Techniques, Observation/Experimental Design, Geometrical Calculations, 2- & 3-Dimensional Figures, Equations & Inequalities, Evaluating Expressions, Using Statistics, Properties and Notations, Practical Applications, Expository Writing Sample, Conventions of Written English, Writing as a Process, Understanding Literature, Reading Analytically, Reading Critically), Cluster (Social Sciences, History, Fundamental Concepts, Laboratory & Field Work, Geometry, Algebra, General Mathematics, Writing, Reading & Literature), Subject (Social Studies, Science, Mathematics, English), Composite.

Administration: Group.

Price Data, 2016: $92 per 50 test booklets; $52 per 50 answer booklets (includes examiner's manual).

Time: 45 minutes per subject; 40 minutes for optional essay; plus 20 minutes for administration time.

Comments: "Criterion-referenced"; 180 multiple-choice items, optional essay assignment; All four subjects may be administered or any combination of 1-3 subjects; accommodations packages are available for students with special needs; additional technical reports and data files may be ordered by special request.

Author: Steven J. Osterlind.

Publisher: Assessment Resource Center, University of Missouri-Columbia.

Cross References: See T5:570 (1 reference); for reviews by William E. Coffman and Delwyn L. Harnisch, see 11:76.

[476]

College Student Inventory [part of the Retention Management System].

Purpose: Designed to assess "a variety of motives and background information related to college success," improved student retention, and enhancing student advising effectiveness.

Population: First-year undergraduate college students.

Publication Date: 1988.

Acronym: CSI.

Scores, 4: Academic Motivation (Study Habits, Intellectual Interests, Academic Confidence, Desire to Finish College, Attitude Toward Educators), Social Motivation (Self-Reliance, Sociability, Leadership), General Coping Ability (Ease of Transition, Family Emotional Support, Openness, Career Planning, Sense of Financial Security), Receptivity to Support Services (Academic Assistance, Personal Counseling, Social Enhancement, Career Counseling).

Administration: Group.

Price Data: Available from publisher.

Time: (60) minutes.

Author: Michael L. Stratil.

Publisher: Noel-Levitz.

Cross References: For reviews by Michael H. Campbell and Thomas P. Hogan, see 16:59.

[477]

College Survival and Success Scale, Second Edition.

Purpose: Designed "to identify the concerns college students are experiencing or the concerns that prospective college students can anticipate."

Population: Prospective college or university students.

Publication Dates: 2006-2011.

Acronym: CSSS.

Scores, 5: Commitment to Education, Self- and Resource-Management Skills, Interpersonal and Social Skills, Academic Success Skills, Career Planning Skills.

Administration: Individual or group.

Price Data, 2016: $63.95 per package of 25 consumable booklets; volume discount available. Administrator's guide (2011, 8 pages) available for download from publisher's website.

Time: (20) minutes.

Comments: Self-scored and interpreted.

Author: John J. Liptak.

Publisher: JIST/EMC Publishing.

Cross References: Reviews are scheduled for *The Twentieth Mental Measurements Yearbook*. For a review by Heidi M. Carty of the original edition, see 17:50.

[478]

College-to-Career Transition Inventory.

Purpose: Designed to "help students pinpoint the false beliefs and potential gaps in knowledge and skills that might prevent them from finding a job, further advancing their education, and succeeding in their career."

Population: Individuals transitioning to the workplace from high school, college, vocational, technical, and training programs.

Publication Date: 2010.

Acronym: CCTI; C2C.

Scores, 5: Life Management, Emotional Intelligence, Job Search, Transition to Work, Career Management.

Administration: Group.

Price Data, 2015: $35.67 per 25 assessment booklets.

Time: (20-25) minutes.

Comments: The administrator's guide (14 pages) is available for download on the publisher's web site.

Author: John J. Liptak.

Publisher: JIST Publishing, Inc.

Cross References: For reviews by Michael Bunch and Tracey Wyatt, see 19:39.

[479]

Color Trails Test.

Purpose: Designed as a test of sustained visual attention and simple sequencing.

Population: Ages 18 and over.

Publication Dates: 1994–1996.

Acronym: CTT.

Scores, 10: Color Trails 1, Color Trails 1 Errors, Color Trails 1 Near-Misses, Color Trails 1 Prompts, Color Trails 2, Color Trails 2 Color Errors, Color Trails 2 Number Errors, Color Trails 2 Near-Misses, Color Trails 2 Prompts, Interference Index.

Administration: Individual.

Forms, 8: Color Trails 1: A, B, C, D; Color Trails 2: A, B, C, D.

Price Data, 2015: $146 per introductory kit including professional manual (1996, 88 pages), 25 record forms, and 25 administrations of the CCT Form A, Trials 1 and 2 test sheets.

Time: (10) minutes

Comments: The CTT was developed to be free from the influence of language, and is an analogue of the Trail Making Test (TMT). Administration instructions in Spanish and English are provided in the manual. Respondents must be able to recognize Arabic numerals 1–25.

Authors: Louis F. D'Elia, Paul Satz, Craig Lyons Uchiyama, and Travis White.

Publisher: Psychological Assessment Resources, Inc.

Cross References: For reviews by James C. Reed and Surendra P. Singh, see 15:56.

[480]

Colored Overlay Assessment Kits.

Purpose: Designed to help determine the effectiveness of each colored overlay in improving the ease and accuracy of seeing the printed word while reading.

Population: Individuals experiencing reading and writing problems due to suspected visual perception problems.

Publication Date: 1993.

Scores: Not scored.

Administration: Individual.

Price Data, 2005: Available from publisher.

Time: Administration time varies from student to student.

Author: Marie Carbo.

Publisher: National Reading Styles Institute, Inc.

[481]

Combined Basic Skills.

Purpose: To evaluate literacy and cognitive skills.

Population: Applicants and incumbents for jobs requiring literacy and cognitive skills.

Publication Dates: 1998–2014.

Scores, 4: Reading, Arithmetic, Inspection and Measurement, Process Monitoring & Problem Solving.

Administration: Group.

Price Data, 2015: $16 per consumable self-scoring test booklet or $17 per online test administration (minimum order of 20); $24.95 per manual.

Foreign Language Editions: Available in Spanish.

Time: (48) minutes.

Comments: Self-scoring instrument; two alternate equivalent forms; available for online test administration; test publisher advises changes in form names indicate minor revisions and updating.

Author: Roland T. Ramsay.

Publisher: Ramsay Corporation.

Cross References: For a review by Cher N. Edwards and Scott F. Beers of Forms LCS-C and B-C (2010), see 17:51.

[482]

The Common-Metric Questionnaire.

Purpose: "Designed to describe, analyze, and evaluate jobs of all types from both public and private sector organizations."

Population: Job incumbents, supervisors, job analysts.

Publication Dates: 1990–1992.

Acronym: CMQ.

Scores: 6 sections: General Background, Contacts With People, Making Decisions, Physical and Mechanical Activities, Work Setting, Selection Test Scores.

Administration: Group.

Price Data: Available from publisher.

Time: (180–240) minutes.

Authors: Robert J. Harvey (questionnaire) and The Psychological Corporation (manuals).

Publisher: Robert J. Harvey (the author) [No reply from publisher; status unknown].

Cross References: For a review by Gerald A. Rosen, see 13:75.

[483]

Communication Activities of Daily Living, Second Edition.

Purpose: "To assess the functional communication skills of adults with neurogenic communication disorders."

Population: Aphasic adults.

Publication Dates: 1980–1999.

Acronym: CADL-2.

Scores: Total score only.

Administration: Individual.

Price Data, 2015: $233 per complete kit; $31 per 25 patient response forms; $68 per examiner record booklets; $94 per picture book; $68 per examiner's manual.
Time: (25–35) minutes.
Comments: Previous edition entitled Communicative Abilities in Daily Living.
Authors: Audrey Holland, Carol Frattali, and David Fromm.
Publisher: PRO-ED.
Cross References: For reviews by Carolyn Mitchell Person and Katharine Snyder, see 14:84; for a review by Rita Sloan Berndt of an earlier edition, see 10:69 (2 references).

[484]

Communication and Symbolic Behavior Scales Developmental Profile: First Normed Edition.

Purpose: Designed to "evaluate communication and symbolic abilities of children whose functional communication is between 6 months and 2 years."
Population: Ages 6–24 months
Publication Dates: 1995–2002.
Acronym: CSBS DP.
Scores, 11: Social Composite (Emotion and Eye Gaze, Communication, Gestures, Total); Speech Composite (Sounds, Words, Total); Symbolic Composite (Understanding, Object Use, Total); Total.
Administration: Individual.
Forms, 3: Infant-Toddler Checklist, Caregiver Questionnaire, Behavior Sample.
Price Data, 2016: $399 per complete kit including manual (2002, 188 pages), 20 infant-toddler checklists, 20 caregiver questionnaires, 20 caregiver questionnaire scoring worksheets, 20 behavior sample scoring worksheets, 20 caregiver perception rating forms, 1 of each (Part 1 and Part 2) sampling and scoring DVDs, and toy kit; $199.95 per test kit including manual, 20 infant-toddler checklists, 20 caregiver questionnaires, 20 caregiver questionnaire scoring worksheets, 20 of each (Part 1 and Part 2) sampling and scoring DVDs; $259.95 per toy kit; $65 per manual; $40 per 20 of each infant-toddler checklists, caregiver questionnaires, caregiver questionnaire scoring worksheets, behavior sample scoring worksheets, and caregiver perception rating forms; $25 per 50 caregiver questionnaires; $99 per sampling and scoring videos 1 and 2 on DVD; $99.95 for Infant-Toddler Checklist and Easy-Score CD-ROM with instructional user's guide.
Comments: May be used with children "up to 5–6 years if their developmental level of functioning is younger than 24 months."
Authors: Amy M. Wetherby and Barry M. Prizant.
Publisher: Paul H. Brookes Publishing Co., Inc.
a) INFANT-TODDLER CHECKLIST.
Time: (5–10) minutes.

Comments: A screening tool completed by a caregiver; computer scoring available; may be administered independent of other components.
b) CAREGIVER QUESTIONNAIRE.
Time: (15–20) minutes.
Comments: Companion to the behavior sample completed by caregiver.
c) BEHAVIOR SAMPLE.
Time: (30) minutes.
Comments: A "face to face evaluation tool" conducted by professional evaluator with the caregiver present. The caregiver questionnaire is designed to "determine whether a child has a developmental delay or disability in the areas measured."
Cross References: For a review by Karen T. Carey, see 16:60; see also T5:630 (1 reference); for reviews by Steven H. Long and Dolores Kluppel Vetter of the original edition, see 13:76 (3 references).

[485]

Communication Preference Profile.

Purpose: Designed to identify four habitual communication styles.
Population: Employees.
Publication Dates: 2011-2014.
Acronym: CPP.
Scores, 4: People-Oriented, Action-Oriented, Content-Oriented, Technology-Oriented.
Administration: Individual or group.
Manual: No manual.
Price Data, 2016: $14.99 per single administration; $130 per 10 administrations; $1,200 per 100 administrations; $75 per 1 CPP administration, facilitator's guide, and 20-minute feedback call.
Time: Administration time not reported.
Authors: Michelle K. Johnston, Larry L. Barker, and Kittie W. Watson.
Publisher: Innolect, Inc.

[486]

Communication Response Style: Assessment.

Purpose: To assess an individual's communication response style.
Population: Adults.
Publication Dates: 1981–1987.
Scores, 4: Empathic Response Score, Critical Response Score, Searching Response Score, Advising Response Score.
Administration: Group or individual.
Manual: No manual.
Price Data, 2016: $59.95; volume discounts available.
Time: (20) minutes.
Comments: Self-administered, self-scored.
Author: Madelyn Burley-Allen.
Publisher: HRD Press, Inc.
Cross References: For reviews by Janet Norris and Gargi Roysircar Sodowsky, see 11:78.

[487]
Communication Skills Assessment.

Purpose: Designed to assess "how well a person communicates with others" and "whether he or she has any problem areas that can potentially inhibit the communication process."
Population: Under age 17 through adult.
Publication Date: 2011.
Acronym: COMSA-R2.
Scores, 5: Overall Score, Insightfulness, Verbal Expression, Assertiveness, Listening Skills, Emotional Management.
Administration: Individual.
Price Data: Available from publisher.
Time: (15) minutes.
Comments: Self-administered online assessment. The test publisher provides clients with information about the methods and theoretical basis used in the development of the test as well as benchmarks for relevant industries and racial/ethnic group comparison data.
Author: PsychTests AIM, Inc.
Publisher: PsychTests AIM, Inc. [Canada].
Cross References: For reviews by Ric Brown and Monica Gordon Pershey, see 19:40.

[488]
Communication Skills Profile.

Purpose: "Designed to help people who want to gain a thorough knowledge of the processes of communication and to improve their effectiveness as communicators."
Population: Individuals or teams within organizations.
Publication Date: 1997.
Scores: 6 scales: Slowing My Thought Processes, Making Myself Understood, Testing My Conclusions, Listening Constructively, Getting to the Essence, Exploring Disagreement.
Administration: Group.
Price Data: Available from publisher.
Time: Administration time not reported.
Author: Elena Tosca.
Publisher: Jossey-Bass, A Wiley Company.
Cross References: For reviews by Robert Brown and Thomas P. Hogan, see 14:86.

[489]
Community-Based Social Skill Performance Assessment Tool.

Purpose: Designed to assess students' social skill performance in the home and in the community.
Population: Ages 14–21 years, with emotional or behavioral disorders.
Publication Date: Not dated.
Acronym: CBSP.
Scores, 5: Positive Social Behavior, Social Skills Mechanics, Anti-Social Behavior, Self-Control, Total.

Administration: Group.
Forms, 2: Male, Female.
Price Data: Price data available from publisher for set including teaching guide and script (no date, 34 pages), male and female testing materials, response form, and response interpretation/scoring guide.
Time: (45) minutes.
Author: Michael Bullis.
Publisher: James Stanfield Co., Inc.

[490]
Community College Student Experiences Questionnaire, Second Edition.

Purpose: Designed to assess community college students' "quality of effort" toward maximizing college opportunities and achieving their goals.
Population: Community college students.
Publication Dates: 1990–2001.
Acronym: CCSEQ-2.
Scores: 9 scales: Quality of Effort (Course Activities, Library Activities, Faculty-Student Acquaintances, Art, Music and Theater, Writing Activities, Science Activities, Vocational Skills), Satisfaction.
Administration: Group.
Price Data: Available from publisher.
Time: (20–30) minutes.
Comments: For use with students fluent in English.
Authors: C. Robert Pace, Patricia H. Murrell, Jack Friedlander, Penny W. Lehman; Corinna A. Ethington, Anne Marie Guthrie, and Penny W. Lehman (test manual, 3rd edition).
Publisher: Center for the Study of Higher Education, The University of Memphis.
Cross References: For reviews by Candice Haas Hollingsead and James P. Van Haneghan, see 14:87; for reviews by Charles Houston and by Rosemary E. Sutton and Hinsdale Bernard of the original edition, see 12:87.

[491]
Community Oriented Programs Environment Scale [Fourth Edition Manual].

Purpose: Designed to "assess the social environments of community-based psychiatric treatment programs, day programs, sheltered workshops, rehabilitation centers and community care homes."
Population: Patients and staff of community oriented psychiatric facilities.
Publication Dates: 1974-2009.
Acronym: COPES.
Scores: 10 in 3 dimensions: Relationship (Involvement, Support, Spontaneity), Treatment Program (Autonomy, Practical Orientation, Personal Problem Orientation, Anger and Aggression), System Maintenance (Order and Organization, Program Clarity, Staff Control).
Administration: Individual or group.

Forms, 4: R (Real), I (Ideal), E (Expectations), S (Short).

Price Data, 2015: $50 for manual (2009, 107 pages), including review-only copy of test form; $2 per Remote Online Survey License (minimum 50); $2 per License to Reproduce (minimum 50); $10 per user's guide.

Foreign Language Editions: Translations available in French, Italian, Japanese, Norwegian, Spanish, and Swedish.

Time: Administration time not reported.

Comments: A part of the Social Climate Scales.

Author: Rudolf H. Moos.

Publisher: Mind Garden, Inc.

Cross References: See T5:637 (3 references), T4:605 (11 references) and T3:542 (6 references); for a review by Richard I. Lanyon of the original edition, see 8:525 (17 references). For a review of the Social Climate Scales, see 8:681.

[492]

Competency-Based Performance Improvement: Organizational Assessment Package.

Purpose: Used to assess an organization's performance improvement program/s and to improve planning for future programs.

Population: Business managers.

Publication Date: 1995.

Scores, 7: 6 categories (Strategic Goals and Business Objectives, Needs Analysis/Assessment/Planning, Competency Modeling, Curriculum Planning, Learning Intervention Design and Development, Evaluation), Total.

Administration: Group.

Price Data, 2016: $39.95; volume discounts available.

Time: Administration time not reported.

Author: David D. Dubois.

Publisher: HRD Press, Inc.

Cross References: For reviews by Stephen F. Davis and Jerry M. Lowe, see 14:88.

[493]

The Competent Speaker Speech Evaluation Form, Second Edition.

Purpose: Designed to measure public speaking competency.

Population: Post-secondary students.

Publication Date: 1993-2007.

Scores, 9: Chooses and Narrows a Topic Appropriately for the Audience and Occasion, Communicates the Thesis/Specific Purpose in a Manner Appropriate for Audience and Occasion, Uses an Organizational Pattern Appropriate to Topic/Audience/Occasion and Purpose, Provides Appropriate Supporting Material Based on the Audience and Occasion, Uses Language That is Appropriate to the Audience/Occasion and Purpose, Uses Vocal Variety in Rate/Pitch and Intensity to Heighten and Maintain Interest, Uses Pronunciation/Grammar and Articulation Appropriate to the Designated Audience, Uses Physical Behaviors that Support the Verbal Message, Total.

Administration: Individual.

Price Data: Available at no charge from test publisher.

Time: Administration time not reported.

Author: Speech Communication Association.

Publisher: National Communication Association.

Cross References: For reviews by Sandra M. Ketrow and Julia Y. Porter of an earlier edition, see 14:89.

[494]

Compliance with Supervisor's Wishes.

Purpose: Measures employees' attitudinal and behavioral compliance with supervisors' wishes.

Population: Employees.

Publication Date: 1993.

Acronym: CSW.

Scores, 2: Attitudinal Compliance, Behavioral Compliance.

Administration: Group.

Manual: No manual.

Price Data: Available from publisher.

Time: Administration time not reported.

Author: M. Afzal Rahim.

Publisher: Center for Advanced Studies in Management.

[495]

Comprehensive Addictions and Psychological Evaluation–5.

Purpose: Designed as a structured interview with items derived from the DSM-5 diagnostic criteria for use in mental health and substance abuse disorder assessment.

Population: Adults.

Publication Dates: 2000-2013.

Acronym: CAAPE-5.

Scores, 15: Substance Use Disorders, Mental Health Conditions (Major Depressive Episode, Manic Episode, Panic, Posttraumatic Stress, Anxiety and Phobias, Obsessions/Compulsions, Psychosis), Personality Disorders (Conduct Disorder, Antisocial Personality, Paranoid Personality, Schizoid Personality, Borderline Personality, Dependent Personality, Obsessive-Compulsive Personality).

Administration: Individual.

Price Data, 2015: $67.50 per 25 booklets, $20 per manual (2013, 56 pages).

Time: [35-50] minutes.

Author: Norman G. Hoffman.

Publisher: The Change Companies.

Cross References: Reviews are scheduled for *The Twentieth Mental Measurements Yearbook*. For reviews by Tony Cellucci and William E. Martin, Jr., of an earlier (DSM-IV) edition, see 18:31.

[496]
Comprehensive Adult Student Assessment System—Third Edition.

Purpose: Designed to provide a measure to "place students in the appropriate program, level or test, diagnose student learning needs, monitor student progress and certify student proficiency levels."

Population: Adults.

Publication Dates: 1980-2004.

Acronym: CASAS.

Administration: Group.

Restricted Distribution: Agency training is required before test can be provided.

Price Data: Available from publisher.

Time: Administration times vary.

Comments: Third edition includes new technical manual; computer scoring and individual and class score profiles available.

Author: CASAS.

Publisher: CASAS.

a) APPRAISAL TESTS.

1) *ESL Appraisal (English as a Second Language).*
Scores: 4 tests: Listening, Reading, Speaking, Writing.
Comments: Appraisal determines level of pretests of CASAS Life Skills Series to be administered.

2) *Life Skills Appraisal.*
Scores: 2 tests: Reading, Math.
Comments: Appraisal determines level of CASAS Life Skills Series Pre-Test to be administered.

3) *ECS Appraisal (Employability Competency System).*
Scores: 2 tests: Reading, Math.
Forms, 2: 120, 130.
Comments: Appraisal determines level of CASAS Basic Skills for Employability Pre-Test to be administered.

b) CASAS TESTS FOR MONITORING PROGRESS.
Comments: All tests serve as pre/post tests.

1) *Employability Competency Series.*
(a) Reading.
Levels, 4: A, B, C, and D each with 2 forms.
(b) Math.
Levels, 4: A, B, C, and D each with 2 forms.
(c) *Listening.*
Levels, 3: A, B, and C each with 2 forms.

2) *Life Skills Series.*
(a) Reading.
Levels, 5: (Beginning Literacy, A, B, C, D), Beginning Literacy, Levels C and D each have 2 forms; Levels A and B have 3 forms.
(b) Math.
Levels, 4: A, B, C, and D each with 2 forms.
(c) Listening.
Levels, 3: A, B, and C each with 2 forms.

Cross References: For reviews by Terri Flowerday and Carol S. Parke, see 16:61; see also T5:645 (1 reference); for reviews by Ralph O. Mueller and Patricia K. Freitag and by William D. Schafer of a previous edition, see 13:78 (2 references).

[497]
Comprehensive Aphasia Test.

Purpose: Designed for use in "diagnosis of impairment and impairment-based treatment planning" to assess language performance and to screen for associated cognitive deficits.

Population: Persons with aphasia.

Publication Date: 2004.

Acronym: CAT.

Scores, 34: Cognitive Screen (Line Bisection, Semantic Memory, Word Fluency, Recognition Memory, Gesture Object Use, Arithmetic), Language Battery (Comprehension of Spoken Words, Comprehension of Written Words, Comprehension of Spoken Sentences, Comprehension of Written Sentences, Comprehension of Spoken Paragraphs, Repetition of Words, Repetition of Complex Words, Repetition of Nonwords, Repetition of Digit Strings, Repetition of Sentences, Naming Objects, Naming Actions, Spoken Picture Description, Reading Words, Reading Complex Words, Reading Function Words, Reading Nonwords, Writing/Copying, Writing Picture Names, Writing to Dictation, Written Picture Description), Disability Questionnaire (Talking, Understanding, Reading, Writing, Intrusion, Self-Image, Emotional Consequences).

Administration: Individual.

Parts, 3: Cognitive Screen, Language Battery, Disability Questionnaire.

Price Data, 2015: $320 per test pack including manual (2004, 186 pages), Disability Questionnaire, Cognitive Screen, Language Battery, and 10 scoring books.

Time: (90-120) minutes.

Comments: May be administered in two sessions.

Authors: Kate Swinburn, Gillian Porter, and David Howard.

Publisher: Routledge Psychology.

Cross References: Reviews are scheduled for *The Twentieth Mental Measurements Yearbook.*

[498]
Comprehensive Assessment of Mathematics Strategies.

Purpose: Designed to "identify and assess a student's level of mastery in each of 12 mathematics strategies."

Population: Grades 1–8.

Publication Dates: 2000-2011.

Acronym: CAMS.

Scores, 12: Building Number Sense, Using Estimation, Applying Addition, Applying Subtraction, Applying Multiplication, Applying Division, Converting Time and Money, Converting Customary and Metric Measures, Using Algebra, Using Geometry, Determining Probability and Averages, Interpreting Graphs and Charts.

Administration: Group.

Levels, 8: Grade 1, Grade 2, Grade 3, Grade 4, Grade 5, Grade 6, Grade 7, Grade 8.

Price Data, 2016: $39.90 per 10 student books; $5.95 per teacher guide (for each level).
Time: (60) minutes.
Comments: Testing materials include practice lessons, self-assessments, and teacher assessments; self-assessments (both of which are completed after the student is exposed to and practices lessons 1–5, and again after the student is exposed to each practices lessons 6–10); class performance chart available; Teacher Assessment 1 "assesses a student's performance for each of the 12 mathematics' strategies"; Teacher Assessment 2 compares a student's level of mastery in the criteria for the 12 mathematics' strategies.
Author: Robert G. Forest.
Publisher: Curriculum Associates, LLC.

[499]

Comprehensive Assessment of Reading Strategies.

Purpose: Designed to "identify and assess a student's level of mastery with each of 12 reading strategies."
Population: Grades 1-8.
Publication Dates: 1998–2011.
Acronym: CARS.
Scores, 13: Finding Main Idea, Recalling Facts and Details, Understanding Sequence, Recognizing Cause and Effect, Comparing and Contrasting, Making Predictions, Finding Word Meaning in Context, Drawing Conclusions and Making Inferences, Distinguishing Between Fact and Opinion, Identifying Author's Purpose, Interpreting Figurative Language, Distinguishing Between Real and Make-Believe [Books 1-4], Summarizing [Books 5–8].
Administration: Group.
Levels, 8: Grades 1, 2, 3, 4, 5, 6, 7, 8.
Price Data, 2016: $39.90 per 10 student books $5.95 per teacher's guide (specify grade).
Time: (45) minutes.
Comments: Testing materials include practice lessons, self-assessments, and teacher assessments; self-assessment and teacher assessment are completed after student is exposed to and practices the lessons presented in the test materials; class performance charts available; assessment consists of 2 assessments to be given at separate times.
Authors: Deborah Adcock and Courtney Bolser (contributing author to test booklet).
Publisher: Curriculum Associates, LLC.

[500]

Comprehensive Assessment of Spoken Language.

Purpose: Designed to measure the processes of comprehension, expression, and retrieval in oral language.
Population: Ages 3–21.
Publication Date: 1999.
Acronym: CASL.

Scores: 15 tests: Basic Concepts, Antonyms, Synonyms, Sentence Completion, Idiomatic Language, Syntax Construction, Paragraph Comprehension, Grammatical Morphemes, Sentence Comprehension, Grammaticality Judgment, Nonliteral Language, Meaning from Context, Inference, Ambiguous Sentences, and Pragmatic Judgment; plus Core Composite scores, Category Index scores (Lexical/Semantic, Syntactic, Supralinguistic); Processing Index scores (Expressive, Receptive).
Administration: Individual.
Forms, 2: 1, 2.
Price Data, 2016: $522.50 per complete kit, including 3 test books, 24 record forms (12 each of forms 1 and 2, for ages 3 to 6 and 7 to 21, respectively), manual, and norms book; $654 for complete kit plus Assist Scoring Software; $344.50 per Assist Scoring Software CD-ROM; $39 per 12 record forms for ages 3-6 (volume discounts available); $44 per 12 record forms for ages 7-21; $53 per manual; $53 per norms book; $131.50 test book 1: Lexical/Semantics Tests; $131.50 Test Book 2: Syntactic Tests; $131.50 test book 3: Supralinguistic & Pragmatic Tests.
Author: Elizabeth Carrow-Woolfolk.
Publisher: Western Psychological Services.
Cross References: For reviews by Katharine A. Snyder and Gabrielle Stutman, see 15:58.

[501]

Comprehensive Assessment of Symptoms and History.

Purpose: "Designed as a structured interview and recording instrument for documenting the signs, symptoms, and history of subjects evaluated in research studies of the major psychoses and affective disorders."
Population: Psychiatric patients.
Publication Date: 1987.
Acronym: CASH.
Scores: Interview divided into 3 major sections: Present State (Sociodemographic Data, Evaluation of Current Condition, Psychotic Syndrome, Manic Syndrome, Major Depressive Syndrome, Treatment, Cognitive Assessment, Global Assessment Scale, Diagnosis for Current Episode), Past History (History of Onset and Hospitalization, Past Symptoms of Psychosis, Characterization of Course, Past Symptoms of Affective Disorder), Lifetime History (History of Somatic Therapy, Alcoholism, Drug Use and Abuse and Dependence, Modified Premorbid Adjustment Scale, Premorbid or Intermorbid Personality, Functioning During Past Five Years, Global Assessment Scale, Diagnosis for Lifetime).
Administration: Individual.
Price Data: Available free of charge from test publisher.
Time: [60–180] minutes.
Comments: The CASH is one component of a modular assessment battery available from the publisher.
Author: Nancy C. Andreasen.

Publisher: Nancy C. Andreasen.

Cross References: See T5:650 (16 references); for reviews by Patricia A. Bachelor and Barbara J. Kaplan, see 12:88 (12 references); see also T4:612 (4 references).

[502]

Comprehensive Executive Function Inventory.

Purpose: Designed to "measure behaviors that are associated with Executive Function in children and youths."

Population: Ages 5–18.

Publication Date: 2013.

Acronym: CEFI.

Scores, 13: Attention, Emotion Regulation, Flexibility, Inhibitory Control, Initiation, Organization, Planning, Self-Monitoring, Working Memory, Full Scale, Consistency Index, Negative Impression, Positive Impression.

Administration: Individual or group.

Forms, 3: Self-Report (ages 12–18), Parent, Teacher.

Price Data, 2015: $92 per manual (195 pages); $344 per complete online kit including manual and 25 Self-Report/Parent/Teacher online forms; $549 per scoring software kit including manual, scoring software program (USB key), and 25 Self-Report/Parent/Teacher response forms; $269 per handscored kit, including manual and 25 Self-Report/Parent/Teacher QuikScore forms.

Foreign Language Edition: Spanish edition available.

Time: (15) minutes.

Comments: Online and paper-and-pencil administration available.

Authors: Jack A. Naglieri and Sam Goldstein.

Publisher: Multi-Health Systems, Inc.

Cross References: For reviews by Joe W. Dixon and Tawnya Meadows, see 19:41.

[503]

Comprehensive Identification Process [Revised].

Purpose: "Designed to identify children who may have medical, psychological or learning problems that could interfere with their success in school."

Population: Ages 2–6.5.

Publication Date: 1975–1997.

Acronym: CIP.

Administration: Individual.

Price Data, 2015: $301.50 per screening kit/Form 750R; $34.50 per 35 forms (specify parent interview forms; observation of behavior forms; or speech and expressive language forms); $53.50 per 35 child record folders; $34.50 per screening booklet; $55 per symbol booklet; $33 per interviewer's manual; $33 per administrator's manual; $21 per circle pad.

Foreign Language Edition: Spanish materials available.

Time: Varies.

Comments: CIP screening team should include at least one member who has a background in early childhood education of the disabled and is skilled in screening and evaluation; alternatives to the standard screening, such as in-home screening or bilingual screening available.

Authors: R. Reid Zehrbach (test), and Joan Good Erickson (Speech and Expressive Language Record Form).

Publisher: Scholastic Testing Service, Inc.

    a) CHILD: RECORD FOLDER.

    Scores, 5: Hearing, Vision, Perceptual Motor, Cognitive-Verbal, Gross Motor.

    Comment: Materials for hearing and vision screening must be obtained locally.

    b) SPEECH AND EXPRESSIVE LANGUAGE RECORD FORM.

    Scores, 6: Articulation/Phonology, Voice, Fluency, Expressive Language, Associated Factors, Total.

    Author: Joan Good Erickson.

    c) OBSERVATION OF BEHAVIOR FORM.

    Scores, 7: Hearing, Vision, Physical/Motor Speech and Expressive Language, Social Behavior (Responses, Interaction), Affective Behavior.

    d) PARENT INTERVIEW FORM.

    Scores, 7: Pregnancy/Birth/Hospitalization, Walking/Toilet Training, Hearing, Vision, Speech and Expressive Language, Medical, Social Affect.

    Comments: History and ratings by parent.

Cross References: For a review by J. Jeffrey Grill, see 14:91; see also T4:616 (1 reference); for reviews by Robert P. Anderson and Phyllis L. Newcomer of an earlier version, see 8:425 (1 reference).

[504]

Comprehensive Mathematical Abilities Test.

Purpose: Developed to "assess a broad spectrum of mathematical abilities in the areas of comprehension (reasoning), calculation and application."

Population: Ages 7:0 to 18:11.

Publication Date: 2003.

Acronym: CMAT.

Scores: (10–18): General Mathematics (Basic Calculations, composed of Addition, Subtraction, Multiplication, Division, and Mathematical Reasoning, composed of Problem Solving, Charts/Tables/and Graphs); Advanced Calculations (Algebra, Geometry, Rational Numbers) [supplemental]; Practical Applications (Time, Money, Measurement) [supplemental]; Global Mathematics Ability.

Administration: Individual.

Price Data, 2015: $341 per complete kit including examiner's manual (199 pages), picture book, 25 profile/examiner record booklets, 25 student response booklet I, 25 student response booklet II, and information sheet; $109 per examiner's manual; $91 per picture book; $48 per pack of 25 profile/examiner record booklets; $57 per pack of 25 student response booklet I or II; $131 per CMAT scoring and reporting software, Version 1.23; $435 for CMAT Print & Software COMBO kit including examiner's manual, picture book, 25 profile/examiner record booklets, 25 student response booklet I, 25 student response booklet II, and scoring and reporting software, Version 1.23.

Time: 45–60 minutes.

Comments: Computer scoring available.

Authors: Wayne P. Hresko, Paul L. Schlieve, Shelley R. Herron, Colleen Swain, and Rita J. Sherbenou.

Publisher: PRO-ED.

Cross References: For reviews by George Engelhard, Jr. and Suzanne Lane, see 16:62.

[505]
Comprehensive Personality Profile.

Purpose: Designed to provide a comprehensive assessment of job-relevant personality characteristics that impact the successful fulfillment of job requirements; used within organizations to identify individuals whose personality characteristics are compatible with job demands.

Population: Ages 15 and up.

Publication Dates: 1985–2002.

Acronym: CPP.

Scores, 48: Primary Scales (Emotional Intensity, Intuition, Recognition Motivation, Sensitivity, Assertiveness, Trust, Exaggeration), Secondary Traits (Ego Drive, Interpersonal Warmth, Stability, Empathy, Objectivity, Independence, Aggressiveness, Decisiveness, Tolerance, Efficiency), Interaction Traits (Temperament, Ego Style, Social Style), Management Performance Traits (Ability To Make Unpopular Decisions, Decisiveness To Act Without Precedent, Ingenuity To Create New Ideas, Ability To Motivate Others To Act, Vision To Plan Ahead On A Large Scale, Self-Discipline To Efficiently Manage Time, Communicates With Frankness And Humility, Tolerance For Corporate Red Tape Or Politics, Delegates Responsibility Or Authority, Caution In Making Policy Commitments), Sales Performance Traits (Goal Oriented Drive Toward Immediate Results, Insight To Perceive The Buyer's Need, Ability To Close Sales Without Hesitation, Ability To Make New Contacts (Call Courage), Overcomes Objections With Tact And Diplomacy, Desire To Provide After-The-Sale Service, Desire To Compete And Win At All Costs, Ability To Keep Positive Attitude (Optimism), Ability To Control Emotional Ups And Downs, Ability To Handle Sales Rejection), Administrative Performance Traits (Tolerance To Stay At One Work Station, Desire To Conform To Management Objectives, Ability To Cope With Change And Disruption, Satisfaction To Stay At Job Level Attained, Ability To Be Diplomatic And Cooperative, Patience To Follow Detailed Instructions, Capacity To Follow Systems), Summary Profile.

Administration: Group or individual.

Price Data: Available from publisher.

Foreign Language Editions: Available in French and Spanish.

Time: (15–25) minutes.

Comments: Title on questionnaire is CPP Compatibility Questionnaire; online administration available.

Authors: Wonderlic, Inc. and Larry L. Craft (questionnaire).

Publisher: Wonderlic, Inc.

Cross References: For reviews by Sanford J. Cohn and Ira Stuart Katz, see 14:92; see also T4:617 (1 reference). For reviews by Sanford J. Cohn and Ira Stuart Katz, see 14:92; see also T4:617 (1 reference).

[506]
Comprehensive Receptive and Expressive Vocabulary Test–Third Edition.

Purpose: Designed to "identify individuals with below-average oral proficiency skills, to recognize any discrepancy between receptive and expressive oral vocabulary, and to document progress in oral proficiency."

Population: Ages 5 through 89.

Publication Dates: 1994-2013.

Acronym: CREVT-3.

Scores, 3: Receptive Vocabulary, Expressive Vocabulary, General Vocabulary.

Administration: Individual.

Forms, 2: A, B.

Price Data, 2014: $316 per complete kit including examiner's manual (2013, 94 pages), photo album picture booklet, 25 Form A examiner record booklets, 25 Form B examiner record booklets; $99 per examiner's manual; $59 per 25 examiner's record booklets (Form A or Form B); $99 per photo album picture book.

Time: (20-30) minutes.

Authors: Gerald Wallace and Donald D. Hammill.

Publisher: PRO-ED.

Cross References: Reviews are scheduled for *The Twentieth Mental Measurements Yearbook.* For reviews by Luanne Andersson and Gretchen Owens of the second edition, see 15:59; see T5:655 (CREVT, 1 reference) and T5:656 (CREVT); for reviews by Alan S. Kaufman and Mary J. McLellan of the CREVT, see 13:80 (1 reference); for reviews by Margaret E. Malone and Wayne H. Slater of the CREVT-A, see 14:93 (1 reference).

[507]
Comprehensive Test of Nonverbal Intelligence–Second Edition.

Purpose: Designed "to estimate the general intelligence of children and adults whose performance on traditional intelligence tests might be adversely affected by subtle or overt impairments involving language or motor abilities."

Population: Ages 6 through 89.

Publication Dates: 1996-2009.

Acronym: CTONI-2.

Scores, 9: Pictorial Scale (Pictorial Analogies, Pictorial Categories, Pictorial Sequences, Total), Geometric Scale

(Geometric Analogies, Geometric Categories, Geometric Sequences, Total), Full Scale.

Administration: Individual.

Price Data, 2014: $457 per complete kit including examiner's manual (2009, 137 pages), analogies picture book, categories picture book, sequences picture book, and 25 examiner record forms; $105 per examiner's manual; $100 per picture book (analogies, categories, or sequences); $56 per 25 record forms.

Foreign Language Editions: Manual includes oral instructions in Spanish, Simplified Chinese, French, Tagalog, Vietnamese, German, and Korean.

Time: (5-10) minutes per subtest; (40-60) minutes for all subtests.

Authors: Donald D. Hammill, Nils A. Pearson, and J. Lee Wiederholt.

Publisher: PRO-ED.

Cross References: Reviews are scheduled for *The Twentieth Mental Measurements Yearbook*. See T5:662 (1 reference); for reviews by Glen P. Aylward and Gabriele van Lingen of the original edition, see 13:82.

[508]

Comprehensive Test of Phonological Processing–Second Edition.

Purpose: Designed to measure "phonological processing abilities related to reading."

Population: Ages 4 through 24.

Publication Dates: 1999-2013.

Acronym: CTOPP-2.

Administration: Individual.

Price Data, 2015: $330 per complete kit including examiner's manual (2013, 136 pages), 25 examiner record booklets for ages 4 through 6, 25 examiner record booklets for ages 7 through 24, picture book, and two CDs; $75 per manual; $69 per 25 examiner record booklets (ages 4-6 or 7-24); $63 per picture book; $27 per core subtest CD-ROM; $27 per supplemental subtest CD-ROM.

Time: (30) minutes for core battery.

Authors: Richard K. Wagner, Joseph K. Torgesen, Carol A. Rashotte, and Nils A. Pearson.

Publisher: PRO-ED.

a) AGES 4-6.

Scores, 14: Phonological Awareness (Elision, Blending Words, Sound Matching), Phonological Memory (Memory for Digits, Nonword Repetition), Rapid Symbolic Naming (Rapid Digit Naming, Rapid Letter Naming), Rapid Non-Symbolic Naming (Rapid Color Naming, Rapid Object Naming), Blending Nonwords (supplemental subtest).

b) AGES 7-24.

Scores, 13: Phonological Awareness (Elision, Blending Words, Phoneme Isolation), Phonological Memory (Memory for Digits, Nonword Repetition), Rapid Symbolic Naming (Rapid Digit Naming, Rapid Letter Naming), Alternate Phonological Awareness (Blending Nonwords, Segmenting Nonwords).

Cross References: Reviews are scheduled for *The Twentieth Mental Measurements Yearbook*. For reviews by

David P. Hurford and Claudia R. Wright of the original edition, see 15:60.

[509]

Comprehensive Test of Visual Functioning.

Purpose: Designed to identify and differentiate type of visual perceptual dysfunction.

Population: Ages 8 and over.

Publication Date: 1990.

Acronym: CTVF.

Scores, 9: Visual/Letter Integration, Visual/Writing Integration, Nonverbal Visual Closure, Nonverbal Visual Reasoning/Memory, Spatial Orientation/Memory/Motor, Spatial Orientation/Motor, Visual Design/Motor, Visual Design/Memory/Motor, Total.

Administration: Individual.

Price Data, 2016: $175.25 per complete kit including manual (64 pages), stimulus cards/easel, and stimulus items; $50.25 per manual; $68.50 per examiner's directions and scoring protocol (18 pages); $49 per 25 examinee test booklets; $49 per stimulus cards/easel.

Time: (25) minutes.

Comments: "Norm-referenced"; includes 4 additional subtests (Visual Acuity, Visual Processing/Figure-Ground, Visual Tracking, Reading Word Analysis) which do not contribute to the overall visual performance quotient.

Authors: Sue L. Larson, Evelyn Buethe, and Gary J. Vitali.

Publisher: Slosson Educational Publications, Inc.

Cross References: For reviews by Stephen R. Hooper and Douglas J. McRae, see 12:89.

[510]

Comprehensive Testing Program 4.

Purpose: Summative tests designed to provide instructionally useful information about student performance in key areas of the school curriculum" in Language Arts, Mathematics, and Science.

Population: Grades 1–2, 2–3, 3–4, 4–5, 5–6, 6–7, 7–8, 8–9, 9–10, 10–11.

Publication Dates: 1974–2004.

Acronym: CTP 4.

Administration: Group.

Levels, 10: 1–10.

Price Data: Available from publisher.

Time: (300) minutes for total battery; time for each grade level varies.

Comments: Classroom administration in schools; partial battery is an option; allows for nonstandard administration; the test can be administered online and paper; multiple choice tests are machine scored; optional constructed response sections available for Mathematics and Reading Comprehension and are scored by hand.

Author: Educational Records Bureau.

Publisher: Educational Records Bureau.

a) LEVEL 1.
Population: Grade 1 spring or Grade 2 fall.
Scores, 4: Auditory Comprehension, Reading Comprehension, Word Analysis, Mathematics Achievement.
b) LEVEL 2.
Population: Grade 2 spring or Grade 3 fall.
Scores, 5: Same as for Level 1 plus Writing Mechanics.
c) LEVEL 3.
Population: Grade 3 spring or Grade 4 fall.
Scores, 7-8: Verbal Reasoning, Auditory Comprehension, Reading Comprehension, Writing Mechanics, Writing Concepts and Skills, Mathematics Achievement, Quantitative Reasoning plus Science offered online only.
d) LEVEL 4.
Population: Grade 4 spring or Grade 5 fall.
Scores, 7-8: Verbal Reasoning, Vocabulary, Reading Comprehension, Writing Mechanics, Writing Concepts and Skills, Mathematics Achievement, Quantitative Reasoning plus Science offered online only.
e) LEVEL 5.
Population: Grade 5 spring or Grade 6 fall.
Scores, 7-8: Same as for Level 4.
f) LEVEL 6.
Population: Grade 6 spring or Grade 7 fall.
Scores, 7-8: Same as for Levels 4 and 5.
g) LEVEL 7.
Population: Grade 7 spring or Grade 8 fall.
Scores, 7-8: Same as for Levels 4, 5, and 6.
h) LEVEL 8.
Population: Grade 8 spring or Grade 9 fall.
Scores, 8-9: Same as for Levels 4, 5, 6, and 7 plus Algebra 1.
i) LEVEL 9.
Population: Grade 9 spring or Grade 10 fall.
Scores, 8-9: Same as for Level 8.
j) LEVEL 10.
Population: Grade 10 spring or Grade 11 fall.
Scores, 7-8: Same as for Levels 8 and 9 except for omission of Algebra 1.
Cross References: For reviews by Koressa Kutsick Malcolm and William D. Schafer of an earlier version, see 17:52.

[511]

Comprehensive Trail-Making Test.
Purpose: Developed for the evaluation and diagnosis of brain injury and other forms of central nervous system compromise.
Population: Ages 8 to 74-11.
Publication Date: 2002.
Acronym: CTMT.
Scores, 6: Trail 1, Trail 2, Trail 3, Trail 4, Trail 5, Composite Index.
Administration: Individual.
Price Data, 2015: $138 per complete kit; $67 per 10 record booklets; $79 per examiner's manual (79 pages).
Time: (5–12) minutes.
Author: Cecil R. Reynolds.
Publisher: PRO-ED.
Cross References: For a review by Nora M. Thompson, see 15:61.

[512]

Computer Career Assessment Test.
Purpose: Measures aptitude for work in the computer field.
Population: Any adult without prior computer experience.
Publication Date: 2000.
Acronym: CCAT.
Scores, 3: Total Score, Narrative Evaluation, Ranking.
Administration: Group.
Price Data: Available from publisher.
Time: (60) minutes.
Author: Bruce A. Winrow.
Publisher: Walden Personnel Testing & Consulting Inc. [Canada].
Cross References: For reviews by Michael B. Bunch and Thomas R. O'Neill, see 16:63.

[513]

Computer Literacy Skills Profile.
Purpose: To evaluate computer literacy potential.
Population: Candidates whose job responsibilities will include utilizing common software packages.
Publication Date: 1996.
Acronym: COMPLIT.
Scores: Total Score, Narrative Evaluation, Ranking, Recommendation.
Administration: Group.
Price Data: Available from publisher.
Time: (110) minutes.
Author: Bruce A. Winrow.
Publisher: Walden Personnel Testing & Consulting Inc. [Canada].

[514]

Computer Operator Aptitude Battery.
Purpose: Predict "ability to perform computer operator job and potential for learning computer programming."
Population: Experienced computer operators and trainees.
Publication Dates: 1973–1974.
Acronym: COAB.
Scores, 4: Sequence Recognition, Formal Checking, Logical Thinking, Total.
Administration: Individual or group.
Price Data: Available from publisher.
Time: 45 minutes.
Author: General Dynamics Information Technology.
Publisher: General Dynamics Information Technology.

[515]

Computer Programmer Aptitude Battery.
Purpose: To "measure abilities related to success in computer programmer and systems analysis fields."

Population: Students, programmer trainees, entry-level and experienced.

Publication Dates: 1964–1993.

Acronym: CPAB.

Scores, 6: Verbal Meaning, Reasoning, Letter Series, Number Ability, Diagramming, Total.

Administration: Individual or group.

Forms, 2: A, B.

Price Data: Available from publisher.

Time: 79 minutes; 55 minutes for short form.

Comments: Short form contains Reasoning and Diagramming sections and can be used for all levels of programmers; short form norms available only for entry level.

Author: Science Research Associates.

Publisher: General Dynamics Information Technology.

Cross References: For reviews by Roderick K. Mahurin and William D. Schafer, see 11:85; see also T3:557 (1 reference); for additional information and a review by Nick L. Smith, see 8:1079 (3 references); see also T2:2334 (2 references); for reviews by Richard T. Johnson and Donald J. Veldman, see 7:1089 (2 references).

[516]

Computerized Oral Proficiency Instrument.

Purpose: Designed to assess students' oral language proficiency in Arabic, Spanish, or Mandarin Chinese.

Population: Native English speaking upper high school students, college students, and professionals who are learning the target language.

Publication Date: 2008.

Acronym: COPI.

Scores: 10 ratings: Novice Low, Novice Mid, Novice High, Intermediate Low, Intermediate Mid, Intermediate High, Advanced Low, Advanced Mid, Advanced High, Superior.

Administration: Group.

Editions, 3: Spanish, Arabic, Mandarin Chinese.

Levels: 4 proficiency levels: Novice, Intermediate, Advanced, Superior.

Price Data, 2016: $125 per test kit including Test Administration Program on CD-ROM, Training and Rating CD-ROM, and manual (51 pages).

Time: (45-60) minutes.

Comments: Computer-based, semi-adaptive test; publisher recommends using with rater training programs, available separately; also available on USB.

Author: Center for Applied Linguistics.

Publisher: Center for Applied Linguistics.

Cross References: For reviews by Sandra T. Acosta and by Elvis Wagner and Antony John Kunnan, see 19:42.

[517]

Computerized Test of Information Processing.

Purpose: Designed to "measure the degree to which various neurological injuries impact the speed at which information is processed" and to detect "whether a traumatic brain injury patient is putting forth maximum effort."

Population: Ages 15-74.

Publication Date: 2008.

Acronym: CTiP.

Scores, 3: Simple Reaction Time, Choice Reaction Time, Semantic Search Reaction Time.

Administration: Individual.

Price Data, 2015: $289 per V.5 software kit including manual and unlimited use software; $59 per technical/software manual.

Time: (15) minutes.

Comments: Version 5 software package requires Microsoft Windows 98 SE through Windows XP; provides the ability to administer assessments and score and generate reports; scoring is automatic and the test can be administered multiple times to the same individual without high practice effects.

Authors: Tom N. Tombaugh and Laura M. Rees.

Publisher: Multi-Health Systems, Inc.

Cross References: For reviews by Brad M. Merker and Jeremy R. Sullivan, see 18:32.

[518]

Comrey Personality Scales.

Purpose: Developed to measure major personality characteristics.

Population: Ages 16 and over.

Publication Date: 1970.

Acronym: CPS.

Scores, 10: Trust vs. Defensiveness (T), Orderliness vs. Lack of Compulsion (O), Social Conformity vs. Rebelliousness (C), Activity vs. Lack of Energy (A), Emotional Stability vs. Neuroticism (S), Extraversion vs. Introversion (E), Mental Toughness vs. Sensitivity (M), Empathy vs. Egocentrism (P), Validity Check (V), Response Bias (R).

Administration: Group.

Price Data, 2016: $31 per 25 reusable test booklets; $20.50 per 50 answer sheets (hand-scoring); $22.50 per 50 answer sheets (machine-scoring); $6.50 per hand-scoring instructions for the CPS; $47 per specimen set including a manual and one copy of all forms; $36.75 per manual & handbook of interpretations.

Time: (35–50) minutes.

Comments: Comrey Personality Scales, Short Form is also available with same scales and prices.

Author: Andrew L. Comrey.

Publisher: EdITS/Educational and Industrial Testing Service.

Cross References: See T5:672 (6 references), T4:628 (21 references), 9:261 (8 references), and T3:558 (22 references); for a review by Edgar Howarth, see 8:527 (27 references); for reviews by R. G. Demaree and M. Y. Quereshi, see 7:59 (20 references).

[519]

Comrey Personality Scales—Short Form.

Purpose: To provide a comprehensive, multidimensional assessment instrument for measuring eight personality dimensions.

Population: High school, college, and adults.

Publication Dates: 1993–1995.

Acronym: CPS Short Form.

Scores, 10: Trust vs. Defensiveness, Orderliness vs. Lack of Compulsion, Social Conformity vs. Rebelliousness, Activity vs. Lack of Energy, Emotional Stability vs. Neuroticism, Extraversion vs. Introversion, Mental Toughness vs. Sensitivity, Empathy vs. Egocentrism, Validity Check, Response Bias.

Administration: Group.

Price Data, 2016: $90.50 per 50 Short Form Booklets with Answer Sheets Combined (hand-scoring) [$126 per 100, $449.75 per 500]; $20.50 per 50 Profile Sheets [$38 per 100, $171.25 per 500]; $36.75 per manual & handbook of interpretations.

Time: Administration time not reported.

Comments: Includes same scales as the Comrey Personality Scales (518) but has fewer items per scale.

Author: Andrew L. Comrey.

Publisher: EdITS/Educational and Industrial Testing Service.

[520]

Concept Assessment Kit—Conservation.

Purpose: To "determine child's level of conservation by his conservation behavior and his comprehension of the principle involved."

Population: Ages 4–7.

Publication Date: 1968.

Acronym: CAK.

Administration: Individual.

Price Data, 2016: $79.50 per kit; $15.25 per 25 recording forms [$52 per 100, $197 per 500]; $6.25 per manual.

Authors: Marcel L. Goldschmid and Peter M. Bentler.

Publisher: EdITS/Educational and Industrial Testing Service.

  a) FORMS A AND B.

  Scores, 13: 2 scores (Behavior, Explanation) in each of 6 areas (2-Dimensional Space, Number, Substance, Continuous Quantity, Weight, Discontinuous Quantity), Total.

  Time: (15) minutes per form.

  b) FORM C.

  Scores, 13: 2 scores (Behavior, Explanation) in each of 3 areas and 3 lengths, Total.

Cross References: See T5:674 (5 references), T4:630 (11 references), T3:559 (17 references), 8:238 (32 references), and T2:549 (5 references); for a review by J. Douglas Ayers, and excerpted reviews by Rheta DeVries and Lawrence Kohlberg, by Vernon C. Hall and Michael Mery, and by Charles D. Smock, see 7:437 (5 references).

[521]

Concussion Vital Signs.

Purpose: Designed as a web-based neurocognitive assessment for baseline testing and measuring and monitoring an athlete following a sports concussion.

Population: Athletes ages 10 to 25.

Publication Dates: 2003-2015.

Acronym: CVS.

Scores, 8: Verbal Memory, Visual Memory, Psychomotor Speed, Executive Function, Cognitive Flexibility, Continuous Performance Test Correct Responses, Reaction Time, Neurocognitive Index.

Subtests, 7: Verbal Memory, Visual Memory, Finger Tapping, Symbol Digit Coding, Stroop, Shifting Attention, Continuous Performance.

Administration: Individual.

Price Data, 2016: Free to all schools, colleges, and providers that support them within the United States; prices for other users, training, and support services available from publisher.

Foreign Language Edition: Spanish version available.

Time: (30) minutes.

Comments: Computer administered and scored; includes Concussion Symptom Severity Scale and self-report concussion history; cognitive tests in the battery are a subset of CNS Vital Signs Computerized Cognitive Battery (456) tests.

Author: CNS Vital Signs.

Publisher: CNS Vital Signs.

Cross References: Reviews are scheduled for *The Twentieth Mental Measurements Yearbook.*

[522]

Conduct Disorder Scale.

Purpose: "To identify persons with Conduct Disorder by evaluating the characteristic behaviors that define this condition."

Population: Ages 5–22 years.

Publication Date: 2002.

Acronym: CDS.

Scores, 5: 4 subscales (Aggressive Conduct, Hostility, Deceitfulness/Theft, Rule Violations), Conduct Disorder Quotient.

Administration: Individual

Price Data, 2015: $107 per complete kit including examiner's manual (41 pages), and 50 summary/response forms, all in a storage box; $63 per examiner's manual; $48 per 50 summary/response forms.

Time: (5–10) minutes.

Comments: Based on the diagnostic criteria for conduct disorder specified by the Diagnostic and Statistical Manual of Mental Disorders—Fourth Edition—Text Revision (DSM-IV-TR); provides interpretation guide for classifying degree of severity of conduct disorder (severe, moderate, mild, not applicable).

Author: James E. Gilliam.
Publisher: PRO-ED.
Cross References: For reviews by Michael J. Furlong and Jenne Simental and by Steven I. Pfeiffer, see 16:64.

[523]
Conflict Analysis Battery.

Purpose: Designed to "assess a person's conflict resolution process, qualitatively, quantitatively and graphically along a range of four relational modalities and a symbolic system consisting of a six step dialectic of formal and energetic intertransformations."
Population: School age and adults.
Publication Date: 1988.
Acronym: CAB.
Scores, 11: The personality inventory (Relational Modality Evaluation Scale), projective tests (Balloon Portraits and Story, Conflictual Memories Test, Dream Analysis), Transparent Mask Test, Animal Metaphor Test, Fairy Tale Metaphor Test, Short Story Metaphor, Intensified Animal Metaphor Test, House-Tree-Person Metaphor Test, Scribble Metaphor.
Administration: Individuals and group.
Price Data: Available from publisher.
Time: Administration time not reported.
Comments: Self-administered inventory and projective test battery; developed for use with Conflict Analysis Training: A Concise Program of Emotional Education.
Author: Albert J. Levis.
Publisher: The Institute of Conflict Analysis and the Museum of the Creative Process.
Cross References: For reviews by Susan M. Brookhart and Carl Isenhart, see 16:65.

[524]
Conflict Management Survey.

Purpose: "Designed to provide information about the various ways people react to and try to manage the differences between themselves and others."
Population: Adults.
Publication Dates: 1969–1996.
Acronym: CMS.
Scores, 20: 5 conflict management styles (9/1 Win-Lose, 1/9 Yield-Lose, 1/1 Lose-Leave, 5/5 Compromise, 9/9 Synergistic) for each of 4 contexts (Personal Orientation, Interpersonal Relationships, Small Group Relationships, Intergroup Relationships).
Administration: Group.
Price Data, 2016: $12.95 per instrument.
Time: Administration time not reported.
Comments: Self-ratings.
Author: Jay Hall.
Publisher: Teleometrics International, Inc.
Cross References: For reviews by Frederick Bessai and Douglas J. McRae, see 12:91; for a review by Frank J. Landy of an earlier edition, see 8:1173 (2 references).

[525]
Conflict Style Inventory.

Purpose: Designed to assess an individual's approach to conflict resolution.
Population: Adults.
Publication Dates: 1990–1995.
Acronym: CSI.
Scores, 15: Total Score, Individual [one-on-one] Conflict Situations, Group/Team Conflict Situations on 5 styles: (Avoiding, Smoothing, Bargaining, Forcing, Problem Solving).
Administration: Group.
Price Data, 2016: $59.95; volume discounts available.
Time: (20) minutes.
Comments: Self-scored.
Author: Marshall Sashkin.
Publisher: HRD Press, Inc.
Cross References: For reviews by Trenton R. Ferro and Scott T. Meier, see 14:96.

[526]
Conflict Tactics Scales.

Purpose: Designed to obtain reports of domestic violence among abusive adult partners and "physical maltreatment and neglect of children by parents, as well as nonviolent modes of discipline."
Population: Adults.
Publication Date: 2003.
Administration: Individual.
Price Data, 2016: $105 per complete kit including Handbook (146 pages), 10 CTS2 AutoScore forms, and 10 CTSPC AutoScore forms; $52.50 per 25 AutoScore forms (CTS2 or CTSPC); $72 per Handbook.
Authors: Murray A. Straus, Sherry L. Hamby, and W. Louise Warren.
Publisher: Western Psychological Services.
   a) REVISED CONFLICT TACTICS SCALES.
   Acronym: CTS2.
   Scores, 5: Negotiation, Psychological Aggression, Physical Assault, Injury, Sexual Coercion.
   Time: (10-15) minutes.
   b) CONFLICT TACTICS SCALES: PARENT-CHILD VERSION.
   Acronym: CTSPC.
   Scores, 6: Nonviolent Discipline, Psychological Aggression, Physical Assault, Weekly Discipline, Neglect, Sexual Abuse.
   Time: (10) minutes.
Cross References: For reviews by Meghan Davidson and John J. Vacca, see 19:43.

[527]
Conners' Adult ADHD Diagnostic Interview for DSM-IV.

Purpose: Empirically based structured interview that assists the process of diagnosing ADHD.

Population: Age 18 and older.
Publication Date: 2001.
Acronym: CAADID.
Scores: Childhood and Adult ADHD Diagnosis (specifies Inattentive vs. Hyperactive Impulsive).
Administration: Individual.
Price Data, 2015: $179 per complete kit including manual (2001, 52 pages), 10 patient history forms, and 10 diagnostic criteria interview forms; $64 per technical manual; $63 per 10 patient history forms; $63 per 10 diagnostic criteria interview forms.
Time: (60–90) minutes for Interview; (30–60) minutes for Self-Report.
Authors: Jeff Epstein, Diane Johnson, and C. Keith Conners.
Publisher: Multi-Health Systems, Inc.
Cross References: For reviews by George J. Demakis and Timothy J. Makatura, see 16:66.

[528]
Conners' Adult ADHD Rating Scales.
Purpose: Designed to assess "psychopathology and problem behaviors associated with adult ADHD."
Population: Ages 18 and over.
Publication Date: 1999.
Administration: Individual or group.
Forms, 6: Self-Report: Long (CAARS-S:L); Self-Report: Short (CAARS-S:S); Self-Report: Screening (CAARS-S:SV); Observer: Long (CAARS-O:L); Observer: Short (CAARS-O:S); Observer: Screening (CAARS-O: SV).
Price Data, 2015: $379 per complete kit including manual (144 pages) and 25 QuikScore™ forms for each of the 6 forms; $81 per technical manual; $55 per 25 of any one of the 6 Screening QuikScore™ forms; $104 per online profile report kit including manual and 3 profile reports; $109 per online interpretive report kit including manual and 3 interpretive reports; $6 per online profile report; $8 per online interpretive report; Software also available.
Comments: Observer rating and/or self-report. Correctional Setting norms supplement is available.
Authors: C. Keith Conners, Drew Erhardt, and Elizabeth Sparrow.
Publisher: Multi-Health Systems, Inc.
   a) CAARS—SELF-REPORT: LONG; CAARS—OBSERVER: LONG.
   Scores, 9: Inattention/Memory Problems, Hyperactivity/Restlessness, Impulsivity/Emotional Lability, Problems with Self-Concept, DSM-IV Inattentive Symptoms, DSM-IV Hyperactive-Impulsive Symptoms, DSM-IV Total ADHD Symptoms, ADHD Index, Inconsistency Index.
   Time: (20) minutes.
   b) CAARS—SELF-REPORT: SHORT; CAARS—OBSERVER: SHORT.
   Scores, 6: Inattentive/Memory Problems, Hyperactivity/Restlessness, Impulsivity/Emotional Lability, Problems with Self-Concept, ADHD Index, Inconsistency Index.
   Time: (10) minutes.

   c) CAARS—SELF-REPORT: SCREENING; CAARS—OBSERVER: SCREENING.
   Scores, 4: DSM-IV Inattentive Symptoms, DSM-IV Hyperactive/Impulsivity Symptoms, DSM-IV Total ADHD Symptoms, ADHD Index.
   Time: (10) minutes.
Cross References: For reviews by Andrew S. Davis and Rik Carl D'Amato and by Ronald J. Ganellen, see 15:65.

[529]
Conners Comprehensive Behavior Rating Scales.
Purpose: Designed to "assess a wide range of behavioral, emotional, social, and academic concerns" in order to diagnose, develop, and monitor treatment plans for children and adolescents.
Population: Ages 6-18.
Publication Dates: 2008-2015.
Acronym: Conners CBRS; Conners CI.
Administration: Individual or group.
Price Data, 2015: $689 per software kit including manual (English), unlimited-use scoring program, 25 item booklets for each of Conners CBRS-P, CBRS-T, and CBRS-SR (specify English or Spanish); $349 per online assessment report kit including manual (English), 25 parent/teacher/self-report online forms (specify English or Spanish); $440 per scoring software; $104 per manual (English).
Forms, 6: Conners CBRS-Teacher, Conners CBRS-Parent, Conners CBRS-Self-Report, Conners Clinical Index-Teacher, Conners Clinical Index-Parent, Conners Clinical Index-Self-Report.
Foreign Language Edition: Spanish edition available.
Comments: "The Conners Clinical Index (Conners CI) is extracted from the Conners CBRS form; the same 24 items used to calculate the Conners Clinical Index score on the Conners CBRS form are used on the Conners CI"; The Conners CBRS and Conners CI forms can be administered and scored online; paper-and-pencil forms can also be scored online and can be scored using the Conners CBRS scoring software program by entering responses from a completed paper-and-pencil administration but cannot be administered through the software. Updated with a scoring option for the DSM-5 Symptom Scales.
Author: C. Keith Conners.
Publisher: Multi-Health Systems Inc.
   a) CONNERS COMPREHENSIVE BEHAVIOR RATING SCALE-TEACHER.
   Population: Ages 6-18.
   Acronym: Conners CBRS-T.
   Scores, 44: Emotional Distress, Upsetting Thoughts/Physical Symptoms, Social Anxiety, Defiant/Aggressive Behaviors, Academic Difficulties, Academic Difficulties: Language, Academic Difficulties: Math, Hyperactivity, Social Problems, Separation Fears, Perfectionistic and Compulsive

Behaviors, Violence Potential Indicator, Physical Symptoms, ADHD Hyperactive/Impulsive, ADHD Inattentive, ADHD Combined, Conduct Disorder, Oppositional Defiant Disorder, Major Depressive Episode, Manic Episode, Mixed Episode, Generalized Anxiety Disorder, Separation Anxiety Disorder, Social Phobia, Obsessive-Compulsive Disorder, Autistic Disorder, Asperger's Disorder, Positive Impression, Negative Impression, Inconsistency Index, Conners Clinical Index, Bullying Perpetration, Bullying Victimization, Enuresis/Encopresis, Panic Attack, Post Traumatic Stress Disorder, Specific Phobia, Substance Use, Tics, Trichotillomania, Impairment in Schoolwork/Grades, Impairment in Friendships/Relationships, Severe Conduct, Self-Harm.

Time: (20) minutes.

b) CONNERS COMPREHENSIVE BEHAVIOR RATING SCALE-PARENT.

Population: Ages 6-18.

Acronym: Conners CBRS-P.

Scores, 46: Emotional Distress, Upsetting Thoughts, Worrying, Defiant/Aggressive Behaviors, Academic Difficulties, Academic Difficulties: Language, Academic Difficulties: Math, Hyperactivity/Impulsivity, Social Problems, Separation Fears, Perfectionistic and Compulsive Behaviors, Violence Potential Indicator, Physical Symptoms, ADHD Hyperactive/Impulsive, ADHD Inattentive, ADHD Combined, Conduct Disorder, Oppositional Defiant Disorder, Major Depressive Episode, Manic Episode, Mixed Episode, Generalized Anxiety Disorder, Separation Anxiety Disorder, Social Phobia, Obsessive-Compulsive Disorder, Autistic Disorder, Asperger's Disorder, Positive Impression, Negative Impression, Inconsistency Index, Conners Clinical Index, Bullying Perpetration, Bullying Victimization, Enuresis/Encopresis, Panic Attack, Pica, Post Traumatic Stress Disorder, Specific Phobia, Substance Use, Tics, Trichotillomania, Impairment in Schoolwork/Grades, Impairment in Friendships/Relationships, Impairment in Home Life, Severe Conduct, Self-Harm.

Time: Same as *a* above.

c) CONNERS COMPREHENSIVE BEHAVIOR RATING SCALE-SELF-REPORT.

Population: Ages 8-18.

Acronym: Conners CBRS-SR.

Scores, 38: Emotional Distress, Defiant/Aggressive Behaviors, Academic Difficulties, Hyperactivity/Impulsivity, Separation Fears, Violence Potential Indicator, Physical Symptoms, ADHD Hyperactive/Impulsive, ADHD Inattentive, ADHD Combined, Conduct Disorder, Oppositional Defiant Disorder, Major Depressive Episode, Manic Episode, Mixed Episode, Generalized Anxiety Disorder, Separation Anxiety Disorder, Social Phobia, Obsessive-Compulsive Disorder, Positive Impression, Negative Impression, Inconsistency Index, Conners Clinical Index, Bullying Perpetration, Bullying Victimization, Panic Attack, Pervasive Developmental Disorder, Pica, Post Traumatic Stress Disorder, Specific Phobia, Substance Use, Tics, Trichotillomania, Impairment in Schoolwork/Grades, Impairment in Friendships/Relationships, Impairment in Home Life, Severe Conduct, Self-Harm.

Time: Same as *a* above.

d) CONNERS CLINICAL INDEX-TEACHER.

Population: Ages 6-18.

Acronym: Conners CI-T.

Scores, 6: Overall Conners Clinical Index Score, Disruptive Behavior Indicator, Learning and Language Disorder Indicator, Mood Disorder Indicator, Anxiety Disorder Indicator, ADHD Indicator.

Time: (10) minutes.

e) CONNERS CLINICAL INDEX-PARENT.

Population: Ages 6-18.

Acronym: Conners CI-P.

Scores: Same as *d* above.

Time: Same as *d* above.

f) CONNERS CLINICAL INDEX-SELF-REPORT.

Population: Ages 8-18.

Scores: Same as *d* above.

Time: Same as *d* above.

Cross References: For reviews by Jeremy R. Sullivan and John J. Vacca, see 18:33.

[530]

Conners Continuous Auditory Test of Attention.

Purpose: Computerized test designed to assess "auditory processing and attention-related problems."

Population: Ages 8 and older.

Publication Date: 2014.

Acronym: Conners CATA.

Scores, 12: 9 scores grouped into 3 clusters: Inattentiveness (Detectability, Omissions, Commissions, Hit Reaction Time, Hit Reaction Time Standard Deviation), Impulsivity (Hit Reaction Time, Commissions, Perseverative Commissions), Sustained Attention (Hit Reaction Time Block Change, Omissions by Block, Commissions by Block) plus Auditory Laterality, Auditory Mobility, Response Style.

Administration: Individual or group.

Price Data, 2015: $399 per unlimited use kit including manual (112 pages), software, and unlimited uses; $299 per pay-per-use kit including manual, software, and 10 uses; $100 per 10 additional uses after purchase of pay-per-use kit; $99 per manual.

Time: (14) minutes.

Comments: "Designed to yield both complementary and unique information to the visually-based Conners Continuous Performance Test 3rd Edition" (531); computer administered and scored.

Author: C. Keith Conners.

Publisher: Multi-Health Systems Inc.

Cross References: Reviews are scheduled for *The Twentieth Mental Measurements Yearbook*.

[531]

Conners Continuous Performance Test 3rd Edition.

Purpose: Computerized test designed to assess "attention-related problems" to "facilitate diagnostic decisions and guide treatment planning."

Population: Ages 8 and older.

Publication Dates: 1992-2014.

Acronym: Conners CPT 3.

Scores, 14: 13 scores grouped into 4 clusters: Inattentiveness (Detectability, Omissions, Commissions, Hit Reaction Time, Hit Reaction Time Standard Deviation, Variability), Impulsivity (Hit Reaction Time, Commissions, Perseverations), Sustained Attention (Hit Reaction Time Block Change, Omissions by Block, Commissions by Block), Vigilance (Hit Reaction Time Inter-Stimulus Interval Change, Omissions by Inter-Stimulus Interval, Commissions by Inter-Stimulus Interval), plus Response Style.

Administration: Individual or group.

Price Data, 2015: $1,199 per unlimited use kit including manual (2014, 120 pages), software, and unlimited uses; $999 per pay-per-use kit including manual, software, and 10 uses; $99 per manual; $100 per 10 pay-per-use software administrations.

Time: 14 minutes.

Comments: Computer administered and scored.

Author: C. Keith Conners.

Publisher: Multi-Health Systems Inc.

Cross References: Reviews are scheduled for *The Twentieth Mental Measurements Yearbook.* For reviews by Beverly M. Klecker and Wesley E. Sime of the second edition, see 15:66; for a review by James Ysseldyke of the original edition, see 14:97; see also T5:679 (2 references).

[532]

Conners Early Childhood.

Purpose: Designed to "assess a wide range of behavioral, emotional, and social concerns and developmental milestones in preschool-aged children."

Population: Ages 2-6.

Publication Date: 2009.

Acronym: Conners EC.

Administration: Individual or group.

Forms: 5 form options per rater (Parent, Teacher/Childcare Provider).

Price Data, 2015: $419 per Complete Scoring Software kit including 25 each of the Parent and Teacher response booklets, manual (242 pages), and unlimited use scoring software; $254 per Online Kit including 25 of the Parent/Teacher/Self-Report Online Forms, and Manual; $189 per Global Index Handscored Kit including 25 of the Parent and Teacher QuikScore forms and manual; $60 per 25 behavior-teacher, behavior-parent, teacher, or parent response booklets; $55 per 25 GI-Parent, or GI-Teacher QuickScore forms; $55 per 25 developmental milestones-parent, developmental milestones-teacher, behavior-parent short, or behavior-teacher short response booklets. $93 per manual; $231 per unlimited scoring software (USB); prices are identical for the equivalent Spanish forms.

Foreign Language Edition: Spanish version available for all forms.

Comments: Administration available in paper-and-pencil or online format; scoring available online or using the scoring software (Global Index QuikScore form can also be hand-scored).

Author: C. Keith Conners.

Publisher: Multi-Health Systems, Inc.

a) CONNERS EARLY CHILDHOOD FULL-LENGTH FORMS.

Acronyms: Conners EC-P; Conners EC-T.

Scores: 22 scores per parent; 21 scores per Teacher, including 11 Behavior scores (Inattention/Hyperactivity, Defiance/Temper, Aggression, Defiant/Aggressive Behaviors Total, Social Functioning, Atypical Behaviors, Social Functioning/Atypical Behaviors Total, Anxiety, Mood and Affect, Physical Symptoms, Sleep Problems, parent only), 5 Developmental Milestone scores (Adaptive Skills, Communication, Motor Skills, Play, Pre-Academic/Cognitive), 3 Validity scores (Positive Impression, Negative Impression, Inconsistency Index), and 3 Global Index scores (Restless-Impulsive, Emotional Lability, Total).

Time: (25) minutes.

Comments: Scoring report also includes item ratings for Other Clinical Indicators and Impairment Items, and rater's responses to two additional open-ended questions.

b) CONNERS EARLY CHILDHOOD BEHAVIOR FORMS.

Acronyms: Conners EC BEH-P; Conners EC BEH-T.

Scores: 17 scores per parent; 16 scores per teacher, including 11 Behavior scores (Inattention/Hyperactivity, Defiance/Temper, Aggression, Defiant/Aggressive Behaviors Total, Social Functioning, Atypical Behaviors, Social Functioning/Atypical Behaviors Total, Anxiety, Mood and Affect, Physical Symptoms, Sleep Problems, parent only), 3 Validity scores (Positive Impression, Negative Impression, Inconsistency Index), and 3 Global Index scores (Restless-Impulsive, Emotional Lability, Total).

Time: (15) minutes.

Comments: Scoring report also includes item ratings for Other Clinical Indicators and Impairment Items, and rater's responses to two additional open-ended questions.

c) CONNERS EARLY CHILDHOOD DEVELOPMENTAL MILESTONES FORMS.

Acronyms: Conners EC DM-P; Conners EC DM-T.

Scores: 5 Developmental Milestones scores per rater: Adaptive Skills, Communication, Motor Skills, Play, Pre-Academic/Cognitive.

Time: (10) minutes.

Comments: Scoring report also includes item ratings for Impairment Items, and rater's responses to two additional open-ended questions.

d) CONNERS EARLY CHILDHOOD BEHAVIOR SHORT FORMS.

Acronyms: Conners EC BEH-P[S]; Conners EC BEH-T[S].

Scores: 8 scores per rater, including 6 Behavior scores (Inattention/Hyperactivity, Defiant/Aggressive Behaviors Total, Social Functioning/Atypical Behaviors Total, Anxiety, Mood and Affect, Physical Symptoms), and 2 Validity scores (Positive Impression, Negative Impression).

Time: (10) minutes.

Comments: Scoring report also includes rater's responses to two additional open-ended questions.

e) CONNERS EARLY CHILDHOOD GLOBAL INDEX FORMS.
Acronyms: Conners ECGI-P; Conners ECGI-T.
Scores: 3 Global Index scores per rater: Restless-Impulsive, Emotional Lability, Total.
Time: (5) minutes.
Cross References: For reviews by Sherry K. Bain and Kathleen B. Aspiranti and by Jean N. Clark, see 18:34.

[533]

Conners Kiddie Continuous Performance Test 2nd Edition.

Purpose: Designed to "assess attention-related problems in children."
Population: Ages 4 through 7.
Publication Dates: 2001-2015.
Acronym: Conners K-CPT 2.
Scores, 14: Response Style, Detectability (d-prime), Ommissions, Commissions, Persevertions, Hit Reaction Time (HRT), Hit Reaction Time Standard Deviation, Variability, HRT Block Change, Omissions by Block, Commissions by Block, HRT Inter-Stimulus Interval (ISI) Change, Ommissions by ISI, Commissions by ISI.
Administration: Individual.
Price Data, 2016: $599 per unlimited use kit including manual (2015, 108 pages) and software; $399 per pay-per-use kit including manual, software, and 10 uses; $100 per 10 additional uses after purchase of pay-per-use kit; $99 per manual.
Time: 7.5 minutes.
Comments: Administered and scored via computer.
Authors: C. Keith Conners and Multi-Health Systems, Inc. staff.
Publisher: Multi-Health Systems, Inc.
Cross References: Reviews are scheduled for *The Twentieth Mental Measurements Yearbook*. For reviews by Brian F. French and by Scott A. Napolitano and Courtney Miller of the original edition, see 16:67.

[534]

Conners 3rd Edition.

Purpose: Designed to be an assessment of "Attention-Deficit/Hyperactivity Disorder (ADHD) and its most common comorbid problems and disorders in children and adolescents."
Population: Ages 6-18.
Publication Dates: 1989-2008.
Acronym: Conners 3.
Administration: Individual or group.
Forms, 11: Conners 3-Parent Full, Conners 3-Parent Short, Conners 3-Teacher Full, Conners 3-Teacher Short, Conners 3-Self-Report Full, Conners 3-Self-Report Short, Conners 3 ADHD Index-Teacher, Conners 3 ADHD Index-Parent, Conners 3 ADHD Index-Self-Report, Conners 3 Global Index-Teacher, Conners 3 Global Index-Parent.

Price Data, 2015: $449 per Handscored kit including manual (2008, 470 pages), 25 parent/teacher/self-report QuikScore™ forms, and 25 parent/teacher/self-report short QuikScore™ forms; $349 per Reorder Kit including 25 parent/teacher/self-report QuikScore™ forms, and 25 parent/teacher/self-report short QuikScore™ forms; $104 per manual; $65 per package of 25 parent, teacher, or self-report QuikScore™ forms; $60 per package of 25 parent, teacher, or self-report (short) QuikScore™ forms; $349 per Online Kit including manual, 25 Parent/Teacher/ self-report online forms; $3.50 per Online form; $759 per Conners 3 Software Kit including manual, unlimited use scoring software program (USB Key), 25 Parent/Teacher/Self-Report response booklets, and 25 Parent/Teacher/Self-Report (Short) QuikScore™ forms; $15 per paper copy of DSM-5 Supplement.
Foreign Language Edition: Spanish versions available for Parent and Self-Report forms.
Time: (20) minutes for full length form; (10) minutes for short forms.
Comments: All forms are available in QuikScore™ format; can also be completed and scored online; paper-and-pencil forms can also be scored online; can also be scored using the scoring software program by entering responses from a completed pencil-and-paper administration but cannot be administered through the software; new scoring options are available based on diagnostic criteria in the Diagnostic and Statistical Manual of Mental Disorders, Fifth Edition (DSM-5).
Author: C. Keith Conners.
Publisher: Multi-Health Systems, Inc.
a) CONNERS 3-PARENT.
Population: Ages 6-18.
Full-Length Scores, 22: Inattention, Hyperactivity/Impulsivity, Learning Problems, Executive Functioning, Defiance/Aggression, Peer Relations, DSM-IV-TR ADHD Hyperactive-Impulsive, DSM-IV-TR ADHD Inattentive, DSM-IV-TR ADHD Combined, DSM-IV-TR Conduct Disorder, DSM-IV-TR Oppositional Defiant Disorder, Positive Impression, Negative Impression, Inconsistency Index, Conners 3 ADHD Index, Conners 3 Global Index, Anxiety, Depression, Impairment in Schoolwork/Grades, Impairment in Friendships/Relationships, Impairment in Home Life, Severe Conduct.
Forms, 4: Full, Short, ADHD Index, Global Index.
b) CONNERS 3-TEACHER.
Population: Ages 6-18.
Full-Length Scores, 22: Inattention, Hyperactivity/Impulsivity, Learning Problems, Executive Functioning, Learning Problems/Executive Functioning, Defiance/Aggression, Peer Relations, DSM-IV-TR ADHD Hyperactive-Impulsive, DSM-IV-TR ADHD Inattentive, DSM-IV-TR ADHD Combined, DSM-IV-TR Conduct Disorder, DSM-IV-TR Oppositional Defiant Disorder, Positive Impression, Negative Impression, Inconsistency Index, Conners 3 ADHD Index, Conners 3 Global Index, Anxiety, Depression, Impairment in Schoolwork/Grades, Impairment in Friendships/Relationships, Severe Conduct.
Forms, 4: Full, Short, ADHD Index, Global Index.

c) CONNERS 3-SELF-REPORT.
Population: Ages 8-18.
Full-Length Scores, 20: Inattention, Hyperactivity/Impulsivity, Learning Problems, Defiance/Aggression, Family Relations, DSM-IV-TR ADHD Hyperactive/Impulsive, DSM-IV-TR ADHD Inattentive, DSM-IV-TR ADHD Combined, DSM-IV-TR Conduct Disorder, DSM-IV-TR Oppositional Defiant Disorder, Positive Impression, Negative Impression, Inconsistency Index, Conners 3 ADHD Index, Anxiety, Depression, Impairment in Schoolwork/Grades, Impairment in Friendships/Relationships, Impairment in Home Life, Severe Conduct.
Forms, 3: Full, Short, ADHD Index.
Cross References: For reviews by Sharon Arffa and Thomas M. Dunn, see 18:35; for reviews by Allen K. Hess and Howard M. Knoff of an earlier edition, see 14:98; see also T5:681 (99 references) and T4:636 (50 references); for reviews by Brian K. Martens and Judy Oehler-Stinnett of the original edition, see 11:87 (83 references).

[535]
Constructive Thinking Inventory.

Purpose: "Evaluates an individual's experiential intelligence and coping skills."
Population: Ages 18–81 years.
Publication Date: 2001.
Acronym: CTI.
Scores, 9: Emotional Coping (Self-Acceptance, Absence of Negative Overgeneralization, Nonsensitivity, Absence of Dwelling), Behavioral Coping (Positive Thinking, Action Orientation, Conscientiousness), Personal Superstitious Thinking, Categorical Thinking (Polarized Thinking, Distrust of Others, Intolerance), Esoteric Thinking (Belief in the Unusual, Formal Superstitious Thinking), Naive Optimism (Over-Optimism, Stereotypical Thinking, Polyanna-ish Thinking), Defensiveness, Validity, Global Constructive Thinking
Administration: Individual or group.
Price Data, 2015: $190 per introductory kit including CD ROM-based scoring program with on-screen user's manual, professional manual (59 pages), and 25 test booklets.
Time: (15–30) minutes.
Author: Seymour Epstein.
Publisher: Psychological Assessment Resources, Inc.

[536]
Contextual Memory Test.

Purpose: Designed to assess awareness of memory capacity, strategy use, and recall in adults with memory dysfunction.
Population: Adults.
Publication Date: 1993.
Acronym: CMT.
Scores, 12: Recall Score (Immediate Recall, Delayed Recall, Total Recall), Cued Recall, Recognition, Awareness Score (Prediction, Estimation of Performance Following Recall, Response to General Questioning [Prior to Recall, Following Recall]), Strategy Use (Effect of Context, Order of Recall, Total Strategy Score).
Administration: Individual.
Price Data, 2015: $152.75 per complete kit including manual (138 pages), 2 test cards, 14 cut-apart sheets of 80 picture cards, 25 score sheets (12 pages), and carrying case; $59.70 per 25 score sheets; $75.60 per manual; $16.40 per picture cards; $11.30 per 2 test cards.
Time: (10–20) minutes.
Author: Joan P. Toglia.
Publisher: Pearson.
Cross References: For reviews by Karen Mackler and Alan J. Raphael, see 14:99.

[537]
Continuous Visual Memory Test [Revised].

Purpose: Constructed to assess visual memory.
Population: Ages 7–80+.
Publication Dates: 1983–1997.
Acronym: CVMT.
Scores, 6: Acquisition (Hits, False Alarms, d-Prime, Total), Delayed Recognition, Visual Discrimination.
Administration: Individual.
Price Data, 2015: $216 per kit including manual (1988, 22 pages), manual supplement, stimulus cards, and 50 scoring forms.
Time: (45–50) minutes.
Authors: Donald E. Trahan and Glenn J. Larrabee.
Publisher: Psychological Assessment Resources, Inc.
Cross References: For reviews by Michael B. Brown and Alice J. Corkill, see 14:100; see also T5:687 (4 references); for reviews by Nancy B. Bologna and Stephen F. Davis of an earlier edition, see 12:93; see also T4:642 (4 references).

[538]
The Conversational Skills Rating Scale: An Instructional Assessment of Interpersonal Competence.

Purpose: "To assess the skills domain of conversational competence."
Population: Secondary and post-secondary students.
Publication Date: 1995.
Acronym: CSRS.
Scores, 5: Altercentricism, Composure, Expressiveness, Interaction Management, Total.
Administration: Group.
Forms, 7: Rating of Partner Form, Rating of Self Form, Instructor Rating of Student Form, Self Frequency Version, Partner Frequency Version, Self Trait Rating Form, Other Trait Rating Form.
Price Data: Available at no charge from test publisher.
Time: (5–15) minutes.

Author: Brian H. Spitzberg.
Publisher: National Communication Association.
Cross References: For reviews by Sandra M. Ketrow and Julia Y. Porter, see 14:101.

[539]
Coolidge Assessment Battery.

Purpose: Designed to assess personality disorders and neuropsychological functioning.
Population: Ages 15 and older.
Publication Date: 1999.
Acronym: CAB.
Scores, 46: 7 Axis I scales (Anxiety, Depression, Post-Traumatic Stress, Psychotic Thinking, Schizophrenia, Social Phobia, Withdrawal); 14 Axis II scales (Antisocial, Avoidant, Borderline, Dependent, Depressive, Histrionic, Narcissistic, Obsessive-Compulsive, Paranoid, Passive-Aggressive, Sadistic, Schizoid, Schizotypal, Self-Defeating); 4 Neuropsychological Dysfunction scales (Overall Neuropsychological, Language Functions, Memory and Concentration, Neurosomatic Functions); 4 Executive Functions of the Frontal Lobe scales (Overall Executive Functions, Decision Difficulty, Planning Problems, Task Completion Difficulty); 5 Personality Change due to Medical Condition scales (Aggression, Apathy, Disinhibition, Emotional Lability, Paranoid); 3 Hostility scales (Anger, Dangerousness, Impulsiveness); 5 Normative scales (Apathy, Emotional Lability, Indecisiveness, Maladjustment, Introversion-Extroversion); 4 Validity scales (Answer Choice Frequency, Random Responding, Tendency to Look Good or Bad, Tendency to Deny Blatant Pathology).
Administration: Group or individual.
Price Data, 2015: $55 per manual (1999, 54 pages); $155 per Windows software installation package, includes 10 scoring coupons.
Time: 40 minutes.
Comments: Originally published as the Coolidge Axis II Inventory (14:102); software scoring.
Author: Frederick L. Coolidge.
Publisher: SIGMA Assessment Systems, Inc.
Cross References: For reviews by Mark A. Staal and Peter Zachar, see 15:68; for reviews by Kevin L. Moreland and Paul Retzlaff of an earlier edition, see 14:102; see also T5:690 (3 references).

[540]
The Cooperative Institutional Research Program.

Purpose: "A national longitudinal study of the American higher educational system" based on freshman survey data.
Population: First-time, full-time entering college freshmen.
Publication Dates: 1966–1994.
Acronym: CIRP.
Scores: No scores.
Administration: Group.
Price Data: Available from publisher.
Time: (40) minutes.
Comments: Test titled Student Information Form (T3:2333); national norms reported annually.
Authors: Alexander W. Astin, William S. Korn, and Ellyne R. Riggs.
Publisher: Higher Education Research Institute. [Efforts to obtain updated information from the test publisher were unsuccessful. An updated edition of this test appears on the test publisher's website.]
Cross References: See T5:692 (1 reference) and T4:645 (8 references); for a review by Harvey Resnick, see 9:266. For a review by Albert B. Hood of the Student Information Form, see 8:397 (15 references).

[541]
Coopersmith Self-Esteem Inventories.

Purpose: "Designed to measure evaluative attitudes toward the self in social, academic, family, and personal areas of experience."
Population: Ages 8-15, 16 and above
Publication Date: 1981-2002.
Acronym: CSEI.
Administration: Individual and group.
Forms, 2: School, Adult.
Price Data, 2015: $50 per manual, including review-only copies of the test forms; $2.40 per online administration license (minimum 50); $2 per License to Reproduce (minimum 50).
Foreign Language Editions: Both forms available in Spanish. School form available in Arabic, Chinese, German and Greek.
Time: (10) minutes.
Author: Stanley Coopersmith.
Publisher: Mind Garden, Inc.

  a) SCHOOL FORM.
  Population: Ages 8–15.
  Acronym: CSEI-SC.
  Scores, 6: General Self, Social Self-Peers, Home-Parents, School-Academic, Total Self Score, Lie.
  Comments: Separate answer sheets may be used; school short form also available.
  b) ADULT FORM.
  Population: Ages 16 and above.
  Acronym: CSEI-AD.
  Score: Total score only.
Cross References: See T5:694 (134 references) and T4:647 (106 references); for reviews by Christopher Peterson and James T. Austin and by Trevor E. Sewell, see 9:267 (32 references).

[542]

Coping Inventory: A Measure of Adaptive Behavior.

Purpose: "Assess the behavior patterns and skills used to meet personal needs and to adapt to the demands of the environment."
Population: Ages 3-16; Ages 15-Adult.
Publication Date: 1985.
Scores, 9: 3 scores (Productive, Active, Flexible) for Coping with Self, Coping with Environment, plus Adaptive Behavior Index.
Administration: Individual.
Price Data, 2015: $60 per starter set (observation form version); $25 per manual (observation form version); $15.50 per manual (self-rated form version); $42 per 20 observation forms; $40.85 per starter set (self-rated form version); $21.65 per 10 self-rated forms.
Time: Administration time not reported.
Author: Shirley Zeitlin.
Publisher: Scholastic Testing Service, Inc.
  a) SELF-RATED FORM.
  Population: Ages 15-Adult.
  Comments: Self-report ratings of adaptive behavior.
  b) OBSERVATION FORM.
  Population: Ages 3–16.
  Comments: Ratings of adaptive behavior by adult informant.
Cross References: See T5:695 (3 references) and T4:648 (1 reference).

[543]

Coping Inventory for Stressful Situations, Second Edition.

Purpose: Designed as a "scale for measuring coping styles."
Population: Adolescents ages 13–18, adults age 18 and over.
Publication Dates: 1990-1999.
Acronym: CISS.
Scores, 5: Task-Oriented Coping, Emotion-Oriented Coping, Avoidance-Oriented Coping, Distraction, Social Diversion.
Administration: Individual or group.
Forms, 3: Adult, Adolescent, Situation-Specific Coping (CISS:SSC).
Price Data, 2015: $158 per CISS Adult Version Complete Kit Plus including 25 Adult QuikScore™ forms, 25 SSC QuikScore™ forms, and manual (1999, 75 pages); $97 per CISS Adolescent Version Complete Kit including 25 Adolescent QuikScore™ forms and manual (1999, 75 pages); $55 per 25 QuikScore™ forms (specify Adult, Adolescent, or SSC); $57 per manual.
Foreign Language Editions: French (European), French (Quebec), Arabic, Armenian, Danish, German, Greek, Hebrew, Icelandic, Italian, Japanese, Korean, Malaysian, Norwegian, Polish, Russion, Spanish (U.S.), and Spanish (European) translations available.
Time: (10) minutes.
Comments: Self-report.
Authors: Norman S. Endler and James D. A. Parker.
Publisher: Multi-Health Systems, Inc.
Cross References: For a review by William C. Tirre, see 15:69; for reviews by E. Thomas Dowd and Stephanie Stein of an earlier edition, see 14:104, see also T5:696 (2 references).

[544]

Coping Operations Preference Enquiry.

Purpose: Designed to measure a person's preference for using each of five coping mechanisms, or mechanisms of defense.
Population: Adults.
Publication Dates: 1962-1978.
Acronyms: COPE, FCPE.
Scores, 5: Denial, Isolation, Projection, Regression, Turning-Against-the-Self.
Administration: Individual or group.
Forms, 2: Male, Female.
Price Data, 2016: $50 per PDF manual (1978, 24 pages including test forms and scoring keys), including review-only copy of test form; $2 per Remote Online Survey License or License to Reproduce (minimum 50).
Time: [10] minutes.
Comments: Previously included in The FIRO Scales (7:78).
Authors: Will Schutz.
Publisher: Mind Garden, Inc.

[545]

Coping Resources Inventory [Revised].

Purpose: Developed to assess a person's resources for coping with stress.
Population: Middle school-age to adult.
Publication Dates: 1987-2004.
Acronym: CRI.
Scores, 6: Cognitive, Social, Emotional, Spiritual/Philosophical, Physical, Total.
Administration: Individual or group.
Price Data, 2016: $50 per manual (2004, 55 pages), including review-only copy of the CRI form; $2.40 per online administration license (minimum 50); $$2 per Remote Online Survey License (minimum 50); $15 per Individual Report; $15 Report About Me.
Foreign Language Edition: Available in Portuguese.
Time: (10) minutes.
Authors: M. Susan Marting and Allen L. Hammer.
Publisher: Mind Garden, Inc.
Cross References: See T5:697 (6 references); for reviews by Roger A. Boothroyd and Larry Cochran of the original edition, see 12:95 (1 reference); see also T4:649 (2 references).

[546]
Coping Responses Inventory—Adult and Youth.

Purpose: Constructed to "identify and monitor coping strategies in adults and adolescents."

Population: Ages 12–18, 18 and older.

Publication Date: 1993.

Acronym: CRI.

Scores, 8: Logical Analysis, Positive Reappraisal, Seeking Guidance and Support, Problem Solving, Cognitive Avoidance, Acceptance or Resignation, Seeking Alternative Rewards, Emotional Discharge.

Administration: Group.

Levels, 2: Adult and Youth.

Forms, 2: Ideal, Actual.

Price Data, 2015: $207 per CRI-Adult introductory kit including CRI-Adult professional manual (44 pages), 10 reusable item booklets, 50 answer sheets, and "Coping Responses Inventory"; $207 per CRI-Youth introductory kit including CRI-Youth professional manual, 10 reusable item booklets, 50 answer sheets, and "Coping Responses Inventory."

Time: (10–15) minutes.

Author: Rudolf H. Moos.

Publisher: Psychological Assessment Resources, Inc.

Cross References: For reviews by Ashraf Kagee and Everett V. Smith, Jr., see 14:105; see also T5:699 (5 references).

[547]
Coping Scale for Adults.

Purpose: Designed as a self-report inventory that examines coping behavior and facilitates development of coping strategies.

Population: Ages 18 and over.

Publication Date: 1997.

Acronym: CSA.

Scores, 19: Seek Social Support, Focus on Solving the Problem, Work Hard, Worry, Improve Relationships, Wishful Thinking, Tension Reduction, Social Action, Ignore the Problem, Self-Blame, Keep to Self, Seek Spiritual Support, Focus on the Positive, Seek Professional Help, Seek Relaxing Diversions, Physical Recreation, Protect Self, Humor, Not Cope.

Administration: Group.

Forms, 2: Short Form, Long Form.

Price Data, 2016: A$36.95 per 10 short forms; A$52.95 per 10 long forms; A$19.95 per 10 scoring sheets; A$19.95 per 10 profile charts; A$79.95 per manual (60 pages); A$19.95 per 0-99 administrations of Long Form Online; A$16.95 per 0-99 administrations of Short Form Online; volume discounts available.

Time: (20-30) minutes for Long Form; (10-15) minutes for Short Form.

Authors: Erica Frydenberg and Ramon Lewis.

Publisher: Australian Council for Educational Research Ltd. [Australia].

Cross References: For reviews by Peter Miles Berger and M. Allan Cooperstein, see 15:70.

[548]
Coping Skills Assessment.

Purpose: Designed to "evaluate whether an individual uses healthy or unhealthy coping mechanisms to deal with stress."

Population: Below 17 through adulthood.

Publication Date: 2011.

Acronym: COSA.

Scores, 16: Overall Score, Problem-Focused Coping, Emotion-Focused Coping, Hang-Ups, Problem Solving, Information Seeking, Negotiation, Social Support, Positive Cognitive Restructuring, Emotional Regulation, Distraction, Rumination, Avoidance, Helplessness, Social Withdrawal, Opposition.

Administration: Individual.

Price Data: Available from publisher.

Time: (20) minutes.

Comments: Self-administered online assessment. The test publisher provides clients with information about the methods and theoretical basis used in the development of the test as well as benchmarks for relevant industries and racial/ethnic group comparison data.

Author: PsychTests AIM, Inc.

Publisher: PsychTests AIM, Inc. [Canada].

Cross References: For reviews by Susan N. Kushner Benson and Romeo Vitelli, see 19:44.

[549]
Coping With Health Injuries and Problems.

Purpose: "Helps you quickly identify an individual's typical coping styles and suggests strategies that will best help the individual cope with and overcome his/her health problems."

Population: Adults.

Publication Dates: 1992–2000.

Acronym: CHIP.

Scores, 4: Distraction, Palliative, Instrumental, Emotional Preoccupation.

Administration: Individual or Group.

Price Data, 2015: $109 per complete kit including manual (2000, 66 pages) and 25 Quikscore forms; $55 per 25 Quikscore forms; $64 per technical manual.

Time: (15) minutes.

Comments: Self-report.

Authors: Norman S. Endler and James D. A. Parker.

Publisher: Multi-Health Systems, Inc.

Cross References: For reviews by Linda K. Bunker and by Leonard Handler and Amanda Jill Clements, see 15:71.

[550]
Coping With Stress.
Purpose: Constructed as a self-assessment tool to identify sources of stress and responses to stress.
Population: Adults.
Publication Date: 1989.
Scores, 9: Reaction to Stress (Obsessive, Hysteria, Anxiety, Phobia, Total, Normal), Adjustment to Stress (Healthy, Unhealthy), Sources of Stress.
Administration: Group.
Price Data, 2016: $195; quantity discounts available.
Time: [20] minutes administration; [10] minutes scoring; [30] minutes interpretation.
Comments: Self-administered, self-scored; now sold as part of the Training House Assessment Kit.
Author: Training House, Inc.
Publisher: HRD Press, Inc.
Cross References: For a review by Bert W. Westbrook and Suzanne Markel-Fox, see 12:96.

[551]
COPSystem Picture Inventory of Careers.
Purpose: To measure career interest for persons with reading or language difficulties.
Population: Elementary through adult-non-verbal.
Publication Date: 1993.
Acronym: COPS-PIC.
Scores: Interest scores in 14 COPSystem Career Clusters: Science—Professional, Science—Skilled, Technology—Professional, Technology—Skilled, Consumer Economics, Outdoor, Business—Professional, Business—Skilled, Clerical, Communication, Arts—Professional, Arts—Skilled, Service—Professional, Service—Skilled.
Administration: Group.
Price Data, 2016: $45.25 per 25 booklets and answer sheets combined (quantity discounts available); $35 per hand-scoring keys.
Time: (30) minutes.
Comments: Test publisher indicates materials have been updated; description will be updated when those materials are received.
Author: Lisa Knapp-Lee.
Publisher: EdITS/Educational and Industrial Testing Service.

[552]
The Cornell Class-Reasoning Test, Form X.
Purpose: "A multiple-choice deductive logic class-reasoning test."
Population: Grades 4–12.
Publication Date: 1964.
Scores: Deductive Logic.
Administration: Group.
Manual: No manual.
Price Data: Available at no charge from test publisher.

Time: Untimed.
Comments: Subtitle on test booklet is Cornell Critical Thinking Test Series.
Authors: Robert H. Ennis, William L. Gardiner, Richard Morrow, Dieter Paulus, and Lucille Ringel.
Publisher: Illinois Critical Thinking Project.
Cross References: See T2:1753 (1 reference).

[553]
The Cornell Conditional-Reasoning Test, Form X.
Purpose: Designed as "a multiple-choice deductive logic conditional-reasoning test."
Population: Grades 4–12.
Publication Date: 1964.
Scores: Deductive Logic.
Administration: Group.
Manual: No manual.
Price Data: Available at no charge from test publisher.
Time: Untimed.
Comments: Subtitle on test booklet is Cornell Critical Thinking Test Series.
Authors: Robert H. Ennis, William L. Gardiner, John Gazzetta, Richard Morrow, Dieter Paulus, and Lucille Ringel.
Publisher: Illinois Critical Thinking Project.
Cross References: See T2:1754 (1 reference).

[554]
Cornell Critical Thinking Tests, Fifth Edition.
Purpose: Designed to assess general critical thinking ability including induction, deduction, observation, credibility (of statements made by others), assumptions, and meaning.
Population: Students in Grade 4 through adults.
Publication Dates: 1961-2005.
Acronym: CCTT.
Score: Total score only for each level.
Administration: Group.
Levels: 2 levels.
Price Data, 2015: $19.99 per specimen set including manual (Fifth Edition, Revised, 2005, 54 pages), 1 Level X test, and 1 Level Z test; $29.99 per 10 test booklets (Level X or Level Z); $8.99 per manual (2005, 54 pages); $9.99 per 10 answer sheets (Level X and Level Z).
Time: (50) minutes.
Comments: May be administered in two or more sessions; additional administration time may be needed for elementary students; Fifth Edition, Revised Administration Manual (2005) includes results from additional empirical studies and an updated validity section.
Authors: Robert H. Ennis, Jason Millman, and Thomas N. Tomko.
Publisher: The Critical Thinking Co.

a) LEVEL X.
Population: Students in Grades 4-14.
b) LEVEL Z.
Population: Advanced and gifted high school students, college students, graduate students, and other adults.
Cross References: Reviews are scheduled for *The Twentieth Mental Measurements Yearbook*. See T5:705 (10 references) and T4:655 (1 reference); for reviews by Jan N. Hughes and Koressa Kutsick Malcolm of an earlier edition, see 11:88 (3 references); see also 9:269 (1 reference), T3:606 (7 references), T2:1755 (2 references), and 7:779 (10 references).

[555]

The Cornell Inventory for Student Appraisal of Teaching and Courses.

Purpose: "Provides teachers with feedback of student opinion."
Population: College teachers.
Publication Dates: 1972–1973.
Scores: Item norms only.
Administration: Group.
Price Data: Available from distributor.
Time: (15–20) minutes.
Authors: James B. Maas and Thomas R. Owen (manual).
Publisher: James B. Maas [Test distributed through the Test Collection at ETS].
Cross References: For a review by Wilbert J. Mc-Keachie, see 8:367.

[556]

Correa-Barrick Depression Scale.

Purpose: Designed to "measure the severity of depression" and to assess "changes in depression over time to evaluate treatment response."
Population: Ages 18 and older.
Publication Date: 2015.
Acronym: CBDS.
Score: Total score only.
Administration: Individual or group.
Price Data, 2015: $125 per complete kit including manual (10 pages) and 25 record forms; $55 per 25 record forms; $70 per manual.
Time: (5) minutes.
Comments: Separate measure of postpartum depression (Correa-Barrick Postpartum Depression Scale [557]) is available.
Authors: Christina B. Barrick and Elsa I. Correa.
Publisher: Stoelting Co.
Cross References: Reviews are scheduled for *The Twentieth Mental Measurements Yearbook*.

[557]

Correa-Barrick Postpartum Depression Scale.

Purpose: Designed to screen for postpartum depression.

Population: Postpartum mothers (within four weeks of giving birth).
Publication Date: 2015.
Acronym: CBPDS.
Score: Total score only.
Administration: Individual.
Price Data, 2015: $125 per complete kit including manual (10 pages) and 25 record forms; $70 per manual; $55 per 25 record forms.
Time: (5-10) minutes.
Comments: Designed to be used by primary-care providers and nurses, as well as maternity and public health nurses; adapted from the Correa-Barrick Depression Scale (556).
Authors: Christina B. Barrick and Elsa I. Correa.
Publisher: Stoelting Co.
Cross References: Reviews are scheduled for *The Twentieth Mental Measurements Yearbook*.

[558]

Correctional Institutions Environment Scale, Second Edition.

Purpose: Designed to measure the "social climate of juvenile and adult correctional programs."
Population: Residents and staff of correctional facilities.
Publication Dates: 1974–1987.
Acronym: CIES.
Scores, 9: Involvement, Support, Expressiveness, Autonomy, Practical Orientation, Personal Problem Orientation, Order and Organization, Clarity, Staff Control.
Administration: Group.
Forms, 4: Real (R), Ideal (I), Expectations (E), Short (S).
Price Data: 2015: $50 manual; $2 Remote Online Survey License; $2 License to Reproduce; $10 User's Guide.
Foreign Language Edition: Canadian French.
Time: Administration time not reported.
Comments: Part of the Social Climate Scales.
Author: Rudolf H. Moos.
Publisher: Mind Garden, Inc.
Cross References: For reviews by Kevin J. McCarthy and M. David Miller, see 14:106; see also T4:660 (3 references) and T3:612 (1 reference); for a review by Kenneth A. Carlson of an earlier version, see 8:531 (16 references). For a review of the Social Climate Scales, see 8:681.

[559]

Correctional Officers' Interest Blank.

Purpose: Designed for research in the development of selection techniques for correctional officers.
Population: Correctional officer applicants.
Publication Dates: 1953-2001.
Acronym: COIB.
Scores: Total score only.
Administration: Group or individual.

Price Data: Available from publisher.
Time: (10) minutes.
Author: Harrison G. Gough.
Publisher: Mind Garden, Inc.
Cross References: For reviews by Robert J. Howell and R. Lynn Richards and by Samuel Roll, see 10:75.

[560]
Cortical Vision Screening Test.

Purpose: "Designed to detect visual impairments in individuals with normal (corrected) or near-normal vision."
Population: Ages 18–80.
Publication Date: 2001.
Acronym: CORVIST.
Scores, 10: Symbol Acuity, Shape Discrimination, Size Discrimination, Shape Detection, Hue Discrimination, Scattered Dot Counting, Fragmented Numbers, Word Reading, Face Perception, Crowding.
Administration: Individual.
Price Data, 2015: £169 per complete kit including manual/stimulus book (40 pages) and 25 scoring sheets; £18.50 per 25 scoring sheets; £152 per manual/stimulus book.
Time: Untimed.
Authors: Merle James, Gordon T. Plant, and Elizabeth K. Warrington.
Publisher: Pearson Assessment [England].

[561]
The Couples BrainMap™.

Purpose: "To help partners gain new perspective of, and value for, their relationship."
Population: Couples.
Publication Dates: 1981-1986.
Scores, 4: I-Organize, I-Explore, I-Pursue, I-Preserve.
Administration: Group.
Price Data: Available from publisher.
Time: 40(50) minutes.
Comments: Self-administered, self-scored.
Authors: Sherry Lynch, Dudley Lynch, Phyllis Miller, and Sherod Miller.
Publisher: Brain Technologies Corporation.
Cross References: For a review by Alicia Skinner Cook and Richard E. Guest, see 11:91.

[562]
Course Finder.

Purpose: Assesses "students' interests and preferences, and identifies suitable higher education courses at appropriate universities/colleges in Great Britain."
Population: Students entering higher education.
Publication Dates: 1992–1993.
Acronym: CF.
Administration: Group.
Price Data: Available from publisher.

Time: (45–60) minutes.
Comments: For use in Great Britain; was listed in a previous *MMY* as Course Finder 2000; however, is updated each year.
Authors: Malcolm Morrisby, Glen Fox, and Mark Parkinson.
Publisher: The Morrisby Organisation [England].
Cross References: For a review by Colin Cooper, see 13:85.

[563]
CPF [Second Edition].

Purpose: "To assess extroversion and preference for social contact."
Population: Ages 16–adult.
Publication Dates: 1954–1992.
Acronym: CPF.
Scores, 3: Validity Scores (Uncertainty, Good Impression), Total Extroversion.
Administration: Group or individual.
Price Data, 2015: $37 per introductory kit including manual (1992, 10 pages), 20 test booklets, and scoring key; $32 per 20 test booklets; $10 per manual.
Foreign Language Edition: Spanish edition is available.
Time: (5–10) minutes.
Comments: Previously listed as a subtest of the Employee Attitude Series of the Job Tests Program (T3:1219).
Author: Samuel E. Krug.
Publisher: Industrial Psychology International Ltd.
Cross References: For reviews by Michael R. Harwell and Allen K. Hess, see 12:97.

[564]
CPI 260.

Purpose: "The goal of the inventory is to give a true-to-life description of the respondent, in clear, everyday language, in formats that can help the client to achieve a better understanding of self."
Population: Ages 13 and up.
Publication Date: 2002.
Acronym: CPI 260.
Scores, 29: Dominance, Capacity for Status, Sociability, Social Presence, Self-Acceptance, Independence, Empathy, Responsibility, Social Conformity, Self-Control, Good Impression, Communality, Well-Being, Tolerance, Achievement via Conformance, Achievement via Independence, Conceptual Fluency, Insightfulness, Flexibility, Sensitivity, Managerial Potential, Work Orientation, Creative Temperament, Leadership, Amicability, Law Enforcement Orientation, Orientation Toward Others, Orientation Toward Societal Values, Orientation Toward Self.
Administration: Individual or group.

Price Data, 2015: $34.95 each for CPI 260 Client Feedback Report online administration; $39.95 each for CPI 260 Coaching Report for Leaders online administration; $71.95 each for CPI 260 Client Feedback Report and Coaching Report for Leaders online administration; $96 each for CPI 260 Manual; $44 ea. for CPI 260 Coaching Report for Leaders User's Guide; $44 each for CPI 260 Client Feedback Report Guide for Interpretation.
Time: (25-30) minutes.
Comments: Abbreviated version derived from the California Psychological Inventory (15:43).
Authors: Harrison G. Gough and Pamela Bradley; Sam Manoogian (Coaching Report for Leaders); Robert J. Devine (Client Feedback Report).
Publisher: CPP, Inc.
Cross References: For reviews by Gary J. Dean and Stephen J. Freeman, see 18:36.

[565]

Creativity and Problem-Solving Aptitude Test.

Purpose: "Designed to evaluate a person's creative problem-solving potential based on pertinent personality traits."
Population: Under age 17 through adult.
Publication Date: 2011.
Acronym: CAPSAT.
Scores, 5: Comfort with Decision Making, Flexibility, Openness to Creativity, Sense of Self-Efficacy, Overall Score.
Administration: Individual.
Price Data: Available from publisher.
Time: (15) minutes.
Comments: Self-administered online assessment. The test publisher provides clients with information about the methods and theoretical basis used in the development of the test as well as benchmarks for relevant industries and racial/ethnic group comparison data.
Author: PsychTests AIM, Inc.
Publisher: PsychTests AIM, Inc. [Canada].
Cross References: For reviews by Merith Cosden and Allen I. Huffcutt, see 19:45.

[566]

Creativity Assessment Packet.

Purpose: To assess creative potential.
Population: Ages 6 through 18.
Publication Date: 1980.
Acronym: CAP.
Administration: Group.
Price Data, 2015: $143 per complete kit including 25 of each test (Form A and B), 25 test of divergent feeling forms, 25 Williams scale forms and manual (1980, 24 pages); $37 per manual; $31 per 25 test of

divergent thinking form A or B; $31 per 25 divergent feeling forms; $31 per 25 Williams scale.
Author: Frank Williams.
Publisher: PRO-ED.
   a) TEST OF DIVERGENT THINKING.
   Scores, 6: Fluency, Flexibility, Originality, Elaboration, Vocabulary, Comprehension.
   Forms, 2: A, B.
   Price Data: $29 per 25 tests (specify Form A or Form B).
   Time: 20 (25) minutes for grades 6-12; 25 (30) minutes for grades 3-5.
   b) TEST OF DIVERGENT FEELING.
   Scores, 5: Curiosity, Imagination, Complexity, Risk-Taking, Total.
   Price Data: $29 per 25 tests.
   Time: 10 (20) minutes.
   c) THE WILLIAMS SCALE.
   Scores, 9: Fluency, Flexibility, Originality, Elaboration, Curiosity, Imagination, Complexity, Risk-Taking, Total.
   Price Data: $29 per 25 tests.
   Time: Administration time not reported.
   Comments: Ratings by parents and teachers.
Cross References: See T5:724 (6 references) and T4:682 (3 references); for reviews by Fred Damarin and Carl L. Rosen, see 9:280.

[567]

The Creatrix Inventory [Revised].

Purpose: Determines a person's "creative risk-taking propensity."
Population: Members of organizations.
Publication Dates: 1971–2006.
Scores, 2: Creativity, Risk Taking; plotted on matrix to determine 1 of 8 orientations: Sustainer, Modifier, Challenger, Practicalizer, Innovator, Synthesizer, Dreamer, Planner.
Administration: Group.
Price Data: Available from publisher.
Time: Administration time not reported.
Comments: Online administration and scoring; designed for self-assessment and educational purposes.
Authors: Richard E. Byrd and Jacqueline L. Byrd.
Publisher: Creatrix.
Cross References: For reviews by Harrison G. Gough and John F. Wakefield of an earlier version, see 11:95.

[568]

Cree Questionnaire.

Purpose: "To measure an individual's overall creative potential."
Population: Individuals in a variety of occupations; clients in vocational and career counseling.
Publication Dates: 1957–1995.
Acronym: CQ.
Scores, 11: Overall Creative Potential, plus 10 factorially determined dimension scores grouped under 4

broad headings: Social Orientation, Work Orientation, Internal Functioning, and Interests.
Administration: Individual or group.
Price Data: Available from publisher.
Time: No limit (approximately 20 minutes).
Authors: T. G. Thurstone and J. Melinger.
Publisher: General Dynamics Information Technology.
Cross References: See T5:728 (1 reference); for a review by Janet M. Stoppard, see 9:282; see also T2:1149 (1 reference) and P:53 (3 references); for reviews of an earlier edition by Allyn Miles Munger and Theodor F. Naumann, see 6:84.

[569]

Crichton Vocabulary Scale.

Purpose: Designed to provide an index of a child's "acquired fund of verbal information."
Population: Ages 4.5–11.
Publication Dates: 1950–1988.
Acronym: CVS.
Scores, 3: Definitions of Set One, Definitions of Set Two, Total.
Administration: Individual.
Price Data, 2015: A$99 per manual; A$98 per 25 record forms/answer sheets.
Time: Administration time not reported.
Comments: Designed for use with Raven's Progressive Matrices (1688).
Author: J. C. Raven.
Publisher: Pearson Clinical Assessment [Australia and New Zealand].
Cross References: See T4:687 (3 references), T3:632 (2 references), and T2:491 (3 references); for a review by Morton Bortner, see 6:518 (1 reference); for reviews by Charlotte Banks and W. D. Wall, see 4:337.

[570]

Crisis Stabilization Scale.

Purpose: Designed as a clinician-rated instrument to "track progress and stabilization for adolescents in crisis, inform clinical decisions, and indicate treatment or program effectiveness."
Population: Adolesents in crisis.
Publication Date: 2014.
Acronym: CriSS.
Scores, 2: Coping, Commitment to Follow-Up.
Administration: Individual.
Price Data, 2016: $50 per PDF manual including review-only copy of form (31 pages); $60 per paper manual; $2 per Remote Online Survey License or $2 License to Reproduce (minimum 50).
Time: (10) minutes.
Comments: Completed by clinician; previously titled Goal Attainment Scale of Stabilization.
Author: Richard S. Balkin.
Publisher: Mind Garden, Inc.

[571]

Criterion Test of Basic Skills [2002 Edition].

Purpose: Developed to assess "the basic reading and arithmetic skills of individual students."
Population: Ages 6 through 11-11.
Publication Dates: 1976–2002.
Acronym: CTOBS-2.
Administration: Individual.
Price Data, 2015: $112 per test kit including manual (2002, 136 pages), 25 Arithmetic recording forms, 25 Reading assessment records, 25 Math problem sheets, and test plates in portfolio folder; $25 per manual; $25 per 25 Arithmetic recording forms; $25 per 25 Reading assessment records; $12 per 25 Math problem sheets; $25 per set of test plates.
Time: (15–20) minutes.
Comments: "Criterion referenced."
Authors: James Evans, Kerth Lundell, and William Brown.
Publisher: Academic Therapy Publications.
  a) READING.
  Scores, 7: Letter Recognition, Letter Sounding, Blending and Sequencing, Phonics Patterns, Multisyllable Words, Sight Words, Letter Writing.
  b) ARITHMETIC.
  Scores, 14: Correspondence, Numbers and Numerals, Addition, Subtraction, Multiplication, Division, Measurement, Telling Time, Symbols, Fractions, Decimals and Percents, Geometric Concepts, Pre-Algebra, Rounding and Estimations.
Cross References: See T3:635 (1 reference).

[572]

Criterion Validated Written Test for Emergency Medical Practitioner.

Purpose: Intended for the selection of paramedic personnel.
Population: Prospective paramedics.
Publication Dates: 1995-1999.
Scores: 7 subtests and total: Interest, Teamwork, Problem Solving—Common Sense, Problem Solving—Map Reading, Problem Solving—Logical Thinking, Problem Solving—Relevancy, Attentiveness, Total.
Administration: Group.
Form, 1: EMP 90.
Restricted Distribution: Distribution restricted to civil service commissions and qualified municipal officials.
Price Data: Available from publisher.
Time: 110 minutes.
Author: McCann Associates, Inc.
Publisher: McCann Associates [No reply from publisher; status unknown].

[573]

Critical Reasoning Test Battery.

Purpose: To assist students in subject and career choices and employers with the selection of job candidates.

Population: Students and employees ages 15 and over.
Publication Dates: 1981–1983.
Acronym: CRTB.
Administration: Group.
Restricted Distribution: Distribution restricted to persons who have completed the publisher's training course or members of the Division of Occupational Psychology of the British Psychological Society.
Price Data: Available from publisher.
Comments: 3 subtests available as separates.
Authors: Peter Saville, Roger Holdsworth, Gill Nyfield, David Hawkey, Susan Bawtree, and Ruth Holdsworth.
Publisher: CEB.
    a) VERBAL EVALUATION.
    Publication Dates: 1982–1983.
    Acronym: VC1.
    Time: 30(35) minutes.
    b) INTERPRETING DATA.
    Publication Dates: 1982–1983.
    Acronym: NC2.
    Time: 30(35) minutes.
    c) DIAGRAMMATIC SERIES.
    Publication Dates: 1982–1983.
    Acronym: DC3.
    Time: 20(25) minutes.

[574]
Cross-Cultural Adaptability Inventory.

Purpose: "Designed to provide information to an individual about his or her potential for cross-cultural effectiveness."
Population: Trainers and professionals who work with culturally diverse and cross-culturally oriented populations.
Publication Dates: 1987–2015.
Acronym: CCAI.
Scores: 4 scales: Emotional Resilience, Flexibility/Openness, Perceptual Acuity, Personal Autonomy.
Administration: Group.
Price Data: Available from publisher.
Time: 30 minutes.
Authors: Colleen Kelley and Judith Meyers.
Publisher: HRDQ.
Cross References: For reviews by Lynn L. Brown and Wendy Naumann, see 14:107.

[575]
Cultural Competence Self-Assessment Instrument.

Purpose: Designed "to help agencies measure their cultural competency in agency policymaking, administrative procedures, and practices."
Population: Business staff and clients of child welfare agencies
Publication Date: 1993.
Scores: Not scored.
Administration: Group.

Price Data: Price information available from publisher for instrument including manual (48 pages).
Time: Administration time not reported.
Author: Child Welfare League of America, Inc.
Publisher: Child Welfare League of America.

[576]
Culture-Free Self-Esteem Inventories, Third Edition.

Purpose: "A set of self-report inventories used to determine the level of self-esteem in students ages 6-0 through 18-11."
Population: Ages 0-6 through 11-18.
Publication Dates: 1981–2002.
Acronym: CFSEI-3.
Administration: Individual or group.
Levels, 3: Primary, Intermediate, Adolescent.
Price Data, 2015: $220 per complete kit including manual (2002, 60 pages); $34 per 50 primary/examiner record forms; $34 per 50 intermediate profile/scoring forms; $34 per 50 intermediate student response forms; $34 per 50 adolescent profile/scoring forms; $34 per 50 adolescent student response forms; $63 per manual.
Time: (15–20) minutes.
Comments: Newly normed revision of Culture-Free Self-Esteem Inventories, Second Edition; all levels include Defensiveness Score (a lie scale); previous editions titled Culture-Free Self-Esteem Inventories for Children and Adults; derivative titled North American Depression Inventories for Children and Adults (T5:1803).
Author: James Battle.
Publisher: PRO-ED.
    a) PRIMARY.
    Population: Ages 6–8.
    Score: Global Self-Esteem Quotient.
    Price Data: $32 per 50 primary examiner/record forms.
    b) INTERMEDIATE.
    Population: Ages 9–12.
    Scores, 5: Academic, General, Parental/Home, Social, Global Self-Esteem Quotient.
    Price Data: $32 per 50 intermediate profile/scoring forms; $32 per 50 intermediate student response forms.
    c) ADOLESCENT.
    Population: Ages 13–18.
    Scores, 6: Academic, General, Parental/Home, Social, Personal, Global Self-Esteem Quotient.
    Price Data: $32 per 50 adolescent profile/scoring forms, $28 per 50 adolescent student response forms.
Cross References: For reviews by Bethany A. Brunsman and Y. Evie Garcia, see 15:72; see T5:746 (4 references); for reviews by Michael G. Kavan and Michael J. Subkoviak of a previous edition, see 12:100 (7 references); see also T4:700 (9 references); for reviews by Gerald R. Adams and Janet Morgan Riggs of the original edition, see 9:291 (1 reference); see also T3:644 (1 reference). For reviews by Patricia A. Bachelor and Michael G. Kavan of the North American Depression Inventories for Children and Adults, see 11:265 (1 reference).

[577]

Customer Reaction Survey.

Purpose: Assesses customers' perceptions of salespeople's interpersonal skills.
Population: Salespeople.
Publication Dates: 1972-1995.
Acronym: CRS.
Scores, 4: Observed Exposure, Observed Feedback, Preferred Exposure, Preferred Feedback.
Administration: Group.
Price Data: Available from publisher.
Time: Administration time not reported.
Comments: Ratings by customers; also called Customer Reaction Index; based on the Johari Window Model of interpersonal relations.
Authors: Jay Hall and C. Leo Griffith.
Publisher: Teleometrics International, Inc.

[578]

Customer Service Applicant Inventory.

Purpose: "Evaluates skills and attitudes to help hire customer service oriented, honest, safe, and productive employees."
Population: Job applicants.
Publication Date: 1996.
Acronym: CSAI.
Scores, 12: Validity Scales (Candidness, Accuracy), Interpersonal Scales (Customer Service, Teamwork, Communication, Stress Tolerance), Core Values (Honesty, Drug Avoidance, Safety), Supplemental Scales (Applied Math, Training Readiness), Composite (Employability Index).
Administration: Group or individual.
Price Data: Available from publisher.
Time: (45) minutes.
Comments: Paper-and-pencil or computer administration available.
Author: General Dynamics Information Technology.
Publisher: General Dynamics Information Technology.

[579]

Customer Service Aptitude Profile.

Purpose: Designed to "assist in the selection, placement, and development of people to work in customer service roles."
Population: Ages 15 and over.
Publication Date: 2002.
Acronym: Customer Service AP.
Scores, 21: Self-Enhancement, Self-Criticism, Inconsistent Responding Index, Sales Disposition, Initiative-Cold Calling, Sales Closing, Achievement, Motivation, Competitiveness, Goal Orientation, Planning, Initiative-General, Team Player, Managerial, Assertiveness, Personal Diplomacy, Extroversion, Cooperativeness, Relaxed Style, Patience, Self-Confidence.

Administration: Group.
Price Data, 2016: $148 per CD good for 10 uses ($999 per CD good for 100 uses); $23 per Employers' Guide (24 pages); $18 per 100 PC answer sheets.
Time: (20) minutes.
Comments: Self-report format.
Authors: Sander I. Marcus, Jotham G. Friedland, and Harvey P. Mandel.
Publisher: Multi-Health Systems, Inc.
Cross References: For reviews by Michael Bunch and Cleborne D. Maddux, see 19:46.

[580]

Customer Service Profile [General Dynamics Information Technology].

Purpose: Designed to "identify qualified people for service positions by measuring important attitudes and aptitudes."
Population: Ages 18 and over.
Publication Date: 1994.
Acronym: CSP.
Scores, 6: Validity-Candidness, Validity-Accuracy, Customer Service Attitude, Customer Service Aptitude, Sales Aptitude, Customer Service Index.
Administration: Individual or group.
Price Data: Available from publisher.
Time: (20–25) minutes.
Comments: Test can be scored using operator-assisted telephone scoring, touch-test telephone scoring, Quanta-based scoring, or mail-in scoring.
Author: General Dynamics Information Technology.
Publisher: General Dynamics Information Technology.

[581]

Customer Service Profile [PsychTests AIM, Inc.].

Purpose: Designed to "assess whether a test-taker's skills and personality traits match those required to work in the customer service field."
Population: Under age 17 through adult.
Publication Date: 2011.
Acronym: CSP.
Scores, 20: Soft Skills (Communication Skills, Conflict Resolution, Social Skills, Patience, Self-Control, Hostility, Negative Reaction to Intimidation, Negative Reaction to Criticism), Psychological Strength (Coping Skills, Positive Attitude, Mental Toughness, Perspective), Work Habits (Organizational Skills, Conscientiousness, Self-Motivation), Impression Management, Overall Score.
Administration: Individual.
Price Data: Available from publisher.
Time: (30) minutes.
Comments: Self-administered online assessment. The test publisher provides clients with information about the methods and theoretical basis used in the development

of the test as well as benchmarks for relevant industries and racial/ethnic group comparison data.
Author: PsychTests AIM, Inc.
Publisher: PsychTests AIM, Inc. [Canada].
Cross References: For reviews by Michael Bunch and Cleborne D. Maddux, see 19:46.

[582]

Customer Service Simulator.

Purpose: "Designed to identify individuals who can solve problems while projecting responsiveness and sensitivity, and who avoid making common interpersonal errors in dealing with customers."
Population: Any position requiring public contact.
Publication Date: 1993.
Acronym: CSS.
Scores, 3: Customer Service Orientation, Interpersonal Sensitivity, Total.
Administration: Group.
Forms, 3: Customer Service Representative Version, Team Leader Version, Supervisor Version.
Restricted Distribution: Clients may be required to pay a nominal one-time overhead/sign-up fee.
Price Data, 2015: $295 per candidate for rental/scoring and feedback report.
Time: 90 minutes.
Comments: All versions are available for online administration.
Author: Richard C. Joines.
Publisher: Management & Personnel Systems, Inc.

[583]

Customer Service Skills Inventory.

Purpose: Designed to "assess customer service skills across a variety of customer-contact jobs."
Population: Ages 18 and over.
Publication Dates: 1993–1995.
Acronym: CSSI.
Scores, 8: Pressure Tolerance, Realistic Orientation, Time Appraisal, Independent Judgment, Responsiveness, Sensitivity, Balanced Judgment, Precision Orientation.
Administration: Group or individual.
Price Data: Available from publisher.
Time: (25–30) minutes.
Comments: Test can be administered online or via paper and pencil; can be scored via Internet, QUANTA software, or self-scoring.
Authors: Juan I. Sanchez and Simon L. Fraser.
Publisher: General Dynamics Information Technology.

[584]

Customer Service Skills Test.

Purpose: To evaluate technical and interpersonal skills of persons for the customer service position; available also to measure computer use skills.

Population: Candidates for customer service positions.
Publication Date: 1992.
Acronym: BASLCUS.
Scores: Total Score, Narrative Evaluation, Ranking, Recommendation.
Administration: Group.
Price Data: Available from publisher.
Foreign Language Edition: Available in French.
Time: (70) minutes.
Author: Walden Personnel Performance, Inc.
Publisher: Walden Personnel Testing & Consulting Inc. [Canada].
Cross References: For reviews by Wayne J. Camara and Jean Powell Kirnan, see 16:68.

[585]

d2 Test of Attention.

Purpose: Designed to measure processing speed, rule compliance, and quality of performance, allowing for a neuropsychological estimation of individual attention and concentration performance.
Population: Children, adolescents, and adults.
Publication Date: 1998.
Acronym: d2 Test.
Scores: Score information available from publisher.
Administration: Individual or group.
Price Data, 2016: $137 per complete test including 20 recording blanks, set of 2 scoring keys, and manual (1998, 80 pages); $19 per 50 recording blanks; $41 per set of 2 scoring keys; $104 per manual.
Time: (8) minutes.
Comments: Originally conceived to assess individuals' suitability for driving, the test has also been used as a part of personnel selection in other workplace environments where high levels of visual attention and concentration are demanded.
Authors: Rolf Brickenkamp and Eric Zillmer.
Publisher: Hogrefe Ltd [United Kingdom].
Cross References: For reviews by Phillip L. Ackerman and Elaine Clark, see 15:87.

[586]

DABERON-2: Screening for School Readiness, Second Edition.

Purpose: Developed to provide a standardized assessment of school readiness.
Population: Ages 4 through 6.
Publication Dates: 1972–1991.
Scores: Total score only.
Administration: Individual.
Price Data, 2015: $203 per complete kit including 24 presentation cards, 25 screen forms, 25 readiness reports, 5 classroom summary forms, object kit of manipulatives, and administration manual (1991, 38 pages); $20 per set of 24 presentation cards; $43 per 25 screen forms; $43 per 25 readiness reports; $20 per 5 classroom summary

forms; $43 per object kit of manipulatives; $62 per administration manual.

Time: (20-40) minutes.

Authors: Virginia A. Danzer, Mary Frances Gerber, Theresa M. Lyons, and Judith K. Voress.

Publisher: PRO-ED.

Cross References: For reviews by Stephen N. Axford and Selma Hughes, see 11:100 (1 reference).

[587]

A Dating Scale.

Purpose: To measure "liberalism of attitudes toward dating."

Population: Adolescents and adults.

Publication Dates: 1962–1988.

Scores: Total score only.

Administration: Group.

Manual: No manual.

Price Data, 2015: $2 per scale.

Time: [10] minutes.

Comments: Supplementary article available.

Author: Panos D. Bardis.

Publisher: Donna Bardis.

Cross References: For additional information and a review by Charles F. Warnath, see 8:335 (3 references).

[588]

Davidson Trauma Scale.

Purpose: "Developed to assess post traumatic stress disorder (PTSD) symptoms and aid in treatment."

Population: Adults who have been exposed to a serious trauma.

Publication Date: 1996.

Acronym: DTS.

Scores, 4: Intrusion, Avoidance/Numbing, Hyperarousal, Total.

Administration: Individual or group.

Price Data, 2015: $115 per complete kit including manual (32 pages), and 25 QuikScore™ forms; $55 per 25 QuikScore™ forms; $74 per manual.

Foreign Language Edition: French-Canadian QuikScore™ forms available.

Time: (10) minutes.

Comments: Self-report.

Author: Jonathan Davidson.

Publisher: Multi-Health Systems, Inc.

Cross References: For reviews by Janet F. Carlson and William E. Martin, Jr., see 14:110.

[589]

Dean-Woodcock Neuropsychological Battery.

Purpose: Designed to provide a "comprehensive assessment of sensory-motor functioning."

Population: Ages 4-0 and over.

Publication Date: 2003.

Acronym: DWNB.

Administration: Individual.

Price Data, 2015: $422.10 per complete kit including manual (269 pages), stimulus book, 25 test records, 25 interview forms, 25 emotional status forms, and a plastic storage box containing a comb, scissors, key, candle, nail, paper clip, pen, ball, plastic fork, plastic spoon, stylus, eye occluder, and three blindfolds; $70.20 per 25 test records; $57.35 per 25 interview forms; $83.05 per 25 emotional status forms.

Comments: Examiner's manual provides verbal instructions in Spanish and English.

Authors: Raymond S. Dean and Richard W. Woodcock.

Publisher: Houghton Mifflin Harcourt.

a) DEAN-WOODCOCK SENSORY-MOTOR BATTERY.

Acronym: DWSMB.

Scores, 21: Sensory (Near Point Visual Acuity, Visual Confrontation, Naming Pictures of Objects, Auditory Acuity), Tactile (Palm Writing, Object Identification, Finger Identification, Simultaneous Localization, Total), Motor (Lateral Preference, Gait and Station, Romberg, Construction, Coordination, Mime Movements, Left-Right Movements, Finger Tapping, Expressive Speech, Grip Strength, Total), Impairment Index.

Time: (30–45) minutes.

b) DEAN-WOODCOCK STRUCTURED NEURO-PSYCHOLOGICAL INTERVIEW.

Scores: Not scored.

Time: (30) minutes.

Comments: Structured interview can be administered to the subject, a parent, or "other informant who knows the subject well."

c) DEAN-WOODCOCK EMOTIONAL STATUS EXAMINATION.

Scores: Not scored.

Time: (30) minutes.

Comments: May be administered to subject or to an informant.

Cross References: For reviews by Rik Carl D'Amato and Justin M. Walker and by W. Joel Schneider, see 17:54.

[590]

Decision-making and Self-regulation Assessor.

Purpose: Designed to measure "a person's decision-making competence, decision-making style and ability to self-regulate."

Population: Adults.

Publication Date: 2015.

Acronym: DASA.

Scores, 12: Mental Energy, Self-Discipline, Procrastination, Advancement Focus, Protection Focus, Decision Avoidance, Spontaneous Choice, Deliberation, Option Generation, Decision-Making Confidence, General Self-Regulation, Decision-Making Competence.

Administration: Individual.

Price Data, 2016: £75 per manual (52 pages); £65 per online administration with Technical Report & Personal Insight Report (subscription discounts available).
Time: (10) minutes.
Comments: Administered online.
Author: Chris Dewberry.
Publisher: Hogrefe Ltd [United Kingdom].

[591]
Decision Making Inventory.

Purpose: "Designed to assess an individual's preferred style of decision making."
Population: High school and college, working adults.
Publication Dates: 1983–1986.
Acronym: DMI.
Scores, 4: Information Gathering Style (Spontaneous, Systematic), Information Processing Style (Internal, External).
Administration: Group.
Forms, 2: H, I.
Price Data, 2015: $19 per assessment.
Time: (10) minutes.
Authors: William C. Coscarelli, Richard Johnson (test), and JaDean Johnson (test).
Publisher: John Wiley & Sons, Inc.
Cross References: See T5:768 (2 references); for reviews by George Domino and Barbara A. Kerr, see 10:77 (3 references).

[592]
Decision-Making Strategies Inventory.

Purpose: Designed to help "discover your current decision-making pattern."
Population: Adults.
Publication Date: 1983.
Scores, 5: Bargaining, Collaboration, Decide-By-Rule, Unilateral, Total Score.
Administration: Group.
Price Data: Available from publisher.
Time: (15) minutes.
Author: Herbert S. Kindler.
Publisher: The Center for Management Effectiveness, Inc.

[593]
Decoding and Spelling Proficiency Test-Revised.

Purpose: Designed to provide "a detailed profile of crucial literacy skills that underlie reading and spelling."
Population: Ages 6-25.
Publication Dates: 1982-2010.
Acronym: DSPT-R.
Scores, 4: Decoding, Visual Recognition, Auditory-Visual Recognition, Spelling.
Administration: Group.

Forms, 2: Parallel Forms A and B.
Price Data, 2015: $155 per test kit including manual (2010, 219 pages), 25 record Forms A, 25 record Forms B, 25 test booklets Form A, and 25 test booklets Form B; $65 per manual.
Time: (25-40) minutes.
Comments: "The current version…is a revision of the Diagnostic Spelling Potential test"; the four parts can be administered separately or in conjunction with one another.
Authors: Michael Milone and John Arena.
Publisher: Academic Therapy Publications.
Cross References: For reviews by Timothy Shanahan and Kay B. Stevens, see 19:48; for information regarding the Diagnostic Spelling Potential Test, see T4:790 (1 reference); for reviews by Marcee J. Meyers and Ruth Noyce of the Diagnostic Spelling Potential Test, see 9:345 (1 reference).

[594]
Decoding-Encoding Screener for Dyslexia.

Purpose: Designed to "quickly assess a student's specific reading difficulties."
Population: Grades 1-8.
Publication Date: 2006.
Acronym: DESD.
Scores, 5: DESD Grade Level, Reading Raw Score, Reading Standard Score, Sight-Word Spelling Raw Score, Phonetic Spelling Raw Score.
Administration: Individual.
Price Data, 2016: $137 per kit including stimulus booklet, 100 spelling response forms, 100 record sheets, and manual (63 pages); $33 per stimulus booklet; $11.50 per 100 spelling response forms; $52.50 per 100 record sheets; $65.50 per manual.
Time: (5-10) minutes.
Authors: John R. Griffin, Howard N. Walton, and Garth N. Christenson.
Publisher: Western Psychological Services.
Cross References: For reviews by Mildred Murray-Ward and Monica Gordon Pershey, see 19:49.

[595]
Decoding Skills Test.

Purpose: Measures the reading levels and decoding skills of elementary school readers and identifies reading disabled children and provides a diagnostic profile of their decoding skill development.
Population: Children who read at 1st-5th grade levels.
Publication Date: 1985.
Acronym: DST.
Scores: 3 subtests yielding 12 scores: Basal Vocabulary (Instructional Level, Frustration Level), Phonic Patterns (Monosyllabic, Polysyllabic), Contextual Decoding (Instructional Level [Reading Rate, Error Rate, Phonic Words, Comprehension], Frustration

Level [Reading Rate, Error Rate, Phonic Words, Comprehension]).
Administration: Individual.
Price Data, 2016: $190.50 per complete kit including reusable Presentation Book, 10 scoring booklets, and manual; $90 per 1 reusable Presentation Book; $46.50 per 10 scoring booklets; $65.50 per manual.
Time: 15-30 minutes.
Comments: "Criterion-referenced."
Authors: Ellis Richardson and Barbara DiBenedetto.
Publisher: Western Psychological Services.
Cross References: See T5:769 (8 references); for reviews by Stephen N. Elliott and Timothy S. Harts-horne, see 10:78.

[596]
Defendant Questionnaire.
Purpose: "Designed for defendant (misdemeanor or felony) assessment in court settings."
Population: Defendants (misdemeanor or felony).
Publication Date: 1997.
Acronym: DQ.
Scores: 7 scales: Truthfulness, Alcohol, Drugs, Substance Abuse/Dependency, Violence (Lethality), Antisocial, Stress Coping Abilities.
Administration: Group.
Price Data: Available from publisher.
Foreign Language Editions: Available in English and Spanish.
Time: Administration time not reported.
Comments: Can be administered via paper and pencil test booklet, directly on computer screen, optically scanned answer sheet, human voice audio via headset and computer.
Author: Risk & Needs Assessment, Inc.
Publisher: Behavior Data Systems, Ltd.

[597]
Defining Issues Test.
Purpose: "Gives information about the process by which people judge what ought to be done in moral dilemmas."
Population: Grades 9-12 and college and adults.
Publication Dates: 1979-1987.
Acronym: DIT.
Scores, 12: Consistency Check, M (meaningless items) score, P (principled moral thinking) score, U (utilizer) score, D (composite) score, A (antiestablishment) score, and stage scores (2, 3, 4, 5A, 5B, and 6).
Administration: Group.
Forms, 2: Short form, long form.
Price Data, 2016: $31 per 15 paper and pencil copies (volume discounts available); $26.25 per 15 copies for online administration (extra charge for scoring; volume discounts available).

Time: (30-40) minutes for short form; (40-50) minutes for long form.
Comments: 2 optional companion booklets available: Development in Judging Moral Issues from the Center for the Study of Ethical Development, and Moral Development: Advances in Theory and Research from Praeger Press.
Authors: James R. Rest, with model computer scoring programs by Steve Thoma, Mark Davison, Stephen Robbins, and David Swanson.
Publisher: Center for the Study of Ethical Development.
Cross References: See T5:771 (28 references) and T4:724 (10 references); for reviews by Rosemary E. Sutton and by Bert W. Westbrook and K. Denise Bane, see 11:104 (34 references); for reviews by Robert R. McCrae and Kevin L. Moreland, see 9:304 (22 references); see also T3:666 (8 references).

[598]
DeGangi-Berk Test of Sensory Integration.
Purpose: "Designed to overcome problems in detecting sensory integrative dysfunction in the early years."
Population: Ages 3–5.
Publication Date: 1983.
Acronym: TSI.
Scores, 4: Postural Control, Bilateral Motor Integration, Reflex Integration, Total.
Administration: Individual.
Price Data, 2016: $238 per complete kit including set of test materials, 25 star design sheets, 25 protocol booklets, and manual (48 pages) in a carrying case; $35.50 per 100 star designs; $35.50 per 25 protocol booklets; $54 per manual.
Time: (30) minutes.
Comments: Other test materials (e.g., stopwatch, carpeted scooter board, hula hoop) must be supplied by examiner.
Authors: Georgia A. DeGangi and Ronald A. Berk.
Publisher: Western Psychological Services.
Cross References: See T5:772 (2 references); for a review by R. A. Bornstein, see 10:80.

[599]
Degrees of Reading Power [Primary and Standard Test Forms J & K and Advanced Test Forms T & U].
Purpose: Designed to provide direct criterion-referenced, performance measures of reading comprehension.
Population: Grades 1–12 and over.
Publication Dates: 1979–2002.
Acronym: DRP.
Scores: Total score only.
Administration: Group.
Levels, 3: Primary, Standard, Advanced.

Price Data: Available from publisher.

Time: (45) minutes.

Comments: Practice exercises provided; provides readability analysis of instructional material in print; computer or hand scored; group profiles, optional reports, services, and software also available.

Authors: Touchstone Applied Science Associates (TASA), Inc.

Publisher: Questar Assessment, Inc.

a) PRIMARY.

Purpose: To provide a measure of how well students understand the meaning of text.

Population: Grades 1–3.

Forms, 2: J, K.

Levels, 2: 0, 9.

b) STANDARD.

Purpose: To provide a measure of how well students understand the meaning of text.

Population: Grades 3–12 and over.

Forms, 2: J, K.

Levels, 5: 8, 7, 6, 4, 2.

c) ADVANCED.

Purpose: To assess how well students are able to reason with textual materials.

Population: Grades 6–12 and over.

Forms, 2: T, U.

Levels, 2: 4, 2.

Cross References: For reviews by Jeffrey K. Smith and Keith F. Widaman, see 16:69; for reviews by Felice J. Green and Howard Margolis of a previous edition, see 14:111; see also T5:773 (5 references); for reviews by Darrell N. Caulley, Elaine Furniss, and Michael McNamara and by Lawrence Cross of an earlier edition, see 12:101 (9 references); see also T4:726 (14 references); for reviews by Roger Bruning and Gerald S. Hanna of an earlier edition, see 9:305 (1 reference).

[600]

Delis-Kaplan Executive Function System.

Purpose: To "comprehensive assess ... the key components of executive functions believed to be mediated primarily by the frontal lobe."

Population: 8–89 years.

Publication Date: 2001.

Acronym: D-KEFS.

Scores: 9 tests: Trail Making Test, Verbal Fluency Test, Design Fluency Test, Color-Word Interference Test, Sorting Test, 20 Questions Test, Word Context Test, Tower Test, Proverb Test.

Administration: Individual.

Price Data, 2015: $614 per complete kit in box including manual (388 pages), stimulus booklet, sorting cards (3 sets of 6 cards each), 1 tower stand with 5 color disks, 25 record forms, 25 Design Fluency Response booklets, 25 Trail Making response booklet sets (each set contains 25 response booklets for the 5 Trail Making conditions; $665 per complete kit with soft-side case; $819 per complete kit in box with

Scoring Assistant CD-ROM for Windows; $870.25 per complete kit in a soft-side case with Scoring Assistant; $240.90 per D-KEFS Scoring Assistant (CD-ROM); $271.60 per examiner's and technical manual; $142.50 per examiner's manual; $129.15 per technical manual (144 pages); $51.25 per 25 record forms; $51.25 per 25 Sorting or Color-Word Interference test record forms; $28.70 per 25 sets of Trail Making Test response booklets (each set contains 25 different response booklets for the 5 Trail Making conditions); $35 per 25 Design Fluency Test record forms; $51.25 per 25 Verbal Fluency, 20 Questions, or Word Context test record forms; $51.25 per 25 Tower or Proverb test record forms; $77.90 per 3 sets of 6 cards each of alternate record forms for Sorting; $76.90 per Sorting Test set of cards including 2 sets of standard sorting cards, and 2 practice sets; $179.40 per stimulus book.

Time: (90) minutes for all 9 tests.

Comments: Each test assesses a different executive-function domain; tests may be administered alone or in combination; hand-scorable; D-KEFS Scoring Assistant software available; scoring software generates reports in table or graphical format; for system requirements contact publisher.

Authors: Dean C. Delis, Edith Kaplan, and Joel H. Kramer.

Publisher: Pearson.

a) D-KEFS TRAIL MAKING TEST.

Purpose: Assesses "flexibility of thinking on a visual-motor task."

Form, 1: Standard Record Form.

Scores, 6: Visual Scanning, Number Sequencing, Letter Sequencing, Number-Letter Switching, Motor Speed, Composite Score.

b) D-KEFS VERBAL FLUENCY TEST.

Purpose: Assesses "fluent productivity in the verbal domain."

Forms, 2: Standard Record Form, Alternate Record Form.

Scores, 3: Letter Fluency, Category Fluency, Category Switching.

c) D-KEFS DESIGN FLUENCY TEST.

Purpose: Assesses "fluent productivity in the spatial domain."

Form, 1: Standard Record Form.

Scores, 3: Filled Dots, Empty Dots Only, Switching.

d) D-KEFS COLOR-WORD INTERFERENCE TEST.

Purpose: Assesses "verbal inhibition."

Form, 1: Standard Record Form.

Scores, 4: Color Naming, Word Reading, Inhibition, Inhibition/Switching.

e) D-KEFS SORTING TEST.

Purpose: Assesses "problem-solving, verbal and spatial concept formation, flexibility of thinking on a conceptual task."

Forms, 2: Standard Record Form, Alternate Record Form.

Scores, 2: Free Sorting, Sort Recognition.

Comments: Alternate set of scoring cards available.

f) D-KEFS TOWER TEST.

Purpose: Assesses "planning and reasoning in the spatial modality [and] impulsivity."

Form, 1: Standard Record Form.

Score: Total Achievement Score.

g) D-KEFS 20 QUESTIONS TEST.

Purpose: Assesses "hypothesis testing, verbal and spatial abstract thinking, [and] impulsivity."

Forms, 2: Standard Record Form, Alternate Record Form.

Score: Initial Abstraction Score.

h) D-KEFS WORD CONTEXT TEST.

Purpose: Assesses "deductive reasoning [and] verbal abstract thinking."

Form, 1: Standard Record Form.

Score: Total Consecutively Correct.

i) D-KEFS PROVERB TEST.

Purpose: Assesses "metaphorical thinking, generating versus comprehending abstract thought."

Form, 1: Standard Record Form.

Scores, 2: Total Achievement scores: Free Inquiry, Multiple Choice.

Cross References: For reviews by Anthony T. Dugbartey and Pamilla Ramsden, see 15:74.

[601]
Delis Rating of Executive Functions.

Purpose: Designed to "assess behaviors that may reflect difficulties with executive functioning."

Population: Ages 5-18.

Publication Date: 2012.

Acronym: D-REF.

Scores, 8: Behavioral Functioning, Emotional Functioning, Executive Functioning, Total Composite, Attention/Working Memory, Activity Level/Impulse Control, Compliance/Anger Management, Abstract Thinking/Problem-Solving.

Administration: Individual.

Forms, 3: Parent Rating, Teacher Rating, Self Rating.

Price Data, 2015: Manual (154 pages) available as download from publisher's website; $2 per report usage including administration, scoring, and reporting; $99 per print starter kit including manual, 10 response books each for parent, teacher, and self, plus 10 score reports; $49 per manual, $50 per 25 response books with score reports (parent, teacher, or self).

Time: (10) minutes.

Comments: Parent and teacher forms designed for rating children/adolescents ages 5-18 years; self-rating form designed for youth 11-18 years.

Author: Dean C. Delis.

Publisher: Pearson.

Cross References: Reviews are scheduled for *The Twentieth Mental Measurements Yearbook.*

[602]
Dementia Rating Scale—2.

Purpose: To measure and track "mental status in adults with cognitive impairment."

Population: Adults ages 56–89 and older.

Publication Dates: 1973–2001.

Acronym: DRS-2.

Scores, 6: Attention, Initiation/Perseveration, Construction, Conceptualization, Memory, Total.

Administration: Individual.

Price Data, 2015: $312 per introductory kit including professional manual (2001, 47 pages), 50 scoring booklets, 50 profile forms, and 1 set of stimulus cards; $274 per Alternate Form introductory kit; $460 per software (CD-ROM) with on-screen help and quick start guide.

Time: (15–30) minutes.

Comments: Revised version of the DRS; DRS-2 stimulus cards same as for original DRS; can be administered bedside by appropriately trained personnel; alternate form is also available.

Authors: Steven Mattis (professional manual, stimulus cards, scoring booklet), Paul J. Jurica, and Christopher L. Leitten (professional manual).

Publisher: Psychological Assessment Resources, Inc.

Cross References: For reviews by Iris Phillips and Pamilla Ramsden, see 15:75; see T5:776 (63 references); for a review by R. A. Bornstein of an earlier edition, see 11:107 (2 references).

[603]
Dementia Rating Scale-2 Alternate Form.

Purpose: Designed as an alternate form of the Dementia Rating Scale-2, a measure of cognitive status, to reduce "the practice effects that occur with serial administrations of the DRS-2."

Population: Ages 56-105.

Publication Dates: 1973-2004.

Acronym: DRS-2: AF.

Scores, 6: Attention, Initiation/Perseveration, Construction, Conceptualization, Memory, Total.

Administration: Individual.

Price Data, 2015: $274 per introductory kit, including 50 scoring booklets, 50 profile forms, 1 set of stimulus cards, and professional manual supplement (2004, 29 pages); $148 per 50 scoring booklets; $48 per 50 profile forms; $47 per set of stimulus cards; $64 per professional manual supplement.

Time: [15-30] minutes.

Comments: As noted in the Dementia Rating Scale-2 Alternate Form professional manual supplement, "The Professional Manual Supplement contains information on the development, reliability, and validity of the DRS-2: AF, as well as instructions for administration and scoring. However, this Professional Manual Supplement should be considered an adjunct to the DRS-2 Professional Manual," which must be purchased separately.

Authors: Kara S. Schmidt and Steven Mattis.

Publisher: Psychological Assessment Resources, Inc.

Cross References: For a review by Matthew E. Lambert, see 19:50; for reviews by Iris Phillips and

Pamilla Ramsden of the Dementia Rating Scale-2, see 15:75; see also T5:776 (63 references); for a review by R. A. Bornstein of the original Dementia Rating Scale, see 11:107 (2 references).

[604]
Dental Admission Test.

Purpose: "Designed to measure general academic achievement, comprehension of scientific information, and perceptual ability."
Population: United States dental school applicants.
Publication Dates: 1950–2006.
Acronym: DAT.
Scores, 8: Natural Sciences (Biology, General Chemistry, Organic Chemistry, Total), Reading Comprehension, Quantitative Reasoning, Perceptual Ability, Academic Average.
Administration: Group.
Price Data: Available from publisher.
Time: 255(270) minutes.
Comments: Formerly called Dental Aptitude Testing Program; computer-based test administered throughout the year at centers approved by publisher.
Author: Department of Testing Services.
Publisher: American Dental Association.
Cross References: For reviews by Janet Baldwin and Jerry S. Gilmer, see 12:102; for reviews by Henry M. Cherrick and Linda M. DuBois of an earlier edition, see 9:308; see also T3:673 (2 references); for reviews by Robert L. Linn and Christine H. McGuire of an earlier edition, see 8:1085 (7 references); see also T2:2337 (8 references), 7:1091 (28 references), 5:916 (6 references), and 4:788 (2 references).

[605]
Dental Assistant Test.

Purpose: Developed to help screen for dental assistant positions.
Population: Dental assistant applicants.
Publication Date: 1975.
Scores: 8 tests: Attention to Details, Organization Skills, Perception of Objects in Space, Perception of Spatial Perspective, Following Directions, Detail Judgments, Dexterity, Logic and Reasoning.
Administration: Group.
Price Data: Available from publisher.
Time: (40-45) minutes.
Comments: Self-administered.
Authors: Mary Meeker and Robert Meeker.
Publisher: SOI Systems.

[606]
Dental Receptionist Test.

Purpose: Developed to help screen for dental receptionist positions.

Population: Dental receptionist applicants.
Publication Date: 1975.
Scores: 8 tests: Attention to Details, Vocabulary, Verbal Reasoning, Following Directions, Management of Details, Management of Numerical Information, Dexterity, Logic and Reasoning.
Administration: Group.
Price Data: Available from publisher.
Time: (45-50) minutes.
Comments: Self-administered.
Authors: Mary Meeker and Robert Meeker.
Publisher: SOI Systems.

[607]
Depressive Experiences Questionnaire.

Purpose: Designed to assess an individual's depressive experience.
Population: Adolescents and adults (patients and normals).
Publication Dates: 1976–1989.
Acronym: DEQ.
Scores, 3: Dependency, Self-Criticism, Efficacy.
Administration: Group.
Forms, 2: DEQ, DEQ-A.
Manual: No manual.
Price Data: Available for free from publisher.
Time: Administration time not reported.
Authors: Sidney J. Blatt, Carrie E. Schaffer, Susan A. Bers, and Donald M. Quinlan.
Publisher: Sidney J. Blatt [c/o Dr. David C. Zuroff].
Cross References: See T5:790 (29 references), T4:744 (30 references), 9:316 (2 references), and T3:682 (1 reference).

[608]
Derogatis Affects Balance Scale [Revised].

Purpose: Designed as a multidimensional mood and affects inventory to "measure the affects profile of community, medical, and psychiatric respondents."
Population: Adults.
Publication Dates: 1975–1996.
Acronym: DABS.
Scores, 13: Joy, Contentment, Vigor, Affection, Anxiety, Depression, Guilt, Hostility, Positive Score Total, Negative Score Total, Affects Balance Index, Affects Expressiveness Index, Positive Affects Ratio.
Administration: Individual.
Forms, 2: DABS, DABS-SF (Short Form).
Price Data, 2016: $90 per 50 tests; $25 per 50 profiles; $30 per manual (1996, 58 pages); $1.75 per 1 website scoring.
Time: (5) minutes (DABS); (2–3) minutes (Short Form).
Comments: Self-report inventory, for clinical or research uses; formerly published as the Affects Balance Scale (ABS).
Author: Leonard R. Derogatis.

Publisher: Clinical Psychometric Research, Inc.
Cross References: For reviews by Mark J. Atkinson and Carlen Hennington, see 14:112; see also T5:791 (16 references), T4:132 (6 references), and 9:61 (6 references).

[609]

Derogatis Interview for Sexual Functioning.

Purpose: "A brief semistructured interview designed to provide an estimate of the quality of an individual's current sexual functioning in quantitative terms."
Population: Adults.
Publication Dates: 1987–1989.
Scores, 6: Sexual Cognition/Fantasy, Sexual Arousal, Sexual Behavior/Experience, Orgasm, Sexual Drive/Relationship, Total Score.
Administration: Individual.
Price Data, 2016: $112.50 per 50 DISF-SR booklets; $2 per 1 DSF-SR website scoring.
Foreign Language Editions: Polish, French, Finnish, and German editions available.
Time: (15–20) minutes for DISF; (10–15) minutes for DISF-SR.
Author: Leonard R. Derogatis.
Publisher: Clinical Psychometric Research, Inc.
  a) DEROGATIS INTERVIEW FOR SEXUAL FUNCTIONING.
  Acronym: DISF.
  Time: (15–20) minutes.
  Comments: Semistructured interview format using a 4-point Likert scale.
  b) DEROGATIS INTERVIEW FOR SEXUAL FUNC-TIONING—SELF REPORT.
  Acronym: DISF-SR.
  Time: (10–15) minutes.
  Comments: Paper-and-pencil format using Likert scales; may be used to gain evaluations of patient's sexual functioning by the patient or the patient's spouse.
Cross References: For a review by Sheri Bauman, see 15:76.

[610]

Derogatis Sexual Functioning Inventory.

Purpose: Multidimensional assessment of sexual functioning.
Population: Adults.
Publication Dates: 1975–1979.
Acronym: DSFI.
Scores, 12: Information, Experience, Drive, Attitudes, Psychological Symptoms, Affects, Gender Role, Definition, Fantasy, Body Image, Sexual Satisfaction, Total, Patient's Evaluation of Current Functioning.
Administration: Individual.
Price Data, 2016: $150 per starter kit, including 10 DSFI booklets and 10 website scorings; $200 per 25 DSFI booklets; $25 per 50 DSFI profile forms; $14 per 1 DSFI manual (1979, 36 pages); $10 per 1 DSFI website scoring.

Time: (45–60) minutes.
Author: Leonard R. Derogatis.
Publisher: Clinical Psychometric Research, Inc.
Cross References: See T5:793 (24 references) and T4:746 (10 references); for reviews by Edward S. Herold and David L. Weis, see 9:317 (3 references); see also T3:683 (6 references).

[611]

Derogatis Stress Profile.

Purpose: "Designed to assess and represent stress at three distinct but related levels of measurement."
Population: Adults.
Publication Dates: 1984–1986.
Acronym: DSP.
Scores: 3 domains: Environmental Events, Emotional Response, Personality Mediators; 11 dimensions: Time Pressure, Driven Behavior, Attitude Posture, Relaxation Potential, Role Definition, Vocational Satisfaction, Domestic Satisfaction, Health Posture, Hostility, Anxiety, Depression; 2 global scores: Subjective Stress, Total Stress.
Administration: Individual.
Price Data, 2016: $150 per 50 tests; $20 per 1 DSP online administration and scoring; $65 per 50 DSP score/profile forms; $15 per 1 set DSP scoring instructions (1986, 14 pages); $5 per 1 DSP website scoring.
Time: 10(15) minutes.
Author: Leonard R. Derogatis.
Publisher: Clinical Psychometric Research, Inc.
Cross References: See T5:794 (2 references); for reviews by Mariela C. Shirley and Paul D. Werner, see 13:93 (4 references); see also T4:747 (1 reference).

[612]

Detailed Assessment of Posttraumatic Stress.

Purpose: Designed as a comprehensive diagnostic measure of trauma exposure and posttraumatic stress and associated functions, including dissociative symptoms, substance abuse, and suicidality.
Population: Adults 18 and over who have undergone a significant psychological stressor.
Publication Date: 2001.
Acronym: DAPS.
Scores: 2 validity scales (Positive Bias and Negative Bias) and 11 scales in 3 clusters: Trauma Specification (Relative Trauma Exposure, Peritraumatic Distress, Peritraumatic Dissociation), Posttraumatic Stress (Re-experiencing, Avoidance, Hyperarousal, Posttraumatic Stress—Total, Posttraumatic Impairment), Associated Features (Trauma-Specific Dissociation, Substance Abuse, Suicidality).
Administration: Individual or group.
Price Data, 2015: $258 per introductory kit including professional manual (56 pages), 10 item booklets, 50 hand-scorable answer sheets, and 50 male/female profile forms; $460 per DAPS-IR CD-ROM based software kit.

Time: (20–30) minutes.
Comments: Self-administered; CD-ROM based software with Interpretive Report also available (DAPS-IR).
Author: John Briere.
Publisher: Psychological Assessment Resources, Inc.
Cross References: For reviews by Roger A. Boothroyd and Larissa Smith, see 15:77.

[613]
Detention Promotion Tests—Complete Service.

Purpose: Designed as a custom-made test to fit duties and responsibilities for promotion of detention personnel.
Population: Detention workers under consideration for promotion.
Publication Dates: 1990–1998.
Scores: 6 subtests: Detention-Related Technical Knowledges, Knowledge of the Behavioral Sciences and Human Relations, Supervisory and Managerial Knowledges, Administrative Knowledges, Knowledge of Inmate Legal Rights, Comprehension Ability, Total.
Administration: Group.
Price Data: Available from publisher.
Time: [210] minutes.
Author: McCann Associates, Inc.
Publisher: McCann Associates [No reply from publisher; status unknown].

[614]
Detroit Tests of Learning Aptitude, Fourth Edition.

Purpose: Designed to measure both general intelligence and discrete ability areas.
Population: Ages 0-6 to 0-17.
Publication Dates: 1935–1998.
Acronym: DTLA-4.
Scores: 10 subtest scores: Word Opposites, Design Sequences, Sentence Imitation, Reversed Letters, Story Construction, Design Reproduction, Basic Information, Symbolic Relations, Word Sequences, Story Sequences; and 16 composite scores: General Mental Ability Composite, Optimal Composite, Domain Composites (Verbal, Nonverbal, Attention-Enhanced, Attention-Reduced, Motor-Enhanced, Motor-Reduced, Total), Theoretical Composites (Fluid Intelligence, Crystallized Intelligence, Associative Level, Cognitive Level, Simultaneous Processing, Successive Processing, Verbal Scale, Performance Scale, Total).
Administration: Individual.
Price Data, 2015: $437 per complete kit including examiner's manual (1998, 247 pages), Picture Books 1 and 2, 25 Profile/Summary forms, 25 Examiner Record Booklets, 25 response forms, Story Sequence Chips, and Design Sequence Cubes; $97 per examiner's manual; $117 per Picture Book 1 (for Design Sequences, Design Reproduction and Symbolic Relations); $62 per Picture Book 2 (for Story Sequences and Story Construction); $37 per 25 Profile/Summary forms; $62 per 25 Examiner Record Booklets; $37 per 25 response forms; $25 per Story Sequence Chips; $29 per 15 Spanish version examiner record booklets; $13 per 15 Spanish version profile forms; $13 per 15 Spanish version response forms.
Time: (40–120) minutes.
Author: Donald D. Hammill.
Publisher: PRO-ED.
Cross References: For reviews by Jeffrey K. Smith and Ross E. Traub, see 14:113; see also T5:798 (27 references); for reviews by William A. Mehrens and Michael Poteat of an earlier edition, see 12:107 (4 references); see also T4:752 (7 references); for reviews by Arthur B. Silverstein and Joan Silverstein of an earlier edition, see 10:85 (15 references); see also 9:320 (11 references), and T3:691 (20 references); for a review by Arthur B. Silverstein of an earlier edition, see 8:213 (14 references); see also T2:493 (3 references), and 7:406 (10 references); for a review by F. L. Wells, see 3:275 (1 reference); for reviews by Anne Anastasi and Henry Feinburg and an excerpted review by D. A. Worcester and S. M. Corey, see 1:1058.

[615]
Detroit Tests of Learning Aptitude–Primary, Third Edition.

Purpose: "Measures general aptitude."
Population: Ages 0-3 through 9-11.
Publication Dates: 1986–2005.
Acronym: DTLA-P:3.
Scores, 7: Verbal-Enhanced, Verbal-Reduced, Attention-Enhanced, Attention-Reduced, Motor-Enhanced, Motor-Reduced, General Ability.
Administration: Individual.
Price Data, 2015: $239 per complete kit including examiner's manual (2005, 128 pages), picture book, 25 examiner record booklets, and 25 response forms; $75 per picture book; $45 per 25 response forms; $62 per 25 examiner record booklets; $72 per manual.
Time: (15–45) minutes.
Comments: Adaptation of the Detroit Tests of Learning Aptitude—Second Edition (T5:779).
Authors: Donald D. Hammill and Brian R. Bryant.
Publisher: PRO-ED.
Cross References: For reviews by Bethany A. Brunsman and Shawn Powell, see 17:55; see also T5:799 (2 references); for reviews by Terry A. Ackerman and Robert T. Williams of an earlier edition, see 12:106 (1 reference); for reviews by Cathy F. Telzrow and Stanley F. Vasa of an earlier edition, see 10:84 (1 reference).

[616]
Developing the Leader Within.

Purpose: Designed for self-assessment of leadership skills.
Population: Management personnel.
Publication Date: 1995.
Scores: 4 dimensions: Developing Within, Helping Others Excel, Improving Critical Processes, Showing Commitment to the Team.
Administration: Individual or group.
Manual: No manual.
Price Data, 2015: $15 Individual Report, $15 Report About Me.
Time: Administration time not reported.
Author: L. Phillips-Jones.
Publisher: Mind Garden, Inc.

[617]
Developmental Activities Screening Inventory, Second Edition.

Purpose: To provide early detection of developmental disabilities in children functioning between the ages of birth and 60 months.
Population: Ages birth to 60 months.
Publication Dates: 1977–1984.
Acronym: DASI-II.
Scores: Total score only.
Administration: Individual.
Price Data, 2015: $31 per 50 record forms.
Time: (25-30) minutes.
Comments: Behavior checklist; some test materials (form board, bell) must be supplied by examiner.
Authors: Rebecca R. Fewell and Mary Beth Langley.
Publisher: PRO-ED.
Cross References: See T5:803 (3 references); for reviews by Dennis C. Harper and William B. Michael, see 10:87; see also 9:323 (1 reference); for a reviews by Carl J. Dunst of the original edition, see 9:322 (1 reference).

[618]
Developmental Assessment for Individuals with Severe Disabilities, Third Edition.

Purpose: Designed "as a criterion-referenced assessment" to measure specific skill levels in people with severe disabilities.
Population: Individuals with disabilities and children who are functioning chronologically from birth to 7 years of age.
Publication Dates: 1980-2012.
Acronym: DASH-3.
Scores: 5 scales: Sensory-Motor, Language, Social-Emotional, Activities of Daily Living, Academics.
Administration: Individual.
Price Data, 2015: $239 per complete Kit including examiner's manual (2012, 46 pages), 25 Comprehensive Program record forms, 25 Intervention Planning Worksheets, 25 Cumulative Summary Sheets, 10 Academics Scales, 10 Activities of Daily Living Scales, 10 Language Scales, 10 Sensory-Motor Scales, and 10 Social-Emotional Scales; $53 per examiner's manual; $47 per 10 Academics Scales; $47 per 10 Activities of Daily Living Scales; $47 per 10 Language Scales; $47 per 10 Sensory-Motor Scales; $47 per 10 Social-Emotional Scales; $25 per 25 Comprehensive Program record forms; $25 per 25 Cumulative Summary Sheets; $25 per 25 Intervention Planning Worksheets.
Time: (120-180) minutes.
Comments: Criterion-referenced assessment.
Authors: Mary Kay Dykes and Daniel W. Mruzek.
Publisher: PRO-ED.
Cross References: Reviews are scheduled for *The Twentieth Mental Measurements Yearbook*. See T5:804 (1 reference); for reviews by Harvey N. Switzky and David P. Wacker of the original edition, see 9:324.

[619]
Developmental Assessment of Young Children–Second Edition.

Purpose: Designed to measure children's developmental level in the domains of cognition, communication, social-emotional development, physical development, and adaptive behavior.
Population: Children from birth through age 5.
Publication Dates: 1998-2013.
Acronym: DAYC-2.
Scores, 8: Cognitive, Communication (Receptive Language, Expressive Language, Total), Social-Emotional, Physical Development (Gross Motor, Fine Motor, Total), Adaptive Behavior, General Development Index.
Administration: Individual.
Forms, 5: Cognitive Domain, Communication Domain, Social-Emotional Domain, Physical Development Domain, Adaptive Behavior Domain.
Price Data, 2016: $345 per complete kit including examiner's manual, scoring forms (25 for each of domain), a 25 early child development charts, and 25 examiner summary sheets; $72 per examiner's manual (2013, 133 pages); $199 per first-year Base Online Scoring and Report System/$69 annual renewal.
Time: (10-20) minutes per domain.
Comments: "The domains can be assessed independently, so examiners may test only the domains that interest them or test all five domains when a measure of general development is desired."
Authors: Judith K. Voress and Taddy Maddox.
Publisher: PRO-ED.
Cross References: Reviews are scheduled for *The Twentieth Mental Measurements Yearbook*. For reviews by Billy T. Ogletree and T. Steuart Watson of the original edition, see 14:115.

Developmental Assessment Resource for Teachers (DART) English.

Purpose: Designed to "assist teachers of upper primary and middle primary in their assessment of students' viewing, reading, listening, speaking and writing skills."
Population: Australian students in years 3–4, 5–6.
Publication Dates: 1994–1997.
Scores, 5: Viewing, Reading, Listening, Speaking, Writing.
Administration: Group.
Forms, 2: Form A, Form B.
Publisher: Australian Council for Educational Research Ltd. [Australia].
    a) DART MIDDLE PRIMARY ENGLISH.
    Population: Students in years 3–4 in Australian classrooms.
    Publication Date: 1997.
    Time: (40–190) minutes per section.
    Authors: Wendy Bodey, Lynne Darkin, Margaret Forster, and Geoff Masters.
    b) DART UPPER PRIMARY ENGLISH.
    Population: Students in years 5–6 in Australian classrooms.
    Publication Date: 1994.
    Time: (40–190) minutes per section.
    Authors: Margaret Forster, Juliette Mendelovits, and Geoff Masters.
Cross References: For reviews by Valentina McInerney and by Gretchen Owens and Jan Harting-McChesney, see 15:78.

Developmental Assessment Resource for Teachers (DART) Mathematics.

Purpose: "Provides an estimate of a student's level of achievement on each of four strands of the [Australian] national mathematics profile … and on each of three strands of the national benchmark framework."
Population: Australian students in years 5–6.
Publication Date: 1998.
Acronym: DART MATHEMATICS.
Scores, 5: Number, Space, Measurement, Chance and Data, Data Sense.
Administration: Group.
Forms, 2: Form A, Form B.
Price Data, 2016: A$78.95 per kit including video, manual (160 pages), 30 grid sheets, 30 measurement sheets, and photocopy master answer booklet and stimulus for all tests.
Time: (60) minutes per section.
Authors: Eve Recht, Margaret Forster, and Geoff Masters.
Publisher: Australian Council for Educational Research Ltd. [Australia].
Cross References: For reviews by Carlen Henington and Judith A. Monsaas, see 15:79.

Developmental History Checklist for Children.

Purpose: To document the developmental history of children.
Population: Ages 5–12.
Publication Date: 1989.
Scores: 7 Content Areas: Presenting Information, Personal Information/Family Background, Early Developmental History, Educational History, Medical History/Health Status, Family History, Current Behavior/Relationships.
Administration: Individual.
Manual: No manual.
Price Data, 2015: $62 per package of 25.
Time: Administration time not reported.
Comments: Designed to be completed by a parent, guardian, or clinician.
Authors: Edward H. Dougherty and John A. Schinka.
Publisher: Psychological Assessment Resources, Inc.

Developmental Indicators for the Assessment of Learning–Fourth Edition.

Purpose: Designed to "identify children ages 2:6 through 5:11 who are in need of intervention or diagnostic assessment in the following areas: motor, concepts, language, self-help, and social-emotional skills."
Population: Ages 2:6-5:11.
Publication Dates: 1983–2011.
Acronym: DIAL-4.
Scores: 9 regular form: Motor, Concepts, Language, DIAL-4 Total, Behavioral Observations, Parent Self-Help Development, Parent Social-Emotional Development, Teacher Self-Help Development, Teacher Social-Emotional Development; Speed DIAL-4: Total Score only.
Administration: Individual.
Forms, 2: Regular Form, Short Form.
Price Data, 2015: $655 per complete kit including manual (2011, 131 pages), 50 record forms (English), 1 record form (Spanish), 50 cutting cards, 50 Parent Questionnaires (English), 25 Teacher Questionnaires (English), manipulatives, dials, Operator's Handbooks in English and Spanish for Motor, Concepts, and Language Areas plus the Speed DIAL, Training Packet, and Training DVD; $48.65 per 50 Speed DIAL record forms; $296.95 per Speed DIAL kit in English/Spanish.
Foreign Language Edition: Available in Spanish.
Time: (30-45) minutes, regular form; (20) minutes, short form.
Authors: Carol Mardell and Dorothea S. Goldenberg.
Publisher: Pearson.
Cross References: For reviews by Sherry K. Bain and Michelle P. Black and by Claudia R. Wright, see 19:51; for reviews by Gregory J. Cizek and Doreen

Ward Fairbank of the third edition, see 14:116; see also T5:809 (2 references); for reviews by Darrell L. Sabers and Scott Spreat of the revised/AGS edition, see 12:110 (1 reference); see also T4:762 (6 references); for reviews by David W. Barnett and G. Michael Poteat of an earlier revised version, see 10:89 (6 references); see also 9:326 (1 reference) and T3:696 (2 references); for reviews by J. Jeffrey Grill and James J. McCarthy of an earlier edition, see 8:428 (3 references).

[624]

Developmental Observation Checklist System.

Purpose: "For the assessment of very young children with respect to general development (DC), adjustment behavior (ABC), and parent stress and support (PSSC)."

Population: Birth through age 6.

Publication Date: 1994.

Acronym: DOCS.

Scores, 12: Developmental Checklist (Cognition, Language, Social, Motor, Total); Adjustment Behavior Checklist (Mother, Father, Both Parents, Teacher); Parental Stress and Support Checklist (Mother, Father, Both Parents).

Administration: Individual.

Parts, 3: Developmental Checklist, Adjustment Behavior Checklist, Parental Stress and Support Checklist.

Price Data, 2015: $198 per complete kit including examiner's manual (91 pages), 25 profile/record forms, 25 DC profile/record forms, 25 ABC profile/record forms, and 25 PSSC profile/record forms; $73 per manual; $25 per 25 cumulative profile/record forms; $62 per 25 DC profile/record forms; $25 per ABC or PSSC profile/record forms.

Time: (30) minutes.

Authors: Wayne P. Hresko, Shirley A. Miguel, Rita J. Sherbenou, and Steve D. Burton.

Publisher: PRO-ED.

Cross References: For reviews by Frank M. Bernt and Gene Schwarting, see 13:95.

[625]

Developmental Profile 3.

Purpose: "Designed to assess the development and functioning of children from birth through age 12."

Population: Ages 0-0 to 12-11.

Publication Dates: 1972-2007.

Acronym: DP-3.

Scores: 5 scales: Physical, Adaptive Behavior, Social-Emotional, Cognitive, Communication, plus General Development Score.

Administration: Individual.

Forms, 2: Interview Form, Parent/Caregiver Checklist.

Price Data, 2016: $272 per complete kit including 25 Interview Forms; 25 Parent/Caregiver Checklists, and manual (2007, 195 pages); $95 per 25 Interview Forms; $95 per 25 English Parent/Caregiver Checklists; $38 per 10 print Spanish Interview Forms; $38 per 10 print Spanish Parent/Caregiver Checklists; $100 per manual; $471.50 per software kit with unlimited-use scoring and interpretation CD; $332 per DP-3 CD with unlimited-use scoring and interpretation; $272 per online kit including 25 uses of Interview Online Form, 25 Uses of Parent/Caregiver Online Checklist and online manual; $19 per 5 online English Interview Forms; $19 per 5 online English Parent/Caregiver Checklists; $95 per 25 online English Interview Forms; $38 per 10 online Spanish Interview Forms; $38 per 10 online Spanish Parent/Caregiver Checklists; $100 per online manual.

Foreign Language Edition: Spanish Interview Form and Parent/Caregiver Checklist available.

Time: (20-40) minutes.

Comments: The Interview Form is the preferred method of administration; the Parent/Caregiver Checklist, which contains the same content as the Interview may be used when administering the Interview is not possible because of time constraints or clinical/research needs.

Author: Gerald D. Alpern.

Publisher: Western Psychological Services.

Cross References: For reviews by Rosemary Flanagan and Carlen Henington, see 18:38; see T5:811 (14 references) and T4:764 (1 reference); for reviews by A. Dirk Hightower and E. Scott Huebner of an earlier edition, see 10:90 (3 references); for reviews by Dennis C. Harper and Sue White of an earlier edition, see 9:327; see also T3:698 (5 references); for a review by Jane V. Hunt of the original edition, see 8:215 (1 reference).

[626]

Developmental Scoring System for the Rey-Osterrieth Complex Figure.

Purpose: Designed "to provide developmental guidelines for interpretation of the ROCF," which is a "measure [of] visuospatial ability and visuospatial memory."

Population: Ages 5-14.

Publication Dates: 1986-1996.

Acronym: DSS-ROCF.

Scores: 12 scores, 3 ratings: 4 scores (Organization, Structural Elements Accuracy, Incidental Elements Accuracy, Errors) and 1 rating (Style) per ROCF production (Copy, Immediate Recall, Delayed Recall).

Administration: Individual.

Price Data, 2015: $214 per introductory kit including professional manual (1996, 87 pages), ROCF stimulus card, 25 scoring booklets, and 50 response sheets; $80 per 25 scoring booklets; $58 per 50 response sheets; $18 per ROCF stimulus card; $71 per professional manual.

Time: [35] minutes, including 1 15-20 minute delay.

Authors: Jane Holmes Bernstein and Deborah P. Waber.

Publisher: Psychological Assessment Resources, Inc.

Cross References: For reviews by Stefan C. Dombrowski and Gabrielle Stutman, see 18:39.

[627]

Developmental Tasks for Kindergarten Readiness—II.

Purpose: Designed to provide "objective data about the school-readiness of pre-kindergarten children so that effective educational programming can be planned for them."

Population: Pre-kindergarten children.

Publication Dates: 1978–1994.

Acronym: DTKR-II.

Scores, 19: Composite Score (Social Interaction, Name Printing, Body Concepts—Awareness, Body Concepts—Use, Auditory Sequencing, Auditory Association, Visual Discrimination, Visual Memory, Visual Motor, Color Naming, Relational Concepts, Number Counting, Number Use, Number Naming, Alphabet Knowledge), Acquired Knowledge, Verbal-Conceptual, Visual Skills.

Administration: Individual.

Price Data, 2015: $162 per kit including manual (1994, 97 pages), materials book (cards), and 25 test booklets; $56 per 25 test booklets; $43 per materials book; $70 per test manual.

Time: (20–30) minutes.

Comments: Administered by school personnel for diagnostic-remedial purposes.

Authors: Walter J. Lesiak and Judi Lucas Lesiak.

Publisher: PRO-ED.

Cross References: For reviews by Joseph O. Prewitt and Theresa Graham, see 14:117; see also T4:766 (1 reference); for reviews by Carol A. Gray and Sue White of an earlier edition, see 9:328.

[628]

Developmental Teaching Objectives and Rating Form-Revised, 5th Edition.

Purpose: Designed "for assessing social and emotional development of children and youth."

Population: Ages 0-16.

Publication Dates: 1992-2007.

Acronym: DTORF-R.

Scores, 4: Behavior (Doing), Communication (Saying), Socialization (Relating), Cognition (Thinking).

Administration: Individual.

Levels, 5: Stage I, Stage II, Stage III, Stage IV, Stage V.

Forms, 3: Early Childhood, Elementary, Secondary.

Price Data, 2015: $200 annual fee per district/program with up to five locations/schools and $8 per student for secure data entry, record management, group summaries, analysis, and reports (www.dtorf.com). Additional resources: textbook, $91 (available from PRO-ED); DTORF-R user's manual, $12 (from Developmental Therapy Institute); introductory staff training online course, Developmental Teaching for Students with Special Needs, Module 2: Developmental Assessment (from The University of Georgia Center for Continuing Education).

Foreign Language Editions: Publisher indicates full or partial translations of the DTORF-R are available in Chinese, Dutch, German, Korean, Italian, Norwegian, and Spanish.

Time: [30] minutes per individual student.

Comments: Textbook (2007, 346 pages) and CD distributed by PRO-ED, Inc.; User's manual (2012, 32 pages) distributed by Developmental Therapy Institute, Inc.; rating form filled out by people familiar with the child, following observations; older children (and their parents) participate in their own team ratings.

Authors: Mary M. Wood, Constance A. Quirk, and Faye L. Swindle.

Publisher: Developmental Therapy Institute, Inc.

Cross References: For reviews by Andrew A. Cox and by Rebecca Gokiert and Rebecca Georgis, see 19:52; for a review by Sharon H. deFur of the Developmental Teaching Objectives and Rating Form-Revised, see 14:118.

[629]

Developmental Test of Auditory Perception.

Purpose: Designed to "identify school-age individuals who may have auditory problems."

Population: Ages 6 through 18.

Publication Date: 2008.

Acronym: DTAP.

Scores, 5: Language Auditory Perception Index, Nonlanguage Auditory Perception Index, Background Noise Index, No Background Noise Index, Composite Auditory Perception Index.

Administration: Individual or group.

Price Data, 2016: $186 per complete kit including examiner's manual (79 pages), administration audio CD, 25 examiner record forms, and 25 student record forms; $83 per examiner's manual; $46 per administration audio CD; $47 per 25 examiner record forms; $47 per 25 student record forms.

Time: 30 minutes.

Authors: Cecil R. Reynolds, Judith K. Voress, and Nils A. Pearson.

Publisher: PRO-ED.

Cross References: Reviews are scheduled for *The Twentieth Mental Measurements Yearbook*.

[630]

Developmental Test of Visual Perception— Adolescent and Adult.

Purpose: "To document the presence and degree of visual perceptual or visual-motor difficulties in individual adolescents and adults."

Population: Ages 11-0 to 74-11 years.

Publication Date: 2002.

Acronym: DTVP-A.

Scores, 9: Motor-Reduced Visual Perception (Figure-Ground, Visual Closure, Form Constancy, Motor-

Reduced Visual Perception Index), Visual-Motor Integration (Copying, Visual-Motor Search, Visual-Motor Speed, Visual-Motor Integration Index), General Visual Perception Index.

Administration: Individual.

Price Data, 2015: $239 per complete kit including examiner's manual (135 pages), picture book, 25 profile/examiner record forms, 25 response booklets, all in a sturdy storage box; $85 per examiner's manual; $67 per picture book; $37 per 25 profiler/examiner record forms; $65 per 25 response booklets.

Time: (25) minutes.

Comments: Upward extension and redevelopment of the Developmental Test of Visual Perception, Second Edition (DTVP-2); designed to identify candidates for referral to special education, cognitive rehabilitation, or occupational therapy; may be used to distinguish true visual-perception deficits from problems solely with complex eye-hand or perceptual-motor actions; may assist in differential diagnosis of various dementias.

Authors: Cecil R. Reynolds, Nils A. Pearson, and Judith K. Voress.

Publisher: PRO-ED.

Cross References: For reviews by James M. Hodgson and Ralph G. Leverett, see 16:70.

[631]

Developmental Test of Visual Perception–Third Edition.

Purpose: Designed to measure "visual perception and visual-motor abilities."

Population: Ages 4 through 12.

Publication Dates: 1961-2014.

Acronym: DTVP-3.

Scores, 8: Eye-Hand Coordination, Copying, Figure-Ground, Visual Closure, Form Constancy, Motor-Reduced Visual Perception, Visual-Motor Integration, General Visual Perception.

Administration: Individual.

Price Data, 2014: $257 per complete kit including examiner's manual (2014, 113 pages), picture book, 25 response booklets, 25 examiner record books, and copying scoring template; $75 per examiner's manual; $81 per 25 response booklets; $39 per 25 examiner record books.

Time: (20-40) minutes.

Authors: Donald D. Hammill, Nils A. Pearson, and Judith K. Voress.

Publisher: PRO-ED.

Cross References: Reviews are scheduled for *The Twentieth Mental Measurements Yearbook*. See T5:816 (1 reference); for reviews by Nancy B. Bologna and Gerald Tindal of the second edition, see 12:112 (1 reference); see also T4:767 (2 references); for reviews by Richard E. Darnell and David A. Sabatino of an earlier edition titled Marianne Frostig Developmental Test of Visual Perception, Third Edition, see 9:650 (4 references); see

also T3:1371 (25 references), 8:882 (72 references), and T2:1921 (43 references); for reviews by Brad S. Chissom, Newell C. Kephart, and Lester Mann, see 7:871 (117 references); for reviews by James M. Anderson and Mary C. Austin, see 6:553 (7 references).

[632]

Devereux Behavior Rating Scale—School Form.

Purpose: To evaluate "behaviors typical of children and adolescents with moderate to severe emotional disturbance."

Population: Ages 5–18.

Publication Dates: 1990–1993.

Acronym: BRSS.

Scores, 4: Interpersonal Problems, Inappropriate Behaviors/Feelings, Depression, Physical Symptoms/Fears.

Administration: Individual or group.

Forms, 2: Children, Adolescents.

Price Data, 2015: $256.15 per complete kit including manual (1993, 142 pages), 25 answer documents 5–12, and 25 ready score answer documents 13–18; $135.40 per manual; $67.95 per 25 ready score answer documents 5–12; $67.95 per 25 ready score answer documents 13–18.

Time: (5–10) minutes.

Comments: Ratings by parents and teachers.

Authors: Jack A. Naglieri, Paul A. LeBuffe, and Steven I. Pfeiffer.

Publisher: Pearson.

Cross References: For reviews by Lisa Bloom and Richard F. Farmer, see 13:96 (8 references); see also T5:817 (1 reference); for additional information on the Devereux Adolescent Behavior Rating Scale, see T3:702 (1 reference); for a review by Carl F. Jesness, see 7:66; see also P:60 (1 reference). For reviews by Lisa Bloom and Richard F. Farmer, see 13:96 (8 references). For additional information on the Devereux Child Behavior Rating Scale, see T3:203 (6 references); see also T2:1158 (1 reference); for a review by Allan G. Barclay, see 7:67; see also P:61 (3 references).

[633]

Devereux Early Childhood Assessment.

Purpose: "To assess preschool children's protective factors and behavioral concerns."

Population: Ages 2–5.

Publication Date: 1999.

Acronym: DECA.

Scores, 5: Initiative, Self-Control, Attachment, Total Protective Factors, Behavioral Concerns.

Administration: Individual.

Price Data, 2016: $199.95 per kit including 40 record forms, user's guide (65 pages), technical manual (42 pages), classroom strategies guide, 20 parent guides, and classroom observation journal.

Foreign Language Edition: Parent guides and record forms also available in Spanish.

Time: (10) minutes.

Comments: Ratings by teachers and parents.

Authors: Paul A. LeBuffe and Jack A. Naglieri.

Publisher: Kaplan Early Learning Company.

Cross References: For reviews by Eric S. Buhs and Mary M. Chittooran, see 15:81.

[634]

Devereux Early Childhood Assessment—Clinical Form.

Purpose: Designed to evaluate "behaviors related to both social and emotional resilience as well as social and emotional concerns in preschool children."

Population: Ages 2:0–5:11.

Publication Dates: 2002–2003.

Acronym: DECA-C.

Scores, 9: Protective Factors (Initiative, Self-Control, Attachment, Total), Behavioral Concerns (Withdrawal/Depression, Emotional Control Problems, Attention Problems, Aggression, Total).

Administration: Individual.

Price Data: Prices for the manual, record forms, and norms reference card available from publisher.

Time: Administration time not reported.

Comments: Behavior rating scale may be completed by parent or family member or teacher.

Authors: Paul A. LeBuffe and Jack A. Naglieri.

Publisher: Kaplan Early Learning Company.

Cross References: For reviews by Joan C. Ballard and Sandra A. Loew, see 16:71.

[635]

Devereux Early Childhood Assessment for Infants and Toddlers.

Purpose: "Assesses protective factors and screens for social and emotional risks in very young children."

Population: Ages 1 month to 36 months.

Publication Dates: 2007-2009.

Acronym: DECA-I/T.

Scores, 7: 3 Infant scores: Initiative, Attachment/Relationships, Total Protective Factors (composite of previous 2 scale scores), and 4 Toddler scores: Initiative, Attachment/Relationships, Self-Regulation, Total Protective Factors (composite of previous 3 scale scores).

Administration: Group.

Forms, 2: Infant (1 month to 18 months), Toddler (18 months to 36 months).

Price Data, 2016: $199.95 per complete kit including 20 Infant Record Forms, 30 Toddler Record Forms, 5 reproducible Parent/Teacher Profile Masters for 5 different age ranges (1 mo. to 3 mos., 3 mos. to 6 mos., 6 mos. to 9 mos., 9 mos. to 18 mos., 18 mos. to 36 mos.), User's Guide (2007, 111 pages), Strategies Guide (2009, 158 pages), 20 Parent Strategy Guides ("For Now and

Forever"), 3 Adult Resilience Journals ("Building Your Bounce: Simple Strategies For a Resilient You"), and Forms CD (including Technical Manual [2007, 51 pages], Reproducible Planning Forms, and Scoring Profiles); $19.95 per 20 Infant Record Forms; $29.95 per 30 Toddler Record Forms; $12.95 per 5 reproducible Parent/Teacher Profile Masters; $39.95 per User's Guide; $49.95 per Strategies Guide; $99.95 per CD Scoring Assistant; technical manual is free to print from publisher's website.

Time: Administration time not reported.

Comments: Ratings by parents, other family members, or childcare providers; scoring completed by hand or with separately sold CD Scoring Assistant; DECA-I/T is "part of an integrated, comprehensive five-step system" that involves implementing strategies and evaluating progress; other tests in the Devereux series include: the Devereux Early Childhood Assessment (DECA; 633), the Devereux Early Childhood Assessment-Clinical Form (DECA-C; 634), and the Devereux Student Strengths Assessment (DESSA; 637).

Authors: Mary Mackrain, Paul A. LeBuffe, and Gregg Powell; Kristin Tenney-Blackwell (Strategies Guide only).

Publisher: Kaplan Early Learning Co.

Cross References: For reviews by Jean N. Clark and Mary J. McLellan, see 18:40.

[636]

Devereux Scales of Mental Disorders.

Purpose: Constructed for "evaluating behaviors associated with psychopathology."

Population: Ages 5–12, 13–18.

Publication Dates: 1993–1996.

Acronym: DSMD.

Scores, 10: Conduct, Attention/Delinquency, Anxiety, Depression, Autism, Acute Problems, Internalizing Composite, Externalizing Composite, Critical Pathology Composite, Total.

Administration: Group or individual.

Forms, 2: Child Form, Adolescent Form.

Price Data, 2015: $311.55 per complete kit including manual (1994, 300 pages) and 25 ReadyScore™ answer documents for each Child Form and Adolescent Form; $116.60 per ReadyScore™ answer documents (specify form); $135.40 per manual.

Time: (15) minutes.

Comments: Revision of Devereux Child Behavior Rating Scale (T3:703) and Devereux Adolescent Behavior Rating Scale (T3:702); ratings by parents, teachers, or other professionals; Scoring Assistant available to provide narrative interpretive reports and other information.

Authors: Jack A. Naglieri, Paul A. LeBuffe, and Steven I. Pfeiffer.

Publisher: Pearson.

Cross References: For reviews by Colin Cooper and Charles A. Peterson, see 14:120; see also T5:818 (1 reference).

[637]
Devereux Student Strengths Assessment.
Purpose: "Developed to provide a measure of social-emotional competencies."
Population: Grades K-8.
Publication Dates: 2008-2009.
Acronym: DESSA.
Scores, 9: Personal Responsibility, Optimistic Thinking, Goal-Directed Behavior, Social-Awareness, Decision Making, Relationship Skills, Self-Awareness, Self-Management, Total (Social-Emotional Composite).
Administration: Group.
Price Data, 2016: $120 per complete kit including 25 record forms, manual (2009, 161 pages), and norms reference card; $42 per 25 record forms; price information for online administration, scoring, and individual student reports available from publisher.
Time: [10] minutes or less.
Comments: Test is part of a series that includes: the Devereux Early Childhood Assessment for Infants and Toddlers (DECA-I/T; 635), the Devereux Early Childhood Assessment (DECA; 633), and the Devereux Early Childhood Assessment-Clinical Form (DECA-C; 634); ratings "by parents, teachers, or staff at schools and child-serving agencies"; individual and classroom profiles available.
Authors: Paul A. LeBuffe, Valerie B. Shapiro, and Jack A. Naglieri.
Publisher: Apperson, Inc.
Cross References: For reviews by Jeffrey A. Atlas and Koressa Kutsick Malcolm, see 18:41.

[638]
Devereux Student Strengths Assessment–mini.
Purpose: Designed to "measure and track a subset of predictors of future mental, emotional, and behavioral disorders in order to make early intervention more possible."
Population: Students in kindergarten through Grade 8.
Publication Date: 2014.
Acronym: DESSA-mini.
Score: Social-Emotional Total.
Administration: Individual.
Forms: 4 parallel forms: 1, 2, 3, 4.
Price Data, 2015: $104.95 per kit including manual (92 pages), 25 copies of each record forms (1-4), and 25 ongoing progress monitoring forms; $7.95 per 25 forms (1, 2, 3, or 4); $7.95 per 25 ongoing progress monitoring forms.
Foreign Language Edition: Spanish forms available.
Time: (1) minute.
Comments: Ratings completed by teachers or staff at schools and child-serving agencies. Items selected from the Devereux Student Strengths Assessment (18:41).
Authors: Jack A. Naglieri, Paul A. LeBuffe, and Valerie B. Shapiro.

Publisher: Apperson, Inc.
Cross References: Reviews are scheduled for *The Twentieth Mental Measurements Yearbook*.

[639]
The Devine Inventory [Revised].
Purpose: Designed as a comprehensive measure of work-related behaviors to assist in employee selection and development.
Population: Employees and prospective employees.
Publication Dates: 1989–2005.
Scores, 29: Self-Responsibility, Role Clarity, Approaches Problems Realistically, Openness to Change And Experience, Growth And Development/Learning, Response to Crisis, Trust in Self, Trust in Others, Dominance/Leadership, Negotiating, Decisiveness, Thinking, Detail Mindedness, Structure, Follow-Through, Diligence/Work Ethic, Goal Orientation, Response to Change, Mobility, Energy, Quiescence, Assertiveness, Authority Relationships/Loyalty, Following Rules and Procedures, Recognition, Sociability/Gregariousness, Belonging, Intimacy, Dependability.
Administration: Individual.
Price Data: Available from publisher.
Foreign Language Editions: Available in Spanish, French, and German.
Time: (25–30) minutes.
Comments: Administered and scored online.
Author: Donald W. Devine.
Publisher: The Devine Group, Inc.
Cross References: For reviews by Theodore L. Hayes and Paul M. Muchinsky, see 17:56; for reviews by Phillip Benson and William L. Deaton of an earlier edition, see 12:113.

[640]
Diagnosing Organizational Culture.
Purpose: "Designed to help consultants and organizational members identify the shared values and beliefs that constitute an organization's culture."
Population: Adults.
Publication Dates: 1992–1993.
Scores: 5 scores (Power, Role, Achievement, Support, Total) in each of two areas: Existing Culture, Preferred Culture.
Administration: Group.
Price Data: Price information available from publisher for complete kit including trainer's manual (1993, 58 pages) and instrument (1992, 30 pages).
Time: (45–60) minutes.
Authors: Roger Harrison and Herb Stokes (instrument only).
Publisher: Jossey-Bass, A Wiley Company.
Cross References: For a review by John W. Fleenor, see 13:97.

[641]

Diagnostic Achievement Battery–Fourth Edition.

Purpose: Designed "to measure aspects of the elementary and middle school curriculum ... in five major achievement domains ... important to the identification of learning disabilities."
Population: Students ages 6 through 14.
Publication Dates: 1984-2014.
Acronym: DAB-4.
Scores, 13: Spoken Language (Listening Comprehension, Synonyms), Reading (Alphabet/Phonics/Word Identification, Reading Comprehension), Writing (Punctuation/Capitalization, Spelling), Mathematics (Mathematics Reasoning, Mathematics Calculation), Total Basic Academic Skills.
Administration: Individual.
Price Data, 2014: $372 per complete kit including manual (2014, 124 pages), student booklet, 25 examiner record booklets, 25 student response booklets, assessment probes, and audio CD; $99 per manual; $73 per 25 examiner record booklets; $65 per student booklet; $59 per 25 student response booklets; $49 per assessment probes; $27 per audio CD.
Time: (60-90) minutes for entire battery.
Comments: Entire battery or selected subtests may be administered; Spelling, Punctuation/Capitalization, and Mathematics Calculation subtests may be administered in small groups.
Authors: Phyllis L. Newcomer.
Publisher: PRO-ED.
Cross References: Reviews are scheduled for *The Twentieth Mental Measurements Yearbook*. For reviews by Michael B. Bunch and Cleborne D. Maddux of the third edition, see 15:82, see T5:821 (2 references); for reviews by Jean-Jacques Bernier and Martine Hebert and by Ric Brown of the second edition, see 12:114 (2 references); see also T4:774 (1 reference); for a review by William J. Webster of the original edition, see 9:333.

[642]

Diagnostic Achievement Battery–Intermediate.

Purpose: Designed to assess "spoken language, reading, writing mechanics, and mathematics" achievement.
Population: Students ages 13 through 17.
Publication Dates: 1986-2013.
Acronym: DAB-I.
Scores, 13: Spoken Language (Word Relationships, Grammatic Sentences), Reading (Word Identification, Reading Comprehension), Writing (Spelling, Punctuation/Capitalization), Mathematics (Math Calculation, Math Reasoning), Basic Academic Skills.
Administration: Individual.
Price Data, 2014: $238 per complete kit including manual (2013, 85 pages), reusable student booklet, 25

profile/examiner record booklets, and 25 student response booklets; $75 per 25 examiner record booklets; $75 per manual; $43 per reusable student booklet; $45 per 25 student response booklets.
Time: (60-90) minutes.
Comments: Battery is the "renamed third edition of the Diagnostic Achievement Test for Adolescents." Spelling, Punctuation/Capitalization, and Math Calculation subtests may be administered in small groups.
Author: Phyllis L. Newcomer.
Publisher: PRO-ED.
Cross References: Reviews are scheduled for *The Twentieth Mental Measurements Yearbook*. For reviews by Jerrilyn V. Andrews and Gerald E. DeMauro of an earlier edition titled Diagnostic Achievement Test for Adolescents, Second Edition, see 13:98 (1 reference); for reviews by Randy W. Kamphaus and James E. Ysseldyke of the original edition, see 10:92.

[643]

Diagnostic Assessments of Reading™, Second Edition.

Purpose: Designed to function as an assessment of individual reading ability for the DARTTS testing and teaching program.
Population: Grades K-12.
Publication Dates: 1992-2006.
Acronym: DAR™-2.
Scores, 10: Word Recognition, Oral Reading Accuracy, Oral Reading Fluency (optional), Silent Reading Comprehension, Spelling, Word Meaning, Print Awareness, Phonological Awareness, Letters and Sounds, Word Analysis.
Administration: Individual.
Forms, 2: Form A, Form B (equivalent forms).
Price Data, 2015: $272 per classroom kit (Form A or B) including student book (57 pages), 30 response record forms, teacher's manual (27 pages), and 5-user license for Trial Teaching Strategy (TTS) program; $82 per student book; $82 per 15 response records; $32 per teacher's manual; $42 per technical manual (2006, 159 pages); $133 per scoring software; $514 per Combo kit including forms A and B with TTS.
Time: (40) minutes.
Authors: Florence G. Roswell, Jeanne S. Chall, Mary E. Curtis, and Gail Kearns.
Publisher: PRO-ED.
Cross References: For reviews by Timothy R. Konold and Camille Lawrence and by Natalie Rathvon, see 18:42; for reviews by Kevin D. Crehan and Gene Schwarting of an earlier edition, see 12:115.

[644]

Diagnostic English Language Tests.

Purpose: Designed to measure "ability to cope with the English language demands of upper secondary school in Australia."

Population: Non-English-speaking students entering Australian secondary schools at years 10 and 11
Publication Date: 1994.
Acronym: DELTA.
Scores, 3: Reading, Writing, Listening.
Administration: Group.
Price Data, 2016: A$169.95 per complete set; A$24.95 per 10 copies Reading Test; A$24.95 per 10 copies Listening Test.
Time: (180) minutes.
Authors: Joy McQueen and Cecily Aldous.
Publisher: Australian Council for Educational Research Ltd. [Australia].
Cross References: For a review by Alfred Longo, see 15:83.

[645]
Diagnostic Evaluation of Language Variation-Norm Referenced.

Purpose: Designed "to be used by clinicians to identify speech and language disorders (or delays) in children."
Population: Ages 4-0 to 9-11.
Publication Date: 2005.
Acronym: DELV-Norm Referenced.
Scores, 5: Total Language Composite, Syntax, Pragmatics, Semantics, Phonology.
Administration: Individual.
Price Data, 2015: $375.15 per complete test kit including examiner's manual (209 pages), stimulus book, and 25 record forms; $205 per examiner's manual; $107.65 per stimulus book; $69.70 per 25 record forms.
Time: (45) minutes.
Comments: Appropriate for use with children for whom English is their first and primary language.
Authors: Harry N. Seymour, Thomas W. Roeper, and Jill de Villiers.
Publisher: Pearson.
Cross References: For reviews by Donna Kelly and Thomas Guyette and by Aimee Langlois, see 17:57.

[646]
Diagnostic Evaluation of Language Variation™—Screening Test.

Purpose: Designed to "distinguish variations due to normal developmental language changes or to regional and cultural patterns of language difference from true markers of language disorder or delay."
Population: Ages 4-0 to 12-11.
Publication Date: 2003.
Acronym: DELV—Screening Test.
Administration: Individual.
Parts, 2: Part I, Part II.
Price Data, 2015: $184.50 per complete test; $107.65 per examiner's manual (122 pages), $107.65 per stimulus manual; $30.75 per 25 record forms.

Time: (15–20) minutes.
Comments: "Criterion-referenced."
Authors: Harry N. Seymour, Thomas W. Roeper, and Jill de Villiers with contributions by Peter A. de Villiers.
Publisher: Pearson.
  a) PART I.
  Population: Ages 4-0 to 12-11.
  Scores: Language Variation Status.
  b) PART II.
  Population: Ages 4-0 to 9-11.
  Scores: Diagnostic Risk Status.
Cross References: For reviews by Aimee Langlois and Sheila Pratt, see 16:72.

[647]
Diagnostic Mathematics Assessment.

Purpose: Designed to "evaluate areas of strengths and weaknesses in mathematics."
Population: Grades 1-3.
Publication Date: 2008.
Acronym: DMA.
Scores, 16: Number Sense, Algebra and Functions, Measurement and Geometry, Statistics/ Data Analysis/ and Probability, Mathematical Reasoning, Overall Readiness Score Number Sense, Overall Readiness Score Algebra and Functions, Overall Readiness Score Measurement and Geometry, Overall Readiness Score Statistics, Overall Readiness Score Data Analysis and Probability, Overall Readiness Score Mathematical Reasoning, Standards-Based Readiness Rating Number Sense, Standards-Based Readiness Rating Algebra and Functions, Standards-Based Readiness Rating Measurement and Geometry, Standards-Based Readiness Rating Statistics/ Data Analysis/ and Probability, Standards-Based Readiness Rating Mathematical Reasoning, Overall Readiness Rating.
Administration: Group.
Levels, 2: Grade 1, Grade 2.
Parts, 5: Number Sense, Algebra and Functions, Measurement and Geometry, Statistics/ Data Analysis/ and Probability, Mathematical Reasoning.
Price Data, 2015: $53.30 per starter set (specify Grade 1 or Grade 2) including user's manual (20 pages), answer key, 20 test booklets, class record sheet, and class summary report; $14.35 per user's manual; $36.90 per 20 test booklets, 1 class record sheet, and 1 class summary report.
Time: (60) minutes.
Authors: Fredricka K. Reisman.
Publisher: Scholastic Testing Service, Inc.

[648]
Diagnostic Reading Assessment.

Purpose: Designed to "evaluate areas of strengths and weaknesses in reading."
Population: Grade 1.
Publication Date: 2010.

Acronym: DRA.
Scores, 16: Word Analysis/Decoding, Vocabulary, Comprehension, Language Arts, Reference Skills, Overall Readiness Score Word Analysis/Decoding, Overall Readiness Score Vocabulary, Overall Readiness Score Comprehension, Overall Readiness Score Language Arts, Overall Readiness Score Reference Skills, Standards-Based Readiness Rating Word Analysis/Decoding, Standards-Based Readiness Rating Vocabulary, Standards-Based Readiness Rating Comprehension, Standards-Based Readiness Rating Language Arts, Standards-Based Readiness Rating Reference Skills, Overall Readiness Rating.
Administration: Group.
Parts, 5: Word Analysis/Decoding, Vocabulary, Comprehension, Language Arts, Reference Skills.
Price Data, 2015: $53.30 per starter set including manual (15 pages), answer key, 20 test booklets, class record sheet, and class summary report; $36.90 per additional package of 20 test booklets, 1 class record sheet, and 1 class summary report; $14.35 per user's manual; $27.70 per Instructional Strategies manual (21 pages).
Time: (60) minutes.
Author: Ann Bates.
Publisher: Scholastic Testing Service, Inc.

[649]
Diagnostic Screening Test: Achievement.

Purpose: Designed "for estimating practical data about student's overall school achievement level in general, and achievement in Science, Social Studies, and Literature and the Arts more specifically."
Population: Grades K–12.
Publication Date: 1977.
Acronym: DSTA.
Scores, 5: Science, Social Studies, Literature and the Arts, Practical Knowledge, Total Achievement.
Administration: Group.
Price Data, 2016: $71.25 per complete kit including manual (12 pages) and 25 test forms; $28 per 25 test forms.
Time: (5–10) minutes.
Authors: Thomas D. Gnagey and Patricia A. Gnagey.
Publisher: Slosson Educational Publications, Inc.
Cross References: For a review by Edward F. Iwanicki, see 9:339.

[650]
Diagnostic Screening Test: Language, Second Edition.

Purpose: Designed "for estimating over-all achievement level in written language."
Population: Grades 1–12.
Publication Date: 1977.
Acronym: DSTL.
Scores, 8: Punctuation, Grammar, Spelling Rules, Sentence Structure, Capitalization, Formal Knowledge of Language, Applied Knowledge of Language, Total Language.
Administration: Group.
Price Data, 2016: $71.25 per complete kit including manual (12 pages) and 25 test forms; $28 per 25 test forms.
Time: (5–10) minutes.
Authors: Thomas D. Gnagey and Patricia A. Gnagey.
Publisher: Slosson Educational Publications, Inc.
Cross References: For reviews by Janice Arnold Dole and Edward F. Iwanicki, see 9:340.

[651]
Diagnostic Screening Test: Math, Third Edition.

Purpose: Designed for estimating practical data about students' mathematical skills.
Population: Grades 1–11.
Publication Date: 1980.
Acronym: DSTM.
Scores, 31: Basic Process Scores (Addition, Subtraction, Multiplication, Division, Total), Specialized Process Scores (Money, Time, Percent, U.S. Measurement, Metric Measurement, Total), Concept Scores (Process, Sequencing, Simple Computation, Complex Computation, Special Manipulations, Use of Zero, Decimals, Simple Fractions, Manipulation in Fractions), 11 consolidation index scores.
Administration: Group.
Price Data, 2015: $100 per complete kit including manual (17 pages), 25 test Form A, and 25 test Form B; $30 per 50 test Form A; $30 per 50 test Form B.
Time: (5–20) minutes.
Author: Thomas D. Gnagey.
Publisher: Slosson Educational Publications, Inc.
Cross References: For reviews by Edward F. Iwanicki and Stanley F. Vasa, see 9:341.

[652]
Diagnostic Screening Test: Reading, Third Edition.

Purpose: Designed "for estimating practical data about students' reading skills."
Population: Grades 1–12.
Publication Date: 1979.
Acronym: DSTR.
Scores, 16: Comfort Reading Level, Instructional Reading Level, Frustration Reading Level, Comprehension Reading Level, Listening Level, Phonics/Sight Ratio, Word Attack Skill Analysis (c-v/c, v-r, v-l, v-v, c-v-c, Silent e, Mix, Sight, Total), Consolidation Index.
Administration: Individual.
Price Data, 2015: $100 per complete kit including manual (13 pages), 25 test Form A, and 25 test Form B; $30 per 25 test Form A; $30 per 25 test Form B.

Time: (5–10) minutes.
Authors: Thomas D. Gnagey and Patricia A. Gnagey.
Publisher: Slosson Educational Publications, Inc.
Cross References: For a review by Edward F. Iwanicki, see 9:342; for a review by P. David Pearson of an earlier edition, see 8:755.

[653]
Diagnostic Screening Test: Spelling, Third Edition.

Purpose: Designed to gather diagnostic information regarding spelling skills.
Population: Grades 1–12.
Publication Date: 1979.
Acronym: DSTS.
Scores, 12: 3 scores (Verbal, Written, Total) for each of 3 categories (Phonics, Sight, Total); 3 Consolidation Index scores (Phonics Written, Sight Written, Total Spelling Written).
Administration: Group.
Price Data, 2016: $95.25 per complete kit including manual (13 pages), 25 test Form A, and 25 test Form B; $28 per 25 test Form A; $28 per 25 test Form B.
Time: (5–10) minutes.
Author: Thomas D. Gnagey.
Publisher: Slosson Educational Publications, Inc.
Cross References: For reviews by Edward F. Iwanicki and Robert E. Schafer, see 9:343 (4 references).

[654]
Diagnostic Supplement to the WJ III® Tests of Cognitive Abilities.

Purpose: Designed to expand "the diagnostic capabilities of the [Woodcock-Johnson III Tests of Cognitive Abilities] for educational, clinical, or research purposes."
Population: Ages 2–90+.
Publication Date: 2003.
Acronym: WJ III® Diagnostic Supplement to the Tests of Cognitive Abilities.
Scores, 11: Memory for Names, Visual Closure, Sound Patterns—Voice, Number Series, Number Matrices, Cross Out, Memory for Sentences, Block Rotation, Sound Patterns—Music, Memory for Names—Delayed, Bilingual Verbal Comprehension—English/Spanish.
Administration: Individual.
Price Data: Available from publisher.
Time: (5–10) minutes per subtest.
Comments: Tests from the Diagnostic Supplement can be combined with other tests from the Woodcock-Johnson III® Tests of Cognitive Abilities Standard and Extended Batteries and the WJIII® Tests of Achievement to provide 14 additional interpretive cluster; a normative update was published in 2005.
Authors: Richard W. Woodcock, Kevin S. McGrew, Nancy Mather, and Fredrick A. Schrank.

Publisher: Houghton Mifflin Harcourt.
Cross References: For reviews by Timothy Sares and Donald L. Thompson, see 16:275.

[655]
Diagnostic Test for High School Mathematics.

Purpose: Designed to "provide diagnostic information on the competencies of individual students in various areas of basic, high school math."
Population: High school students.
Publication Dates: 2001-2003.
Acronym: DT-HSM.
Scores, 20: Whole Numbers, Common Fractions, Decimal Fractions, Percentages, Signed Numbers, Powers and Roots, Substitution, Setting up Equations, Solving Algebraic Equations, Geometry, Graphs, Tables, Estimation, Probability, Statistics, Order of Operations, Ratios, Math Vocabulary, Word Problems, Miscellaneous.
Administration: Group.
Price Data, 2016: $60 per technical manual (2003, 23 pages); $90 per specimen set including one test, one answer sheet, and sample reports.
Time: (90) minutes.
Author: Joel P. Wiesen.
Publisher: APR Testing Services.
Cross References: For reviews by Thomas P. Hogan and Michael S. Trevisan, see 18:43.

[656]
Diagnostic Test for Pre-Algebra Mathematics.

Purpose: Designed to "provide diagnostic information on the competencies of individual students in various areas of basic math."
Population: 8th grade students.
Publication Dates: 2001-2003.
Acronym: DT-PAM.
Scores, 21: Whole Numbers, Common Fractions, Decimal Fractions, Percentages, Units of Measurement, Signed Numbers, Simple Powers, Substitution, Setting up Equations, Solving Equations, Geometry, Comparisons, Graphs, Tables, Estimation, Probability, Statistics, Order of Operations, Ratios, Math Vocabulary, Word Problems.
Administration: Group.
Price Data, 2016: $90 per specimen set, including test, answer sheet and sample reports; $60 manual (2001).
Time: Administration time not reported.
Comments: Available in both print and online administration formats.
Author: APR Testing Services.
Publisher: APR Testing Services.
Cross References: For reviews by George Engelhard, Jr., and Mary L. Garner, see 18:44.

DIBELS: Dynamic Indicators of Basic Early Literacy Skills, Sixth Edition.

Purpose: Designed to assess "growth and development of early literacy skills."

Population: Grades K–6.

Publication Dates: 2002–2003.

Acronym: DIBELS.

Scores, 7: Initial Sound Fluency, Letter Naming Fluency, Phoneme Segmentation Fluency, Nonsense Word Fluency, Oral Reading Fluency, Oral Retelling Fluency, Word Use Fluency.

Administration: Individual.

Levels, 7: K, 1, 2, 3, 4, 5, 6.

Parts, 2: Benchmark Assessment, Progress Monitoring.

Price Data: Available from publisher.

Time: (10–15) minutes.

Comments: Benchmark Assessments administered to whole class three times per year; progress monitoring components used with at-risk students on a week-to-week basis to determine progress. The test publisher has indicated there is a newer edition of this test; description will be updated when complete test materials are received.

Authors: Roland H. Good III, Ruth A. Kaminski, and Louisa C. Moats (overview only).

Publisher: Voyager Sopris Learning.

a) LETTER NAMING FLUENCY.
Population: Grades K–1.
Authors: Ruth A. Kaminski and Roland H. Good III.

b) INITIAL SOUND FLUENCY.
Population: Grade K.
Forms: 20 alternate forms.
Authors: Roland H. Good III, Deborah Laimon, Ruth A. Kaminski, and Sylvia Smith.

c) PHONEME SEGMENTATION FLUENCY.
Population: Grades K–1.
Forms: 20 alternate forms.
Authors: Roland H. Good III, Ruth A. Kaminski, and Sylvia Smith.

d) NONSENSE WORD FLUENCY.
Population: Grades K–2.
Forms: 20 alternate forms.
Authors: Roland H. Good III and Ruth A. Kaminski.

e) ORAL READING FLUENCY.
Population: Grades 1–6.
Forms: 20 alternate forms.
Authors: Roland H. Good III, Ruth A. Kaminski, and Sheila Dill.

f) ORAL RETELLING FLUENCY.
Population: Grades 1–6.
Authors: Roland H. Good III, Ruth A. Kaminski, and Sheila Dill.

g) WORD USE FLUENCY.
Population: Grades K–3.
Authors: Roland H. Good III, Ruth A. Kaminski, and Sylvia Smith.

Cross References: For reviews by Bethany A. Brunsman and Timothy Shanahan, see 16:73.

Differential Ability Scales-Second Edition.

Purpose: "To profile a child's strengths and weaknesses in a wide range of cognitive abilities."

Population: Ages 2-6 to 17-11.

Publication Dates: 1979-2007.

Acronym: DAS-II.

Subtests: Core, Diagnostic.

Administration: Individual.

Levels, 2: Early Years Battery, School-Age Battery.

Price Data, 2015: $1,250 per comprehensive kit including administration manual (2007, 309 pages), normative data tables manual (2007, 165 pages), technical manual (2007, 309 pages), 15 Preschool record forms, 15 School-Age record forms, 10 each of speed of information processing booklets (versions A, B, and C), 4 stimulus books, object recall cards, picture similarities cards, phonological process and signed sentences CD, manipulatives, and scoring assistant.

Author: Colin D. Elliott.

Publisher: Pearson.

a) EARLY YEARS BATTERY.
Foreign Language Edition: Early Years Spanish Supplement available.

1) *Lower Level Early Years Battery.*
Population: Ages 2-6 to 3-5.
Time: (20) minutes.
Scores, 8: Verbal Ability (Verbal Comprehension, Naming Vocabulary), Nonverbal Ability (Picture Similarities, Pattern Construction), Diagnostic Subtests (Recall of Digits Forward, Recognition of Pictures, Early Number Concepts), General Conceptual Ability.

2) *Upper Level Early Years Battery.*
Population: Ages 3-6 to 6-11.
Time: (31) minutes.
Scores, 19: Verbal Ability (Verbal Comprehension, Naming Vocabulary), Nonverbal Reasoning Ability (Picture Similarities, Matrices), Spatial Ability (Pattern Construction, Copying), Special Nonverbal Composite, School Readiness (Early Number Concepts, Matching Letter-like Forms, Phonological Processing), Working Memory (Recall of Sequential Order, Recall of Digits Backward), Processing Speed (Speed of Information Processing, Rapid Naming), Recall of Objects-Immediate, Recall of Objects-Delayed, Recall of Digits Forward, Recognition of Pictures, General Conceptual Ability.

b) SCHOOL-AGE BATTERY.
Population: Ages 7-0 to 17-11 (and optionally down to age 5-0).
Time: (39) minutes.
Scores, 17: Verbal Ability (Word Definitions, Verbal Similarities), Nonverbal Reasoning Ability (Matrices, Sequential and Quantitative Reasoning), Spatial Ability (Recall of Designs, Pattern Construction), Special Nonverbal Composite, Working Memory (Recall of Sequential Order, Recall of Digits Backward), Processing Speed (Speed of Information Processing, Rapid Naming), Phonological Processing, Recall of Objects-Immediate, Recall of Objects-Delayed, Recall

of Digits Forward, Recognition of Pictures, General Conceptual Ability.

Cross References: For reveiws by Andrew S. Davis and W. Holmes Finch and by Gerald Tindal, see 18:45; see T5:837 (14 references) and T4:800 (3 references); for reviews by Glen P. Aylward and Robert C. Reinehr of an earlier edition, see 11:111 (1 reference).

[659]

Differential Aptitude Tests for Personnel and Career Assessment.

Purpose: Designed to measure ability to learn in eight aptitude areas.
Population: Adult.
Publication Dates: 1972–1991.
Acronym: DAT for PCA.
Scores, 8: General Cognitive Abilities Tests (Verbal Reasoning, Numerical Ability, Total), Perceptual Abilities Tests (Abstract Reasoning, Mechanical Reasoning, Space Relations), Clerical and Language Tests (Spelling, Language Usage, Clerical Speed and Accuracy).
Administration: Group or individual.
Price Data, 2015: $93 per technical manual; $23 per adminstration/scoring directions; $196 per 25 test booklets (Abstract Reasoning, Language Usage, Mechanical Reasoning, Numerical Ability, Space Relations, or Verbal Reasoning); $151 per 50 answer sheets; $99 per scoring key.
Time: 114(144) minutes.
Comments: Abbreviated form of the Differential Aptitude Tests, Form V/W.
Authors: George K. Bennett, Harold G. Seashore, and Alexander G. Wesman.
Publisher: Pearson.
Cross References: For reviews by Victor L. Willson and Hilda Wing, see 12:119.

[660]

Differential Scales of Social Maladjustment and Emotional Disturbance.

Purpose: Designed to "differentiate between individuals with social maladjustment and those with emotional disturbances."
Population: Ages 6-0 to 17-11.
Publication Date: 2009.
Acronym: DSSMED.
Scores, 2: Social Maladjustment, Emotional Disturbance.
Administration: Individual.
Price Data, 2015: $142 per examiner's manual (53 pages), 25 summary/rating forms, and 25 scoring overlays. $68 examiner's manual; $46 per 25 scoring overlays; $35 per 25 summary/rating forms.
Time: (5-10) minutes.
Comments: To be completed by a teacher or professional who knows the student well and has observed their behavior in a classroom setting for at least 4 weeks.

Authors: David J. Ehrler, Ronnie L. McGhee, Carol G. Phillips, and Elizabeth A. Allen.
Publisher: PRO-ED.
Cross References: For reviews by Sherry K. Bain and Kathleen B. Aspiranti and by Richard F. Farmer, see 18:46.

[661]

Differential Test of Conduct and Emotional Problems.

Purpose: "Designed to effect differentiations between conduct problem, emotionally disturbed and noninvolved populations."
Population: Grades K–12.
Publication Dates: 1990–1991.
Acronym: DT/CEP.
Scores, 2: Emotional Disturbance Scale, Conduct Problem Scale.
Administration: Group.
Price Data, 2016: $135 per complete set including manual (1990, 58 pages), score forms, and scoring template; $56.50 per 50 score forms; $19 per set of 2 scoring templates.
Time: (15–20) minutes.
Comments: Ratings by teachers.
Author: Edward J. Kelly.
Publisher: Slosson Educational Publications, Inc.
Cross References: For reviews by Richard Brozovich and Alida S. Westman, see 12:120; see also T4:804 (1 reference).

[662]

Digit Vigilance Test.

Purpose: Designed to measure vigilance during rapid visual tracking and accurate selection of target stimuli.
Population: Ages 20–80.
Publication Date: 1995.
Acronym: DVT.
Scores, 2: Total Time, Total Errors.
Administration: Individual.
Forms, 2: 6s, 9s.
Price Data, 2015: $175 per kit including professional user's guide (12 pages), 50 test booklets, and scoring keys.
Time: (10) minutes.
Author: Ronald F. Lewis.
Publisher: Psychological Assessment Resources, Inc.
Cross References: For reviews by Raymond S. Dean and Scott Kristian Hill and by Daniel C. Miller, see 14:122.

[663]

Dimensional Assessment for Patient Placement Engagement and Recovery–3rd Edition.

Purpose: Designed to "focus the clinician's attention on those areas most likely to influence placement and

planning decisions and to document the foundation for those decisions"when treating individuals with substance abuse problems.
Population: Adults and adolescents.
Publication Dates: 2000-2015.
Acronym: DAPPER-3.
Scores, 6: Intoxication/Withdrawal, Biomedical Conditions/Complications, Emotional/Behavioral/Cognitive Conditions, Readiness to Change, Relapse/Continued Use/Problem Potential, Recovery Environment.
Administration: Individual.
Price Data, 2016: $78.75 per 25 copies; $25 per manual (2015, 16 pages).
Time: Administration time not reported.
Comments: May be used up to 6 times with the same person; compatible with ASAM criteria for patient placement.
Authors: Norman G. Hoffmann, David Mee-Lee, and Gerald D. Shulman.
Publisher: The Change Companies.

[664]

Dimensional Assessment of Personality Pathology-Basic Questionnaire.

Purpose: Designed to "provide a comprehensive assessment of the basic dimensions of personality disorder and clinically relevant personality traits."
Population: Ages 18 and over.
Publication Date: 2009.
Acronym: DAPP-BQ.
Scores, 18: Affective Lability, Anxiousness, Callousness, Compulsivity, Conduct Problems, Cognitive Dysregulation, Identity Problems, Insecure Attachment, Intimacy Problems, Low Affiliation, Narcissism, Oppositionality, Rejection, Restricted Expression, Self-Harm, Stimulus Seeking, Submissiveness, Suspiciousness.
Administration: Group.
Price Data, 2015: $290 per hand-scoring examination kit including manual (149 pages), 10 test booklets, 25 answer sheets, 25 scoring sheets, 25 profile sheets, and 5 online administrations; $39 per test manual; $37 per 10 test booklets; $80 per 10 response sheets (includes 10 answer sheets & 10 scoring sheets); $19 per 10 profile sheets; $155 per software package (software and 10 coupons); $12-$15 (depending on volume) per online administration.
Time: (35-50) minutes.
Authors: W. John Livesley and Douglas N. Jackson.
Publisher: SIGMA Assessment Systems, Inc.
Cross References: For reviews by Nicholas F. Benson and Peter Zachar, see 19:53.

[665]

Dimensions of Excellence Scales [1991 Edition].

Purpose: Designed to identify, describe and validate successful programs and practices of a school district, as well as to forecast future needs.

Population: Schools or districts.
Publication Dates: 1988–1990.
Acronym: DOES.
Administration: Group.
Price Data: Available as free download from test publisher's website.
Comments: Ratings by students, parents, and school staff.
Authors: Russel A. Dusewicz and Francine S. Beyer.
Publisher: Research for Better Schools, Inc.
    a) STUDENT SCALE.
    Scores: 4 dimensions: School Climate, Teacher Behavior, Monitoring and Assessment, Student Discipline and Behavior.
    Time: (30) minutes.
    b) PARENT SCALE.
    Scores, 8: Same as *a* above plus Leadership, Curriculum, Staff Development, Parent Involvement.
    Time: (20–30) minutes.
    c) SCHOOL STAFF SCALE.
    Scores, 8: Same as *b* above.
    Time: (45) minutes.
Cross References: For a review by Andrew A. McConney, see 14:123; for reviews by Janet F. Carlson and William P. Erchul of an earlier edition, see 11:112.

[666]

Dimensions of Self-Concept.

Purpose: Designed to "measure non-cognitive factors associated with self-esteem or self-concept in a school setting."
Publication Dates: 1976–1989.
Acronym: DOSC.
Administration: Group.
Price Data, 2016: $15.75 per 25 forms; $7.75 per 25 profile sheets (specify grade level for norms); $7 per manual; $12.25 per specimen set including a manual and one copy of all forms; quantity discounts available.
Comments: Self-report instrument; test publisher indicates materials have been updated; description will be updated when those test materials are received.
Authors: William B. Michael, Robert A. Smith, and Joan J. Michael.
Publisher: EdITS/Educational and Industrial Testing Service.
    a) FORM E.
    Population: Grades 4–6.
    Scores, 5: Level of Aspiration, Anxiety, Academic Interest and Satisfaction, Leadership and Initiative, Identification vs. Alienation.
    Time: (20–40) minutes.
    b) FORM S.
    Population: Grades 7–12.
    Scores: Same as for *a* above.
    Time: (15–35) minutes.
    c) FORM H.
    Population: College.
    Scores: Same as for *a* above.
    Time: (15–35) minutes.

d) FORM W.

Population: Adult workers.

Scores, 5: Aspiration, Anxiety, Job Interest and Satisfaction, Identification vs. Alienation, Level of Job Stress.

Time: Administration time not reported.

Cross References: See T5:844 (6 references) and T4:806 (1 reference); for a review by Sharon Johnson-Lewis, see 11:113 (10 references); for reviews by Herbert G. W. Bischoff and Alfred B. Heilbrun, Jr., see 9:353 (4 references); see also T3:734 (5 references).

[667]
DiSC Classic.

Purpose: Designed to "help adults better understand themselves and others."

Population: Adults

Publication Dates: 1996–2003.

Scores, 4: Dominance, Influence, Steadiness, Conscientiousness.

Administration: Individual or group.

Price Data: Available from publisher.

Time: (7–10) minutes.

Comments: Update of the Personal Profile System; self-report, self-scored instrument; related scripted seminar available from publisher.

Author: Inscape Publishing.

Publisher: Wiley Publishing.

Cross References: For a review by Collie W. Conoley and Linda Castillo, see 16:74.

[668]
The Discipline Index.

Purpose: "Systematically obtains information from a child about the child's overall perceptions of each parent's disciplinary practices."

Population: Ages 6–17.

Publication Dates: 1999–2002.

Acronym: DI.

Scores, 6: Mother and Father scores for: Clear Expectations, Effectively Monitors, Consistently Enforces, Fairness, Attunement, Moderates Anger, plus Mother Total, Father Total.

Administration: Individual.

Price Data, 2016: $289 per complete kit including handbook (2000, 140 pages), 8 sets response cards, 8 scoring summaries, stylus-pen, placement dots, updates, and 3-year update service; $159 per 10 response cards with summaries (volume discount available); $289 per computer scoring program (CD-ROM); $179 per handbook.

Time: (35 minutes).

Authors: Anita K. Lampel, Barry Bricklin, and Gail Elliot.

Publisher: Village Publishing.

Cross References: For reviews by Patti L. Harrison and Darrell L. Sabers, see 15:86.

[669]
Dissemination Self-Inventory.

Purpose: "To help people involved in NIDILRR-funded disability research and development projects bridge the gap between the creation of disability research outcomes and their use."

Population: Organizations.

Publication Date: 2002.

Scores, 4: Organizational Structure and Policies, Research Design, Dissemination Plan, Evaluation.

Administration: Individual.

Price Data: Online version available at no charge from test publisher.

Time: [20–35] minutes.

Author: National Center for the Dissemination of Disability Research (NCDDR).

Publisher: American Institutes for Research (formerly Southwest Educational Development Laboratory).

[670]
Dissociative Experiences Scale.

Purpose: "Developed to serve as a clinical tool to help identify patients with dissociative psychopathology and as a research tool to provide a means of quantifying dissociative experiences."

Population: Late adolescent–adult.

Publication Date: 1986.

Acronym: DES.

Scores: Total score only.

Administration: Group or individual.

Price Data, 2016: $12 per PDF download.

Foreign Language Editions: Available in French, Spanish, Italian, Dutch, Hindi, Cambodian, Czech, Swedish, Norwegian, Japanese, Hebrew, Chinese (Mandarin, Traditional Character, and Simplified Character), Finnish, Korean, Polish, and Turkish.

Time: [10] minutes.

Comments: Self-report inventory.

Authors: Eve Bernstein Carlson and Frank W. Putnam.

Publisher: The Sidran Institute.

Cross References: See T5:846 (26 references); for reviews by Samuel Juni and Niels G. Waller, see 12:122 (16 references); see also T4:809 (1 reference).

[671]
Dissociative Features Profile.

Purpose: Developed to "help uncover dissociative pathology in children and adolescents."

Population: Children and adolescents.

Publication Date: 1996.

Acronym: DFP.

Scores, 22: Part I: Evidence of Amnesia, Staring Episodes, Odd Movements, Fluctuations/Relatedness, Fluctuations/Language, Fearfulness, Anger, Physical Complaints, Dividedness (1), Dividedness (2), Total;

Part II: Multiplicity, Malevolent Religiosity, Dissociative Coping, Depersonalized Humans, Explicit Emotional Confusion, Categories of Good and Bad, Mutilation, Torture, Magical Transformations, Total; Combined Part I and Part II Total.
Administration: Individual.
Parts, 2: Behaviors, Markers.
Price Data, 2016: $12 per PDF download.
Time: Untimed.
Comments: "Developed to be used with a typical psychological testing battery" (at least 2 other psychological tests given in conjunction with this test); profile completed by psychological professionals about juvenile clients.
Author: Joyanna L. Silberg.
Publisher: The Sidran Institute.

[672]

Diversity Awareness Profile, Second Edition.

Purpose: Designed to "give people an opportunity to take a snapshot of their behaviors as they are interacting with others" to help assess "how free of bias, prejudice, and discrimination" their behavior is.
Population: Employees or managers.
Publication Dates: 1991-2007.
Acronym: DAP.
Score: Total score only.
Administration: Individual or group.
Price Data, 2016: $60 per facilitator's guide (2007, 48 pages), including assessment form; $20.95 per form.
Time: Administration time not reported.
Authors: Karen M. Stinson.
Publisher: John Wiley & Sons, Inc.
Cross References: For reviews by Donald B. Pope-Davis and Jonathan G. Dings and by Gargi Roysircar Sodowsky of an earlier edition, see 12:123.

[673]

Domestic Violence Inventory.

Purpose: "Designed specifically for risk and needs assessment of people who have committed physical, emotional and verbal abuse."
Population: Ages 12–18, adults.
Publication Dates: 1991–1995.
Acronym: DVI.
Scores: 6 scales: Truthfulness, Violence, Alcohol, Drugs, Control, Stress Coping Ability.
Administration: Group.
Forms, 2: Adult, Juvenile.
Price Data, 2016: $9.95 per test.
Foreign Language Edition: Spanish version available.
Time: (30) minutes.
Author: Risk & Needs Assessment, Inc.
Publisher: Behavior Data Systems, Ltd.
Cross References: For reviews by Carol Collins and by David M. Kaplan and Molly L. Vanduser, see 14:125.

[674]

Doors and People.

Purpose: Designed to "provide comparable measures of visual and verbal memory" and "test both recall and recognition."
Population: Ages 16–80.
Publication Date: 1994.
Scores, 14: Verbal Recall (People), Visual Recognition (Doors), Visual Recall (Shapes), Verbal Recognition (Names), Overall, Combined Visual Memory, Combined Verbal Memory, Combined Recall, Combined Recognition, Forgetting (Verbal), Forgetting (Visual), Overall Forgetting, Visual-Verbal Discrepancies, Recall-Recognition Discrepancies.
Administration: Individual.
Price Data, 2015: £348 per complete kit including manual (20 pages), 25 scoring sheets, and 3 stimulus books; £22.50 per 25 scoring sheets; £81.50 per stimulus book - names; £141.50 per stimulus book - doors; £59 per stimulus book - people; £48 per manual.
Time: [35-40] minutes.
Authors: Alan Baddeley, Hazel Emslie, and Ian Nimmo-Smith.
Publisher: Pearson Assessment [England].
Cross References: For a review by William K. Wilkinson, see 17:58.

[675]

Drafter (CAD Operator) (Form DDC).

Purpose: For selecting CAD operator candidates.
Population: Applicants for drafter positions.
Publication Date: 2005.
Scores, 3: Print Reading, Computer Aided Design, Total.
Administration: Group.
Price Data, 2015: $24 per consumable self-scoring test booklet; $26 per online test administration (minimum order of 20).
Time: 30(45) minutes.
Comments: Packet of supplemental sheets included and required for test administration; available for online test administration.
Author: Roland T. Ramsay.
Publisher: Ramsay Corporation.

[676]

Draw-A-Person Intellectual Ability Test for Children, Adolescents, and Adults.

Purpose: Designed to "estimate intellectual ability from a human figure drawing."
Population: Ages 4-0 to 89-11.
Publication Date: 2004.
Acronym: DAP: IQ.
Scores: DAP IQ.
Administration: Individual or group.

Price Data, 2015: $119 per kit including examiner's manual (75 pages), 50 administration/scoring forms, and 50 drawing forms; $56 per examiner's manual; $48 per 50 administration/scoring forms; $31 per 50 drawing forms.
Time: (10-12) minutes.
Authors: Cecil R. Reynolds and Julia A. Hickman.
Publisher: PRO-ED.
Cross References: For reviews by Robert W. Hiltonsmith and Jonathan Sandoval, see 17:59.

[677]

Draw A Person: Screening Procedure for Emotional Disturbance.

Purpose: Designed to screen for children who may have emotional disorders and require further evaluation.
Population: Ages 6–17.
Publication Date: 1991.
Acronym: DAP:SPED.
Scores: Total score only.
Administration: Group and individual.
Price Data, 2015: $168 per complete kit including 25 record forms, manual (77 pages), and 10 scoring templates; $56 per 25 record forms; $79 per manual; $48 per 10 scoring templates.
Time: 20 minutes.
Authors: Jack A. Naglieri, Timothy J. McNeish, and Achilles N. Bardos.
Publisher: PRO-ED.
Cross References: See T5:852 (1 reference); for reviews by Merith Cosden and Gale M. Morrison, see 12:124 (2 references); see also T4:816 (1 reference).

[678]

Driver Risk Inventory—II.

Purpose: "Designed for DUI/DWI offender screening."
Population: Convicted DUI and DWI offenders.
Publication Dates: 1986–1997.
Acronym: DRI-II.
Scores, 6: Truthfulness, Alcohol, Driver Risk, Drug, Stress Coping, Dependency.
Price Data: Available from publisher.
Time: (30–35) minutes.
Comments: Self-administered, computer-scored test.
Author: Behavior Data Systems Ltd.
Publisher: Behavior Data Systems Ltd. [Efforts to obtain updated information from the test publisher were unsuccessful. An newer edition of this test appears on the test publisher's website.]
Cross References: For reviews by Tony Cellucci and Kevin J. McCarthy, see 14:127; for a review by Frank Gresham of an earlier version, see 12:125.

[679]

Drug Abuse Screening Test.

Purpose: To assess "potential involvement with drugs."
Population: Clients of addiction treatment.
Publication Date: 1982.
Acronym: DAST-20.
Scores: Total score only.
Administration: Group.
Price Data, 2016: C$14.45 per pad of 100.
Foreign Language Edition: Available in French.
Time: (5–10) minutes.
Comments: Self-report inventory.
Author: Harvey A. Skinner.
Publisher: Centre for Addiction and Mental Health [Canada].
Cross References: For reviews by Philip Ash and Jeffrey S. Rain, see 13:104.

[680]

Drug-Taking Confidence Questionnaire.

Purpose: "As an assessment tool, the DTCQ identifies a client's coping self-efficacy in relation to 50 drinking or drug-taking situations."
Population: Clients of addiction treatment.
Publication Date: 1997.
Acronym: DTCQ.
Scores: Situation profiles in two areas: Personal States, Situations Involving Other People; 8 subscales: Unpleasant Emotions, Physical Discomfort, Pleasant Emotions, Testing Personal Control, Urges and Temptations to Use, Conflict with Others, Social Pressure to Use, Pleasant Times with Others.
Administration: Group.
Price Data, 2016: C$34.95 per user's guide; C$16.45 per 30 questionnaires (specify alcohol or drug); C$39.95 per sample pack including user's guide and 40 questionnaires (10 alcohol and 30 drug).
Time: (15) minutes.
Comments: User's guide written in both English (160 pages) and French (69 pages); "French versions of DTCQ have not been scientifically validated."
Authors: Helen M. Annis, Sherrilyn M. Sklar, and Nigel E. Turner.
Publisher: Centre for Addiction and Mental Health [Canada].
Cross References: For reviews by Michael H. Campbell and Glenn B. Gelman, see 14:128.

[681]

Drug Use Screening Inventory—Revised.

Purpose: Designed to quantify "severity of mental health and substance use problems in multiple domains of health, behavior, and psychosocial development" and to predict likelihood of mental health disorder, adverse outcomes, and violence proneness.
Population: Youth (ages 10 to 17); Adult (age 18 and over).
Publication Dates: 1990–2011.
Acronym: DUSI-R.

Scores: 10 Domains: Drug and Alcohol Use, Substance Use, Behavior Patterns, Health Status, Psychiatric Disorder, Social Competence, Family System, School Performance, Work Adjustment, Peer Relationships, Leisure/Recreation; also Overall Problem Severity Index and validity/lie scale scores, plus prediction of 6 mental health disorders (ADHD, SUD, Anxiety, Depression, Conduct/Anti-sociality) and prediction of adverse outcomes (DUI, Car Accident, Sell/Deal Drugs, Head Injury, STD), and Violence Proneness.

Administration: Individual or group.

Levels, 2: Youth, Adult.

Parts, 3: Full Assessment (20min), Short Screen (7min), Brief Screen (2min).

Forms, 3: Past Year, Past Month, Past Week.

Price Data, 2016: $10 per client for unlimited use of Initial Intake Assessment and follow-up monitoring of progress during treatment/post-treatment.

Foreign Language and Other Special Editions: Available in Chinese, Danish, Dutch, Flemish, Belgian French, Finnish, French, German, Norwegian, Portuguese, Russian, Spanish, Swedish, Turkish, and English. Audio version available for clients whose reading level is below Grade 5.

Time: Full Assessment, 20 minutes; Short Screen, 7 minutes; Brief Screen, 2 minutes.

Comments: Client self-report inventory; covers both mental health and substance use; subscales within each domain and related subscale questions mapped to DSM; online system provides automated scoring and ability to monitor client progress during treatment, monitor client during aftercare. Recommended and current uses include: detection of high risk youths, intake evaluation (youth/adult), intervention/treatment progress monitoring, outcome assessment, program evaluation, and clinical trials.

Author: Ralph E. Tarter.

Publisher: eCenter Research, Inc.

Cross References: For a review by Tony Cellucci, see 16:76.

[682]

DSST Exams.

Purpose: Gives colleges and universities the opportunity to offer non-traditional learners college credit for knowledge acquired outside the traditional classroom.

Population: Non-traditional students wishing to earn college credit by examination.

Publication Dates: 1983–2016.

Acronym: DSST.

Administration: Group.

Price Data: Available from publisher.

Time: (120) minutes to complete, requiring approximately (90) minutes per test.

Author: Prometric.

Publisher: Prometric.

a) MATH.

Scores: Total score for each of 2 tests:
1) *Fundamentals of College Algebra.*
2) *Principles of Statistics.*

b) SOCIAL SCIENCES.

Scores: Total score for each of 12 tests:
1) *A History of the Vietnam War.*
2) *Human/Cultural Geography.*
3) *Lifespan Developmental Psychology.*
4) *General Anthropology.*
5) *Introduction to Law Enforcement.*
6) *Criminal Justice.*
7) *Fundamentals of Counseling.*
8) *Art of the Western World.*
9) *Substance Abuse.*
10) *The Civil War and Reconstruction.*
11) *Foundations of Education.*
12) *History of the Soviet Union.*

c) PHYSICAL SCIENCE.

Scores: Total score for each of 4 tests:
1) *Astronomy.*
2) *Health & Human Development.*
3) *Environment and Humanity: The Race to Save the Planet.*
4) *Principles of Physical Science I.*

d) BUSINESS.

Scores: Total score for each of 11 tests:
1) *Business Ethics and Society.*
2) *Business Mathematics*
3) *Human Resource Management.*
4) *Introduction to Business.*
5) *Introduction to Computing.*
6) *Management Information Systems.*
7) *Money and Banking.*
8) *Organizational Behavior.*
9) *Personal Finance.*
10) *Principles of Finance.*
11) *Principles of Supervision.*

e) TECHNOLOGY.

Scores: Total score for each of 2 tests:
1) *Technical Writing.*
2) *Fundamentals of Cybersecurity.*

f) HUMANITIES.

Scores: Total score for each of 3 tests:
1) *Ethics in America.*
2) *Principles of Public Speaking.*
3) *Introduction to World Religions.*

Cross References: For reviews by Laura L. B. Barnes and William A. Mehrens of an earlier edition under the title DSST/DANTES Subject Standardized Tests, see 11:103.

[683]

Dyadic Adjustment Scale.

Purpose: Designed to measure the quality of adjustment in marriage and similar dyadic relationships.

Population: People who have any committed couple relationship including unmarried cohabitation.

Publication Dates: 1989-2001.

Acronym: DAS.

Scores, 5: Dyadic Consensus, Dyadic Satisfaction, Affectional Expression, Dyadic Cohesion, Dyadic Adjustment.

Administration: Group or individual.

Price Data, 2015: $88 per complete kit including test manual (54 pages) and 20 QuikScore™ forms (for 10 couples); $57 per 20 QuikScore™ forms (for 10 couples); $43 per manual; $62 per DAS for Windows preview version (includes software manual and 3 reports); $6 per profile report (minimum purchase of 50).

Time: (5-10) minutes.

Comments: Self-report.

Author: Graham B. Spanier.

Publisher: Multi-Health Systems, Inc.

Cross References: See T5:863 (94 references) and T4:824 (37 references); for reviews by Karen S. Budd and Nancy Heilman and by Richard B. Stuart, see 11:117 (17 references).

[684]

Dyadic Parent-Child Interaction Coding System.

Purpose: For use in assessing the quality of parent-child social interaction, discriminating between parent-child interactions of children with and without disruptive behavior disorders and their parents, and evaluating change after parent training interventions for young children with behavior problems.

Population: Children ages 2-10 and their parents.

Publication Dates: 1981-2005.

Acronym: DPICS.

Scores: 24 behavioral categories that provide frequency scores: parent and child positive and negative verbalization and physical touch categories, child negative vocalization categories (whine, yell), and child responses to parent commands and questions.

Administration: Individual dyads.

Price Data: Available from publisher.

Time: 15(20) minutes.

Comments: Behavioral coding by clinician in three standard 5-minute situations that vary in amount of parent control required: child-led play; parent-led play; clean-up; abridged version available for clinical use; workbook to assist coder training available.

Authors: Sheila M. Eyberg, Melanie M. Nelson, Maura Duke, and Stephen R. Boggs.

Publisher: Sheila M. Eyberg. [Efforts to obtain updated information from the test publisher were unsuccessful. An updated edition of this test appears on the test publisher's website.]

Cross References: See T5:864 (3 references) and T4:825 (11 references); for reviews by Robert J. McMahon and Phillip S. Strain, see 9:361 (1 reference); see also T3:768 (1 reference).

[685]

Dynamic Assessment of Test Accommodations.

Purpose: "Designed to assist the teacher in determining the appropriate accommodations that will allow students with learning disabilities to demonstrate academic ability independent of their handicapping conditions."

Population: Students with special needs in Grades 2 to 7.

Publication Date: 2003.

Acronym: DATA.

Administration: Individual or group.

Levels, 3: Grades 2–3, Grades 4–5, Grades 6–7.

Price Data, 2015: $217 per complete kit including manual, and 3 test booklets (specify level); $8 per Reading Screener card; $22 per 25 Reading Screener score sheets; $8 per Workbook Symbols card; $106.50 per manual, $39 per 25 Math booklets (specify level); $68 per 25 Reading booklets (specify level).

Comments: Student must be capable of reading basic text at a rate of at least 10 words per minute before Reading Comprehension is assessed.

Authors: Lynn Fuchs, Douglas Fuchs, Susan Eaton, and Carol Hamlett.

Publisher: Pearson.

a) READING COMPREHENSION.

Scores, 4: Large Print Gain, Extended Time Gain, Read Aloud Gain, No Accommodation.

Time: 40(45) minutes.

b) MATH COMPUTATION.

Scores, 2: Extended Time Gain, No Accommodation.

Time: 24(29) minutes.

c) MATH APPLICATION.

Scores, 4: Extended Time Gain, Calculator Condition Gain, Reader Condition Gain, No Accommodation.

Time: (42) minutes.

Cross References: For reviews by Michelle Athanasiou and Bethany A. Brunsman, see 16:77.

[686]

Dynamic Factors Survey.

Purpose: Designed to measure general motivational factors to assess personality.

Population: Age 16 and older.

Publication Dates: 1954–1993.

Acronym: DFSV.

Scores, 10: Need for Attention, Liking for Thinking, Adventure vs. Security, Self-Reliance vs. Dependence, Aesthetic Appreciation, Cultural Conformity, Need for Freedom, Realistic Thinking, Need for Precision, Need for Diversion.

Administration: Individual or group.

Price Data, 2015: $50 per manual, including review-only copy of the DFS form; $2 per Remote Online Survey License 9minimum 50); $2 License to Reproduce (minimum 50).

Time: (45) minutes.

Authors: J. P. Guilford, Paul R. Christensen, and Nicholas A. Bond, Jr.
Publisher: Mind Garden, Inc.
Cross References: See T2:1151 (7 references) and P:54 (12 references); for reviews by Andrew R. Baggaley, John W. French, and Arthur W. Meadows, see 5:45.

[687]

Dyscalculia Screener.

Purpose: To screen pupil(s) to establish whether a pupil has low attainment because of a dyscalculic deficit.
Population: Ages 6–14.
Publication Date: 2003.
Scores: 4 tests: Dot Enumeration, Number Comparison (Numerical Stroop), Arithmetic Achievement, Simple Reaction Time.
Administration: Group.
Price Data: Available from publisher.
Time: (15–30) minutes.
Comments: Administered online.
Author: Brian Butterworth.
Publisher: GL Assessment [England].
Cross References: For reviews by Cleborne D. Maddux and Gretchen Owens, see 16:78.

[688]

Dyslexia Adult Screening Test.

Purpose: To assess strengths and weaknesses often associated with dyslexia.
Population: 16 years 5 months to adult.
Publication Date: 1998.
Acronym: DAST.
Scores, 12: Rapid Naming, One Minute Reading, Postural Stability, Nonverbal Reasoning, Phonemic Segmentation, Two Minute Spelling, Backwards Span, Verbal Fluency, Semantic Fluency, Nonsense Passage Reading, One Minute Writing, Total.
Administration: Individual.
Price Data, 2015: £199 per complete kit; £56 per 50 record forms; £45.50 per manual.
Time: 30 minutes.
Authors: Angela J. Fawcett and Rod I. Nicolson.
Publisher: Pearson Assessment [England].
Cross References: For reviews by Manuela H. Habicht and William K. Wilkinson, see 16:79.

[689]

Dyslexia Determination Test, Second Edition.

Purpose: To identify individuals who exhibit dyslexic patterns of responding in the areas of reading, writing, and spelling.
Population: Grades 2–12.
Publication Dates: 1980-1987.
Acronym: DDT.

Scores: 6 subtests: Dysnemkinesia (Writing of Numbers, Writing of Letters), Dysphonesia (Decoding, Encoding), Dyseidesia (Decoding, Encoding).
Administration: Individual.
Price Data: Available from publisher.
Time: (15–20) minutes.
Authors: John R. Griffin and Howard N. Walton.
Publisher: Optometric Extension Program Foundation.
Cross References: For a review by Fred M. Grossman, see 9:362.

[690]

Dyslexia Early Screening Test [Second Edition].

Purpose: "Designed to pick out children who are 'at risk' of reading failure early enough to allow them to be given extra support at school."
Population: Ages 4 years, 6 months to 6 years, 5 months.
Publication Dates: 1996-2004.
Acronym: DEST-2.
Scores, 13: Tests of Attainment (Digit Naming, Letter Naming), Diagnostic Tests (Rapid Naming, Bead Threading, Phonological Discrimination, Postural Stability, Rhyme/First Letter, Forwards Digit Span, Sound Order, Shape Copying, Corsi Frog, Vocabulary), At Risk Quotient.
Administration: Individual.
Price Data, 2015: £177 per complete kit including examiner's manual (2004, 106 pages), envelope 1 (containing 7 subtest cards and sample permission letter), envelope 2 (containing score keys), Forward Digit Span tape, Sound Order tape, Corsi Frog, beads, cord, blindfold, balance tester, scoring software with manual, and 50 score sheets in a carrying case; £83 per upgrade kit including examiner's manual, envelope 1 (containing 7 subtest cards and sample permission letter), envelope 2 (containing score keys), Corsi Frog, scoring software with manual, and 50 score sheets in carrying case; £54.50 per 50 score sheets.
Time: (30) minutes.
Authors: Rod I. Nicolson and Angela J. Fawcett.
Publisher: Pearson Assessment [England].
Cross References: For reviews by Lorraine Cleeton and Katharine Snyder, see 17:61; for reviews by Kathleen M. Johnson and William K. Wilkinson of the earlier edition, see 15:88.

[691]

Dyslexia Screening Instrument.

Purpose: Designed to identify students with dyslexia.
Population: Grades 1–12, ages 6–21.
Publication Date: 1994.
Scores, 4: Passed, Failed, Inconclusive, Cannot Be Scored.

Administration: Individual.
Price Data, 2015: $122.85 per complete kit including teacher rating scale, manual (40 pages), and scoring program software; $28.50 per 25 rating forms; $71.25 per manual; $50.70 per scoring program CD.
Time: (15–20) minutes.
Comments: Rating form is completed by student's teacher; computer scored.
Authors: Kathryn B. Coon, Mary Jo Polk, and Melissa McCoy Waguespack.
Publisher: Pearson.
Cross References: For reviews by Janet E. Spector and Betsy Waterman, see 14:130.

[692]

Dysphagia Evaluation Protocol.

Purpose: Developed to "assist in evaluating swallowing functioning in adult patients."
Population: Adult patients.
Publication Date: 1997.
Acronym: DEP.
Scores: 14 ratings: History and Observations (Feeding History, Nutritional Status, Respiratory Status), Clinical Evaluation of Swallowing (Observations, Oral Control, Primitive and Abnormal Reflexes, Pharyngeal Control), Feeding Trial (Appetite/Willingness to Participate, Ability to Swallow Without Food Bolus, Oral State, Pharyngeal Stage), Impressions (Summary, Functional Level, Recommendations/Plan).
Administration: Individual.
Price Data, 2015: $100 per complete kit including 15 record forms, pocket manual (40 pages), and manual (64 pages); $25 per 15 record forms; $54 per pocket manual; $46 per manual.
Time: (30) minutes.
Authors: Wendy Avery-Smith, Abbey Brod Rosen, and Donna M. Dellarosa.
Publisher: Pearson.
Cross References: For a review by Maynard D. Filter, see 14:131.

[693]

Early Childhood Attention Deficit Disorders Evaluation Scale.

Purpose: Designed to document behaviors and measure the characteristics of ADHD in school and home environments.
Population: Males, ages 24–84 months; Females ages 24–83 months.
Publication Date: 1995.
Acronym: ECADDES.
Scores, 3: Inattentive, Hyperactive-Impulsive, Total Percentile Rank.
Administration: Individual.
Forms, 3: Home, School, ECADDES/DSM-IV.

Price Data, 2015: $205.50 per complete kit including 50 School Version rating forms, 50 Home Version rating forms, 50 ECADDES/DSM-IV forms, School Version technical manual (42 pages), Home Version technical manual (42 pages), ECADDES Intervention manual (147 pages), and Parent's Guide (134 pages); $44 per 50 rating forms (specify School Version or Home Version); $44 per 50 Home Version Spanish rating forms; $25 per 50 ECADDES/DSM-IV forms; $21 per technical manual (specify School Version or Home Version); $31 per ECADDES Intervention manual; $19.50 per Parent's Guide; $46 per computerized Quick Score program (Windows).
Time: (15–20) minutes.
Foreign Language Edition: Home version Spanish rating form available.
Comments: Ratings by persons familiar with the child's behavior patterns in home or school settings.
Authors: Stephen B. McCarney and Nancy W. Johnson (Intervention Manual and Parent's Guide).
Publisher: Hawthorne Educational Services, Inc.
Cross References: For reviews by Libby G. Cohen and Harold R. Keller, see 14:132.

[694]

The Early Childhood Behavior Scale.

Purpose: Designed to assess behaviors related to early childhood emotional disturbance and behavior disorder.
Population: 36–72 months.
Publication Dates: 1991–1994.
Acronym: ECBS.
Scores, 4: Academic Progress, Social Relationships, Personal Adjustment, Total Percentile Rank.
Administration: Individual.
Price Data, 2015: $134 per complete kit including technical manual (1994, 36 pages), intervention manual (1991, 130 pages), 50 pre-referral ECBS checklists, and 50 ratings forms; $21 per technical manual; $31 per intervention manual; $44 per 50 rating forms; $38 per 50 pre-referral checklists.
Time: (15–20) minutes.
Comments: Ratings by teachers.
Author: Stephen B. McCarney.
Publisher: Hawthorne Educational Services, Inc.
Cross References: For reviews by Kathleen D. Paget and Jonathan Sandoval, see 13:105.

[695]

Early Childhood Environment Rating Scale, Third Edition.

Purpose: Designed to assess the quality of the environments in early childhood programs.
Population: Early childhood programs or classrooms (children ages 3-5 years).
Publication Dates: 1980-2015.

Acronym: ECERS-3.

Scores, 42: 35 items in 6 subscales: Space and Furnishings (Indoor Space, Furnishings for Care/Play/Learning, Room Arrangement for Play and Learning, Space for Privacy, Child-Related Display, Space for Gross Motor Play, Gross Motor Equipment), Personal Care Routines (Meals/Snacks, Toileting/Diapering, Health Practices, Safety Practices), Language and Literacy (Helping Children Expand Vocabulary, Encouraging Children to use Language, Staff Use of Books with Children, Encouraging Children's Use of Books, Becoming Familiar with Print), Learning Activities (Fine Motor, Art, Music and Movement, Blocks, Dramatic Play, Nature/Science, Math Materials and Activities, Math in Daily Events, Understanding Written Numbers, Promoting Acceptance of Diversity, Appropriate Use of Technology), Interaction (Supervision of Gross Motor, Individualized Teaching and Learning, Staff-Child Interaction, Peer Interaction, Discipline), Program Structure (Transitions and Waiting Games, Free Play, Whole-Group Activities for Play and Learning), plus Total Score.

Administration: Individual classrooms.

Price Data, 2015: $22.95 per manual with complete test (2015, 104 pages).

Time: (180) minutes minimum for observation.

Authors: Thelma Harms, Richard M. Clifford, and Debby Cryer.

Publisher: Teachers College Press.

Cross References: Reviews are scheduled for *The Twentieth Mental Measurements Yearbook*. For reviews by Kathleen D. Paget and Gene Schwarting of the revised edition, see 14:133; see also T5:875 (11 references) and T4:833 (7 references); for reviews by Richard Elardo and Cathy Fultz Telzrow of the original version, see 9:365.

---

[696]

Early Childhood Inventory–5.

Purpose: Constructed to assess the "behavioral, affective, and cognitive symptoms of childhood psychiatric disorders."

Population: Ages 3–6.

Publication Dates: 1996–2014.

Acronym: ECI-5.

Scores, 28: AD/HD Inattentive, AD/HD Hyperactive-Impulsive, AD/HD Combined, Oppositional Defiant Disorder, Conduct Disorder, Peer Conflict Scale, Separation Anxiety Disorder, Specific Phobia, Obsessions, Compulsions, Motor Tics, Vocal Tics, Generalized Anxiety Disorder, Selective Mutism, Hair Pulling, Skin Picking, Major Depressive Episode, Persistent Depressive Disorder, Adjustment Disorder, Social Anxiety Disorder, Sleep Problems, Elimination Problems, Posttraumatic Stress Disorder, Feeding Problems, Reactive Attachment Disorder, Disinhibited Social Engagement Disorder, Autistic Disorder (DSM-IV), Asperger's Disorder (DSM-IV).

Administration: Individual.

Forms, 2: Parent Checklist, Teacher Checklist.

Price Data, 2015: $124 per kit including screening manual (2000, 117 pages), norms manual (1997, 184 pages), 25 parent checklists, 25 teacher checklists, 50 parent score sheets, and 50 teacher score sheets; $63 per 50 checklists and score sheets (parent or teacher); $27 per screening manual; $27 per norms manual.

Foreign Language Edition: Spanish edition available.

Time: (10–15) minutes.

Comments: Instrument is designed to correspond to the DSM-5 classification system.

Authors: Kenneth D. Gadow and Joyce Sprafkin.

Publisher: Checkmate Plus, Ltd.

Cross References: For a review by Robert C. Reinehr of the original edition, see 14:134.

---

[697]

Early Childhood Physical Environment Observation Schedules and Rating Scales.

Purpose: "Intended for the systematic assessment of the quality of the physical environment of child care centers and related early childhood environments."

Population: Directors and staff of child care centers, early childhood teachers.

Publication Dates: 1982–1994.

Scores: 9 scales: Early Childhood Teacher Style and Dimensions of Education Rating Scales (Early Childhood Teacher Style Rating Scale, Early Childhood Dimensions of Education Rating Scale, Teacher Style and Dimensions of Education Validity Check), Early Childhood Physical Environment Scales (Pattern 905: Spatial Organization, Pattern 908: Behavior Settings), Playground and Neighborhood Observation Behavior Maps (Playground Observation Behavior Map, Neighborhood Observation Behavior Map, Neighborhood Observation Supplementary Coding Sheet), Environment/Behavior Observation Schedule for Early Childhood Environments.

Administration: Group.

Time: [10–30] minutes per scale.

Comments: For research purposes only; the publisher advised in March 2006 that this test is no longer commercially available; it can be downloaded free of charge from the UW-Milwaukee Golda Meir Library e-reserve and is available in hard copy at that library and the Library of Congress.

Author: Gary T. Moore.

Publisher: Center for Architecture and Urban Planning Research, University of Wisconsin-Milwaukee.

Cross References: For reviews by Lisa G. Bischoff and Patricia B. Keith, see 13:106.

---

[698]

Early Coping Inventory.

Purpose: Measures coping related behaviors.

Population: Mental age 4–36 months.

Publication Date: 1988.

Scores, 4: Sensorimotor Organization, Reactive Behavior, Self-Initiated Behavior, Total.

Administration: Individual.

Price Data, 2015: $60 per starter set including manual and 20 forms; $25 per manual; $42 per 20 forms.

Time: Administration time varies.

Comments: Downward extension of the Coping Inventory (542); ratings of adaptive behavior by an adult.

Authors: Shirley Zeitlin and G. Gordon Williamson with Margery Szczepanski.

Publisher: Scholastic Testing Service, Inc.

Cross References: See T5:878 (1 reference); for reviews by Harlan J. Stientjes and by Logan Wright and Wade L. Hamil, see 11:120.

[699]

Early Intervention Developmental Profile.

Purpose: Designed to yield information for planning comprehensive developmental programs for children with all types of disabilities.

Population: Children who are at developmental ages of 0–36 months.

Publication Dates: 1977–2006.

Scores, 8: Perceptual/Fine Motor, Cognition, Language, Social/Emotional, Self-Care (Feeding, Toileting, Dressing), Gross Motor.

Administration: Individual.

Price Data: Available from publisher.

Time: (50–60) minutes.

Comments: Stimulation activities manual included; see Preschool Developmental Profile (1592) for developmental ages from 36 months to 5 years.

Authors: D. Sue Schafer, Martha S. Moersch, Sally J. Rogers, Diane B. D'Eugenio, Sara L. Brown, Carol M. Donovan, and Eleanor Whiteside Lynch.

Publisher: University of Michigan Press.

Cross References: For reviews by Barbara A. Rothlisberg and Gary J. Stainback, see 13:107 (1 reference); see also T4:835 (1 reference).

[700]

Early Language & Literacy Classroom Observation Tool, K-3, Research Edition.

Purpose: Designed to assess "the quality of both the classroom environment and teachers' practices" for language and literacy instruction.

Population: Kindergarten through third-grade classrooms.

Publication Date: 2008.

Acronym: ELLCO K-3.

Scores, 7: General Classroom Environment (Classroom Structure, Curriculum, Total), Language and Literacy (The Language Environment, Books and Reading, Print and Writing, Total).

Administration: Individual.

Price Data, 2015: $55 per user's guide (100 pages) and set of 5 observation tools; $32 per user's guide; $32 per 5 observation tools.

Time: (210) minutes.

Authors: Miriam W. Smith, Joanne P. Brady, and Nancy Clark-Chiarelli.

Publisher: Paul H. Brookes Publishing Co., Inc.

Cross References: For reviews by Amanda Nolen and Gretchen Owens, see 19:54.

[701]

Early Language & Literacy Classroom Observation Tool, Pre-K.

Purpose: Designed as a way for educators and researchers "to examine the literacy-related features of classrooms."

Population: Center-based classrooms for 3- to 5-year-old children.

Publication Dates: 2008-2012.

Acronym: ELLCO Pre-K.

Scores, 7: General Classroom Environment (Classroom Structure, Curriculum, Total), Language and Literacy (The Language Environment, Books and Book Reading, Print and Early Writing, Total).

Administration: Individual.

Price Data, 2015: $55 per user's guide (101 pages) and 5 observation tools; $32 per 5 observation tools; $32 per user's guide.

Time: (210) minutes.

Authors: Miriam W. Smith, Joanne P. Brady, and Louisa Anastasopoulos.

Publisher: Paul H. Brookes Publishing Co., Inc.

Cross References: For reviews by S. Kathleen Krach and Jeffrey K. Smith, see 19:55.

[702]

Early Language Milestone Scale, Second Edition.

Purpose: To assess speech and language development during infancy and early childhood.

Population: Birth to 36 months.

Publication Dates: 1983–1993.

Acronym: ELM Scale-2.

Scores, 4: Auditory Expressive, Auditory Receptive, Visual, Global Language.

Administration: Individual.

Price Data, 2015: $192 per complete kit including manual (1993, 95 pages), object kit, and 100 records; $72 per manual; $67 per 100 record forms; $63 per object kit.

Time: (1–10) minutes.

Author: James Coplan.

Publisher: PRO-ED.

Cross References: See T5:880 (1 reference) for reviews by Philip Backlund and Sherwyn Morreale and by Betsy Waterman, see 13:108; for a review by Ruth M. Noyce of an earlier edition, see 10:99 (2 references).

[703]
Early Literacy Skills Assessment.
Purpose: "Designed to provide preschool programs and teachers with an authentic and meaningful way to assess young children's early literacy skills."
Population: Ages 3-5 years.
Publication Dates: 2005–2007.
Acronym: ELSA.
Scores: 12 scores in 4 areas: Comprehension (Prediction, Retelling, Connection to Real Life), Phonological Awareness (Rhyming, Segmentation, Phonemic Awareness), Alphabetic Principle (Sense of Word, Alphabet Letter Recognition, Letter-Sound Correspondence), Concepts About Print (Orientation, Story Beginning, Direction of Text).
Administration: Individual.
Price Data, 2015: $149.95 per complete kit including 2 copies of Violet's Adventure or Dante Grows Up, user guide (48 pages), 60 score sheets, 60 child summary forms, 12 class summary forms, and 60 family report forms; $149.95 per Spanish version complete kit including 2 copies of La Aventura de Violeta or El Cambio en Dante, user guide, 60 score sheets, 60 child summary forms, 12 class summary forms, and 60 family report forms; $39.95 per Violet's Adventure or La Aventura de Violeta; $39.95 per Dante Grows Up or El Cambio en Dante; $29.97 per DVD Scoring the ELSA: Establishing Reliability; $49.95 per ELSA Reports on CD-ROM, which allows user to enter score sheet results to automatically create child, class and family reports.
Foreign Language Edition: Spanish edition (2006) available.
Time: (15-20) minutes; (20–25) minutes for Spanish edition.
Author: Andrea DeBruin-Parecki.
Publisher: High/Scope Educational Research Foundation.
Cross References: For a review by Rick Eigenbrood, see 17:62.

[704]
Early Math Diagnostic Assessment.
Purpose: Designed to "screen and identify children at risk for math difficulties."
Population: Prekindergarten to Grade 3.
Publication Date: 2002.
Acronym: EMDA.
Scores: 2 subtests: Math Reasoning, Numerical Operations.
Administration: Individual.
Price Data, 2015: $254 per complete kit including examiner's manual (84 pages), stimulus book, 25 record forms, 25 response booklets, and 30 "Thumbs Up" worm stickers; $47 per examiner's manual; $139.40 per stimulus book; $54.35 per 25 record forms; $49 per 25 response booklets.

Time: (20–30) minutes.
Comments: Items selected to "address mathematical domains identified by" the Principles and Standards for School Mathematics (2002) set forth by the National Council of Teachers of Mathematics.
Author: The Psychological Corporation.
Publisher: Pearson.
Cross References: For reviews by Mark J. Gierl and Xuan Tan and by Arturo Olivarez, Jr., see 16:81.

[705]
Early Memories Procedure.
Purpose: "Method of exploring personality organization, especially current life concerns, based on an individual's memory of the past."
Population: Ages 10 and over with at least a fourth-grade reading level.
Publication Dates: 1989–1992.
Scores: No scores.
Administration: Group.
Price Data: Available from publisher.
Time: (90–240) minutes.
Comments: Instrument may be interpreted according to a Freudian, Adlerian, Ego-Psychological, or Cognitive-Perceptual model.
Author: Arnold R. Bruhn.
Publisher: Arnold R. Bruhn and Associates.
Cross References: For reviews by Karl R. Hanes and LeAdelle Phelps, see 13:109; see also T4:840 (1 reference).

[706]
Early Reading Assessment.
Purpose: Designed to identify "young children who are significantly behind their age mates in print knowledge and early reading skills."
Population: Ages 4 through 7.
Publication Date: 2012.
Acronym: ERA.
Scores, 6: Early Reading Index (Written Word Vocabulary, Rapid Orthographic Naming, Silent Orthographic Efficiency, Total), Phonological Awareness, Receptive Vocabulary.
Administration: Individual.
Price Data, 2016: $275 per complete kit including examiner's manual (71 pages), picture book, 25 examiner record forms, rapid orthographic naming stimulus card, 25 silent orthographic efficiency student response forms; $91 per manual; $57 per 25 examiner record forms; $31 per 25 silent orthographic efficiency student response forms; $95 per picture book; $28 per stimulus card.
Time: [10-15] minutes.
Comments: Phonological Awareness and Receptive Vocabulary are supplemental subtests.
Authors: Donald D. Hammill, Nils A. Pearson, Wayne P. Hresko, and John J. Hoover.
Publisher: Hammill Institute on Disabilities.

Cross References: Reviews are scheduled for *The Twentieth Mental Measurements Yearbook.*

[707]

Early Reading Diagnostic Assessment—Second Edition.

Purpose: Designed to evaluate "the essential components of reading defined by Reading First—phonemic awareness, phonics, fluency, vocabulary and comprehension."

Population: Grades K–3.

Publication Dates: 2002–2003.

Acronym: ERDA Second Edition.

Administration: Individual.

Levels, 4: Grades K, 1, 2, and 3.

Price Data: 2015: $385.40 per kit (Grade K, 1, 2, or 3); $64 per technical manual; $46 per administration manual; $103.50 per 25 record forms (Grade K, 1, 2, or 3).

Author: The Psychological Corporation.

Publisher: Pearson.

a) GRADE K.

Population: Kindergarten.

Scores, 11: Letter Recognition, Story Retell, Phonological Awareness (Rhyming, Phonemes, Syllables, Composite), Vocabulary (Receptive, Expressive, Composite), Reading Comprehension, Passage Fluency.

Time: (65–75) minutes.

b) GRADE 1.

Population: Grade 1.

Scores, 14: Word Reading, Pseudoword Decoding, Letter Recognition, Listening Comprehension, Phonological Awareness (Phonemes, Rimes, Syllables, Composite), Reading Comprehension, Vocabulary (Receptive, Expressive, Word Opposites, Composite), Passage Fluency.

Time: (90–95) minutes.

c) GRADE 2.

Population: Grade 2.

Scores, 23: Brief Vocabulary (Receptive, Expressive, Composite), Reading Comprehension, Listening Comprehension, Phonological Awareness (Phonemes, Rimes, Syllables, Comprehension), Word Reading, Pseudoword Decoding, Rapid Automatic Naming (Letters, Words, Digits, Words and Digits, Composite), Full Vocabulary (Brief Vocabulary Composite, Synonyms, Word Definitions, Multiple Meanings, Composite), Passage Fluency (Narrative, Informational).

Time: (110) minutes.

d) GRADE 3.

Population: Grade 3.

Scores, 23: Same as Grade 2.

Time: (110) minutes.

Cross References: For reviews by Marie Miller-Whitehead and Steven R. Shaw, see 16:82.

[708]

Early School Personality Questionnaire.

Purpose: Measures personality dimensions of young children; useful in the treatment of emotional and conduct problems in schools and clinical settings.

Population: Ages 6–8

Publication Date: 1966.

Acronym: ESPQ.

Scores, 17: 13 Primary Factors (Warmth, Abstract Thinking, Emotional Stability, Excitability, Dominance, Enthusiasm, Conformity, Boldness, Sensitivity, Withdrawal, Shrewdness, Apprehension, Tension), 4 Second-Order Factors (Extraversion, Anxiety, Tough Poise, Independence).

Administration: Group or individual.

Price Data: Available from publisher.

Time: (30–50) minutes for each of two parts (untimed).

Authors: Richard W. Coan and Raymond B. Cattell.

Publisher: Institute for Personality and Ability Testing, Inc. (IPAT)

Cross References: See T4:843 (3 references and T3:772 (4 references); for reviews by Jacob O. Sines and Robert L. Thorndike, see 8:540 (8 references); see also T2:1163 (3 references); for a review by Lovick C. Miller, see 7:71 (8 references); see also P:66 (7 references).

[709]

Early Screening Inventory—Revised [2008 Edition].

Purpose: Designed to identify children at risk for possible school failure.

Population: Ages 3-0 to 5-11.

Publication Dates: 1976–2008.

Acronym: ESI-R.

Scores, 3: Visual-Motor/Adaptive, Language and Cognition, Gross Motor.

Administration: Individual.

Levels, 2: Preschool (3 to 4 1/2 years old), Kindergarten (4 1/2 to 6 years old).

Price Data, 2015: $153.20 per preschool kit including examiner's manual, screening materials, 30 score sheets, and 30 parent questionnaires in carry bag; $149.45 per kindergarten kit; $65.60 per examiner's manual; $36.90 per 30 score sheets (preschool or kindergarten); $31.05 per 30 parent questionnaires.

Foreign Language Edition: Spanish versions available for score sheets, parent questionnaire, and the administration and scoring chapter of the manual.

Time: (15–20) minutes.

Comments: Originally introduced as the Eliot-Pearson Screening Inventory.

Authors: Samuel J. Meisels, Dorothea B. Marsden, Martha Stone Wiske, and Laura W. Henderson.

Publisher: Pearson.

Cross References: For reviews by Ernest Kimmel and Kathleen D. Paget of the 1997 edition, see 14:135; see also T5:889 (1 reference); for reviews by Denise M. Dezolt and Kevin Menefee of an earlier edition, see 11:122 (1 reference).

[710]

Early Screening Profiles.

Purpose: A comprehensive, brief, multidimensional screening instrument for children.
Population: Ages 2-0 to 6-11.
Publication Date: 1990.
Acronym: ESP.
Scores: 3 Profile Scores: Cognitive/Language, Motor, Self-Help/Social (Parent or Teacher), and 4 Survey Scores: Articulation, Home, Behavior, Health History.
Administration: Individual.
Price Data, 2015: $399.75 per complete kit including manual (297 pages), motor administration manual (16 pages), test easel, 25 test records, 25 Self-Help/Social Profile Questionnaires, 25 Score Summaries, Sample Home/Health History Survey, tape measure, beads; $46.15 per 25 test records; $25.60 per 25 Self-Help/Social Profile questionnaires; $25.65 per 25 Home/Health History surveys; $17.45 per 25 score summary forms; $88.65 per manual; $15.90 per motor administration manual; $148.65 per training video.
Time: (15–40) minutes.
Comments: Two levels of scoring: Level I scores are 6 "screening indexes" and 3 descriptive categories; Level II scores are standard scores, percentile ranks, normal curve equivalents (NCEs), stanines, and age equivalents; ecological assessment with ratings by parents and teachers as well as direct assessment of the child; previously listed as AGS Early Screening Profiles.
Authors: Patti L. Harrison (coordinating author and manual author), Alan S. Kaufman (Cognitive/Language Profile), Nadeen L. Kaufman (Cognitive/Language Profile), Robert H. Bruininks (Motor Profile), John Rynders (Motor Profile), Steven Ilmer (Motor Profile), Sara S. Sparrow (Self-Help/Social Profile), and Domenic V. Cicchetti (Self-Help/Social Profile).
Publisher: Pearson.
Cross References: See T5:124 (1 reference); for reviews by David W. Barnett and Cathy Telzrow, see 12:24 (1 reference); see also T4:134 (2 references).

[711]

Early Speech Perception Test [2012 Update].

Purpose: Designed as a battery of tests of speech perception for children who are profoundly deaf for use in establishing objectives for auditory training and/or measuring effectiveness of a hearing aid or cochlear implant in terms of its impact on speech perception abilities.
Population: Young profoundly hearing-impaired children who have limited vocabulary and language skills.
Publication Dates: 1990-2012.
Acronym: ESP.
Scores, 3: Pattern Perception, Spondee Identification, Monosyllable Identification.
Subtests, 2: Pattern Perception, Word Identification.
Administration: Individual.

Forms, 2: Standard, Low-Verbal.
Price Data, 2016: $250 per complete kit including manual (2012, 44 pages), 25 Standard Forms, 25 Low-Verbal Forms, picture cards, CD, and box of toys; $15 per 25 forms (Standard or Low-Verbal).
Time: (20) minutes.
Comments: Test unchanged from original version; manual has been updated, and speech stimuli are now on single compact disc.
Authors: Jean S. Moog and Ann E. Geers (original test); Lisa Davidson, Marie Richter, Jennifer Manley, and Kim Readmond (2012 manual and CD).
Publisher: CID - Central Institute for the Deaf.
Cross References: See T5:891 (1 reference); for a review by Arlene E. Carney of the original version, see 12:128.

[712]

Earning Capacity Assessment Form-Second Edition.

Purpose: Designed to "facilitate the systematic analysis and appraisal of loss of earning capacity."
Population: Birth to 99.
Publication Date: 2010.
Acronym: ECAF-2.
Scores: 1 rating: Impairment to Earning Capacity.
Administration: Individual.
Price Data, 2015: $100 per complete kit, including manual (46 pages) and 25 rating forms; $38 per 25 rating forms; $64 per manual.
Time: [5-10] minutes.
Author: Michael Shahnasarian.
Publisher: Psychological Assessment Resources.
Cross References: For reviews by Martin W. Anderson and Gary J. Dean, see 19:56.

[713]

EARS® Evaluation of Auditory Responses to Speech.

Purpose: Designed as a battery of tests to "evaluate auditory perception development in severely and profoundly hearing-impaired children who have received cochlear implants, to provide support for device fitting and the rehabilitation of these children, and to provide an instrument for the long-term assessment of children with cochlear implants."
Administration: Individual.
Levels, 3: EARS, LittlEARS, TeenEARS.
Price Data: Available from publisher.
Publisher: MED-EL.
  a) EARS®
  Population: Children ages 3 and older who have received cochlear implants.
  Publication Date: 2012.
  Acronym: EARS.

Scores, 20: Listening Progress Profile, Monosyllabic Trochee Polysyllabic (MTP) 3 Patterns, MTP 3 Words, MTP 6 Patterns, MTP 6 Words, MTP 12 Patterns, MTP 12 Words, Closed-Set Words 4, Closed-Set Words 12, Closed-Set Sentence Test A, Closed-Set Sentence Test B1, Closed-Set Sentence Test B2, Closed-Set Sentence Test C, Open-Set Words: Phoneme, Open-Set Words: Word, Glendonald Auditory Screening Procedure, Meaningful Auditory Integration Scale: Parent, Meaningful Auditory Integration Scale: Teacher, Meaningful Use of Speech Scale: Parent, Meaningful Use of Speech Scale: Teacher.

Subtests, 7: Listening Progress Profile, Monosyllabic Trochee Polysyllabic Word Test, Monosyllable Closed-Set Test, Common Objects Token Test, Tyler Holstad Closed-Set Sentence Test, Monosyllable Open-Set Test, Glendonald Auditory Screening Procedure, plus Meaningful Auditory Integration Scale and Meaningful Use of Speech Scale.

Foreign Language Editions: Available in Arabic, Bulgarian, Croatian, Dutch, Finnish, French, German, Greek, Hungarian, Italian, Korean, Malay, Mandarin, Polish, Portuguese, Romanian, Russian, Spanish, Tagalog, Tamil, and Turkish.

Time: (5-40) minutes per subtest.

Comments: The test publisher suggests the use of different subtests at different time intervals (i.e., pre-operative, near initial fitting, 1 month, 3 months, 6 months, 12 months, 18 months, yearly).

Author: Diane Allum-Mecklenburg.

b) LittlEARS® AUDITORY QUESTIONNAIRE.

Purpose: "Designed to reflect the most important milestones of preverbal auditory behavior ... emphasizing the response to sounds, particularly the response to linguistic stimuli, and takes into account infants' preference for these stimuli."

Population: Ages 3 years and younger.

Publication Date: 2011.

Acronym: LEAQ.

Score: Total score only.

Foreign Language Editions: Available in Afrikaans, Arabic, Bosnian, Bulgarian, Croatian, Finnish, Flemish, French, German, Greek, Gujarati, Hebrew, Hindi, Hungarian, Indonesian, Italian, Japanese, Korean, Mandarin, Marathi, Norwegian, Polish, Portuguese, Quebecois, Romanian, Russian, Serbian, Slovak, Slovenian, Spanish, Swedish, Tagalog and Turkish.

Time: (10) minutes.

Authors: Frans Coninx, Viktor Weichbold, Labriana Tsiakpini, and Heike Kühn-Inacker.

c) TeenEARS®.

Purpose: Designed as a battery of seven tests and one questionnaire covering "differing levels of language skills, as well as auditory skills and psycho-social issues."

Population: Teenagers who have cochlear implants.

Publication Date: 2008.

Subtests, 7: Listening Skills Screening, Common Phrases Test, Categories of Auditory Performance, Speech Intelligibility Rating, Paediatric Telephone Profile, 1990 UCH Environmental Sounds Test, TesTrax, plus Manchester Teens Questionnaire.

Foreign Language Editions: Available in French, German, and Spanish.

Time: (5-20) minutes per subtest.

Comments: May be used "as a follow-on from the EARS® test battery, or as a stand-alone assessment battery for newly implanted teens."

Authors: Ilona Anderson, Lucy Phillips, Lynne Roberts, Lyn Jamieson, Anne Costa, and Sarie Cross.

Cross References: Reviews are scheduled for *The Twentieth Mental Measurements Yearbook.*

[714]

easyCBM.

Purpose: An online system designed to provide "reading and math Benchmark and Progress Monitoring assessments and reports for districts, schools, and teachers."

Population: Students in kindergarten through eighth grade.

Publication Date: 2014.

Scores, 14: Letter Names, Letter Sounds, Phoneme Segmentation, Word Reading Fluency, Passage Reading Fluency, Vocabulary, Multiple Choice Reading Comprehension, Common Core State Standards (CCSS) Reading, CCSS Math, National Council of Teachers of Mathematics (NCTM) Math, Spanish Measures (Syllable Segmenting, Syllable Reading, Word Reading, Sentence Reading).

Administration: Individual and group.

Price Data, 2015: $4 per individual student license (minimum purchase of 200 licenses as an initial purchase).

Foreign Language Edition: Spanish literacy measures available for kindergarten through second grade; text and audio for CCSS math are also available in Spanish.

Time: Varies by subtest.

Comments: "Individually administered fluency measures are typically administered using paper-and-pencil tests, while the group-administered measures are normally administered online. The (test) publisher recommends administering measures online whenever possible." Paper-and-pencil tests must be computer scored.

Authors: Daniel Anderson, Julie Alonzo, Gerald Tindal, Dan Farley, P. Shawn Irvin, Cheng-Fei Lai, Jessica L. Saven, Kraig A. Wray.

Publisher: Houghton Mifflin Harcourt.

Cross References: Reviews are scheduled for *The Twentieth Mental Measurements Yearbook.*

[715]

Eating Disorder Inventory-3.

Purpose: Designed to "provide a standardized clinical evaluation of symptomatology associated with eating disorders."

Population: Females ages 13 to 53 years.

Publication Dates: 1984–2004.

Acronym: EDI-3.

Administration: Group.

Price Data, 2015: $330 per introductory kit including professional manual (2004, 223 pages), referral form manual (2004, 36 pages), 25 item booklets, 25 answer

sheets, 25 percentile/T-score profile forms, 25 symptom checklists, and 25 referral forms; $310 per software (CD-ROM) with on-screen help and quick start guide.
Author: David M. Garner.
Publisher: Psychological Assessment Resources, Inc.

a) EATING DISORDER INVENTORY-3.
Population: Females ages 13 to 53 years.
Scores, 21: 6 composite scores (Eating Disorder Risk Composite, Ineffectiveness Composite, Interpersonal Problems Composite, Affective Problems Composite, Overcontrol Composite, General Psychological Maladjustment Composite), 12 primary scores (Drive for Thinness, Bulimia, Body Dissatisfaction, Low Self-Esteem, Personal Alienation, Interpersonal Insecurity, Interpersonal Alienation, Interoceptive Deficits, Emotional Dysregulation, Perfectionism, Asceticism, Maturity Fears), 3 response style indicators (Inconsistency, Infrequency, Negative Impression).
Time: (20) minutes.
Comments: Full battery.

b) EATING DISORDER INVENTORY-3 REFERRAL FORM.
Population: Adolescents and adults ages 13 and older.
Acronym: EDI-3 RF.
Scores, 4: Drive for Thinness, Bulimia, Body Dissatisfaction, BMI.
Time: (10) minutes.
Comments: Abbreviated referral form of Eating Disorder Inventory-3 "used to identify individuals who are at risk for eating disorders."

c) EATING DISORDER INVENTORY-3 SYMPTOM CHECKLIST.
Population: Adolescents and adults.
Acronym: EDI-3 SC.
Scores: Frequency ratings.
Time: (10) minutes.
Comments: Symptom checklist used as an aid in the diagnosis of eating disorders.

Cross References: For reviews by Jeffrey A. Atlas and Ashraf Kagee, see 17:64; see also T5:893 (54 references); for reviews by Phillip Ash and Steven Schinke of an earlier edition, see 12:130 (38 references); see also T4:847 (38 references); for a review by Cabrini S. Swassing of an earlier edition, see 10:100 (16 references).

[716]
Eating Inventory.
Purpose: To assess "three dimensions of eating behavior found to be important in recognizing and treating eating-related disorders: cognitive control of eating, disinhibition, and hunger."
Population: Ages 17 and older.
Publication Dates: 1983–1988.
Scores, 3: Cognitive Restraint of Eating, Disinhibition, Hunger.
Administration: Group or individual.
Price Data, 2015: $238 per complete kit including 25 questionnaires, 25 answer sheets, and manual (1988, 37 pages); $114.80 per 25 questionnaires; $114.80 per 25 answer sheets; $123 per manual.

Time: (15–20) minutes.
Authors: Albert J. Stunkard and Samuel Messick.
Publisher: Pearson.
Cross References: For reviews by Lisa Bloom and Sandra D. Haynes, see 13:111 (3 references); see also T4:848 (1 reference).

[717]
Edinburgh Reading Tests.
Purpose: To assess pupil progress in reading.
Population: Ages 7-0 to 9-0, 8-6 to 10-6, 10-0 to 12-6, 12-0 to 16-6.
Publication Dates: 1972–2002.
Administration: Group.
Levels, 4: Stages 1, 2, 3, 4.
Price Data: Available from publisher.
Publisher: Hodder Education [United Kingdom].

a) STAGE 1 [THIRD EDITION].
Population: Ages 7-0 to 9-0.
Publication Dates: 1977–2002.
Scores, 5: Vocabulary, Syntax, Sequences, Comprehension, Total.
Forms, 2: A, B.
Time: (30–55) minutes.
Author: Educational Assessment Unit, University of Edinburgh.

b) STAGE 2 [FOURTH EDITION].
Population: Ages 8-6 to 10-6.
Publication Dates: 1972–2002.
Scores, 5: Vocabulary, Comprehension of Sequences, Use of Context, Comprehension of Essential Ideas, Total.
Time: (40) minutes for part I; (35) minutes for part II.
Author: Educational Assessment Unit, University of Edinburgh.

c) STAGE 3 [FOURTH EDITION].
Population: Ages 10-0 to 12-6.
Publication Dates: 1973–2002.
Scores, 5: Reading for Facts and Comprehension of Sequences, Main Ideas, Comprehension of Points of View, Vocabulary, Total.
Time: (40) minutes for part I; (35) minutes for part II.
Author: Educational Assessment Unit, University of Edinburgh.

d) STAGE 4 [THIRD EDITION].
Population: Ages 11-7 to 16+.
Publication Dates: 1977–2002.
Scores, 6: Skimming, Vocabulary, Reading for Facts, Points of View, Comprehension, Total.
Time: 60(70) minutes.
Author: Educational Assessment Unit, University of Edinburgh.

e) SHORTENED EDINBURGH READING TEST.
Purpose: Designed as a survey and screening instrument of written language attainment.
Population: Ages 10-0 to 11-6.
Scores, 3: Vocabulary, Syntax and Sequence, Comprehension.
Time: (40) minutes.
Comments: Questions selected from items in the full Edinburgh Reading Tests.

Authors: Godfrey Thomson Unit for Educational Research, Moray House Institute of Education, and the Child Health and Education Study, University of Bristol.

Cross References: See T5:901 (2 references) and T4:855 (1 reference); for reviews by Nancy L. Roser and Byron H. Van Roekel of previous editions, see 9:374 (1 reference); see T3:775 (2 references); for reviews by Douglas A. Pidgeon and Earl F. Rankin of the first editions of Stages 2 and 3, see 8:724.

[718]

Educational Development Series.

Purpose: A battery of ability and achievement tests and questions on interests and plans.

Population: Grades K-12.

Publication Dates: 1963-2014.

Acronym: EDS.

Administration: Group.

Price Data: Available from publisher.

Authors: O. F. Anderhalter, R. H. Bauernfeind, V. M. Cashew, Mary E. Greig, Walter M. Lifton, George Mallinson, Jacqueline Mallinson, Joseph F. Papenfuss, and Neil Vail.

Publisher: Scholastic Testing Service, Inc.

a) LEVEL 10G.

Population: Grade K.

Publication Date: 1999.

Scores, 8: Cognitive Skills (Verbal, Nonverbal, Total), Basic Skills (Reading, Language, Mathematics, Total), Battery Average.

Time: (190) minutes in 5 sessions.

b) LEVEL 11J.

Population: Grade 1.

Publication Date: 2013.

Scores, 10: Cognitive Skills (Verbal, Quantitative, Total), Basic Skills (Reading, Language, Mathematics, Total), Science, Social Studies, Battery Average.

Time: (260) minutes in 4 sessions.

c) LEVEL 12J.

Population: Grade 2.

Publication Date: 2013.

Scores, 10: Cognitive Skills (Verbal, Quantitative, Total), Basic Skills (Reading, Language Arts, Mathematics, Total), Science, Social Studies, Battery Average.

Time: (260) minutes in 4 sessions.

d) LEVEL 13J.

Population: Grade 3.

Publication Date: 2013.

Scores, 13: Cognitive Skills (Verbal, Quantitative, Total), Basic Skills (Reading, Language Arts, Mathematics, Total), Career Interests, School Plans, School Interests, Science, Social Studies, Battery Average.

Time: (320) minutes in 3 sessions.

e) LEVEL 14J.

Population: Grade 4.

Publication Date: 2013.

Scores, 14: Cognitive Skills (Verbal, Quantitative, Total), Basic Skills (Reading, Language Arts, Mathematics, Total), Career Interests, School Plans, School Interests, Science, Social Studies, Battery Average, Career Interests, School Plans, School Interests.

Time: (335) minutes in 3 sessions.

f) LEVEL 15J.

Population: Grade 5.

Publication Date: 2013.

Scores, 14: Same as for e above.

Time: (335) minutes in 3 sessions.

g) LEVEL 15K.

Population: Grade 6.

Publication Date: 2013.

Scores, 14: Same as for e above.

Time: (335) minutes in 3 sessions.

h) LEVEL 16K.

Population: Grade 7.

Publication Date: 2013.

Scores, 14: Same as for e above.

Time: (335) minutes in 3 sessions.

i) LEVEL 16K.

Population: Grade 8.

Publication Date: 2013.

Scores, 14: Same as for e above.

Time: (335) minutes in 3 sessions.

j) LEVEL 17J.

Population: Grade 9.

Publication Date: 2010.

Scores, 14: Same as for e above.

Time: (335) minutes in 3 sessions.

k) LEVEL 17K.

Population: Grade 10/11.

Publication Date: 2010.

Details: Same as for j above.

l) LEVEL 18J.

Population: Grade 11/12.

Publication Date: 2010.

Details: Same as for j above.

m) LEVEL 18K.

Population: Grade 12.

Publication Date: 2014.

Details: Same as for j above.

Time: (335) minutes in 3 sessions.

Cross References: See T4:858 (2 references); for a review by Esther E. Diamond of the 1992 edition, see 9:376; see also T3:2325 (1 reference); for reviews by Samuel T. Mayo and William A. Mehrens of forms copyrighted 1976 and earlier see 8:27; see also T2:33 (1 reference); for a review by Robert D. North of forms copyrighted 1968 and earlier see 7:22.

[719]

Ego Function Assessment.

Purpose: Designed as a "mental status examination" to assess ego function.

Population: Adults.

Publication Date: 1989.

Acronym: EFA.

Scores, 12: Reality Testing, Judgment, Sense of Reality, Regulation and Control of Drives, Object Relations, Thought Processes, Adaptive Regression in the Service of the Ego, Defensive Functions, Stimulus Barrier, Autonomous Functions, Synthetic Functions, Mastery-Competence.

Administration: Individual.
Price Data, 2015: $6.99 per manual (64 pages); $30 per 10 blanks.
Time: Administration time not reported.
Author: Leopold Bellak.
Publisher: C.P.S. Publishing, LLC
Cross References: For reviews by Beth Doll and Samuel Juni, see 13:112.

[720]

Eidetic Parents Test.

Purpose: To provide stimuli meant to arouse eidetic images of parents to aid in exploring emotional attachments that affect current functioning.
Population: Clinical patients and marriage and family counselees.
Publication Date: 1972.
Acronym: EPT.
Scores: No scores; verbal reporting by individuals of subjective visual images (called eidetics) of increasingly surrealistic situations.
Administration: Individual.
Price Data, 2016: $35 per hard cover; $15 per spiral-bound paperback.
Time: (60) minutes for brief report; "many hours" for comprehensive report.
Author: Akhter Ahsen.
Publisher: Brandon House, Inc. [Eidetic Image Psychology, distributor].
Cross References: For additional information and a review by Charles Warnath and excerpted reviews by Gregory Sarmousakis, Barry Bricklin, and Manas Raychaudhuri, see 8:546 (8 references).

[721]

Einstein Evaluation of School-Related Skills.

Purpose: "To identify children who are at risk for, or are experiencing, learning difficulties; and who therefore should be referred for a comprehensive evaluation."
Population: Grades K–5.
Publication Date: 1988.
Administration: Individual.
Levels, 6: Kindergarten, First Grade, Second Grade, Third Grade, Fourth Grade, Fifth Grade.
Price Data: Available from publisher.
Time: (10) minutes.
Authors: Ruth L. Gottesman and Frances M. Cerullo.
Publisher: Slosson Educational Publications, Inc.
  a) KINDERGARTEN LEVEL.
  Scores, 5: Language/Cognition, Letter Recognition, Auditory Memory, Arithmetic, Visual-Motor Integration.
  b) FIRST GRADE LEVEL.
  Scores, 7: Language/Cognition, Word Recognition, Oral Reading, Reading Comprehension, Auditory Memory, Arithmetic, Visual-Motor Integration.
  c) SECOND GRADE LEVEL.
  Scores: Same as *b* above.

  d) THIRD GRADE LEVEL.
  Scores: Same as *b* above.
  e) FOURTH GRADE LEVEL.
  Scores: Same as *b* above.
  f) FIFTH GRADE LEVEL.
  Scores: Same as *b* above.
Cross References: See T5:916 (1 reference) and T4:871 (1 reference); for a review by Gloria A. Galvin, see 11:126 (1 reference).

[722]

Ekwall/Shanker Reading Inventory—Third Edition.

Purpose: "Designed to assess the full range of students' reading abilities."
Population: Grades 1–9.
Publication Dates: 1979–1993.
Acronym: ESRI.
Administration: Individual.
Price Data: Available from publisher.
Authors: Eldon E. Ekwall and James L. Shanker.
Publisher: Pearson Education. [Efforts to obtain updated information from the test publisher were unsuccessful. An updated edition of this test appears on the test publisher's website.]
  a) GRADED WORD LIST.
  Purpose: "To obtain a quick estimate of the student's independent, instructional, and frustration reading levels."
  Acronym: GWL.
  Scores, 3: Independent Reading Level, Instructional Reading Level, Frustration Level.
  Time: (5–10) minutes.
  b) ORAL AND SILENT READING.
  Purpose: To obtain an assessment of the student's independent, instructional, and frustration reading levels in oral and silent reading.
  Scores, 3: 3 scores (Independent Reading Level, Instructional Reading Level, Frustration Level) in each of two areas (Oral, Silent Reading).
  Time: (10–30) minutes.
  c) LISTENING COMPREHENSION.
  Purpose: "To obtain the level at which a student can understand material when it is read to him or her."
  Score: Listening Comprehension Level.
  Time: (5–10) minutes.
  d) THE BASIC SIGHT WORDS AND PHRASES TEST.
  Purpose: To determine basic sight words and basic sight word phrases that can be recognized and pronounced instantly by the student.
  Scores, 2: Basic Sight Words, Basic Sight Phrases.
  Time: (5–12) minutes.
  e) LETTER KNOWLEDGE.
  Purpose: "To determine if the student can associate the letter symbols with the letter names."
  Scores, 2: Letters (Auditory), Letters (Visual).
  Time: Administration time not reported.
  f) PHONICS.
  Purpose: "To determine if the student has mastered letter-sound (phonics)."

Scores, 9: Initial Consonants, Initial Blends and Digraphs, Ending Sounds, Vowels, Phonograms, Blending, Substitution, Vowel Pronunciation, Application in Context.
Time: Administration time not reported.
g) STRUCTURAL ANALYSIS.
Purpose: "To determine if the student can use structural analysis skills to aid in decoding unknown words."
Scores, 10: Hearing Word Parts, Inflectional Endings, Prefixes, Suffixes, Compound Words, Affixes, Syllabication, Application in Context (Part I, Part II, Total).
Time: Administration time not reported.
h) KNOWLEDGE OF CONTRACTIONS TEST.
Purpose: "To determine if the student has knowledge of contractions."
Scores, 3: Number of Words Pronounced, Number of Words Known, Total.
Time: Administration time not reported.
i) EL PASO PHONICS SURVEY.
Purpose: "To determine if the student has the ability to pronounce and blend 90 phonic elements."
Scores, 4: Initial Consonant Sounds, Ending Consonant, Initial Consonant Clusters, Vowels, Vowel Teams, and Special Letter Combinations.
Time: Administration time not reported.
j) QUICK SURVEY WORD LIST.
Purpose: "To determine quickly if the student has mastered phonics and structural analysis."
Score: Comments.
Time: Administration time not reported.
k) READING INTEREST SURVEY.
Purpose: "To assess the student's attitude toward reading and school, areas of reading interest, reading experiences, and conditions affecting reading in the home."
Score: Comments.
Time: Administration time not reported.
Cross References: For reviews by Koressa Kutsick Malcolm and by Blaine R. Worthen and Richard R. Sudweeks, see 13:113 (2 references); see also T4:872 (3 references); for reviews by Lynn S. Fuchs and Mary Beth Marr of an earlier edition, see 9:380.

[723]

ElecTest.

Purpose: For selecting electrical repair and maintenance candidates.
Population: Applicants and incumbents for jobs requiring practical electrical knowledge and skills.
Publication Dates: 1997-2014.
Scores, 10: Motors, Digital & Analog, Electronics, Schematics & Print Reading and Control Circuits, Basic AC/DC Theory and Electrical Maintenance, Computers & PLC and Test Instruments, Power Supplies, Power Distribution and Construction & Installation, Mechanical and Hand & Power Tools, Total.
Administration: Group.
Forms: Parallel forms available.
Price Data, 2015: $24 per consumable self-scoring test booklet; $26 per online test administration (minimum order of 20); $24.95 per manual (2014, 28 pages).

Foreign Language Edition: Available in Spanish.
Time: (60-70) minutes.
Comments: Self-scoring instrument; online version available; test publisher advises changes in form names indicate minor revisions and updating.
Author: Roland T. Ramsay.
Publisher: Ramsay Corporation.
Cross References: For a review by John K. Hawley of the ElecTest (Form AR-C & Form B), see 19:57; for a review by Eugene P. Sheehan of the ElecTest (Form A, Form A-C, & Form B), see 18:47.

[724]

Electrical Aptitude Test (Form EA2-C and Form BR).

Purpose: For evaluating electrical aptitude skills.
Population: Applicants for jobs that require the ability to learn electrical skills.
Publication Dates: 2003–2014.
Scores: Total score only for 6 areas: Mathematics, Electrical Concepts, Electrical Schematics, Process Flow, Signal Flow, Electrical Sequences.
Administration: Group.
Price Data, 2015: $24 per consumable self-scoring test booklet or $26 per online test administration (minimum order of 20); $24.95 per manual (2014, 19 pages).
Foreign Language Edition: Available in Spanish.
Time: (18) minutes.
Comments: Self-scoring instrument; available for online test administration; Form BR is an alternate equivalent of Form EA2-C.
Author: Roland T. Ramsay.
Publisher: Ramsay Corporation.
Cross References: For a review by Martin W. Anderson of an earlier form (Form EA-R-C), see 17:65.

[725]

Electrical Maintenance Trainee–Form UKE-1RC.

Purpose: Designed for selecting or evaluating electrical trainees with one year of training or experience.
Population: Applicants for jobs requiring electrical knowledge and skills.
Publication Dates: 1991-2013.
Scores, 12: Motors, Digital and Analog Electronics, Schematics and Electrical Print Reading, Control, Power Supplies, Basic AC/DC Theory, Construction Installation and Distribution, Test Instruments, Mechanical/Equipment Operation/Hand and Power Tools, Computers and PLC, Electrical Maintenance, Total.
Administration: Group.
Price Data, 2015: $24 per consumable self-scoring test booklet; $26 per online administration, scoring, and reports (20 minimum); $24.95 per manual (2013, 22 pages).

Time: (60-70) minutes.
Comments: Self-scoring instrument; available for online test administration.
Author: Roland T. Ramsay.
Publisher: Ramsay Corporation.
Cross References: For reviews by Eleanor E. Sanford-Moore and Eugene P. Sheehan, see 19:58; for a review by David C. Roberts of an earlier edition, see 13:114.

[726]

ElectronTest.

Purpose: Designed for selecting or evaluating candidates for industrial electronics jobs.
Population: Electronic technicians and applicants for electronics jobs.
Publication Dates: 1987-2013.
Scores, 7: Digital & Analog Electronics, AC/DC Theory & Schematics, Motors/Regulators/Electronic Equipment/Power Distribution, Power Supplies, Test Instruments, Computers and PLC, Total.
Administration: Group.
Price Data, 2015: $24 per consumable self-scoring test booklet or $26 per online test administration (minimum 20); $24.95 per manual.
Time: (60-70) minutes.
Comments: Test publisher advises changes in form names indicate minor revisions and updating.
Author: Roland T. Ramsay.
Publisher: Ramsay Corporation.
Cross References: For reviews by Phillip L. Ackerman and Paul Muchinsky of Form HR-C, see 19:59; for reviews by K. Hattrup and Eugene (Geno) Pichette of an earlier edition, see 13:116.

[727]

Emergenetics Profile.

Purpose: Designed as a "business personality tool" to measure "thinking and behavioral preferences."
Population: Adults.
Publication Date: 2014.
Scores, 7: 4 Thinking Attributes (Analytical, Structural, Social, Conceptual), 3 Behavioral Attributes (Expressiveness, Assertiveness, Flexibility).
Administration: Individual.
Price Data: Available from publisher.
Foreign Language Editions: Translations available in Bahasa (Indonesia and Malaysia), Chinese (Simplified and Traditional), Danish, Dutch, Finnish, French, German, Italian, Japanese, Korean, Norwegian, Portuguese, Romanian, Russian, Spanish, Swedish, and Thai.
Time: (20) minutes.
Comments: Administered online.
Authors: R. Wendell Williams and Geil Browning.
Publisher: Emergenetics International.
Cross References: Reviews are scheduled for *The Twentieth Mental Measurements Yearbook*.

[728]

Emo Questionnaire.

Purpose: "Designed to assess an individual's personal-emotional adjustment."
Population: Clinical and research applications.
Publication Dates: 1958–1998.
Scores: 10 diagnostic dimensions: Rationalization, Inferiority Feelings, Hostility, Depression, Fear and Anxiety, Organic Reaction, Projection, Unreality, Sex Problems, Withdrawal, 3 key adjustment factors: Internal, External, Somatic, and 4 normative level adjustment factors: Internal, External, Somatic, General.
Administration: Individual or group.
Forms, 2: A, B.
Price Data: Available from publisher.
Time: No limit (approximately 20 minutes).
Authors: George O. Baehr and Melany E. Baehr.
Publisher: General Dynamics Information Technology.
Cross References: See T5:927 (1 reference) and T4:883 (1 reference); for reviews by Allan L. LaVoie and Paul McReynolds, see 9:383; see also T2:1170 (1 reference); for reviews by Bertram D. Cohen and W. Grant Dahlstrom, see 6:90 (1 reference).

[729]

Emotional and Behavior Problem Scale—Second Edition.

Purpose: "Developed to contribute to the early identification and service delivery for students with behavior disorders/emotional disturbance."
Population: Ages 5–18.
Publication Dates: 1989–2001.
Acronym: EBPS-2.
Scores, 10: Theoretical (Learning Problems, Interpersonal Relations, Inappropriate Behavior, Unhappiness/Depression, Physical Symptoms/Fears), Empirical (Social Aggression/Conduct Disorder, Social-Emotional Withdrawal/Depression, Learning/Comprehension Disorder, Avoidance/Unresponsiveness, Aggressive/Self-Destructive).
Administration: Individual.
Price Data: Available from publisher.
Time: (15) minutes.
Comments: Ratings by teachers and/or parents/guardians. The test publisher has indicated there is a newer edition of this test; description will be updated when complete test materials are received.
Authors: Stephen B. McCarney and Tamara J. Arthaud.
Publisher: Hawthorne Educational Services, Inc.
Cross References: For reviews by Adrienne Garro and Judy Oehler-Stinnett, see 16:83; for reviews by J. Jeffrey Grill and Robert C. Reinehr of the original edition, see 12:134.

[730]
Emotional and Behavioral Screener.
Purpose: Designed to use "teachers' ratings to identify students at risk for emotional and behavioral problems."
Population: Students ages 5 through 17.
Publication Date: 2013.
Acronym: EBS.
Score: Total score only.
Administration: Individual.
Forms, 2: Rating Form, Decision Summary Form.
Price Data, 2014: $125 per complete kit including examiner's manual (37 pages), 50 rating forms, and 50 decision summary forms; $55 per manual; $35 per 50 rating forms; $35 per 50 decision summary forms.
Time: [1-2] minutes.
Comments: "Rater should be a classroom, special, or remedial teacher or related professional who is well acquainted with the student's behavior."
Authors: Douglas Cullinan and Michael H. Epstein.
Publisher: PRO-ED.
Cross References: Reviews are scheduled for T*he Twentieth Mental Measurements Yearbook.*

[731]
Emotional and Social Competence Inventory.
Purpose: "Designed to assess emotional intelligence (the ability to recognize and manage emotions [yours and others])."
Population: Coaches, executive coaches, mid to senior level managers.
Publication Dates: 1999–2002.
Acronym: ECI.
Scores: 4 clusters, 18 competencies: Self-Awareness (Emotional Self-Awareness, Accurate Self-Assessment, Self-Confidence); Self-Management (Emotional Self-Control, Transparency, Adaptability, Achievement Orientation, Initiative, Optimism); Social Awareness (Empathy, Organizational Awareness, Service Orientation); Relationship Management (Developing Others, Inspirational Leadership, Influence, Change Catalyst, Conflict Management, Teamwork & Collaboration).
Administration: Group or individual.
Price Data, 2016: $3,500 Accreditation (2-day program); $2,000 Accreditation (one-day master class for participants already accredited in a multirater tool); once accredited online assessments are $110 per participant for self-service and $235 per participant for full-service (this includes unlimited raters); online development tool available for $75 annual subscription.
Time: (50–60) minutes.
Comments: Accreditation required; multirater assessment to be administered by accredited consultants only; accreditation programs run approximately every other month; previously titled Emotional Competence Inventory.
Authors: Daniel Goleman, Richard Boyatzis, and the Hay Group.
Publisher: Hay Group.
Cross References: For reviews by T. Steuart Watson and Tonya S. Watson, see 17:66.

[732]
Emotional Behavioral Checklist.
Purpose: To assess an individual's overt emotional behavior.
Population: Ages 16 and over.
Publication Date: 1986.
Acronym: EBC.
Scores, 8: Impulsivity-Frustration, Anxiety, Depression-Withdrawal, Socialization, Self-Concept, Aggression, Reality Disorientation, Total EBC.
Administration: Individual.
Manual: No manual.
Price Data, 2016: $55 per 25 checklists.
Time: Administration time not reported.
Comments: Included in the Auxiliary Component of the McCarron-Dial System (1225).
Authors: Jack G. Dial, Carolyn Mezger, Theresa Massey, and Lawrence T. McCarron.
Publisher: McCarron-Dial Systems, Inc.
Cross References: For reviews by William A. Stock and Hoi K. Suen, see 11:130.

[733]
Emotional Disturbance Decision Tree.
Purpose: To "assist in the identification of children who qualify for the Special Education category of Emotional Disturbance based on federal criteria."
Population: Ages 5-18.
Publication Date: 2007.
Acronym: EDDT.
Scores, 10: Inability to Build or Maintain Relationships Scale, Inappropriate Behaviors or Feelings Scale, Pervasive Mood/Depression Scale, Physical Symptoms or Fears Scale, Emotional Disturbance Decision Tree Total Score, Attention-Deficit Hyperactivity Disorder Cluster, Possible Psychosis/Schizophrenia Cluster, Social Maladjustment Cluster, Level of Severity Cluster, Educational Impact Cluster.
Administration: Group.
Price Data, 2015: $170 per introductory kit including professional manual (139 pages), 25 reusable item booklets, 25 response booklets, and 25 score summary booklets.
Time: (20) minutes.
Author: Bryan L. Euler.
Publisher: Psychological Assessment Resources, Inc.
Cross References: For reviews by Jonathan Sandoval and by Christopher A. Sink and Nyaradzo H. Mvududu, see 18:48.

[734]
Emotional Disturbance Decision Tree-Parent Form.

Purpose: Designed to help identify "children who qualify for the federal Special Education category of Emotional Disturbance."

Population: Ages 5-18.

Publication Date: 2010.

Acronym: EDDT-PF.

Scores, 11: Inability to Build or Maintain Relationships Scale, Inappropriate Behaviors or Feelings Scale, Pervasive Mood/Depression Scale, Physical Symptoms or Fears Scale, Emotional Disturbance Characteristic Scale Total Score, Resilience Scale, Attention-Deficit Hyperactivity Disorder Cluster, Possible Psychosis Cluster, Social Maladjustment Cluster, Severity Cluster, Motivation Cluster.

Administration: Group or individual.

Price Data, 2015: $170 per introductory kit including 25 response booklets, 25 reusable item booklets, 25 score summary booklets, and manual (151 pages); $66 per 25 response booklets; $35 per 25 reusable item booklets; $25 per 25 score summary booklets; $64 per manual.

Foreign Language Edition: Spanish version available.

Time: (15-20) minutes.

Comments: Ratings by parents/guardians; modeled after the EDDT-TF (18:48; called EDDT in its own listing).

Author: Bryan L. Euler.

Publisher: Psychological Assessment Resources, Inc.

Cross References: For reviews by Jeffrey A. Atlas and Tony C. Wu, see 19:60.

[735]
Emotional Eating Behavior Assessment.

Purpose: "Designed to assess a person's tendency to eat for reasons other than hunger and evaluate the underlying reasons for overeating."

Population: Under 17 through adult.

Publication Date: 2011.

Acronym: EMEBA.

Scores, 37: Health Locus of Control, Self-Discipline, Reward Dependence, Sense of Self-Efficacy, Depression, Anxiety, Resilience, Anger Control, Tolerance for Frustration, Eating Trigger (Deal with Emotional Pain, Avoid Confrontation, Loneliness, Boredom, Satisfy Need for Intimacy, Early Childhood Deprivation, Rebellion, Avoid New Challenges, Avoid Intimacy Due to Child Abuse, Feel Carefree, Fear of Other's Expectations, Self-Sabotaging Beliefs, Shame), Problem Solving, Information Seeking, Negotiation, Support Seeking, Positive Cognitive Restructuring, Emotional Regulation, Distraction, Rumination, Avoidance, Helplessness, Opposition, Social Withdrawal, Triggers, Coping Skills, Overall Score.

Administration: Individual.

Price Data: Available from publisher.

Time: (40) minutes.

Comments: Self-administered online assessment. The test publisher provides clients with information about the methods and theoretical basis used in the development of the test as well as benchmarks for relevant industries and racial/ethnic group comparison data.

Author: PsychTests AIM, Inc.

Publisher: PsychTests AIM, Inc. [Canada].

Cross References: For reviews by Tony Cellucci and Lesley Lutes and by Andrew A. Cox, see 19:61.

[736]
Emotional Intelligence Questionnaire.

Purpose: "Designed to provide information about a person's emotional skills and competencies."

Population: Ages 16 to 70.

Publication Date: 2014.

Acronym: EIQ16.

Scores, 22: Reading People (Self-Analysis, Analysis of Others, Self-Expression, Discrimination), Using Emotions (Thinking, Judgment, Sensitivity, Problem Solving), Understanding Emotions (Symptoms, Causes, Complexity, Transitions), Managing Emotions (Openness, Monitoring, Self-Control, Managing Others), Emotional Intelligence Level, Impression Management.

Administration: Individual or group.

Price Data, 2015: $19.95 per online administration.

Time: (20) minutes.

Author: MySkillsProfile.

Publisher: MySkillsProfile [United Kingdom].

Cross References: Reviews are scheduled for *The Twentieth Mental Measurements Yearbook*.

[737]
Emotional Judgment Inventory.

Purpose: "Developed to assess emotional intelligence for use in employee selection and development in organizational contexts."

Population: Ages 16 and over.

Publication Dates: 2000–2003.

Acronym: EJI.

Scores, 8: Being Aware of Emotions, Identifying Own Emotions, Identifying Others' Emotions, Managing Own Emotions, Managing Others' Emotions, Using Emotions in Problem Solving, Expressing Emotions Adaptively, Impression Management.

Administration: Group or individual; online or paper-and-pencil.

Price Data: Available from publisher.

Time: (15) minutes.

Author: Scott Bedwell.

Publisher: OPP, Ltd.

Cross References: For reviews by Phillip L. Ackerman and by Deniz S. Ones and Stephan Dilchert, see 16:84.

[738]

Emotional or Behavior Disorder Scale— Revised.

Purpose: "Designed to document those behaviors most indicative of emotional or behavioral disorders and the behavior problems which exceed the norms of any student in the environment."

Population: Ages 5–18.

Publication Dates: 1991–2003.

Acronym: EBDS-R.

Scores, 6: Behavioral Component (Academic Progress, Social Relationships, Personal Adjustment), Vocational Component (Work Related, Interpersonal Relations, Social/Community Expectations).

Administration: Individual.

Price Data, 2015: $107 per complete kit including technical manual (2003, 66 pages), 50 rating forms, and intervention manual (2003, 407 pages); $21 per technical manual; $44 per 50 rating forms; $42 per intervention manual; $46 per Quick Score; $225 per intervention manual (Windows).

Time: Administration time not reported.

Comments: Behavior rating scale completed by observers familiar with the student; derived from the Emotional or Behavior Disorder Scale School Version and the Work Adjustment Scale (T6:2743); accompanied by Intervention manual; computer scoring software available.

Authors: Stephen B. McCarney (scale and manuals) and Tamara J. Arthaud (technical manual).

Publisher: Hawthorne Educational Services, Inc.

Cross References: For reviews by Amy M. Rees and T. Steuart Watson, see 16:85; for reviews by Patti L. Harrison and Steven W. Lee of the original edition, see 13:117.

[739]

Emotional Problems Scales.

Purpose: "To assess emotional and behavioral problems in individuals with mild mental retardation or borderline intelligence."

Population: Ages 14 and over.

Publication Dates: 1984–2010.

Acronym: EPS.

Price Data, 2015: $177 per introductory kit including manual (1991, 31 pages), 25 BRS test booklets, 25 SRI test booklets, SRI scoring keys, and 25 profile forms.

Comments: Previous editions titled Prout-Strohmer Personality Inventory and Strohmer-Prout Behavior Rating Scale.

Authors: H. Thompson Prout and Douglas C. Strohmer.

Publisher: Integrated Assessment, LLC.

   a) BEHAVIOR RATING SCALES.

   Acronym: BRS.

   Scores, 12: Thought/Behavior Disorder, Verbal Aggression, Physical Aggression, Sexual Maladjustment, Distractibility, Hyperactivity, Somatic Concerns, Depression, Withdrawal, Low Self-Esteem, Externalizing Behavior Problems, Internalizing Behavior Problems.

   Administration: Individual.

   Time: [20–50] minutes.

   b) SELF-REPORT INVENTORY.

   Acronym: SRI.

   Scores, 7: Positive Impression, Thought/Behavior Disorder, Impulse Control, Anxiety, Depression, Low Self-Esteem, Total Pathology.

   Administration: Individual.

   Time: (30–35) minutes.

Cross References: For reviews by S. Alvin Leung and John A. Mills, see 13:118. For reviews by Richard Brozovich and Ernest A. Bauer and by Peter F. Merenda of the Prout-Strohmer Personality Inventory, see 11:311.

[740]

Emotional Processing Scale.

Purpose: Designed to "identify, quantify and differentiate different types of emotional processing styles in normal healthy individuals and those with psychological disorders."

Population: Ages 18 and older.

Publication Date: 2015.

Acronym: EPS.

Scores, 6: Suppression, Signs of Unprocessed Emotion, Controllability of Emotion, Avoidance, Emotional Experience, Total.

Administration: Individual.

Price Data, 2016: £137 per kit including manual, norms booklet, and 25 test booklets; £53 per manual (2015, 106 pages); £37 per norms booklet-version 1; £53 per 25 booklets/scoring forms.

Time: (5-10) minutes.

Authors: Roger Baker, Peter Thomas, Sarah Thomas, Mariaelisa Santonastaso, and Eimear Corrigan.

Publisher: Hogrefe Ltd [United Kingdom].

[741]

Emotional Quotient Inventory 2.0.

Purpose: Designed to measure emotional intelligence.

Population: Ages 18 and older.

Publication Dates: 1997-2011.

Acronym: EQ-i 2.0.

Scores: 21 content scores: Composite Scale Scores (Total EI, Self-Perception, Self-Expression, Interpersonal, Decision Making, Stress Management), Self-Perception Subscale Scores (Self-Regard, Self-Actualized, Emotional Self-Awareness), Self-Expression Subscale Scores (Emotional Expression, Assertiveness, Independence), Interpersonal Subscale Scores (Interpersonal Relationships, Empathy, Social Responsibility), Decision Making Subscale Scores (Problem Solving, Reality Testing, Impulse Control), Stress Management Subscale Scores (Flexibility, Stress Tolerance, Optimism), plus 1 Well-Being Indicator (Happiness) and 2 Response Style Indicators (Positive/Negative Impression, Inconsistency Index).

Administration: Individual or group.

Price Data: Available from publisher.

Foreign Language Editions: Translations available in Simplified Chinese, German, Spanish (European), French (Canadian and European), and Arabic.

Time: (20-30) minutes.

Author: Multi-Health Systems, Inc.

Publisher: Multi-Health Systems, Inc.

Cross References: For reviews by James C. DiPerna and Lia E. Sandilos, see 19:62; for reviews by Andrew A. Cox and Robert M. Guion of an earlier edition titled the BarOn Emotional Quotient Inventory, see 14:32.

[742]

Emotional Quotient Inventory: Youth Version.

Purpose: "Designed to measure emotional intelligence in young people aged 7 to 18 years."

Population: Ages 7–18.

Publication Date: 2000.

Acronym: EQ-i: YV.

Scores, 8: Intrapersonal Scale, Interpersonal Scale, Adaptability Scale, Stress Management Scale, Total EQ, General Mood Scale, Positive Impression Scale, Inconsistency Index.

Administration: Individual or group.

Forms, 2: EQ-i:YV Long Form; EQ-i:YV(S) Short Form.

Price Data, 2015: $225 per kit including manual (86 pages) and 25 Quikscore forms for each EQ-i:YV and EQ-i:YV(S); $100 per manual; $70 per 25 EQ-i:YV Quikscore forms; $68 per 25 EQ-i:YV(S)Quikscore forms. $237 per online kit including manual, 25 online forms for each EQ-i:YV and EQ-i:YV(S).

Foreign Language Edition: Spanish edition available upon special request.

Time: (20–25) minutes.

Comments: Self-report; previously listed as BarOn Emotional Quotient Inventory: Youth Version.

Authors: Reuven Bar-On and James D. A. Parker.

Publisher: Multi-Health Systems, Inc.

Cross References: For reviews by Joan C. Ballard and Frederick T. L. Leong, see 15:26.

[743]

Emotional Quotient-360.

Purpose: Designed to provide a "multiperspective view of [an] individual's emotional functioning."

Population: Ages 16 and over.

Publication Date: 2003.

Acronym: EQ-360

Scores, 21: Intrapersonal (Self-Regard, Emotional Self-Awareness, Assertiveness, Independence, Self-Actualization, Total), Interpersonal (Empathy, Social Responsibility, Interpersonal Relationship, Total), Stress Management (Stress Tolerance, Impulse Control, Total), Adaptability (Reality Testing, Flexibility, Problem Solving, Total), General Mood (Optimism, Happiness, Total), Total EQ.

Administration: Individual.

Price Data: Available from publisher.

Time: (30) minutes.

Comments: Designed for use in conjunction with the EQ-i (770); multi-informant rating scale available for paper-and-pencil or online administration.

Authors: Reuven Bar-On and Rich Handley.

Publisher: Multi-Health Systems, Inc.

Cross References: For reviews by Deborah L. Bandalos and Ric Brown, see 16:21.

[744]

Empirically-Statistically Validated (ESV) Written Tests for Fire Medic.

Purpose: Intended for the selection of cross-trained firefighter/fire medic candidates.

Population: Prospective firefighter/fire medic candidates.

Publication Dates: 1995-2010.

Scores: 7 subtests and total: Interest, Teamwork, Problem Solving—Common Sense, Problem Solving—Mechanical, Problem Solving—Logical Thinking, Problem Solving—Relevancy, Attentiveness, Total.

Administration: Group.

Form, 1: ESV-100.

Restricted Distribution: Distribution restricted to civil service commissions and qualified municipal officials.

Price Data: Available from publisher.

Time: 121 minutes.

Author: McCann Associates, Inc.

Publisher: McCann Associates [No reply from publisher; status unknown].

[745]

Empirically-Statistically Validated (ESV) Written Tests for Firefighter.

Purpose: For the selection of firefighter candidates.

Population: Prospective firefighters.

Publication Dates: 1976–2010.

Scores: 7 subtests: Interest in Firefighting, Teamwork/Compatibility, Map Reading, Spatial Visualization, Attentiveness (Visual Pursuit), Understanding and Interpreting Table and Text Material About Firefighting, Mechanical Aptitude.

Administration: Group.

Forms, 2: Form ESV-100, M-100.

Restricted Distribution: Distribution restricted to civil service commissions and qualified municipal officials.

Price Data: Available from publisher.

Time: 121 minutes.
Author: McCann Associates.
Publisher: McCann Associates [No reply from publisher; status unknown].

[746]

Empirically-Statistically Validated (ESV) Written Tests for Police Officer.

Purpose: Designed for the selection of police officer candidates.
Population: Prospective police officers.
Publication Dates: 1980–2010.
Scores: 7 subtests and total: Observational Ability, Ability to Exercise Judgment and Common Sense, Interest in Police Work, Ability to Exercise Judgment—Map Reading, Ability to Exercise Judgment—Dealing With People, Ability to Read and Comprehend Police Test Material, Reasoning Ability, Total.
Administration: Group.
Forms, 2: Form ESV 100, Form N-100.
Restricted Distribution: Distribution restricted to civil service commissions and qualified municipal officials.
Price Data: Available from publisher.
Time: 170 minutes.
Author: McCann Associates.
Publisher: McCann Associates [No reply from publisher; status unknown].

[747]

Employability Maturity Interview.

Purpose: "Developed to assess readiness for the vocational rehabilitation planning process."
Population: Rehabilitation clients.
Publication Date: 1987.
Acronym: EMI.
Scores: Total score only.
Administration: Individual.
Price Data: Available as free download from Educational Resources Information Center (ERIC) database.
Time: (15–20) minutes.
Comments: Based upon the Adult Vocational Maturity Assessment Interview.
Authors: Richard Roessler and Brian Bolton.
Publisher: The National Center on Employment & Disability.
Cross References: See T5:936 (1 reference); for a review by William R. Koch, see 11:132.

[748]

Employability Skills Inventory.

Purpose: Designed to help people "pinpoint competencies and personal qualities that might help them to secure and maintain employment."
Population: Teenaged and adult job seekers and career planners.

Publication Date: 2010.
Acronym: ESI.
Scores, 8: Basic Skills, Thinking Skills, Personal Qualities, Resource Management, Information Skills, Interpersonal Skills, Systems Management, Technology Use.
Administration: Individual or group.
Price Data, 2016: $47.95 per package of 25 consumable booklets; volume discount available. Administrator's guide (16 pages) available for download from publisher's website.
Time: (20-25) minutes.
Comments: Self-scored and interpreted.
Authors: John J. Liptak.
Publisher: JIST/EMC Publishing.
Cross References: Reviews are scheduled for *The Twentieth Mental Measurements Yearbook*.

[749]

Employee Aptitude Survey, Second Edition.

Purpose: Designed to predict future job performance.
Population: Ages 16 to adult
Publication Dates: 1952–2000.
Acronym: EAS.
Administration: Group or individual.
Price Data: Price data available from publisher for test materials including User's Manual (2005, 64 pages), Technical Manual (1994, 91 pages), Technical Addendum: Fairness of the EAS (2000, 11 pages), and Supplemental Norms Report (1995, 92 pages).
Time: 5-10(10-15) minutes.
Comments: Tests available separately; computerized versions available; transportability procedure available.
Authors: G. Grimsley (*a–h*), F. L. Ruch (*a–g, i, j*), N. D. Warren (*a–g*), and J. S. Ford (*a, c, e–g*).
Publisher: PSI Services LLC.
 a) TEST 1, VERBAL COMPREHENSION.
 Publication Dates: 1956–1984.
 Scores: Total score only.
 b) TEST 2, NUMERICAL ABILITY.
 Publication Dates: 1952–1963.
 Scores: Total score only.
 c) TEST 3, VISUAL PURSUIT.
 Publication Date: 1956.
 Scores: Total score only.
 d) TEST 4, VISUAL SPEED AND ACCURACY.
 Publication Dates: 1952–1980.
 Scores: Total score only.
 e) TEST 5, SPACE VISUALIZATION.
 Publication Dates: 1952–1980.
 Scores: Total score only.
 f) TEST 6, NUMERICAL REASONING.
 Publication Dates: 1957–1985.
 Scores: Total score only.
 g) TEST 7, VERBAL REASONING.
 Publication Dates: 1952–1963.
 Scores: Total score only.
 h) TEST 8, WORD FLUENCY.
 Publication Dates: 1953–1963.
 Scores: Total score only.

i) TEST 9, MANUAL SPEED AND ACCURACY.
Publication Dates: 1953–1963.
Scores: Total score only.
j) TEST 10, SYMBOLIC REASONING.
Publication Dates: 1957–1985.
Scores: Total score only.
Cross References: For reviews by Brian Engdahl and Paul M. Muchinsky, see 14:137; see also T5:937 (4 references), T4:894 (1 reference), T3:799 (4 references), and T2:1071 (14 references); for reviews by Paul F. Ross and Erwin K. Taylor, and an excerpted review by John O. Crites of an earlier edition, see 6:769 (4 references); for reviews by Dorothy C. Adkins and S. Rains Wallace of an earlier edition, see 5:607.

[750]

Employee Assistance Program Inventory.

Purpose: "Designed as an intake or screening tool for professionals who provide counseling and other services in working adults."
Population: Adults seeking vocational counseling.
Publication Date: 1994.
Acronym: EAPI.
Scores: 10 scales: Anxiety, Depression, Self-Esteem Problems, Marital Problems, Family Problems, External Stressors, Interpersonal Conflict, Work Adjustment, Problem Minimization, Effects of Substance Abuse.
Administration: Group.
Price Data, 2015: $154 per introductory kit including manual (44 pages), 25 reusable item booklets, and 25 answer sheet/profiles.
Time: (20) minutes.
Authors: William D. Anton and James R. Reed.
Publisher: Psychological Assessment Resources, Inc.
Cross References: For reviews by Michael G. Kavan and David J. Pittenger, see 14:138.

[751]

Employee Attitude and Personality Test.

Purpose: "Designed to evaluate whether a person has the traits and skills needed to be a productive and successful worker."
Population: Under age 19 through adult.
Publication Date: 2011.
Acronym: EAPT.
Scores, 45: Social Skills, Forcefulness, Industriousness/Assiduity, Openness to Improvement, Openness to Change, Conformity, Resilience, Level-Headedness, Need for Supervision, Compliance, Trainability, Steadiness, Conscientiousness, Integrity, Approval-Seeking, Adaptability, Coping Skills, Emotional Stability, Creativity, Open-Mindedness, Innovation, Drive/Success Orientation, Calculated Risk-Taking, Street Smarts, Initiative, Independence, Leadership Potential, Dominance, Authoritarianism, Extroversion, Soft Skills, Agreeableness, Dynamism, Fair-Mindedness, Abrasiveness, Tension/Nervous Energy, Accident Proneness, Hotheadedness, Generalist, Specialist, Technical Skill, Kinesthetic Skill, Visual/Spatial Skill, Linguistic Skill, Analytical Thinking.
Administration: Individual.
Price Data: Available from publisher.
Time: (20) minutes.
Comments: Self-administered online assessment. The test publisher provides clients with information about the methods and theoretical basis used in the development of the test as well as benchmarks for relevant industries and racial/ethnic group comparison data.
Author: PsychTests AIM, Inc.
Publisher: PsychTests AIM, Inc. [Canada].
Cross References: For a review by Stephen B. Johnson, see 19:63.

[752]

Employee Involvement Survey.

Purpose: Assesses employees' actual and desired opportunities for personal involvement and influence in the workplace.
Population: Business and industry employees.
Publication Date: 1988.
Acronym: EIS.
Scores, 5: Basic Creature Comfort, Safety and Order, Belonging and Affiliation, Ego-Status, Actualization and Self-Expression.
Administration: Group.
Price Data: Available from publisher.
Time: Administration time not reported.
Comments: Self-administered, self-scored.
Author: Jay Hall.
Publisher: Teleometrics International, Inc.

[753]

Employee Productivity Index.

Purpose: "Designed to aid in hiring productive and responsible employees."
Population: Job applicants.
Publication Date: 1989.
Acronym: EPI.
Scores, 7: Dependability Scale, Interpersonal Cooperation Scale, Drug Avoidance Scale, Safety Scale, Validity/Accuracy Scale, Productivity Index, Significant Behavioral Indicators.
Administration: Individual or group.
Forms, 6: Quanta Touch Test, Quanta Software for Windows, Online, Scan, Quanta-Fax, Optical Scoring.
Price Data: Available from publisher.
Foreign Language Edition: Available in Spanish.
Time: [20–40] minutes.
Author: General Dynamics Information Technology.
Publisher: General Dynamics Information Technology.

[754]

Employee Reliability Inventory.

Purpose: Designed to be used as a preemployment instrument for assessing a number of different dimensions of work behavior skills, each of which are associated with reliable and productive work behavior.

Population: Job applicants.

Publication Dates: 1986–1998.

Acronym: ERI.

Scores, 7: Freedom from Disruptive Alcohol and Illegal Drug Use, Courtesy, Emotional Maturity, Conscientiousness, Trustworthiness, Long Term Job Commitment, Safe Job Performance.

Administration: Individual or group.

Price Data, 2016: $25 or less (depending on the number and scoring method used), including questionnaire, user's manual (1998, 52 pages), all documentation, training, toll-free technical support, and consultation; $55 per Americans With Disabilities Act Kit including user's manual addendum (1992, 19 pages), audio version, Braille version, and large print version.

Foreign Language and Other Special Editions: Available in Spanish and French, as well as braille, large print and audio versions.

Time: (12–15) minutes.

Comments: Individual applicant scores are compared to a position specific profile; can be administered online, at a stand alone computer terminal, or by paper and pencil; results for online administration are stored in a database, which is user accessible, and can be used to generate a range of reports.

Author: Gerald L. Borofsky.

Publisher: Bay State Psychological Associates, Inc.

Cross References: See T5:944 (1 reference); for reviews by Robert M. Guion and Lawrence M. Rudner, see 12:137 (3 references); see also T4:899 (2 references).

[755]

Employee Safety Inventory.

Purpose: Designed to "assess the safety attitudes of job applicants and current employees."

Population: Job applicants and employees.

Publication Dates: 1989–1994.

Acronym: ESI.

Scores, 7: Survey Scales (Safety Control, Risk Avoidance, Stress Tolerance), Validity Scales (Validity/Distortion, Accuracy), Composite Score (Safety Index), Supplemental Scale (Driver Attitude).

Administration: Group or individual.

Price Data: Available from publisher.

Time: (45) minutes.

Comments: Paper-and-pencil or computer administration available.

Author: General Dynamics Information Technology.

Publisher: General Dynamics Information Technology.

[756]

Employee Screening Questionnaire.

Purpose: "A personality-based selection measure designed to provide employers with a technique for identifying superior job candidates and to screen out dishonest and unproductive ones."

Population: Ages 16 and over.

Publication Dates: 2001–2002.

Acronym: ESQ.

Scores, 15: Customer Service, Productivity, Accuracy, Commitment/Job Satisfaction, Promotability, Risk of Counter-Productive Behavior, Alcohol and Substance Abuse, Bogus Sick Days, Driving Delinquency, Lateness, Loafing, Sabotage of Employer's Production or Property, Safety Infractions, Theft, Overall Hiring Recommendation.

Administration: Individual or group.

Price Data, 2015: $25 per test manual; $2 per test booklet; $15-$20 (depending on volume) per administration (online or fax-in).

Time: 15 minutes.

Foreign Language Editions: French, Spanish, Puerto Rican Spanish, and Portuguese materials available.

Comments: Internet administration or fax-in scoring service available; recommended by publisher for use in conjunction with the Personnel Assessment Form (PAF).

Author: Douglas N. Jackson.

Publisher: SIGMA Assessment Systems, Inc.

Cross References: For reviews by Paul M. Muchinsky and Frank Schmidt, see 16:86.

[757]

Employee Wellness Evaluation.

Purpose: Designed to "identify potential problems in several areas of significance for employees" as a clinical aid for referral for counseling or "to provide indications of problem prevalence in a workforce."

Population: Employees seeking counseling.

Publication Dates: 1994-1999.

Acronym: EWE.

Scores, 7: Alcohol, Depression, Stress, Anger, Morale, Management, Family Stress.

Administration: Individual and group.

Price Data, 2016: $52.50 per 25 assessments; $15 per EWE guide (1999, 5 pages).

Time: (10-15) minutes.

Author: Norman G. Hoffmann.

Publisher: The Change Companies.

Cross References: For reviews by Elizabeth Bigham and Thomas M. Dunn, see 18:49.

[758]

Employment Inventory.

Purpose: Designed to identify job applicants who will be likely to be productive, exhibit helpful and positive

behaviors in interacting with customers, and to stay on the job at least three months.
Population: Job applicants.
Publication Dates: 1985–1993.
Acronym: EI.
Scores, 4: Performance, Tenure, Customer Service, Sales.
Administration: Group.
Price Data: Available from publisher.
Foreign Language Editions: Foreign and bilingual editions available include American Spanish/English, French-Canadian English, Mexican Spanish, British English, and Vietnamese/English.
Time: (30) minutes.
Comments: Online inventory of attitudes and self-descriptions; computer-scored.
Authors: George E. Paajanen, Timothy L. Hansen, and Richard A. McLellan.
Publisher: CEB.
Cross References: For reviews by Gordon C. Bruner II and Annie W. Ward, see 14:278.

[759]
The Encouragement Index.

Purpose: Designed to help people "develop a picture of [their] strengths and opportunities for improvement in the leadership practice of Encouraging the Heart."
Population: Persons in leadership roles.
Publication Date: 2011.
Score: Total score only.
Administration: Group.
Price Data, 2016: $12 per assessment; $91 per facilitator's guide (2011, 78 pages); $19.95 per revised workbook (2011, 119 pages).
Time: Administration time not reported.
Comments: Focuses on the leadership practice Encourage the Heart from the Five Practices of Exemplary Leadership® in the Leadership Practices Inventory, Fourth Edition (1121).
Authors: James M. Kouzes and Barry Z. Posner.
Publisher: The Leadership Challenge, A Wiley Brand.

[760]
Endicott Work Productivity Scale.

Purpose: "Designed to describe types of behavior and subjective feelings that are highly likely to reduce productivity and efficiency in work activities."
Population: Adults.
Publication Dates: 1994–1997.
Acronym: EWPS.
Scores: Total score only.
Administration: Individual.
Manual: No manual.
Price Data: Available from publisher.
Time: [3–5] minutes.
Author: Jean Endicott.

Publisher: Department of Research Assessment and Training.
Cross References: For reviews by Andrew A. Cox and William C. Tirre, see 14:140.

[761]
English as a Second Language Oral Assessment, Second Edition.

Purpose: Measures the "learner's ability to speak and understand English."
Population: Adult nonnative speakers of English.
Publication Dates: 1978–1996.
Acronym: ESLOA.
Scores, 4: Auditory Comprehension, Basic Vocabulary and Grammatical Structures, Complex Grammatical Structures and Communicating Meaning and Comprehension, Comprehension and Fluency and Pronunciation.
Administration: Individual.
Levels, 4: 1, 2, 3, 4.
Price Data: Now available at no charge from test publisher.
Time: Administration time not reported.
Authors: Joye Coy Shaffer and Teri McLean.
Publisher: ProLiteracy Worldwide.
Cross References: For reviews by James D. Brown and Charlene Rivera of an earlier edition, see 11:136.

[762]
English Placement Test [Forms D, E, F].

Purpose: Designed to "place ESL students into homogeneous ability levels" and to assess "general receptive language proficiency by measuring performance" in listening comprehension, grammatical knowledge, vocabulary range, and reading comprehension.
Population: ESL students.
Publication Dates: 1972-2013.
Acronym: CaMLA EPT.
Scores: Total score only.
Administration: Group for paper-and-pencil version; individual for computer-delivered version.
Forms, 3: D, E, F.
Price Data, 2015: $845 for complete package including 20 booklets each of Forms D, E, and F, scoring stencils for Forms D, E, and F, audio CDs containing listening prompts for each form, administration manual (2013, 9 pages), and reproducible answer sheet; computer-delivered version: $5.95 per test, minimum order of 25.
Time: (60) minutes.
Comments: Specific cut scores must be set at individual institutions; CEFR linking study shows score ranges for levels A2 to C1; publisher recommends that only overall scores be used for placement decisions; computer administration available.
Author: Cambridge Michigan Language Assessments.
Publisher: Cambridge Michigan Language Assessments.

Cross References: Reviews are scheduled for *The Twentieth Mental Measurements Yearbook*. For a review by James Dean Brown of the 1993 form, see 17:67; see also T4:908 (3 references); for a review by John L. D. Clark of the 1972 form, see 8:102.

[763]
English Skills Assessment.
Purpose: ACER adaptation of STEP Series and DTLS by Educational Testing Service and The College Board.
Population: Grades 11-12 and first year of post-secondary education.
Publication Dates: 1969-1982.
Acronym: ESA.
Scores, 11: Part I (Spelling, Punctuation and Capitalization, Comprehension I, Total), Part II (Comprehension II, Usage, Vocabulary, Sentence Structure, Logical Relationships [optional], Total), Total.
Administration: Group.
Price Data, 2016: A$5.95 per Part I test booklet; A$5.95 per Part II test booklet; A$25.95 per 10 answer sheets; A$5.95 per score key; A$23.95 per manual.
Time: 50(70) minutes for Part I; 60(70) minutes for Part II.
Author: Australian Council for Educational Research Ltd. (adaptation).
Publisher: Australian Council for Educational Research Ltd. [Australia].
Cross References: See T4:910 (1 reference); for a review by John C. Sherwood, see 9:389.

[764]
Ennis-Weir Critical Thinking Essay Test.
Purpose: "To help evaluate a person's ability to appraise an argument and to formulate in writing an argument in response, thus recognizing a creative dimension in critical thinking ability."
Population: High school and college.
Publication Dates: 1983-1985.
Scores: Critical Thinking Ability.
Administration: Group.
Price Data: Available at no charge from test publisher.
Time: (40) minutes.
Comments: Supplementary information also available from author's website.
Authors: Robert H. Ennis and Eric Weir.
Publisher: Robert H. Ennis (the author).
Cross References: See T5:959 (2 references); for reviews by James A. Poteet and Gail E. Tompkins, see 10:107.

[765]
The Enright Forgiveness Inventory.
Purpose: "To measure the degree to which one person forgives another who has hurt him or her deeply and unfairly."

Population: High school and college and adults.
Publication Dates: 2000-2004.
Acronym: EFI.
Scores, 10: 3 Affect scores (Positive Affect, Negative Affect, Total Affect), 3 Behavior scores (Positive Behavior, Negative Behavior, Total Behavior), 3 Cognition scores (Positive Cognition, Negative Cognition, Total Cognition), Total.
Administration: Group or individual.
Foreign Language Edition: Dutch, Farsi, Filipino, German, Hungarian, Italian, Norwegian, Brazilian Portuguese, Spanish, Taiwanese, Thai, and Turkish.
Price Data, 2015: $50 per manual/sample set (63 pages); $15 for individual Report: "Letting it Go"; $15 for Report About Me: "Letting it Go"; $20 Individual Report: Multi-Incident; $2.40 Transform Survey Hosting; $2 Remote Online Survey License; $2 License to Reproduce.
Time: (40) minutes.
Authors: Robert D. Enright and Julio Rique.
Publisher: Mind Garden, Inc.
Cross References: For reviews by Laura L. B. Barnes and by James Fauth and Scott T. Meier, see 15:89.

[766]
Entrepreneurial Aptitude Profile.
Purpose: Designed to "assess whether a test-taker's skills and personality traits match those required" to work as an entrepreneur.
Population: Potential entrepreneurs.
Publication Date: 2011.
Acronym: EntAP.
Scores, 19: Drive to Succeed (Independence, Passion, Goal-Orientation, Conscientiousness), Social Network (Social Skills, Leadership, Mentoring/Support), Outlook on Success (Self-Efficaciousness, Optimism, Status-Seeking), Openness to New Ideas (Interest in Knowledge, Innovation, Adaptability, Risk-Taking), Overall Score.
Administration: Individual.
Price Data: Available from publisher.
Time: (30) minutes.
Comments: Self-administered online assessment. The test publisher provides clients with information about the methods and theoretical basis used in the development of the test as well as benchmarks for relevant industries and racial/ethnic group comparison data.
Author: PsychTests AIM, Inc.
Publisher: PsychTests AIM, Inc. [Canada].
Cross References: For reviews by Steven W. Schmidt and Chockalingam Viswesvaran, see 19:65.

[767]
Entrepreneurial Personality Assessment.
Purpose: Designed to "provide information about which aspects of a person's personality are well suited to owning a business, and which aspects could be problematic."

Population: Under age 17 through adult.
Publication Date: 2011.
Acronym: EPA.
Scores, 7: Self-Sufficiency, Conscientiousness, Drive Orientation, Social Skills, Optimism, Risk-Taking, Networking Ability.
Administration: Individual.
Price Data: Available from publisher.
Time: (15) minutes.
Comments: Self-administered online assessment. The test publisher provides clients with information about the methods and theoretical basis used in the development of the test as well as benchmarks for relevant industries and racial/ethnic group comparison data.
Author: PsychTests AIM, Inc.
Publisher: PsychTests AIM, Inc. [Canada].
Cross References: For reviews by Robert K. Gable and Meghan Kiley and by Frederick T. L. Leong and Dzenana Husremovic, see 19:66.

[768]

Entrepreneurial Style and Success Indicator [Revised].

Purpose: Designed to help individuals identify their preferred entrepreneurial style and its related strengths and weaknesses, as well as comparing their background to the background of other successful entrepreneurs.
Population: Adults.
Publication Dates: 1988-2006.
Acronym: ESSI.
Scores, 4: Behavioral/Action, Cognitive/Analysis, Interpersonal/Harmony, Affective/Expression, plus 28 Entrepreneurial Success Factors.
Administration: Individual or group.
Price Data, 2015: $25 per test booklet (32 pages); $20 per interpretations booklet (48 pages); $49 per code for online version; $75 per Professional's Guide (62 pages); $40 per Trainer's Guidelines (18 pages); $26 per participant workbook (64 pages).
Foreign Language Edition: Online version is available in Simplified Chinese.
Time: [120-180] minutes for Basic; [360-720] minutes for Advanced.
Comments: Self-administered and self-scored.
Authors: Ken Keis, Terry D. Anderson, and Howard Shenson.
Publisher: Consulting Resource Group International, Inc.
Cross References: For reviews by Frederick T. L. Leong and Myra N. Womble, see 17:68; for a review by Stephen F. Davis of an earlier edition, see 13:120.

[769]

Eosys Word Processing Aptitude Battery.

Purpose: For use in selection, allocation, and development of word processor operators.

Population: Job candidates for work processor operator positions.
Publication Date: 1983.
Acronym: WPAB.
Scores, 5: Verbal Skills (WP1), Checking Skills (WP2), Written Instructions (WP3), Coded Information (WP4), Numerical Computation (WP5).
Administration: Group.
Price Data: Available from publisher.
Time: (10) minutes per WP1, WP2, WP5; (12) minutes per WP3; (15) minutes per WP4.
Authors: Gill Nyfield, Susan Bawtree, Michael Pearn (test), David Hawkey (test), and Emma Bird (manual).
Publisher: CEB.

[770]

EQ Index.

Purpose: Measures organizational leaders' emotional intelligence (EQ) at work, specifically their EQ ability as opposed to their personality.
Population: Organizational leaders, managers, and supervisors.
Publication Date: 2002.
Acronym: EQI.
Scores, 5: Self-Awareness, Self-Regulation, Motivation, Empathy, Social Skills.
Administration: Group.
Manual: No manual.
Price Data: Available from publisher.
Time: Administration time not reported.
Comments: Observer or self-rating.
Authors: M. Afzal Rahim, Clement Psenicka, Panagiotis Polychroniou, Jing-Hua Zhao, C. S. Yu, K. A. Chan, K. W. Yee, M. G. Alves, C. W. Lee, M. S. Rahman, S. Ferdausy, and R. V. Wyk.
Publisher: Center for Advanced Studies in Management.

[771]

ERB Writing Assessment Program [Revised].

Purpose: Designed to assess six domains of writing proficiency in a chosen genre.
Population: Grades 3–4, 5–6, 7–8, 9–10, 11–12.
Publication Dates: 1989–2016.
Acronym: ERB WrAP.
Scores: 6 writing traits: Overall Development, Organization, Support, Sentence Structure, Word Choice, Mechanics.
Administration: Group.
Price Data: Available from publisher. Discount for combination WrAP and online Writing Practice Program (WPP) when ordered together.
Comments: Non-stimulus (short prompts with pre-writing and editing suggestions) and stimulus (prompts with text passages) prompt options available for all levels; WrAP writing essays for both prompt types are scored by Measurement Incorporated; online WPP provides immedi-

ate computer scoring and tutorials and is a complementary formative tool; a 6-point scoring rubric provides analytic scores of 1-6 on each of six writing traits offering detailed information on students' writing skills. Raw scores show growth across grades within a test level; scale scores based on a student's raw score may be compared across grades and test levels; percentile ranks and stanines allow comparison of students' scores on same grade to suburban/public, independent, and international school norms.

Author: Educational Records Bureau.

Publisher: Educational Records Bureau.

> *a*) ELEMENTARY LEVEL.
> **Population:** Grades 3 and 4.
> **Time:** Two [40–60] minute sessions. Two (75) minute sessions (stimulus).
> *b*) INTERMEDIATE LEVEL.
> **Population:** Grades 5 and 6.
> **Time:** Two [40–50] minute sessions. Two (75) minute sessions (stimulus).
> *c*) MIDDLE SCHOOL LEVEL.
> **Population:** Grades 7 and 8.
> **Time:** Same as *b* above.
> *d*) SECONDARY LEVEL.
> **Population:** Grades 9 and 10.
> **Time:** Same as *b* above.
> *e*) COLLEGE PREP LEVEL.
> **Population:** Grades 11 and 12.
> **Time:** Same as *b* above.

Cross References: For reviews by Thomas P. Hogan and Bruce G. Rogers of an earlier (2004) version, see 17:69; for reviews by G. Michael Poteat and Wayne H. Slater of an earlier edition, see 13:122.

[772]

Erotometer: A Technique for the Measurement of Heterosexual Love.

Purpose: Designed to measure attitudes toward heterosexual love.

Population: Adults.

Publication Dates: 1971–1988.

Scores: Total score only.

Administration: Group.

Manual: No manual.

Price Data, 2015: $2 per test.

Time: [10] minutes.

Comments: Supplementary article available.

Author: Panos D. Bardis.

Publisher: Donna Bardis.

Cross References: For additional information, see 8:337 (1 reference).

[773]

Evaluating Acquired Skills in Communication–Third Edition.

Purpose: Designed to assess "prelinguistic skills, semantics, syntax, morphology, and pragmatics for students functioning under the language and cognitive level of the average 6-year-old."

Population: Ages 3 months to 6 years.

Publication Dates: 1984-2009.

Acronym: EASIC-3.

Administration: Individual.

Levels, 5: Prelanguage, Receptive I, Expressive I, Receptive II, Expressive II.

Price Data, 2016: $193 per complete kit including manual (2009, 92 pages), picture book, picture cards, 10 Prelanguage Inventory Booklets, 10 Receptive I Inventory Booklets, 10 Receptive II Inventory Booklets, 10 Expressive I Inventory Booklets, 10 Expressive II Inventory Booklets, 10 Prelanguage Profile Forms, 10 Receptive I Profile Forms, 10 Receptive II Profile Forms, 10 Expressive I Profile Forms, 10 Expressive II Profile Forms, developmental age chart and goals and objectives list; $40 per refill kit (Expressive I, Expressive II, Prelanguage, Receptive I, or Receptive II).

Time: [15-30] minutes.

Author: Anita Marcott.

Publisher: PRO-ED.

> *a*) PRELANGUAGE.
> **Scores:** Ratings in 9 areas: Sensory Stimulation, Object Relations, Means-End Causality, Motor Imitation, Matching, Rejection/Negation/Affirmation, Comprehension and Use of Communicative Gestures, Social Interaction, Nonverbal Pragmatic Analysis.
> *b*) RECEPTIVE I.
> **Scores:** Ratings in 12 areas: Noun Labels, Visuospatial Regard, Commands, Matching, Noun Labels and Picture Identification, Verbs and Action Commands, Sequencing Pictures, Comprehension of Two-Word Phrases, Prepositional and Noun Location Commands, Classification/Categorization/Association, Adjectives and Attributes, Interrogatives.
> *c*) EXPRESSIVE I.
> **Scores:** Ratings in 9 areas: Noun Labels, Actions and Verbs, Nonexistence/Affirmation/Negation, Noun Locations and Prepositions, Adjectives and Attributes, Two-Word Phrases, Interrogatives, Social Interaction, Pragmatic Analysis.
> *d*) RECEPTIVE II.
> **Scores:** Ratings in 11 areas: Labels: Nouns and Pronouns, Visuospatial Regard, Verbs and Action Commands, Comprehension of Three-Word Phrases, Affirmation and Negation, Prepositional Location Commands, Comprehension of Singular and Plural, Adjectives and Attributes, Money Concepts, Categorization and Association, Interrogatives.
> *e*) EXPRESSIVE II.
> **Scores:** Ratings in 13 areas: Labels: Nouns and Pronouns, Verbs, Affirmation and Negation, Locations and Prepositions, Plurals, Categorization, Adjectives and Attributes, Three-Word Phrases, Interrogatives, Social Interactions, Sequencing and Sentence Structure, Connected Language Analysis, Pragmatic Analysis.

Cross References: For reviews by William O. Haynes and John H. Kranzler of the revised edition, see 12:329; for reviews by Barry W. Jones and Robert E. Owens, Jr. of the original edition, see 10:109.

[774]

Evaluation of Basic Skills.

Purpose: Designed to provide a concept-based measurement of reading, writing, and mathematics.
Population: Ages 3 to 18.
Publication Dates: 1995–1996.
Scores, 3: Reading, Writing, Mathematics.
Administration: Individual.
Price Data, 2016: $89.95 per complete start-up kit including administration manual (1995, 27 pages), 50 test forms, and 25 pre-test/post-test word tests; $15.95 per administration manual; $12 per 2-tape audio cassette set "Administering the Test"; $195 per application fee as test administrator; $50 per 50 test forms; $40 per 50 pre-test/post-test word tests.
Time: (10) minutes for Mathematics section; untimed for Reading and Writing sections.
Author: Lee Havis.
Publisher: Trust Tutoring.
Cross References: For reviews by Eleanor E. Sanford and Loraine J. Spenciner, see 14:142.

[775]

Evaluation of Competency to Stand Trial—Revised.

Purpose: "Designed for specialized forensic evaluations related to competency to stand trial."
Population: Ages 18 and over.
Publication Date: 2004.
Acronym: ECST-R.
Scores, 8: Competency Scales (Factual Understanding of Courtroom Proceedings, Rational Understanding of Courtroom Proceedings, Consult with Counsel), Atypical Presentation Scales (Realistic, Psychotic, Nonpsychotic Impairment, Both [Psychotic and Nonpsychotic combined]).
Administration: Individual.
Price Data, 2015: $290 per introductory kit including professional manual (2004, 176 pages), binder with interview booklet, 25 record forms, and 25 profile/summary forms in a soft-sided attaché case.
Time: Untimed.
Comments: Semistructured interview format.
Authors: Richard Rogers, Chad E. Tillbrook, and Kenneth W. Sewell.
Publisher: Psychological Assessment Resources, Inc.
Cross References: For reviews by D. Ashley Cohen and Robert A. Leark, see 16:87.

[776]

Everyday Life Activities: Photo Series.

Purpose: Designed as a photo series for "language training, teaching, testing and remediation of word-, sentence-, and text/discourse-level abilities."
Population: Children with delay in language development, autistic children, and adults with a language or speech impairment sequel to brain damage.
Publication Date: 1994.
Acronym: ELA.
Scores: Available from publisher.
Administration: Individual.
Price Data: Available from publisher.
Time: Administration time not reported.
Author: Jacqueline Stark.
Publisher: Jacqueline Stark [Austria].

[777]

Examination for the Certificate of Competency in English.

Purpose: Designed as a test of general language proficiency in a variety of contexts; it assesses linguistic, discoursal, sociolinguistic, and pragmatic elements of the English language.
Population: Nonnative speakers of English.
Publication Dates: 1995-2015.
Acronym: ECCE.
Scores, 5: Writing, Listening Comprehension, GVR (Grammar/Vocabulary/Reading), Speaking, Overall Score.
Administration: Group.
Forms: 4 per year.
Price Data: Available from publisher.
Time: (30) minutes for Listening; (80) minutes for Grammar/Vocabulary/Reading; (30) minutes for Writing; (15) minutes for Speaking.
Comments: Offered 4 times per year at CaMLA test centers; Designed for nonnative speakers of English who would like official documentary evidence of intermediate proficiency in the English language, particularly for academic and professional purposes; Aims at the B2 level of the Common European Framework of Reference.
Author: Cambridge Michigan Language Assessments.
Publisher: Cambridge Michigan Language Assessments.
Cross References: For reviews by Antony John Kunnan and Elvis Wagner and by Judith A. Monsaas, see 19:68.

[778]

Examination for the Certificate of Proficiency in English.

Purpose: Designed "as a test of general language proficiency in a variety of contexts; it assesses linguistic, discoursal, sociolinguistic, and pragmatic elements of the English language."
Population: English language learners.
Publication Dates: 1953-2015.
Acronym: ECPE.
Scores, 5: Writing, Listening Comprehension, Grammar/Cloze/Vocabulary/Reading, Speaking, Overall Score.

Administration: Group.
Forms: 4 forms per year.
Price Data: Available from publisher.
Time: (150) minutes.
Comments: Administered four times per year at approved test centers around the world; aimed at the C2 level of the Common European Framework of Reference; designed for English language learners who would like official documentary evidence of advanced proficiency in the English language, particularly for academic and professional purposes.
Author: Cambridge Michigan Language Assessments.
Publisher: Cambridge Michigan Language Assessments.
Cross References: For reviews by Jorge E. Gonzalez and Brenda Lagunas and by María Del R. Medina-Díaz, see 19:69.

[779]
Examining for Aphasia, Third Edition.

Purpose: "For evaluating possible aphasic language impairments and other acquired impairments that are often closely related to language functions."
Population: Adolescents and adults.
Publication Dates: 1946–1994.
Acronym: EFA-3.
Scores, 41: Agnosias (Common Objects, Pictures, Colors, Geometric Forms, Numerals, Letters, Printed Words, Almost Alike Pictures, Printed Sentences, Nonverbal Noises, Object Identification, Total); Aphasias (Word Identification, Comprehension of Sentences, Comprehension of Multiple Choice, Oral Paragraphs, Silent Reading Sentences, Silent Reading Paragraphs, Total); Apraxias (Body Parts, Simple Skills, Pretend Action, Numerals, Words, Sentences, Total), Aphasios (Automatic Speech, Writing Numerals, Writing Letters, Spelling, Writing from Dictation, Naming Body Parts, Word Finding, Arithmetic Computations, Arithmetic Problems, Total); Composites (Receptive, Expressive, Subaphasic, Aphasia, Total).
Administration: Individual.
Price Data: Available from publisher.
Time: (30–120) minutes.
Comments: Shortened version of test may be administered for screening purposes; the publisher advises that a Fourth Edition is now available.
Author: Jon Eisenson.
Publisher: PRO-ED.
Cross References: For a review by Helen Kitchens, see 13:124: see also T4:940 (2 references), T2:2071 (3 references), and P:76 (2 references); for excerpted reviews by Louis M. DiCarlo and Laurance F. Shaffer, see 5:52 (3 references); for a review by D. Russell Davis and excerpted reviews by Nolan D. C. Lewis and one other, see 4:42; for a review by C. R. Strother and an excerpted review, see 3:39.

[780]
The Executive Control Battery.

Purpose: "To document the presence and extent of the 'executive dyscontrol' or 'frontal lobe' syndrome."
Population: Adults.
Publication Date: 1999.
Acronym: ECB.
Administration: Individual.
Price Data: Available from publisher.
Comments: Neuropsychological battery; subtests can be administered independently.
Authors: Elkhonon Goldberg, Kenneth Podell, Robert Bilder, and Judith Jaeger.
Publisher: Psych Press [Australia].
a) THE GRAPHICAL SEQUENCES TEST.
Purpose: "Designed to elicit perseverations … and various behavioural stereotypies."
Scores, 7: Hyperkinetic Motor Perseverations (Occurrences), Perseveration of Elements (Occurrences, Repetitions), Perseveration of Features (Occurrences, Repetitions), Perseverations of Activities (Occurrences, Repetitions).
Time: (15–20) minutes.
b) COMPETING PROGRAMS TEST.
Purpose: "Designed to elicit various types of echopraxia, behavioural stereotypies, and disinhibition."
Scores, 8: Simple Go/No-Go (Random, Simple Stereotype, Alternating Stereotype, Total Errors), Simple Conflict—Visual (Random, Simple Stereotype, Alternating Stereotype, Total Errors).
Time: (12–15) minutes.
c) MANUAL POSTURES TEST.
Purpose: "Designed to elicit various types of echopraxia."
Scores: 3 ratings: Correct, Full Mirroring, Other.
Time: (10–15) minutes.
d) MOTOR SEQUENCES TEST.
Purpose: "Designed to elicit various types of motor perseverations, stereotypies, and other deficits of sequential motor organisation."
Parts, 2: Dynamic Praxis, Bimanual Coordination.
Time: (10–15) minutes.
   1) *Dynamic Praxis.*
   Scores, 6: Two Stage Movement (Imitation, Continuation, Without Model), Reversal of Two State Movement (Imitation, Continuation Without Model), Three Stage Movement (Imitation, Continuation Without Model.
   2) *Bimanual Coordination.*
   Scores, 6: Distal (Imitation, Continuation Without Model), Proximal (Imitation, Continuation Without Model), Mixed (Imitation, Continuation Without Model).
Cross References: For reviews by Anthony T. Dugbartey and by Shawn Powell and David McCone, see 15:92.

[781]
Executive Leadership Survey.

Purpose: Designed to aid in executive development and long-term succession planning.

Population: Top-level executives and managers; board members.
Publication Dates: 1988-2006.
Acronym: ELS.
Scores, 19: Leadership Vision, Risk Taking/Innovation, Engagement, Business & Financial Acumen, Industry & Market Insight, Organizational Savvy, Judgment, Customer Focus, Speed &Decisiveness, Talent & Team Development, Perseverance, Awareness of Others, Self-Awareness, Delivering World-Class Results, Push/Pressure, Self Management, Sharing Credit, Trust, Effectiveness/Outcomes.
Administration: Individual.
Price Data: Available from publisher.
Time: 20-30 minutes.
Comments: Publisher suggests allowing 2-3 weeks to collect feedback.
Authors: Paul M. Connolly and Clark L. Wilson.
Publisher: The Clark Wilson Group, Inc. (subsidiary of The Booth Company, Inc.).

[782]
Experience and Background Inventory (Form S).
Purpose: "Provides quantitative measures of past performance and experience."
Population: Adults [industry].
Publication Dates: 1980–1996.
Acronym: EBI.
Scores: 9 factors: School Achievement, Choice of a College Major, Aspiration Level, Drive/Career Progress, Leadership and Group Participation, Vocational Satisfaction, Financial Responsibility, General Responsibility, Relaxation Pursuits.
Administration: Group.
Price Data: Available from publisher.
Time: Administration time not reported.
Authors: Melany E. Baehr and Ernest C. Froemel.
Publisher: General Dynamics Information Technology.
Cross References: For reviews by F. Felicia Ferrara and Chantale Jeanrie, see 15:93.

[783]
The Experiencing Scale.
Purpose: Assess the degree to which a patient communicates and employs a personal, phenomenological perspective in a therapy session.
Population: Counselors and counselor trainees.
Publication Date: 1969.
Acronym: EXP.
Scores, 2: Mode, Peak; based on a 7-point rating scale.
Administration: Individual.
Price Data, 2015: $100 for Volume I and II and 10 CDs.
Time: Administration time not reported.

Comments: "Evaluating the quality of patient self-involvement in psychotherapy directly from tape recordings or typescripts of the therapy session"; tape or transcript of session required; rated by trained raters from tapes (audio or video).
Authors: M. H. Klein, P. L. Mathieu, E. T. Gendlin, and D. J. Kiesler.
Publisher: The Focusing Institute.
Cross References: See T5:991 (3 references) and T4:943 (1 reference).

[784]
Expression, Reception and Recall of Narrative Instrument.
Purpose: Designed to test "a person's ability to relate a story, comprehend it, and remember it after a delay" in order to measure "expressive language and story comprehension."
Population: Ages 4 and older; "most useful" with ages 6 and older.
Publication Date: 2004.
Acronym: ERRNI.
Scores, 5: Ideas: Initial Story-Telling, Ideas: Recall, Forgetting, Comprehension, Mean Length of Utterance in words (MLUw).
Administration: Individual.
Forms: 2 parallel forms: Version 1, Version 2.
Price Data, 2015: £154 per kit including manual (147 pages), stimulus book, 25 Version 1 record forms, and 25 Version 2 record forms in bag; £88.50 per manual; £80 per stimulus book; £39 per 25 record forms (Version 1 or Version 2).
Time: [8-10] minutes plus 10-30 minute delay.
Comments: Narrative must be audio recorded and transcribed.
Authors: D. V. M. Bishop.
Publisher: Pearson Clinical Assessment, a division of Pearson Education Ltd. [England].
Cross References: Reviews are scheduled for *The Twentieth Mental Measurements Yearbook*.

[785]
Expressive One-Word Picture Vocabulary Test–4: Spanish-Bilingual Edition.
Purpose: Designed to assess "an individual's ability to name–in either Spanish or English–objects, actions, and concepts shown in color illustrations."
Population: Ages 2–70+.
Publication Dates: 2001–2013.
Acronym: EOWPVT-4: SBE.
Score: Total score only.
Administration: Individual.
Price Data, 2015: $185 per test kit including manual (2013, 105 pages), test plates, and 25 record forms, in portfolio; $65 per manual; $40 per 25 record forms; $80 per test plates.

Time: (20) minutes.
Comments: Co-normed with the Receptive One-Word Picture Vocabulary Test–4: Spanish-Bilingual Edition (1700).
Author: Nancy A. Martin.
Publisher: Academic Therapy Publications.
Cross References: For a review by Michael S. Matthews, see 19:70; for a review by Jill Ann Jenkins of an earlier edition, see 16:88.

[786]

Expressive One-Word Picture Vocabulary Test, 4th Edition.

Purpose: Designed to measure an individual's English-speaking vocabulary.
Population: Ages 2 to 80 years and older.
Publication Dates: 1979-2011.
Acronym: EOWPVT-4.
Scores: Total score only.
Administration: Individual.
Price Data, 2015: $185 per test kit including manual (2011, 99 pages), 25 record forms, and test plates, in portfolio; $80 per set of test plates; $40 per 25 record forms; $65 per manual.
Foreign Language Edition: Spanish-Bilingual version available.
Time: (20) minutes.
Authors: 1990 and earlier edition by Morrison F. Gardner; 2000 edition by Rick Brownell; 4th Edition by Nancy A. Martin and Rick Brownell.
Publisher: Academic Therapy Publications.
Cross References: For reviews by Sandra M. Harris and Kathleen M. Johnson, see 19:71; for a review by Alfred Longo of the 2000 edition, see 15:95; see also T5:994 (53 references) and T4:946 (23 references); for reviews by Gregory J. Cizek and Larry B. Grantham of an earlier edition, see 12:147 (6 references); for reviews by Jack A. Cummings and Gilbert M. Spivack of the Lower Level, see 9:403 (2 references).

[787]

Expressive Vocabulary Test, Second Edition.

Purpose: Designed to assess "expressive vocabulary and word retrieval for Standard American English."
Population: Ages 2:6 to 90+ years.
Publication Dates: 1997-2007.
Acronym: EVT-2™.
Scores: Total score only.
Administration: Individual.
Forms, 2: A, B.
Price Data, 2015: $452.70 per complete kit (A & B) including 25 form A and form B record forms, and manual (2007, 238 pages); $55.15 per 25 record forms (specify A or B); form kits (specify A or B) are also available.
Time: (10-20) minutes.

Comments: Also includes a growth scale value (GSV) to specifically measure progress over time; conormed with the Peabody Picture Vocabulary Test-4 (1478); EVT-2 and PPVT-4 standard scores allow direct comparisons between expressive and receptive vocabulary; items are categorized for multiple levels and types of descriptive analysis; scoring and reporting software (ASSIST) allows for multiple types of individual and group reporting, including aggregation and disaggregation options; evidence-based interventions are embedded within the ASSIST.
Author: Kathleen T. Williams.
Publisher: Pearson.
Cross References: For reviews by Theresa Graham and Natalie Rathvon, see 18:51; for reviews by Frederick Bessai and Orest Eugene Wasyliw of a previous edition, see 14:143.

[788]

Extended Complex Figure Test.

Purpose: Designed to measure both perceptual organization and visual memory in persons with brain injury.
Population: Ages 6 and older.
Publication Date: 2003.
Acronym: ECFT.
Scores, 14: Copy Total Correct, Copy Time, Immediate Recall Total Correct, Immediate Recall Time, Delayed Recall Total Correct, Delayed Recall Time, Recognition Total Correct, Recognition Global, Recognition Detail, Recognition Left Detail, Recognition Right Detail, Matching Total Correct, Matching Left Detail, Matching Right Detail.
Administration: Individual.
Price Data, 2016: $197 per kit including manual (94 pages), stimulus booklet, and administration scoring booklets; $83.50 per stimulus booklet; $59 per 25 administration and scoring booklets; $72 per manual.
Time: (15–20) minutes plus 30-minute delay.
Author: Philip S. Fastenau.
Publisher: Western Psychological Services.
Cross References: For reviews by Mary "Rina" M. Chittooran and Daniel C. Miller, see 16:89.

[789]

Eyberg Child Behavior Inventory and Sutter-Eyberg Student Behavior Inventory—Revised.

Purpose: Designed "to measure conduct problems in children ages 2 through 16 years."
Population: Ages 2–16.
Publication Dates: 1978–1999.
Acronym: ECBI; SESBI-R.
Scores, 2: Intensity, Problem.
Administration: Group or individual.
Forms, 2: Eyberg Child Behavior Inventory; Sutter-Eyberg Student Behavior Inventory—Revised.

Price Data, 2015: $214 per introductory kit including professional manual (1999, 64 pages), 50 ECBI test sheets, and 50 SESBI-R test sheets.
Foreign Language Edition: Spanish version of the Eyberg Child Behavior Inventory form available.
Time: (10) minutes.
Comments: ECBI is a rating form completed by parents; SESBI-R is a rating form completed by teachers.
Authors: Sheila Eyberg (SESBI-R, ECBI, and professional manual), Joseph Sutter (SESBI-R), and Donna Pincus (professional manual).
Publisher: Psychological Assessment Resources, Inc.
Cross References: For reviews by Joyce Meikamp and by Susan C. Whiston and Jennifer C. Bouwkamp, see 15:96; for information on the Eyberg Child Behavior Inventory, see T5:997 (30 references) and T4:948 (26 references); for a review by Michael L. Reed of an earlier edition, see 9:404 (6 references); see also T3:858 (2 references). For information on the Sutter-Eyberg Student Behavior Inventory, see T5:2595 (2 references) and T4:2668 (1 reference); for a review by T. Steuart Watson of an earlier edition, see 11:410 (2 references).

[790]

Eysenck Personality Inventory.

Purpose: Measures two independent dimensions of personality: Extraversion-Introversion and Neuroticism-Stability.
Population: Adults.
Publication Dates: 1963–1969.
Acronym: EPI.
Scores, 3: Extraversion, Neuroticism, Lie.
Administration: Group.
Time: (10–15) minutes.
Comments: Revision of Maudsley Personality Inventory; for revised edition of EPI, see Eysenck Personality Questionnaire [Revised] (791); no reliability data for Lie scores; authors recommend use of both forms to obtain adequate reliability for individual measurements; U.S. and British Editions are identical except for three words and directions.
Authors: H. J. Eysenck and Sybil B. G. Eysenck.
  a) UNITED STATES EDITION.
  Population: Grades 9–16 and adults.
  Publication Dates: 1963–1969.
  Forms, 2: A, B.
  Price Data, 2016: $14.50 per 25 EPI Inventories (specify Form B or Form A-I) ; $6.75 per manual; $13.75 per hand-scoring keys; $12.25 per specimen set including manual and one copy of all forms.
  Foreign Language Edition: Spanish edition (1972) available.
  Comments: A printing with the title Eysenck Personality Inventory is available for industrial use.
  Publisher: EdITS/Educational and Industrial Testing Service.
  b) BRITISH EDITION.
  Population: Adults.

Publication Dates: 1963–1964.
Forms, 2: A, B.
Price Data: Available from publisher.
Comments: This test is now superseded by Eysenck Personality Questionnaire [Revised] (791) except where parallel forms are required.
Publisher: Hodder Education [United Kingdom].
Cross References: See T5:998 (135 references), T4:949 (226 references), 9:405 (91 references), and T3:859 (245 references); for a review by Auke Tellegen, see 8:553 (405 references); see also T2:1174 (140 references); for reviews by Richard I. Lanyon and excerpted reviews by A. W. Heim and James Linder, see 7:776 (121 references); see also P:77 (52 references); for a review by James C. Lingoes, see 6:93 (1 reference).

[791]

Eysenck Personality Questionnaire [Revised].

Publication Dates: 1975–1994.
Acronym: EPQ-R.
Scores, 5: Psychoticism or Tough-Mindedness, Extraversion, Neuroticism or Emotionality, Lie, Addiction.
Administration: Group.
Foreign Language Edition: Spanish edition available.
Time: (10–15) minutes.
Comments: Revision of the Eysenck Personality Inventory (790).
Authors: H. J. Eysenck and Sybil B. G. Eysenck.
  a) UNITED STATES EDITION.
  Purpose: Designed to measure four dimensions of personality in adults.
  Population: College and general adults including those with lower education levels.
  Publication Dates: 1975–1994.
  Price Data, 2016: $22.25 per 25 EPQ-R or EPQ-R short form inventories [$82 per 100, $306.50 per 500]; $35 per manual; $54.25 per hand-scoring keys; $45.50 per specimen set including a manual and one copy of all forms.
  b) BRITISH EDITION.
  Purpose: Measures three main personality factors: Psychoticism, Extraversion, and Neuroticism.
  Population: Ages 7–15, 16 and over.
  Publication Dates: 1975–1991.
  Price Data: Available from publisher.
  Publisher: Hodder Education [United Kingdom].
Cross References: See T5:999 (195 references), T4:950 (190 references), 9:406 (32 references), and T3:860 (72 references); for reviews by Jack Block, Paul Kline, Lawrence J. Stricker, and Auke Tellegen, see 8:554 (84 references).

[792]

FACES IV (Family Adaptability and Cohesion Evaluation Scale).

Purpose: To determine the dynamics of the family in terms of family cohesion and family flexibility in order to plot the family on the Circumplex Model.

Population: Couples and families.
Publication Dates: 1985-2010.
Acronym: FACES IV.
Scores: 2 major dimensions: Family Cohesion, Family Flexibility; 6 scales with 2 balanced scales (Balanced Cohesion and Balanced Flexibility) and 4 unbalanced scales (Disengaged and Enmeshed, Rigid and Chaotic).
Administration: Individual or group.
Price Data, 2015: $95 for FACES IV Package, which includes unlimited use (package includes manual [2010, 21 pages], scales, and scoring procedures as well as the Family Communication Scale and the Family Satisfaction Scale, both of which are also available separately).
Time: (15-20) minutes.
Comments: FACES II and FACES III are no longer available but are integrated into FACES IV; also known as Family Adaptability & Cohesion Evaluation Scales; self-report instrument; additional information available at www.facesiv.com.
Author: David H. Olson.
Publisher: Life Innovations, Inc.
Cross References: Reviews are scheduled for T*he Twentieth Mental Measurements Yearbook*. See T5:1000 (110 references), T4:951 (31 references), and 11:140 (26 references).

[793]

Facial Action Coding System.

Purpose: Constructed to assess facial movements or expressions.
Population: Adults.
Publication Date: 1978.
Acronym: FACS.
Scores: 66 Action Units.
Administration: Individual.
Price Data: Available from publisher.
Time: Administration time not reported.
Comments: The test publisher has indicated there is a newer edition of this test; description will be updated when complete test materials are received.
Authors: Paul Ekman and Wallace V. Friesen.
Publisher: Paul Ekman Group.
Cross References: See T5:1001 (17 references); for reviews by Kathryn M. Benes and Thomas F. Donlon, see 12:149 (7 references); see also T4:952 (11 references).

[794]

The Fairy Tale Test, 2nd Edition.

Purpose: A projective test designed to help assess personality variables in children.
Population: Ages 6-12 years.
Publication Dates: 2003-2013.
Acronym: FTT.
Scores, 30: Desire for Material Things, Desire for Help, Desire for Superiority, Oral Needs, Need for Affiliation, Need to Give and/or Receive Affection, Need

for Approval, Need for Protection, Sexual Preoccupation, Bizarres, Oral Aggression, Instrumental Aggression, Impulsive Aggression, Aggression as Defense, Aggression as Dominance, Aggression as Envy, Aggression as Jealousy, Aggression as Retaliation, Relationship with Mother, Relationship with Father, Fear of Aggression, Anxiety, Depression, Ambivalence, Self-Esteem, Morality, Sense of Property, Sense of Privacy, Adaptation to Fairy Tale Content, Repetitions.
Administration: Individual.
Price Data, 2016: $193 per complete kit including manual (2013, 298 pages), 21 test cards, and 10 recording sheets; $111 per manual; $48 per 21 test cards; $34 per 10 recording sheets.
Time: (45) minutes.
Comments: Norms based on sample of children from regions of India.
Authors: Carina Coulacoglou.
Publisher: Hogrefe Ltd [United Kingdom].
Cross References: For reviews by Frederic J. Medway and Peter Zachar of the original edition (norms based on sample of children from Greece), see 16:90.

[795]

A Familism Scale.

Purpose: Measures attitudes related to family.
Population: Adolescents and adults.
Publication Dates: 1959–1988.
Scores, 3: Nuclear, Extended, Total.
Administration: Group.
Manual: No manual.
Price Data, 2015: $2 per scale.
Time: (8) minutes.
Comments: Supplementary article available.
Author: Panos D. Bardis.
Publisher: Donna Bardis.
Cross References: See T4:957 (1 reference).

[796]

Family Assessment Form: A Practice-Based Approach to Assessing Family Functioning.

Purpose: Constructed to "standardize the assessment of family functioning and service planning for families receiving home-based services."
Population: Families receiving home-based services
Publication Date: 1997.
Acronym: FAF.
Scores, 6: Parent-Child Interactions, Living Conditions, Caregiver Interactions, Supports for Parents, Financial Conditions, Developmental Stimulation.
Administration: Group.
Price Data: Price information available from publisher for test booklet/manual (79 pages).
Time: (60–90) minutes.
Comments: Ratings by child welfare practitioners.

Author: Children's Bureau of Southern California.
Publisher: Child Welfare League of America.
Cross References: For reviews by Cindy Carlson and Mary Lou Kelley, see 14:144; see also T5:1007 (1 reference).

[797]

Family Assessment Measure Version III.

Purpose: "Provides quantitative indices of family strengths and weaknesses."
Population: Families.
Publication Dates: 1993–1995.
Acronym: FAM-III.
Scores, 26: General scale (Task Accomplishment, Role Performance, Communication, Affective Expression, Involvement, Control, Values and Norms, Social Desirability, Defensiveness, Total), Dyadic Relationships (Task Accomplishment, Role Performance, Communication, Affective Expression, Involvement, Control, Values and Norms, Total), Self-Rating (Task Accomplishment, Role Performance, Communication, Affective Expression, Involvement, Control, Values and Norms, Total).
Administration: Individual.
Price Data, 2015: $289 per FAM-III complete kit including manual (1995, 90 pages), 25 General Scale QuikScore™ forms, 25 Dyadic Relationship Scale QuikScore™ forms, 25 Self-Rating Scale QuikScore™ forms, and 15 ColorPlot Profile of Family Perceptions; $289 per Brief FAM complete kit including manual, 25 Brief FAM General Scale QuikScore™ forms, 25 Brief FAM Dyadic Relationship Scale QuikScore™ forms, 25 Brief FAM Self-Rating Scale QuikScore™ forms, and 15 Progress ColorPlots; $55 per 25 General Scale QuikScore™ forms (English, Spanish, or French-Canadian); $55 per 25 Dyadic Relationship Scale QuikScore™ forms (English, Spanish, or French-Canadian); $55 per 25 Self-Rating Scale QuikScore™ forms (English, Spanish, or French-Canadian); $55 per 25 Brief General Scale QuikScore™ forms (English, Spanish, or French-Canadian); $55 per 25 Brief FAM Dyadic Relationship Scale QuikScore™ forms (English, Spanish, or French-Canadian); $55 per 25 Brief FAM Self-Rating Scale QuikScore™ forms (English, Spanish, or French-Canadian); $47 per 15 Progress Color Plot Profiles; $47 per 15 Color Plot Profile of Family Perceptions; $91 per technical manual; software also available; $11 per FAM-III profile report; $8 per Brief profile report; $62 per FAM-III preview version including 3 profile reports and software manual.
Foreign Language Editions: Spanish and French-Canadian QuikScore™ forms available.
Time: (30–40) minutes.
Authors: Harvey A. Skinner, Paul D. Steinhauer, and Jack Santa-Barbara.
Publisher: Multi-Health Systems Inc.

Cross References: For reviews by Kenneth J. Manges and Stephen A. Spilland, see 14:145; see also T5:1008 (3 references).

[798]

Family Child Care Environment Rating Scale, Revised Edition.

Purpose: Designed to assess program quality and to quantify "what is observed to be happening in a family child care home."
Population: Consumers of day care services, day care providers, agency supervisors, and researchers.
Publication Dates: 1989-2007.
Acronym: FCCERS-R.
Scores, 46: 38 items in 7 subscales: Space and Furnishing (Indoor Space Used for Childcare, Furniture for Routine Care/Play/Learning, Provision for Relaxation and Comfort, Arrangement of Indoor Space for Child Care, Display for Children, Space for Privacy), Personal Care Routines (Greeting/Departing, Nap/Rest, Meals/Snacks, Diapering/Toileting, Health Practices, Safety Practices), Listening and Talking (Helping Children Understand Language, Helping Children Use Language, Using Books), Activities (Fine Motor, Art, Music and Movement, Blocks, Dramatic Play, Math/Number, Nature/Science, Sand and Water Play, Promoting Acceptance of Diversity, Use of TV/Video/Computer, Active Physical Play), Interaction (Supervision of Play and Learning, Provider-Child Interaction, Discipline, Interactions Among Children), Program Structure (Schedule, Free Play, Group Time, Provisions for Children with Disabilities), Parents and Provider (Provisions for Parents, Balancing Personal and Caregiving Responsibilities, Opportunities for Professional Growth, Provisions for Professional Needs), plus Total Score.
Administration: Individual family child care homes.
Price Data, 2015: $22.95 per manual with complete test (2007, 88 pages).
Foreign Language Edition: Spanish version available.
Time: (180) minutes minimum for observation.
Comments: Revision of Family and Day Care Rating Scale; may be used as self-assessment or by outside observers for program monitoring, program evaluation, program improvement, or research.
Authors: Thelma Harms, Debby Cryer, and Richard M. Clifford.
Publisher: Teachers College Press.
Cross References: Reviews are scheduled for *The Twentieth Mental Measurements Yearbook*. For a review by Annette M. Iverson of an earlier edition titled Family and Day Care Rating Scale, see 11:141.

[799]

Family Communication Scale.

Purpose: Designed to measure family communication.

Population: Families.
Publication Dates: 2000-2010.
Scores: Family Communication for individual family members.
Administration: Individual or group.
Price Data, 2015: $30 per manual (7 pages) and scale (unlimited rights for duplication).
Time: (10-15) minutes.
Comments: Included in FACES IV package (792).
Authors: David H. Olson and Howard Barnes.
Publisher: Life Innovations, Inc.

[800]
Family Environment Scale [Third Edition Manual].

Purpose: Designed to assess family members' perceptions of their family environment.
Population: Ages 11–adult.
Publication Dates: 1974–2002.
Acronym: FES.
Scores: 10 in 3 dimensions: Relationship (Cohesion, Expressiveness, Conflict), Personal Growth (Independence, Achievement Orientation, Intellectual-Cultural Orientation, Active-Recreational Orientation, Moral-Religious Emphasis), System Maintenance (Organization, Control).
Administration: Individual or group.
Forms, 3: Real (Form R), Ideal (Form I), Expectations (Form E).
Price Data, 2015: $50 per manual, including review-only copy of FES forms; $15 per Individual Report; $15 per Report About Me; $100 per Group Report: Real Form; $2.40 per online administration license (minimum 50); $2 per Remote Online Survey License (minimum 50); $2 per License to Reproduce (minimum 50).
Foreign Language Edition: Translated materials available for Arabic, Traditional Chinese, Danish, Dutch, Finnish, French, Greek, Hebrew, Hindi, Italian, Japanese, Korean, Polish, Portuguese, Swedish, and Thai. Form R only available in Farsi, Malay, Norwegian, and Slovenian. Form R and E available in Spanish.
Time: (15–20) minutes.
Comments: One component of the Social Climate Scales (T5:2445); Children's version available.
Authors: Rudolf H. Moos and Bernice S. Moos.
Publisher: Mind Garden, Inc.
Cross References: For reviews by Jay A. Mancini and Michael J. Sporakowski, see 14:146; see also T5:1010 (138 references); for reviews by Julie A. Allison and Brenda H. Loyd of an earlier edition, see 12:151 (76 references); see also T4:961 (136 references); for reviews by Nancy A. Busch-Rossnagel and Nadine M. Lambert of an earlier edition, see 9:408 (18 references); see also T3:872 (14 references); for a review by Philip H. Dreyer, see 8:557 (4 references). For a review of the Social Climate Series, see 8:681.

[801]
Family Relations Test: Children's Version.

Purpose: "To assess the relative importance that different family members have for children" and to explore the child's emotional relations with his family.
Population: Ages 3–15.
Publication Date: 1976.
Administration: Individual.
Levels, 2: Form for Young Children, Form for Older Children.
Price Data, 2016: £350 for complete set including manual (1985, 59 pages), test figures and item cards, scoring and record sheets for older children, and record/score sheets for young children.
Time: 25(40) minutes.
Authors: Eva Bene (test and revised manual) and James Anthony (test).
Publisher: GL Assessment [England].
   a) FORM FOR YOUNG CHILDREN.
   Population: Ages 3–7.
   Scores, 8: Outgoing Feelings (Positive Total, Negative Total), Incoming Feelings (Positive Total, Negative Total), Dependency Feelings, Sum of Positive, Sum of Negative, Total Involvement.
   b) FORM FOR OLDER CHILDREN.
   Population: Ages 7–15.
   Scores, 12: Sum of Outgoing Positive, Sum of Outgoing Negative, Sum of Incoming Positive, Sum of Incoming Negative, Total Involvement, Sum of Positive Mild, Sum of Positive Strong, Sum of Negative Mild, Sum of Negative Strong, Maternal Overprotection, Paternal Overindulgence, Maternal Overindulgence.
Cross References: See T5:1012 (2 references); for reviews by Cindy I. Carlson and Steven I. Pfeiffer, see 11:142; for information on the complete test, see 9:409 (3 references), T3:874 (33 references), 8:558 (18 references), and T2:1182 (4 references); for an excerpted review by B. Semeonoff of the Children's Version and the Adult Version, see 7:79 (7 references); see also P:81 (2 references); for reviews by John E. Bell, Dale B. Harris, and Arthur R. Jensen of the Children's Version, see 5:132 (1 reference).

[802]
Family Relationship Inventory.

Purpose: "Method of examining family relationships, designed to clarify individual feelings and interpersonal behavior"; within the family, the FRI identifies who feels closest to whom and who feels most distant and provides a Self-Esteem score for each family member.
Population: Young children age 5 and above, adolescents, and adults.
Publication Dates: 1972–1984.
Acronym: FRI.
Scores, 2: Positive, Negative, for each family member.
Administration: Individual or family groups.
Price Data, 2015: $250 per complete kit including item cards, 25 scoring forms, 50 tabulating forms, 50

individual relationship wheel forms, 25 familygram forms, and test manual (1982, 36 pages); $66.50 per set of item cards; $43.50 per 100 scoring forms; $49.50 per 100 tabulating forms; $49.50 per 100 individual relationship wheels; $49.50 per 100 familygrams.
Time: Administration time not reported.
Comments: Based upon Family Relationship Scale.
Authors: Ruth B. Michaelson, Harry L. Bascom, Louise Nash, W. Lee Morrison, and Robert M. Taylor.
Publisher: Psychological Publications, Inc.
Cross References: See T5:1013 (2 references) and T4:964 (2 references); for a review by Mary Henning-Stout, see 10:112.

[803]

Family Satisfaction Scale [Revised].

Purpose: Designed to measure satisfaction on the dimensions of family cohesion and family adaptability.
Population: Families.
Publication Dates: 1982-2010.
Scores: Family Satisfaction for individual family members.
Administration: Individual or group.
Price Data, 2015: $30 per manual (7 pages) and scale (unlimited rights for duplication).
Time: (10-15) minutes.
Comments: Included in FACES IV package (792).
Authors: David H. Olson.
Publisher: Life Innovations, Inc.
Cross References: See T5:1014 (7 references).

[804]

Family-Supportive Supervisor's Behaviors.

Purpose: Designed to address "how supervisors can help workers ease the stress of work and non-work life."
Population: Working adults.
Publication Date: 2014.
Acronym: FSSB.
Scores, 4: Emotional Support, Instrumental Support, Role Modeling, Creative Work-Family Management.
Administration: Individual or group.
Price Data, 2016: $50 per PDF manual including review-only copy of form (27 pages); $60 per paper manual; $2 per Remote Online Survey License or License to Reproduce (minimum 50); $15 per Individual Report; $250 per Group Report.
Time: (5) minutes.
Authors: Leslie B. Hammer and Ellen E. Kossek.
Publisher: Mind Garden, Inc.

[805]

A Family Violence Scale.

Purpose: To indicate the occurrence of family violence in one's childhood.
Population: Adolescents and adults.
Publication Dates: 1973–1988.

Scores: Total Family Violence Score.
Administration: Group.
Manual: No manual.
Price Data, 2015: $2 per scale.
Time: Administration time not reported.
Comments: Supplementary article available.
Author: Panos D. Bardis.
Publisher: Donna Bardis.
Cross References: See 8:340 (1 reference).

[806]

Fear Survey Schedule.

Purpose: "Designed to identify and quantify patients' reactions to a variety of sources of maladaptive emotional reactions."
Population: College and adults.
Publication Dates: 1964–1977.
Acronym: FSS.
Scores: Total score only.
Administration: Group.
Price Data, 2016: $19 per 25 response forms and manual; $52.75 per 50 response forms and manual.
Time: (15) minutes.
Comments: Self-rating.
Authors: Joseph Wolpe and Peter J. Lang.
Publisher: EdITS/Educational and Industrial Testing Service.
Cross References: See T5:1021 (48 references), T4:974 (30 references), 9:411 (23 references), and T3:883 (53 references); for a review by Charles D. Spielberger, see 8:559 (32 references); see also T2:1185 (14 references); for a review by R. G. Demaree, see 7:80 (17 references).

[807]

Feelings, Attitudes, and Behaviors Scale for Children.

Purpose: "Designed to assess a range of emotional and behavioral problems."
Population: Ages 6–13.
Publication Date: 1996.
Acronym: FAB-C.
Scores, 7: Conduct Problems, Self Image, Worry, Negative Peer Relationships, Antisocial, Lie (validity), Problem Index.
Administration: Individual or Group.
Price Data, 2015: $116 per complete kit including manual (47 pages), and 25 QuikScore™ forms; $55 per 25 QuikScore™ forms; $81 per manual; $89 per online profile report kit including manual and 3 profile reports; $6 per online profile report.
Time: (10) minutes.
Comments: Self-report.
Author: Joseph H. Beitchman.
Publisher: Multi-Health Systems, Inc.
Cross References: For reviews by Patti L. Harrison and Mary Lou Kelley, see 14:147.

[808]

Figure Classification Test.

Purpose: Designed to "measure abstract reasoning ability."
Population: Applicants for industrial work with 7 to 9 years of schooling.
Publication Date: 1976.
Scores: Total score only.
Administration: Group.
Price Data: Price information available from publisher for test materials including manual (21 pages).
Foreign Language Edition: Manual written in both English and Afrikaans.
Time: 60(70) minutes.
Comments: Separate answer sheets must be used.
Author: T. R. Taylor.
Publisher: Human Sciences Research Council [South Africa].
Cross References: See T4:978 (1 reference).

[809]

The Filipino Work Values Scale.

Purpose: "Constructed to measure work values."
Population: Filipino employees and students.
Publication Dates: 1987–1988.
Acronym: FWVS.
Scores, 10: Environmental, Familial, Intellectual-Achievement Oriented, Interpersonal, Managerial, Material, Occupational, Organizational, Religious, Variety.
Administration: Group or individual.
Forms, 2: Employee, Student.
Price Data: Available from publisher.
Foreign Language Editions: English, Thai; Philippine languages editions: Cebuano, Filipino, Pangasinense.
Time: (15–20) minutes.
Author: Vicentita M. Cervera.
Publisher: MAVEC Specialists Foundation, Inc. [Philippines] [No reply from publisher; status unknown].
Cross References: For reviews by Gary J. Dean and William I. Sauser, Jr., see 14:148.

[810]

Fire Promotional Tests (Custom).

Purpose: "Fully-customized content-valid written promotional assessments to test the duties and responsibilities of firefighters."
Population: Firefighters.
Publication Dates: 1979–2010.
Scores: 11 subtests: Knowledge of Fire Protection/Prevention Practices, Fire Investigation Practices, Size-Up and Command Practices, Emergency Scene Practices–All Companies, Emergency Scene Practices–Truck Companies, Emergency Scene Practices–Engine Companies, Emergency Scene Practices–EMS Companies, Supervisory and Managerial Practices, Administrative Practices, Ability to Comprehend Hypothetical Fire Codes, Ability to Read and Comprehend Fire-Service Related Tables and Texts.
Administration: Group.
Price Data: Available from publisher.
Time: (210) minutes.
Author: McCann Associates.
Publisher: McCann Associates [No reply from publisher; status unknown].

[811]

Firefighter Learning Simulation.

Purpose: Designed to "simulate the learning process required of entry-level firefighters in Fire Academies."
Population: Applicants for firefighter trainee positions.
Publication Dates: 1983-1998.
Acronym: FLS.
Scores: Total score only.
Administration: Group or individual.
Price Data: Price information available from publisher for test material including Administration Guide and Technical Manual (11 pages), and Training Manual (26 pages).
Time: 90(95) minutes.
Comments: Simulated training manual is provided to examinees in advance of the test.
Author: Psychological Services, Inc.
Publisher: PSI Services LLC.
Cross References: For reviews by JoEllen V. Carlson and James W. Pinkney, see 15:102.

[812]

Firefighter Selection Test [Revised].

Purpose: "To rank-order applicants according to their probability of success in training and success on the job" as a firefighter.
Population: Applicants for firefighter trainee positions.
Publication Dates: 1983–1998.
Acronym: FST.
Scores: Total score only.
Administration: Group or individual.
Price Data: Price data available from publisher for test material including Technical Manual (1998, 22 pages), Administrator's Guide (1998, 6 pages), and Study Guide (1998, 16 pages).
Time: 150(165) minutes.
Comments: Measures mechanical comprehension, reading comprehension, and report interpretation.
Author: Psychological Services, Inc.
Publisher: PSI Services LLC.
Cross References: For reviews by Chantale Jeanrie and Deniz S. Ones, see 15:103; for reviews by David O. Anderson and Cynthia Ann Druva-Roush of an earlier edition, see 11:143.

[813]

Firestone Assessment of Self-Destructive Thoughts and Firestone Assessment of Suicide Intent.

Purpose: Designed to assess "a wide range of self-destructive behaviors—from self-denial, to extreme self-hate, addictions, self-mutilation, and ... suicide."

Population: Ages 16 to 70 years.

Publication Dates: 1996-2006.

Administration: Individual or group.

Price Data, 2015: $218 per kit including manual (2006, 119 pages), 25 FAST rating forms, 25 FAST scoring summary/profile forms, and 25 FASI rating forms/scoring summary; $74 per manual; $70 per 25 FAST rating forms; $23 per 25 FAST scoring summary/profile forms; $54 per 25 FASI rating forms/scoring summary.

Authors: Robert W. Firestone and Lisa A. Firestone.

Publisher: Psychological Assessment Resources, Inc.

   a) FIRESTONE ASSESSMENT OF SELF-DE-STRUCTIVE THOUGHTS.

   Acronym: FAST.

   Scores, 15: Self-Defeating (Self-Depreciation, Self-Denial, Cynical Attitudes, Isolation, Self-Contempt, Total), Self-Annihilating (Addictions, Hopelessness, Giving Up, Self-Harm, Suicide Plans, Suicide Injunctions, Total), Suicide Intent, Total.

   Time: (15-20) minutes.

   b) FIRESTONE ASSESSMENT OF SUICIDE IN-TENT.

   Purpose: Derived from the FAST as a "brief screener focusing on suicide risk."

   Acronym: FASI.

   Score: Total score only.

   Time: (5-10) minutes.

Cross References: For reviews by William E. Martin and Robert C. Reinehr of the Firestone Assessment of Self-Destructive Thoughts, see 14:149.

[814]

Firestone Assessment of Violent Thoughts.

Purpose: "Designed to assess the underlying thoughts that predispose violent behavior."

Population: Ages 18+.

Publication Dates: 1999-2008.

Acronym: FAVT.

Scores, 10: Paranoid/Suspicious, Persecuted Misfit, Self-Depreciating/Pseudo-Independent, Overtly Aggressive, Self-Aggrandizing, Total, Theoretical Subscale scores (Instrumental/Proactive Violence, Hostile/Reactive Violence), Validity scores (Negativity, Inconsistency).

Administration: Group.

Price Data, 2015: $146 per introductory kit including professional manual (2008, 148 pages), 25 rating forms, and 25 score summary/profile forms; $70 per 25 rating forms; $23 per 25 score summary/profile forms; $60 per professional manual.

Time: (15-20) minutes.

Comments: Scores normed for Younger Men (ages 18-39), Older Men (ages 40-75), Younger Women (ages 18-39), and Older Women (ages 40-75).

Authors: Robert W. Firestone and Lisa A. Firestone.

Publisher: Psychological Assessment Resources, Inc.

Cross References: For reviews by Stephen Axford and M. Meghan Davidson, see 18:52.

[815]

Firestone Assessment of Violent Thoughts-Adolescent.

Purpose: To "assess the underlying thoughts that predispose violent behavior in adolescents."

Population: Ages 11-18.

Publication Dates: 1999-2008.

Acronym: FAVT-A.

Scores, 9: Paranoid/Suspicious, Persecuted Misfit, Self-Depreciating/Pseudo-Independent, Overtly Aggressive, Total, Instrumental/Proactive Violence, Hostile/Reactive Violence, Inconsistency, Negativity.

Administration: Individual.

Price Data, 2015: $138 per introductory kit including professional manual (2008, 167 pages), 25 rating forms, and 25 score summary/profile forms; $60 per professional manual; $70 per 25 rating forms; $23 per 25 score summary/profile forms.

Time: 15 minutes.

Authors: Robert W. Firestone and Lisa A. Firestone.

Publisher: Psychological Assessment Resources, Inc.

Cross References: For reviews by David F. Ciampi and Jeremy R. Sullivan, see 19:72.

[816]

FIRO-B® [Fundamental Interpersonal Relations Orientation—Behavior™].

Purpose: Designed "to measure behavior that derives from interpersonal needs."

Population: Age 13 and over.

Publication Dates: 1958–2000.

Acronym: FIRO-B™.

Scores, 7: 2 Overall Behavior scores (Expressed, Wanted) for each of 3 dimensions (Inclusion, Control, Affection) plus Overall Need score.

Administration: Individual or group.

Price Data, 2016: $16.95 per FIRO-B® Profile online administration; $139.50 per 10 FIRO-B® Self-Scorable forms; $14.95 per FIRO-B® Interpretive Report for Organizations online administration; $25.95 per Leadership Report Using the FIRO-B® and MBTI® Instruments online administration; $61 per FIRO-B® Technical Guide; $124.50 per 10 Introduction to the FIRO-B® Instrument; $124.50 per 10 Introduction to the FIRO-B® Instrument in Organizations; $124.50 per 10 Participating in Teams (Using Your FIRO-B® Results to Improve Interpersonal Effectiveness); $99.50 per 10 Understanding Your FIRO-B® Results.

Time: (10–15) minutes.

Comments: May be administered via paper-pencil or online at skillsone.com; earlier versions titled FIRO Awareness Scales.

Authors: William Schutz (original test), Allen L. Hammer (technical guide), and Eugene R. Schnell (technical guide).

Publisher: CPP, Inc.

Cross References: For reviews by Michelle Athanasiou and Donald Oswald, see 15:104; see T5:1036 (13 references) and T4:982 (18 references); for a review by Peter D. Lifton of an earlier edition, see 9:416 (12 references); see also T3:890 (45 references), 8:555 (147 references), and T2:1176 (58 references); for a review by Bruce Bloxom, see 7:78 (70 references); see also P:79 (30 references) and 6:94 (15 references).

[817]

FIRO Business® [Fundamental Interpersonal Relations Orientation].

Purpose: Designed "to provide a measure of interpersonal needs" and "to predict future interactions with others based on level of expressed or wanted needs."

Population: Ages 18 and older.

Publication Dates: 2009-2010.

Scores, 12: Total Involvement, Total Influence, Total Connection, Total Expressed Needs, Total Wanted Needs, Expressed Involvement, Wanted Involvement, Expressed Influence, Wanted Influence, Expressed Connection, Wanted Connection, Overall Score.

Administration: Individual.

Price Data, 2016: $20.95 per FIRO® Business Leadership Report; $31.95 per FIRO® Business Leadership Report with FIRO Business® Profile; $124.50 per 10 Introduction to the FIRO Business® Instrument; $71 per FIRO Business® Technical Guide; $31 per FIRO Business® Leadership Report User's Guide.

Foreign Language Editions: Available in Arabic, Chinese (Simplified and Traditional), Danish, Dutch, English (U.K.), Finnish, French, German, Greek, Italian, Japanese, Korean, Norwegian, Polish, Portuguese (Brazilian and European), Russian, Spanish (European and Latin American), and Swedish.

Time: [8] minutes.

Comments: The FIRO Business® instrument is "an extension and updated version of the original FIRO-B® assessment"; computer-administered and scored.

Authors: Nicole A. Herk, Richard C. Thompson, Michael L. Morris, and Nancy A. Schaubhut (Technical Guide); Judith A. Waterman and Jenny Rogers (Introduction to the FIRO Business® Instrument); Eugene R. Schnell and Allen L. Hammer (Leadership Report User's Guide).

Publisher: CPP, Inc.

Cross References: Reviews are scheduled for *The Twentieth Mental Measurements Yearbook*.

[818]

FirstSTEP: Screening Test for Evaluating Preschoolers.

Purpose: "Designed to identify preschool children who are at risk for developmental delays in the five areas mandated by IDEA (PL 99-457)."

Population: Preschool children.

Publication Dates: 1990–1993.

Scores, 7: Cognitive, Language, Motor, Composite, Social-Emotional, Adaptive Behavior, Parent/Teacher.

Administration: Individual.

Levels, 3: Ages 1–2, Ages 3–4, Ages 5–7.

Price Data, 2015: $305.30 per complete kit including 5 record forms each for levels 1, 2, and 3, 25 Social-Emotional/Adaptive Behavior booklets, 25 Parent booklets, manipulatives, and manual (1993, 166 pages); $58.85 per 25 record forms (specify level); $30.35 per 25 Social-Emotional Scale/Adaptive Behavior checklists; $30.35 per 25 Parent/Teacher Scales; $147.75 per manual; $35.25 per manipulatives; $96.20 per stimulus booklet.

Foreign Language Edition: Spanish version titled PrimerPASO was published in 2003.

Time: (15–20) minutes.

Author: Lucy J. Miller.

Publisher: Pearson.

Cross References: For a review by Terry Overton, see 13:126.

[819]

Fitness Interview Test-Revised.

Purpose: A screening instrument that provides "a structured interview for assessing competency to stand trial."

Population: Juveniles and adults.

Publication Date: 2006.

Acronym: FIT-R.

Scores: Individual item scores only.

Subtests, 3: Understand the Nature or Object of Proceedings, Understand the Possible Consequences, Communicate with Counsel.

Administration: Individual.

Price Data, 2015: $60 per manual (64 pages) and CD-ROM.

Time: Administration time not reported.

Comments: Designed to correspond with case law in the U.S., U.K., and Canada.

Authors: Ronald Roesch, Patricia A. Zapf, and Derek Eaves.

Publisher: Professional Resource Press.

Cross References: For reviews by Rita Budrionis and Joe W. Dixon, see 18:53.

[820]

Five-Factor Personality Inventory–Children.

Purpose: Developed to "measure personality dispositions in children and adolescents" in order to "identify children who are at risk for adjustment problems at school and in their community."

Population: Ages 9-0 to 18-11.

Publication Date: 2007.

Acronym: FFPI-C.

Scores, 5: Agreeableness, Extraversion, Openness to Experience, Conscientiousness, Emotional Regulation.

Administration: Individual or group.

Price Data, 2015: $166 per complete kit including examiner's manual (69 pages), and 25 administration and scoring forms. $85 per examiner's manual; $85 per 25 administration and scoring forms.

Time: (15-40) minutes.

Comments: Descriptive ratings for each of the five scores are provided to aid in the interpretation of personality characteristics as they relate to a child's risk for experiencing adjustment problems.

Authors: Ronnie L. McGhee, David J. Ehrler, and Joseph A. Buckhalt.

Publisher: PRO-ED.

Cross References: For reviews by Merith Cosden and H. Dennis Kade, see 18:54.

---

[821]

Five Factor Wellness Inventory (2nd Edition Manual).

Purpose: Designed to "assess characters of wellness as a basis for helping individuals make choices for healthier living."

Population: Elementary students, high school students, and adults.

Publication Dates: 2005-2014.

Acronym: FFWEL, 5F-WEL.

Scores, 28: Wellness (Creative Self [Thinking, Emotions, Control, Positive Humor, Work], Coping Self [Realistic Beliefs, Stress Management, Self-Worth, Leisure], Social Self [Friendship, Love], Essential Self [Spirituality, Self-Care, Gender Identity, Cultural Identity], Physical Self [Exercise, Nutrition]), Local Context, Institutional Context, Global Context, Chronometrical Context, Life Satisfaction Index.

Administration: Individual or group.

Levels, 3: Elementary, Teen, Adult.

Forms, 3: FFWEL-E, FFWEL-T, FFWEL-A2.

Price Data, 2016: $50 per PDF manual, including review-only copy of forms and scoring key (2014, 88 pages); $15 per individual report; $2 per Remote Online Survey License or License to Reproduce (minimum 50).

Foreign Language Editions: Translations available from test publisher.

Time: (10-20) minutes.

Comments: Original adult form (Form A) was revised in 2014 to alter one item on the Self-Care scale; 2nd edition manual includes norms for teenagers and adults.

Authors: Jane E. Myers and Thomas J. Sweeney.

Publisher: Mind Garden, Inc.

Cross References: For reviews by Gerald E. DeMauro and Susan Lonborg of the original version, see 17:74.

---

[822]

The Five P's (Parent/Professional Preschool Performance Profile) [2002 Update].

Purpose: Constructed to collect teacher and parent ratings of child's observed performance across all domains of development to create a comprehensive profile of child's current level of functioning, to link assessment to goal setting and remediation, to monitor change over time, and to promote home/school collaboration.

Population: Children with disabilities between the ages of 6 and 59 months.

Publication Dates: 1982–2004.

Scores: Standard Index and Percentile scores may be prepared separately in five domains of development: Self Help (Toileting and Hygiene, Mealtime Behaviors, Dressing), Language Development (Communicative Competence, Receptive Language, Expressive Language), Social Development (Emerging Self, Relationships to Adults, Relationships to Children, Classroom Adjustment), Motor Development (Gross Motor/Balance/Coordination Skills, Perceptual/Fine Motor Skills), Cognitive Development; Interfering Behaviors for each of the five domains are scored separately.

Administration: Individual.

Price Data, 2004: $150 per materials for class of 10 children including 10 sets of scales, 1 user manual (2002, 40 pages), 10 Information and Directions, 10 graphic profiles, 1 copy of The Five P's Preschool Annual Goals and Short-Term Instructional Objectives; $45 per training video (25 minutes); $10 per user manual; $25 per copy of The Five P's Preschool Annual Goals and Short-Term Instructional Objectives (bound copy); $45 per technical manual, which includes Index and Percentile Score Tables (2004, 132 pages); $85 per sample packet including assessment packet, training video, research papers, and The Five P's Preschool Annual Goals and Short-Term Instructional Objectives.

Foreign Language Edition: Spanish edition available.

Time: (60) minutes.

Comments: Teacher and Parent Observer training protocol and training video available. The test publisher has indicated there is a newer edition of this test; description will be updated when complete test materials are received.

Authors: Judith Simon Bloch, John S. Hicks, and Janice L. Friedman.

Publisher: Variety Child Learning Center.

Cross References: For reviews by Kimberly A. Blair and Lisa F. Smith, see 16:91; for reviews by Annie W. Ward and Steven Zucker of an earlier edition, see 13:127; for a review by Barbara Perry-Sheldon, see 10:116.

[823]

Flanagan Aptitude Classification Tests.

Purpose: Measurement of aptitudes for 16 on-the-job skills.

Population: Individuals in a variety of lower-level industrial or mechanical positions.

Publication Dates: 1951–1994.

Acronym: FACT.

Scores: Total score only for each test.

Administration: Individual or group.

Price Data: Available from publisher.

Author: John C. Flanagan.

Publisher: General Dynamics Information Technology.

a) FACT 1A, INSPECTION.
Publication Dates: 1953–1956.
Time: 6 minutes.

b) FACT 2A AND 2B, CODING.
Publication Dates: 1953–1956.
Forms, 2: A, B.
Time: 10 minutes.

c) FACT 3A AND 3B, MEMORY.
Publication Dates: 1953–1956.
Forms, 2: A, B.
Time: 4 minutes.

d) FACT 4A, PRECISION.
Publication Dates: 1953–1956.
Time: 8 minutes.

e) FACT 5A, ASSEMBLY.
Publication Dates: 1953–1956.
Time: 12 minutes.

f) FACT 6A, SCALES.
Publication Dates: 1953–1956.
Time: 16 minutes.

g) FACT 7A, COORDINATION.
Publication Dates: 1953–1956.
Time: 2 minutes, 40 seconds.

h) FACT 8A, JUDGEMENT AND COMPREHENSION.
Publication Dates: 1953–1956.
Time: No limit (approximately 35 minutes).

i) FACT 9A, ARITHMETIC.
Publication Dates: 1953–1956.
Time: 10 minutes.

j) FACT 10A, PATTERNS.
Publication Dates: 1953–1956.
Time: 20 minutes.

k) FACT 11A, COMPONENTS.
Publication Dates: 1953–1956.
Time: 20 minutes.

l) FACT 12A, TABLES.
Publication Dates: 1953–1956.
Time: 10 minutes.

m) FACT 13A AND 13B, MECHANICS.
Publication Dates: 1953–1956.
Forms, 2: A, B.
Time: 20 minutes.

n) FACT 14A, EXPRESSION.
Publication Dates: 1953–1956.
Time: No limit (approximately 30 minutes).

o) FACT 15A, REASONING.
Publication Dates: 1957–1960.
Time: 24 minutes.

p) FACT 16A, INGENUITY.
Publication Dates: 1957–1960.
Time: 24 minutes.

Cross References: See T3:899 (2 references), and T2:1072 (1 reference); for an excerpted review by Harold D. Murphy (with John P. McQuary), see 7:675 (10 references); for reviews by Norman Frederiksen and William B. Michael, see 6:770 (7 references); for reviews by Harold P. Bechtoldt, Ralph F. Berdie, and John B. Carroll, see 5:608.

[824]

Flanagan Industrial Tests.

Purpose: Measurement of aptitudes for eighteen on-the-job skills.

Population: Supervisory, technical, office, skilled labor, and other industrial positions.

Publication Dates: 1960–1975.

Acronym: FIT.

Scores: Total score only for each test.

Administration: Individual or group.

Price Data: Available from publisher.

Author: John C. Flanagan.

Publisher: General Dynamics Information Technology.

a) ARITHMETIC.
Time: 5(7) minutes.

b) ASSEMBLY.
Time: 10(13) minutes.

c) COMPONENTS.
Time: 10(12) minutes.

d) COORDINATION.
Time: 5(7) minutes.

e) ELECTRONICS.
Time: 15(17) minutes.

f) EXPRESSION.
Time: 5(8) minutes.

g) INGENUITY.
Time: 15(18) minutes.

h) INSPECTION.
Time: 5(9) minutes.

i) JUDGMENT AND COMPREHENSION.
Time: 15(17) minutes.

j) MATHEMATICS AND REASONING.
Time: 15(18) minutes.

k) MECHANICS.
Time: 15(18) minutes.

l) MEMORY.
Time: 10(19) minutes.

m) PATTERNS.
Time: 5(7) minutes.

n) PLANNING.
Time: 15(18) minutes.

o) PRECISION.
Time: 5(8) minutes.

p) SCALES.
Time: 5(7) minutes.

q) TABLES.
Time: 5(8) minutes.

r) VOCABULARY.
Time: 15(17) minutes.

Cross References: See T5:1043 (1 reference) and T4:989 (1 reference); for reviews by David O. Herman and Arthur C. MacKinney, see 8:981 (3 references); for reviews by C. J. Adcock and Robert C. Droege and an excerpted review by John L. Horn, see 7:977 (1 reference).

[825]

Fleishman Job Analysis Survey [Revised].

Purpose: "A means for analyzing the knowledge, skills and abilities needed to perform jobs."
Population: Adults.
Publication Dates: 1992–1996.
Acronym: F-JAS.
Scores: 52 Abilities Scales: Cognitive (Oral Comprehension, Written Comprehension, Oral Expression, Written Expression, Fluency of Ideas, Originality, Memorization, Problem Sensitivity, Mathematical Reasoning, Number Facility, Deductive Reasoning, Inductive Reasoning, Information Ordering, Category Flexibility, Speed of Closure, Flexibility of Closure, Spatial Orientation, Visualization, Perceptual Speed, Selective Attention, Time Sharing), Psychomotor (Control Precision, Multilimb Coordination, Response Orientation, Rate Control, Reaction Time, Arm-Hand Steadiness, Manual Dexterity, Finger Dexterity, Wrist-Finger Speed, Speed of Limb Movement), Physical (Static Strength, Explosive Strength, Dynamic Strength, Trunk Strength, Extent Flexibility, Dynamic Flexibility, Gross Body Coordination, Gross Body Equilibrium, Stamina), Sensory/Perceptual (Near Vision, Far Vision, Visual Color Discrimination, Night Vision, Peripheral Vision, Depth Perception, Glare Sensitivity, Hearing Sensitivity, Auditory Attention, Sound Localization, Speech Recognition, Speech Clarity).
Administration: Group.
Levels, 3: Job-Level Analysis, Job Dimension-Level Analysis, Task-Level Analysis.
Price Data: Available from publisher.
Time: (40) minutes.
Comments: Previously referred to as the Task Assessment Scales, Ability Requirement Scale, Manual for the Ability Requirement Scales (MARS); Handbook of Human Abilities brings together ability definitions, tasks, and jobs requiring each ability, and test descriptions and tests available to measure each ability.
Authors: Edwin A. Fleishman, Maureen E. Reilly, and David P. Costanza.
Publisher: Management Research Institute, Inc.
  a) SOCIAL/INTERPERSONAL ABILITIES.
  Publication Date: 1996.
  Acronym: F-JAS-2.
  Scores: 21 Social/Interpersonal Skill Scales: Agreeableness, Behavior Flexibility, Coordination, Dependability, Assertiveness, Negotiation, Persuasion, Sociability, Social Conformity, Social Sensitivity, Self Control, Social Confidence, Coaching, Oral Fact Finding, Achieve-ment Striving, Openness to Experience, Self Sufficiency, Perseverance, Resistance to Premature Judgment, Oral Defense, Resilience.
  Time: (20) minutes.
  b) KNOWLEDGES/SKILLS.
  Publication Date: 1992.
  Acronym: F-JAS-3.
  Scores: 33 Knowledge Scales: Administration and Management, Clerical, Economics and Accounting, Sales and Marketing, Customer and Personal Service, Personnel and Human Resources, Production and Processing, Food Production, Computers and Electronics, Engineering and Technology, Design, Building and Construction, Mechanical, Mathematics, Physics, Chemistry, Biology, Psychology, Sociology and Anthropology, Geography, Medicine and Dentistry, Therapy and Counseling, Education and Training, English Language, Foreign Language, Fine Arts, History and Archeology, Philosophy and Theology, Public Safety and Security, Law/Government and Jurisprudence, Telecommunications, Communications and Media, Transportation.
  Time: (25) minutes.
Cross References: For reviews by Jeffrey S. Rain and Ross E. Traub, see 12:153.

[826]

Flex Style Negotiating.

Purpose: Designed to profile participants' preferred negotiation styles and to define legitimate versus illegitimate behaviors.
Population: Employees and managers.
Publication Date: 1997.
Scores, 3: Social Dimension, Emotional Dimension, Cognitive Dimension.
Administration: Group.
Price Data: Available from publisher.
Time: (25) minutes.
Author: Alexander Watson Hiam.
Publisher: HRD Press, Inc.

[827]

Flow Scales.

Purpose: Designed "to assess flow in two ways: general tendency to experience flow, as well as particular incidence (or non-incidence) of flow characteristics during a particular event."
Population: Ages 12 and older.
Publication Date: 2010.
Administration: Individual or group.
Price Data, 2016: $50 per PDF manual (85 pages including sample forms and scoring information); $60 per print manual; $2.40 per Transform Survey Hosting (minimum 50); $2 per Remote Online Survey License (minimum 50); $2 per License to Reproduce (minimum 50).
Foreign Language Editions: Some forms available in Hindi, Hungarian, Finnish, French, Greek, and Spanish.

Authors: Susan A. Jackson, Robert C. Eklund, and Andrew J. Martin.
Publisher: Mind Garden, Inc.
  a) LONG FLOW SCALES.
  Purpose: Designed to "provide a detailed assessment of the dimensional flow model."
  Scores, 11: Challenge-Skill Balance, Merging of Action and Awareness, Clear Goals, Unambiguous Feedback, Concentration on the Task at Hand, Sense of Control, Loss of Self-Consciousness, Transformation of Time, Autotelic Experience, Total.
  Forms, 2: General (adaptable to a wide range of settings), Physical (to be used in sport and performance settings).
  Time: (10) minutes.
    1) *LONG Dispositional Flow Scale-2.*
    Acronym: DFS-2.
    Foreign Language Editions: Available in Chinese, Croation (general form), German (physical form), Japanese (physical form), and Russian (general form).
    2) *LONG Flow State Scale-2.*
    Acronym: FSS-2.
    Foreign Language Editions: Available in Chinese, Croation (general form), Indonesian (general form), Japanese (physical form), and Swedish (general form).
  b) SHORT FLOW SCALES.
  Purpose: Designed to "provide a flow assessment that focuses on a holistic concept of flow as one coherent experience ... drawn from the nine flow dimensions."
  Scores: Same as *a* above.
  Time: (5) minutes.
    1) *SHORT Dispositional Flow Scale.*
    Acronym: S DFS.
    2) *SHORT Flow State Scale.*
    Acronym: S FSS.
  c) CORE FLOW SCALES.
  Purpose: "Designed to describe what it is like to be in flow from the perspective of the person in flow."
  Score: Total score only.
  Time: (5) minutes.
    1) *CORE Dispositional Flow Scale.*
    Acronym: C DFS.
    2) *CORE Flow State Scale.*
    Acronym: C FSS.

[828]

Fluharty Preschool Speech and Language Screening Test—Second Edition.

Purpose: Designed to identify preschool children whose speech and language skills warrant a comprehensive communication evaluation.
Population: Ages 3-0 to 6-11.
Publication Dates: 1978–2000.
Acronym: FLUHARTY-2.
Scores, 8: Articulation, Repeating Sentences, Following Directives and Answering Questions, Describing Actions, Sequencing Events, Receptive Language, Expressive Language, General Language.

Administration: Individual.
Price Data, 2015: $201 per complete kit including examiner's manual (2000, 65 pages), picture book, 25 profile/record forms, and a set of 12 colored blocks; $43 per 25 profile/examiner record forms; $37 per set of blocks; $67 per picture book; $67 per examiner's manual.
Time: (10) minutes.
Author: Nancy Buono Fluharty.
Publisher: PRO-ED.
Cross References: For reviews by David P. Hurford and Rebecca McCauley, see 15:105; see T5:1047 (7 references) and T4:993 (2 references); for reviews by Nicholas W. Bankson and Harold A. Peterson of an earlier edition, see 9:422 (1 reference).

[829]

Franchisee Personality Profile Abridged–general version.

Purpose: Designed to assess "how well a person's personality and attitude fit the ideal franchisee profile."
Population: Potential franchise owners.
Publication Date: 2011.
Acronym: FPP-Ab.
Scores, 15: Leadership, Comfort with Sharing Cost and Profit, Self-Efficacy, Management Skills, Rule-Abiding, Community/Family Values, Go-Getter, Diligence, Innovation, Determination, Approachability, Self-Confidence, Positive Mindset, Entrepreneurial Spirit, Overall Score.
Administration: Individual.
Price Data: Available from publisher.
Time: (15) minutes.
Comments: Self-administered online assessment. The test publisher provides clients with information about the methods and theoretical basis used in the development of the test as well as benchmarks for relevant industries and racial/ethnic group comparison data.
Author: PsychTests AIM, Inc.
Publisher: PsychTests AIM, Inc. [Canada].
Cross References: For reviews by Frank M. Bernt and Eugene P. Sheehan, see 19:73.

[830]

Frenchay Dysarthria Assessment–Second Edition.

Purpose: Designed to provide a "measurement, differential description, and diagnosis of dysarthria."
Population: Ages 12 to adult.
Publication Dates: 1983-2008.
Acronym: FDA-2.
Scores, 7: Reflexes, Respiration, Lips, Palate, Laryngeal, Tongue, Intelligibility.
Administration: Individual.
Price Data, 2015: $157 per complete kit including 25 rating forms, Intelligibility cards, and examiner's

manual (2008, 45 pages); $47 per 25 rating forms; $48 per Intelligibility cards; $76 per examiner's manual.
Time: (30) minutes.
Comments: Additional items required for administration include: tongue depressor, stopwatch, tape recorder, glass of water, cookie, sterile gloves, and calipers.
Authors: Pamela Enderby and Rebecca Palmer.
Publisher: PRO-ED.
Cross References: For reviews by Jeff Berry and Steven Long and by Patricia Brazier-Carter, see 18:55; see T5:1056 (2 references); for reviews by Steven B. Leder and Malcolm R. McNeil of a previous edition, see 12:154; see also T4:1007 (2 references).

[831]
Friedman Well-Being Scale.
Purpose: "Designed to assess the level of well-being of an individual."
Population: Adults.
Publication Dates: 1992–1994.
Acronym: FWBS.
Scores, 6: Composite/Total, Sociability, Self-Esteem, Joviality, Emotional Stability, Happiness.
Administration: Group.
Price Data, 2015: $50 for manual, including a review-only copy of the FWBS form; $2 per Remote Online Survey License (minimum 50); $2 per License to Reproduce (minimum 50).
Time: (2–3) minutes.
Comments: Scale for rating perception of others or for self-rating; self-administered, administrator scored.
Author: Philip H. Friedman.
Publisher: Mind Garden, Inc.
Cross References: For a review by John W. Fleenor, see 14:152.

[832]
Frontal Systems Behavior Scale.
Purpose: "Identifies and quantifies behavioral problems associated with frontal lobe lesions."
Population: Ages 18–95.
Publication Date: 2001.
Acronym: FrSBe.
Scores, 4: Apathy (subscale A), Disinhibition (subscale D), Executive Dysfunction (subscale E), Total Score.
Administration: Individual or group.
Forms, 2: Family Rating Form, Self-Rating Form.
Price Data, 2015: $258 per introductory kit including professional manual (109 pages), 25 hand-scorable Self-Rating test booklets, 25 hand-scorable Family Rating test booklets, 25 Self-Rating profile forms, and 25 Family Rating profile forms.
Time: 10 minutes to administer; 10–15 minutes to score.
Comments: Revision of the Frontal Lobe Personality Scale; available in paper-and-pencil form only; obtains

ratings of patient's behavior before and after an injury or illness.
Authors: Janet Grace and Paul F. Malloy.
Publisher: Psychological Assessment Resources, Inc.
Cross References: For reviews by Harrison D. Kane and Shawn K. Acheson and by Nora M. Thompson, see 15:106.

[833]
Fuld Object-Memory Evaluation.
Purpose: Designed to "evaluate memory and learning under conditions that virtually guarantee attention and minimize anxiety."
Population: Ages 70–90 regardless of language and sensory handicaps.
Publication Date: 1977.
Acronym: FOME.
Scores, 5: Total Recall, Storage, Consistency of Retrieval, Ability to Benefit from Reminding, Ability to Say Words in Categories.
Administration: Individual.
Forms, 2: Record Form I, II.
Price Data, 2015: $97 per complete kit; $30 per 30 record forms; $25 per manual (24 pages).
Time: Administration time not reported.
Author: Paula Altman Fuld.
Publisher: Stoelting Co.
Cross References: See T5:1058 (9 references) and T4:1009 (6 references); for a review by Eric F. Gardner, see 9:427.

[834]
Full Range Test of Visual Motor Integration.
Purpose: Designed to assess the ability of individuals to "accurately relate visual stimuli to motor responses" and "to assist in differentiating normal from pathological aging."
Population: Ages 5-0 through 74-0.
Publication Dates: 1996-2006.
Acronym: FRTVMI.
Scores: Total score only.
Administration: Group or individual.
Price Data, 2015: $202 per complete kit including examiner's manual (2006, 102 pages), 25 profile/examiner record forms for ages 5-10, 25 profile/examiner record forms for ages 11-74, and scoring transparency; $63 per examiner's manual; $71 per 25 profile/examiner record forms for ages 5-10; $71 per 25 profile/examiner record forms for ages 11-74; $9 per scoring transparency.
Time: (5-15) minutes
Comments: Extensive revision and redevelopment of the Test of Visual-Motor Integration.
Authors: Donald D. Hammill, Nils A. Pearson, Judith K. Voress, and Cecil R. Reynolds.
Publisher: PRO-ED.

Cross References: For reviews by Rik Carl D'Amato and Jamie E. Vannice and by Katharine Snyder, see 17:75; for a review by Deborah Erickson of the Test of Visual-Motor Integration, see 14:395; see also T5:2722 (1 reference).

[835]

Functional Assessment and Intervention System: Improving School Behavior.

Purpose: "Designed to enable interdisciplinary staff (school psychologists, teachers, counselors, and support staff) to systematically identify the intent or function of a student's challenging behaviors and gain a clear understanding of his or her needs."

Population: Early childhood through high school.

Publication Date: 2004.

Acronym: FAIS.

Scores: No scores.

Administration: Individual.

Forms, 2: Social Competence Performance Checklist, Classroom Competence Observation Form.

Price Data, 2015: $114.25 per complete kit including manual (177 pages), 25 record forms, and 25 social competence performance checklists.

Time: (10) minutes for Social Competence Performance Checklist; (15–30) minutes for observation and support plan development.

Comments: Components of the FAIS can be used with Outcomes: Planning, Monitoring, Evaluating (1441) for planning interventions.

Author: Karen Callan Stoiber.

Publisher: Pearson.

Cross References: For reviews by Robert W. Hiltonsmith and Daniel C. Miller, see 16:93.

[836]

Functional Evaluation for Assistive Technology.

Purpose: To identify "the most appropriate and effective assistive technology (AT) devices to help individuals with learning problems compensate for their difficulties and meet the demands of specific tasks and contexts."

Population: "Individuals with learning problems (of all ages)."

Publication Date: 2002.

Acronym: FEAT.

Scores: Not scored; "examiner interprets the FEAT on a 'per item' basis."

Administration: Individual and group.

Price Data, 2016: $169 per complete kit including 25 of each of the following forms: Contextual Matching Inventory, Checklist of Strengths and Limitations, Checklist of Technology Experiences, Technology Characteristics Inventory, Individual-Technology Evaluation Scale, and Summary and Recommendations Booklet, and 1 examiner's manual (78 pages).

Time: Administration time not reported.

Comments: The FEAT should be used by an AT evaluation team rather than a single evaluator; "examiner" is the head of the evaluation team; total number of parts administered depends on "individual's AT needs."

Authors: Marshall H. Raskind and Brian R. Bryant.

Publisher: Psycho-Educational Services.

a) CONTEXTUAL MATCHING INVENTORY.

Purpose: To identify "the tasks in which the individual is typically engaged across settings … and [to determine] whether the [assistive] technology will be successful across those settings."

Comments: Ratings "based on interviews with… teachers, employers, family members, and/or [the] student or employee" being evaluated.

b) CHECKLIST OF STRENGTHS AND LIMITATIONS.

Purpose: To "provide information concerning academic behaviors associated with listening, speaking, reading, writing, mathematics, memory, organization, physical/motor, and behavior."

Administration: Group.

Comments: Ratings by "teachers, employers, family members, and/or [the] student or employee" being evaluated.

c) CHECKLIST OF TECHNOLOGY EXPERIENCES.

Purpose: "To identify the individual's familiarity with [AT] devices that may be evaluated."

Comments: Ratings based on an interview with the student or employee being evaluated.

d) TECHNOLOGY CHARACTERISTICS INVENTORY.

Purpose: "To evaluate [AT] device-specific characteristics such as its reliability/dependability, operational ease, and so forth."

Comments: Ratings by examiner.

e) INDIVIDUAL-TECHNOLOGY EVALUATION SCALE AND RELATED WORKSHEETS.

Purpose: "To obtain "information about the person's interaction with the AT device that is being evaluated."

Forms: 5 additional worksheets "to be used in conjunction with the Individual-Technology Evaluation Scale:" Optical Character Recognition/Speech Synthesis, Speech Synthesis/Screen Reading Systems, Speech Recognition Systems, Word Prediction Software, Spell Checkers.

Comments: Individual-Technology Evaluation Worksheets are reproducible and found in Appendix B of Examiner's Manual; ratings by examiner.

f) SUMMARY AND RECOMMENDATIONS BOOKLET.

Purpose: "To summarize the assessment information, make recommendations, and arrange for follow-ups to assess for effective implementation."

Comments: Completed by examiner.

Cross References: For reviews by Marta Coleman and Suzanne Young, see 18:56.

[837]

Functional Linguistic Communication Inventory.

Purpose: "Designed to quantify the functional linguistic communication skills of moderately and severely demented individuals."

Population: Adults diagnosed with Alzheimer's disease.

Publication Date: 1994.

Acronym: FLCI.

Scores, 10: Greeting and Naming, Question Answering, Writing, Comprehension of Signs and Object-to-Picture Matching, Word Reading and Comprehension, Following Commands, Pantomime, Gesture, Conversation, Total.

Administration: Individual.

Price Data, 2015: $239 per complete kit including manual (31 pages), 25 response record forms, 25 score forms, stimulus book (50 pages), and 3 objects (comb, pencil, mask); $31 per 25 response record forms; $25 per 25 score sheets; $72 per manual; $121 per stimulus book; $20 per object kit.

Time: (30) minutes.

Authors: Kathryn A. Bayles and Cheryl K. Tomoeda.

Publisher: PRO-ED.

Cross References: For reviews by Cameron J. Camp and Jennifer A. Brush and by Wilfred G. Van Gorp, see 13:129.

[838]

Functional Skills Screening Inventory, Individual Edition.

Purpose: "To be used in natural settings to assess critical living and working skills in persons with moderate to severe handicapping conditions."

Population: Age 6 through adult.

Publication Dates: 1984-1986.

Acronym: FSSI.

Scores, 9: Categorized into 3 priority levels: Basic Skills and Concepts, Communication, Personal Care, Homemaking, Work Skills and Concepts, Community Living, Social Awareness, Functional Skills Subtotal, Problem Behaviors.

Administration: Individual.

Price Data, 2015: $190 per master print copy including assessment booklet for unlimited assessments, hand-scoring sheets, and user guide (1986, 117 pages); $450 per site license for Windows interactive computer version; web site provides demo with documentation.

Time: [60-120] minutes per assessment.

Comments: A domain-referenced behavioral checklist; Employment Edition and Environmental Edition are also available in Windows format.

Authors: Heather Becker, Sally Schur, Michele Paoletti-Schelp, and Ed Hammer.

Publisher: Functional Resources.

Cross References: See T5:1067 (1 reference); for reviews by Diane Browder and G. Michael Poteat, see 10:123 (3 references).

[839]

Functional Vision and Learning Media Assessment.

Purpose: Designed to provide a "framework for systematic ... assessment of a student's visual functioning and the need for adapted educational media to access information available in print."

Population: Students with visual impairments who are pre-academic or academic.

Publication Date: 2012.

Acronym: FVLMA.

Scores: Not scored.

Administration: Individual.

Price Data, 2016: $67 per kit including practitioner's guidebook (130 pages), screening forms, and protocols; $22 per protocols; $45 per practitioner's guidebook.

Time: Administration time not reported.

Comments: Includes assessment protocols for interviews and observations, functional vision assessment, and learning media assessment. "The examiner should be a certified teacher of students who are visually impaired (TVI) and have had preservice and/or inservice training regarding techniques for assessing functional vision and learning media."

Authors: LaRhea Sanford, Rebecca Burnett, and Elaine Kitchel.

Publisher: American Printing House for the Blind, Inc.

[840]

Gambler Addiction Index.

Purpose: Designed for "gambler assessment in clinics, employee assistance programs, counseling settings, courts, probation departments, mental health professionals, and service provider offices."

Population: Ages 17-74.

Publication Dates: 1982-2004.

Acronym: GAI.

Scores, 7: Truthfulness, Gambler Severity, DSM-IV Gambling, Alcohol, Drugs, Suicide, Stress Coping Abilities.

Administration: Group.

Price Data, 2016: $9.95 per test; volume discounts available.

Foreign Language Edition: Spanish version available.

Time: (35) minutes.

Comments: May be administered via paper and pencil, computer, or human voice audio.

Author: Behavior Data Systems, Ltd.

Publisher: Behavior Data Systems, Ltd.

[841]

Garos Sexual Behavior Inventory.

Purpose: "Designed to assist forensic specialists and mental health professionals in making assessments and treatment decisions about individuals with problems related to sexuality and sexual behavior."

Population: Ages 18 and over.

Publication Date: 2008.

Acronym: GSBI.

Scores, 8: Discordance, Sexual Obsession, Permissiveness, Sexual Stimulation, Sexual Control Difficulties, Sexual Excitability, Sexual Insecurity, Inconsistent Responding.

Administration: Individual or group.

Price Data, 2016: $118.50 per complete kit including 25 AutoScore forms, 5 reusable administration cards, and manual (63 pages); $52.50 per 25 AutoScore forms; $33 per 5 reusable administration cards; $65.50 per manual.

Time: (20-30) minutes.

Comments: Administration card is titled Sexual Attitudes Inventory.

Author: Sheila Garos.

Publisher: Western Psychological Services.

Cross References: For reviews by Norman A. Constantine and Nancy Berglas and by M. Meghan Davidson, see 19:74.

[842]

Gates-MacGinitie Reading Tests®, Fourth Edition, Forms S and T.

Purpose: Designed to assess students' "general level of reading achievement."

Population: Grades K.7–12 and adults.

Publication Dates: 1926–2000.

Acronym: GMRT®.

Scores, 11: Literacy Concepts, Oral Language Concepts, Letters and Letter/Sound Correspondences, Listening Comprehension, Initial Consonants and Consonant Clusters, Final Consonants and Consonant Clusters, Vowels, Basic Story Words, Word Decoding, Vocabulary/Word Knowledge, Comprehension.

Administration: Group.

Levels, 11: PR (Pre-Reading), BR (Beginning Reading), 1, 2, 3, 4, 5, 6, 7/9, 10/12, AR (Adult Reading).

Forms, 2: S, T.

Price Data, 2015: $103.40 per hand-scorable test booklet package (Levels PR–3, specify level and form) including 25 test booklets, 1 Directions for Administration, 1 Booklet Scoring Key, 1 Class Summary Record, and 1 Decoding Skills Analysis form (for Levels 1 and 2 only); $144.25 per machine-scorable test booklet package (Levels BR–3, specify level and form); $170.35 per Level PR machine-scorable test booklet package (scored by publisher for an additional fee) including 25 test booklets, 1 Directions for Administration, and materials needed for machine scoring; $103.40 per reusable test booklet package (Levels 4–10/12 and AR) including 25 test booklets, 1 Directions for Administration, 1 Booklet Scoring Key, and 1 Class Summary Record; $146.55 per machine-scorable answer sheet package (Levels 4–10/12 and AR; scored by publisher for an additional fee) including 100 answer sheets and materials for machine scoring (specify level); $55.10 per self-scorable answer sheet package (Levels 4–10/12 and AR) including 25 answer sheets and 1 Class Summary Record (specify level); $491.75 per self-scorable answer sheet package (Levels 4–10/12 and AR) including 250 answer sheets (specify level); $14.05 per copy of Directions for Administration (specify level); $28.15 per Manual for Scoring and Interpretation (specify level); $18.75 per Linking Testing to Teaching: A Classroom Resource for Reading Assessment and Instruction (specify level); $52.85 per Technical Report.

Time: (55–100) minutes.

Comments: Norms tables available on CD-ROM.

Authors: Walter H. MacGinitie, Ruth K. MacGinitie, Katherine Maria, and Lois G. Dreyer.

Publisher: Houghton Mifflin Harcourt.

Cross References: For reviews by Kathleen M. Johnson and Patrick P. McCabe, see 16:94; see also T5:1072 (55 references) and T4:1022 (13 references); for a review by Mark E. Swerdlik of the third edition, see 11:146 (78 references); for reviews by Robert Calfee and William H. Rupley of an earlier edition, see 9:430 (15 references); see also T3:932 (77 references) and 8:726A (34 references); for reviews by Carolyn L. Burke and Byron H. Van Roekel and an excerpted review by William R. Powell of an earlier edition, see 7:689.

[843]

Gates-MacGinitie Reading Tests, 2nd Canadian Edition.

Purpose: Constructed to assess reading achievement.

Population: Grades K.7–12.

Publication Dates: 1978-1992.

Administration: Group.

Forms, 2: 3, 4.

Price Data: Available from publisher.

Comments: Levels PRE, R, and A are each available as Form 3; Levels B through F have two parallel forms (3, 4).

Authors: Walter H. MacGinitie and Ruth K. MacGinitie.

Publisher: Nelson Education Ltd. [Canada].

a) LEVEL PRE.
Population: Grades K.7-1.2.
Scores: Total score only.
Time: (90) minutes.
b) LEVEL R.
Population: Grades 1.0-1.9.
Scores: Total score only.
Time: (70) minutes.

c) LEVEL A.
Population: Grades 1.3-1.9.
Scores, 3: Vocabulary, Comprehension, Total.
Time: 55 minutes.
d) LEVEL B.
Population: Grade 2.
Scores, 3: Same as for *c* above.
Time: Same as for *c* above.
e) LEVEL C.
Population: Grade 3.
Scores, 3: Same as for *c* above.
Time: Same as for *c* above.
f) LEVEL D 4.
Population: Grade 4.
Scores, 3: Same as for *c* above.
Time: Same as for *c* above.
g) LEVEL D 5/6.
Population: Grades 5-6.
Scores, 3: Same as for *c* above.
h) LEVEL E.
Population: Grades 7-9.
Scores, 3: Same as for *c* above.
Time: Same as for *c* above.
i) LEVEL F.
Population: Grades 10-12.
Scores, 3: Same as for c above.
Time: Same as for *c* above.

Cross References: See T5:1071 (5 references) and T4:1021 (6 references); for reviews by Mariam Jean Dreher and Susanna W. Pflaum of an earlier edition, see 9:431.

Comments: Administered via computer at sites authorized by test publisher.
Authors: GED Testing Service.
Publisher: GED Testing Service.
    a) GED READY®
    Purpose: "To provide a practice opportunity for test-takers" and to serve as an indicator of how they might perform on the operational test.
    Scores: Total score interpreted using 3 performance reporting zones (Not Likely to Pass, Too Close to Call, Likely to Pass).
    Comments: An abbreviated version of the operational GED test; administered online except in correctional settings.

Cross References: Reviews are scheduled for *The Twentieth Mental Measurements Yearbook*. See T4:2816 (2 references); for reviews by Bruce G. Rogers and Michael S. Trevisan of the fourth series (2002), see 11:447 (2 references); for reviews by J. Stanley Ahmann and A. Harry Passow of the second series (1978), see 9:1284 (1 reference); see also T3:2485 (2 references), 8:35 (20 references), and 7:34 (21 references); for a review by Robert J. Solomon of earlier forms, see 5:27 (39 references); for a review by Gustav J. Froehlich, see 4:26 (27 references); for reviews by Herbert S. Conrad and Warren G. Findley, see 3:20 (11 references). For reviews by Charlotte W. Croon of an earlier form of the expression subtest, see 3:122; for reviews by W. E. Hall and C. Robert Pace of an earlier form of the social studies reading subtest, see 3:528.

---

[844]

GED® Test [2014 Series].

Purpose: Designed to measure "foundational academic skills and knowledge" necessary for high school graduation, to provide information about an examinee's "performance on career- and college-readiness standards," and "to provide evidence of readiness to enter workforce training programs, some careers, or post-secondary education."
Population: Adults who do not have a traditional high school diploma.
Publication Dates: 1944–2014.
Acronym: GED.
Scores: Total scores in 4 sections: Reasoning Through Language Arts, Mathematical Reasoning, Science, Social Studies.
Administration: Individual or group.
Forms: 3 equivalent English forms and 3 equivalent Spanish forms.
Price Data: Available from publisher.
Foreign Language and Special Editions: Spanish version available; various special editions (e.g., paper, audio, screen reader, Braille) for adults with disabilities are available through an accommodations request process.
Time: 150 minutes for Reasoning Through Language Arts; 115 minutes for Mathematical Reasoning; 90 minutes for Science; 90 minutes for Social Studies.

[845]

The Geist Picture Interest Inventory.

Purpose: Designed to "assess quantitatively eleven male and twelve female general interest areas and identify motivating forces behind occupational choice."
Population: Grade 8–adulthood.
Publication Dates: 1959–1971.
Acronym: GPII.
Scores: 18 (males) or 19 (females) scores: 11 or 12 Interest scores (Persuasive, Clerical, Mechanical, Musical, Scientific, Outdoor, Literary, Computational, Artistic, Social Service, Dramatic, Personal Service–females only), and 7 Motivation scores (Family, Prestige, Financial, Intrinsic and Personality, Environmental, Past Experience, Could Not Say).
Administration: Group or individual.
Forms, 2: M (male), F (female).
Price Data, 2016: $110.50 per kit including 10 tests of each form (male or female), and manual (1971, 42 pages plus tests and motivation questionnaires); $46.50 per 20 tests of male form; $45 per 20 tests of female form; $72 per manual; $19 per 20 motivation questionnaires of male form; $13.50 per 20 motivation questionnaires of female form.
Time: 10–20 minutes.
Author: Harold Geist.
Publisher: Western Psychological Services.

Cross References: See T2:2180 (18 references); for reviews by Milton E. Hahn and Benjamin Shimberg, and an excerpted review by David V. Tiedeman, see 6:1054 (12 references)

[846]
General Ability Measure for Adults.
Purpose: "Designed to evaluate intellectual ability using abstract designs."
Population: Ages 18–96.
Publication Date: 1997.
Acronym: GAMA.
Scores, 5: Matching, Analogies, Sequences, Construction, GAMA IQ Score.
Administration: Individual and/or group.
Price Data, 2015: $74.20 per manual (1997, 97 pages); $197.60 per 10 softcover test booklets; $95.60 per 25 hand-scored answer sheets (test items included); $24.10 per 25 Q Local answer sheets (test items included); $11.85 per Q Local report; quantity discounts available for the reports.
Time: (25) minutes.
Comments: May be self-administered.
Authors: Jack A. Naglieri and Achilles N. Bardos.
Publisher: Pearson.
Cross References: For reviews by Robert Fitzpatrick and Bert A. Goldman, see 14:153.

[847]
General Clerical Test.
Purpose: Developed to assess clerical speed and accuracy, numerical skills, and language-related skills.
Population: Clerical applicants and workers.
Publication Dates: 1972–1988.
Acronym: GCT.
Scores, 4: Clerical, Numerical, Verbal, Total.
Administration: Group or individual.
Price Data, 2016: $252 per starter pack including manual and 25 Clerical/Numerical/Verbal test booklets; $291 per 25 Clerical/Numerical/Verbal test booklets; $157 per 25 Clerical/Numerical test booklets; $115 per 25 Verbal test booklets; $150 per handscoring answer key; $82 per manual.
Time: 60 minutes.
Author: The Psychological Corporation.
Publisher: Pearson.
Cross References: See T5:1078 (1 reference); for reviews by Dianna L. Newman and Alfred L. Smith, Jr., see 12:158.

[848]
General Management In-Basket.
Purpose: "Designed to assess supervisory/managerial skills independent of any particular management position, from entry management up through top management positions; may be used for selection and/or career development."
Population: Managers.
Publication Dates: 1985–2011.
Acronym: GMIB.
Scores, 5: Leadership Style and Practices, Handling Priorities and Sensitive Situations, Managing Conflict, Organizational Practices/Management Control, Total.
Administration: Group.
Forms, 4: Private and public sector forms include Executive Version, Engineer Version, Police Versions for each managerial level from Police Sergeant to Police Chief, and Fire Versions for each managerial level from Fire Captain to Fire Chief.
Restricted Distribution: Clients may be required to pay a one-time overhead/sign-up fee.
Price Data, 2015: $575-$625 per candidate (depending on particular version) for rental/scoring and detailed Career Development Report identifying strengths, weaknesses, and developmental needs with specific learning objectives for each of the four factors measured by the test.
Time: 165 minutes.
Comments: All versions are available for online administration.
Author: Richard C. Joines.
Publisher: Management & Personnel Systems, Inc.
Cross References: For reviews by S. David Kriska and William J. Waldron, see 12:160.

[849]
General Processing Inventory.
Purpose: Designed to identify learning disabilities.
Population: Ages 5–75 years.
Publication Dates: 1986–2015.
Acronym: GPI.
Scores, 7: Graphomotor, Short Term Memory Retrieval, Long Term Memory Retrieval, Visual (Dyslexia), Auditory, Speech (Dysphasia), Total.
Subtests, 2: General Elementary Inventory of Language Skills (GEILS), General Elementary Inventory of Mathematics and Numeration (GEIMAN).
Administration: Individual.
Levels, 4: One (5 years old), Two (Above 6 years), Three (Above 8 years), Four (Above 10 years).
Price Data, 2015: $2,500 for mandatory training including 4 test administrations and scoring.
Time: (60–180) minutes.
Comments: Training required; psychologists and other licensed test administrators will learn to tabulate errors and may send their results to publisher for report writing. There is a fee for report writing dependent on volume; manual updated in 2015, but instrument did not change.
Author: Ruth M. Geiman.
Publisher: Ruth M. Geiman, Ph.D.
Cross References: For reviews by Sherry K. Bain and Stephen A. Spillane, see 14:154.

[850]

Generic Children's Quality of Life Measure.

Purpose: Designed to assess "how a child views his/her life, and how the child would like it to be, based upon self-reports of what the child considers to be important indicators of quality of life."
Population: Ages 6-14.
Publication Date: 2008.
Acronym: GCQ.
Scores, 3: Perceived-Self, Preferred-Self, Total Quality of Life.
Administration: Individual or group.
Price Data, 2016: £118 per starter set including manual (75 pages), 10 boy item booklets with score sheets, and 10 girl item booklets with score sheets; £69 per manual; £32 per 10 item booklets with score sheets (boy or girl).
Time: (10-30) minutes.
Authors: Jacqueline Collier and Dorothy MacKinlay.
Publisher: Hogrefe Ltd [United Kingdom].

[851]

Gesell Developmental Observation–Revised.

Purpose: Designed as a comprehensive developmental screening that measures social/emotional/adaptive skills, physical/neurological growth, language skills, and cognitive behaviors such as thinking, memory, perception, attention to task, ability to follow directions, short term visual and auditory memory, cognitive-perceptual thinking, organizational skills, logical mathematical thinking skills, and application of what is learned.
Population: Ages 2.5 through 9 years.
Publication Dates: 1964-2012.
Acronym: GDO-R.
Scores: 26 tasks: Cubes, Interview, Name and Numbers, Copy Forms, Incomplete Man, Right and Left, Visual I, Visual III, Naming Animals, Interests, Prepositions, Digit Repetition, Comprehension Questions, Color Forms, Three-Hole Form Board, Action Agents, Identifying Letters and Numbers, Numeracy, Counting, One-to-One Correspondence, Conservation, Calculations, Fine Motor, Gross Motor, Overt Behavior, Social/Emotional/Adaptive.
Administration: Individual.
Levels, 2: Ages 2.5 to 6.5; ages 7 to 9.
Price Data, 2015: $298.90 per complete kit, including 30 GDO-R child recording forms, 30 parent/guardian questionnaires, and 30 teacher questionnaires, plus non-consumable examiner's script and manipulatives; $306.40 for Spanish complete kit; $64.25 per 30 child recording forms; $24.60 per 30 teacher questionnaires; $24.60 per 30 parent/guardian questionnaires; $32.10 per 30 Spanish language parent/guardian Questionnaires for 30 families; $191.80 per examiner's manual (2011, 230 pages); $96.40 per examiner's script; price information for technical manual available from publisher.

Foreign Language Edition: Parent/Guardian Questionnaires are available in Spanish.
Time: Untimed; (20-45) minutes.
Comments: 5 strands: A (Developmental Tasks), B (Letters/Numbers), C (Language/Comprehension), D (Visual/Spatial Discrimination), E (Social/Emotional/Adaptive); original version of the test was called The Gesell School Readiness Test.
Author: The Gesell Institute of Child Development.
Publisher: Gesell Institute of Child Development.
Cross References: For reviews by Theresa Graham Laughlin and Timothy R. Konold, see 19:75; see T5:1085 (4 references) and T4:1035 (13 references); for reviews by Robert H. Bradley and Everett Waters of an earlier version, see 9:438; see also T3:953 (6 references) and T2:1703 (4 references); for excerpted reviews by L. J. Borstelmann and Edith Meyer Taylor, see 7:750 (5 references).

[852]

Gesell Early Screener.

Purpose: Designed as a brief developmental screening instrument to "identify children who may have a learning problem or condition that could affect his or her potential to learn."
Population: Ages 3-6.
Publication Dates: 2011-2012.
Acronym: GES.
Scores: 14 scores in 4 strands: Cognitive Strand (Cubes, Copy Forms, Prepositions, One-to-One Correspondence, Conservation, Identifying Numbers), Language Strand (Interview), Motor Strand (Tiptoe, Balance on One Foot, Hop on One Foot Forward, Skip, Catch, Throw), Social/Emotional/Adaptive.
Administration: Individual.
Price Data, 2015: $257.05 per complete kit including 30 child recording forms, 30 parent/guardian questionnaires, 30 teacher questionnaires, copy form cards, Numbers cards, 10 hardwood cubes, beanbag, tote bag, examiner's manual (2011, 78 pages); $262.40 per complete kit plus Spanish parent/guardian questionnaires; $37.45 per 30 child recording forms; $85.65 per examiner's manual; price data for technical report (2012, 104 pages) available from publisher.
Foreign Language Edition: Parent/guardian questionnaires are available in Spanish.
Time: (15-20) minutes.
Author: Gesell Institute of Child Development.
Publisher: Gesell Institute of Child Development.
Cross References: For reviews by Jean N. Clark and Joseph C. Kush, see 19:76.

[853]

Get Ready to Read!-Revised.

Purpose: Designed as a screening tool to measure preschool students' "understanding of books, printed letters, and words," as well as "the relationship between letters and speech sounds and how sounds can combine to form words" to "determine if they have the necessary early literacy skills to become successful readers."

Population: Ages 3-0 to 5-11.

Publication Dates: 2000-2009.

Acronym: GRTR!.

Scores: Total score only.

Administration: Individual.

Price Data, 2015: $92.25 per kit; $19 per 25 child record forms; $1.10 per summary form; $54.65 per stimulus easel; $29.60 per Early Literacy Manual.

Foreign Language Edition: A Spanish version of the complete test kit is available.

Time: (10-15) minutes.

Comments: Should not be used to screen the same student more than three times in 1 year and at least 3 months should separate screening dates; a summary form is included for administrators to record screening scores at different time points for each student in a particular class or group; the Total score is interpreted using Step Scores or Performance Levels provided in the manual and on the back of the answer sheet; there are four (1-4) Step Scores (providing information about the student's pre-literacy skill level) that correspond to a range of Total scores.

Author: National Center for Learning Disabilities.

Publisher: Pearson.

Cross References: For reviews by Zandra S. Gratz and Timothy Shanahan, see 18:57.

[854]

Gifted and Talented Evaluation Scales–Second Edition.

Purpose: Designed as a norm-referenced screening instrument for identifying students who are gifted and talented.

Population: Ages 5 through 18.

Publication Dates: 1996-2015.

Acronym: GATES-2.

Scores, 5: General Intellectual Ability, Academic Skills, Creativity, Leadership, Artistic Talent.

Administration: Individual.

Price Data, 2015: $135 per kit including examiner's manual (2015, 57 pages) and 50 summary/response forms; $81 per manual; $65 per 50 summary/response forms.

Time: [5-10] minutes.

Comments: Rating scale should be completed by parent, guardian, teacher, or related professional who has had regular, sustained contact with the student for at least a month.

Authors: James E. Gilliam and Olga Jerman.

Publisher: PRO-ED.

Cross References: Reviews are scheduled for *The Twentieth Mental Measurements Yearbook*. For reviews by Linda E. Brody and Carolyn M. Callahan of the original edition, see 17:77.

[855]

Gifted Evaluation Scale, Second Edition.

Purpose: Designed to help identify gifted students.

Population: Ages 5–18.

Publication Dates: 1987–2000.

Acronym: GES-2.

Scores, 8: 6 subscales (Intellectual, Creativity, Specific Academic Aptitude, Leadership Ability, Performing and Visual Arts, Motivation [optional]), Quotient Score, Percentile Score.

Administration: Individual.

Price Data, 2015: $104 per complete kit including technical manual (1998, 60 pages), 50 rating forms, and Gifted Intervention Manual (1990, 107 pages); $11.50 per 50 motivation scoring forms; $29 per technical manual; $44 per 50 rating forms; $31 per Gifted Intervention Manual; $46 per Quick Score (Windows®).

Time: (15–20) minutes.

Comments: Ratings by "anyone familiar with the student's behavior patterns and specific skills … (e.g., teacher, counselor, etc.)." The test publisher has indicated there is a newer edition of this test; description will be updated when complete test materials are received.

Authors: Diana Henage (The Gifted Intervention Manual), Stephen B. McCarney and Paul D. Anderson (technical manual and subscale percentile tables).

Publisher: Hawthorne Educational Services, Inc.

Cross References: For reviews by Douglas K. Smith and John W. Young, see 14:156; see also T5:1089 (2 references); for reviews by Carolyn M. Callahan and Ross E. Traub of an earlier edition, see 12:162 (1 reference).

[856]

Gifted Rating Scales.

Purpose: Designed to "assess observable student behaviors indicating giftedness."

Publication Date: 2003.

Acronym: GRS.

Administration: Individual.

Price Data, 2015: $182.50 per complete kit including manual (86 pages), 25 Early Child record forms, and 25 School Age record forms; $108.75 per manual; $58.85 per 25 Early Child record forms; $58.85 per 25 School Age record forms.

Comments: Norm-referenced, teacher-completed rating scale.

Authors: Steven I. Pfeiffer and Tania Jarosewich.

Publisher: Pearson.

a) GIFTED RATING SCALE—PRESCHOOL AND KINDERGARTEN.

Population: Ages 4:0 to 6:11.

Acronym: GRS-P.

Scores, 5: Intellectual Ability, Academic Ability, Creativity, Artistic Talent, Motivation.

Time: (10) minutes.

b) GIFTED RATING SCALE—SCHOOL.
Population: Ages: 6:0 to 13:11.
Acronym: GRS-S.
Scores, 6: Same as *a* above with the addition of Leadership Ability.
Time: (15) minutes.
Cross References: For a review by Sandra A. Ward, see 16:95.

[857]

Gilliam Asperger's Disorder Scale [2003 Update].

Purpose: Designed to evaluate children with unique behavioral problems who may have Asperger's Disorder.
Population: Ages 3–0 through 22-0 years.
Publication Date: 2001-2003.
Acronym: GADS.
Scores, 4: Social Interaction, Restricted Patterns of Behavior, Cognitive Patterns, Pragmatic Skills.
Administration: Individual.
Price Data, 2015: $121 per complete kit including examiner's manual (52 pages) and 25 summary/response forms; $72 per examiner's manual; $56 per 25 summary/response booklets.
Time: (5–10) minutes.
Authors: James E. Gilliam.
Publisher: PRO-ED.
Cross References: For reviews by Connie T. England and Carol M. McGregor, see 16:96; for reviews by Donald Oswald and Theresa Volpe-Johnstone of an earlier edition, see 15:108.

[858]

Gilliam Autism Rating Scale—Third Edition.

Purpose: Designed "to identify individuals ... who have severe behavioral problems that may be indicative of autism."
Population: Ages 3 through 22.
Publication Dates: 1995-2014.
Acronym: GARS-3.
Scores, 7: Restricted/Repetitive Behaviors, Social Interaction, Social Communication, Emotional Responses, Cognitive Style, Maladaptive Speech, Autism Index.
Administration: Individual.
Price Data, 2014: $163 per complete kit including examiner's manual (2014, 65 pages), 50 summary/response forms, and instructional objectives guide; $73 per examiner's manual, $35 per instructional objectives guide; $59 per 50 summary/response forms.
Time: (5-10) minutes.
Comments: "The rater is usually a classroom teacher, parent, or other caregiver who has had regular sustained contact with the individual for at least 2 weeks."
Author: James E. Gilliam.
Publisher: PRO-ED.

Cross References: Reviews are scheduled for *The Twentieth Mental Measurements Yearbook*. For reviews by Doreen Ward Fairbank and Adrienne Garro of the second edition, see 17:78; for reviews by Donald P. Oswald and Steven Welsh of the original edition, see 13:130.

[859]

Giotto.

Purpose: To provide a wide-ranging measure of personal integrity for use in staff selection.
Population: Unspecified.
Publication Dates: 1996–1997.
Scores: 7 scales: Prudence, Fortitude, Temperance, Justice, Faith, Charity, Hope.
Administration: Group or individual.
Price Data, 2015: £80.40 per starter kit including 20 question and answer booklets, scoring software, and manual (1997, 79 pages); £113.50 per manual.
Time: (15) minutes.
Comments: Computer scored.
Author: John Rust.
Publisher: Pearson Assessment [England].
Cross References: For reviews by Eugene V. Aidman and by Deniz S. Ones and Stephan Dilchert, see 16:97.

[860]

Global Assessment Scale.

Purpose: "For evaluating the overall functioning of a subject during a specified time period on a continuum from psychological or psychiatric sickness to health."
Population: Psychiatric patients and possible psychiatric patients.
Publication Dates: 1976-1985.
Acronym: GAS.
Scores: Mental Health-Illness rating of individual on a continuum of 1 to 100.
Administration: Individual.
Price Data: Available from publisher.
Authors: Robert L. Spitzer, Miriam Gibbon, and Jean Endicott.
Publisher: Department of Research Assessment and Training.
Cross References: See T5:1093 (116 references) and T4:1043 (62 references); for a review by Michael J. Subkoviak, see 11:147 (22 references).

[861]

Goal-Oriented Assessment of Lifeskills.

Purpose: Designed to be "an evaluation of fundamental motor abilities needed for daily living."
Population: Ages 7 to 17.
Publication Date: 2013.
Acronym: GOAL.
Scores, 3: Fine Motor, Gross Motor, Progress Score.
Administration: Individual.

Price Data, 2016: $353 per kit including 1 set of test materials, 25 record forms, pad of 25 paper box sheets, stimulus easel, and manual (115 pages); $52.50 per 25 record forms; $21 per 25 paper box sheets, $77 per stimulus easel, $77 per manual.
Time: (45-60) minutes.
Authors: Lucy Jane Miller, Thomas Oakland, and David S. Herzberg.
Publisher: Western Psychological Services.

[862]

Goldman-Fristoe Test of Articulation, Third Edition.

Purpose: Designed to "measure speech sound abilities in the area of articulation in children, adolescents, and young adults."
Population: Ages 2-0 through 21-11.
Publication Dates: 1969-2015.
Acronym: GFTA-3.
Scores: Total scores in two sections: Sounds-in-Words, Sounds-in-Sentences; 3 Supplemental Measures: Error Analysis, Intelligibility, Stimulability.
Administration: Individual.
Parts, 2: Sounds-in-Words (all ages), Sounds-in-Sentences (Ages 4-0 through 21-11).
Price Data, 2015: $299 per complete kit including manual (2015, 273 pages), stimulus book, 25 record forms, and soft carrying case; $99 per manual; $199 per stimulus book; $40 per 25 record forms.
Time: (12) minutes for Sounds-in-Words, (4) minutes for Sounds-in-Sentences.
Authors: Ronald Goldman and Macalyne Fristoe.
Publisher: Pearson.
Cross References: Reviews are scheduled for *The Twentieth Mental Measurements Yearbook*. For reviews by Steven Long and Katharine A. Snyder of the second edition, see 15:109; see T5:1095 (48 references) and T4:1045 (15 references); for a review by Donald E. Mowrer of an earlier (1986) edition, see 10:126 (7 references); see also T3:960 (21 references); for reviews by Margaret C. Byrne and Ralph L. Shelton, and an excerpted review by Dorothy Sherman of the original edition, see 7:952 (4 references).

[863]

The Gordon Diagnostic System.

Purpose: Aids in the evaluation of Attention Deficit Hyperactivity Disorder as well as useful in titrating stimulant medication; is also used in the neuropsychological assessment of disorders such as subclinical hepatic encephalopathy, AIDS dementia complex, post concussion syndrome, closed head injury, and neurotoxicity.
Population: Children, adolescents, and adults.
Publication Dates: [1982–1996].
Acronym: GDS.

Scores: 11 tests: Standard Vigilance Task, Standard Distractibility Test, Delay Task, Preschool Delay Task, Preschool Vigilance "0" Task, Preschool Vigilance "1" Task, Vigilance "3/5" Task, Adult Vigilance Task, Adult Distractibility Task, Auditory Vigilance Task, Auditory Interference Task.
Administration: Individual.
Price Data, 2015: $1,695 per GDS III microprocessor-based portable unit including all tasks, capacity for automatic output to a printer, instruction manual (1996, 102 pages), interpretive guide, 50 record forms, 4 issues of the ADHD REPORT, and 1-year warranty; $300 plus shipping per 2-month trial rental; $299 plus shipping per optional GDS compatible printer; $35 per 50 GDS record forms; $225 plus shipping per optional auditory module.
Time: (9) minutes per task.
Comments: A portable, microprocessor-based unit that administers tests of attention and impulse control; FDA approved as a medical device.
Author: Michael Gordon.
Publisher: Gordon Systems, Inc.
Cross References: See T5:1099 (5 references); for reviews by Robert G. Harrington and Judy J. Oehler-Stinnett, see 13:132 (6 references); see also T4:1051 (6 references).

[864]

Gordon Personal Profile—Inventory™ [Revised].

Purpose: Pre-employment assessment for all roles; nine "normal" personality traits are measured.
Population: Grades 9–12 and college and adults.
Publication Dates: 1951–1993.
Acronym: GPP-I.
Administration: Group.
Price Data, 2015: $133 per 25 hand-scorable test booklets; $113 per manual; $150 per score key; $75 per interpretive guide; $24 online administration.
Time: (20–25) minutes.
Comments: Combination of Gordon Personal Profile and Gordon Personal Inventory; separate booklet editions still available.
Author: Leonard V. Gordon.
Publisher: Pearson.
   a) GORDON PERSONAL PROFILE.
   Scores, 5: Ascendancy, Responsibility, Emotional Stability, Sociability, Self-Esteem (Total).
   b) GORDON PERSONAL INVENTORY.
   Scores, 4: Cautiousness, Original Thinking, Personal Relations, Vigor.
Cross References: See T5:1101 (2 references); for reviews by Robert M. Guion and Allen K. Hess, see 13:133 (4 references); see also T4:1053 (2 references); for reviews by Douglas Fuchs and Alfred B. Heilbrun, Jr. of an earlier edition, see 10:128 (4 references); see also 9:444 (1 reference), T3:966 (6 references), 8:568

(34 references), 8:569 (52 references), T2:1194 (56 references), and P:93 (23 references); for reviews by Charles F. Dicken and Alfred B. Heilbrun, Jr., see 6:102 (13 references) and 6:103 (25 references); for reviews by Benno G. Fricke and John A. Radcliffe and excerpted reviews by Laurance F. Shaffer and Laurence Siegel, see 5:58 and 5:59 (16 references).

[865]

Goyer Organization of Ideas Test, Form S (Revised).

Purpose: Intended to assess the ability to organize ideas.
Population: College and adults.
Publication Dates: 1966–1993.
Acronym: GOIT, Form S (Rev.).
Scores: Total score only.
Administration: Individual or group.
Manual: No manual.
Price Data: Available from publisher.
Time: [20–40] minutes.
Author: Robert S. Goyer.
Publisher: Robert S. Goyer [Test distributed through the Test Collection at ETS].
Cross References: For reviews of an earlier edition by Ric Brown and Robert B. Frary, see 9:445; see also 8:817 (1 reference).

[866]

Graded Word Spelling Test, Second Edition.

Purpose: Designed to measure spelling achievement.
Population: Ages 6-0 to adults.
Publication Dates: 1977–1998.
Scores: Total Words Correct.
Administration: Group.
Price Data: Available from publisher.
Time: (20–30) minutes.
Comments: The test publisher has indicated there is a newer edition of this test; description will be updated when complete test materials are received.
Author: P. E. Vernon.
Publisher: Hodder Education [United Kingdom].
Cross References: For a review by Deborah L. Bandalos, see 14:157; see also T5:1105 (1 reference); for a review by Carol E. Westby of an earlier edition, see 12:165 (3 references); see also T4:1056 (2 references).

[867]

Graduate and Managerial Assessment.

Purpose: Designed as assess cognitive skills among elite graduates for employee selection and development.
Population: Undergraduate and graduate students.
Publication Date: 1985.
Acronym: GMA.
Scores: 3 tests: Numerical, Abstract, Verbal.
Administration: Group.

Forms, 2: A, B.
Price Data: Available from publisher.
Time: 30(35) minutes per test.
Comments: Online administration available.
Author: Psychometric Research Unit, The Hatfield Polytechnic.
Publisher: Psychometric Research & Development Ltd. [England].
Cross References: See T5:1106 (1 reference); for reviews by Philip G. Benson and Rhonda L. Gutenberg, see 10:129.

[868]

Graduate Management Admission Test.

Population: Applicants to study in graduate management education.
Publication Dates: 1954-2016.
Acronym: GMAT.
Scores, 5: Verbal, Quantitative, Integrated Reasoning, Analytical Writing, Total.
Administration: Group.
Price Data, 2016: $250 registration fee.
Time: 210 minutes.
Comments: Computer based testing administered year-round at test centers established by the test publisher; Integrated Reasoning Section added July 2012.
Author: Graduate Management Admission Council.
Publisher: Pearson VUE.
Cross References: See T5:1107 (10 references) and T4:1058 (6 references); for reviews by Lawrence A. Crosby and James Ledvinka, see 9:447 (1 reference); see also T3:973 (6 references), 8:1074 (11 references), and T2:2325 (5 references); for reviews by Jerome E. Doppelt and Gary R. Hanson of earlier forms, see 7:1080 (10 references).

[869]

The Graduate Record Examinations Biochemistry, Cell and Molecular Biology Test.

Purpose: Designed to measure the qualifications of graduate school applicants for advanced study and for fellowships in biochemistry, cell biology, molecular biology, and genetics, along with related programs such as microbiology and genetics.
Population: Graduate school candidates.
Publication Dates: 1990–2016.
Acronym: GRE.
Scores, 4: Biochemistry, Cell Biology, Molecular Biology and Genetics, Total.
Administration: Group.
Price Data: Available from publisher.
Time: (170) minutes.
Comments: Test administered 3 times annually (September, October, April) at centers established by publisher.
Author: Educational Testing Service.
Publisher: Educational Testing Service.

Cross References: For reviews of the GRE program, see 7:667 (1 review) and 5:601 (1 review).

[870]

The Graduate Record Examinations Biology Test.

Purpose: Designed to measure the qualifications of graduate school applicants for advanced study and for fellowships in Biology.
Population: Graduate school candidates.
Publication Dates: 1939–2016.
Acronym: GRE.
Scores, 4: Cellular and Molecular Biology, Organismal Biology, Ecology and Evolution, Total.
Administration: Group.
Price Data: Available from publisher.
Time: (170) minutes.
Comments: Test administered 3 times annually (September, October, April) at centers established by publisher.
Author: Educational Testing Service.
Publisher: Educational Testing Service.
Cross References: See T5:1110 (1 reference); for a review by Clark W. Horton of an earlier form, see 5:727. For reviews of the GRE program, see 7:667 (1 review) and 5:601 (1 review).

[871]

The Graduate Record Examinations Chemistry Test.

Purpose: Designed to measure the qualifications of graduate school applicants for advanced study and for fellowships in chemistry.
Population: Graduate school candidates.
Publication Dates: 1939–2016.
Acronym: GRE.
Scores: Total score only.
Administration: Group.
Price Data: Available from publisher.
Time: (170) minutes.
Comments: Test administered 3 times annually (September, October, April) at centers established by publisher.
Author: Educational Testing Service.
Publisher: Educational Testing Service.
Cross References: See T4:1060 (1 reference), 8:852 (1 reference), and 7:848 (1 reference); for a review by Max D. Engelhart of an earlier form, see 6:919. For reviews of the GRE program, see 7:667 (1 review) and 5:601 (1 review).

[872]

The Graduate Record Examinations—General Test.

Purpose: "Designed to assess the verbal reasoning, quantitative reasoning, critical thinking, and analytical writing abilities of graduate school applicants."

Population: Graduate school candidates.
Publication Dates: 1949–2016.
Acronym: GRE.
Scores, 3: Verbal Reasoning, Quantitative Reasoning, Analytical Writing.
Administration: Individual
Price Data: Available from publisher.
Time: (225) minutes for computer-administered test.
Author: Educational Testing Service.
Publisher: Educational Testing Service.
Cross References: See T5:1115 (29 references) and T4:1076 (31 references); for reviews by Sanford J. Cohn and Richard M. Jaeger, see 9:448 (9 references); see also T3:995 (26 references), 8:188 (45 references), T2:382 (15 references), and 7:353 (43 references); for reviews by Robert L. French and Warren W. Willingham of an earlier edition, see 6:461 (17 references); for a review by John T. Dailey, see 5:336 (7 references); for reviews by J. P. Guilford and Carl I. Hovland, see 4:293 (2 references). For reviews of the GRE program, see 7:667 (1 review) and 5:601 (1 review).

[873]

The Graduate Record Examinations Literature in English Test.

Purpose: Designed to measure the qualifications of graduate school applicants for advanced study and for fellowships in literature in English.
Population: Graduate school candidates.
Publication Dates: 1939–2016.
Acronym: GRE.
Scores: Total score only.
Administration: Group.
Price Data: Available from publisher.
Time: (170) minutes.
Comments: Test administered 3 times annually (September, October, April) at centers established by publisher.
Author: Educational Testing Service.
Publisher: Educational Testing Service.
Cross References: See T5:1118 (1 reference); for a review by Edward M. White, see 8:69; see also 7:219 (1 reference); for a review by Robert C. Pooley of an earlier form, see 5:215. For reviews of the GRE program, see 7:667 (1 review) and 5:601 (1 review).

[874]

The Graduate Record Examinations Mathematics Test.

Purpose: Designed to measure the qualifications of graduate school applicants for advanced study and for fellowships in mathematics.
Population: Graduate school candidates.
Publication Dates: 1939–2016.
Acronym: GRE.
Scores: Total score only.

Administration: Group.
Price Data: Available from publisher.
Time: (170) minutes.
Comments: Test administered 3 times annually (September, October, April) at centers established by publisher.
Author: Educational Testing Service.
Publisher: Educational Testing Service.
Cross References: See T4:1069 (1 reference) and 8:272 (1 reference); for a review by Paul C. Rosenbloom of an earlier form, see 6:578; for a review by Eric F. Gardner, see 5:427 (1 reference). For reviews of the GRE program, see 7:667 (1 review) and 5:601 (1 review).

[875]

The Graduate Record Examinations Physics Test.

Purpose: Designed to measure the qualifications of graduate school applicants for advanced study and for fellowships in physics.
Population: Graduate school candidates.
Publication Dates: 1939–2016.
Acronym: GRE.
Scores: Total score only.
Administration: Group.
Price Data: Available from publisher.
Time: (170) minutes.
Comments: Test administered 3 times annually (September, October, April) at centers established by publisher.
Author: Educational Testing Service.
Publisher: Educational Testing Service.
Cross References: See 8:866 (1 reference); for a review by Theodore G. Phillips, see 6:931; for a review by Leo Nedelsky, see 5:754. For reviews of the GRE program, see 7:667 (1 review) and 5:601 (1 review).

[876]

The Graduate Record Examinations Psychology Test.

Purpose: Designed to measure the qualifications of graduate school applicants for advanced study and for fellowships in psychology.
Population: Graduate school candidates.
Publication Dates: 1939–2016.
Acronym: GRE.
Scores, 3: Experimental Psychology, Social Psychology, Total.
Administration: Group.
Price Data: Available from publisher.
Time: (170) minutes.
Comments: Test administered 3 times annually (September, October, April) at centers established by publisher. All GRE Psychology Test editions given at Subject Test administrations adhere to the terminology, criteria and classifications referred to in the DSM-5.
Author: Educational Testing Service.

Publisher: Educational Testing Service.
Cross References: See T5:1122 (2 references), T4:1073 (3 references), 8:461 (3 references), T2:1005 (2 references), and 7:644 (9 references); for a review by Harold Seashore of an earlier form, see 5:583. For reviews of the GRE program, see 7:667 (1 review) and 5:601 (1 review).

[877]

Graduate Record Examinations: Subject Tests.

Purpose: Designed to measure the qualifications of graduate school applicants in specific fields of study.
Population: Graduate school candidates.
Publication Dates: 1939–2016.
Acronym: GRE.
Scores: 8 tests: Biochemistry/Cell and Molecular Biology, Biology, Chemistry, Literature in English, Mathematics, Physics, Psychology.
Administration: Group.
Price Data: Available from publisher.
Time: (170) minutes.
Comments: Test administered 3 times annually (September, October, April) at centers established by publisher.
Author: Educational Testing Service.
Publisher: Educational Testing Service.
Cross References: See T4:1075 (2 references), T3:994 (5 references), and 8:476 (6 references); for a review by Leona E. Tyler of an earlier program, see 7:667 (10 references); see also 6:762 (1 reference); for a review by Harold Seashore, see 5:601 (12 references); see also 4:527 (24 references).

[878]

Grandparent Strengths and Needs Inventory.

Purpose: Designed "to help grandparents recognize their favorable qualities and identify aspects of their family relationships in which further growth is needed."
Population: Grandparents of children 6 and over.
Publication Date: 1993.
Acronym: GSNI.
Scores, 6: Satisfaction, Success, Teaching, Difficulty, Frustration, Information Needs.
Administration: Group.
Price Data: Available from publisher.
Time: Administration time not reported.
Comments: Parent and grandchild inventories included for comparison purposes.
Authors: Robert D. Strom and Shirley K. Strom.
Publisher: Robert Strom.
Cross References: See T5:1128 (4 references); for reviews by Roger A. Boothroyd and Dianna L. Newman, see 13:134 (2 references).

[879]

Gravidometer.

Purpose: Measures knowledge about human pregnancy.
Population: Adolescents and adults.
Publication Dates: 1974–1988.
Scores: Total score only.
Administration: Group.
Manual: No manual.
Price Data, 2015: $2 per test.
Time: [10] minutes.
Comments: Supplementary article available.
Author: Panos D. Bardis.
Publisher: Donna Bardis.

[880]

Gray Diagnostic Reading Tests—Second Edition.

Purpose: Designed as "a comprehensive measure of reading skills … to determine strengths and weaknesses, document progress in reading programs, [and] help diagnose specific reading problems."
Population: Ages 6-0 to 13-11.
Publication Dates: 1991-2004.
Acronym: GDRT-2.
Scores: 7 subtests: Letter/Word Recognition, Phonetic Analysis, Reading Vocabulary, Meaningful Reading, Listening Vocabulary, Rapid Naming, Phonological Awareness; and 3 composites: Decoding, Comprehension, General Reading.
Administration: Individual.
Forms: 2 equivalent forms: A, B.
Price Data, 2015: $299 per complete kit including examiner's manual (2004, 113 pages), Adventures in Fancyland Storybook, Student Book Form A, Student Book Form B, 25 Examiner/Record Forms A, 25 Examiner/Record Forms B; $89 per examiner's manual; $62 per Student Book (Form A or Form B); $8 per Adventures in Fancyland Storybook; $58 per 25 record forms (A or B).
Time: (45-60) minutes.
Comments: Norm-referenced; revision of the Gray Oral Reading Tests-Diagnostic.
Authors: Brian R. Bryant, J. Lee Wiederholt, and Diane Pedrotty Bryant.
Publisher: PRO-ED.
Cross References: For reviews by Howard Margolis and Antonia D'Onofrio and by Lisa F. Smith, see 17:80; see also T5:1130 (2 references); for reviews by William R. Merz, Sr. and Steven A. Stahl of the original edition, see 11:149 (1 reference).

[881]

Gray Oral Reading Tests–Fifth Edition.

Purpose: Designed to "identify students with reading difficulty, diagnose reading disabilities, determine strengths and weaknesses, and evaluate students' progress in reading."

Population: Ages 6 through 23.
Publication Dates: 1963-2012.
Acronym: GORT-5.
Scores, 5: Oral Reading Index (Fluency [Rate, Accuracy, Total], Comprehension).
Administration: Individual.
Forms, 2: A, B.
Price Data, 2014: $275 per complete kit including examiner's manual (129 pages), 25 examiner record booklets Form A, 25 examiner record booklets Form B, and student book; $92 per examiner's manual; $59 per 25 examiner record booklets (Form A or Form B); $65 per student book.
Time: [20-30] minutes.
Authors: J. Lee Wiederholt and Brian R. Bryant.
Publisher: PRO-ED.
Cross References: Reviews are scheduled for *The Twentieth Mental Measurements Yearbook*. For reviews by Nancy L. Crumpton and Marie Miller-Whitehead of the fourth edition, see 15:111; see T5:1131 (18 references); for reviews by John D. King and Deborah King Kundert of the third edition, see 12:166 (5 references); see also T4:1084 (9 references); for reviews by Julia A. Hickman and Robert J. Tierney of the revised edition, see 10:131 (15 references); for reviews by Emery P. Bliesmer, Albert J. Harris, and Paul R. Lohnes of the original edition, see 6:842.

[882]

Gray Silent Reading Tests.

Purpose: "Designed to assess silent reading comprehension."
Population: Ages 7–25.
Publication Date: 2000.
Acronym: GSRT.
Scores: Silent Reading Quotient.
Administration: Group.
Forms, 2: A, B.
Price Data, 2015: $192 per complete kit including 25 profile/response forms, 10 each of reading book Forms A and B, and manual (101 pages); $31 per 25 profile/response forms; $43 per 10 reading books (specify Form A or Form B); $86 per manual.
Time: (15–30) minutes.
Comments: Developed to be used as an adjunct to the Gray Oral Reading Tests (881) or independently.
Authors: J. Lee Wiederholt and Ginger Blalock.
Publisher: PRO-ED.
Cross References: For reviews by Harold R. Keller and Darrell L. Sabers, see 15:112.

[883]

Green's Emotional Perception Test.

Purpose: Designed to measure "the ability to judge emotion expressed in another person's tone of voice."
Population: Ages 6 to 90.

Publication Dates: 1986-2008.
Acronym: EPT.
Scores: Total score only.
Administration: Individual.
Price Data, 2010: $200 per 20 test uses and manual (2008, 44 pages); $4 per individual use.
Time: (6) minutes.
Comments: Administered using Microsoft Windows; Nonsense version available for non-English speakers.
Authors: Paul Green, Lloyd Flaro, and Roger Gervais.
Publisher: Green's Publishing Inc. [Canada].
Cross References: For reviews by George Engelhard, Jr. and Aminah Perkins and by Tracey Wyatt, see 19:77.

[884]

Green's Medical Symptom Validity Test.

Purpose: Designed as a computerized "verbal memory screening test with built-in effort testing."
Population: Ages 6 to 68.
Publication Dates: 2003-2004.
Acronym: MSVT.
Scores, 5: Primary Effort (Immediate Recognition, Delayed Recognition, Consistency), Memory (Paired Associates, Free Recall).
Administration: Individual.
Price Data, 2013: $340 per manual (2004, 102 pages), program on CD for use with Microsoft Windows, and 30 test uses; $6 per individual use.
Foreign Language Editions: Available in Danish, Dutch, French, German, Norwegian, Portuguese, Spanish, and Swedish.
Time: [5-15] minutes.
Author: Paul Green.
Publisher: Green's Publishing Inc. [Canada].
Cross References: For a review by Mark A. Albanese, see 19:78.

[885]

Green's Non-Verbal Medical Symptom Validity Test.

Purpose: Designed as a "computerized nonverbal memory-screening test, which allows the person's effort on testing to be measured."
Population: Children and adults.
Publication Dates: 2006-2008.
Acronym: NV-MSVT.
Scores, 7: Primary Effort (Immediate Recognition, Delayed Recognition, Consistency, Delayed Recognition-Variations, Delayed Recognition-Archetypes), Memory (Paired Associates, Free Recall).
Administration: Individual.
Price Data, 2010: $300 per manual (2008, 116 pages), program on CD for use with Microsoft Windows, and 30 test uses; $6 per individual use.
Time: [5-15] minutes.
Author: Paul Green.

Publisher: Green's Publishing, Inc. [Canada].
Cross References: For reviews by Matthew E. Lambert and Janet S. Reed, see 19:79.

[886]

Green's Word Memory Test.

Purpose: Designed to "measure verbal and nonverbal memory."
Population: Ages 7 and over.
Publication Dates: 1995-2005.
Acronym: WMT.
Scores, 6: Immediate Recognition, Delayed Recognition, Multiple Choice, Paired Associates, Free Recall, Long Delayed Free Recall.
Administration: Individual.
Price Data, 2010: $300 per Green's WMT for Windows first year (unlimited use).
Foreign Language Editions: Oral, Spanish, French, German, Dutch, Portuguese, Turkish, Russian, Danish, and Hebrew translations available.
Time: Administration time not reported.
Comments: Two scores are designed to be sensitive to "poor effort or exaggeration of cognitive difficulties, yet they are insensitive to ... cognitive impairment."
Author: Paul Green.
Publisher: Green's Publishing Inc. [Canada].
Cross References: For reviews by Sandra D. Haynes and Anita M. Hubley, see 19:80; for reviews by M. Allan Cooperstein and Michael P. Gamache of an earlier version, see 14:424.

[887]

Greenspan Social-Emotional Growth Chart.

Purpose: Designed to help determine a child's social-emotional development and growth.
Population: Birth to 3.5 years.
Publication Date: 2004.
Scores, 3: Total Growth Chart Score, Sensory Processing Score, Highest Stage Mastered.
Administration: Individual.
Price Data, 2015: $112.15 per kit including manual, 25 caregiver reports, and 25 questionnaires; $92.85 per manual; $45.80 per 25 caregiver reports or questionnaires.
Time: (5-15) minutes.
Comments: It is recommended that the questionnaire be administered at each developmental stage.
Author: Stanley I. Greenspan.
Publisher: Pearson.
Cross References: For reviews by Carol M. McGregor and Gretchen Owens, see 17:81.

[888]

Gregorc Style Delineator.

Purpose: "Designed to aid an individual to recognize and identify the channels through which he/she receives and expresses information."

Population: Adults.

Publication Dates: 1982–2002.

Scores, 4: Concrete Sequential score, Abstract Sequential score, Abstract Random score, Concrete Random score.

Administration: Group.

Price Data, 2016: $85 per presenter's package including An Adult's Guide to Style (2002, 110 pages), Mind Styles Model: Theory Principles and Practice (1998, 28 pages), Mind Styles FAQs Book (2001, 152 pages), Relating with Style (1997, 170 pages), test, Extenda-Charts, Phoenix bookmark, and Careful Use audio tape; $18.95 per technical manual (1982, 46 pages); $75 per 25 instrument packets; $9.95 per audio tape on careful use; $17.95 per An Adult's Guide to Style; $22.95 per Mind Styles FAQs Book; $22.95 per Relating with Style; $9 per Mind Styles Model: Theory, Principles, and Practice.

Time: 3 minutes.

Comments: Self-assessment instrument.

Author: Anthony F. Gregorc.

Publisher: Gregorc Associates, Inc.

Cross References: See T5:1132 (1 reference); for reviews by Stephen L. Benton and Trenton R. Ferro, see 12:167 (3 references); see also T4:1086 (2 references).

[889]
Griffiths Mental Development Scales [Revised].

Purpose: Designed to measure trends of development that are indicative of intelligence/mental growth.

Publication Dates: 1951–1996.

Administration: Individual.

Forms, 2: Scale 1 (0–2 years), Scale 2 (2–8 years).

Restricted Distribution: Restricted to persons who qualify by attending an approved course; details available from distributor.

Price Data, 2016: £792 per 2-8 years starter pack, including revised items, administration manual, analysis manual, 40 record and drawing books and a leather carrying case; £617 per 2-8 years 2006 revised mental development scales kit; £155 Griffiths 2-8 years revised items; £50 per administration manual; £50 per analysis manual; £34 per record books and drawing books; £88 per carrying case; £6 per administration key; £75 per software starter pack, including user guide, 20 uses of Griff-it and 20 drawing sheets.

Authors: Ruth Griffiths and Michael Huntley (Birth–2 years Scale [Scale 1] and manual, 1996 Revision).

Publisher: Hogrefe Ltd [United Kingdom].

a) SCALE 1: BIRTH TO 2 YEARS.

Population: Ages 0–2 years.

Publication Dates: 1951–1996.

Scores, 6: Locomotor, Personal-Social, Hearing and Speech, Eye and Hand, Performance, Total.

Time: (20–40) minutes.

b) SCALE 2: (2 TO 8 YEARS).

Population: Ages 2–8 years.

Publication Dates: 1951–1978.

Scores, 7: Same as Scale 1 above plus Practical Reasoning.

Time: Administration time not reported.

Cross References: See T5:1134 (8 references), T4:1088 (10 references), and 9:450 (1 reference); for a review by C. B. Hindley of an earlier version of Scale 2, see 6:523 (4 references); for a review by Nancy Bayley of Scale 1, see 5:404 (3 references).

[890]
Grooved Pegboard Test.

Purpose: To assess manipulative dexterity.

Population: Ages 5 to 8-12, 9 to 14-12, 15 to adult.

Publication Date: 1989.

Scores, 3: Total Time, Number of "Drops," Total Pegs Correctly Placed.

Administration: Individual.

Price Data, 2016: $95 per test.

Time: Trial discontinued after 5 minutes.

Comments: Ages 5 to 8-12 only complete first two rows of the Pegboard; "this test requires more complex visual-motor coordination than most pegboards."

Author: Ronald Trites (manual).

Publisher: Lafayette Instrument.

Cross References: See T5:1135 (27 references); for reviews by Roderick K. Mahurin and Erin McClure and Richard K. Stratton, see 12:169 (14 references); see also T4:1089 (2 references).

[891]
Group Achievement Identification Measure.

Purpose: "To determine the degree to which children exhibit the characteristics of underachievers so that preventative or curative efforts may be administered."

Population: Grades 5-12.

Publication Date: 1986.

Acronym: GAIM.

Scores, 6: Competition, Responsibility, Achievement Communication, Independence/Dependence, Respect/Dominance, Total.

Administration: Group.

Price Data, 2015: $15 per specimen set; $120 per class set of 30 inventories including prepaid computer scoring by publisher; manual for administration and interpretation (12 pages) included with test orders.

Time: (30) minutes.

Comments: Student self-report inventory.

Author: Sylvia B. Rimm.

Publisher: Educational Assessment Service Inc.

Cross References: See T5:1136 (1 reference); for reviews by Robert K. Gable and Jeffrey Jenkins, see 11:150.

[892]

Group Embedded Figures Test [Second Edition Manual].

Purpose: Designed to "assess the field dependence-independence (FDI) cognitive style construct."

Population: Older children, adolescents, and adults.

Publication Dates: 1971-2014.

Acronym: GEFT.

Score: Total score only.

Administration: Group.

Price Data, 2016: $50 per PDF manual (2014, 129 pages); $60 per paper manual; $2.40 per Transform Survey Hosting (minimum 50); $250 per Group Report; $50 per 25 Booklet Pack; $15 per Individual Report; $15 per Report About Me.

Foreign Language Editions: Available in Dutch, German, Mandarin, and Turkish.

Time: (20) minutes.

Comments: Adaptation of the individually administered Embedded Figures Test (T6:900); manual has been revised; assessment content has not changed.

Authors: Herman A. Witkin, Philip K. Oltman, Evelyn Raskin, Stephen A. Karp, and Jack Demick (manual).

Publisher: Mind Garden, Inc.

Cross References: See T5:1140 (60 references), T4:1094 (95 references), 9:452 (41 references), and T3:1013 (88 references); for reviews by Leonard D. Goodstein and Alfred E. Hall, see 8:572 (47 references); see also T2:1201 (3 references); for references to reviews of the individual test, see 8:548.

[893]

Group Environment Scale [Third Edition Manual].

Purpose: Designed to "measure the actual, preferred, and expected, social environments of task-oriented, social, psychotherapy, and self-help groups."

Population: Group members and leaders; clinicians, consultants, and program evaluators.

Publication Dates: 1974–2002.

Acronym: GES.

Scores: 10 in 3 dimensions: Relationship (Cohesion, Leader Support, Expressiveness), Personal Growth (Independence, Task Orientation, Self-Discovery, Anger and Aggression), System Maintenance and Change (Order and Organization, Leader Control, Innovation).

Administration: Group.

Forms, 3: Real (R), Ideal (I), Expectations (E).

Price Data, 2015: $50 per manual, including a review-only copy of the GES form; $2.40 per online administration license (minimum 50); $250 Group Report; $2 per Remote Online Survey License or License to Reproduce (minimum 50); $10 user's guide.

Foreign Language Edition: Translations available for French, Hebrew, Italian, Japanese, and Spanish.

Time: [15-20] minutes.

Comments: A component of the Social Climate Scales.

Author: Rudolf H. Moos.

Publisher: Mind Garden, Inc.

Cross References: For reviews by Laura L. B. Barnes and Malinda Hendricks Green, see 17:82; see also T5:1141 (5 references) and T4:1095 (5 references); for a review by Arthur M. Nezu of an earlier edition, see 10:132 (6 references); for reviews by Michael J. Curtis and Robert J. Illback, see 9:435 (4 references); for reviews by David P. Campbell and Robyn M. Dawes, see 8:573; see also T3:1015 (1 reference); for a review of the Social Climate Scales, see 8:681.

[894]

Group Inventory for Finding Creative Talent.

Purpose: "Identify students with attitudes and values usually associated with creativity."

Population: Grades K-2, 3-4, 5-6

Publication Dates: 1976-2010.

Acronym: GIFT.

Scores, 4: Imagination, Independence, Many Interests, Total.

Administration: Group or individual.

Levels, 3: Primary (Grades K-2), Elementary (Grades 3-4), Upper Elementary (Grades 5-6).

Price Data, 2015: $160 per 30 test booklets and scoring service (scoring must be done by publisher); $15 per specimen set.

Foreign Language Edition: Spanish edition available.

Time: (20-45) minutes.

Author: Sylvia B. Rimm.

Publisher: Educational Assessment Service, Inc.

Cross References: See T5:1142 (5 references); for reviews by Patricia L. Dwinell and Dan Wright, see 9:454 (1 reference); see also T3:1016 (1 reference).

[895]

Group Inventory For Finding Interests.

Purpose: "Identify students with attitudes and interests usually associated with creativity."

Population: Grades 6-12.

Publication Dates: 1979-2010.

Acronym: GIFFI.

Scores: 5 dimensional scores: Creative Arts and Writing, Challenge-Inventiveness, Confidence, Imagination, Many Interests.

Administration: Group or individual.

Levels, 2: Level 1: Grades 6-9; Level 2: Grades 9-12.

Price Data, 2005: $120 per 30 test booklets and scoring service (scoring must be done by publisher); $15 per specimen set.

Foreign Language Edition: Spanish edition available.

Time: (20-40) minutes.

Authors: Sylvia B. Rimm and Gary A. Davis.
Publisher: Educational Assessment Service Inc.
Cross References: See T5:1143 (2 references); for a review by M. O'Neal Weeks, see 9:455 (1 reference).

[896]
Group Mathematics Assessment and Diagnostic Evaluation.

Purpose: A group-administered diagnostic mathematics test that measures individual skills in key areas, including concepts, operations, computation, and applications.
Population: Grades K–12.
Publication Date: 2004.
Acronym: G•MADE.
Administration: Group.
Forms: 2 parallel forms, A or B, for each of 9 levels.
Price Data, 2015: $125-$200 per Form A classroom sets (specify Level) including administration, scoring, and interpretation manual and 30 student booklets; $220–$330 per Forms A & B classroom sets (specify Level); $35 per norms supplement (specify age-based or grade-based out-of-level); $40 per technical manual (122 pages). Scoring options and prices available from publisher.
Time: (50–90) minutes per level.
Author: Kathleen T. Williams.
Publisher: Pearson.
a) LEVEL R.
Population: Ages 5-0 to 7-11.
Scores, 3: Concepts and Communication, Process and Applications, Total.
b) LEVEL 1.
Population: Ages 6-0 to 8-11.
Scores, 4: Same as *a* above plus Operations and Computation.
c) LEVEL 2.
Population: Ages 6-0 to 9-11.
Scores, 4: Same as *b* above.
d) LEVEL 3.
Population: Ages 7-0 to 10-11.
Scores, 4: Same as *b*.
e) LEVEL 4.
Population: Ages 8-0 to 12-11.
Scores, 4: Same as *b*.
f) LEVEL 5.
Population: Ages 9-0 to 18-0 and above.
Scores, 4: Same as *b*.
g) LEVEL 6.
Population: Ages 10-0 to 18-0 and above.
Scores, 4: Same as *b*.
h) LEVEL M.
Population: Ages 11-0 to 18-0 and above.
Scores, 4: Same as *b*.
i) LEVEL H.
Population: Ages 12-0 to 18-0 and above.
Scores, 4: Same as *b*.
Cross References: For reviews by Joseph C. Ciechalski and Kevin D. Crehan, see 17:83.

[897]
Group Process Questionnaire.

Purpose: "Designed to help groups assess how effective they are."
Population: Adults.
Publication Dates: 1988-1994.
Scores, 29 to 145: My Rating, Group Rating, and How I Did scores for Behavior Scale (Task Behavior, Maintenance Behavior), for Total Scale, and for 12 optional categories (Initiating, Seeking Information or Opinions, Giving Information or Opinions, Clarifying and Elaborating, Summarizing, Consensus-Testing, Listening, Harmonizing, Gatekeeping, Encouraging, Compromising, Standard Setting/Testing), and My Rating and Group Rating scores for 5 additional optional categories (Leadership, Time Utilization, Results, Acceptance, Inclusion).
Administration: Group.
Price Data: Available from publisher.
Time: (60) minutes.
Comments: Scale for ratings by group members and for self-ratings.
Authors: Richard Hill, D. Joseph Fisher, Tom Webber, and Kathleen A. Fisher.
Publisher: Aviat.

[898]
Group Reading Assessment and Diagnostic Evaluation.

Purpose: Designed to pinpoint students' individual reading levels.
Population: Pre-K through adult.
Publication Dates: 2001-2002.
Administration: Individual or group.
Levels, 11: P (pre-kindergarten and kindergarten), K (kindergarten and first grade), 1 (kindergarten through second grade), 2, 3, 4, 5, 6, M (middle school, grades 5–9), H (high school, grades 9–12), A (grades 11 to postsecondary).
Forms, 2: Form A, Form B.
Price Data, 2015: $235 per Levels 1, 2, or 3 Classroom Set with Forms A and B including 30 each of Form A and Form B student booklets, 1 teacher's administration manual, and 2 scoring and interpretative manual; $245 per Levels P and K Classroom Set with Forms A and B; $345 per Levels 4, 5, 6, M, H, or A Classroom Set with Forms A and B; $35 per 10 student booklets (each of Levels P–A); $50 per Forms A and B hand-scoring templates (each of Levels 4–A); $11 per 10 answer sheets (each of Levels 4-A); $25 per teacher's administration manual (each of Levels P–A); $25 per scoring and interpretative manual (each of Levels P–A); $40 per technical manual (for all levels); $40 per Out of Level Norms Supplement (205 page book of norm tables); $130 per GRADE Resource Library (each of Levels P–A); $450 per GRADE Scoring and Report-

ing Software (single PC version); $2000 per GRADE Scoring and Reporting Software.
Time: (45–90) minutes.
Comments: May be hand scored or computer scored.
Author: Kathleen T. Williams.
Publisher: Pearson.

a) LEVEL P.
Scores, 8: Picture Matching, Picture Differences, Verbal Concepts, Picture Categories, Sound Matching, Rhyming, Listening Comprehension, Total Score.
b) LEVEL K.
Scores, 9: Sound Matching, Rhyming, Print Awareness, Letter Recognition, Same and Different Words, Phoneme-Grapheme Correspondence, Word Reading, Listening Comprehension, Total Score.
c) LEVEL 1, 2.
Scores, 6: Word Reading, Word Meaning, Sentence Comprehension, Passage Comprehension, Listening Comprehension, Total Score.
d) LEVEL 3.
Scores, 6: Word Reading, Vocabulary, Sentence Comprehension, Passage Comprehension, Listening Comprehension, Total Score.
e) LEVEL 4–A.
Scores, 5: Vocabulary, Sentence Comprehension, Passage Comprehension, Listening Comprehension, Total Score.
Cross References: For reviews by Mark H. Fugate and Betsy B. Waterman, see 15:113.

[899]

Group Reading Test, Fourth Edition.

Purpose: Designed to measure "the reading of single words and of simple sentences."
Population: Ages 6:4 to 8:11 and less able children 8:0 to 11:11.
Publication Dates: 1968–1999.
Acronym: GRT.
Scores: Total score only.
Administration: Group.
Forms, 2: A, B.
Price Data, 2016: £16.50 per 20 Form A or Form B; £28 per manual (1999, 27 pages).
Time: (20) minutes.
Author: Dennis Young.
Publisher: Hodder Education [United Kingdom].
Cross References: For reviews by Gretchen Owens and John W. Young, see 14:158; for reviews by William R. Merz, Sr., and Diane J. Sawyer of an earlier edition, see 12:171 (1 reference); see also T4:1102 (4 references); for reviews by Patrick Groff and Douglas A. Pidgeon of the Second Edition, see 9:458 (1 reference); for a review by Ralph D. Dutch of the original edition, see 8:729.

[900]

Group Reading Test II (6–14).

Purpose: Designed to monitor progress in reading and to screen and identify pupils who require further diagnostic assessment.

Population: Ages 6 years to 15 years 9 months.
Publication Dates: 1985–2000.
Acronym: GRT II (6–14).
Scores, 2: Sentence Completion, Context Comprehension.
Administration: Group.
Forms, 6: A and B; C and D; X and Y.
Price Data: Price data for teacher's guide (2000, 75 pages), At-a-Glance Guide, group record sheet, and record forms available from publisher.
Time: (30) minutes.
Comments: Computer and publisher scoring service available; originally published as Macmillan Group Reading Test.
Author: NFER-Nelson Publishing Co., Ltd.
Publisher: GL Assessment [England; Efforts to obtain updated information from the test publisher were unsuccessful. An updated edition of this test appears on the test publisher's website].
Cross References: For reviews by C. Dale Carpenter and Alice J. Corkill, see 16:98; for reviews by Koressa Kutsick and Gail E. Tompkins of the Macmillan Reading Test, see 10:179.

[901]

Group Shorr Imagery Test.

Purpose: Designed as a projective measure of personality conflict.
Population: Adults.
Publication Date: 1977.
Acronym: GSIT.
Scores, 6: Item scores in 5 areas (Human, Animal, Inanimate, Botanical, Others) plus Total score for Conflict.
Administration: Group.
Price Data: Available from publisher.
Time: Administration time not reported.
Comments: Tape cassette used for administration; group form of the Shorr Imagery Test (1869).
Author: Joseph E. Shorr.
Publisher: Institute for Psycho-Imagination Therapy.

[902]

Group Styles Inventory.

Purpose: Designed to "assess the particular style or styles of your work group following a simulated or real problem-solving session or meeting."
Population: Group members.
Publication Dates: 1990–1993.
Acronym: GSI.
Scores: 12 styles in 3 general clusters: Constructive (Achievement, Self-Actualizing, Humanistic-Encouraging, Affiliative), Passive/Defensive (Approval, Conventional, Dependent, Avoidance), Aggressive/Defensive (Oppositional, Power, Competitive, Perfectionistic).
Administration: Group.
Price Data: Available from publisher.

Time: [10–15] minutes.

Comments: The test publisher has indicated there is a newer edition of this test; description will be updated when complete test materials are received.

Authors: Robert A. Cooke and J. Clayton Lafferty.

Publisher: Human Synergistics International.

Cross References: For reviews by Lawrence M. Aleamoni and Bert A. Goldman, see 12:172.

[903]

Gudjonsson Suggestibility Scales.

Purpose: "Developed in order to measure objectively the vulnerability or proneness of people [to suggestive influence and/or] to give erroneous accounts when interviewed," particularly in forensic contexts.

Population: Ages 6 and over.

Publication Date: 1997.

Scores, 7: Immediate Recall, Delayed Recall, Yield 1, Yield 2, Shift, Total Suggestibility, Confabulation.

Administration: Individual.

Forms: 2 parallel forms: GSS1, GSS2.

Price Data, 2016: £250 per manual, 25 scoresheets, and CD; £50 per 25 scoresheets.

Time: Administration time not reported.

Author: Gisli H. Gudjonsson.

Publisher: Routledge Psychology.

Cross References: For reviews by Marc Janoson and Bruce Frumkin and by Romeo Vitelli, see 17:84.

[904]

H-T-P: House-Tree-Person Projective Technique.

Purpose: "To provide psychologists and psychiatrists … with an examining procedure with which to acquire diagnostically and prognostically significant data concerning a subject's total personality."

Population: Ages 3 and over

Publication Dates: 1946–1993.

Acronym: H-T-P.

Scores: Total score only.

Administration: Individual.

Price Data, 2016: $238 per complete kit including The House-Tree-Person Projective Drawing Technique: Manual and Interpretive Guide, House-Tree-Person Drawings: An Illustrated Diagnostic Handbook, Catalog for the Qualitative Interpretation of the House-Tree-Person (H-T-P), 25 H-T-P Interpretation Booklets, and 25 H-T-P Drawing Forms; $90 for The House-Tree-Person Projective Drawing Technique: Manual and Interpretive Guide (165 pages); $54 for a Catalog for the Qualitative Interpretation of the House-Tree-Person (191 pages); $54 for the House-Tree-Person Drawings: An Illustrated Diagnostic Handbook (108 pages); $28 per 25 H-T-P Interpretation Booklets; $28 per 25 H-T-P Person Drawing/Interpretation Booklets; $21 per 25 H-T-P Drawing Forms (volume discounts available).

Foreign Language Edition: Spanish edition available.

Time: (60–90) minutes.

Authors: John N. Buck, W. L. Warren (revision), Isaac Jolles (interpretive catalog), L. Stanley Wenck (diagnostic handbook), and Emmanuel F. Hammer (clinical research manual).

Publisher: Western Psychological Services.

Cross References: See T5:1160 (4 references), T4:1183 (6 references), T2:1469 (61 references), and P:437 (24 references); for a review by Mary R. Haworth of an earlier edition, see 6:215 (32 references); for a review by Philip L. Harriman, see 5:139 (61 references); for reviews by Albert Ellis and Ephraim Rosen and an excerpted review, see 4:107 (14 references); for reviews by Morris Krugman and Katherine N. Wilcox, see 3:47 (5 references).

[905]

Hairstylist Aptitude Personality & Attitude Profile.

Purpose: Designed to "assess whether a test-taker's skills and personality traits match those required to work in the hairdressing industry."

Population: Hairstylists and prospective employees in hairdressing industry.

Publication Date: 2011.

Acronym: HAPAP.

Scores, 18: Competitiveness, Willingness to Learn New Skills, Integrity, Passion, Time Management, Neatness, Physical Hardiness, Stress Management, Self-Efficacy, Social Skills, Self-Control, Reliability, Creative Problem-Solving, Self-Motivation, Networking, Common Sense, Entrepreneurial Spirit, Overall Score.

Administration: Individual.

Price Data: Available from publisher.

Time: (30) minutes.

Comments: Self-administered online assessment. The test publisher provides clients with information about the methods and theoretical basis used in the development of the test as well as benchmarks for relevant industries and racial/ethnic group comparison data.

Author: PsychTests AIM, Inc.

Publisher: PsychTests AIM, Inc. [Canada].

Cross References: For a review by John S. Geisler, see 19:81.

[906]

Hall Occupational Orientation Inventory, Form II and Young Adult/College/Adult Form (Fourth Edition).

Purpose: Designed to help individuals understand their values, needs, interests, and preferred life-styles, and how these relate to career goals and future educational plans.

Population: Junior high students–adults, high school students–adults.
Publication Dates: 1968–2002.
Administration: Group or individual.
Price Data, 2015: $36.90 per 20 inventory booklets (Form II); $108.35 per 20 self-interpretive digests (Form II); $25.60 per 20 response sheets (Form II); $18.05 per 1 professional manual (Form II); $41.30 per 20 inventory booklets (Young adult/college/adult form); $29.35 per 20 self-interpretive folders (Young adult/college/adult form); $28 per 20 response forms (Young adult/college/adult form); $20.10 per counselor/user's manual (Young adult/college/adult form).
Time: (45–60) minutes.
Author: Lacy G. Hall.
Publisher: Scholastic Testing Service, Inc.

   a) YOUNG ADULT/COLLEGE/ADULT FORM.
   Population: High school–adults.
   Publication Dates: 1968–2002.
   Scores, 29: Creativity-Independence, Information-Knowledge, Belongingness, Security, Aspiration, Esteem, Self-Actualization, Personal Satisfaction, Routine-Dependence, People-Social-Accommodating, Data-Information, Things-Physical, People-Business-Influencing, Ideas-Scientific, Aesthetics-Arts, Geographic Location, Abilities, Monetary-Compensation, Workplace, Coworkers, Time, Qualifications, Risk, Subjective External Authority, Objective External Authority, Subjective Internal Authority, Shaping/Autonomy/and Self-Empowerment, Interdependent, Procrastination.
   b) FORM II.
   Population: Junior high students–adults.
   Publication Dates: 1968–1989.
   Scores, 15: Creativity-Independence, Information-Knowledge, Belongingness, Security, Aspiration, Esteem, Self-Actualization, Personal Satisfaction, Routine-Dependence, People-Social-Accommodating, Data-Information, Things-Physical, People-Business-Influencing, Ideas-Scientific, Aesthetics-Arts.
Cross References: For reviews by John S. Geisler and Joseph G. Law, Jr., see 16:100; for reviews by Gregory Schraw and Hilda Wing of an earlier edition, see 12:175 (1 reference); see also T3:1051 (4 references); for reviews by Robert H. Dolliver and Austin C. Frank of an earlier edition, see 8:1003 (5 references); see also T2:2187 (3 references); for a review by Donald G. Zytowski of the original edition, see 7:104 (4 references).

[907]
Halpern Critical Thinking Assessment.

Purpose: Designed to assess "critical thinking skills."
Population: Ages 15 and over.
Publication Date: 2010.
Acronym: HCTA.
Scores: 3 scores for each dimension of critical thinking (Verbal Reasoning, Argument Analysis, Thinking as Hypothesis Testing, Likelihood and Uncertainty, Decision Making and Problem Solving): Total Critical Thinking Score, Critical Thinking Score-Constructed Responses, Critical Thinking Score-Forced Choice Responses.
Administration: Group or individual.
Forms, 2: Form S1 (Standard version), Form S2 (Multiple-choice short version).
Price Data: Available from publisher.
Foreign Language Editions: The management software is available in 13 languages; translations of the HCTA are available in 10 languages including Chinese, Spanish, Dutch, and Turkish.
Time: (20) minutes for short-form recognition items; (60-80) minutes constructed response and recognition items.
Comments: Computer administered and scored using the Vienna Test System; single user, server license, or Internet testing.
Author: Diane F. Halpern.
Publisher: Schuhfried GmbH [Austria].
Cross References: For reviews by Julia Y. Porter and Gerald Tindal, see 19:82.

[908]
Halstead-Reitan Neuropsychological Test Battery.

Purpose: "Developed to evaluate the brain-behavior functioning of individuals."
Population: Ages 5-8, 9-14, 15 and over.
Publication Dates: 1979-1993.
Scores: 1 combined score for each battery and for areas of function, plus scores for individual tests.
Price Data: Available from publisher.
Comments: Consists of three neuropsychological test batteries, one for each age level; each battery includes a Neuropsychological Deficit Scale, which provides normative ranges for each test, for areas of function, and for the entire battery in addition to cut-off scores (brain impairment versus normal brain status) for each variable, area, and summary score.
Author: Ralph M. Reitan.
Publisher: Reitan Neuropsychology Laboratory.

   a) REITAN-INDIANA NEUROPSYCHOLOGICAL TEST BATTERY FOR YOUNG CHILDREN.
   Population: Ages 5-8.
   1) *Category.*
   Comments: Projection box with slide projector and slides necessary for administration.
   2) *Tactual Performance.*
   Scores, 3: Total Time, Memory, Localization.
   Comments: 6-figure board.
   3) *Finger Tapping.*
   Comments: Electronic finger tapper necessary for administration.
   4) *Matching Pictures.*
   5) *Individual Performance.*
   Subtests, 4: Matching Figures, Star, Matching V's, Concentric Squares.
   6) *Marching.*
   7) *Progressive Figures.*

8) *Color Form.*
Scores, 2: Total Time, Errors.
9) *Lateral Dominance Examination.*
10) *Target.*
11) *Aphasia Screening.*
12) *Sensory Perceptual.*
Subtests, 6: Imperception (Tactile, Auditory, Visual), Tactile Finger Recognition, Finger-Tip Symbol Writing and Recognition, Tactile Form Recognition.
13) *Grip Strength.*
Scores, 2: Preferred Grip, Nonpreferred Grip.
Comments: Hand dynamometer necessary for administration.
14) *Name Writing.*
b) HALSTEAD-REITAN NEUROPSYCHOLOGICAL TEST BATTERY FOR OLDER CHILDREN.
Population: Ages 9-14.
1) *Category.*
Comments: Similar to *a* above.
2) *Tactual Performance.*
Comments: Same as *a* above.
3) *Seashore Rhythm Test.*
4) *Speech-Sounds Perception.*
5) *Trail Making.*
6) *Finger Tapping.*
Comments: Manual finger tapping apparatus necessary for administration.
7) *Aphasia Screening.*
8) *Sensory-Perceptual.*
Subtests, 5: Sensory Imperception (Tactile, Auditory, Visual), Finger Agnosia, Finger-Tip Number Writing.
9) *Tactile Form Recognition.*
10) *Grip Strength.*
Scores, 2: Preferred Grip, Nonpreferred Grip.
Comments: Hand dynamometer necessary for administration.
11) *Lateral Dominance.*
12) *Name Writing.*
c) HALSTEAD-REITAN NEUROPSYCHOLOGICAL TEST BATTERY FOR ADULTS.
Population: Ages 15 and over.
Comments: Battery has 11 tests same as b above with a number of changes in equipment, administration, and scoring forms for this level.
Cross References: See T5:1164 (187 references) and T4:1119 (159 references); for reviews by Raymond S. Dean and Manfred J. Meier, see 9:463 (79 references); see also T3:1052 (4 references).

[909]

Halstead Russell Neuropsychological Evaluation System.

Purpose: Provides "comprehensive measures of the functions relevant to neuropsychological assessment."
Population: Adults.
Publication Date: 1993.
Acronym: HRNES.
Scores, 3: Percent Impaired Score, Average Index Score, Lateralization Key.
Administration: Individual.

Price Data, 2016: $656.50 per complete kit including manual (99 pages), 10 recording booklets, and unlimited-use HRNES-R disk; $68.50 per 10 recording booklets; $72 per manual.
Time: Administration time not reported.
Comments: HRNES computer program compiles raw scores from up to 22 tests, corrects them for age and education, and converts them to scaled scores; includes unlimited use disk.
Authors: Elbert W. Russell and Regina I. Starkey.
Publisher: Western Psychological Services.
Cross References: For reviews by Roderick K. Mahurin and Paul Retzlaff, see 12:176 (1 reference).

[910]

Hammill Multiability Achievement Test.

Purpose: Designed as a "measure of school achievement."
Population: Ages 7-0 to 17-11.
Publication Date: 1998.
Acronym: HAMAT.
Scores, 5: Reading, Writing, Arithmetic, Facts, General Achievement Quotient.
Administration: Individual.
Forms, 2: A, B.
Price Data, 2015: $250 per complete kit including examiner's manual (116 pages), 25 each Form A and Form B response booklets, and 25 each Form A and Form B record forms; $56 per student response booklets (Form A or B); $37 per profile/examiner record forms (Form A or B); $86 per examiner's manual.
Time: (30–60) minutes.
Authors: Donald D. Hammill, Wayne P. Hresko, Jerome J. Ammer, Mary E. Cronin, and Sally S. Quinby.
Publisher: PRO-ED.
Cross References: For reviews by Jeffrey A. Jenkins and Eleanor E. Sanford, see 14:159.

[911]

The Hand Test [Revised].

Purpose: Designed as a projective technique that uses pictures of hands; may be used to measure action tendencies—particularly acting-out and aggressive behavior—in adults and children.
Population: Ages 5 and older.
Publication Dates: 1959–1991.
Scores, 41: 24 quantitative scores: Interpersonal (Affection, Dependence, Communication, Exhibition, Direction, Aggression, Total), Environmental (Acquisition, Active, Passive, Total), Maladjustive (Tension, Crippled, Fear, Total), Withdrawal (Description, Bizarre, Failure, Total), Experience Ratio, Acting Out Ratio, Pathological, Average Initial Response Time, High Minus Low Score, plus 17 qualitative scores: Ambivalent, Automatic Phrase, Cylindrical, Denial, Emotion, Gross, Hiding,

Immature, Inanimate, Movement, Oral, Perplexity, Sensual, Sexual, Original, Repetition.
Administration: Individual.
Price Data, 2016: $209 per complete kit including manual (1983, 94 pages), manual supplement: Interpreting Child and Adolescent Responses (1991, 41 pages), 25 scoring booklets, and 1 set of picture cards; $35.50 per 25 scoring booklets; $54 per set of picture cards; $72 per manual; $59.50 per manual supplement: Interpreting Child and Adolescent Responses.
Time: (10) minutes.
Author: Edwin E. Wagner.
Publisher: Western Psychological Services.
Cross References: For reviews by Colin Cooper and Susana Urbina, see 14:161; see also T5:1169 (6 references) and T4:1121 (17 references); for a review by Marcia B. Shaffer of an earlier edition, see 10:134 (5 references); see also 9:464 (16 references), T3:1053 (21 references), 8:575 (29 references), T2:1470 (15 references), and P:438 (12 references); for a review by Goldine C. Gleser and an excerpted review by Irving R. Stone of an earlier edition, see 6:216 (6 references).

[912]

Hand-Tool Dexterity Test.

Purpose: Intended to "provide a measure of proficiency in using ordinary mechanic's tools."
Population: Adolescents and adults.
Publication Dates: 1946–1981.
Acronym: HTDT.
Scores: Total score only.
Administration: Individual.
Price Data, 2015: $650 per complete set including all necessary equipment and manual (1981, 19 pages).
Time: (5–10) minutes.
Comments: Examinee's score based on time it takes to finish test.
Author: George K. Bennett.
Publisher: Pearson.
Cross References: See T3:1054 (1 reference) and 7:1044 (4 references); for reviews by C. H. Lawshe, Jr. and Neil D. Warren, see 3:649 (2 references).

[913]

Hare P-Scan.

Purpose: Designed as a "tool for assessing psychopathy and managing risk for antisocial, criminal, and violent behavior."
Population: Ages 13 and older
Publication Date: 1999.
Scores, 4: Interpersonal Facet, Affective Facet, Lifestyle Facet, Total.
Administration: Individual or group.
Price Data, 2015: $94 per complete kit including 25 QuikScore™ forms, 1 manual, and 1 book "Without Conscience"; $39 per 25 QuikScore™ forms; $44 per manual.

Time: (10–15) minutes.
Comments: Ratings by evaluator.
Authors: Robert D. Hare and Hugues F. Herve.
Publisher: Multi-Health Systems, Inc.

[914]

Hare Psychopathy Checklist–Revised: 2nd Edition.

Purpose: Designed for "the assessment of psychopathy in research, clinical and forensic settings."
Population: Ages 18 and over
Publication Dates: 1990–2003.
Acronym: PCL-R.
Scores, 7: Factor 1 (Interpersonal, Affective, Total), Factor 2 (Lifestyle, Antisocial, Total), Total.
Administration: Individual.
Forms, 2: Rating Booklet, Interview Guide.
Price Data, 2015: $439 per complete kit including manual (2003, 231 pages), 1 rating booklet, 25 QuikScore™ forms, and 25 interview guides; $149 per technical manual; $83 per rating booklet (reusable, hardcover); $94 per 25 QuikScore™ forms; $154 per 25 interview guides; $209 per preview set including manual, 1 rating booklet, 2 QuikScore forms, and 2 interview guides; $389 for software kit (V.5) including manual and 25 profile reports.
Time: (90–120) minutes for interview; (60) minutes for collateral review, (15-20) minutes for assessment.
Comments: Rating scale based on responses to semi-structured interview and collateral information review. Expands previous edition for use with female and African American offenders, substance abusers, and offenders in countries other than the U.S.
Author: Robert D. Hare.
Publisher: Multi-Health Systems, Inc.
Cross References: For reviews by Shawn K. Acheson and Joshua W. Payne and by D. Joe Olmi, see 16:101; see also T5:1174 (1 reference); for reviews by Solomon M. Fulero and Gerald L. Stone of a previous edition, see 12:177 (5 references); see also T4:1127 (3 references).

[915]

Hare Psychopathy Checklist: Screening Version.

Purpose: To screen for psychopathy in forensic and nonforensic settings.
Population: Adults age 18 and over.
Publication Date: 1995.
Acronym: PCL:SV.
Scores, 3: Part 1, Part 2, Total.
Administration: Individual.
Price Data, 2015: $229 per kit including 25 interview guides, 25 QuikScore™ forms, and manual (82 pages); $159 per 25 interview guides/QuikScore™ forms; $84 per 25 interview guides; $84 per 25 QuikScore™ forms; $79 per manual.

Time: (30–60) minutes; case history review and scoring require further (20–30) minutes.
Comments: Interview format; shortened version of Hare Psychopathy Checklist—Revised (914).
Authors: Stephen D. Hart, David N. Cox, and Robert D. Hare.
Publisher: Multi-Health Systems, Inc.
Cross References: For reviews by Ronald J. Ganellen and by Nathaniel J. Pallone and James J. Hennessy, see 14:162.

[916]

Hare Psychopathy Checklist: Youth Version.

Purpose: Designed for "the assessment of psychopathic traits in adolescents."
Population: Ages 12–18
Publication Date: 2003.
Acronym: PCL:YV.
Scores, 5: Interpersonal, Affective, Behavioral, Antisocial, Total.
Administration: Individual.
Forms, 2: Interview Guide, QuikScore™ Rating Form.
Price Data, 2015: $419 per complete kit including manual, rating booklet, 25 QuikScore forms, and 25 interview guides; $114 per technical manual; $88 per rating booklet (reusable, hardcover); $89 per 25 QuikScore forms; $149 per 25 interview guides.
Time: (90-120) minutes for interview, (60) minutes for collateral interview, (10-20) minutes for completing assessment and scoring.
Comments: Adapted from the Hare Psychopathy Checklist—Revised (914); expert-completed rating scale based on responses to semistructured interview and collateral information review.
Authors: Adelle E. Forth, David S. Kosson, and Robert D. Hare.
Publisher: Multi-Health Systems, Inc.
Cross References: For a review by John W. Fleenor, see 16:102.

[917]

Harmonic Improvisation Readiness Record and Rhythm Improvisation Readiness Record.

Purpose: Designed to "help determine objectively whether individual students have the necessary harmonic and rhythmic readiness to learn to improvise" music.
Population: Grades 3 through music graduate school.
Publication Date: 1998.
Scores, 2: Harmonic Readiness, Rhythmic Readiness.
Administration: Group.
Price Data, 2015: $110 per complete kit including 100 harmonic answer sheets, 100 rhythm answer sheets, scoring masks, compact disc, and manual (1998); $20 per 100 answer sheets (specify harmonic or rhythm); $20 per scoring masks; $25 per compact disc.

Time: (20) minutes per test.
Comments: Can be machine scored.
Author: Edwin E. Gordon.
Publisher: GIA Publications, Inc.

[918]

The Harrington-O'Shea Career Decision-Making System—Revised, 2005 Update.

Purpose: An interest inventory that provides an assessment of career interests, job choices, school subjects, future plans, values, and abilities.
Population: Grade 7 and over.
Publication Dates: 1976-2005.
Acronym: CDM-R.
Administration: Individual or group.
Price Data, 2015: $74.30 per hand-scored edition (Level 1 or 2), including 25 booklets, directions. $38.95 per manual.
Foreign Language Edition: Available in Spanish.
Comments: Hand scored or computer scored; updated every 2 years to reflect changes in occupational forecasts and titles.
Authors: Thomas F. Harrington and Arthur J. O'Shea.
Publisher: Pearson.
 a) LEVEL 1.
 Population: Middle school students, and other students and adults with reading difficulty.
 Publication Dates: 1992–2000.
 Scores: 6 Career Interest Areas: Crafts, Scientific, The Arts, Social, Business, Office Operations; 18 Career Clusters: Manual, Skilled Crafts, Technical, Math-Science, Medical-Dental, Literary, Art, Music, Entertainment, Customer Service, Personal Service, Social Service, Education, Sales, Management, Legal, Clerical, Data Analysis.
 Time: (20–25) minutes.
 b) LEVEL 2.
 Population: High school and college students and adults with average or better reading level.
 Publication Dates: 1976–2000.
 Scores: Same as *a* above and questions in 5 areas: Career Choices, School Subjects, Future Plans, Values, Abilities.
 Time: (30–45) minutes.
Cross References: For reviews by Kevin R. Kelly and Mark L. Pope, see 16:103; see also T5:1177 (2 references); for reviews by Debra Neubert and Marcia B. Shaffer of an earlier edition, see 12:179; see also T4:1128 (1 reference); for a review by Caroline Manuele-Adkins of an earlier edition, see 10:136 (1 reference); see also T3:1054 (3 references); for a review by Carl G. Willis of an earlier edition, see 8:1004.

[919]

Harris Infant Neuromotor Test.

Purpose: Developed as a "family-focused screening tool" for use "in clinical and research settings for the early identification of developmental disorders in infants."
Population: 2.5 months to 12.5 months.
Publication Dates: 2009-2010.

Acronym: HINT.
Score: Total score only.
Administration: Individual.
Price Data, 2015: $36 per manual (2010, 39 pages); $60 per 50 test forms.
Time: (15-25) minutes.
Comments: Additional materials required for administration, but not included: brightly colored ring with string attached, black and white contrasting pictures or designs, disposable paper tape measures for measuring head circumference; after getting a total raw score, it is possible to obtain standard scores based on age norms.
Authors: Susan R. Harris, Antoinette M. Megens, and Linda E. Daniels.
Publisher: Infant Motor Performance Scales, LLC.
Cross References: For reviews by Leslie R. Hawley and Mary J. McLellan, see 19:83.

[920]

Hassles and Uplifts Scales.

Purpose: To identify sources of stress and positive aspects of daily living that help counteract the damaging effects of stress.
Population: Adults.
Publication Date: 1989.
Acronym: HSUP.
Administration: Group.
Price Data, 2015: $50 for manual, including a review-only copy of the HSUP forms; $2.40 per license (minimum 50) to use Transform Survey Hosting: Combined Scale, Daily Hassles Scale, Daily Uplifts Scale; $2 per Remote Online Survey License or License to Reproduce (minimum 50); $15 per Individual Report: Combined Scale; $15 per Report About Me: Combined Scale.
Foreign Language Editions: Available in Creole, French, and Spanish.
Time: (10-15) minutes per test.
Comments: Self-administered; tests available as separates.
Authors: Richard S. Lazarus and Susan Folkman.
Publisher: Mind Garden, Inc.
  a) THE DAILY HASSLES SCALE.
  Scores, 2: Frequency, Severity.
  b) THE UPLIFTS SCALE.
  Scores, 2: Frequency, Intensity.
  c) THE COMBINED HASSLES AND UPLIFTS SCALES.
  Scores, 2: Hassles, Uplifts.
Cross References: See T5:1178 (17 references) and T4:1132 (2 references); for reviews by Karen S. Budd and Nancy Heilman and by Barbara A. Reilly, see 11:155 (6 references).

[921]

Hay Aptitude Test Battery [Revised].

Purpose: Designed to assess perceptual speed and accuracy.

Population: Applicants for positions that place a heavy emphasis on information processing speed and accuracy.
Publication Dates: 1947-2004.
Scores, 2: Number of Correct Responses, Number of Incorrect Responses.
Administration: Group or individual.
Price Data: Available from publisher.
Foreign Language Editions: French and Spanish versions available.
Author: Edward N. Hay.
Publisher: Wonderlic, Inc.
  a) WARM-UP TEST.
  Purpose: Designed to reduce test-taker anxiety and help acclimate the test taker to the testing setting.
  Time: (1) minute.
  b) NUMBER PERCEPTION TEST.
  Purpose: Designed to assess short-term memory and accuracy with numerical detail.
  Time: (4) minutes.
  c) NAME FINDING TEST.
  Purpose: Assesses short-term memory and accuracy with alphabetical detail.
  Time: (4) minutes.
  d) NUMBER SERIES COMPLETION TEST.
  Purpose: Assesses numerical comprehension, logical thinking, and the ability to perceive patterns and relationships.
  Time: (4) minutes.
Cross References: For reviews by Mark A. Albanese and Michael Kane, see 14:164; for reviews by Sue M. Legg and M. David Miller of an earlier edition, see 12:179; for a review by Robert P. Vecchio of an earlier edition, see 9:470; see also T2:2132 (2 references) and 5:849 (2 references); for reviews by Reign H. Bittner and Edward E. Cureton, see 4:725 (8 references).

[922]

The Hayling and Brixton Tests.

Purpose: Designed to assess executive functions.
Population: Ages 18-80.
Publication Date: 1997.
Administration: Individual.
Price Data, 2015: £189.50 per complete kit including manual (20 pages), stimulus book, and 25 scoring sheets; £27.50 per 25 scoring sheets; £51 per manual; £117 per stimulus book.
Authors: Paul W. Burgess and Tim Shallice.
Publisher: Pearson Assessment [England].
  a) HAYLING TEST.
  Scores, 4: Response Latency, Error Score, Time Taken to Respond, Total.
  Time: [5] minutes.
  Comments: Administered verbally; requires no reading or writing.
  b) BRIXTON TEST.
  Score: Total score only.
  Time: [5-10] minutes.
Cross References: For reviews by Kathleen D. Allen and Eugene P. Sheehan, see 17:85.

[923]
HCR-20V3: Assessing Risk for Violence.

Purpose: Designed to "facilitate assessments of risk for interpersonal violence defined as actual, attempted, or threatened infliction of bodily harm on another person."
Population: Adults ages 18 and older.
Publication Dates: 1997-2013.
Acronym: HCR-20 V3.
Scores: 20 risk factors in 3 scales: Historical Factors, Clinical Factors, Risk Management Factors; Risk for Future Violence, Risk for Serious Physical Harm, Risk for Imminent Violence.
Administration: Individual.
Price Data: Available from publisher.
Time: Administration time not reported.
Authors: Kevin S. Douglas, Stephen D. Hart, Christopher D. Webster, and Henrik Belfrage.
Publisher: Mental Health, Law, and Policy Institute, Simon Fraser University [Canada].
Cross References: Reviews are scheduled for *The Twentieth Mental Measurements Yearbook*. For reviews by Paul A. Arbisi and Colin Cooper of Version 2, see 15:115.

[924]
Health and Daily Living Form [Second Edition Manual].

Purpose: To examine the influence of extra treatment factors on treatment outcome as well as to explore the social resources and coping processes people use to prevent and adapt to stressful life circumstances.
Population: Students ages 12-18, Adults.
Publication Dates: 1984-1990.
Acronym: HDLF.
Administration: Individual or group.
Forms, 2: Youth Form, Adult Form B.
Price Data, 2015: $50 for manual, including review-only copy of HDLF form; $2 per Remote Online Survey License (minimum 50); $2 License to Reproduce (minimum 50).
Time: (30-45) minutes.
Comments: May be administered as an interview or as a questionnaire.
Authors: Rudolf H. Moos, Ruth C. Cronkite, and John W. Finney.
Publisher: Mind Garden, Inc.
a) YOUTH FORM.
   Population: Students ages 12-18.
   Scores: 9 indices: Health-Related (Self-Confidence, Positive Mood, Distressed Mood, Physical Symptoms, Medical Conditions, Health—Risk Behaviors), Social Functioning (Family Activities, Activities with Friends, Social Integration in School).
   Time: [5-10] minutes.
b) ADULT FORM B.
   Population: Adults.
   Scores: 41 indices: Health-Related Functioning (Self-Confidence, Physical Symptoms, Medical Conditions,

Global Depression, Depressive Mood and Ideation, Endogenous Depression, Depressive Features, Depressed Mood/Past 12 Months, Alcohol Consumption—Quantity, Alcohol Consumption—Quantity/Frequency, Drinking Problems, Smoking Symptoms, Medication Use), Social Functioning and Resources (Social Activities with Friends, Network Contacts, Number of Close Relationships, Quality of Significant Relationship), Family Functioning and Home Environment (Family Social Activities, Family Task Sharing, Tasks Performed by Self, Tasks Performed by Partner, Family Arguments, Negative Home Environment), Children's Health and Functioning (Children's Physical Health Problems, Children's Psychological Health Problems, Children's Total Health Problems, Children's Behavioral Problems, Children's Health—Risk Behaviors), Life Change Events (Negative Life Change Events, Exit Events, Positive Life Change Events), Help-Seeking (Mental Health Professional [past 12 months], Mental Health Professional [ever gone], Non-Mental Health Professional [past 12 months], Non-Mental Health Professional [ever gone]), Family Level Composite (Quality of Conjugal Relationship, Family Social Activities, Family Agreement on Task Sharing, Family Agreement on Household Tasks, Family Arguments, Negative Home Environment).
   Time: [15-20] minutes.
Cross References: For reviews by Sandra D. Haynes and Ashraf Kagee, see 15:116; see T5:1181 (28 references) and T4:1135 (19 references); for reviews by Arthur M. Nezu and Steven P. Schinke, see 10:137 (8 references).

[925]
Health Dynamics Inventory.

Purpose: Developed to assess mental health status.
Population: Ages 3-18 (Parent Form), Ages 16-84 (Self Form).
Publication Date: 2003.
Acronym: HDI.
Scores, 13: Morale, Global Symptoms, Global Impairment, Depression, Anxiety, Attention Problems, Psychotic Thinking, Eating Disorders, Substance Abuse, Behavioral Problems, Occupational/Task Impairment, Relationship Impairment, Self-Care Impairment.
Administration: Group or individual.
Forms, 2: Parent, Self.
Price Data, 2015: $394 per complete kit including manual (152 pages), 10 HDI-P (Parent) and HDI-S (Self) item booklets, 25 HDI-P and HDI-S background information questionnaires, and 25 HDI-P and HDI-S response forms; $93 per technical manual; $32 per 10 item booklets (specify HDI-P or HDI-S); $74 per 25 background information questionnaires (specify HDI-P or HDI-S); $55 per 25 response forms (specify HDI-P or HDI-S); $249 per Interpretive report kit including manual, V.5 getting started guide, and 25 interpretive reports; $229 per Health summary report kit including manual, V.5 getting started guide, and 25 Health summary reports.
Time: (15) minutes.
Comments: Parent form is completed for children ages 3–18 by parent.

Authors: Stephen M. Saunders and James V. Wojcik.
Publisher: Multi-Health Systems, Inc.
Cross References: For reviews by Rik Carl D'Amato and Gregory C. Wochos and by Jeffrey A. Jenkins, see 16:104.

[926]
Health Problems Checklist.

Purpose: To facilitate "the rapid assessment of the health status and potential health problems of clients typically seen in psychotherapy settings."
Population: Adults.
Publication Dates: 1984-1989.
Scores: Items in 13 areas: General Health, Cardiovascular/Pulmonary, Endocrine/Hematology, Gastrointestinal, Dermatological, Visual, Auditory/Olfactory, Mouth/Throat/Nose, Orthopedic, Neurological, Genitourinary, Habits, History; no formal scoring procedure.
Administration: Individual or group.
Manual: No manual.
Price Data, 2015: $62 per package of 50.
Time: (10–20) minutes.
Author: John A. Schinka.
Publisher: Psychological Assessment Resources, Inc.
Cross References: See T5:1186 (1 reference); for a review by Robert M. Kaplan and Michelle T. Toshima of an earlier version, see 10:138.

[927]
The Health Sciences Reasoning Test.

Purpose: "Was developed for use by educators and researchers to assess the critical thinking skills of health science professionals and health science students."
Population: Health science professionals and students.
Publication Dates: 2006-2007.
Acronym: HSRT.
Scores, 6: Analysis, Evaluation, Inference, Deductive Reasoning, Inductive Reasoning, Total.
Administration: Group.
Price Data: Available from publisher.
Time: (45) minutes.
Comments: This test can be administered online or via paper and pencil.
Authors: Noreen C. Facione and Peter A. Facione.
Publisher: Insight Assessment-The California Academic Press LLC.
Cross References: For reviews by Brian F. French and Sandra D. Haynes, see 18:58.

[928]
Healthcare Customer Service Test.

Purpose: Selects customer service oriented workers for hospitals and healthcare settings.
Population: Hospital employees (service, skilled, professional, nursing, administrative, physician, technicians, environmental services).

Publication Dates: 1996–1997.
Acronym: HCST.
Scores, 5: Collaborate, Accommodate, Respect, Engage, Total.
Administration: Group.
Price Data: Available from publisher.
Time: (25–35) minutes, untimed.
Comments: Used for selection; subtests can be used for interview probes; may be administered online.
Author: Healthcare Testing, Inc.
Publisher: Silverwood Enterprises, LLC.
Cross References: For a review by Ronald A. Berk, see 16:106.

[929]
HELP® 3–6 (2nd Edition).

Purpose: Designed as "a curriculum-based assessment" of developmental skills/behaviors for use in identifying "strengths and needs, and the services appropriate to meet those needs" as well as in documenting growth and progress, at home and in educational settings.
Population: Children ages 3-6 years.
Publication Dates: 1987-2010.
Scores: Item scores in 6 developmental areas: Cognitive, Language, Gross Motor, Fine Motor, Social, Self-Help.
Administration: Individual.
Price Data, 2016: $57.95 per Assessment Manual (2010, 400 pages); $62.95 per Activities at Home book; $39.95 per Curriculum Guide; $3.50 per charts; $3.50 per checklist; $3.50 per Assessment Strands; volume discounts available.
Time: Administration time not reported.
Comments: Adaptation of Behavioral Characteristics Progression (BCP; 234); upward extension of HELP Strands (Hawaii Early Learning Profile): Ages 0-3 (930); "criterion-referenced"; formerly titled Help for Preschoolers.
Author: VORT Corporation.
Publisher: VORT Corporation.
Cross References: For reviews by Harlan J. Stientjes and Gerald Tindal of the original edition titled Help for Special Preschoolers Assessment Checklist: Ages 3-6 (1987) see 11:158.

[930]
HELP Strands (Hawaii Early Learning Profile): Ages birth-3.

Purpose: Assesses developmental skills/behaviors.
Population: Ages birth-3 years.
Publication Dates: 1984-2004.
Acronym: HELP Strands.
Scores: Item scores only; 6 developmental areas: Cognitive, Language, Gross Motor, Fine Motor, Social, Self-Help.
Administration: Individual.
Price Data: Available from publisher.

Time: Administration time not reported.
Comments: Ratings by professionals; previous version titled HELP Checklist (Hawaii Early Learning Profile).
Authors: Stephanie Parks (based on original work by Setsu Furuno, Katherine A. O'Reilly, Carol M. Hosaka, Takayo T. Inatsuka, Barbara Zeisloft-Falbey, and Toney Allman).
Publisher: VORT Corporation.
Cross References: For reviews by William Steven Lang and Koressa Kutsick Malcolm of an earlier edition, see 11:157.

[931]
Herrmann Brain Dominance Instrument [Revised].
Purpose: Designed to measure "a person's preference both for right-brained or left-brained thinking and for conceptual or experiential thinking."
Population: Adults
Publication Dates: 1981–1995.
Acronym: HBDI®.
Scores, 12: Left Mode Preference, Right Mode Preference, Quadrant (Upper Left, Lower Left, Upper Right, Lower Right), Adjective Pairs (subset of 4 Quadrant Scores), Upper (Cerebral) Mode Preference, Lower (Limbic Mode) Preference.
Administration: Group.
Manual: No manual.
Price Data: Available from publisher.
Time: (15–20) minutes.
Comments: Administered via computer; scored by publisher and interpreted by a certified practitioner; hard copy version is available for special needs.
Author: Ned Herrmann.
Publisher: Herrmann International
Cross References: For reviews by F. Felicia Ferrara and Gabriele van Lingen, see 14:165; see also T5:1197 (1 reference); for a review by Rik Carl D'Amato of an earlier edition, see 11:159 (7 references).

[932]
High Level Battery: Test A/75.
Purpose: To provide "measures of general intelligence, arithmetical ability and certain language abilities."
Population: Adults with at least 12 years of education.
Publication Dates: 1960–1972.
Scores: Total scores only for 4 tests in a single booklet: Mental Alertness, Arithmetic Problems, Reading Comprehension (English, Afrikaans), Vocabulary (English, Afrikaans).
Administration: Group.
Price Data: Available from publisher.
Time: 197 (215) minutes.
Comments: Formerly listed as National Institute for Personnel Research High Level Battery.

Author: D. P. M. Beukes (manual).
Publisher: Human Sciences Research Council [South Africa]. [Efforts to obtain updated information from the test publisher were unsuccessful. This test could not be found on the test publisher's website; its status is unknown.]
Cross References: See 6:778 (1 reference).

[933]
High Level Figure Classification Test.
Purpose: Designed to assess intellectual ability.
Population: Grades 10–12.
Publication Date: 1983.
Acronym: HL FCT.
Scores: Total score only.
Administration: Group.
Price Data: Available from publisher.
Foreign Language Edition: Test printed in both English and Afrikaans.
Time: 30(40) minutes.
Authors: M. Werbeloff and T. R. Taylor.
Publisher: Human Sciences Research Council [South Africa].

[934]
High School Placement Test-Open Edition.
Purpose: Designed as a measure of cognitive and basic skills to assist in placement decisions for entering freshmen.
Population: Eighth grade students.
Publication Dates: 1982–2004.
Acronym: HSPT.
Scores, 5: Verbal Skills, Quantitative Skills, Reading, Mathematics, Language.
Administration: Group.
Restricted Distribution: Available for school purchase only.
Price Data: Available from publisher.
Time: 150 minutes plus (15–25) minutes per optional test.
Comments: Optional tests available including Science, Mechanical Aptitude, and Catholic Religion.
Author: Scholastic Testing Service, Inc.
Publisher: Scholastic Testing Service, Inc.
Cross References: For reviews by John O. Anderson and Geneva D. Haertel, see 14:166.

[935]
Hilson Career Satisfaction Index.
Purpose: Designed to identify "stress symptoms, drug/alcohol abuse, and disciplinary history to inform conditional-offer selection and fitness-for-duty decisions."
Population: Public safety/security officers
Publication Date: 1989.
Acronym: HCSI.

Scores, 10: 9 in 3 scales: Stress Patterns (Stress Symptoms, Drug/Alcohol Abuse, Lack of Interpersonal Support), Anger/Hostility Patterns (Disciplinary History, Excusing Attitudes, Aggression/Hostility), Dissatisfaction with Career (Dissatisfaction with Supervisor, Relationship with Co-Workers, Dissatisfaction with Job), plus Defensiveness (validity scale).
Administration: Individual or group.
Price Data: Available from publisher.
Time: 20 minutes.
Author: Robin Inwald.
Publisher: Institute for Personality and Ability Testing, Inc. (IPAT).
Cross References: See T4:1166 (1 reference).

[936]

Hilson Personnel Profile/Success Quotient.
Purpose: Designed to aid in the assessment of the qualifications needed for long term career success (e.g., emotional IQ, drive, work ethic, social skills and communication skills).
Population: Age 16 and above or as determined by a psychologist.
Publication Date: 1988.
Acronym: HPP/SQ.
Scores, 16: Candor, Achievement History, Social Ability, "Winner's" Image, Initiative, Success Quotient, Extraversion, Popularity/"Charisma," Sensitivity, Competitive Spirit, Self-Worth, Family Achievement Expectations, Drive, Preparation Style, Goal Orientation, Anxiety about Organization.
Administration: Individual or group.
Price Data: Available from publisher.
Time: 20 minutes.
Author: Robin E. Inwald.
Publisher: Institute for Personality and Ability Testing, Inc. (IPAT).
Cross References: For a review by Joseph G. Law, Jr., see 11:162.

[937]

Hodson Assessment of Phonological Patterns—Third Edition.
Purpose: Designed to "assess and analyze phonological deviations of children with highly unintelligible speech."
Population: Ages 3 to 8.
Publication Dates: 1986-2004.
Acronym: HAPP-3.
Scores, 14: Word/Syllable Structures Omissions (Syllables, Consonant Sequences/Clusters, Prevocalic Singletons, Intervocalic Singletons, Postvocalic Singletons, Total), Consonant Category Deficiencies (Liquids, Nasals, Glides, Stridents, Velars, Anterior Nonstridents, Total), Total Occurrences of Major Phonological Deviations.
Administration: Individual.

Levels, 3: Comprehensive Phonological Evaluation, Preschool Phonological Screening, Multisyllabic Word Screening.
Price Data, 2015: $227 per complete kit including examiner's manual (2004, 64 pages), 25 Comprehensive Phonological Evaluation Record Forms, 25 Major Phonological Deviations Analysis Forms, 25 Substitutions and Other Strategies Analysis Forms, 50 Preschool Phonological Screening Record Forms, 50 Multisyllabic Word Screening Record Forms, 1 Multisyllabic Word Screening Picture Sheet, 30-piece Object Kit, and 13 Picture Cards; $43 per 25 Comprehensive Phonological Evaluation Record Forms; $37 per 25 Major Phonological Deviations Analysis Forms; $37 per 25 Substitutions and Other Strategies Analysis Forms; $25 per 50 Preschool Phonological Screening Record Forms; $25 per 50 Multisyllabic Word Screening Record Forms; $12 per 1 Multisyllabic Word Screening Picture Sheet; $62 per object kit; $13 per picture card kit; $73 per examiner's manual.
Time: (15–20) minutes.
Comments: Norm referenced and "criterion referenced"; formerly called The Assessment of Phonological Processes.
Author: Barbara Williams Hodson.
Publisher: PRO-ED.
Cross References: For reviews by David P. Hurford and Vincent J. Samar, see 17:87; see also T5:214 (19 references); for reviews of an earlier version by Allen O. Diefendorf, Michael K. Wynne, and Kathy Kessler and by Kathryn W. Kenney, see 12:36; see also T4:220 (4 references); for a review by Sheldon L. Stick, see 9:91 (1 reference).

[938]

Hogan Development Survey [Revised].
Purpose: Designed to assess 11 personality dimensions that may inhibit career success.
Population: Adults.
Publication Dates: 1995-2009.
Acronym: HDS.
Scores, 11: Excitable, Skeptical, Cautious, Reserved, Leisurely, Bold, Mischievous, Colorful, Imaginative, Diligent, Dutiful.
Administration: Group.
Price Data: Available from publisher.
Foreign Language Editions: List of translations available from publisher.
Time: (15-20) minutes.
Comments: Available for online administration.
Authors: Robert Hogan and Joyce Hogan (manual).
Publisher: Hogan Assessment Systems, Inc.
Cross References: For reviews by Stephen Axford and Theodore L. Hayes, see 19:84; for reviews by Glen Fox and E. Scott Huebner of an earlier edition, see 14:168.

[939]

Hogan Personality Inventory [Revised].

Purpose: Measure of normal personality designed for use in personnel selection, individualized assessment, and career-related decision making.
Population: Adults.
Publication Dates: 1985–1995.
Acronym: HPI.
Scores: 7 primary scale scores (Inquisitive, Adjustment, Ambition, Sociability, Interpersonal Sensitivity, Prudence, Learning Approach), 6 occupational scale scores (Service Orientation, Stress Tolerance, Reliability, Clerical Potential, Sales Potential, Managerial Potential), and Validity scale score.
Administration: Group.
Price Data: Available from publisher.
Foreign Language Editions: List of translations available from publisher.
Time: (15–20) minutes.
Comments: Web-based administration.
Authors: Robert Hogan and Joyce Hogan (manual).
Publisher: Hogan Assessment Systems, Inc.
Cross References: See T5:1212 (1 reference); for reviews by Stephen N. Axford and Steven G. LoBello, see 13:138 (2 references); see also T4:1169 (7 references); for reviews by James J. Hennessy and Rolf A. Peterson of an earlier edition, see 10:140.

[940]

Holden Psychological Screening Inventory.

Purpose: "To provide a very brief measure of psychiatric symptomatology, social symptomatology, and depression."
Population: Ages 14 and older.
Publication Date: 1996.
Acronym: HPSI.
Scores, 4: Psychiatric Symptomatology, Social Symptomatology, Depression, Total.
Administration: Individual or group.
Price Data, 2015: $114 per complete kit including manual (50 pages) and 25 QuikScore™ forms; $55 per 25 QuikScore™ forms; $69 per manual; $79 per online profile report kit; $6 per online profile report.
Foreign Language Edition: French-Canadian QuikScore™ forms available.
Time: (5–7) minutes.
Comments: Self-report; computer administration and scoring available.
Author: Ronald R. Holden.
Publisher: Multi-Health Systems, Inc.
Cross References: For reviews by Stephen N. Axford and Janet F. Carlson, see 14:169; see also T5:1213 (1 reference).

[941]

Holtzman Inkblot Technique.

Purpose: Designed as a projective personality test.

Population: Ages 5 and over.
Publication Dates: 1958–1972.
Acronym: HIT.
Scores, 20–22: Reaction Time (*a* only), Rejection, Location, Space, Form Definiteness, Form Appropriateness, Color, Shading, Movement, Pathognomic Verbalization, Integration, Content (Human, Animal, Anatomy, Sex, Abstract), Anxiety, Hostility, Barrier, Penetration, Balance (*a* only), Popular.
Administration: Group or individual.
Price Data, 2015: $27.70 per 25 Hill clinical summary forms; $66.35 per Workbook for the Holtzman Inkblot Technique.
Author: Wayne H. Holtzman.
Publisher: Pearson.
a) INDIVIDUAL TEST.
Publication Dates: 1958–1972.
Forms, 2: A, B.
Price Data: $784 per complete set for Forms A and B combined including 47 inkblots, 25 record forms with summary sheets, and scoring guide; $425 per complete set (specify Form A or B).
b) GROUP TEST.
Publication Dates: 1958–1972.
Manual: No manual.
Price Data: $53.80 per 50 Gorham-Holtzman group record forms; $50.75 per normative item statistics.
Comments: Administration slides for either form must be constructed locally.
Author: Donald R. Gorham (record form).
Cross References: See T4:1170 (12 references); for reviews by Bert P. Cundick and David M. Dush, see 9:480 (17 references); see also T3:1106 (25 references); for a review by Rolf A. Peterson, see 8:578 (96 references); see also T2:1471 (42 references); for excerpted reviews by Raymond J. McCall and David G. Martin, see 7:169 (106 references); see also P:439 (90 references); for reviews by Richard N. Coan, H. J. Eysenck, Bertram R. Forer, and William N. Thetford, see 6:217 (22 references).

[942]

Home & Community Social Behavior Scales.

Purpose: Designed to evaluate social competence and antisocial behavior.
Population: Ages 5–18 (Grades K-12).
Publication Date: 2008.
Acronym: HCSBS.
Scores, 6: Peer Relations, Self-Management/Compliance, Social Competence Total, Defiant/Disruptive, Antisocial/Aggressive, Antisocial Behavior Total.
Administration: Individual.
Price Data, 2016: $49.95 per user's guide (120 pages); $39.95 per 25 test forms.
Time: (5–10) minutes.
Comments: Companion to the School Social Behavior Scales (1817); rated by parent or other home- or community-based rater.
Authors: Kenneth W. Merrell and Paul Caldarella.

Publisher: Paul H. Brookes Publishing Co., Inc.
Cross References: For reviews by Theodore Coladarci and by Stephanie Stein and Phil Diaz, see 16:107.

[943]

Home Observation for Measurement of the Environment.

Purpose: Designed to measure the quality and quantity of stimulation and support available to a child in the home environment.
Population: Birth to age 3, early childhood, middle childhood, early adolescent.
Publication Dates: 1978–2003.
Acronym: HOME Inventory.
Administration: Individual.
Price Data, 2016: $50 per comprehensive manual; $40 per standard manual (without Disability Adapted or Child Care HOME); $30 per Child Care HOME Manual; $15 per pad of Infant Toddler forms; $25 per 50 Early Childhood forms; $12.50 per 25 Middle and Early Adolescent forms.
Time: (60) minutes.
Comment: Focus is on the child in the home environment as a recipient of inputs from objects, events, and transactions occurring in connection with the family surroundings.
Authors: Bettye M. Caldwell and Robert H. Bradley.
Publisher: Home Inventory LLC.
  a) INFANT/TODDLER HOME INVENTORY.
  Population: Birth-3 years.
  Scores, 7: Responsivity, Acceptance, Organization, Learning Materials, Involvement, Variety, Total.
  b) EARLY CHILDHOOD HOME INVENTORY.
  Population: 3-6 years.
  Scores, 9: Learning Materials, Language Stimulation, Physical Environment, Responsivity, Academic Stimulation, Modeling, Variety, Acceptance, Total.
  c) MIDDLE CHILDHOOD HOME INVENTORY.
  Population: 6-10 years.
  Scores, 8: Responsivity, Encouragement of Maturity, Acceptance, Learning Materials, Enrichment, Family Companionship, Paternal Involvement, Total.
  d) EARLY ADOLESCENT HOME INVENTORY.
  Population: Early adolescents.
  Scores 7: Physical Environment, Learning Materials, Modeling, Instructional Activities, Regular Activities, Variety of Experience and Acceptance, Responsivity.
Cross References: See T5:1216 (113 references) and T4:1172 (42 references); for a review by Ann E. Boehm, see 9:481 (13 references); see also T3:1108 (14 references).

[944]

Home-Visit Kit.

Purpose: Yields information regarding home safety and life-style issues necessary in child custody evaluations.
Population: Families involved in child custody situations.
Publication Dates: 1997–2002.

Scores: Unscored.
Administration: Group.
Price Data, 2016: $289 per kit including 8 Home-Visit booklets, instruction booklet (42 pages), and up-date service; $159 per 10 Home-Visit booklets (volume discounts available); $149 per Home-Visit instruction booklet.
Time: Administration time not reported.
Comments: Previously listed as The Bricklin/Elliot Child Custody Evaluation.
Authors: Barry Bricklin and Gail Elliot.
Publisher: Village Publishing.

[945]

The Hooper Visual Organization Test.

Purpose: Measures an individual's ability to organize visual stimuli.
Population: Ages 5 years and over.
Publication Dates: 1957–1983.
Acronym: VOT.
Scores: Total score only.
Administration: Group or individual.
Price Data, 2016: $256.50 per complete kit including 4 reusable test pictures booklets, manual (1983, 39 pages), 25 test booklets, 100 answer sheets, and scoring key; $35 per 25 test booklets; $50.50 per reusable test pictures booklet; $20.50 per scoring key; $35 per 100 answer sheets; $59.50 per manual.
Time: (15) minutes.
Author: H. Elston Hooper.
Publisher: Western Psychological Services.
Cross References: See T5:1218 (19 references); for reviews by Kathy E. Green and Wilfred G. Van Gorp, see 12:182 (7 references); see also T4:1174 (28 references), T3:1109 (6 references), T2:1216 (5 references), and P:111 (7 references); for reviews by Ralph M. Reitan and Otfried Spreen of an earlier edition, see 6:116 (4 references).

[946]

HOPE Teacher Rating Scale.

Purpose: Designed to "aid in the identification of gifted and talented students."
Population: Students in kindergarten through Grade 12.
Publication Date: 2015.
Acronym: HOPE Scale.
Scores, 2: Academic, Social.
Administration: Individual.
Price Data, 2015: $110 per kit, including administration manual (56 pages) and 50 forms; $60 per manual; $55 per 50 forms.
Time: Administration time not reported.
Comments: Test publisher recommends that teachers complete the scale on each of their students, one class at a time.

Authors: Marcia Gentry, Nielsen Pereira, Scott J. Peters, Jason S. McIntosh, and C. Matthew Fugate.
Publisher: Prufrock Press Inc.
Cross References: Reviews are scheduled for *The Twentieth Mental Measurements Yearbook.*

[947]

Hopkins Verbal Learning Test—Revised.

Purpose: A "brief assessment of verbal learning and memory (immediate recall, delayed recall, delayed recognition)."
Population: Ages 16 years and older.
Publication Dates: 1991–2001.
Acronym: HVLT-R.
Scores, 4: Total Recall, Delayed Recall, Retention, Recognition Discrimination Index.
Administration: Individual.
Forms, 6: 1–6.
Price Data, 2015: $340 per introductory kit including professional manual (2001, 55 pages), professional manual supplement, and 25 each of 6 test booklets (Forms 1–6).
Time: (5–10) minutes with a 25-minute delay.
Comments: Forms 1–6 are very similar psychometrically and can be used to eliminate practice effects on repeated administration.
Authors: Jason Brandt and Ralph H. B. Benedict.
Publisher: Psychological Assessment Resources, Inc.
Cross References: For reviews by Timothy Z. Keith and Wendy J. Steinberg, see 16:108.

[948]

The Hospital Anxiety and Depression Scale with the Irritability-Depression-Anxiety Scale and the Leeds Situational Anxiety Scale.

Purpose: Designed to detect and distinguish "between anxiety and depression and measures the severity of emotional disorder."
Population: Adults.
Publication Date: 1994.
Acronym: HADS.
Scores, 3: Irritability, Anxiety, Depression.
Administration: Individual.
Price Data, 2016: £110 per complete set, including manual and 100 record forms; £75 per record forms; £45 per manual.
Foreign Language Edition: Available in 115 languages, including French, Dutch, Italian, Spanish, Chinese and Arabic.
Time: (5) minutes.
Authors: R. P. Snaith and A. S. Zigmond.
Publisher: GL Assessment [England].
Cross References: For reviews by Michael H. Campbell and William E. Martin, Jr., see 15:118.

[949]

House-Tree-Person and Draw-A-Person as Measures of Abuse in Children: A Quantitative Scoring System.

Purpose: Developed to "evaluate possible child sexual abuse."
Population: Ages 7–11.
Publication Date: 1994.
Acronym: H-T-P/D-A-P.
Scores, 4: Preoccupation with Sexually Relevant Concepts, Aggression and Hostility, Withdrawal and Guarded Accessibility, Alertness for Danger/Suspiciousness and Lack of Trust.
Administration: Individual.
Price Data, 2015: $130 per H-T-P/D-A-P Quantitative Scoring System Kit including "H-T-P/D-A-P as Measures of Abuse in Children," and 25 scoring booklets.
Time: Administration time not reported.
Comments: A projective drawing instrument; for related instruments see The Draw-A-Person, Draw A Person: A Quantitative Scoring System, Draw-A-Person Quality Scale, and Draw A Person: Screening Procedure for Emotional Disturbance.
Author: Valerie Van Hutton.
Publisher: Psychological Assessment Resources, Inc.
Cross References: See T5:1219 (1 reference); for reviews by E. Thomas Dowd and Howard M. Knoff, see 13:139 (2 references).

[950]

How Am I Doing? A Self-Assessment for Child Caregivers.

Purpose: Designed to identify areas of strength and skill development needs of caregivers of children with disabilities.
Population: Caregivers of children with disabilities.
Publication Date: 1993.
Scores: 8 sections: Arrival and Departure, Free Choice Play, Structured Group Activities, Outside Play, Meal Time, Toileting, Nap Time, Throughout the Day.
Administration: Group.
Price Data, 2016: $14.95 per assessment.
Time: Administration time not reported.
Author: Irene Carney.
Publisher: Child Development Resources.
Cross References: For reviews by Lisa G. Bischoff and by Frederic J. Medway and Karen Fay, see 13:140.

[951]

How I Think about Drugs and Alcohol Questionnaire.

Purpose: Designed to "measure adolescents' behaviors and attitudes related to drug use."
Population: Grades 9-12.

Publication Date: 2008.
Acronym: HIT-D&A.
Scores, 16: Behavior Scale (Soft Drug Use, Hard Drug Use, Drug Abuse, Drug Dependence), Attitude Scale [3 Cognitive Distortion Referent subscales (Self-Centered, Blaming Others and Assuming the Worst, Minimizing and Mislabeling) or 4 Drug Referent subscales (Alcohol, Nicotine, Marijuana, Hard Drugs)], Validity Screener, Drug Use Screener, Drug of Choice Ranking.
Administration: Group.
Price Data, 2015: $25.99 per manual (65 pages) and 20 questionnaires, $23.99 per 20 questionnaires.
Time: (5-10) minutes.
Authors: Alvaro Q. Barriga (test and manual), John C. Gibbs, Granville Bud Potter, M. Konopisos, and K. T. Barriga.
Publisher: Research Press.
Cross References: For reviews by Collie W. Conoley and Elisa Vasquez and by Robert K. Gable and Meghan Kiley, see 19:85.

[952]

How I Think Questionnaire.

Purpose: Designed to "measure self-serving cognitive distortion."
Population: Ages 12–21.
Publication Date: 2001.
Acronym: HIT.
Scores, 11: Hit Questionnaire, Overt, Covert, Self-Centered, Blaming Others, Minimizing/Mislabeling, Assuming the Worst, Opposition-Defiance, Physical Aggression, Lying, Stealing, Anomalous Responding.
Administration: Individual.
Price Data, 2015: $34.99 per 20 questionnaires and manual (44 pages); $32.99 per 20 additional questionnaires.
Time: (5–15) minutes.
Authors: John C. Gibbs, Alvaro Q. Barriga, Granville Bud Potter, and Albert K. Kiau.
Publisher: Research Press.
Cross References: For reviews by Jack E. Gebart-Eaglemont and Joseph C. Kush, see 15:119.

[953]

HRR Pseudoisochromatic Plates for Detecting and Classifying Color Vision Deficiency.

Purpose: Designed to test for color vision; distinguishes those with normal color vision from those with defective color vision. For those with defective color vision, indicates the type (Protan, Deutan, or Tritan) and the degree of defect (mild, medium, or strong).
Population: People who may have color vision deficiency and occupational settings where the work requires a known level of color vision.
Publication Dates: 1991-2002.

Scores, 3: Normal Color Vision, Defective Color Vision (Red-Green Deficiency, Blue-Yellow Deficiency).
Administration: Individual.
Price Data: Available from publisher.
Time: (1–3) minutes.
Authors: Richmond Products, Inc.; LeGrand H. Hardy (manual), Gertrude Rand (manual), and M. Catherine Rittler (manual); J. Neitz (Fourth Edition), and J. Bailey (Fourth Edition).
Publisher: Richmond Products, Inc.
Cross References: For a review by Ayres G. D'Costa, see 15:120.

[954]

Human Information Processing Survey.

Purpose: "Assesses processing preference--left, right, integrated, or mixed [brain functioning]."
Population: Adults.
Publication Date: 1984.
Acronym: HIP Survey.
Scores, 3: Right, Left, Integrated.
Administration: Group.
Editions, 2: Research Edition, Professional Edition.
Price Data: Available from publisher.
Time: [40] minutes.
Authors: E. Paul Torrance, William Taggart (manual), and Barbara Taggart.
Publisher: Scholastic Testing Service, Inc.
Cross References: See T5:1227 (2 references) and T4:1186 (1 reference); for a review by J. P. Das, see 10:144 (1 reference).

[955]

Humanics National Child Assessment Form [Revised].

Purpose: To serve as developmental checklists of skills and behavior that occur during the first 9 years of life.
Population: Ages 0–3, 3–6, 6–9.
Dates: 1981–2002.
Administration: Group.
Levels, 3: Birth to age 3, ages 3 to 6, ages 6 to 9.
Price Data, 2016: $34.95 per 25 assessment forms (specify level).
Time: Administration time varies.
Comments: Behavior checklists to be completed by parents or teachers.
Publisher: Green Publishing.
   a) BIRTH TO THREE.
   Scores, 5: Social-Emotional, Language, Cognitive, Gross Motor, Fine Motor.
   Authors: Marsha Kaufman (checklist), T. Thomas McMurrain (checklist), Jane A. Caballero (handbook), and Derek Whordley (handbook).
   b) AGES THREE TO SIX.
   Scores, 5: Same as *a* above.
   Authors: Derek Whordley (handbook) and Rebecca J. Doster (handbook).

c) AGES SIX TO NINE.
Scores, 5: Same as *a* above.
Comments: Title on form is Humanics National After-School Assessment Form.
Authors: Jackson Rabbit (checklist), Sylvia B. Booth (checklist), and Marilyn L. Perling (checklist).
Cross References: For reviews by Arthur S. Ellen and David MacPhee of an earlier edition, see 11:170.

[956]

The Hundred Pictures Naming Test.

Purpose: "A confrontation naming test designed to evaluate rapid naming ability."
Population: Ages 4-6 to 11-11.
Publication Date: 1992.
Acronym: HPNT.
Scores, 3: Error, Accuracy, Time.
Administration: Individual.
Price Data, 2016: A$104.50 per complete kit including manual (84 pages), test book, and 25 response forms.
Time: (6) minutes.
Authors: John P. Fisher and Jennifer M. Glenister.
Publisher: Australian Council for Educational Research Ltd. [Australia].
Cross References: For reviews by Jeffrey A. Atlas and Stephen Jurs, see 12:183.

[957]

I Can Do Maths.

Purpose: Designed "to inform teachers and parents about children's development in numeracy in the early years of schooling."
Population: Children in the first 3 years of Australian and New Zealand school systems.
Publication Dates: 2000–2001.
Scores, 4: Number, Measurement, Space, Total.
Administration: Group.
Price Data, 2016: A$61.95 per specimen set including one Level A test booklet, one Level B test booklet, one Level A Ezi-guide, one Level B Ezi-guide, and teacher's guide (36 pages).
Time: (30–40) minutes.
Authors: Brian Doig and Marion de Lemos.
Publisher: Australian Council for Educational Research Ltd. [Australia].
   a) LEVEL A.
   Population: Children in the first 2 years of school.
   b) LEVEL B.
   Population: Children in the second and third years of school.
Cross References: For a review by Theresa Graham, see 16:109.

[958]

i-Ready K-12 Diagnostic and K-8 Instruction.

Purpose: Designed to identify student strengths and weaknesses in reading and math through computer adaptive testing and to provide differentiated online instruction.
Population: Grades K-12 (Diagnostic) and K-8 (Instruction).
Publication Dates: 2011-2015.
Scores, 15: Reading (Overall Scale Score, Placement Level, Phonological Awareness [K-1], Phonics [K-4], High-Frequency Words [K-3], Vocabulary [K-12], Comprehension—Literary Text [K-12], Comprehension—Informational Text [K-12]), Mathematics (Overall Scale Score, Placement Level, Number and Operations [K-8], Algebra and Algebraic Thinking [K-12], Measurement and Data [K-8], Geometry [K-8], Geometry and Measurement [9-12]).
Administration: Group.
Price Data, 2015: $30 per 1-year Diagnostic and Instruction subscription per student (reading or math); $6 per 1-year Diagnostic subscription per student (reading or math); 150 license minimum per subject for new customers; site license and multiyear pricing available.
Time: (35-60) minutes per diagnostic (reading or math).
Comments: Diagnostic test may be purchased with or without instruction component.
Author: Curriculum Associates, LLC.
Publisher: Curriculum Associates, LLC.
Cross References: Reviews are scheduled for *The Twentieth Mental Measurements Yearbook*. For reviews by Ric Brown and Jennifer N. Mahdavi of an earlier (2011) edition, see 19:86.

[959]

I-SPEAK Your Language™: A Survey of Personal Styles.

Purpose: Designed to teach employees how to identify and modify their communication style to work best with others in a variety of situations.
Population: Employees.
Publication Dates: 1972–1999.
Scores, 8: Favorable Conditions (Intuitor, Thinker, Feeler, Senser), Stress Conditions (Intuitor, Thinker, Feeler, Senser).
Administration: Group or individual.
Price Data: Available from publisher.
Foreign Language Editions: Available (except Self-Development Exercises manual) in Spanish, French, German, Portugese, Arabic, Norwegian, Bhasa Indonesian.
Time: (20) minutes.
Author: Drake Beam Morin, Inc.
Publisher: Lee Hecht Harrison. [No reply from publisher; status unknown].
Cross References: For reviews by Mary Anne Bunda and Kimberly A. Lawless, see 13:141.

IDEA Student Ratings of Instruction.

Purpose: Designed to provide student ratings of college instructors.
Population: College faculty.
Publication Dates: 1975–1998.
Scores: 5-part report compiled from ratings data: Overall Measures of Teaching Effectiveness, Student Ratings of Progress in Specific Objectives, Teaching Methods/Style, Course Description/Context, Statistical Detail.
Administration: Group.
Price Data: Available from publisher.
Time: (10–20) minutes.
Comments: Available for use in the classroom and in online classes.
Authors: Donald P. Hoyt, William H. Pallett, Amy B. Gross, Richard E. Owens, William E. Cashin (technical reports), Glenn R. Sixbury (technical reports, numbers 7–10), Yih-Fen Chen (technical report number 11).
Publisher: IDEA.
Cross References: For reviews by Raoul A. Arreola and Jennifer J. Fager, see 14:172; see also T4:1195 (1 reference); for a review by John C. Ory of an earlier edition, see 9:493 (2 references).

[961]

IDEAS: Interest Determination, Exploration and Assessment System™.

Purpose: "To be used as an introduction to career exploration for students and adults."
Population: Grades 7–12 and adults.
Publication Dates: 1977–1994.
Acronym: IDEAS™.
Scores, 16: Mechanical/Fixing, Protective Services, Nature/Outdoors, Mathematics, Science, Medical, Creative Arts, Writing, Community Service, Educating, Child Care, Public Speaking, Business, Sales, Office Practices, Food Service.
Administration: Group or individual.
Price Data, 2015: $86.85 per 50 test booklets (Youth or Adult); $26.65 per manual (1990, 80 pages); $27.95 per starter kit with self-scored reports; quantity discounts available for the reports.
Foreign Language Edition: Spanish version available.
Time: (40–45) minutes.
Comments: Self-administered, self-scored.
Author: Charles B. Johansson.
Publisher: Pearson.
Cross References: For a review by Robert J. Miller, see 11:172; for a review by M. O'Neal Weeks of an earlier edition, see 9:516.

Illinois Test of Psycholinguistic Abilities, Third Edition.

Purpose: Designed "to help children who have weakness in various linguistic processes including spoke or written language."
Population: Ages 5-0 to 12-11.
Publication Dates: 1961–2001.
Acronym: ITPA-3.
Scores, 12: Spoken Analogies, Spoken Vocabulary, Morphological Closure, Syntactic Sentences, Sound Deletion, Rhyming Sequences, Sentence Sequencing, Written Vocabulary, Sight Decoding, Sound Decoding, Sight Spelling, Sound Spelling.
Administration: Individual.
Price Data, 2015: $213 per kit including 25 profile/examiner record booklets, 25 student response booklets, manual (2001, 165 pages), and an CD; $62 per 25 profile/examiner record booklets; $56 per 25 student response booklets; $86 per examiner's manual; $25 per CD.
Time: (45–60) minutes.
Authors: Donald D. Hammill, Nancy Mather, and Rhia Roberts.
Publisher: PRO-ED.
Cross References: For a review by Roger L. Towne, see 15:122; see T5:1240 (51 references), T4:1201 (53 references), 9:496 (37 references), and T3:1126 (145 references); for reviews by James Lumsden and J. Lee Wiederholt of an earlier edition, and an excerpted review by R. P. Waugh, see 8:431 (269 references); see also T2:981 (113 references); for reviews by John B. Carroll and Clinton I. Chase, see 7:442 (239 references); see also 6:549 (22 references).

[963]

The Impact Message Inventory—Circumplex.

Purpose: Designed for assessing any two-person interaction "including that between patient and physician, student and teacher, husband and wife; between two siblings, family members, friends, acquaintances or strangers, and other dyads."
Population: Ages 16 and older.
Publication Dates: 1975-2006.
Acronym: IMI-C.
Scores, 10: 8 Octant Scores: Dominant, Hostile-Dominant, Hostile, Hostile-Submissive, Submissive, Friendly-Submissive, Friendly, Friendly Dominant; 2 Axis Scores: Control, Affiliation.
Administration: Individual or group.
Forms, 2: Male Target, Female Target.
Price Data: Available from publisher.
Foreign Language Editions: Available in Dutch and Japanese.
Time: [10-15] minutes.
Comments: Brief Version (28 items) may be administered by modifying question booklets.

Authors: Donald J. Kiesler and James A. Schmidt.
Publisher: Mind Garden, Inc.
Cross References: See T4:1205 (13 references); for reviews by Stephen L. Benton and Steven G. LoBello of the Impact Message Inventory, Research Edition, see 12:186 (4 references); for reviews by Fred H. Borgen and Stanley R. Strong of the Impact Message Inventory: Form II, see 9:500 (1 reference); see also T3:1130 (1 reference).

[964]

Implicitly.

Purpose: Designed to "measure the strength of attitude towards other groups through the strength of the hidden (or implicit) attitudes that people hold."
Population: Employed persons and job candidates.
Publication Date: 2009.
Scores, 2: Risk of Propensity for Prejudiced Behavior (Low, Mid-Range, Elevated, High), plus Robustness score.
Administration: Individual or group.
Forms, 9: Ethnic Origin (White/Black), Ethnic Origin (White/Asian), Ethnic Origin (White/SE Asian), Age, Gender, Gender Leadership, Disability, Sexual Orientation (Homosexual/Heterosexual Woman), Sexual Orientation (Homosexual/Heterosexual Man).
Price Data, 2016: £65 per manual (57 pages); £8 per test credit.
Time: [5] minutes per test.
Comments: Administered online; available as individual tests or as a suite.
Author: Pete Jones.
Publisher: Hogrefe Ltd [United Kingdom].

[965]

Incentives Management Index.

Purpose: Designed to make explicit sales managers' "assumptions, theories, and practices in the realm of sales motivation."
Population: Sales managers.
Publication Dates: 1972–1995.
Acronym: IMI.
Scores, 5: Basic Creative Comfort, Safety and Order, Belonging and Affiliation, Ego-Status, Actualization and Self-Expression.
Administration: Group.
Price Data, 2016: $9.95 per instrument (1995, 24 pages).
Time: Administration time not reported.
Comments: Self-administered; self-scored.
Authors: Jay Hall and Norman J. Seim.
Publisher: Teleometrics International, Inc.
Cross References: For reviews by Leslie H. Krieger and Patricia H. Wheeler, see 14:173.

[966]

Independent Living Scales.

Purpose: Designed to assess adults' competence in instrumental activities of daily living.
Population: Adults with cognitive impairments.
Publication Date: 1996.
Acronym: ILS.
Scores, 6: Memory/Orientation, Managing Money, Managing Home and Transportation, Health and Safety, Social Adjustment, Total.
Administration: Individual.
Price Data, 2015: $353.65 per complete kit including manual (119 pages), 25 record forms, stimulus booklet, and a pouch containing a facsimile of a driver's license, credit card, and key; $67.65 per 25 record forms.
Time: (45) minutes.
Comments: Four screening items are used to determine whether the examinee has a vision, speech, or hearing impairment; the stimulus booklet is designed for adults who can hear and those with a hearing impairment.
Author: Patricia Anderten Loeb.
Publisher: Pearson.
Cross References: For reviews by Libby G. Cohen and Jack A. Cummings, see 14:174.

[967]

Independent School Entrance Exam, 3rd Edition.

Purpose: Designed to "assess verbal reasoning, quantitative reasoning, reading comprehension, and mathematics achievement for use in admissions into independent schools."
Population: Grades 1-11, or candidates for Grades 2–12.
Publication Dates: 1989-2016.
Acronym: ISEE.
Scores, 6: Verbal Reasoning, Quantitative Reasoning, Reading Comprehension, Mathematics Achievement, Reading, Mathematics.
Administration: Group.
Levels, 6: Primary 2, Primary 3, Primary 4, Lower, Middle, Upper.
Price Data: Available from publisher.
Time: (53) minutes for Primary 2; (60) minutes for Primary 3 and 4; (140) minutes for Lower Level; (160) minutes for Middle and Upper Levels.
Comments: Test booklet title is ISEE.
Author: Educational Records Bureau.
Publisher: Educational Records Bureau.
Cross References: For reviews by Dale Carpenter and Thanos Patelis of an earlier version, see 19:87; for reviews by Mary Anne Bunda and Joyce R. McLarty of an earlier edition, see 11:174.

[968]

Index of Teaching Stress.

Purpose: Designed to "assess the effects of a specific student's behavior on a teacher's stress level and self-perception."
Population: Teachers from preschool to 12th grade.
Publication Dates: 2003–2004.
Acronym: ITS.
Scores, 12: Total Stress Score, Attention-Deficit/Hyperactivity Disorder, Student Characteristics (Emotional Lability/Low Adaptability, Anxiety/Withdrawal, Low Ability/Learning Disability, Aggressive/Conduct Disorder, Total); Teacher Characteristics (Sense of Competence/Need for Support, Loss of Satisfaction From Teaching, Disruption of the Teaching Process, Frustration Working With Parents, Total).
Administration: Group.
Price Data, 2015: $56 per ITS e-Manual; $46 per 25 hand scorable answer sheets; $46 per 25 reusable item booklets; $25 per 25 profile forms.
Time: (20–25) minutes.
Authors: Richard R. Abidin, Ross W. Greene, and Timothy R. Konold.
Publisher: Psychological Assessment Resources, Inc.
Cross References: For a review by Mildred Murray-Ward, see 17:88.

[969]

Individual Directions Inventory™.

Purpose: Designed to provide insight into a wide range of personal motivations; useful in individual and organizational development.
Population: Adults.
Publication Dates: 1988–2001.
Acronym: IDI.
Scores: 17 dimensions: Types of Emotional Satisfaction (Giving, Receiving, Belonging, Expressing, Gaining Stature, Entertaining, Creating, Interpreting, Excelling, Enduring, Structuring, Maneuvering, Winning, Controlling, Stability, Independence, Irreproachability).
Administration: Group.
Price Data: Available from publisher.
Foreign Language Editions: Available in Arabic, British English, Danish, Dutch, French, German, Italian, Swedish, and Spanish.
Time: (30) minutes.
Comments: Training or credential review required.
Authors: James T. Mahoney (test) and Robert I. Kabacoff (manual).
Publisher: Management Research Group.

[970]

Individual Employment Plan with 84-Item Employability Assessment.

Purpose: To help service organizations gather information about clients' employability status and assist clients in creating and completing a training and services plan.

Population: Participants in employment programs
Publication Date: 2002.
Acronym: IEP.
Scores, 7: Personal Issues and Considerations, Health and Physical Considerations, Work Orientation, Career and Life Planning Skills, Job Seeking Skills, Job Adaptation Skills, Education and Training.
Administration: Individual.
Price Data, 2016: $47.95 per 25 inventories including free administrator's guide (8 pages).
Time: (30) minutes.
Comments: Eight-panel foldout.
Authors: LaVerne L. Ludden and Bonnie R. Maitlen.
Publisher: JIST Publishing, Inc.

[971]

Individual Outlook Test.

Purpose: Designed to assess codependent orientation.
Population: Adults.
Publication Date: 1993.
Acronym: IOT.
Scores, 6: Codependent Orientation, Externally Derived Sense of Self Worth, Anxiety, Dysfunctional Family of Origin, Dependency within Relationships, Dysfunctional Relationships.
Administration: Group or individual.
Price Data: Available from publisher.
Time: (15–20) minutes.
Authors: Laurie A. Sim and Eugene E. Fox (test and manual); Michelle J. Worth and Donald Macnab (manual).
Publisher: Psychometrics Canada Ltd. [Canada].
Cross References: For reviews by Jeffrey A. Atlas and by Susan C. Whiston and Wendi L. Tai, see 16:111.

[972]

Individual Style Survey.

Purpose: "Intended to be an educational tool for self and interpersonal development."
Publication Dates: 1989–1990.
Administration: Group.
Price Data: Available from publisher.
Time: (60–90) minutes.
Comments: Self-administered, self-scored survey.
Author: Norman Amundson.
Publisher: Psychometrics Canada Ltd. [Canada] [No reply from publisher; status unknown].
  a) INDIVIDUAL STYLE SURVEY.
  Population: Adults.
  Publication Date: 1989.
  Acronym: ISS.
  Scores, 14: 8 categories of behavior (Forceful, Assertive, Outgoing, Spontaneous, Empathetic, Patient, Reserved, Analytical) yielding 4 styles (Dominant, Influencing, Harmonious, Cautious) that combine to form 2 summary scores (People/Task Orientation, Introspective/Interactive Stance).

b) MY PERSONAL STYLE.
Population: Ages 10–18.
Publication Date: 1990.
Acronym: MPS.
Scores, 14: 8 categories (Carefree, Outgoing, Straight Forward, Forceful, Precise, Reserved, Patient, Sensitive) yielding 4 styles (Influencing, Strong Willed, Cautious, Peaceful) that combine to form 2 summary scores (People/ Task Orientation, Expressive/Thoughtful Stance).
Comments: Simplified version of the Individual Style Survey for use with young people.
Cross References: For reviews by Jeffrey A. Atlas and William I. Sauser, see 13:144.

[973]
Industrial Reading Test.
Purpose: "Measures an individual's ability to comprehend written technical materials."
Population: Grade 9 and above vocational students and applicants or trainees in technical or vocational training programs.
Publication Dates: 1976-1989.
Acronym: IRT.
Scores: Total score only.
Administration: Group or individual.
Forms, 2: A, B.
Restricted Distribution: Distribution of Form A restricted to business and industry.
Price Data, 2015: $15 per online administration and report; manual available for download at test publisher's website.
Time: 40 minutes.
Author: The Psychological Corporation.
Publisher: Pearson.
Cross References: For a review by Darrell L. Sabers, see 9:504.

[974]
Industrial Test Battery.
Purpose: Intended to assess an individual's conceptual reasoning and spatial abilities.
Population: Individuals with less than 7 years of formal schooling.
Publication Date: 1986.
Acronym: ITB.
Scores: Total score only for each test.
Subtests, 3: Anomalous Concept Test (ACT), Anomalous Figure Test (AFT), Series Induction Test (SIT).
Administration: Group.
Price Data: Available from publisher.
Foreign Language Edition: Tests printed in both English and Afrikaans.
Time: 20(30) minutes for ACT; 25(35) minutes for AFT; 30(40) minutes for SIT.
Author: T. R. Taylor.
Publisher: Human Sciences Research Council [South Africa]. [Efforts to obtain updated information from the test publisher were unsuccessful. This test could not be found on the test publisher's website; its status is unknown.]

[975]
The Infanib.
Purpose: Designed to provide a systematic scorable method to assess the neurological status of infants, especially infants who are premature or have special conditions.
Population: Infants from 4 to 18 months corrected gestational age.
Publication Date: 1994.
Scores, 20: Hands Open, Hands Closed, Scarf Sign, Heel-To-Ear, Popliteal Angle, Leg Abduction, Dorsiflexion of the Foot, The Foot Grasp, Tonic Labyrinthine Supine, Asymmetric Tonic Neck Reflex, Pull-To-Sitting, Body Denotative, Body Rotative, All-Fours, Tonic Labyrinthine Prone, Sitting, Sideways Parachute, Backwards Parachute, Standing-Positive Support Reaction, Forward Parachute.
Administration: Individual.
Price Data, 2015: $131.20 per complete kit including 50 screening forms and manual (131 pages); $44 per 50 screening forms; $100.45 per manual.
Time: Untimed.
Comments: "Criterion-referenced" test with ratings determined by therapist.
Author: Patricia H. Ellison.
Publisher: Pearson.
Cross References: For reviews by Jill Ann Jenkins and John J. Vacca, see 14:175.

[976]
Infant Development Inventory.
Purpose: Designed "for screening or assessing the development of infants in the first eighteen months."
Population: Birth to 18 months.
Publication Dates: 1980–1995.
Acronym: IDI.
Scores, 5: Social, Self-Help, Gross Motor, Fine Motor, Language.
Administration: Individual.
Manual: Brief Instructions only.
Price Data, 2015: $45 per 75 parent questionnaires.
Foreign Language Edition: The questionnaire is available in Spanish.
Time: [5–10] minutes.
Comments: New version of the Minnesota Infant Development Inventory (T4:1642).
Author: Harold Ireton.
Publisher: Child Development Review - Behavior Science Systems, Inc.
Cross References: For reviews by Alan S. Kaufman and John J. Vacca, see 14:176; see also T5:1259 (2 references); for information on the earlier edition, see T4:1642 (1 reference); for a review by Bonnie W. Camp of the earlier edition, see 9:714.

[977]

The Infant-Toddler and Family Instrument.

Purpose: Designed as "a relatively short survey of family and child functioning" to "help in making a judgment about whether a child and family need further services and referrals."

Population: Families with infants and toddlers 6–36 months

Publication Date: 2001.

Acronym: ITFI.

Scores, 4: Caregiver Interview, Developmental Map, Checklist for Evaluating Concern, Plan for the Child and Family.

Administration: Individual.

Price Data, 2015: $55 per Infant-Toddler and Family Instrument manual and instrument set; $30 per manual; $30 per instrument (packages of 5).

Time: (150–165) minutes.

Authors: Nancy H. Apfel and Sally Provence.

Publisher: Paul H. Brookes Publishing Co., Inc.

[978]

Infant-Toddler Developmental Assessment.

Purpose: Constructed as "an integrated family-centered assessment process that addresses the health and development of children." It is designed to improve the early identification of children (birth to 3 years) who are developmentally at risk.

Population: Birth to 36 months.

Publication Date: 1995.

Acronym: IDA.

Scores: 8 developmental domains: Gross Motor, Fine Motor, Relationship to Inanimate Objects (Cognitive), Language Communication, Self-Help, Relationship to Persons, Emotions and Feeling States (Affects), Coping.

Administration: Individual.

Price Data, 2015: $740 per complete kit including administration manual (223 pages), foundations and study guide, readings, 25 parent report forms (English), 25 health record guides, and 25 record forms all in a canvas carrying case along with manipulatives in a separate carrying case; $100 per administration manual; $100 per foundations and study guide; $42 per 25 parent report forms (English or Spanish); $33 per 25 health record guides; $73 per 25 record forms; $70 per 25 Spanish record forms; $434 per manipulatives kit; $83 per readings (supplemental reading manual).

Time: Varies.

Comments: Ratings by multidisciplinary team; the test publisher advises that a second edition is scheduled for release in 2016.

Authors: Sally Provence, Joanna Erikson, Susan Vater, and Saro Palmeri.

Publisher: PRO-ED.

Cross References: For reviews by Melissa M. Groves and E. Jean Newman, see 13:146.

[979]

Infant/Toddler Environment Rating Scale-Revised Edition.

Purpose: Designed to assess programs for children from birth to 30 months of age in group care settings.

Population: Infant/toddler day care centers.

Publication Dates: 1990-2006.

Acronym: ITERS-R.

Scores, 8: Space and Furnishings, Personal Care Routines, Listening and Talking, Activities, Interaction, Program Structure, Parents and Staff, Total.

Administration: Individual.

Price Data, 2016: $23.95 per rating scale (2006, 79 pages) including administration and scoring instructions and score sheet and profile that may be photocopied.

Time: (180) minutes to observe and rate.

Authors: Thelma Harms, Debby Cryer, and Richard M. Clifford.

Publisher: Teachers College Press.

Cross References: For reviews by Karen Carey and Joseph C. Kush, see 17:89; see also T5:1264 (6 references); for reviews by Norman A. Constantine and Annette M. Iverson of an earlier edition, see 12:188.

[980]

Influence Strategies Exercise.

Purpose: Designed to identify and develop influence techniques.

Population: Managers and employees.

Publication Date: 1993.

Acronym: ISE.

Scores, 9: Empowerment, Interpersonal Awareness, Bargaining, Relationship Building, Organizational Awareness, Common Vision, Impact Management, Logical Persuasion, Coercion.

Administration: Individual or group.

Parts, 3: Participant Version, Profile and Interpretative Notes, and Feedback Version (optional).

Price Data, 2016: $152 per complete kit including 10 exercises and 10 profiles and interpretive notes (19 pages); $70 per 10 feedback version exercises.

Time: (20–25) minutes.

Comments: Self-administered questionnaire; administered via paper and pencil or online.

Author: Hay Group.

Publisher: Hay Group.

Cross References: For reviews by Collie W. Conoley and Paul M. Muchinsky, see 13:147.

[981]

The Influence Styles Inventory.

Purpose: Designed to identify and examine the styles and strategies used in "day-to-day problems managers face."

Population: Managers.

Publication Dates: 1997–1998.

Scores, 3: Aggressive, Assertive, Passive.
Administration: Group.
Price Data, 2016: $59.95; volume discounts available.
Time: (20) minutes.
Author: Marshall Sashkin.
Publisher: HRD Press, Inc.

[982]

Informeter: An International Technique for the Measurement of Political Information.

Purpose: Designed to measure political information.
Population: Adults.
Publication Date: 1972.
Scores, 5: Local, National, International, Miscellaneous, Total.
Administration: Group.
Manual: No manual.
Price Data, 2015: $2 per scale.
Time: [15] minutes.
Comments: Supplementary article available.
Author: Panos D. Bardis.
Publisher: Donna Bardis.

[983]

InQ: Assessing Your Thinking Profile.

Purpose: Designed to "measure individual preferences in the way people think…it is a wide-ranging tool for both individual and group development, and for planning for more effective contacts with others."
Population: Business and industry.
Publication Dates: 1997-2001.
Acronym: InQ.
Scores, 5: Synthesist, Idealist, Pragmatist, Analyst, Realist.
Administration: Group.
Price Data: Available from publisher for manual (2001, 73 pages) and questionnaires.
Foreign Language Edition: Spanish edition available.
Time: (20) minutes.
Comments: Self-administered version of the Inquiry Mode Questionnaire (984), which is the trainer-administered version.
Author: InQ Educational Materials, Inc.
Publisher: InQ Educational Materials, Inc.
Cross References: For reviews by Patricia A. Bachelor and Ayres D'Costa, see 18:59.

[984]

Inquiry Mode Questionnaire: A Measure of How You Think and Make Decisions.

Purpose: Developed to measure "individual preferences in the way people think."
Population: Business and industry.
Publication Dates: 1977–1989.

Acronym: INQ.
Scores, 5: Synthesist, Idealist, Pragmatist, Analyst, Realist.
Administration: Group or individual.
Price Data: Available from publisher.
Time: (20) minutes.
Comments: Manual title is INQ Styles of Thinking.
Authors: Allen F. Harrison and Robert M. Bramson.
Publisher: INQ Educational Materials Inc.
Cross References: For reviews by Philip Benson and Tamela Yelland, see 12:189.

[985]

Insight.

Purpose: Designed "to screen for cognitive exceptionalities in students."
Population: Students in Grades 2 through 7.
Publication Dates: 2011-2015.
Scores, 11: 7 subtest scores: Crystallized Knowledge, Visual Processing, Fluid Reasoning, Short-Term Memory, Long-Term Memory Retrieval, Auditory Processing, Processing Speed; 4 index scores: Ability, General Ability, Thinking, Memory/Processing.
Administration: Group.
Levels, 3: Level 1 (Grades 2-3), Level 2 (Grades 4-5), Level 3: (Grades 6-7).
Price Data: Available from publisher.
Time: (84-89) minutes.
Comments: Administered via DVD, requires computer, projector, and projection screen.
Authors: A. Lynne Beal (test, examiner's manual); David Galati and Zhimei Gu (validation report).
Publisher: Canadian Test Centre [Canada].
Cross References: Reviews are scheduled for The Twentieth Mental Measurements Yearbook.

[986]

INSIGHT Inventory [2015 Revision].

Purpose: Designed to help individuals identify their personality strengths, clarify how they may behave differently in various situations, and better understand themselves and others.
Population: Adults ages 21 and over, students ages 16–20.
Publication Dates: 1988–2015.
Scores: 4 traits: Influencing (Direct, Indirect), Responding (Reserved, Outgoing), Pacing (Urgent, Steady), Organizing (Unstructured, Precise).
Administration: Group or individual.
Forms, 3: Self, Team, Student.
Price Data, 2015: $17.95 per Self Form (hard copy, self-scorable); $19.95 per Team Form (hard copy, self-scorable); $14.95 per Student Form (hard copy, self-scorable); $19.95 per online digital Self report; $8.95 per online Observer report; $19.95 per online Team Map report; training guide, technical manual,

and other resources available as free downloads from test publisher's website.

Time: [10–15] minutes.

Comments: Self-ratings and optional observer ratings provide 360-degree perspective; self-scorable paper booklets and online digital reports available.

Author: Patrick Handley.

Publisher: Insight Institute, Inc.

Cross References: For reviews by Sanford J. Cohen and Elizabeth L. Jones of an earlier version, see 14:179; for a review by Susana Urbina, see 13:149.

[987]

Instructional Style Indicator [Revised].

Purpose: Designed to identify "instructional preferences and learning effectiveness with others."

Population: Adults.

Publication Dates: 1996-2006.

Acronym: ISI.

Scores, 4: Behavioral/Action/Independent, Cognitive/Analysis/Visual, Interpersonal/Harmony/Auditory, Affective/Expression/Experiential.

Administration: Individual or group.

Price Data, 2016: $25 per test booklet (2006, 16 pages); $15 per In-Depth Interpretation booklet (2006, 28 pages); $45 per online version; $40 per Trainer's Guidelines (1996, 28 pages).

Time: (30) minutes (90-180 minutes program options).

Comments: Self-administered and self-scored; can be used in conjunction with the Learning Style Indicator (1133).

Authors: Ken Keis, Everett T. Robinson, and Terry D. Anderson.

Publisher: Consulting Resource Group International, Inc.

[988]

Instrument for Disability Screening [Developmental Edition].

Purpose: To screen for learning disabilities.

Population: Primary grade children.

Publication Date: 1980.

Acronym: IDS.

Scores, 9: Hyperactive/Aggression, Visual, Speech/Auditory, Reading, Drawing/Writing, Inactivity, Concepts, Psychomotor Development, Total.

Administration: Individual.

Manual: No manual.

Price Data: Available from publisher.

Time: (5-15) minutes.

Author: James R. Beatty.

Publisher: James R. Beatty.

Cross References: See T3:1161 (3 references); for reviews by Norman A. Buktenica and Stephen I. Pfeiffer, see 9:515.

[989]

Instrument Timbre Preference Test.

Purpose: "To act as an objective aid to the teacher and the parent in helping a student choose an appropriate woodwind or brass instrument to learn to play in beginning instrumental music and band."

Population: Grades 4-12.

Publication Dates: 1984-1985.

Acronym: ITPT.

Scores, 7: Flute, Clarinet, Saxophone and French Horn, Oboe/English Horn/Bassoon, Trumpet and Cornet, Trombone/Baritone/French Horn, Tuba and Sousaphone.

Administration: Group.

Price Data, 2015: $59 per complete kit including 100 test sheets, scoring masks, compact disc, and manual (1984, 53 pages); $15 per 100 test sheets; scoring service available from publisher.

Time: (30) minutes.

Author: Edwin E. Gordon.

Publisher: GIA Publications, Inc.

Cross References: For reviews by Richard Colwell and Paul R. Lehman, see 10:150.

[990]

InstrumenTest (Form AIT-C).

Purpose: For selecting instrument technicians.

Population: Applicants and incumbents for jobs requiring technical knowledge and skills of instrumentation.

Publication Dates: 2001–2005.

Scores, 8: Mathematics & Basic AC/DC Theory, Analog & Digital Electronics and Power Supplies, Schematics & Electrical Print Reading, Process Control, Test Instruments, Mechanical and Hand & Power Tools, Computers & PLC, Total.

Administration: Group.

Price Data, 2015: $24 per consumable self-scoring test booklet; $26 per online test administration (minimum order of 20); $24.95 per manual (2005, 15 pages).

Time: (60-70) minutes.

Comments: Self-scoring instrument; available for online administration.

Author: Roland T. Ramsay.

Publisher: Ramsay Corporation.

Cross References: For a review by Suzanne Young, see 17:90.

[991]

Insurance Selection Inventory.

Purpose: Designed to "evaluate skills and attitudes that are generally appropriate for insurance claims examiner/adjuster, correspondence representative or customer service representative positions."

Population: Ages 18 and over.

Publication Date: 2002.

Acronym: ISI.

Scores, 11: Number Comparison, Verbal Reasoning, Arithmetic Computation, Error Recognition, Applied Arithmetic, Drive, Interpersonal Skills, Cognitive Skills, Self-Discipline, Writing Skills, Work Preference.
Administration: Group.
Forms, 2: Timed, Untimed.
Price Data: Available from publisher.
Time: (45) minutes.
Comments: Test can be scored via Touch Test, Internet, or Optical Scanning Software.
Author: General Dynamics Information Technology.
Publisher: General Dynamics Information Technology.

[992]

Integrated Writing Test.

Purpose: "Designed to evaluate major components of good writing in students' writing samples."
Population: Grades 2–12.
Publication Date: 1993.
Acronym: IWT.
Scores, 7: Productivity, Clarity, Vocabulary, Spelling, Punctuation, Legibility, Total Test Language Quotient.
Administration: Group.
Levels, 5: Grades 2/3, Grade 4, Grades 5/6, Grades 7 to 9, Grades 10 to 12.
Price Data, 2015: $131.95 per kit including manual (66 pages) and 35 booklets for each grade level; $22.95 per package of 35 booklets; $22.95 per manual.
Time: 15(20) minutes.
Comments: Academic extension of the Beery-Buktenica Developmental Test of Visual-Motor Integration (217); also based upon the National Assessment of Educational Progress Writing Test.
Authors: Keith E. Beery with assistance from the Integrated Teaching Team.
Publisher: Golden Educational Center.
Cross References: For reviews by C. Dale Carpenter and Richard M. Wolf, see 14:181.

[993]

Integrative Child Temperament Inventory.

Purpose: Designed to "assess aspects of a child's temperament."
Population: Children ages 2 through 8.
Publication Date: 2013.
Acronym: ICTI.
Scores, 5: Frustration, Behavioral Inhibition, Activity Level, Attention/Persistence, Sensory Sensitivity.
Administration: Individual.
Price Data, 2016: £130 per starter set including manual and 20 response booklets; £75 per manual (90 pages), £60 per 20 response booklets.
Foreign Language Edition: German version available.
Time: (5) minutes.
Authors: Marcel Zentner and Feng Wang.

Publisher: Hogrefe Ltd [United Kingdom].
Cross References: Reviews are scheduled for *The Twentieth Mental Measurements Yearbook.*

[994]

Intelligence Structure Test.

Purpose: Designed to measure intelligence.
Population: Ages 15 and older.
Publication Date: 2010.
Acronym: IST-R.
Scores, 13 to 19: Verbal Intelligence (Sentence Completion, Verbal Analogies, Verbal Similarities), Numerical Intelligence (Calculations, Number Series, Numerical Signs), Figural Intelligence (Figure Selection, Cubes, Matrices), Reasoning; Extended Module adds Verbal Knowledge, Numerical Knowledge, Figural Knowledge, Knowledge Total, Fluid Intelligence (gf), Crystallized Intelligence (gc).
Administration: Individual or group.
Forms, 2: A, B.
Price Data, 2016: £98 per manual (91 pages); £33 per online administration with standard report (subscription rates available).
Time: (90) minutes for Basic Module; (140) minutes for Extended Module.
Comments: Administered via paper and pencil, computer (offline), or Internet; translated and adapted from the German Intelligenz-Struktur-Test 2000R.
Authors: André Beauducel, Detlev Liepmann, Sierk Horn, and Burkhard Brocke.
Publisher: Hogrefe Ltd [United Kingdom].

[995]

Interest-A-Lyzer Family of Instruments.

Purpose: Series of instruments "designed to assess various aspects of student interests."
Population: Students in Grades K-12.
Publication Dates: 1982–1997.
Scores, 10: Performing Arts, Creative Writing and Journalism, Mathematics, Business Management, Athletics, History, Social Action, Fine Arts and Crafts, Science, Technology.
Administration: Group.
Forms, 3: Primary, Secondary, Art.
Price Data, 2015: $19.95 per manual (1997, 80 pages); $39.95 per 30 Interest-A-Lyzer Forms.
Time: Untimed.
Author: Joseph S. Renzulli.
Publisher: Prufrock Press Inc.

[996]

Intermediate Measures of Music Audiation.

Purpose: "To identify children with exceptionally high music aptitude … who can profit from the opportunity to participate in additional group study and special

private instruction ... to evaluate the comparative tonal and rhythm aptitudes of each child with exceptionally high music aptitude."
Population: Grades 1-4.
Publication Dates: 1978-1982.
Acronym: IMMA.
Scores, 3: Tonal, Rhythm, Composite.
Administration: Group.
Price Data, 2015: $100 per complete kit containing 1 tonal and rhythm compact disc, 100 tonal answer sheets, 100 rhythm answer sheets, 2 sets of scoring masks, 100 profile cards, 4 class record sheets, research monographs, and test manual (1982, 44 pages); $25 per CD; $10 per 100 tonal answer sheets; $10 per 100 rhythm answer sheets; $43 per 500 tonal answer sheets; $43 per 500 rhythm answer sheets; $10 per set of tonal or rhythm scoring masks; $15.50 per 100 profile cards; $2 per 10 class record sheets; $20 per manual. Also available on CD-ROM: $49.95 for single computer, volume discounts available.
Foreign Language Edition: Available in Portuguese.
Time: (20) minutes per Tonal test; (20) minutes per Rhythm test.
Comments: Advanced version of the Primary Measures of Music Audiation (1606); tests administered by CD.
Author: Edwin E. Gordon.
Publisher: GIA Publications, Inc.

[997]

Internalized Shame Scale.

Purpose: Developed to measure an individual's feelings of shame and the negative response patterns that result from internalized chance.
Population: Age 13 and older.
Publication Date: 2001.
Acronym: ISS.
Scores, 2: Shame, Self-Esteem.
Administration: Individual or group.
Price Data, 2015: $69 per technical manual; $38 per 25 patient handouts.
Time: 15 minutes.
Comments: Self-completed.
Author: David R. Cook.
Publisher: Multi-Health Systems, Inc.
Cross References: For reviews by Sean P. Reilley and by Susan M. Swearer and Kelly Brey Love, see 16:113.

[998]

International Personality Disorder Examination.

Purpose: To "diagnose personality disorders using DSM-IV or ICD-10 criteria."
Population: Adults.
Publication Dates: 1988–1999.
Acronym: IPDE.

Scores: 11 scores for DSM-IV version: Paranoid, Schizoid, Schizotypal, Antisocial, Borderline, Histrionic, Narcissistic, Avoidant, Dependent, Obsessive-Compulsive, Not Otherwise Specified; 10 scores for ICD-10 version: Paranoid, Schizoid, Dissocial, Emotionally Unstable/Impulsive Type, Emotionally Unstable/Borderline Type, Histrionic, Anankastic, Anxious (Avoidant), Dependent, Unspecified.
Administration: Individual.
Parts, 2: DSM-IV Module, ICD-10 Module.
Price Data, 2015: $234 per introductory kit including professional manual, 25 screening questionnaires (specify for DSM-IV or ICD-10), 15 scoring booklets (specify DSM-IV or ICD-10), and 50 answer sheets (specify DSM-IV or ICD-10).
Time: [60–120] minutes.
Comments: Complete administration includes a self-administered questionnaire as well as a clinical interview with client/subject.
Author: Armand W. Loranger.
Publisher: Psychological Assessment Resources, Inc.
Cross References: For reviews by Felito Aldarondo and Kwong-Liem Karl Kwan and by Gregory J. Boyle, see 15:126.

[999]

International Teaching Assistant Speaking Assessment.

Purpose: Designed to assess "a nonnative English speaker's competence and effectiveness in the type of communication commonly required of international teaching assistants (ITAs) in North America."
Population: Potential international teaching assistants.
Publication Date: 2013.
Acronym: ITASA.
Scores: Total score only.
Administration: Individual.
Price Data: Available from publisher.
Time: (14-15) minutes.
Comments: A live performance test, administered by two or three evaluators and scored in real time.
Author: Cambridge Michigan Language Assessments.
Publisher: Cambridge Michigan Language Assessments.
Cross References: Reviews are scheduled for *The Twentieth Mental Measurements Yearbook.*

[1000]

Interpersonal Adjective Scales.

Purpose: "A self-report instrument designed to measure two important dimensions of interpersonal transactions: Dominance and Nurturance."
Population: Ages 18 and up.
Publication Date: 1995.
Acronym: IAS.

Scores, 10: Assured-Dominant, Arrogant-Calculating, Cold-hearted, Aloof-Introverted, Unassured-Submissive, Unassuming-Ingenious, Warm-Agreeable, Gregarious-Extraverted, Dominance, Nurturance.
Administration: Individual or group.
Price Data, 2015: $152 per kit including manual (143 pages), 25 test booklets, 25 scoring booklets, and 25 glossaries.
Time: (15–20) minutes.
Comments: Separate norms are available for college students and adults; glossary is included to be used by subjects during testing.
Author: Jerry S. Wiggins.
Publisher: Psychological Assessment Resources, Inc.
Cross References: For reviews by Steven J. Lindner and Gerald R. Schneck, see 14:184; see also T5:1288 (2 references).

[1001]

Interpersonal Behavior Survey.

Purpose: "Developed to distinguish assertive behaviors from aggressive behaviors."
Population: Adolescents and adults.
Publication Date: 1980.
Acronym: IBS.
Scores, 21: Denial, Infrequency, Impression Management, General Aggressiveness—Rational, Hostile Stance, Expression of Anger, Disregard for Rights, Verbal Aggressiveness, Physical Aggressiveness, Passive Aggressiveness, General Assertiveness—Rational, Self-Confidence, Initiating Assertiveness, Defending Assertiveness, Frankness, Praise, Requesting Help, Refusing Demands, Conflict Avoidance, Dependency, Shyness, plus additional scores (General Aggressiveness—Empirical, General Assertiveness—Empirical) and 10 short-form scores.
Administration: Group.
Price Data, 2016: $178.50 per complete kit including 5 reusable administration booklets, 50 profile forms, 50 answer sheets, set of scoring keys, manual (78 pages), and 25 Autoscore forms for the short form; $33.50 per 10 administration booklets; $42 per set of scoring keys; $35.50 per 100 answer sheets; $35.50 per 100 profiles; $65.50 per manual; $48 per 25 short form AutoScore forms.
Time: 45 minutes.
Comments: Self-report inventory.
Authors: Paul A. Mauger, David R. Adkinson, Suzanne K. Zoss (test), Gregory Firestone (test), and J. David Hook (test).
Publisher: Western Psychological Services.
Cross References: See T5:1290 (4 references) and T4:1251 (5 references); for reviews by Stephen L. Franzoi and Robert R. Hutzell, see 9:518.

[1002]

Interpersonal Relations Questionnaire.

Purpose: "To identify specific problems in connection with interpersonal relations and identity formation."

Population: "White pupils" in Standards 5–7 in South African schools.
Publication Dates: 1981–1988.
Acronym: IRQ.
Scores, 13: Self-Confidence, Self-Esteem, Self-Control, Nervousness, Health, Family Influences, Personal Freedom, Sociability A, Sociability T, Sociability D, Moral Sense, Formal Relations, Lie Scale.
Administration: Group.
Price Data: Available from publisher.
Time: (105–120) minutes.
Comments: Supplementary manual in English and Afrikaans.
Authors: Marianne Joubert and Dawn Schlebusch (supplementary manual).
Publisher: Human Sciences Research Council [South Africa].

[1003]

Interpersonal Trust Surveys.

Purpose: Designed to measure an individual's "propensity to trust and to build trust with other people."
Population: Adults.
Publication Dates: 1996–1997.
Acronym: ITS; ITS-O; OTS.
Administration: Group.
Scores, 6: Shares Information, Reduces Control, Allows for Mutual Influences, Clarifies Expectations, Meets Others' Expectations, Total.
Forms, 3: Interpersonal Trust Survey, Interpersonal Trust Survey—Observer, Organizational Trust Survey.
Price Data: Available from publisher.
Time: Administration time not reported.
Comments: Scored for "My Behavior" and "Others' Behavior"; can be used as part of an educational workshop in interpersonal trust or as a tool for counseling; based on the "behavioral model of interpersonal trust"; scoring software available (must be run with Microsoft Excel).
Author: Guy L. DeFuria.
Publisher: Jossey-Bass, A Wiley Company.
Cross References: For a review by Mark E. Sibicky, see 14:185.

[1004]

Intuitive Mechanics (Weights & Pulleys).

Purpose: "To measure the ability to understand mechanical relationships, to visualize internal movement in a mechanical system."
Population: Industrial positions.
Publication Dates: 1956–1984.
Scores: Total score only.
Administration: Individual or group.
Price Data: Available from publisher.
Time: (3) minutes.
Authors: L. L. Thurstone and T. E. Jeffrey.
Publisher: General Dynamics Information Technology.

Cross References: For a review by William A. Owens, see 9:523.

[1005]
Inventory for Client and Agency Planning.
Purpose: Developed "to assess the status, adaptive functioning, and service needs of clients."
Population: Infant to adult.
Publication Date: 1986.
Acronym: ICAP.
Scores, 10: Maladaptive Behavior Indexes (Internalized, Asocial, Externalized, General), Adaptive Behavior (Motor Skills, Social and Communication Skills, Personal Living Skills, Community Living Skills, Total), Broad Independence Service Level Index.
Administration: Individual.
Price Data, 2015: $236.40 per complete program (specify English or Spanish) including examiner's manual (165 pages) and 25 response booklets; $91.20 per 25 response booklets (specify English or Spanish).
Foreign Language Edition: Also available in Spanish.
Time: (20–30) minutes.
Comments: Statistically related to the Scales of Independent Behavior (1794) and the Woodcock-Johnson Psycho-Educational Battery (2264); to be completed by "a respondent who has known a client for at least 3 months and who sees him or her on a day-to-day basis."
Authors: Robert H. Bruininks, Bradley K. Hill, Richard F. Weatherman, and Richard W. Woodcock.
Publisher: Houghton Mifflin Harcourt.
Cross References: See T5:1300 (11 references) and T4:1260 (3 references); for reviews by Ronn Johnson and Richard L. Wikoff, see 10:152.

[1006]
Inventory of Altered Self-Capacities.
Purpose: Designed to assess difficulties in relatedness, identity, and affect control.
Population: Age 18 and above.
Publication Dates: 1998–2000.
Acronym: IASC.
Scores, 11: Interpersonal Conflicts, Idealization—Disillusionment, Abandonment Concerns, Identity Impairment, Self-Awareness, Identity Diffusion, Susceptibility to Influence, Affect Dysregulation, Affect Skill Deficits, Affect Instability, Tension Reduction Activities.
Administration: Group or individual.
Price Data, 2015: $228 per kit including 25 reusable item booklets, 50 hand-scorable answer sheets, 50 profile forms, and professional manual (2000, 49 pages).
Time: [15–20] minutes.
Author: John Briere.
Publisher: Psychological Assessment Resources, Inc.
Cross References: For a review by Rosemary Flanagan, see 15:127.

[1007]
Inventory of Drinking Situations.
Purpose: "Designed to assess situations in which a client drank heavily over the past year."
Population: Ages 18 to 75.
Publication Date: 1987.
Acronym: IDS.
Scores, 8: Personal Status (Unpleasant Emotions, Physical Discomfort, Pleasant Emotions, Testing Personal Control, Urges and Temptations), Situations Involving Other People (Conflict with Othears, Social Pressure to Drink, Pleasant Times with Others).
Administration: Group.
Forms, 2: IDS-100, IDS-42 (Brief Version).
Price Data: Available from publisher.
Foreign Language Edition: Both forms available in French.
Time: (20–25) minutes.
Comments: IDS-42 (Brief Version) is for research use only.
Authors: Helen M. Annis, J. Martin Graham, and Christine S. Davis.
Publisher: Centre for Addiction and Mental Health [Canada].
Cross References: See T5:1304 (1 reference); for reviews by Merith Cosden and Kevin L. Moreland, see 13:155 (3 references); see also T4:1265 (2 references).

[1008]
Inventory of Drug Taking Situations.
Purpose: "Designed primarily as an assessment instrument, the IDTS generates an individualized profile detailing situations in which a client has used alcohol and/or other drugs over the past year."
Population: Drug or alcohol users.
Publication Date: 1997.
Acronym: IDTS.
Scores: Situation profiles in three areas: Negative Situations, Positive Situations, Temptation Situations; 8 subscales: Unpleasant Emotions, Physical Discomfort, Pleasant Emotions, Testing Personal Control, Urges/Temptations to Use, Conflict with Others, Social Pressure to Use, Pleasant Times with Others.
Administration: Group.
Price Data, 2016: C$34.95 per user's guide; C$16.45 per 30 questionnaires (specify alcohol or drug); C$39.95 per sample pack including user's guide, and 40 questionnaires (10 alcohol and 30 drug).
Time: (15) minutes per each drug class.
Comments: User's guide written in both English (150 pages) and French (72 pages); French version of IDTS has not been scientifically validated; "The IDTS is administered separately for each of the client's major substances of abuse, not once for the client's overall use of drugs."
Authors: Helen M. Annis, Nigel E. Turner, and Sherrilyn M. Sklar.

Publisher: Centre for Addiction and Mental Health [Canada].
Cross References: For reviews by Tony Cellucci and Glenn B. Gelman, see 14:186.

[1009]
Inventory of Interpersonal Problems.

Purpose: "A self-report instrument that identifies a person's most salient interpersonal problems."
Population: Adults ages 18 and over.
Publication Date: 2000.
Acronym: IIP.
Scores, 9: Domineering/Controlling, Vindictive/Self-Centered, Cold/Distant, Socially Inhibited, Nonassertive, Overly Accommodating, Self-Sacrificing, Intrusive/Needy, Total.
Administration: Individual or group.
Price Data, 2015: $50 for manual, including a review-only copy of the IIP form; $15 Individual Report; $15 Report About Me; $2.40 Transform Survey Hosting: 64 and 32; $2 Remote Online Survey License; $2 License to Reproduce.
Foreign Language Editions: Finnish, Malay, Polish, and Spanish.
Time: (10–15) minutes for Full Version; (5–10) minutes for Short Version.
Comments: Full version (IIP-64) contains 64 items; short version (IIP-32), intended for screening, contains 32 items.
Authors: Leonard M. Horowitz, Lynn E. Alden, Jerry S. Wiggins, and Aaron L. Pincus.
Publisher: Mind Garden, Inc.
Cross References: For reviews by Joshua M. Gold and Brian Hess, see 15:128.

[1010]
Inventory of Learning Processes—R.

Purpose: To measure learning styles of college and university students.
Population: College and university students.
Publication Dates: 1977–1992.
Acronym: ILP-R.
Scores, 14: Academic Self-Concept (Intrinsic Motivation, Self-Efficacy, Non-reiterative Processing, Self-Esteem, Total), Reflective Processing (Deep Processing, Elaborative Processing, Self-Expression, Total), Agentic Processing (Conventional, Serial Processing, Fact Retention, Total), Methodical Study.
Administration: Group.
Price Data: Available at no charge from test publisher.
Time: Administration time not reported.
Authors: Ronald R. Schmeck and Elke Geisler-Bernstein.
Publisher: Ronald R. Schmeck (the author).
Cross References: For reviews by Kusum Singh and Gerald L. Stone, see 13:156 (5 references).

[1011]
Inventory of Legal Knowledge.

Purpose: "Designed to assist the forensic examiner in assessing response styles of defendants undergoing evaluations of adjudicative competence" and to measure "a defendant's approach to inquiries about his or her legal knowledge."
Population: Ages 12 and over.
Publication Date: 2010.
Acronym: ILK.
Scores: Total score only.
Administration: Individual.
Price Data, 2015: $146 per complete kit including 10 reusable item booklets, 25 response sheets, and manual (56 pages); $43 per 10 reusable item booklets; $59 per 25 response sheets; $49 per manual.
Time: (15) minutes.
Comments: "The ILK is not a test of adjudicative competence….The ILK is solely a measure of response style; more specifically, it is a measure of a defendant's approach to inquiries about his or her legal knowledge."
Authors: Randy K. Otto and Jeffrey E. Musick; Christina B. Sherrod (manual only).
Publisher: Psychological Assessment Resources, Inc.
Cross References: For reviews by Rosemary Flanagan and Jeffrey A. Jenkins, see 19:88.

[1012]
Inventory of Offender Risk, Needs, and Strengths.

Purpose: Designed "to identify static, dynamic, and protective factors related to offender risk, treatment need, and management."
Population: Ages 18 and older.
Publication Date: 2006.
Acronym: IORNS.
Scores, 28: Overall Risk Index, Static Risk Index, Criminal Orientation, Psychopathy, Intra/Interpersonal Problems, Alcohol Drug Problems, Aggression, Negative Social Influence, Dynamic Need Index, Personal Resources, Environmental Resources, Protective Strength Index, Favorable Impression, Procriminal Attitudes, Irresponsibility, Manipulativeness, Impulsivity, Angry Detachment, Esteem Problems, Relational Problems, Hostility, Aggressive Behaviors, Negative Friends, Negative Family, Cognitive/Behavioral Regulation, Anger Regulation, Education/Training, Inconsistent Response Style.
Administration: Individual or group.
Price Data, 2015: $180 per introductory kit including professional manual (129 pages), 25 response forms, and 25 scoring summary/profile forms.
Time: (20) minutes.
Author: Holly A. Miller.
Publisher: Psychological Assessment Resources, Inc.

Cross References: For reviews by Sheri Bauman and by Geoffrey L. Thorpe and Lindsay R. Owings, see 18:61.

[1013]

Inventory of Perceptual Skills.

Purpose: "Assesses visual and auditory perceptual skills."
Population: Ages 5–10.
Publication Date: 1983.
Acronym: IPS.
Scores, 11: Visual Perception Skills (Visual Discrimination, Visual Memory, Object Recognition, Visual-Motor Coordination, Total), Auditory Perception Skills (Auditory Discrimination, Auditory Memory, Auditory Sequencing, Auditory Blending, Total), Total.
Administration: Individual.
Price Data, 2015: $45 per complete kit including manual (16 pages), stimulus cards, student workbook, and record booklets; $25 per 10 student record booklets; $15 per stimulus cards; $6 per student workbook.
Time: (15) minutes.
Author: Donald R. O'Dell.
Publisher: Stoelting Co.
Cross References: For reviews by Donna Spiker and by Logan Wright, Tim Eck, and Natasha Gwartney, see 12:193.

[1014]

Inventory of Suicide Orientation-30.

Purpose: "To assess and help identify adolescents who are at risk for suicide orientation by measuring the strength of their suicide orientation."
Population: Adolescents.
Publication Dates: 1988–1994.
Acronym: ISO-30.
Scores, 2: Final Raw Score, Final Critical Item Score.
Administration: Group.
Price Data, 2015: $44.50 per hand-scoring starter kit, including manual and three answer sheets; $68 per 25 answer sheets; $44 per manual.
Foreign Language Edition: Spanish answer sheets are available.
Time: [10] minutes.
Authors: John D. King and Brian Kowalchuk.
Publisher: Pearson.
Cross References: For a review by George Domino, see 13:158.

[1015]

InView.

Purpose: "A cognitive abilities test ... measur[ing] selected verbal, nonverbal, and quantitative reasoning abilities ... important for success in an educational program."
Population: Grades 2–12.
Publication Date: 2001.
Scores, 8: 5 subtest scores (Sequences, Analogies, Quantitative Reasoning, Verbal Reasoning—Words, Verbal Reasoning—Context); 3 composite scores (Verbal Composite, Nonverbal Composite, Total Test Scale Score).
Administration: Group.
Levels, 6: 1 (Grades 2–3), 2 (Grades 4–5), 3 (Grades 6–7), 4 (Grades 8–9), 5 (Grades 10–11), 6 (Grades 11–12).
Price Data, 2016: $155.25 per 25 InView-1 consumable test books; $121 per 25 test books levels 2-6; $53.20 per 50 InView 2–6 answer sheets; $38.35 per InView 2–6 stencil set (specify level); $32.90 per examiner's manual (specify level); $58.80 per Teacher's Guide to InView, Technical Bulletin 1, Technical Report (CD-ROM version), or Norms Book (all levels); $4.55 per Class Record Sheet for Handscoring.
Time: 95 minutes.
Comments: Replaces the Test of Cognitive Skills, Second Edition (TCS/2); conormed with the Primary Test of Cognitive Skills (PTCS; 1607) and with TerraNova, The Second Edition (see 2072); Level 1 students record answers in test books; Levels 2–6 students use separate answer sheets; variety of score report formats available; on-line feedback on test performance available, contact publisher for details.
Author: CTB/McGraw-Hill.
Publisher: DRC.
Cross References: For reviews by Russell N. Carney and Bruce Thompson, see 16:114; see T5:2677 for information on the Test of Cognitive Skills, Second Edition; for a review by Randy W. Kamphaus of an earlier edition, see 13:325 (8 references); see also T4:2745 (4 references); for reviews by Timothy Z. Keith and Robert J. Sternberg of an earlier edition, see 9:1248; for a review by Lynn H. Fox and an excerpted review by David M. Shoemaker of the Short Form Test of Academic Aptitude, see 8:202 (9 references).

[1016]

Inwald Personality Inventory [Revised].

Purpose: "To aid public safety/law enforcement and security agencies in selecting new officers."
Population: Public safety, security, and law enforcement applicants (post-conditional job offer only)
Publication Dates: 1980-1992.
Acronym: IPI.
Scores, 26: Guardedness, Externalized Behavior Measures (Actions [Alcohol, Drugs, Driving Violations, Job Difficulties, Trouble with the Law and Society, Absence Abuse], Attitudes [Substance Abuse, Antisocial Attitudes, Hyperactivity, Rigid Type, Type A]), Internalized Conflict Measures (Illness Concerns, Treatment Programs, Anxiety, Phobic Personality, Obsessive Personality, Depression, Loner, Unusual Experiences/Thoughts), Interpersonal Conflict Measures (Lack of Assertiveness, Interpersonal Difficulties, Undue Suspiciousness, Family Conflicts, Sexual Concerns, Spouse/Mate Conflicts).
Administration: Individual or group.
Price Data: Available from publisher.

Time: (30–45) minutes.

Comments: The test publisher has indicated there is a newer edition of this test; description will be updated when complete test materials are received.

Author: Robin Inwald.

Publisher: Institute for Personality and Ability Testing, Inc. (IPAT).

Cross References: See T5:1313 (2 references) and T4:1275 (1 reference); for reviews by Brian Bolton and Richard I. Lanyon, see 12:194; for reviews by Samuel Juni and Niels G. Waller of an earlier edition, see 11:183 (2 references); for reviews by Brian Bolton and Jon D. Swartz of an earlier edition, see 9:530.

[1017]
Inwald Survey 5–Revised.

Purpose: Designed to aid in pre-offer screening by identifying a job candidate's lack of integrity, anger patterns, job performance problems, and domestic difficulties.

Population: All occupations including public safety/security, clerical, managerial, sales, and entry-level.

Publication Date: 1992.

Acronym: IS5-R.

Scores, 17: Lack of Insight/Candor, Frustration/Anger Patterns, Distrust of Others, Work Adjustment Difficulties, Attitudes (Antisocial Behaviors), Behavior Patterns (Integrity Concerns), Lack of Competitive Motivation, Work Effort Concerns, Lack of Sensitivity, Leadership Avoidance, Introverted Personality Style, Domestic Difficulties, Lack of Service Orientation, Lack of Employee Reliability, Lack of Conscientiousness/Reliability, Lack of Work Ethic, Lack of Social Initiative.

Administration: Individual or group.

Price Data: Available from publisher.

Time: 15-20 minutes.

Comments: "Appropriate under ADA and can be administered pre-employment."

Authors: Robin Inwald.

Publisher: Institute for Personality and Ability Testing, Inc. (IPAT)

[1018]
Iowa Algebra Aptitude Test™, Fifth Edition.

Purpose: Designed to "help teachers and counselors make the most informed decisions possible regarding the initial placement of students in the secondary mathematics curriculum."

Population: Grades 7-8.

Publication Dates: 1931-2006.

Acronym: IAAT.

Scores, 5: Pre-Algebraic Number Skills and Concepts, Interpreting Mathematical Information, Representing Relationships, Using Symbols, Total.

Administration: Group or individual.

Forms, 2: A, B.

Price Data, 2015: $49 per manual Forms A and B; $123.30 per 25 test booklets (Form A or B); $11 per Directions for Administration booklet (Forms A and B); $55.35 per 25 self-scoring answer sheets (Forms A and B); $154.95 per 100 scannable answer sheets (Forms A and B); $52.20 per 25 Report to Families booklets (Forms A and B); $1,975.55 per Licensed Norms (Forms A and B).

Time: 40 minutes for the battery (i.e., 10 minutes for each of four subtests) plus approximately 10 minutes for distribution and collection of materials.

Comments: "Designed to be used in conjunction with other indicators of student progress, such as grades and teacher evaluations."

Authors: Harold L. Schoen and Timothy N. Ansley.

Publisher: Houghton Mifflin Harcourt.

Cross References: For reviews by David Morse and Bruce G. Rogers, see 17:92; for reviews by John W. Fleenor and Judith A. Monsaas of an earlier edition, see 12:195; see also T2:681 (7 references); for reviews by W. L. Bashaw and Cyril J. Hoyt, and an excerpted review by Russell A. Chadbourn of an earlier edition, see 7:505 (8 references); for reviews by Harold Gulliksen and Emma Spaney of an earlier edition, see 4:393; for a review by David Segel, see 3:327 (2 references); for reviews by Richard M. Drake and M. W. Richardson, see 2:144 (1 reference).

[1019]
Iowa Assessments™, Form E.

Purpose: Designed to measure achievement based on national core standards in several key areas including vocabulary, word analysis, listening, language, mathematics, social studies, and science.

Population: Students in Grades K-12.

Publication Dates: 1955-2012.

Administration: Group.

Levels, 13: 5-18.

Price Data: Available from publisher.

Foreign Language Edition: Spanish version available.

Comments: Testing program replaces the Iowa Tests of Basic Skills (Grades K-8) and the Iowa Tests of Educational Development (Grades 9-12); provides scores for both norm-referenced and criterion-referenced interpretations.

Author: Iowa Testing Programs.

Publisher: Houghton Mifflin Harcourt.

a) LEVELS 5/6.

Population: Grades K-1.

Scores, 12: 6 test scores: Reading, Language, Vocabulary, Word Analysis, Listening, Mathematics; 6 total scores: English Language Arts Total, Extended English Language Arts Total, Core Composite with English Language Arts Total and Mathematics, Core Composite with Extended English Language Arts Total and Mathematics, Reading Total, Language Total.

Time: Untimed; approximate working time 160 minutes.

b) LEVEL 7.
Population: Grades 1-2.
Scores, 22: 9 test scores: Same as *a* above plus Computation, Science, Social Studies; 13 total scores: English Language Arts Total, Extended English Language Arts Total, Mathematics Total, Core Composite with English Language Arts Total/Mathematics and Computation, Core Composite with Extended English Language Arts Total/Mathematics and Computation, Core Composite with English Language Arts Total and Mathematics (no Computation), Core Composite with Extended English Language Arts Total and Mathematics (no Computation), Complete Composite with English Language Arts Total/Mathematics and Computation, Complete Composite with Extended English Language Arts Total/Mathematics and Computation, Complete Composite with English Language Arts Total and Mathematics (no Computation), Complete Composite with Extended English Language Arts Total and Mathematics (no Computation), Reading Total, Language Total.
Time: Untimed; approximate working time 200 minutes for Core Battery, 250 minutes for Complete Battery.
c) LEVEL 8.
Population: Grades 2-3.
Scores, 22: Same as *b* above.
Time: Untimed; approximate working time 200 minutes for Core Battery, 250 minutes for Complete Battery.
d) LEVEL 9.
Population: Grade 3.
Scores, 28: 14 test scores: Same as *a* above plus Mathematics, Written Expression, Computation, Science, Social Studies, Spelling, Capitalization, Punctuation; 14 total scores: Same as *b* above plus Conventions of Writing.
Time: Untimed; approximate working time 270 minutes for Core Battery, 340 minutes for Complete Battery.
e) LEVELS 10-14.
Population: Grades 4-9.
Scores, 28: Same as *d* above.
Time: Untimed; approximate working time 225 minutes for Core Battery, 295 minutes for Complete Battery.
f) LEVELS 15-17/18.
Population: Grades 9-12.
Scores, 15: 7 test scores: Reading, Written Expression, Vocabulary, Mathematics, Computation, Science, Social Studies; 8 total scores: English Language Arts Total, Mathematics Total, Core Composite with Mathematics and Computation, Core Composite with Mathematics (no Computation), Complete Composite with Mathematics and Computation, Complete Composite with Mathematics (no Computation), Reading Total, Language Total.
Time: Untimed; approximate working time 155 minutes for Core Battery, 235 minutes for Complete Battery.
Cross References: Reviews are scheduled for *The Twentieth Mental Measurements Yearbook*. For reviews by George Engelhard, Jr. and Suzanne Lane of the Iowa Tests of Basic Skills, Forms A and B, see 17:93; see also T5:1318 (24 references); for reviews by Susan M. Brookhart and Lawrence H. Cross of Forms K, L and M, see 13:159 (110 references); see also T4:1280 (33) references; for reviews by Suzanne Lane and Nambury S. Raju of Form J, see 11:184 (24 references); for reviews by Robert L. Linn and Victor L. Willson of Forms G

and H, see 10:155 (45 references); for reviews by Peter W. Airasian and Anthony J. Nitko of Forms 7 and 8, see 9:533 (29 references); see also T3:1192 (97 references); for reviews by Larry A. Harris and Fred Pyrczak of Forms 5 and 6, see 8:19 (58 references); see T2:19 (87 references) and 6:13 (17 references); for reviews by Virgil E. Herrick, G.A.V. Morgan, and H. H. Remmers, and an excerpted review by Laurence Siegel of Forms 1-2, see 5:16. For reviews of the modern mathematics supplement, see 7:481 (2 reviews). For reviews by Alan C. Bugbee, Jr. and William D. Schafer of the Iowa Tests of Educational Development, Forms A and B, see 16:116; for reviews by William A. Mehrens and Michael J. Subkoviak of Forms K, L, and M, see 13:160 (7 references); see also T4:1281 (4 references); for a review by S. E. Phillips of the eighth edition, see 10:156 (3 references); for reviews by Edward Kifer and James L. Wardrop of the seventh edition, see 9:534 (5 references); see also T3:1193 (14 references) for reviews by C. Mauritz Lindvall and John E. Milholland of the SRA Assessment Survey, see 8:20 (15 references); see T2:20 (85 references); for reviews by Ellis Batton Page and Alexander G. Wesman of earlier forms, see 6:14 (23 references); for reviews by J. Murray Lee and Stephen Wiseman, see 5:17 (9 references); for a review by Eric Gardner, see 4:17 (3 references); for reviews by Henry Chauncey, Gustav J. Froelich, and Lavone A. Hanna, see 3:12.

[1020]

Iowa Gambling Task.

Purpose: Designed to detect impaired decision making that is mediated by the prefrontal cortex.
Population: Ages 18 and over.
Publication Dates: 1992-2007.
Acronym: IGT.
Scores, 4: Block Net, Total Money, Deck Selection Frequency, Net Total.
Administration: Individual.
Price Data, 2015: $560 per introductory kit including professional manual (2007, 71 pages), administration card, and software (CD-ROM) with on-screen help and quick start guide; $54 per professional manual.
Time: [15-20] minutes to administer and score.
Comments: Administered and scored via computer.
Author: Antoine Bechara.
Publisher: Psychological Assessment Resources, Inc.
Cross References: For reviews by Anita M. Hubley and Matthew E. Lambert, see 18:62.

[1021]

Iowa Parent Behavior Inventory.

Purpose: Designed "to measure parental behavior in relation to a child."
Population: Parents.
Publication Dates: 1976–1979.
Acronym: IPBI.

Administration: Group.

Price Data: Available at no charge from test author.

Time: Administration time not reported.

Authors: Sedahlia Jasper Crase, Samuel G. Clark, and Damaris Pease.

Publisher: Iowa State University Research Foundation, Inc.

   a) MOTHER FORM.

   Publication Date: 1977.

   Scores, 6: Parental Involvement, Limit Setting, Responsiveness, Reasoning Guidance, Free Expression, Intimacy.

   b) FATHER FORM.

   Publication Date: 1977.

   Scores, 5: Parental Involvement, Limit Setting, Responsiveness, Reasoning Guidance, Intimacy.

Cross References: See T5:1316 (2 references) and T4:1278 (3 references); for reviews by Verna Hart and Richard L. Wikoff, see 9:531 (1 reference).

[1022]

Iowa Social Competency Scales.

Purpose: To provide an "easily administered and objectively scored individual rating instrument for parents relative to the social behavior (competencies) of normal children."

Population: Ages 3–12.

Publication Dates: 1976–1982.

Acronym: ISCS.

Administration: Group.

Price Data: Available at no charge from test author.

Time: Administration time not reported.

Comments: Ratings by parents.

Authors: Damaris Pease, Samuel G. Clark, and Sedahlia Jasper Crase.

Publisher: Iowa State University Research Foundation, Inc.

   a) PRESCHOOL.

   Population: Ages 3–6.

     1) *Mother.*

   Scores, 5: Social Activator, Hypersensitivity, Reassurance, Uncooperativeness, Cooperativeness.

     2) *Father.*

   Scores, 5: Social Activator, Hypersensitivity, Reassurance, Social Ineptness, Attentiveness.

     3) *Combined.*

   Scores, 3: Social Activator, Hypersensitivity, Reassurance.

   b) SCHOOL-AGE.

   Population: Ages 6–12.

   Comments: Adaptation of Devereux Elementary School Behavior Rating Scale.

     1) *Mother.*

   Scores, 6: Task Oriented, Disruptive, Leader, Physically Active, Affectionate Toward Parent, Apprehensive.

     2) *Father.*

   Scores, 5: Capable, Defiant, Leader, Active with Peers, Affectionate Toward Parent.

Cross References: For a review by Gloria E. Miller, see 10:154; see also 9:532 (2 references).

[1023]

Iowa Tests of Music Literacy, Revised.

Purpose: Assesses "a student's comparative strengths and weaknesses in six dimensions of tonal and rhythm audiation and notational audiation" and compares these scores to the student's "music aptitude."

Population: Grades 4–12.

Publication Dates: 1970–1991.

Scores, 9: Tonal Concepts (Audiation/Listening, Audiation/Reading, Audiation/Writing, Total), Rhythm Concepts (Audiation/Listening, Audiation/Reading, Audiation/Writing, Total), Total.

Administration: Group.

Price Data, 2015: $350 per complete kit for all six levels including manual, six CDs, 50 answer sheets, six record folders, and scoring masks; $90 per complete kit for Level One only including manual, one CD, scoring masks, 50 answer sheets, and 6 record folders; $8 per 50 tonal answer sheets; $8 per 50 rhythm answer sheets; $15 per 50 cumulative record folders; $3 per 6 class record sheets; $15 per manual; $25 per CD (specify level).

Time: 36(45) minutes for Tonal Concepts; 36(45) minutes for Rhythm Concepts.

Author: Edwin E. Gordon.

Publisher: GIA Publications, Inc.

Cross References: For a review by Rudolf E. Radocy, see 13:161; for a review by Paul R. Lehman of an earlier edition, see 8:97 (16 references); see also T2:199 (5 references) and 7:245 (2 references).

[1024]

IPI Job-Tests Program.

Purpose: "Screening, selection, and promotion of job applicants and employees."

Population: Job applicants and employees in industry.

Publication Dates: 1948–1997.

Administration: Group or individual.

Foreign Language Editions: French and Spanish editions available.

Comments: Program is composed of 19 tests "used in different combinations to form specific batteries for each of the job-test fields"; job fields include Sales Personnel, Medical Office Assistant, Clerical Staff, Dental Technician, and Production/Mechanical.

Author: Industrial Psychology International Ltd.

Publisher: Industrial Psychology International Ltd.

   a) OFFICE TERMS.

   Price Data, 2015: $32 per 20 test booklets; $37 per introductory kit including 20 test booklets, technical manual, and scoring key.

   Time: (6) minutes.

   b) NUMBERS.

   Price Data: Same as *a* above.

   Time: (6) minutes.

   c) PERCEPTION.

   Price Data: Same as *a* above.

   Time: Same as *a* above.

d) JUDGMENT.
Price Data: Same as *a* above.
Time: Same as *a* above.
e) FLUENCY.
Price Data: Same as *a* above.
Time: Same as *a* above.
f) PARTS.
Price Data: Same as *a* above.
Time: Same as *a* above.
g) MEMORY.
Price Data: $46 per 20 test booklets; $51 per kit including 20 test booklets, technical manual, and scoring key.
Time: Same as *a* above.
h) BLOCKS.
Price Data: Same as *a* above.
Time: Same as *a* above.
i) DEXTERITY.
Price Data: Same as *a* above.
Time: (3) minutes.
j) DIMENSION.
Price Data: Same as *a* above.
Time: Same as *a* above.
k) PRECISION.
Price Data: Same as *a* above.
Time: Same as *a* above.
l) TOOLS.
Price Data: Same as *a* above.
Time: Same as *a* above.
m) MOTOR.
Price Data: $32 per 20 record booklets; $37 per kit including 20 record booklets and technical manual; $160 per motor board.
Time: Same as *a* above.
n) SALES TERMS.
Price Data: Same as *a* above.
Time: (5) minutes.
o) APPLIED MATH.
Price Data: Same as *a* above.
Time: (12) minutes.
p) READING COMPREHENSION.
Price Data: $22 per 10 reusable test booklets; $34 per 20 answer/score sheets; $42 per kit including 5 reusable test booklets, 20 answer/score sheets, and technical manual.
Time: Same as *o* above.
q) CPF SECOND EDITION.
Acronym: CPF.
Price Data: Same as *a* above.
Time: (5-10) minutes.
Author: Samuel E. Krug.
r) NPF SECOND EDITION.
Acronym: NPF.
Price Data: Same as *a* above.
Time: Same as *q* above.
Author: Same as *q* above.
Cross References: For reviews by Laura L. B. Barnes and Mary A. Lewis, see 11:185; see also T2:1078 (12 references); for reviews by William H. Helme and Stanley I. Rubin, see 6:774; for a review by Harold P. Bechtoldt of the Factored Aptitude Series, see 5:602; for a review by D. Welty Lefever and an excerpted review by Laurance F. Shaffer of an earlier edition of this series, see 4:712 (1 reference).

[1025]

IPT English Early Literacy Test, Third Edition.

Purpose: Designed to "assess the skill development of English learners in kindergarten and first grade on the continuum of literacy development."

Population: Students in Kindergarten and Grade 1 who speak English as a second language.

Publication Dates: 2000-2011.

Administration: Small groups of no more than five students.

Price Data, 2016: $340 per test set including 50 Reading test booklets, 50 Writing test booklets, and examiner's manual (2011, 116 pages); $151 per 50 Reading test booklets; $114 per 50 Writing test booklets; $103 per examiner's manual; $80 per technical manual (2011, 76 pages).

Foreign Language Edition: Spanish version available for "students who speak Spanish as a first language, heritage language, or second language."

Comments: Assesses students' developmental stages of reading and writing; designed for "initial identification, program placement, progress monitoring, and redesignation in school."

Author: Nathalie Longree-Guevara.

Publisher: Ballard & Tighe, Publishers.

a) READING.
Scores, 9: Visual Recognition, Letter Recognition, Phonemic Awareness-Initial Sounds, Phonics-Initial Blends and Digraphs (Grade 1 only), Reading Vocabulary, Reading for Life Skills, Reading for Understanding Sentences, Reading for Understanding Stories (Grade 1 only), Total Reading.
Time: (15-30) minutes.
b) WRITING.
Scores, 5: Copy Letters, Write a Word and Copy the Sentence, Write a Story, Spelling (Grade 1 only), Total Writing.
Time: (5-30) minutes.

Cross References: For reviews by Merith Cosden and Patti L. Harrison of an earlier edition, see 17:94.

[1026]

IPT English Reading & Writing Tests, Third Edition.

Purpose: Designed to "assess students' reading and writing skills in English in order to identify English language learners who need language support ... for purposes of placement, progress monitoring, and redesignation."

Population: Students in Grades 2-12 whose native language is not English.

Publication Dates: 1992-2015.

Scores, 10: Reading (Vocabulary, Vocabulary in Context, Reading for Understanding, Reading for Life Skills, Language Usage, Total), Writing (Conventions, Write a Story, Write Your Own Story, Total).

Administration: Group.

Levels, 3: IPT 1, IPT 2, IPT 3.

Foreign Language Edition: Spanish version available for "students who speak Spanish as a first language, heritage language, or second language."

Time: (45-75) minutes for Reading; (25-60) minutes for Writing.

Comments: Administered via paper and pencil or online.

Authors: Beverly Amori, Enrique F. Dalton, and Phyllis L. Tighe.

Publisher: Ballard & Tighe, Publishers.

a) IPT 1.

Population: Students in Grades 2-3.

Forms, 2: 1C, 1D.

Price Data: $312 per test set including 50 Reading test booklets, 50 Writing test booklets and examiner's manual (2015, 130 pages); $72 per technical manual (2015, 114 pages).

b) IPT 2.

Population: Students in Grades 4-6.

Forms, 2: 2C, 2D.

Price Data: $396 per test set including 50 Reading test booklets, 50 Reading Test answer sheets, 50 Writing test booklets, Reading test scoring template, and examiner's manual (2015, 142 pages); $72 per technical manual (2015, 128 pages).

c) IPT 3.

Population: Students in Grades 7-12.

Forms, 2: 3C, 3D.

Price Data: $396 per test set including 50 Reading test booklets, 50 Reading Test answer sheets, 50 Writing test booklets, Reading test scoring template, and examiner's manual (2015, 141 pages); $72 per technical manual (2015, 113 pages).

Cross References: For reviews by James Dean Brown and Alan Garfinkel of an earlier edition titled IDEA Reading and Writing Proficiency Test, see 13:142.

[1027]

IPT Oral English Test.

Purpose: Designed to "evaluate students' oral proficiency in English" for program placement, progress monitoring, and/or redesignation after completion of a language development program.

Population: Students in pre-kindergarten through Grade 12 who speak English as a second language.

Publication Dates: 1983-2010.

Scores, 8: Vocabulary, grammar, Comprehension, Verbal Expression, Listening Skills, Speaking Skills, Basic Interpersonal Communication Skills, Cognitive Academic Language Proficiency.

Administration: Individual.

Foreign Language Edition: Spanish version available for "students who speak Spanish as a first language, heritage language, or second language."

Comments: Administered via paper and pencil or online.

Publisher: Ballard & Tighe, Publishers.

a) PRE-IPT ORAL ENGLISH, FOURTH EDITION.

Population: Ages 3-5.

Price Data, 2016: $323 per paper-based test set including 50 test booklets, story board with story pieces and box, examiner's manual (2010, 37 pages), 50 test level summaries in English, and 50 test level summaries in Spanish; $110 per 50 online test credits (story board [$67] and story pieces [$63] required for online administration; examiner's manuals provided free online); $58 per technical manual.

Time: (15-20) minutes.

Author: Robin Stevens.

b) IPT I.

Population: Students in kindergarten to Grade 6.

Forms, 2: G, H.

Price Data: $295 per paper-based test set including 50 test booklets, 1 book of test pictures, examiner's manual (2010, 50 pages), 50 test level summaries in English, and 50 test level summaries in Spanish; $110 per 50 online test credits (picture book [$127 for Form G or Form H] required for online administration; examiner's manuals provided free online); $58 per technical manual.

Time: (14) minutes.

Authors: Corie De Anda and Bill Eilfort.

c) IPT II.

Population: Students in Grades 6-12.

Scores, 9: Same as above plus Morphology.

Forms, 2: E, F.

Price Data: $295 per paper-based test set including 50 test booklets, 1 book of test pictures, examiner's manual (2010, 48 pages), 50 test level summaries in English, and 50 test level summaries in Spanish; $110 per 50 online test credits (picture book [$127 for Form E or Form F] required for online administration; examiner's manuals provided free online); $58 per technical manual.

Time: (14) minutes.

Authors: Bill Eilfort and Corie De Anda.

Cross References: For reviews by Emilia C. Lopez and Salvador Hector Ochoa of an earlier edition titled IDEA Oral Language Proficiency Test, see 14:171; see also T5:1234 (5 references).

[1028]

IRAOS: Interview for the Retrospective Assessment of the Onset and Course of Schizophrenia and Other Psychoses.

Purpose: Designed to provide "a retrospective assessment of symptoms, disability and social development in schizophrenic and affective illness."

Population: Adults who have schizophrenia.

Publication Dates: 1987–2003.

Acronym: IRAOS.

Scores: Item scores only.

Subtest, 5: General Information, Socio-Demographic and Case History Information, Episodes and Intervals of Mental Disorder, Indicators of Psychiatric Illness, Evaluation of Success of Information.

Administration: Individual.

Price Data, 2011: $334 per kit including manual (2003, 60 pages), 5 interview booklets, 50 score sheets,

50 IND forms, 50 TREAT forms, 50 EPIS forms, 50 time schedules, and 50 calendars of episodes.
Time: (90–120) minutes.
Authors: Heinz Häfner, Walter Löffler, Kurt Maurer, Anita Riecher-Rössler, and Astrid Stein.
Publisher: Hogrefe Ltd [United Kingdom].
Cross References: For reviews by Allen K. Hess and Janet V. Smith, see 16:117.

[1029]

Irenometer.
Purpose: Measures attitudes toward peace.
Population: Adults.
Publication Dates: 1984–1985.
Scores: Total score only.
Administration: Group.
Manual: No manual.
Price Data, 2015: $2 per scale
Time: [12] minutes.
Comments: Supplementary article available.
Author: Panos D. Bardis.
Publisher: Donna Bardis.

[1030]

Irritation Index for the Assessment of Work-Related Strain [UK Version].
Purpose: Designed to assess "subjectively perceived emotional and cognitive strain in occupational contexts."
Population: Adults.
Publication Date: 2009.
Scores, 3: Emotional Irritation, Cognitive Irritation, Global Irritation Index.
Administration: Individual or group.
Price Data, 2016: £40 per manual (2009, 47 pages); £18 per 25 item/response sheets; £17 per 25 scoring sheets; £20 per manual supplement.
Foreign Language Editions: Originally published in German; manual supplements available in Spanish, Belgian, Dutch, and Swedish.
Time: [10] minutes.
Authors: Gisela Mohr, Thomas Rigotti, and Andreas Müller.
Publisher: Hogrefe Ltd [United Kingdom].

[1031]

Ishihara's Tests for Colour-Deficiency.
Purpose: To identify congenital color vision deficiency.
Population: Ages 4 and over.
Publication Dates: 1917–2015.
Scores: Total score only.
Administration: Individual.
Price Data, 2015: $335 per 38 plate (Complete Edition) book; $311 per 24 plate (Abridged Edition) book; $223 per 14 plate (Concise Edition) book; $200 per 10 plate (Unlettered Persons and Children) book.

Time: Administration time not reported.
Author: Shinobu Ishihara.
Publisher: Graham-Field Health Products, Inc. (North American distributor).
Cross References: See T5:2658 (2 references), T4:2729 (3 references), T3:2419 (1 reference), T2:1932 (29 references), 7:882 (13 references), and 6:962 (58 references).

[1032]

IT Aptitude Personality & Attitude Profile.
Purpose: "Designed to assess certain aspects of a person's work habits, work attitudes, and analytical skills that pertain to success in a career in the IT industry."
Population: Under age 17 through adult.
Publication Date: 2011.
Acronym: ITAPAP.
Scores, 21: Meticulousness, Concentration, Prioritization, Attitude Towards Team Work, Team vs. Individual Preference, Adaptability, Pattern Recognition, Classification, Analogies, Logic, Creative Problem-Solving, Patience, Time Management, Reaction to Stress, Attitude Towards Dishonesty, Impression Management, Acquiescence, Work Habits, Work Attitudes, Analytical Skills, Overall Score.
Administration: Individual.
Price Data: Available from publisher.
Time: (30) minutes.
Comments: Self-administered online assessment. The test publisher provides clients with information about the methods and theoretical basis used in the development of the test as well as benchmarks for relevant industries and racial/ethnic group comparison data.
Author: PsychTests AIM, Inc.
Publisher: PsychTests AIM, Inc. [Canada].
Cross References: For reviews by Laura L. B. Barnes and Tracy Kantrowitz, see 19:89.

[1033]

ITSEA/BITSEA: Infant-Toddler and Brief Infant-Toddler Social and Emotional Assessment.
Purpose: Designed to identify children "who may have social-emotional and behavioral problems and/or delays, or deficits in social-emotional competence."
Population: Ages 12-0 to 35-1 months.
Publication Date: 2006.
Administration: Individual.
Parts: 2 assessments: Brief Infant Toddler Social Emotional Assessment, Infant Toddler Social Emotional Assessment.
Forms, 2: Parent, Childcare Provider.
Price Data, 2015: $278.15 per ITSEA/BITSEA combo kit including ITSEA manual, BITSEA manual, 25 ITSEA Parent Forms, 25 ITSEA Childcare Provider

Forms, 25 BITSEA Parent Forms, and 25 BITSEA Childcare Provider Forms.

Foreign Language Editions: Parent and Childcare Provider Forms available in Spanish.

Comments: These tests are to be completed by a parent/guardian and a childcare provider; the parent form may be completed as an interview.

Publisher: Pearson.

   a) BRIEF INFANT TODDLER SOCIAL EMOTIONAL ASSESSMENT.

   Acronym: BITSEA.

   Scores, 2: Problem Total, Competence Total.

   Price Data, 2015: $118.90 per complete kit including BITSEA manual (2006, 62 pages), 25 BITSEA Parent Forms, and 25 BITSEA Childcare Provider Forms; $63 per BITSEA manual; $45.60 per 50 BITSEA Parent Forms; $45.60 per 50 BITSEA Childcare Provider Forms.

   Time: (5-10) minutes.

   Authors: Margaret J. Briggs-Gowan and Alice S. Carter.

   b) INFANT TODDLER SOCIAL EMOTIONAL ASSESSMENT.

   Acronym: ITSEA.

   Scores, 20: Externalizing (Activity/Impulsivity, Aggression/Defiance, Peer Aggression), Internalizing (Depression/Withdrawal, General Anxiety, Separation Distress, Inhibition to Novelty), Dysregulation (Sleep, Negative Emotionality, Eating, Sensory Sensitivity), Competence (Compliance, Attention, Imitation/Play, Mastery Motivation, Empathy, Prosocial Peer Relations), Maladaptive Item Cluster, Social Relatedness Cluster, Atypical Item Cluster.

   Price Data, 2015: $187.20 per complete kit including ITSEA manual (2006, 62 pages), 25 ITSEA Parent Forms and 25 ITSEA Childcare Provider Forms; $101 per ITSEA manual; $57.25 per 25 ITSEA F Parent Forms; $57.25 per 25 ITSEA Childcare Provider Forms.

   Time: (20-30) minutes.

   Authors: Alice S. Carter and Margaret J. Briggs-Gowan.

Cross References: For reviews by Abigail Baxter and Timothy R. Konold, see 17:95.

[1034]

IVA+Plus [Integrated Visual and Auditory Continuous Performance Test].

Purpose: "Designed primarily to help in the diagnosis and quantification of the symptoms of Attention-Deficit/Hyperactivity Disorders (ADHD)."

Population: Ages 6 to adult.

Publication Dates: 1993–2010.

Acronym: IVA+Plus CPT.

Scores, 30: Auditory Response Control Quotient, Prudence Auditory, Consistency Auditory, Stamina Auditory, Visual Response Control Quotient, Prudence Visual, Consistency Visual, Stamina Visual, Full Scale Response Control Quotient, Auditory Attention Quotient, Vigilance Auditory, Focus Auditory, Speed Auditory, Visual Attention Quotient, Vigilance Visual, Focus Visual, Speed Visual, Full Scale Attention Quotient, Fine Motor Regulation Quotient (Hyperactivity), Balance, Readiness Auditory, Readiness Visual, Comprehension Auditory, Comprehension Visual, Persistence Auditory, Persistence Visual, Sensory/Motor Auditory, Sensory/Motor Visual, Sustained Visual Attention, Sustained Auditory Attention.

Administration: Individual.

Price Data, 2010: Option 1: $499 per starter kit with Investigator including CD-ROM, interpretation, administration and technical support manuals (included on CD), and 10 testing administrations (licensed for use at one computer); $249 per 10 additional test administrations for starter kit preferred customer ($399 per 25); Option 2: $1,895 per unlimited use kit with Investigator including CD-ROM, interpretation, administration, and technical support manuals (included on CD), and unlimited testing administrations at one computer station; $99 per preferred customer plan; $25 for a two test trial version; $349 per Interpretive Report Writer Kit; $249 per 10 additional reports; $349 per 25 additional reports $649 per 100 additional reports; discounts apply for customers who choose to participate in the preferred customer plan.

Foreign Language Editions: Option available to allow the test stimuli to be spoken in a foreign language (Arabic, Danish, Dutch, French, German, Greek, Hebrew, Hindi, Indonesian, Italian, Japanese, Mandarin, Pashto, Polish, Portuguese, Russian, Spanish, Swahili, Swedish, Taiwanese Dialect, Turkish, Vietnamese, and Welsh) for an additional fee.

Time: 13[20] minutes.

Comments: Computer administered; optional analyses (Investigator and Special Analyses) and report writers (Standard Report, ADHD Report) may be added to software; the Preferred Customer Plan provides software and normative updates, free technical support for one year, and discounts on the cost of additional testing administrations and Add-Ons. The test publisher has indicated there is a newer edition of this test; description will be updated when complete test materials are received.

Authors: Joseph A. Sandford and Ann Turner.

Publisher: BrainTrain.

Cross References: For reviews by Cleborne D. Maddux and Wes Sime, see 17:96; for reviews by Harrison Kane and Susan C. Whiston and by Martin J. Wiese of an earlier edition, see 14:180.

[1035]

Jackson Personality Inventory—Revised.

Purpose: Designed as a "modern measure of normal personality, useful in counseling and business settings."

Population: Adolescents and adults.

Publication Dates: 1976–1997.

Acronym: JPI-R.

Scores: 15 scales in 5 clusters: Analytical (Complexity, Breadth of Interest, Innovation, Tolerance), Emotional (Empathy, Anxiety, Cooperativeness), Extroverted (Sociability, Social Confidence, Energy Level), Opportunistic

(Social Astuteness, Risk Taking), Dependable (Organization, Traditional Values, Responsibility).
Administration: Group or individual.
Price Data, 2015: $97 per examination kit including manual on CD (1994, 138 pages), 5 test booklets, 5 Quick Score answer sheets, 5 profile sheets, and coupon and machine-scorable answer sheet for one Basic Report; $25 per manual on CD; $65 per 25 reusable test booklets; $80 per 25 Quick Score answer sheets; $50 per 25 profile sheets; $67–$77 (depending on volume) per 10 machine-scorable answer sheets and coupons for Basic Reports; $155 per software package including installation package and 10 coupons for computer reports; $12-$20 (depending on volume) per online password.
Foreign Language Edition: French Test Booklets available, as well as French administration through online platform www.SigmaTesting.com.
Time: 45 minutes.
Author: Douglas N. Jackson.
Publisher: SIGMA Assessment Systems, Inc.
Cross References: See T5:1333 (8 references); for reviews by David J. Pittenger and Peter Zachar, see 13:162 (21 references); see also T4:1296 (28 references) and T3:1203 (6 references); for reviews by Lewis R. Goldberg and David T. Lykken of an earlier edition, see 8:593 (6 references).

[1036]

Jackson Vocational Interest Survey [1999 Revision].

Purpose: "Designed to yield ... a set of scores representing interests and preferences relevant to work ..., conceptualized as work roles and work styles."
Population: High school and above.
Publication Dates: 1977–2000.
Acronym: JVIS.
Scores, 50: 34 Basic Interest Scales (Creative Arts, Performing Arts, Mathematics, Physical Science, Engineering, Life Science, Social Science, Adventure, Nature—Agriculture, Skilled Trades, Personal Service, Family Activity, Medical Service, Dominant Leadership, Job Security, Stamina, Accountability, Teaching, Social Service, Elementary Education, Finance, Business, Office Work, Sales, Supervision, Human Relations Management, Law, Professional Advising, Author—Journalism, Academic Achievement, Technical Writing, Independence, Planfulness, Interpersonal Confidence); 10 General Occupational Themes (Expressive, Logical, Inquiring, Practical, Assertive, Socialized, Helping, Conventional, Enterprising, Communicative); 3 Administrative Indices (Unscorable Responses, Response Consistency Index, Infrequency Index); Academic Satisfaction; Similarity to College Students; Similarity to Occupational Classifications.
Administration: Group or individual.
Price Data, 2015: $119 per examination kit including manual on CD (2000, 149 pages), JVIS Applica-

tions Handbook, JVIS Occupations Guide, machine-scorable answer sheet for Extended Report, reusable test booklet, hand-scorable answer and profile sheets, and jvis.com password; $25 per test manual on CD; $55 per JVIS Applications Handbook; $45 per JVIS Occupations Guide; $65 per 25 reusable test booklets; $55 per 25 hand-scorable answer sheets; $55 per 25 profile sheets; $97-$107 per 10 Mail-in Extended Report; $66-$76 per 10 Mail-in Basic Report; $155 per SigmaSoft JVIS for Windows installation package and 10 coupons; $8-$10 (depending on volume) per online password.
Foreign Language Editions: Spanish booklets available. French available for hand scoring, mail-in scoring, software administration, and online administration.
Time: 45 minutes.
Comments: Former edition no longer available; available in paper-and-pencil format (hand scoring or mail-in scoring), software administration and scoring available using SigmaSoft JVIS for Windows software; system requirements: SigmaSoft JVIS for Windows also can be used for scoring data scanned by an optical mark reader using SigmaSoft Scanning Utility; SigmaSoft JVIS for Windows produces Basic Report, Extended Report, and Data Report. Online scoring available.
Authors: Douglas N. Jackson and Marc Verhoeve (applications handbook).
Publisher: SIGMA Assessment Systems, Inc.
Cross References: For reviews by Eleanor E. Sanford and Wendy J. Steinberg, see 15:129; see T5:1334 (5 references and T4:1297 (1 reference); for reviews by Douglas T. Brown and John W. Shepard of a previous edition, see 10:158 (1 reference); for reviews by Charles Davidshofer and Ruth G. Thomas, see 9:542; see also T3:1204 (1 reference).

[1037]

James Madison Test of Critical Thinking.

Purpose: "Designed to evaluate the in-depth critical thinking ability of middle school students through adults."
Population: Grades 7-12+.
Publication Date: 2004.
Acronym: JMTCT.
Scores: Total score only.
Administration: Individual or group.
Forms, 2: A, B.
Price Data: Available from publisher.
Time: 50 minutes.
Comments: Both forms can be used as a pretest or posttest; formerly known as the Comprehensive Test of Critical Thinking.
Authors: Don Fawkes, Bill O'Meara, and Dan Flage.
Publisher: The Critical Thinking Co.
Cross References: For reviews by Jerrell C. Cassady and Suzanne Young, see 17:97.

[1038]

Jesness Behavior Checklist.

Purpose: "Designed as a multiple rating scale to be used by self and others that measures individuals at risk for antisocial behavior."

Population: Delinquents ages 13-20.

Publication Dates: 1970-1971.

Scores, 14: Unobtrusiveness/Obtrusiveness, Friendliness/Hostility, Responsibility/Irresponsibility, Considerateness/Inconsiderateness, Independence/Dependence, Rapport/Alienation, Enthusiasm/Depression, Sociability/Poor Peer Relations, Conformity/Non-Conformity, Calmness/Anxiousness, Effective Communications/Inarticulateness, Insight/Unawareness and Indecisiveness, Social Control/Attention-Seeking, Anger Control/Hypersensitivity.

Administration: Individual.

Editions, 2: Observer, Self-Appraisal.

Price Data, 2015: $259 per complete kit including 10 Observer item booklets, 25 Observer QuikScore™ forms, 10 Self-Appraisal item booklets, 25 Self-Appraisal QuikScore™ forms, and manual (1971, 32 pages); $46 per 10 Observer item booklets; $59 per 25 Observer QuikScore™ forms; $46 per 10 Self-Appraisal item booklets; $59 per 25 Self-Appraisal QuikScore™ forms; $72 per manual.

Time: (10-20) minutes.

Comments: Software also available (observer and self-appraisal entry sheets).

Author: Carl F. Jesness.

Publisher: Multi-Health Systems, Inc.

Cross References: See T5:1340 (5 references); for reviews by Dorcas Susan Butt and Edwin I. Megargee, see 8:594 (3 references).

[1039]

Jesness Inventory—Revised.

Purpose: Designed to be used as a personality inventory for delinquent and conduct-disordered youths and adults.

Population: Ages 8 and over

Publication Dates: 1962–2003.

Acronym: JI-R.

Scores, 24: Randomness Scale, Lie Scale, Asocial Index, Social Maladjustment, Value Orientation, Immaturity, Autism, Alienation, Manifest Aggression, Withdrawal-Depression, Social Anxiety, Repression, Denial, Conduct Disorder, Oppositional Defiant Disorder, Undersocialized/Active [Unsocialized/Aggressive], Undersocialized/Passive [Unsocialized/Passive], Conformist [Immature Conformist], Group Oriented [Cultural Conformist], Pragmatist [Manipulator], Autonomy-Oriented [Neurotic/Acting-Out], Introspective [Neurotic/Anxious], Inhibited [Situational], Adaptive [Cultural Identifier].

Administration: Individual or Group.

Price Data, 2015: $284 per complete kit including manual, 10 item booklets, 25 QuikScore forms, and scoring templates; $99 per technical manual; $34 per 10 reusable item booklets; $69 per 25 QuikScore forms; $99 for scoring templates; $259 per online kit including manual and 25 online forms; $7.25 per online form (specify English or Spanish); $299 per software kit (V.5) including manual, V.5 getting started guide, and 25 interpretive report uses; $8.25 per profile report (minimum 50); $14 per interpretive report (minimum 25).

Foreign Language Edition: Spanish edition available.

Time: (20-30) minutes.

Comments: Software version available; Web administration available.

Author: Carl F. Jesness.

Publisher: Multi-Health Systems, Inc.

Cross References: For reviews by Elizabeth Kelley Rhoades and Georgette Yetter, see 16:118; for reviews by Robert M. Guion and Susana Urbina of a previous edition, see 14:188; see also T5:1341 (3 references) and T3:1209 (9 references); for a review by Dorcas Susan Butt of an earlier edition, see 8:595 (14 references); see also T2:1249 (5 references); for a review by Sheldon A. Weintraub of the Youth Edition of the earlier edition, see 7:94 (10 references); see also P:133 (3 references).

[1040]

Job and Vocational Attitudes Assessment Questionnaire and Interview.

Purpose: Designed to assess an employee's readiness to return to work following a positive drug screening or addiction treatment.

Population: Employees.

Publication Dates: 1994-2003.

Acronym: JAVAA.

Scores, 9: Recognition/Status, Job Attitudes, Work Relationships, Desire to Work, Recovery Strategy, Emotional Well-being, Anger Resolution, Insight, Support.

Administration: Individual.

Forms, 2: Questionnaire, Interview Guide.

Price Data, 2016: $62.50 per 25 questionnaire forms; $62.50 per 25 interview forms; $37.50 per 25 summary forms; $15 per manual (2003, 29 pages).

Time: Administration time not reported.

Comments: Materials for questionnaire and interview form are purchased separately.

Author: Norman G. Hoffmann.

Publisher: The Change Companies.

[1041]

Job Challenge Profile.

Purpose: "Designed to help managers better understand and see their job assignments as opportunities for learning and growth."

Population: Managers, leaders, and executives.
Publication Date: 1999-2015.
Acronym: JCP.
Scores, 10: Unfamiliar Responsibilities, New Directions, Inherited Problems, Problems with Employees, High Stakes, Scope and Scale, External Pressure, Influence Without Authority, Work Across Cultures, Work Group Diversity.
Administration: Individual.
Price Data, 2015: $50 per Facilitator's Guide (76 pages); $30 per Participant's Workbook/Survey (49 pages); $16 per survey.
Time: 15-20 minutes.
Comments: Revision of the Developmental Challenge Profile (DCP; no longer available); self-scored; Facilitator's Guide includes details of workshop procedures, reproducible overheads, and handout masters; Participant's Workbook contains test items and action guide.
Authors: Cynthia D. McCauley (Facilitator's Guide, Participant Workbook/Survey), Patricia J. Ohlott (Facilitator's Guide, Survey), and Marian N. Ruderman (Facilitator's Guide, Survey).
Publisher: Center for Creative Leadership.
Cross References: For reviews by Laura L. B. Barnes and Jean Powell Kirnan, see 16:119; for reviews by Jean Powell Kirnan and Kristen Wojcik and by Eugene P. Sheehan of The Developmental Challenge Profile, see 13:94 (2 references).

[1042]
A Job Choice Decision-Making Exercise.

Purpose: Serves as a behavioral decision theory measurement approach to need for affiliation, need for power, and need for achievement.
Population: High school and college and adults.
Publication Dates: 1981–1986.
Acronym: JCE.
Scores, 3: Affiliation, Power, Achievement.
Administration: Group.
Price Data, 2015: $4 per exercise booklet; $35 per Managerial and Technical Motivation book (1986, 178 pages, available from Praeger Publishers, in lieu of manual).
Time: [15–20] minutes.
Authors: Michael J. Stahl and Anil Gulati (scoring software and scoring manual).
Publisher: Assessment Enterprises.
Cross References: For a review by Nicholas A. Vacc and J. Scott Hinkle, see 11:187.

[1043]
Job Descriptive Index (2009 Revision) and The Job in General Scales (2009 Revision).

Purpose: To measure job satisfaction (facet and/or overall).
Population: Employees.

Publication Dates: 1969–2009.
Acronym: JDI; JIG.
Scores: Five facets (Work on Present Job, Pay, Opportunities for Promotion, Supervision, and People on Your Present Job) and the Job in General.
Administration: Group or individual.
Price Data, 2015: There is no charge to use the copyrighted scales; prices for user manuals, scoring services, and national norms available from publisher.
Time: 5-15 minutes.
Authors: Patricia C. Smith, Lorne M. Kendall, and Charles L. Hulin (1969 edition); William K. Balzer, Jenifer A. Kihm, Patricia C. Smith, Jennifer L. Irwin, Peter D. Bachiochi, Chet Robie, Evan F. Sinar, and Luis F. Parra (1997 edition). Gillespie, J., Balzer, W., Gillespie, M., & Brodke, M. et al. (2009 edition).
Publisher: Bowling Green State University.
Cross References: For a review by Michael R. Harwell, see 15:130; see T5:1348 (16 references); for reviews by Charles K. Parsons and Norman D. Sundberg for an earlier edition of the Job Descriptive Index and Retirement Descriptive Index, see 12:199 (33 references); see also T4:1312 (63 references); for reviews by John O. Crites and Barbara A. Kerr of an earlier edition of the Job Descriptive Index, see 9:550 (49 references).

[1044]
Job Observation and Behavior Scale.

Purpose: Designed as "a work performance evaluation for supported and entry level employees."
Population: Ages 15 and above.
Publication Dates: 1998–2000.
Acronym: JOBS.
Scores, 4: Work-Required Daily Living Activities, Work-Required Behavior, Work-Required Job Duties, Quality of Performance Composite/Total.
Administration: Individual.
Price Data, 2015: $75 per complete test kit including 25 record forms and manual (1998, 28 pages); $30 per 25 record forms; $50 per manual.
Time: (30) minutes.
Authors: Howard Rosenberg and Michael Brady.
Publisher: Stoelting Co.
Cross References: For reviews by Ayres G. D'Costa and Sheldon Zedeck, see 15:131.

[1045]
Job Search Attitude Inventory, Fifth Edition.

Purpose: Designed to "make job seekers more aware of their self-directed and other-directed attitudes about their searches for employment."
Population: Adult and teen job seekers and career planners.
Publication Dates: 2002-2015.
Acronym: JSAI.

Scores, 5: Luck vs. Planning, Uninvolved vs. Involved, Help from Others vs. Self-Help, Passive vs. Active, Pessimistic vs. Optimistic.
Administration: Individual or group.
Price Data, 2016: $60.95 per 25 inventories; administrator's guide (2015, 19 pages) may be downloaded at no charge.
Time: (20) minutes.
Comments: Self-administered, self-scored, and self-interpreted.
Author: John J. Liptak.
Publisher: JIST/EMC Publishing.
Cross References: For reviews by John W. Fleenor and Thomas R. O'Neill of the second edition, see 16:120.

[1046]
Job Search Knowledge Scale, Third Edition.
Purpose: Designed to assess a person's knowledge about finding a job.
Population: Job seekers.
Publication Dates: 2005-2015.
Acronym: JSKS.
Scores, 5: Identifying Job Leads, Direct Application to Employers, Resumes and Cover Letters, Employment Interviews, Following Up.
Administration: Group.
Price Data, 2016: $60.95 per 25 scales; administrator's guide (2015, 14 pages) available as free download from test publisher.
Time: (20) minutes.
Comments: Self-administered, self-scored, and self-interpreted.
Author: John J. Liptak.
Publisher: JIST/EMC Publishing.
Cross References: For reviews by Gary J. Dean and K. Hattrup of the original edition, see 17:98.

[1047]
Job Seeking Skills Assessment.
Purpose: "For assessing clients' ability to complete a job application form and participate in the employment interview, and to serve as a guide for integrating the results into program planning."
Population: Vocational rehabilitation clients.
Publication Date: 1988.
Acronym: JSSA.
Scores, 2: Job Application, Employment Interview.
Administration: Group.
Price Data: Available as free download from Educational Resources Information Center (ERIC) database.
Time: Administration time not reported.
Comments: Designed as a component of the Diagnostic Employability Profile (DEP).
Authors: Suki Hinman, Bob Means, Sandra Parkerson, and Betty Odendahl.

Publisher: The National Center on Employment & Disability.
Cross References: For reviews by Paul M. Muchinsky and William I. Sauser, Jr., see 12:201.

[1048]
Job Stress Survey.
Purpose: "Designed to assess generic sources of occupational stress encountered by men and women employed in a variety of work settings."
Population: Adults ages 18 and older.
Publication Dates: 1991–1999.
Acronym: JSS.
Scores, 9: Job Stress Index, Job Stress Severity, Job Stress Frequency, Job Pressure Index, Job Pressure Severity, Job Pressure Frequency, Lack of Organizational Support Index, Lack of Organizational Support Severity, Lack of Organizational Support Frequency.
Administration: Group.
Forms, 2: Form HS (Hand-Scorable), Form SP (Scoring Program).
Price Data, 2015: $215 per introductory kit including professional manual (1999, 72 pages), 50 test booklets, and 50 profile forms.
Foreign Language Edition: Spanish version available: Cuestionario de Estrés Laboral.
Time: (10–15) minutes.
Comments: Computer scoring program available; Forms HS and SP are identical in content.
Authors: Charles D. Spielberger and Peter R. Vagg.
Publisher: Psychological Assessment Resources, Inc.
Cross References: For reviews by Peter M. Berger and James W. Pinkney, see 15:132.

[1049]
Job Style Indicator [Revised].
Purpose: Designed to help understand "the work behavioral style and task requirements" of a job and to provide "a job compatibility rating when used with the following CRG Style assessments: Personal, Sales, Instructional, Entrepreneurial, and Quick."
Population: Adults.
Publication Dates: 1988-2006.
Acronym: JSI.
Scores, 4: Behavioral/Action, Cognitive/Analysis, Interpersonal/Harmony, Affective/Expression.
Administration: Individual or group.
Price Data, 2016: $12 per test; $75 per professional's guide (2006, 64 pages).
Foreign Language Edition: Swedish version available.
Time: [30-60] minutes.
Comments: Self-administered and self-scored; may be used in conjunction with Personal Style Indicator (1516), Sales Style Indicator (1772), Quick Style Indicator (1681), Entrepreneurial Style and Success Indicator

(768), and the Instructional Style Indicator (987); online administration available.

Authors: Ken Keis, Terry D. Anderson, and Everett T. Robinson.

Publisher: Consulting Resource Group International, Inc.

Cross References: For a review by M. David Miller, see 17:99; for reviews by Neal Schmitt and David M. Williamson of an earlier edition, see 13:164.

[1050]

Job Survival and Success Scale, Second Edition.

Purpose: Designed to "identify a person's attitudes and knowledge about keeping a job and getting ahead in the workplace."

Population: Job seekers.

Publication Dates: 2005-2009.

Acronym: JSSS.

Scores, 5: Dependability, Responsibility, Human Relations, Ethical Behavior, Getting Ahead.

Administration: Group.

Price Data, 2016: $55.95 per 25 scales; administrator's guide (2009, 15 pages) available as free download from test publisher.

Time: (20) minutes.

Comments: Self-administered, self-scored, and self-interpreted.

Author: John J. Liptak.

Publisher: JIST/EMC Publishing.

Cross References: For reviews by James T. Austin and Stephanie D. Tischendorf and by Stephen B. Johnson of the original edition, see 17:100.

[1051]

Jordan Left-Right Reversal Test, 3rd Edition.

Purpose: Designed "to identify children who may have difficulty recognizing the correct orientation of letters and numbers, or who may reverse words or other letter sequences."

Population: Ages 5-0 through 18-11.

Publication Dates: 1973-2011.

Acronym: Jordan-3.

Scores, 2: Accuracy, Error.

Administration: Group.

Levels, 2: 2 levels (ages 5 through 8, ages 9 through 18).

Forms: 1 form.

Price Data, 2015: $120 per test kit, including manual (2011, 88 pages), 25 record forms, 25 Remedial Checklists (optional), and 25 Laterality Checklists (optional); $35 per 25 record forms; $20 per 25 Remedial Checklists; $20 per 25 Laterality Checklists; $45 per manual.

Time: (20-30) minutes.

Author: Brian T. Jordan.

Publisher: Academic Therapy Publications.

Cross References: For reviews by Darrell L. Sabers and James P. van Haneghan, see 19:90; for reviews by Christine W. Burns and Jeffrey H. Snow of the 1990 Edition, see 12:203 (1 reference); see also T4:1326 (4 references); for reviews by Mary S. Poplin and Joseph Torgesen of the Second Revised Edition, see 9:557; see also T3:1224 (2 references); for reviews by Barbara K. Keogh and Richard J. Reisboard, and excerpted reviews by Alex Bannatyne and Alan Krichev, see 8:434 (5 references).

[1052]

Joseph Picture Self-Concept Scale.

Purpose: Designed to measure "self-concept in children" and "identify children whose negative self-appraisals signal that they are at risk for academic and behavioral difficulties."

Publication Date: 2004.

Scores: Total Self-Concept Score.

Administration: Individual.

Parts, 4: Light-Skin Boys, Dark-Skin Boys, Light-Skin Girls, Dark-Skin Girls.

Price Data, 2016: $238 for complete kit for younger children including 2 stimulus booklets, 20 AutoScore forms, and manual (86 pages); $149.50 for complete kit for older children including 2 stimulus booklets, 20 AutoScore forms, and manual; $59.50 per manual; $48 per 20 AutoScore forms (specify Form Y [younger] or Form O [older]); $77.50 for choice of Form Y stimulus booklets; $35.50 for choice of Form O stimulus booklet.

Time: (5-10) minutes.

Comments: Both forms of this test allow participants to "respond using pictures rather than words."

Author: Jack Joseph.

Publisher: Western Psychological Services.

    a) FORM Y-YOUNG CHILD INTERVIEW.

    Population: Ages 3-0 to 7-11 years.

    b) FORM O-OLDER CHILD INTERVIEW.

    Population: Ages 7-0 to 13-11 years.

Cross References: For reviews by Eugene V. Aidman and Carlen Henington, see 17:101.

[1053]

Joseph Pre-School and Primary Self-Concept Screening Test.

Purpose: Constructed as an early screen for learning problems.

Population: Ages 3-5 to 9-11.

Publication Date: 1979.

Scores: Global Self Concept.

Administration: Individual.

Price Data, 2015: $150 per complete kit including manual (66 pages), 56 stimulus cards, 100 identity reference drawings, and 100 record forms; $30 per 50 record forms; $35 per set of identity drawings (specify boy or girl).

Time: (5–7) minutes.
Comments: May be used with non-verbal children.
Author: Jack Joseph.
Publisher: Stoelting Co.
Cross References: See T5:1363 (2 references); for reviews by Kathryn Clark Gerken and Cathy Fultz Telzrow, see 9:558.

[1054]

Jung Personality Questionnaire.

Purpose: "To assist pupils in choosing a career."
Population: Standards 7 and 8 and 10 in South African school system.
Publication Date: 1983.
Acronym: JPQ.
Scores, 4: Extraversion vs. Introversion, Thinking vs. Feeling, Sensation vs. Intuition, Judgement vs. Perception.
Administration: Group.
Price Data: Available from publisher.
Foreign Language Edition: Afrikaans edition available.
Time: (25–35) minutes.
Comments: "Criterion-referenced."
Author: L. B. H. duToit.
Publisher: Human Sciences Research Council [South Africa].

[1055]

Jungian Type Survey: The Gray-Wheelwrights Test (16th Revision).

Purpose: "Designed to delineate types of personality structure."
Population: Adults.
Publication Date: 1964.
Scores, 6: Introversion, Extraversion, Intuition, Sensation, Thinking, Feeling.
Administration: Group.
Price Data: Price information available from publisher for reusable question sheet, answer sheet, and manual (8 pages).
Foreign Language Editions: Available in German, French, Italian, and Spanish.
Time: (20) minutes.
Authors: Horace Gray (test only), Joseph B. Wheelwright (test and manual), Jane H. Wheelwright (test and manual), and John A. Bueler (manual only).
Publisher: C. G. Jung Institute of San Francisco, Inc.

[1056]

Junior Eysenck Personality Inventory.

Purpose: "Designed to measure ... neuroticism or emotionality, and extraversion-introversion in children."
Population: Ages 7–16.
Publication Dates: 1963–1970.
Acronym: JEPI.
Scores, 3: Extraversion, Neuroticism, Lie.

Administration: Group.
Price Data: Available from publisher.
Foreign Language Edition: Spanish edition available.
Time: [15–20] minutes.
Comments: Test publisher indicates materials have been updated; description will be updated when those test materials are received.
Author: Sybil B. G. Eysenck.
Publisher: EdITS/Educational and Industrial Testing Service.
Cross References: See T5:1367 (7 references), T4:1331 (13 references), 9:561 (10 references), T3:1229 (24 references), 8:596 (36 references), and T2:1252 (14 references); for reviews by Maurice Chazan and Robert D. Wirt and excerpted reviews by Gertrude H. Keir and B. Semeonoff, see 7:96 (19 references); see also P:135 (7 references).

[1057]

Junior South African Individual Scales.

Purpose: Measures general intellectual level.
Population: South African children ages 3.0–7.11.
Publication Dates: 1981–1988.
Acronym: JSAIS.
Scores, 27: Verbal (Vocabulary, Reading Knowledge, Story Memory, Picture Riddles, Word Association, Social Reasoning, Picture Analogies, Word Fluency), Numerical (Number and Quantity A, Number and Quantity B, Number and Quantity A & B, Memory for Digits A, Memory for Digits B, Memory for Digits A & B), Visual-Spatial (Form Board, Block Designs, Absurdities A, Absurdities B, Form Discrimination A & B, Grouping, Gestalt Completion, Picture Series, Picture Puzzles, Visual Memory A, Visual Memory B, Visual Memory A & B, Copying).
Administration: Individual.
Price Data: Available from publisher.
Foreign Language Edition: Afrikaans edition available.
Time: (60–90) minutes.
Authors: Elizabeth M. Madge (manuals, Parts 1-3), A. R. vandenBerg (manual, Part 3), Maryna Robinson (manual, Part 3), and J. Landman (appendix to manuals).
Publisher: Human Sciences Research Council [South Africa].
Cross References: See T5:1370 (1 reference) and T4:1335 (1 reference).

[1058]

Just-in-Time Training Assessment Instrument.

Purpose: "Intended to measure ... perceptions of how frequently and how effectively [an] organization has created a work environment that supports JITT."

Population: Adults.
Publication Date: 1996.
Acronym: JITT.
Scores, 2: Frequency, Effectiveness.
Administration: Group.
Price Data, 2016: $195; quantity discounts available.
Time: (15–20) minutes.
Comments: Now sold as part of the Training House Assessment Kit.
Author: William J. Rothwell.
Publisher: HRD Press, Inc.

[1059]

Juvenile Automated Substance Abuse Evaluation.

Purpose: Intended to "measure adolescent alcohol and drug use/abuse ... attitudes and life-stress issues."
Population: Adolescents.
Publication Dates: 1989–1997.
Acronym: JASAE.
Scores, 6: Test Taking Attitude, Life Circumstance Evaluation, Drinking Evaluation Category, Alcohol Addiction Evaluation, Drug Use Evaluation, Summary.
Administration: Individual or group.
Price Data: Available from publisher.
Foreign Language Edition: Available in Spanish.
Time: (20) minutes.
Comments: Self-administered; computer scored; provides DSM–5 classification for alcohol and drug use and ASAM patient placement criteria for treatment recommendations.
Author: ADE Incorporated.
Publisher: ADE Incorporated.
Cross References: For reviews by Mark Pope and Jody L. Swartz-Kulstad, see 14:190.

[1060]

Juvenile Substance Abuse Profile.

Purpose: "Designed for troubled youth ... assessment in juvenile courts, screening programs, schools systems, and treatment agencies."
Population: Troubled youth.
Publication Date: 2002.
Acronym: JSAP.
Scores, 5: Truthfulness, Aggressiveness, Alcohol, Drugs, Stress Coping Abilities.
Administration: Group.
Price Data, 2016: $9.95 per test; volume discounts available.
Foreign Language Edition: Spanish version available.
Time: (20) minutes.
Author: Behavior Data Systems, Ltd.
Publisher: Behavior Data Systems, Ltd.

[1061]

Kaplan Baycrest Neurocognitive Assessment.

Purpose: "Test of neurocognitive functioning."
Population: Ages 20–89.
Publication Date: 2000.
Acronym: KBNA.
Scores: 8 index scores: Attention/Concentration, Immediate Memory Recall, Delayed Memory Recall, Delayed Memory Recognition, Spatial Processing, Verbal Fluency, Reasoning/Conceptual Shifting, Total Index.
Administration: Individual.
Price Data, 2015: $281.90 per complete kit including manual (188 pages), stimulus book (94 pages), response chips (set of 8), 25 response booklets, 25 record forms, and response grid; $117.90 per manual; $138.40 per stimulus book; $56.40 per 25 response booklets; $87.15 per 25 record forms; $22.55 per response grid.
Time: (60–90) minutes.
Comments: Test contains 25 subtests (Orientation, Sequences, Numbers, Word Lists 1, Complex Figure 1, Motor Programming, Auditory Signal Detection, Symbol Cancellation, Clocks, Word Lists 2, Complex Figure 2, Picture Naming, Sentence Reading—Arithmetic, Reading Single Words, Spatial Location, Verbal Fluency, Praxis, Picture Recognition, Expression of Emotion, Practical Problem Solving, Conceptual Shifting, Picture Description—Oral, Auditory Comprehension, Repetition, Picture Description—Written); detailed analysis of neurocognitive functioning can be obtained through examination of 94 component Process Scores; Process Scores are categorized as below average, equivocal, or average.
Authors: Larry Leach, Edith Kaplan, Dmytro Rewilak, Brian Richards, and Guy-B. Proulx.
Publisher: Pearson.
Cross References: For reviews by Raymond S. Dean and John J. Brinkman, Jr., and by Harrison D. Kane and Shawn K. Acheson, see 16:121.

[1062]

Kaufman Assessment Battery for Children, Second Edition.

Purpose: Designed to measure the "processing and cognitive abilities of children and adolescents."
Population: Ages 3-18.
Publication Dates: 1983-2004.
Acronym: KABC-II.
Scores, 7–23: Sequential (Number Recall, Word Order, Hand Movements, Total), Simultaneous (Block Counting, Conceptual Thinking, Face Recognition, Pattern Reasoning [Ages 5 and 6], Rover, Story Completion [Ages 5 and 6], Triangles, Gestalt Closure, Total), Planning [Ages 7–18 only] (Pattern Reasoning, Story Completion, Total), Learning (Atlantis, Rebus, Atlantis Delayed, Rebus Delayed, Total), Knowledge (Expressive Vocabulary, Riddles, Verbal Knowledge, Total), Nonverbal Index, Mental Processing Index, Fluid-Crystallized Index.

Administration: Individual.
Price Data, 2015: $935 per complete kit including 4 easels, 1 manual, all necessary stimulus and manipulative materials, and 25 record forms; $70.75 per 25 record forms; $75 per manual. $302 per CD-ROM software.
Time: (25-70) minutes.
Comments: Nonverbal scale available for hearing impaired, speech-and-language disordered, and non-English-speaking children (an adaptation that examiners can make when verbal concerns are present).
Authors: Alan S. Kaufman and Nadeen L. Kaufman.
Publisher: Pearson.
Cross References: For reviews by Jeffery P. Braden and Sandye M. Ouzts and by Robert M. Thorndike, see 16:123; see also T5:1379 (103 references) and T4:1343 (114 references); for reviews by Anne Anastasi, William E. Coffman, and Ellis Batten Page of an earlier edition, see 9:562 (3 references).

[1063]
Kaufman Brief Intelligence Test, Second Edition.
Purpose: Intended as a brief measure of verbal and nonverbal intelligence.
Population: Ages 4-90.
Publication Dates: 1990–2004.
Acronym: KBIT-2.
Scores: 3: Verbal, Nonverbal, IQ Composite.
Subtests: 3: Verbal Knowledge, Riddles, Matrices.
Administration: Individual.
Price Data, 2015: $256.25 per complete kit including stimulus easel, manual (2004, 147 pages), 25 individual test record forms, and carry bag; $55.85 per 25 individual test records; $75.85 per scoring and administration manual.
Time: (15–30) minutes.
Comments: Examiners are encouraged to teach individuals, using teaching items, how to solve the kinds of items included in subtests.
Authors: Alan S. Kaufman and Nadeen L. Kaufman.
Publisher: Pearson.
Cross References: For reviews by Ronald A. Madle and Steven R. Shaw, see 17:102; see also T5:1380 (21 references); for reviews by M. David Miller and John W. Young of an earlier version, see 12:205 (9 references); see also T4:1344 (4 references).

[1064]
Kaufman Developmental Scale.
Purpose: Designed to assess the "level of development … and an overall level of functioning."
Population: Birth to age 9 and mentally retarded of all ages.
Publication Dates: 1972–1975.
Acronym: KDS.

Scores, 7: Gross Motor, Fine Motor, Receptive, Expressive, Personal Behavior, Inter-Personal Behavior, Total.
Administration: Individual.
Price Data, 2015: $425 per complete kit including test materials, manual (1974, 83 pages), 25 record forms, and carrying case; $55 per 25 evaluation booklets; $30 per 25 record forms; $55 per manual.
Time: (30) minutes.
Author: H. Kaufman.
Publisher: Stoelting Co.
Cross References: For a review by Dorothy H. Eichorn, see 8:218.

[1065]
Kaufman Infant and Preschool Scale.
Purpose: Designed to measure "early, high-level cognitive thinking, and indicates possible need for intervention."
Population: Ages 1 month–48 months and mentally retarded individuals whose preacademic functioning age does not exceed 48 months.
Publication Date: 1979.
Acronym: KIPS.
Scores: Tasks in 3 areas: General Reasoning, Storage, Verbal Communication.
Administration: Individual.
Price Data, 2015: $210 per complete kit including all manipulatives, stimulus cards, and 10 evaluation booklets; $23.10 per 10 evaluation booklets; $14 per set of stimulus cards; $19.60 per manual (40 pages).
Time: (20-30) minutes.
Author: H. Kaufman.
Publisher: Stoelting Co.
Cross References: For reviews by Roy A. Kress and Phyllis Anne Teeter, see 9:563.

[1066]
Kaufman Short Neuropsychological Assessment Procedure.
Purpose: A brief, individually administered measure of the cognitive functioning of adolescents and adults.
Population: Ages 11 through 85+.
Publication Date: 1994.
Acronym: K-SNAP.
Scores, 5: Gestalt Closure, Number Recall, Four-Letter Words, Recall/Closure Composite, K-SNAP Composite.
Administration: Individual.
Price Data, 2015: $275.75 per complete kit including manual (128 pages), easel, and 25 record forms; $60.50 per 25 record forms; $204 per easel; $85.15 per manual.
Time: 30 minutes.
Authors: Alan S. Kaufman and Nadeen L. Kaufman.
Publisher: Pearson.
Cross References: See T5:1384 (2 references); for reviews by Karen Geller and Martine Hebert, see 13:167 (2 references).

[1067]

Kaufman Survey of Early Academic and Language Skills.

Purpose: Designed as an easy-to-administer measure of children's language skills (expressive and receptive vocabulary), numerical skills, and articulation.
Population: 3-0 to 6-11.
Publication Date: 1993.
Acronym: K-SEALS.
Scores, 3: Vocabulary; Numbers, Letters, and Words; Articulation Survey.
Administration: Individual.
Price Data, 2015: $365.95 per complete kit including manual (109 pages), easel, 25 test records, and carrying bag; $46.80 per 25 record booklets; $59 per manual; $231.10 per easel.
Time: (15–25) minutes.
Comments: The Early Academic Scales can be interpreted only for ages 5-0 to 6-11.
Authors: Alan S. Kaufman and Nadeen L. Kaufman.
Publisher: Pearson.
Cross References: For reviews by Phillip L. Ackerman and by Laurie Ford and Kerri Turk, see 12:206.

[1068]

Kaufman Test of Educational Achievement, Third Edition.

Purpose: Designed to measure academic achievement in reading, mathematics, written language, and oral language.
Population: Ages 4 through 25 years.
Publication Dates: 1985-2014.
Acronym: KTEA-3.
Scores, 33: 19 subtest scores: Letter & Word Recognition, Nonsense Word Decoding, Reading Comprehension, Reading Vocabulary, Word Recognition Fluency, Decoding Fluency, Silent Reading Fluency, Math Concepts & Applications, Math Computation, Math Fluency, Written Expression, Spelling, Writing Fluency, Listening Comprehension, Oral Expression, Associational Fluency, Phonological Processing, Object Naming Facility, Letter Naming Facility; 4 core composite scores: Reading, Math, Written Language, Academic Skills Battery; 10 supplemental composite scores: Sound-Symbol, Decoding, Reading Fluency, Reading Understanding, Oral Language, Oral Fluency, Comprehension, Expression, Orthographic Processing, Academic Fluency.
Administration: Individual.
Forms: 2 parallel forms: A and B.
Price Data, 2014: $740 per Form A and Form B combined kit for manual scoring; $940 per Form A and Form B combined kit with 100 Q-global score reports; $410 per manual scoring kit (Form A or Form B) including administration manual (2014, 78 pages), scoring manual (2014, 208 pages), 2 stimulus books, USB Flash drive (contains technical manual, audio files, scoring keys, hand scoring forms, letter checklist, qualitative observations form, and error analysis forms), 25 record forms, 25 response booklets, and written expression booklets in soft-sided carrying bag; $610 per Q-Global scoring kit (Form A or Form B) including 100 Q-Global score reports; $164 per stimulus book; $82 per 25 record forms and response booklets; $60 per USB flash drive; $51 per administration manual; $51 per scoring manual; $14 per written expression booklet.
Time: (2-23) minutes per subtest; (10-35) minutes for each of the three core academic composites; (15-85) minutes for the Academic Skills Battery; administration times vary by age.
Comments: Computer and hand scoring available. Not all 19 subtests are administered at every age or grade level: "Examiners may choose to administer a single subtest or any combination of subtests to assess an examinee's academic achievement in one or more domains, or to obtain the desired composite score(s)."
Authors: Alan S. Kaufman, Nadeen L. Kaufman, and Kristina C. Breaux (manuals only).
Publisher: Pearson.
Cross References: Reviews are scheduled for *The Twentieth Mental Measurements Yearbook*. For reviews by Mike Bonner and C. Dale Carpenter of the second edition, see 16:124; for reviews by John Poggio and William D. Schafer of the 1998 normative update, see 14:191; see also T5:1386 (26 references) and T4:1348 (5 references); for reviews by Elizabeth J. Doll and Jerome M. Sattler of the original edition, see 10:161.

[1069]

Keegan Type Indicator.

Purpose: Measures perception, judgment, and attitude (extraversion/introversion) based on C. G. Jung's theory of psychological types.
Population: Adults.
Publication Dates: 1980–2006.
Acronym: KTI.
Scores, 3: Extraversion vs. Introversion, Sensation vs. Intuition, Thinking vs. Feeling.
Administration: Group.
Price Data: Price data, including user's manual (1980, 12 pages) and instructor's manual (1980, 21 pages), available from publisher.
Time: [20] minutes.
Author: Warren J. Keegan.
Publisher: Keegan & Company LLC.
Cross References: For a review by Arlene C. Rosenthal, see 10:162.

[1070]

Keirsey Temperament Sorter II.

Purpose: Designed to be used "for assessing temperament, character, and personality."
Population: College and adult.

Publication Dates: 1978–2003.
Acronym: KTS-II.
Scores, 16: Artisan-Promoter (ESTP), Artisan-Crafter (ISTP), Artisan-Performer (ESFP), Artisan-Composer (ISFP), Guardian-Supervisor (ESTJ), Guardian-Inspector (ISTJ),Guardian-Provider (ESFJ), Guardian-Protector (ISFJ), Rational-Fieldmarshal (ENTJ), Rational-Mastermind (INTJ), Rational-Inventor (ENTP), Rational-Architect (INTP), Idealist-Teacher (ENFJ), Idealist-Counselor (INFJ), Idealist-Champion (ENFP), Idealist-Header (INFP).
Administration: Group.
Price Data, 2016: Individual consumers may take the KTS-II free online; $14.95 per Classic Temperament Report; $19.95 per Career Temperament Report; $14.95 Learning Styles Temperament Report; $24.95 Corporate Temperament Report; Team Temperament Report (pricing depends on size of team); $19.95 per "Please Understand Me II" (1998, 352 pages).
Foreign Language Editions: Available in American English, Spanish, French, German, Italian, Polish, Portuguese, and Japanese.
Time: (10–15) minutes.
Authors: David Keirsey (instrument and "Please Understand Me II") and Alpine Media Corporation (Statistical Study).
Publisher: Keirsey.com.
Cross References: For a review by Peter Zachar, see 16:125.

[1071]

Kent Inventory of Developmental Skills [1996 Standardization].

Purpose: Designed to assess the developmental status and progress of healthy infants, infants at risk, and young children with developmental disabilities.
Population: Infants up to 15 months of age and children up to age 6 when severe developmental disabilities are present.
Publication Dates: 1978–1999.
Acronym: KIDS.
Scores, 12: Developmental Ages and Standard Scores for: Cognitive, Motor, Language, Self-Help, Social Domains, Full Scale.
Administration: Individual.
Price Data, 2016: $143.50 per complete kit including 25 profile sheets, 25 answer sheets, reusable administration and scoring booklet, 5 scoring templates, set of developmental timetables, manual; $150.50 per 10-use administration, scoring and interpretation CD, $66 per manual; $12 per 5 scoring templates; $33 per 5 reusable administration booklets; $24 per 25 answer sheets; $24 per 25 profile sheets; $24 per 25 developmental timetables.
Time: (45) minutes.
Comments: Relies on caregiver report; also yields individualized developmental timetables; includes hand-scoring materials and an expanded computer report, including a list of developmentally appropriate activities selected to match each child's specific competencies; earlier editions titled The Kent Infant Development Scale.
Authors: Jeanette Reuter with Lewis Katoff and Jeffrey Wozniak (3rd edition of the test manual and user's guide) and James Whiteman (computer-scoring disk).
Publisher: Western Psychological Services.
Cross References: For reviews by Diane J. Sawyer and Gary J. Stainback, see 14:192; see also T5:1391 (2 references); for reviews by Candice Feiring and Edward S. Shapiro of an earlier edition, see 10:163 (2 references); for a review by Candice Feiring of an earlier version, see 9:567; see also T3:1246 (1 reference).

[1072]

Kent Visual Perceptual Test.

Purpose: Designed to "identify and characterize visual processing deficits in school or neuropsychological settings."
Population: Ages 5–11.
Publication Dates: 1995–2000.
Acronym: KVPT.
Administration: Individual.
Price Data, 2015: $210 per complete kit including 10 copy tests, memory test stimuli, discrimination test stimuli, 10 scoring and error analysis booklets, and professional manual (2000, 128 pages).
Time: (25–30) minutes.
Author: Lawrence E. Melamed.
Publisher: Melamed & Melamed Psycho-Educational and Neuropsychological Services.
  a) KENT VISUAL PERCEPTION TEST—DISCRIMINATION.
  Purpose: Designed to assess visual discrimination skills.
  Acronym: KVPT-D.
  Scores, 2: Error Analysis, Total.
  b) KENT VISUAL PERCEPTION TEST—COPY.
  Purpose: Designed to assess visual reproduction skills.
  Acronym: KVPT-C.
  Scores, 4: KVPT-C1, KVPT-C2, KVPT-C3, Total.
  c) VISUAL PERCEPTION TESTS—IMMEDIATE MEMORY.
  Purpose: Designed to assess immediate memory.
  Acronym: KVPT-M.
  Scores, 2: Error Analysis, Total.
Cross References: For reviews by Ralph G. Leverett and Katharine A. Snyder, see 16:126; for a review by Annie W. Ward of an earlier edition, see 14:193.

[1073]

KeyMath-3 Diagnostic Assessment.

Purpose: Designed to assess understanding and applications of mathematics concepts and skills.
Population: Ages 4-6 to 21-11.
Publication Dates: 1971-2007.
Acronym: KeyMath-3 DA.

Scores, 14: Basic Concepts (Numeration, Algebra, Geometry, Measurement, Data Analysis and Probability, Total), Operations (Mental Computation and Estimation, Addition and Subtraction, Multiplication and Division, Total), Applications (Foundations of Problem Solving, Applied Problem Solving, Total), Total.
Administration: Individual.
Forms, 2: A, B.
Price Data, 2015: $808 per Form A and B combined starter kit including manual (2007, 371 pages), easels 1 and 2 for both Form A and B, 25 Form A & Form B record forms, and carrying bag; $457 per single form (specify form A or B) kit including manual, easel 1, easel 2, 25 record forms, and carrying bag; $88.15 per 25 record forms (specify form); $302.40 per KeyMath-3 ASSIST software.
Time: (30-40) minutes Grades PK-2; (75-90) minutes Grades 3 and up.
Author: Austin J. Connolly.
Publisher: Pearson.
Cross References: For reviews by Theresa Graham and by Suzanne Lane and Debra Moore, see 18:63; for reviews by G. Gage Kingsbury and James A. Wollack of a previous edition, see 14:194; see also T5:139 (15 references) and T4:1355 (5 references); for reviews by Michael D. Beck and Carmen J. Finley of an earlier edition, see 11:191 (26 references); see also T3:1250 (12 references); for an excerpted review by Alex Bannatyne of an earlier edition, see 8:305 (10 references).

[1074]
KEYS® to Creativity and Innovation.

Purpose: Designed to assess "the climate within a work group or organization" and to measure "elements in the work environment that can have an impact on creativity."
Population: Employees.
Publication Dates: 1995-2010.
Acronym: KEYS.
Scores: 10 work environment dimensions: Freedom, Challenging Work, Managerial Encouragement, Work Group Supports, Organizational Encouragement, Lack of Organizational Impediments, Sufficient Resources, Realistic Workload, Pressure, Creativity, Productivity.
Administration: Group.
Price Data, 2016: $2000 including up to 100 invitations sent on the same start date, overall report, up to 2 comparison reports, administration access, and access to online user's guide (2010, 75 pages) and other facilitator materials (quantity discounts available).
Time: [15-20] minutes.
Comments: Previously titled KEYS to Creativity; new edition of manual; assessment content has not changed.
Authors: Teresa M. Amabile and Center for Creative Leadership.
Publisher: Center for Creative Leadership.

Cross References: For a review by Carolyn M. Callahan of KEYS to Creativity, see 14:195; see also T5:1393 (1 reference).

[1075]
Khan-Lewis Phonological Analysis, Third Edition.

Purpose: Designed "to analyze an individual's production of target words for any sound changes and to identify the phonological processes used to produce those sound changes."
Population: Ages 2-0 through 21-11.
Publication Dates: 1986-2015.
Acronym: KLPA-3.
Scores, 13: 12 Core Phonological Processes: Manner (Deaffrication, Gliding of Liquids, Stopping of Fricatives and Affricates, Stridency Deletion, Vocalization), Place (Palatal Fronting, Velar Fronting), Reduction (Cluster Simplification, Deletion of Final Consonant, Syllable Reduction), Voicing (Final Devoicing, Initial Voicing) plus Total Score.
Administration: Individual.
Price Data, 2015: $179 per kit including manual (2015, 192 pages) and 25 analysis forms; $99 per manual; $59 per 25 analysis forms; $39 per Sound Change Booklet.
Time: (10-30) minutes.
Comments: A companion tool to the Goldman-Fristoe Test of Articulation 3 (GFTA-3; 862); scores based on completely transcribed responses to the Sounds-in-Words subtest of the GFTA-3; to complete the KLPA-3, examiner needs both complete KLPA-3 kit and GFTA-3 stimulus book; although not used to derive the standard score, analyses of Supplemental Phonological Processes and Other Phonological Processes may be conducted along with Vowel Analysis and Consonant Analysis.
Authors: Linda M. L. Khan and Nancy P. Lewis.
Publisher: Pearson.
Cross References: Reviews are scheduled for *The Twentieth Mental Measurements Yearbook*. For reviews by Carlos Inchaurralde and Steven Long of the second edition, see 16:127; see also T5:1394 (13 references) and T4:1356 (1 reference); for a review by Donald E. Mowrer of the original edition, see 10:164.

[1076]
Khatena-Morse Multitalent Perception Inventory.

Purpose: Identifies giftedness in music, art, and leadership.
Population: Age 6–adult.
Publication Dates: 1985–1994.
Acronym: KMMPI.
Scores, 6: Artistic, Musical, Creative Imagination, Initiative, Leadership, Versatility.
Administration: Group.
Forms, 2: A, B.

Price Data, 2015: $60 per starter set (Form A or Form B) including scoring and administration guide/norms-technical manual, 35 questionnaires, and 35 profile charts; $30 per 35 questionnaires and 35 profile charts (Form A or Form B); $30 per scoring and administration guide/norms-technical manual.
Time: (30–45) minutes.
Authors: Joe Khatena and David T. Morse.
Publisher: Scholastic Testing Service, Inc.
Cross References: For reviews by Carolyn M. Callahan and William Steve Lang, see 13:169.

[1077]

Khatena-Torrance Creative Perception Inventory.

Purpose: Developed as measures of creative personality.
Population: Age 12–adult.
Publication Dates: 1976–1998.
Acronym: KTCPI.
Administration: Group.
Price Data, 2015: $42 per 35 SAM checklists, 35 WKOPAY checklists, and 35 scoring worksheets.
Time: (10–20) minutes per checklist.
Comments: Includes 2 self-report checklists designed to identify candidates for creativity programs.
Publisher: Scholastic Testing Service, Inc.
  a) WHAT KIND OF PERSON ARE YOU?
  Purpose: Designed to "yield an index of the individual's disposition or motivation to function in creative ways."
  Acronym: WKOPAY?
  Scores: 5 factors: Acceptance of Authority, Self-Confidence, Inquisitiveness, Awareness of Others, Disciplined Imagination.
  Author: E. Paul Torrance.
  b) SOMETHING ABOUT MYSELF.
  Purpose: Designed as an autobiographical "screening device for the identification of creative people."
  Acronym: SAM.
  Scores: 6 factors: Environmental Sensitivity, Initiative, Self-Strength, Intellectuality, Individuality, Artistry.
  Author: Joe Khatena.
Cross References: For reviews by Carolyn M. Callahan and Gregory Schraw, see 16:128; see also T5:1396 (5 references); for reviews by David L. Bolton and William Steve Lang of a previous edition, see 13:168 (2 references); for a review by Philip E. Vernon of an earlier edition, see 9:569 (3 references).

[1078]

Kilmann-Saxton Culture-Gap Survey [Revised].

Purpose: Assesses "actual versus desired cultural norms."
Population: Work team members, employees.
Publication Dates: 1983–1991.
Acronym: CGS.
Scores, 4: Task Support, Social Relationships, Task Innovation, Personal Freedom.

Administration: Group.
Price Data, 2016: $25 per online survey; $12.95 per print booklet.
Time: (30) minutes.
Authors: Ralph H. Kilmann and Mary J. Saxton.
Publisher: Kilmann Diagnostics.
Cross References: For reviews by Russell N. Carney and Norman D. Sundberg, see 13:170; for reviews by Andres Barona and Gargi Roysircar Sodowsky of an earlier edition, see 11:192.

[1079]

Kilmanns Organizational Belief Survey.

Purpose: Assesses beliefs about one's level of control in their organizational surroundings.
Population: Employees.
Publication Date: 1991.
Scores, 8: Control Score, My Work Group, My Department, My Organization, Individual Profile, Work Group Profile, Department Profile, Organizational Profile.
Administration: Group.
Price Data, 2016: $12.95 per questionnaire/booklet.
Time: Administration time not reported.
Comments: A component of the Workshop for Implementing the Five Tracks, part of a completely integrated set of materials for creating and maintaining long-term organizational success; self-scored.
Authors: Ralph H. Kilmann and Ines Kilmann.
Publisher: Kilmann Diagnostics.

[1080]

Kindergarten Diagnostic Instrument—Second Edition.

Purpose: "Designed to assess developmental readiness skills in children."
Population: Children ages 4–6 years or older children with known or suspected developmental delays.
Publication Date: 2000.
Acronym: KDI-2.
Scores, 22: 13 subtest scores (Body Awareness, Concept Mastery, Form/Letter Identification, General Information, Gross Motor, Memory for Sentences, Number Skills, Phonemic Awareness, Verbal Associations, Visual Discrimination, Visual Memory, Visual-Motor Integration, Vocabulary), 6 subskills (Form Identification, Letter Identification, Verbal Associations—Similarities, Verbal Associations—Opposites, Visual Discrimination—Similarities, Visual Discrimination—Differences), Nonverbal Factor Score, Verbal Factor Score, Total Test Score.
Administration: Individual.
Price Data, 2016: $275 per complete test kit including administration manual (146 pages), 3 stimulus booklets, 13 1-inch wooden blocks, and 25 student response booklets in a carrying case; $45 per 25 student response booklets; $300 per KDI-2 Scoring Program for

Windows (one-time license fee, additional cost applies for sites screening more than 300 children annually); quantity discounts available on all items.
Time: (35–45) minutes.
Comments: KDI-2 Scoring Program for Windows stores students' pre-kindergarten and kindergarten data, generates local schoolwide norms, assesses performance compared to local norms, generates individual reports, test-retest reports; contact publisher for KDI-2 Scoring Program system requirements.
Authors: Daniel C. Miller.
Publisher: Schoolhouse Educational Services, LLC.
Cross References: For reviews by Glen P. Aylward and Lisa F. Smith, see 16:129.

[1081]

Kindergarten Essential Skills Assessment.

Purpose: "Designed to measure the critical skills that predict end-of-year kindergarten success" in order "to identify children who are at risk for academic failure."
Population: Ages 4:0 through 5:11.
Publication Dates: 2000-2015.
Acronym: KESA.
Score: Total score only.
Administration: Individual.
Price Data, 2015: $169 per kit including manual (2015, 108 pages), 25 record forms, 25 examinee workbooks, test plates, timer, transparency, 8 building blocks, 1" masking tape, and 8 crayon box in messenger bag; $50 per 25 record forms; $40 per test plates, $70 per manual; $40 per 25 examinee workbooks.
Time: (25-30) minutes.
Comments: "A revision and expansion of the Pre-Kindergarten Screen."
Authors: Raymond E. Webster and Angela H. Matthews.
Publisher: Academic Therapy Publications.
Cross References: Reviews are scheduled for *The Twentieth Mental Measurements Yearbook*. For reviews by Mary M. Chittooran and Mary Lou Kelley of an earlier edition titled Pre-Kindergarten Screen, see 15:194.

[1082]

Kindergarten Language Screening Test, Second Edition.

Purpose: Designed to help identify children "who need further diagnostic testing to determine whether or not they have language deficits that will accelerate academic failure."
Population: Ages 4-0 through 6-11.
Publication Dates: 1978–1998.
Acronym: KLST-2.
Scores: Total score only.
Administration: Individual.
Price Data, 2015: $157 per complete kit including examiner's manual (1998, 30 pages), 50 profile/examiner

record forms, picture book, and 3 picture cards; $48 per examiner's manual; $56 per 50 profile/examiner record forms; $48 per picture book; $16 per 3 picture cards.
Time: (5) minutes.
Authors: Sharon V. Gauthier and Charles L. Madison.
Publisher: PRO-ED.
Cross References: For reviews by Timothy R. Konold and Leslie Eastman Lukin, see 14:196; see also T4:1359 (2 references).

[1083]

Kindergarten Readiness Test [Slosson Educational Publications, Inc.].

Purpose: Determines the readiness of children to begin kindergarten.
Population: Ages 4–6.
Publication Date: 1988.
Acronym: KRT.
Scores: Total score only.
Administration: Individual.
Price Data, 2016: $205 per complete kit; $68 per manual (39 pages); $102.50 per 25 test booklets; $26.75 per 25 performance grid sheets; $26.75 per 25 letter to parent; $26.75 per 25 scoring interpretation; $37.50 per stimulus items.
Time: (15) minutes.
Authors: Sue L. Larson and Gary J. Vitali.
Publisher: Slosson Educational Publications, Inc.
Cross References: For reviews by Michael D. Beck and by Rosemary E. Sutton and Catharine C. Knight, see 12:207.

[1084]

Kindergarten Readiness Test, Second Edition [Scholastic Testing Service, Inc.].

Purpose: Designed to "assist in determining a student's readiness for beginning kindergarten."
Population: Children who are at the end of preschool or before their third full week of kindergarten.
Publication Dates: 2006-2015.
Acronym: KRT.
Scores, 9: Letter Recognition, Visual Discrimination, Phonemic Awareness, Listening Comprehension, Vocabulary, Numbers and Operations, Measurement, Geometric Concepts, Overall Readiness.
Administration: Individual.
Restricted Distribution: Sold only to schools and school districts.
Price Data, 2016: $61 per starter set including user's manual (2014, 22 pages), answer key, and 20 test booklets; $48.75 per 20 test booklets; $15.50 per user's manual; $4.35 per answer key; $22 per 20 parent/teacher reports for presenting test results to parents.
Time: (45) minutes total in 2 sessions.

Comments: May be administered to small groups of up to 3 students; test publisher recommends that test be administered in 2 sittings on 2 mornings.
Author: Scholastic Testing Service, Inc.
Publisher: Scholastic Testing Service, Inc.
Cross References: Reviews are scheduled for *The Twentieth Mental Measurements Yearbook.* For reviews by Kathleen M. Johnson and by Mark E. Swerdlik and Kathryn E. Hoff of the original edition, see 18:64.

[1085]
Kinetic Drawing System for Family and School: A Handbook.

Purpose: Designed "as a projective technique which assesses a child's perceptions of relationships among the child, peers, family, school, and significant others."
Population: Ages 5-20.
Publication Date: 1985.
Scores: 5 diagnostic categories: Actions of and Between Figures, Figure Characteristics, Position/Distance/Barriers, Style, Symbols.
Administration: Individual.
Price Data, 2016: $101.50 per complete kit including 25 scoring booklets and handbook (65 pages); $48 per 25 scoring booklets.
Time: (20-40) minutes.
Comments: A combination of the Kinetic Family Drawing and Kinetic School Drawing.
Authors: Howard M. Knoff and H. Thompson Prout (handbook).
Publisher: Western Psychological Services.
Cross References: See T5:1401 (4 references) and T4:1362 (2 references); for reviews by Bert P. Cundick and Richard A. Weinberg, see 10:166 (4 references).

[1086]
Kirton Adaption-Innovation Inventory [2003 Edition].

Purpose: Designed as a measure of one's preferred cognitive style of problem solving (creativity and decision making) so that one can distinguish between cognitive style and capacity.
Population: British and U.S. adults and teenagers over age 14.
Publication Dates: 1976–2003.
Acronym: KAI.
Scores, 4: Sufficiency v. Proliferation of Originality, Efficiency, Rule/Group Conformity, Total.
Administration: Individual or group.
Price Data, 2016: $320 per 50 inventories (minimum order) including feedback booklets and delivery (volume discounts available); manual (200 pages) given in certification course; $125 per book Adaption-Innovation In the Context of Diversity and Change (2003; reprinted 2011, 410 pages); $125 per book Adaptors & Innovators.

Foreign Language Editions: Translations available in Dutch, French, Italian, Portuguese, Slovak, and Spanish.
Time: (10-15) minutes.
Comments: See publisher website (www.kaicentre.com) for expanded information on theory and research and for access to extensive reference/publication list; administered via paper and pencil and online.
Author: M. J. Kirton.
Publisher: Occupational Research Centre [England].
Cross References: For reviews by Lynn L. Brown and Ric Brown of the 1998 Edition, see 14:198; see also T5:1404 (15 references) and T4:1364 (9 references); for reviews by Gregory J. Boyle and Gerald E. DeMauro of an earlier (1977) edition, see 11:193 (8 references).

[1087]
Kit of Factor Referenced Cognitive Tests.

Purpose: "To provide research workers with a means of identifying certain aptitude factors in factor-analytic studies."
Population: Various grades 6-college level.
Publication Dates: 1954–1978.
Administration: Group.
Price Data, 2016: $45 per complete set including 72 tests and manual (1976, 230 pages); a license agreement is required for the use of the tests ($.15 per copy with a minimum of $40 for graduate students, $.30 a copy with a minimum of $55 for other researchers).
Time: Administration time given separately for each test.
Comments: Formerly called the Kit of Reference Tests for Cognitive Factors.
Authors: Tests and manual written by Ruth B. Ekstrom, John W. French, Harry H. Harman, and Diran Dermen.
Publisher: Educational Testing Service.
- *a)* FACTOR CF: FLEXIBILITY OF CLOSURE.
  - 1) *Hidden Figures Test.*
  - 2) *Hidden Patterns Test.*
  - 3) *Copying Test.*
- *b)* FACTOR CS: SPEED OF CLOSURE.
  - 1) *Gestalt Completion Test.*
  - 2) *Concealed Words Test.*
  - 3) *Snowy Pictures.*
- *c)* FACTOR CV: VERBAL CLOSURE.
  - 1) *Scrambled Words.*
  - 2) *Hidden Words.*
  - 3) *Incomplete Words.*
- *d)* FACTOR FA: ASSOCIATIONAL FLUENCY.
  - 1) *Controlled Associations Test.*
  - 2) *Opposites Test.*
  - 3) *Figures of Speech.*
- *e)* FACTOR FE: EXPRESSIONAL FLUENCY.
  - 1) *Making Sentences.*
  - 2) *Arranging Words.*
  - 3) *Rewriting.*
- *f)* FACTOR FF: FIGURAL FLUENCY.
  - 1) *Ornamentation Test.*
  - 2) *Elaboration Test.*
  - 3) *Symbols Test.*

g) FACTOR FI: IDEATIONAL FLUENCY.
  1) *Topics Test.*
  2) *Theme Test.*
  3) *Thing Categories Test.*
h) FACTOR FW: WORD FLUENCY.
  1) *Word Endings Test.*
  2) *Word Beginnings Test.*
  3) *Word Beginnings and Endings Test.*
i) FACTOR I: INDUCTION.
  1) *Letter Sets Test.*
  2) *Locations Test.*
  3) *Figure Classifications.*
j) FACTOR IP: INTEGRATIVE PROCESSES.
  1) *Calendar Test.*
  2) *Following Directions.*
k) FACTOR MA: ASSOCIATIVE MEMORY.
  1) *Picture-Number Test.*
  2) *Object-Number Test.*
  3) *First and Last Names Test.*
l) FACTOR MS: MEMORY SPAN.
  1) *Auditory Number Span Test.*
  2) *Visual Number Span Test.*
  3) *Auditory Letter Span Test.*
m) FACTOR MV: VISUAL MEMORY.
  1) *Shape Memory Test.*
  2) *Building Memory.*
  3) *Map Memory.*
n) FACTOR N: NUMBER.
  1) *Addition Test.*
  2) *Division Test.*
  3) *Subtraction and Multiplication Test.*
  4) *Addition and Subtraction Correction.*
o) FACTOR P: PERCEPTUAL SPEED.
  1) *Finding A's Test.*
  2) *Number Comparison Test.*
  3) *Identical Pictures Test.*
p) FACTOR RG: GENERAL REASONING.
  1) *Arithmetic Aptitude Test.*
  2) *Mathematics Aptitude Test.*
  3) *Necessary Arithmetic Operations Test.*
q) FACTOR RL: LOGICAL REASONING.
  1) *Nonsense Syllogisms Test.*
  2) *Diagramming Relationships.*
  3) *Inference Test.*
  4) *Deciphering Languages.*
r) FACTOR S: SPATIAL ORIENTATION.
  1) *Card Rotations Test.*
  2) *Cube Comparisons Test.*
s) FACTOR SS: SPATIAL SCANNING.
  1) *Maze Tracing Speed Test.*
  2) *Choosing a Path.*
  3) *Map Planning Test.*
t) FACTOR V: VERBAL COMPREHENSION.
  1) *Vocabulary Test I.*
  2) *Vocabulary Test II.*
  3) *Extended Range Vocabulary Test.*
  4) *Advanced Vocabulary Test I.*
  5) *Advanced Vocabulary Test II.*
u) FACTOR VZ: VISUALIZATION.
  1) *Form Board Test.*
  2) *Paper Folding Test.*
  3) *Surface Development Test.*
v) FACTOR XF: FIGURAL FLEXIBILITY.
  1) *Toothpicks Test.*
  2) *Planning Patterns.*
  3) *Storage Test.*
w) FACTOR XU: FLEXIBILITY OF USE.
  1) *Combining Objects.*
  2) *Substitute Uses.*
  3) *Making Groups.*
  4) *Different Uses.*

Cross References: See T5:1405 (40 references), T4:1365 (92 references), 9:572 (27 references), T3:1257 (78 references), and T2:561 (103 references).

[1088]

Klein Group Instrument® for Effective Leadership and Participation in Teams.

Purpose: Designed "to assess a range of behaviors that are essential for effective leadership and teamwork."
Population: Team and group participants of ages 14+.
Publication Date: 2008.
Acronym: KGI®.
Scores, 13: Leadership (Assertiveness, Group Facilitation, Initiative, Total), Negotiation Orientation (Perspective Taking, Constructive Negotiation Approach, Total), Task Focus (Task Analysis, Task Implementation, Total), Interpersonal Focus (Positive Group Affiliation, Feeling Orientation, Total).
Administration: Group or Individual.
Price Data, 2015: $30 per individual online administration including a downloadable User's Guide and Individual Profile of results; $50 per group online administration (plus $25 per group member) including a downloadable User's Guide, Individual Profile, and Group Profile per group member, and 1 downloadable administration manual per group; $50 per administration manual (138 pages).
Time: (25-30) minutes.
Comments: Available online.
Author: Robert R. Klein.
Publisher: Center for Applications of Psychological Type, Inc.
Cross References: For reviews by Philip G. Benson and Myra N. Womble, see 18:65.

[1089]

Knox's Cube Test-Revised.

Purpose: A nonverbal mental test designed to measure attention span and memory of children and adults.
Population: Ages 3 and over.
Publication Dates: 1980–2002.
Acronym: KCT-R.
Scores: Total score only.
Administration: Individual.
Price Data, 2015: $105 per complete kit including manual, tapping cubes, and 15 test/record booklets; $25 per 15 report booklets.

Time: (10-15) minutes.
Comments: Items unchanged from previous edition; Junior and Senior forms have been eliminated.
Author: Mark H. Stone.
Publisher: Stoelting Co.
Cross References: For reviews by Carolyn M. Callahan and Anita M. Hubley, see 16:131; see also T5:1407 (5 references) and T4:1367 (7 references); for reviews by Raymond S. Dean and Jerome M. Sattler of the previous edition, see 9:574 (2 references).

[1090]

Kohlberg's Moral Judgment Interview.

Purpose: To identify stages of moral development.
Population: Ages 10 and over.
Publication Date: 1983.
Scores: Moral Development Stages.
Price Data: Available from publisher.
Time: Administration time not reported.
Authors: Anne Colby and Lawrence Kohlberg.
Publisher: Cambridge University Press.
Cross References: See T5:1408 (9 references), T4:1368 (9 references), and T3:1262 (2 references).

[1091]

The Kohlman Evaluation of Living Skills.

Purpose: "An occupational therapy evaluation that is designed to determine a person's ability to function in basic living skills."
Population: Occupational therapy clients with living skill deficits.
Publication Dates: 1981–1992.
Acronym: KELS.
Scores: 5 areas: Self-care, Safety and Health, Money Management, Transportation and Telephone, Work and Leisure.
Administration: Individual.
Price Data, 2016: $140 per book.
Time: (30–45) minutes.
Comments: Evaluation combines interview questions and tasks; can be used with the elderly, with persons who have cognitively disabling conditions, in court for the determination of commitment, and in discharge planning at acute-care hospitals.
Author: Linda Kohlman Thomson.
Publisher: The American Occupational Therapy Association, Inc.
Cross References: For a review by Gabriele van Lingen, see 14:199.

[1092]

The Kohs Block-Design Test.

Purpose: Designed as "performance tests that have been standardized to measure intelligence."
Population: Mental ages 5–20.

Publication Date: [1919].
Scores: Total score only.
Administration: Individual.
Price Data, 2015: $140 per complete kit including cubes, cards, manual (20 pages), and 50 record blanks; $25 per 50 record blanks; $20 per set of design cards; $115 per set of blocks; $25 per manual.
Time: (30-40) minutes.
Comments: Formerly called The Block-Design Test; modifications appear in Arthur Point Scale of Performance Tests, New Guinea Performance Scales, Ohwaki-Kohs Tactile Block Design Intelligence Test for the Blind, and Pacific Design Construction Test.
Author: S. C. Kohs.
Publisher: Stoelting Co.
Cross References: See T5:1410 (4 references), T4:1370 (5 references), T3:1265 (4 references), and T2:545 (74 references).

[1093]

Kolbe Index.

Purpose: Designed to focus on the "predisposition of a subject to respond to specific behavioral settings with certain patterns of behavior."
Publication Dates: 1987–1997.
Administration: Group or individual.
Price Data: Available from publisher.
Foreign Language Editions: Available in French, German, and Spanish.
Comments: A series of instruments designed to enhance personnel selection and increase self-awareness about instructive talent and potential.
Author: Kathy Kolbe.
Publisher: Kolbe Corp.
   a) KOLBE A™ INDEX.
   Purpose: Designed to measure conative style.
   Population: Adults.
   Acronym: KCI-A.
   Scores, 4: Fact Finder, Follow Thru, Quick Start, Implementor.
   Time: (25) minutes.
   b) KOLBE B™ INDEX.
   Purpose: Designed to "identify the characteristics perceived as necessary to succeed in a given job."
   Population: Job applicants.
   Acronym: KCI-B.
   Time: (15–20) minutes.
   c) KOLBE C™ INDEX.
   Purpose: Designed to "identify the characteristics necessary to function successfully in a specific job."
   Population: Supervisors.
   Acronym: KCI-C.
   d) KOLBE Y™ INDEX.
   Purpose: Designed to assist the respondent in identifying his/her "talent for certain types of activities."
   Population: Youth (5th grade reading level).
   Acronym: KCI-Y.
Cross References: For reviews by Raoul A. Arreola and Chockalingam Viswesvaran, see 14:200; for reviews

by Collie Wyatt Conoley and Frank Gresham of an earlier edition, see 12:208.

[1094]

Koppitz Developmental Scoring System for the Bender Gestalt Test, Second Edition.

Purpose: Designed "to document the presence and degree of visual-motor difficulties in individual examinees."
Population: Ages 5-7, 8-85+.
Publication Dates: 1963-2007.
Acronym: KOPPITZ-2.
Scores: Total score only.
Administration: Individual.
Levels, 2: Ages 5-7, 8-85+.
Price Data, 2015: $249 per complete kit including 25 examiner record forms ages 5-7, 25 examiner record forms ages 8-85+, 25 emotional indicators record forms, Bender Gestalt II stimulus cards, examiner's manual (2007, 192 pages), and scoring template; $47 per 25 examiner record forms (specify ages 5-7 or 8-85+); $30 per 25 emotional indicators record forms; $64 per Bender Gestalt II stimulus cards set; $95 per examiner's manual (2007, 200 pages); $12 per scoring template.
Time: (6-20) minutes.
Comments: An update of the Bender Gestalt Test for Young Children; current edition utilizes drawings from the Bender Visual-Motor Gestalt Test, Second Edition (16:30).
Author: Cecil R. Reynolds.
Publisher: PRO-ED.
Cross References: For reviews by Joseph C. Kush and Katharine A. Snyder, see 18:66.

[1095]

Krantz Health Opinion Survey.

Purpose: "To measure attitudes toward different treatment approaches."
Population: College, healthy adults, and chronic disease populations.
Publication Date: 1980.
Acronym: KHOS.
Scores, 3: Information, Behavioral Involvement, Total.
Administration: Group.
Manual: No manual.
Price Data: Test materials now available free of charge from author.
Foreign Language Edition: Swedish version available.
Time: (10-15) minutes.
Authors: David S. Krantz, Andrew Baum, and Margaret V. Wideman.
Publisher: David S. Krantz.
Cross References: See T5:1412 (4 references) and T4:1373 (1 reference); for a review by James A. Blumenthal, see 9:578 (1 reference); see also T3:1267 (1 reference).

[1096]

Kuder Career Interests Assessment.

Purpose: Designed to "determine the relative level of interest a respondent has in each of six Holland areas of interest" to suggest possibly satisfying occupations.
Population: Middle school students to adults.
Publication Date: 2012.
Acronym: KCIA.
Scores, 6: Realistic, Investigative, Artistic, Social, Enterprising, Conventional.
Administration: Individual or group.
Forms, 2: KCIA-32, KCIA-L (Likert).
Price Data: Available from publisher.
Time: (10) minutes.
Authors: Frederic Kuder and Donald G. Zytowski.
Publisher: Kuder, Inc.

[1097]

Kuder Skills Confidence Assessment.

Purpose: Designed to "determine the relative self-efficacy of respondent in each of six areas" to identify possibly satisfying occupations.
Population: Middle school students through adults.
Publication Date: 2012.
Acronym: KSCA.
Scores, 6: Realistic, Investigative, Artistic, Social, Enterprising, Conventional.
Administration: Individual or group.
Levels, 2: Kuder Skills Confidence Assessment, Kuder Skills Confidence Assessment–Adult.
Price Data: Available from publisher.
Time: (7) minutes.
Authors: Donald G. Zytowski and Darrell Luzzo.
Publisher: Kuder, Inc.

[1098]

Kuhlmann-Anderson Tests, Eighth Edition.

Purpose: "Designed to provide a measure of an individual's academic potential through assessing cognitive skills related to the learning process."
Population: Grades K, 1, 2–3, 3–4, 5–6, 7–9, 9–12.
Publication Dates: 1927–1982.
Acronym: KA.
Scores, 6: 3 raw scores (Verbal, Nonverbal, Full) and 3 derived scores.
Administration: Group.
Price Data: Available from publisher.
Levels, 7: K, A, BC, CD, EF, G, and H.
Manual: Separate manual of directions for each level.
Authors: F. Kuhlmann (fourth and earlier editions) and Rose G. Anderson.
Publisher: Scholastic Testing Service, Inc.
   a) LEVEL K.
   Population: Kindergarten.
   Time: 28(50–75) minutes in 2 days.

b) LEVEL A.
Population: Grade 1.
Time: 28(50–75) minutes in 2 days.
c) LEVEL BC.
Population: Grades 2, 3.
Time: 28(50–75) minutes in 2 days.
d) LEVEL CD.
Population: Grades 3, 4.
Time: 35(50–75) minutes.
e) LEVEL EF.
Population: Grades 5, 6.
Time: 40(50–75) minutes.
f) LEVEL G.
Population: Grades 7–9.
Time: 40(50–75) minutes.
g) LEVEL H.
Population: Grades 9–12.
Time: 40(50–75) minutes.
Cross References: See T4:1377 (2 references); for reviews by Michael D. Hiscox and Ronald C. Rodgers, see 9:579 (2 references); see T3:1272 (13 references) and T2:398 (53 references); for reviews by William B. Michael and Douglas A. Pidgeon, and an excerpted review by Frederick B. Davis of the seventh edition, see 6:466 (11 references); see also 5:348 (15 references); for reviews by Henry E. Garrett and David Segel of an earlier edition, see 5:302 (10 references); for reviews by W. G. Emmett and Stanley S. Maryolf, see 3:236 (25 references); for a review by Henry E. Garrett, see 2:1404 (15 references); for reviews by Psyche Cattell, S. A. Courtis, and Austin H. Turney, see 1:1049.

[1099]
Language Arts Objective Sequence.

Purpose: "Helps evaluate students' current [language arts] performance levels and identify specific goals and objectives."
Population: Grades 1–12.
Publication Date: 2001.
Scores: 9 ratings/objectives: Readiness (Level 3), Listening (Levels 3, 2), Speaking (Levels 3, 2, 1), Reading—Word Recognition (Level 3), Reading—Comprehension (Levels 3, 2, 1), Writing—Handwriting (Level 3), Writing—Spelling (Levels 3, 2), Writing Process (Levels 3, 2, 1), Writing—Grammar (Levels 3, 2, 1).
Administration: Individual.
Levels, 3: 1, 2, 3.
Price Data, 2015: $36 per assessment manual (120 pages) including 24 reproducible forms and checklists.
Time: Administration time not reported.
Comments: Intended to be used by teachers as an informal "curriculum guide, bank of objectives, rubric guide, or structured observation system"; some objectives do not include all 3 levels.
Authors: Jacqueline Robertson and Sheldon Braaten.
Publisher: Behavioral Institute for Children and Adolescents.

[1100]
Language Assessment Scales, 2nd Edition—Oral.

Purpose: Designed to "measure those English and language skills necessary for functioning in a mainstream academic environment."
Population: Grades 1–6, 7-12.
Publication Dates: 1987–1991.
Acronym: LAS-O.
Scores, 6: Vocabulary, Listening Comprehension, Story Retelling, Minimal Sound Pairs, Phonemes, Total.
Administration: Individual.
Levels, 2: 1, 2.
Parts, 2: Oral Language (for Level 1 & 2), Pronunciation (for Grades 2–12).
Forms, 2: C, D.
Price Data: Available from publisher.
Foreign Language Edition: Spanish edition (1990) available.
Time: [15] minutes.
Comments: Language Proficiency Score also incorporates Language Assessment Scales, Reading and Writing. The test publisher has indicated there is a newer edition of this test; description will be updated when complete test materials are received.
Authors: Edward A. DeAvila and Sharon E. Duncan.
Publisher: DRC.
Cross References: See T5:1420 (1 references); for reviews by Natalie L. Hedberg and Pamela S. Tidwell, see 12:210 (1 reference); for a review of the Language Assessment Scales by Lyn Haber, see 9:584 (1 reference).

[1101]
Language Assessment Scales, 2nd Edition, Reading and Writing.

Purpose: Designed to measure "English language skills in reading and writing necessary for functioning in a mainstream academic environment."
Population: Language-minority students in Grades 2–3, 4–6, 7–11.
Publication Dates: 1988–2000.
Acronym: LAW R/W.
Scores, 3: Reading, Writing, Total.
Administration: Group.
Levels, 3: 1, 2, 3.
Forms, 2: A, B.
Price Data: Available from publisher.
Time: (50–75) minutes for Level 1; (49–87) minutes for Level 2; (53–86) minutes for Level 3.
Comments: May be used in conjunction with LAS Oral, 2nd Edition. The test publisher has indicated there is a newer edition of this test; description will be updated when complete test materials are received.
Authors: Sharon E. Duncan and Edward A. DeAvila.
Publisher: DRC.

Cross References: See T5:1421 (4 references); for reviews by C. Dale Carpenter and Thomas W. Guyette, see 12:211; see also T4:1386 (5 references).

[1102]

Language Assessment Skills Links Benchmark Assessment.

Purpose: Designed to "measure students' skills in speaking, listening, reading and writing."
Population: Grades K-12.
Publication Date: 2005.
Acronym: LAS Links Benchmark Assessment.
Scores, 6: Speaking, Listening, Reading, Writing, Comprehension, Oral.
Administration: Individual or group.
Levels, 5: Grades K-1; Grades 2-3; Grades 4-5; Grades 6-8; Grades 9-12.
Price Data, 2016: $38.30 per 10 student books; $22.55 per student answer documents (specify book number and grades); $22.40 per examiner's guide (99-111 pages, specify level); $26.20 per 10 student profile sheets (specify grades).
Comments: Test is designed for English language learners.
Author: CTB/McGraw-Hill.
Publisher: DRC.
 a) SPEAKING.
 Time: (2-8) minutes.
 Subtests, 4: Speak in Words, Speak in Sentences, Make Conversation, Tell a Story.
 b) LISTENING.
 Time: (5-15) minutes.
 Subtests, 3: Listen for Information, Listen in the Classroom, Listen/Comprehend.
 c) READING.
 Time: (10-20) minutes.
 Subtests, 3: Analyze Words, Read Words, Read for Understanding.
 d) WRITING.
 Time: (5-15) minutes.
 Subtests, 3-4: Use Conventions, Write About, Write Why, Write in Detail (not included in Grades K-1).

[1103]

Language Assessment Skills Links K-12 Assessments.

Purpose: Designed to "measure students' skills in speaking, listening, reading, writing, and comprehension."
Population: Grades K-12.
Publication Date: 2005.
Acronym: LAS Links K-12.
Scores, 7: Speaking, Listening, Reading, Writing, Overall, Comprehension, Oral.
Levels, 5: Grades K-1; Grades 2-3; Grades 4-5; Grades 6-8; Grades 9-12.
Price Data: Available from publisher.

Comments: Test is designed for English language learners. The test publisher has indicated there is a newer edition of this test; description will be updated when complete test materials are received.
Author: CTB/McGraw-Hill.
Publisher: DRC.
 a) SPEAKING.
 Administration: Individual.
 Time: (5-15) minutes.
 Subtests, 4: Speak in Words, Speak in Sentences, Make Conversation, Tell a Story.
 b) LISTENING.
 Administration: Individual or group.
 Time: (10-20) minutes.
 Subtests, 3: Listen for Information, Listen in the Classroom, Listen/Comprehend.
 c) READING.
 Administration: Individual or group.
 Time: (35-45) minutes.
 Subtests, 3: Analyze Words, Read Words, Read for Understanding.
 d) WRITING.
 Administration: Individual or group.
 Time: (35-45) minutes.
 Subtests, 3: Use Conventions, Write About, Write Why, Write in Detail [not included in Grades K-1].

[1104]

Language Processing Test 3: Elementary.

Purpose: Designed to identify "students' language processing strengths and weaknesses in a hierarchical framework."
Population: Ages 5-0 to 11-11.
Publication Dates: 1985-2005.
Acronym: LPT-3:E.
Scores, 8: Labeling, Stating Functions, Associations, Categorization, Similarities, Differences, Multiple Meanings, Attributes.
Administration: Individual.
Price Data, 2016: $159.95 per kit including examiner's manual and 20 test forms; $41.95 per 20 forms.
Time: (35) minutes.
Authors: Gail J. Richard and Mary Anne Hanner.
Publisher: PRO-ED.
Cross References: For a review by Natalie Rathvon, see 17:103; see also T5:1424 (5 references); for reviews by Thomas W. Guyette and Lyn Haber of an earlier edition, see 10:169.

[1105]

Language Proficiency Test Series.

Purpose: Designed to aid in student placement and the evaluation of student language proficiency in reading, writing, listening, and speaking.
Population: Grades K–12, specifically ELL students.
Publication Dates: 1998-2001.
Acronym: LPTS.
Scores, 3: Reading, Writing, Listening/Speaking.
Administration: Individual or group.

Forms, 24: Listening/Speaking: L/S 1–Grades K–2, L/S 2—Grades 3–5, L/S 3—Grades 6–8, L/S 4—Grades 9–12, Reading: R1—Grades K–2, R2—Grades 3–5, R3—Grades 6–8, R4—Grades 9–12, Writing: W1—Grades K–2, W2—Grades 3–5, W3—Grades 6–8, W4—Grades 9–12; alternate forms available for all subjects and grade clusters.

Price Data, 2015: $32 per administrator's sample set including Administration and Scoring Guide plus one test booklet each for Reading, Writing, and Listening/Speaking at grade level of choice (K-2, 3–5, 6–8, or 9–12); $59.50 per 25 Grades K–2 or for Grades 3–5 (Form A or B) Reading Test booklets; $51.50 per 25 Grades 6–8 or Grades 9–12 (Form A or B) Reading Test booklets; $12.50 per 25 scannable answer sheets for Reading Test (Grades 6–12 only); $1.25 each for scoring Reading Test booklet; $26.50 per 25 Writing Test booklets (Grades K-2, 3–5, 6–8, or 9–12, Form A or B); $1.25–$2.30 each for scoring Writing Test booklet; $26.50 per 25 Listening/Speaking Test booklets (Grades K-2, 3–5, 6–8, or 9–12, Form A or B); $1.25–$2.85 each for scoring Listening/Speaking Test booklet; $59.50 per technical manual (2004, 36 pages).

Time: (25) minutes average per test.

Author: MetriTech, Inc.

Publisher: MetriTech, Inc.

Cross References: For reviews by Marie Miller-Whitehead and Judith A. Monsaas, see 15:134.

[1106]
Law Enforcement Applicant Inventory.

Purpose: Designed to "identify individuals who have the integrity and attitudes important to become model law enforcement officers and security personnel."

Population: Ages 18 and over.

Publication Dates: 1991–1996.

Acronym: LEAI.

Scores, 12: Honesty, Nonviolence, Drug Avoidance, Risk Avoidance, Safety, Stress Tolerance, Validity/Distortion, Validity/Accuracy, Candidate Potential Index, Criminal Justice Orientation, Background and Work Experience, Narrative Information.

Administration: Individual or group.

Price Data: Available from publisher.

Time: (30–45) minutes.

Comments: Test can be scored via Touch Test, Internet, or Optical Scanning Software.

Author: General Dynamics Information Technology.

Publisher: General Dynamics Information Technology.

[1107]
Law School Admission Test.

Purpose: "To measure skills that are considered essential for success in law school."

Population: Law school entrants.

Publication Dates: 1948–2015.

Acronym: LSAT.

Scores: Total score plus unscored writing sample.

Administration: Group.

Price Data, 2016: $175 per LSAT; $90 per late registration; $90 per test center change; $90 per test date change; $270 per nonpublished test center (U.S.A., Canada, Puerto Rico); $360 per nonpublished test center (all other countries); $100 per hand scoring.

Foreign Language Edition: A Spanish LSAT is administered once per year at 2 test centers in Puerto Rico for applicants to law schools in Puerto Rico only.

Time: 175 minutes; 35 minutes per writing sample.

Comments: Test administered 4 times annually (June, September/October, December, February) at centers established by the test publisher.

Author: Law School Admission Council, Inc.

Publisher: Law School Admission Council, Inc.

Cross References: See T5:1434 (2 references); for reviews by James B. Erdmann and by Robert F. Mc-Morris, Elizabeth L. Bringsjord, and Wei-Ping Liu, see 13:174 (8 references); see also T4:1400 (4 references); for a review by Gary B. Melton of an earlier edition, see 9:594 (2 references); see also T3:1292 (6 references), 8:1093 (7 references), and T2:2349 (7 references); for a review by Leo A. Munday of earlier forms, see 7:1098 (23 references); see also 5:928 (7 references); for a review by Alexander G. Wesman, see 4:815 (6 references).

[1108]
Leader Behavior Analysis II.

Purpose: Developed to assess leadership style.

Population: Middle and upper level managers.

Publication Date: 1991.

Acronym: LBAII.

Scores, 6: Style Flexibility, Style Effectiveness, Directing Style, Coaching Style, Supporting Style, Delegating Style.

Administration: Group.

Editions, 2: Self, Other.

Price Data: Available from publisher.

Time: [15-20] minutes.

Comments: Ratings by employees and self-ratings; instrument is available in conduction with Situational Leadership II Concepts program or SLII Experience.

Authors: Drea Zigarmi, Douglas Forsyth, Kenneth Blanchard, and Ronald Hambleton (tests).

Publisher: The Ken Blanchard Companies.

Cross References: See T5:1436 (1 reference); for reviews by H. John Bernardin and Donna K. Cooke and by Sharon McNeely, see 12:212; see also T4:1402 (1 reference).

[1109]
Leader Behavior Questionnaire, Revised.

Purpose: Constructed as a measure of "organizational leadership."

Population: Managers and employees.
Publication Dates: 1988–1996.
Acronym: LBQ.
Scores: Visionary Leadership Behavior Scales (Clear Leadership, Communicative Leadership, Consistent Leadership, Caring Leadership, Creative Leadership) Visionary Leadership Characteristics Scales (Confident Leadership, Empowered Leadership, Visionary Leadership), Visionary Culture Building Scales (Organizational Leadership, Cultural Leadership).
Administration: Group.
Forms, 2: Self, Other.
Price Data: Available from publisher.
Time: (10–20) minutes.
Author: Marshall Sashkin.
Publisher: HRD Press, Inc.
Cross References: For reviews by Janet Barnes-Farrell and Hilda Wing, see 14:202.

[1110]

Leader Efficacy Questionnaire.

Purpose: Designed to "assess leaders' perceptions of their own level of confidence in their capabilities" and for comparing how "self-ratings coincide with others' ratings of the level of leader efficacy they display."
Population: Adults.
Publication Date: 2013.
Acronym: LEQ.
Scores, 4: Leader Action Self-Efficacy, Leader Means Efficacy, Leader Self-Regulation Efficacy, Total.
Administration: Individual or group.
Forms, 2: Self Form, External Rating Form.
Manual: No manual.
Price Data, 2016: $5 per Transform Survey Hosting: Multi-rater Form ($100 set up fee); $2.40 per Transform Survey Hosting: Self Form (minimum 50); $2 per Remote Online Survey License (minimum 50); $2 per License to Reproduce (minimum 50).
Foreign Language Editions: Available in Indonesian and Korean.
Time: [5-10] minutes.
Authors: Sean T. Hannah and Bruce J. Avolio.
Publisher: Mind Garden, Inc.

[1111]

Leadership and Self-Development Scale.

Purpose: Measurement of the effectiveness of a leadership workshop for college women.
Population: College.
Publication Dates: 1976-1979.
Scores, 9: Assertiveness, Risk Taking, Self-Concept, Setting Goals, Decision Making, Obtaining a Followership, Conflict Resolution, Group Roles, Evaluation.
Administration: Group.
Manual: No manual; mimeographed research report (1976, 20 pages).

Price Data: Available in the Southern Illinois University Archives at the Morris Library at Southern Illinois University.
Time: Administration time not reported.
Authors: Virginia Hoffman and Patricia B. Elmore.
Publisher: Patricia B. Elmore.
Cross References: For a review by Robert R. McCrae, see 9:597; see also T3:1298 (2 references).

[1112]

Leadership Competencies for Managers.

Purpose: Designed to assess management development intended to add thought leadership to the traditional role.
Population: First-line and middle managers.
Publication Dates: 1998-2006.
Acronym: LCM.
Scores, 16: Envisioning Opportunities, Communicating Effectively, Innovation & Risk-Taking, Problem Solving & Decision Making, Planning and Collaboration, Managing Conflict, Team Development, Coaching, Providing Feedback, Standards of Performance, Personal Drive, Delegation, Goal Pressure, Recognition of Good Performance, Tension Level, Overall Effectiveness.
Administration: Individual.
Price Data: Available from publisher.
Time: 20-30 minutes.
Comments: Publisher suggests allowing 2-3 weeks to collect feedback.
Authors: Paul M. Connolly, Daniel Booth, and Clark L. Wilson.
Publisher: The Clark Wilson Group, Inc. (subsidiary of The Booth Company, Inc.).

[1113]

Leadership Development Report.

Purpose: "An expert system providing insight into how a manager's personality affects his or her performance and how to modify a manager's behavior within his or her natural limits."
Population: Adults.
Publication Dates: 1996–2000.
Acronym: LDR.
Scores, 34: Impulsivity, Understanding, Complexity, Risk Taking, Breadth of Interests, Innovation, Endurance, Cognitive Structure, Order, Organization, Play, Self-Esteem, Anxiety, Tolerance, Change, Achievement, Aggression, Responsibility, Abasement, Value Orthodoxy, Energy Level, Harm Avoidance, Affiliation, Dominance, Exhibition, Interpersonal Affect, Succorance, Social Participation, Social Adroitness, Conformity, Defendence, Social Recognition, Nurturance, Autonomy.
Administration: Group or individual.
Price Data, 2015: $25 per test manual; $6 per test booklet; $70-$98 (depending on volume) per report available through fax-in scoring system or online.
Time: 40 minutes.

Comments: Includes items from the Jackson Personality Inventory—Revised (1035), The Personality Research Form (1528), and The Survey of Work Styles (2030) (all still available for sale). The LDR can be administered in two ways: answer sheets can be faxed to publisher, bound reports are returned via courier or sent by email; or test can be administered and scored directly through a www.sigmatesting.com account.
Authors: Douglas N. Jackson and Julie Carswell.
Publisher: SIGMA Assessment Systems, Inc.
Cross References: For a review by Mark A. Staal, see 15:135.

[1114]

Leadership Effectiveness Analysis™.
Purpose: Developed to identify leadership skills and behaviors in a 360 degree context.
Population: Managers, supervisors, individual contributors at all levels.
Publication Dates: 1981–2001.
Acronym: LEA.
Scores, 23: Conservative, Innovative, Technical, Self, Strategic, Persuasive, Outgoing, Excitement, Restraint, Structuring, Tactical, Communication, Delegation, Control, Feedback, Management Focus, Dominant, Production, Cooperation, Consensual, Authority, Empathy, Exaggeration.
Administration: Group.
Price Data: Available from publisher.
Foreign Language Editions: Available in English (American), English (British), Czech, Chinese (Simplified characters), Chinese (Traditional characters), Danish, Dutch, Finnish, French, German, Italian, Japanese, Norwegian, Polish, Portuguese (Brazil), Spanish, and Swedish.
Time: (45) minutes.
Comments: Requires training by publisher before purchase and use.
Authors: James T. Mahoney (test) and Robert I. Kabacoff (manual).
Publisher: Management Research Group

[1115]

Leadership EQ.
Purpose: Designed to provide feedback for development programs for managers and staff professionals.
Population: Professionals responsible for initiating and leading change.
Publication Date: 2005.
Acronym: LEQ.
Scores, 15: Leadership Vision, Risk Taking, Organizational Effectiveness, Collaborative Planning, Talent Development, Communicates with Impact, Self-Awareness, Awareness of Others, Delivers Results, Push/Pressure, Self Management, Passion/Enthusiasm, Sharing Credit, Trustworthiness/Integrity, Effectiveness/Outcomes.

Administration: Individual.
Price Data: Available from publisher.
Time: 20-30 minutes.
Comments: Publisher suggests allowing 2-3 weeks to collect feedback.
Authors: Paul M. Connolly, Daniel Booth, and Clark L. Wilson.
Publisher: The Clark Wilson Group, Inc. (subsidiary of The Booth Company, Inc.).

[1116]

Leadership/Impact.
Purpose: Provides people in leadership with information about their current performance as well as insights into ways they can enhance their effectiveness through the leadership strategies they employ and the impact they have on others.
Population: Leaders at the executive level.
Publication Date: 1996.
Acronym: L/I.
Scores: 3 Dimensions of Effectiveness: Organizational Effectiveness, Personal Effectiveness, Balance; 12 Types of Impact on Others: Impact (Achievement, Self-Actualizing, Humanistic-Encouraging, Affiliative), Passive/Defensive (Approval, Conventional, Dependent, Avoidance), Aggressive/Defensive (Oppositional, Power, Competitive, Perfectionistic); 10 Domains of Leadership: Personal Focus (Envisioning, Role Modeling), Interpersonal Focus (Mentoring, Stimulating Thinking, Referring, Monitoring, Providing Feedback), Organizational Focus (Reinforcing, Influencing, Creating a Setting).
Administration: Individual or group.
Price Data: Available from publisher.
Foreign Language Editions: Available in Bulgarian, Chinese (Simplified), Chinese (Traditional), Danish, Dutch, French (Canadian), French (European), German, Hungarian, Japanese, Polish, Portuguese (European), Romanian, Serbian, Spanish (Castilian), Spanish (Latin American), and Swedish.
Time: Administration time not reported.
Comments: Ratings by self and at least three coworkers; in the United States, accreditation is required to purchase and debrief the assessment. The test publisher has indicated there is a newer edition of this test; description will be updated when complete test materials are received.
Author: Robert A. Cooke.
Publisher: Human Synergistics International.

[1117]

Leadership Judgement Indicator (2nd Edition).
Purpose: Designed to measure "accuracy of judgement when dealing with leadership situations, including the degree to which strength of preference for one decision making strategy over others impacts the ability to adapt leadership style to different situations."

Population: Adults who have, or who are being considered for, leadership positions.
Publication Date: 2014.
Acronym: LJI-2.
Scores, 13: 5 Judgement scores: Overall, Directive, Consultative, Consensual, Delegative; 4 Preference scores: Directive, Consultative, Consensual, Delegative; 4 Leadership Orientations: Task, Involvement, Control, Empowerment.
Administration: Individual or group.
Price Data, 2015: £498 per starter set including manual (90 pages), 5 item booklets, 25 answer sheets, 25 profile sheets, 5 administration cards, 5 personal development planners, 5 candidate briefing booklets, and £360 in software credits; £66 per manual; £20 per online test completion; £12 per 5 personal development planners; £42 per 5 item booklets; £16 per 5 administration cards; £48 per 25 response sheets.
Time: (40 minutes).
Comments: Online and paper-and-pencil versions available; both formats must be computer scored.
Authors: Michael Lock, Robert Wheeler, and Nick Burnard.
Publisher: Hogrefe Ltd [United Kingdom].
Cross References: Reviews are scheduled for *The Twentieth Mental Measurements Yearbook*.

[1118]

Leadership Opinion Questionnaire.

Purpose: To measure supervisory leadership dimensions.
Population: Supervisors and prospective supervisors.
Publication Dates: 1960–1989.
Acronym: LOQ.
Scores, 2: Structure, Consideration.
Administration: Individual or group.
Price Data: Available from publisher.
Time: No limit (approximately 10–15 minutes).
Author: Edwin A. Reishman.
Publisher: General Dynamics Information Technology.
Cross References: See T5:1444 (4 references), T4:1409 (7 references), T3:1300 (10 references), 8:1177 (52 references), and T2:2454 (15 references); for a review by Cecil A. Gibb, see 7:1149 (41 references); for reviews by Jerome E. Doppelt and Wayne K. Kirchner, see 6:1190 (6 references).

[1119]

Leadership Potential Assessment.

Purpose: Designed "to measure whether one has the right attitudes, behaviors, and skills to be an effective leader."
Population: Under 17 through adult.
Publication Date: 2011.
Acronym: LEAP.
Scores, 20: Transactional Leadership, Transformational Leadership, Leadership Potential, Delegating, Giving Feedback, Goal Setting, Rewarding Performance, Motivating, Coaching, Problem Solving, Vision, Collaboration, Setting an Example, Agreeableness, Conscientiousness, Open-Mindedness, Extroversion, Emotional Stability, Impression Management, Overall Score.
Administration: Individual.
Price Data: Available from publisher.
Time: (30) minutes.
Comments: Self-administered online assessment. The test publisher provides clients with information about the methods and theoretical basis used in the development of the test as well as benchmarks for relevant industries and racial/ethnic group comparison data.
Author: PsychTests AIM, Inc.
Publisher: PsychTests AIM, Inc. [Canada].
Cross References: For reviews by John K. Hawley and Karl N. Kelley, see 19:91.

[1120]

Leadership Potential Indicator.

Purpose: "Designed to help individuals in management and leadership positions identify their current areas of competency, and decide where they should focus their developmental efforts."
Population: Ages 16 to 65.
Publication Date: 2015.
Acronym: LPI.
Scores, 25: Managing Change (Initiating Activity, Taking Risks, Creating and Innovating, Adapting to Change), Planning and Organizing (Analyzing and Interpreting, Making Decisions, Planning and Prioritizing, Monitoring Quality), Interpersonal Skills (Communicating, Listening and Supporting, Relating and Networking, Team Working), Results Orientation (Achieving Goals, Meeting Customer Needs, Focusing on the Business, Learning and Developing), Leadership (Persuading and Influencing, Motivating and Empowering, Coaching Others, Coping with Pressure).
Administration: Individual.
Price Data, 2015: $19.95 per online administration; user's manual (57 pages) available for download from test publisher's website.
Time: [15] minutes.
Comments: Administered online.
Author: MySkillsProfile.
Publisher: MySkillsProfile [United Kingdom].
Cross References: Reviews are scheduled for *The Twentieth Mental Measurements Yearbook*.

[1121]

Leadership Practices Inventory, Fourth Edition.

Purpose: Designed "as a measure of the frequency of specific leadership behaviors ... to help leaders gain perspective into how they see themselves as leaders, how others view them, and what actions they can take to improve their effectiveness."

Population: Individuals at all organizational levels; primarily used at middle management level.

Publication Dates: 1990-2013.

Acronym: LPI.

Scores, 5: Model the Way, Inspire a Shared Vision, Challenge the Process, Enable Others to Act, Encourage the Heart.

Administration: Group.

Forms, 2: Self, Observer.

Price Data, 2016: $230 per facilitator's guide set including facilitator's guide (2013, 200 pages), Self-Assessment Form, Observer Form, workbook (2013, 47 pages), Leadership Development Planner (2013, 95 pages), flash drive with presentation slides and scoring software, article, poster, and reminder card.

Time: (10-20) minutes.

Comments: Observer form can be completed by up to 10 people for 360-degree feedback; administered via paper and pencil or online.

Authors: James M. Kouzes and Barry Z. Posner.

Publisher: The Leadership Challenge, A Wiley Brand.

> *a*) STUDENT LEADERSHIP PRACTICES INVENTORY, SECOND EDITION.
> **Population:** High school and college students.
> **Publication Date:** 2013.
> **Acronym:** Student LPI.
> **Price Data:** $6 per print Self Assessment; $14 per online 360-degree assessment; $38 per scoring software on CD.

Cross References: See T5:1448 (1 reference); for reviews by John M. Enger and L. Carolyn Pearson of an earlier version titled Leadership Practices Inventory—Individual Contributor [Second Edition], see 14:204; for reviews by Jeffrey B. Brookings and William J. Waldron of The Team Leadership Practices Inventory, see 13:317; for reviews by Frederick T. L. Leong and Mary A. Lewis of an earlier version (1992) of the Leadership Practices Inventory, see 12:213; see also T4:1411 (2 references).

[1122]
Leadership Skills Inventory [Revised].

Purpose: Designed to benchmark 60 leadership competencies and skills required for effective leadership; also offers 360° feedback with the LSI-Others version.

Population: Adults.

Publication Dates: 1992-2006.

Acronym: LSI.

Scores, 6: Self-Management Skills, Interpersonal Communication Skills, Coaching/Counseling and Problem Management Skills, Skills for Developing Teams and Organizations, Versatility and Organizational Development Skills, Total Score.

Administration: Individual or group.

Price Data, 2016: $35 per Leadership Skills Inventory-Self (2006, 20 pages); $40 per Online Leadership Skills Inventory-Self; $15 per Leadership Skills Inventory-Others (2006, 8 pages); $40 per Trainer's Guidelines (1996, 18 pages); $75 per Transforming Leadership Book.

Editions, 2: Self, Others.

Time: (30) minutes.

Comments: Self-administered and self-scored.

Authors: Ken Keis and Terry D. Anderson.

Publisher: Consulting Resource Group International, Inc.

> *a*) LEADERSHIP SKILLS INVENTORY-OTHERS.
> **Acronym**: LSI-O.
> **Price Data:** $15 per test booklet.
> *b*) LEADERSHIP SKILLS INVENTORY-SELF.
> **Acronym**: LSI-S.
> **Price Data:** $35 per test booklet; $40 per online assessment.

Cross References: For reviews by Alan D. Moore and Nambury S. Raju of an earlier edition, see 16:134; for reviews by Mary Henning-Stout and George C. Thornton, III of an earlier edition, see 13:176.

[1123]
Leadership Skills Profile.

Purpose: Designed to analyze "the strengths and weaknesses of managerial and executive candidates."

Population: Ages 18 and over.

Publication Date: 2003.

Acronym: LSP.

Scores, 42: Leadership Dimensions: Technical Orientation, Analytical Orientation, Decisiveness, Creativity, Thoroughness, Objectivity, Risk Taking, Open-Mindedness, First Impression, Interpersonal Relations, Sensitivity, Social Astuteness, Conflict Management, Communication, Formal Presentation, Persuasiveness, Negotiation, Listening, Achievement/Motivation, Self Discipline, Flexibility, Independence, Self Esteem, Emotional Control, Dependability, Ambition, General Leadership Effectiveness, Assuming Responsibility, Vision, Emphasizing Excellence, Organizational Spokesperson, Subordinate Involvement, Facilitating Teamwork, Inspirational Role Model, Short-Term Planning, Strategic Planning, Organizing the Work of Others, Delegation, Monitoring and Controlling, Motivating Others, Attracting Staff, Productivity.

Administration: Individual or group.

Price Data, 2015: $25 per test manual; $6 per test booklet; $80-$300 per test (depending on volume and type of report purchased), available through fax-in scoring or online scoring at www.SigmaTesting.com.

Time: 40 minutes.

Comments: Publisher scoring services provided via Internet or fax. Two reports available: Selection and Development.

Author: Douglas N. Jackson.

Publisher: SIGMA Assessment Systems, Inc.

Cross References: For reviews by Philip G. Benson and John S. Geisler, see 16:135.

[1124]

Leadership Spectrum Profile.

Purpose: To identify leadership business priorities in a given situation, develop business acumen, improve team effectiveness, enhance strategic thinking, and to reflect that leadership requirements change by context or circumstance.

Population: Senior leaders, teams, and individuals in leadership positions.

Publication Dates: 1998–2000.

Acronym: LSP.

Scores: 6 choices: Inventor (new products/services), Catalyst (market growth), Developer (reduce risk and improve accountabilities), Performer (increase efficiency, quality, and resource utilization), Protector (build culture and develop talent), and Challenger (position for the future, check assumptions and trends) .

Administration: Group.

Price Data, 2016: $45.95 per online administration with personalized report; $45.95 per manual/test booklet (2000, 31 pages); $45 per Priority Balancing Handbook (110 pages); volume discounts available.

Foreign Language Edition: Japanese language version is available.

Time: (12–18) minutes.

Comments: Results reflect the business priorities that are currently driving the leader; online version is available at www.leadershipspectrum.com.

Author: Mary Lippitt.

Publisher: Enterprise Management Ltd.

Cross References: For reviews by Janet F. Carlson and by L. Carolyn Pearson and Sharon Ann Richardson, see 17:104.

[1125]

Leadership Style Workbook.

Purpose: Measures individuals' perception of how they manage based on the assessment of six managerial styles.

Population: Persons in managerial situations.

Publication Dates: 1980–1996.

Acronym: LSW.

Scores, 6: Directive, Visionary, Affiliative, Participative, Pacesetting, Coaching.

Administration: Group or individual.

Price Data, 2016: $152 per 10 questionnaires, profiles, and interpretive notes.

Time: [30–40] minutes.

Comments: Self-scored instrument; Previously titled Managerial Style Questionnaire; the test publisher advises that the name and some terminology have been updated, but the test itself has not changed.

Author: Hay Group.

Publisher: Hay Group.

Cross References: For a review by H. John Bernardin and Joan E. Pynes of the Managerial Style Questionnaire (1980), see 10:185.

[1126]

Leadership Versatility Index.

Purpose: Designed to measure "versatility on two complementary pairs of leadership dimensions: forceful and enabling, and strategic and operational."

Population: Managers, executives.

Publication Dates: 2001-2007.

Acronym: LVI.

Scores, 7: Overall Versatility, Forceful-Enabling Versatility, Strategic-Operational Versatility, Specific Leadership Behavior Items, Team Productivity, Team Vitality, Overall Effectiveness.

Administration: Group.

Forms, 2: Standard LVI 360, LVI 360-plus.

Restricted Distribution: Special authorization from publisher is required to use the LVI.

Price Data, 2015: $335 per complete Standard LVI 360 test kit; $410 per LVI 360-plus kit including open-ended questions.

Time: (20) minutes.

Comments: The Standard LVI 360 includes only numerical feedback and the LVI 360-plus includes open-ended questions. The test publisher has indicated there is a newer edition of this test; description will be updated when complete test materials are received.

Authors: Robert E. Kaplan and Robert B. Kaiser.

Publisher: Kaiser Leadership Solutions, LLC.

Cross References: For reviews by Mark A. Staal and Matt Vassar, see 18:67.

[1127]

Learning Accomplishment Profile Diagnostic Edition.

Purpose: "Designed to provide the teacher of the young child with a simple criterion-referenced tool for systematic assessment of the child's existing skills."

Publication Dates: 1992–1997.

Administration: Individual or group.

Parts, 4: LAP-D Normed Assessment, LAP-D Screen, LAP (Revised Edition), Early LAP.

Price Data: Available from publisher.

Comments: May be administered in station or individual format. The test publisher has indicated there is a newer edition of this test; description will be updated when complete test materials are received.

Publisher: Kaplan Early Learning Company.

a) LEARNING ACCOMPLISHMENT PROFILE DIAGNOSTIC EDITION NORMED ASSESSMENT.

Purpose: "Facilitates standardized, norm referenced assessment … of developmental skills."

Population: Ages 30–60 months.

Publication Date: 1992.

Acronym: LAP-D.

Scores, 8: 4 development areas: Fine Motor (Writing, Manipulation), Language (Comprehension, Naming), Gross Motor (Body Movement, Object Movement), Cognitive (Counting, Matching).

Time: (45–90) minutes.

Comments: "Designed to assist in making relevant educational decisions with regard to young children and to enable the teacher to develop developmentally appropriate instructional objectives and strategies."

Authors: Aubrey D. Nehring, Ema F. Nehring, John R. Bruni, Jr., and Patricia L. Randolph.

b) LEARNING ACCOMPLISHMENT PROFILE DIAGNOSTIC EDITION NORMED SCREEN.

Purpose: "Quick initial developmental instruments designed as entry level to the diagnostic process."

Population: Ages 3–5 years.

Publication Date: 1997.

Acronym: LAP-D Screen.

Scores, 6: 4 developmental areas: Fine Motor (Writing, Manipulation), Language (Comprehension, Naming), Gross Motor, Cognitive.

Time: (12–15) minutes, untimed.

Comments: Designed to be completed by the child's classroom teacher; items selected from LAP-D Standardized Assessment.

Author: Kaplan Press.

c) LEARNING ACCOMPLISHMENT PROFILE— REVISED EDITION.

Purpose: "A systematic, ongoing, criterion-referenced assessment of a child's existing skills in fine and gross motor, cognitive/language, personal/social, and self-help skills."

Population: Ages 3–6 years.

Publication Date: 1995.

Acronym: LAP-R.

Ratings, 7: Gross Motor, Fine Motor, Pre-Writing, Cognitive, Language, Self-Help, Personal/Social.

Time: Administration time not reported.

Authors: Anne R. Sanford and Janet G. Zelman.

d) EARLY LEARNING ACCOMPLISHMENT PROFILE.

Purpose: "An ongoing, criterion-referenced assessment system covering gross motor, fine motor, cognitive, language, self-help, and social/emotional domains."

Population: Birth to 36 months.

Publication Date: 1995.

Acronym: E-LAP.

Ratings, 6: Gross Motor, Fine Motor, Cognitive, Language, Self-Help, Social/Emotional.

Time: Administration time not reported.

Authors: M. Elayne Glover, Jodi L. Preminger, and Anne R. Sanford.

Cross References: For a review by Loraine J. Spenciner, see 16:136.

[1128]

Learning and Study Strategies Inventory— High School Version.

Purpose: Designed to assist high school students "in determining their study skills strategies, problems and attitudes, and learning practices."

Population: Grades 9–12.

Publication Date: 1990.

Acronym: LASSI-HS.

Scores, 10: Attitude, Motivation, Time Management, Anxiety, Concentration, Information Processing,

Selecting Main Ideas, Study Aids, Self Testing, Test Strategies.

Administration: Group.

Price Data, 2015: $4 per test (1-99 copies); $3.50 per test (100 copies or more); free user's manual.

Time: (25–30) minutes.

Authors: Claire E. Weinstein and David R. Palmer.

Publisher: H & H Publishing Co., Inc.

Cross References: For reviews by Kenneth A. Kiewra and Robert T. Williams, see 13:177 (4 references).

[1129]

Learning and Study Strategies Inventory, Second Edition.

Purpose: Designed to assess "students' awareness about and use of learning and study strategies related to skill, will and self-regulation components of strategic learning."

Population: Grades 9 and over.

Publication Dates: 1987-2002.

Acronym: LASSI.

Scores, 10: Anxiety Scale, Attitude Scale, Concentration Scale, Information Processing Scale, Motivation Scale, Self-Testing Scale, Selecting Main Ideas Scale, Study Aids Scale, Time Management Scale, Test Strategies Scale.

Administration: Individual or group.

Price Data, 2016: $4 per test (quantity 1-99); $3.50 per test (100 or more).

Time: (15-20) minutes.

Comments: This test can be self-administered and self-scored; can be computer administered and scored.

Authors: Claire E. Weinstein, Ann C. Schulte, and David R. Palmer.

Publisher: H&H Publishing Company, Inc.

> *a)* COLLEGE VERSION.
> **Population:** College students.
> **Foreign Language Edition:** Spanish version available.
> *b)* HIGH SCHOOL VERSION.
> **Population:** Grades 9-12.

Cross References: For reviews by Heidi M. Carty and Claudia R. Wright, see 17:105; see also T5:1455 (13 references) and T4:1417 (1 reference); for reviews by Martha W. Blackwell and Steven C. Hayes of an earlier edition, see 11:198 (3 references).

[1130]

Learning Disabilities Diagnostic Inventory.

Purpose: Designed to identify specific learning disabilities and to help diagnose dysphasia, dyslexia, dysgraphia, dyscalculia, and disorders in executive function.

Population: Ages 8-0 to 17-11.

Publication Date: 1998.

Acronym: LDDI.

Scores, 6: Listening, Speaking, Reading, Writing, Mathematics, Reasoning.

Administration: Individual.

Price Data, 2015: $143 per complete kit including examiner's manual (106 pages) and 50 rating summary booklets; $62 per examiner's manual; $91 per 50 rating summary booklets.

Time: (10–20) minutes.

Authors: Donald D. Hammill and Brian R. Bryant.

Publisher: PRO-ED.

Cross References: For reviews by Terry B. Gutkin and John MacDonald, see 14:206.

[1131]

Learning Disability Evaluation Scale (Renormed).

Purpose: "Developed to aid in diagnosis, placement, and planning for learning disabled children and adolescents."

Population: Grades K–12.

Publication Dates: 1983–1996.

Acronym: LDES.

Scores, 7: Listening, Thinking, Speaking, Reading, Writing, Spelling, Mathematical Calculations.

Administration: Individual.

Price Data: Available from publisher.

Time: (15–20) minutes.

Comments: Ratings by teacher; the 1996 edition is renormed but content is not revised. The test publisher has indicated there is a newer edition of this test; description will be updated when complete test materials are received.

Authors: Stephen B. McCarney (test and manual) and Angela Marie Bauer (manual).

Publisher: Hawthorne Educational Services, Inc.

Cross References: For reviews by Patricia B. Keith and Loraine J. Spenciner, see 14:207; for reviews by Glen P. Aylward and Scott W. Brown of an earlier edition, see 12:214 (1 reference).

[1132]

Learning Skills Profile.

Purpose: To assess the gap between personal aptitudes and critical skills required by a job.

Population: Junior high to adults.

Publication Date: 1993.

Acronym: LSP.

Scores, 36: 3 scores: Personal Learning Skill, Job Skill Demand, and Learning Gap in each of 12 skill areas: Interpersonal Skills (Leadership Skill, Relationship Skill, Help Skill), Analytical Skills (Theory Skill, Quantitative Skill, Technology Skill), Information Skills (Sense-Making Skill, Information-Gathering Skill, Information Analysis Skill), Behavioral Skills (Goal Setting Skill, Action Skill, Initiative Skill).

Administration: Group or individual.

Price Data, 2016: $25 per online administration.

Time: [45–60] minutes.

Comments: Online only.

Authors: Richard E. Boyatzis and David A. Kolb.

Publisher: Hay Group.

Cross References: See T5:1467 (1 reference); for a review by David O. Herman, see 13:179.

[1133]

Learning Style Indicator [Revised].

Purpose: Designed to identify "preferred learning style and preferences."

Population: Ages 15 years and over.

Publication Dates: 1996-2006.

Acronym: LSI.

Scores, 4: Behavioral/Action/Independent, Cognitive/Analysis/Visual, Interpersonal/Harmony/Auditory, Affective/Expression/Experiential.

Administration: Individual or group.

Price Data, 2016: $20 per test booklet (2006, 12 pages); $15 per In-Depth Interpretations booklet (2006, 28 pages); $35 per online version; $40 per Trainer's Guidelines (1996, 28 pages).

Time: (30) minutes (90-180 minutes program options).

Comments: Self-administered and self-scored; can be used in conjunction with the Instructional Style Indicator (987).

Authors: Ken Keis and Everett T. Robinson.

Publisher: Consulting Resource Group International, Inc.

[1134]

Learning Style Inventory [Price Systems, Inc.].

Purpose: Identifies "the conditions under which an individual is most likely to learn, remember, and achieve."

Population: Grades 3–12.

Publication Dates: 1975-2009.

Acronym: LSI.

Scores: 22 areas: Noise Level, Light, Temperature, Design, Motivation, Persistent, Responsible, Structure, Learning Alone/Peer Oriented, Authority Figures Present, Learn in Several Ways, Auditory, Visual, Tactile, Kinesthetic, Requires Intake, Evening/Morning, Late Morning, Afternoon, Needs Mobility, Parent Figure Motivated, Teacher Motivated, plus a Consistency score.

Administration: Group or individual.

Price Data, 2015: $22.50 per 10 answer sheets for Grades 3 & 4 or for Grade 5 thru 12 (includes scoring); $7.50 or less per group and subscale summaries available from publisher only in addition to individual profiles; $.60 per individual interpretative booklet; $16 per manual (1997, 100 pages); $3.25 per research report; $395 per computerized self-administered inventory program in English ($495 for multi-language version) with 100 administrations (Windows); $495 for Scanwin program permitting schools to scan and profile forms on site (includes multi-language capability); $.60 per answer form to use with Scanwin.

Time: (20–30) minutes.

Comments: PC compatible computer required for (optional) computerized administration; NCS Pearson Optical Mark Reader with dual pencil reader; Scrantron 8000, 8200, 8400, or SCANMARK 2550, 2660, 2800, 4000 or 5500 Scanner with dual pencil read for Scanwin; online administration available.
Authors: Rita Dunn, Kenneth Dunn, and Gary E. Price.
Publisher: Price Systems, Inc.
Cross References: See T5:1470 (5 references); for reviews by Thomas R. Knapp and Craig S. Shwery, see 13:180 (9 references); see also T4:1432 (3 references); for reviews by Jan N. Hughes and Alida S. Westman of an earlier edition, see 11:203 (6 references).

[1135]
Learning Style Inventory, Version 3.1.

Purpose: Identifies an individual's learning preference and explores the opportunities that different learning styles present.
Population: Ages 18–60.
Publication Dates: 1976–2005.
Acronym: LSI3.1.
Scores, 4: Concrete Experience, Active Experimentation, Reflective Observation, Abstract Conceptualization; plus 4 learning styles: Accommodating, Diverging, Converging, Assimilating.
Administration: Group or individual.
Price Data, 2016: $158 per 10 self-scoring booklets; $53 per facilitator's guide to learning (2000, 81 pages); $35 per online administration.
Foreign Language Editions: Available in Czech, Finnish, French (Canadian), German, Korean, Portuguese (Brazil), and Spanish (Argentina).
Time: [20–30] minutes.
Author: David A. Kolb.
Publisher: Hay Group.
Cross References: For reviews by Cecil R. Reynolds and David Shum, see 15:136; see T5:1469 (13 references) and T4:1438 (12 references); for a review by Noel Gregg of an earlier edition, see 10:173 (17 references); see also 9:607 (7 references).

[1136]
Learning Style Questionnaire.

Purpose: Developed to "help individuals measure their preferences for learning."
Population: Adults.
Publication Date: 1999.
Acronym: LSQ.
Scores, 4: Participation, Reflecting, Structuring, Experiencing.
Administration: Group.
Price Data, 2016: $59.95; volume discounts available.
Time: (20–30) minutes.
Author: Chris Hutcheson.
Publisher: HRD Press, Inc.

[1137]
Learning Styles Inventory [Piney Mountain Press].

Purpose: Designed to identify learning needs of students.
Population: Grades 6–12.
Publication Dates: 1988–2000.
Scores: 9 subtopics in 2 areas: Learning (Auditory Language, Visual Language, Auditory Numerical, Visual Numerical, Auditory-Visual-Kinesthetic), Working (Group Learner, Individual Learner, Oral Expressive, Written Expressive).
Administration: Individual or group.
Price Data, 2016: $195 per single station software; $495 per multistation software including instructor guide and Windows multimedia CD; $1,495 for Network version.
Time: [11] minutes.
Author: Al Babich.
Publisher: Piney Mountain Press.
Cross References: For reviews by Kevin D. Crehan and Mark H. Fugate, see 12:218.

[1138]
Learning Styles Inventory [Western Psychological Services].

Purpose: Provides a quick measure of learning preferences.
Population: Junior High School, High School, College, Adults in business settings.
Publication Dates: 1976–1988.
Acronym: LSI.
Scores, 21: Conditions for Learning (Peer, Organization, Goal Setting, Competition, Instructor, Detail, Independence, Authority), Area of Interest (Numeric, Qualitative, Inanimate, People), Mode of Learning (Listening, Reading, Iconic, Direct Experience), Expectation for Course Grade (A-expectation, B-expectation, C-expectation, D-expectation, Total expectation).
Administration: Group.
Forms, 4: A (College), B (High School), C (Junior High School), E (College-Easy).
Price Data, 2016: $137 per complete kit including 3 each of Forms A, B, C, and E inventory booklets, and manual (1988, 76 pages); $72 per 10 inventory booklets (specify form A, B, C, or E); $65.50 per manual; $15 per form (specify A, B, C, or E).
Time: (15–20) minutes.
Comments: Previously listed as Canfield Learning Styles Inventory.
Author: Albert A. Canfield.
Publisher: Western Psychological Services.
Cross References: See T5:392 (2 references) and T4:378 (5 references); for a review by Stephen L. Benton, see 11:57 (2 references); for reviews by John Biggs and C. Dean Miller of an earlier edition, see 9:609 (1 reference).

[1139]

Learning Tactics Inventory.

Purpose: "Provides … individuals with information about how they learn and illustrates behaviors that they can adopt to become more versatile learners."

Population: Managers, leaders, executives.

Publication Date: 1999.

Acronym: LTI.

Scores: 4 learning tactics: Action, Thinking, Feeling, Accessing Others.

Administration: Individual.

Price Data, 2016: $50 per Facilitator's Guide (41 pages); $28 per Participant's Workbook/Survey; quantity discounts available.

Time: 15 minutes.

Comments: An inventory of the behaviors individuals have reported using when engaged in the task of learning from experience; self-scored; Facilitator's Guide includes details of workshop procedures, reproducible overheads, and handout masters.

Authors: Maxine Dalton.

Publisher: Center for Creative Leadership.

Cross References: For reviews by Kathleen A. Dolgos and William B. Michael, see 15:137.

[1140]

Learning/Working Styles Inventory.

Purpose: "Developed to assess learning styles and preferred working conditions."

Population: Grades 7–12 and adults.

Publication Dates: 1989–2000.

Scores: 25 subtopics in 5 areas: Physical Domain (Kinesthetic, Visual, Tactile, Auditory), Social Domain (Group, Individual), Environmental Domain (Formal Design, Informal Design, Bright Lights, Dim Lights, Warm Temperature, Cool Temperature, With Sound, Without Sound), Mode of Expression Domain (Oral Expressive, Written Expressive), Work Characteristics Domain (Outdoors, Indoors, Sedentary, Non-Sedentary, Lifting, Non-Lifting, Data, People, Things).

Administration: Group and individual.

Price Data, 2016: $195 per single station software, $495 per multistation software including instructor guide and multimedia CD for Windows; $1,495 per Network version; $495 per web-based version with 1-year license.

Time: [15] minutes.

Comments: Previously titled Vocational Learning Styles.

Author: Helena Hendrix-Frye.

Publisher: Piney Mountain Press.

Cross References: For reviews by Leo M. Harvill and Craig N. Mills of the earlier edition (Vocational Learning Styles), see 12:410.

[1141]

Leatherman Leadership Questionnaire [Revised].

Purpose: "To aid in selecting leaders, providing specific feedback to participants on their leadership knowledge for career counseling, conducting accurate needs analysis, and screening for assessment centers or giving pre/post assessment feedback."

Population: Managers, supervisors, team leaders, and potential leaders.

Publication Dates: 1987–1992.

Acronym: LLQ.

Scores, 28: Assigning Work, Career Counseling, Coaching Employees, Oral Communication, Managing Change, Handling Employee Complaints, Dealing with Employee Conflicts, Counseling Employees, Helping an Employee Make Decisions, Delegating, Taking Disciplinary Action, Handling Emotional Situations, Setting Goals/Planning with Employees, Handling Employee Grievances, Conducting Employee Meetings, Giving Positive Feedback, Negotiating, Conducting Performance Appraisals, Establishing Performance Standards, Persuading/Influencing Employees, Making Presentations to Employees, Problem Solving with Employees, Conducting Selection Interviews, Team Building, Conducting Termination Interviews, Helping an Employee Manage Time, One-on-One Training, Total.

Subtests, 2: May be administered in separate parts.

Administration: Group.

Price Data: Available from publisher.

Time: (300–325) minutes for battery; (150–165) minutes per part.

Comments: Complete test administered in 2 parts; machine scored by publisher. The test publisher has indicated there is a newer edition of this test; description will be updated when complete test materials are received.

Author: Richard W. Leatherman.

Publisher: Edge Training Systems, Inc.

Cross References: For reviews by Jeffrey S. Rain and Lawrence M. Rudner, see 12:219; for reviews by Walter Katkovsky and William D. Porterfield of an earlier edition, see 11:205.

[1142]

Leisure Interest Inventory.

Purpose: Designed to assess "preferred leisure activities."

Population: College students.

Publication Date: 1969.

Acronym: LII.

Scores, 5: Sociability, Games, Art, Mobility, Immobility.

Administration: Group.

Price Data: Available from publisher.

Time: (20-25) minutes.

Author: Edwina E. Hubert.

Publisher: Edwina E. Hubert, Ph.D.

[1143]

Leisure/Retirement Activities Card Sort.

Purpose: "To introduce a new perspective on adult development and a model of understanding the process of change as it relates to retirement; to stimulate personal thinking on handling retirement; and to assist participants to identify and begin planning for avenues of new growth or expanded satisfaction in retirement living" and "to incorporate leisure activities into your life style."

Population: Adults.

Publication Dates: 1977-2005.

Scores: Item scores only.

Administration: Group or individual.

Price Data, 2016: $12 per card sort deck and worksheet; $10 per manual; $24 per 24 pack of worksheets.

Time: (75–120) minutes.

Comments: Previously known as Retirement Activities Card Sort Planning Kit; 8 supplementary activities included in manual; distributors are available in Canada, Australia, Egypt, and U.S.A.

Author: Richard L. Knowdell.

Publisher: Career Research & Testing, Inc.

Cross References: For reviews by M. Allan Cooperstein and Robert B. Frary of the Retirement Activities Card Sort Planning Kit, see 13:262.

[1144]

Leiter International Performance Scale–Third Edition.

Purpose: Designed to "measure nonverbal intelligence and abilities as well as attention and memory functioning."

Population: Ages 3 to 75 years and older.

Publication Dates: 1936-2013.

Acronym: Leiter-3.

Scores, 19: 11 subtest scores: Figure Ground, Form Completion, Classification/Analogies, Sequential Order, Visual Patterns (Optional), Attention Sustained, Forward Memory, Reverse Memory, Nonverbal Stroop Incongruent Correct, Nonverbal Stroop Congruent Correct, Nonverbal Stroop Effect; 3 composite scores: Nonverbal IQ, Nonverbal Memory, Processing Speed; 5 supplemental scores: Attention Sustained Errors, Attention Divided Correct, Attention Divided Incorrect, Nonverbal Stroop Congruent Incorrect, Nonverbal Stroop Incongruent Incorrect.

Administration: Individual.

Price Data, 2015: $1,095 per complete kit including all manipulatives (frame, blocks, foam shapes, stimulus cards, attention divided bowls), easel book, stimulus book, scoring keys, administration gestures laminate, record forms, response booklets, manual, timer, and purple marker in a rolling backpack; $73 per 20 record forms; $84 per 20 response booklets; $225 per scoring software.

Time: (30-45) minutes for cognitive battery; (30) minutes for attention/memory battery.

Authors: Gale H. Roid, Lucy J. Miller, Mark Pomplun, and Chris Koch.

Publisher: Stoelting Co.

> *a*) EXAMINER RATING SCALE.
> **Purpose:** "Developed to provide information about … behavioral characteristics that can impact reasoning, visualization, memory, and attention."
> **Scores, 10:** Cognitive/Social (Attention, Organization/Impulse Control, Activity Level, Sociability, Total), Emotions/Regulations (Energy and Feelings, Regulation, Anxiety, Sensory Reaction, Total).

Cross References: Reviews are scheduled for *The Twentieth Mental Measurements Yearbook*. For reviews by Gary L. Marco and Terry A. Stinnett of the revised edition, see 14:211; see also T5:1485 (64 references), T4:1446 (33 references), T3:1319 (16 references), and T2:505 (18 references); for a review by Emmy E. Werner of the original version, see 6:526 (10 references); see also 5:408 (17 references); for a review by Gwen F. Arnold and an excerpted review by Laurance F. Shaffer, see 4:349 (25 references).

[1145]

Level of Service/Case Management Inventory: An Offender Assessment System.

Purpose: Designed to help "determine an offender's risk/needs level so that an appropriate level of service can be provided."

Population: Offenders ages 16 and over.

Publication Date: 2004.

Acronym: LS/CMI.

Scores, 9: Total Score plus 8 Risk/Need factors: Criminal History, Education/Employment, Family/Marital, Leisure/Recreation, Companions, Alcohol/Drug Problem, Procriminal Attitude/Orientation, Antisocial Pattern.

Administration: Individual.

Price Data, 2015: $389 per complete kit including user's manual (228 pages), scoring guide, and 25 each of interview guides, offender history forms, QuikScore forms, ColorPlot profile forms, and case management protocols; $259 per reorder kit including 25 each of interview guides, offender history forms, QuikScore forms, ColorPlot profile forms, and case management protocols; $104 per user's manual; $109 per 25 interview guides; $24 per 25 offender history forms; $69 per 25 QuikScore forms; $33 per 25 ColorPlot profile forms; $281 per V.5 software kit including user's manual, V.5 getting started guide, and 25 profile reports.

Time: (20–30) minutes plus interview.

Comments: Online version available.

Authors: D. A. Andrews, James L. Bonta, and J. Stephen Wormith.

Publisher: Multi-Health Systems, Inc.

Cross References: For reviews by Sheri Bauman and Geoffrey L. Thorpe, see 17:108.

[1146]

Level of Service Inventory—Revised: Screening Version.

Purpose: Designed to provide "a risk/needs assessment important to offender treatment planning."
Population: Ages 16 and older.
Publication Date: 1998.
Acronym: LSI-R:SV.
Scores: Total score only.
Administration: Individual.
Price Data, 2015: $179 per complete kit including 25 interview guides, 25 QuikScore™ forms, and manual (1998, 26 pages); $104 per 25 interview guides/QuikScore™ forms; $44 per 25 interview guides; $69 per 25 QuikScore™ forms; $79 per manual.
Time: (10–15) minutes.
Authors: Don Andrews and James Bonta.
Publisher: Multi-Health Systems, Inc.
Cross References: For reviews by Ira S. Katz and Kevin J. McCarthy, see 15:138.

[1147]

The Level of Service Inventory—Revised [2003 Norms Update].

Purpose: Designed as a "quantitative survey of attributes of offenders and their situations relevant to level of service decisions."
Population: Ages 16 and older.
Publication Dates: 1995–2003.
Acronym: LSI-R.
Scores: Total score only.
Administration: Individual.
Price Data, 2015: $309 per U.S. Norms complete kit including manual (2001, 63 pages), U.S. Norms Supplement (2003, 16 pages), 25 interview guides, 25 QuikScore forms, and 25 U.S. ColorPlot profiles; $199 per 25 interview guides/QuikScore forms/ColorPlot profiles; $109 per 25 interview guides; $69 per 25 QuikScore forms; $34 per 25 U.S. Norms ColorPlot profile forms; $299 per software kit including manual, V.5 getting started guide, and 25 profile report uses.
Foreign Language Edition: LSI-R is available in Spanish but the U.S. ColorPlot profile forms are not.
Time: (30–45) minutes.
Comments: Software version also available.
Authors: Don A. Andrews and James L. Bonta.
Publisher: Multi-Health Systems, Inc.
Cross References: For reviews by David F. Ciampi and Andrew A. Cox, see 17:107; for reviews by Solomon M. Fulero and Romeo Vitelli of an earlier edition, see 14:212.

[1148]

Level of Service/Risk, Need, Responsivity.

Purpose: "Designed to assist professionals in management and treatment planning with adult and late adolescent male and female offenders in justice, forensic, correctional, prevention, and related agencies."
Population: "Male and female offenders 16 years of age and older."
Publication Date: 2008.
Acronym: LS/RNR.
Scores, 9: Criminal History, Education/Employment, Family/Marital, Leisure/Recreation, Companions, Procriminal Attitude/Orientation, Alcohol/Drug Problem, Antisocial Pattern, Total (General Risk/Need Factors).
Administration: Individual.
Parts, 2: Interview Guide, QuikScore; Sections, 8: Specific Risk/Need Factors, Prison Experience-Institutional Factors, Other Client Issues, Special Responsivity Considerations, Risk/Need Summary and Override, Risk/Need Profile, and Program/Placement Decision.
Price Data, 2015: $229 per complete kit including 25 interview guides, 25 QuikScore forms, 25 ColorPlot forms, and scoring guide (63 pages); $109 per 25 interview guides; $69 per 25 QuikScore forms; $34 per 25 ColorPlot profile forms; $42 per scoring guide.
Time: [40-120] minutes.
Comments: Test is part of the LSI family of instruments including the Level of Service Inventory-Revised (LSI-R; 1147), the Level of Service Inventory-Revised: Screening Version (LSI-R:SV; 1146), the Youth Level of Service/Case Management Inventory (YLS/CMI; 2309), and the Level of Service/Case Management Inventory (LS/CMI; 1145); the Interview Guide is a semi-structured interview used to obtain ratings for the QuikScore form; Sections 2 through 8 provide additional information that is not numerically scored.
Authors: D. A. Andrews, James L. Bonta, and J. Stephen Wormith.
Publisher: Multi-Health Systems, Inc.
Cross References: For reviews by Jeffrey A. Jenkins and Mark H. Stone, see 18:68.

[1149]

Life Attitudes Schedule: A Risk Assessment for Suicidal and Life-Threatening Behaviors.

Purpose: Designed to "measure the cognitive, affective, and action-oriented components of suicide proneness."
Population: Ages 15–20.
Publication Date: 2004.
Administration: Individual or group.
Forms, 2: Life Attitudes Schedule, Life Attitudes Schedule: Short.
Price Data, 2015: $199 per complete kit including manual (70 pages), 10 item booklets, and 25 Quikscore forms for LAS and LAS:S; $66 per technical manual; $35 per 10 item booklets (reusable); $55 per 25 Quikscore forms for LAS or LAS:S.
Authors: Peter M. Lewinsohn, Jennifer Langhinrichsen-Rohling, Paul Rohde, and Richard A. Langford.
Publisher: Multi-Health Systems, Inc.

a) LIFE ATTITUDES SCHEDULE.
Acronym: LAS.
Scores, 12: Composite Scores (Physical, Psychological), Content Scales (Health-Related, Death-Related, Injury-Related, Self-Related), Modality Type Scales (Actions, Thoughts, Feelings), Valence Scales (Negative, Positive), Total.
Time: (30) minutes.
b) LIFE ATTITUDES SCHEDULE: SHORT.
Acronym: LAS:S.
Scores, 3: Physical, Psychological, Total.
Time: (10) minutes.
Cross References: For reviews by Thomas P. Hogan and Janet Smith, see 17:109.

[1150]

Life Stressors and Social Resources Inventory—Adult Form.

Purpose: "Provides an integrated picture of an individual's current life context" including "stable life stressors and social resources."
Population: Healthy adults, psychiatric patients, and medical patients.
Publication Dates: 1988–1994.
Acronym: LISRES-A.
Scores: 16 scales: 9 Life Stressor Scales (Physical Health, Home/Neighborhood, Financial, Work, Spouse or Partner, Children, Extended Family, Friends, Negative Life Events); 7 Social Resources Scales (Financial, Work, Spouse or Partner, Children, Extended Family, Friends, Positive Life Events).
Administration: Individual or group.
Price Data, 2015: $216 per introductory kit including manual (1994, 40 pages), 10 reusable item booklets, and 50 hand-scorable answer/profile forms.
Time: [10] minutes.
Comments: May be administered using either a self-report or a structured interview format.
Authors: Rudolf H. Moos (instrument and manual) and Bernice S. Moos (manual).
Publisher: Psychological Assessment Resources, Inc.
Cross References: See T5:1495 (1 reference); for reviews by M. Allan Cooperstein and Richard B. Stuart, see 13:184 (1 reference).

[1151]

Life Stressors and Social Resources Inventory—Youth Form.

Purpose: "Provides an integrated picture of a youth's current life context … assesses stable life stressors and social resources as well as changes in them over time."
Population: Ages 12–18.
Publication Dates: 1990–1994.
Acronym: LISRES-Y.
Scores, 16: 9 Life Stressors Scales (Physical Health, Home and Money, Parents, Siblings, Extended Family, School, Friends, Boyfriend/Girlfriend, Negative Life

Events); 7 Social Resources Scales (Parents, Siblings, Extended Family, School, Friends, Boyfriend/Girlfriend, Positive Life Events).
Administration: Individual or Group.
Editions, 2: Youth, Adult.
Price Data, 2015: $216 per introductory kit including manual (1994, 38 pages), 10 item booklets, and 50 hand-scorable answer/profile forms.
Time: (45) minutes for self-report; (45–90) minutes for structured interview.
Comments: Available as self-report or structured interview; structured interview "allows an interviewer to use the inventory with youths whose reading and comprehension skills are below a sixth-grade level."
Authors: Rudolf H. Moos and Bernice S. Moos.
Publisher: Psychological Assessment Resources, Inc.
Cross References: See T5:1496 (1 reference); for reviews by Kevin D. Crehan and Albert Oosterhof, see 13:185 (1 reference).

[1152]

Life Styles Inventory.

Purpose: Designed to assess an individual's thinking and behavioral styles.
Population: Adults.
Publication Dates: 1973–1990.
Acronym: LSI.
Administration: Individual.
Price Data: Available from publisher.
Foreign Language Editions: Available in Arabic, Bulgarian, Chinese (Simplified and Traditional), Croatian, Danish, Dutch, Finnish, French (Canadian and European), German, Greek, Hungarian, Italian, Japanese, Korean, Polish, Portuguese (Brazilian and European), Romanian, Russian, Serbian, Spanish (Castilian and Latin American), Swedish, Thai, Turkish.
Time: (20-25) minutes.
Comments: The test publisher has indicated there is a newer edition of this test; description will be updated when complete test materials are received.
Author: J. Clayton Lafferty.
Publisher: Human Synergistics International.
   a) LSI1: LIFE STYLES INVENTORY (SELF DESCRIPTION).
   Scores, 12: Constructive Styles (Achievement, Self-Actualizing, Humanistic-Encouraging, Affiliative), Passive/Defensive Styles (Approval, Conventional, Dependent, Avoidance), Aggressive/Defensive Styles (Oppositional, Power, Competitive, Perfectionistic).
   b) LSI2: LIFE STYLES INVENTORY (DESCRIPTION BY OTHERS).
   Scores, 12: Same as for *a* above.
   Comments: Administered to manager and 4 or 5 others.
Cross References: For reviews by Gregory J. Boyle and Patricia Schoenrade, see 12:222; see also T4:1459 (6 references); for reviews by Henry M. Cherrick and Linda M. DuBois, see 9:620 (1 reference).

[1153]

Light's Retention Scale, 5th Edition.

Purpose: Developed to assist in determining whether grade retention will have a positive or negative outcome for a particular student.

Population: Students in kindergarten through Grade 12.

Publication Dates: 1981-2015.

Acronym: LRS-5.

Scores: Total score only.

Administration: Individual.

Price Data, 2015: $120 per test kit including manual (2015, 96 pages), 25 record forms, 25 parent guides in English, and principal's guide to grade retention and promotion (2013, 32 pages); $45 per manual; $35 per 25 record forms; $25 per 25 parent guides (English or Spanish); $15 per principal's guide.

Foreign Language Edition: Parent guide available in Spanish.

Time: (10-15) minutes.

Comments: A nonpsychometric instrument used as a counseling tool with a specific retention candidate.

Authors: H. Wayne Light (scale and principal's guide) and Jill DelConte (principal's guide).

Publisher: Academic Therapy Publications.

Cross References: Reviews are scheduled for *The Twentieth Mental Measurements Yearbook*. For reviews by Loraine J. Spenciner and Hoi K. Suen of the 2006 Revision, see 18:69; for reviews by Bruce K. Alcorn and Frederic J. Medway of the 1991 Revision, see 11:208 (2 references); for reviews by Michael J. Hannafin and Patti L. Harrison of the 1981 Revision, see 9:622, see also T3:1328 (1 reference).

[1154]

Lindamood Auditory Conceptualization Test—Third Edition.

Purpose: Designed to measure "the ability to (a) discriminate one speech sound or phoneme from another and (b) segment a spoken word into its constituent phonemic units."

Population: Ages 5-0 through 18-11.

Publication Dates: 1971–2004.

Acronym: LAC-3.

Scores, 6: Isolated Phoneme Patterns, Tracking Phonemes, Counting Syllables, Tracking Syllables, Tracking Syllables and Phonemes, Total.

Administration: Individual.

Price Data, 2015: $227 per complete kit including examiner's manual, 25 examiner record booklets, 24 blocks, 6 felts, and 1 audio CD; $111 per examiner's manual and CD; $83 per 25 examiner record booklets; $31 per blocks kit; $10 per felt kit.

Time: (20–30) minutes.

Comments: "Criterion referenced"; requires no reading by examinees.

Authors: Patricia C. Lindamood and Phyllis Lindamood.

Publisher: PRO-ED.

Cross References: For reviews by Vincent J. Samar and Dolores Kluppel Vetter, see 17:110; see also T5:1503 (16 references) and T4:1465 (2 references); for reviews by Nicholas G. Bountress and James R. Cox of a previous edition, see 9:623 (1 reference).

[1155]

Listener Preference Profile.

Purpose: Designed to identify "four habitual listening responses."

Population: Adults.

Publication Dates: 1993-2015.

Scores, 4: People-Oriented, Action-Oriented, Content-Oriented, Time-Oriented.

Administration: Individual.

Price Data, 2016: $32.95 per facilitator's guide and sample instrument; $9.95 per profile; $15.95 per online assessment (quantity discounts available).

Time: Administration time not reported.

Authors: Kittie W. Watson, Larry L. Barker, and James B. Weaver III.

Publisher: Innolect, Inc.

[1156]

The Listening Inventory.

Purpose: Developed as an initial screener for students "who may be at risk for having (Central) Auditory Processing Disorder."

Population: Ages 4-17.

Publication Date: 2006.

Acronym: TLI.

Scores, 7: Linguistic Organization, Decoding & Language Mechanics, Attention & Organization, Sensory-Motor Skills, Social & Behavioral Skills, Auditory Processes, Total Score.

Administration: Individual.

Price Data, 2015: $90 per test kit including 25 listening inventory forms, 25 profile forms, and manual (64 pages); $30 per 25 record forms; $20 per 25 profile forms; $40 per manual.

Time: 15 minutes.

Authors: Donna Geffner and Deborah Ross-Swain.

Publisher: Academic Therapy Publications.

Cross References: For reviews by Tiffany L. Hutchins and Sandra Ward, see 18:70.

[1157]

Listening Skills Inventory.

Purpose: Designed "to evaluate one's listening abilities."

Population: Under age 18 through adult.

Publication Date: 2011.

Acronym: LiSI.

Scores, 10: Physical Attentiveness (External Distractions, Conversation Flow, Speaker to Listener Transition, Body Language), Mental Attentiveness (Internal Distractions, Attention Span, Hearing a Person Out), Overall Score.
Administration: Individual.
Price Data: Available from publisher.
Time: (15) minutes.
Comments: Self-administered online assessment. The test publisher provides clients with information about the methods and theoretical basis used in the development of the test as well as benchmarks for relevant industries and racial/ethnic group comparison data.
Author: PsychTests AIM, Inc.
Publisher: PsychTests AIM, Inc. [Canada].
Cross References: For reviews by Victoria A. Comerchero and Ray Fenton, see 19:92.

[1158]
Literature Tests/Objective and Essay.

Purpose: To assess students' literal and interpretive comprehension of over 200 works of contemporary and classical literature.
Population: Middle school and high school.
Publication Dates: 1929–1990.
Scores: Total score only.
Administration: Group.
Manual: No manual.
Price Data, 2016: $4.95 per 50-question test; $5.95 per 100-question test; $5.95 per essay test.
Time: Administration time not reported.
Comments: Over 700 tests on specific literary works; formerly called Book Review Tests and Objective Tests in English.
Author: Perfection Learning Corp.
Publisher: Perfection Learning Corp.

[1159]
Location Learning Test–Revised Edition.

Purpose: Designed to measure visuospatial memory performance using both immediate and delayed recall.
Population: Ages 18-96.
Publication Dates: 2000-2011.
Acronym: LLT.
Scores, 6: Displacement, Total Displacement, Delayed Recall, Delayed Recognition, Discrimination Index, Learning Index.
Administration: Individual.
Forms, 2: Version A, Version B.
Price Data, 2016: £242 per kit including manual (2001, 49 pages), test grid, practice grid, 22 picture cards, 20 Version A scoring forms, and 10 Version B scoring forms; £57 per manual; £26 per 20 Version A scoring forms; £14 per 10 Version B scoring forms; £143 per digital scoring program.

Time: 15 seconds or 30 seconds per trial; 15 minute or 20-30 minute delay, depending on administration procedure.
Authors: Romola S. Bucks, Jonathan R. Willison, Lucie M. T. Byrne, and Roy P. C. Kessels.
Publisher: Hogrefe Ltd [United Kingdom].
Cross References: For reviews by Anita M. Hubley and Claudia R. Wright of an earlier edition, see 17:111.

[1160]
Loewenstein Occupational Therapy Cognitive Assessment.

Purpose: "A cognitive battery of tests for both primary assessments and ongoing evaluation in the occupational therapy treatment of brain-injured patients."
Population: Ages 6 to 12 and brain-injured adults.
Publication Date: 1990.
Acronym: LOTCA.
Scores: 21 tests in 4 areas: Orientation (Orientation for Place, Orientation for Time), Visual and Spatial Perception (Object Identification, Shapes Identification, Overlapping Figures, Object Constancy, Spatial Perception, Praxis), Visual Motor Organization (Copying Geometric Forms, Reproduction of a Two-Dimensional Model, Pegboard Construction, Colored Block Design, Plain Block Design, Reproduction of a Puzzle, Drawing a Clock), Thinking Operations (Categorization, ROC Unstructured, ROC Structured, Pictorial Sequence A, Pictorial Sequence B, Geometric Sequence).
Administration: Individual.
Price Data: Price data available from publisher for complete kit including manual (56 pages), test booklet, and other materials packed in a plastic carrying case.
Time: (30–45) minutes.
Authors: Loewenstein Rehabilitation Hospital; Malka Itzkovich (manual), Betty Elazar (manual), Sarah Averbuch (manual), Naomi Katz (principal researcher), and Levy Rahmani (advisor).
Publisher: Maddak Inc.
Cross References: For reviews by Elaine Clark and Stephen R. Hooper, see 13:187.

[1161]
The Lollipop Test: A Diagnostic Screening Test of School Readiness--Revised.

Purpose: "A screening test to identify the child's deficits (and strengths) in readiness skills."
Population: First grade entrants.
Publication Dates: 1981–2002.
Scores, 5: Identification of Colors and Shapes and Copying Shapes, Picture Description and Position and Spatial Recognition, Identification of Numbers and Counting, Identification of Letters and Writing, Total.
Administration: Individual.

Price Data, 2015: $75 per complete kit including 25 test booklets, stimulus cards, and manual (1989, 35 pages).
Foreign Language Edition: Available in Spanish.
Time: (15–20) minutes.
Author: Alex L. Chew.
Publisher: Green Dragon Publishing.
Cross References: See T5:1515 (1 reference) and T4:1477 (2 references); for reviews by Sylvia T. Johnson and Albert C. Oosterhof, see 11:210 (5 references); for reviews by Isabel L. Beck and Janet A. Norris of an earlier edition, see 9:629.

[1162]

LSI Conflict.

Purpose: Enables individuals to identify and understand how their thinking patterns and coping behaviors influence their ability to deal with conflict situations.
Population: Adults.
Publication Date: 1990.
Scores: 12 patterns of thinking and behavior: Constructive (Pragmatist, Self-Empowered, Conciliator, Relationship Builder), Passive/Defensive (Accommodator, Regulator, Insulator, Avoider), Aggressive/Defensive (Escalator, Dominator, Competitor, Perfectionist).
Administration: Individual or group.
Price Data: Price data for test materials including Self-Development Guide and Leader's Guide available from publisher.
Foreign Language Editions: Available in French (Canadian), Romanian, and Serbian.
Time: Administration time not reported.
Author: J. Clayton Lafferty.
Publisher: Human Synergistics International.

[1163]

MAC Checklist for Evaluating, Preparing, and/or Improving Standardized Tests for Limited English Speaking Students.

Purpose: Aids in the review, critique, or preparation of ESL assessment instruments.
Population: ESL test developers, reviewers, and users.
Publication Date: 1981.
Scores: 5 criterion categories: Evidence of Validity, Evidence of Examinee Appropriateness, Evidence of Proper Item Construction, Evidence of Technical Merit, Evidence of Administrative Excellence.
Administration: Group.
Price Data: Available from publisher.
Time: Administration time not reported.
Author: Jean D'Arcy Maculaitis.
Publisher: Questar Assessment, Inc.
Cross References: For reviews by Eugene E. Garcia and Charles W. Stansfield, see 10:177.

[1164]

MacArthur-Bates Communicative Development Inventories, Second Edition.

Purpose: Designed as parent-completed assessments "of key language milestones" yielding "information on the course of language development."
Publication Dates: 1993-2007.
Acronym: CDI.
Administration: Individual.
Price Data, 2016: $121.95 per complete kit, including 20 Words and Gestures forms, 20 Words and Sentences forms, CDI III, and user's guide (2007, 207 pages); $99.95 per kit including 20 Words and Gestures forms, 20 Words and Sentences forms, and user's guide; $25 per 20 Words and Gestures forms; $25 per 20 Words and Sentences forms; $20 per 25 CDI-III forms; $59.95 per manual.
Foreign Language Edition: Spanish edition available.
Time: (20-40) minutes.
Comments: Previous version known as MacArthur Communicative Development Inventories.
Authors: Larry Fenson, Virginia A. Marchman, Donna J. Thal, Philip S. Dale, J. Steven Reznick, and Elizabeth Bates.
Publisher: Paul H. Brookes Publishing Co., Inc.
   a) WORDS AND GESTURES.
   Population: Ages 8-18 months.
   Scores, 7: Early Words (First Signs of Understanding, Phrases Understood, Starting to Talk, Vocabulary Checklist), Actions and Gestures (Early Gestures, Later Gestures, Total Gestures).
   b) WORDS AND SENTENCES.
   Population: Ages 16-30 months.
   Scores, 7: Words Children Use (Vocabulary Checklist, How Children Use Words), Sentences and Grammar (Word Endings/Part 1, Word Forms, Word Endings/Part 2), Combining Words (Examples of the Child's Three Longest Sentences, Complexity).
   c) CDI-III.
   Population: Ages 30-37 months.
   Scores, 3: Vocabulary Checklist, Sentences, Using Language.
Cross References: For reviews by Tiffany L. Hutchins and Hoi K. Suen, see 19:93; see T5:1528 (8 references); for a review by Carol Westby of the MacArthur Communicative Development Inventories, see 13:188 (14 references).

[1165]

The MacArthur Competence Assessment Tool–Criminal Adjudication.

Purpose: Designed to evaluate an individual's "competence to proceed to adjudication."
Population: English-speaking adults ages 18 and older.
Publication Date: 1999.
Acronym: MacCAT-CA.
Scores, 3: Understanding, Reasoning, Appreciation.

Administration: Individual.
Price Data, 2015: $228 per introductory Kit including professional manual (63 pages) and 20 interview booklets; $94 per 10 interview booklets; $54 per manual.
Time: (25-55) minutes.
Authors: Norman G. Poythress, Robert Nicholson, Randy K. Otto, John F. Edens, Richard J. Bonnie, John Monahan, and Steven K. Hoge.
Publisher: Psychological Assessment Resources, Inc.
Cross References: Reviews are scheduled for *The Twentieth Mental Measurements Yearbook*.

[1166]

Machinist Test.

Purpose: Designed for selecting or evaluating applicants or incumbents for machine shop jobs.
Population: Machinist job applicants or incumbents.
Publication Dates: 1981-2014.
Scores, 10: Heat Treating, Layout/Cutting and Assembly, Print Reading, Steel/Metals and Materials, Rigging, Mechanical Principles and Repair, Machine Tools, Tools/Material and Equipment, Machine Shop Lubrication, Total.
Administration: Group.
Price Data, 2015: $24 per consumable self-scoring test booklet (20 minimum order); $24.95 per manual (2014, 19 pages).
Time: (60-70) minutes.
Comments: Self-scoring instrument; previously listed as Ramsay Corporation Job Skills-Machinist Test; available for online test administration; test publisher advises changes in form names indicate minor revisions and updating.
Author: Roland T. Ramsay.
Publisher: Ramsay Corporation.
Cross References: For reviews by Susan M. Brookhart and Carolyn H. Suppa of Form AR-C (2007), see 19:94; for reviews by John Peter Hudson, Jr. and James W. Pinkney of an earlier edition, see 13:253.

[1167]

Maculaitis Assessment of Competencies II.

Purpose: "A comprehensive assessment of English Language proficiency for students ... whose first language is not English."
Population: Grades K–12.
Publication Dates: 1982–2001.
Acronym: MAC II.
Scores, 5: 4 subtests (Speaking, Listening, Reading, Writing), Total Battery.
Forms, 2: A, B.
Price Data: Available from publisher.
Comments: Updated and revised version of Maculaitis Assessment of Competencies (MAC).
Author: Jean D'Arcy Maculaitis.
Publisher: Questar Assessment, Inc. [Efforts to obtain updated information from the test publisher were unsuc-cessful. An updated edition of this test appears on the test publisher's website.]
a) RED LEVEL.
Population: Grades K–1.
Administration: Individual.
Time: (25) minutes.
b) BLUE LEVEL.
Population: Grades 2–3.
Administration: Individual or group.
Time: (75) minutes.
c) ORANGE LEVEL.
Population: Grades 4–5.
Administration: Individual or group.
Time: (121) minutes.
d) IVORY LEVEL.
Population: Grades 6–8.
Administration: Individual or group.
Time: (126) minutes.
e) TAN LEVEL.
Population: Grades 9–12.
Administration: Individual or group.
Time: (131) minutes.

[1168]

Maintenance Electrician A Test.

Purpose: Designed for selecting manufacturing or processing maintenance candidates.
Population: Applicants and incumbents for jobs requiring electrical knowledge and skills at the highest level.
Publication Dates: 2000-2013.
Scores, 8: Motors, Digital Electronics and Analog Electronics, Schematics & Print Reading and Control Circuits, Power Supplies/Power Distribution and Construction & Installation, Basic AC/DC Theory and Electrical Maintenance & Troubleshooting, Test Instruments and Computers & PLC, Mechanical Maintenance, Total.
Administration: Group.
Price Data, 2015: $24 per consumable self-scoring test booklet; $26 per online test administration (minimum order of 20); $24.95 per manual (22 pages).
Time: (60-70) minutes.
Comments: Self-scoring instrument; available for online test administration; test publisher advises changes in form names indicate minor revisions and updating.
Author: Roland T. Ramsay.
Publisher: Ramsay Corporation.
Cross References: For a review by Emily Bullock-Yowell of Form BTA-RC (2009), see 19:95; for a review by Kevin R. Kelly of an earlier edition, see 17:112.

[1169]

Maintenance Electrician B Test (Form BTB-C).

Purpose: For selecting manufacturing or processing maintenance candidates.
Population: Applicants and incumbents for jobs requiring electrical knowledge and skills.
Publication Dates: 2000–2012.

Scores, 8: Motors, Digital Electronics and Analog Electronics, Schematics & Print Reading and Control Circuits, Power Supplies/Power Distribution and Construction & Installation, AC/DC Theory and Electrical Maintenance, Test Instruments and Computers & PLC, Mechanical Maintenance and Hand & Power Tools, Total.
Administration: Group.
Price Data, 2015: $24 per consumable self-scoring test booklet; $26 per online test administration (minimum order of 20); $24.95 per manual (22 pages).
Time: (60-70) minutes.
Comments: Self-scoring instrument; available for online test administration; test publisher advises changes in form names indicate minor revisions and updating.
Author: Roland T. Ramsay.
Publisher: Ramsay Corporation.
Cross References: For a review by Jay R. Stewart of Form BTB-C (2005), see 17:113.

[1170]

MAINTEST.

Purpose: Measures practical mechanical and electrical knowledge.
Population: Applicants and incumbents for jobs requiring practical mechanical and electrical knowledge and skills.
Publication Dates: 1991–2012.
Scores, 22: Hydraulics, Pneumatics, Welding, Power Transmission, Lubrication, Pumps, Piping, Rigging, Mechanical Maintenance, Shop Machines and Tools & Equipment, Combustion, Motors, Digital Electronics, Schematics & Print Reading, Control Circuits, Power Supplies, Basic AC & DC Theory, Power Distribution, Test Instruments, Computers & PLC, Electrical Maintenance, Total.
Administration: Group.
Forms: Parallel forms available.
Price Data, 2015: $65 per paper-and-pencil test or online test administration (minimum order of 10, quantity discounts available) no charge for manual (30 pages).
Foreign Language Edition: Available in Spanish.
Time: (130-170) minutes.
Comments: Tests scored by publisher; test publisher advises changes in form names indicate minor revisions and updating.
Author: Roland T. Ramsay.
Publisher: Ramsay Corporation.
Cross References: For a review by Michael J. Zickar of Form NL-1, Form NL-1R, Form B, and Form C, see 17:114; for reviews by Nambury S. Raju and William J. Waldron of an earlier edition, see 13:189.

[1171]

Major Field Tests.

Purpose: Designed to measure the basic knowledge and understanding achieved by students in a major field of study.

Population: Undergraduate students completing an academic major program and MBA.
Publication Dates: 1988–2006.
Acronym: MFT.
Scores: Total score only.
Administration: Group.
Price Data: Available from publisher.
Time: (120) minutes for associate and bachelor degree programs; (180) minutes for MBA program.
Comments: Objective, end-of-program content tests in 16 disciplines; yields individual scores and subscores, group mean scores, and "assessment indicators" (group reliable subscores); delivered in two formats: online and paper-and-pencil; because there are no preset test administration dates, institutions and departments may schedule testing at their convenience; colleges and academic departments can choose where to administer the exams, as long as it is in a proctored environment, and with Internet connections for the online tests.
Author: Educational Testing Service.
Publisher: Educational Testing Service.

[1172]

Making a Terrific Career Happen.

Purpose: Designed for use in guiding examinees in self-evaluation and exploration of careers.
Population: High school graduates, college students, and adults.
Publication Date: 1992.
Acronym: MATCH.
Scores: Science-Professional, Science-Skilled, Technology-Professional, Technology-Skilled, Consumer Economics, Outdoor, Business-Professional, Business-Skilled, Clinical, Communication, Arts-Professional, Arts-Skilled, Service-Professional, Service-Skilled.
Administration: Group.
Price Data, 2016: $19.50 per self-scoring form; $175.50 per 10 self-scoring forms. Each self-scoring form includes all COPSystem Booklets: COPS interests, CAPS abilities, COPES values, and Self-Evaluation Guide.
Time: Administration time varies.
Comments: Self-administered and interpreted; test publisher indicates materials have been updated; description will be updated when those test materials are received.
Author: Lisa Knapp-Lee.
Publisher: EdITS/Educational and Industrial Testing Service.

[1173]

Malingering Probability Scale.

Purpose: Designed to "assess whether an individual is attempting to produce false evidence of psychological distress."
Population: Ages 17 and over
Publication Date: 1998.
Acronym: MPS.

Scores, 6: Depression and Anxiety, Dissociative Disorders, Post-Traumatic Stress, Schizophrenia, Inconsistency, Malingering.
Administration: Individual.
Price Data, 2016: $536.50 per kit for on-site computer scoring including reusable administration card, 20-use CD, 100 PC answer sheets, and manual; $35.50 per five pack of reusable administration cards; $72 per manual; $475.50 per 20-use scoring CD; $20.50 per 100 PC answer sheets.
Time: (20) minutes.
Authors: Leigh Silverton and Chris Gruber (manual).
Publisher: Western Psychological Services.
Cross References: For reviews by Solomon M. Fulero and Radhika krishnamurthy, see 14:216.

[1174]
Management and Graduate Item Bank.
Purpose: "For use in the selection, development or guidance of personnel at graduate level or in management positions."
Population: Graduate level and senior management applicants for the following areas: finance, computing, engineering, corporate planning, purchasing, personnel, and marketing.
Publication Dates: 1985–1987.
Acronym: MGIB.
Scores, 2: Verbal Critical Reasoning, Numerical Critical Reasoning.
Administration: Group.
Price Data: Available from publisher.
Time: 60(65) minutes.
Comments: Abbreviated adaptation of the Advanced Test Battery (85); subtests available as separates.
Authors: Saville & Holdsworth Ltd. and Linda Espey (supplementary norms manual).
Publisher: CEB.
Cross References: For reviews by James T. Austin and H. John Bernardin and by R. W. Faunce, see 11:213.

[1175]
Management and Leadership Questionnaire [2015 Manual].
Purpose: "Designed to provide information about an individual's management and leadership competencies and skills."
Population: Ages 16 and older.
Publication Dates: 2011-2015.
Acronym: MLQ30.
Scores, 30: Thinking and Managing Globally, Developing Strategy and Acting Strategically, Managing Knowledge and Information, Creating and Innovating, Managing Costs and Financial Performance, Attracting and Managing Talent, Motivating People and Inspiring Them to Excel, Coaching and Developing People, Managing Culture and Diversity, Making Sound Decisions, Displaying Initiative and Drive, Showing courage and Strength, Learning and Developing Continuously, Managing and Implementing Change, Adapting and Coping with Pressure, Executing Strategies and Plans, Improving Processes and Systems, Managing Customer Relationships and Services, Analyzing Issues and Problems, Managing Plans and Projects, Communicating and Presenting, Facilitating and Improving Communication, Influencing and Persuading People, Managing Feelings and Emotions, Speaking with Confidence and Presenting to Groups, Writing and Reporting, Relating and Networking, Listening and Showing Understanding, Building Trust and Modeling Integrity, Identifying and Resolving Conflict, Cultivating Teamwork and Collaboration.
Administration: Individual.
Forms, 2: Normative, Ipsative.
Price Data, 2015: $19.95 per online administration; manual (2015, 77 pages) available for download from test publisher's website.
Time: [20] minutes.
Comments: Administered online.
Authors: John Beazer and Allan Cameron.
Publisher: MySkillsProfile [United Kingdom].
Cross References: Reviews are scheduled for *The Twentieth Mental Measurements Yearbook*. For reviews by Patricia A. Bachelor and by Janet Houser and Lynn Wimett of an earlier edition, see 19:96.

[1176]
Management and Organizational Skills Test.
Purpose: Measures "an individual's knowledge and understanding of how relatively complex organizations function as well as knowledge of the competencies and skills required for success in management and executive positions."
Population: Job applicants.
Publication Date: 2004.
Acronym: MOST.
Scores: Total score only.
Administration: Group.
Price Data: Available from publisher.
Time: (45–60) minutes.
Comments: Web-based test version is self-administering.
Authors: E. P. Prien and Leonard D. Goodstein.
Publisher: HRD Press, Inc.
Cross References: For reviews by Paul M. Muchinsky and by L. Carolyn Pearson and Ibrahim Duyar, see 17:115.

[1177]
Management Appraisal Survey.
Purpose: "An assessment of managerial practices and attitudes as viewed through the eyes of employees."
Population: Employees.
Publication Dates: 1967-1996.

Scores, 5: Overall Leadership Style, Philosophy, Planning, Implementation, Evaluation.
Administration: No manual.
Price Data, 2016: $12.95 per instrument.
Time: Administration time not reported.
Comments: Self-administered survey.
Authors: Jay Hall, Jerry B. Harvey, and Martha S. Williams.
Publisher: Teleometrics International, Inc.
Cross References: For reviews by H. John Bernardin and George C. Thornton, III, see 10:182; see also T3:2351 (1 reference); for a review by Abraham K. Korman of the Styles of Leadership and Management, see 8:1185 (8 references).

[1178]

Management Aptitude Test.
Purpose: Designed to "evaluate critical thinking skills typically relevant to management positions."
Population: Age 18 and over.
Publication Date: 1993.
Acronym: MAT.
Scores, 7: Administrative Skills, Business Control, Communication, Planning/Organizing, Problem Solving, Supervisory Skills, Manager Potential Index.
Administration: Group or individual.
Price Data: Available from publisher.
Time: (90–100) minutes.
Comments: Test can be scored using operator-assisted telephone scoring, touch-test telephone scoring, and Quanta-based scoring.
Author: General Dynamics Information Technology.
Publisher: General Dynamics Information Technology.

[1179]

Management Development Questionnaire [Hogrefe Ltd].
Purpose: Designed "to help individuals in managerial and professional positions identify their current areas of competency and decide where they should focus their development efforts."
Population: Managers and leaders.
Publication Date: 2006.
Acronym: MDQ.
Administration: Individual or group.
Forms, 3: MDQn (normative); MDQi (semi-ipsative); MDQ360 (360-degree format).
Price Data, 2016: £226 per starter set including manual (2006, 83 pages), 5 MDQn item booklets, 10 MDQn response sheets, 10 MDQn profile sheets, 10 MDQn/i feedback charts, 10 MDQ360 rater assessment/item response sheets, 10 MDQ360 self assessment/item/response sheets, 5 MDQi item booklets, 10 MDQi response sheets, 10 MDQi profile sheets, 10 introductory leaflets for test takers; £64 per manual.

Comments: Administered via computer or paper and pencil.
Author: Allan Cameron.
Publisher: Hogrefe Ltd [United Kingdom].
a) MDQn.
Purpose: Designed to help "managers benchmark themselves against other managers."
Scores, 26: Managing Change (Initiative, Risk Taking, Creativity & Innovation, Adaptability), Planning & Organising (Analytical Thinking, Decision Making, Planning, Quality Management), Interpersonal Skills (Communicating, Listening & Supporting, Relating & Networking, Teamwork), Results Orientation (Achieving Goals, Customer Focus, Business Awareness, Learning Orientation), Leadership (Authority & Influence, Motivating & Empowering, Developing Others, Coping with Pressure), plus Impression Management.
Time: (20-30) minutes.
b) MDQi.
Purpose: Designed to generate information "about specific competency elements that the test taker identifies as priorities for development."
Scores: Same as *a* above.
Time: (20-30) minutes.
c) MDQ360.
Purpose: Designed to "help a manager understand how their bosses, peers, and subordinates assess their strengths and weaknesses."
Scores, 30: Managing Change (Initiative, Risk Taking, Creativity & Innovation, Adaptability, Strategic Thinking), Planning & Organising (Analytical Thinking, Decision Making, Planning, Quality Management, Financial Management), Interpersonal Skills (Oral Communication, Listening & Supporting, Relating & Networking, Teamwork, Emotional Awareness), Results Orientation (Achieving Goals, Customer Focus, Business Awareness, Learning Orientation, Written Communication), Leadership (Authority & Influence, Motivating & Empowering, Developing Others, Coping with Pressure, Ethics).
Time: (5-10) minutes.

[1180]

Management Development Questionnaire [HRD Press, Inc.].
Purpose: A personal competence assessment instrument "designed to help managers identify their weakness and strengths and decide what they need to do to develop themselves."
Population: Managers.
Publication Date: 1997.
Acronym: MDQ.
Scores, 20: Initiative, Risk Taking, Innovation, Flexibility/Adaptability, Analytical Thinking, Decision Making, Planning, Quality Focus, Oral Communication, Sensitivity, Relationships, Teamwork, Achievement, Customer Focus, Business Awareness, Learning Orientation, Authority/Presence, Motivating Others, Developing People, Resilience.
Administration: Individual.
Price Data, 2016: $59.95; volume discounts available.

Time: (35) minutes.
Author: Alan Cameron.
Publisher: HRD Press, Inc.
Cross References: For reviews by Samuel Hinton and Eugene P. Sheehan, see 15:140.

[1181]
Management Effectiveness Profile System.
Purpose: "Identifies managers' current strengths and weaknesses and provides direction for individual development."
Population: Managers and coworkers.
Publication Dates: 1983–1993.
Acronym: MEPS.
Scores: 2 scores (Self, Other) in 14 management skill areas: Problem Solving, Time Management, Planning, Goal Setting, Performance Leadership, Organizing, Team Development, Delegation, Participation, Integrating Differences, Providing Feedback, Stress Processing, Maintaining Integrity, Commitment.
Administration: Individual or group.
Forms, 2: Self Description, Description by Others.
Price Data: Available from publisher.
Comments: Originally called Management Practices Audit; administered to manager and 4 or 5 coworkers.
Author: Human Synergistics International.
Publisher: Human Synergistics International.

[1182]
Management Interest Inventory.
Purpose: "To assist both organizations and individuals in making decisions relating to selection, placement, and career development at management level."
Population: Managers.
Publication Dates: 1983–1986.
Scores, 54: Management Functions Preference Scores and Experience Scores (Production Operations, Technical Services, Research and Development, Distribution, Purchasing, Sales, Marketing Support, Personnel and Training, Data Processing, Finance, Legal and Secretarial, Administration, Total, Spread Across Functions); Management Skills Preference Scores and Experience Scores (Information Collecting, Information Processing, Problem-Solving, Decision-Making, Modelling, Communicating Orally, Communicating in Writing, Organising Things, Organising People, Persuading, Developing, Representing, Total).
Administration: Group.
Price Data: Available from publisher.
Time: (20–40) minutes.
Authors: Roger Holdsworth (test), Ruth Holdsworth (test), Lisa Cramp (test), and Miranda Blum (manual).
Publisher: CEB.
Cross References: For a review by David M. Saunders, see 11:216.

[1183]
Management of Differences Inventory.
Purpose: To provide feedback to an individual concerning his/her manner of handling differences in managerial situations.
Population: Business managers.
Publication Dates: 1981–1994.
Acronyn: MODI.
Scores, 9: Maintain, Smooth, Dominate, Decide by Rule, Coexist, Bargain, Yield, Release, Collaborate.
Administration: Group.
Forms, 2: Self, Feedback.
Price Data, 2016: $10.95 per form (Self or Feedback); minimum 20; volume discounts available.
Time: (20) minutes.
Comments: Self-administered; self-scored.
Author: Herbert S. Kindler.
Publisher: The Center for Management Effectiveness, Inc.

[1184]
Management Practices Update.
Purpose: To provide individuals with information about managerial behavior in areas of interpersonal relationships, the management of motivation, and personal "style" of management.
Population: Individuals involved in the management of others.
Publication Date: 1987.
Acronym: MPU.
Scores, 12: Section I (Exposure, Feedback), Section II (Basic, Safety, Belonging, Ego Status, Actualization), Section III (Team Management, Middle-of-the-Road Management, Task Management, Country Club Management, Impoverished Management).
Administration: Group.
Parts, 3: I (Interpersonal Relationships), II (Management of Motivation), III (Analysis of Management Style).
Price Data: Available from publisher.
Time: Administration time not reported.
Comments: Represents a shortened version of Personnel Relations Survey (1533), Management of Motives Index, and Styles of Management Inventory (2001).
Author: Jay Hall.
Publisher: Teleometrics International, Inc.

[1185]
Management Readiness Profile.
Purpose: Designed to "measure the attitudes and aptitudes that are commonly critical to management success."
Population: Ages 18 and over.
Publication Dates: 1989–2000.
Acronym: MRP.
Scores, 9: Managerial Interest, Leadership, Energy Level, Practical Thinking, Interpersonal Skills, Business Ethics, Management Readiness Index, Candidness, Accuracy.

Administration: Group or individual.
Price Data: Available from publisher.
Foreign Language Editions: Available in Spanish and French Canadian.
Time: (20–25) minutes.
Comments: Test can be scored over Touch Test, Internet, and Optical Scanning Software.
Author: General Dynamics Information Technology.
Publisher: General Dynamics Information Technology.

[1186]

Management Relations Survey.

Purpose: To assess employees' perceptions of their practices toward their managers.
Population: Subordinates to managers.
Publication Dates: 1970-1995.
Acronym: MRS.
Scores, 2: Exposure, Feedback.
Administration: Group.
Price Data, 2016: $12.95 per instrument.
Time: Administration time not reported.
Comments: Companion instrument to Personnel Relations Survey (1533); based on the Johari Window Model of interpersonal relations.
Author: Jay Hall.
Publisher: Teleometrics International, Inc.
Cross Reference: For a review by Walter C. Borman, see 8:1178 (1 reference).

[1187]

Management Skills and Styles Assessment.

Purpose: Designed to assess "basic managerial functions" to "determine an individual's overall management skills and style."
Population: Under 17 through adult.
Publication Date: 2011.
Acronym: MANSSA.
Scores, 40: Intrapersonal Skills (Comfort with Authority, Concentration, Coping Skills, Decision-Making, Locus of Control, Optimism, Perfectionism [Self-Directed], Self-Confidence, Integrity), Interpersonal Skills (Communication Skills, Flexibility, Soft Skills, Perfectionism [Other-Directed], Self-Monitoring, Sensitivity to Social Cues), Executive Skills (Creativity, Drive, Goal-Setting, Time Management, Vision, Risk-Taking, Organizational Skills, Cognitive Ability), Transactional Leadership (Delegating, Giving Feedback, Rewarding Performance), Transformational Leadership (Coaching, Motivating, Problem-Solving, Communicating Vision, Collaboration), Leadership Ability, Impression Management, Setting an Example, Overall Score.
Administration: Individual.
Price Data: Available from publisher.
Time: (45) minutes.
Comments: Self-administered online assessment. The test publisher provides clients with information about the methods and theoretical basis used in the development of the test as well as benchmarks for relevant industries and racial/ethnic group comparison data.
Author: PsychTests AIM, Inc.
Publisher: PsychTests AIM, Inc. [Canada].
Cross References: For reviews by Frederick L. Oswald and Richard Reilly, see 19:97.

[1188]

Management Style Inventory.

Purpose: "This exercise is designed to give you some insights into your management style and how it affects others."
Population: Industry.
Publication Dates: 1986–1987.
Scores, 5: Team Builder, Soft, Hard, Middle of Road, Ineffective.
Administration: Group or individual.
Price Data, 2016: $195; quantity discounts available.
Time: (20) minutes.
Comments: Self-administered, self-scored; now sold as part of the Training House Assessment Kit.
Author: Training House, Inc.
Publisher: HRD Press, Inc.
Cross References: For reviews by Ernest J. Kozma and Charles K. Parsons, see 11:220.

[1189]

Management Styles Inventory.

Purpose: Assesses individual management style under a variety of conditions.
Population: Adults.
Publication Dates: 1964-1995.
Scores, 5: Philosophy, Planning and Goal Setting, Implementation, Performance Evaluation, Total.
Administration: Group.
Price Data, 2016: $12.95 per instrument.
Time: Untimed.
Comments: Self-administered survey.
Authors: Jay Hall, Jerry B. Harvey, and Martha S. Williams.
Publisher: Teleometrics International Inc.
Cross References: For reviews by Ralph F. Darr, Jr. and Charles K. Parsons, see 12:227.

[1190]

Management Success Profile.

Purpose: "Provides a standardized measure of potential for success in management and is an ideal instrument for selecting supervisors, unit managers, and team leaders. The MSP assesses the individual's interest in, motivation toward, and knowledge about management positions."
Population: Adults (management position candidates).
Publication Date: 1996.
Acronym: MSP.

Scores: Validity (Candidness, Accuracy), Management Focus (Work Background, Leadership), Motivation and Attitudes (Management Responsibility, Productivity, Customer Service Orientation), Management Style (Practical Thinking, Adaptability, Coaching), Stability and Risk (Business Ethics, Job Commitment), Overall Management Profile Index.
Administration: Group.
Price Data: Available from publisher.
Time: (45) minutes.
Author: General Dynamics Information Technology.
Publisher: General Dynamics Information Technology.

[1191]

Management Transactions Audit.

Purpose: Assesses "one's interpersonal transactions and their implications for managerial effectiveness."
Population: Managers.
Publication Dates: 1973–1997.
Acronym: MTA.
Scores, 9: Transaction Scores (Parent Subsystem, Adult Subsystem, Child Subsystem); Tension Index Scores (Subordinates [Disruptive, Constructive], Colleagues [Disruptive, Constructive], Superiors [Disruptive, Constructive]).
Administration: Group.
Manual: No manual.
Price Data: Available from publisher.
Time: [15-30] minutes.
Comments: Self-administered survey.
Authors: Jay Hall and C. Leo Griffith.
Publisher: Teleometrics International, Inc.
Cross References: For reviews by Stephan J. Motowidlo and Ronald N. Taylor, see 8:1180.

[1192]

Manager Style Appraisal.

Purpose: A measure of managerial style.
Population: Adults.
Publication Dates: 1967-1995.
Scores, 5: Philosophy, Planning and Goal Setting, Implementation, Performance Evaluation, Total.
Administration: Group.
Price Data, 2016: $12.95 per instrument.
Time: Untimed.
Comments: Self-administered survey.
Authors: Jay Hall, Jerry B. Harvey, and Martha S. Williams.
Publisher: Teleometrics International, Inc.
Cross References: For reviews by Kenneth N. Anchor and Claudia J. Morner, see 12:228.

[1193]

Managerial and Professional Job Functions Inventory.

Purpose: "For defining the basic dimensions of jobs and assessing their relative importance for the job" and "assessing one's ability to perform them."

Population: Middle and upper level managers and higher-level professionals.
Publication Dates: 1978–1997.
Acronym: MPJFI.
Scores, 16: Setting Organizational Objectives, Financial Planning and Review, Improving Work Procedures and Practices, Interdepartmental Coordination, Developing and Implementing Technical Ideas, Judgment and Decision-Making, Developing Teamwork, Coping with Difficulties and Emergencies, Promoting Safety Attitudes and Practices, Communications, Developing Employee Potential, Supervisory Practices, Self-Development and Improvement, Personnel Practices, Promoting Community-Organization Relations, Handling Outside Contacts.
Administration: Individual or group.
Price Data: Available from publisher.
Time: No limit (approximately 40–60 minutes).
Authors: Melany E. Baehr, Wallace G. Lonergan, and Bruce A. Hunt.
Publisher: General Dynamics Information Technology.
Cross References: For reviews by L. Alan Witt and Sheldon Zedeck, see 11:222.

[1194]

Managerial Assessment of Proficiency MAP™.

Purpose: "Shows a participant's strengths and weaknesses in twelve areas of managerial competency and two dimensions of management style."
Population: Managers.
Publication Dates: 1985–1988.
Acronym: MAP.
Scores, 19: Administrative Competencies (Time Management and Prioritizing, Setting Goals and Standards, Planning and Scheduling Work, Administrative Composite), Communication Competencies (Listening and Organizing, Giving Clear Information, Getting Unbiased Information, Communication Composite), Supervisory Competencies (Training/Coaching/Delegating, Appraising People and Performance, Disciplining and Counseling, Supervisory Composite), Cognitive Competencies (Identifying and Solving Problems, Making Decisions/Weighing Risk, Thinking Clearly and Analytically, Cognitive Composite), Proficiency Composite, Theory X Style (Parent-Child), and Theory Y Style (Adult-Adult).
Administration: Group.
Price Data, 2016: $125.
Time: (360–420) minutes.
Comments: May be purchased with licensing agreement, contracted for in-house administration, or used by attending a public workshop provided by publisher; administered in part by videocassette.
Author: Scott B. Parry.
Publisher: HRD Press, Inc.
Cross References: For a review by Jerard F. Kehoe, see 11:223.

[1195]

Managerial Competence Index.

Purpose: "To assess the probable competence of one's approach to management."
Population: Individuals who manage or are being assessed for their potential to manage others.
Publication Dates: 1980-1989.
Acronym: MCI.
Scores, 5: Team Management, Middle-of-the-Road Management, Task Management, Country Club Management, Impoverished Management.
Administration: Group.
Price Data: Available from publisher.
Time: Administration time not reported.
Author: Jay Hall.
Publisher: Teleometrics International, Inc.
Cross References: For a review by Kurt F. Geisinger, see 11:224.

[1196]

Managerial Competence Review.

Purpose: To identify a manager's preferred managerial style and assess the relative competence of his/her approach to management.
Population: Subordinates to managers.
Publication Dates: 1980–1989.
Acronym: MCR.
Scores, 5: Relative measures of concern for people and concern for production ("9/9," "1/9," "5/5," "9/1," "1/1").
Administration: Group.
Price Data: Available from publisher.
Time: Administration time not reported.
Comments: Companion instrument for Managerial Competence Index (1195).
Author: Jay Hall.
Publisher: Teleometrics International, Inc.

[1197]

Managerial Philosophies Scale.

Purpose: Surveys the "manager's assumptions and working theories about the nature of those whose activities he or she coordinates."
Population: Managers.
Publication Dates: 1975–1995.
Acronym: MPS.
Scores, 2: Theory X (Reductive Management Beliefs), Theory Y (Developmental Management Beliefs).
Administration: Group.
Manual: No manual.
Price Data, 2016: $12.95 per instrument.
Time: [15-30] minutes.
Comments: Self-administered survey.
Authors: Jacob Jacoby and James R. Terborg.
Publisher: Teleometrics International, Inc.
Cross References: See T3:1366 (1 reference).

[1198]

Manifest Needs Questionnaire.

Purpose: "Measures the relative power of four work-related motivation factors: the need for achievement, for affiliation, for autonomy, and for dominance."
Population: Adult employees of a company or organization.
Publication Date: [No date].
Acronym: MNQ.
Scores, 4: Need for Achievement, Need for Affiliation, Need for Autonomy, Need for Dominance.
Administration: Group.
Price Data: Available from publisher.
Time: Administration time not reported.
Author: InQ Educational Materials, Inc.
Publisher: InQ Educational Materials, Inc.

[1199]

Manifestation of Symptomatology Scale.

Purpose: Designed "to identify problems of children and adolescents."
Population: Ages 11–18.
Publication Date: 1999.
Acronym: MOSS.
Scores, 20: Validity Scores (Inconsistent Responding, Random Responding, Faking Good, Faking Bad), Summary Index (Affective State, Home, Acting Out), Content Scales (Sexual Abuse, Alcohol and Drugs, Suspiciousness, Thought Process, Self-Esteem, Depression, Anxiety, Mother, Father, Home Environment, Impulsivity, School, Compliance).
Administration: Group or individual.
Price Data, 2016: $118 per kit including 25 AutoScore forms and manual (69 pages); $59 per 25 AutoScore forms; $65.50 per manual; $20.50 per 100 PC answer sheets; $178.50 per 10-use scoring and interpretation CD.
Time: (15–20) minutes.
Comments: Self-report inventory; publisher indicates that this test is specifically designed for adolescents who may not have the reading skills and concentration required by other broadband measures of personality and behavior.
Author: Neil L. Mogge.
Publisher: Western Psychological Services
Cross References: For reviews by Ronald A. Berk and Richard B. Stuart, see 15:143.

[1200]

The Manson Evaluation, Revised Edition.

Purpose: Identifies alcoholics and potential alcoholics.
Population: Adults.
Publication Dates: 1948–1987.
Scores, 8: Anxiety, Depressive Fluctuations, Emotional Sensitivity, Resentfulness, Incompleteness, Aloneness, Interpersonal Relations, Total.

Administration: Individual or group.
Price Data, 2016: $101.50 per complete kit including 25 AutoScore™ test profile forms and manual (1987, 28 pages); $48 per 25 AutoScore™ test booklets/profiles (1987); $62.50 per manual.
Time: 5–10 minutes.
Comments: Self-administered.
Authors: Morse P. Manson and George J. Huba.
Publisher: Western Psychological Services.
Cross References: For reviews by Tony Toneatto and Jalie A. Tucker, see 11:226; see also T2:1271 (2 references) and P:152 (1 reference); for a review by Dugal Campbell, see 6:137 (5 references); for reviews by Charles H. Honzik and Albert L. Hunsicker, see 4:68 (4 references).

[1201]
Manual Dexterity Test.

Purpose: Designed to provide "a measure of manual speed and skill."
Population: Ages 16 and over.
Publication Date: 2009.
Acronym: MDT.
Scores, 4: Speed, Speed and Skill, Manual Speed (average scale score of Speed, Speed and Skill), Manual Skill (difference between Speed, Speed and Skill scale scores).
Administration: Group.
Price Data: Available from publisher.
Time: 2 minutes and 15 seconds (8 minutes).
Author: Educational & Industrial Test Services Ltd.
Publisher: The Morrisby Organisation [England].

[1202]
MAPP: Motivational Appraisal of Personal Potential.

Purpose: Intended to measure "an individual's potential and motivation for given areas of work."
Population: Employees at all levels.
Publication Date: 1995.
Acronym: MAPP.
Scores, 13: Interest in Job Content, Temperament for the Job, Aptitude for the Job, Orientation to People, Affinity for Objects and Things, Approach to Data and Information, Reasoning and Thinking Style, Mathematical Capability, Language Levels, Personal Style, Personal Traits, Interpersonal and Social Tendencies, Learning Style.
Administration: Group.
Price Data: Available from publisher.
Foreign Language Editions: Available in Swedish, German, Polish, Spanish, Italian, Portuguese, Arabic, Korean, Russian, Romanian, Bulgarian, Turkish, Chinese, and Iranian.
Time: (20–25) minutes.
Author: International Assessment Network.

Publisher: International Assessment Network.
Cross References: For reviews by Martha E. Hennen and Abbot Packard, see 14:218.

[1203]
Marital Evaluation Checklist.

Purpose: "Provides a brief yet comprehensive survey of the most common characteristics and problem areas in a marital relationship."
Population: Married couples in counseling.
Publication Date: 1984.
Acronym: MEC.
Scores: 3 areas: Reasons for Marrying, Problems of the Current Relationship, Motivation for Counseling.
Administration: Group.
Price Data, 2015: $62 per package of 50.
Time: (30-40) minutes.
Comments: Self-administered checklist.
Author: Leslie Navran.
Publisher: Psychological Assessment Resources, Inc.
Cross References: See T5:1581 (1 reference); for a review by Richard B. Stuart, see 10:187.

[1204]
Marital Satisfaction Inventory—Revised.

Purpose: Designed to "identify, separately for each partner in a relationship, the nature and extent of distress along several key dimensions of their relationship."
Population: 18 years and up; couples who are married or living together.
Publication Dates: 1979–1998.
Acronym: MSI-R.
Scores, 13: Conventionalization, Global Distress, Affective Communication, Problem-Solving Communication, Aggression, Time Together, Disagreement About Finances, Sexual Dissatisfaction, Role Orientation, Family History of Distress, Dissatisfaction with Children, Conflict over Child Rearing, Inconsistency.
Administration: Group.
Price Data, 2016: $149.50 per complete kit including 40 AutoScore™ answer forms and manual (1997, 126 pages); $52.50 per 20 AutoScore™ answer forms; $72 per manual; $149.50 per 20-use scoring CD; $20.50 per 100 PC answer sheets; $357 per 20-use scoring and interpretation CD.
Foreign Language Edition: Spanish research edition administration booklet available but without separate norms.
Time: 20 to 25 minutes.
Comments: 150-item self-report inventory; hand or computer scoring available; computer-generated interpretation available.
Author: Douglas K. Snyder.
Publisher: Western Psychological Services.
Cross References: For reviews by Frank Bernt and Mary Lou Bryant Frank, see 14:219; see also T5:1582

(15 references) and T4:1538 (7 references); for reviews by David N. Dixon and E. M. Waring of an earlier edition, see 9:652 (2 references).

[1205]

The Maroondah Assessment Profile for Problem Gambling.

Purpose: Designed as "an instrument that assists counselors in developing treatment intervention for their clients with gambling problems."
Population: People with gambling problems.
Publication Date: 1999.
Acronym: G-MAP.
Scores, 17: Beliefs About Winning (Control, Prophecy, Uninformed), Feelings (Good Feelings, Relaxation, Boredom, Numbness), Situations (Oasis, Transition, Desperation, Mischief), Attitudes to Self (Low Self-Image, "Winner," Entrenchment, Harm to Self), Social (Shyness, Friendship).
Administration: Group or individual.
Price Data, 2016: A$264.95 per kit including 10 questionnaires, manual (2000, 234 pages), 10 answer sheets, 18 photocopiable action sheet masters, 10 profile sheets, 10 response reports, and computer scoring program disk.
Time: (20) minutes.
Comments: Self-report inventory; Scoring program calculates scores for all factors and provides unlimited scoring.
Authors: Tim Loughnan, Mark Pierce, and Anastasia Sagris-Desmond.
Publisher: Australian Council for Educational Research Ltd. [Australia].
Cross References: For reviews by George Engelhard, Jr. and Michael G. Kavan, see 15:144.

[1206]

Martin and Pratt Nonword Reading Test.

Purpose: Designed to "investigate the [phonological] recoding skills of students."
Population: Ages 6–16.
Publication Date: 2001.
Score: Total score only.
Administration: Individual.
Forms, 2: A, B.
Price Data, 2016: A$179.95 per starter set including record booklet, stimulus book, and manual (60 pages).
Time: (5–10) minutes.
Authors: Frances Martin and Chris Pratt.
Publisher: Australian Council for Educational Research Ltd. [Australia].
Cross References: For reviews by Kris L. Baack and Annabel J. Cohen, see 16:139.

[1207]

Maryland Addictions Questionnaire.

Purpose: Intended to survey "issues relevant to the severity of patients' alcohol and drug abuse history."

Population: Ages 17 and older.
Publication Date: 1997.
Acronym: MAQ.
Scores, 15: Validity (Response Inconsistency, Defensiveness), Summary (Emotional Distress, Resistance to Treatment, Admission of Problems), Substance Abuse (Alcoholism Severity, Drug Abuse Severity, Craving, Substance Abuse Control, Resentment), Treatment (Motivation for Treatment, Social Anxiety, Antisocial Behaviors, Cognitive Symptoms, Affective Disturbance).
Administration: Group.
Price Data, 2016: $118 per complete kit including manual (102 pages) and 25 AutoScore™ answer sheets; $59.50 per 25 AutoScore™ answer sheets; $20.50 per 100-pad PC answer sheets; $72 per manual; $405.50 per 25-use CD-ROM for scoring and interpretation.
Time: (15–20) minutes.
Comments: Author suggests should be administered as an intake measure for individuals entering addiction treatment programs.
Authors: William E. O'Donnell, Clinton B. DeSoto, and Janet L. DeSoto.
Publisher: Western Psychological Services.
Cross References: For reviews by Carl Isenhart and John A. Mills, see 14:220.

[1208]

Maryland Parent Attitude Survey.

Purpose: Designed to measure child-rearing attitudes.
Population: Parents.
Publication Dates: [1957-1966].
Acronym: MPAS.
Scores, 4: Disciplinarian, Indulgent, Protective, Rejecting.
Administration: Group.
Price Data: Available from distributor.
Time: [20–60] minutes.
Comments: For research use only; tests may be reproduced locally.
Author: Donald K. Pumroy.
Publisher: Donald K. Pumroy [Test distributed through the Test Collection at ETS].
Cross References: See T4:1551 (1 reference).

[1209]

Maslach Burnout Inventory [Third Edition Manual].

Purpose: Constructed to measure three aspects of burnout.
Population: Working adults.
Publication Dates: 1981–1996.
Scores, 3: Emotional Exhaustion, Depersonalization, Personal Accomplishment.
Administration: Individual or group.
Price Data, 2015: $50 for manual, including review-only copy of MBI forms; $15 per individual reports;

$250 per group reports; $2.40 per online administration license (minimum 50); $2 per Remote Online Survey License (minimum 50); $2 per License to Reproduce (minimum 50).

Authors: Wilmar B. Schaufeli, Michael P. Leiter, Christina Maslach, Susan E. Jackson, and Richard L. Schwab.

Publisher: Mind Garden, Inc.

   a) HUMAN SERVICES SURVEY.

   Acronym: MBI-HSS.

   Population: Staff members in the Human Services profession.

   Time: (10–15) minutes.

   b) EDUCATORS SURVEY.

   Acronym: MBI-ES.

   Population: Educators.

   Time: (5–10) minutes.

   c) GENERAL SURVEY.

   Acronym: MBI-GS.

   Population: Working adults.

   Foreign Language Edition: Spanish translation of HSS and ES forms available.

   Time: (10-15) minutes.

Cross References: For reviews by Robert Fitzpatrick and Claudia R. Wright, see 16:140; see also T5:1590 (69 references) and T4:1552 (30 references); for reviews by David S. Hargrove and Jonathan Sandoval of an earlier edition, see 10:189 (34 references).

[1210]
Massachusetts Youth Screening Instrument- Version 2.

Purpose: "To identify youths with potential mental, emotional, or behavioral problems at entry points in the juvenile justice system."

Population: Ages 12-17.

Publication Dates: 1998-2006.

Acronym: MAYSI-2.

Administration: Individual.

Forms, 2: Male, Female.

Restricted Distribution: To use the MAYSI-2 one must be registered with the National Youth Screening Assistance Project.

Price Data, 2015: $279.95 per manual and MAYSI-WARE software; $125 per manual, includes CD-ROM with printable versions of all forms.

Foreign Language Editions: Spanish language paper-and-pencil version is available; MAYSIWARE software presents the items in Spanish, on screen and with audio; MAYSI-2 Translated Edition contains translations in Arabic, Catalan, Dutch, French, German, Italian, Portuguese, Russian, and Spanish. ·

Time: (15) minutes.

Authors: Thomas Grisso and Richard Barnum.

Publisher: Professional Resource Press.

   a) MALE.

   Scores, 7: Alcohol/Drug Use, Angry-Irritable, Depressed-Anxious, Somatic Complaints, Suicide Ideation, Thought Disturbance, Traumatic Experiences.

   b) FEMALE.

   Scores, 6: Alcohol/Drug Use, Angry-Irritable, Depressed-Anxious, Somatic Complaints, Suicide Ideation, Traumatic Experiences.

Cross References: For reviews by Randy G. Floyd and by Renee M. Tobin and Corinne Zimmerman, see 18:71.

[1211]
Matching Assistive Technology & Child.

Purpose: A series of instruments designed to assess "infants' and childrens' need for assistive technology" to determine the most appropriate child-technology match.

Population: Children with disabilities, ages 0–5.

Publication Date: 1997.

Administration: Individual.

Price Data: Available from publisher.

Time: (90) minutes for entire battery.

Comments: To be used by Early Intervention and Special Education professionals with parents.

Author: Marcia J. Scherer.

Publisher: Institute for Matching Person & Technology, Inc.

   a) TECHNOLOGY UTILIZATION WORKSHEET FOR MATCHING ASSISTIVE TECHNOLOGY & CHILD.

   Purpose: Designed to "review technologies the child is currently using, has used in the past, and needs."

   Scores: No formal scores; examines perceptions in 10 areas: Communication, Mobility/Gross Motor, Vision, Hearing, Fine Motor Skills, Daily Living, Health Maintenance, Play, Self-Care, Learning/Cognition.

   Comments: Completed by parent and/or educator.

   b) WORKSHEET FOR MATCHING ASSISTIVE TECHNOLOGY & CHILD.

   Purpose: Designed to "obtain parent perspectives of a child's particular limitations, goals, and interventions as well as strengths which can be built upon in planning interventions."

   Scores: No scores; examines perceptions of 10 areas: Communication, Mobility/Gross Motor, Vision, Hearing, Fine Motor Skills, Daily Living, Health Maintenance, Play, Self-Care, Learning/Cognition.

   Comments: Completed by the child's parent.

   c) SURVEY OF TECHNOLOGY USE.

   Purpose: Designed to "help identify technologies and technology functions/features a child is likely to feel comfortable or successful in using."

   Acronym: SOTU.

   Scores: No formal scores.

   Comments: Completed by educator and/or parent.

   d) MATCHING ASSISTIVE TECHNOLOGY & CHILD.

   Purpose: Designed to help "select the most appropriate assistive technology for a child's use while pinpointing areas for training and further assessment."

   Acronym: MATCH.

   Scores: No formal scores.

   Comments: Completed by caregiver or educator.

Cross References: For reviews by Libby G. Cohen and by T. Steuart Watson and R. Anthony Doggett, see 15:145.

[1212]

Matching Assistive Technology to Child–Augmentative Communication Evaluation Simplified.

Purpose: Designed as a progression of instruments to match assistive technology to students' needs.
Population: Students eligible for special education and/or 504 services who need assistive technology to help them achieve their individualized education plan.
Publication Dates: 2010-2014.
Acronym: MATCH-ACES.
Administration: Individual.
Parts, 6: Student Information and Needs Analysis, Predisposition to Technology, History of Technology Use, AT/AAC Device Features, MATCH-ACES Assessment Interpretation/Scoring & Considerations, Recommendations.
Price Data: Available from publisher.
Time: (90-120) minutes.
Comments: Developed for educational settings but can be used in health care, home, and adult rehabilitation settings.
Authors: Susan A. Zapf, Debby McBride, and Marcia J. Scherer.
Publisher: Children's Journey to Shine, Inc.

a) NEEDS ANALYSIS FORM.
Purpose: Designed "to determine the child's current level of performance and area of need for AT [assistive technology] in their educational plan."
Scores: Ratings in 15 areas of possible need: Positioning, Mobility, Vision, Hearing, Sensory Processing, Use of Classroom Materials, Communication Skills, Self-Help, Physical Motor Performance, Recreation/Leisure, Social/Behavioral, Academic Development, Writing Skills, Learning/Study Skills, Vocational Skills.
b) PREDISPOSITION TO TECHNOLOGY FORM.
Purpose: Designed to assess the student and teacher/parent predispositions to technology use.
Scores, 3: Child Technology Experience, Personality Characteristics, Teacher and Parent Perspective.
c) MATCH-ACES SCORE FORM.
Purpose: Designed "to determine the level of the match" between the child's skills, abilities, and resources and the recommended AT device features.
Scores: Ratings in 8 areas: Physical Demands, Care/Maintenance Demands, Expense, Support and Training Service, Service Delivery, Cognitive Demands, Psychosocial Demands, Expectations, plus Total Score.

Cross References: Reviews are scheduled for *The Twentieth Mental Measurements Yearbook*.

[1213]

Matching Person and Technology.

Purpose: Designed for "selecting and evaluating technologies used in rehabilitation, education, the workplace and other settings."
Population: Clients, patients, students, or employees, and those professionals working with them.
Publication Dates: 1991–2005.
Acronym: MPT.

Administration: Individual or group.
Forms, 2: Consumer, Professional.
Price Data: Available from publisher.
Foreign Language Editions: Available in Brazilian, Portuguese, French, Italian, Korean and German.
Time: (15) minutes per test.
Comments: CD version (2005) is available with additional administration tools and supplemental resources.
Author: Marcia J. Scherer.
Publisher: Institute for Matching Person & Technology, Inc.

a) SURVEY OF TECHNOLOGY USE.
Purpose: Constructed to measure "the consumer's present use of, experiences with, and feelings toward technological devices."
Acronym: SOTU.
Scores, 4: Experience with Current Technologies, Perspectives on Technologies, Typical Activities, Personal/Social Characteristics.
b) ASSISTIVE TECHNOLOGY DEVICE PREDISPOSITION ASSESSMENT.
Purpose: Designed to "help individuals select appropriate assistive technologies."
Acronym: ATD PA.
Scores, 4: Subjective View of Capabilities, Subjective Well-Being/Quality of Life, Temperament and Psychosocial Characteristics, Device and Person Degree of Match.
c) EDUCATIONAL TECHNOLOGY PREDISPOSITION ASSESSMENT.
Purpose: Designed "for teachers who are helping students use technology to reach educational goals."
Acronym: ET PA.
Scores, 4: Educational Goal, The Student, Educational Technology, Educational Environment.
d) WORKPLACE TECHNOLOGY PREDISPOSITION ASSESSMENT.
Purpose: "Designed to assist employers in identifying factors that might inhibit the acceptance or use of a new technology in the workplace."
Acronym: WT PA.
Scores, 4: The Technology, The Employee Being Trained to Use the Technology, The Workplace Environment, Match Between Person and Technology.
e) HEALTH CARE TECHNOLOGY PREDISPOSITION ASSESSMENT.
Purpose: "Developed to assist health care professionals in identifying factors that might inhibit the acceptance or appropriate use of health care technologies."
Acronym: HCT PA.
Scores, 5: Health Problem, Consequences of HCT Use, Characteristics of the Health Care Technology, Personal Issues, Attitudes of Others.

Cross References: For reviews by Patricia A. Bachelor and by Laura L. B. Barnes and Carrie L. Winterowd, see 14:221.

[1214]

MATE [Marital Attitude Evaluation].

Purpose: "Designed to explore the relation between two people who have close contact with each other."

Population: Couples.
Publication Date: 1989.
Acronym: MATE.
Scores: 5 scales: Inclusion Behavior, Inclusion Feelings, Control Behavior, Control Feelings, Affection.
Administration: Individual and group.
Manual: Information included in manual of FIRO Awareness Scales (816).
Price Data, 2015: $50 for manual, including review-only copy of the MATE form; $2 Remote Online Survey License; $2 License to Reproduce.
Time: Administration time not reported.
Comments: Based on FIRO Awareness Scales (816).
Author: Will Schutz.
Publisher: Mind Garden, Inc.

[1215]
Math-Level Indicator.
Purpose: Designed to survey the basic mathematical skills of students.
Population: Grades 4–12.
Publication Date: 2003.
Acronym: MLI.
Scores: Total score only.
Administration: Group.
Price Data, 2016: $162 per starter set including manual, 1 package (25) Red forms, 1 package (25) Blue forms, 2 hand-scoring templates, and 2 scannable answer sheets packages (25 each); $30 per manual; $40 per 25 forms (specify Red or Blue).
Time: (30) minutes.
Comments: Designed to work with the Group Mathematics Assessment and Diagnostic Evaluation (G•MADE; 896).
Author: Kathleen T. Williams.
Publisher: Pearson.
Cross References: For reviews by Zandra S. Gratz and Dixie McGinty, see 16:141.

[1216]
Mathematical Olympiads.
Purpose: Constructed "to discover and challenge secondary school students with outstanding mathematical talent."
Population: Secondary school.
Publication Dates: 1972-2016.
Scores: Total score only.
Administration: Group.
Manual: No manual.
Price Data: Available from publisher.
Author: Committee on the American Mathematics Competitions.
Publisher: MAA American Mathematics Competition.
a) USA MATHEMATICAL OLYMPIAD.
Acronym: USAMO.
Time: 9 hours over 2 days.

Comments: Test administered annually in April; selection to participate is based on AMC12 and AIME scores.
b) INTERNATIONAL MATHEMATICAL OLYMPIAD.
Acronym: IMO.
Time: 9 hours over 2 days.
Comments: Test administered annually in the summer; selection to participate is based on USAMO scores and other scores obtained during the training session.
Cross References: For reviews by Phillip L. Ackerman and William R. Koch, see 11:228.

[1217]
Mathematics Attitude Inventory.
Purpose: "To measure the attitudes toward mathematics of secondary school and college students."
Population: Grades 7-12 and undergraduate students.
Publication Date: 1979.
Acronym: MAI.
Scores, 6: Perception of the Mathematics Teacher, Anxiety Toward Mathematics, Value of Mathematics in Society, Self-Concept in Mathematics, Enjoyment of Mathematics, Motivation in Mathematics.
Administration: Group.
Price Data: Test, scoring key, and manual (26 pages) available at no charge from test publisher.
Time: 15 minutes.
Comments: Tests may be reproduced locally.
Author: Richard S. Sandman.
Publisher: Quantitative Methods in Education, University of Minnesota.
Cross References: See T5:1599 (6 references); for reviews by Harvey Resnick and Richard F. Schmid, see 9:664 (3 references); see also T3:1410 (1 reference).

[1218]
Mathematics Competency Test.
Purpose: Designed to assess "mathematics achievement."
Population: Ages 11 to adult.
Publication Date: 1996.
Scores: Total score only.
Administration: Group.
Price Data, 2016: A$19.95 per 10 test booklets; A$38.95 per manual; £15.50 per 10 test booklets; £25 per manual.
Time: (40) minutes.
Authors: P. E. Vernon, K. M. Miller, and J. F. Izard.
Publisher: Australian Council for Educational Research Ltd. [Australia]; Hodder Education [England].
Cross References: For reviews by Joseph C. Ciechalski and G. Michael Poteat, see 14:222.

[1219]
Mathematics Self-Efficacy Scale.
Purpose: Intended to measure beliefs regarding ability to perform various math-related tasks and behaviors.

Population: College students.
Publication Date: 1993.
Acronym: MATH.
Scores, 3: Mathematics Task Self-Efficacy, Math-Related School Subjects Self-Efficacy, Total Mathematics Self-Efficacy Score.
Administration: Individual or group.
Forms, 2: A, B.
Price Data, 2015: $50 for manual including review-only copy of MATH form; $2.40 per Transform Survey Hosting license (minimum 50); $2 per Remote Online Survey license (minimum 50); $2 License to Reproduce.
Time: (15) minutes.
Authors: Nancy E. Betz and Gail Hackett.
Publisher: Mind Garden, Inc.
Cross References: For reviews by Joseph C. Ciechalski and Everett V. Smith, Jr., see 14:223; see also T5:1602 (1 reference).

[1220]
MATRICS Consensus Cognitive Battery.

Purpose: "A self-contained battery that includes copyrighted materials from various sources" that is designed "to provide a relatively brief evaluation of key cognitive domains that are relevant to schizophrenia and related disorders."
Population: Adults with schizophrenia and related disorders.
Publication Date: 2006.
Acronym: MCCB.
Scores, 18: Speed of Processing [Brief Assessment of Cognition in Schizophrenia: Symbol Coding, Category Fluency: Animal Naming (Fluency), Trail Making Test: Part A], Attention/Vigilance [Continuous Performance Test—Identical Pairs], Working Memory [Wechsler Memory Scale—Third Edition: Spatial Span, Letter-Number Span], Verbal Learning [Hopkins Verbal Learning Test—Revised], Visual Learning [Brief Visuospatial Memory Test—Revised], Reasoning and Problem Solving [Neuropsychological Assessment Battery: Mazes], Social Cognition [Mayer-Salovey-Caruso Emotional Intelligence Test: Managing Emotions], Overall Composite Score.
Administration: Individual.
Price Data, 2012: $1,275 per complete kit, including manual (2006, 163 pages), 25 MCCB administrator's forms, 25 MCCB respondent's booklets, 2 software discs in plastic sleeves [one with the CPT-IP and the second with the MSCEIT™ and MCCB scoring programs], 1 Scoring Template for the BACS Symbol Coding Task, 1 WMS-III™ Spatial Span board, 25 HVLT-R test booklets–Form 1, 1 BVMT-R Recall Stimulus booklet, 25 Executive Functions Module response booklets–Form 1, and 25 NAB Mazes Test record forms–Form 1, in an MCCB box; $510 per Retest Packet, including 25 MCCB administrator's forms, 25 MCCB respondent's booklets, 25 NAB Executive Functions Module response booklets, 25 NAB Mazes Test record forms, and 25 HVLT-R test booklets.
Foreign Language Editions: Simplified Chinese, German, Hebrew, Hindi, Italian, Japanese, Kannada, Marathi, Romanian, Russian, Spanish (Central and South American), Spanish (Spain), Tamil, and Telugu versions available.
Time: (90) minutes.
Comments: Distributed by Psychological Assessment Resources, Inc., 16204 N. Florida Ave., Lutz, FL 33549-8119; Multi-Health Systems, Inc., P. O. Box 950, North Tonawanda, NY 14120-0950; Pearson Assessments, Inc., P. O. Box 599700, San Antonio, TX 78259.
Authors: Keith H. Nuechterlein and Michael F. Green.
Publisher: MATRICS Assessment, Inc.
Cross References: For reviews by Thomas P. Hogan and Oren Meyers, see 19:98; for reviews of Brief Visuospatial Memory Test—Revised by Anita M. Hubley and Terry A. Stinnett, see 15:40; see also T8:367. For reviews of Hopkins Verbal Learning Test—Revised by Timothy Z. Keith and Wendy J. Steinberg, see 16:108; see also T8:1264. For reviews of Mayer-Salovey-Caruso Emotional Intelligence Test by S. Alvin Leung and by Catherine Cook-Cottone and Scott T. Meier, see 16:143; see also T8:1634. For reviews of Wechsler Memory Scale—Third Edition by Erik Carl D'Amato and Cecil R. Reynolds, see 14:416; see also T6:2695.

[1221]
Matrix-Predictive Uniform Law Enforcement Selection Evaluation Inventory.

Purpose: Designed to "assess the future job-performance liabilities of law enforcement officer candidates."
Population: Law enforcement officer candidates.
Publication Date: 2008.
Acronym: M-PULSE.
Scores, 47: Interpersonal Difficulties, Off-Duty Misconduct, Property Damage, Motor Vehicle Accidents, Inappropriate Use of Weapon, Excessive Force, Sexually Offensive Conduct, Potential for Reprimands/Suspensions, Potential for Resignation, Potential for Termination, Chemical Abuse/Dependency, Procedural and Conduct Mistakes, Misuse of Vehicle, Discharge of Weapon, Unprofessional Conduct, Racially Offensive Conduct, Lawsuit Potential, Criminal Conduct, Impression Management, Negative Self-Issues, Negative Emotions, Egocentrism, Inadequate Views of Police Work, Poor Emotional Controls, Negative Perceptions of Law Enforcement, Inappropriate Attitudes About the Use of Force, Overly Traditional Officer Traits, Suspiciousness, Unethical Behavior, Lack of Personal Integrity, Negative Views of Department/Leadership, Amorality, Unpredictability, Risk Taking, Novelty Seeking, Social Incompetence, Lack of Teamwork, Unreliability, Reckless-Impulsivity, Rigidity, Lack of Integrity/Ethics, Emotional

Instability-Stress Intolerance, Poor Decision-Making and Judgment, Passivity-Submissiveness, Poor Service Orientation, Substance Abuse.
Administration: Individual or group.
Price Data, 2015: $69 per technical manual (58 pages); $54 per 10 item booklets; $37 per 50 data entry sheets; $25 per online profile reports.
Time: (60-80) minutes.
Comments: Can be administered online or via paper and pencil.
Authors: Robert D. Davis and Cary D. Rostow.
Publisher: Multi-Health Systems, Inc.
Cross References: For reviews by J. M. Blackbourn, Conn Thomas, and Jennifer G. Fillingim and by Gary J. Dean, see 18:72.

[1222]
Mayer-Salovey-Caruso Emotional Intelligence Test.

Purpose: Designed to assess emotional intelligence, measuring a person's capacity for reasoning with emotional information.
Population: Age 17 and older.
Publication Date: 2002.
Acronym: MSCEIT.
Scores, 4: Managing Emotions, Understanding Emotions, Using Emotions, Perceiving Emotions.
Administration: Individual or group.
Price Data, 2015: $75 per user's manual; $70 per package of 3 item booklets; $110 per online personal summary report kit including user's manual and 1 personal summary report; $50 per online personal summary reports; $57 per online resource reports; $105 per software preview version including getting started guide and 3 personal summary reports.
Foreign Language Editions: Spanish edition available.
Time: (30-45) minutes.
Comments: Self-completed.
Authors: John D. Mayer, Peter Salovey, and David R. Caruso.
Publisher: Multi-Health Systems, Inc.
Cross References: For reviews by S. Alvin Leung and by Catherine Cook-Cottone and Scott T. Meier, see 16:143.

[1223]
The MbM Questionnaire: Managing by Motivation, Third Edition.

Purpose: Designed for "helping managers understand their own needs" and "to identify the needs of their employees."
Population: Managers and supervisors.
Publication Dates: 1986–1996.
Acronym: The MbM Questionnaire.

Scores: 4 scales: Safety/Security, Social/Belonging, Self-Esteem, Self-Actualization.
Administration: Group.
Price Data, 2016: $59.95; volume discounts available.
Time: (10) minutes.
Author: Marshall Sashkin.
Publisher: HRD Press, Inc.
Cross References: For reviews by John W. Fleenor and Robert K. Gable, see 14:225.

[1224]
McCall-Crabbs Standard Test Lessons in Reading.

Purpose: Measurement of reading progress.
Population: Reading level grades 3-8.
Publication Dates: 1926–1979.
Scores: Item and grade equivalent scores.
Administration: Group.
Levels, 6: Overlapping levels labeled A, B, C, D, E, F.
Price Data, 2016: $12 per test booklet (any level); $8.95 per manual/answer key (1979, 16 pages).
Time: 3 minutes for any one test; 180 minutes for each booklet (60 tests per booklet).
Comments: Fourth edition.
Authors: William A. McCall and Lelah Crabbs Schroeder; revision by Robert P. Starr.
Publisher: Teachers College Press.
Cross References: See T4:1568 (1 reference); for a review by Brendan John Bartlett, see 9:669.

[1225]
McCarron-Dial System.

Purpose: A battery of neurometric and behavioral measures to be used for vocational, educational, and neuropsychological assessment particularly in meeting the programming needs of handicapped persons.
Population: Normal and handicapped individuals ages 3 to adult.
Publication Dates: 1973-2005.
Acronym: MDS.
Scores: 5 factors: Verbal-Spatial-Cognitive, Sensory, Motor, Emotional, Integration-Coping.
Administration: Individual.
Parts: 3 components (Auxiliary Component, Haptic Visual Discrimination Test [HVDT], McCarron Assessment of Neuromuscular Development [MAND]).
Price Data, 2016: $4,190 per complete System including Auxiliary, HVDT, and MAND Components; price data for software for computer-assisted programs supporting the MDS available from publisher; price information for workshops and training available from publisher.
Comments: "A commitment to receive training is required for all purchasers of the McCarron-Dial System"; components available as separates.

Authors: Lawrence McCarron and Jack G. Dial.
Publisher: McCarron-Dial Systems, Inc.

   a) AUXILIARY COMPONENT.
Publication Dates: 1973-2005.
Price Data: $670 per set of materials in carrying case; $55 per 50 IEP forms; $55 per 25 IPP forms; $210 per manual (2005, 259 pages).
Comments: Manual title is Revised McCarron-Dial Evaluation System Manual; kit includes Bender Visual Motor Gestalt Test, and Koppitz Scoring Manual for The Bender Gestalt Test for Young Children, the McCarron-Dial System Individual Evaluation Profile (IEP), the McCarron-Dial Individual Program Plan (IPP), the Observational Emotional Inventory, the Emotional Behavioral Checklist, and the Dial Behavior Rating Scale.

   1) Dial Behavior Rating Scale.
Purpose: To provide an abbreviated assessment of essential personal, social, and work adjustment behaviors that relate to vocational placement, adjustment to work, and personal-social adjustment.
Publication Dates: 1973-1986.
Acronym: BRS.
Price Data: $55 per 25 forms.
Author: Jack G. Dial.

   2) Observational Emotional Inventory.
Publication Date: 1986.
Acronym: OEI.
Price Data: $55 per 25 forms.
Time: 120 minutes on each of 5 days.
Comments: Behavior checklist.

   3) Emotional Behavioral Checklist.
Purpose: To assess an individual's overt emotional behavior.
Publication Date: 1986.
Acronym: EBC.
Price Data: $55 per 25 forms.
Comments: Behavior Checklist (alternate to OEI).

   b) HAPTIC VISUAL DISCRIMINATION TEST.
Purpose: To measure an individual's haptic-visual integration skills.
Publication Dates: 1976-1988.
Acronym: HVDT.
Scores, 4: Shape, Size, Texture, Configuration.
Price Data: $1,575 per complete kit including score forms, photographic plates, folding screen, sets of shapes, sizes, textures, and configurations, manual (1988, 261 pages) in a carrying case; $57.50 per 50 score forms; $98 per manual.
Time: (10-15) minutes per hand.
Comments: Manual title is Sensory Integration: The Haptic Visual Processes.

   c) McCARRON ASSESSMENT OF NEUROMUSCULAR DEVELOPMENT.
Purpose: "A standardized and quantitative procedure for assessing fine and gross motor abilities."
Population: Ages 3.5 to adult.
Publication Dates: 1976–1997.
Acronym: MAND.
Scores, 3: Fine Motor, Gross Motor, Total.
Price Data: $1,945 per complete kit including score forms, a dynamometer, stopwatch-timer, components for fine and gross motor testing, and manual (1997, 221 pages) in carrying case; $75 per 25 score forms; $105 per manual.
Time: (15) minutes.

Comments: Manual title is Revised McCarron Assessment of Neuromuscular Development Manual.
Author: Lawrence T. McCarron.
Cross References: For reviews by Calvin P. Garbin and David C. Solly, see 11:231 (1 reference).

[1226]
McDowell Vision Screening Kit.

Purpose: "Designed for screening children's vision problems."
Population: 2 1/2 to 5 1/2 years.
Publication Date: 1994.
Scores, 15: Distance Vision, Near Point Vision, Ocular Alignment/Motility (Cover/Uncover, Light Reflex), Color Perception, Ocular Function (Pupils, Scanning, Shifts Attention, Blink, Tracking, Convergence, Conjugate Gaze, Visual Fields, Distant/Near Accommodation, Nystagmus).
Administration: Individual.
Price Data, 2016: $190 per kit including all test materials, 100 recording forms, and manual (40 pages); $42 per 100 recording forms; $62.50 per manual.
Time: (10–20) minutes.
Comments: Recording form for use in screening very young or severely disabled children; administrator scored.
Authors: P. Marlene McDowell and Richard L. McDowell.
Publisher: Western Psychological Services.
Cross References: For a review by Cynthia A. Rohrbeck, see 14:226.

[1227]
McGhee-Mangrum Inventory of School Adjustment.

Purpose: Designed to be used by school counselors to assess interpersonal and academic behaviors associated with student success in the classroom.
Population: Students ages 5 through 18.
Publication Date: 2007.
Acronym: MISA.
Scores, 5: Attention and Academic Problems, Hyperactivity and Impulsivity, Anxiety, Oppositional Behavior, Aggressive Behavior.
Administration: Individual.
Price Data, 2014: $131 per complete kit including examiner's manual (2007, 78 pages) and 25 record forms.
Time: (5-10) minutes.
Authors: Ronnie L. McGhee and Lori Mangrum.
Publisher: PRO-ED.
Cross References: Reviews are scheduled for *The Twentieth Mental Measurements Yearbook*.

[1228]
The mCircle™ Instrument.

Purpose: "Tests for and explores appropriate uses for five strategies routinely used by individuals to solve problems and reach resolution in human interaction."

Population: Business and industry.
Publication Date: 1986.
Scores, 5: Get Out, Give In, Take Over, Trade Off, Breakthrough.
Administration: Group.
Price Data, 2016: $19.95 per assessment (volume discounts available).
Time: (30-40) minutes.
Comments: Self-administered, self-scored. The test publisher has indicated there is a newer edition of this test; description will be updated when complete test materials are received.
Authors: Paul Kordis and Dudley Lynch.
Publisher: Brain Technologies Corporation.
Cross References: For reviews by Stephen Jurs and Rick Lindskog, see 11:232.

[1229]

MDS Vocational Interest Exploration System.

Purpose: "A computer-assisted interest exploration process that facilitates the discovery of personal preferences and job opportunities."
Population: High school–adults.
Publication Date: 1991.
Acronym: VIE.
Scores: 3 steps: Selection of Jobs Based on Work Preferences, Occupational Exploration, Job Review Comparison.
Administration: Individual.
Price Data, 2016: $490 per set including computer program 4 VIE job manuals, instructor's manual (135 pages), 25 VIE system guides with work preference questionnaires and job review forms.
Time: Administration time not reported.
Comments: Three supplementary forms are also provided with materials: Pre-Post Job Knowledge Form, Understanding of Self and Job Questionnaire, and Vocational Goal Planning Exercise.
Authors: Lawrence T. McCarron and Harriette P. Spires.
Publisher: McCarron-Dial Systems, Inc.
Cross References: For reviews by Douglas J. McRae and Myra N. Womble, see 13:194.

[1230]

Meadow-Kendall Social-Emotional Assessment Inventory for Deaf and Hearing Impaired Students.

Purpose: "Can be used to flag students who need extra attention in particular areas . . . . useful in communicating with parents who are reluctant to admit that their child needs special attention … helpful in implementing an individualized program so that social and emotional areas are emphasized in the curriculum for the child who needs them."
Population: Ages 3–6, 7–21.
Publication Date: 1983.

Acronym: SEAI.
Administration: Group.
Levels: 2 levels.
Price Data, 2015: $10 per 10 forms; $15 per manual (37 pages).
Time: Administration time not reported.
Comments: Behavior checklist to be completed by adult informant.
Authors: Kathryn P. Meadow and others listed below.
Publisher: Laurent Clerc National Deaf Education Center.
　　a) PRE-SCHOOL.
　　　Population: Ages 3-6.
　　　Scores, 5: Sociable/Communicative Behaviors, Impulsive Dominating Behaviors, Developmental Lags, Anxious/Compulsive Behaviors, Special Items.
　　　Authors: Kathryn P. Meadow, Pamela Getson, Chi K. Lee, Linda Stamper, and the Center for Studies in Education and Human Development.
　　b) SCHOOL-AGE.
　　　Population: Ages 7-21.
　　　Scores, 3: Social Adjustment, Self Image, Emotional Adjustment.
　　　Authors: Kathryn P. Meadow, Michael A. Karchmer, Linda M. Petersen, and Lawrence Rudner.
Cross References: See T5:1618 (3 references) and T4:1579 (2 references); for reviews by Marilyn E. Demorest and Kenneth L. Sheldon, see 10:194 (1 reference).

[1231]

Measure of Questioning Skills.

Purpose: Designed "to measure the quantity and quality of questions."
Population: Grades 3–10.
Publication Dates: 1986–1993.
Scores, 4: Gathering Information, Organizing Information, Extending Information, Composite.
Administration: Group.
Forms, 2: A, B.
Price Data: Available from publisher.
Time: (20) minutes.
Authors: Ralph Himsl and Garnet W. Millar.
Publisher: Scholastic Testing Service, Inc.
Cross References: For a review by Darrell R. Sabers, see 14:228.

[1232]

The Measurement of Moral Judgment.

Purpose: Measures moral judgment through dilemma interviews.
Population: Ages 10 and over.
Publication Date: 1984.
Scores: 1 score dichotomized as moral stage (I to V) and moral type (A: Heteronomous or B: Autonomous).
Administration: Individual.
Forms, 3: Parallel Forms A, B, and C consist of 3 standard dilemmas each.

Price Data: Available from publisher.
Time: (10-15) minutes.
Authors: Anne Colby, Lawrence Kohlberg, John Gibbs, and Marcus Lieberman.
Publisher: Cambridge University Press.
Cross References: See T5:1625 (1 reference), 9:681 (9 references), and T3:1262 (2 references).

[1233]

Measures of Academic Progress.

Purpose: Designed to provide "educators the information they need to improve teaching and learning" in the areas of reading, language usage, mathematics, and science as well as develop instructional strategies and promote school improvement.
Population: Grades 2-12.
Publication Dates: 2003-2016.
Acronym: MAP.
Administration: Group.
Restricted Distribution: To administer MAP assessments, professionals must have completed MAP training requirements.
Price Data: Available from publisher.
Time: Untimed (typically 60 to 75 minutes).
Comments: MAP tests are computer administered and adaptive; sublistings vary by state, typical example below.
Author: Northwest Evaluation Association.
Publisher: Northwest Evaluation Association.
   a) LANGUAGE.
    Scores, 6: Writing Process, Composition Structure, Grammar/Usage, Punctuation, Capitalization, Total.
   b) MATHEMATICS.
    Scores, 9: Number/Numeration Systems, Operations/ Computation, Equations/Numerals, Geometry, Measurement, Problem Solving, Statistics/Probability, Applications, Total.
   c) READING.
    Scores, 5: Word Meaning, Literal Comprehension, Interpretive Comprehension, Evaluative Comprehension, Total.
   d) SCIENCE CONCEPTS.
    Scores, 3: Concepts, Processes, Total.
   e) GENERAL SCIENCE.
    Scores, 4: Life Sciences, Earth/ Space Sciences, Physical Sciences, Total.
Cross References: For reviews by Gregory J. Cizek and by Mark J. Gierl and Cecilia B. Alves, see 18:73.

[1234]

Measures of Psychosocial Development.

Purpose: "Assesses personality development through eight stages of life."
Population: Ages 13–86 years.
Publication Dates: 1980-1988.
Acronym: MPD.
Scores, 27: 8 Positive scores (Trust [P1], Autonomy [P2], Initiative [P3], Industry [P4], Identity [P5], Intimacy [P6], Generativity [P7], Ego Integrity [P8]),

8 Negative scores (Mistrust [N1], Shame and Doubt [N2], Guilt [N3], Inferiority [N4], Identity Confusion [N5], Isolation [N6], Stagnation [N7], Despair [N8]), 8 Resolution scale scores (R1, R2, R3, R4, R5, R6, R7, R8), 3 Total scores (Total Positive [TP], Total Negative [TN], Total Resolution [TR]).
Administration: Individual or group.
Price Data, 2015: $200 per introductory kit including 25 reusable item booklets, 50 answer sheets, 25 male profile forms, 25 female profile forms, and manual (1988, 31 pages).
Time: (15-20) minutes.
Comments: Based upon Erikson's theory of human development.
Author: Gwen A. Hawley.
Publisher: Psychological Assessment Resources, Inc.
Cross References: See T5:1631 (4 references); for reviews by James C. Carmer and Robert K. Gable, see 11:233.

[1235]

Mechanic Evaluation Test.

Purpose: Designed for selecting or evaluating industrial mechanics.
Population: Mechanic job applicants or incumbents.
Publication Dates: 1992-2014.
Administration: Group.
Levels, 3: C Mechanic, B Mechanic, A Mechanic.
Price Data, 2015: $24 per consumable self-scoring booklet; $26 per online test administration (20 minimum order); $24.95 per manual (20 pages).
Foreign Language Edition: Available in Spanish.
Time: (60-70) minutes.
Comments: Self-scoring instrument; available for online test administration; test publisher advises changes in form names indicate minor revisions and updating.
Author: Roland T. Ramsay.
Publisher: Ramsay Corporation.
   a) A MECHANIC.
    Scores: 6 areas: Welding & HVAC, Pneumatics and Lubrication, Print Reading and Shop, Electrical, Mechanical & Miscellaneous, Total.
   b) B MECHANIC.
    Scores: 5 areas: Welding/ Plumbing & HVAC, Pneumatics and Lubrication, Print Reading/ Mechanical & Shop, Electrical, Total.
   c) C MECHANIC.
    Scores: 6 areas: Welding/ Plumbing & HVAC, Pneumatics and Lubrication, Mechanical & Print Reading, Electrical, Shop/ Tools & Machines, Rigging & Miscellaneous, Total.
Cross References: For reviews by Stephen B. Johnson and Charles A. Scherbaum of Forms A1R-C, B1-C, C1-C, C1R-C (2013), see 19:99; for reviews by David O. Anderson and Alan C. Bugbee of an earlier edition, see 13:254.

[1236]

Mechanical and Technical Understanding Test.

Purpose: "Designed to test the respondent's mechanical comprehension."
Population: Ages 13-58 years.
Publication Dates: 1958-2015.
Acronym: MTVT.
Score: Total score only.
Administration: Individual or group.
Price Data, 2016: £28 per online administration with technical report and electronic copy of manual (2015, 19 pages); subscription discount available.
Foreign Language Edition: Originally published in German.
Time: 45 minutes.
Comments: Administered online.
Author: G. A. Lienert.
Publisher: Hogrefe Ltd [United Kingdom].

[1237]

Mechanical Aptitude Test.

Purpose: Designed for evaluating mechanical aptitude.
Population: Applicants for jobs that require the ability to learn mechanical skills.
Publication Dates: 2002-2015.
Scores: Total score only covering 4 areas: Household Objects, Work-Production and Maintenance, School-Science and Physics, Hand and Power Tools.
Administration: Group.
Price Data, 2016: $24 per consumable self-scoring test booklet; $26 per online test administration (minimum order of 20); $24.95 per manual.
Foreign Language Edition: Available in Spanish and French.
Time: 20(30) minutes.
Comments: Self-scoring instrument; available for online administration; test publisher advises changes in form names indicate minor revisions and updating.
Author: Roland T. Ramsay.
Publisher: Ramsay Corporation.
Cross References: For reviews by James T. Austin and Karl N. Kelley of Form MAT-3-C (2010), see 19:100; for a review by M. David Miller of an earlier edition, see 17:116.

[1238]

Mechanical Aptitudes.

Purpose: Measures ability to learn and succeed in an industrial, mechanical or maintenance position.
Population: Applicants for industrial positions, training programs, and vocational counseling.
Publication Dates: 1947–1995.
Scores, 4: Mechanical Knowledge, Space Relations, Shop Arithmetic, Total.

Administration: Individual or group.
Price Data: Available from publisher.
Time: 35 minutes.
Comments: Previously listed as SRA Mechanical Aptitudes.
Author: Richardson, Bellows, Henry & Co., Inc.
Publisher: General Dynamics Information Technology.
Cross References: See T2:2267 (8 references); for reviews by Alec Rodger and Douglas G. Schultz, see 4:764.

[1239]

Mechanical Maintenance Trainee.

Purpose: Designed for selecting mechanical maintenance trainees.
Population: Applicants with mechanical training and experience necessary for entry into a training program.
Publication Dates: 1998-2014.
Scores, 13: Hydraulics, Pneumatics, Print Reading, Welding, Power Transmission, Lubrication, Pumps, Piping, Rigging, Maintenance, Shop Machines, Tools/Material & Equipment, Total.
Administration: Group.
Price Data, 2015: $24 per consumable self-scoring test booklet; $26 per online test administration (minimum order of 20); $24.95 per manual (2014, 20 pages).
Time: (60-70) minutes.
Comments: Self-scoring instrument; available for online test administration; test publisher advises changes in form names indicate minor revisions and updating.
Author: Roland T. Ramsay.
Publisher: Ramsay Corporation.
Cross References: For reviews by Patricia A. Bachelor and Kate Hattrup of Form UKM-1C, see 19:101; for a review by Kevin J. McCarthy of an earlier edition, see 17:117.

[1240]

Mechanical Movements.

Purpose: Assesses the ability to visualize a mechanical system where there is internal movement or displacement of parts.
Population: Assesses the ability to visualize a mechanical system where there is internal movement or displacement of parts.
Publication Dates: 1959–1963.
Scores: Total score only.
Administration: Individual or group.
Price Data: Available from publisher.
Time: 14 minutes.
Authors: L. L. Thurstone and T. E. Jeffrey.
Publisher: General Dynamics Information Technology.
Cross References: For a review by William A. Owens, see 6:1089.

[1241]
Mechanical Technician A.

Purpose: Designed for selecting or evaluating above journey level maintenance technicians for jobs in the metals or manufacturing industry.

Population: Applicants and incumbents for jobs requiring mechanical maintenance knowledge and skills at the highest level.

Publication Dates: 2003-2009.

Scores, 6: Hydraulics & Pneumatics, Print Reading, Power Transmission & Lubrication, Pumps & Piping, Mechanical Maintenance Principles, Total.

Administration: Group.

Forms: Parallel forms available.

Price Data, 2015: $24 per consumable self-scoring test booklet or $26 per online test administration (minimum order of 20); $24.95 per manual (2009, 24 pages).

Time: (60-70) minutes.

Comments: Self-scoring instrument; available for online test administration; test publisher advises changes in form names indicate minor revisions and updating.

Author: Roland T. Ramsay.

Publisher: Ramsay Corporation.

Cross References: For reviews by Allen I. Huffcutt and Yuanzhong Zhang of Forms AR-XC (2009) and MTA-YC (2003), see 19:102; for reviews by Michael D. Biderman and Bart L. Weathington and by Mary L. Garner of an earlier edition, see 17:118.

[1242]
Mechanical Technician B.

Purpose: For selecting or evaluating mid-journey level maintenance technicians for jobs in the metals or manufacturing industry.

Population: Applicants and incumbents for jobs requiring mechanical maintenance knowledge and skills.

Publication Dates: 2003–2011.

Scores, 8: Hydraulics & Pneumatics, Print Reading, Burning/Fabricating/Welding & Rigging, Power Transmission & Lubrication, Pumps & Piping, Mechanical Maintenance Principles, Shop Equipment & Tools, Total.

Administration: Group.

Forms: Parallel forms available.

Price Data, 2015: $24 per consumable self-scoring test booklet; $26 per online test administration (minimum order of 20); $24.95 per manual (26 pages).

Time: (60-70) minutes (untimed).

Comments: Self-scoring instrument; test publisher advises changes in form names indicate minor revisions and updating.

Author: Roland T. Ramsay.

Publisher: Ramsay Corporation.

Cross References: For a review by Gregory J. Cizek of Forms MTB-XC and MTB-YC (2005), see 17:119.

[1243]
Mechanical Technician C.

Purpose: For selecting or evaluating entry-journey level maintenance technicians for jobs in the metals or manufacturing industry.

Population: Applicants and incumbents for jobs requiring mechanical knowledge and skills.

Publication Dates: 2003-2011.

Scores, 8: Hydraulics & Pneumatics, Print Reading, Burning/Fabricating/Welding & Rigging, Power Transmission & Lubrication, Pumps & Piping, Mechanical Maintenance Principles, Shop Equipment & Tools, Total.

Administration: Group.

Forms: Parallel forms available.

Price Data, 2015: $24 per consumable self-scoring test booklet or $26 per online test administration (minimum order of 20); $24.95 per manual (26 pages).

Time: (60-70) minutes.

Comments: Self-scoring instrument; test publisher advises changes in form names indicate minor revisions and updating.

Author: Roland T. Ramsay.

Publisher: Ramsay Corporation.

Cross References: For reviews by James A. Athanasou and Christa E. Washington of Forms CR-XC and MTC-YC (2011), see 19:103; for a review by Russell W. Smith of an earlier edition, see 17:120.

[1244]
Mechanical Understanding Test.

Purpose: Designed to assess how well people understand "the basic principles of physics and mechanics that determine success in handling and manipulating objects and machines."

Population: Adults.

Publication Date: 2004.

Acronym: MUT.

Scores: Total score only.

Administration: Group.

Price Data, 2016: $39.95 per administrator manual; $75 per 25 answer sheets; $59.95 per 10 test booklets.

Time: (30–40) minutes.

Authors: Erich P. Prien, Leonard D. Goodstein, and Kristin O. Prien.

Publisher: HRD Press, Inc.

Cross References: For reviews by Phillip L. Ackerman and Michael B. Bunch, see 17:121.

[1245]
MecTest.

Purpose: Designed for selecting or evaluating journey-level maintenance mechanics.

Population: Applicants and incumbents for maintenance jobs.

Publication Dates: 1991–2014.

Scores, 9: Hydraulics and Pneumatics, Print Reading, Welding and Rigging, Power Transmission, Lubrication, Pumps and Piping, Mechanical Maintenance, Shop Machines/Tools/Equipment, Total.
Administration: Group.
Price Data, 2015: $24 per consumable self-scoring test booklet (20 minimum order); $26 per online administration; $24.95 per manual (28 pages).
Foreign Language Edition: Available in Spanish.
Time: (60-70) minutes.
Comments: Self-scoring instrument; available for online test administration; test publisher advises changes in form names indicate minor revisions and updating.
Author: Roland T. Ramsay.
Publisher: Ramsay Corporation.
Cross References: For reviews by Nancy T. Tippins and Sheldon Zedeck of Forms AU-C and BV-R (2012), see 19:104; for a review by Robert J. Drummond of an earlier edition, see 13:197.

[1246]
Medical College Admission Test.

Purpose: Designed to test examinees "on the skills and knowledge medical educators and physicians have identified as key prerequisites for success in medical school and the practice of medicine."
Population: Applicants for admission to a health-professionals school.
Publication Dates: 1946-2016.
Acronym: MCAT.
Scores, 5: Biological and Biochemical Foundations of Living Systems, Chemical and Physical Foundations of Biological Systems, Psychological/Social/Biological Foundations of Behavior, Critical Analysis and Reasoning Skills, Total.
Administration: Group.
Price Data: Available from publisher.
Time: (375) minutes.
Comments: A new version of the MCAT was launched in April 2015; administered at testing centers established by test publisher.
Author: Constructed under the direction of the Association of American Medical Colleges.
Publisher: Administered at the direction of the Association of American Medical Colleges.
Cross References: See T5:1638 (3 references), T4:1600 (11 references), 9:691 (9 references), T3:1576 (40 references), 8:1101 (40 references), and T2:2355 (30 references); for reviews by Nancy S. Cole and James M. Richards, Jr. of earlier forms, see 7:1100 (57 references); for reviews by Robert L. Ebel and Philip H. DuBois, see 6:1137 (43 references); for a review by Alexander G. Wesman, see 5:932 (4 references); for a review by Morey J. Wantman, see 4:817 (11 references).

[1247]
Medical Ethics Inventory.

Purpose: Designed to provide "profiles of the value preferences of medical students regarding medical ethical dilemmas."
Population: First year medical students.
Publication Date: 1982.
Acronym: MEI.
Scores, 6: Social, Economic, Theoretical, Political, Religious, Aesthetic.
Administration: Group.
Price Data: This measure is now available at no charge; contact the test publisher for more information.
Time: [30-40] minutes.
Authors: Cynthia J. Stolman and Rodney L. Doran.
Publisher: Rodney L. Doran.
Cross References: For reviews by Joseph D. Matarazzo and Gary B. Melton, see 10:197.

[1248]
Meeker Behavioral Correlates.

Purpose: Assesses "major dimensions of intellectual abilities and personality characteristics" for management matching of teams.
Population: Industry.
Publication Date: 1981.
Scores: Ratings by self in 6 areas: Comprehension, Memory, Leadership, Convergent Production Skills, Creativity, Team Contributions.
Administration: Group.
Price Data: Available from publisher.
Time: [20] minutes.
Comments: Self-ratings.
Author: Mary Meeker.
Publisher: SOI Systems.
Cross Reference: For a review by William I. Sauser, Jr., see 10:198.

[1249]
Memory Assessment Scales.

Purpose: Developed to provide a comprehensive battery that assesses short- and long-term verbal and visual (nonverbal) memory.
Population: Ages 18 and over.
Publication Date: 1991.
Acronym: MAS.
Scores, 16: Short-Term Memory (Verbal Span, Visual Span, Total), List Acquisition, Delayed List Recall, Delayed Prose Recall, Global Memory Scale (Verbal Memory [List Recall, Immediate Prose Recall, Total], Visual Memory [Visual Reproduction, Immediate Visual Recognition, Total], Total), Delayed Visual Recognition, Names-Faces (Immediate, Delayed) and 7 Verbal Process scores: Total Intrusions, List Clustering (Acquisition, Recall, Delayed Recall), Cued List Recall (Recall, Delayed Recall), List Recognition.

Administration: Individual.
Price Data, 2015: $29 per 25 scoring forms.
Time: [40-45] minutes.
Author: J. Michael Williams.
Publisher: Brainmetric.
Cross References: See T5:1644 (1 reference); for reviews by Ronald A. Berk and John W. Young, see 12:229.

[1250]

Memory for Intentions Test.

Purpose: Designed to measure "everyday aspects" of prospective memory performance.
Population: Ages 18 to 95.
Publication Date: 2010.
Acronym: MIST.
Scores, 8: 2-Minute Time Delay, 15-Minute Time Delay, Time Cue, Event Cue, Verbal Response, Action Response, Prospective Memory Total, Retrospective Recognition Total; 1 optional score: Delayed Prospective Memory Task.
Administration: Individual.
Forms, 2: A, B.
Price Data, 2015: $270 per comprehensive kit including 25 Form A record forms, 25 Form B record forms, 25 Form A word search sheets, 25 Form B word search sheets, 25 score summary sheets, 25 request for records forms, digital clock, carrying case, and manual (62 pages); $205 per introductory kit including 25 Form A record forms, 25 Form A word search sheets, 25 score summary sheets, 25 request for records forms, digital clock, carrying case, and manual; $45 per 25 record forms (Form A or Form B); $28 per 25 word search sheets (Form A or Form B); $33 per 25 score summary sheets; $28 per 25 request for records forms; $18 per digital clock; $74 per manual.
Time: (30) minutes.
Comments: Additional materials required for administration, but not included in test materials: red pen, postcard, envelope, tape recorder.
Authors: Sarah Raskin, Carol Buckheit, and Christina Sherrod (manual).
Publisher: Psychological Assessment Resources, Inc.
Cross References: For reviews by Jeanette W. Farmer and by Michael J. Furlong and Victoria M. Gonzalez, see 19:105.

[1251]

Memory Test for Older Adults.

Purpose: Designed as a brief instrument to assess verbal and visuospatial learning and memory in older adults.
Population: Ages 55–84.
Publication Date: 2002.
Acronym: MTOA, MTOA:S, MTOA:L.
Scores, 8: Free Recall Word List Total Score, Free Recall Word List Retention, Free Recall + Cued Recall Word List Total Score, Free Recall + Cued Recall Word List Retention Score, Recognition Score, Geometric Figure Total Score, Geometric Figure Retention Score, Geometric Figure Copy Score.
Administration: Individual.
Forms, 2: Long, Short.
Price Data, 2015: $223 per kit including 1 MTOA:L and 1 MTOA:S geometric card, 25 MTOA:L record forms, 25 MTOA:S record forms, and manual; $66 per 25 record forms (specify MTOA:L or MTOA:S); $81 per technical manual.
Time: Administration time not reported.
Authors: Anita M. Hubley and Tom M. Tombaugh.
Publisher: Multi-Health Systems, Inc.
Cross References: For reviews by Stephen J. Freeman and by W. Joel Schneider and Mark E. Swerdlik, see 16:144.

[1252]

Memory Validity Profile.

Purpose: Designed for use by "clinicians who administer cognitive, academic, or neuropsychological assessments to children, adolescents, and young adults" to detect "whether an examinee is providing valid test scores."
Population: Ages 5-21.
Publication Date: 2015.
Acronym: MVP.
Scores, 3: Visual, Verbal, Total.
Administration: Individual.
Price Data, 2016: $175 per introductory kit including professional manual (52 pages) with fast guide, 25 record forms, and stimulus book; $60 per professional manual; $99 per stimulus book; $40 per 25 record forms.
Time: (5-7) minutes.
Comments: Conormed with the Child and Adolescent Memory Profile (389).
Authors: Elisabeth M. S. Sherman and Brian L. Brooks.
Publisher: Psychological Assessment Resources, Inc.

[1253]

Menometer.

Purpose: Designed to measure "knowledge of the physical aspects of human menstruation."
Population: Adolescents and adults.
Publication Dates: 1974–1988.
Scores: Total score only.
Administration: Group.
Manual: No manual.
Price Data, 2015: $2 per scale.
Time: [10] minutes.
Comments: For a supplementary source, see Panos D. Bardis, "Research Instruments for Population Studies," Society and Culture, July 1974, 5(2), 177-191.
Author: Panos D. Bardis.
Publisher: Donna Bardis.

[1254]

Menstrual Distress Questionnaire.
Purpose: Designed as "a self-report inventory for use in the diagnosis and treatment of premenstrual and menstrual distress."
Population: Women.
Publication Dates: 1968–2010.
Acronym: MDQ.
Scores, 8: Pain, Water Retention, Autonomic Reactions, Negative Affect, Impaired Concentration, Behavior Change, Arousal, Control.
Administration: Group or individual.
Forms, 2: Form C, Form T.
Price Data, 2015: $50 per manual, including review-only copy of the MDQ form; $2.40 per online administration license (minimum 50); $2 per Remote Online Survey License (minimum 50); $2 per License to reproduce (minimum 50).
Foreign Language Edition: Translations available in Dutch (Netherlands and non-specific), French (Belgium, Canada, and France), Portuguese (Brazil), Czech, Danish, Finnish, German (Switzerland and Germany), Hungarian, Italian, Malay, Norwegian, Polish, Spanish (Argentina, Chile, Mexico, U.S. and non-specific), Swedish, and Korean, and Thai (Form C only).
Time: (15) minutes for Form C; (5) minutes for Form T.
Author: Rudolph H. Moos.
Publisher: Mind Garden, Inc.
Cross References: See T5:1647 (4 references); for reviews by Jennifer J. Fager and Donna L. Sundre, see 12:230 (12 references); see T4:1608 (7 references), 9:695 (6 references), and T3:1466 (4 references).

[1255]

Mental Status Checklist for Adolescents.
Purpose: To assist professionals in the assessment of adolescents' mental status.
Population: Ages 13–17.
Publication Date: 1988.
Scores: Item scores only.
Administration: Individual.
Price Data, 2015: $62 per package of 25.
Time: Administration time not reported.
Comments: Reliability and validity data not reported; problems checklist.
Authors: Edward H. Dougherty and John A. Schinka.
Publisher: Psychological Assessment Resources, Inc.
Cross References: For a review by Julian Fabry, see 11:234.

[1256]

Mental Status Checklist for Adults, 1988 Revision.
Purpose: "Surveys items that are commonly included in a comprehensive mental status examination."

Population: Adults.
Publication Dates: 1986–1988.
Scores: 10 Content Areas: Presenting Problems, Behavioral/Physical Descriptions, Emotional State, Mental Status, Health and Habits, Legal Issues, Current Living Situation, Diagnoses, Treatment Recommendations, Disposition.
Administration: Individual.
Manual: No manual.
Price Data, 2015: $62 per package of 25.
Time: Administration time not reported.
Author: John A. Schinka.
Publisher: Psychological Assessment Resources, Inc.

[1257]

Mental Status Checklist for Children.
Purpose: Assess childhood problems and plan for treatment approaches.
Population: Ages 5–12.
Publication Date: 1989.
Scores: Item scores only.
Administration: Individual.
Manual: No manual.
Price Data, 2015: $62 per package of 25.
Time: (10–20) minutes.
Comments: Downward extension of the Mental Status Checklist for Adults (1256); scale for ratings by parents, caregivers, or self-ratings.
Authors: Edward H. Dougherty and John A. Schinka.
Publisher: Psychological Assessment Resources, Inc.
Cross References: For reviews by David Lachar and Marcia B. Shaffer, see 11:235.

[1258]

Mentoring Style Indicator™.
Purpose: Assesses 4 mentoring styles (Informational, Guiding, Collaborative, Confirming) and associated mentoring behaviors; identifies the style of mentoring that mentors prefer to provide and proteges prefer to receive.
Population: Mentors and proteges.
Publication Dates: 1987–2005.
Acronym: MSI.
Scores, 6: Informational Mentoring, Guiding Mentoring, Collaborative Mentoring, Confirming Mentoring, Preferred Mentoring Style.
Administration: Individual and group.
Price Data: Available from publisher; discounts on bulk orders.
Time: (20-25) minutes.
Comments: Versions available for new hires, career development, leadership development, generic, sales, healthcare, youth, new teachers, college students, college faculty, and educational administrators; Preferred Mentoring Style and an interpretation is printed out.
Author: William A. Gray.
Publisher: Corporate Mentoring Solutions® Inc.

a) MSI FOR MENTORING NEW HIRES.

Population: Mentors and proteges wanting orientation.

b) MSI FOR CAREER DEVELOPMENT.

Population: Mentors and proteges wanting to explore career options.

c) MSI FOR LEADERSHIP DEVELOPMENT.

Population: Mentors and proteges wanting to become leaders.

d) MSI–GENERIC.

Population: Mentors and proteges wanting to handle generic work challenges.

e) MSI FOR SALES.

Population: Mentors and proteges wanting to handle common sales challenges.

f) MSI FOR HEALTHCARE PROFESSIONALS.

Population: Mentors and proteges wanting to handle healthcare challenges.

g) MSI FOR MENTORING NEW TEACHERS.

Population: Mentors and new teachers wanting induction into the profession.

h) MSI FOR EDUCATIONAL ADMINISTRATORS.

Population: Educational administrators and proteges wanting to become administrators.

i) MSI FOR MENTORING COLLEGE/UNIVERSITY STUDENTS.

Population: Mentors and college students wanting to handle freshman and transfer challenges.

j) MSI FOR MENTORING COLLEGE/UNIVERSITY FACULTY.

Population: Mentors and proteges wanting to get tenured and promoted.

k) MSI FOR MENTORING YOUTH.

Population: Mentors and youthful proteges wanting adult assistance.

Cross References: For reviews by Raoul A. Arreola and Russell N. Carney, see 13:198.

[1259]

Merrill-Palmer-Revised Scales of Development.

Purpose: Designed to assess cognitive, social-emotional, self-help, and fine and gross motor development in infants and children.

Population: Ages 0-1 to 6-6 years.

Publication Dates: 1926-2004.

Acronym: M-P-R.

Administration: Individual.

Price Data, 2015: $925 per complete kit including manual (2004, 267 pages), infant stimuli book, easel book, Fido book, choke-safe toys and manipulatives, and 20 each of all necessary forms in a rolling bag; $55 per manual; $30 per 20 Cognitive Battery record forms; $10 per 20 Social Emotional Development Parent Scales; $10 per 20 Social Emotional Temperament Style Parent Forms; $20 per 20 Gross Motor Record Forms; $10 per 20 Self-Help/Adaptive Development Scale Parent Forms; $10 per 20 Expressive Language Evaluator Forms; $10 per 20 Expressive Language Parent Forms; $20 per 20 Summary Reports/Growth Score Profiles; $2.50 per 20 Copying Response (specify Sheets A or Sheets B).

Time: (40-50) minutes.

Comments: Portions of this test are to be completed by a parent/guardian; previous edition entitled Merrill-Palmer Scale of Mental Tests.

Authors: Gale H. Roid and Jackie L. Sampers.

Publisher: Stoelting Co.

a) EXPRESSIVE LANGUAGE-EXAMINER FORM.

   1) *Element of Attire, Body Parts, Verbs.*

   Population: Ages 1-1 years and older.

   2) *Adverbs, Adjectives, Prepositions, Pronouns.*

   Population: Ages 1-6 years and older.

b) EXPRESSIVE LANGUAGE-PARENT REPORT.

Scores: 2 scales, 4 subscales: 0-12 months, 13 months and older (Word Combination, Word Meanings/Semantics, Gestural, Expressive Verbal).

c) SELF-HELP/ADAPTIVE-PARENT.

Forms, 5: 0-11 months, 12-23 months, 24-35 months, 36-37 months, 48-78 months.

d) GROSS MOTOR-EXAMINER.

Scores: 7 scales, 23 subscales: 0-12 months (Lifts Head, Supported Sitting, Reaching, Rolls, Balance Responses, Independent Sitting, Stomach Creep, Hand/Knee Creep), 13-24 months (Pull to Standing, Cruises Furniture, Independent Walking), 25-36 months (Child Squats to Pick Up Toy, Climbing Into Chair, Stairs, Special Walking), 37-48 months (Running, Jumping #1), 49-78 months (Throwing/Catching, Kicking, Dynamic Walking, Static Balance, Jumping #2, Hopping Movements), Quality of Movement, Tone.

e) SOCIAL-EMOTIONAL DEVELOPMENTAL-PARENT.

Forms, 5: Same as *c* above.

f) SOCIAL-EMOTIONAL TEMPERAMENT-PARENT.

Forms, 2: 0-17 months, 18-78 months.

g) COGNITIVE BATTERY-EXAMINER.

Scores, 6: Cognitive, Memory, Fine Motor, Speed, Receptive Language, Visual Motor; 8 scales, 49 subscales: 1-5 months (Warm-up, Visual Regard, Small Rattle Play, Visual Preference), 6-12 months (Spin Toy, Large Rattle Play, Dangle Toy, Push-Spin Toy, Object Permanence), 13-23 months (Novel Problem, Blocks, Chips in the Box, Round Peg Board (A), Body Parts, Pop Out, Simple Puzzle, Square Peg Board (B), Fido Book), 24-35 months (Ring Stack, Color Matching, Identifies Emotions, Picture Details, Goodnight Baby, Bead Stringing, Two Puzzles, Find It, Goes Together, Square Pegs, Same), 36-47 months (Fingers, Questions, Where Do They Go?, Word Pictures, See It?, Shapes Puzzle), 48-59 months (Puzzle Fun, Big/Small, Touch Picture, Draw It, Hidden Picture, Different Pictures), 60-78 months (Find 'em, High/Low, Count 'em, Fun with Cards, Touch 'em, What's Next?, Different Pictures, Let's Draw It).

   1) *Testing Behaviors-Examiner.*

   Scores: 4 scales, 6 subscales: 1-5 months (Emotionality), 6-11 months (Attention), 12-17 months (Fearful/Cautious), 18-78 months (Organized/Cooperative, Active/Eager, Angry/Oppositional).

h) SUMMARY REPORT-EXAMINER.

   1) *Developmental Index.*

   Scores, 7: Developmental Index, Cognitive, Fine Motor, Receptive Language, Memory (ages 1-4 years and older), Speed (ages 1-4 years and older),

Visual Motor.

2) *Gross Motor.*

Score: Gross Motor.

3) *Language.*

Scores, 2: Overall Expressive Language, Overall Language.

4) *Social-Emotional.*

Score: Social-Emotional.

5) *Self-Help.*

Score: Self-Help/Adaptive.

Cross References: For reviews by Sandra Loew and by Loraine J. Spenciner and Dolores J. Appl, see 17:122; see also T5:1653 (29 references) and T4:1614 (19 references); for a review by Jack A. Naglieri of an earlier edition, see 9:697 (4 references).

[1260]
Meta-Motivation Inventory.

Purpose: Designed to measure personal and managerial style.

Population: Managers and persons in leadership positions.

Publication Date: 1979.

Acronym: MMI.

Scores, 32: Motivation for Achievement, Perfection, Assertiveness, Independence, Achievement, Meta-Achievement, Deterministic, Approval, Conventional, Dependent, Avoidance, Helplessness, Need for Control, Persuasiveness, Manipulation, Reactive, Authoritarian, Exploitive, Concern for People, Cooperation, Affiliation, Humanistic, Synergy, Meta-Humanistic, Self-Actualization, Stress, Repression, Anger, Judgemental, Creativity, Growth Potential, Fun Scale.

Administration: Group.

Price Data, 2016: $12.

Time: Administration time not reported.

Comments: Self-administered.

Author: John A. Walker.

Publisher: Meta-Visions.

Cross References: For reviews by John K. Butler, Jr. and Denise M. Rousseau, see 9:698.

[1261]
Michigan Alcoholism Screening Test.

Purpose: Designed as a screening test for assessing alcohol abuse.

Population: Adults.

Publication Dates: 1971–1980.

Acronym: MAST.

Scores: Total score only.

Administration: Group or individual.

Manual: No manual available.

Price Data, 2015: $40 per scoring key, which includes permission to duplicate the test.

Foreign Language Editions: French, Japanese, Spanish, and Vietnamese versions available.

Time: (10) minutes.

Comments: Can be self-administered.

Author: Melvin L. Selzer.

Publisher: Melvin L. Selzer.

Cross References: For reviews by Jane Close Conoley and Jeff Reese and by Janice W. Murdoch, see 14:232; see also T5:1661 (85 references).

[1262]
Michigan English Language Assessment Battery.

Purpose: Designed "to evaluate the advanced level English language proficiency of adult non-native speakers of English."

Population: Adult non-native speakers of English.

Publication Dates: 1985–2015.

Acronym: MELAB.

Scores, 5: Writing, Listening, GCVR [includes Grammar, Cloze Reading, Vocabulary, Reading], Final Score, Speaking Test (optional).

Administration: Group or individual.

Forms: 12 per year.

Price Data: Available from publisher.

Time: (145–160) minutes for complete battery; (30) minutes for Writing; (35) minutes for Listening; (80) minutes for Grammar/Cloze/Vocabulary/Reading; (15) minutes for optional oral interview.

Comments: Administered monthly; "Used primarily to draw inferences about a test-taker's ability to study in an institution where English is the medium of instruction" or for test takers who require evidence of English language ability for professional purposes; candidates register to take exam through authorized test centers; publisher scores all examinations and issues official score report directly to institutions selected by examinee.

Author: Cambridge Michigan Language Assessments.

Publisher: Cambridge Michigan Language Assessments.

Cross References: For reviews by Ayres D'Costa and Alan Garfinkel, see 14:233.

[1263]
Michigan English Test.

Purpose: Designed to assess "general English language proficiency" by measuring "listening, reading, grammar, and vocabulary skills in personal, public, occupational, and educational contexts."

Population: Adolescents and adults at or above a secondary level of education.

Publication Dates: 2009-2015.

Acronym: MET.

Scores, 3: Section I: Listening, Section II: Reading and Grammar, Final Score.

Administration: Group.

Forms: 18 per year, 1-2 per month.

Price Data: Available from publisher.

Time: (135) minutes.

Comments: A paper-and-pencil test that is administered monthly, except December, only at authorized test centers.

Author: Cambridge Michigan Language Assessments.

Publisher: Cambridge Michigan Language Assessments.

Cross References: For reviews by Sandra T. Acosta and Mildred Murray-Ward, see 19:106.

[1264]

MicroCog: Assessment of Cognitive Functioning.

Purpose: "Assesses important neurocognitive functions in adults."

Population: Ages 18–89.

Publication Dates: 1993–2004.

Scores: 9 areas: Attention/Mental Control, Memory, Reasoning/Calculation, Spatial Processing, Reaction Time, Information Processing Accuracy, Information Processing Speed, General Cognitive Functioning, General Cognitive Proficiency.

Administration: Individual.

Price Data, 2016: $210 per complete kit including manual (1993, 106 pages), user's guide (2004, 94 pages), CD-ROM Windows software with booklet insert, and 10 report credits; $135 per 10 report credits; bulk discounts available for report credits.

Time: (50–60) minutes for Standard form; (30) minutes for Brief form.

Comments: Computer administered and scored.

Authors: Douglas Powell, Edith Kaplan, Dean Whitla, Sandra Weintraub, Randolph Catlin, and Harris Funkenstein.

Publisher: Pearson.

Cross References: For reviews by Charles J. Long and Stephanie L. Cutlan and by Cynthia A. Rohrbeck, see 13:199.

[1265]

The MIDAS: Multiple Intelligences Developmental Assessment Scales [Revised].

Purpose: "A self-report designed to provide an objective measure of the multiple intelligences using a process approach."

Publication Dates: 1994-2011.

Acronym: MIDAS.

Administration: Group or individual.

Price Data, 2015: $250 per Professional kit including MIDAS Questionnaire (select 2 age groups-reproducible), 50 MIDAS Profiles (pre-paid bulk scoring), The MIDAS: A Professional Manual (rev ed., 2007, 136 pages), and 1 interpretative workbook (reproducible); $350 per Classroom kit including MIDAS Questionnaire (select 1 age group-reproducible), 100 MIDAS Profiles (bulk pre-paid mail-in scoring included), The MIDAS Teacher's Handbook, Common Miracles in Your School, Select 1 of the two (2) reproducible workbooks above, 1 hour technical support, and discount bulk scoring rate; $900 per Guidance kit including MIDAS Questionnaires for Teens and Adults (reproducible), 200 MIDAS Profiles (pre-paid bulk scoring), The MIDAS: Professional Manual, The Challenge! Guide to Career Development, Student High Impact Project (SHIP) reproducible, and 1 hour technical support; $2,500 per School kit including MIDAS Questionnaires for 2 age groups-reproducible, bulk scoring for 1,000 profiles, on-site DOS scoring program (upon request during checkout), The MIDAS: A Professional Manual, Common Miracles in Your School (bulk pricing available), Student High Impact Project (SHIP) (reproducible), Teacher's Handbook for MI in the Classroom (bulk pricing available), Stepping Stones: A Teacher's Workbook (reproducible), Stepping Stones: Student Workbook for MI (reproducible), The Challenge! Guide to Career Success (reproducible), 2 hours on-site training (plus travel expenses), and 3 hours of telephone (free), Discounted Bulk Scoring Rate; $500 per Staff Development kit including MIDAS Questionnaire for adults (reproducible), 100 MIDAS Profiles (pre-paid bulk scoring), Teacher's Handbook: Multiple Intelligences in the Classroom, Common Miracles in Your School, Stepping Stones Workbook for Teachers (reproducible), 1 hour of technical support, Staff Development Packet (reproducible)-forthcoming, inquire; $40 per MIDAS preview package including 3 profiles, 1 book, interpretative packet, and Teacher's Handbook for MI in the Classroom; $45 per Teacher's Profile Package including Teacher's Handbook for MI in the Classroom, Common Miracles in Your School, and 1 MIDAS Adult Profile; $150 per The Basic Research kit, 100 MIDAS profiles, Professional Manual or Teacher's Handbook, Brief Interpretative Packet, data imported into database (either SPSS or Excel database-upon request), and 1 workbook (upon request); $300 per 100 MIDAS Profiles (with kit purchase); $400 per 100 MIDAS Profiles (without kit purchase); $100 per MIDAS Database; $7 per MIDAS Personal Profile (with purchase of book or package); $15 per MIDAS profile (bulk discounts available); $20 per Teacher's Handbook: Multiple Intelligences in the Classroom; $40 per The MIDAS: A Professional Manual (rev ed.).

Foreign Language Editions: Korean (MIDAS-K) and Chinese (C-MIDAS); research editions available: Greek, Singaporean, Spanish, Malaysian, Romanian, Farsi, Arabic, Turkish, Icelandic, and Bahasa; test items and instructions for the MIDAS, Teen MIDAS, MIDAS Kids: "All About Me," and MIDAS Kids: "My Young Child" are available in Spanish.

Time: (25-35) minutes via self-completion using Online MIDAS System (OMS) or paper questionnaire; (60-90) minutes via structured interview.

Comments: This assessment can be administered via self-completion or as a structured interview; can be completed by an individual who is close to the subject; parents complete the MIDAS-KIDS: My Young Child version; the web-based administrative system automatically scores the responses and returns the profile via email within minutes.

Author: C. Branton Shearer.

Publisher: Multiple Intelligences Research and Consulting, Inc.

a) MIDAS.

Population: Ages 20 and up.

Scores: 11 scales and 26 subscales: Basic Scales: Musical (Appreciation, Vocal Ability, Instrumental Skill, Composing), Kinesthetic (Athletics, Dexterity), Logical-Mathematical (Strategy Games, Everyday Skills with Math, Everyday Problem Solving, School Math), Spatial (Spatial Awareness, Artistic Design, Working with Objects), Linguistic (Rhetorical Skill, Expressive Sensitivity, Written/Academic Ability), Interpersonal (Social Sensitivity, Social Persuasion, Interpersonal Work), Intrapersonal (Personal Knowledge/Efficacy, Self/Other Efficacy, Calculations, Spatial Problem-Solving), Naturalist (Animal Care, Plant Care, Science), Intellectual Style Scales: Leadership (Social Adeptness, Communication Skill, Managerial Skill), Innovation (Musical, Kinesthetic, Logical-Mathematical, Spatial, Linguistic, Interpersonal, Intrapersonal), General Logic (Logical-Mathematical, Spatial, Interpersonal, Intrapersonal).

b) TEEN-MIDAS.

Population: Ages 15-19.

Scores: Same as *a* above.

c) MIDAS-KIDS: ALL ABOUT ME.

Population: Ages 10-14.

Scores: 10 scales and 24 subscales: Basic Scales: Musical (Musicality, Vocal, Appreciation, Instrument), Kinesthetic (Physical Ability, Dance, Working with Hands), Logical-Mathematical (Problem Solving, Calculations), Spatial (Artistic, Constructions, Imagery), Linguistic (Linguistic Sensitivity, Writing, Reading), Interpersonal (Leadership, Understanding People, Getting Along with Others), Intrapersonal (Self Knowledge, Managing Feelings, Effective Relationships, Goal Achievement), Naturalist (Animal Care, Earth Science), Intellectual Style Scales: Technical, Innovative.

d) MIDAS-KIDS: MY VIEW.

Population: Ages 8-9.

Scores: Same as *c* above.

e) MIDAS-KIDS: MY YOUNG CHILD.

Population: Ages 4-8.

Scores: Same as *c* above, except without Intellectual Style Scales.

Cross References: For reviews by Robert W. Hiltonsmith and W. Joel Schneider, see 17:123; for reviews by Abbot Packard and Michael S. Trevisan of an earlier version, see 14:234.

[1266]
The Middle Infant Screening Test.

Purpose: Designed to screen for reading and writing difficulties in first year school children.

Population: Ages 5-8 and over.

Publication Date: 1993.

Acronym: MIST.

Scores, 5: Listening Skills, Letter Sounds, Written Vocabulary, Three-Phoneme Words, Sentence Dictation.

Administration: Group.

Price Data, 2016: £80.95 per complete kit; £15.49 per activity book; £15.49 per pack of 10 pupil booklets; £59.95 per teacher guide pack.

Time: (50–60) minutes.

Comments: "Criterion referenced"; designed for use with the Forward Together skills recovery program.

Author: Sybil Hannavy.

Publisher: GL Assessment [England].

[1267]
The Middlesex Elderly Assessment of Mental State.

Purpose: "Developed as a screening test to detect gross impairment of specific cognitive skills in the elderly."

Population: Adults.

Publication Date: 1989.

Acronym: MEAMS.

Scores, 12: Orientation, Name Learning, Naming, Comprehension, Remembering Pictures, Arithmetic, Spatial Construction, Fragmented Letter Perception, Unusual Views, Usual Views, Verbal Fluency, Motor Perseveration.

Administration: Individual.

Forms, 2: Version A, Version B.

Price Data, 2015: £185 per complete kit including manual (14 pages), 25 scoring sheets, and 2 stimulus books; £21.50 per 25 scoring sheets; £42 per manual; £61 per stimulus book A or B.

Time: [10] minutes.

Author: Evelyn Golding.

Publisher: Pearson Assessment [England].

Cross References: For reviews by Stephen J. Freeman and Matthew E. Lambert, see 17:124.

[1268]
MILCOM Patient Data Base System.

Purpose: Designed to record a patient's medical history.

Population: Medical patients.

Publication Dates: 1971–1985.

Scores: Item scores only.

Administration: Individual.

Manual: No manual.

Price Data: Available from publisher.

Foreign Language Edition: Spanish version available.

Time: Administration time not reported.

Comments: Questionnaire includes health questionnaire and 18-part physical exam.

Author: MILCOM Systems, A Division of Hollister, Inc.

Publisher: Briggs Healthcare.

[1269]

Military Environment Inventory.

Purpose: "Asesses the social environment of varied types of military contexts."
Population: Military personnel.
Publication Date: 1986.
Acronym: MEI.
Scores: 7 in 3 dimensions: Relationship (Involvement, Peer Cohesion, Officer Support), Personal Growth (Personal Status), System Maintenance (Order and Organization, Clarity, Officer Control).
Administration: Individual or group.
Forms, 4: Real Form (Form R), Short Form (Form S), Ideal Form (Form I), Expectations Form (Form E).
Price Data, 2015: $50 per manual, including review-only copy of test; $2 per Remote Online Survey License or License to Reproduce (minimum 50); $10 per user's guide.
Time: Administration time not reported.
Comments: One of 10 Social Climate Scales.
Author: Rudolf H. Moos.
Publisher: Mind Garden, Inc.
Cross References: For reviews by David O. Herman and Alfred L. Smith, Jr., see 11:237 (1 reference).

[1270]

Mill Hill Vocabulary Scale.

Purpose: Provides a measure of acquired verbal knowledge.
Population: Ages 6.5-16.5, Ages 18–adult.
Publication Dates: 1943–1998.
Acronym: MHV.
Scores: Total score only.
Administration: Group or individual.
Forms, 2: 1, 2.
Price Data: Available from publisher.
Time: (15–40) minutes.
Comments: To be used in conjunction with the Raven's Progressive Matrices (1688); short-form also available.
Authors: J. C. Raven, J. H. Court, and J. Raven.
Publisher: Pearson Clinical Assessment [Australia and New Zealand].
    a) JUNIOR.
    Population: Ages 6.5–16.5.
    b) SENIOR.
    Population: Ages 18–adult.
Cross References: See T5:1671 (8 references); for reviews by Theodore L. Hayes and William K. Wilkinson, see 13:200 (30 references); see also T4:1629 (51 reference), 9:705 (8 references), T3:1485 (29 references), and T2:402 (32 references); for a review by Morton Bortner of an earlier edition, see 6:471 (16 references); see also 4:303 (7 references); for a review by David Wechsler, see 3:239 (3 references).

[1271]

Miller Analogies Test.

Purpose: Measures background knowledge and analytical abilities critical to the commencement of study in graduate school.
Population: Graduate school applicants.
Publication Dates: 1926–2006.
Acronym: MAT.
Scores: Total score only.
Administration: Group or individual.
Price Data: Available from publisher.
Time: 60 minutes.
Comments: Paper-and-pencil or computer-based.
Author: Harcourt Assessment, Inc.
Publisher: Pearson.
Cross References: See T5:1672 (5 references); for reviews by Robert B. Frary and Stephen H. Ivens, see 12:235 (2 references); see also T4:1630 (1 reference), T3:1486 (16 references), 8:192 (31 references), T2:404 (15 references), and 7:363 (57 references); for reviews by Lloyd G. Humphreys, William B. Schrader, and Warren W. Willingham, see 6:472 (26 references); for a review by John T. Dailey, see 5:352 (28 references); for reviews by J. P. Guilford and Cart I. Hovland, see 4:304 (16 references).

[1272]

Miller Assessment for Preschoolers.

Purpose: Designed "to identify children who exhibit moderate 'preacademic' problems."
Population: Ages 2-9 to 5-8.
Publication Date: 1982.
Acronym: MAP.
Scores, 6: Foundations, Coordination, Verbal, Non-Verbal, Complex Tasks, Total.
Administration: Individual.
Levels: 6 developmental levels (ages 2-9 to 3-2, 3-3 to 3-8, 3-9 to 4-2, 4-3 to 4-8, 4-9 to 5-2, 5-3 to 5-8).
Price Data, 2015: $881.50 per complete kit including manual (220 pages), score sheets, and all items needed for administration and scoring; $164 per examiner's manual; $57.50 per 25 score sheets (specify age level); $55.85 per 25 drawing booklets; $57.50 per 25 record booklets.
Time: (20–30) minutes.
Author: Lucy Jane Miller.
Publisher: Pearson.
Cross References: See T5:1673 (11 references) and T4:1631 (6 references); for reviews by Dennis J. Deloria and William B. Michael, see 9:706.

[1273]

Miller Forensic Assessment of Symptoms Test.

Purpose: Designed to "provide information regarding the probability that an individual is malingering psychiatric illness."

Population: Ages 18 and over.
Publication Dates: 1995–2001.
Acronym: M-FAST.
Scores, 8: Reported vs. Observed, Extreme Symptomatology, Rare Combinations, Unusual Hallucinations, Unusual Symptom Course, Negative Image, Suggestibility, Total.
Administration: Individual.
Price Data, 2015: $184 per introductory kit including professional manual and 25 interview booklets.
Time: (5–10) minutes.
Author: Holly A. Miller.
Publisher: Psychological Assessment Resources, Inc.
Cross References: For reviews by Marc Janoson and by Nathaniel J. Pallone and James J. Hennessy, see 15:155.

[1274]
Miller Function and Participation Scales.

Purpose: Designed "to determine if a child has a developmental delay in the functional motor abilities needed to participate in early school years."
Population: Ages 2.6-7.11.
Publication Date: 2006.
Acronym: M-FUN.
Administration: Individual.
Parts, 2: Performance Assessment, Participation Assessment.
Price Data, 2015: $440.75 per complete kit with manipulatives.
Time: (40-60) minutes.
Author: Lucy J. Miller.
Publisher: Pearson.
  a) PERFORMANCE ASSESSMENT.
  Levels, 3: Ages 2.6-3.11, Ages 4.0-5.11, Ages 6.0-7.11.
  Forms, 2:, Ages 2.6-3.11, Ages 4.0-7.11.
    1) *Ages 2.6–3.11.*
    Scores, 21: Follow the Path, Flying Birds, Clouds, Hidden Forks, Find the Rabbits, Copying Shapes, Writing, Visual Motor Behavior Rating, Clay Play, Penny Bank, Origami, Snack Time, Fine Motor Behavior Rating, Statue, Throw and Catch, Soccer, Jumping, Gross Motor Behavior Rating, Visual Motor, Fine Motor, Gross Motor.
    2) *Ages 4.0-5.11.*
    Scores, 22: Amazing Mazes, Race Car, Hidden Forks, Find the Puppies, Draw a Kid, Writing, Go Fishing (1-4), Visual Motor Behavior Rating, Go Fishing (5-7), Clay Play, Penny Bank, Origami, Snack Time, Fine Motor Behavior Rating, Statue, Ball Balance, Soccer, Jumping, Gross Motor Behavior Rating, Visual Motor, Fine Motor, Gross Motor.
    3) *Ages 6.0-7.11.*
    Scores, 23: Amazing Mazes, Race Car, Hidden Forks, Find the Puppies, Draw a Kid, Writing, Go Fishing (1-4), Visual Motor Behavior Rating, Go Fishing (5-7), Clay Play, Penny Bank, Origami, Snack Time, Fine Motor Behavior Rating, Statue, Ball Balance, Bouncing Ball, Soccer, Jumping, Gross Motor Behavior Rating, Visual Motor, Fine Motor, Gross Motor.

  b) PARTICIPATION ASSESSMENT.
  Scores, 3: Home Observations, Classroom Observations, Test Observations.
  Population: Ages 2.6-7.11.
Cross References: For reviews by Abigail Baxter and C. Dale Carpenter, see 18:74.

[1275]
Millon Adolescent Clinical Inventory.

Purpose: Designed to assess "an adolescent's personality, along with self-reported concerns and clinical syndromes."
Population: Ages 13–19.
Publication Date: 1993.
Acronym: MACI.
Scores, 27: Personality Patterns (Introversive, Inhibited, Doleful, Submissive, Dramatizing, Egotistic, Unruly, Forceful, Conforming, Oppositional, Self-Demeaning, Borderline Tendency), Expressed Concerns (Identify Diffusion, Self-Devaluation, Body Disapproval, Sexual Discomfort, Peer Insecurity, Social Insensitivity, Family Discord, Childhood Abuse), Clinical Syndromes (Eating Dysfunctions, Substance Abuse Proneness, Delinquent Predisposition, Impulsive Propensity, Anxious Feelings, Depressive Affect, Suicidal Tendency), and 3 Modifying Indices (Disclosure, Desirability, Debasement).
Administration: Individual or group.
Price Data, 2015: $128.75 per computer (Q Local) starter kit including manual (123 pages), 3 answer sheets with test items, and three interpretive report administrations; $33.30 per individual computer interpretive report administrations (quantity discounts available); $407.95 per hand-scoring starter kit including manual, hand-scoring user's guide, 10 test booklets, 50 answer sheets, 50 profile forms, and answer keys; $59.45 per audio CD; $49.45 per manual.
Foreign Language Edition: Spanish materials available.
Time: (25-30) minutes.
Comments: Self-report personality inventory; paper-and-pencil and on-line administration available; computer (Q Local), mail-in scoring, and hand-scoring options; available in profile and interpretive report formats; Facet scales also available, contact publisher for details.
Authors: Theodore Millon, Carrie Millon, Roger Davis, and Seth Grossman.
Publisher: Pearson.
Cross References: See T5:1685 (2 references); for reviews by Paul Retzlaff and Richard B. Stuart, see 12:236 (6 references); see also T4:1633 (14 references); for reviews by Douglas T. Brown and Thomas A. Widiger of the Millon Adolescent Personality Inventory, see 9:707.

[1276]
Millon Adolescent Personality Inventory.

Purpose: Designed to assess an adolescent's personality.
Population: Ages 13-18.

Publication Dates: 1976-1982.

Acronym: MAPI.

Scores: 20 scales: Personality Styles (Introversive, Inhibited, Cooperative, Sociable, Confident, Forceful, Respectful, Sensitive) Expressed Concerns (Self-Concept, Personal Esteem, Body Comfort, Sexual Acceptance, Peer Security, Social Tolerance, Family Rapport, Academic Confidence) Behavioral Correlates (Impulse Control, Social Conformity, Scholastic Achievement, Attendance Consistency).

Administration: Group or individual.

Price Data, 2015: $133.25 per software-based starter kit including manual, 3 answer sheets, 1 test booklet, and 3 administrations; $130 per web-based starter kit including manual, 3 answer sheets, 1 test booklet, and 3 administrations; $142.48 per mail-in scoring and reporting starter kit including manual, 3 answer sheets, 1 test booklet, and 3 administrations with interpretive reports; $49.20 per manual.

Foreign Language Edition: Spanish version available.

Time: (20-30) minutes.

Authors: Theodore Millon, Catherine J. Green, and Robert B. Meagher, Jr.

Comments: Self-report personality inventory; paper-and-pencil and computer administration available.

Publisher: Pearson.

Cross References: For reviews by Douglas T. Brown and Thomas A. Widiger, see 9:707.

[1277]

Millon Behavioral Medicine Diagnostic.

Purpose: Designed to "assess psychological factors that can influence the course of treatment of medically ill patients ... especially for patients in which psychosocial factors may play a role in the course of the disease and treatment outcome."

Population: Clinical and rehabilitation patients ages 18–85.

Publication Date: 2001.

Acronym: MBMD.

Scores, 39: Validity Indicator, Response Patterns (Disclosure, Desirability, Debasement), Negative Health Habits (Alcohol, Drug, Eating, Caffeine, Inactivity, Smoking), Psychiatric Indications (Anxiety-Tension, Depression, Cognitive Dysfunction, Emotional Lability, Guardedness), Coping Styles (Introversion, Inhibited, Dejected, Cooperative, Sociable, Confident, Nonconforming, Forceful, Respectful, Oppositional, Denigrated), Stress Moderators (Illness Apprehension, Functional Deficits, Pain Sensitivity, Social Isolation, Future Pessimism, Spiritual Absence), Treatment Prognostics (Interventional Fragility, Medication Abuse, Information Discomfort, Utilization Excess, Problematic Compliance), Management Guides (Adjustment Difficulties, Psych Referral).

Administration: Individual or group.

Price Data, 2015: $110 per Q Local starter kit with interpretive reports including manual, softcover test booklet, 3 answer sheets with test items to conduct and receive 3 interpretive Q Local administrations; $28 per 25 Q Local answer sheets with test items; $60.50 per manual (183 pages); $59.45 per compact disc; $35.90 per Q Local bariatric interpretive report; $23.85 per Q Local bariatric profile report; $23.85 per general medical profile report; $34.35 per general medical interpretive reports; $23.85 per pain patient profile reports; $37.95 per pain patient interpretive reports; $382.35 per manual scoring service starter kit including manual, manual-scoring user's guide, 50 answer sheets, 50 worksheets and 50 profile forms (general medical/bariatric), 10 soft cover test booklets, and answer keys; $36.40 per mail-in interpretive report (test items and answer sheets included); $26.15 per mail-in profile reports (test items and answer sheets included); $34.35 per 10 hand-scoring test booklets; $61.50 per 50 large print answer sheets; quantity discounts available.

Foreign Language Edition: Test booklets and audio CD are available in Spanish.

Time: (20–25) minutes.

Comments: Upgrading of the Millon Behavioral Health Inventory (T5:1686); self-administered; may be administered in paper-and pencil format, via computer, or via audiocassette; interpretive reports with healthcare provider summary and profile available; scoring options include handscoring, mail-in, Q Local Assessment System software.

Authors: Theodore Millon, Michael Antoni, Carrie Millon, Sarah Minor, and Seth Grossman.

Publisher: Pearson.

Cross References: For reviews by Mark J. Atkinson and John C. Caruso, see 15:164; for information regarding the original Millon Behavioral Health Inventory, see T5:1686 (7 references) and T4:1634 (6 references); for reviews of the Millon Behavioral Health Inventory by Mary J. Allen and Richard I. Lanyon, see 9:708 (1 reference).

[1278]

Millon Clinical Multiaxial Inventory-IV.

Purpose: Designed to "help clinicians assess personality and psychopathy in adults ... who are undergoing psychological or psychiatric assessment or treatment."

Population: Ages 18 and older.

Publication Dates: 1976-2015.

Acronym: MCMI-IV.

Scores, 25: Clinical Personality Patterns (Schizoid, Avoidant, Melancholic, Dependent, Histrionic, Turbulent, Narcissistic, Antisocial, Sadistic, Compulsive, Negativistic, Masochistic), Severe Personality Pathology (Schizotypical, Borderline, Paranoid), Clinical Syndromes (Generalized Anxiety, Somatic Symptom, Bipolar Spectrum, Persistent Depression, Alcohol Use, Drug Use, Post-Traumatic

Stress), Severe Clinical Syndromes (Schizophrenic Spectrum, Major Depression, Delusional).

Administration: Individual or group.

Price Data, 2016: $61.50 per manual (2015, 125 pages); $44 per Q-global interpretive report; $22.25 per Q-global profile report; $28 per Q step-down answer sheet (includes test items); $48.20 per mail-in interpretive report answer sheet (includes test items and scoring); $28.20 per mail-in profile report answer sheet (includes test items and scoring); $59.50 per audio CD.

Foreign Language Edition: Spanish version available.

Time: (30) minutes.

Comments: Designed to align with DSM-5 categories of personality disorders and clinical syndromes; administered digitally or via paper and pencil; computer scored.

Authors: Theodore Millon, Seth Grossman, and Carrie Millon.

Publisher: Pearson.

Cross References: Reviews are scheduled for *The Twentieth Mental Measurements Yearbook*. For reviews by James P. Choca and Thomas A. Widiger of the Millon Clinical Multiaxial Inventory—III [Manual Third Edition], see 14:236; see also T5:1687 (47 references); for reviews by Allen K. Hess and Paul Retzlaff of the third edition, see 13:201 (81 references); see also T4:1635 (104 references); for reviews by Thomas M. Haladyna and Cecil R. Reynolds of the second edition, see 11:239 (74 references); for reviews by Allen K. Hess and Thomas A. Widiger of the original edition, see 9:709 (1 reference); see also T3:1488 (3 references).

[1279]

Millon College Counseling Inventory.

Purpose: Designed to "help counselors identify, predict, and understand a broad range of psychological issues that are common among college students seen primarily in college counseling settings."

Population: College students ages 16-40.

Publication Date: 2006.

Acronym: MCCI.

Scores, 36: Personality Style Scales (Introverted, Inhibited, Dejected, Needy, Sociable, Confident, Unruly, Conscientious, Oppositional, Denigrated), Severe Personality Tendencies Scale (Borderline), Expressed Concerns Scales (Mental Health Upset, Identity Quandaries, Family Disquiet, Peer Alienation, Romantic Distress, Academic Concerns, Career Confusion, Abusive Experiences, Living Arrangement Problems, Financial Burdens, Spiritual Doubts), Clinical Signs Scales (Suicidal Tendencies, Depressive Outlook, Anxiety/Tension, Post-Traumatic Stress, Eating Disorders, Anger Dyscontrol, Attention [Cognitive] Deficits, Obsessions/Compulsions, Alcohol Abuse, Drug Abuse), Response Tendency Scales (Validity, Disclosure, Desirability, Debasement), plus 7 Noteworthy Responses (Risky Behaviors, Homesickness, Expectation

Pressures, Escapist Distractions, Minority Prejudice, Somatic Concerns, Reality Distortions).

Administration: Group or individual.

Price Data, 2015: $198.50 per manual-scoring starter kit, including 50 answer sheets, answer keys, and manual (2006, 115 pages); $47 per 50 manual-scoring answer sheets; $58 per audio CD; $34.50 per manual; $70 per computer (Q-Local) starter kit with interpretive reports, including manual, 3 answer sheets, and 3 Q Local administrations (does not include Q Local software); $28 per 25 Q Local answer sheets; $17.50 per administration for Q Local interpretive report; $84 per mail-in starter kit with interpretive reports including 3 answer sheets, manual, and all materials necessary to conduct 3 assessments and receive interpretive reports using the mail-in scoring service; $21.50 per mail-in interpretive report (price includes answer sheet and scoring).

Time: (20-25) minutes.

Comments: Self-report personality inventory; paper-and-pencil and on-line administration available; computer (Q Local), mail-in scoring, and hand-scoring options.

Authors: Theodore Millon, Stephen N. Strack, Carrie Millon, and Seth Grossman.

Publisher: Pearson.

Cross References: For reviews by Mark A. Albanese and Georgia Hinman and by Andrew A. Cox, see 18:75.

[1280]

Millon Index of Personality Styles Revised.

Purpose: "Designed to measure personality styles of normally functioning adults."

Population: 18 years and older.

Publication Dates: 1994-2004.

Acronym: MIPS Revised.

Scores, 28: 6 Motivating Styles (Pleasure-Enhancing, Pain-Avoiding, Actively Modifying, Passively Accommodating, Self-Indulging, Other-Nurturing), 8 Thinking Styles (Externally Focused, Internally Focused, Realistic/Sensing, Imaginative/Intuiting, Thought-Guided, Feeling-Guided, Conservation-Seeking, Innovation-Seeking), 10 Behavior Styles (Asocial/Withdrawing, Gregarious/Outgoing, Anxious/Hesitating, Confident/Asserting, Unconventional/Dissenting, Dutiful/Conforming, Submissive/Yielding, Dominant/Controlling, Dissatisfied/Complaining, Cooperative/Agreeing), 3 Validity Indices (Positive Impression, Negative Impression, Consistency), Clinical Index.

Administration: Group or individual.

Form: 1 form with 2 reporting options: Interpretive, Profile.

Price Data, 2015: $53.80 per manual (2004, 176 pages); $212.20 per manual-scoring starter kit, including manual, 10 test booklets, 50 answer sheets, and answer keys; $113.80 per Q Local starter kit, including manual, 3 answer sheets, 1 test booklet, and 3 Q Local administrations; $24.60 per Q Local interpretive report.

Time: (25–30) minutes.

Comments: Self-report personality inventory; paper-and-pencil and on-line administration available; computer (Q Local), mail-in scoring, and hand-scoring options; available in profile and interpretive report formats.

Authors: Theodore Millon.

Publisher: Pearson.

Cross References: For reviews by S. Alvin Leung and David J. Pittenger, see 17:125; see also T5:1688 (1 reference); for reviews by James P. Choca and Peter Zachar of an earlier version, see 13:202.

[1281]

Millon Pre-Adolescent Clinical Inventory.

Purpose: To "identify, predict, and understand a broad range of psychological disorders that are common in 9–12 year olds seen in clinical settings."

Population: Ages 9–12.

Publication Date: 2005.

Acronym: M-PACI.

Scores: 16 scales: Emerging Personality Patterns (Confident, Outgoing, Conforming, Submissive, Inhibited, Unruly, Unstable), Current Clinical Signs (Anxiety/Fears, Attention Deficits, Obsessions/Compulsions, Conduct Disorder, Disruptive Behaviors, Depressive Moods, Reality Distortions), Response Validity Indicators (Invalidity, Response Negativity).

Administration: Individual or group.

Price Data, 2015: $302 per manual-scoring starter kit including manual (115 pages), 50 answer sheets, 50 profile forms, and answer keys; $59.45 per audio CD; $47.15 per manual; $113.80 per computer (Q Local) starter kit including manual, 3 answer sheets with test items, and 3 Q local administrations; $28.20 per Q Local interpretive reports.

Time: (15–20) minutes.

Comments: Self-report personality inventory; paper-and-pencil and on-line administration available; computer (Q Local), mail-in scoring, and hand-scoring options; available in profile and interpretive report formats.

Authors: Theodore Millon, Robert Tringone, Carrie Millon, and Seth Grossman.

Publisher: Pearson.

Cross References: For a review by Jeffrey A. Atlas and Steven I. Pfeiffer, see 17:126.

[1282]

Mind Body Wellness Geriatric Rehabilitation and Restorative Assessment System.

Purpose: Designed to "assess pathology and general quality of life for residents who need assisted living or nursing home care based on their levels of behavioral, emotional, and illness symptoms."

Population: Ages 55 and up.

Publication Date: 2008.

Acronym: GRRAS.

Administration: Individual.

Scores: 3 subtests: Psychological Resistance to Activities of Daily Living Index, Geriatric Multidimensional Pain and Illness Inventory, Geriatric Level of Dysfunction Scale.

Price Data, 2015: $238 per introductory kit including professional manual (117 pages), 25 PRADLI rating forms, 25 GMPI rating forms, 25 GLDS rating Forms, and 25 GRRAS profile forms in a soft-sided attaché case; $82 per professional manual; $29 per 25 profile forms; $350 per software (CD-ROM) with on-screen help and quick start guide.

Authors: P. Andrew Clifford, Kristi D. Roper, and Daisha J. Cipher.

Publisher: Psychological Assessment Resources, Inc.

a) PSYCHOLOGICAL RESISTANCE TO ACTIVITIES OF DAILY LIVING INDEX.

Acronym: PRADLI.

Price Data: $40 per 25 PRADLI rating forms; $125 per PRADLI kit including professional manual, 25 PRADLI rating forms, and 25 profile forms.

Time: (15) minutes.

b) GERIATRIC MULTIDIMENSIONAL PAIN AND ILLNESS INVENTORY.

Acronym: GMPI.

Price Data: $40 per 25 GMPI rating forms; $125 per GMPI kit including professional manual, 25 GMPI rating forms, and 25 profile forms.

Time: (15) minutes.

c) GERIATRIC LEVEL OF DYSFUNCTION SCALE.

Acronym: GLDS.

Price Data: $45 per 25 GLDS rating forms; $130 per GLDS kit including professional manual, 25 GLDS rating forms, and 25 profile forms.

Time: (15) minutes.

Cross References: For reviews by John J. Brinkman and Amber Carter and by Timothy J. Makatura, see 18:76.

[1283]

Mindex: Your Thinking Style Profile.

Purpose: Designed to measure "thinking style," an individual's "unique way of processing ideas and deriving meaning" from experience.

Population: Adults.

Publication Date: 1983.

Scores, 20: Thinking Style Preference (Red Earth, Blue Earth, Red Sky, Blue Sky), Sensory Mode Preference (Kinesthetic, Visual, Auditory), Structure Preference (Time Orientation, Detail Orientation, Technical Orientation, Goal Orientation), Mental Flexibility (Tolerance for Ambiguity, Opinion Flexibility, Semantic Flexibility, Positive Orientation, Sense of Humor, Investigative Orientation, Resistance to Enculturation), Thinking Fluency (Idea Fluency, Logical Fluency).

Administration: Individual.

Price Data, 2015: $495 per licensing fee; $20 per profile booklet or online profile, volume discounts available.

Foreign Language Editions: Print version available in Spanish and Japanese; Spanish version also available online.

Time: Administration time not reported.

Comments: Licenses available to practitioners (trainers, consultants, coaches) in the human development field.

Author: Karl Albrecht.

Publisher: Karl Albrecht International.

[1284]
MindMaker6™.

Purpose: To determine personality or personal style using hemispheric dominance theories for use in training, consulting, and counseling clients.

Population: Adults.

Publication Dates: 1985-1987.

Scores, 6: Kins-Person, Loner, Loyalist, Achiever, Involver, Choice-Seeker.

Administration: Group.

Price Data, 2016: $19.95 per assessment (volume discounts available).

Time: (30-40) minutes.

Comments: The test publisher has indicated there is a newer edition of this test; description will be updated when complete test materials are received.

Authors: Kenneth L. Adams and Dudley Lynch.

Publisher: Brain Technologies Corporation.

Cross References: For a review by Thomas A. Wrobel, see 11:240.

[1285]
Miner Sentence Completion Scale.

Purpose: Intended for use in "selection, vocational and career guidance, identifying talent supplies, and evaluating training primarily."

Population: Workers and prospective workers in management, professional, and entrepreneurial or task-oriented occupations.

Publication Dates: 1961–1986.

Acronym: MSCS.

Administration: Group.

Forms, 3: Form H (Management domain), Form P (Professional domain), Form T (Task domain).

Price Data, 2015: $30 per 50 tests with scoring sheets; $10 per scoring guide (Form H, 1964, 64 pages, with 1977 supplement, 15 pages, and 1989 supplement, 4 pages; Form P, 1981, 49 pages; Form T, 1986, 56 pages).

Time: (20–30) minutes.

Comments: Form H available as free-response or multiple-choice version; directions included for scoring rare response patterns.

Author: John B. Miner.

Publisher: Organizational Measurement Systems Press.

   a) FORM H.

   Scores, 9: Authority Figures, Competitive Games, Competitive Situations, Assertive Role, Imposing Wishes, Standing Out from Group, Routine Administrative Functions, Supervisory Job, Total.

   b) FORM P.

   Scores, 6: Acquiring Knowledge, Independent Action, Accepting Status, Providing Help, Professional Commitment, Total.

   c) FORM T.

   Scores, 6: Self Achievement, Avoiding Risks, Feedback of Results, Personal Innovation, Planning for the Future, Total.

Cross References: See T5:1689 (4 references) and T4:1637 (1 reference); for reviews by Frederick T. L. Leong and Linda F. Wightman, see 11:241 (2 references); see also T2:1484 (4 references); for a review by C. J. Adcock, see 7:172 (2 references); see also P:450 (3 references) and 6:230a (2 references).

[1286]
Mini-ICF-APP Social Functioning Scale.

Purpose: Designed "to assess the extent to which a patient's activities and capacities are limited in terms of performance and ability, along with what is hindering the patient."

Population: Adults with mental disorders.

Publication Date: 2014.

Acronym: Mini-ICF-APP.

Scores, 13: Adherence to Regulations, Structuring of Tasks, Flexibility, Competency, Judgment, Endurance, Assertiveness, Contact with Others, Group Integration, Intimate Relationships, Spontaneous Activities, Self Care, Mobility.

Administration: Individual.

Price Data, 2016: £95 per complete kit including reference manual (2014, 70 pages), short manual with U.K. data, 50 forms, and case; £50 per reference manual; £40 per short manual; £35 per 50 scoring forms.

Foreign Language Edition: Originally published in German.

Time: (10-15) minutes.

Authors: Michael Linden, Stefanie Baron, Beate Muschalla, and Andrew Molodynski (U.K. Adaptor).

Publisher: Hogrefe Ltd [United Kingdom].

[1287]
Mini Inventory of Right Brain Injury, Second Edition.

Purpose: Designed for "screening neurocognitive deficits associated with right hemisphere lesions."

Population: Ages 20-80.

Publication Dates: 1989–2000.

Acronym: MIRBI-2.

Scores, 10: Visual Scanning, Integrity of Gnosis, Integrity of Body Image, Visuoverbal Processing, Visuosymbolic Processing, Integrity of Visuomotor Praxis, Higher-Level Language Skills, Expressing Emotion, General Affect, General Behavior.

Administration: Individual.

Price Data, 2015: $195 per complete kit; $43 per 25 examiner record booklets; $43 per 25 response forms; $25 per 25 response sheets; $25 per caliper; $72 per manual (2000, 58 pages).
Time: (15–30) minutes.
Authors: Patricia A. Pimental and Jeffrey A. Knight.
Publisher: PRO-ED.
Cross References: For reviews by Daniel C. Miller and David Shum, see 15:165; for reviews of an earlier edition by R. A. Bornstein and by John E. Obrzut and Carol A. Boliek, see 11:242.

[1288]
Mini-Mental State Examination, 2nd Edition.

Purpose: Designed "as an aid to the clinical cognitive mental state examination ... to screen for cognitive impairment and to track patients' progress over time."
Population: Ages 18 and older.
Publication Dates: 1975-2010.
Acronym: MMSE-2.
Administration: Individual.
Forms: Each version has 2 equivalent forms (red, blue).
Price Data, 2015: $155 per standard version kit including user's manual (2010, 101 pages), 25 MMSE-2:SV blue forms, 25 MMSE-2:SV red forms, 10 MMSE-2:BV blue forms, 10 MMSE-2:BV red forms, and pocket norms guide; $196 per expanded version kit including user's manual, 25 MMSE-2:EV blue forms, 25 MMSE-2:EV red forms, 2 processing speed scoring templates (blue and red), and pocket norms guide; $78 per user's manual; $16 per 25 brief forms (blue or red); $33 per 25 standard forms (blue or red); $46 per 25 expanded forms (blue or red).
Foreign Language Editions: Translations available in Dutch, French, German, Hindi, Italian, Spanish (European, Latin American, and U.S.), Russian, and Simplified Chinese.
Authors: Marshal F. Folstein, Susan E. Folstein, Travis White, and Melissa A. Messer.
Publisher: Psychological Assessment Resources, Inc.
a) MMSE-2: BRIEF VERSION.
  Purpose: Designed "for screening large populations and for screening individuals in clinical practice who have not been referred because of cognitive complaints."
  Acronym: MMSE-2:BV.
  Scores: Total score only from 4 tasks: Registration, Orientation to Time, Orientation to Place, Recall.
  Time: (5) minutes.
b) MMSE-2: STANDARD VERSION.
  Purpose: Designed to "be given first to individuals who are referred because of a complaint of cognitive decline or who, when asked about their memory, reply that it is not as good as in the past."
  Acronym: MMSE-2:SV.
  Scores: Total score only from 11 tasks: Registration, Orientation to Time, Orientation to Place, Recall, Attention and Calculation, Naming, Repetition, Comprehension, Reading, Writing, Drawing.
  Time: [10-15] minutes.

c) MMSE-2: EXPANDED VERSION.
  Purpose: Designed to extend the test's ceiling, "increasing the screening sensitivity for individuals with less severe cognitive impairment."
  Acronym: MMSE-2:EV.
  Scores: Total score only from 13 tasks: Registration, Orientation to Time, Orientation to Place, Recall, Attention and Calculation, Naming, Repetition, Comprehension, Reading, Writing, Drawing, Story Memory, Processing Speed.
  Time: (20) minutes.
Cross References: Reviews are scheduled for *The Twentieth Mental Measurements Yearbook*. For reviews by Mark A. Albanese and Sandra B. Ward of the original edition, see 15:166.

[1289]
Minnesota Clerical Test.

Purpose: Designed to measure speed and accuracy in clerical work.
Population: Grades 8–12 and adults.
Publication Dates: 1933–1979.
Acronym: MCT.
Scores, 2: Number Comparison, Name Comparison.
Administration: Group or individual.
Price Data, 2015: $150 per kit including manual, 25 test booklets, and key; $113 per key for hand scoring test booklets; $75 per manual.
Time: 15(20) minutes.
Authors: Dorothy M. Andrew, Donald G. Paterson, and Howard P. Longstaff.
Publisher: Pearson.
Cross References: See T5:1693 (3 references) and T4:1640 (3 references); for reviews by Michael Ryan and Ruth G. Thomas, see 9:713 (2 references); see also T3:1493 (5 references), T2:2135 (23 references), and 6:1040 (10 references); for a review by Donald E. Super, see 5:850 (46 references); for reviews by Thelma Hunt, R. B. Selover, Erwin K. Taylor, and E. F. Wonderlic, see 3:627 (22 references); for a review by W. D. Commins, see 2:1664 (18 references).

[1290]
Minnesota Handwriting Assessment.

Purpose: "Used to assess manuscript and D'Nealian handwriting of students."
Population: Grades 1–2.
Publication Date: 1999.
Acronym: MHA.
Scores, 6: Rate, Legibility, Form, Alignment, Size, Spacing.
Administration: Group or individual.
Price Data, 2015: $89.20 per complete kit including 25 manuscript sheets, 25 D'Nealian sheets, and manual (99 pages).
Time: (2.5–10) minutes.
Author: Judith Reisman.

Publisher: Pearson.

Cross References: For reviews by Kathy J. Bohan and Andrew A. Cox, see 16:149.

[1291]
Minnesota Importance Questionnaire.

Purpose: "To measure twenty psychological needs and six underlying values that have been found to be relevant to work adjustment, specifically to satisfaction with work."

Population: Ages 16 and over.

Publication Dates: 1967-1981.

Acronym: MIQ.

Scores, 21: Ability Utilization, Achievement, Activity, Independence, Variety, Compensation, Security, Working Conditions, Advancement, Recognition, Authority, Social Status, Co-workers, Social Services, Moral Values, Company Policies, Supervision-Human Relations, Supervision-Technical, Creativity, Responsibility, Autonomy (ranked form only).

Administration: Group.

Forms, 2: Ranked form (1975, 9 pages), paired form (1975, 18 pages).

Price Data: Available from publisher.

Time: (15-25) minutes for ranked form; (30-40) minutes for paired form.

Authors: James B. Rounds, Jr., George A. Henly, René V. Dawis, Lloyd H. Lofquist, and David J. Weiss.

Publisher: Vocational Psychology Research.

Cross References: See T5:1694 (10 references) and T4:1641 (3 references); for reviews by Barbara Lachar and Wilbur L. Layton, see 11:243 (4 references); for reviews by Lewis E. Albright and Sheldon Zedeck, see 8:1050 (40 references); see also T3:1495 (14 references), T2:2283 (8 references), and 7:1063 (29 references).

[1292]
Minnesota Manual Dexterity Test.

Purpose: "Measures the capacity for simple but rapid eyehand coordination as well as arm-hand dexterity."

Population: Ages 13–adult.

Publication Date: [Undated].

Scores: Total time for each of two tests.

Administration: Group.

Tests, 2: Placing Test, Turning Test.

Price Data, 2016: $250 per test.

Time: Administration time not reported.

Author: Lafayette Instrument.

Publisher: Lafayette Instrument.

Cross References: For reviews by Deborah Erickson and Alida S. Westman, see 12:237.

[1293]
Minnesota Multiphasic Personality Inventory-Adolescent.

Purpose: Designed for use with adolescents to assess a number of the major patterns of personality and emotional disorders.

Population: Ages 14-18

Publication Date: 1992.

Acronym: MMPI-A.

Scores, 68: 8 Validity Scales (Cannot Say (?), Lie (L), Infrequency 1 (F1), Infrequency 2 (F2), Infrequency (F), Defensiveness (K), Variable Response Inconsistency (VRIN), True Response Inconsistency (TRIN); 10 Clinical Scales (Hypochondriasis, Depression, Hysteria, Psychopathic Deviate, Masculinity-Femininity, Paranoia, Psychasthenia, Schizophrenia, Hypomania, Social Introversion); 28 Harris-Lingoes Subscales (Subjective Depression, Psychomotor Retardation, Physical Malfunctioning, Mental Dullness, Brooding, Denial of Social Anxiety, Need for Affection, Lassitude-Malaise, Somatic Complaints, Inhibition of Aggression, Familial Discord, Authority Problems, Social Imperturbability, Social Alienation, Self-Alienation, Persecutory Ideas, Poignancy, Naivete, Social Alienation, Emotional Alienation, Lack of Ego Mastery-Cognitive, Lack of Ego Mastery-Conative, Lack of Ego Mastery-Defective Inhibition, Bizarre Sensory Experiences, Amorality, Psychomotor Acceleration, Imperturbability, Ego Inflation); 3 Si Subscales (Shyness/Self-Consciousness, Social Avoidance, Alienation); 15 Adolescent Content Scales (Anxiety, Obsessiveness, Depression, Health Concerns, Alienation, Bizarre Mentation, Anger, Cynicism, Conduct Problems, Low Self-Esteem, Low Aspirations, Social Discomfort, Family Problems, School Problems, Negative Treatment Indicators); 6 Supplementary Scales (Anxiety, Repression, MacAndrew Alcoholism Scale—Revised, Alcohol/Drug Problem Acknowledgment, Alcohol/Drug Problem Proneness, Immaturity).

Administration: Group or individual.

Price Data, 2016: $64.45 per manual; $37 per manual supplement (2006); $44.90 per Adolescent Interpretive System User's Guide; $44.35 per 10 softcover test booklets; $67.60 per 1 hardcover test booklet; $63.35 per audio CD; $114 hand-scoring materials package (50 answer sheets, 50 Validity/Clinical scales profile forms); $57.55 per 50 profile and record forms; price information for scoring and interpretive reports available from Pearson Assessments.

Foreign Language Edition: Spanish version available.

Time: 45–60 minutes.

Authors: James N. Butcher, Carolyn L. Williams, John R. Graham, Robert P. Archer, Auke Tellegen, Yossef S. Ben-Porath, and Beverly Kaemmer (manual).

Publisher: University of Minnesota Press; distributed by Pearson.

Cross References: See T5:1698 (28 references); for reviews by Charles D. Claiborn and Richard I. Lanyon, see 12:238 (4 references); see also T4:1646 (4 references).

[1294]

Minnesota Multiphasic Personality Inventory-2.

Purpose: "Designed to assess a number of the major patterns of personality and emotional disorders."
Population: Ages 18 and over.
Publication Dates: 1942–1990.
Acronym: MMPI-2.
Scores, 75: 7 Validity Indicators: Cannot Say (?), Lie (L), Infrequency (F), Correction (K), Back F (FB), Variable Response Inconsistency (VRIN), True Response Inconsistency (TRIN); 10 Clinical Scales: Hypochondriasis (Hs), Depression (D), Conversion Hysteria (Hy), Psychopathic Deviate (Pd), Masculinity-Femininity (Mf), Paranoia (Pa), Psychasthenia (Pt), Schizophrenia (Sc), Hypomania (Ma), Social Introversion (Si); 15 Supplementary Scales: Anxiety (A), Repression (R), Ego Strength (Es), MacAndrew Alcoholism Scale-Revised (MAC-R), Overcontrolled Hostility (O-H), Dominance (Do), Social Responsibility (Re), College Maladjustment (Mt), Gender Role-Masculine (GM), Gender Role-Feminine (GF), 2 Post-Traumatic Stress Disorder Scales (PK & PS); Marital Distress Scale (MDS), Addiction Potential Scale (APS), Addiction Admission Scale (AAS); 15 Content Scales: Anxiety (ANX), Fears (FRS), Obsessiveness (OBS), Depression (DEP), Health Concerns (HEA), Bizarre Mentation (BIZ), Anger (ANG), Cynicism (CYN), Antisocial Practices (ASP), Type A (TPA), Low Self-Esteem (LSE), Social Discomfort (SOD), Family Problems (FAM), Work Interference (WRK), Negative Treatment Indicators (TRT); 3 Si subscales: Shyness/Self-Consciousness (Si1), Social Avoidance (Si2), Alienation-Self and Others (Si3); 28 Harris-Lingoes Subscales: Subjective Depression (D1), Psychomotor Retardation (D2), Physical Malfunctioning (D3), Mental Dullness (D4), Brooding (D5), Denial of Social Anxiety (Hy1), Need for Affection (Hy2), Lassitude-Malaise (Hy3), Somatic Complaints (Hy4), Inhibition of Aggression (Hy5), Familial Discord (Pd1), Authority Problems (Pd2), Social Imperturbability (Pd3), Social Alienation (Pd4), Self-Alienation (Pd5), Persecutory Ideas (Pa1), Poignancy (Pa2), Naivete (Pa3), Social Alienation (Sc1), Emotional Alienation (Sc2), Lack of Ego Mastery, Cognitive (Sc3), Conative (Sc4), Defective Inhibition (Sc5), Bizarre Sensory Experiences (Sc6), Amorality (Ma1), Psychomotor Acceleration (Ma2), Imperturbability (Ma3), Ego Inflation (Ma4).
Administration: Group or individual.
Price Data, 2016: $44.35 per 10 reusable softcover test booklets; $67.85 per reusable hardcover test booklet; $58.10 per 50 hand-scorable answer sheets and profile forms; $63.35 per audio CD; $57.55 per 50 profile forms;

$94 per answer keys (specify scale and for softcover or hardcover test booklets); $63.85 per manual; price data available from publisher for various scoring options and interpretive reports.
Foreign Language Editions: May be administered in Spanish, Hmong, and French (Canadian).
Time: (90) minutes.
Comments: Revision of the Minnesota Multiphasic Personality Inventory; may be administered via computer, CD, or paper and pencil.
Authors: James N. Butcher, W. Grant Dahlstrom, John Graham, Auke Tellegen, and Beverly Kaemmer.
Publisher: Published by University of Minnesota Press; distributed by Pearson.
Cross References: See T5:1697 (600 references) and T4:1645 (504 references); for reviews by Robert P. Archer and David S. Nichols, see 11:244 (637 references); see also 9:715 (339 references) and T3:1498 (749 references); for reviews by Henry A. Alker and Glen D. King of the original version, see 8:616 (1,188 references); see also T2:1281 (549 references); for reviews by Malcolm D. Gynther and David A. Rodgers, see 7:104 (831 references); see also P:166 (1,066 references); for a review by Arthur L. Benton, see 4:71 (211 references); for reviews by Arthur L. Benton, H. J. Eysenck, L. S. Penrose, and Julian B. Rotter, and an excerpted review, see 3:60 (76 references).

[1295]

Minnesota Multiphasic Personality Inventory–2–Restructured Form.

Purpose: Designed to "provide information on the individual test taker's clinical symptoms, personality characteristics, behavioral tendencies, interpersonal functioning, and interests."
Population: Ages 18 and older.
Publication Dates: 2008-2011.
Acronym: MMPI-2-RF.
Scores, 51: Variable Response Inconsistency, True Response Inconsistency, Infrequent Responses, Infrequent Psychopathology Responses, Infrequent Somatic Responses, Symptom Validity, Response Bias Scale, Uncommon Virtues, Adjustment Validity, Emotional/Internalizing Dysfunction, Thought Dysfunction, Behavioral/Externalizing Dysfunction, Demoralization, Somatic Complaints, Low Positive Emotions, Cynicism, Antisocial Behavior, Ideas of Persecution, Dysfunctional Negative Emotions, Aberrant Experiences, Hypomanic Activation, Malaise, Gastrointestinal Complaints, Head Pain Complaints, Neurological Complaints, Cognitive Complaints, Suicidal/Death Ideation, Helplessness/Hopelessness, Self-Doubt, Inefficacy, Stress/Worry, Anxiety, Anger Proneness, Behavior-Restricting Fears, Multiple Specific Fears, Juvenile Conduct Problems, Substance Abuse, Aggression, Activation, Family Problems, Interpersonal Passivity, Social Avoidance, Shy-

ness, Disaffiliativeness, Aesthetic-Literary Interests, Mechanical-Physical Interests, Aggressiveness-Revised, Psychoticism-Revised, Disconstraint-Revised, Negative Emotionality/Neuroticism-Revised, Introversion/Low Positive Emotionality-Revised.

Administration: Individual.

Price Data, 2014: $459 per complete kit including administration and technical manuals, 25 answer sheets, 5 sets of profile forms, 5 sets of answer keys, and 5 softcover test booklets; $83 per administration (2011, 157 pages) and technical (2011, 436 pages) manuals; $42.50 per user's guide for reports; $22 per 5 softcover test booklets.

Time: (35-50) mintues.

Comments: A revised, 338-item version of the MMPI-2 (1294) with the restructured clinical (RC) scales at its core. Scoring and reporting may be done manually or via mail-in, software-based, and web-based methods.

Authors: Yossef S. Ben-Porath and Auke Tellegen.

Publisher: Published by University of Minnesota Press; distributed by Pearson.

Cross References: Reviews are scheduled for *The Twentieth Mental Measurements Yearbook*. For reviews by Robert P. Archer and David S. Nichols of the MMPI-2, see 11:244 (637 references); see also 9:715 (339 references) and T3:1498 (749 references); for reviews by Henry A. Alker and Glen D. King of the MMPI, see 8:616 (1,188 references); see also T2:1281 (549 references); for reviews by Malcolm D. Gynther and David A. Rodgers of the MMPI, see 7:104 (831 references); see also P:166 (1,066 references); for a review by Arthur L. Benton of the MMPI, see 4:71 (211 references); for reviews by Arthur L. Benton, H. J. Eysenck, L. S. Penrose, and Julian B. Rotter, and an excerpted review of the MMPI, see 3:60 (76 references).

[1296]
Minnesota Satisfaction Questionnaire.

Purpose: "Designed to measure an employee's satisfaction with his/her job."

Population: Business and industry.

Publication Dates: 1963-1977.

Acronym: MSQ.

Administration: Group.

Price Data: Available from publisher.

Authors: David J. Weiss, René V. Dawis, George W. England, and Lloyd H. Lofquist.

Publisher: Vocational Psychology Research.

a) LONG FORM.

Scores, 21: Ability Utilization, Achievement, Activity, Advancement, Authority, Company Policies and Practices, Compensation, Coworkers, Creativity, Independence, Moral Values, Recognition, Responsibility, Security, Social Service, Social Status, Supervision-Human Relations, Supervision-Technical, Variety, Working Conditions, General Satisfaction.

Editions, 2: 1967 revision, 1977 edition.

Time: (15-20) minutes.

b) SHORT FORM.

Scores, 3: Intrinsic, Extrinsic, General.

Time: (5-10) minutes.

Cross References: See T5:1701 (56 references), T4:1649 (49 references), 9:721 (21 references), and T3:1508 (27 references); for a review by Robert M. Guion, see 8:1052 (82 references); see also T2:2285 (11 references); for reviews by Lewis E. Albright and John P. Foley, Jr., see 7:1064 (18 references).

[1297]
Miranda Rights Comprehension Instruments.

Purpose: Designed to "assess an individual's basic understanding [at the time of the forensic evaluation] of the meaning of the Miranda rights and appreciation of the consequences of waiving those rights."

Population: Adolescent and adult offenders.

Publication Dates: 1998-2014.

Acronym: MRCI.

Administration: Individual.

Parts, 4: Comprehension of Miranda Rights-II, Comprehension of Miranda Rights-Recognition-II, Function of Rights in Interrogation, Comprehension of Miranda Vocabulary-II.

Price Data, 2016: $134.95 per adult and juvenile kit including manual (2014, 195 pages), easel, and 10 forms; $50 per manual; $25 per 10 forms; $75 per easel.

Comments: Revision of the Instruments for Assessing Understanding & Appreciation of Miranda Rights.

Authors: Naomi E. S. Goldstein, Heather Zelle, and Thomas Grisso.

Publisher: Professional Resource Press.

a) COMPREHENSION OF MIRANDA RIGHTS-II.

Purpose: Designed to assess "the examinee's understanding of the Miranda warnings as measured by the examinee's explanations of the warnings."

Acronym: CMR-II.

Score: Total score only.

Time: (15) minutes.

b) COMPREHENSION OF MIRANDA RIGHTS-RECOGNITION-II.

Purpose: Designed to assess "the examinee's understanding of the Miranda warnings by measuring the examinee's ability to identify whether various interpretations of each warning ... are the same as or different from the warnings presented."

Acronym: CMR-R-II.

Score: Total score only.

Time: (5-10) minutes.

c) FUNCTION OF RIGHTS IN INTERROGATION.

Purpose: Designed to assess "the examinee's grasp of the significance of the Miranda rights in the context of interrogation."

Acronym: FRI.

Score: Total score only.

Time: (15-20) minutes.

d) COMPREHENSION OF MIRANDA VOCABULARY-II.
Purpose: Designed to assess "the examinee's ability to define ... words often used in Miranda warnings."
Acronym: CMV-II.
Score: Total score only.
Time: (15) minutes.
Cross References: Reviews are scheduled for *The Twentieth Mental Measurements Yearbook*. For reviews by Joe W. Dixon and by Marc Janoson and Thomas Lazzaro of an earlier edition titled Instruments for Assessing Understanding & Appreciation of Miranda Rights, see 18:60.

[1298]

Missouri Kindergarten Inventory of Developmental Skills, Alternate Form.

Purpose: A screening battery providing a comprehensive assessment measure to use at or before kindergarten entrance.
Population: Ages 48-72 months.
Publication Date: 1982.
Acronym: KIDS.
Scores: 6 areas: Number Concepts, Auditory Skills, Language Concepts, Paper and Pencil Skills, Visual Skills, Gross Motor Skills.
Administration: Individual.
Price Data, 2016: $1.44 per Student Packet (including Pupil Record Sheet, Answer Sheets, and Parent/Guardian Questionnaire); $13.94 for Manual Packet (includes Administration and Scoring Manual, Color Cards, and one Student Packet); $4.91 for the Instructional Guidebook; $17.30 per specimen set (includes Manual Packet and Instructional Guidebook).
Time: 35 minutes.
Comments: Can be given anytime within the year preceding kindergarten as well as at kindergarten entrance.
Author: Missouri Department of Elementary and Secondary Education.
Publisher: Assessment Resource Center, University of Missouri-Columbia
Cross References: For reviews by Mary Henning-Stout and James E. Ysseldyke, see 11:246.

[1299]

MKM Binocular Preschool Test.

Purpose: To evaluate "the near point performance of preschool and other nonreading children."
Population: Preschool.
Publication Dates: 1963–1965.
Scores: Item scores only.
Administration: Individual.
Price Data: Available from publisher.
Time: [1–2] minutes.
Comments: Stereoscope necessary for administration.
Authors: Leland D. Michael, James W. King, and Arlene Moorhead (instructions).
Publisher: MKM Reading Systems.

[1300]

MKM Monocular and Binocular Reading Test.

Purpose: "To detect children who are likely to have reading problems associated with poor binocular coordination and macular suppression."
Population: Grades 1–2, 3 and over.
Publication Dates: 1963–1964.
Scores: Item scores only.
Administration: Individual.
Levels, 2: 1, 2.
Price Data: Available from publisher.
Time: [3–10] minutes.
Comments: Stereoscope necessary for administration.
Authors: Leland D. Michael, James W. King, and Arlene Moorhead (instructions).
Publisher: MKM Reading Systems.
Cross References: See T2:1920 (1 reference).

[1301]

The MLR Visual Diagnostic Skills Test.

Purpose: Designed to "provide an objective measure of one's ability to identify common technical-physical performance problems and to prescribe appropriate remedies."
Population: Undergraduate through graduate school.
Publication Dates: 1983-2008.
Scores: Total score only.
Subtests, 2: Woodwind, Brass.
Administration: Group.
Price Data, 2015: $50 per Visual Diagnostic Skills Test CD-ROM, including composite test, brass subtest, woodwind subtest, test manual, and answer sheets.
Time: (45) minutes.
Comments: This test can be used as a pre-test/post-test companion to the Visual Diagnostic Skills Program; the two additional subtests (Woodwind, Brass) are provided to accommodate pretest/posttest visual diagnostic skills assessment but no studies have been undertaken to determine the subtests' reliability, content validity, and construct validity.
Authors: James O. Froseth and John R. Woods.
Publisher: GIA Publications, Inc.
Cross References: For reviews by Mary L. Garner and Christopher Johnson, see 19:107.

[1302]

Modern Occupational Skills Tests, Second Edition.

Purpose: Developed to assess skills in checking, numeracy, verbal skills, and office administration skills for use in "recruitment, selection and development of clerical and related staff."
Population: Potential and current office employee.
Publication Dates: 1989-2001.

Acronym: MOST.
Scores: Total score only for each test.
Administration: Group.
Editions, 2: British, Australian.
Price Data: Available from publisher.
Foreign Adaptation: Australian Edition available from Australian Council for Educational Research Ltd. [Australia].
Comments: Some parts of this series are available for online administration at www.gma-online.com.
Authors: Charles Johnson, Steve Blinkhorn, Robert Wood, and Jonathan Hall.
Publisher: Psychometric Research & Development Ltd. [England].

    a) NUMERICAL ESTIMATION.
    Time: 12 minutes.
    b) NUMERICAL AWARENESS.
    Time: 8 minutes.
    c) NUMERICAL CHECKING.
    Time: 8 minutes.
    d) TECHNICAL CHECKING.
    Time: 12 minutes.
    e) WORD MEANINGS.
    Time: 12 minutes.
    f) VERBAL CHECKING.
    Time: 8 minutes.
    g) DECISION MAKING.
    Time: 15 minutes.
    h) SPELLING AND GRAMMAR.
    Time: 8 minutes.
    i) FILING.
    Time: 12 minutes.
Cross References: For reviews by Joseph C. Ciechalski and Bikkar S. Randhawa of the original edition, see 12:239.

[1303]
Modified Wisconsin Card Sorting Test.

Purpose: Designed "to assess problem solving and the ability to shift cognitive strategies in response to changing environmental contingencies."
Population: Ages 18 to 92.
Publication Date: 2010.
Acronym: M-WCST.
Scores, 5: Number of Categories Correct, Number of Perseverative Errors, Number of Total Errors, Percent of Perseverative Errors, Executive Function Composite.
Administration: Individual.
Price Data, 2015: $246 per introductory kit including professional manual (102 pages), 50 record forms, and one card deck; $49 per 25 record forms; $70 per card deck; $92 per professional manual.
Time: (10-15) minutes.
Comments: A modification of the original Wisconsin Card Sorting Test that eliminates all 80 cards from the original 128-card deck that share more than one attribute with a stimulus card.
Author: David J. Schretlen.

Publisher: Psychological Assessment Resources, Inc.
Cross References: For reviews by Anita M. Hubley and by Denise E. Maricle and Amanda Gray, see 19:108.

[1304]
The Mooney Problem Check Lists, 1950 Revision.

Purpose: "Intended to help individuals express their personal problems."
Population: Junior high–adults.
Publication Dates: 1941–1950.
Acronym: MPCL.
Administration: Group.
Price Data, 2015: $22.75 per adult manual; $22.75 per junior high/high school/college manual; $71 per 25 checklists (choose among college, junior high, high school, adult).
Time: (35) minutes.
Authors: Ross L. Mooney and Leonard V. Gordon (manuals, c, and d).
Publisher: Pearson.

    a) JUNIOR HIGH SCHOOL FORM.
    Population: Grades 7–9.
    Publication Dates: 1942–1950.
    Scores, 7: Health and Physical Development, School, Home and Family, Money-Work-The Future, Boy and Girl Relations, Relations to People in General, Self-Centered Concerns.
    b) HIGH SCHOOL FORM.
    Population: Grades 9–12.
    Publication Dates: 1941–1950.
    Scores, 11: Health and Physical Development, Finances-Living Conditions-Employment, Social and Recreational Activities, Social-Psychological Relations, Personal-Psychological Relations, Courtship-Sex-Marriage, Home and Family, Morals and Religion, Adjustment to School Work, The Future-Vocational and Educational, Curriculum and Teaching Procedure.
    c) COLLEGE FORM.
    Population: Grades 13–16.
    Publication Dates: 1941–1950.
    Scores, 11: Same as for High School Form.
    d) ADULT FORM.
    Population: Adults.
    Publication Date: 1950.
    Scores, 9: Health, Economic Security, Self-Improvement, Personality, Home and Family, Courtship, Sex, Religion, Occupation.
Cross References: See T5:1716 (5 references), T4:1667 (14 references), T3:1531 (19 references), 8:626 (48 references), T2:1289 (92 references), and P:173 (55 references); for a review by Thomas C. Burgess, see 6:145 (25 references); see also 5:89 (26 references); for reviews by Harold E. Jones and Morris Krugman, see 4:73 (13 references); for reviews by Ralph C. Bedell and Theodore F. Lentz of an earlier form of a-c, see 3:67 (17 references).

[1305]

Moral Potency Questionnaire.

Purpose: Designed to "measure moral potency," defined as "the capacity to generate responsibility and motivation to take moral action in the face of adversity and persevere through challenges."
Population: Adults.
Publication Date: 2010.
Acronym: MPQ.
Scores, 3: Moral Courage, Moral Ownership, Moral Efficacy.
Administration: Individual or group.
Forms, 2: Self, Rater.
Manual: No manual.
Price Data, 2016: $5 per Transform Survey Hosting: Multi-rater Form ($100 set up fee); $2.40 per Transform Survey Hosting: Self Form (minimum purchase of 50); $2 per Remote Online Survey License (minimum purchase of 50); $2 per License to Reproduce (minimum purchase of 50).
Foreign Language Editions: Available in Chinese, Finnish, Italian (Self Form only), and Spanish.
Time: [5-10] minutes.
Authors: Sean T. Hannah and Bruce J. Avolio.
Publisher: Mind Garden, Inc.

[1306]

Morel Emotional Numbing Test for Post-traumatic Stress Disorder, 3rd Edition.

Purpose: Designed as "a symptom validity test ... to detect simulated symptoms of PTSD."
Population: Ages 18-75.
Publication Dates: 1998-2012.
Acronym: MENT.
Score: Total score only.
Administration: Individual.
Price Data, 2014: $327 per complete kit including unlimited test uses, stimulus book, 25 record forms, scoring form, normative data form, and manual (2012, 50 pages).
Foreign Language Editions: German, Turkish, and Vietnamese language versions available.
Time: (15) minutes.
Author: Kenneth R. Morel.
Publisher: Kenneth R. Morel.
Cross References: Reviews are scheduled for *The Twentieth Mental Measurements Yearbook*.

[1307]

Morrisby Profile.

Purpose: "Designed to give a complete statement, in objective terms, about the basic mental structure of a person."
Population: Age 14–adults.
Publication Dates: 1955–1992.

Acronym: MP.
Scores: 12 tests: Compound Series, General Abilities-Verbal, General Abilities-Numerical, General Abilities-Perceptual, Shapes, Mechanical Ability, Speed Tests 1–4 (Modal Profile), Speed Tests 5–6 (Dexterity).
Administration: Group.
Price Data: Available from publisher.
Time: (165–180) minutes.
Comments: Although more commonly used as a battery of tests to provide a profile of an individual's attributes, often for vocational guidance, component tests can be used in isolation for selection purposes (e.g., the Compound Series test is used to measure Abstract Reasoning, and the three General Ability tests are used together to identify relative strengths in verbal, numerical, and perceptual abilities).
Author: The Morrisby Organisation.
Publisher: The Morrisby Organisation [England].
Cross References: For a review by Patricia A. Bachelor, see 16:151; for information on the Differential Test Battery, see T3:733 (2 references) and T2:1070 (6 references); for reviews by E. A. Peel, Donald E. Super, and Philip E. Vernon, see 5:606.

[1308]

Motivated Skills Card Sort.

Purpose: To identify skills that are central to personal and career satisfaction and success by rank ordering skills on two dimensions: Competency and Motivation.
Population: Adults
Publication Dates: 1977-2005.
Scores: Skills Ratings Matrix.
Administration: Group or individual.
Price Data, 2016: $12 per one deck of cards and one worksheet; $10 per manual; $24 per 24 pack of worksheets.
Foreign Language Editions: Available in Arabic and Korean.
Time: (45–60) minutes.
Comments: Distributors are available in Canada, Australia, Egypt, and U.S.A. List of distributor information is available from publisher.
Author: Richard L. Knowdell.
Publisher: Career Research & Testing, Inc.
Cross References: For reviews by Albert M. Bugaj and Gary J. Robertson, see 13:204.

[1309]

Motivated Strategies for Learning Questionnaire.

Purpose: "To assess college students' motivational orientations and their use of different learning strategies for a college course."
Population: College students
Publication Date: 1991.
Acronym: MSLQ.

Scores, 15: 3 Motivation Scales [Value Component (Intrinsic Goal Orientation, Extrinsic Goal Orientation, Task Value), Expectancy Component (Control of Learning Beliefs, Self-Efficacy for Learning and Performance), Affective Component (Test Anxiety)]; 2 Learning Strategies Scales [Cognitive and Metacognitive Strategies (Rehearsal, Elaboration, Organization, Critical Thinking, Metacognitive Self-Regulation), Resource Management Strategies (Time and Study Environment, Effort Regulation, Peer Learning, Help Seeking)].
Administration: Group.
Price Data: Available from publisher.
Time: (20–30) minutes.
Authors: Paul R. Pintrich, David A. F. Smith, Teresa Garcia, and Wilbert J. McKeachie.
Publisher: Combined Program in Education and Psychology, University of Michigan
Cross References: See T5:1720 (5 references); for reviews by Jeri Benson and Robert K. Gable, see 13:205 (5 references).

[1310]
Motivation Assessment Scale.

Purpose: Designed to assess the motivation underlying problem behaviors so as to curb those behaviors.
Population: People with mental disabilities.
Publication Date: 1992.
Scores, 4: Sensory, Escape, Attention, Tangible.
Administration: Individual.
Price Data: Available from publisher.
Foreign Language Edition: Spanish version available.
Time: 10 minutes.
Comments: A rating tool designed and validated to provide results equivalent to a functional assessment of behavior; may be administered to or completed by someone in close contact with the target individual; can be completed by paper and pencil or as an interview; results identify the maintaining consequence for the target behavior given the particular setting and rater; also available in electronic and Internet subscription versions, which score and summarize results.
Authors: V. Mark Durand and Daniel B. Crimmins.
Publisher: Monaco & Associates Incorporated.
Cross References: For reviews by Roger A. Boothroyd and James P. Van Haneghan, see 14:239; see also T5:1722 (2 references).

[1311]
Motives, Values, Preferences Inventory.

Purpose: Designed to assess 10 core motives and values and the degree of fit between individual values and organizational cultures.
Population: Adults.
Publication Dates: 1987–1996.
Acronym: MVPI.

Scores: 10 scales: Aesthetics, Affiliation, Altruistic, Commerce, Hedonism, Power, Recognition, Science, Security, Tradition.
Administration: Group.
Price Data: Available from publisher.
Foreign Language Editions: List of translations available from publisher.
Time: (20) minutes.
Authors: Joyce Hogan and Robert Hogan (manual).
Publisher: Hogan Assessment Systems, Inc.
Cross References: For reviews by Brent W. Roberts and Sheldon Zedeck, see 14:240.

[1312]
Motor-Free Visual Perception Test–4.

Purpose: Designed to assess "visual-perceptual skills commonly used in everyday activities" including spatial relationships, visual discrimination, figure-ground, visual closure, and visual memory.
Population: Ages 4 to 80 years and older.
Publication Dates: 1972-2015.
Acronym: MVPT-4.
Score: Total score only.
Administration: Individual.
Price Data, 2015: $160 per kit including manual (2015, 78 pages), test plates, and 25 record forms; $45 per manual; $75 per test plates; $40 per 25 record forms.
Time: (20-30) minutes.
Authors: Ronald P. Colarusso and Donald D. Hammill.
Publisher: Academic Therapy Publications.
Cross References: Reviews are scheduled for *The Twentieth Mental Measurements Yearbook*. For reviews by Gary L. Canivez and John D. King of the third edition, see 16:152; for reviews by Nancy B. Bologna and Theresa Volpe-Johnstone of the revised edition, see 14:241; see also T5:1725 (8 references) and T4:1677 (6 references); for a review by Carl L. Rosen of the original edition and an excerpted review by Alan Krichev, see 8:883 (9 references).

[1313]
Movement Assessment Battery for Children.

Purpose: Designed to assess motor skills and motor development difficulties.
Population: Ages 4–12 years.
Publication Dates: 1972–1992.
Acronym: Movement ABC.
Administration: Individual.
Price Data: Available from publisher.
Comments: This test is now available in a second edition; description will be updated when test materials are received.
Authors: Sheila E. Henderson and David A. Sugden.
Publisher: Pearson Assessment [England].
   a) MOVEMENT ABC.
   Scores, 3: Manual Dexterity, Ball Skills, Static and Dynamic Balance.

Administration: Individual.

Levels, 4: Age Band 1 (Ages 4–6); Age Band 2 (Ages 7–8); Age Band 3 (Ages 9–10); Age Band 4 (Ages 11–12).

Time: (20–30) minutes.

Comments: Developed from the Test of Motor Impairment (9:1265).

b) MOVEMENT ABC CHECKLIST.

Scores, 5: Child Stationary/Environment Stable, Child Moving/Environment Stable, Child Stationary/Environment Changing, Child Moving/Environment Changing, Behavioral Problems Related to Motor Difficulties.

Administration: Group or individual.

Time: Administration time not reported.

Comments: Behavior Checklist used by teachers, parents, and other professionals.

Cross References: For reviews by Larry M. Bolen and Carol E. Kessler, see 14:243; see also T5:1725 (8 references); for a review by Jerome D. Pauker of an earlier edition, see 8:881 (2 references); see also T2:1904 (4 references).

[1314]

Mullen Scales of Early Learning.

Purpose: A comprehensive measure of cognitive functioning for infants and preschool children.

Population: Birth to 68 months.

Publication Dates: 1984–1995.

Scores, 6: Gross Motor Scale, Cognitive Scales (Visual Reception, Fine Motor, Receptive Language, Expressive Language), Early Learning Composite.

Administration: Individual.

Price Data, 2015: $870.90 per complete kit; $46.95 per 25 record forms; $168.10 per Mullen ASSIST CD-ROM.

Time: (15–60) minutes.

Comments: Previous editions titled Infant Mullen Scales of Early Learning and Preschool Mullen Scales of Early Learning.

Author: Eileen M. Mullen.

Publisher: Pearson.

Cross References: For reviews by Mary Mathai Chittooran and Carol E. Kessler, see 14:244; see also T5:1728 (2 references); for a review by Verna Hart of an earlier edition titled Infant Mullen Scales of Early Learning, see 11:177.

[1315]

Multi-Craft Aptitude Test.

Purpose: To evaluate mechanical and electrical aptitude.

Population: Applicants for jobs that require the ability to learn mechanical and electrical skills.

Publication Dates: 2004–2013.

Scores: Total score only covering 9 areas: General Science, Power Tools, Hand Tools, Household Items, Electrical Concepts, Electrical Schematic Maze, Process Flow, Signal Flow, Electrical Sequences.

Administration: Group.

Forms: Parallel forms available.

Price Data, 2015: $24 per consumable self-scoring test booklet; $26 per online test administration (minimum order of 20); $24.95 per manual (22 pages).

Time: 24(30) minutes.

Comments: Test publisher advises changes in form names indicate minor revisions and updating.

Author: Roland T. Ramsay.

Publisher: Ramsay Corporation.

Cross References: For a review by Kevin J. McCarthy of Form A (2005), see 17:127.

[1316]

Multi-dimensional Emotional Intelligence Quotient, 7th Revision.

Purpose: Designed to assess "the ability to recognize and understand emotions, understand sentiments in oneself and to handle one's feelings in a productive manner, as well as the ability to understand what it takes to motivate oneself."

Population: Below 18 through adult.

Publication Date: 2011.

Acronym: MEIQ-R7.

Scores, 36: Emotional Identification/ Perception/ and Expression, Emotional Facilitation of Thought, Emotional Understanding, Emotional Management, Moderating Emotional Intelligence Factors, Emotional Self-Awareness, Awareness of Strengths and Limitations, Impulse Control, Self-Control, Resilience/Hardiness, Rumination, Comfort with Emotions, Assertiveness, Coping Skills, Problem Solving, Self-Esteem, Contentment, Values Integrity, Positive Mindset, Independence, Self-Motivation, Goal Setting, Striving, Emotional Selectivity, Social Responsibility, Flexibility, Empathy, Adaptable Social Skills, Conflict Management Behavior, Social Insight, Recognition of Other's Emotions, Emotional Integration, Conflict Management Knowledge, Emotional Reflection, Impression Management.

Administration: Individual.

Price Data: Available from publisher.

Time: (60) minutes.

Comments: Self-administered online assessment. The test publisher provides clients with information about the methods and theoretical basis used in the development of the test as well as benchmarks for relevant industries and racial/ethnic group comparison data.

Author: PsychTests AIM, Inc.

Publisher: PsychTests AIM, Inc. [Canada].

Cross References: For reviews by Nina W. Brown and by James C. DiPerna and Christopher Anthony, see 19:110.

[1317]

Multi-Dimensional Intelligence Test.

Purpose: Designed to measure "several factors of intelligence, including logical reasoning, math skills, language

abilities, spatial relations skills, knowledge retained and the ability to solve novel problems."
Population: Below 17 through older adult.
Publication Date: 2011.
Acronym: MIT.
Scores, 15: Overall Score, Fluid Intelligence, Crystallized Intelligence, Vocabulary, Analogies, Arithmetic, Graphs & Charts, Matrices, 2D/3D Images, Arguments, Puzzles, Verbal, Numeric, Spatial, Logical.
Administration: Individual.
Price Data: Available from publisher.
Time: (40) minutes.
Comments: Self-administered online assessment. The test publisher provides clients with information about the methods and theoretical basis used in the development of the test as well as benchmarks for relevant industries and racial/ethnic group comparison data.
Author: PsychTests AIM, Inc.
Publisher: PsychTests AIM, Inc. [Canada].
Cross References: For reviews by Jason C. Immekus and William Schafer, see 19:111.

[1318]
Multiaxial Diagnostic Inventory-Revised Edition.

Purpose: "Developed to serve as a criterion-referenced diagnostic screening instrument designed to assess personality disorders and clinical syndromes."
Population: Children, adolescents, adults.
Publication Dates: 1989-1994.
Acronym: MDI-R.
Administration: Individual or group.
Levels, 4: Personality Scales, Adult Clinical Scales, Adolescent Clinical Scales, Child Clinical Scales.
Price Data, 2015: $74.95 per manual and 10 copies of each scale.
Time: Administration time not reported.
Comments: "Criterion-referenced."
Author: William F. Doverspike.
Publisher: Professional Resource Press.
  a) PERSONALITY SCALES.
  Population: Adults.
  Scores, 12: Paranoid, Schizoid, Schizotypal, Borderline, Histrionic, Narcissistic, Antisocial, Avoidant, Dependent, Obsessive-Compulsive, Passive-Aggressive, Depressive.
  b) ADULT CLINICAL SCALES.
  Population: Adults.
  Scores, 13: Dysthymic Disorder, Major Depressive Disorder, Bipolar Disorder, Psychotic Disorder, Dissociative Disorder, Posttraumatic Stress, Anxiety Disorder, Panic Disorder, Somatoform Disorder, Anorexia Nervosa, Bulimia Nervosa, Alcohol Abuse, Substance Abuse.
  c) ADOLESCENT CLINICAL SCALES.
  Population: Ages 10-12.
  Scores, 12: Attention-Deficit/Hyperactivity Disorder, Oppositional Defiant Disorder, Conduct Disorder, Alcohol Abuse, Substance Abuse, Dysthymic Disorder,

Major Depressive Disorder, Anxiety, Separation Anxiety, Psychotic Disorder, Anorexia Nervosa, Bulimia Nervosa.
  d) CHILD CLINICAL SCALES.
  Population: Children.
  Scores, 12: Attention-Deficit/Hyperactivity Disorder, Oppositional Defiant Disorder, Conduct Disorder, Alcohol Abuse, Substance Abuse, Dysthymic Disorder, Major Depressive Disorder, Anxiety, Separation Anxiety, Psychotic Disorder, Anorexia Nervosa, Bulimia Nervosa.
Cross References: For reviews by Ashraf Kagee and Robert Wright, see 18:77.

[1319]
MultiCraft Trainee Test.

Purpose: For selecting MultiCraft (mechanical and electrical) trainees.
Population: Applicants for jobs where some knowledge and skill in mechanical and electrical areas is needed.
Publication Dates: 2004-2011.
Scores, 8: Hydraulics & Pneumatics, Welding/Cutting & Rigging, Power Transmission/Lubrication/Mechanical Maintenance & Shop Machines and Tools & Equipment, Pumps/Piping & Combustion, Motors/Control Circuits and Schematics & Print Reading, Digital & Analog Electronics/Power Supplies/Computers & PLC and Test Instruments, Basic AC/DC Theory/Power Distribution and Electrical Maintenance, Total.
Administration: Group.
Price Data, 2015: $24 per consumable self-scoring test booklet or $26 per online administration (minimum order of 20); $24.95 per manual.
Foreign Language Edition: Available in Spanish.
Time: 60-70 minutes.
Comments: Test publisher advises changes in form names indicate minor revisions and updating.
Author: Roland T. Ramsay.
Publisher: Ramsay Corporation.
Cross References: For reviews by Nancy L. Crumpton and Frederick L. Oswald of Form A, see 19:112.

[1320]
MultiCraftTest.

Purpose: Designed for selecting or evaluating maintenance employees.
Population: Applicants and incumbents for jobs requiring mechanical and electrical knowledge and skills.
Publication Dates: 2000-2011.
Scores, 8: Hydraulics & Pneumatics, Welding & Rigging, Power Transmission/Lubrication/Mechanical Maintenance & Shop Machines/Tools and Equipment, Pumps/Piping & Combustion, Motors/Control Circuits & Schematics and Print Reading, Digital Electronics/Power Supplies/Computers & PLC and Test Instruments, Basic AC & DC Theory/Power Distribution and Electrical Maintenance, Total.
Administration: Group.

Forms: Parallel forms available.
Price Data, 2015: $24 per consumable self-scoring test booklet or $26 per online test administration (minimum order of 20); $24.95 per manual.
Foreign Language Edition: Available in Spanish.
Time: (60-70) minutes.
Comments: Self-scoring instrument; available for online test administration; test publisher advises changes in form names indicate minor revisions and updating.
Author: Roland T. Ramsay.
Publisher: Ramsay Corporation.
Cross References: For reviews by Bruce Biskin and M. David Miller of an earlier edition (2009) titled Multi-CrafTest (Forms MC-C and B), see 19:109; for a review by Vicki S. Packman of an earlier edition (2002) titled Multi-CrafTest, see 17:128.

[1321]
Multicultural Tasks of Emotional Development Test.

Purpose: "Designed to assess the social and emotional development and adjustment of children" by means of projective techniques.
Population: Ages 6 through 18.
Publication Dates: 1960-2015.
Acronym: MultiTED.
Scores: Perception, Outcome, Affect, Motivation, Psychosocial Function and Task Score for each of 14 photo tasks.
Administration: Individual.
Price Data: Available from publisher.
Time: Administration time not reported.
Comments: An updated version of the Tasks of Emotional Development Test (2042).
Authors: Edward E. Gotts, Haskel Cohen, and Daniel J. Williams.
Publisher: MultiTED Publishing.
Cross References: Reviews are scheduled for *The Twentieth Mental Measurements Yearbook*. For information about the original Tasks of Emotional Development Test, see T5:2614 (2 references) and T4:2686 (1 reference); for excerpted reviews by Edward Earl Gotts and by C. H. Ammons and R. B. Ammons of the Tasks of Emotional Development Test, see 8:691 (7 references); see also T2:1517 (2 references) and P:481 (1 reference).

[1322]
The Multidimensional Addictions and Personality Profile.

Purpose: Designed as "an objective measure of substance abuse and personal adjustment problems."
Population: Adolescents and adults experiencing substance abuse and mental health disorders.
Publication Dates: 1988–2006.
Acronym: MAPP.

Scores, 15: Substance Abuse Subscales (Psychological Dependence, Abusive/Secretive/Irresponsible Use, Interference, Signs of Withdrawal, Total), Personal Adjustment Subscales (Frustration Problems, Interpersonal Problems, Self-Image Problems, Total), Defensiveness and Inconsistency Scores (Defensiveness, Inconsistency, Total); Minimizing Response Pattern Scales (Substance Abuse, Personal Adjustment, Total).
Administration: Group and individual.
Price Data: Available from publisher.
Foreign Language Editions: French and Spanish translation package available (including printed questions with audio tape).
Time: (20–25) minutes.
Comments: Previous edition titled The COMPASS.
Authors: John R. Craig and Phyllis Craig.
Publisher: Diagnostic Counseling Services, Inc. [No reply from publisher; status unknown].
Cross References: For reviews by Carl Isenhart and Keith F. Widaman, see 14:245.

[1323]
Multidimensional Anxiety Questionnaire.

Purpose: Designed "for the evaluation of anxiety symptoms in adults."
Population: Ages 18–89.
Publication Date: 1999.
Acronym: MAQ.
Scores, 5: Physiological-Panic, Social Phobia, Worry-Fears, Negative Affectivity, Total.
Administration: Group or individual.
Price Data, 2015: $158 per introductory kit including 25 hand-scorable booklets, professional manual (94 pages), and 50 profile forms.
Time: (10) minutes.
Author: William M. Reynolds.
Publisher: Psychological Assessment Resources, Inc.
Cross References: For reviews by Stephanie Stein and Robert E. Wall, see 15:169.

[1324]
Multidimensional Anxiety Scale for Children 2nd Edition.

Purpose: Designed as "a comprehensive, multi-rater assessment of anxiety dimensions in children and adolescents…to [aid] in the early identification, diagnosis, treatment planning and monitoring of anxiety-prone youth."
Population: Ages 8–19.
Publication Dates: 1997–2013.
Acronym: MASC 2.
Scores, 13: Separation Anxiety/Phobias, Generalized Anxiety Disorder (GAD) Index, Social Anxiety: Total (Humiliation/Rejection Subscale, Performance Fears Subscale, Total), Obsessions & Compulsions, Physical Symptoms: Total (Panic Subscale, Tense/Restless Sub-

scale, Total), Harm Avoidance, Anxiety Probability Score, Inconsistency Index (response style), Total Score.
Administration: Individual or Group.
Forms, 2: Self-Report, Parent.
Price Data, 2015: $189 per complete handscored kit including manual, 25 each of self-report and parent QuikScore™ forms; $88 per manual (2013, 136 pages); $226 per complete online kit including manual, 25 self-report, and parent online forms; $329 per complete scoring software kit including manual, scoring software (USB key), 25 each of self-report and parent response forms).
Time: (15) minutes.
Comments: Revision includes addition of parent form, new norms, and some new scales. Online and paper/pencil versions available.
Author: John S. March.
Publisher: Multi-Health Systems, Inc.
Cross References: For reviews by Jerrell C. Cassady and by Merilee McCurdy and Jill Holtz, see 19: 113; for reviews by John C. Caruso and Robert Christopher of an earlier edition, see 14:246.

[1325]

Multidimensional Aptitude Battery-II.

Purpose: Designed "to provide a measure of general cognitive ability or intelligence."
Population: Ages 16 and over.
Publication Dates: 1984–1998.
Acronym: MAB-II.
Scores, 13: Verbal (Information, Comprehension, Arithmetic, Similarities, Vocabulary, Total); Performance (Digit Symbol, Picture Completion, Spatial, Picture Arrangement, Object Assembly, Total), Total.
Administration: Group or individual.
Price Data, 2015: $85 per mail-in scoring examination kit including 1 Verbal and Performance booklet, manual on CD (1998, 107 pages), 1 Verbal and Performance answer sheet, and one coupon for computerized scoring; $117 per hand-scoring examination scoring kit including 1 Verbal and Performance booklet, manual on CD (1998, 107 pages), 1 Verbal and Performance answer sheet, record form, and set of scoring templates; $25 per test manual on CD; $70 per 10 Verbal or Performance test booklets; $70 per 25 Verbal or Performance answer sheets; $55 per 25 record forms; $50 per scoring templates; $87–$97 (depending on volume) per 10 machine-scorable answer sheets and coupons for Mail-in Extended Reports; $107–$117 (depending on volume) per 10 machine-scorable answer sheets and coupons for Mail-in Clinical Reports; $155 per software installation package, includes 10 coupons for computer reports.
Time: 100 minutes.
Foreign Language Edition: French booklets and mail-in scoring answer sheets are available.
Comments: Paper-and-pencil or computer administration available.

Author: Douglas N. Jackson.
Publisher: SIGMA Assessment Systems, Inc.
Cross References: For reviews by Donald L. Thompson and Keith F. Widaman, see 15:170; see T5:1731 (3 references), and T4:1678 (13 references); for reviews by Sharon B. Reynolds and Arthur B. Silverstein of an earlier edition, see 10:202 (5 references).

[1326]

Multidimensional Health Profile.

Purpose: Developed to provide a brief but comprehensive assessment of psychosocial and health functioning for general use in health-related settings.
Population: Ages 18–90.
Publication Dates: 1992–1998.
Administration: Group or Individual.
Forms, 2: Psychosocial Functioning (MHP-P), Health Functioning (MHP-H).
Price Data, 2015: $196 per kit including professional manual, 25 MHP-P booklets, and 25 MHP-H booklets.
Time: (15) minutes for either form.
Authors: Linda S. Ruehlman, Richard I. Lanyon, and Paul Karoly.
Publisher: Psychological Assessment Resources, Inc.
a) MULTIDIMENSIONAL HEALTH PROFILE—PSYCHOSOCIAL FUNCTIONING.
Acronym: MHP-P.
Scores, 17: Number of Stressful Events, Perceived Stress, Coping Skills, Total Social Support, Emotional Support, Informational Support, Tangible Support, Negative Social Exchange, Total Psychological Distress, Depressed Affect, Guilt, Motor Retardation, Anxious Affect, Somatic Complaints, Cognitive Disturbance, Life Satisfaction, Global Stress.
Comments: 58-item self-report questionnaire to assess psychosocial functioning.
b) MULTIDIMENSIONAL HEALTH PROFILE—HEALTH FUNCTIONING.
Acronym: MHP-H.
Scores, 20: Self-Help, Professional Help, Help from Friends, Spiritual Help, Positive Health Habits, Negative Health Habits, Self-Efficacy, Health Vigilance, Health Values, Trust in Health Care Personnel, Trust in Health Care System, Hypochondriasis, Overall Health, Recent Health, Presence of a Chronic Illness, Impairment Due to a Chronic Illness, Office Visits, Overnight Hospital Treatment, Emergency Room Treatment, Over the Counter Medication.
Comments: 69-item self-report questionnaire to assess health functioning.
Cross References: For reviews by Wendy Naumann and Terri L. Weaver, see 14:247.

[1327]

Multidimensional Perfectionism Scale.

Purpose: Designed to assess "different aspects of perfectionism."
Population: Ages 18 and over.
Publication Date: 2004.

Acronym: MPS.
Scores: 3 subscales: Self-Oriented Perfectionism, Other-Oriented Perfectionism, Socially Prescribed Perfectionism.
Administration: Individual or group.
Price Data, 2015: $125 per complete kit including manual (88 pages) and 25 QuikScore forms; $83 per technical manual; $55 per 25 QuikScore forms; $99 per Online Profile Report Kit including manual and 3 profile reports; $6 per each online Profile report (min. purchase of 50); $99 per Online Interpretive Report Kit including manual and 3 interpretive reports; $8 per each online Interpretive report (minimum 25); $185 per software kit including manual, V.5 getting started guide, and 25 interpretive reports; $6 per V.5 software Profile report (minimum 50); $8 per V.5 software Interpretive report (minimum 25).
Time: (15) minutes.
Comments: Self-report inventory.
Authors: Paul L. Hewitt and Gordon L. Flett.
Publisher: Multi-Health Systems, Inc.
Cross References: For a review by Collie Conoley, see 17:129.

[1328]
Multidimensional Self Concept Scale.

Purpose: Designed to provide a multidimensional assessment of self concept in clinical and research settings.
Population: Grades 5–12.
Publication Date: 1992.
Acronym: MSCS.
Scores, 7: Social, Competence, Affect, Academic, Family, Physical, Total.
Administration: Group or individual.
Price Data, 2015: $133 per complete set; $72 per 50 record booklets; $67 per examiner's manual (82 pages).
Time: (20) minutes.
Author: Bruce A. Bracken.
Publisher: PRO-ED.
Cross References: See T5:1734 (6 references); for reviews by Francis X. Archambault, Jr. and W. Grant Willis, see 12:246 (1 reference); see also T4:1682 (1 reference).

[1329]
The Multidimensional Self-Esteem Inventory.

Purpose: "Measures global self-esteem and its eight components."
Population: Adults.
Publication Dates: 1983–1988.
Acronym: MSEI.
Scores, 11: Competence, Lovability, Likability, Self-control, Personal Power, Moral Self-approval, Body Appearance, Body Functioning, Identity Integration, Defensive Self-enhancement, Global Self-esteem.

Administration: Individual or group.
Price Data, 2015: $216 per introductory kit including manual (1988, 22 pages), 25 reusable test booklets, 50 rating forms, and 50 profile forms.
Time: (15-30) minutes.
Comments: Originally called Self-Report Inventory.
Authors: Edward J. O'Brien and Seymour Epstein.
Publisher: Psychological Assessment Resources, Inc.
Cross References: See T5:1735 (12 references) and T4:1683 (2 references); for reviews by Barbara J. Kaplan and Joseph G. Ponterotto, see 11:250 (1 reference).

[1330]
Multidimensional Verbal Intelligence Test.

Purpose: Designed "to evaluate a person's verbal ability."
Population: Under age 17 through adult.
Publication Date: 2011.
Acronym: MVIT.
Scores, 7: Definitions, Antonyms, Sentence Completions, Analogies, Reading Comprehension, Vocabulary, Overall Score.
Administration: Individual.
Price Data: Available from publisher.
Time: (30) minutes.
Comments: Self-administered online assessment. The test publisher provides clients with information about the methods and theoretical basis used in the development of the test as well as benchmarks for relevant industries and racial/ethnic group comparison data.
Author: PsychTests AIM, Inc.
Publisher: PsychTests AIM, Inc. [Canada].
Cross References: For reviews by Thanos Patelis and Kathleen Quinn, see 19:114.

[1331]
Multifactor Leadership Questionnaire [Third Edition Manual].

Purpose: Measures a broad range of leadership types; identifies the characteristics of a transformational leader and helps individuals discover how they measure up in their own eyes and in the eyes of those with whom they work.
Population: Researchers, consultants, leaders, supervisors, colleagues, peers, direct reports.
Publication Dates: 1990–2004.
Acronym: MLQ.
Scores, 12: 12: Transformational Leadership (Idealized Attributes, Idealized Behaviors, Inspirational Motivational, Intellectual Stimulation, Individualized Consideration), Transactional Leadership (Contingent Reward, Management-by-Exception: Active), Passive-Avoidant Behaviors (Management-by-Exception: Passive, Laissez-Faire), Outcomes of Leadership (Extra Effort, Effectiveness, and Satisfaction with the Leadership).
Administration: Individual or group.

Forms, 4: Multirater, Rater, Self, and Actual/Ought.
Price Data: Available from publisher.
Foreign Language Editions: Paper-and-pencil translations are available for Czech, German, Spanish, French, Italian, Portuguese, Russian, and Turkish (Multi-Rater); German and Turkish (Rater only); and Spanish (Actual/Ought). Online translations are available for Albanian, Arabic, Bulgarian, Chinese (Mandarin and Cantonese), Croatian, Czech, Danish, Dutch, Farsi, Filipino, Finnish, French, German, Greek, Hebrew, Icelandic, Indonesian, Italian, Japanese, Korean, Lao, Lithuanian, Malay, Burmese, Norwegian, Polish, Portuguese, Romanian, Russian, Serbian, Slovene, Spanish, Swahili, Swedish, Turkish, Urdu, and Vietnamese.
Time: (15) minutes.
Comments: Both paper form-based and Web-based forms are available; scoring and reporting provided by publisher (including both multirater and an Actual vs Ought Feedback Report); previous edition listed as Multifactor Leadership Questionnaire for Research, Second Edition.
Authors: Bruce J. Avolio and Bernard M. Bass.
Publisher: Mind Garden, Inc.
Cross References: For reviews by John W. Fleenor and Eugene P. Sheehan, see 17:130; for a review by David J. Pittenger of an earlier edition, see 14:248; see also T5:1736 (5 references); for reviews by Frederick Bessai and Jean Powell Kirnan and Brooke Snyder of an earlier edition, see 12:247 (5 references); see also T4:1684 (5 references).

[1332]
Multilingual Aphasia Examination, Third Edition.
Purpose: Designed to evaluate the presence, severity, and qualitative aspects of aphasic disorder.
Population: Ages 6–69.
Publication Dates: 1978–1994.
Acronym: MAE.
Scores, 11: Visual Naming, Sentence Repetition, Controlled Word Association, Oral Spelling, Written Spelling, Block Spelling, MAE Token Test, Aural Comprehension of Words and Phrases, Reading Comprehension of Words and Phrases, Rating of Articulation, Rating of Praxic Features of Writing.
Administration: Individual.
Price Data, 2015: $500 per introductory kit including professional manual, reading stimulus cards, visual stimulus cards, set of tokens and letters, and 100 each of all record forms.
Foreign Language Edition: Spanish edition available.
Time: Administration time not reported.
Authors: A. L. Benton, deS. Hamsher, and A. B. Sivan.
Publisher: Psychological Assessment Resources, Inc.

Cross References: For reviews by Nancy B. Bologna and by Malcolm R. McNeil and Wiltrud Fassbinder, see 14:249; see also T5:1740 (36 references).

[1333]
Multimodal Life History Inventory.
Purpose: To provide "therapists with an in-depth assessment tool for adult counseling."
Population: Adult counseling clients.
Publication Dates: 1980-1991.
Scores: No scores.
Administration: Group.
Manual: No manual.
Price Data, 2015: $34.99 per set of 20 inventories.
Foreign Language Edition: Spanish version available.
Time: Administration time not reported.
Comments: Self-report to be completed in the client's "own time"; previously listed as Multimodal Life History Questionnaire.
Authors: Arnold A. Lazarus and Clifford N. Lazarus.
Publisher: Research Press.

[1334]
Multiphasic Sex Inventory II.
Purpose: "To assess a wide range of psychosexual characteristics of the sexual offender."
Population: Adult males, ages 18–84.
Publication Dates: 1984–2003.
Acronym: MSI II.
Scores: 42 scales and indices: Suicide, Sexual Ethics, Sex Knowledge and Beliefs, Repeated Items, Infrequency, Social Sexual Desirability, Sexual Obsessions, Dissimulation, Lie, Molester Comparison, Rapist Comparison, Child Molest, Rape, Exhibitionism, Voyeurism, Sex Harassment, Net Sex, Obscene Call, Pornography, Transvestism, Fetishism & NOS Paraphilias, Bondage Discipline, Sexual Sadism, Masochism, Physiologic Dysfunction, Desire, Premature Ejaculation, Body Image, Social Sexual Inadequacies, Emotional Neediness, Cognitive Distortion and Immaturity, Antisocial Behavior, Conduct Disorder, Sociopathy, Domestic Violence, Substance Abuse, Denial, Justification, Scheming, Superoplimism, Gender Identity, Treatment Attitudes.
Administration: Group.
Price Data: Available from publisher.
Foreign Language Edition: Spanish language version available.
Time: (45–120) minutes.
Comments: May be administered via audio cassette or paper-pencil; computer scoring done by publisher.
Authors: H. R. Nichols and Ilene Molinder.
Publisher: Nichols & Molinder Assessments.
Cross References: For reviews by Paul A. Arbisi and Albert Bugaj, see 16:153; see also T5:1744 (8 references) and T4:1689 (2 references).

[1335]
Multiple Affect Adjective Check List–Revised.

Purpose: "To measure both state and affect traits."
Population: Ages 20–79.
Publication Dates: 1960–1999.
Acronym: MAACL-R.
Scores, 7: Anxiety, Depression, Hostility, Positive Affect, Sensation Seeking, Dysphoria, Positive Affect and Sensation Seeking.
Administration: Group.
Price Data, 2016: $14.50 per 25 form checklists (specify State or Trait); $20.75 per hand-scoring keys; $36.50 per manual (1999, 71 pages); $39.25 per specimen set including manual and 1 copy of all forms.
Time: 5(10) minutes.
Authors: Marvin Zuckerman and Bernard Lubin.
Publisher: EdITS/Educational and Industrial Testing Service.
Cross References: For reviews by Gerald E. De-Mauro and Paul Retzlaff, see 16:154; see also T5:1745 (89 references) and T4:1690 (96 references); for a review by John A. Zarske of an earlier edition, see 10:205 (84 references); see also 9:734 (47 references), T3:1547 (108 references), 8:628 (102 references), and T2:1293 (56 references); for reviews by E. Lowell Kelly and Edwin I. Megargee of an earlier edition, see 7:112 (60 references); see also P:176 (28 references).

[1336]
Multiscale Dissociation Inventory.

Purpose: To assess the clinical severity of dissociative disturbance.
Population: Ages 18 and older.
Publication Dates: 1998–2002.
Acronym: MDI.
Scores, 6: Disengagement, Depersonalization, Derealization, Emotional Constriction, Memory Disturbance, Identity Dissociation.
Administration: Individual or group.
Price Data: Available for free from publisher for qualified researchers or licensed clinicians.
Time: (5–10) minutes.
Comments: Self-report; requires 6th grade reading level; normed on 440 adults with a histories of at least one DSM-IV-TR "Criterion A" traumatic event.
Author: John Briere.
Publisher: John Briere.
Cross References: For reviews by Frederick T. L. Leong and Paul Retzlaff, see 16:156.

[1337]
Multiscore Depression Inventory for Children.

Purpose: Designed to assess depression and "features related to depression."

Population: Ages 8–17
Publication Date: 1996.
Acronym: MDI-C.
Scores, 9: Anxiety, Self-Esteem, Sad Mood, Instrumental Helplessness, Social Introversion, Low Energy, Pessimism, Defiance, Total.
Administration: Group.
Price Data, 2016: $143.50 per complete kit, including 25 AutoScore™ test forms, 25 profile forms, and manual; $52.50 per 25 AutoScore™ test forms; $65.50 per manual; $33 per 50 profile forms; $448 per 25-use CD-ROM for scoring and interpretation.
Time: (15–20) minutes.
Authors: David J. Berndt and Charles F. Kaiser.
Publisher: Western Psychological Services.
Cross References: For reviews by Jill Ann Jenkins and Michael G. Kavan, see 14:250.

[1338]
Murphy-Meisgeier Type Indicator for Children® [Revised].

Purpose: "Intended to help students develop greater awareness of their preferred ways for processing information, making decisions, and forming relationships."
Population: Grades 2-12.
Publication Dates: 1987-2008.
Acronym: MMTIC™.
Scores, 4: Extraversion or Introversion, Sensing or Intuition, Thinking or Feeling, Judging or Perceiving.
Administration: Individual or group.
Price Data, 2015: $8 per online assessment including scoring and a personalized student report; $4 per additional Professional report (designed for counselors); $4 per additional Career Report; $4 for additional Verified Type Report; $39 per year for access to the MMTIC Facilitator Interface, which allows quantity purchases, set up and management of different groups and individuals, report generation, data management, and free downloadable support materials (including MMTIC manual, 2008, 96 pages).
Time: (15-20) minutes.
Comments: Each report provides the indicated preference for the respondent on the four dichotomies that are scored.
Authors: Elizabeth Murphy and Charles Meisgeier.
Publisher: Center for Applications of Psychological Type, Inc.
Cross References: For reviews by Joyce Meikamp and Jeanette Lee-Farmer and by David Morse, see 18:78; see T5:1750 (1 reference); for reviews by Joanne Jensen and Norman Constantine and by Hoi K. Suen of an earlier edition, see 12:249.

[1339]
Music Appreception Test.

Purpose: Designed for application in "clinical, educational, organizational and neuropsychology, art and creativity, and language and cognition."

Population: Ages 8 to 45.
Publication Date: 2007.
Acronym: MAT.
Scores, 39: Response Latency, Fluency (Compositional Fluency, Post-Compositional Fluency, Run-on Fluency, Total), Content Categories (Human, Human Mythic, Human Group, Participant Observer, Total Human, Animal, Animal Mythic, Total Animal, Natural, Man Made, Abstract, Morbid, Total Other), Interaction (Solitary, Mutual, Conflict, Detach), Tangential Response (Self, Music Centered, Other, Total Non-Story Reference), Affective Fit (Hedonic Tone, Affect Expressed, Common Theme, Common Interaction, Common Setting, Total), Narrative Style (Logical, Balanced, Kinetic/Imagistic, Disorganized/Other), Morbid Content, Adaptive Response to Change, Time to Termination.
Administration: Individual.
Forms, 4: Standard, Extended, Short Form (A, B).
Price Data, 2016: $191 per starter kit including manual (2007, 125 pages), manual supplement (2007, 115 pages), 20 record forms, administration CD, and carrier bag; $38 per 20 record forms; $48 per manual; $38 per manual supplement; $89 per administration CD.
Time: (8-25) minutes.
Comments: Test administered via CD; requires the use of a playback device, such as an MP3 player, speaker or recorder.
Author: Leland van den Daele.
Publisher: Psychodiagnostics, Inc.
Cross References: For reviews by Mary L. Garner and Jeffrey K. Smith, see 18:79.

[1340]
Music Teacher Self-Assessment.

Purpose: Designed to provide means for music teachers to view and analyze their teaching.
Population: Music teachers.
Publication Date: 1996.
Administration: Individual.
Scores: No scores.
Price Data, 2015: $34.95 per workbook (36 pages), self-assessment, and DVD.
Time: Administration time not available.
Authors: James O. Froseth and Molly A. Weaver.
Publisher: GIA Publications.

[1341]
Musical Aptitude Profile [1995 Revision].

Purpose: Designed to evaluate music aptitude.
Population: Grades 4–12.
Publication Dates: 1965–1995.
Scores, 11: Tonal Imagery (Melody, Harmony, Total), Rhythm Imagery (Tempo, Meter, Total), Musical Sensitivity (Phrasing, Balance, Style, Total), Total.
Administration: Group.

Price Data, 2015: $140 per complete kit; $25 per 100 answer sheets; $30 per 100 profile cards; $2 per class record sheet; $25 per sensitivity compact disc; $25 per tonal and rhythm compact disc; $20 per scoring masks (with school purchase order only); $20 per manual (1995, 162 pages).
Time: (110) minutes.
Comments: Test must be scored manually.
Author: Edwin E. Gordon.
Publisher: GIA Publications, Inc.
Cross References: For reviews by Christopher M. Johnson and James W. Sherbon, see 16:157; see also T5:1752 (1 reference); for reviews by Annabel J. Cohen and James W. Sherbon of an earlier edition, see 12:251; see also T4:1697 (2 references); T3:1552 (4 references); 8:98 (25 references), and T2:209 (11 references); for reviews by Robert W. Lundin and John McLeish, see 7:249 (33 references).

[1342]
My Vocational Situation.

Purpose: Designed to diagnose difficulties in vocational decision-making.
Population: High school and college and adult.
Publication Date: 1980.
Acronym: MVS.
Scores, 3: Vocational Identity, Occupational Information, Barriers.
Administration: Group.
Price Data: Available at no charge from test publisher.
Time: (5-10) minutes.
Authors: John L. Holland, Denise Daiger, and Paul G. Power.
Publisher: University of Maryland.
Cross References: See T5:1754 (27 references) and T4:1701 (24 references); for a review by Bert W. Westbrook, see 9:738 (1 reference).

[1343]
My Worst Experience Scale.

Purpose: Designed to "assess youngsters' reports of their most stressful experiences and their thoughts, behaviors, and feelings associated with those experiences."
Population: Ages 9–18.
Publication Date: 2002.
Acronym: MWES.
Scores, 12: DSM IV PTSD Criterion Subscales (Impact of the Event, Re-experience of the Trauma, Avoidance and Numbing, Increased Arousal), Symptoms Subscales (Depression, Hopelessness, Somatic Symptoms, Oppositional Conduct, Hypervigilance, Dissociation and Dreams, General Maladjustment), Total.
Administration: Group or individual.
Price Data, 2016: $59.50 per manual (78 pages); $19.50 per 25 answer booklets for use with scoring CD; $31.50 per 100 school alienation and trauma survey forms; $369.50 per 25-use scoring CD.

Time: (20–30) minutes.
Comments: Self-report questionnaire; computer administration and scoring available.
Authors: Irwin A. Hyman, and Pamela A. Snook (scale and manual), J. M. Berna, M. A. Kohr, J. DuCette, and G. Britton (scale).
Publisher: Western Psychological Services.
Cross References: For reviews by Frederic J. Medway and Heidi K. Moore, see 16:158.

[1344]
Myers-Briggs Type Indicator®, Form M.

Purpose: Designed for "the identification of basic preferences on each of the four dichotomies specified or implicit in Jung's theory" and "the identification and description of the 16 personality types that result from interactions among the preferences."
Population: Ages 14 and older.
Publication Dates: 1943–1998.
Acronym: MBTI®.
Scores, 4: Extraversion vs. Introversion, Sensing vs. Intuition, Thinking vs. Feeling, Judging vs. Perceiving.
Administration: Individual or group.
Price Data, 2016: $42.95 per complete online administration with interpretation; $159.50 per 10 self-scorable forms; $18.95 per Profile online administration; $22.95 per Interpretative Report online administration; $29.95 per Interpretive Report for Organizations online administration; $16.95 per MBTI Career Report online administration; $27.95 per Team Report online administration; $27.95 per MBTI Comparison: Work Styles Report online administration; $27.95 per Decision-Making Styles Report online administration; $27.95 per Stress Management Report online administration; $28.95 per Communication Style Report online administration; $147.00 per manual (1998, 440 pages).
Foreign Language Editions: U.S. English, U.K. English, Latin American Spanish, Japanese, Chinese - Traditional, Chinese - Simplified, Danish, Dutch, French, German, Swedish, European Spanish, Brazilian Portuguese, Argentine Spanish, Canadian French, Norwegian, Italian, Greek, Portuguese, Finnish, Indonesian, Korean, Polish, Russian, Turkish.
Time: (15–25) minutes.
Comments: Scoring options: Online, self-scorable, template scoring, software on-site scoring, mail-in scoring; Extensive support materials are available, visit www.cpp. com to review all MBTI(R)-related products.
Authors: Katharine C. Briggs, Isabel Briggs Myers, Mary H. McCaulley (revised manual), Naomi L. Quenk (revised manual), and Allen L. Hammer (revised manual).
Publisher: CPP, Inc.
Cross References: For reviews by John W. Fleenor and Paul M. Mastrangelo, see 14:251; see also T5:1755 (78 references) and T4:1702 (45 references); for a review by Jerry S. Wiggins of an earlier edition, see 10:206 (42 references); for a review by Anthony J. DeVito of an earlier edition, see 9:739 (19 references); see also T3:1555 (42 references); for a review by Richard W. Coan, of an earlier edition, see 8:630 (115 references); see also T2:1294 (120 references) and P:177 (56 references); for reviews by Gerald A. Mendelsohn and Norman D. Sundberg and an excerpted review by Laurence Siegel, see 6:147 (10 references).

[1345]
Myers-Briggs Type Indicator® Step III.

Purpose: Designed to provide "individualized descriptions of a person's current uses of perception and judgment, as well as suggestions for enhancing effectiveness."
Population: Adults ages 18 and older.
Publication Date: 2009.
Acronym: MBTI® Step III.
Scores: Individualized report results based on 3 Sufficiency scales (Confidence, Stamina, Compensatory Strain) and 26 Developmental scales (Acceptance, Application, Appreciation, Cynicism, Defensiveness, Dependence, Enjoyment, Evidence of Failure, Faith, Flexibility, Freedom of Expression, Friendship, Grievance, Group Sociability, Harmony, Indecisiveness, Logic, Planning, Relatedness, Resistance, Self-focus, Shyness, Spontaneity, Stubbornness, Warmth, Worry).
Administration: Individual.
Restricted Distribution: Available for purchase and use only by those who have successfully completed certification program.
Price Data, 2016: $129 per manual (168 pages); $10 per question booklet; $10 per answer sheet.
Time: (40-50) minutes.
Comments: Administered via paper and pencil or online; computer-scored; CPP, Inc. publishes the Step III manual, question book, and answer sheets; the Center for Applications of Psychological Type (CAPT) retains ownership of the scoring and content of the reports.
Authors: Isabel Briggs Myers, Mary H. McCaulley, Naomi L. Quenk, Allen L. Hammer, and Wayne D. Mitchell.
Publisher: CPP, Inc.
Cross References: Reviews are scheduled for *The Twentieth Mental Measurements Yearbook*. For reviews by Allen K. Hess and Kevin Lanning, of Step II, see 15:172; for reviews by John W. Fleenor and Paul M. Mastrangelo of Form M, see 14:251 (1 reference); for a review by Jerry S. Wiggins, see 10:206 (42 references); for a review by Anthony J. DeVito, see 9:739 (19 references); see also T3:1555 (42 references); for a review by Richard Coan, see 8:630 (115 references); see also T2:1294 (120 references) and P:177 (56 references); for reviews by Gerald A. Mendelsohn and Norman D. Sundberg and an excerpted review by Laurence Siegel, see 6:147 (10 references).

[1346]
Myers-Briggs Type Indicator® Step II (Form Q).

Purpose: "Provides an in-depth personalized account of personality preferences."

Population: Age 12 and over.

Publication Date: 2001.

Acronym: MBTI Step II—Form Q.

Scores, 24: Four dichotomies (Extraversion vs. Introversion, Sensing vs. Intuition, Thinking vs. Feeling, Judging vs. Perceiving), 20 facets: 5 Extraversion—Introversion facets (Initiating—Receiving, Expressive—Contained, Gregarious—Intimate, Active—Reflective, Enthusiastic—Quiet), 5 Sensing—Intuition facets (Concrete—Abstract, Realistic—Imaginative, Practical—Conceptual, Experiential—Theoretical, Traditional—Original), 5 Thinking—Feeling facets (Logical—Empathetic, Reasonable—Compassionate, Questioning—Accommodating, Critical—Accepting, Tough—Tender), 5 Judging—Perceiving facets (Systematic—Casual, Planful—Open-Ended, Early Starting—Pressure-Prompted, Scheduled—Spontaneous, Methodical—Emergent).

Administration: Individual or group.

Price Data, 2016: $29.95 each for MBTI® Step II™ Profile online administration; $46.95 each for MBTI® Step II™ Interpretive Report online administration; $132.00 each for MBTI® Step II™ manual; $63.00 each for MBTI® Step II™ User's Guide; $21.95 each for Understanding Your MBTI® Step II™ Results.

Foreign Language Editions: Available in U.S. English, U.K. English, Latin American Spanish, Japanese, Chinese Traditional, Chinese Simplified, Danish, Dutch, French, German, Swedish, European Spanish, Canadian French, Korean, Polish, Brazilian Portuguese, Russian.

Time: (25–35) minutes.

Comments: Includes all items comprising Step I, Form M of MBTI® (14:251); can be used to generate all reports produced by Step I, Form M of MBTI®; provides advice for enhancing communication, conflict and change management, and decision making skills; computer or web-administered scoring available.

Authors: Katharine C. Briggs, Isabel Briggs Myers, Naomi L. Quenk (Profile Form, Interpretive Form, MBTI Step II Manual), Jean Kummerow (Profile Form, Interpretive Form), Allen L. Hammer (MBTI Step II Manual), and Mark S. Major (MBTI Step II Manual).

Publisher: CPP, Inc.

Cross References: For reviews by Allen K. Hess and Kevin Lanning, see 15:172; for information about other components of this program, see T5:1755 (78 references) and T4:1702 (45 references); for reviews by John W. Fleenor and Paul M. Mastrangelo of Form M, see 14:251 (1 reference); for a review by Jerry S. Wiggins, see 10:206 (42 references); for a review by Anthony J. DeVito, see 9:739 (19 references); see also T3:1555 (42 references); for a review by Richard Coan, see 8:630 (115 references); see also T2:1294 (120 references) and P:177 (56 references); for reviews by Gerald A. Mendelsohn and Norman D. Sundberg and an excerpted review by Laurence Siegel, see 6:147 (10 references).

[1347]
Naglieri Nonverbal Ability Test—Individual Administration.

Purpose: Designed to provide a brief nonverbal measure of general ability.

Population: Ages 5-0 to 17-11.

Publication Date: 2003.

Acronym: NNAT-I.

Scores: Total score only.

Administration: Individual.

Price Data, 2015: $323 per complete kit including manual (139 pages), stimulus book, 25 parent reports, and 25 each of record forms A and B; $157.85 per stimulus book; $80.75 per manual; $83.50 per 25 record forms (specify Form A or B); $80 per 25 parent reports (Spanish or English).

Foreign Language Edition: Parent Report available in Spanish.

Time: (25–30) minutes.

Comments: This test and the Naglieri Nonverbal Ability Test (Multilevel Form) are the second editions of the still in-print Matrix Analogies Test (Expanded Form and Short Form).

Author: Jack A. Naglieri.

Publisher: Pearson.

Cross References: For reviews by Connie T. England and Brian F. French, see 16:159; see also T5:1607 (15 references) and T4:1566 (8 references); for a review by Robert F. McMorris, David L. Rule, and Wendy J. Steinberg of the Matrix Analogies Test, see 10:191 (1 reference).

[1348]
Naglieri Nonverbal Ability Test–Second Edition.

Purpose: Designed as "a nonverbal measure of general ability" for use in identifying "students whose low general ability may indicate potential academic problems, as well as identifying gifted and talented students with high general ability."

Population: Students in kindergarten through Grade 12.

Publication Dates: 1996-2011.

Acronym: NNAT2.

Score: Total score only.

Administration: Group.

Levels, 7: A (Kindergarten), B (Grade 1), C (Grade 2), D (Grades 3-4), E (Grades 5-6), F (Grades 7-9), G (Grades 10-12).

Price Data, 2015: $56 per 10 consumable/machine-scorable test packs (Levels A-D); $46 per 10 reusable test booklets (Levels C-G); $50 per 30 answer documents; $9.95 per online test and report; $58 per technical manual (2011, 71 pages); $35 per gifted teachers guide (2008, 139 pages); $20 per administration directions (35 pages).
Foreign Language Edition: Directions for administration are printed in English and Spanish; home report available in Spanish.
Time: (30) minutes.
Comments: May be administered online or via paper and pencil.
Authors: Jack A. Naglieri (test and teacher's guide), Dina Brulles (teacher's guide), and Kim Lansdowne (teacher's guide).
Publisher: Pearson.
Cross References: Reviews are scheduled for *The Twentieth Mental Measurements Yearbook*. For reviews by Terry A. Stinnett and Michael S. Trevisan, see 14:252.

[1349]
National Assessment of Educational Progress—Released Exercises.

Purpose: "A continuing, congressionally mandated national survey of knowledge, skills, and understanding, of young Americans" in the fields of mathematics, science, reading, writing, U.S. history, geography, and other subject areas.
Population: Grades 4, 8, and 12 (main NAEP); Ages 9, 13, and 17 (Long-Term Trend NAEP).
Publication Dates: 1983–2002.
Acronym: NAEP.
Scores: No individual scores, scaled results (average proficiency) are provided for designated reporting subgroups.
Administration: Group.
Price Data: Released items available on the NAEP website.
Comments: Released-exercise set, which is approximately one-third to one-half of the complete assessment package; administered to national samples of specified age groups biennially since 1969 (1969–1998 now out of print); released exercises are in the public domain and may be copied without restriction following receipt of permission from the author (NCES); student, teacher, and school questionnaires are also available; details of the assessments, procedures, analyses, and results can be found in a series of reports available from the author and publisher; ETS has served as the primary NAEP contractor since 1983.
Authors: National Assessment of Educational Progress; National Center for Education Statistics; Office of Educational Research and Improvement; U.S. Dept. of Education.
Publisher: Educational Testing Service [Efforts to obtain updated information from the test publisher were unsuccessful. An updated edition of this test appears on the test publisher's website.]

a) MATHEMATICS.
Scores: 5 content areas (Numbers and Operations, Measurement, Geometry, Data Analysis/Statistics and Probability, Algebra and Functions), Estimation Skills; 3 process areas (Conceptual Understanding, Procedural Knowledge, Problem Solving).
Comments: Assessment dates: 1986, 1990, 1992, 1996.
b) SCIENCE.
Scores: 3 content areas (Life Sciences, Physical Sciences, Earth & Space Sciences); 3 thinking skills/areas (Conducting Inquiries, Solving Problems, Knowing Science).
Comments: Assessment dates: 1986, 1990.
c) READING.
Scores: 3 purposes (Reading for Literary Experience, Reading to Gain Information, Reading to Perform a Task); 4 stances (Initial Understanding, Developing Interpretation, Personal Reflection and Response, Demonstrating a Critical Stance).
Comments: Assessment dates: 1984, 1986, 1988, 1990, 1992, 1994, 1998, 2000, 2002.
d) WRITING.
Scores: 3 purposes (Informative, Narrative, Persuasive).
Comments: Assessment dates: 1984, 1988, 1992, 1998, 2002.
e) U.S. HISTORY.
Scores: 4 themes (Change and Continuity in American Democracy, The Gathering and Interaction of Peoples/Cultures/and Ideas, Economic and Technological Changes and Their Relation to Society/Ideas/and the Environment, The Changing Role of America in the World).
Comments: Assessment dates: 1988, 1994, 2001.
f) GEOGRAPHY.
Scores: 3 content areas (Space and Place, Environment and Society, Spatial Dynamics and Dimensions).
Comments: Assessment dates: 1988, 1994, 2001.
g) FINE ARTS.
Scores: 4 content areas (Music, Dance, Theatre, Visual Arts).
Comments: Assessment date: 1997.
Cross References: See T5:1759 (18 references).

[1350]
National German Examination for High School Students.

Purpose: To evaluate students' achievement in German study, may be used as a diagnostic tool.
Population: 2, 3, or 4 years high school.
Publication Dates: 1960-2016.
Scores: Total score only.
Administration: Group.
Levels, 3: Second Year, Third Year, Fourth Year.
Price Data, 2016: $6 per student; $80 non-member sponsor fee.
Time: 60(65) minutes.
Comments: Also called AATG National Standardized Testing Program; formerly called AATG German Test and National German Contest for High School Students; tests administered online annually in December and January under auspices of high school guidance departments and administration; test is new each year.

Author: American Association of Teachers of German.
Publisher: American Association of Teachers of German, Inc.
Cross References: For reviews by Gilbert C. Kettelkamp and Theodor F. Naumann of an earlier edition, see 6:382.

[1351]
National Institute for Personnel Research Normal Battery.

Purpose: "Designed as a selection device for use mainly with Bantu clerks in various industrial and government organizations."
Population: South African Standards 6–10 and job applicants with 8–11 years of education.
Publication Dates: 1960–1973.
Subtests, 5: Mental Alertness, Reading Comprehension, Vocabulary, Spelling, Computation.
Administration: Group.
Price Data: Price information available from publisher for test materials including manual (1969, 129 pages).
Author: S. M. A. Waterhouse (manual).
Publisher: Human Sciences Research Council [South Africa]. [Efforts to obtain updated information from the test publisher were unsuccessful. This test could not be found on the test publisher's website; its status is unknown.]
Cross References: See T2:1085 (2 references) and 6:779.

[1352]
National Police Officer Selection Test.

Purpose: Measures skills critical to the successful performance of entry-level officers.
Population: Police officer candidates.
Publication Dates: 1991–1992.
Acronym: POST.
Partial Batteries: POST III or POST IV.
Administration: Group.
Restricted Distribution: Available to authorized police personnel only.
Price Data: Price information available from publisher for administration guide (1991, 12 pages), examiner's manual (1992, 13 pages; required with first purchase), and study guide.
Comments: Test may be self-scored or scored by Stanard & Associates, Inc.
Author: Stanard & Associates, Inc.
Publisher: Stanard & Associates, Inc.
 a) POST III.
  Scores, 4: Mathematics, Reading Comprehension, Grammar, Total.
  Price Data: Price information available from publisher for 1-250 POST III (scored by publisher) and 1–250 POST III (self-scored).
  Time: 66 (71) minutes.

 b) POST IV.
  Scores, 5: Mathematics, Reading Comprehension, Grammar, Incident Report Writing, Total.
  Price Data: Price information available from publisher for 1-250 POST IV (scored by publisher) and 1–250 POST IV (self-scored).
  Time: 83 (88) minutes.
Cross References: See T5:1763 (1 reference); for reviews by Jim C. Fortune and Abbot Packard and by Kurt F. Geisinger, see 12:253.

[1353]
National Spanish Examinations.

Purpose: Designed "to measure proficiency and achievement of students who are studying Spanish as a second language."
Population: Grades 6-12.
Publication Dates: 1957-2005 (written), 2006-2016 (online).
Acronym: NSE.
Scores, 7: Vocabulary, Grammar, Achievement, Reading Comprehension, Listening Comprehension, Proficiency, Overall.
Administration: Individual or group.
Levels, 6: 01, 1, 2, 3, 4, 5, 6; Levels vary by years of exposure to Spanish as a second language.
Parts, 2: Achievement (Vocabulary and Grammar), Proficiency (Reading Comprehension and Listening Comprehension).
Price Data, 2015: $3 per students; $75 for each teacher administering the exam; AATSP members do not have to pay the teacher fee.
Time: Two 40-minute sessions.
Comments: The NSE is administered and taken entirely online through the NSE's online test provider Quia/IXL Learning. The test is not intended for native Spanish speakers.
Author: Teacher members of the American Association of Teachers of Spanish and Portuguese (AATSP).
Publisher: National Spanish Exam.
Cross References: See 8:168 (2 references); for a review by Walter V. Kalfers of earlier forms, see 7:323 (1 reference); see also 6:428 (8 references).

[1354]
National Survey of Student Engagement.

Purpose: Designed to provide colleges and universities information about the student experience and institutional performance to use to improve undergraduate education, inform accountability and accreditation efforts, and facilitate national and sector benchmarking efforts.
Population: First-year and senior undergraduate students at 4-year colleges and universities.
Publication Dates: 2000–2016.
Acronym: NSSE.

Scores, 21: 10 Engagement Indicators in 4 themes: Academic Challenge (Higher-Order Learning, Reflective & Integrative Learning, Learning Strategies, Quantitative Reasoning), Learning with Peers (Collaborative Learning, Discussions with Diverse Others), Experiences with Faculty (Student-Faculty Interaction, Effective Teaching Practices), Campus Environment (Quality of Interactions, Supportive Environment), 6 High-Impact Practices (Learning Community, Service-Learning, Research with Faculty, Internship, Study Abroad, Culminating Senior Experience), Overall Experience.
Administration: Group.
Price Data, 2016: Base cost includes a $300 non-refundable registration fee plus an administration fee determined by undergraduate enrollment. This fee ranges from $2,100 to $8,000. Additional charges may apply.
Foreign Language Editions: Available in U.S. Spanish, Canadian English, and Canadian French.
Time: Administration time not reported.
Comments: Updated survey launched in 2013.
Author: Trustees of Indiana University.
Publisher: Indiana University Center for Postsecondary Research
Cross References: For reviews by William I. Sauser, Jr. and Eugene P. Sheehan of an earlier version, see 16:160.

[1355]

Neale Analysis of Reading Ability: Second Revised British Edition.

Purpose: Designed to measure reading accuracy, comprehension and rate and to provide diagnostic information about children's reading difficulties.
Population: Ages 6-0 to 12-11.
Publication Dates: 1958–1997.
Acronym: NARA II.
Scores, 3: Comprehension, Accuracy, Rate; plus 4 supplementary diagnostic scores (Discrimination of Initial and Final Sounds, Names and Sounds of the Alphabet, Graded Spelling, Auditory Discrimination and Blending).
Administration: Individual.
Forms, 3: 1, 2, Diagnostic Tutor Form (not norm referenced).
Price Data: Available from publisher.
Time: (20) minutes.
Comments: Revision includes new norms and larger standardization sample.
Authors: Marie D. Neale (test and manual); Second Revised British Edition and standardization by Chris Whetton, Louise Caspall, and Kay McCulloch.
Publisher: GL Assessment [England].
Cross References: For reviews by Marie Miller-Whitehead and Elizabeth Kelley Rhoades, see 16:161; see also T5:1765 (36 references) and T4:1714 (7 references); for reviews by Cleborne D. Maddux and G. Michael Poteat of an earlier edition, see 11:257 (41 references); see also T3:1567 (13 references) and T2:1683 (7 refer-

ences); for reviews by M. Alan Brimer and Magdalen D. Vernon, and an excerpted review, see 6:843.

[1356]

Neale Analysis of Reading Ability, 3rd Edition [Australian Standardisation].

Purpose: Designed to "assess reading progress objectivity [and] to obtain structured diagnostic observations of an individual's reading behaviour."
Population: Ages 6 to 12.
Publication Dates: 1958–1999.
Scores, 3: Accuracy, Comprehension, Rate.
Administration: Individual.
Forms, 2: 1, 2.
Price Data, 2016: A$170.95 per specimen set including manual (1999, 141 pages), test booklet reader, record standardised test form 1, record standardised test form 2, record diagnostic tutor form A, record diagnostic tutor form B, and DVD.
Time: (20) minutes.
Comments: Includes six supplementary diagnostic tests (Discrimination of Initial and Final Sounds, Names and Sounds of the Alphabet, Graded Spelling, Auditory Discrimination and Blending, Word Lists, and Silent Reading/Writing).
Authors: Marie D. Neale, Michael McKay, and John Barnard.
Publisher: Australian Council for Educational Research Ltd. [Australia].
Cross References: For reviews by Valentina McInerney and Bruce G. Rogers, see 15:173.

[1357]

NEEDS Survey.

Purpose: Designed "to provide a concise but comprehensive profile of an individual's functioning" relative to the treatment of substance abuse.
Population: Adults.
Publication Date: 1994.
Acronym: NEEDS.
Scores, 10: Test Taking Attitude, Basic Problem Solving and Reading, Emotional Stability, Substance Abuse, Employment, Personal Relationship and Support System, Physical Health, Education, Criminal History, Overall "Needs."
Administration: Individual or group.
Price Data: Available from publisher.
Foreign Language Edition: Available in Spanish.
Time: (26) minutes.
Comments: Self-administered; computer-scored; provides DSM-5 classification for alcohol and drug abuse and ASAM patient placement criteria for treatment recommendations.
Author: ADE Incorporated.
Publisher: ADE Incorporated.

Cross References: For reviews by Anita M. Hubley and Paul M. Mastrangelo, see 14:253.

[1358]
Negotiation Aptitude Profile.
Purpose: Designed to assess "ability to negotiate effectively in a business environment."
Population: Under 17 through adult.
Publication Date: 2011.
Acronym: NAP.
Scores, 35: Memory for Faces, Memory for Names, Stress Management, Patience, Anger Control, Perspective, Self-Monitoring, Communication Skills, Listening Skills, Social Skills, Persuasiveness, Conflict-Resolution Skills, Assertiveness, Networking Skills, Social Insight, Empathy, Flexibility, Willingness to Withhold Judgment, Integrity, Use of "Dirty" Tactics, Mental Speed, Problem-Solving Skills, Knowledge of Negotiation Tactics, Knowledge of Negotiation Principles/Terminology, Preparation and Planning, Clarification and Justification, Bargaining and Problem-Solving, Closure and Implementation, Memory Skills, Self-Control, People Skills, Agreeableness, Cognitive Acuity, Knowledge of the Negotiation Process, Overall Scores.
Administration: Individual.
Price Data: Available from publisher.
Time: (30) minutes.
Comments: Self-administered online assessment. The test publisher provides clients with information about the methods and theoretical basis used in the development of the test as well as benchmarks for relevant industries and racial/ethnic group comparison data.
Author: PsychTests AIM, Inc.
Publisher: PsychTests AIM, Inc. [Canada].
Cross References: For reviews by Nora P. Reilly and F. Staskon, see 19:115.

[1359]
Nelson-Denny Reading Test CD-ROM Version 1.2.
Purpose: "To provide a trustworthy assessment of student ability in three areas of academic achievement: vocabulary, reading comprehension, and reading rate."
Population: Grades 9–16 and adults.
Publication Dates: 1929–2000.
Scores, 4: Vocabulary, Comprehension, Total, Reading Rate.
Administration: Group.
Forms, 2: G and H.
Price Data, 2015: $28 per Manual for Scoring and Interpretation; $10 per administration for 25 to 499 test administrations; $9 per administration for 500-999 test administrations; $8 per administration for 1000+ administrations.
Time: 35(56) minutes.

Comments: Requires Windows 95, 98, NT, or 2000; creates reports including the Individual Narrative, Individual Longitudinal, Group Longitudinal, Group Longitudinal Summary, List of Student Scores, and the Group Summary; a computerized alternative identical in content to paper-pencil Forms G and H and considered by the publisher to be parallel forms.
Authors: James I. Brown, Vivian Vick Fishco, and Gerald S. Hanna.
Publisher: PRO-ED
Cross References: For reviews by Alice Corkill and by Darrell L. Sabers and Amy M. Olson, see 17:132; see also T5:1767 (9 references); for reviews by Mildred Murray-Ward and Douglas K. Smith of Forms G and H, see 13:206 (52 references); see also T4:1715 (30 references); for reviews by Robert J. Tierney and James E. Ysseldyke of Forms E and F, see 9:745 (12 references); see also T3:1568 (38 references); for reviews by Robert A. Forsyth and Alton L. Raynor of Forms C and D, see 8:735 (31 references); see also T2:1572 (46 references); for reviews by David B. Orr and Agatha Townsend and an excerpted review by John O. Crites of Forms A and B, see 6:800 (13 references); for a review by Ivan A. Booker, see 4:544 (17 references); for a review by Hans C. Gordon, see 2:1557.

[1360]
Nelson-Denny Reading Test, Forms G and H.
Purpose: "To assess student achievement and progress in vocabulary, comprehension, and reading rate."
Population: Grades 9–16 and adult
Publication Dates: 1929–1993.
Scores, 4: Vocabulary, Comprehension, Total, Reading Rate.
Administration: Group.
Price Data, 2015: $213 per complete kit, which includes 25 Form G Test Booklets, 25 Form H Test Booklets, 50 Self-Scorable Answer Sheets, Directions for Administration, and a Manual for Scoring and Interpretation.
Time: 35 minutes; 56 minutes for extended time administration.
Comments: Computer-administered version is available on CD-ROM in Windows format.
Authors: James I. Brown, Vivian Vick Fishco, and Gerald S. Hanna.
Publisher: PRO-ED.
Cross References: See T5:1767 (9 references); for reviews by Mildred Murray-Ward and Douglas K. Smith, see 13:206 (52 references); see also T4:1715 (30 references); for reviews by Robert J. Tierney and James E. Ysseldyke of Forms E and F, see 9:745 (12 references); see also T3:1568 (38 references); for reviews by Robert A. Forsyth and Alton L. Raynor of Forms C and D, see 8:735 (31 references); see also T2:1572 (46 references); for reviews by David B. Orr and Agatha Townsend and

an excerpted review by John O. Crites of Forms A and B, see 6:800 (13 references); for a review by Ivan A. Booker, see 4:544 (17 references); for a review by Hans C. Gordon, see 2:1557.

[1361]
NEO–4.

Purpose: Designed as a four-factor version of the Revised NEO Personality Inventory.
Population: Ages 17 and older.
Publication Date: 1998.
Scores, 28: Extraversion (Warmth, Gregariousness, Assertiveness, Activity, Excitement-Seeking, Positive Emotions, Total); Openness to Experience (Fantasy, Aesthetics, Feelings, Actions, Ideas, Values, Total); Agreeableness (Trust, Straightforwardness, Altruism, Compliance, Modesty, Tender-Mindedness, Total); Conscientiousness (Competence, Order, Dutifulness, Achievement Striving, Self-Discipline, Deliberation, Total).
Administration: Group or individual.
Forms, 2: Form S (self-reports), Form R (observer ratings).
Price Data, 2015: $280 per introductory kit including NEO-4 manual supplement (19 pages), 10 each Form S and Form R reusable item booklets, 25 hand-scorable answer sheets, 25 profile forms, 25 style graph booklets, and 25 Your NEO-4 summary forms.
Time: [25–35] minutes.
Comments: Questionnaire items, scoring keys, and scale norms are identical to those found in the Revised NEO Personality Inventory (NEO PI-R; 12:330) for the four factors of Extraversion, Openness to Experience, Agreeableness, and Conscientiousness and users are encouraged to consult the professional manual for the NEO PI-R.
Authors: Paul T. Costa and Robert R. McCrae.
Publisher: Psychological Assessment Resources, Inc.
Cross References: For reviews by Theresa M. Bahns and Carlen Hennington, see 14:254.

[1362]
NEO Personality Inventory–3.

Purpose: Designed to measure "the five major dimensions, or domains, of personality and the most important traits or facets that define each domain."
Population: Ages 12 and older.
Publication Dates: 1978-2010.
Administration: Group.
Price Data, 2015: $346 per complete NEO-PI-3 Adult Comprehensive Kit including NEO Inventories professional manual (2010, 145 pages), 10 reusable Form S item booklets, 10 reusable Form R item booklets (5 male and 5 female), 25 handscorable answer sheets, 25 Form S Adult profile forms, 25 Form R Adult profile forms, 25 Adult Combined-Gender profile forms (Form S/Form R), and 25 Your NEO Summary feedback sheets in a soft-sided attaché case; $346 per complete NEO-PI-3 Adolescent Comprehensive Kit including NEO Inventories professional manual, 10 reusable Form S item booklets, 10 reusable Form R item booklets (5 male and 5 female), 25 handscorable answer sheets, 25 Form S Adolescent profile forms, 25 Form R Adolescent profile forms, 25 Adolescent Combined-Gender profile forms (Form S/Form R), and 25 Your NEO Summary feedback sheets in a soft-sided attaché case; $70 per NEO Inventories professional manual: NEO-PI-3, NEO-FFI-3, NEO PI-R.
Comments: A major innovation of this edition is the modification of the NEO PI-R in which 37 items were replaced; the NEO-PI-3 is now "suitable for assessing personality in middle school-aged children and adolescents, as well as adults"; clinicians may continue using the NEO PI-R; "The NEO-FFI-3 is a revision of the NEO-FFI in which 15 … items have been replaced to improve readability and psychometric properties."
Authors: Robert R. McCrae and Paul T. Costa, Jr.
Publisher: Psychological Assessment Resources, Inc.
  a) NEO PERSONALITY INVENTORY-3.
  Acronym: NEO-PI-3.
  Scores, 35: 30 facets in 5 domains: Neuroticism (Anxiety, Angry Hostility, Depression, Self-Consciousness, Impulsiveness, Vulnerability), Extraversion (Warmth, Gregariousness, Assertiveness, Activity, Excitement-Seeking, Positive Emotions), Openness (Fantasy, Aesthetics, Feelings, Actions, Ideas, Values), Agreeableness (Trust, Straightforwardness, Altruism, Compliance, Modesty, Tender-Mindedness), Conscientiousness (Competence, Order, Dutifulness, Achievement Striving, Self-Discipline, Deliberation).
  Forms, 2: Form S (self-report), Form R (observer ratings).
  Time: (30-40) minutes.
  b) REVISED NEO PERSONALITY INVENTORY.
  Acronym: NEO PI-R.
  Scores, 35: 30 facets in 5 domains: Neuroticism (Anxiety, Angry Hostility, Depression, Self-Consciousness, Impulsiveness, Vulnerability), Extraversion (Warmth, Gregariousness, Assertiveness, Activity, Excitement-Seeking, Positive Emotions), Openness (Fantasy, Aesthetics, Feelings, Actions, Ideas, Values), Agreeableness (Trust, Straightforwardness, Altruism, Compliance, Modesty, Tender-Mindedness), Conscientiousness (Competence, Order, Dutifulness, Achievement Striving, Self-Discipline, Deliberation).
  Forms, 2: Form S (self-report), Form R (observer ratings).
  Time: (30-40) minutes.
  c) NEO FIVE-FACTOR INVENTORY-3.
  Acronym: NEO-FFI-3.
  Scores, 5: Neuroticism, Extraversion, Openness, Agreeableness, Conscientiousness.
  Forms, 4: Form S (self-report), Form R (observer ratings), Adolescent, Adult.
  Time: (5-10) minutes.
Cross References: For reviews by Nicholas F. Benson and Annette S. Kluck, see 19:116; see also T5:2218 (135 references); for reviews by Michael D. Botwin and Samuel

Juni of the Revised Edition, see 12:330 (50 references); see also T4:2263 (49 references); for reviews by Allen K. Hess and Thomas A. Widiger of an earlier edition, see 11:258 (5 references); for a review by Robert Hogan of an earlier edition, see 10:214 (6 references).

[1363]

NEO Personality Inventory-3 (UK Edition).

Purpose: Designed to measure "the five broad domains of personality and specific salient traits, or facets, associated with each domain."

Population: Ages 16 and older.

Publication Dates: 2006-2015.

Acronym: NEO-PI-3 (UK Edition).

Scores, 35: 30 facets in 5 domains: Neuroticism (Anxiety, Angry Hostility, Depression, Self-Consciousness, Impulsiveness, Vulnerability), Extraversion (Warmth, Gregariousness, Assertiveness, Activity, Excitement Seeking, Positive Emotions), Openness (Fantasy, Aesthetics, Feelings, Actions, Ideas, Values), Agreeableness (Trust, Straightforwardness, Altruism, Compliance, Modesty, Tender-Mindedness), Conscientiousness (Competence, Order, Dutifulness, Achievement Striving, Self-Discipline, Deliberation).

Administration: Individual or group.

Price Data, 2016: £250 per complete print kit including manual (2015, 81 pages), norms booklet, item booklets, response sheets, profile sheets, and feedback charts; £50 per manual; £85 per Technical Report and Personal Insight Report (includes online administration); £70 per Technical Report (includes online administration); £95 per Primary Colours Leadership Report (includes online administration); subscription discounts available; £120 per NEO Cards.

Time: Administration time not reported.

Comments: A U.K. adaptation of the U.S. version of the NEO Personality Inventory-3 (1362); administered online or via paper and pencil.

Authors: Robert R. McCrae and Paul T. Costa, Jr. (test); UK adaptation by Wendy Lord.

Publisher: Hogrefe Ltd [United Kingdom].

Cross References: For reviews by Nicholas F. Benson and Annette S. Kluck of the U.S. version, see 19:116.

[1364]

Neonatal Behavioral Assessment Scale, 4th Edition.

Purpose: Designed to assess an infant's behavioral and neurological status.

Population: Ages 3 days through 2 months.

Publication Dates: 1973-2011.

Acronym: NBAS.

Scores: 53 in 3 domains: Behavioral (Response Decrement to Light, Response Decrement to Rattle, Response Decrement to Bell, Response Decrement to Foot, Animate Visual, Animate Visual and Auditory, Inanimate Visual, Inanimate Visual and Auditory, Animate Auditory, Inanimate Auditory, Alertness, General Tone, Motor Maturity, Pull-to-Sit, Defensive, Activity Level, Peak of Excitement, Rapidity of Build-up, Irritability, Lability of States, Cuddliness, Consolability, Self-Quieting, Hand-to-Mouth, Tremulousness, Startles, Lability of Skin Color, Smiles), Supplementary (Quality of Alertness, Cost of Attention, Examiner Facilitation, General Irritability, Robustness/Endurance, State Regulation, Examiner's Emotional Response), Reflex (Plantar Grasp, Babinski, Ankle Clonus, Rooting, Sucking, Glabella, Passive Resistance—Legs, Passive Resistance—Arms, Palmar Grasp, Placing, Standing, Walking, Crawling, Incurvation, Tonic Dev. Head/Eyes, Nystagmus, Tonic Neck Reflex, Moro).

Administration: Individual.

Price Data, 2016: $65 per hardcover book (2011, 200 pages).

Time: (12-20) minutes.

Comments: A 53-item rating scale of infant behavior and reflexes; not for use with infants recovering from illness or premature birth; to be administered by clinicians trained in neonatal behavior.

Authors: T. Berry Brazelton and J. Kevin Nugent.

Publisher: John Wiley and Sons, Inc.

Cross References: For reviews by Carol M. McGregor and Hoi K. Suen of the third edition, see 14:255; see also T5:1770 (17 references), T4:321 (9 references), 9:157 (9 references), and T3:311 (31 references); for a review by Anita Miller Sostek and an excerpted review by Stephen Wolkind of an earlier edition titled Brazelton Neonatal Behavioral Assessment Scale, see 8:208 (15 references).

[1365]

NEPSY-II-Second Edition.

Purpose: "Designed to assess neuropsychological development."

Population: Ages 3-0 to 16-11.

Publication Dates: 1998-2007.

Acronym: NEPSY-II.

Scores, 32: Attention/Executive Functioning (Animal Sorting, Auditory Attention and Response Set, Clocks, Design Fluency, Inhibition, Statue), Language (Body Part Naming and Identification, Comprehension of Instructions, Oromotor Sequences, Phonological Processing, Repetition of Nonsense Words, Speeded Naming, Word Generation), Memory and Learning (List Memory, Memory for Designs, Memory for Faces, Memory for Names, Narrative Memory, Sentence Repetition, Word List Interference), Sensorimotor (Fingertip Tapping, Imitating Hand Positions, Manual Motor Sequences, Visuomotor Precision), Social Perception (Affect Recognition, Theory of Mind), Visuospatial Processing (Arrows, Block Construction, Design Copying, Geometric Puzzles, Picture Puzzles, Route Finding).

Administration: Individual.

Forms, 2: Ages 3-4, Ages 5-16.

Price Data, 2015: $921.50 per kit including administration manual (2007, 183 pages), clinical and interpretive manual (2007, 290 pages), 2 stimulus books, 25 record forms (ages 3-4), 25 record forms (ages 5-16), 25 response booklets (ages 3-4), 25 response booklets (ages 5-16), memory for designs card set, memory for names card set, animal sorting card set, memory grid, 1 scoring template, 12 red blocks set, black pencil in box, and training CD; $70.75 per 25 record forms (ages 3-4); $91.25 per 25 record forms (ages 5-16); $59 per 25 response booklets (ages 3-4); $79 per 25 response booklets (ages 5-16); $25.65 per scoring template; $76.90 per card sets (3 sets and box); $43 per memory grid; $117.90 per administration manual; $163 per clinical and interpretive scoring manual; $173.25 per stimulus book (specify I or II); $70.75 per training CD.

Time: (45-90) minutes for ages 3-4; (60-180) minutes for ages 5-16.

Comments: Also contains optional qualitative behavioral observations and supplemental scores; earlier edition titled: NEPSY: A Developmental Neuropsychological Assessment.

Authors: Marit Korkman, Ursula Kirk, and Sally Kemp.

Publisher: Pearson.

Cross References: For reviews by Rik Carl D'Amato and Jonathan E. Titley and by Scott A. Napolitano, see 18:80; for reviews by Sandra D. Haynes and Daniel C. Miller of an earlier edition, see 14:256.

[1366]
Neurobehavioral Functioning Inventory.

Purpose: "Designed to measure the frequency of neurobehavioral problems associated with traumatic brain injury and other neurological disorders."

Population: Patients ages 17 and older.

Publication Date: 1999.

Acronym: NFI.

Scores, 6: Depression, Somatic, Memory/Attention, Communication, Aggression, Motor.

Administration: Individual or group.

Price Data, 2015: $204 per complete kit including manual (120 pages), 25 Family record forms, and 25 Patient record forms; $138 per manual; $81 per 25 record forms (Family or Patient).

Time: (30) minutes.

Comments: Self-scoring self-report forms.

Authors: Jeffrey S. Kreutzer, Ronald T. Seel, and Jennifer H. Marwitz.

Publisher: Pearson.

Cross References: For reviews by Raymond S. Dean and John J. Brinkman, Jr., and by Thomas McKnight, see 16:162.

[1367]
Neuropsychiatry Unit Cognitive Assessment Tool.

Purpose: Designed to "assist in the diagnosis and management of cognitive disorders and serve as a guide to more in-depth formal neuropsychological testing."

Population: Ages 18+.

Publication Date: 2008.

Acronym: NUCOG.

Scores, 6: Attention, Memory, Executive Function, Language, Visuoconstructional Function, Total.

Administration: Individual.

Price Data: Available from publisher.

Time: (20) minutes.

Authors: Mark Walterfang and Dennis Velakoulis.

Publisher: Australian Council for Educational Research Ltd. [Australia].

Cross References: For a review by Anthony T. Dugbartey, see 18:81.

[1368]
Neuropsychological Assessment Battery.

Purpose: "Developed for the assessment of a wide array of cognitive skills and functions in adults with known or suspected disorders of the central nervous system."

Population: Ages 18–97.

Publication Dates: 2001–2003.

Forms, 2: Form 1, Form 2 (equivalent forms).

Price Data: 2015: $1,995 per NAB complete kit including 33 tests, NAB administration, scoring, and interpretation manual, NAB psychometric and technical manual, NAB demographically corrected Norms manual, NAB U.S. census-matched norms manual, 50 score summary/profile forms, 2 sets of manipulatives, NAB-SP–CD-ROM, video training program–DVD, Form 1 materials, and Form 2 materials.

Time: Administration time not reported.

Comments: Modules may be purchased and administered individually; NAB Training Program on DVD is included with each module; software portfolio available for use on CD-ROM.

Authors: Robert A. Stern and Travis White.

Publisher: Psychological Assessment Resources, Inc.

   a) SCREENING MODULE.

   Scores, 6: Attention, Language, Memory, Spatial, Executive Function, Total.

   Comments: May be used to determine whether more in-depth, followup examinations are necessary.

   b) ATTENTION MODULE.

   Scores, 12: Digits (2), Dots, Numbers & Letters (7), Driving Scenes, Total.

   c) LANGUAGE MODULE.

   Scores, 6: Oral Production, Auditory Comprehension, Naming, Writing, Bill Payment, Total.

   d) MEMORY MODULE.

   Scores, 5: List Learning, Shape Learning, Story Learning, Daily Living Memory, Total.

Comments: Also available as a stand-alone test with a separate manual.
e) SPATIAL MODULE.
Scores, 5: Visual Discrimination, Design Construction, Figure Drawing, Map Reading, Total.
f) EXECUTIVE FUNCTIONS.
Scores, 5: Mazes, Judgment, Categories, Word Generation, Total.
Cross References: For reviews by Timothy J. Makatura and by Wilfred G. Van Gorp and Jason Hassenstab, see 16:163.

[1369]
The Neuropsychological Impairment Scale.
Purpose: Designed to screen for "neuropsychological symptoms."
Population: Ages 18–88 years.
Publication Date: 1994.
Acronym: NIS.
Scores, 14: Defensiveness, Affective Disturbance, Response Inconsistency, Subjective Distortion Index, Global Measure of Impairment, Total Items Circled, Symptom Intensity Measure, Critical Items, Cognitive Efficiency, Attention, Memory, Frustration Tolerance, Learning-Verbal, Academic Skills.
Administration: Group.
Forms, 3: Self-Report, Observer Report, Senior Interview.
Price Data, 2016: $185.50 per complete kit including 25 self-report AutoScore™ answer forms, 25 observer-report AutoScore™ answer forms, and manual (71 pages) with Senior Interview Response Card; $59 per 25 self-report AutoScore™ answer forms; $59 per 25 observer-report AutoScore™ answer forms; $77.50 per manual; $118 per Senior Interview kit including 25 Senior Interview AutoScore™ answer forms, 1 manual with Senior Interview Supplement and Response Card; $59 per 25 Senior Interview AutoScore™ answer forms; $227 per 10 use scoring CD-ROM for use with self report, observer report, and senior interview; $19.50 per 100 PC Answer Sheets.
Time: (15–20) minutes.
Comments: Self-Report form and Observer-Report form both utilize the 14 scores listed above, Senior Interview provides Global Measure of Impairment and scores for Defensiveness, Affective Disturbance, and Inconsistency.
Authors: William E. O'Donnell, Clinton B. DeSoto, Janet L. DeSoto, and Don McQ. Reynolds.
Publisher: Western Psychological Services.
Cross References: For a review by Robert A. Leark, see 14:257; see also T5:1775 (3 references).

[1370]
Neuropsychological Status Exam.
Purpose: Designed to organize data useful in neuro-psychological assessment.

Population: Neuropsychological patients.
Publication Date: 1983.
Acronym: NSE.
Scores: Checklists in 13 areas: Patient Data, Referral Data, Tentative Findings, Neuropsychological Symptom Checklist, Premorbid Status, Physical Status, Emotional Status, Cognitive Status, Test Administration, Results of Neuropsychological Testing, Diagnostic Comments, Effects on Patient Functioning, Treatment Recommendations.
Administration: Individual.
Price Data, 2015: $84 per complete kit including 25 NSE and 25 NSC (Checklist) forms and manual (13 pages).
Time: Administration time not reported.
Author: John A. Schinka.
Publisher: Psychological Assessment Resources, Inc.

[1371]
Neuropsychology Behavior and Affect Profile–Dementia.
Purpose: Designed to assess "symptoms of a neuro-degenerative process, such as dementia, by measuring changes in emotional levels and in behavior."
Population: Ages 15 and older.
Publication Dates: 1989-2009.
Acronym: NBAP–D.
Scores, 10: Indifference (Before, Now), Inappropriateness (Before, Now), Pragnosia (Before, Now), Depression (Before, Now), Mania (Before, Now).
Administration: Individual.
Forms, 2: Self, Other.
Price Data: Available from publisher.
Time: Administration time not reported.
Authors: Linda D. Nelson, Paul Satz, and Louis F. D'Elia.
Publisher: Mind Garden, Inc.
Cross References: For a review by Surendra P. Singh of an earlier edition, see 14:258.

[1372]
New Technology Tests: Computer Rules.
Purpose: To "provide a measure of aptitude for those entering employment or training in occupations where computers are used as a basic operational tool … the emphasis in this test is primarily on following rules."
Population: Applicants for computer-related jobs.
Publication Date: 1987.
Scores: Total score only.
Administration: Group.
Price Data: Available from publisher.
Time: 30[35] minutes.
Comments: New Technology Tests: Computer Commands (11:260) also available.
Author: Psychometric Research & Development Ltd.

Publisher: Psychometric Research & Development Ltd. [England].
Cross References: For a review by Bruce W. Hall, see 11:261.

[1373]
New York Longitudinal Scales Adult Temperament Questionnaire, Second Edition.

Purpose: Designed to measure the nine NYLS dimensions of temperament in adulthood.
Population: Ages 13-89.
Publication Dates: 1995-2008.
Acronym: ATQ2.
Scores, 9: Activity Level, Rhythmicity, Adaptability, Approach, Intensity, Mood, Persistence, Distractibility, Threshold.
Administration: Group.
Price Data: Available from publisher.
Time: (10-15) minutes.
Comments: Self-report ratings; online scoring available. The test publisher has indicated there is a newer edition of this test; description will be updated when complete test materials are received.
Authors: Stella Chess and Alexander Thomas.
Publisher: Behavioral-Developmental Initiatives.
Cross References: For reviews by Gypsy M. Denzine and Gregory A. Lobb, see 19:117; for reviews by James A. Athanasou and Stephen N. Axford of the original edition, see 16:166.

[1374]
NICU Network Neurobehavioral Scale.

Purpose: Designed to examine "the neurobehavioral organization, neurologic reflexes, motor development, and active and passive tone as well as signs of stress and withdrawal of the at-risk or drug-exposed infant."
Population: Infants between 30 to 48 weeks corrected or conceptional age.
Publication Date: 2005.
Acronym: NNNS.
Scores, 13: Habituation, Attention, Handling, Quality of Movement, Regulation, Nonoptimal Reflexes, Asymmetry, Stress/Abstinence, Arousal, Hypertonicity, Hypotonicity, Excitability, Lethargy.
Administration: Individual.
Restricted Distribution: Examiners must obtain training and certification from the publisher to administer the test.
Price Data: Available from publisher.
Time: (20) minutes.
Comments: Examiners are instructed to gather observations and then complete the scoring sheet; scores should not be completed while conducting the examination. The standardized administration procedures are designed to accommodate the current state of arousal and age of the infant being assessed. The authors state that the scale is

"not appropriate for infants who are younger than 30 weeks gestational age."
Authors: Barry M. Lester and Edward Z. Tronick.
Publisher: Women & Infants Hospital.
Cross References: For reviews by Janet S. Reed and Catherine Ruth Solomon Scherzer, see 19:118.

[1375]
19 Field Interest Inventory.

Purpose: Measures vocational interests in 19 broad vocational areas.
Population: Standards 8–10 in South African school system and college and adults.
Publication Dates: 1970–1971.
Acronym: 19FII.
Scores, 21: Fine Arts, Performing Arts, Language, Historical, Service, Social Work, Sociability, Public Speaking, Law, Creative Thought, Science, Practical-Male, Practical-Female, Numerical, Business, Clerical, Travel, Nature, Sport, Work-Hobby, Active-Passive.
Administration: Group.
Price Data: Available from publisher.
Time: (45) minutes.
Authors: F. A. Fouche and N. F. Alberts.
Publisher: Human Sciences Research Council [South Africa].
Cross References: For additional information, see 7:1027.

[1376]
NOCTI Experienced Worker Assessments.

Purpose: "Designed to measure an individual's knowledge of higher-level concepts, theories, and applications in the related occupation."
Population: Career and technical education teachers, potential teachers, and journey workers.
Publication Dates: 1993–2002.
Scores: Duty category scores and total scores are reported for 52 Written and Performance tests: Advertising and Design, Air Cooled Gas Engine Repair, Appliance Repair, Architectural Drafting, Audio Visual Communications Technology, Automotive Technician, Building and Home Maintenance Services, Building Construction Occupations, Building Trades Maintenance, Cabinetmaking and Millwork, Carpentry, Collision Repair, Collision Repair/Refinishing Technology, Computer Programming, Computer Technology, Cosmetology, Diesel Engine Repair, Diesel Mechanics, Drafting Occupations, Early Child Care and Education, Electrical Construction, Electrical Installation, Electromechanical Technology, Electronic Product Servicing, Electronics Communications, Electronics Technology, Graphic Imaging Technology, Heating/Ventilation & Air Conditioning (HVAC), Heating/Ventilation/Air Conditioning & Refrigeration (HVAC/R), Heavy Equipment Mechanics, Hospitality Management—Food & Beverage, Hospitality

Management—Lodging, Industrial Electrician, Industrial Electronics, Industrial Technology, Marine Mechanics, Masonry, Materials Handling, Metalworking Occupations, Motorcycle Mechanics, Painting and Decorating, Plumbing, Precision Machining, Quantity Food Preparation, Quantity Foods, Refinishing Technology, Retail Commercial Baking, Retail Trades, Sheet Metal, Technical Drafting, Tool and Die Making, Welding.

Administration: Group.

Parts, 2: Written, Performance.

Price Data, 2016: $180 per complete test including written and performance parts, instructions for administration, scoring and reporting services and certificates of competence, if applicable.

Time: (180) minutes for all written tests; (1.5–6) hours for performance tests.

Comments: The National Occupational Competency Testing Institute (NOCTI) is a not-for-profit organization with a primary mission to serve all levels of the career-technical education field and to assist in developing a world-class workforce. NOCTI's assessment services include customization of assessments to better meet client needs. Assessments are designed to meet psychometric standards that utilize the psychomotor, cognitive, and affective domains of learning to assess competence. Most standardized assessments have both written (cognitive) and performance (psychomotor) components.

Author: National Occupational Competency Testing Institute.

Publisher: National Occupational Competency Testing Institute/The Whitener Group.

Cross References: For a review of an earlier version of the NOCTI program, see 8:1153 (6 references). Reviews and references for previous separate NOCTI TOCT tests: Appliance Repair: For reviews by Geneva D. Haertel and Cyril J. Sadowski, see 13:208; for a review by Richard C. Erickson, see 10:227; Architectural Drafting: See 9:776 (1 reference); for a review by Gary E. Lintereur, see 8:1131; Audio-Visual Communications Technology: For reviews by JoEllen V. Carlson and Anne L. Harvey, see 11:262; for reviews by Patricia A. Bachelor and Connie Kubo Della-Piana, see 13:209; Auto Body Repair: For reviews by Robert J. Drummond and Dale P. Scannell, see 13:210; see also 9:777 (1 reference); Automotive Technician: For reviews by Dale P. Scannell and George C. Thornton III, see 13:211; see also 9:778 and T3:1595 (1 reference); for a review by Charles W. Pendleton, see 8:1133; Brick Masonry: For a review by Thomas S. Baldwin, see 10:229; Building and Home Maintenance Services: For a review by Gary E. Lintereur, see 10:230; Cabinet Making and Millwork: See 9:782 (1 reference); for a review by Gary E. Lintereur, see 8:1134; Carpentry: See 9:783 (1 reference); for a review by Daniel L. Householder, see 8:1535; Child Care and Guidance: For reviews by Patricia B. Keith and by Jean Powell Kirnan and Jennifer DeNicolis, see 12:255; Commercial Art: For a review by Gary E. Lintereur, see

10:231; Diesel Engine Repair: See 9:786 (1 reference); for a review by Charles W. Pendleton, see 8:1138; Electrical Installation: See 9:788 (1 reference) and T3:1601 (1 reference); for a review by Alan R. Suess, see 8:1139 (1 reference); Electronics Communications: See 9:789 (1 reference); for a review by Emil H. Hoch, see 8:1140; Industrial Electrician: See 9:792 (1 reference); for a review by Alan R. Suess, see 8:1141; Industrial Electronics: See 9:793 (1 reference); for a review by Emil H. Hoch, see 8:1142; Machine Drafting: See 9:794 (1 reference); for a review by Tim L. Wentling, see 8:1143; Machine Trades: For a review by Thomas S. Baldwin, see 10:239; see also 9:795 (1 reference) and 8:1144 (1 reference); Masonry: See 9:797 (1 reference); Mechanical Technology: For reviews by Bruce K. Alcorn and David O. Anderson, see 12:256; Microcomputer Repair: For reviews by Kurt F. Geisinger and David O. Herman, see 12:257; Plumbing: See 9:801 (1 reference); for a review by Richard C. Erickson, see 8:1147; Quantity Food Preparation: See 9:804 (1 reference); Scientific Data Processing: For reviews by Jim C. Fortune and Myra N. Womble, see 13:212; for a review by William M. Bart, see 11:263; Sheet Metal; See 9:807 (1 reference) and T3:1612 (1 reference); for a review by Daniel L. Householder, see 8:1150; Small Engine Repair: See 9:808 (1 reference); for a review by Kenneth E. Poucher, see 8:1151; Welding: See 9:809 (1 reference); for a review by Richard C. Erickson, see 8:1152.

[1377]

NOCTI Job Ready Assessments.

Purpose: "Designed to measure an individual's knowledge of basic processes including the identification and use of terminology and tools."

Population: Students in career and technical education programs.

Publication Dates: 1983–2005.

Scores: Duty category and total scores are reported for 85 Written and Performance tests: Accounting, Administrative Assisting, Advertising and Design, Agriculture Mechanics, Air Cooled Gas Engine Repair, Appliance Repair, Architectural Drafting, Audio-Visual Communications, Auto Diesel Mechanics, Automotive Technician, Building Construction Occupations, Building Trades Maintenance, Business and Information Processing, CAD/CAM, Cabinetmaking, Carpentry, Clothing and Textiles Management and Production, Collision Repair, Collision Repair/Refinishing Technology, Commercial Foods, Computer Networking Fundamentals, Computer Programming, Computer Repair Technology, Computer Technology, Construction Electricity, Construction Masonry–Blocklaying, Construction Masonry—Bricklaying, Construction Masonry–Stone, Cosmetology, Criminal Justice, Dental Assisting, Dental Lab Technology, Diesel Engine Mechanics, Early Childhood Care & Education, Electrical Construction, Electrical Occupations,

Electronic Product Servicing, Electronic Technology, Electronics, Floriculture, Food Production Management and Services, Forestry Products and Processing, General Drafting and Design, Graphic Communications Tech, Health Assisting, Heating/Ventilation & Air Conditioning, Heating/Ventilation/Air Conditioning & Refrigeration, Heavy Equipment Maintenance and Repair, Home Health Aide, Horticulture-Landscaping, Horticulture—Olericulture, Hospitality Management—Food & Beverage, Hospitality Management—Lodging, Industrial Electricity, Industrial Electronics, Industrial Maintenance Mechanic, Manufacturing Technology, Marine Mechanics, Medical Assisting, Metalworking and Fabrication, Motorcycle Mechanics, Nursing Assisting, Painting and Decorating, Plumbing, Practical Nursing, Pre-Engineering/Engineering Technology, Precision Machining, Production Agriculture, Refinishing Technology, Retail Commercial Baking, Retail Trades, Robotics Technology, Technical Drafting, Television Broadcasting, Truck and Bus Mechanics, Visual Communications, Warehousing Services, Welding, Workplace Readiness.
Administration: Group.
Parts, 2: Written, Performance.
Price Data, 2016: $20 per complete online test (Written and Performance) including instructions for administration, scoring and reporting services, and certificates of completion, if applicable; $17.50 if purchased separately (Written only or Performance only); $25 per complete paper/pencil test combination; $23 if purchased separately.
Time: (180) minutes for most Written tests; (1–5) hours for Performance tests.
Comments: The National Occupational Competency Testing Institute (NOCTI) is a not-for-profit organization with a primary mission to serve all levels of the career-technical education field and to assist in developing a world-class workforce. NOCTI's assessment services include customization of assessments to better meet client needs. Assessments meet psychometric standards that utilize the psychomotor, cognitive, and affective domains of learning to assess competence. Most standardized assessments have both written (cognitive) and performance (psychomotor) components. Assessments are reviewed for revision every 2 years.
Author: National Occupational Competency Testing Institute.
Publisher: National Occupational Competency Testing Institute/The Whitener Group.

[1378]

Noncognitive Variables and Questionnaire.
Purpose: To aid in admission decisions and advising regarding minority college student applicants.
Population: Minority college student applicants.
Publication Dates: 1978–1998.
Acronym: NCQ.

Scores, 8: Positive Self-Concept or Confidence, Realistic Self-Appraisal, Understands and Deals with Racism, Prefers Long-Range Goals to Short-Term or Immediate Needs, Availability of Strong Support Person, Successful Leadership Experience, Demonstrated Community Service, Knowledge Acquired in a Field.
Administration: Group.
Manual: No manual.
Price Data: This test is now available at no charge from the test publisher.
Time: [20] minutes.
Author: William E. Sedlacek.
Publisher: William E. Sedlacek.
Cross References: For reviews by Gregory J. Marchant and Lisa F. Smith, see 14:259.

[1379]

Non-Reading Intelligence Tests, Levels 1–3.
Purpose: Measures "aspects of language and thinking that are not fully represented in the earlier stages of learning in reading and mathematics."
Population: Ages 6-4 to 8-3, 7-4 to 9-3, 8-4 to 10-11.
Publication Dates: 1989–1992.
Acronym: NRIT.
Scores, 5: Total score for each of four subtests (A, B, C, D), Grand Total.
Administration: Group.
Levels: 3 overlapping levels.
Price Data: Available from publisher.
Time: (60) minutes for Levels 1 and 2; (45–60) minutes for Level 3.
Comments: Incorporates the Non-Readers Intelligence Test (9:811) as Level 1 and the Oral Verbal Intelligence Test (8:197) as Level 3, along with a newer intermediate test as Level 2. The test publisher has indicated there is a newer edition of this test; description will be updated when complete test materials are received.
Author: Dennis Young.
Publisher: Hodder Education [United Kingdom].
Cross References: For reviews by Carole M. Krauthamer and Esther E. Diamond, see 12:258; see also T4:1816 (1 reference). For a review by A. E. G. Pilliner of the Oral Verbal Intelligence Test, see 8:197; for reviews by Calvin O. Dyer and Steven I. Pfeiffer of the Non-Readers Intelligence Test, Third Edition, see 9:811.

[1380]

Nonverbal Form.
Purpose: Measures general learning ability independent of language and reading skills.
Population: Adults.
Publication Dates: 1946–1986.
Scores: Total score only.
Administration: Individual or group.
Price Data: Available from publisher.
Time: 10 minutes.

Comments: Previously listed as SRA Nonverbal Form.
Authors: Robert N. McMurray and Joseph E. King.
Publisher: General Dynamics Information Technology.
Cross References: See T2:449 (12 references); for a review by W. D. Commins, see 4:318; for an excerpted review, see 3:261 (incorrectly listed under 3:260 in the first printing of *The Third Mental Measurements Yearbook*).

[1381]

Non-verbal IQ Test.

Purpose: "Designed to test intelligence while minimizing cultural or educational background unfairness."
Population: Below age 17 through adult.
Publication Date: 2011.
Acronym: NVIQT.
Scores: Overall Score only.
Administration: Individual.
Price Data: Available from publisher.
Time: (30) minutes.
Comments: Self-administered online assessment. The test publisher provides clients with information about the methods and theoretical basis used in the development of the test as well as benchmarks for relevant industries and racial/ethnic group comparison data.
Author: PsychTests AIM, Inc.
Publisher: PsychTests AIM, Inc. [Canada].
Cross References: For reviews by Stephan Dilchert and Stefan C. Dombrowski, see 19:119.

[1382]

Nonverbal Personality Questionnaire and Five-Factor Nonverbal Personality Questionnaire.

Purpose: Designed to "measure normal personality characteristics" with the use of pictures instead of words.
Population: Ages 18 and over.
Publication Date: 2004.
Administration: Group or individual.
Price Data, 2010: $24 per test manual (72 pages)
Comments: Tests can be administered together and use the same manual; can be used in research, counseling, and business settings.
Authors: Sampo V. Paunonen, Douglas N. Jackson, and Michael C. Ashton (manual).
Publisher: SIGMA Assessment Systems, Inc.
  a) NONVERBAL PERSONALITY QUESTION-NAIRE.
  Acronym: NPQ.
  Scores, 17: Achievement, Affiliation, Aggression, Autonomy, Dominance, Endurance, Exhibition, Thrill-Seeking, Impulsivity, Nurturance, Order, Play, Sentience, Social Recognition, Succorance, Understanding, Deviation.
  Price Data: $50 per handscorable examination kit including test manual, picture booklet, 5 answer sheets, and 5 profile sheets; $60 per 10 picture booklets; $75 per 25 answer sheets; $50 per 25 profile sheets; $8-$14

(depending on volume) per online administration at www.SigmaTesting.com.
  Time: (20–35) minutes.
  Authors: Sampo V. Paunonen and Douglas N. Jackson.
  b) FIVE-FACTOR NONVERBAL PERSONALITY QUESTIONNAIRE.
  Acronym: FF-NPQ.
  Scores, 5: Extraversion, Agreeableness, Conscientiousness, Neuroticism, Openness to Experience.
  Price Data, 2015: $25 per test manual (72 pages); $55 per handscorable examination kit (includes manual, 1 picture booklet, 5 answer sheets, 5 profile sheets, and 1 online password); $65 per 10 picture booklets; $80 per 25 NPQ answer sheets; $70 per 25 FF-NPQ answer sheets; $55 per 25 profile sheets; $8-$14 (depending on volume) per NPQ online test administration; $6-$12 (depending on volume) per FF-NPQ online test administration.
  Time: (10–15) minutes.
  Authors: Sampo Paunonen, Douglas N. Jackson, and Michael C. Ashton.
Cross References: For reviews by Ashraf Kagee and Sean Reilley, see 17:133.

[1383]

Nonverbal Reasoning.

Purpose: "To measure the capacity to reason logically as indicated by solutions to pictorial problems."
Population: Individuals in a variety of occupations.
Publication Dates: 1957–1986.
Scores: Total score only.
Administration: Individual or group.
Price Data: Available from publisher.
Time: No limit (approximately 20 minutes).
Author: Raymond J. Corsini.
Publisher: General Dynamics Information Technology.
Cross References: See T4:1817 (1 reference) and T2:414 (2 references); for reviews by James E. Kennedy and David G. Ryans, see 6:478.

[1384]

Non-Verbal Reasoning.

Purpose: Designed to assess "a pupil's ability to recognise similarities, analogies and patterns in unfamiliar designs."
Population: Ages 7.3-15.3.
Publication Date: 1993.
Scores: Total score only.
Administration: Group.
Levels, 3: Age 8 and 9; Age 10 and 11; Ages 12–14.
Price Data: Available from publisher.
Comments: Available in paper-and-pencil and digital format.
Time: (40–45) minutes.
Authors: Pauline Smith and Neil Hagues.
Publisher: GL Assessment [England].
Cross References: For reviews by Sally Kuhlenschmidt and Julia Y. Porter, see 16:167.

[1385]
Nonverbal Stroop Card Sorting Test.

Purpose: Designed "to identify deficits in executive functioning and attention processes."
Population: Ages 3 to 75 and older.
Publication Date: 2012.
Acronym: NSCST.
Scores, 5: Color Congruent Time, Color Congruent Ratio, Color Incongruent Time, Color Incongruent Ratio, Stroop Effect.
Administration: Individual.
Price Data, 2015: $140 per kit including two sets of cards, laminate sorting sheet, 25 record forms, timer, and manual (54 pages).
Time: (5-10) minutes.
Comments: Co-normed with Leiter International Performance Scale–Third Edition (1144).
Authors: Chris Koch and Gale Roid.
Publisher: Stoelting Co.
Cross References: Reviews are scheduled for *The Twentieth Mental Measurements Yearbook.*

[1386]
Norris Educational Achievement Test.

Purpose: Designed to assess educational ability.
Publication Dates: 1991–1992.
Acronym: NEAT.
Administration: Individual.
Forms, 2: A, B.
Price Data, 2016: $188 per complete kit including 10 test booklets (5 Form A, 5 Form B), administration and scoring manual (1992, 234 pages), and technical manual (1992, 86 pages).
Authors: Janet Switzer and Christian P. Gruber (manuals).
Publisher: Western Psychological Services.
  a) READINESS.
  Population: Ages 4-0 to 6-11.
  Scores, 4: Fine Motor Coordination, Math Concepts, Letters, Total.
  Time: (10–15) minutes.
  b) ACHIEVEMENT.
  Population: Ages 6-0 to 17-11.
  Scores, 4-6: Word Recognition, Spelling, Arithmetic, Total plus 2 supplemental scores (Oral Reading and Comprehension, Written Language).
  Time: (20–30) minutes for basic battery; (30–40) minutes for entire battery.
Cross References: See T5:1802 (1 reference); for reviews by A. Harry Passow and Michael S. Trevisan, see 12:260.

[1387]
Novaco Anger Scale and Provocation Inventory.

Purpose: "Designed to assess anger as a problem of psychological functioning and physical health and to assess therapeutic change."
Population: Ages 9–84 years.
Publication Date: 2003.
Acronym: NAS-PI.
Administration: Individual or group.
Price Data, 2016: $118 per complete kit including 25 AutoScore test forms and manual (64 pages); $72 per manual; $52.50 per 25 AutoScore test forms; $190.50 per 25-use scoring CD-ROM; $20.50 per 100 PC answer sheets.
Comments: Can be administered as a whole or as two separate parts.
Author: Raymond W. Novaco.
Publisher: Western Psychological Services.
  a) THE NOVACO ANGER SCALE.
  Purpose: Designed to assess "how an individual experiences anger."
  Scores: Cognitive, Arousal, Behavior, NAS Total, Anger Regulation.
  Time: (10-20) minutes.
  b) THE PROVOCATION INVENTORY.
  Purpose: Designed to identify "the kinds of situations that lead to anger."
  Scores: PI Total.
  Time: (5-15) minutes.
Cross References: For reviews by Albert Bugaj and Geoffrey L. Thorpe, see 17:134.

[1388]
NPF [Second Edition].

Purpose: "To assess stress tolerance and overall adjustment."
Population: Ages 16-adult.
Publication Dates: 1955-1992.
Acronym: NPF.
Scores, 3: Validity Scores (Uncertainty, Good Impression), Total Adjustment.
Administration: Group or individual.
Price Data, 2015: $37 per introductory kit including manual (1992, 10 pages), 20 test booklets, and scoring key; $32 per 20 test booklets; $10 per manual.
Time: (5-10) minutes.
Comments: Previously listed as a subtest of the Employee Attitude Series of the Job-Tests Program (T3:1219).
Author: Samuel E. Krug.
Publisher: Industrial Psychology International Ltd.
Cross References: For reviews by Charles D. Claiborn and Howard M. Knoff, see 12:261.

[1389]
NSight Aptitude/Personality Questionnaire.

Purpose: A "method for measuring a person's work-related characteristics … [that can be used] for hiring and promoting people who are similar to those already successful in the job."
Population: Adults.
Publication Dates: 1990–2002.

Acronym: NAPQ.

Scores, 26: 3 Cognitive Characteristics (Verbal Reasoning/Comprehension, Numerical Reasoning, Word Knowledge); 1 Achievement Characteristic (Visual Perception); 19 Personality Characteristics measured along 6 subtopics: Thinking Style (Emotional Decision Maker, Analytical Thinker, Logical Thinker, Practical), Drives (Security Oriented, Cooperative, Rule Bound), Stress (Anxious, Tolerant, Apprehensive), Communication (Serious, Reserved, Assuming), Leadership (Passive, Submissive, Suspicious), Reliability (Indifferent, Changeable, Expedient); 3 Validity Scales (Lie, Faking Bad, Faking Good).

Administration: Group.

Price Data, 2016: $178 per assessment including 11-page report and telephone consultation; quantity discounts available.

Time: (120) minutes for Cognitive Characteristics Inventory; Personality Inventory untimed.

Author: Stephen Overcash.

Publisher: Directional Insight International, Inc.

Cross References: For a review by John S. Geisler, see 15:174.

[1390]

Number Sense Screener, K-1, Research Edition.

Purpose: Designed "for screening early numerical competencies in kindergarten and early first grade."

Population: Students in kindergarten and first grade.

Publication Date: 2012.

Acronym: NSS.

Scores, 7: Counting Skills, Number Recognition, Number Comparisons, Nonverbal Calculation, Story Problems, Number Combinations, Total Score.

Administration: Individual.

Price Data, 2016: $89.95 per kit including user's guide (66 pages), stimulus book, quick script for administrators, and 25 record sheets; $25 per 25 record sheets.

Time: (15-20) minutes.

Authors: Nancy C. Jordan, Joseph J. Glutting, and Nancy Dyson.

Publisher: Paul H. Brookes Publishing Co.

Cross References: For reviews by Arturo Olivárez, Jr. and Norma Martinez and by G. Michael Poteat, see 19:120.

[1391]

O*NET Career Interests Inventory, Third Edition.

Purpose: Designed to help individuals "identify their work interests."

Population: Teenagers and adults who are involved in career exploration.

Publication Dates: 2002-2012.

Scores, 6: Realistic, Investigative, Artistic, Social, Enterprising, Conventional.

Administration: Individual or group.

Price Data, 2016: $59.95 per package of 25 consumable booklets; volume discount available. Administrator's guide (2012, 8 pages) available for download from publisher's website.

Time: (30) minutes.

Comments: Self-scored and interpreted; based on the O*NET Work Importance Locator developed by the U.S. Department of Labor.

Author: JIST/EMC Publishing.

Publisher: JIST/EMC Publishing.

Cross References: Reviews are scheduled for *The Twentieth Mental Measurements Yearbook*. For reviews by Mark Pope and Eleanor E. Sanford, see 16:172.

[1392]

O*NET Career Values Inventory: Based on the "O*NET Work Importance Locator" developed by the U.S. Department of Labor, Third Edition.

Purpose: Designed to allow users to rank six work values and relate them to specific careers.

Population: Youth and adults.

Publication Dates: 2002-2012.

Scores, 6: Achievement, Independence, Recognition, Relationships, Support, Working Conditions.

Administration: Individual or group.

Price Data, 2016: $59.95 per package of 25 consumable booklets; volume discount available. Administrator's guide (2012, 8 pages) available for download from publisher's website.

Time: (30) minutes.

Author: JIST/EMC Publishing.

Publisher: JIST/EMC Publishing.

Cross References: For reviews by Kathy Green and Richard E. Harding of an earlier edition, see 16:173.

[1393]

O*NET Interest Profiler.

Purpose: Designed to provide information about one's vocational personality type and to foster career awareness.

Population: Age 14 and older.

Publication Dates: 1985–2000.

Acronym: IP.

Scores, 11: Interest Areas (Realistic, Investigative, Artistic, Social, Enterprising, Conventional), Job Zones (Little or No Preparation Needed, Some Preparation Needed, Medium Preparation Needed, High Preparation Needed, Extensive Preparation Needed).

Administration: Individual.

Price Data: This test is available for free online from My Next Move, which is sponsored by the U.S. Department of Labor.

Time: (20–60) minutes.

Comments: Replaces the Job Search Inventory (T5:1351); self-administered and self-scored; part of the O*NET Career Exploration Tools; intended for career exploration, planning, and counseling purposes only; results should not be used for employment or hiring decisions.

Author: U.S. Department of Labor, Employment and Training Administration.

Publisher: U.S. Department of Labor, Employment and Training Administration.

Cross References: For reviews by Michael B. Brown and William B. Michael, see 16:174; for reviews by Ralph O. Mueller and Sheldon Zedeck of the Job Search Inventory, see 13:163.

[1394]
O*NET Work Importance Locator.

Purpose: "Helps users identify what is important to them in a job."

Population: Ages 16 and older.

Publication Date: 2000.

Acronym: WIL.

Scores, 6: Achievement, Independence, Recognition, Relationships, Support, Working Conditions.

Administration: Individual.

Price Data: Available as free download from the O*NET Resource Center, a program sponsored by the U.S. Department of Labor.

Time: (30) minutes.

Comments: Available in paper-and-pencil format or computerized version; intended for career exploration, planning, and counseling purposes only; results should not be used for employment or hiring decisions.

Author: U.S. Department of Labor, Employment and Training Administration.

Publisher: U.S. Department of Labor, Employment and Training Administration.

Cross References: For reviews by Karl N. Kelley and William B. Michael, see 16:175.

[1395]
The OAD Survey.

Purpose: "Measures seven work-related personality traits and seven perceptions of how an individual believes he/she must behave in his/her job."

Population: Employees.

Publication Dates: 1990-2002.

Acronym: OAD.

Scores, 7: Autonomy, Extroversion, Patience, Detail, Versatility Level, Emotional Control, Creativity.

Administration: Individual and group.

Restricted Distribution: Completion of a 3-day seminar required for participants to administer and use.

Price Data: Available from publisher.

Foreign Language Editions: Available in 10 languages.

Time: Not timed.

Comments: Web-based scoring available.

Author: Michael J. Gray.

Publisher: Organization Analysis and Design LLC.

Cross References: For reviews by Arthur S. Ellen and Jeffrey A. Jenkins, see 17:135.

[1396]
OARS Multidimensional Functional Assessment Questionnaire.

Purpose: Designed to assess individual functioning in the elderly.

Population: Ages 65 and over.

Publication Dates: 1975–1988.

Acronym: OARS MFAQ.

Scores: One of 6 ratings (Excellent, Good, Mildly Impaired, Moderately Impaired, Severely Impaired, Totally Impaired) for 5 scales: Social Resources, Economic Resources, Mental Health, Physical Health, Activities of Daily Living.

Administration: Individual.

Price Data, 2016: $75 per training video; $40 per manual (2005, electronic); $5 per questionnaire.

Comments: Orally administered to the subject or to someone who knows the subject well.

Author: Center for the Study of Aging and Human Development.

Publisher: Center for the Study of Aging and Human Development, Duke University Medical Center.

Cross References: See T5:1808 (3 references) and T4:1855 (9 references); for reviews by Keith S. Dobson and Bruce R. Fretz, see 9:847 (4 references); see also T3:1659 (1 reference).

[1397]
Oaster Stressors Scales.

Purpose: Designed to index an individual's level of stressors by using derived trait scales.

Population: Adults.

Publication Date: 1983.

Scores: 4 profiles: Classic/Overload Stressor Pattern of Type A Behavior, Overload Stressor Pattern, Underload Stressor Pattern/Goal-Blocked Type A, Type B Behavior Pattern.

Administration: Group.

Price Data: Available from distributor.

Time: Administration time not reported.

Author: Thomas R. Oaster.

Publisher: Thomas R. Oaster [Test distributed through the Test Collection at ETS].

[1398]
Object-Oriented Programmer Analyst Staff Selector.

Purpose: To measure knowledge of object-oriented terminology and C++.

Population: Candidates for the position of object-oriented programmer analyst.
Publication Date: 1994.
Acronym: OOPS.
Scores, 4: Total Score, Narrative Evaluation, Ranking, Recommendation.
Administration: Group.
Price Data: Available from publisher.
Time: (120) minutes.
Comments: Scored by publisher.
Author: Bruce A. Winrow.
Publisher: Walden Personnel Testing & Consulting Inc. [Canada].
Cross References: For reviews by Dennis Doverspike and Matthew E. Lambert, see 16:170.

[1399]

Observation Ability Test for the Police Service.

Purpose: Designed as a testing instrument for police jobs or any other jobs with high observational requirements.
Population: Candidates for police entry-level positions.
Publication Dates: 1980-2010.
Scores, 1: Observation Ability.
Administration: Group.
Restricted Distribution: Distribution restricted to civil service commissions and qualified municipal officials.
Price Data: Available from publisher.
Time: (35) minutes.
Comments: Typically utilized as a portion of the Empirically-Statistically Validated (ESV) Written Tests for Police Officer.
Author: McCann Associates.
Publisher: McCann Associates [No reply from publisher; status unknown].

[1400]

An Observation Survey of Early Literacy Achievement, Third Edition.

Purpose: "Designed for systematic observation of young children as they learn to read and write."
Population: Students in kindergarten through Grade 3.
Publication Date: 2013.
Administration: Individual.
Price Data, 2015: $29.50 per book (214 pages); $14 per book of master forms that may be copied.
Author: Marie M. Clay.
Publisher: Heinemann Publishing.
   a) CONCEPTS ABOUT PRINT.
   Purpose: Designed to give teachers information about what the student is attending to on the printed page.
   Score: Total score only.
   Time: Administration time not reported.
   b) RUNNING RECORDS.
   Purpose: Designed to provide an assessment of text reading and to provide evidence of how well children are learning to direct their knowledge of letters, sounds, and words to understanding the messages in text.
   Scores, 3: Error Ratio, Accuracy Rate, Self-Correction Ratio.
   Time: Administration time not reported.
   c) LETTER IDENTIFICATION.
   Purpose: Designed for determining "which alphabetic symbols [students] are noticing."
   Score: Total score only.
   Time: (5-10) minutes.
   d) WORD READING.
   Purpose: Designed to indicate reading vocabulary of frequently used words during a child's first year at school.
   Score: Total score only.
   Time: (2) minutes.
   e) WRITING VOCABULARY.
   Purpose: Designed to indicate "how fast a child is building control over a basic writing vocabulary."
   Score: Total score only.
   Time: 10 minutes.
   f) HEARING AND RECORDING SOUNDS IN WORDS.
   Purpose: Designed to "capture the child's control of sound-to-letter links."
   Score: Total score only.
   Time: Administration time not reported.
Cross References: Reviews are scheduled for *The Twentieth Mental Measurements Yearbook*.

[1401]

Observational Assessment of Temperament.

Purpose: Assesses temperamental characteristics, primarily in industrial/organizational settings.
Population: Higher level specialized and managerial personnel.
Publication Dates: 1979–1996.
Acronym: CAT.
Scores: 3 behavior factors: Extroversive/Impulsive vs. Introversive/Reserved, Emotional/Responsive vs. Nonemotional/Controlled, Self-Reliant/Individually Oriented vs. Dependent/Group Oriented.
Administration: Group.
Price Data: Available from publisher.
Time: (10) minutes.
Comments: Can be used as a self-assessment or for the assessment of the observed behavior of others; assesses the three behavior factors measured by the Temperament Comparator (2070).
Author: Melany E. Baehr.
Publisher: General Dynamics Information Technology.
Cross References: For reviews by Stephen J. DePaola and David J. Pittenger, see 15:175.

[1402]

Observational Emotional Inventory—Revised.

Purpose: "Provides a stucture for observing and rating overt emotional behaviors which interfere with educational or vocational potential."

Population: Students and adults.
Publication Date: 1986.
Acronym: OEI-R.
Scores, 8: Impulsivity-Frustration, Anxiety, Depression-Withdrawal, Socialization, Self-Concept, Aggression, Reality Disorientation, Total Score.
Administration: Group.
Price Data, 2016: $71.50 per package of 25 inventories.
Time: 120 minutes each day for 5 days.
Comments: Problems checklist.
Authors: Lawrence T. McCarron and Jack G. Dial.
Publisher: McCarron-Dial Systems, Inc.
Cross References: For a review by Joseph G. Ponterotto, see 11:266.

[1403]
Occupational Aptitude Survey and Interest Schedule—Third Edition.

Purpose: To assist in career development.
Population: Grades 8–12 and adults.
Publication Dates: 1983–2002.
Acronym: OASIS-3:AS.
Administration: Group or individual.
Time: (30–45) minutes per survey.
Comments: Machine scoring is available.
Author: Randall M. Parker.
Publisher: Hammill Institute on Disabilities.

a) APTITUDE SURVEY.
Acronym: OASIS-3:AS.
Scores, 6: General Ability, Verbal Aptitude, Numerical Aptitude, Spatial Aptitude, Perceptual Aptitude, Manual Dexterity.
Price Data, 2016: $191 per kit kit including examiner's manual (2002, 45 pages), 10 student test booklets, 50 handscorable answer sheets, 50 student profiles, scoring key vocabulary and computation transparencies and 1 sample interpretation workbook; $51 per 10 student test booklets; $51 per 50 handscorable answer sheets; $31 per 50 profile sheets; $67 per examiner's manual.
b) INTEREST SCHEDULE.
Acronym: OASIS-3:IS.
Scores, 12: Artistic, Scientific, Nature, Protective, Mechanical, Industrial, Business Detail, Selling, Accommodating, Humanitarian, Leading-Influencing, Physical Performing.
Price Data: $206 per complete kit including 25 student test booklets, 50 handscorable answer sheets, 50 profile sheets, 50 scoring forms, and examiner's manual (2002, 53 pages); $51 per 25 student test booklets; $31 per 50 handscorable answer sheets; $31 per 50 profile sheets; $31 per scoring forms; $67 per examiner's manual; $67 per 25 Interpretation Workbooks.
Cross References: For reviews by Michael B. Bunch and William B. Michael, see 16:171; for reviews by Laura L. B. Barnes and Thomas E. Dinero of an earlier version of the Aptitude Survey, see 12:263 (2 references); see also T4:1862 (2 references). For reviews by Robert J. Miller and Donald G. Zytowski of an earlier version of the Interest Schedule, see 12:264; see also T4:1863 (2 references); for reviews by Christopher Borman and Ruth G. Thomas of an earlier edition, see 20:244 (1 reference).

[1404]
Occupational Interest Inventories.

Purpose: Interest assessment to be used in career guidance, placement, selection, and counseling.
Population: Adults.
Publication Date: 1982.
Administration: Group.
Price Data: Available from publisher.
Time: (25–45) minutes per inventory.
Authors: Ruth Holdsworth and Lisa Camp (manual and user's guide).
Publisher: CEB.

a) GENERAL OCCUPATIONAL INTEREST INVENTORY.
Population: Adults of average educational level.
Acronym: GOII.
Scores, 18: Medical, Welfare, Personal Services, Selling Goods, Selling Services, Supervision, Clerical, Office Equipment, Control, Leisure, Art and Design, Crafts, Plants, Animals, Transport, Construction, Electrical, Mechanical.
b) ADVANCED OCCUPATIONAL INTEREST INVENTORY.
Population: Adults of above average educational level.
Acronym: AOII.
Scores, 19: Medical, Welfare, Education, Control, Commercial, Managerial, Administration, Legal, Financial, Data Processing, Information, Media, Art and Design, Biological Sciences, Physical Sciences, Process, Mechanical, Electrical/Electronic, Construction.

[1405]
Occupational Interests Card Sort.

Purpose: To identify and rank occupational interests.
Population: Adults.
Publication Dates: 1977-2009.
Scores: Interests Work Sheet.
Administration: Group or individual.
Price Data, 2016: $18 per deck of cards and worksheet; $10 per manual; $24 per 24 pack of worksheets.
Time: (20–30) minutes.
Comments: Distributors are available in Canada, Australia, Egypt, and U.S. List of distributor information available from test publisher.
Author: Richard L. Knowdell.
Publisher: Career Research & Testing, Inc.
Cross References: For reviews by Michael B. Bunch and Donald Thompson, see 13:213.

[1406]
Occupational Stress Inventory—Revised Edition.

Purpose: Designed as a "measure of three dimensions of occupational adjustment: occupational stress, psychological strain, and coping resources."

Population: Age 18 years and over.
Publication Dates: 1981–1998.
Acronym: OSI-R.
Scores, 14: Occupational Roles Questionnaire (Role Overload, Role Insufficiency, Role Ambiguity, Role Boundary, Responsibility, Physical Environment); Personal Strain Questionnaire (Vocational Strain, Psychological Strain, Interpersonal Strain, Physical Strain); Personal Resources Questionnaire (Recreation, Self-Care, Social Support, Rational Cognitive Coping).
Administration: Individual or group.
Price Data, 2015: $230 per introductory kit including professional manual, 25 reusable item booklets, 50 rating sheets, 50 gender-specific profile forms, and 50 generic profile forms.
Time: (30) minutes.
Comments: Self-administered.
Author: Samuel H. Osipow.
Publisher: Psychological Assessment Resources, Inc.
Cross References: For reviews by Patricia K. Freitag and Robert Wall, see 14:260; see also T5:1825 (7 references) and T4:1870 (4 references); for reviews by Mary Ann Bunda and Larry Cochran of an earlier edition, see 11:269 (1 reference).

[1407]

Offender Assessment Index.

Purpose: Designed "for evaluating misdemeanor and felony defendants" in adult courts.
Population: Adult defendants.
Publication Dates: 1985-1997.
Acronym: OAI.
Scores, 7: Truthfulness, Resistance, Violence, Alcohol, Drugs, Substance Abuse/Dependency, Stress Coping Abilities.
Administration: Group.
Price Data, 2016: $9.95 per test; volume discounts available.
Foreign Language Edition: Spanish version available.
Time: (30-35) minutes.
Author: Risk & Needs Assessment, Inc.
Publisher: Behavior Data Systems, Ltd.

[1408]

Offender Reintegration Scale, Second Edition.

Purpose: "A self-report assessment designed to measure the concerns and potential barriers faced by offenders and ex-offenders" regarding re-entry into society.
Population: Offenders in various statuses, including incarceration, work release, probation, or parole.
Publication Dates: 2008-2016.
Acronym: ORS.
Scores, 5: Basic Needs, Job Search, Family, Wellness, Career Development.

Administration: Individual or group.
Price Data, 2016: $52.95 per 25 scales; administrator's guide (2016, 17 pages) may be downloaded at no charge.
Time: (20) minutes.
Comments: Self-administered, self-scored, and self-interpreted.
Author: John J. Liptak.
Publisher: JIST/EMC Publishing.
Cross References: For reviews by Michael G. Kavan and Romeo Vitelli of the original edition, see 19:121.

[1409]

Office Arithmetic Test (Form CA).

Purpose: For evaluating the ability to perform arithmetic computations at various levels of difficulty.
Population: Applicants and incumbents for jobs requiring the ability to calculate computations generally found in an office environment.
Publication Dates: 1990-2005.
Scores: Total score only.
Administration: Group.
Price Data, 2015: $12 per paper-and-pencil test administration (answer key provided).
Time: 30(45) minutes.
Author: Roland T. Ramsay.
Publisher: Ramsay Corporation.
Cross References: For reviews by Frederick Bessai and Anita Tesh, see 13:255.

[1410]

Office Proficiency Assessment and Certification [OPAC System].

Purpose: "Assess[es] the knowledge, skills, and abilities of … job candidates [and students]" "for corporate, government, and educational environments."
Population: Ages 18 and over.
Publication Dates: 1994–2016.
Acronym: OPAC System.
Scores: 45 in 8 categories: Keyboarding/Data-Entry (10-Key, Keyboarding, Keyboarding 2, Data Entry 1-Vendor, Data Entry 2-Inventory, Data Entry 3-Invoice), Clerical (Alphabetic Filing, Numeric Filing, Composing Minutes, Formatting a Letter, Proofreading 1, Proofreading 2, Proofreading Practice, Reading Comprehension, Sentence Clarity, Spelling, Transcription), Computer Applications (Database, Editing/Formatting from a Rough Draft, Editing/Formatting from Rough Draft [Advanced], Spreadsheet), Microsoft Applications (Basic Excel, Intermediate Excel, Outlook, PowerPoint, Windows, Basic Word, Intermediate Word), Microsoft Pre-Assessment (Word 2000, Word XP, Excel 2000, Excel XP), Customer Service (Telephone, Telephone Order Entry, Applying Policies, Record Locating), Professional (Legal/Medical Keyboarding, Legal/Medical Terminology, Legal/Medical Proofreading, Legal/

Medical Transcription), Financial (Bank Deposit, Bank Reconciliation, Basic Math, Petty Cash, QuickBooks).
Administration: Individual or group.
Price Data: OPAC Testing Software is licensed for unlimited testing on an unlimited number of stations based upon the number of employees in an organization. The annual license includes the OPAC Testing Software, unlimited training and technical support, software updates, and software upgrades. Prices available from publisher.
Time: Time limits for OPAC tests set by administrator.
Comments: Computer administered; self-administered, self-scored; test administrator selects tests to be administered; test writer provides custom test development in-house, enabling user to create additional tests in other content areas; Validation Wizard assists user in determining cutoff scores and examining basic content validity; personality assessments (optional); OPAC Certificates (additional fee).
Author: International Association of Administrative Professionals.
Publisher: Biddle Consulting Group Inc.

[1411]
Office Reading Test.

Purpose: "Measures the ability to read, comprehend, and answer questions based on a printed passage."
Population: Applicants or incumbents in an office environment where the ability to read and comprehend is a job requirement.
Publication Dates: 1990–2009.
Scores: Total score only.
Administration: Group.
Price Data, 2015: $12 per pencil-and-paper test administration (with scoring key provided); $24.95 per manual (14 pages).
Time: 30(45) minutes.
Comments: Test publisher advises changes in form names indicate minor revisions and updating.
Author: Roland T. Ramsay.
Publisher: Ramsay Corporation.
Cross References: For reviews by Laura L. B. Barnes and Steven J. Osterlind of an earlier edition titled Ramsay Corporation Job Skills–Office Reading Test, see 13:256 (1 reference).

[1412]
Office Skills Assessment Battery.

Purpose: Designed to "provide objective information to aid in your hiring and placement decisions."
Population: Administrative support and clerical position applicants.
Publication Date: 1991.
Acronym: OSAB.
Administration: Individual or group.
Forms, 5: Quanta Touch Test, Quanta Software for Windows—administration and scoring, Quanta

Software for Windows—scoring only, RLH Online, Mail-in Scoring.
Price Data: Available from publisher.
Author: General Dynamics Information Technology.
Publisher: General Dynamics Information Technology.
    a) OFFICE SKILLS ASSESSMENT BATTERY—SKILLS.
    Acronym: OSAB-S.
    Scores, 9: Number Comparison, Checking, Filing, Grammar, Office Vocabulary, Spelling, Punctuation/Capitalization, Career Development, Office Skills Index.
    Time: (50–70) minutes for battery; 3(8) minutes for Sessions 1, 2, and 4; 5(10) minutes for Session 3.
    b) OFFICE SKILLS ASSESSMENT BATTERY—ATTITUDES.
    Acronym: OSAB-A.
    Scores, 12: Work Conduct, Work Accountability, Work Performance, Office Practices, Tenure, Energy Level, Stress Tolerance, Career Interests, Background/Education/Work Experience, Office Attitudes Index, Candidness, Accuracy.
    Time: [10–20] minutes.

[1413]
Office Skills Tests.

Purpose: Designed for measurement of aptitudes for twelve on-the-job skills.
Population: Applicants for clerical positions.
Publication Dates: 1977–1984.
Acronym: OST.
Scores: Total score only for each of 12 tests: Checking, Coding, Filing, Forms Completion, Grammar, Numerical Skills, Oral Directions, Punctuation, Reading Comprehension, Spelling, Typing, Vocabulary.
Administration: Individual or group.
Forms, 2: A, B for each test.
Price Data: Available from publisher.
Time: (3–10) minutes.
Author: Science Research Associates.
Publisher: General Dynamics Information Technology.
Cross References: See T5:1836 (1 references); for reviews by Benjamin Shimberg and Paul W. Thayer, see 9:857.

[1414]
Older Persons Counseling Needs Survey.

Purpose: To assess the needs of older persons and their desires for counseling.
Population: Ages 60 and over.
Publication Date: 1993.
Scores, 3: Needs, Desires, Total.
Administration: Individual.
Price Data: Available from publisher.
Time: (10–15) minutes.
Author: Jane E. Myers.
Publisher: Mind Garden, Inc.
Cross References: For reviews by Dennis C. Harper and Lawrence J. Ryan, see 14:264.

[1415]

Oliver Organization Description Questionnaire.

Purpose: Describes occupational organizations along four dimensions.

Population: Adults.

Publication Date: 1981.

Acronym: OODQ.

Scores, 4: H (Hierarchy), P (Professional), T (Task), G (Group).

Administration: Group.

Price Data, 2015: $30 per 50 tests with scoring sheets; $5 per scoring guide (1981, 13 pages).

Time: (15–20) minutes.

Author: John E. Oliver, Jr.

Publisher: Organizational Measurement Systems Press.

Cross References: For a review by Peter Villanova and H. John Bernardin, see 11:271.

[1416]

OMNI Personality Inventory and OMNI-IV Personality Disorder Inventory.

Purpose: "Comprehensive self-report instruments for measuring normal and abnormal personality traits."

Population: Ages 18–74 years.

Publication Date: 2001.

Administration: Individual or group.

Price Data, 2015: $260 per OMNI introductory kit including OMNI professional manual (75 pages), 25 OMNI test booklets, OMNI CD-ROM software system with on-screen manual, and 5 free on-screen administrations of the OMNI; $218 per OMNI-IV Introductory kit including OMNI professional manual (75 pages), 25 OMNI-IV test booklets, OMNI-IV CD-ROM software system with on-screen manual, and 5 free on-screen administrations of the OMNI-IV.

Comments: Paper-and-pencil and computer administration available; computer-scored only (cannot be hand-scored); CD-ROM based scoring software generates interpretive report.

Author: Armand W. Loranger.

Publisher: Psychological Assessment Resources, Inc.

a) OMNI PERSONALITY INVENTORY.

Acronym: OMNI.

Scores, 44: 2 Validity Scales: Variable Response Inconsistency (VRIN), Current Distress (CD); 25 Normal Scales: Aestheticism (AE), Ambition (AM), Anxiety (AN), Assertiveness (AS), Conventionality (CO), Depression (DE), Dutifulness (DU), Excitement (EC), Exhibitionism (EH), Energy (EN), Flexibility (FL), Hostility (HS), Impulsiveness (IM), Intellect (IT), Irritability (IR), Modesty (MD), Moodiness (MO), Orderliness (OR), Self-Indulgence (SI), Sincerity (SN), Sociability (SO), Self-Reliance (SR), Tolerance (TO), Trustfulness (TR), Warmth (WR); 10 Personality Disorder Scales: Paranoid (PAR), Schizoid (SCH), Schizotypal (SCT), Antisocial (ANT), Borderline (BOR), Histrionic (HIS) Narcissistic (NAR), Avoidant (AVD), Dependent (DEP), Obsessive-Compulsive (OBC); 7 Personality Factor Scales: Agreeableness (AGRE), Conscientiousness (CONC), Extraversion (EXTR), Narcissism (NARC), Neuroticism (NEUR), Openness (OPEN), Sensation-Seeking (SENS).

Time: (60–90) minutes.

Comments: 375-item self-report inventory; measure both normal and abnormal personality traits as specified in DSM-IV.

b) OMNI-IV PERSONALITY DISORDER INVENTORY.

Acronym: OMNI-IV.

Scores, 12: 2 Validity Scales: Variable Response Inconsistency (VRIN), Current Distress (CD); 10 Personality Disorder Scales: Paranoid (PAR), Schizoid (SCH), Schizotypal (SCT), Antisocial (ANT), Borderline (BOR), Histrionic (HIS), Narcissistic (NAR), Avoidant (AVD), Dependent (DEP), Obsessive-Compulsive (OBC).

Time: (35–45) minutes.

Comments: 210 items taken from the OMNI; assesses personality disorders as specified in DSM-IV.

Cross References: For a review by Kevin Lanning, see 15:177.

[1417]

Opinions About Deaf People Scale.

Purpose: To measure hearing adults' beliefs about the capabilities of deaf adults.

Population: Adults.

Publication Date: Undated.

Scores: Total score only.

Administration: Group.

Price Data: Available as free download from Educational Resources Information Center (ERIC) database.

Time: Administration time not reported.

Authors: Paul James Berkay, J. Emmett Gardener, and Patricia L. Smith.

Publisher: National Clearinghouse of Rehabilitation Training Materials.

Cross References: For reviews by Jeffery P. Braden and by Vincent J. Samar and Ila Parasnis, see 14:265.

[1418]

Opposite Strengths Inventory of Strengths.

Purpose: "To identify eight patterns of human strengths."

Population: Managers and adults in organizational settings.

Publication Dates: 1977– 2014.

Acronym: OSIS

Scores: Core Strengths.

Administration: Individual.

Forms, 2: Self-report (1977, 2 pages, for self-ratings), Other-report (1977, 2 pages, for ratings by unlimited numbers of others).

Restricted Distribution: Inventory and all reports available only to Opposite Strengths Certified Executive Coaches and Certified Facilitators.

Price Data, 2016: Scoring service, part of executive coaching or culture transformation service; otherwise $375; online printing only.
Time: (10) minutes.
Authors: J. W. Thomas, Clyde C. Mayo (manual), and T. J. Thomas (interpretive reports).
Publisher: Opposite Strengths, Inc.

[1419]
OPQ32.

Purpose: A "personality questionnaire ... designed to give information on individual styles or preferences at work."
Population: Employees and job applicants.
Publication Dates: 1984-2011.
Scores: 32 Personality Characteristics in 3 Domains, plus Consistency Scale: Relationships with People (Persuasive, Controlling, Outspoken, Independent Minded, Outgoing, Affiliative, Socially Confident, Modest, Democratic, Caring), Thinking Style (Data Rational, Evaluative, Behavioral, Conventional, Conceptual, Innovative, Variety Seeking, Adaptable, Forward Thinking, Detail Conscious, Conscientious, Rule Following), Feelings and Emotions (Relaxed, Worrying, Tough Minded, Optimistic, Trusting, Emotionally Controlled, Vigorous, Competitive, Achieving, Decisive).
Administration: Group.
Forms, 3: OPQ32r, OPQ32n, OPQ32i.
Price Data: Available from publisher
Foreign Language Editions: Available in more than 30 languages; contact publisher for information.
Time: (30) minutes.
Comments: Training required; a previous edition was titled Occupational Personality Questionnaire.
Author: SHL Group Ltd.
Publisher: CEB.
Cross References: For reviews by S. Alvin Leung and Sameano F. Porchea, see 19:122; see T5:1822 (7 references); for a review by Thomas M. Haladyna of an earlier edition, see 11:267.

[1420]
Optometry Admission Testing Program.

Purpose: "Designed to measure general academic ability and comprehension of scientific information."
Population: Optometry school applicants.
Publication Dates: 1987-2006.
Acronym: OAT.
Scores, 8: Academic Average, Quantitative Reasoning, Reading Comprehension, Physics, Biology, General Chemistry, Organic Chemistry, Total Science.
Administration: Group.
Price Data: Available from publisher.
Time: 245(285) minutes.
Comments: Administered via computer at testing centers.
Author: Optometry Admission Testing Program.

Publisher: Optometry Admission Testing Program.
Cross References: For reviews by Alan C. Bugbee, Jr. and James E. Carlson, see 12:269; for a review by Penelope Kegel-Flom of the Optometry College Admission Test, see 8:1104 (3 references).

[1421]
OQ-45.2 (Outcome Questionnaire).

Purpose: Designed to measure "patient progress in therapy."
Population: Adult therapy patients.
Publication Dates: 1996–2004.
Scores, 4: Symptom Distress, Interpersonal Relations, Social Role, Total.
Administration: Individual.
Price Data, 2015: $250 per annual license fee per clinician includes unlimited administrations; $25 per manual (2004, 54 pages).
Foreign Language Editions: Software version available in French (Canadian), Norwegian, Spanish, and Swedish; paper-and-pencil version available in Arabic, Armenian, Chinese (Simplified and Traditional), Danish, Dutch, Farsi, Finnish, German, Hebrew, Hungarian, Italian, Japanese, Korean, Lithuanian, Norwegian, Polish, Romanian, Russian, Slovak, Slovene, Spanish, Swedish, Tagalog, Thai, Turkish, Ukranian, and Vietnamese.
Time: (5–15) minutes.
Comments: Designed for repeated administration over the course of therapy; computer scoring available; may be administered orally.
Authors: Michael J. Lambert, Jared S. Morton, Derick Hatfield, Cory Harmon, Stacy Hamilton, Rory C. Reid, Kenichi Shumokawa, Cody Christopherson, and Gary Burlingame.
Publisher: OQ Measures LLC.
Cross References: For reviews by William E. Hanson and Brad M. Merker and by Steven I. Pfeiffer, see 16:176.

[1422]
OQ-10.2 [A Brief Screening & Outcome Questionnaire].

Purpose: "Designed as a brief screening instrument ... intended to alert the physician to the possibility that the patient was experiencing enough psychological distress to consider follow-up with other specific diagnostic tests or interviews."
Population: Ages 17-80 years.
Publication Dates: 1998-2000.
Acronym: OQ-10.2.
Scores: Total score only.
Administration: Individual or group.
Restricted Distribution: Requires licensure from OQ Measures LLC.

Price Data, 2015: $250 per annual license fee per clinician includes unlimited administrations; $25 per manual (1998, 10 pages).

Foreign Language Editions: Spanish and French editions available.

Time: (1-5) minutes.

Authors: Michael J. Lambert, Arthur M. Finch, John Okishi, Gary M. Burlingame (manual only), Celeste McKelvey (manual only), and Curtis W. Reisinger.

Publisher: OQ Measures LLC.

Cross References: For reviews by Jody L. Kulstad and Michael J. Scheel, see 17:136.

[1423]

OQ-30.2 [Outcome Questionnaire for Adults].

Purpose: Designed to "measure patient progress following psychological and medical interventions."

Population: Ages 17-80 years.

Publication Dates: 2001-2003.

Acronym: OQ-30.2.

Scores: Total score only.

Administration: Individual or group.

Restricted Distribution: Requires licensure from OQ Measures LLC.

Price Data, 2016: License fee is $250 per clinician per year.

Foreign Language Editions: Software version available in Spanish and French (Canadian); paper-and-pencil version available in Chinese, Dutch, French, Korean, Spanish, and Swedish.

Time: (2-15) minutes.

Comments: Test can be administered orally.

Authors: Michael J. Lambert, Derek R. Hatfield, David A. Vermeersch (manual only), Gary M. Burlingame, Curtis W. Resinger, and G. S. (Jeb) Brown (manual only).

Publisher: OQ Measures LLC.

Cross References: For reviews by Collie Conoley and Pam Ramsden of the OQ-30.1, see 17:137.

[1424]

Oral and Written Language Scales, Second Edition: Listening Comprehension and Oral Expression.

Purpose: Designed to measure oral language "across receptive and expressive processes."

Publication Dates: 1995-2011.

Acronym: OWLS-II LC; OWLS-II OE.

Scores, 5: Listening Comprehension, Oral Expression, Oral Language Composite, [Receptive Language Composite, Expressive Language Composite (when used with OWLS-II Listening Comprehension and Oral Expression Scales)].

Administration: Individual.

Price Data, 2016: $565 per software kit including 10 LC/OE record forms, LC easel, OE easel, unlimited-use computer-scoring CD, Foundations of Language Assessment handbook, LC/OE manual (2011, 282 pages), and carrying case; $450 per hand-scored kit (includes everything except computer-scoring CD); $60 per 25 LC/OE record forms; $155 per easel (LC or OE); $68.50 per Foundations of Language Assessment handbook; $77.50 per LC/OE manual.

Time: [10-30] minutes per scale.

Comments: May be used alone or in combination with OWLS-II Reading Comprehension and Written Expression (1425).

Author: Elizabeth Carrow-Woolfolk.

Publisher: Western Psychological Services.

a) FORM A.

Population: Ages 3-21.

b) FORM B.

Purpose: Designed as a parallel form for retesting.

Population: Ages 5-21.

Price Data: $268.50 per Form B pack, including 10 LC/OE record forms-Form B, LC easel-Form B, OE easel-Form B; $60 per 25 LC/OE record forms-Form B; $155 per Form B easel (LC or OE).

Cross References: For reviews by Bethany Brunsman and Carolyn Mitchell-Person, see 19:123; for reviews by Steve Graham and Koressa Kutsick Malcolm of an earlier edition, see 14:266.

[1425]

Oral and Written Language Scales, Second Edition: Reading Comprehension and Written Expression.

Purpose: Designed to measure "written language across receptive and expressive processes."

Population: Ages 5-21.

Publication Dates: 1996-2011.

Acronym: OWLS-II RC; OWLS-II WE.

Scores, 5: Reading Comprehension, Written Expression, Written Language Composite, [Receptive Language Composite, Expressive Language Composite (when used with OWLS-II Listening Comprehension and Oral Expression Scales)].

Administration: Individual.

Price Data, 2016: $565 per software kit including RC/WE manual (2011, 443 pages), 10 RC/WE record forms, 10 WE response booklets, RC easel, WE easel, unlimited-use computer-scoring CD, and carrying case; $450 per hand-scored kit; $60 per 25 RC/WE record forms; $30 per 25 WE response booklets; $155 per easel (RC or WE); $77.50 per RC/WE manual.

Time: [10-30] minutes per scale.

Comments: May be used alone or in combination with OWLS-II Listening Comprehension and Oral Expression (1424).

Authors: Elizabeth Carrow-Woolfolk (test and manual) and Kathleen T. Williams (Written Expression scale and manual).

Publisher: Western Psychological Services.

    a) FORM B.

    Purpose: Designed as a parallel form for retesting.

    Price Data: $268.50 per Form B pack, including 10 RC/WE record forms-Form B, 10 WE response booklets-Form B, RC easel-Form B, WE easel-Form B; $60 per 25 RC/WE record forms-Form B; $30 per 25 WE response booklets-Form B, $155 per Form B easel (RC or WE).

Cross References: For reviews by Sharon Hall deFur and Sandra Ward, see 19:124; for reviews by C. Dale Carpenter and Koressa Kutsick Malcolm of an earlier edition, see 14:267.

[1426]

Oral English/Spanish Placement Test.

Purpose: Designed as a measure of bilingualism to aid in placing children properly for efficient instruction.

Population: Ages 4–20.

Publication Dates: 1974–1976.

Acronym: OE/SPPT.

Scores: Total score and grade level equivalents.

Administration: Individual.

Tests, 2: English, Spanish.

Price Data, 2015: $20 per packet (includes manual and 1 English and 1 Spanish rating/answer sheets); permission to copy answer sheets is included.

Time: (1–2) minutes for children with little or no proficiency; (2–5) minutes for children with slightly better proficiency.

Comments: Performance rated by examiner; no reading by examinees.

Author: Steve Moreno.

Publisher: Moreno Educational Co.

Cross References: For a review by Stephen Powers, see 9:902.

[1427]

Oral-Motor/Feeding Rating Scale.

Purpose: Constructed to assess "oral-motor movement/ feeding dysfunction."

Population: Ages 1 and over.

Publication Date: 1990.

Scores: Item scores only.

Administration: Individual.

Price Data, 2015: $59 per complete kit including 25 progress charts and manual (26 pages); $35.50 per 25 progress charts; $40 per manual.

Time: (60) minutes or less.

Comments: Ratings by professional.

Author: Judy Michels Jelm.

Publisher: Pearson.

Cross References: For reviews by Glen E. Ray and Donna Spiker, see 12:271.

[1428]

Oral Speech Mechanism Screening Examination, Third Edition.

Purpose: "To provide the speech-language pathologist and other professionals with a method for assessing the adequacy of the oral mechanism for speech and related functions."

Population: Age 5 through adults.

Publication Dates: 1981–2000.

Acronym: OSMSE-3.

Scores: 9 areas: Lips, Tongue, Jaw, Teeth, Hard Palate, Soft Palate, Pharynx, Breathing, Diadochokinesis.

Administration: Individual.

Price Data, 2015: $122 per complete kit; $37 per 50 scoring forms; $25 per audio CD; $68 per examiner's manual.

Time: (10–15) minutes.

Authors: Kenneth O. St. Louis and Dennis M. Ruscello.

Publisher: PRO-ED

Cross References: For a review by Roger L. Towne, see 14:268; see also T5:1852 (6 references) and T4:1900 (4 references); for reviews by Charles Wm. Martin and Malcolm R. McNeil of an earlier edition, see 11:272.

[1429]

Organic Dysfunction Survey Schedules.

Purpose: To assist in discovering psychological and medical factors that may contribute to treatment.

Population: Adult clients.

Publication Date: 1981.

Acronym: ODSS.

Scores: 22 survey schedules: Arthritis, Asthma, Cancer, Cardiac, Covert Thermal, Cues for Tension and Anxiety, Dysmenorrhea, Gastrointestinal, Guidelines for Cardiac Rehabilitation, Headache, Hypertension, Nutrition, Organic Dysfunction-Medical, Organic Dysfunction-Psychological, Pain, Physical Complaint, Reactions Toward Illness, Renal Failure, Seizure, Stress, Stroke, Vomiting.

Administration: Group or individual.

Manual: No manual.

Price Data, 2016: $79.95 per set of schedules.

Time: Administration time not reported.

Author: Joseph R. Cautela.

Publisher: Cambridge Center for Behavioral Studies.

Cross References: See T5:1853 (1 reference); for reviews by Julian Fabry and George N. Prigitano, see 9:909.

[1430]

Organizational Beliefs Questionnaire.

Purpose: "Intended to give concerned managers a deeper understanding of their own organization's culture."

Population: Organizations.

Publication Date: 1997.

Acronym: OBQ.

Scores, 10: Work Can Be As Much Fun As Play, Seek Constant Improvement, Accept Specific And Difficult Goals, Accept Responsibility For Your Actions, Care About One Another, Quality Is Crucially Important, Work Together To Get The Job Done, Have Concern For Measures Of Our Success, There Must Be Hands-On Management, A Strong Set Of Shared Values And Beliefs Guide Our Actions.
Administration: Group.
Price Data: Available from publisher.
Time: Administration time not reported.
Comments: Computerized interpretive information provided by publisher, including scale summaries and individual item analyses.
Author: Marshall Sashkin.
Publisher: HRD Press, Inc.
Cross References: For reviews by Cynthia A. Larson-Daugherty and Mary Roznowski, see 14:269.

[1431]
Organizational Change-Readiness Scale.

Purpose: Constructed "to analyze the ability of an organization to manage change effectively and to plan improvement actions."
Population: Employees.
Publication Date: 1996.
Acronym: OCRS.
Scores: 5 scales: Structural Readiness, Technological Readiness, Climatic Readiness, Systemic Readiness, People Readiness.
Administration: Group.
Price Data, 2016: $195; quantity discounts available.
Time: (20) minutes.
Comments: Redevelopment of Organizational Change-Readiness Survey; now sold as part of the Training House Assessment Kit.
Authors: John E. Jones and William L. Bearley.
Publisher: HRD Press, Inc.
Cross References: For reviews by Gary J. Dean and Eugene P. Sheehan, see 14:270.

[1432]
Organizational Character Index.

Purpose: Designed to determine the character of a department, team, or organization.
Population: Adults working for an organization.
Publication Date: 2000.
Acronym: OCI.
Scores, 4: Extroversion or Introversion, Sensing or Intuition, Thinking or Feeling, Judging or Perceiving.
Administration: Individual or group.
Price Data, 2016: $8.75 per Organizational Character Index self-scorable test booklet; $77.50 per package of 10.
Time: (15) minutes.
Comments: Can be self-administered and scored; book titled The Character of Organizations serves as manual.

Author: William Bridges.
Publisher: CPP, Inc.

[1433]
Organizational Climate Workbook.

Purpose: Assesses the current climate within an organization/department versus how one thinks it should be.
Population: Work groups.
Publication Dates: 1991–1993.
Acronym: OCW.
Scores, 12: Actual Organizational Climate and Ideal Organizational Climate on 6 dimensions: Flexibility, Responsibility, Standards, Rewards, Clarity, Team Commitment.
Administration: Group or individual.
Price Data, 2016: $152 per complete kit including 10 questionnaires and 10 profiles and interpretive notes (11 pages).
Foreign Language Editions: Available in French (Canadian) and Japanese.
Time: [30] minutes.
Comments: Self-scored instrument; previously titled Organizational Climate Exercise II.
Author: Hay Group.
Publisher: Hay Group.
Cross References: For reviews by Mary Anne Bunda and Erich P. Prien of the of the Organizational Climate Exercise II, see 13:217.

[1434]
Organizational Culture Inventory.

Purpose: Designed to measure an organization's current and ideal norms and expectations.
Population: Organizational members.
Publication Dates: 1987–1989.
Acronym: OCI.
Scores: 12 culture styles: Constructive Cultures (Achievement, Self-Actualizing, Humanistic-Encouraging, Affiliative), Passive/Defensive Cultures (Approval, Conventional, Dependent, Avoidance Style), Aggressive/Defensive Cultures (Oppositional, Power, Competitive, Perfectionistic).
Administration: Group or individual.
Forms, 2: OCI Ideal, OCI Current.
Price Data: Available from publisher.
Foreign Language Editions: Available in Arabic, Bulgarian, Chinese (Simplified), Chinese (Traditional), Croatian, Czech, Danish, Dutch, Farsi, Finnish, French (Canadian), French (European), German, Greek, Hungarian, Indonesian, Italian, Japanese, Korean, Malaysian, Polish, Portuguese (Brazilian), Portuguese (European), Romanian, Russian, Serbian, Slovak, Slovenian, Spanish (Castilian), Spanish (Latin American), Swedish, Thai, and Turkish.
Time: [15-20] minutes.

Comments: Certification is required to purchase and debrief the OCI. The test publisher has indicated there is a newer edition of this test; description will be updated when complete test materials are received.
Authors: Robert A. Cooke and J. Clayton Lafferty.
Publisher: Human Synergistics International.
Cross References: See T5:1862 (2 references); for reviews by Charlene M. Alexander and Gargi Roysircar Sodowsky, see 12:272 (1 reference).

[1435]

Organizational Description Questionnaire.

Purpose: Designed to "measure how often each member of the organization perceives the culture of their unit/department/organization to be using a full range of specific leadership factors."
Population: Working adults.
Publication Date: 1992.
Acronym: ODQ.
Scores, 2: Transactional, Transformational.
Administration: Individual or group.
Price Data: 2015: $50 per manual, including review-only copy of ODQ form; $2.40 per online administration license (minimum 50); $250 Group Report; $2 per Remote Online Survey License (minimum 50); $2 per License to Reproduce (minimum 50).
Foreign Language Editions: Translated materials available in German and Indonesian.
Time: (10-15) minutes.
Authors: Bernard M. Bass and Bruce J. Avolio.
Publisher: Mind Garden, Inc.

[1436]

Organizational Effectiveness Inventory.

Purpose: Determines the impact of organizational, group, and job level factors on organizational effectiveness.
Population: Organization members.
Publication Date: 1997.
Acronym: OEI.
Scores: 41 Outcomes and Causal Factors: Mission and Philosophy (Articulation of Mission, Customer-Service Focus), Structures (Empowerment, Employee Involvement), Systems (Selection /Placement, Training and Development, Respect for Members, Fairness of Appraisals, Use of Rewards, Use of Punishment, Goal Clarity, Goal Challenge, Participative Goal Setting, Goal Acceptance), Technology (Autonomy, Skill Variety, Feedback, Task identity, Significance, Interdependence), Skills/Qualities (Upward Communication, Downward Communication, Communication for Learning, Interaction Facilitation, Task Facilitation, Goal Emphasis, Consideration, Personal Bases of Power, Organizational Bases of Power), Individual Outcomes—Positive Indices (Role Clarity, Motivation, Satisfaction, Intention to Stay), Individual Outcomes—Negative Indices (Role Conflict, Job Insecurity, Stress), Group Outcomes (Intra-Unit Cooperation, Inter-Unit Coordination, Departmental—Level Quality), Organizational Outcomes (Organizational—Level Quality, External Adaptability).
Administration: Individual or group.
Price Data: Available from publisher.
Time: Administration time not reported.
Foreign Language Editions: Arabic, Bulgarian, Chinese (Simplified and Traditional), Croatian, Danish, Dutch, Finnish, French (Canadian and European), German, Greek, Hungarian, Italian, Japanese, Korean, Polish, Portuguese (Brazilian and European), Romanian, Russian, Serbian, Spanish (Castilian and Latin American), Swedish, Thai, Turkish.
Author: Robert A. Cooke.
Publisher: Human Synergistics International.

[1437]

Organizational Justice Inventory.

Purpose: Measures employees' perception of their organization's commitment to justice.
Population: Employees.
Publication Date: 2000.
Acronym: OJI.
Scores, 4: Procedural Justice, Distributive Justice, Interpersonal Justice, Informational Justice.
Administration: Group.
Manual: No manual.
Price Data: Available from publisher.
Time: Administration time not reported.
Authors: M. Afzal Rahim, Nace R. Magner, and Debra L. Shapiro.
Publisher: Center for Advanced Studies in Management.

[1438]

Orleans-Hanna Algebra Prognosis Test, Third Edition.

Purpose: Designed to "determine algebra readiness" and as a predictor of student success in first-year algebra.
Population: Grades 7–11.
Publication Dates: 1928–1998.
Scores: Total score only.
Administration: Group.
Price Data, 2016: $31 per manual (1998, 55 pages); $45 per 25 hand-scorable answer documents including class record; $26.50 per key to use with hand-scorable answer documents; $38.50 per 25 student report forms; $45 per 25 machine-scorable answer documents.
Time: 35(40) minutes.
Author: Gerald S. Hanna.
Publisher: Pearson.
Cross References: For reviews by Joseph C. Ciechalski and Kevin D. Crehan, see 17:138; see also T4:1910 (3 references); for reviews by Dietmar Küchemann and Charles Secolsky of an earlier edition, see 9:912 (1 refer-

ence); see also T2:688 (11 references); for reviews by W. L. Bashaw and Cyril J. Hoyt of an earlier edition, see 7:510 (3 references); for reviews by Harold Gulliksen and Emma Spany, see 4:396 (1 reference); for a review by S. S. Wilks, see 2:1444 (4 references).

[1439]
Otis-Lennon School Ability Test, Eighth Edition.

Purpose: "Designed to measure those verbal, quantitative, and figural reasoning skills that are most closely related to scholastic achievement."
Population: Ages 4-6 to 18-2.
Publication Dates: 1977-2003.
Acronym: OLSAT 8.
Scores, 3: Verbal, Nonverbal, Total.
Administration: Group.
Levels, 7: A, B, C, D, E, F, G.
Forms, 1: 5.
Restricted Distribution: OLSAT 8 is sold only to accredited schools and school districts.
Price Data, 2016: $8 per directions for administering for the practice test (Form 5, Levels A-F); $10 per 10 practice test packs (Form 5, Levels A-F); $20 per directions for administering (Form 5, Levels A, B, C, and D and E/F/G combined); $56 per 10 machine-scorable test packs (Form 5, Levels A-D); $46 per 10 reusable test packs (Form 5, Levels E-G); $43 per 30 machine-scorable answer documents (Form 5, Levels E/F/G combined); $28 per response keys for hand scoring (Form 5, Levels A-G); $75 per norms book (specify spring [2003, 94 pages] or fall [2003, 94 pages]); $55 per technical manual (2003, 65 pages).
Time: (77) minutes over 2 sessions for Levels A-B; (72) minutes over 2 sessions for Level C; 50 (60) minutes over 1 session for Level D; 40 (60) minutes over 1 session for Levels E-G.
Comments: Administered orally at Levels A-B; Level C is partially self-administered; Levels D-G are self-administered; Levels D-G available online; originally titled Otis-Lennon Mental Ability Test.
Author: Pearson.
Publisher: Pearson.
Cross References: For reviews by Cleborne D. Maddux and David Morse, see 18:82; for reviews by Lizanne DeStefano and Bert A. Goldman of the Seventh Edition, see 14:271; see also T5:1866 (45 references) and T4:1913 (8 references); for reviews by Anne Anastasi and Mark E. Swerdlik of an earlier edition, see 11:274 (48 references); for reviews by Calvin O. Dyer and Thomas Oakland of an earlier edition, see 9:913 (7 references); see also T3:1754 (64 references), 8:198 (35 references), and T2:424 (10 references); for a review by John E. Milholland and excerpted reviews by Arden Grotelueschen and Arthur E. Smith of an earlier edition, see 7:370 (6 references).

[1440]
Outcome Assessment and Reporting System.

Purpose: Designed to provide "relevant longitudinal data," throughout the treatment period, documenting "observations that are related to positive outcomes for the treatment of substance dependence."
Population: Adolescents and adults.
Publication Date: 2005.
Acronym: OAARS.
Scores, 13: Emotional Volatility, Ability to Focus on Treatment, Affective and Anxiety Problems/Disorders, Awareness and Understanding of the Condition, Openness and Personal Commitment to Change, Willingness to Involve Others in Treatment, Indication of Ability to Follow-Through on the Treatment Plan, Level of Engagement in Treatment, Social/Interpersonal Supports, The Recovery Environment, Discharge/Program Completion Status, Engagement, Recovery Status.
Administration: Individual.
Price Data, 2016: $99 per kit; $5 per manual (7 pages).
Time: Administration time not reported.
Comments: The scale is to be completed three times throughout the course of treatment; items to assess treatment effectiveness are to be completed 3 to 6 months after treatment.
Authors: Norman G. Hoffmann, Gerald D. Shulman, and David Mee-Lee.
Publisher: The Change Companies.

[1441]
Outcomes: Planning, Monitoring, Evaluating.

Purpose: "A tool for monitoring student progress toward selected goals."
Population: Grades K–12.
Publication Date: 2002.
Acronym: PME.
Scores: 11 categories: Concern Description, Goals and Benchmarks, Benchmark Sealing, Social-Validation Criteria, Intervention Planning, Progress-Monitoring Procedures, Progress Chart, Progress Analysis, Evaluation of Outcomes, Next-Step Strategies, Special Education Considerations.
Administration: Individual.
Price Data, 2015: $103.10 per complete kit including manual (2002, 139 pages), binder, and 25 record forms; $79.20 per manual; $62.25 per 25 record forms.
Time: Untimed.
Comments: Provides a framework for documenting education professionals' problem-solving efforts; helps identify concerns, describe context of problem, rate baseline performance, operationalize goals, plan intervention, monitor and graph student progress, evaluate intervention outcomes, plan next steps.

Authors: Karen Callan Stoiber and Thomas R. Kratochwill.
Publisher: Pearson.
Cross References: For a review by Gypsy M. Denzine, see 15:178.

[1442]

Overall Assessment of the Speaker's Experience of Stuttering.

Purpose: Designed to "provide clinicians with a measure of the overall impact of stuttering on a person's life."
Population: Individuals 18 and over who stutter.
Publication Date: 2008.
Acronym: OASES.
Scores, 4: General Information, Your Reaction to Stuttering, Communication in Daily Situations, Quality of Life.
Administration: Individual or group.
Price Data, 2015: $78.95 per hand-scoring starting kit including technical manual (41 pages) and 25 record forms (ages 7-12); $38.20 per 25 hand-scoring record forms; $67.45 per Q local starter kit including technical manual, 3 record forms, and 3 Q local administrations; $32.15 per Q local record forms; $3.25 per profile report; $67.45 per mail-in scoring starter kit including technical manual, 3 record forms, and 3 interpretive reports; $5.40 per mail-in scoring interpretive report; $5.40 per mail-in scoring profile report.
Foreign Language Edition: Record forms are available in Spanish.
Time: (15-20) minutes.
Authors: J. Scott Yaruss and Robert W. Quesal.
Publisher: Stuttering Therapy Resources, Inc.
Cross References: For reviews by Sandra D. Haynes and by Jeanette Lee-Farmer and Joyce Meikamp, see 18:83.

[1443]

Overeating Questionnaire.

Purpose: Designed to measure "key habits, thoughts, and attitudes related to obesity."
Population: Ages 9–98 years.
Publication Date: 2004.
Acronym: OQ.
Scores, 12: 2 Validity scores (Inconsistent Responding, Defensiveness), 6 Eating-Related Habits and Attitudes scores (Overeating, Undereating, Craving, Expectations About Eating, Rationalizations, Motivation to Lose Weight), 4 general Health Habits and Psychosocial Functioning scores (Health Habits, Body Image, Social Isolation, Affective Disturbance).
Administration: Group or individual.
Price Data, 2016: $112.50 per complete kit including 25 AutoScore answer sheets and manual (51 pages); $52.50 per 25 AutoScore answer sheets; $68.50 per manual; $369.50 per 25-use scoring CD-ROM; $19.50 per 100 PC answer sheets.
Time: 20 minutes.

Comments: Written for individuals with a fourth-grade reading level and higher.
Authors: William E. O'Donnell and W. L. Warren.
Publisher: Western Psychological Services.
Cross References: For reviews by James P. Donnelly and Sandra D. Haynes, see 17:139.

[1444]

P-BDQ Police Officer Background Data Questionnaire.

Purpose: Assesses backgrounds and personal characteristics of entry-level police officer candidates.
Population: Entry-level police officer candidates.
Publication Dates: 1999-2000.
Acronym: P-BDQ.
Scores: 5 biodata subtypes: Background, Lifestyle, Interest, Personality, Ability.
Administration: Individual or group.
Price Data: Available from publisher.
Time: 30 minutes.
Comments: "It is recommended that this test be used in conjunction with one of IPMA-HR's other entry-level police officer tests."
Authors: International Public Management Association for Human Resources & Bruce Davey Associates.
Publisher: International Public Management Association for Human Resources (IPMA-HR).
Cross References: For a review by Thomas R. O'Neill, see 18:84.

[1445]

P.C. User Aptitude Test.

Purpose: To evaluate the practical and analytical skills required for the effective use of personal computers.
Population: Applicants for positions involving the use of personal computers.
Publication Date: 1986.
Acronym: WMICRO.
Scores: Total Score, Narrative Evaluation, Ranking, Recommendation.
Administration: Group.
Price Data: Available from publisher.
Foreign Language Edition: Available in French.
Time: 75 minutes.
Comments: Graded by publisher; must be proctored; previously listed as Microcomputer User Aptitude Test.
Author: Richard Label.
Publisher: Walden Personnel Testing & Consulting Inc. [Canada].
Cross References: For a review by Robert Fitzpatrick, see 11:473.

[1446]

Pain Patient Profile.

Purpose: "Designed to identify patients who are experiencing emotional distress associated with primary

complaints of pain and assess the severity of distress in comparison to community and pain patient population national sample."
Population: Pain patients aged 17–76.
Publication Dates: 1992–1995.
Acronym: P-3®.
Scores, 4: Depression, Anxiety, Somatization, Validity Index.
Administration: Group.
Price Data, 2015: $71.25 per Q Local interpretive starter kit including manual (1995, 89 pages) and 3 answer sheets with test items to conduct and receive 3 Q Local administrations (starter kits with 10 or 30 Q Local administrations available); $77.90 per mail-in scoring starter kit including manual and 3 answer sheets with test items to conduct and receive 3 interpretive reports; $111.45 per 50 hand-scorable answer sheets; $13.50 per Q Local interpretive report; $16.70 per mail-in interpretive report including answer sheet with test items; $41 per manual; quantity discounts available for the reports.
Foreign Language Edition: Test booklets are available in Spanish.
Time: (10–15) minutes.
Authors: C. David Tollison and Jerry C. Langley.
Publisher: Pearson.
Cross References: For reviews by Gregory J. Boyle and Ronald J. Ganellen, see 14:273.

[1447]

Pair Attraction Inventory.

Purpose: "Designed to measure both complementarity and symmetry in pair relationships."
Population: College and adults.
Publication Dates: 1970–1971.
Acronym: PAI.
Scores, 7: Mother-Son, Daddy-Doll, Bitch-Nice Guy, Master-Servant, Hawks, Doves, Person-Person.
Administration: Individual.
Price Data, 2016: $29.75 per 25 booklets (specify male or female); $19 per 50 answer sheets (same for male or female); $17.75 per 50 profile sheets (same for male or female); $29.75 per kit of materials; $6.75 per manual.
Time: (20-30) minutes.
Author: Everett L. Shostrom.
Publisher: EdITS/Educational and Industrial Testing Service.
Cross References: For a review by James R. Clopton, see 8:349 (10 references).

[1448]

Panic and Agoraphobia Scale.

Purpose: "Determine[s] the severity of panic disorder with or without agoraphobia and … monitor[s] treatment efficacy."
Population: Age 16 and older.
Publication Date: 1999.

Acronym: PAS.
Scores, 5: Panic Attacks, Agoraphobic Avoidance, Anticipatory Anxiety, Disability, Worries About Health.
Administration: Individual and group.
Forms, 2: Observer-rated, self-rated.
Price Data, 2016: $110 per kit including manual (88 pages), 50 observer-rated scales, and 50 patient questionnaires.
Foreign Language Editions: Available in Arabic, Danish, Dutch, French, German, Greek, Hebrew, Hungarian, Italian, Japanese, Portuguese, Serbocroat, Spanish, Swedish, and Turkish.
Time: (5–10) minutes for observer-rated scale.
Comments: Self-administered; computerized version of self-rated scale in preparation; compatible with DSM-IV and ICD-10 classifications.
Author: Borwin Bandelow.
Publisher: Hogrefe Ltd [United Kingdom].
Cross References: For reviews by C. G. Bellah and by James Donnelly and Scott T. Meier, see 15:179.

[1449]

Paper and Pencil Games.

Purpose: Constructed to measure "figural, quantitative and verbal skills closely related to scholastic achievement."
Population: Pupils in their second, third and fourth years in South African school system.
Publication Date: 1996.
Acronym: PPG.
Administration: Group.
Levels, 2: 2, 3.
Price Data: Available from publisher.
Foreign Language Editions: Available in Afrikaans, Ndebele, Northern Sotho, Swati, Southern Sotho, Tsonga, Tswana, Venda, Xhosa, and Zulu.
Time: (150–180) minutes including 20-minute break.
Author: N. C. W. Claassen.
Publisher: Human Sciences Research Council [South Africa].
   a) LEVEL 2.
   Population: School years 2–3.
   Scores, 5: Classification, Verbal and Quantitative Reasoning, Figure Series, Comprehension, Pattern Completion.
   b) LEVEL 3.
   Population: School years 3–4.
   Scores, 5: Figure Series, Verbal and Quantitative Reasoning, Pattern Completion, Comprehension, Number Series.
Cross References: For a review by Gary L. Marco, see 14:274.

[1450]

PAR: Proficiency Assessment Report.

Purpose: Developed to identify proficiency in 22 abilities associated with effective management.
Population: Supervisors and managers.
Publication Date: 1989.

Scores, 24: 22 Ability Scores, 2 Style Scores.
Administration: Group or individual.
Manual: No manual.
Price Data, 2016: $195; quantity discounts available.
Time: (30) minutes.
Comments: Ratings by manager and self; administered prior to training program and then discussed in pairs; now sold as part of the Training House Assessment Kit.
Author: Training House, Inc.
Publisher: HRD Press, Inc.
Cross References: For reviews by Stephen F. Davis and S. Alvin Leung, see 12:276.

[1451]

Parallel Spelling Tests, Second Edition.

Purpose: Designed to help "chart children's progress in spelling."
Population: Ages 6 to 13 years.
Publication Dates: 1983–1998.
Scores: Total score only.
Administration: Group.
Price Data, 2016: £33 per test booklet/manual (1998, 40 pages).
Time: (20) minutes per test.
Comments: Teachers create tests from two banks of items: A (for ages 6 to 10) and B (for ages 9 to 13).
Author: Dennis Young.
Publisher: Hodder Education [United Kingdom].
Cross References: For reviews by Theresa G. Siskind and Lisa F. Smith, see 14:275; for reviews by Steven R. Shaw and Mark E. Swerdlik and by Claudia R. Wright of an earlier edition, see 12:277.

[1452]

Parent Adolescent Relationship Questionnaire.

Purpose: Designed to "examine and understand the parent-adolescent relationship."
Population: Parents of adolescents ages 11-18 and adolescents ages 11-18.
Publication Date: 2009.
Acronym: PARQ.
Scores, 31: Conventionalization, Global Distress, Communication, Problem Solving, School Conflict, Sibling Conflict, Eating Conflict, Malicious Intent, Perfectionism, Ruination, Cohesion, Coalitions, Mother-Father Coalition, Spouse-Adolescent Coalition, Parent-Adolescent Coalition, Triangulation, Adolescent in Middle, Parent in Middle, Spouse in Middle (Parent Form), Mother Communication, Father Communication, Mother Problem Solving, Father Problem Solving, Mother School Conflict, Father School Conflict, Autonomy, Unfairness, Father-Adolescent Coalition, Mother-Adolescent Coalition, Father in the Middle, Mother in the Middle (Adolescent Form).
Administration: Group.

Forms, 2: Parent Profile Form, Adolescent Profile Form.
Price Data, 2015: $290 per introductory kit including professional manual (171 pages), 10 parent reusable item booklets, 25 parent response booklets, 25 parent profile forms, 10 adolescent reusable item booklets, 25 adolescent response booklets, 25 adolescent profile forms; $74 per professional manual; scoring software is available from publisher.
Time: (15-20) minutes, Parent Form; (15-20) minutes, Adolescent Form.
Authors: Arthur L. Robin, Thomas Koepke, Ann W. Moye, and Rebecca Gerhardstein.
Publisher: Psychological Assessment Resources, Inc.
Cross References: For reviews by Michael J. Scheel and by Christopher A. Sink and Lauren D. Moore, see 19:125.

[1453]

Parent As A Teacher Inventory [Revised].

Purpose: "Intended to help mothers and fathers of preschool and primary grade children ... recognize their favorable qualities and identify realms in which further personal growth is needed."
Population: Mothers and fathers of children ages 3–9.
Publication Dates: 1984-1995.
Acronym: PAAT.
Scores, 6: Creativity, Frustration, Control, Play, Teaching/Learning, Total.
Administration: Group or individual.
Price Data: Available from publisher.
Foreign Language Edition: Spanish edition available.
Time: (30–45) minutes.
Author: Robert D. Strom.
Publisher: Robert Strom (the author).
Cross References: See T5:1878 (1 reference); for reviews by Alice J. Corkill and Ralph F. Darr, Jr., see 13:218 (4 references); see also T4:1922 (6 references); for a review by Elizabeth A. Robinson of an earlier edition, see 9:917 (1 reference).

[1454]

Parent Awareness Skills Survey.

Purpose: Constructed to identify strengths and weaknesses in a parent's sensitivity to typical child care situations.
Population: Parents involved in custody decisions.
Publication Dates: 1990–2002.
Acronym: PASS.
Scores, 18: 6 categories (Awareness of Critical Issues, Awareness of Adequate Solutions, Awareness of Communicating in Understandable Terms, Awareness of Acknowledging Feelings, Awareness of the Importance of Relevant Aspects of a Child's Past History, Awareness of Feedback Data) for each of the following conditions (Spontaneous Level, Probe Level One, Probe Level Two).

Administration: Individual.

Price Data, 2016: $289 per complete kit including 8 booklets, 8 scoring summaries, answer pen, updates, and manual and scoring guide; $159 per 10 booklets (volume discounts available); $169 per manual and scoring guide.

Time: [30–60] minutes.

Comments: Orally administered.

Author: Barry Bricklin.

Publisher: Village Publishing.

Cross References: For reviews by Lisa G. Bischoff and Debra E. Cole, see 12:279.

[1455]

Parent Behavior Form.

Purpose: "Designed to assess … dimensions of perceived parent behavior."

Population: Parents; ratings by ages 8–12, 12–18 and adults.

Publication Date: No date.

Acronym: PBF.

Scores, 15: Acceptance, Active Involvement, Egalitarianism, Cognitive Independence, Cognitive-Understanding, Cognitive Competence, Lax Control, Conformity, Achievement, Strict Control, Punitive Control, Hostile Control, Rejection, Inconsistent Responding, Social Desirability.

Administration: Group or individual.

Forms, 5: PBF, PBF-S, PBF Elementary, Form A, Form C-B.

Price Data: Available from distributor.

Time: Administration time not reported.

Comments: Ratings of parent behavior by their children; form for parent self-rating available.

Authors: Leonard Worell and Judith Worell.

Publisher: Judith Worell, Ph.D [Test distributed through the Test Collection at ETS].

Cross References: See T5:1881 (3 references) and T4:1925 (1 reference); for reviews by JoEllen V. Carlson and Stephen Olejnik, see 11:277 (1 reference).

[1456]

Parent-Child Relationship Inventory.

Purpose: "Assesses parents' attitudes toward parenting and toward their children."

Population: Parents of 3–15-year-old children.

Publication Date: 1994.

Acronym: PCRI.

Scores, 9: 7 content scales (Parental Support, Satisfaction With Parenting, Involvement, Communication, Limit Setting, Autonomy, Role Orientation), 2 validity indicators (Social Desirability, Inconsistency).

Administration: Group.

Price Data, 2016: $125.50 per complete kit including manual (57 pages) and 25 AutoScore™ answer sheets; $59.50 per 25 AutoScore™ answer sheets; $74 per manual; $448 per 25-use scoring and interpretation

CD (PC with Microsoft Windows); $19.50 per 100 PC answer sheets; $20 per pack of 5 Spanish test forms.

Foreign Language Edition: Test form is available in Spanish.

Time: (15) minutes.

Comments: Self-report.

Author: Anthony B. Gerard.

Publisher: Western Psychological Services.

Cross References: See T5:1883 (1 reference); for reviews by Roger A. Boothroyd and Gregory J. Marchant, see 13:220.

[1457]

Parent Perception of Child Profile.

Purpose: Designed to elicit a parent's knowledge and understanding of a child.

Population: Parents.

Publication Dates: 1991–2002.

Acronym: PPCP.

Scores, 13: Interpersonal Relations, Daily Routine, Health History, Developmental History, School History, Fears, Communication Style, Depth of Knowledge, Scope of Knowledge, Emotional Tone, Value/Philosophy, Areas Needing Attention, Recall.

Administration: Individual.

Price Data, 2016: $289 per kit including directions (1991, 11 pages), 8 Q-books, 8 recall worksheets, 8 summary forms, "answer" pen (black), "other source" pen (red), and updates; $159 per 10 Q-books with recall worksheets and summary sheets (volume discounts available); $149 per directions.

Time: (60) minutes.

Comments: Self- or evaluator-administered.

Authors: Barry Bricklin and Gail Elliot.

Publisher: Village Publishing.

Cross References: For reviews by Robert W. Hiltonsmith and Mary Lou Kelley, see 12:280.

[1458]

Parent Success Indicator [Revised Edition].

Purpose: Designed to "identify favorable qualities of parents and aspects of their behavior where education seems warranted."

Population: Ages 10-14 and parents of ages 10-14.

Publication Dates: 1984-2009.

Acronym: PSI.

Scores, 6: Communication, Use of Time, Teaching, Frustration, Satisfaction, Information.

Administration: Group.

Forms, 2: Parent, Adolescent.

Price Data, 2010: Available from publisher.

Foreign Language Editions: Spanish, Japanese, and Mandarin versions available.

Time: (15-20) minutes.

Comments: Parents provide self-assessments, adolescents provide observations of their parents.

Authors: Robert D. Strom and Paris S. Strom.
Publisher: Paris Strom and Robert Strom (the authors).
Cross References: For reviews by Rosemary Flanagan and Geoffrey L. Thorpe, see 19:126; for reviews by C. Ruth Solomon Scherzer and Suzanne Young of an earlier edition, see 16:179.

[1459]

Parenting Alliance Measure.

Purpose: "Measures the strength of the perceived alliance between parents of children ages 1 to 19 years"; and "reflects the parents' ability to cooperate with each other in meeting the needs of the child."
Population: Parents of children ages 1–19 years.
Publication Dates: 1988–1999.
Acronym: PAM.
Scores: Total score only.
Administration: Group.
Price Data, 2015: $164 per introductory kit including professional manual and 50 hand-scorable test forms.
Time: (5–15) minutes.
Authors: Richard R. Abidin (test) and Timothy R. Konold (manual and test).
Publisher: Psychological Assessment Resources, Inc.
Cross References: For reviews by Cindy I. Carlson and Mary M. Clare, see 15:181.

[1460]

Parenting Interactions with Children: Checklist of Observations Linked to Outcomes.

Purpose: Designed to be "a measure of parenting interactions that predicts children's early social, cognitive, and language development."
Population: Parents of children ages 10 months to 47 months.
Publication Date: 2013.
Acronym: PICCOLO.
Scores, 5: 4 parenting domains (Affection, Responsiveness, Encouragement, Teaching), Total.
Administration: Individual.
Price Data, 2015: $55 per starter kit including user's guide (106 pages) and 25 forms; $25 per 25 forms; $150 per training DVD.
Foreign Language Edition: Spanish version available.
Time: (10) minutes.
Comments: Based on observation of parent-child interaction; the test publisher recommends that observations be video recorded.
Authors: Lori A. Roggman, Gina A. Cook, Mark S. Innocenti, Vonda Jump Norman, Katie Christiansen, and Sheila Anderson.
Publisher: Paul H. Brookes Publishing Co., Inc.
Cross References: Reviews are scheduled for *The Twentieth Mental Measurements Yearbook*.

[1461]

Parenting Relationship Questionnaire.

Purpose: Designed to "capture a parent's perspective of the parent-child relationship."
Population: Parents of children ages 2-5, 6-18.
Publication Date: 2006.
Acronym: PRQ.
Scores, 7: Attachment, Communication (child and adolescent only), Discipline Practices, Involvement, Parenting Confidence, Satisfaction with School (child and adolescent only), Relational Frustration.
Administration: Individual.
Levels, 2: Preschool, Child and Adolescent.
Forms, 3: Parent Feedback Report, Preschool, Child and Adolescent.
Price Data, 2015: $151.10 per hand-scored starter set including 25 of each hand-scored form (preschool, child/adolescent, and parent feedback), and manual (104 pages); $405.90 per PRQ Assist starter set including 25 of each form (preschool, child/adolescent, and parent feedback), manual, and Assist computer scoring software; $37.60 per 25 hand-scored forms (specify preschool or child/adolescent); $31.40 per 25 computer-entry forms (specify preschool or child/adolescent); $50.70 per 25 scannable forms (specify preschool or child/adolescent); $31.40 per 25 parent feedback report forms; $72.70 per manual; $40.80 per test item audio CD; $425.40 per ASSIST Scanning software.
Foreign Language Edition: Available in Spanish.
Time: (10-15) minutes.
Comments: For use in conjunction with the Behavior Assessment System for Children, Second Edition (BASC-2) or as a stand-alone instrument; alternative starter sets and upgrades available for current BASC-2 users, contact publisher for details.
Authors: Randy W. Kamphaus and Cecil R. Reynolds.
Publisher: Pearson.
Cross References: For reviews by Mary M. Clare and Sandra Ward, see 18:87.

[1462]

Parenting Satisfaction Scale™.

Purpose: Designed to assess "parents' attitudes toward parenting."
Population: Adults with dependent children.
Publication Date: 1994.
Acronym: PSS.
Scores, 3: Satisfaction with Spouse/Ex-Spouse Parenting Performance, Satisfaction with the Parent-Child Relationship, Satisfaction with Parenting Performance.
Administration: Group.
Price Data, 2015: $198.65 per comprehensive kit including manual (47 pages) and 25 ReadyScore® answer documents; $79.20 per 25 ReadyScore® answer documents; $132.10 per manual.
Time: (30) minutes.

Authors: John Guidubaldi and Helen K. Cleminshaw.
Publisher: Pearson.
Cross References: For reviews by Ira Stuart Katz and Janet V. Smith, see 14:276; see also T5:1888 (1 reference).

[1463]

Parenting Stress Index, Fourth Edition.

Purpose: "Designed to evaluate the magnitude of stress in the parent-child system."
Population: Parents of children ages 1 month to 12 years.
Publication Dates: 1983-2012.
Administration: Group.
Price Data, 2015: $216 per introductory kit including manual, 10 reusable item booklets, 25 answer sheets and 25 profile forms; $138 per short form kit including manual, and 25 short form record/profile forms.
Foreign Language Editions: Validation studies done for Chinese, Portuguese, French Canadian, Finnish, and Dutch populations.
Author: Richard R. Abidin.
Publisher: Psychological Assessment Resources, Inc.
  a) FULL LENGTH.
  Acronym: PSI-4.
  Scores, 18: Total Stress (Child Domain [Distractibility/Hyperactivity, Adaptability, Reinforces Parent, Demandingness, Mood, Acceptability, Total], Parent Domain [Competence, Isolation, Attachment, Health, Role Restriction, Depression, Spouse/Parenting Partner Relationship, Total], Total), Life Stress, Defensive Responding.
  Time: (20) minutes.
  b) SHORT FORM.
  Acronym: PSI-4-SF.
  Scores, 5: Total Stress (Parental Distress, Parent-Child Dysfunctional Interaction, Difficult Child, Total), Defensive Responding.
  Time: (10) minutes.
Cross References: For reviews by Mary M. Clare and Suzanne Young, see 19:127; see also T5:1889 (20 references); for reviews by Julie A. Allison and by Laura L. B. Barnes and Judy J. Oehler-Stinnett of the Third Edition, see 13:221 (51 references); see also T4:1933 (22 references); for reviews by Frank M. Gresham and Richard A. Wantz of an earlier edition, see 10:271 (2 references).

[1464]

Parents' Observation of Study Behaviors Survey.

Purpose: To measure students' improvement in study habits and behaviors.
Population: Grades 6–13.
Publication Date: 1991.
Scores, 4: Positive Attitudes, Useful Work Habits, Efficient Learning Tools, Effective Test Taking.
Administration: Individual.
Price Data, 2016: $3 per survey.
Time: Administration time not reported.
Comments: Ratings by parents.

Author: The Cambridge Stratford Study Skills Institute.
Publisher: The Cambridge Stratford Study Skills Institute.

[1465]

Parker Team Development Survey.

Purpose: Identifies teams' strengths and weaknesses across 12 characteristics of effective teams, as perceived by teams' participants.
Population: Team and group participants.
Publication Dates: 1992–2003.
Acronym: PTDS.
Scores, 24: 2 scores (Description, Importance) per team characteristic: Clear Purpose, Informality, Participation, Listening, Civilized Disagreement, Consensus Decisions, Open Communication, Clear Roles and Work Assignments, Shared Leadership, External Relations, Style Diversity, Self-Assessment.
Administration: Group.
Manual: No manual.
Price Data, 2016: $69.50 per Parker Team Development Survey kit; $89.50 per Parker Team Development Survey Program.
Time: Administration time not reported.
Comments: For measurement of groups, not individuals.
Authors: Glenn M. Parker.
Publisher: CPP, Inc.

[1466]

Parker Team Player Survey.

Purpose: "Helps individuals identify their primary team player styles."
Population: Employees.
Publication Date: 1991.
Acronym: PTPS.
Scores, 4: Contributor, Collaborator, Communicator, Challenger.
Administration: Group or individual.
Price Data, 2016: $18.50 per Parker Team Player Survey test booklet/manual (23 pages); $18.50 per Parker Team Player Survey Styles test booklet/manual.
Foreign Language Editions: Available in Spanish and French.
Time: (15) minutes.
Comments: Self-scored.
Author: Glenn M. Parker.
Publisher: CPP, Inc.
Cross References: For reviews by Gary J. Dean and Richard B. Stuart, see 13:222 (1 reference).

[1467]

A Partial Index of Modernization: Measurement of Attitudes Toward Morality.

Purpose: Designed to measure attitudes toward morality issues.

Population: Children and adults.
Publication Date: 1972.
Scores: Total score only.
Administration: Group.
Manual: No manual.
Price Data, 2015: $2 per scale.
Time: [8] minutes.
Comments: Supplementary article available.
Author: Panos D. Bardis.
Publisher: Donna Bardis.
Cross References: See 8:464 (1 reference).

[1468]

Participative Management Survey.

Purpose: To assess the extent to which a leader provides opportunities and support for employee involvement.
Population: Individuals involved in a leadership capacity with others.
Publication Date: 1988.
Acronym: PMS.
Scores, 5: Basic Creature Comfort, Safety, Belonging, Ego-Status, Actualization.
Administration: Group or individual.
Price Data: Available from publisher.
Time: Administration time not reported.
Author: Jay Hall.
Publisher: Teleometrics International, Inc.

[1469]

Partners in Play: Assessing Infants and Toddlers in Natural Contexts.

Purpose: Designed "for the identification and follow-up of infants and toddlers … who might be eligible for early intervention services."
Population: Ages 1-36 months.
Publication Date: 2007.
Acronym: PIP.
Scores, 5: Neuromotor Domain, Sensory-Perceptual Domain, Cognitive Domain, Language Domain, Social-Emotional Behavior.
Administration: Individual.
Parts, 5: Initial Caregiver Interview, Caregiver Report of Child Development, Unstructured Caregiver-Child Play, Unstructured Examiner-Child Play, Structured Examiner-Child Play.
Price Data, 2016: $36.50 per book including assessment (219 pages).
Authors: Gail L. Ensher, Tasia P. Bobish, Eric F. Gardner, Carol L. Reinson, Deborah A. Bryden, and Daniel J. Foertsch.
Publisher: Cengage Learning.
  a) CAREGIVER FORMS/INTERVIEWS.
  Time: (30-45) minutes.
    1) *Initial Caregiver Interview.*
    Scores: Not scored.

2) *Caregiver Report of Child Development.*
Scores, 5: Neuromotor Skills, Sensory-Perceptual Skills, Cognitive Domain, Language Skills, Social-Emotional Skills.
b) PLAY INTERACTIONS.
Comments: It is preferable to conduct all play interactions in one session; if they need to be broken up, complete both unstructured interactions in one session, and schedule another session within 5 days for the structured interaction.
  1) *Unstructured Caregiver-Child Play.*
  Scores: 5 scales, 13 subscales: Language Domain (Strategies for Communication, Communication of Needs/Intent, Understanding of Language Communication [3-36 months], Vocalized Turn-Taking [1-18 months], Joint Referencing with Caregiver), Social-Emotional Behavior (Quality of Social Interaction with Caregiver [1-36 months only], Emotional Stability), Cognitive Domain (Play Strategies Observed [5-36 months]), Sensory-Perceptual Domain (Moving/Maneuvering in the Environment [3-36 months], Skill in Eating [1-18 months], Skill in Drinking), Neuromotor Domain (Picking Up Finger Food/Self-Feeding [9-24 months], Self-Feeding with Eating Utensils [11-36 months]).
  Time: (20-30) minutes.
  2) *Unstructured Examiner-Child Play.*
  Scores: 5 scales, 15 subscales: Language Domain (Response to Common Sounds in the Environment, Intelligibility of Speech and Language [1-36 months], Imitation Skills [5-36 months]), Social-Emotional Behavior (Quality of Interaction with Unfamiliar People, Attentiveness to Play Activities, Attention-Gaining Behaviors Observed [5-36 months]), Neuromotor Domain (Quality of Movement [3-36 months], Large Motor Milestones [5-36 months], Hand Skills Observation [3-36 months], Body Symmetry, Transition Into/Out of Various Positions [9-36 months], Protective Responses [5-12 months]), Sensory-Perceptual Domain (Response to Touch), Cognitive Domain (Purposeful Behavior in Play [7-36 months], Problem-Solving Skills [11-36 months]).
  Time: (20-30) minutes.
  3) *Structured Examiner-Child Play.*
  Scores: 5 scales, 15 subscales: Neuromotor Domain (Play with Rattles [3-12 months], Play with Balls [7-36 months]), Sensory-Perceptual Domain (Tracking, Play with Bubble Tumbler [13-36 months], Undressing/Dressing [9-36 months]), Cognitive Domain (Attention to Faces/Designs [1-18 months], Response to Hidden Objects [5-12 months], Early Understanding of Cause/Effect [5-24 months], Play with Blocks/Shape Sorter [9-36 months], Play with Pictures and Point [5-36 months], Advanced Doll Play [13-36 months], Problem-Solving [13-36 months]), Language Domain (Response to Bell, Early Social Games [3-18 months]), Social Emotional Behavior (Adaptability [11-36 months]).
  Time: (30-40) minutes.

[1470]

PASAT 2000 [Poppleton Allen Sales Aptitude Test].

Purpose: "Designed to measure those personality attributes which have a direct relevance to success in sales roles."

Population: Adults.
Publication Date: 1999.
Acronym: PASAT 2000.
Scores: 11 scales: Motivational, Emotional, Social, Adaptability, Conscientious, Emotional Stability, Social Control, Self-Assurance, Attentive Distortion, Adaptive Distortion, Social Distortion.
Administration: Group.
Price Data, 2016: £185 per starter set, including manual, 10 item booklets, 10 self-score response sheet and 10 candidate feedback forms; £61 per manual; £67 per item booklet; £69 per self-score response sheet/integrated profile chart; £20 per candidate feedback form.
Time: (20) minutes.
Authors: Steve Poppleton and Peter Jones.
Publisher: Hogrefe Ltd [United Kingdom].
Cross References: For reviews by Richard E. Harding and John Tivendell, see 15:182; for reviews by Larry Cochran and David O. Herman of an earlier edition of the Poppleton Allen Sales Aptitude Test, see 10:285.

[1471]

PAT: Punctuation and Grammar.

Purpose: Designed to provide "information about student ability to recognize and use the grammatical conventions of standard New Zealand English, including punctuation."
Population: Students in Years 4-10 in New Zealand schools.
Publication Date: 2013.
Score: Total score only.
Administration: Group.
Levels, 7: 1, 2, 3, 4, 5, 6, 7.
Price Data, 2016: NZ$87.50 per starter kit for years 1-7 including manual (83 pages), one of each test booklet, answer sheet, and marking key; NZ$31 per teacher's manual; $4.75 per reusable test booklet; NZ$2.35 per 10 answer sheets; NZ$4.20 per marking key.
Time: (40) minutes.
Comments: Test booklets each aimed at a specific year level, but may be used with adjacent year levels to suit particular students; test is group-administered, but students may be administered different tests because administration, instructions, and example questions are the same.
Authors: Jan Eyre, Elliot Lawes, and Verena Watson.
Publisher: New Zealand Council for Educational Research.
Cross References: Reviews are scheduled for *The Twentieth Mental Measurements Yearbook.*

[1472]

PATH Personality Questionnaire [Version 2.0].

Purpose: Designed to give employers "insight into what motivates and drives individuals, they way they think, how they relate to others, [and] their preferred work style."

Population: Job applicants and incumbents.
Publication Date: 2015.
Acronym: PATH.
Scores, 32: 30 personality measures: Influential, Directing, Motivating, Amiable, Empathetic, Collaborative, Sociable, Socially Aware, Trusting, Accepting, Self-Confident, Adaptable, Composed, Optimistic, Data Driven, Intuitive, Analytical, Strategic, Theoretical, Innovative, Learning Focused, Compliant, Risk Tolerant, Work Focused, Meticulous, Reliable, Energetic, Competitive, Driven, Decisive; 2 response scales: Receptive, Self-Aware.
Administration: Individual.
Price Data: Available from publisher.
Time: (20) minutes.
Comments: Administered online.
Authors: Talegent.
Publisher: Talegent [New Zealand].
Cross References: Reviews are scheduled for *The Twentieth Mental Measurements Yearbook.*

[1473]

Pathways to Independence, Second Edition.

Purpose: Assess skills that contribute to personal and social independence.
Population: Disadvantaged school-aged children and mentally and otherwise handicapped teenagers and adults and rehabilitating brain-damaged and geriatric patients.
Publication Dates: 1982–1998.
Scores: Checklists for recording behavior in 11 areas: Eating and Drinking, Domestic Tasks, Cleanliness and Health, Clothing, Giving Information, Use of Information, Time, Money, Freedom of Movement, Use of Amenities, Leisure.
Administration: Individual.
Manual: No manual.
Price Data, 2016: £39 per 10 checklists, including instructions and profile sheet; £7.50 per specimen copy.
Time: Administration time not reported.
Authors: Dorothy M. Jeffree and Sally Cheseldine.
Publisher: Hodder Education [United Kingdom].
Cross References: See T5:1897 (1 reference) and T4:1940 (2 references).

[1474]

Paulhus Deception Scales: Balanced Inventory of Desirable Responding Version 7.

Purpose: Designed to measure the tendency to give socially desirable responses to tests.
Population: Ages 16 and older.
Publication Dates: 1998–1999.
Acronym: PDS.
Scores, 2: Impression Management, Self-Deceptive Enhancement.

Administration: Individual or group.
Price Data, 2015: $109 per complete kit including 25 QuikScore™ forms and manual; $55 per 25 QuikScore™ forms; $61 per manual.
Time: (5–7) minutes.
Comments: Self-report; software also available; multiple translations available.
Authors: Delroy L. Paulhus.
Publisher: Multi-Health Systems, Inc.
Cross References: For reviews by Kwong-Liem Karl Kwan and Romeo Vitelli, see 15:183; see T5:1898 (1 reference).

[1475]

PDD Behavior Inventory.

Purpose: Designed to assist in the assessment of children who have been diagnosed with a pervasive developmental disorder.
Population: Ages 1-6 to 12-5.
Publication Dates: 1999-2005.
Acronym: PDDBI.
Scores, 51: 29 Approach/Withdrawal Problems scores: Approach/Withdrawal Problems Composite, Receptive/Ritualistic/Pragmatic Problems Composite, Sensory/Perceptual Repetitive Approach Behaviors (Visual Behaviors, Non-Food Taste Behaviors, Touch Behaviors, Proprioceptive/Kinesthetic Behaviors, Receptive Manipulative Behaviors), Ritualism/Resistance to Change (Resistance to Change in the Environment, Resistance to Change in Schedules/Routines, Rituals), Social Pragmatic Problems (Problems with Social Approach, Social Awareness Problems, Inappropriate Reactions to the Approaches of Others), Semantic/Pragmatic Problems (Aberrant Vocal Quality When Speaking, Problems with Understanding Words, Verbal Pragmatic Deficits), Arousal Regulation Problems (Kinesthetic Behaviors, Reduced Responsiveness, Sleep Regulation Problem [extended form only]), Specific Fears (Sadness When Away From Caregiver/Other Significant Figure/or in New Situation, Anxious When Away From Caregiver/Other Significant Figure/or in New Situation, Auditory Withdrawal Behaviors, Fears and Anxieties, Social Withdrawal Behaviors [extended form only]), Aggressiveness (Self-Directed Aggressive Behaviors, Incongruous Negative Affect, Problems When Caregiver or Other Significant Figure Returns From Work/an Outing/or Vacation, Aggressiveness Toward Others, Overall Temperament Problems [extended form only]); 22 Receptive/Expressive Social Communication Abilities scores: Receptive/Expressive Social Communication Abilities Composite, Expressive Social Communication Abilities Composite, Social Approach Behaviors (Visual Social Approach Behaviors, Positive Affect Behaviors, Gestural Approach Behaviors, Responsiveness to Social Inhibition Cues, Social Play Behaviors, Imaginative

Play Behaviors, Empathy Behaviors, Social Interaction Behaviors [parent/caregiver form only], Social Imitative Behaviors), Expressive Language (Vowel Production, Consonant Production at the Beginning/Middle/and End of Words, Diphthong Production, Expressive Language Competence, Verbal Affective Tone, Pragmatic Conversational Skills), Learning/Memory/Receptive Language (General Memory Skills, Receptive Language Competence [extended form only]), Autism Composite, SOCPP-SOCAPP Discrepancy Score, SEMPP-EXPRESS Discrepancy Score.
Administration: Individual or group.
Forms, 4: Parent/Guardian or Teacher, Standard or Extended.
Price Data, 2015: $296 per introductory kit including professional manual (2005, 545 pages), 25 Parent Rating forms, 25 Teacher Rating forms, 25 Parent Score Summary sheets, 25 Teacher Score Summary sheets, and 50 Profile forms; $92 per professional manual; $78 per 25 Parent Rating forms; $78 per 25 Teacher Rating forms; $22 per 25 Parent Score Summary sheets; $22 per 25 Teacher Score Summary sheets; $33 per 50 Profile forms; $280 per software (CD-ROM) with on-screen help and quick start guide.
Time: (30-45) minutes for Extended forms; (20-30) minutes to Standard forms.
Comments: Ratings from both parents and multiple teachers/school personnel is desirable.
Authors: Ira L. Cohen and Vicki Sudhalter.
Publisher: Psychological Assessment Resources, Inc.
Cross References: For reviews by Karen Carey and by Kathryn E. Hoff and Renee M. Tobin, see 17:142.

[1476]

PDD Behavior Inventory-Screening Version.

Purpose: Designed as "a screening tool to help clinicians quickly identify children at risk for" autism and other pervasive developmental disorders.
Population: Ages 1-6 to 12-5.
Publication Dates: 1999-2011.
Acronym: PDDBI-SV.
Scores, 3: Social Pragmatic Problems, Social Approach Behaviors, Social Deficits.
Administration: Group.
Price Data, 2015: $102 per introductory kit, including 50 rating forms and professional manual (2011, 41 pages); $60 per 50 rating forms; $55 per professional manual.
Time: (5-10) minutes.
Comments: Derived from the PDD Behavior Inventory (1475).
Author: Ira L. Cohen.
Publisher: Psychological Assessment Resources, Inc.
Cross References: For reviews by Lucy Barnard-Brak and David M. Richman and by Steven R. Shaw, see 19:128.

[1477]
Peabody Developmental Motor Scales— Second Edition.

Purpose: Designed "to assess gross motor skills and fine motor skills."
Population: Birth to 72 months.
Publication Dates: 1983–2000.
Acronym: PDMS-2.
Scores, 9: Reflexes, Stationary, Locomotion, Object Manipulation, Grasping, Visual-Motor Integration, Gross Motor, Fine Motor, Total Motor.
Administration: Individual.
Price Data, 2016: $530 per complete kit including examiner's manual (2000, 234 pages), 25 profile/summary forms, 25 examiner record booklets, administration guide, motor activities program manual, black-and-white motor development chart, 25 black-and-white motor development parent charts, and manipulatives; $435 per complete test including everything in complete kit except the motor activities program; $85 per 25 examiner record booklets; $37 per 25 profile/summary forms; $97 per motor activities program; $85 per object kit; $19 per shape cards/BLM kit; $111 per guide to item administration; $97 per examiner's manual; $25 per 25 parent charts; $32 per full color charts; $199 per online scoring and report system (1 year base subscription).
Time: (45–60) minutes.
Authors: M. Rhonda Folio and Rebecca R. Fewell.
Publisher: PRO-ED.
Cross References: For reviews by Linda K. Bunker and Peggy Kellers and by Donald Lee Stovall, see 15:184; see T5:1901 (19 references) and T4:1943 (3 references); for a review by Homer B. C. Read, Jr. of an earlier edition, see 9:922.

[1478]
Peabody Picture Vocabulary Test, Fourth Edition.

Purpose: Designed for use as a measure of receptive vocabulary for Standard American English.
Population: Ages 2:6–90+.
Publication Dates: 1959-2007.
Acronym: PPVT-4.
Scores: Total score only.
Administration: Individual.
Forms, 2: A, B.
Price Data, 2015: $452.70 per complete kit (Forms A & B) including A & B easels, 25 record forms for Form A and Form B, and manual (2007, 219 pages); $49.35 per 25 record forms (specify A or B).
Time: (10-15) minutes.
Comments: Also includes a growth scale value (GSV) to specifically measure progress over time; conormed with the Expressive Vocabulary Test-2 (787); PPVT-4 and EVT-2 standard scores allow direct comparisons between receptive and expressive vocabulary; items are categorized for multiple levels of descriptive analysis; evidence-based interventions are embedded in the scoring and reporting software (ASSIST) and allow for multiple individual and group reports with aggregation and disaggregation options.
Authors: Lloyd M. Dunn and Douglas M. Dunn.
Publisher: Pearson.
Cross References: For reviews by Joseph C. Kush and Steven R. Shaw, see 18:88; for reviews by Frederick Bessai and Orest Eugene Wasyliw of the third edition, see 14:280; see also T5:1903 (585 references) and T4:1945 (426 references); for reviews by R. Steve McCallum and Elisabeth H. Wiig of an earlier edition, see 9:926 (117 references); see also T3:1771 (301 references), 8:222 (213 references), T2:516 (77 references), and 7:417 (201 references); for reviews by Howard B. Lyman and Ellen V. Piers, see 6:530 (21 references).

[1479]
Pearson-Marr Archetype Indicator®.

Purpose: Designed to help people discover the stories that define the personal archetypal journey in professional and personal lives; provides a unique perspective that facilitates the understanding of life patterns and how they affect a person's choices, behaviors, and future vision.
Population: Adolescent—adult.
Publication Dates: 1989–2003.
Acronym: PMAI®
Scores, 12: Innocent, Orphan, Warrior, Caregiver, Seeker, Lover, Destroyer, Creator, Ruler, Magician, Saga, Jester.
Administration: Group.
Price Data, 2015: $22 for handscoring version, including Introduction to Archetypes (2003, 64 pages), questionnaire, and individualized scoring sheet; $19 per online administration, including electronic version of Introduction to Archetypes; $35 per manual (2003, 103 pages).
Time: 15 minutes
Comments: Self-administered and self-scored; can also be administered and scored online.
Authors: Carol S. Pearson and Hugh K. Marr.
Publisher: Center for Applications of Psychological Type, Inc.
Cross References: For reviews by Carl Isenhart and William E. Martin, Jr., see 16:180.

[1480]
Pediatric Attention Disorders Diagnostic Screener.

Purpose: Designed to assist clinicians in diagnosing children with ADHD by using multiple sources and multiple types of assessments.
Population: Parent- or school-referred children ages 6-12.

Publication Dates: 2000-2008.
Acronym: PADDS.
Scores, 22: 4 scores per SNAP-IV form (Parent/
Guardian, Teacher): ADHD-Inattention, Hyperactivity/
Impulsivity, ADHD-Combined Type, Total (calculated
as likelihood ratio); Total count of behavioral responses
(Redirection/Re-instruction, Fidgeting, Emotional Re-
action) per Target Test; Raw score and likelihood ratio
per Target Test (Target Recognition, Target Sequence,
Target Tracking); 5 cumulative, Post-test probabilities
of being diagnosed with ADHD (calculated each time
additional assessment is entered into PADDS system).
Administration: Individual.
Parts, 4: SNAP-IV Rating Scale, Computer Administered Diagnostic Interview, Structured Assessment of
Testing Behaviors, Target Tests of Executive Functioning.
Price Data: Available from publisher.
Time: (35-45) minutes; (25-30) minutes to administer
all three Target Tests of Executive Functions; (10-15)
minutes to input data from previously completed CADI
and SNAP-IV forms.
Comments: Also called Pediatric ADHD Screener,
Target Tests of Executive Functioning; testing software
is Windows compatible and requires Adobe Reader
(included) for viewing of summary reports.
Authors: Thomas K. Pedigo, Kenneth L. Pedigo, and
Vann B. Scott, Jr. (Clinical Manual).
Publisher: SenseLabs.

a) SNAP-IV RATING SCALE.
Purpose: Identifies "Parent and teacher ratings [of the
child] of the behavior criteria for ADHD based on criteria
set by the [DSM-IV-R]."
Publication Date: 1992.
Acronym: SNAP-IV.
Scores, 8: 4 scores per form: ADHD-Inattention,
Hyperactivity/Impulsivity, ADHD-Combined Type, Total
(calculated as likelihood ratio).
Administration: Group.
Forms, 2: Parent/Guardian, Teacher.
Foreign Language Editions: Available in Spanish;
contact publisher for availability of other languages.
Time: Administration time not reported.
Comments: Separate ratings by parent/guardian and
teacher.
Authors: James M. Swanson, W. Nolan, and W. E.
Pelham.
b) COMPUTER ADMINISTERED DIAGNOSTIC
INTERVIEW.
Purpose: Screens for "possible co-morbid conditions that
can mimic or exacerbate ADHD symptoms."
Acronym: CADI.
Scores: Not scored; Clinical feedback may be provided
for 6 possible domains: Medical History/Systems Review,
Developmental History, Social/Emotional Functioning,
Depression/Anxiety, Attention/Hyperactivity, Behavior/
School History.
Administration: Group.
Foreign Language Editions: Available in Spanish;
contact publisher for availability of other languages.
Time: Administration time not reported.

Comments: Interview can be computer administered
and completed during child's session, or interview and
protocol can be printed out and completed prior to child's
session. Ratings by Parent/Guardian.
c) STRUCTURED ASSESSMENT OF TESTING
BEHAVIORS.
Purpose: Designed to "help assess and quantify behavior changes in subjects across administration as in
pre-medication and post-medication challenges."
Scores, 3: Total count of behavioral responses (Redi-
rection/Re-instruction, Fidgeting, Emotional Reaction)
per Target Test.
Administration: Individual.
Time: (25-30) minutes.
Comments: Ratings by administrator of Target Tests.
d) TARGET TESTS OF EXECUTIVE FUNCTION-
ING.
Purpose: Computer presented tasks "aimed at provid-
ing objective assessment of a subject's ability to employ
various but not all executive processes: (planning, attend-
ing, organizing input, storing and retrieving information,
modulating emotions and sustaining effort)."
Acronym: TTEF.
Scores, 6: 2 scores (Raw score and likelihood ratio)
per Target Test (Target Recognition, Target Sequence,
Target Tracking).
Administration: Individual.
Time: (25-30) minutes to administer all three Target Tests.
Cross References: For reviews by Rama K. Mishra
and Janet Reed, see 18:89.

[1481]
Pediatric Behavior Rating Scale.
Purpose: "To assist in the identification of serious
emotional dysregulation and related disorders-most
notably early onset bipolar disorder."
Population: Ages 3-18.
Publication Date: 2008.
Acronym: PBRS.
Scores, 10: Atypical, Irritability, Grandiosity, Hyperac-
tivity/Impulsivity, Aggression, Inattention, Affect, Social
Interactions, Total Bipolar Index, Inconsistency Score.
Administration: Group.
Forms, 2: Parent (PBRS-P), Teacher (PBRS-T).
Price Data, 2015: $280 per introductory kit includ-
ing professional manual (128 pages), 25 reusable Parent
item booklets, 25 reusable Teacher item booklets, 25
Parent response booklets, 25 Teacher response booklets,
25 Parent score summary/profile forms, and 25 Teacher
score summary/profile forms; $35 per 25 reusable Parent
item booklets; $35 per 25 reusable Teacher item booklets;
$56 per 25 Parent response booklets; $56 per 25 Teacher
response booklets; $25 per 25 Parent score summary/
profile forms; $25 per 25 Teacher score summary/profile
forms; $58 per professional manual.
Time: [15-20] minutes.
Comments: Pediatric Behavior Rating Scale Scoring
Program (PBRS-SP) offered separately.
Authors: Richard M. Marshall and Berney J. Wilkinson.

Publisher: Psychological Assessment Resources, Inc.
Cross References: For reviews by Janet Reed and Tony C. Wu, see 18:90.

[1482]
Pediatric Evaluation of Disability Inventory.

Purpose: Designed as a "comprehensive clinical assessment instrument that samples key functional capabilities and performance."
Population: Ages 6 months to 7.5 years.
Publication Date: 1992.
Acronym: PEDI.
Scores, 9: Self-Care (Functional Skills, Caregiver Assistance, Modification Frequencies), Mobility (Functional Skills, Caregiver Assistance, Modification Frequencies), Social Function (Functional Skills, Caregiver Assistance, Modification Frequencies).
Administration: Individual.
Price Data, 2016: $125.95 per manual; $45.60 per 25 scoring forms.
Time: (45–60) minutes.
Comments: Should be completed by the person or group of persons familiar with the child's typical performance in the domains surveyed.
Authors: Stephen M. Haley, Wendy J. Coster, Larry H. Ludlow, Jane T. Haltiwanger, and Peter J. Andrellos.
Publisher: Health and Disability Research Institute at Boston University (Distributed by Pearson).
Cross References: For a review by Billy T. Ogletree, see 14:281.

[1483]
Pediatric Test of Brain Injury.

Purpose: Designed to "estimate a child's ability in applying neurocognitive-linguistic skills that are vulnerable to pediatric brain injury and relevant to functioning well in school" and track "recovery starting in the acute phase and continuing until…performance indicates functioning in the normal range."
Population: Ages 6-16 who have sustained traumatic brain injury or acquired brain injury.
Publication Date: 2010.
Acronym: PTBI.
Scores, 11: Orientation, Following Commands, Word Fluency, What Goes Together, Digit Span, Naming, Story Retelling-Immediate, Yes/No/Maybe, Picture Recall, Story Retelling-Delayed, Overall Performance Rating.
Administration: Individual.
Price Data, 2016: $349.95 per complete test kit including examiner's manual (127 pages), stimulus book, and test forms; $49.95 per 10 test forms.
Time: (30-35) minutes.
Comments: Specialists trained to assess children and adolescents with cognitive-communication impairments, including brain injury, are qualified to administer the PTBI. Results from each score are reported in a per-

formance profile pattern and are combined to provide a level of overall performance.
Authors: Gillian Hotz, Nancy Helm-Estabrooks, Nickola W. Nelson, and Elena Plante.
Publisher: Paul H. Brookes Publishing Co., Inc.
Cross References: For reviews by Andrew S. Davis and W. Holmes Finch and by Rama K. Mishra, see 19:129.

[1484]
PEDS Tools [Parents' Evaluation of Developmental Status].

Purpose: Designed to provide "developmental screening and behavioral screening plus ongoing surveillance."
Population: Children from birth to 8 years.
Publication Dates: 1997-2016.
Administration: Individual.
Publisher: PEDStest.com, LLC.
   a) PARENTS EVALUATION OF DEVELOPMENTAL STATUS [2ND EDITION MANUAL].
   Purpose: Designed to elicit and address "parents' concerns about children's language, motor, self-help, early academic skills, behavior and social-emotional/mental health."
   Publication Dates: 1997-2013.
   Acronym: PEDS.
   Scores: 10 areas of concern: Expressive Language and Articulation, Receptive Language, Fine Motor, Gross Motor, Behavior, Social-Emotional, Self-Help, School Skills, Global/Cognitive, Other/Health.
   Price Data, 2016: $42 per complete set including brief administration and scoring guide (2013, 12 pages), pad of 50 response forms, and pad of 50 score/interpretation forms; $5 per brief guide; $19.50 per 50 response forms; $19.50 per 50 score/interpretation forms; $19.50 per 50 response forms in Spanish or Vietnamese; $89.95 per 2nd edition technical manual (2013, 200 pages).
   Foreign Language Editions: Spanish and Vietnamese response forms available; translations available for license in more than 40 additional languages.
   Time: (5) minutes.
   Comments: May be used alone or in conjunction with Parents' Evaluation of Developmental Status–Developmental Milestones (PEDS:DM); items unchanged from original version; 2nd Edition manual includes information from 2013 standardization studies; also available online.
   Author: Frances Page Glascoe.
   b) PARENTS' EVALUATION OF DEVELOPMENTAL STATUS–DEVELOPMENTAL MILESTONES.
   Purpose: Designed as an "indicator of children's skills across developmental domains."
   Publication Dates: 2007-2016.
   Acronym: PEDS:DM.
   Scores: 8 domains: Fine Motor/Writing, Gross Motor, Expressive Language, Receptive Language, Social Emotional, Adaptive Behavior, Reading/Pre-Reading, Math/Pre-Math.
   Price Data: $299 per starter kit (English or Spanish) including reusable laminated forms, 100 recording forms, and binder case with scoring template, family book with items and supplementary measures, professional manual (2016, 190 pages), dry erase marker, and clip; $130 per

family book (English or Spanish); $57 per 100 recording forms; $75 per professional manual.

Foreign Language Editions: Spanish, French (Canadian), and Australian English versions available in print; Chinese, Portuguese, and Arabic versions available for license.

Time: (6) minutes.

Comments: May be used alone or in conjunction with Parents' Evaluation of Developmental Status (PEDS); may be administered by interview, hands-on, or parent report; also available online.

Authors: Frances Page Glascoe and Nicholas S. Robertshaw.

    1) *PEDS:DM Assessment Version*

    Purpose: "Designed for NICU follow-up and early intervention" and "offers a method for tracking progress in each domain over time."

    Scores: 7 domains: Fine Motor, Receptive Language, Expressive Language, Academic, Gross Motor, Self-Help, Social Emotional.

    Price Data: $86 per 25 record booklets (English or Spanish), which are designed to be used repeatedly with the same family.

    Foreign Language Editions: Spanish, Portuguese, French (Canadian), and Chinese versions available.

    Time: (30) minutes.

Cross References: Reviews are scheduled for *The Twentieth Mental Measurements Yearbook*. For reviews by Lisa Bischoff and Mark W. Roberts of the original edition, see 14:277.

[1485]

PEEK—Perceptions, Expectations, Emotions, and Knowledge About College.

Purpose: "Designed to assess prospective student's expectations about what college will be like."

Population: Prospective college students.

Publication Date: 1995.

Acronym: PEEK.

Scores, 3: Academic Expectations, Personal Expectations, Social Expectations.

Administration: Group or individual.

Price Data, 2015: $2.25 per publisher-scored form; $2 per Internet form (volume discounts available).

Time: (15–25) minutes.

Comments: Self-report questionnaire; can be machine scored by publisher or locally via the Internet.

Authors: Claire E. Weinstein, David R. Palmer, and Gary R. Hanson.

Publisher: H & H Publishing Co., Inc.

Cross References: For reviews by David Gillespie and Daniel L. Yazak, see 14:283.

[1486]

Peg Board.

Purpose: Developed to measure manual dexterity.

Population: Applicants for electrical and light engineering assembly jobs.

Publication Date: 1983.

Scores, 4: Preferred Hand, Non-Preferred Hand, Both Hands, Assemblies.

Administration: Group.

Price Data: Available from publisher.

Time: 3 minutes and 50 seconds (7 minutes).

Author: Educational & Industrial Test Services Ltd.

Publisher: The Morrisby Organisation [England].

[1487]

The People Process.

Purpose: Designed to help determine personalities and assist in relating to people "of the same or different personality traits."

Population: Adults.

Publication Date: 1990.

Scores: 4 processes: Energy, Information, Decisions, Actions.

Administration: Group.

Price Data: Available from publisher.

Time: (120–240) minutes.

Author: Pam Hollister.

Publisher: The PEOPLE Process.

[1488]

People Smarts: Behavioral Profiles.

Purpose: Designed to reveal perceptions of behavioral styles in the workplace.

Population: Adults.

Publication Date: 1994.

Scores: 4 profiles: Relater, Socializer, Thinker, Director.

Administration: Group.

Price Data: Price information available from publisher for trainer's package including trainer's guide (100 pages), 1 self-assessment, 1 observer assessment, 1 scoring matrix, 1 reminder card, 1 45-minute videocassette, and 1 People Smarts book (224 pages); participant's package including 1 workbook, 1 self-assessment, 1 scoring matrix, and 5 observer assessments; 1 self-assessment or 1 observer assessment; scoring matrix; reminder card; participant workbook; People Smarts book.

Time: Administration time not reported.

Author: Tony Alessandra.

Publisher: Jossey-Bass, A Wiley Company.

[1489]

Perception-Of-Relationships Test [2014 Manual].

Purpose: A drawing test designed to measure "the degree to which a child seeks psychological 'closeness' (positive interactions) with each parent" and the types of dispositions "the child has had to develop to permit or accommodate interaction with each parent."

Population: Ages 3 and older.

Publication Dates: 1964–2014.

Acronym: PORT.
Scores: No scores.
Administration: Individual.
Price Data, 2016: $289 per complete kit including 8 test/scoring booklets, manual (2014, 109 pages); pen, eraser, and updates; $159 per 10 test/scoring booklets (volume discounts available); $179 per manual; $289 per computer scoring profile (CD-ROM).
Time: [30] minutes.
Comments: Projective test for use in custody decision-making and other settings.
Author: Barry Bricklin.
Publisher: Village Publishing.
Cross References: For reviews by Janet F. Carlson and Judith Conger of an earlier version, see 12:283.

[1490]

Perceptions of Parental Role Scales.

Purpose: "To measure perceived parental role responsibilities."
Population: Parents.
Publication Date: 1982.
Acronym: PPRS.
Scores: 13 areas in 3 domains: Teaching the Child (Cognitive Development, Social Skills, Handling of Emotions, Physical Health, Norms and Social Values, Personal Hygiene, Survival Skills), Meeting the Child's Basic Needs (Health Care, Food/Clothing/Shelter, Child's Emotional Needs, Child Care), Family as an Interface With Society (Social Institutions, the Family Unit Itself).
Administration: Group.
Price Data: This measure is now available at no charge from the test publisher.
Time: (15) minutes.
Comments: Self-administered.
Authors: Lucia A. Gilbert and Gary R. Hanson.
Publisher: Lucia A. Gilbert, Ph.D.
Cross References: For reviews by Cindy I. Carlson and Mark W. Roberts, see 11:282.

[1491]

Perceptual-Motor Assessment for Children & Emotional/Behavioral Screening Program.

Purpose: "Designed for screening visual, auditory and haptic perception; fine and gross motor abilities; and perceptual memory in children."
Population: Ages 4-0 to 15-11.
Publication Date: 1988.
Acronym: P-MAC/ESP.
Scores, 12: 3 scores for the Perceptual Memory Task-Abbreviated (PMT-A): Spatial Relations, Auditory-Visual Colors Recognition, Auditory-Visual Colors Sequence; 3 scores for Haptic Visual Discrimination Test-Abbreviated (HVDT-A): Shape, Size, Texture;

6 scores for McCarron Assessment of Neuromuscular Development-Abbreviated (MAND-A): Beads in Box, Finger Tapping, Nut and Bolt, Hand Strength, Standing on One Foot, Finger-Nose-Finger.
Subtests, 3: PMT-A, HVDT-A, MAND-A.
Administration: Individual.
Price Data, 2016: $2,455 per P-MAC/ESP including P-MAC battery, computer program, manual (219 pages), 25 Protocol/Data Entry Forms, and 5 GEM volumes; $250 per ESP including 25 Behavioral Checklists for Students, computer program, and manual; $59.25 per each of 5 GEM volumes; $77 per 25 P-MAC Protocol/Data Entry Forms; $55 per 25 Behavioral Checklists for Students; $78.75 per P-MAC/ESP manual.
Time: (45) minutes.
Comments: P-MAC battery consists of selected subtests from the MAND, HVDT, and PMT; 5 age-specific volumes of Guides for Educational Management (GEM) that provide expanded recommendations and functional implications; computer software included; Behavioral Checklist for Students for ESP program.
Authors: Jack G. Dial (P-MAC and ESP), Lawrence McCarron (P-MAC), and Garry Amann (P-MAC and ESP).
Publisher: McCarron-Dial Systems, Inc.
Cross References: See T5:1919 (1 reference); for reviews by Barbara A. Rothlisberg and E. W. Testut, see 12:284.

[1492]

Perceptual Speed (Identical Forms).

Purpose: Designed to assess "the ability to rapidly compare visual configurations and identify two figures as similar or identical or to identify some particular detail that is buried in distracting material."
Population: Visual inspectors, proofreaders, clerical personnel.
Publication Dates: 1984–1996.
Scores: Total score only.
Administration: Group or individual.
Price Data: Available from publisher.
Time: 5 minutes.
Comments: Primarily used in industry and governmental organizations (norms provided to these personnel).
Authors: L. L. Thurstone and T. E. Jeffrey.
Publisher: General Dynamics Information Technology.
Cross References: For reviews by John W. Fleenor and Paul M. Mastrangelo, see 15:185.

[1493]

Performance Series.

Purpose: A computer-adaptive assessment of student performance and progress, modified to measure the different academic objectives of individual state standards.
Population: Grades 2-10.
Publication Dates: 2002-2006.

Scores, 21: Reading (Vocabulary, Fiction, Nonfiction, Long Passages, Total), Mathematics (Number & Operations, Algebra, Geometry, Measurement, Data Analysis & Probability, Total), Language Arts (Capitalization, Parts of Speech, Punctuation, Sentence Structure, Total), Science (Ecology, Science Processes, Living Things, Total), Total.
Administration: Group.
Price Data, 2016: $12-$15 per student annual subscription cost.
Time: (60) minutes per subject area.
Comments: Test is administered online.
Author: Scantron Corporation.
Publisher: Scantron Corporation.
Cross References: For reviews by Carlen Henington and David Morse, see 17:143.

[1494]
Performance Skills Leader.

Purpose: Designed to identify "leadership strengths and developmental needs."
Population: Employees in leadership positions.
Publication Date: 1996.
Acronym: PS Leader.
Scores, 24: Strategic Focus (Vision, Business Knowledge, Change Management), Business Focus (Quality Centered, Planning and Executing, Budgeting, Technology Management and Application), Work Force Focus (Coaching, Team Leadership, Creativity and Innovation, Commitment to Work Force Diversity, Human Resource Management), Interpersonal Focus (Interpersonal Skills, Oral Communication, Influencing, Writing, Conflict Resolution and Negotiation), Personal Focus (Self-Development, Action Orientation, Results Focus, Flexibility, Problem Solving and Decision Making, Role Modeling, Time Management).
Administration: Group.
Price Data, 2016: $195; quantity discounts available.
Time: Administration time not reported.
Comments: Now sold as part of the Training House Assessment Kit.
Author: Human Technology, Inc.
Publisher: HRD Press, Inc.
Cross References: For reviews by Trenton R. Ferro and George C. Thornton III, see 14:284.

[1495]
Personal Achievement Formula.

Purpose: Constructed to identify an individual's managerial strategy and his/her view of the organizational culture.
Population: Managers.
Publication Dates: 1976–1997.
Scores: 4 scores (Personal Achievement Formula, Organizational Culture, Group Achievement Formula, Group Assessment of Organization) each falling in one of 4 domains (Human Relations Specialist, Low Achiever, Average Achiever, High Achiever).
Administration: Group.
Price Data: Available from publisher.
Time: Administration time not reported.
Author: Jay Hall.
Publisher: Teleometrics International, Inc.

[1496]
Personal Characteristics Inventory™.

Purpose: Used for selection and developmental purposes; designed to gauge individual standing on the "Big Five" primary dimensions of personality to predict important work, education, and life outcomes and to help organizations identify promising candidates more effectively and provide feedback to individuals regarding strengths and areas where improvement is necessary.
Population: Ages 15 and over.
Publication Dates: 1995–2005.
Acronym: PCI.
Scores, 26: Conscientiousness (Dependability, Achievement Striving, Efficiency, Total), Stability (Even Temperament, Self-Confidence, Total), Extraversion (Sociability, Need for Recognition, Leadership Orientation, Total), Agreeableness (Cooperation, Consideration, Total), Openness (Abstract Thinking, Creative Thinking, Total), Occupational Score (Manager, Sales, Clerical, Production, Driver), Teamwork, Integrity, Learning Orientation, Commitment to Work.
Administration: Group or individual.
Price Data: Available from publisher.
Foreign Language Editions: French and Spanish editions available.
Time: 25–30 minutes.
Comments: Online administration available.
Authors: Michael K. Mount, Murray R. Barrick, and Wonderlic Consulting.
Publisher: Wonderlic, Inc.
Cross References: For reviews by Susan M. Brookhart and Mark L. Pope, see 16:181.

[1497]
Personal Creativity Assessment.

Purpose: Designed "to allow individuals to determine how they measure up in the realm of creativity."
Population: Age 18 and above.
Publication Date: 1999.
Acronym: PCA.
Scores, 2: Enabler, Barrier.
Administration: Group or individual.
Price Data, 2016: $59.95 per facilitator guide and assessment; $59.95 per pack of 5 additional assessments.
Time: (20–25) minutes.
Author: Alexander Watson Hiam.
Publisher: HRD Press, Inc.

[1498]

Personal Directions®.

Purpose: An executive coaching tool designed to aid in the structured exploration of an individual's personal choices regarding life balance issues, career planning, feelings of satisfaction and security, and opportunities for growth and development.

Population: Adults.

Publication Dates: 1997–2001.

Scores: 46 dimensions: Types of Emotional Satisfaction (Giving, Receiving, Belonging, Expressing, Gaining Stature, Entertaining, Creating, Interpreting, Excelling, Enduring, Structuring, Maneuvering, Winning, Controlling, Stability, Independence, Irreproachability), Areas of Emphasis (Career, Economic, Community, Interpersonal, Recreation, Travel, Nature, Palate, Arts, Practical Arts, Home, Romance, Family, Intellectual, Ideological, Physical, Emotional, Spiritual), World Outcomes (Level of Satisfaction, Level of Dissatisfaction, Level of Security, Level of Insecurity, Level of Growth, Balance of World, Level of Present Support, Internal Focus of World, External Focus of World, Flexibility of Boundaries, Level of Public Success).

Administration: Group.

Price Data: Available from publisher.

Foreign Language Editions: Available in English (American), English (British), Danish, Dutch, French, German, Italian, and Swedish.

Time: (45) minutes.

Comments: Purchase and use requires training by publisher.

Authors: James T. Mahoney, Joan W. Chadbourne (test), and Robert I. Kabacoff (manual).

Publisher: Management Research Group.

[1499]

Personal Experience Inventory.

Purpose: "Assesses all forms of substance abuse plus related psychosocial problems and personal risk factors."

Population: Ages 12–18.

Publication Dates: 1988–1989.

Acronym: PEI.

Scores: 45 scores/screens: Chemical Involvement Problem Severity Section: Basic Scales (Personal Involvement with Chemicals, Effects from Drug Use, Social Benefits of Drug Use, Personal Consequences of Drug Use, Polydrug Use), Clinical Scales (Social-Recreational Drug Use, Psychological Benefits of Drug Use, Transsituational Drug Use, Preoccupation with Drugs, Loss of Control), Validity Indicators (Infrequent Responses, Defensiveness, Pattern Misfit), Drug Use Frequency/Duration/Age of Onset (Alcohol, Marijuana, LSD, Psychedelics, Cocaine, Amphetamines, Quaaludes, Barbiturates, Tranquilizers, Heroin, Opiates, Inhalants); Psychosocial Section: Personal Risk Factor Scales (Negative Self-Image, Psychological Disturbance, Social Isolation, Uncontrolled,

Rejecting Convention, Deviant Behavior, Absence of Goals, Spiritual Isolation), Environmental Risk Factor Scales (Peer Chemical Environment, Sibling Chemical Use, Family Pathology, Family Estrangement), Problem Screens (Psychiatric Referral, Eating Disorder, Sexual Abuse, Physical Abuse, Family Chemical Dependency, Suicide Potential), Validity Indicators (Infrequent Responses, Defensiveness).

Administration: Group.

Parts, 2: Chemical Involvement Problem Severity Section, Psychosocial Section.

Price Data, 2015: $193 per kit for on-site computer scoring including 5-use CD (PC with Windows), 5 PC answer booklets, and manual (1989, 103 pages); $68.50 per manual; $426.50 per 25-use scoring CD (PC with Windows); $31 per 10 PC answer booklets.

Time: 45 minutes.

Authors: Ken C. Winters and George A. Henly.

Publisher: Western Psychological Services.

Cross References: See T5:1931 (1 reference) and T4:1971 (2 references); for reviews by Tony Toneatto and Jalie A. Tucker, see 11:284.

[1500]

Personal Experience Inventory for Adults.

Purpose: Designed to yield "comprehensive information about an individual's substance abuse patterns and problems."

Population: Age 19 and older.

Publication Dates: 1995–1996.

Acronym: PEI-A.

Scores, 37: Problem Severity Scales (Personal Involvement with Drugs, Physiological Dependence, Effects of Use, Social Benefits of Use, Personal Consequences of Use, Recreational Use, Transsituational Use, Psychological Benefits of Use, Preoccupation, Loss of Control, Infrequency—1, Self-Deception, Social Desirability—1, Treatment Receptiveness), Psychosocial Scales (Negative Self-Image, Psychological Disturbance, Social Isolation, Uncontrolled, Rejecting Convention, Deviant Behavior, Absence of Goals, Spiritual Isolation, Peer Drug Use, Interpersonal Pathology, Estrangement in the Home, Infrequency—2, Social Desirability—2), Problem Screens (Suicide Risk, Work Environment Risk, Past Family Pathology, Other Impulse-Related Problems, Significant Other Drug Problem, Sexual Abuse Perpetrator, Physical Abuse Perpetrator, Physical/Sexual Abuse Victim, Need for Psychiatric Referral, Miscellaneous).

Administration: Group.

Parts, 2: Problem Severity Scales, Psychosocial Scales.

Price Data, 2015: $193 per kit for 5-use CD, 5 PC booklets and manual (1996, 100 pages); $426.50 per 25-use scoring CD (PC with Windows); $31 per 10 PC answer booklets for use with computer CD; $68.50 per manual.

Time: (45–60) minutes.

Comments: Untimed self-report inventory; computer scored only.
Author: Ken C. Winters.
Publisher: Western Psychological Services.
Cross References: For reviews by Mark D. Shriver and Claudia R. Wright, see 13:225.

[1501]

Personal Experience Screening Questionnaire.

Purpose: "Designed as a brief screening tool to aid ... in the identification of teenagers likely to need a drug abuse assessment referral."
Population: Adolescents 12 to 18 years of age.
Publication Date: 1991.
Acronym: PESQ.
Scores, 3: Infrequency, Defensiveness, Problem Severity.
Administration: Group.
Price Data, 2015: $112.50 per complete kit including 25 AutoScore™ test forms and manual (30 pages); $50 per 25 AutoScore™ test forms; $68.50 per manual.
Time: (10) minutes.
Author: Ken C. Winters.
Publisher: Western Psychological Services.
Cross References: For reviews by Stuart N. Hart and Richard W. Johnson, see 12:286 (1 reference).

[1502]

Personal Experience Screening Questionnaire for Adults.

Purpose: Designed to "screen for the abuse of alcohol and other drugs by adults."
Population: Ages 19 and over.
Publication Date: 2003.
Acronym: PESQ-A.
Scores, 2: Problem Severity, Defensiveness.
Administration: Individual or group.
Price Data, 2016: $118 per kit including 25 Autoscore™ test forms and manual; $52.50 per 25 Autoscore™ test forms; $72 per manual.
Time: (10) minutes.
Comments: Self-report behavior inventory.
Author: Ken C. Winters.
Publisher: Western Psychological Services.
Cross References: For reviews by Jody L. Kulstad and William E. Martin, Jr., see 16:182.

[1503]

Personal History Checklist for Adolescents.

Purpose: To obtain historical information during routine intake procedures.
Population: Adolescent clients of mental health services.
Publication Date: 1989.

Scores: Item scores only.
Administration: Individual.
Manual: No manual.
Price Data, 2015: $62 per package of 25.
Time: Administration time not reported.
Comments: Can be completed by client or clinician.
Authors: Edward H. Dougherty and John A. Schinka.
Publisher: Psychological Assessment Resources, Inc.

[1504]

Personal History Checklist for Adults.

Purpose: To obtain historical information during routine intake procedures.
Population: Adult clients of mental health services.
Publication Date: 1989.
Scores: Item scores only.
Administration: Individual.
Manual: No manual.
Price Data, 2015: $62 per package of 25.
Time: Administration time not reported.
Comments: Checklist can be completed by client or clinician.
Author: John A. Schinka.
Publisher: Psychological Assessment Resources, Inc.
Cross References: For a review by Thomas A. Widiger, see 11:285.

[1505]

Personal Inventory of Needs.

Purpose: Designed as a self-assessment tool to identify the strengths of basic needs.
Population: Employees.
Publication Date: 1990.
Scores, 3: Achievement, Affiliation, Power.
Administration: Group or individual.
Price Data, 2016: $195; quantity discounts available.
Time: [30] minutes administration; [30] minutes interpretation.
Comments: Self-administered, self-scored; based on David McClelland's research at MIT; now sold as part of the Training House Assessment Kit.
Author: Training House, Inc.
Publisher: HRD Press, Inc.
Cross References: For reviews by Gary J. Dean and Trenton R. Ferro, see 12:287.

[1506]

Personal Opinion Matrix.

Purpose: Surveys the impressions and reactions of those who are managed.
Population: Employees.
Publication Dates: 1977-1983.
Scores, 2: Managerial Review, Climate.
Administration: Group.
Manual: No manual.

Price Data: Available from publisher.
Time: Administration time not reported.
Comments: Self-administered survey.
Author: Jay Hall.
Publisher: Teleometrics International, Inc.
Cross References: For a review by Gregory H. Dobbins, see 10:276 (7 references).

[1507]
Personal Orientation Dimensions.

Purpose: Designed to "measure attitudes and values in terms of concepts of the actualizing person."
Population: High school, college, and adults.
Publication Dates: 1975–1977.
Acronym: POD.
Scores, 13: Orientation (Time Orientation, Core Centeredness), Polarities (Strength, Weakness, Anger, Love), Integration (Synergistic Integration, Potentiation), Awareness (Being, Trust in Humanity, Creative Living, Mission, Manipulation Awareness).
Administration: Group.
Price Data, 2016: $30.25 per 25 reusable test booklets; $20.25 per 50 answer sheets (machine-scoring) [$199.50 per 500]; $12.50 per specimen set including manual and one copy of all forms; $6.75 per manual.
Time: (40) minutes.
Comments: A refinement and extension of concepts first measured by the Personal Orientation Inventory (1508); self-administering.
Author: Everett L. Shostrom.
Publisher: EdITS/Educational and Industrial Testing Service.
Cross References: For reviews by Gloria Maccow and Claudia R. Wright, see 14:285; see also T5:1938 (1 reference) and T4:1977 (1 reference).

[1508]
Personal Orientation Inventory.

Purpose: Designed as a "measure of values and behavior seen to be of importance in the development of the self-actualizing person."
Population: High school, college, and adults.
Publication Dates: 1962–1996.
Acronym: POI.
Scores, 12: Time Ratio, Support Ratio, Self-Actualizing Value, Existentiality, Feeling Reactivity, Spontaneity, Self-Regard, Self-Acceptance, Nature of Man, Synergy, Acceptance of Aggression, Capacity for Intimate Contact.
Administration: Group.
Price Data, 2016: $30.25 per 25 reusable test booklets; $20.50 per 50 answer sheets (hand-scoring); $20.50 per 50 answer sheets (machine-scoring for ERAS processing); $17.75 per 50 profile sheets; $60.50 per hand-scoring stencils (set of 14); $33 per handbook for the POI; $7.75 per manual; $12.75 per specimen set including a manual and one copy of all forms.

Foreign Language Editions: Available in Spanish and French.
Time: (30–40) minutes.
Comments: Self-administered.
Author: Everett L. Shostrum.
Publisher: EdITS/Educational and Industrial Testing Service.
Cross References: See T5:1939 (15 references), T4:1978 (42 references), 9:943 (24 references), and T3:1789 (98 references); for an excerpted review by Donald J. Tosi and Cathy A. Lindamood, see 8:641 (433 references); see also T2:1315 (80 references); for reviews by Bruce Bloxom and Richard W. Coan, see 7:121 (97 references); see also P:193 (26 references).

[1509]
Personal Problems Checklist—Adult.

Purpose: "To facilitate the rapid assessment of an individual's problems as seen from that person's point of view."
Population: Adults.
Publication Date: 1985.
Scores: 13 areas: Social, Appearance, Vocational, Family and Home, School, Finances, Religion, Emotions, Sex, Legal, Health and Habits, Attitude, Crises.
Administration: Individual or group.
Manual: No manual.
Price Data, 2015: $62 per package of 25.
Time: (10) minutes.
Author: John A. Schinka.
Publisher: Psychological Assessment Resources, Inc.
Cross References: See T5:1941 (1 reference); for a review by Harold R. Keller, see 10:278.

[1510]
Personal Problems Checklist for Adolescents.

Purpose: "To identify relevant problems, establish rapport, and provide written documentation of presenting problems consistent with community standards of care."
Population: Adolescents.
Publication Dates: 1985–1989.
Acronym: PPC.
Scores: 13 problem areas: Social and Friends, Appearance, Job, Parents, Family and Home, School, Money, Religion, Emotions, Dating and Sex, Health and Habits, Attitudes and Opinions, Crises.
Administration: Individual or group.
Manual: No manual.
Price Data, 2015: $62 per package of 25.
Time: (10–20) minutes.
Comments: Adolescent version of the Personal Problems Checklist (1509).
Author: John A. Schinka.
Publisher: Psychological Assessment Resources, Inc.
Cross References: See T5:1942 (1 reference); for reviews by Brian K. Martens and Toni E. Santmire, see 10:279.

[1511]

Personal Reaction Index.

Purpose: Assesses how people feel regarding the aspects of their work environment.
Population: Employees.
Publication Dates: 1974-1995.
Scores, 6: Degree of Participation, Feelings of Satisfaction, Feelings of Responsibility, Feelings of Commitment, Feelings of Frustration, Perceived Decision Quality.
Administration: Group.
Manual: No manual.
Price Data: Available from publisher.
Time: Administration time not reported.
Comments: Self-administered survey.
Author: Jay Hall.
Publisher: Teleometrics International, Inc.
Cross References: For reviews by Ralph M. Alexander and Daniel G. Spencer, see 9:946.

[1512]

Personal Stress Assessment Inventory.

Purpose: A self-assessment instrument designed to identify those who would most likely benefit from participation in stress-management training.
Population: Adults.
Publication Dates: 1981–1993.
Acronym: PSAI.
Scores, 6: Predisposition, Resilience, Sources of Stress, Overall Stress Factor, Health Symptoms, Personal Reactions.
Administration: Group or individual.
Price Data, 2016: $10.95 per inventory; minimum of 20 (volume discounts available).
Time: (20–30) minutes.
Comments: Self-administered; self-scored.
Author: Herbert S. Kindler.
Publisher: The Center for Management Effectiveness, Inc.
Cross References: For reviews by E. Scott Huebner and Norman D. Sundberg, see 14:286.

[1513]

Personal Stress Navigator.

Purpose: "Samples the magnitude and types of stress [and stress symptoms] experienced by the respondent and assesses relative vulnerability to stress."
Population: Adults.
Publication Dates: 1983-1987.
Scores, 16: Situational (Family, Individual Roles, Social Being, Environment, Financial, Work/School), Symptom (Muscular System, Parasympathetic Nervous System, Sympathetic Nervous System, Emotional, Cognitive System, Endocrine, Immune System), Vulnerability, Total Situational Stress, Total Symptoms.
Administration: Group.

Price Data: Available from publisher.
Time: [20-30] minutes.
Authors: Lyle H. Miller, Alma Dell Smith, and Bruce L. Mehler (manual only).
Publisher: Stress Directions, Inc.
Cross References: For a review by Rolf A. Peterson of an earlier version titled Stress Audit, see 10:347.

[1514]

Personal Style Assessment.

Purpose: To assess an individual's personal style of communication.
Population: Adults.
Publication Dates: 1980–1987.
Scores, 4: Thinker, Intuitor, Sensor, Feeler.
Administration: Group.
Manual: No manual.
Price Data, 2016: $59.95; quantity discounts available.
Time: (15–25) minutes.
Comments: Self-administered, self-scored.
Author: Training House, Inc.
Publisher: HRD Press, Inc.
Cross References: For reviews by Cathy W. Hall and Gerald L. Stone, see 11:287.

[1515]

Personal Style Assessment, Jung-Parry Form.

Purpose: To assess an individual's relative strength on Jung's four personal styles, or "psychological types."
Population: Adults.
Publication Date: 1992.
Scores, 4: Thinker, Intuitor, Sensor, Feeler.
Administration: Group or individual.
Manual: No manual.
Price Data, 2016: $59.95; quantity discounts available.
Time: (20–30) minutes.
Comments: Self-administered; self-scored.
Author: Scott B. Parry.
Publisher: HRD Press, Inc.
Cross References: For a review by Vicki S. Packman, see 13:227.

[1516]

Personal Style Indicator [Revised].

Purpose: Designed to increase mutual understanding, acceptance, and communication among people and to increase self-awareness.
Population: Ages 15 years–adults.
Publication Dates: 1988-2006.
Acronym: PSI.
Scores, 4: Behavioral/Action, Cognitive/Analysis, Interpersonal/Harmony, Affective/Expression.
Administration: Individual or group.

Price Data, 2016: $25 per test booklet (2006, 20 pages); $20 per In-Depth Interpretations booklet (2006, 28 pages); $45 per online version; $75 per Professional's Guide (2006, 64 pages); $40 per Trainer's Guidelines (1996, 70 pages); $30 per participant workbook Building Relationships With Style (2006, 68 pages).
Foreign Language Editions: Available online in Chinese, Indonesian, and Spanish, and in print in Arabic, Danish, Dutch, French, Japanese, Spanish, Swedish, and Vietnamese; the In-Depth interpretations booklet is available in Dutch, French, Japanese, Spanish, Swedish, and Vietnamese.
Time: [90] minutes; [180-720] minutes advanced.
Comments: Self-administered and self-scored.
Authors: Ken Keis, Terry D. Anderson, and Everett T. Robinson.
Publisher: Consulting Resource Group International, Inc.
Cross References: For a review by Gypsy M. Denzine, see 17:144; for reviews by James T. Austin and Kusum Singh of an earlier edition, see 13:228.

[1517]

Personal Styles Inventory [PSI-120] [1999 Revision].

Purpose: Designed to provide a comprehensive assessment of nonpathological personality characteristics in multiple report formats, both graphic and verbal.
Population: Individuals with at least an eighth-grade reading level.
Publication Dates: 1990–2005.
Acronym: PSI-120.
Scores, 24: Styles of Expressing Emotions (Sympathetic, Enthusiastic, Expansive, Confronting, Self-Willed, Reserved, Modest, Patient), Styles of Doing Things (Agreeing, Sociable, Excitement-Seeking, Venturing, Restless, Self-Directed, Self-Motivated, Organizing), Styles of Thinking (Traditional, Dedicated, Imaginative, Inquiring, Individualistic, Analytical, Practical, Focused).
Administration: Group or individual.
Price Data, 2016: $19.95 per single use (packages available).
Time: (10) minutes.
Comments: Administered online.
Authors: Joseph T. Kunce, Corrine S. Cope, and Russel M. Newton.
Publisher: Educational & Psychological Consultants, LLC.
Cross References: For reviews by Frederick Medway and Janet Smith, see 17:145; see also T5:1954 (1 reference); for reviews by Paul A. Arbisi and Mary Henning-Stout of an earlier edition, see 13:229 (2 references); see also T4:1993 (4 references).

[1518]

Personal Values Questionnaire.

Purpose: Measures individuals' "values related to achievement, affiliation, and power."
Population: Adults.
Publication Date: 1993.
Acronym: PVQ.
Scores, 3: Achievement, Affiliation, Power.
Administration: Individual.
Price Data, 2016: $152 per complete kit including 10 questionnaires and 10 profiles and interpretive notes (11 pages).
Time: [30] minutes.
Comments: Self-scored profile; also available online.
Author: Hay Group.
Publisher: Hay Group.
Cross References: For reviews by Brian F. Bolton and Gary J. Dean, see 13:230.

[1519]

Personality Adjective Check List.

Purpose: "Developed primarily as a self-report instrument for measuring personality in normal adults."
Population: Ages 16-adult.
Publication Dates: 1986-2013.
Acronym: PACL.
Scores, 9: Introversive, Inhibited, Cooperative, Sociable, Confident, Forceful, Respectful, Sensitive, PI (indicator of potential personality problems).
Administration: Individual or group.
Price Data, 2015: $50 per manual, including review-only copy of the PDACL form; $2 per Remote Online Survey License (minimum 50); $2 License to Reproduce.
Time: (10-15) minutes.
Comments: Conceived as a tool for measuring the personality styles outlined by Theodore Millon among counseling clients and normal adults.
Author: Stephen Strack.
Publisher: Mind Garden, Inc.
Cross References: See T5:1958 (1 reference); for reviews by Allen K. Hess and Howard M. Knoff, see 12:289 (1 reference); see also T4:1996 (3 references).

[1520]

Personality Advantage Questionnaire.

Purpose: Designed to "identify personality strengths, and set those strengths in a work context."
Population: Employees.
Publication Date: 1998.
Acronym: PAQ.
Scores, 5: Communication Style, Emotions, Drive and Determination, Relationships with People, Thinking Style.
Administration: Individual.
Manual: No manual.
Price Data, 2016: $195; quantity discounts available.

Time: Administration time not reported.
Comments: Now sold as part of the Training House Assessment Kit.
Author: Human Resource Development Press.
Publisher: HRD Press, Inc.

[1521]

Personality Assessment Inventory-Adolescent.

Purpose: An "objective test of personality designed to provide information on critical client variables in professional settings."
Population: Ages 12-18.
Publication Dates: 1990-2007.
Acronym: PAI-A.
Scores, 53: Somatic Complaints (Conversion, Somatization, Health Concerns, Total), Anxiety (Cognitive, Affective, Physiological, Total), Anxiety-Related Disorders (Obsessive-Compulsive, Phobias, Traumatic Stress, Total), Depression (Cognitive, Affective, Physiological, Total), Mania (Activity Level, Grandiosity, Irritability, Total), Paranoia (Hypervigilance, Persecution, Resentment, Total), Schizophrenia (Psychotic Experiences, Social Detachment, Thought Disorder, Total), Borderline Features (Affective Instability, Identity Problems, Negative Relationships, Self-Harm, Total), Antisocial Features (Antisocial behaviors, Egocentricity, Stimulus-Seeking, Total), Alcohol Problems, Drug Problems, Aggression (Aggressive Attitude, Verbal Aggression, Physical Aggression, Total), Suicidal Ideation, Stress, Nonsupport, Treatment Rejection, Dominance, Warmth, Inconsistency, Infrequency, Negative Impression, Positive Impression.
Administration: Group.
Price Data, 2015: $328 per complete kit including professional manual (2007, 190 pages), 2 reusable item booklets, 2 administration folios, 25 hand-scored answer sheets, 25 profile forms-adolescent, and 25 critical items forms-adolescent; $37 per reusable item booklet; $44 per 10 soft cover item booklets; $58 per 25 hand-scored answer sheets; $41 per 25 profile forms-adolescent; $35 per 25 critical items forms-adolescent; $78 per professional manual.
Time: 45(55) minutes.
Comments: Designed to complement its parent instrument, the Personality Assessment Inventory (1522).
Author: Leslie C. Morey.
Publisher: Psychological Assessment Resources, Inc.
Cross References: For reviews by H. Dennis Kade and Jonathan Sandoval, see 18:92.

[1522]

Personality Assessment Inventory [2007 Professional Manual].

Purpose: Designed to provide information relevant to clinical diagnosis, treatment planning, and screening for psychopathology.

Population: Ages 18 and over.
Publication Dates: 1991-2007.
Acronym: PAI.
Scores, 54: Somatic Complaints (Conversion, Somatization, Health Concerns, Total), Anxiety (Cognitive, Affective, Physiological, Total), Anxiety-Related Disorders (Obsessive-Compulsive, Phobias, Traumatic Stress, Total), Depression (Cognitive, Affective, Physiological, Total), Mania (Activity Level, Grandiosity, Irritability, Total), Paranoia (Hypervigilance, Persecution, Resentment, Total), Schizophrenia (Psychotic Experiences, Social Detachment, Thought Disorder, Total), Borderline Features (Affective Instability, Identity Problems, Negative Relationships, Self-Harm, Total), Antisocial Features (Antisocial Behaviors, Egocentricity, Stimulus-Seeking, Total), Alcohol Problems, Drug Problems, Aggression (Aggressive Attitude, Verbal Aggression, Physical Aggression, Total), Suicidal Ideation, Stress, Nonsupport, Treatment Rejection, Dominance, Warmth, Inconsistency, Infrequency, Negative Impression, Positive Impression.
Administration: Group.
Price Data, 2015: $328 per complete kit including professional manual, 2nd Ed., 2 reusable item booklets, 2 administration folios, 25 hand-scored answer sheets, 25 adult profile forms-revised, and 25 critical item forms-revised; $44 per 10 item booklets; $37 per reusable item booklet; $58 per 25 hand-scored answer sheets; $41 per 25 adult profile forms-revised; $37 per 25 college profile forms; $35 per 25 critical item forms-revised; $78 per professional manual, 2nd Ed.; $37 per administration folio.
Time: 55(75) minutes.
Author: Leslie C. Morey.
Publisher: Psychological Assessment Resources, Inc.
Cross References: For reviews by Andrew A. Cox and by Geoffrey L. Thorpe and Rachel D. Burrows, see 18:93; see T5:1959 (8 references); for reviews of a previous edition by Gregory J. Boyle and Michael G. Kavan, see 12:290 (8 references); see also T4:1997 (3 references).

[1523]

Personality Assessment Screener.

Purpose: "Designed to identify individuals in need of further assessment for emotional problems, behavioral problems, or both."
Population: Ages 18 and older.
Publication Dates: 1991–1997.
Acronym: PAS.
Scores, 11: Negative Affect, Acting Out, Health Problems, Psychotic Features, Social Withdrawal, Hostile Control, Suicidal Thinking, Alienation, Alcohol Problem, Anger Control, Total.
Administration: Individual or group.
Price Data, 2015: $148 per complete kit including manual (1997, 69 pages) and 50 hand-scorable response forms.
Time: (5) minutes.

Comments: Screening version of the Personality Assessment Inventory (1522).
Author: Leslie C. Morey.
Publisher: Psychological Assessment Resources, Inc.
Cross References: For a review by Matthew Burns, see 14:288.

[1524]
Personality Disorder Adjective Check List.
Purpose: Designed as a self-report instrument to measure personality disorders.
Population: Ages 18-79.
Publication Date: 2008.
Acronym: PDACL.
Scores, 20: Schizoid, Avoidant, Depressive, Dependent, Histrionic, Narcissistic, Antisocial, Aggressive, Compulsive, Passive-Aggressive (Negativistic), Self-Defeating, Schizotypal, Borderline, Paranoid, plus 6 Validity Scales: Random Index, Number of Adjectives Checked, Number of Positive Adjectives Endorsed, Number of Negative Adjectives Endorsed, Response Consistency, Response Inconsistency.
Administration: Individual or group.
Price Data, 2016: $50 per PDF manual (182 pages) including review-only copy of form; $60 per paper manual; $2 per Remote Online Survey License or License to Reproduce (minimum 50).
Foreign Language Edition: Available in Spanish.
Time: (5-7) minutes.
Comments: Based on DSM-IV criteria.
Author: Robert J. Craig.
Publisher: Mind Garden, Inc.

[1525]
Personality Disorder Interview-IV: A Semi-structured Interview for the Assessment of Personality Disorders.
Purpose: Constructed to "facilitate reliable and valid interview assessments of DSM-IV personality disorders."
Population: Ages 18 and older.
Publication Date: 1995.
Acronym: PDI—IV.
Scores, 21: 12 Personality Disorder Scores (Antisocial, Avoidant, Borderline, Dependent, Histrionic, Narcissistic, Obsessive-Compulsive, Paranoid, Schizoid, Schizotypal, Depressive, Passive-Aggressive); 9 Thematic Content Area Scores (Attitudes Toward Self, Attitudes Toward Others, Security/Comfort with Others, Friendships and Relationships, Conflicts and Disagreements, Work and Leisure, Social Norms, Mood, Appearance and Perception).
Administration: Individual.
Price Data: This test is now available for free from the publisher.
Time: [120] minutes.
Comments: Corresponds with DSM—IV Personality Disorder diagnosis criteria.

Authors: Thomas A. Widiger, Steve Mangine, Elizabeth M. Corbitt, Cynthia G. Ellis, and Glenn V. Thomas.
Publisher: Thomas Widiger.
Cross References: For reviews by Samuel Juni and Paul Retzlaff, see 14:289.

[1526]
Personality Inventory for Children, Second Edition.
Purpose: "Assesses both broad and narrow dimensions of behavioral, emotional, cognitive, and interpersonal adjustment."
Population: Ages 5–19 years (Kindergarten–Grade 12).
Publication Dates: 1977–2001.
Acronym: PIC-2.
Administration: Group.
Forms, 2: Standard Form, Behavioral Summary.
Price Data, 2016: $262.50 per hand scoring kit including manual, 2 reusable administration booklets, 50 answer sheets, set of scoring templates, 25 behavioral summary autoscore forms, 50 standard form profile sheets, 50 critical items summary sheets; $550.50 per computer scoring and interpretation kit including manual, 2 reusable administration booklets, 50 answer sheets, 25 use scoring and interpretation CD; $262.50 per computer scoring kit including manual, 2 reusable administration booklets, 50 answer sheets, 25-use PIC-2/PIY/SBS scoring CD; $38 per reusable administration booklet; $28 per 100 answer sheets; $48 per 25 behavioral summary auto score answer forms; $28 per 100 standard profile (male and female); 28 per 100 critical items summary sheet (male and female); $75 per manual; $50.50 per scoring templates.
Foreign Language Editions: Spanish editions available for both forms.
Comments: Complete revision and restandardization of Personality Inventory for Children, Revised (PIC-R); old edition no longer available; coordinates with Personality Inventory for Youth (PIY, 1526) and Student Behavior Survey (SBS, 1991).
Authors: David Lachar and Christian P. Gruber.
Publisher: Western Psychological Services.

    a) STANDARD FORM.
    Scores, 33: 9 Adjustment Scales and 21 Adjustment Subscales: Cognitive Impairment (Inadequate Abilities, Poor Achievement, Developmental Delay), Impulsivity and Distractibility (Disruptive Behavior, Fearlessness), Delinquency (Antisocial Behavior, Dyscontrol, Noncompliance), Family Dysfunction (Conflict Among Members, Parent Maladjustment), Reality Distortion (Developmental Deviation, Hallucinations and Delusions), Somatic Concern (Psychosomatic Preoccupation, Muscular Tension and Anxiety), Psychological Discomfort (Fear and Worry, Depression, Sleep Disturbance/Preoccupation with Death), Social Withdrawal (Social Introversion, Isolation), Social Skill Deficits (Limited Peer Status, Conflict With Peers), 3 Response Validity Scales (Defensiveness, Dissimulation, Inconsistency).

Price Data: $28 per 100 Standard Form profiles or 100 Critical Items summary sheets.
Time: (40) minutes.
b) BEHAVIORAL SUMMARY.
Scores, 12: 8 Short Adjustment Scales (Impulsivity and Distractibility—Short, Delinquency—Short, Family Dysfunction—Short, Reality Distortion—Short, Somatic Concern—Short, Psychological Discomfort—Short, Social Withdrawal—Short, Social Skill Deficits—Short), 3 Composite Scales (Externalization—Composite, Internalization—Composite, Adjustment—Composite), Total Score.
Price Data: $48 per 25 Behavioral Summary AutoScore answer forms including Behavioral Summary profiles.
Time: (15) minutes.
Comments: "A quick screening version of the Standard Form; focuses on current behavior that can support the development of a treatment plan; can be administered using standard PIC-2 test materials."
Cross References: For reviews by Radhika Krishnamurthy and Susana Urbina, see 16:183; see T5:1962 (23 references) and T4:1998 (21 references); for a review by Howard M. Knoff of an earlier edition, see 10:281 (20 references); for reviews by Cecil R. Reynolds and June M. Tuma of an earlier edition, see 9:949 (5 references); see also T3:1796 (5 references).

[1527]
Personality Inventory for Youth.
Purpose: "Assesses emotional and behavioral adjustment, family character and interaction, and school adjustment and academic ability."
Population: Ages 9–19.
Publication Date: 1995.
Acronym: PIY.
Scores, 37: Validity, Inconsistency, Dissimulation, Defensiveness, Cognitive Impairment (Poor Achievement and Memory, Inadequate Abilities, Learning Problems, Total), Impulsivity and Distractibility (Brashness, Distractibility and Overactivity, Impulsivity, Total), Delinquency (Antisocial Behavior, Dyscontrol, Noncompliance, Total), Family Dysfunction (Parent-Child Conflict, Parent Maladjustment, Marital Discord, Total), Reality Distortion (Feelings of Alienation, Hallucinations and Delusions, Total), Somatic Concern (Psychosomatic Syndrome, Muscular Tension and Anxiety, Preoccupation with Disease, Total), Psychological Discomfort (Fear and Worry, Depression, Sleep Disturbance, Total), Social Withdrawal (Social Introversion, Isolation, Total), Social Skill Deficits (Limited Peer Status, Conflict with Peers, Total).
Administration: Group.
Price Data, 2015: $310 per complete kit including administration and interpretation guide, technical guide, 100 answer sheets, 1 set of scoring templates, 100 profile forms (male and female), 100 critical items summary sheets (male and female), 2 reusable administration booklets, and audio CD; $36 per reusable administration booklet; $32.50 per 5 Spanish Edition reusable administration booklets; $32.50 per 100 answer sheets; $32.50 per 100

profile forms; $32.50 per 100 critical items summary sheets; $310 per 25-use computer scoring kit (PC with Microsoft Windows); $44.50 per set of scoring templates; $20.50 per audio CD; $63 per administration and interpretation guide; $63 per technical guide; $125 manual (administration and interpretation guide and technical guide).
Foreign Language Edition: Spanish version available.
Time: (45) minutes; (15) minutes for screener.
Comments: First 80 items can be used as screening measure.
Authors: David Lachar and Christian P. Gruber.
Publisher: Western Psychological Services.
Cross References: For reviews by Lizanne DeStefano and by Gregory J. Marchant and T. Andrew Ridenour, see 13:231.

[1528]
Personality Research Form, 3rd Edition.
Purpose: Designed as an "extensively validated comprehensive measure of normal personality."
Population: Grade 6-college, adults.
Publication Dates: 1964-1997.
Acronym: PRF.
Administration: Group or individual.
Forms, 5: A, B, AA, BB, and E (Form E sent out unless specified; contact publisher for availability and prices of other forms).
Price Data, 2015: $97 per examination kit including manual on CD (1984, 72 pages), 5 reusable test booklets, 5 hand-scorable answer sheets, 5 profile sheets, scoring template, and one machine-scorable answer sheet and coupon for an Extended Report; $25 per test manual on CD; $65 per 25 reusable test booklets; $55 per 25 hand-scorable answer sheets; $55 per 25 profile sheets; $24 per scoring template; $97–$107 (depending on volume) per 10 machine-scorable answer sheets and coupons for Mail-in Extended Report; $67–$77 (depending on volume) per 10 machine-scorable answer sheets and coupons for Mail-in Basic Report; $155 per software installation package, includes 10 coupons for computer reports; $12-$20 (depending on volume) per online password.
Foreign Language Editions: Spanish booklets available. French booklets and online administration available at test publisher's website.
Comments: Online scoring available.
Author: Douglas N. Jackson.
Publisher: SIGMA Assessment Systems, Inc.
a) FORM A.
Population: Ages 16-adult.
Publication Dates: 1965-1985.
Scores, 15: Achievement, Affiliation, Aggression, Autonomy, Dominance, Endurance, Exhibition, Harmavoidance, Impulsivity, Nurturance, Order, Play, Social Recognition, Understanding, Infrequency.
Time: (30-45) minutes.

b) FORM B.

Comments: Parallel form to Form A.

c) FORM AA.

Population: College students.

Publication Dates: 1965-1985.

Scores, 22: Same as Form A and Form B plus Abasement, Change, Cognitive Structure, Defendence, Sentience, Succorance, Desirability.

Time: (40-70) minutes.

d) FORM BB.

Comments: Parallel form to Form AA.

e) FORM E.

Population: Grade 6-adult.

Publication Dates: 1974-1987.

Scores, 22: Same as Form AA.

Time: 45 minutes.

Cross References: See T5:1965 (86 references) and T4:2000 (45 references); for reviews by Robert Hogan and Jerry S. Wiggins, see 10:282 (68 references); see also 9:950 (42 references) and T3:1798 (116 references); for a review by Robert Hogan of an earlier edition, see 8:643 (132 references); see also T3:1322 (23 references); for reviews by Anne Anastasi, E. Lowell Kelly, and Jerry Wiggins, and excerpted reviews by John O. Crites, Lonnie D. Valentine, Jr., and Ruth Wessler with Jane Loevinger of an earlier edition, see 7:123 (27 references); see also P:201 (13 references).

[1529]

Personalized Achievement Summary System.

Purpose: Designed to provide information useful for monitoring academic progress, selecting curriculum and evaluating and planning instructional programming in home school settings.

Population: Grades 3–8.

Publication Dates: 1987–2006.

Acronym: P.A.S.S.

Scores, 20: Reading (Word Meaning, Literal Comprehension, Interpretive Comprehension, Evaluative Comprehension, Total); Mathematics (Numeration and Number Systems, Fractions, Decimals/Percent/and Currency, Geometry and Measurement, Graphs/Charts/and Statistics, Word Problems and Problem Solving, Computation, Total); Language Usage (Grammar, Capitalization, Punctuation, Composition, Study Skills, Spelling, Total).

Administration: Individual.

Price Data, 2015: $36; volume discounts available.

Time: Untimed.

Comments: Items licensed from the Portland (Oregon) Public Schools.

Author: Hewitt Research Foundation.

Publisher: Hewitt Research Foundation.

Cross References: For reviews by Douglas F. Kauffman and Michael S. Trevisan, see 16:185.

[1530]

Personalysis®.

Purpose: Constructed "to inventory personality characteristics of individuals at five different levels" yielding information on "how to maximize personal, interpersonal, and group effectiveness in the work place."

Population: Leaders, employees, families, individuals.

Publication Dates: 1975–2001.

Scores, 32: Preferred Style—Rational Self (Authoritative, Democratic, Structured, Self Directed), Communication Expectations—Socialized Self (Direction, Involvement, Methodology, Input), Motivational Needs—Instinctive Self (Authority, Influence, Control, Understanding), Defensive Self (Coerce, Provoke, Resist, Reject), Irrational Self (Hostile, Rebellious, Stubborn, Withdrawn); Act, Adapt, Analyze, and Assess scores for Preferred Style—Rational Self, Back-Up Style—Socialized Self, and Functional Stress—Instinctive.

Administration: Individual or group.

Price Data: Available from publisher.

Time: Untimed.

Comments: Self-administered; available online only to certified practitioners.

Author: James R. Noland.

Publisher: Personalysis Corporation.

Cross References: For reviews by Jack Gebart-Eaglemont and S. Alvin Leung, see 16:186; for reviews by George Engelhard, Jr. and L. Alan Witt of an earlier edition, see 12:291.

[1531]

Personnel Assessment Form.

Purpose: To measure mental ability and intelligence for employee selection and placement planning.

Population: Ages 16 and older.

Publication Dates: 2004–2006.

Acronym: PAF.

Scores, 3: Verbal Subtest Score, Quantitative Subtest Score, Total Score.

Subtest: Verbal Subtest, Quantitative Subtest.

Administration: Group and individual.

Forms, 2: A, C.

Price Data, 2015: $25 per manual; $6 per Form A test booklet or Form C test booklet; $15-$20 (depending on volume) per report via fax-in scoring or online administration.

Time: 14 minutes.

Comments: The PAF is available through fax-in scoring and online administration at www.sigmatesting.com.

Author: Douglas N. Jackson.

Publisher: SIGMA Assessment Systems, Inc.

Cross References: For reviews by Jean P. Kirnan and James W. Pinkney, see 17:146.

[1532]

Personnel Reaction Blank.

Purpose: A personality-based integrity test to help in hiring trustworthy, dependable employees.

Population: Ages 15 to adult.

Publication Dates: 1972–2003.

Acronym: PRB.

Scores, 5: Personality Reliability Index, which is a composite of 4 subscales: Sense of Well-Being, Positive Background Indicators, Compliance with Rules and Routines, Conventional Occupational Preferences.

Administration: Group or individual.

Price Data: Available from publisher.

Time: 15 minutes.

Comments: In addition to the scores, the report produces a narrative statement for each score that describes typical behavior of low scorers and high scorers; the summary page of the report provides item responses and number of missing responses for each scale; administered via paper and pencil or online.

Authors: Harrison G. Gough, Richard Arvey, and Pamela Bradley.

Publisher: Institute for Personality and Ability Testing, Inc. (IPAT).

Cross References: For a review by Donna L. Sundre of an earlier version, see 13:232.

[1533]

Personnel Relations Survey [Revised].

Purpose: "Designed to assess the understanding and behavior of managers in their interpersonal relationships."

Population: Managers.

Publication Dates: 1967–2000.

Acronym: PRS.

Scores, 6: Relationships with Employees (Exposure, Feedback); Relationships with Colleagues (Exposure, Feedback); Relationships with Superiors (Exposure, Feedback).

Administration: Group.

Manual: Leader's Guide available.

Price Data, 2016: $12.95 per instrument.

Time: Administration time not reported.

Comments: Self-administered, self-scored; based on the Johari Window Model of interpersonal relationships.

Authors: Jay Hall and Martha S. Williams.

Publisher: Teleometrics International, Inc.

Cross References: For a review by Matthew E. Lambert, see 14:29.

[1534]

Personnel Selection Inventory.

Purpose: Helps identify job applicants who are likely to be honest and have positive attitudes toward work, safety and customer service and provides a valid, fair, and cost effective means of identifying applicants who are likely to be productive and responsible.

Population: Job applicants.

Publication Dates: 1975–1980.

Acronym: PSI.

Scores: 21 scales: Honesty, Supervision Attitudes, Tenure, Drug Avoidance Scale, Nonviolence Scale, Employee/Customer Relations Scale, Risk Avoidance Scale, Stress Tolerance Scale, Safety Scale, Work Values Scale, Math Scale, Responsibility, Productivity, Customer Service Aptitude Scale, Customer Service Attitude Scale, Sales Aptitude Scale, Customer Service Index, Candidness Validity Scale, Employability Index, Detailed Personal and Behavioral History.

Administration: Individual or group.

Forms: 20 versions available including non-integrity test versions.

Price Data: Available from publisher.

Time: Varies based on version.

Comments: Previously listed as London House Personnel Selection Inventory.

Author: General Dynamics Information Technology.

Publisher: General Dynamics Information Technology.

Cross References: See T5:1972 (1 reference) and T4:1478 (1 reference); for a review by William I. Sauser, see 9:631; see also T3:1339 (2 references).

[1535]

Personnel Test Battery.

Purpose: Designed to assess numerical skills, language proficiency, and perceptual accuracy.

Population: Office and sales groups.

Publication Dates: 1979–1981.

Acronym: PTB.

Subtests: Available as separates.

Administration: Group.

Levels, 2: 1, 2.

Restricted Distribution: Restricted to persons who have completed the publisher's training course or members of the Division of Occupational Psychology of the British Psychological Society.

Price Data: Available from publisher.

Authors: Peter Saville, Gill Nyfield, Roger Holdsworth (test), and Ruth Holdsworth (manual).

Publisher: CEB.

   a) LEVEL 1.

   Comments: "Basic skills and comprehension"; 3 tests plus 2 optional tests for Levels 1 and 2.

     1) Verbal Usage.

     Acronym: VPI.

     Time: 10(15) minutes.

     2) Numerical Comprehension.

     Acronym: NP2.

     Time: 7(12) minutes.

     3) Checking.

     Acronym: CP3.

     Time: 7(12) minutes.

     4) Basic Checking.

     Acronym: CP7.

     Time: 5(10) minutes.

     Comments: Optional test for Levels 1 and 2.

     5) Audio Checking.

     Acronym: CP8.

     Time: (15) minutes.

     Comments: Optional test for Levels 1 and 2; test administered by cassette tape.

b) LEVEL 2.
Comments: "Higher-order reasoning skills"; 3 tests plus 2 optional tests for Levels 1 and 2.
   1) *Classification.*
   Acronym: CP4.
   Time: 7(12) minutes.
   2) *Verbal Meaning.*
   Acronym: VP5.
   Time: 10(15) minutes.
   3) *Numerical Reasoning.*
   Acronym: NP6.
   Time: 10(15) minutes.

[1536]

Personnel Tests for Industry.

Purpose: To assist in the selection, placement, training, and promotion of individuals in industrial settings.
Population: Trade school and adults.
Publication Dates: 1945–1995.
Acronym: PTI.
Scores: Total score only.
Administration: Group or individual.
Publisher: Pearson.
   a) PTI-VERBAL TEST.
   Publication Dates: 1952–1969.
   Acronym: PTI-V.
   Forms, 2: A, B.
   Price Data, 2016: $158 per 25 test booklets (specify Form A or B); $523 per 100 test booklets.
   Time: 5(15) minutes.
   Author: Alexander G. Wesman.
   b) PTI-NUMERICAL TEST.
   Publication Dates: 1952–1969.
   Acronym: PTI-N.
   Forms, 2: A, B.
   Price Data: Same as for *a* above.
   Time: 20(25) minutes.
   Author: Jerome E. Doppelt.
   c) PTI-ORAL DIRECTIONS TEST.
   Publication Dates: 1945–1995.
   Acronym: PTI-ODT.
   Comments: For information on revision of this subtest, see 1537.
   Author: Charles R. Langmuir.
Cross References: See T5:1974 (1 reference), T4:2008 (5 references), T3:1808 (3 references), T2:433 (5 references), and 7:373 (3 references); for a review by Erwin K. Taylor, see 5:366; see also 4:309 (1 reference); for reviews by Charles D. Flory, Irving Lorge, and William W. Turnbull on the Oral Directions Test, see 3:245.

[1537]

Personnel Tests for Industry-Oral Directions Test [Second Edition].

Purpose: A test of general ability designed to "assess an individual's ability to follow directions presented orally" and as a selection tool "to predict performance in a variety of vocational and technical training settings."

Population: Adolescents and adults.
Publication Dates: 1974-1995.
Acronym: PTI-ODT.
Scores: Total score only.
Administration: Individual or group.
Forms, 2: S, T.
Price Data, 2015: $372 per complete set Form S including recording, manual (1995, 67 pages), script, key, 100 answer documents and directions for administering, and CD.
Time: (15) minutes.
Comments: Tape-recorded administration; one of three subtests of Personnel Tests for Industry.
Author: Charles R. Langmuir.
Publisher: Pearson.
Cross References: For reviews by Caroline M. Adkins and Bruce Biskin, see 17:147; for information for Personnel Tests for Industry, see T5:1974 (1 reference), T4:2008 (5 references), T3:1808 (3 references), T2:433 (5 references), and 7:373 (3 references); for a review by Erwin K. Taylor, see 5:366; see also 4:309 (1 reference); for reviews by Charles D. Flory, Irving Lorge, and William W. Turnbull of the Oral Directions Test, see 3:245.

[1538]

Pervasive Developmental Disorder in Mental Retardation Scale [Second Revised Edition].

Purpose: "A simple classification and screening instrument designed for the identification of Pervasive Developmental Disorders in persons with mental retardation/intellectual disability."
Population: Ages 2-80.
Publication Dates: 1990-2006.
Acronym: PDD-MRS.
Scores: Total score only.
Administration: Individual.
Price Data, 2016: €68 per manual; €96 per 75 record forms.
Foreign Language Editions: First published in Dutch; English, German, and Italian versions available.
Time: (10-20) minutes.
Comments: Norms of the scale are based on data of 1,230 children, adolescents, and adults in the profound, severe, moderate, and mild ranges of mental retardation.
Author: D. W. Kraijer.
Publisher: Hogrefe Ltd [United Kingdom].
Cross References: For a review by Tawnya Meadows, see 17:148.

[1539]

Pervasive Developmental Disorders Screening Test, Second Edition.

Purpose: Designed as "a clinical screening tool for autism (autistic disorder)/AD and other pervasive developmental disorders, such as pervasive developmental

disorder, not otherwise specified (PDD-NOS) and Asperger's Disorder."
Population: Ages 12 to 48 months.
Publication Date: 2004.
Acronym: PDDST-II.
Scores: Total score only.
Administration: Individual.
Forms, 3: Stage 1—Primary Care Screener, Stage 2—Developmental Clinic Screener, Stage 3—Autism Clinic Severity Screener.
Price Data, 2015: $176.30 per complete kit; $48.35 per 25 record forms (specify Stage 1, 2, or 3).
Time: (10–20) minutes.
Comments: Parent-report screening measure.
Author: Bryna Siegel.
Publisher: Pearson.
Cross References: For reviews by Mary (Rina) M. Chittooran and Theresa Volpe-Johnstone, see 17:149.

[1540]
Pharmacy College Admission Test.
Purpose: Developed to measure the abilities, aptitudes, and skills that pharmacy schools have deemed essential for success in basic pharmacy curricula.
Population: Pharmacy school applicants.
Publication Dates: 1974–2016.
Acronym: PCAT.
Scores, 7: Verbal Ability, Biology, Reading Comprehension, Quantitative Ability, Chemistry, Composite, Writing.
Administration: Group.
Restricted Distribution: Distribution restricted and test administered at testing centers; details may be obtained from publisher.
Price Data: Available from publisher.
Time: 235 minutes.
Author: Pearson.
Publisher: Pearson.
Cross References: For reviews by Mark Albanese and Leo M. Harvill of an earlier edition (1993-94), see 13:233.

[1541]
Phelps Kindergarten Readiness Scale [2012 Restandardization].
Purpose: Designed to assess the academic readiness of children preparing to enroll in kindergarten.
Population: Children in prekindergarten and early kindergarten.
Publication Dates: 1991-2012.
Acronym: PKRS.
Scores, 4: Verbal Processing, Perceptual Processing, Auditory Processing, Total Readiness.
Administration: Individual.
Price Data, 2015: $15 per manual (2012, 48 pages); $4.29 per test set including perceptual processing booklet and record booklet; volume discounts available.

Foreign Language Edition: Spanish version available.
Time: (20) minutes.
Comments: Designed to be administered from the spring before a child enters kindergarten (mid-March) until the following fall (mid-November).
Authors: LeAdelle Phelps.
Publisher: Psychology Press, Inc.
Cross References: Reviews are scheduled for *The Twentieth Mental Measurements Yearbook*. For a review by Theresa H. Elofson of an earlier edition, see 12:292.

[1542]
Phonics-Based Reading Test.
Purpose: "Designed to assess reading skills" and "To measure an individual's ability to apply phonics concepts when reading single words and connected text."
Population: Ages 6-0 through 12-11.
Publication Date: 2002.
Acronym: PRT.
Scores, 4: Decoding, Fluency, Comprehension, Total Reading Standard Score.
Administration: Individual.
Price Data, 2015: $105 per test kit including manual (109 pages), stimulus book, and 25 student test booklets, in portfolio; $30 per stimulus book; $35 per 25 student test booklets; $40 per manual.
Time: (20–30) minutes.
Comments: Norm- and criterion-referenced.
Author: Rick Brownell.
Publisher: Academic Therapy Publications.
Cross References: For reviews by Karen Mackler and Annita Marie Ward, see 16:187.

[1543]
Phonological and Print Awareness Scale.
Purpose: Designed to assess early literacy skills including phonological and print awareness.
Population: Ages 3-6 through 8-11.
Publication Date: 2014.
Acronym: PPA Scale.
Score: Total score only, derived from 6 tasks: Rhyming, Print Knowledge, Initial Sound Matching, Final Sound Matching, Sound-Symbol, Phonemic Awareness.
Administration: Individual.
Forms, 3: Parallel forms: A, B, C.
Price Data, 2015: $475 per comprehensive kit including Form A, Form B, Form C (25 of each form), Easel A, Easel B, Easel C, manual (85 pages), and Building Literacy Skills: Phonological and Print Awareness Activities; $250 per Form A kit including manual, Easel A, Building Early Literacy Skills: Phonological and Print Awareness Activities, and 25 Form A forms; $42.50 per 25 forms (A, B, or C); $100 per Easel (A, B, or C); $70 per manual; $70 per Building Early Literacy Skills: Phonological and Print Awareness Activities.

Time: (10-15) minutes.
Comments: Online evaluation kits available.
Author: Kathleen T. Williams.
Publisher: Western Psychological Services.
Cross References: Reviews are scheduled for *The Twentieth Mental Measurements Yearbook*.

[1544]

Phonological Assessment Battery [Standardised Edition].

Purpose: Designed to identify "those children who need special help by providing an individual assessment of the child's phonological skills."
Population: Ages 6–15.
Publication Date: 1997.
Acronym: PhAB.
Scores: 6 tests: Alliteration, Naming Speed, Rhyme, Spoonerisms, Fluency, Non-Word Reading.
Administration: Individual.
Price Data, 2016: £145 per complete set including 10 record booklets and manual (130 pages); £22 per 10 record booklets.
Time: (30–40) minutes.
Comments: Is also appropriate for children whose first language is not English.
Authors: Norah Frederickson, Uta Frith, and Rea Reason.
Publisher: GL Assessment [England].
Cross References: For a review by Claudia R. Wright, see 15:189.

[1545]

Phonological Awareness Skills Program.

Purpose: "Designed to provide a means for placing students at the appropriate entry points in the Phonological Awareness Skills Program Curriculum."
Population: Ages 4 to 10.
Publication Date: 1999.
Acronym: PASP
Scores: Total score only.
Administration: Individual.
Price Data, 2015: $105 per complete kit including 25 record forms, curriculum manual, and instrument manual (24 pages); $22 per 25 record forms.
Time: (2–4) minutes.
Authors: Jerome Rosner.
Publisher: PRO-ED.
Cross References: For a review by Janet Norris, see 15:190.

[1546]

Phonovisual Diagnostic Tests [1975 Revision].

Purpose: "Designed to test phonetic skills as taught by the Phonovisual Method."

Population: Grades 3-12.
Publication Date: 1975.
Scores: Total score only.
Administration: Group.
Tests: 6 tests consisting of 24 words each.
Price Data, 2016: $9.95 per set of tests and instructions.
Time: Administration time not reported.
Authors: Edna B. Smith and Mazie C. Lloyd.
Publisher: Phonovisual Products, Inc.
Cross References: For reviews by Charles M. Brown and George D. Spache of an earlier edition, see 6:829.

[1547]

Photo Articulation Test, Third Edition.

Purpose: Constructed as a "systematic method for eliciting speech sounds from children and identifying errors in articulation."
Population: Ages 3–8.
Publication Dates: 1969–1997.
Acronym: PAT-3.
Scores: Total score only.
Administration: Individual.
Price Data, 2015: $215 per complete kit; $56 per summary/response forms; $56 per examiner's manual; $79 per photo album picture book; $43 per picture card deck.
Time: (20) minutes.
Authors: Barbara A. Lippke, Stanley E. Dickey, John W. Selmar, and Anton L. Sodor.
Publisher: PRO-ED.
Cross References: For a review by David P. Hurford, see 14:291; see also T5:1982 (15 references), T4:2017 (12 references), 9:957 (2 references), and T3:1814 (5 references); for a review by Lawrence D. Shriberg of an earlier edition, see 8:969 (1 reference); see also 7:962 (2 references).

[1548]

PHSF Relations Questionnaire.

Purpose: Constructed "to measure ... the personal, home, social and formal relations of high school pupils, students and adults, in order to determine the level of adjustment."
Population: Standards 6–10 in South African school system, college, and adults.
Publication Dates: 1969–1971.
Acronym: PHSF.
Scores, 12: Personal (Self-Confidence, Self-Esteem, Self-Control, Nervousness, Health), Home (Family Influences, Personal Freedom), Social (Sociability-Group, Sociability-Specific Person, Moral Sense), Formal Relations, Validity Scale.
Administration: Group.
Price Data: Available from publisher.
Time: (30) minutes.
Comments: Test materials in both English and Afrikaans.

Authors: F. A. Fouche and P. E. Grobbelaar.
Publisher: Human Sciences Research Council [South Africa].

[1549]
Physiological Screening Test.

Purpose: Designed for athletic trainers and sports dieticians to use with collegiate athletes to identify those who may be at risk for eating disorders or disordered eating.
Population: Female collegiate athletes.
Publication Date: 2010.
Acronym: PST.
Score: OK versus Eating Disorder/Disordered Eating.
Administration: Individual.
Price Data, 2015: $39.95 per manual (2010, 116 pages) and CD; scoring conducted by the authors for an additional fee.
Time: (15-20) minutes.
Comments: Title on test form is Physiologic Aspects of Eating Behaviors Questionnaire; developed "for those with a physiological background and who have less or no familiarity with psychological principles (or the DSM manuals) and have not been trained accordingly"; Athletic Milieu Direct Test is a companion test for sport psychologists.
Authors: David R. Black, Larry J. Leverenz, Daniel C. Coster, Laurie J. Larkin, and Rachel A. Clark.
Publisher: Healthy Learning.

[1550]
Pictorial Reasoning Test.

Purpose: Assesses general learning ability independent of language and reading skills.
Population: Entry-level positions in a variety of occupations
Publication Dates: 1966–1994.
Acronym: PRT.
Scores: Total score only.
Administration: Individual or group.
Price Data: Available from publisher.
Time: 15 minutes.
Comments: Previously listed as SRA Pictorial Reasoning Test.
Authors: Robert N. McMurry and Phyllis D. Arnold (test), and Bruce A. Campbell (manual).
Publisher: General Dynamics Information Technology.
Cross References: For reviews by Raymond A. Katzell and John E. Milholland, and an excerpted review by John L. Horn, see 7:381.

[1551]
The Pictorial Scale of Perceived Competence and Social Acceptance for Young Children.

Purpose: Measures "perceived competence and perceived social acceptance" in young children.

Population: Preschool through second grade.
Publication Dates: 1980–1983.
Scores, 4: Cognitive Competence, Peer Acceptance, Physical Competence, Maternal Acceptance.
Administration: Individual.
Forms, 2: Preschool/Kindergarten, First/Second Grade.
Price Data: Available at no charge from test publisher.
Time: Administration time not reported.
Comments: Downward extension of the Perceived Competence Scale for Children.
Authors: Susan Harter and Robin Pike in collaboration with Carole Efron, Christine Chao, and Beth Ann Bierer.
Publisher: Susan Harter, University of Denver.
Cross References: See T5:1987 (23 references) and T4:2022 (6 references); for reviews by William B. Michael and Susan M. Sheridan, see 11:292 (9 references).

[1552]
Pictorial Test of Intelligence, Second Edition.

Purpose: Designed to "identify children who are significantly below their peers in important abilities and to identify children among these who are physically disabled who are more able to think and reason than their traditional communication skills support."
Population: Ages 3–8.
Publication Dates: 1964–2001.
Acronym: PTI-2.
Scores, 4: Verbal Abstractions, Form Discrimination, Quantitative Concepts, Pictorial Intelligence Quotient.
Administration: Individual.
Price Data, 2015: $171 per kit including examiner's manual (2001, 87 pages), picture book, and 25 profile/examiner record booklets; $48 per 25 record booklets; $56 per manual; $73 per picture book.
Time: (15–30) minutes.
Author: Joseph L. French.
Publisher: PRO-ED.
Cross References: For reviews by Michelle Athanasiou and by Dawn P. Flanagan and Leonard F. Caltabiano, see 15:191; see T3:1823 (3 references); for an excerpted review by Thomas A. Smith, see 8:223 (11 references); see also T2:517 (1 reference); for reviews by Philip Himelstein and T. Ernest Newland, see 7:418 (17 references); see also 6:531 (2 references).

[1553]
Picture Interest Career Survey, Second Edition.

Purpose: Designed as a "language-free, self-report vocational interest inventory."
Population: Ages 10-65.
Publication Dates: 2007-2011.
Acronym: PICS-2.
Scores, 6: Realistic, Investigative, Artistic, Social, Enterprising, Conventional.
Administration: Individual or group.

Price Data, 2016: $59.95 per 25 surveys; administrator's guide (2011, 18 pages) may be downloaded at no charge.
Time: [15] minutes.
Comments: Self-administered, self-scored, and self-interpreted.
Author: Robert P. Brady.
Publisher: JIST/EMC Publishing.
Cross References: For reviews by Sheri Bauman and Julia Y. Porter of the original edition, see 18:94.

[1554]

Piers-Harris Children's Self-Concept Scale, Second Edition.

Purpose: Designed to aid in the "assessment of self-concept in children and adolescents."
Population: Ages 7–18.
Publication Dates: 1969–2002.
Acronym: Piers-Harris 2.
Scores, 7: Behavioral Adjustment, Intellectual and School Status, Physical Appearance and Attributes, Freedom From Anxiety, Popularity, Happiness and Satisfaction, Total.
Administration: Group or individual.
Price Data, 2016: $164.50 per complete kit including 20 AutoScore™ answer forms, manual (2002, 135 pages); $57 per 20 AutoScore™ answer forms; $81.50 per manual; $408 per 25-Use scoring and interpretation CD; $21.50 per 100 PC answer sheets.
Foreign Language Edition: Spanish answer forms available.
Time: (10–15) minutes.
Authors: Ellen V. Piers (test and manual), David S. Herzberg (test and manual), and Dale B. Harris (test).
Publisher: Western Psychological Services.
Cross References: For reviews by Mary Lou Kelley and Donald P. Oswald, see 16:188; see also T5:1991 (108 references) and T4:2030 (123 references); for reviews by Jayne H. Epstein and Patrick J. Jeske of an earlier edition, see 9:960 (38 references); see also T3:1831 (107 references), 8:646 (95 references); and T2:1326 (10 references); for a review by Peter M. Bentler of an earlier edition, see 7:124 (8 references).

[1555]

A Pill Scale.

Purpose: Designed to measure attitudes toward oral contraception.
Population: Adults.
Publication Dates: 1969–1988.
Scores: Total score only.
Administration: Group.
Manual: No manual.
Price Data, 2015: $2 per scale.
Time: [10] minutes.

Comments: Supplementary article available.
Author: Panos D. Bardis.
Publisher: Donna Bardis.
Cross References: See 8:350 (3 references).

[1556]

PIM 8–12.

Purpose: Designed "to assess the extent to which children have acquired the mathematical skills and concepts covered by each year's curriculum."
Population: Ages 8–12.
Publication Dates: 1983–1985.
Scores, 5: Understanding, Computation, Application, Factual Recall, Total.
Administration: Group.
Levels, 5: Mathematics 8, Mathematics 9, Mathematics 10, Mathematics 11, Mathematics 12.
Price Data: Price information available from publisher for test booklets (specify Mathematics 8, 9, 10, 11, or 12), Teacher's Guide, and specimen set including 1 each of 8–12 test booklets, teacher's guide, and group record sheet.
Time: (60–80) minutes for each level.
Authors: Alan Brighouse, David Godber, and Peter Patilla.
Publisher: GL Assessment [England; Efforts to obtain updated information from the test publisher were unsuccessful. An updated edition of this test appears on the test publisher's website].

[1557]

PIP Developmental Charts, Second Edition.

Purpose: Assess behaviors to establish several developmental levels.
Population: Mentally handicapped children birth to age 5.
Publication Dates: 1976–1998.
Scores: Profile of 5 areas of development: Physical, Social, Eye-Hand, Development of Play, Language.
Administration: Individual.
Manual: No manual (instructions for administration and scoring included on test).
Price Data, 2016: £25.50 per 10 charts; £8 per specimen copy.
Time: Administration time not reported.
Authors: Dorothy M. Jeffree and Ray McConkey.
Publisher: Hodder Education [United Kingdom].
Cross References: For reviews by Joan F. Goodman and Robert L. Slonaker, see 9:961.

[1558]

Planning, Organizing, & Scheduling Test, Revised Edition.

Purpose: Designed to measure an individual's "ability to plan, organize the actions and resources of, and schedule events around an activity."

Population: Adults.
Publication Date: 2004.
Acronym: POST.
Scores: Total score only.
Administration: Individual or group.
Manual: No manual.
Price Data, 2016: $195; quantity discounts available.
Time: 20(25) minutes.
Comments: Now sold as part of the Training House Assessment Kit.
Authors: Erich P. Prien and Leonard D. Goodstein.
Publisher: HRD Press, Inc.

[1559]
The Play Observation Scale [Revised].

Purpose: To assess the social and cognitive levels of children's play behaviors in natural settings.
Population: Preschool to elementary school children.
Publication Dates: 1989-2001.
Acronym: POS.
Scores: 28 possible ratings: 7 Non-Play (Transition, Unoccupied, Onlooker, Aggression, Rough-and-Tumble, Teacher Conversation, Peer Conversation); 15 Play, 5 cognitive ratings (Functional, Exploratory, Constructive, Dramatic, Games) in each of 3 social areas (Solitary, Parallel, Group); 3 Affective (Positive, Negative, Neutral).
Administration: Individual.
Price Data: Available for free from publisher.
Time: (3) minutes per observation.
Author: Kenneth H. Rubin.
Publisher: Kenneth H. Rubin, Ph.D. (the author).
Cross References: For reviews by Denise M. DeZolt and Mark H. Fugate of an earlier edition, see 13:234.

[1560]
Police Promotional Tests (Custom).

Purpose: "Fully-customized content-valid written promotional assessments to test the duties and responsibilities of police officers."
Population: Police officers.
Publication Dates: 1979–2010.
Scores: 7 subtests: Technical Police Knowledge, Investigative Knowledge, Legal Knowledge, Supervisory and Managerial Knowledge, Administrative Knowledge, Deductive Reasoning in Police Situations, Ability to Read and Comprehend Police Related Tables and Texts.
Administration: Group.
Restricted Distribution: Distribution restricted to civil service commissions and qualified municipal officials.
Price Data: Available from publisher.
Time: (210) minutes.
Author: McCann Associates.
Publisher: McCann Associates [No reply from publisher; status unknown].

[1561]
Police Selection Test.

Purpose: "Designed to measure abilities important for successful performance in training and on-the-job" as a police officer.
Population: Police officer applicants.
Publication Dates: 1989–2005.
Acronym: PST.
Scores: Total score only.
Administration: Group or individual.
Forms, 3: A, A-1, B-1.
Price Data: Price information available from publisher for test material including Technical manual (1990, 17 pages), Technical Report Addendum: The Development of PST Short Forms A-1 & B-1 (2005, 9 pages), User's Manual (2005, 10 pages), Study Guide and sample questions (1990, 21 pages).
Time: 120(125) minutes for long form; 60(65) minutes for short forms.
Comments: Measures reading comprehension, quantitative problem solving, data interpretation, writing skills, and verbal problem solving.
Author: Psychological Services, Inc.
Publisher: PSI Services LLC.
Cross References: For reviews by Jim C. Fortune and Deniz S. Ones, see 14:292.

[1562]
Portable Tactual Performance Test.

Purpose: Designed to assess the speed of movement, tactile perception, and problem-solving ability.
Population: Ages 5 to adult.
Publication Date: 1984.
Acronym: P-TPT.
Scores, 3: Dominant Hand, Non-dominant Hand, Both Hands.
Administration: Individual.
Price Data, 2015: $520 per introductory kit including 50 record forms, 6-hole and 10-hole boards, administration case, and manual.
Time: (10-15) minutes per trial (three trial limit).
Comments: A portable alternative to the original Tactual Performance Test for use with the Halstead-Reitan Neuropsychological Test Battery (908).
Author: Psychological Assessment Resources, Inc.
Publisher: Psychological Assessment Resources, Inc.
Cross References: For a review by Calvin P. Garbin, see 11:295.

[1563]
Porteus Mazes.

Purpose: "Designed to examine the individual's ability or … tendency to use planning capacity, prudence and mental alertness in a new situation of a concrete nature."
Publication Dates: 1914–1965.

Scores, 2: Quantitative, Qualitative.
Administration: Group.
Price Data, 2016: $49.50 per 100 score sheets.
Comments: Formerly called The Porteus Maze Test.
Author: S. D. Porteus.
Publisher: Pearson.
  a) VINELAND REVISION.
  Population: Ages 3–12, 14, adult.
  Price Data: $362.50 per basic set including mazes and 100 score sheets.
  Time: Untimed.
  b) PORTEUS MAZE EXTENSION.
  Population: Ages 7–12, 14, adult.
  Price Data: Available from publisher.
  Time: [25] minutes.
  Comments: For use only as a practice-free retest of *a*.
  c) PORTEUS MAZE SUPPLEMENT.
  Population: Ages 7–12, 14, adult.
  Price Data: $285 per basic set including 100 each of 8 mazes.
  Time: [25] minutes.
  Comments: For use only as a third retest after *a* and *b*.
Cross References: See T5:2010 (24 references), T4:2051 (25 references), 9:965 (19 references), T3:1853 (34 references), 8:224 (25 references), and T2:518 (52 references); for reviews by Richard F. Docter and John L. Horn, and excerpted reviews by William D. Altus, H. B. Gibson, D. C. Kendrick, and Laurance F. Shaffer, see 7:419 (67 references); see also 6:532 (38 references) and 5:412 (28 references); for reviews by C. M. Louttit and Gladys C. Schwesinger, see 4:356 (56 references).

[1564]

Portland Digit Recognition Test.

Purpose: "Designed for neuropsychological assessment of exaggeration and malingering."
Population: Adults.
Publication Dates: 1989-1992.
Acronym: PDRT.
Scores, 3: Easy Items, Hard Items, Total.
Administration: Individual.
Price Data: Available from publisher.
Time: (40-50) minutes.
Author: Laurence M. Binder.
Publisher: Laurence M. Binder (the author)
Cross References: For reviews by Charles J. Long and Stephanie Western and by Orest E. Wasyliw, see 12:297 (1 reference); see also T4:2052 (1 reference).

[1565]

Portland Problem Behavior Checklist—Revised.

Purpose: "Developed to aid school and mental health personnel to identify problem behaviors, make classification or diagnostic decisions, and evaluate counseling, intervention, or behavior consultation procedures."

Population: Grades K–12.
Publication Dates: 1980–1992.
Acronym: PPBC-R.
Administration: Individual.
Price Data, 2015: $45 per complete kit including manual and 25 each of male and female forms; $20 per 25 male or female forms; $15 per manual.
Time: Untimed.
Comments: Respondents are professionals working with children; scoring form also includes opportunity to report on "other" problems (those not specifically included as a subscale).
Author: Steven A. Waksman.
Publisher: Enrichment Press.
  a) FORM FOR FEMALES, GRADES K–6.
  Scores, 4: Conduct Problems, Peer Problems, Personal Problems, Total.
  b) FORM FOR FEMALES, GRADES 7–12.
  Scores, 5: Academic Problems, Personal Problems, Conduct Problems, Anxiety Problems, Total.
  c) FORM FOR MALES, GRADES K–6.
  Scores, 5: Conduct Problems, Academic Problems, Anxiety Problems, Peer Problems, Total.
  d) FORM FOR MALES, GRADES 7–12.
  Scores, 6: Academic Problems, Anxiety Problems, Peer Problems, Conduct Problems, Personal Problems, Total.
Cross References: For reviews by Thomas McKnight and Robert Spies, see 14:293; for reviews by Terry A. Stinnett and John G. Svinicki of an earlier edition, see 10:287 (1 reference).

[1566]

Position Analysis Questionnaire.

Purpose: Constructed to analyze "jobs in terms of work activities and work-situation variables."
Population: Business and industrial jobs.
Publication Dates: 1969–1989.
Acronym: PAQ.
Scores: 45 dimensions in 7 divisions: Information Input, Mental Processes, Work Output, Relationships with Other Persons, Job Context, Other Job Characteristics, Overall Dimensions.
Administration: Individual.
Price Data: Available from publisher.
Time: Administration time not reported.
Comments: Ratings by 2 or more analysts; also provides estimates of selected employment tests useful for personnel selection and job evaluation points.
Authors: Ernest J. McCormick, Robert C. Mecham, and P. R. Jeanneret.
Publisher: PAQ Services, Inc.
Cross References: See T5:2016 (2 references); for reviews by Ronald A. Ash and George C. Thornton III, see 12:299 (2 references); see also T4:2054 (17 references) and T3:1855 (12 references); for a review by Alan R. Bass, see 8:983 (17 references).

[1567]
Position Classification Inventory.

Purpose: Designed "as an inventory for classifying positions and occupations" to assess the demands, rewards, and opportunities of work environments.
Population: Adults.
Publication Date: 1991.
Acronym: PCI.
Scores, 6: Realistic, Investigative, Artistic, Social, Enterprising, Conventional.
Administration: Individual or group.
Price Data, 2015: $120 per introductory kit including manual, 25 reusable item booklets, and 25 answer sheets/prhofile forms; $42 per manual; $44 per 25 reusable item booklets; $46 per 25 answer sheets/profile forms.
Time: (10) minutes.
Authors: Gary D. Gottfredson and John L. Holland.
Publisher: Psychological Assessment Resources, Inc.
Cross References: For a review by K. Hattrup, see 17:150.

[1568]
Positive and Negative Syndrome Scale.

Purpose: "Designed to assist in the assessment of schizophrenia."
Population: Psychiatric patients.
Publication Dates: 1986–2006.
Acronym: PANSS.
Scores: Standard Model: Positive, Negative, Composite Index, General Psychopathology, Anergia, Thought Disturbances, Activation, Paranoid/Belligerence, Depression, Supplemental; Pentagonal Model: Positive, Negative, Activation, Dysphoric Mood, Autistic Preoccupation.
Administration: Individual.
Price Data, 2015: $299 per complete kit including manual (2006, 76 pages), 25 QuikScore™ forms, 25 Structured Clinical Interview (SCI-PANNS) forms, and 25 Informant Questionnaire (IQ-PANSS) forms; $55 per 25 QuikScore™ forms; $106 per 25 SCI-PANSS forms; $96 per 25 IQ-PANSS forms; $73 per Preview set including manual, 3 QuikScore™ forms, and 3 SCI-PANSS forms.
Time: (30-40) minutes.
Comments: Completed by clinician.
Authors: Stanley R. Kay, Lewis A. Opler, and Abraham Fiszbein.
Publisher: Multi-Health Systems, Inc.
Cross References: See T5:2017 (17 references); for reviews by Barbara J. Kaplan and Cecil R. Reynolds, see 12:300 (15 references); see also T4:2055 (1 reference).

[1569]
Post-Assault Traumatic Brain Injury Interview and Checklist.

Purpose: "Designed to assist in treatment planning for neuropsychological and neurological evaluation, treatment, and rehabilitation."

Population: Assault victims.
Publication Date: 1997.
Acronym: P-TBI-IC.
Scores: 13 symptom areas: Hallmarks of Brain Injury Alertness, Prosody, Memory, Sensorimotor Functions, Speech, Academic Abilities, Cognitive Problem Solving, Organic Depression, Organic Anxiety, Organic Impulsivity, Laterality, Treatment Problems.
Administration: Group or individual.
Price Data, 2015: $80 per complete kit including manual (11 pages), and 10 test booklets; $55 per 10 test booklets; $35 per manual; volume discounts available.
Time: Administration time not reported.
Comments: Ratings by health care professionals, shelter personnel, sexual assault center personnel, and from data obtained from client, significant others, and other health care professionals.
Authors: Martha E. Banks and Rosalie J. Ackerman.
Publisher: ABackans DCP, Inc.
Cross References: For reviews by James C. Reed and by Wilfred G. Van Gorp and Colleen A. Ewing, see 15:192.

[1570]
Postpartum Depression Screening Scale.

Purpose: Designed to assess the presence, severity, and type of postpartum depression symptoms.
Population: New mothers.
Publication Date: 2002.
Acronym: PDSS.
Scores, 10: Inconsistent Responding Index, Sleeping/Eating Disturbances, Anxiety/Insecurity, Emotional Lability, Mental Confusion, Loss of Self, Guilt/Shame, Suicidal Thoughts, Short Total Score, Total Score.
Administration: Group.
Price Data, 2016: $101.50 per kit including manual (59 pages) and 25 AutoScore™ test forms; $44.50 per 25 AutoScore™ test forms; $65.50 per manual.
Foreign Language Edition: Spanish version available.
Time: (5–10) minutes; (1–2) minutes for short form.
Comments: May be orally administered; allows for detection of women in need of psychiatric evaluation; short form consists of 7 items and yields a short total score.
Authors: Cheryl Tatano Beck and Robert K. Gable.
Publisher: Western Psychological Services.
Cross References: For reviews by Paul A. Arbisi and Delores D. Walcott, see 16:190.

[1571]
Posttraumatic Stress Diagnostic Scale.

Purpose: Designed to identify the presence and symptom severity of posttraumatic stress disorder.
Population: Ages 18-65.
Publication Date: 1995.
Acronym: PDS.

Scores: 5: Symptom Severity Score, Number of Symptoms Endorsed, Symptom Severity Rating, Level of Impairment in Functioning, PTSD Diagnosis.
Administration: Group.
Price Data, 2015: $84 per 50 hand-scoring answer sheets; $84 per 50 scoring worksheets; $5 per hand-scoring directions; $42 per manual; $19.25 per 5 test booklets.
Time: (10–15) minutes.
Author: Edna B. Foa.
Publisher: Pearson.
Cross References: For reviews by Stephen N. Axford and Beth Doll, see 14:294; see also T5:2018 (1 reference).

[1572]

Posture and Fine Motor Assessment of Infants.

Purpose: Designed to identify motor delays in infants and to monitor progress in the first year of life.
Population: Ages 2–12 months.
Publication Date: 2000.
Acronym: PFMAI.
Scores, 2: Posture, Fine Motor.
Administration: Individual.
Levels, 2: PFMAI-I (2–6 months), PFMAI-II (6–12) months.
Price Data, 2015: $76 per manual (96 pages).
Time: (25–30) minutes.
Authors: Jane Case-Smith and Rosemarie Bigsby.
Publisher: Pearson.
Cross References: For reviews by Linda K. Bunker, B. Ann Boyce, and Gregory Hanson, and by John J. Venn, see 16:191.

[1573]

Power and Performance Measures.

Purpose: Battery of nine aptitude and ability tests designed to measure both potential and achievement in a wide range of occupational settings.
Population: Ages 16 and over.
Publication Dates: 1990–1996.
Acronym: PPM.
Scores, 9: Verbal Reasoning, Verbal Comprehension, Perceptual Reasoning, Spatial Ability, Numerical Reasoning, Numerical Computation, Mechanical Understanding, Clerical Speed and Accuracy, Applied Logic.
Administration: Group or individual.
Price Data, 2016: £62 per technical handbook (1996, 54 pages); £8 per question booklet; £168 per specimen set.
Time: (3–12) minutes.
Author: James S. Barrett.
Publisher: Hogrefe Ltd [United Kingdom].
Cross References: For a review by Kurt F. Geisinger, see 16:192.

[1574]

Power Base Inventory.

Purpose: Assesses the techniques individuals use to influence others.
Population: Work team members, leaders, managers, supervisors.
Publication Dates: 1985–1999.
Acronym: PBI.
Scores, 6: Information, Expertise, Goodwill, Authority, Reward, Discipline.
Administration: Group or individual.
Price Data, 2016: $18.50 per inventory.
Time: (15) minutes.
Comments: Self-scored.
Authors: Kenneth W. Thomas and Gail Fann Thomas.
Publisher: CPP, Inc.
Cross References: For a review by Judy L. Elliott, see 13:235.

[1575]

Power Management Inventory.

Purpose: "Designed to assess a manager's characteristic management of influence dynamics; that is, how a given manager prefers to handle situations calling for the exercise of power and authority."
Population: Managers.
Publication Dates: 1981–2000.
Acronym: PMI.
Scores, 4: Power Motive (Personalized, Socialized, Affiliative), Power Style.
Administration: Group.
Manual: No manual.
Price Data, 2016: $12.95 per instrument.
Time: Administration time not reported.
Comments: Self-administered survey; companion to Power Management Profile (1576).
Authors: Jay Hall and James Hawker.
Publisher: Teleometrics International, Inc.
Cross References: For reviews by Philip G. Benson and William A. Owens, see 9:967.

[1576]

Power Management Profile.

Purpose: Assesses "the methods and reasons which most characterize your manager's handling of power situations."
Population: Managers.
Publication Dates: 1981–1995.
Acronym: PMP.
Scores, 5: Power Motive (Personalized, Socialized, Affiliative), Power Style, Moral.
Administration: Group.
Manual: No manual.
Price Data, 2016: $12.95 per instrument.
Time: Administration time not reported.

Comments: Self-administered survey; companion to Power Management Inventory (1575).
Authors: Jay Hall and James Hawker.
Publisher: Teleometrics International, Inc.
Cross References: For a review by Rhonda L. Gutenberg, see 9:968.

[1577]
Power Reading Assessment Kit.
Purpose: Created to "determine a student's reading level and best entry level into the Power Reading Program."
Population: Students.
Publication Date: 2005.
Scores, 3: Reading Accuracy, Comprehension, Fluency.
Administration: Individual.
Levels, 24: Reading levels from Primer (.3) to 10th grade (10.8).
Price Data: Available from publisher.
Time: (5-10) minutes.
Author: Marie Carbo.
Publisher: National Reading Styles Institute, Inc.

[1578]
Practical Adolescent Dual Diagnosis Interview–5.
Purpose: A structured interview designed to cover DSM-5 diagnostic criteria for substance use disorders and certain mental health conditions.
Population: Adolescents.
Publication Dates: 2000-2013.
Acronym: PADDI-5.
Scores, 15: Intellectual Function Screen, Major Depressive Episode, Dangerousness to Self, Dangerous to Others, Manic Episode, Mixed Episode, Psychotic Symptoms, Child Abuse Victim–Physical/Sexual/Emotional, Panic Attacks, Anxiety and Phobias, Posttraumatic Stress, Obsessions/Compulsions, Conduct Disorder, Oppositional Defiant Disorder, Atttention-Deficit/Hyperactive Disorder.
Administration: Individual.
Price Data, 2015: $67.50 per 25 assessments; $20 per manual (2013, 67 pages).
Time: (35-45) minutes.
Authors: Norman G. Hoffmann and Todd W. Estroff.
Publisher: The Change Companies.
Cross References: Reviews are scheduled for *The Twentieth Mental Measurements Yearbook*. For reviews by C. G. Bellah and Michael G. Kavan of an earlier edition, see 16:193.

[1579]
Practical Test of Articulation and Phonology.
Purpose: Designed to help clinicians "make a differential diagnosis between an articulation delay, a phonological disorder, or a combination of both."

Population: Ages 3 and older.
Publication Date: 2009.
Acronym: PTAP.
Scores, 7: Fronting, Stopping, Cluster Reduction, Initial Consonant Deletion, Weak Consonant Deletion, Final Consonant Deletion, Syllable Reduction.
Administration: Individual.
Price Data, 2012: $149 per test kit, including 35 protocols, 35 oral motor exams, and 1 set of pictures; $25 per 30 protocols; $25 per 30 oral motor exams.
Time: (4-10) minutes.
Author: Beth Boozer.
Publisher: Cambridge Speech & Language Pathology, Inc.

[1580]
Pragmatic Language Observation Scale.
Purpose: Designed to assess students' everyday classroom oral language behaviors through teacher ratings.
Population: Ages 8 through 17.
Publication Date: 2009.
Acronym: PLOS.
Score: Total score only.
Administration: Individual.
Price Data, 2016: $88 per complete kit including examiner's manual (42 pages) and 50 summary/rating forms; $51 per manual; $43 per 50 summary/rating forms.
Time: (5-10) minutes.
Authors: Phyllis L. Newcomer and Donald D. Hammill.
Publisher: Hammill Institute on Disabilities.
Cross References: Reviews are scheduled for *The Twentieth Mental Measurements Yearbook*.

[1581]
Pragmatic Language Skills Inventory.
Purpose: Designed to help identify children "who have pragmatic language disabilities."
Population: Ages 5-12.
Publication Date: 2006.
Acronym: PLSI.
Scores: 3 subscales: Classroom Interaction, Social Interaction, Personal Interaction; Pragmatic Language Index.
Administration: Individual
Price Data, 2015: $115 per complete kit including examiner's manual (59 pages) and 25 summary/response forms; $67 per manual; $56 per 25 summary/response forms.
Time: (5-10) minutes.
Comments: Appropriate raters include teachers, parents, teacher assistants, or other qualified persons who work closely with the child and are well acquainted with the child's language characteristics.
Authors: James E. Gilliam and Lynda Miller.
Publisher: PRO-ED.
Cross References: For reviews by Thomas W. Guyette and Donna J. Kelly and by Aimée Langlois, see 17:151.

[1582]

The Praxis Series: Professional Assessments for Beginning Teachers.

Purpose: Includes tests that correspond to two key milestones in the development as a teacher entering a teacher training program and obtaining a license to teach.

Population: Beginning teachers.

Publication Dates: 1993–2016.

Administration: Group.

Price Data: Available from publisher.

Restricted Distribution: Secure instruments administered at centers established by the publisher.

Comments: Tests administered 7 times annually; earlier versions previously available as NTE Programs (1940–1992).

Author: Educational Testing Service.

Publisher: Educational Testing Service.

a) PRAXIS CORE ACADEMIC SKILLS FOR EDU-CATORS.

Purpose: Designed to be taken early in a student's college career to measure reading, writing and mathematical skills.

Time: (40-85) minutes, depending on test.

b) PRAXIS SUBJECT ASSESSMENTS.

Purpose: Measures a student's content knowledge of subjects he or she will teach.

Cross References: For information on earlier editions of the NTE Core Battery, see T4:1824 (5 references), T3:1624 (1 reference), and 8:382 (2 references). For information on earlier editions of the Pre-Professional Skills Test, see T4:2071 (6 references); for reviews by Don B. Oppenheim and Edys S. Quellmalz of an earlier edition, see 9:975.

[1583]

PreLAS® 2000.

Purpose: Designed to "assess oral language proficiency and preliteracy skills in young children"; the PreLAS2000 "assesses receptive language and expressive language, which requires all the processing capacities of comprehension plus cognitive organization and the performance of appropriate motor behavior to make the requisite speech sounds"; helps measure the language development of first- and second-language students in both English and Spanish.

Population: Ages 4–6.

Publication Date: 1998.

Scores, 12: Oral Language Component (Simon Says, Art Show, Say What You Hear, Human Body, Story #1, Story #2); Pre-Literacy Component (Letters, Numbers, Colors, Shapes, Reading, Writing).

Administration: Individual.

Parts, 2: Oral Language Component, Pre-Literacy Component.

Price Data: Available from publisher.

Foreign Language Edition: Spanish version available.

Time: (15–25) minutes.

Authors: Sharon E. Duncan and Edward A. De Avila.

Publisher: DRC.

Cross References: For reviews by Sheila Pratt and Annita Marie Ward, see 15:195.

[1584]

PREPARE/ENRICH: Online Customized Version.

Purpose: Designed as a "customized couple assessment completed online that identifies a couple's strength and growth areas."

Population: Premarital and married couples.

Publication Date: 2005.

Scores, 25: Core Relationship Categories (Communication, Conflict Resolution, Partner Style and Habits, Financial Management, Leisure Activities, Sexual Expectations, Family and Friends, Relationship Roles, Spiritual Beliefs), Relationship Dynamics Scales (Assertiveness, Self-Confidence, Avoidance, Partner Dominance), Couple and Family Scales (Couple Closeness, Couple Flexibility, Family Closeness, Family Flexibility), SCOPE Personality Scales (Social, Change, Organized, Pleasing, Emotionally Steady), Overall Satisfaction, Idealistic Distortion, plus customized scales.

Administration: Couples.

Price Data: Available from publisher.

Time: (30-45) minutes.

Comments: Couple discussion guide with exercises available.

Author: David H. Olson.

Publisher: Life Innovations, Inc.

Cross References: Reviews are scheduled for *The Twentieth Mental Measurements Yearbook*. For reviews by Corine Fitzpatrick and Jay A. Mancini of an earlier edition, see 14:295; see also T5:2034 (7 references).

[1585]

Pre-Reading Inventory of Phonological Awareness.

Purpose: "Designed to assess phonological awareness in young students."

Population: Ages 4.0–6.11.

Publication Dates: 2000–2003.

Acronym: PIPA.

Scores, 6: Rhyme Awareness, Syllable Segmentation, Alliteration Awareness, Sound Isolation, Sound Segmentation, Letter–Sound Knowledge.

Administration: Individual.

Price Data, 2015: $190.25 per complete kit including manual (2003, 82 pages), stimulus book, and 25 record forms; $62 per 25 record forms; $142.15 per stimulus book; $104.55 per manual.

Time: (25–30) minutes.

Authors: Barbara Dodd, Sharon Crosbie, Beth McIntosh, Tania Teitzel, and Anne Ozanne.

Publisher: Pearson.
Cross References: For reviews by David P. Hurford and Maura Jones Moyle, see 17:152.

[1586]
Pre-Referral Intervention Manual-Third Edition.

Purpose: To provide appropriate intervention strategies for learning and behavior problems.
Population: Grades K-12.
Publication Dates: 1988-2006.
Acronym: PRIM-3.
Scores: Not scored.
Administration: Individual.
Price Data: Available from publisher.
Time: Administration time not reported.
Comments: The test publisher has indicated there is a newer edition of this test; description will be updated when complete test materials are received.
Publisher: Hawthorne Educational Services, Inc.
Cross References: For a review by Rosemary Flanagan, see 17:153; for reviews by Anthony W. Paolitto and Gabriele van Lingen of an earlier form, see 13:236.

[1587]
Preschool and Kindergarten Behavior Scales, Second Edition.

Purpose: "Designed for use in evaluating social skills and problem behaviors of preschool and kindergarten-age children."
Population: Ages 3–6.
Publication Dates: 1994–2002.
Acronym: PKBS-2.
Scores, 12: Social Skills (Social Cooperation, Social Interaction, Social Independence, Total), Problem Behavior (Externalizing Problems, Internalizing Problems, Total), Supplemental Problem Behavior Subscales (Self-Control/Explosive, Attention Problems/Overactive, Antisocial/Aggressive, Social Withdrawal, Anxiety/Somatic Problems).
Administration: Individual.
Price Data, 2015: $133 per complete kit including test manual (2002, 103 pages) and 50 test forms; $86 per examiner's manual; $49 per 50 test forms.
Foreign Language Edition: Spanish version available.
Time: (8–12) minutes.
Comments: Ratings by home-based raters or school-based raters; Supplemental Problem Behavior Subscales can be used to identify more specific symptoms of emotional and behavioral problems.
Author: Kenneth W. Merrell.
Publisher: PRO-ED.
Cross References: For reviews by Doreen Ward Fairbank and Ronald A. Madle, see 16:194; see also

T5:2036 (1 reference); for reviews by David MacPhee and T. Steuart Watson of an earlier edition, see 13:237.

[1588]
Preschool and Kindergarten Interest Descriptor.

Purpose: "Identify children with attitudes and interests usually associated with preschool and kindergarten creativity."
Population: Ages 3-6.
Publication Date: 1983.
Acronym: PRIDE.
Scores: 4 dimension scores: Originality, Imagination-Playfulness, Independence-Perseverance, Many Interests.
Administration: Group.
Price Data, 2015: $120 per complete set including manual (10 pages) and 30 scales; $15 per specimen set.
Time: (20-35) minutes.
Comments: Downward extension of the Group Inventory for Finding Creative Talent (9:454); scale for rating by parents.
Author: Sylvia B. Rimm.
Publisher: Educational Assessment Service, Inc.
Cross References: For reviews by Gloria A. Galvin and Sue White, see 10:289.

[1589]
Preschool and Primary Inventory of Phonological Awareness.

Purpose: "Designed to identify children who have poor phonological awareness" and are at risk for literacy problems.
Population: Ages 3 years to 6 years, 11 months.
Publication Date: 2000.
Acronym: PIPA.
Scores: 6 subtests: Syllable Segmentation, Rhyme Awareness, Alliteration Awareness, Phoneme Isolation, Phoneme Segmentation, Letter Knowledge.
Administration: Individual.
Price Data, 2015: £132.50 per complete kit including record forms, stimulus manual, and manual (54 pages); £50 per examiner's manual; £63 per stimulus manual; £42 per 25 record forms.
Time: (25–30) minutes; (5) minutes per subtest.
Authors: Barbara Dodd, Sharon Crosbie, Beth McIntosh, Tania Teitzel, and Anne Ozanne.
Publisher: Pearson Assessment [England].
Cross References: For reviews by Carlos Inchaurralde and Gene Schwarting, see 16:195.

[1590]
Pre-School Behavior Checklist.

Purpose: "To help identify children with emotional and behavioral problems by providing a tool for the systematic and objective description of behavior."

Population: Ages 2 through 5.
Publication Date: 1988.
Acronym: PBCL.
Scores: Total score only.
Administration: Group.
Price Data, 2015: $80 per test kit including manual, 25 recording forms, scoring acetate, and 50 Developmental Activities Checklist forms, in vinyl folder; $25 per 25 recording forms; $10 per scoring acetate; $20 per 50 Developmental Activities Checklist forms; $25 per manual.
Time: (8–10) minutes.
Comments: Behavior checklist.
Authors: Jacqueline McGuire and Naomi Richman.
Publisher: GL Assessment [England]; licensed to Academic Therapy Publications.
Cross References: See T5:2038 (5 references); for reviews by Roger D. Carlson and Gary Stoner, see 11:299.

[1591]
The Preschool Behavior Questionnaire.

Purpose: Designed as a screening tool to identify emotional/behavioral problems in children.
Population: Ages 3-6.
Publication Date: 1974.
Acronym: PBQ.
Scores, 4: Hostile-Aggressive, Anxious-Fearful, Hyperactive-Distractible, Total.
Administration: Group.
Price Data, 2015: $30 per 50 questionnaires, 50 scores sheets, and manual (16 pages).
Foreign Language Editions: Spanish, Hebrew, and Turkish versions available.
Time: [5-10] minutes.
Comments: Modification of Michael A. Rutter's 1967 unpublished Children's Behavior Questionnaire.
Authors: Lenore Behar and Samuel Stringfield.
Publisher: Lenore Behar.
Cross References: See T5:2039 (24 references) and T4:2077 (15 references); for a review by Robert A. Fox, see 9:978 (6 references).

[1592]
Preschool Developmental Profile.

Purpose: "Designed to write an individualized education program and to serve as a way of measuring a child's developmental progress."
Population: Children who function at the 3–6-year developmental age.
Publication Dates: 1977–2006.
Scores, 10: Perceptual/Fine Motor, Cognition (Classification, Number, Space, Seriation, Time), Speech and Language, Social Emotional, Self-Care, Gross Motor.
Administration: Individual.
Price Data: Available from publisher.
Time: (50–60) minutes.

Comments: See Early Intervention Developmental Profile (699) for developmental ages of 0 to 36 months.
Authors: Diane B. D'Eugenio, Martha S. Moersch, Sara L. Brown, Judith E. Drews, B. Suzanne Haskin, Eleanor Whiteside Lynch, and Sally J. Rogers.
Publisher: University of Michigan Press.
Cross References: For reviews by Doreen Ward Fairbank and David MacPhee, see 13:239.

[1593]
Preschool Evaluation Scale.

Purpose: Designed to assess behavior related to developmental delays.
Population: Birth–72 months.
Publication Dates: 1991–1992.
Acronym: PES.
Scores, 6: Large Muscle Skills, Small Muscle Skills, Cognitive Thinking, Expressive Language Skills, Social/Emotional, Self-Help Skills.
Administration: Individual.
Levels, 2: Birth–35 months, 36–72 months.
Price Data: Available from publisher.
Time: (20–25) minutes.
Comments: Ratings by parents or child care providers. The test publisher has indicated there is a newer edition of this test; description will be updated when complete test materials are received.
Author: Stephen B. McCarney.
Publisher: Hawthorne Educational Services, Inc.
Cross References: For reviews by Mary Mathai Chittooran and Lena R. Gaddis, see 13:240.

[1594]
Preschool Language Assessment Instrument—Second Edition.

Purpose: Designed to test "children's discourse abilities" in "aspects of early educational exchanges."
Population: Ages 3-0 to 5-11.
Publication Dates: 1978–2003.
Acronym: PLAI-2.
Administration: Individual.
Forms, 2: Age 3 years, Ages 4–5 years.
Price Data, 2015: $236 per complete kit including examiner's manual (2003, 71 pages), picture book, 25 profile/examiner record booklets—3-year-olds, and 25 profile/examiner record booklets—4/5-year-olds; $64 per examiner's manual; $93 per picture book; $48 per 25 profile/examiner's record booklets for 3-year-olds; $48 per 25 profile/examiner's record booklets for 4/5-year-olds.
Time: (30) minutes.
Comments: Includes nonstandardized procedures for analyzing adequacy of response and interfering behaviors.
Authors: Marion Blank, Susan A. Rose, and Laura J. Berlin.
Publisher: PRO-ED.

a) AGES 3 YEARS.
Scores, 6: Discourse Ability (Matching, Selective Analysis, Reordering and Reasoning, Receptive, Expressive, Total).
b) AGES 4–5 YEARS.
Scores, 7: Discourse Ability (Matching, Selective Analysis, Reordering, Reasoning, Receptive, Expressive, Total).
Cross References: For reviews by Koressa Kutsick Malcolm and Rebecca McCauley, see 16:197; see also T5:2044 (6 references) and T4:2083 (2 references); for reviews by William O. Haynes and Kenneth G. Shipley of a previous edition, see 9:979.

[1595]
Preschool Language Scales, Fifth Edition.
Purpose: Designed to "identify children who have a language delay or disorder."
Population: Ages birth to 7-11.
Publication Dates: 1969-2011.
Acronym: PLS-5.
Scores, 5: Auditory Comprehension, Expressive Communication, Total Language; 2 optional scores: Articulation, Mean Length of Utterance.
Administration: Individual.
Price Data, 2015: $358.75 per complete kit with manipulatives including examiner's manual (2011, 119 pages), administration and scoring manual (2011, 191 pages), picture manual, 15 record forms, and 25 Home Communication Questionnaires; $299 per basic kit without manipulatives including examiner's manual, administration and scoring manual, picture manual, 15 record forms, and 25 Home Communication Questionnaires; $139.40 per complete set of manipulatives; $60 per 15 record forms; $10.75 per 25 Home Communication Questionnaires; $60.50 per examiner's manual; $179.40 per picture manual; $113.80 per administration and scoring manual.
Foreign Language Edition: Spanish edition available.
Time: (25-50) minutes.
Comments: Fifth edition includes some new items, scoring changes, and norms based on 2008 U.S. Census data.
Authors: Irla Lee Zimmerman, Violette G. Steiner, and Roberta Evatt Pond.
Publisher: Pearson.
  a) ARTICULATION SCREENER.
  Purpose: Designed to evaluate articulation in single words.
  Population: Ages 2-6 to 7-11.
  Scores: Total score only.
  Comments: "Criterion-referenced" optional subtest.
  b) LANGUAGE SAMPLE CHECKLIST.
  Purpose: Designed to evaluate spontaneous speech.
  Population: Ages 1 to 7-11.
  Scores: Mean Length of Utterance.
  Comments: Supplemental measure to help validate information obtained from the Expressive Communication scale.

c) HOME COMMUNICATION QUESTIONNAIRE.
Purpose: Designed to give "the caregiver's perspective of a child's communication behaviors" at home, preschool, or daycare.
Population: Ages birth to 2-11.
Scores: Not scored.
Time: (10-15) minutes.
Comments: Supplemental questionnaire.
Cross References: For reviews by Thomas McKnight and Kathy L. Shapley, see 19:130; for reviews by Terri Flowerday and Hoi K. Suen of the fourth edition, see 16:198; see also T5:2045 (6 references); for reviews by J. Jeffrey Grill and Janet A. Norris of the third edition, see 13:241 (26 references); see also T4:2084 (24 references); for an excerpted review by Barton B. Proger of a previous edition, see 8:929 (3 references); see also T2:2024 (1 reference); for a review by Joel Stark and an excerpted review by C. H. Ammons, see 7:965.

[1596]
Preschool Language Scales—Fifth Edition Screening Test.
Purpose: Designed "to assist in the identification of children who may need in-depth assessment of their speech and language abilities."
Population: Ages birth to 7-11.
Publication Date: 2012.
Acronym: PLS-5 Screening Test.
Administration: Individual.
Levels and Forms: 8 forms, 10 levels.
Price Data, 2015: $159 per kit including stimulus book/test manual (251 pages) and 25 record forms for each age; $138.40 per stimulus book/test manual; $37.40 per 25 record forms (age birth to 11 months, age 1, age 2, age 3, age 4, age 5, age 6, or age 7).
Foreign Language Edition: Spanish edition available.
Time: (5-10) minutes.
Authors: Irla Lee Zimmerman, Violette G. Steiner, and Roberta Evatt Pond.
Publisher: Pearson.
  a) AGE BIRTH TO 0:11.
  Scores, 3: Language, Feeding, Social/Interpersonal.
  Comments: Form is subdivided into two levels: ages 0-0 to 0-5 and 0-6 to 0-11.
  b) AGE 1.
  Scores, 3: Language, Feeding, Social/Interpersonal.
  c) AGE 2.
  Scores, 3: Language, Social/Interpersonal, Articulation (ages 2-6 to 2-11).
  d) AGE 3.
  Scores, 6: Language, Articulation, Connected Speech, Social/Interpersonal, Fluency, Voice.
  e) AGE 4.
  Scores, 6: Language, Articulation, Connected Speech, Social/Interpersonal, Fluency, Voice.
  f) AGE 5.
  Scores, 6: Language, Articulation, Connected Speech, Social/Interpersonal, Fluency, Voice.

g) AGE 6.

Scores, 6: Language, Articulation, Connected Speech, Social/Interpersonal, Fluency, Voice.

h) AGE 7.

Scores, 6: Language, Articulation, Connected Speech, Social/Interpersonal, Fluency, Voice.

Cross References: For reviews by Aimée Langlois and by Shawn Powell and Maria I. Kuznetsova, see 19:131.

[1597]

Preschool Language Scales—Fifth Edition Spanish.

Purpose: A "dual-language assessment" designed "to identify a language delay or disorder in children who are monolingual Spanish speakers or bilingual Spanish-English speakers."

Population: Children from birth to age 7-11 whose primary language is Spanish.

Publication Date: 2012.

Acronym: PLS-5 Spanish.

Scores, 5: Auditory Comprehension, Expressive Communication, Total Language; 2 optional scores: Articulation, Mean Length of Utterance in Words.

Administration: Individual.

Price Data, 2015: $398.75 per complete kit with manipulatives including examiner's manual (135 pages), picture manual, administration and scoring manual (217 pages), 15 record forms, and 25 Home Communication Questionnaires; $339 per basic kit without manipulatives including examiner's manual, picture manual, administration/scoring manual, 15 record forms, and 25 Home Communication Questionnaires; $11.30 per package of two Spanish children's books; $67.50 per 15 record forms; $10.75 per 25 Home Communication Questionnaires; $59.45 per examiner's manual; $179.40 per picture manual; $113.80 per administration and scoring manual.

Foreign Language Edition: English edition available.

Time: (30-65) minutes.

Comments: Administrators need "native or near-native proficiency in Spanish"; examiner's manual is written in English; administration and scoring manual is written in English and Spanish; normative data based on children whose primary language is Spanish, including the bilingual Spanish-English speakers in the sample; the English edition (PLS-5; 1595) should be administered to children whose primary language is English.

Authors: Irla Lee Zimmerman, Violette G. Steiner, and Roberta Evatt Pond.

Publisher: Pearson.

a) ARTICULATION SCREENER.

Purpose: Designed to evaluate articulation in single words.

Population: Ages 2-6 to 7-11.

Score: Total score only.

Comments: "Criterion-referenced" optional subtest included in the record form.

b) LANGUAGE SAMPLE CHECKLIST.

Purpose: Designed to evaluate spontaneous speech.

Score: Mean Length of Utterance in Words.

Comments: Supplemental measure included in the record form to help validate information obtained from the Expressive Communication scale.

c) HOME COMMUNICATION QUESTIONNAIRE.

Purpose: Designed to give "the caregiver's perspective" of a child's communication behaviors at home, preschool, or daycare.

Population: Ages birth to 2-11.

Scores: Not scored.

Time: (10-15) minutes.

Comments: Supplemental questionnaire.

Cross References: For a review by Arturo Olivárez, Jr. and Norma Martinez, see 19:132.

[1598]

Preschool Language Scales—Fifth Edition Spanish Screening Test.

Purpose: A "dual language assessment" designed to identify "monolingual Spanish or bilingual Spanish-English-speaking children who may need in-depth assessment of their speech and language abilities."

Population: Children from birth to age 7-11 whose primary language is Spanish.

Publication Date: 2012.

Acronym: PLS-5 Spanish Screening Test.

Administration: Individual.

Levels and Forms: 8 forms, 9 levels.

Price Data, 2015: $170.65 per kit including stimulus book/test manual (282 pages) and 25 record forms for each age; $148.65 per stimulus book/test manual; $37.40 per 25 record forms (age birth to 11 months, age 1, age 2, age 3, age 4, age 5, age 6, or age 7).

Foreign Language Edition: English edition available.

Time: (5-10) minutes.

Comments: Normative data based on children whose primary language is Spanish and who understand and converse fluently in Spanish or Spanish and English; publisher "highly recommends" examiners who administer the assessment to monolingual Spanish speakers be fluent or near-fluent Spanish speakers; examiners who administer the test to bilingual Spanish-English speakers should be bilingual themselves. If an examiner does not have fluent or near-fluent proficiency in Spanish, the test can be administered in collaboration with a trained and qualified interpreter.

Authors: Irla Lee Zimmerman, Violette G. Steiner, and Roberta Evatt Pond.

Publisher: Pearson.

a) AGE BIRTH TO 0:5 MONTHS.

Scores, 3: Language, Feeding, Social/Interpersonal.

b) AGE 0:6 TO 0:11 MONTHS.

Scores, 3: Language, Feeding, Social/Interpersonal.

c) AGE 1.

Scores, 3: Language, Feeding, Social/Interpersonal.

d) AGE 2.

Scores, 3: Language, Social/Interpersonal, Articulation (ages 2-6 to 2-11).

e) AGE 3.

Scores, 6: Language, Articulation, Connected Speech, Social/Interpersonal, Fluency, Voice.

f) AGE 4.

Scores, 6: Language, Articulation, Connected Speech, Social/Interpersonal, Fluency, Voice.

g) AGE 5.

Scores, 6: Language, Articulation, Connected Speech, Social/Interpersonal, Fluency, Voice.

h) AGE 6.

Scores, 6: Language, Articulation, Connected Speech, Social/Interpersonal, Fluency, Voice.

i) AGE 7.

Scores, 6: Language, Articulation, Connected Speech, Social/Interpersonal, Fluency, Voice.

Cross References: For reviews by María Del R. Medina-Díaz and by Richard Ruth, Benjamin Morsa, and Laura W. Reid, see 19:133.

[1599]
Preschool Program Quality Assessment, Second Edition.

Purpose: "Designed to evaluate the quality of early childhood programs and identify staff training needs."

Population: Center-based early childhood education settings.

Publication Dates: 1998-2003.

Acronym: PQA.

Administration: Individual or group.

Forms, 2: A, B.

Price Data, 2015: $27.95 per Starter Pak, which includes administration manual (2003, 32 pages), 1 Form A-Classroom Items, and 1 Form B-Agency Items; $13.95 per administration manual; $7.95 per Form B-Agency items; $7.95 per Form A-Classroom Items; $1.95 per index tab set; $29.95 per classroom for premium online version; $19.95 per classroom for basic online version.

Time: Administration time not reported.

Comments: "Based on classroom observations and interviews with teaching and administrative staff."

Author: High/Scope Educational Research Foundation.

Publisher: High/Scope Educational Research Foundation.

a) FORM A-CLASSROOM ITEMS.

Scores, 5: Learning Environment, Daily Routine, Adult-Child Interaction, Curriculum Planning/Assessment, Classroom Score.

b) FORM B-AGENCY ITEMS.

Scores, 4: Parent Involvement/Family Services, Staff Qualifications/Development, Program Management, Agency Score.

Cross References: For reviews by Abigail Baxter and Stephen B. Johnson, see 17:155; for reviews by Michael B. Bunch and William J. Sauser, Jr. of an earlier version, see 15:198.

[1600]
Preschool Screening Instrument.

Purpose: Designed to identify potential learning problems in prekindergarten children.

Population: Ages 3-0 to 5-3.

Publication Date: 1979.

Acronym: PSSI.

Scores, 6: Human Figure Drawing, Visual Motor Perception/Fine Motor, Gross Motor, Language Development, Speech, Behavior.

Administration: Individual.

Price Data, 2015: $90 per complete kit including 25 student record forms, 25 parental questionnaires, story card, manipulatives, and manual (40 pages).

Time: (5–8) minutes.

Author: Stephen Paul Cohen.

Publisher: Stoelting Co.

Cross References: For a review by Gene Schwarting, see 9:981.

[1601]
Preschool-Wide Evaluation Tool™ (Pre-SET™), Research Edition.

Purpose: Designed "to measure an early childhood program's implementation fidelity of program-wide positive behavior intervention and support."

Population: Evaluators and other observers of early childhood programs.

Publication Date: 2012.

Acronym: PreSET.

Scores, 9: Expectations Defined, Behavioral Expectations Taught, Responses to Appropriate and Challenging Behavior, Organized and Predictable Environment, Monitoring and Decision Making, Family Involvement, Management, Program Support, Total Percent Implemented.

Administration: Individual programs.

Price Data, 2015: $99.95 per CD-ROM that includes all necessary printable forms; $50 per manual (125 pages).

Time: (60) minutes.

Comments: Administration time applies to programs with 1-2 classrooms; time will increase approximately 20 minutes for each additional classroom; intended for use with early childhood programs that implement the program-wide positive behavior intervention and support (PW-PBIS) model.

Authors: Elizabeth A. Steed, Tina M. Pomerleau, and Robert H. Horner (forms).

Publisher: Paul H. Brookes Publishing Co., Inc.

Cross References: For reviews Malinda Hendricks Green and Giuliana Losapio, see 19:134.

[1602]
Present State Examination.

Purpose: Clinical interview questionnaire for ratings of psychiatric symptoms reported by patient during preceding month.

Population: Adult psychiatric patients.
Publication Dates: 1967–1974.
Acronym: PSE.
Scores: 38 syndrome scores and various derived scores.
Administration: Individual.
Price Data: Available from publisher.
Time: (45–60) minutes.
Authors: J. K. Wing, J. E. Cooper, and N. Sartorius.
Publisher: Cambridge University Press.
Cross References: See T5:2050 (142 references), T4:2091 (237 references), 9:985 (71 references), and T3:1883 (70 references); for a review by Jack Zusman, Isabel C. A. Moyes, Clive A. Sims, and David Goldberg, see 8:649.

[1603]

The Press Test.
Purpose: Measures how well an individual performs tasks when experiencing stress.
Population: Managers and high-level professionals.
Publication Dates: 1959–1987.
Scores, 5: Reading Speed, Color-Naming Speed, Color-Naming Speed With Distraction, Difference Between Color-Naming Speed With and Without Distraction, Difference Between Reading Speed and Color-Naming Speed.
Administration: Individual or group.
Price Data: Available from publisher.
Time: (6–10) minutes.
Authors: Melany E. Baehr and Raymond J. Corsini.
Publisher: General Dynamics Information Technology.
Cross References: For a review by Robert P. Vecchio, see 9:986; see also T3:1884 (2 references), T2:1333 (1 reference), and P:213 (1 reference); for reviews by William H. Helme and Allyn Miles Munger, see 6:163.

[1604]

The Prevocational Assessment and Curriculum Guide.
Purpose: Designed to "assess and identify the prevocational training needs of handicapped persons."
Population: Mentally retarded individuals.
Publication Dates: 1978–1993.
Acronym: PACG.
Scores: 9 categories: Attendance/Endurance, Independence, Production, Learning, Behavior, Communication, Social Skills, Grooming/Eating, Toileting.
Administration: Individual.
Price Data, 2016: $12 per complete kit including 10 inventories, summary profile sheets, curriculum guides, and one manual (6 pages); $8 per set of 10 additional forms.
Time: [15–20] minutes.
Comments: Ratings by professional acquainted with individual; title on test is PACG Inventory.

Authors: Dennis E. Mithaug, Deanna K. Mar, and Jeffrey E. Stewart.
Publisher: Exceptional Education — Jeff Stewart's Teaching Tools.
Cross References: For reviews by Richard A. Wantz and Jean M. Williams, see 12:304.

[1605]

Prevocational Assessment Screen.
Purpose: "Designed to assess a student's motor and perceptual abilities in relation to performance requirements within a local vocational training program."
Population: Grades 8-12.
Publication Dates: 1985–2000.
Acronym: PAS.
Scores, 16: Time and Error scores for 8 modules: Alphabetizing, Etch A Sketch Maze, Calculating, Small Parts, Pipe Assembly, O Rings, Block Design, Color Sort.
Administration: Individual.
Price Data, 2016: $1,995 per complete kit including manual (50 pages) and computer software for use in scoring and reporting; web-based version available.
Time: (50) minutes.
Author: Michele Rosinek.
Publisher: Piney Mountain Press.
Cross References: For reviews by Stephen L. Koffler and James B. Rounds, see 12:305.

[1606]

Primary Measures of Music Audiation.
Purpose: To assess basic music aptitudes.
Population: K-3.
Publication Date: 1979.
Acronym: PMMA.
Scores, 3: Tonal, Rhythm, Composite.
Administration: Group.
Price Data, 2015: $100 per complete kit including 1 tonal and rhythm compact disc, 100 total answer sheets and 100 rhythm answer sheets, 1 set of scoring masks, 100 profile cards, 4 class record sheets, and test manual (107 pages); $25 per CD; $10 per 100 tonal or rhythm answer sheets; $43 per 500 tonal or rhythm answer sheets; $10 per set of scoring masks; $15.50 per 100 profile cards; $2 per 10 class record sheets; $20 per manual. Also available on CD-ROM: $49.95 for single computer, volume discounts available.
Time: (20) minutes for tonal and (20) minutes for rhythm.
Comments: For upward extension, see Intermediate Measures of Music Audiation (996); test administered by CD.
Author: Edwin E. Gordon.
Publisher: GIA Publications, Inc.
Cross References: See T4:2099 (2 references); for reviews by Paul R. Lehman and Walter L. Wehner, see 9:988; see also T3:1891 (1 reference).

[1607]

Primary Test of Cognitive Skills.

Purpose: Designed to "measure verbal, spatial, memory, and conceptual abilities."

Population: Grades K–1.

Publication Date: 1990.

Acronym: PTCS.

Scores, 5: Spatial, Memory, Concepts, Verbal, Total.

Administration: Group.

Price Data: Price information available from publisher for test materials including manual (70 pages), norms book (82 pages), and technical bulletin (23 pages); scoring service available from publisher.

Time: Untimed, (30) minutes per subtest; (120) minutes total test.

Authors: Janellen Huttenlocher and Susan Cohen Levine.

Publisher: DRC.

Cross References: For reviews by Sherry K. Bain and Laura L. B. Barnes and David E. McIntosh, see 12:307.

[1608]

Primary Test of Nonverbal Intelligence.

Purpose: Intended for "assessing [nonverbal] reasoning abilities in young children."

Population: Ages 3-0 to 9-11.

Publication Date: 2008.

Acronym: PTONI.

Scores: Total score only.

Administration: Individual.

Price Data, 2015: $229 per complete kit including picture book, 25 examiner/record forms, and examiner's manual (84 pages); $105 per picture book; $53 per 25 record forms; $83 per examiner's manual.

Time: (5-15) minutes.

Comments: Children respond to items by pointing to the correct picture in the picture book.

Authors: David J. Ehrler and Ronnie L. McGhee.

Publisher: PRO-ED.

Cross References: For reviews by Connie Theriot England and Koressa Kutsick Malcolm, see 18:96.

[1609]

Principles of Adult Mentoring Inventory.

Purpose: Designed "to provide a self-assessment instrument for those who have assumed the role of mentor in their contact with adult learners."

Population: Adults.

Publication Date: 1998.

Acronym: PAMI.

Scores, 7: Relationship Emphasis/Trust, information Emphasis/Advice, Facilitative Focus/Alternatives, Confortive Focus/Challenge, Mentor Model/Motivation, Employee Vision/Initiative, Total.

Administration: Individual.

Price Data, 2016: $59.95 per facilitator guide and assessment; $59.95 per pack of 5 additional assessments.

Time: Administration time not reported.

Author: Norman H. Cohen.

Publisher: HRD Press, Inc.

Cross References: For reviews by L. Carolyn Pearson and Trey Martindale and by Cecil R. Reynolds, see 15:197.

[1610]

PrinTest.

Purpose: Designed for selecting or evaluating entry-level production or maintenance employees where the reading of prints and drawings is required.

Population: Applicants or incumbents for jobs requiring print reading abilities.

Publication Dates: 1990-2013.

Acronym: RCJS-PrinTest.

Scores: Total score only.

Administration: Group.

Forms, 2: Decimals, Fractions.

Price Data, 2015: : $24 per consumable self-scoring test booklet; $26 per online test administration; $24.95 per manual (21 pages).

Time: 35(45) minutes.

Comments: Self-scoring instrument; available for online test administration; test publisher advises changes in form names indicate minor revisions and updating.

Author: Roland T. Ramsay.

Publisher: Ramsay Corporation.

Cross References: For reviews by Janet Houser and Chockalingam Viswesvaran of Forms A-C and BR-C, see 19:135; for reviews by James W. Pinkney and Nambury S. Raju of an earlier edition, see 13:258.

[1611]

Prison Inmate Inventory.

Purpose: "Designed for inmate risk assessment and needs identification."

Population: Prison inmates.

Publication Date: 1996.

Acronym: PII.

Scores: 10 scales: Truthfulness, Violence, Antisocial, Adjustment, Self-Esteem, Alcohol, Drugs, Judgment, Distress, Stress Coping Abilities.

Administration: Group.

Price Data, 2016: $9.95 per test; volume discounts available.

Foreign Language Edition: Spanish version available.

Time: (35) minutes.

Author: Risk & Needs Assessment, Inc.

Publisher: Behavior Data Systems, Inc.

Cross References: For reviews by R. J. DeAyala and John A. Mills, see 14:297.

[1612]

Problem Behavior Inventory [Adult & Adolescent Screening Forms].

Purpose: Designed to help "clinicians structure and focus the diagnostic interview."
Population: Adults and adolescents.
Publication Date: 1991.
Scores: No scores.
Administration: Group.
Forms, 2: Adult, Adolescent.
Price Data, 2016: $52.50 per 25 inventories (adult or adolescent).
Time: (10-20) minutes.
Author: Leigh Silverton.
Publisher: Western Psychological Services.

[1613]

Problem Experiences Checklist.

Purpose: Developed for use prior to the initial intake interview to identify potential problems for further discussion.
Population: Adolescents, adults.
Publication Date: 1991.
Scores: No scores.
Administration: Individual.
Editions, 2: Adolescent, Adult.
Manual: No manual.
Price Data, 2016: $35.50 per 25 adult checklists.
Time: [10-15] minutes.
Author: Leigh Silverton.
Publisher: Western Psychological Services.
Cross References: For reviews by Mark H. Daniel and Michael J. Sporakowski, see 12:309.

[1614]

The Problem Solving Inventory.

Purpose: "To assess an individual's perceptions of his or her own problem-solving behaviors and attitudes."
Population: Age 16 and above.
Publication Date: 1988.
Acronym: PSI.
Scores, 4: Problem-Solving Confidence, Approach-Avoidance Style, Personal Control, Total.
Administration: Group and individual.
Price Data: Available from publisher.
Foreign Language Editions: Available in Arabic, French, Italian, Japanese, Korean, Mandarin, Spanish, and Turkish.
Time: (10-15) minutes.
Comment: Self-ratings scale.
Author: Puncky Paul Heppner.
Publisher: Puncky Paul Heppner (the author).
Cross References: See T5:2065 (35 references) and T4:2108 (26 references); for reviews by Cameron J. Camp and Steven G. LoBello, see 11:303 (11 references).

[1615]

Process Assessment of the Learner-Second Edition: Diagnostic Assessment for Math.

Purpose: "Designed for measuring the development of math processes in children."
Population: Grades K-6.
Publication Date: 2007.
Acronym: PAL-II M.
Scores: 48 scores across 17 subtests: Numeral Writing (Automatic Legible Numeral Writing at 15 Seconds [NWAL], Legible Numeral Writing [NWL], Total Time [NWTT], Reversals [NWR], Omissions [NOW], Transpositions [NWTR]), Oral Counting (Oral Counting [OC]), Numeric Coding (Numeric Coding [NC]), Fact Retrieval: Look and Write (Addition [FRLW-A], Subtraction [FRLW-S], Mixed Addition and Subtraction [FRLW-AS], Multiplication [FRLW-M], Division [FRLW-D], Mixed Multiplication and Division [FRLW-MD]), Fact Retrieval: Listen and Say, (Addition [FRLS-A], Subtraction [FRLS-S], Mixed Addition and Subtraction [FRLS-AS], Multiplication [FRLS-M], Division [FRLS-D], Mixed Multiplication and Division [FRLS-MD]), Computation Operations (Task A-Spatial Alignment [CO-SA], Task B-Verbal Explanation [CO-VE], Task C-Problem Solution [CO-PS], Computation Operations Composite [COC]), Place Value (Oral [PVO], Written [PVW], Problem Response Written [PVPW], Place Value Composite [PVC]), Part-Whole Relationships (Part-Whole Concepts [PWC], Part-Whole Fractions and Mixed Numbers [PWF], Part-Whole Time [PWT], Part-Whole Relationships Composite [PWRC]), Finding the Bug (Finding the Bug [FB]), Multi-Step Problem Solving (Multi-Step Problem Solving [MSPS]), Quantitative Working Memory (Quantitative Working Memory [QWM]), Spatial Working Memory (Oral [SWMO], Drawing [SWMD]), RAN: Digits (Single Digits Total Time [RAN-DTT], Single Digits Rate Change [RAN-DRC]), RAN: Double Digits (Double Digits Total Time [RAN-DDTT], Double Digits Rate Change [RAN-DDRC]), RAN: Digits and Double Digits Total Scores (Digits + Double Digits Rate Change [RAN-D-DDRC], Digits + Double Digits Total Errors [RAN-D-DDTE], Digits + Double Digits Total Time Composite [RAN-D-DDC]), RAS: Words and Digits (Words and Digits Total Time [RAS-WDTT], Words and Digits Rate Change [RAS-WDRC], Words and Digits Total Errors [RAS-WDTE]), Fingertip Writing (Fingertip Writing [FW]).
Administration: Individual.
Levels, 5: Kindergarten, Grade 1, Grade 2, Grade 3, Grades 4-6.
Price Data, 2015: $382.65 per Math Kit including 10 Response Booklets, 10 Record Forms, Stimulus Book, Stimulus Booklets, Administration and Scoring Manual (141 pages); $86.50 per 25 Response Booklets; $63.50 per

25 Record Forms; $122.85 per Stimulus Book; $88.35 per Stimulus Booklet.

Time: (60-120) minutes to administer all subtests; time limit varies across individual subtests.

Comments: The PAL-II M has three applications: (a) "Tier 1: universal screening for early intervention and prevention," (b) "Tier 2: problem-solving consultation and progress monitoring," (c) "Tier 3: differential diagnosis and treatment planning;" number and type of subtests administered depends on grade level and application.

Author: Virginia Wise Berninger.

Publisher: Pearson.

Cross References: For reviews by Laura Hamilton and by Katherine Ryan and Michael J. Culbertson, see 18:97.

[1616]

Process Assessment of the Learner–Second Edition: Diagnostic Assessment for Reading and Writing.

Purpose: "Designed for measuring reading and writing skills and related processes in children."

Population: Grades K-6.

Publication Dates: 1998-2007.

Acronym: PAL-II RW.

Scores, 83: Alphabet Writing Automatic Legible Letter Writing (AWAL), Alphabet Writing Legible Letter Writing (AWL), Alphabet Writing Total Time (AWTT), Copying Task A Automatic Legible Letter Writing (CPAAL), Copying Task A Legible Letter Writing (CPAL), Copying Task A Total Time (CPATT), Copying Task B Legibility (0-30 seconds) (CPBL-30), Copying Task B Legibility (0-60 seconds) (CPBL-60), Copying Task B Legibility (0-90 seconds) (CPBL-90), Copying Task B Copy Accuracy (CPBCA), Handwriting Total Automatic Letter Legibility Composite (HWGTALC), Handwriting Total Legibility Composite (HWGTLC), Handwriting Total Time Composite (HWGTTC), Handwriting Total Reversals (HWGTRC), Handwriting Total Inversions (HWGTI), Handwriting Total Omissions (HWGTO), Handwriting Total Repetitions (HWGTRP), Handwriting Total Transpositions (HWGTTR), Handwriting Total Case Confusions (HWGTCC), Handwriting Total Format Confusions (HWGTFC), Receptive Coding (RC), Expressive Coding (EC), Orthographic Coding Composite (ORC), Rhyming (RY), Syllables (SY), Phonemes (PN), Rimes (RI), Phonological Coding Composite (PLC), Are They Related? (RR), Does It Fit? (DF), Sentence Structure (ST), Morphological/Syntactic Coding Composite (MSCC), Pseudoword Decoding Fluency at 60 seconds (PDF-60), Pseudoword Decoding Accuracy (PDA), Find the True Fixes (FF), Morphological Decoding Fluency Accuracy (MDFA), Morphological Decoding Fluency (MDF), Morphological Decoding Composite (MDC), Word Choice Accuracy (WCA), Word Choice Fluency (WCF), Sentence Sense Accuracy (SSA), Sentence Sense Fluency (SSF), Compositional Fluency Total Number of Words (CFTW), Compositional Fluency Total Correctly Spelled Words (CFCSW), Compositional Fluency Total Complete Sentences (CFCST), Expository Note Taking Accuracy (NTA), Expository Note Taking Fact Errors (NTFE), Expository Report Writing Quality (RWQ), Expository Report Writing Organizational Quality of Report Writing (RWO), Expository Report Writing Irrelevant Thoughts Added (RWITA), Cross-Genre Compositional and Expository Writing Total Number of Words (CGWTW), Cross-Genre Compositional and Expository Writing Total Correctly Spelled Words (CG-WCSW), Cross-Genre Compositional and Expository Writing Total Complete Sentences (CGWCS), Letters (WML), Words (WMW), Letters and Words Composite (WML-WC), Sentences: Listening (WMSL), Sentences: Writing (WMSW), Sentences: Listening and Sentences: Writing Composite (WMSL-SWC), Verbal Working Memory Composite (WMVC), RAN-Letters Rate Change Raw Score (RAN-LRC), RAN-Letters Total Time (RAN-LTT), RAN-Letter Groups Rate Change Raw Score (RAN-LGRC), RAN-Letter Groups Total Time (RAN-LGTT), RAN-Words Rate Change Raw Score (RAN-WRC), RAN-Words Total Time (RAN-WTT), RAN-Letters -Letter Groups and -Words Total Rate Change Score (RAN-L-LG-WRC), RAN-Letters -Letter Groups and -Words Total Errors (RAN-L-LG-WTE), RAN-Letters -Letter Groups and -Words Total Time Composite (RAN-L-LG-WC), RAS-Words and Digits Total Time (RAS-WDTT), RAS-Words and Digits Rate Change Raw Score (RAS-WDRC), RAS-Words and Digits Total Errors (RAS-WDTE), Oral Motor Planning Total Time (OMT), Oral Motor Planning Total Errors (OME), Finger Repetition-Dominant Hand Total Time (FSRP-DTT), Finger Repetition-Non-Dominant Hand Total Time (FSRP-NTT), Finger Succession-Dominant Hand Total Time (FSS-DTT), Finger Succession-Non-Dominant Hand Total Time (FSS-NTT), Finger Succession Total Errors (FSSTE), Finger Sense Frequent Motoric Overflow (FSFMO), Finger Sense Occasional Motoric Overflow (FSOMO), Finger Localization (FSL), Finger Recognition (FSRC).

Administration: Individual.

Levels, 5: Kindergarten, Grade 1, Grade 2, Grade 3, Grades 4-6.

Price Data, 2015: $526.95 per complete kit including 10 Response Booklets, 10 Record Forms, Stimulus Book, Stimulus Booklets (A and B), and administration and scoring manual (2007, 225 pages); $86.75 per 25 Response Booklets; $92.50 per 25 Record Forms; $122.85 per Stimulus Book; $88.35 per Stimulus Booklet-A; $88.35 per Stimulus Booklet-B.

Time: (60-120) minutes to administer all subtests; time limit varies across individual subtests.

Comments: The PAL-II RW has three applications: (a) "Tier 1: universal screening for early intervention and prevention," (b) "Tier 2: problem-solving consultation and progress monitoring," (c) "Tier 3: differential diagnosis and treatment planning"; number of subtests administered depends on grade level and application; "designed to complement the Wechsler Intelligence Scale for Children-Fourth Edition (WISC-IV) and the Wechsler Individual Achievement Test-Second Edition (WIAT-II Update)"; previous edition entitled Process Assessment of the Learner: Test Battery of Reading and Writing.

Author: Virginia Wise Berninger.

Publisher: Pearson.

Cross References: For reviews by S. Kathleen Krach and Jennifer N. Mahdavi, see 18:98; for a review by Karen E. Jennings of an earlier edition, see 16:199.

[1617]
Productive Practices Survey.

Purpose: "To assess, describe, and pinpoint specific practices of the manager which support—or fail to support—organizational productivity."

Population: Managers.

Publication Dates: 1987–1996.

Acronym: PPS.

Scores, 12: Dimension I (Management Values, Support Structure, Managerial Credibility, Total), Dimension II (Impact, Relevance, Community, Total), Dimension III (Task Environment, Social Context, Problem Solving, Total).

Administration: Group.

Price Data, 2016: $12.95 per instrument.

Time: (30-35) minutes.

Comments: Based on model of organizational functioning called Competence Theory; self ratings; self scored.

Author: Jay Hall.

Publisher: Teleometrics International, Inc.

[1618]
Productivity Assessment Questionnaire.

Purpose: Assesses an employee's opinions about productivity in the organization in which they work.

Population: Employees.

Publication Date: 1984.

Scores: 11 areas: Policy, Leadership, Objectives, Inputs, Performance, Technology, Work Procedures, HRD, Work Quality, Managerial Skills, Quality of Work Life.

Administration: Group.

Price Data: Available from publisher.

Time: (10-12) minutes.

Comments: Self-administered and self-scored; can be made available for electronic administration.

Author: Robert C. Preziosi.

Publisher: Preziosi Partners, Inc.

Cross References: For a review by Robert M. Guion, see 10:297.

[1619]
Productivity Environmental Preference Survey.

Purpose: Identifies "how adults prefer to function, learn, concentrate and perform in their occupational or educational environment."

Population: Adults age 18 and older.

Publication Dates: 1975-2010.

Acronym: PEPS.

Scores, 20: Sound, Light, Temperature, Design, Motivated/Unmotivated, Persistent, Responsible, Structure, Learning Alone/Peer-Oriented Learner, Authority-Oriented Learner, Several Ways, Auditory Preferences, Visual Preferences, Tactile Preferences, Kinesthetic Preferences, Requires Intake, Evening/Morning, Late Morning, Afternoon, Needs Mobility.

Administration: Group or individual.

Price Data, 2015: $22.50 per 10 answer sheets for adults (includes scoring); $7.50 or less per group and subscale summary available from publisher only in addition to individual profiles; $.60 per individual interpretative booklet; $14 per manual (1996, 66 pages); $395 per computerized self-administered inventory program with 100 administrations (multi-language version $495) ($60 per 100 additional administrations) (Windows); $495 for Scanwin program permitting schools and businesses to scan and profile forms on site, includes multi-language capability; $.60 per answer form to use with Scanwin.

Time: (20–30) minutes.

Comments: PC compatible computer required for (optional) computerized administration; NCS Pearson Optical Mark Reader with dual pencil reader; Scrantron 8000, 8200, 8400, or SCANMARK 2550, 2660, 2800, 4000, or 5500 Scanner with dual pencil read for Scanwin; online administration available at www.learningstyle.com.

Authors: Gary E. Price, Rita Dunn, and Kenneth Dunn.

Publisher: Price Systems, Inc.

Cross References: See T5:2069 (3 references); for reviews by Javaid Kaiser and Thaddeus Rozecki, see 13:242 (6 references); see also T4:2114 (2 references); for reviews by Craig N. Mills and Bertram C. Sippola of an earlier edition, see 11:306 (9 references).

[1620]
Professional Employment Test.

Purpose: Designed to measure reading comprehension, reasoning, quantitative problem solving, and data interpretation for use in selecting personnel for professional, administrative, and managerial occupations.

Population: Potential managerial, administrative, and professional employees.

Publication Dates: 1986–2004.

Acronym: PET.
Scores: Total score only.
Administration: Group or individual.
Forms, 8: A, B, C, D, A-1, B-1, C-1, D-1.
Price Data: Price information available from publisher for test material including Technical Manual (2004, 40 pages), Supplemental Technical Manual for Form A-1 (1988, 9 pages), Supplemental Technical Manual for Forms C, D, C-1, and D-1 (2004, 11 pages), and User's Manual (2004, 19 pages).
Time: 80(85) minutes for long form; 40(45) minutes for short form.
Comments: Computerized versions available.
Authors: William W. Ruch, Richard H. McKillip, and Ricki Buckly.
Publisher: PSI Services LLC.
Cross References: For reviews by Gregory J. Cizek and Jayne E. Stake, see 12:312.

[1621]

The Professional Judgment Rating Form.

Purpose: Designed to judge "the extent to which novices approach problems with critical thinking."
Population: "Novice professionals."
Publication Dates: 1998-2006.
Acronym: PJRF.
Scores: Overall Rating.
Administration: Individual.
Price Data: Available from publisher.
Time: Administration time not reported.
Authors: Peter A. Facione, Stephen W. Blohm, Noreen C. Facione, and Carol Ann F. Giancarlo.
Publisher: Insight Assessment-The California Academic Press LLC.

[1622]

Profile of Aptitude for Leadership.

Purpose: To measure an individual's relative strength in each of four leadership styles (or types of leader).
Population: Adults.
Publication Date: 1991.
Acronym: PAL.
Scores, 4: Manager (Administrator), Supervisor (Coach), Entrepreneur (Leader), Technician (Specialist).
Administration: Group or individual.
Manual: No manual.
Price Data, 2016: $195; quantity discounts available.
Time: (20) minutes.
Comments: Self-administered; self-scored; now sold as part of the Training House Assessment Kit.
Author: Training House, Inc.
Publisher: HRD Press, Inc.
Cross References: For reviews by Jack E. Gebart-Eaglemont and Neal Schmitt, see 13:243.

[1623]

Profile of Creative Abilities.

Purpose: "Designed to measure the creative abilities of students."
Population: Ages 5-0 to 14-11.
Publication Date: 2007.
Acronym: PCA.
Scores, 11: Creativity Index, Drawing (New Elements, Originality, Orientation, Perspectives, Total), Categories (Fluency, Flexibility, Total), Home Rating Scale Total, School Rating Scale Total.
Price Data, 2015: $174 per complete kit including 25 Home Rating Scales, 25 School Rating Scales, 25 Student Forms, 25 Summary and Scoring Booklets, Picture Booklet, and examiner's manual (2007, 97 pages); $31 per 25 Home Rating Scales; $31 per 25 School Rating Scales; $31 per 25 Student Forms; $31 per 25 Summary and Scoring Booklets; $12 per Picture Booklet; $56 per examiner's manual.
Author: Gail R. Ryser.
Publisher: PRO-ED.
  a) PCA SUBTESTS.
  Purpose: Designed to "measure two aspects of divergent production."
  Scores: Creativity Index, Drawing (New Elements, Originality, Orientation, Perspective, Total), Categories (Fluency, Flexibility, Total).
  Subtests, 2: Drawing, Categories.
  Administration: Group (Drawing) and individual (Categories).
  Time: (30-40) minutes.
  b) PCA RATING SCALES.
  Purpose: Designed to "measure creative abilities, domain-relevant skills, creativity-relevant skills, and intrinsic task motivation."
  Scores: Total score only for each scale.
  Administration: Group.
  Forms, 2: Home Rating Scale, School Rating Scale.
  Time: Administration time not reported.
  Comments: Home ratings by parents/guardians; school ratings by teachers/educators.
Cross References: For reviews by Steven I. Pfeiffer and John F. Wakefield, see 18:99.

[1624]

Profile of Mood States, Bi-Polar Form.

Purpose: Developed to measure mood dimensions in terms of six bipolar affective states.
Population: 18 and older.
Publication Dates: 1984–2003.
Acronym: POMS-BI.
Scores, 6: Composed—Anxious, Elated—Depressed, Agreeable—Hostile, Energetic—Tired, Clearheaded—Confused, Confident—Unsure.
Administration: Individual or Group.
Price Data, 2015: $72 per POMS technical manual and POMS Bipolar supplement; $33 per POMS Bipolar supplement; $75 per 25 POMS Bipolar QuikScore forms.

Time: (5-10) minutes.
Authors: Maurice Lorr, Douglas M. McNair, and W. P. Heuchert.
Publisher: Multi-Health Systems, Inc.
Cross References: See T5:2077 (9 references).

[1625]
Profile of Mood States, Second Edition.

Purpose: Designed for the "assessment of transient and fluctuating feelings, as well as relatively enduring affect states."
Publication Dates: 1971-2012.
Acronym: POMS2.
Scores, 8: Anger-Hostility, Confusion-Bewilderment, Depression-Dejection, Fatigue-Inertia, Tension-Anxiety, Vigor-Activity, Total Mood Disturbance, Friendliness.
Administration: Individual or Group.
Forms, 4: Adult, Adult Short, Youth, Youth Short.
Price Data, 2015: $369 per complete online kit including manual (2012, 128 pages), 25 adult/adult short/youth/youth short online forms; $88 per manual; $3 per online form.
Authors: Juvia P. Heuchert and Douglas M. McNair.
Publisher: Multi-Health Systems, Inc.
   a) PROFILE OF MOOD STATES 2ND EDITION— ADULT.
   Population: Ages 18 and older.
   Acronym: POMS2—A.
   Time: (8-10) minutes.
   b) PROFILE OF MOOD STATES 2ND EDITION— ADULT SHORT.
   Population: Ages 18 and older.
   Acronym: POMS2—A Short.
   Time: (3-5) minutes.
   c) PROFILE OF MOOD STATES 2ND EDITION— YOUTH.
   Population: Ages 13 to 17.
   Acronym: POMS2—Y.
   Time: (8-10) minutes.
   d) PROFILE OF MOOD STATES 2ND EDITION— YOUTH SHORT.
   Population: Ages 13 to 17.
   Acronym: POMS2—Y Short.
   Time: (3-5) minutes.
Cross References: For reviews by Ira H. Bernstein and Joseph C. Kush, see 19:136; see also T5:2076 (187 references) and T4:2122 (191 references), 9:998 (46 references), and T3:1904 (84 references); for reviews by William J. Eichman and Thaddeus E. Weckowicz of an earlier edition, see 8:651 (33 references); see also T2:1337 (17 references).

[1626]
Profile of Nonverbal Sensitivity.

Purpose: "Designed to measure ability to decode non-verbal cues conveyed by the face, body, and tone of voice."
Population: Grades 3-16 and adults.
Publication Date: 1979.

Acronym: PONS.
Scores: Total score only.
Administration: Group.
Price Data: Now available at no charge from the Northeastern University library.
Authors: Robert Rosenthal, Judith Hall, Dane Archer, Robin DiMatteo, and Peter Rogers.
Publisher: Judith Hall.
   a) THE FULL PONS TEST.
   Purpose: Matching facial expressions, body movements, and tone of voice to situations.
   Time: 45(50) minutes.
   b) AUDIO CASSETTE VERSION.
   Purpose: To test sensitivity to tone of voice.
   Time: 60(65) minutes.
   Comments: Cassette tape includes the audio sections of the Full PONS, male, female, and child speakers.
   c) FACE AND BODY PONS.
   Time: 8(13) minutes.
   Comments: Visual-only-no-sound test; contains 20 face-only and 20 body-only items from the Full PONS test.
   d) BRIEF EXPOSURE PONS.
   Time: 8(13) minutes.
   Comments: Contains same 40 items as *c* but the exposure times are shortened to from 2 seconds to 1/24, 3/24, 9/24, and 27/24 seconds.
   e) NON-VERBAL DISCREPANCY TEST.
   Purpose: Measures how well the viewer detects discrepant audio versus visual signals.
   Time: 30(35) minutes.
Cross References: See T5:2078 (7 references) and T4:2124 (7 references).

[1627]
Profiles of Organizational Influence Strategies.

Purpose: To "measure how people use influence in their organizations."
Population: Working adults.
Publication Dates: 1982-1999.
Acronym: POIS.
Scores, 12 or 14: Friendliness, Bargaining, Reason, Assertiveness, Sanctions (Form S only), Higher Authority, Coalition scores for each of 2 areas (First Attempt to Influence, Attempts to Overcome Resistance to Influence).
Administration: Group.
Forms, 3: M (Manager), C (Co-Workers), S (Subordinates).
Price Data, 2015: $50 per manual, including review-only copy of forms; $15 per Individual Report (Form M, C and S); $20 per user's guide; $2.40 per online administration license (minimum 50); $2 per Remote Online Survey License or License to Reproduce.
Time: (20–30) minutes.
Authors: David Kipnis and Stuart M. Schmidt.
Publisher: Mind Garden, Inc.
Cross References: See T5:1402 (3 references) and T4:1363 (2 references).

[1628]

ProfileXT Assessment.

Purpose: "Multi-purpose assessment that is used for selection, coaching, training, promotion, managing, and succession planning."

Population: Present and potential employees.

Publication Dates: 1999-2007.

Acronym: PXT.

Scores: 21 scores in 4 subgroups: Thinking Style Scale (Learning Index, Verbal Skill, Verbal Reasoning, Numerical Ability, Numeric Reasoning), Behavioral Trait Scales (Energy Level, Assertiveness, Sociability, Manageability, Attitude, Decisiveness, Accommodating, Independence, Objective Judgment), Occupational Interests Scales (Enterprising, Financial/Administrative, People Service, Technical, Mechanical, Creative), Distortion Scale.

Administration: Group or individual.

Forms, 2: Online, Paper and Pencil.

Price Data: Available from publisher.

Time: (50-70) minutes.

Comments: Web-based administration available; 8 result reports: Placement Report, Coaching Report, Individual Report, Succession Planning Report, Candidate Matching Report, Job Profile Summary Report, Job Summary Graph, and Job Analysis Report.

Author: Profiles International, Inc.

Publisher: Profiles International, Inc.

Cross References: For reviews by Caroline Manuele Adkins and by Richard T. Kinnier and Nicole L. Nieset, see 18:100.

[1629]

Program Administration Scale, Second Edition.

Purpose: Designed to measure the leadership and management practices of center-based early childhood programs.

Population: Center-based early childhood programs.

Publication Date: 2011.

Acronym: PAS.

Scores, 27: 25 indicators: Staff Orientation, Supervision and Performance Appraisal, Staff Development, Compensation, Benefits, Staffing Patterns and Scheduling, Facilities Management, Risk Management, Internal Communications, Screening and Identification of Special Needs, Assessment in Support of Learning, Budget Planning, Accounting Practices, Program Evaluation, Strategic Planning, Family Communications, Family Support and Involvement, External Communications, Community Outreach, Technological Resources, Use of Technology, Administrator, Lead Teacher, Teacher, Assistant Teacher/Aide, plus Total Score, Average Item Score.

Administration: Individual.

Price Data, 2015: $23.95 per manual (91 pages), including rating forms.

Time: (120) minutes for interview; (120) minutes for document review.

Comments: Designed to complement the Early Childhood Environment Rating Scale.

Authors: Teri N. Talan and Paula Jorde Bloom.

Publisher: Teachers College Press.

Cross References: Reviews are scheduled for *The Twentieth Mental Measurements Yearbook*.

[1630]

Programmer Analyst Aptitude Test [One-Hour Version].

Purpose: To evaluate the candidate's aptitude and potential for programming and analyzing business problems.

Population: Entry-level and experienced applicants for programmer analyst positions.

Publication Date: 1997.

Acronym: PROGANI.

Scores: Total Score, Narrative Evaluation, Ranking, Recommendation.

Administration: Group.

Price Data: Available from publisher.

Foreign Language Edition: Available in French.

Time: (60) minutes.

Comments: Available in booklet and Internet versions; scored by publisher; must be proctored.

Author: Bruce A. Winrow.

Publisher: Walden Personnel Testing & Consulting Inc. [Canada].

Cross References: For a review by Suzanne Young, see 16:200.

[1631]

Programmer Analyst Aptitude Test [Two-Hour Version].

Purpose: "To evaluate the candidate's aptitude and potential for programming and analyzing business problems."

Population: Applicants for programmer analyst positions.

Publication Date: 1984.

Acronym: PAAT.

Scores, 6: Programming, Analytical, Total, Narrative Evaluation, Ranking, Recommendation.

Administration: Group.

Price Data: Available from publisher.

Time: (120) minutes.

Comments: Tests scored by publisher only; must be proctored.

Author: Bruce Winrow.

Publisher: Walden Personnel Testing & Consulting Inc. [Canada].

Cross References: For reviews by Frederick Bessai and Ralph F. Darr, Jr., see 11:308.

[1632]
Programmer Aptitude Battery.

Purpose: Designed to assess aptitude for programming.

Population: Adults naive to programming task.

Publication Date: 1988.

Acronym: PAB.

Scores, 4: Procedures, Matrices I, Matrices II, Grand Total.

Administration: Group.

Price Data: Available from publisher.

Foreign Language Edition: Test printed in both English and Afrikaans.

Time: 100(135) minutes.

Author: T. R. Taylor.

Publisher: Human Sciences Research Council [South Africa]. [Efforts to obtain updated information from the test publisher were unsuccessful. This test could not be found on the test publisher's website; its status is unknown.]

[1633]
Programmer Aptitude Series.

Purpose: Designed to assess skills needed in the data processing environment.

Population: Computer programming personnel.

Publication Dates: 1979–1983.

Acronym: PAS.

Administration: Group or individual.

Restricted Distribution: Distribution restricted to persons who have completed the publisher's training course or members of the Division of Occupational Psychology of the British Psychological Society.

Price Data: Available from publisher.

Comments: Consists of tests from within the Advanced, Personnel, and Technical Test Batteries; subtests available as separates.

Authors: Peter Saville (VA1, NA2, manual), Gill Nyfield (CP7, manual), Roger Holdsworth (VA3, NA4), David Hawkey (DA5, ST7, DT8, ST9), Sue Bawtree (CP7), Steve Blinkhorn (VA3), and Alan Iliffe (NA4).

Publisher: CEB.

a) LEVEL 1.
Publication Dates: 1979–1981.
Purpose: Basic programming.
1) *Number Series.*
Publication Date: 1980.
Acronym: NA2.
Time: 15(20) minutes.
2) *Diagramming.*
Publication Date: 1980.
Acronym: DA5.
Time: 20(25) minutes.
3) *Verbal Concepts.*
Publication Date: 1980.
Acronym: VA1.
Time: 15(20) minutes.
4) *Basic Checking.*
Publication Dates: 1980–1981.
Acronym: CP7.
Time: 10(15) minutes.
5) *Spatial Recognition.*
Publication Dates: 1980–1981.
Acronym: ST9.
Time: 15(20) minutes.

b) LEVEL 2.
Publication Dates: 1979–1983.
Purpose: Complex programming skills.
1) *Number series.*
Details same as for Level 1.
2) *Diagramming.*
Details same as for Level 1.
3) *Verbal Critical Reasoning.*
Publication Date: 1983.
Acronym: VA3.
Time: 30(35) minutes.
4) *Basic Checking.*
Details same as for Level 1.
5) *Special Reasoning.*
Publication Dates: 1979–1981.
Acronym: ST7.
Time: 20(25) minutes.

c) LEVEL 3.
Publication Dates: 1979–1983.
Population: Systems analysts and management.
1) *Verbal Concepts.*
Details same as for Level 1.
2) *Number Series.*
Details same as for Level 1.
3) *Verbal Reasoning.*
Details same as for Level 2.
4) *Numerical Critical Reasoning.*
Publication Dates: 1979–1983.
Acronym: NA4.
Time: 35(40) minutes.
5) *Diagrammatic Reasoning.*
Publication Dates: 1979–1981.
Acronym: DT8.
Time: 15(20) minutes.

[1634]
Progress in English 5–14.

Purpose: Designed as "a comprehensive standardized English test series that assesses reading and writing skills."

Population: Ages 4.0–15.05.

Publication Dates: 1994–2001.

Acronym: PiE 5–14.

Administration: Group.

Price Data: Available from publisher.

Comments: Assessments linked to curriculum guidelines for England and Wales, Scotland and Northern Ireland.

Publisher: GL Assessment [England; Efforts to obtain updated information from the test publisher were unsuccessful. An updated edition of this test, called Progress Test in English, appears on the test publisher's website].

a) PROGRESS IN ENGLISH 5.
Population: Ages 4.0–6.03.

Scores, 3: Initial Literacy, Understanding of Whole Text, Total.
Time: (40) minutes.
Authors: Lynn Howard, Anne Kispal, and Neil Hagues, National Foundation for Educational Research.
b) PROGRESS IN ENGLISH 6.
Population: Ages 5.0-7.05.
Scores, 5: Early Reading, Early Reading-Spelling, Understanding of Whole Text, Understanding Language in Context.
Time: (40-45) minutes.
Authors: Anne Kispal, and Neil Hagues, National Foundation for Educational Research.
c) PROGRESS IN ENGLISH 7.
Population: Ages 6.0–8.05.
Scores, 5: Understanding of Whole Text, Understanding Language in Context, Grammar, Spelling, Total.
Time: (60) minutes.
Authors: Anne Kispal, and Neil Hagues, National Foundation for Educational Research.
d) PROGRESS IN ENGLISH 8.
Population: Ages 7.0–9.5.
Scores, 5: Spelling, Grammar, Understanding of Whole Text, Understanding Language in Context, Total.
Time: (60) minutes.
Authors: Anne Kispal, Neil Hagues, and Graham Ruddock, National Foundation for Educational Research.
e) PROGRESS IN ENGLISH 9.
Population: Ages 8.0–10.05.
Scores, 6: Same as *d* above.
Time: (60) minutes.
Authors: Anne Kispal, Neil Hagues, and Graham Ruddock, National Foundation for Educational Research.
f) PROGRESS IN ENGLISH 10.
Population: Ages 9.0–11.05.
Scores, 6: Spelling, Grammar, Understanding of Whole Text, Vocabulary (Frequency and Spelling), Style, Total.
Time: (60) minutes.
Authors: Anne Kispal, Neil Hagues, and Graham Ruddock, National Foundation for Educational Research.
g) PROGRESS IN ENGLISH 11.
Population: Ages 10.0–12.05.
Scores, 6: Same as *f* above.
Time: (60) minutes.
Authors: Anne Kispal, Neil Hagues, and Graham Ruddock, National Foundation for Educational Research.
h) PROGRESS IN ENGLISH 12.
Population: Ages 11.0–13.05.
Scores, 6: Same as *f* above.
Time: (60) minutes.
Authors: Anne Kispal, Neil Hagues, and Graham Ruddock, National Foundation for Educational Research.
i) PROGRESS IN ENGLISH 13.
Population: Ages 12.0–14.05.
Scores, 6: Same as *f* above.
Time: (60) minutes.
Authors: Anne Kispal, Neil Hagues, and Graham Ruddock, National Foundation for Educational Research.
j) PROGRESS IN ENGLISH 14.
Population: Ages 13.0–15.05.
Scores, 6: Same as *f* above.
Time: (60) minutes.
Authors: Anne Kispal, and Neil Hagues, National Foundation for Educational Research.

Cross References: For reviews by Andrew A. Cox and Natalie Rathvon, see 16:201.

[1635]

Progressive Achievement Test of Listening Comprehension [2010 Edition].

Purpose: Designed to assess students' comprehension of texts read to them.
Population: Students in Years 3-10 of New Zealand schools.
Publication Dates: 1971-2010.
Acronym: PAT:Listening Comprehension.
Score: Total score only.
Administration: Group.
Levels, 8: 1, 2, 3, 4, 5, 6, 7, 8.
Price Data, 2015: NZ$85 per starter kit for Tests 1-4 including teacher's manual and one of each component; NZ$95 per starter kit for Tests 1-6 including teacher's manual and one of each component; NZ$65 per starter kit for Tests 5-6 or 7-8 including teacher's manual and one of each component; NZ$15.50 per 10 test booklets; NZ$10.50 per CD; NZ$7.75 per teacher script; NZ$18.50 per teacher's manual (2010, 72 pages); NZ$3 per marking key; NZ$2.90 per 10 answer sheets.
Time: (40) minutes.
Authors: Juliet Twist, Hilary Ferral, Verena Watson, Jim McNaughton, Sally Robertson, and Magdalene Lin.
Publisher: New Zealand Council for Educational Research [New Zealand].
Cross References: For a review by Sherwyn Morreale and Philip Backlund of the Progressive Achievement Tests of Listening Comprehension [Revised], see 13:245 (1 reference); see also T4:2140 (2 references) and T3:1910 (1 reference); for a review by Roger A. Richards of the original edition, see 8:453 (2 references).

[1636]

Progressive Achievement Test of Mathematics, 2nd Edition.

Purpose: To assist classroom teachers in determining the mathematics skills of their students.
Population: Ages 8-14.
Publication Dates: 1974-2015.
Acronym: PAT Mathematics.
Scores: Total score only.
Administration: Group.
Levels, 7: Individual tests for 7 year levels.
Forms: Alternate forms available for each level.
Price Data, 2016: NZ$5.20 per test booklet; NZ$2.35 per 10 answer sheets; NZ$26 per teacher's manual (2009, 63 pages); NZ$4.20 per marking key.
Time: (35-45) minutes.
Comments: Electronic marking service available to generate specific reports for each child/classroom/year

level; normative update in 2009; supplementary tests (alternate forms for 6 levels) added in 2015.
Authors: Charles Darr, Alex Neill, Andrew Stephanou, Hilary Ferral, Elliot Lawes, Jess Mazengarb, and Sally Robertson.
Publisher: New Zealand Council for Educational Research [New Zealand].
Cross References: For a review by Mary L. Garner, see 19:137; for reviews by Linda E. Brady and Suzanne Lane of an earlier edition, see 12:313; see also T3:1911 (1 reference); for a review by Harold C. Trimble of an earlier edition, see 8:288; for reviews by James C. Impara and A. Harry Passow of an earlier Australian edition, see 11:309.

[1637]
Progressive Achievement Test of Reading Comprehension and Vocabulary, Second Edition.

Purpose: Designed to "assist classroom teachers to determine the level of achievement attained by their students in reading comprehension and reading vocabulary."
Population: Years 4-10.
Publication Dates: 1969-2008.
Acronym: PAT: Reading
Scores, 2: Reading Comprehension, Reading Vocabulary.
Administration: Group.
Levels, 7: 1, 2, 3, 4, 5, 6, 7.
Price Data, 2015: NZ$60 starter kit tests 1-3; $93 starter kit tests 1-5; $95 per starter kit tests 1-7; $50 per starter kit tests 4+5 and 6+7; $4.20 per marking key (comprehension or vocabulary); $2.35 per pack of 10 answer sheets (comprehension or vocabulary); $31 per teacher manual; $6.80 per test booklet.
Comments: Scores on the tests are converted to scores on the Reading Comprehension and Reading Vocabulary measurement scales. This allows progress to be measured across tests.
Authors: Charles Darr, Sue McDowall, Hilary Ferral, Juliet Twist, and Verena Watson.
Publisher: New Zealand Council for Educational Research [New Zealand].
a) READING COMPREHENSION.
  Acronym: PATC.
  Time: (55) minutes.
b) READING VOCABULARY.
  Acronym: PATV.
  Time: (35) minutes.
Cross References: See T5:2094 (3 references); for a review by Herbert C. Rudman of an earlier edition, see 12:314 (3 references); see also T4:2141 (7 references) and T3:1912 (2 references); for a review by Douglas A. Pidgeon, see 8:738 (1 reference); see also T2:1579 (1 reference); for excerpted reviews by Milton L. Clark and J. Elkins, see 7:699.

[1638]
Progressive Achievement Tests in Mathematics—3rd Edition.

Purpose: Designed "to provide information to teachers about the level of achievement attained by their students in the skills and understanding of mathematics."
Population: Australian students in years 3-10.
Publication Dates: 1983–2005.
Acronym: PATMaths 3rd edition.
Scores: Total score only.
Administration: Group.
Price Data, 2005: A$6.50 per test booklet; A$149.95 per specimen set including one of each test booklet, teacher's manual, answer sheet, and CD-ROM; A$50 per 10 answer sheets–OMR or non-OMR available.
Time: (45) minutes.
Author: Australian Council for Educational Research Press.
Publisher: Australian Council for Educational Research Ltd. [Australia; Efforts to obtain updated information from the test publisher were unsuccessful. An updated edition of this test appears on the test publisher's website].
  a) LEVEL 1.
  Population: Years 4–6.
  b) LEVEL 2.
  Population: Years 6–9.
  c) LEVEL 3.
  Population: Years 7–9.
Cross References: For reviews by Kevin D. Crehan and Cindy M. Walker of an earlier edition, see 15:199; see T5:2091 (5 references); for reviews by James C. Impara and A. Harry Passow of an earlier edition, see 11:309 (2 references). For information on the New Zealand edition, see T3:1911 (1 reference); for additional information and a review by Harold C. Trimble, see 8:288.

[1639]
Progressive Achievement Tests in Reading: Comprehension and Vocabulary—Third Edition.

Purpose: "Tests designed to assist teachers in their assessment of students' reading comprehension skills and vocabulary knowledge."
Population: Years 3-9 in Australian school system.
Publication Dates: 1973–2001.
Acronym: PAT-R.
Scores, 2: Reading Comprehension, Reading Vocabulary.
Administration: Individual or group.
Parts, 2: PAT-R: Comprehension, PAT-R: Vocabulary.
Levels, 4: 4 levels for Comprehension and for Vocabulary: Test Form 1 (Years 3–5), Test Form 2 (Years 4–6), Test Form 3 (Years 6–8), Test Form 4 (Years 7–9).
Price Data, 2006: A$130 per specimen set including revised teacher's manual with score keys (2001, 79 pages), Comprehension test forms 1–4 (reusable), Comprehen-

sion answer sheets (10 each for Forms 1–4), Vocabulary test forms 1–4 (reusable), Vocabulary answer sheets (10 each for Forms 1–4); $85 per revised manual with score keys; $6.30 per Comprehension test form (any of Levels 1–4); $3.85 per Vocabulary test for (any of Levels 1–4); $11 per 10 Comprehension answer sheets or 10 Vocabulary answer sheets (any of Levels 1–4).

Time: 40(55) minutes (Comprehension); 25 minutes (Vocabulary).

Comments: Developed especially, but not exclusively, for use in Australian schools; hand- or machine-scorable; machine scoring performed by publisher; two types of reports available (PAT-R Report, PAT-R Diagnostic Report).

Author: Australian Council for Educational Research, Ltd.

Publisher: Australian Council for Educational Research Ltd. [Australia; Efforts to obtain updated information from the test publisher were unsuccessful. An updated edition of this test appears on the test publisher's website].

Cross References: For a review by Mark H. Fugate, see 15:200; for information on an earlier edition, see T5:2092 (4 references); for reviews by Paul C. Burnett and Richard Lehrer of an earlier edition, see 11:310 (4 references); see also T3:1912 (4 references); for a review by Douglas A. Pidgeon of an earlier edition, see 8:738 (1 reference); see also T2:1579 (1 reference); for excerpted reviews by Milton L. Clark and J. Elkins, see 7:699.

[1640]
Project Implementation Profile.

Purpose: To identify and measure behavioral variables that may be related to project success.

Population: Project managers and team members.

Publication Date: 1992.

Acronym: PIP.

Scores, 11: Project Mission, Top Management Support, Project Schedule, Client Consultation, Personnel, Technical Tasks, Client Acceptance, Monitoring and Feedback, Communication, Trouble-Shooting, Overall Performance.

Administration: Group.

Price Data: Available from publisher.

Time: (20) minutes.

Authors: Jeffrey K. Pinto and Dennis P. Slevin.

Publisher: Innodyne, Inc.

Cross References: For reviews by Sally Kuhlenschmidt and Kimberly A. Lawless, see 13:246.

[1641]
Project Leader Skills Evaluation.

Purpose: To assess essential skills needed for the position of Project Leader.

Population: Candidates for Project Leader position.

Publication Date: 1993.

Scores, 3: Total Score, Narrative Evaluation, Ranking, Recommendation.

Administration: Group.

Price Data: Available from publisher.

Foreign Language Edition: Available in French.

Time: [60] minutes.

Author: Bruce A. Winrow.

Publisher: Walden Personnel Testing & Consulting Inc. [Canada].

Cross References: For reviews by Laura L. B. Barnes and Alan D. Moore, see 16:202.

[1642]
PSACS Public Safety Assessment Center System for Police Sergeant.

Purpose: Designed "to help assess the promotional potential of police officers for the position of police sergeant."

Population: Candidates for promotion to the police sergeant position.

Publication Date: 2006.

Acronym: PSACS.

Scores: 7 competencies: Problem Identification and Analysis, Decision Making/Decisiveness, Oral Communication, Written Communication, Interpersonal and Community Relations, Planning and Supervising, Applied Technical Knowledge.

Administration: Individual or group.

Price Data: Available from publisher.

Time: 2 days.

Comments: Part of Public Safety Assessment Center System; modifications for rank structure or job title for sheriff's departments can be made; system includes subordinate role play exercise, video-based technical exercise, and an in-basket exercise; the system contains multiple simulation exercises, some of which are automated; also includes educational and training materials for jurisdictions to administer the assessment center without incurring the added cost of hiring a consultant; exercises vary by rank and are updated every other year.

Author: International Public Management Association for Human Resources.

Publisher: International Public Management Association for Human Resources (IPMA-HR).

[1643]
PSAT/NMSQT.

Purpose: Designed to measure "reasoning, math problem-solving, and writing skills generally associated with academic achievement in college."

Population: Students in Grades 8-11.

Publication Dates: 1959-2016.

Acronym: PSAT/NMSQT.

Scores, 13: 7 subscores (Command of Evidence, Words in Context, Expression of Ideas, Standard English Conventions, Heart of Algebra, Problem Solving and Data Analysis, Passport to Advanced Math), 3 test scores (Reading, Writing and Language, Math), 2 cross-test scores (Analysis in History/Social Studies, Analysis in Science), Total.

Administration: Group.

Price Data: Available from publisher.

Time: (165) minutes total; (60) minutes for Reading; (35) minutes for Writing and Language; (70) minutes for Math.

Comments: The PSAT/NMSQT was reconfigured in 2016 as part of the SAT Suite of Assessments.

Author: Administered for the College Board and National Merit Scholarship Corporation by Educational Testing Service.

Publisher: The College Board.

a) PSAT 8/9.

Purpose: Designed to help students and their teachers determine what areas to work on in order to be fully prepared for college after high school graduation.

Population: Students in Grades 8-9.

Comments: The PSAT 8/9 tests the same skills and knowledge as the SAT, PSAT/NMSQT and PSAT 10 but does so in a way that is grade-level appropriate; individual schools choose a date to offer the PSAT 8/9, either in the fall between September and January or in the spring between February and April.

b) PSAT 10.

Purpose: Designed to measure what students learn in high school and to determine what will be needed for success in college.

Population: Students in Grade 10.

Comments: The PSAT 10 tests the same skills and knowledge as the SAT, PSAT/NMSQT, and PSAT 8/9 but does so in a way that is grade-level appropriate; individual schools choose a date to offer the PSAT 10 between February and April.

c) PSAT/NMSQT.

Population: Students in Grades 10-11.

Comments: The PSAT/NMSQT and PSAT 10 are the same test, offered at different times of year; scores from the PSAT/NMSQT are used by the National Merit Scholarship Program to find eligible students.

Cross References: See T5:2031 (11 references), T4:2067 (6 references), and T3:1866 (7 references); for reviews by Jerome E. Doppelt and J. Thomas Hastings of Forms XPT1 and XPT2 (1975), see 8:199 (15 references); see also T2:436 (4 references) and 7:375 (10 references); for a review by Wayne S. Zimmerman of Forms HPT2 and KPT (1963), see 6:487 (2 references).

[1644]

PSB Aptitude for Practical Nursing Examination.

Purpose: Designed as a "method of selection, placement, guidance and counseling of incoming practical/vocational nursing students."

Population: Applicants for admission to practical/vocational nursing schools.

Publication Dates: 1961-2006.

Scores, 8: Academic Aptitude (Verbal, Arithmetic, Nonverbal, Total), Spelling, Information in the Natural Sciences, Judgment and Comprehension in Practical Nursing Situations, Vocational Adjustment Index.

Administration: Individual or group.

Price Data: Available from publisher.

Time: (135) minutes.

Authors: Anna S. Evans, Phyllis G. Roumm, and George A. W. Stouffer, Jr., with technical assistance from Psychological Services Bureau, Inc.

Publisher: Psychological Services Bureau, Inc.

Cross References: For reviews by Mark Albanese and Anita Tesh of the Revised PSB Aptitude for Practical Nursing Examination, see 13:264.

[1645]

PSB Health Occupations Aptitude Examination.

Purpose: Measures "abilities, skills, knowledge, and attitudes important for successful performance of students in the allied health education programs."

Population: Candidates for admission to programs of study for the allied health occupations.

Publication Dates: 1978-1999.

Scores, 8: Academic Aptitude (Verbal, Arithmetic, Nonverbal, Total), Spelling, Reading Comprehension, Information in the Natural Sciences, Vocational Adjustment Index.

Administration: Group or individual.

Price Data: Available from publisher.

Time: (135) minutes.

Authors: Psychological Services Bureau, Inc. with consultant contributions.

Publisher: Psychological Services Bureau, Inc.

Cross References: For reviews by Betty Bergstrom and Hilda Wing of the Revised PSB Health Occupations Aptitude Examination, see 13:265; for reviews by Stephen B. Dunbar and Lawrence M. Rudner of an earlier edition, see 11:312.

[1646]

PSB Reading Comprehension Examination.

Purpose: To reveal the examinee's comprehension or understanding of what is read.

Population: Secondary and postsecondary students applying or enrolled in terminal vocational or occupational programs, general population.

Publication Dates: 2000-2006.

Scores: Total score only.

Administration: Group or individual.

Price Data: Available from publisher.

Time: (60) minutes.

Authors: Psychological Services Bureau, Inc., with consultant contributions.

Publisher: Psychological Services Bureau, Inc.

Cross References: For reviews by Ray Fenton and Felice J. Green of the Revised PSB–Reading Comprehension Examination, see 13:267; for reviews by Joseph C. Ciechalski and by Brandon Davis and John A. Glover of an earlier edition, see 11:314.

[1647]
PSB Registered Nursing School Aptitude Examination.

Purpose: Predicts "readiness or suitability for specialized instruction in a school/program of professional nursing."
Population: Prospective nursing students.
Publication Dates: 1978-2006.
Scores, 8: Academic Aptitude (Verbal, Arithmetic, Nonverbal, Total), Spelling, Reading Comprehension, Information in the Natural Sciences, Vocational Adjustment Index.
Administration: Individual or group.
Price Data: Available from publisher.
Time: (105) minutes.
Comments: Previously listed as PSB Nursing School Aptitude Examination (R.N.).
Authors: Anna S. Evans, Phyllis G. Roumm, and George A. W. Stouffer, Jr.
Publisher: Psychological Services Bureau, Inc.
Cross References: For reviews by Mark H. Daniel and William B. Michael of the Revised PSB–Nursing School Aptitude Examination (R.N.), see 13:266; for reviews by Kurt F. Geisinger and James C. Impara of an earlier edition, see 11:313.

[1648]
PSC-Survey ADT.

Purpose: "Evaluates a job applicant's attitudes toward companies, business, work and trust attitudes."
Population: Job applicants.
Publication Date: 1987.
Scores, 4: Alienation, Trustworthiness, Total, False Positives.
Administration: Group or individual.
Price Data: Available from publisher.
Time: (15–20) minutes.
Comments: On-site scoring available.
Authors: Alan L. Strand and Mark L. Strand.
Publisher: Predictive Surveys Corporation.
Cross References: For a review by Chantale Jeanrie, see 13:247.

[1649]
PSC Survey-SA.

Purpose: "Measures attitudes toward the position of supervisor for selection or promotion."
Population: Job applicants or current employees.
Publication Date: 1987.

Scores, 6: Attitudes Toward Companies and Business, Attitudes Toward Managers and Executives, Attitudes Toward Peers and Associates, Attitudes Toward Being a Supervisor, Attitudes Toward Subordinates, Total.
Administration: Group or individual.
Price Data: Available from publisher.
Time: (10–15) minutes.
Authors: Alan L. Strand and Mark L. Strand.
Publisher: Predictive Surveys Corporation.
Cross References: For reviews by L. Carolyn Pearson and E. Lea Witta, see 13:248.

[1650]
PSI Basic Skills Tests for Business, Industry, and Government.

Purpose: "Designed to assess abilities and skills that are important for clerical, Administrative, and customer service positions."
Population: Prospective administrative, customer service, and clerical employees.
Publication Dates: 1981–1984.
Acronym: BST.
Scores: 15 subtest scores: Language Skills, Reading Comprehension, Vocabulary, Computation, Problem Solving, Decision Making, Following Oral Directions, Following Written Directions, Forms Checking, Reasoning, Classifying, Coding, Filing Names, Filing Numbers, Visual Speed and Accuracy.
Administration: Group or individual.
Price Data: Price information available from publisher for test material including User's Manual (2005, 59 pages), Technical Manual (2001, 61 pages), Technical Report Addendum: Meta-Analysis of the Validity of the Basic Skills Tests (2002, 14 pages), Validation Report (1982, 93 pages).
Time: 1.5-10(5-15) minutes for each test.
Comments: Tests available separately; computerized versions available; transportability procedure available.
Authors: William W. Ruch, Allen N. Shub, Sheryl M. Moinat, and David A. Dye.
Publisher: PSI Services LLC.
Cross References: See T5:2105 (1 reference); for reviews by Michael J. Stahl and Sheldon Zedeck, see 9:1010.

[1651]
PsychEval Personality Questionnaire.

Purpose: "Measures both normal personality and pathology-oriented traits to provide a multidimensional profile of the individual."
Population: Ages 16 and over; adults.
Publication Dates: 2002-2007.
Acronym: PEPQ.
Administration: Individual or group.
Price Data: Available from publisher.

Time: 75-90 minutes.

Comments: Protective Services Report Plus available for post-offer selection and fitness for duty evaluations for personnel in high-risk, public safety professions; PEPQ Interpretation available for use in both personal and vocational counseling.

Authors: Raymond B. Cattell, A. Karen S. Cattell, Heather E. P. Cattell, Mary T. Russell, and Scott Bedwell.

Publisher: Institute for Personality and Ability Testing, Inc. (IPAT).

a) RESPONSE STYLE INDICES.

Scores, 3: Impression Management, Infrequency, Acquiescence.

b) NORMAL PERSONALITY SCALES.

Scores: 16 Primary Factors: Warmth, Reasoning, Emotional Stability, Dominance, Liveliness, Rule-Consciousness, Social Boldness, Sensitivity, Vigilance, Abstractedness, Privateness, Apprehension, Openness to Change, Self-Reliance, Perfectionism, Tension; 5 Global Factors: Extraversion, Anxiety, Tough-Mindedness, Independence, Self-Control.

Comments: Items and norms from the 16PF Fifth Edition (12:354).

c) PATHOLOGY ORIENTED SCALES.

Scores, 12: Psychological Inadequacy, Health Concerns, Suicidal Thinking, Anxious Depression, Low Energy State, Self-Reproach, Apathetic Withdrawal, Paranoid Ideation, Obsessional Thinking, Alienation and Perceptional Distortion, Thrill-Seeking, Threat-Immunity.

d) INDICES.

Scores, 4: Quick-Eval, Depressive Characteristics, Distorted Thought Patterns, Risk-Taking.

e) OCCUPATIONAL INTEREST SECTION.

Scores, 6: Realistic Theme, Investigative Theme, Artistic Theme, Social Theme, Enterprising Theme, Conventional Theme.

Cross References: For reviews by Eugene V. Aidman and Frederick T. L. Leong, see 18:103.

[1652]

Psychiatric Content Analysis and Diagnosis.

Purpose: "For measuring the magnitude of various psychological states and traits from the content analysis of verbal behavior."

Population: Children and adults.

Publication Dates: 1993–2015.

Acronym: PCAD.

Scores, 14: Anxiety Scale, Hostility Scales (Hostility Directed Outward, Hostility Directed Inward, Ambivalent Hostility), Social Alienation—Personal Disorganization Scale, Cognitive and Intellectual Impairment Scale, Depression Scale, Hope Scale, Health-Sickness Scale, Achievement Striving Scale, Human Relations Scale, Dependency Strivings Scale, Quality of Life Scale, Narcissism Scale.

Administration: Individual or group.

Price Data, 2015: $299.95 per software license including manual and software download; academic discount available.

Time: (5) minutes; more if multiple speakers.

Comments: Earlier version listed in previous Buros publications as Psychologic and Neuropsychiatric Assessment Manual.

Authors: Louis A. Gottschalk and Robert Bechtel.

Publisher: GB Software LLC.

Cross References: For a review by William M. Reynolds, see 14:300.

[1653]

Psychiatric Diagnostic Screening Questionnaire.

Purpose: "Designed to screen for the DSM-IV (Diagnostic and Statistical Manual of Mental Disorders, Fourth Edition) Axis I disorders most commonly encountered in medical and outpatient mental health settings."

Population: Adult psychiatric patients ages 18 and older.

Publication Date: 2002.

Acronym: PDSQ.

Scores, 14: Major Depressive Disorder, Posttraumatic Stress Disorder, Bulimia/Binge-Eating Disorder, Obsessive-Compulsive Disorder, Panic Disorder, Psychosis, Agoraphobia, Social Phobia, Alcohol Abuse/Dependence, Drug Abuse/Dependence, Generalized Anxiety Disorder, Somatization Disorder, Hypochondriasis, Total.

Administration: Individual.

Price Data, 2016: $143.50 per test kit including manual, 25 test booklets, 25 summary sheets, and CD containing 13 follow-up interview guides (one for each disorder); $65.50 per manual; $52.50 per 25 test booklets; $35.50 per 100 summary sheets.

Time: (15–20) minutes.

Comments: Self-report questionnaire.

Author: Mark Zimmerman.

Publisher: Western Psychological Services.

Cross References: For reviews by Michael G. Kavan and Sean P. Reilley, see 16:203.

[1654]

Psychoeducational Profile — Third Edition.

Purpose: Designed as a measure of autism and related developmental disabilities.

Population: Ages 6 months to 7 years 5 months

Publication Dates: 1979-2005

Acronym: PEP-3

Administration: Individual

Price Data, 2015: $558 per complete kit including examiner's manual, guide to item administration, picture book, 10 examiner scoring/summary booklets, 10 response booklets, 10 caregiver report forms, and an object kit; $73 per examiner's manual; $49 per guide to item administration; $49 per picture book; $34 per 10 examiner scoring/summary booklets; $24 per 10 response booklets; $24 per 10 caregiver report forms; $347 per object kit.

Time: (45-90) minutes

Comments: Includes a norm-referenced scale and parent/caregiver scale; caregiver "must be an adult who is familiar with the behavior of the child being evaluated."

Authors: Eric Schopler, Margaret D. Lansing, Robert J. Reichler, and Lee M. Marcus

Publisher: PRO-ED.

   a) PERFORMANCE PART.

      1) *Developmental Abilities.*

      Scores: 6 subscales: Cognitive Verbal/Preverbal, Expressive Language, Receptive Language, Fine Motor, Gross Motor, Visual-Motor Imitation.

      2) *Maladaptive Behaviors.*

      Scores: 4 subscales: Affective Expression, Social Reciprocity, Characteristic Motor Behaviors, Characteristic Verbal Behaviors.

      3) *Composites.*

      Scores: 3 subscales: Communication, Motor, Maladaptive Behaviors.

   b) CAREGIVER REPORT.

      1) *Clinical Sections.*

      Scores: 3 subtests: Problem Behaviors, Personal Self-Care, Adaptive Behavior.

Cross References: For reviews by Pat Mirenda and Leah M. Nellis, see 17:156; see also T5:2111 (2 references); for reviews by Pat Mirenda and Gerald Tindal of an earlier edition, see 12:316 (2 references); for reviews by Gerald S. Hanna and Martin J. Wiese of the original edition, see 11:317.

[1655]

Psycholinguistic Assessments of Language Processing in Aphasia.

Purpose: A battery of 60 assessments "designed to help to diagnose language processing difficulties in individuals with acquired brain damage."

Population: Adults with aphasia.

Publication Date: 1992.

Acronym: PALPA.

Scores: 60 tasks in 4 sections: Auditory Processing (Nonword Minimal Pairs, Word Minimal Pairs, Word Minimal Pairs Requiring Written Selection, Word Minimal Pairs Requiring Picture Selection, Auditory Lexical Decision: Imageability x Frequency, Auditory Lexical Decision: Morphological Endings, Repetition: Syllable Length, Repetition: Nonwords, Repetition: Imageability x Frequency, Repetition: Grammatical Class, Repetition: Morphological Endings, Repetition: Sentences, Digit Production/Matching Span, Rhyme Judgments x Pictures, Rhyme Judgments x Words, Phonological Segmentation: Initial Sounds, Phonological Segmentation: Final Sounds), Reading and Spelling (Letter Discrimination: Mirror Reversal, Letter Discrimination: Upper-Lower Case Matching, Letter Discrimination: Lower-Upper Case Matching, Letter Discrimination: Words & Nonwords, Letter Naming & Sounding, Spoken Letter-Written Letter Matching, Visual Lexicon Decision: Legality, Visual Lexicon Decision: Imageability x Frequency, Visual Lexicon Decision: Morphological Endings, Visual Lexicon Decision: Regularity, Homophone Decision, Oral Reading: Letter Length, Oral Reading: Syllable Length, Oral Reading: Imageabilty x Frequency, Oral Reading: Grammatical Class, Oral Reading: Grammatical Class x Imageability, Morphological Endings, Oral Reading: Regularity, Oral Reading: Nonwords, Oral Reading: Sentences, Homophone Definition x Regularity, Spelling to Dictation: Imageabilty x Frequency, Spelling to Dictation: Grammatical Class, Spelling to Dictation: Grammatical Class x Imageability, Spelling to Dictation: Morphological Endings, Spelling to Dictation: Regularity, Spelling to Dictation: Nonwords, Spelling to Dictation: Disambiguated Homophones), Picture & Word Semantics (Spoken Word-Picture Matching, Written Word-Picture Matching, Auditory Synonym Judgments, Written Synonym Judgments, Word Semantic Association, Spoken Word-Written Word Matching, Picture Naming x Oral Reading, Repetition & Written Spelling, Picture Naming x Frequency), Sentence Comprehension (Auditory Sentence Comprehension, Written Sentence Comprehension, Auditory Comprehension of Verbs & Adjectives from the Sentence Set, Auditory Comprehension of Locative Relations, Written Comprehension of Locative Relations, Pointing Span for Noun-Verb Sentences).

Administration: Individual.

Price Data, 2016: $525 per battery.

Time: Administration time not reported.

Authors: Janice Kay, Ruth Lesser, and Max Coltheart.

Publisher: Routledge Psychology.

[1656]

Psychological Capital Questionnaire.

Purpose: Designed to "measure an individual's psychological capital."

Population: Working adults.

Publication Date: 2014.

Acronym: PCQ.

Scores, 4: Hope, Efficacy, Resilience, Optimism.

Administration: Individual or group.

Forms, 3: Self-Rater, Rater, Self-Rater Short.

Price Data, 2016: $50 per PDF manual (41 pages); $60 per paper manual; $75 per Multi-rater Report; $250 per Group Report: Multi-rater; $100 per Trainer's Guide for Developing Psychological Capital; $24 per Individual Report: Self Form; $25 per Report About Me: Self Form; $250 per Group Report: Self Form; $3 per Transform Survey Hosting: Multi-rater ($75 set up fee); $1.92 per Transform Survey Hosting: Self Form (minimum purchase of 50); $1.92 per Transform Survey Hosting: Rater Form (minimum purchase of 50); $1.60 per Remote Online Survey License (minimum purchase of 50); $1.60 per License to Reproduce.

Foreign Language Editions: Both Self and Rater Forms are available in Finnish; Self Form available in

Arabic, Cambodian, Chinese, Dutch, French, French (Canada), German, Greek, Hebrew, Hungarian, Indonesian, Korean, Lithuanian, Norwegian, Persian, Polish, Portuguese, Portuguese (Brazil), Slovenian, Spanish, Thai, and Turkish.
Time: [10-15] minutes.
Authors: Fred Luthans, Bruce J. Avolio, and James B. Avey.
Publisher: Mind Garden, Inc.

[1657]

Psychological Distress Profile.

Purpose: Designed as a self-report screening measure of psychological distress.
Population: Ages 18 and older.
Publication Date: 2015.
Acronym: PDP.
Scores, 5: Depression, Hopelessness, Anxiety, Anger, Total.
Administration: Individual or group.
Price Data, 2016: $50 per PDF manual (41 pages); $60 per paper manual; $15 per Individual Report; $15 per Report About Me; $2.40 per Transform Survey Hosting (minimum purchase of 50); $2 per Remote Online Survey License (minimum purchase of 50); $2 per License to Reproduce (minimum purchase of 50).
Time: (5-10) minutes.
Comments: Title on test form is How I Feel Questionnaire; administered online or via paper and pencil.
Authors: Gary Elkins and Aimee Johnson.
Publisher: Mind Garden, Inc.

[1658]

Psychological Indicator for Assessing Quantities of Love with Regard to Various Types of Love.

Purpose: Designed to assess a person's love for various activities, lifestyles, and people.
Population: Contact publisher for details.
Publication Dates: 2004-2005.
Administration: Group or individual.
Manual: No manual.
Price Data, 2015: $20-50 per survey, based on ability to pay.
Time: Administration time not reported.
Comments: Survey price range is based upon the consumer's ability to pay.
Authors: James T. Struck, with contributions from Marina Garavaglia and Darren Rubin.
Publisher: Dinosaurs, Trees, Religion and Galaxies.

[1659]

Psychological Ownership Questionnaire.

Purpose: Designed to "assess promotive and preventative psychological ownership."

Population: Adults.
Publication Date: 2007.
Acronym: POQ.
Scores, 6: Preventive Psychological Ownership, Promotive Psychological Ownership (Self-Efficacy, Accountability, Sense of Belongingness, Self Identify).
Administration: Individual or group.
Manual: No manual.
Price Data, 2016: $2.40 per Transform Survey Hosting (minimum purchase of 50); $2 per Remote Online Survey License (minimum purchase of 50); $2 per License to Reproduce (minimum purchase of 50).
Foreign Language Editions: Available in Chinese, Dutch, German, Hebrew, Indonesian, Thai, and Turkish.
Time: [10] minutes.
Authors: James B. Avey and Bruce J. Avolio.
Publisher: Mind Garden, Inc.

[1660]

Psychological Processing Checklist–Revised.

Purpose: Designed to assess processing deficits by differentiating "between learning disabilities, underachievement and other disabling conditions" to inform intervention development.
Population: Ages 5-10.
Publication Dates: 2003-2008.
Acronym: PPC-R.
Scores, 7: Auditory Processing, Social Perception, Visual Processing, Organization, Visual-Motor Processing, Attention, Total Score.
Administration: Individual or group.
Price Data, 2015: $127 per complete kit; $79 per technical manual (2008, 84 pages): $55 per 25 Quik-Score forms.
Time: (15) minutes.
Comments: To be completed by the student's regular or special education teacher.
Authors: Mark E. Swerdlik, Peggy Swerdlik, Jeffrey H. Kahn, and Tim Thomas.
Publisher: Multi-Health Systems, Inc.
Cross References: For reviews by Joyce Meikamp and Jeanette Lee-Farmer and by Tawnya J. Meadows and Natasha Segool, see 18:104; for reviews by Bruce A. Bracken and Keith F. Widaman of the earlier edition, see 16:204.

[1661]

Psychological Screening Inventory.

Purpose: Developed to screen for mental health problems.
Population: Ages 16 and over.
Publication Dates: 1973-1978.
Acronym: PSI.
Scores, 5: Alienation, Social Nonconformity, Discomfort, Expression, Defensiveness.
Administration: Group or individual.

Price Data, 2010: $84 per examination kit including manual (1978, 44 pages), 5 question-and-answer sheets, 5 profile sheets, and set of scoring templates; $32 per test manual; $50 per set of scoring templates; $60 per testing kit (including 25 question-and-answer sheets and 25 profile sheets).
Foreign Language Edition: Available in Spanish (question and answer sheets only).
Time: 15 minutes.
Author: Richard I. Lanyon.
Publisher: SIGMA Assessment Systems, Inc.
Cross References: See T5:2115 (6 references), T4:2159 (20 references), 9:1015 (2 references), and T3:1931 (18 references); for a review by Stephen L. Golding, see 8:654 (32 references); see also T2:1342 (7 references).

[1662]

Psychopathic Personality Inventory-Revised.
Purpose: Designed to help "assess psychopathic personality traits."
Population: Ages 18-86.
Publication Date: 2005.
Acronym: PPI-R.
Scores, 15: 8 Content scores (Machiavellian Egocentricity, Rebellious Nonconformity, Blame Externalization, Carefree Nonplanfulness, Social Influence, Fearlessness, Stress Immunity, Coldheartedness), Total, 4 Validity scores (Virtuous Responding, Deviant Responding, Inconsistent Responding 15, Inconsistent Responding 40), 3 Factor scores (Self-Centered Impulsivity, Fearless Dominance, Coldheartedness).
Administration: Individual or group.
Price Data, 2015: $330 per introductory kit including professional manual (166 pages), 25 reusable item booklets, 25 response forms, 25 scoring summary forms, and software (CD-ROM) with on-screen help and quick start guide; $88 per professional manual; $60 per 25 response forms; $70 per 25 reusable item booklets; $58 per 25 scoring summary forms.
Time: (20-30) minutes.
Comments: "PPI-R scores and profiles should not be used as the sole basis for diagnostic and treatment decisions that require the integration of information from varying sources."
Authors: Scott O. Lilienfeld and Michelle R. Widows.
Publisher: Psychological Assessment Resources, Inc.
Cross References: For reviews by Gerald E. De-Mauro and S. Alvin Leung, see 17:157.

[1663]
Psychosocial Adjustment to Illness Scale.
Purpose: "Designed to assess the quality of a patient's psychosocial adjustment to a current medical illness or its residual effects."
Population: Medical patients or their immediate relatives.

Publication Date: 1983.
Acronym: PAIS and PAIS-SR.
Scores, 8: Health Care Orientation, Vocational Environment, Domestic Environment, Sexual Relationship, Extended Family, Social Environment, Psychological Distress, Total.
Administration: Individual.
Editions, 3: Interview, Self-Report, Caretaker version.
Price Data, 2016: $40 per 10 reusable PAIS booklets; $97.50 per 50 PAIS-SR booklets; $25 per 50 PAIS-SR score/profile sheets; $97.50 per 50 PAIS-SR caregiver booklets; $25 per 50 PAIS score/profile sheets; $2 per PAIS-SR website scorings.
Time: (20–30) minutes.
Author: Leonard R. Derogatis.
Publisher: Clinical Psychometric Research, Inc.
Cross References: See T5:2117 (5 references) and T4:2161 (3 references); for a review by Cabrini S. Swassing, see 10:299.

[1664]
Psychosocial Evaluation & Threat Risk Assessment.
Purpose: Designed to "assist school personnel in … determining the nature and degree of violence risk among students."
Population: Ages 11-18.
Publication Date: 2005.
Acronym: PETRA.
Scores, 15: 4 Domain scores (Psychological Domain, Ecological Domain, Resiliency Problems Domain, Total Domain), 8 Cluster scores (Depressed Mood, Alienation, Egocentrism, Aggression, Family/Home, School, Stress, Coping Problems), 2 Response Style Indicator scores (Social Desirability, Inconsistency), PETRA Threat Assessment Matrix score.
Administration: Individual or group.
Price Data, 2015: $150 per introductory kit including professional manual (2005, 85 pages), 25 rating forms, and 25 score summary/profile forms; $64 per professional manual; $66 per 25 rating forms; $32 per 25 score summary/profile forms.
Time: (10-15) minutes.
Author: Jay Schneller.
Publisher: Psychological Assessment Resources, Inc.
Cross References: For reviews by Michael Furlong and Diane Tanigawa and by Georgette Yetter, see 17:158.

[1665]
Psychotherapy Outcome Kit (Including Quality of Emotional Life Self-Report).
Purpose: Designed to assist mental health care providers in collecting treatment outcome data.
Population: Age 15 and under, age 16 and older.
Publication Date: 1994.

Scores: Total score only.
Administration: Individual.
Price Data: Available from publisher.
Time: Average completion time is over several sessions.
Author: David P. Isenberg.
Publisher: Mind Garden, Inc.
  a) CHILD VERSION.
  Population: Age 15 and under.
  Comments: Child Version QELSR completed by parent/guardian. The kit includes the Quality of Emotional Life Self-Report, clinical summary forms, a progress note form, and data sheets to provide a psychotherapy outcome profile.
  b) ADULT VERSION.
  Population: Age 16 and older.
  Comments: Adult Version QELSR completed by patient.
Cross References: For reviews by Matthew Burns and George Domino, see 14:302.

[1666]

PsychProfiler.

Purpose: Assists in the "identification and treatment of disorders in children, adolescents and adults."
Population: Ages 2-18+.
Scores, 54: 22 "Positive Screen Cutoff" conclusions (YES/NO) per population level: Generalised Anxiety Disorder, Obsessive-Compulsive Disorder, Post-Traumatic Stress Disorder, Attention-Deficit/Hyperactivity Disorder (Hyperactive-Impulsive Type, Inattentive Type, Combined Type), Conduct Disorder, Oppositional Defiant Disorder, Expressive Language Disorder, Mixed Receptive-Expressive Language Disorder, Phonological Disorder, Dysthymic Disorder, Anorexia Nervosa, Bulimia Nervosa, Disorder of Written Expression, Mathematics Disorder, Reading Disorder, Asperger's Disorder, Autistic Disorder, Tic Disorder-Motor, Tic Disorder-Vocal, Tourette's Disorder; 1 additional conclusion unique to Child and Adolescent level: Separation Anxiety Disorder; 4 additional conclusions unique to Adult level: Panic Disorder, Specific Phobia, Major Depressive Disorder, Antisocial Personality Disorder; 1 "Reliability Measure" per form per population level (Parent-Report, Self-Report, Teacher-Report [Child and Adolescent]; Self-Report, Observer-Report [Adult]).
Administration: Group.
Price Data, 2016: A$770 per complete kit including manual (2007, 174 pages), online software license, and 10 report forms each APP Self-Report, APP Observer, CAPP Parent, CAPP Self, and CAPP Teacher; A$550 per CAPP or APP complete kit, including manual and 10 of each form; A$77 per manual; A$33 per 10 APP report forms; A$30.80 per 10 CAPP report forms.
Comments: Available for computer or paper-and-pencil administration; test has been updated to incorporate the recent advances in the DSM-5.

Authors: Shane Langsford, Stephen Houghton, and Graham Douglas.
Publisher: Australian Council for Educational Research Ltd. [Australia].
  a) CHILD AND ADOLESCENT PSYCHPROFILER.
  Population: Ages 2-18.
  Publication Dates: 1999-2007.
  Acronym: CAPP.
  Forms, 3: Parent Report, Self-Report (only administered to children ages 10+), Teacher-Report.
  Time: (20) minutes.
  Comments: Formerly called Child and Adolescent Disorder Screening Instrument (CADSI).
  b) ADULT PSYCHPROFILER.
  Population: Ages 18+.
  Publication Date: 2007.
  Acronym: APP.
  Forms, 2: Self-Report, Observer Report.
  Time: (20) minutes.
Cross References: For a review by Mark E. Swerdlik and W. Joel Schneider, see 18:105.

[1667]

PTSD and Suicide Screener.

Purpose: Designed to "screen individuals for post-traumatic stress disorder (PTSD) and suicide risk."
Population: Ages 18 and older.
Publication Dates: 1998-2013.
Acronym: PSS.
Scores, 2: PTSD Risk, Suicide Risk.
Administration: Individual or group.
Price Data, 2015: $82 per kit including manual (2013, 24 pages) and 25 answer sheets; $46 per manual; $38 per 25 answer sheets; $5 per 5 online administrations.
Time: (1-5) minutes.
Comments: Administered via paper and pencil or online. Derived from the Detailed Assessment of Posttraumatic Stress.
Author: John Briere.
Publisher: Psychological Assessment Resources, Inc.
Cross References: Reviews are scheduled for *The Twentieth Mental Measurements Yearbook*.

[1668]

Purdue Pegboard.

Purpose: Measures an individual's ability to move hands, fingers, and arms (gross movement) and to control movements of small objects (finger tip dexterity).
Population: Assembly, general factory and various industrial positions and vocational rehabilitation.
Publication Dates: 1941–1992.
Scores, 5: Right Hand, Left Hand, Both Hands, Right plus Left plus Both Hands, Assembly.
Administration: Individual or group.
Price Data: Available from publisher.
Time: (3–9) minutes.
Author: Purdue Research Foundation.

Publisher: General Dynamics Information Technology.
Cross References: See T5:2125 (30 references), T4:2168 (34 references), T3:948 (13 references), T2:2234 (51 references), and 6:1081 (15 references); for a review by Neil D. Warren, see 5:873 (11 references); see also 4:751 (12 references); for reviews by Edwin F. Ghiselli, Thomas W. Harrell, and Albert Gibson Packard, see 3:666 (3 references).

[1669]

The Pyramids and Palm Trees Test.

Purpose: Designed "to assess a person's ability to access detailed semantic representations from words and from pictures."
Population: Ages 18-80.
Publication Date: 1992.
Scores: Total score only.
Administration: Individual.
Price Data, 2015: $137.35 per kit including manual, 25 scoring sheets, word card, and stimulus book; $17.95 per 25 scoring sheets; $58.45 per manual.
Time: Administration time not reported.
Authors: David Howard and Karalyn Patterson.
Publisher: Pearson Assessment [England].
Cross References: For reviews by Arturo Olivarez, Jr. and Allison Boroda, see 17:160.

[1670]

Quality Culture Assessment.

Purpose: Designed to assess and evaluate organizational practices, policies, and procedures.
Population: Managers and personnel.
Acronym: QCA.
Administration: Group.
Manual: No manual.
Price Data: Available from publisher.
Time: Administration time not reported.
Authors: Juran Institute and Teleometrics International.
Publisher: Teleometrics International, Inc.
  a) QUALITY POTENTIAL ANALYSIS.
  Publication Dates: 1982–1995.
  Acronym: QPA.
  Scores, 2: As It Is Now, As I Would Like It To Be.
  b) QUALITY CULTURE ANALYSIS.
  Publication Date: 1995.
  Acronym: QCA.
  Scores, 9: Quality Values (Senior Leadership, Goals and Objectives, Rewards and Recognition), Empowered Employees (Self-Control, Recovery, Participation), Customer Focus (Individual Customer Focus, Managerial Customer Focus, Organizational Customer Focus).

[1671]

Quality of Life Enjoyment and Satisfaction Questionnaire.

Purpose: Designed to measure the "degree of enjoyment and satisfaction experienced by subjects in various areas of daily functioning."

Population: Adults with mental or medical disorders.
Publication Date: 1990.
Acronym: Q-LES-Q.
Scores, 9: 6 scores (Physical Health, Subjective Feelings, Leisure Time Activities, Social Relationships, General Activities, Overall Life Enjoyment and Satisfaction); 3 optional scores (Work, Household Duties, School/Coursework).
Administration: Group.
Forms, 2: Regular Form, Short Form.
Price Data: Available from publisher.
Time: Regular Form: [5–15] minutes; Short Form: [3–5] minutes.
Comments: Self-report measure.
Author: Jean Endicott.
Publisher: Department of Research Assessment and Training.
Cross References: For reviews by John C. Caruso and Mary Lou Bryant Frank, see 14:303.

[1672]

Quality of Life Inventory.

Purpose: Developed to provide a measure of a person's quality of life and their satisfaction with life.
Population: Ages 18 and over.
Publication Date: 1994.
Acronym: QOLI®.
Scores: 17 scales: Health, Self-Esteem, Goals-and-Values, Money, Work, Play, Learning, Creativity, Helping, Love, Friends, Children, Relatives, Home, Neighborhood, Community, Overall Quality of Life.
Administration: Group or individual.
Price Data, 2015: $122.50 per hand-scoring starter kit including manual (84 pages), 50 answer sheets, and 50 worksheets; $122.50 per Q Local starter kit including 25 answer sheets to conduct and receive 25 Q Local profile reports; $82.50 per hand-scoring reorder kit including 50 answer sheets and 50 worksheets; $23 per Q Local answer sheets; $3 per Q Local profile report; $49.70 per manual; quantity discounts available for the reports.
Time: (5) minutes.
Comments: Useful for outcomes measurement as well as individual counseling.
Author: Michael B. Frisch.
Publisher: Pearson.
Cross References: For reviews by Laura L. B. Barnes and Richard W. Johnson, see 14:304.

[1673]

Quality of Life Questionnaire.

Purpose: "Designed to assess the relationship between the quality of an individual's life and other behaviors and afflictions, such as physical health, psychological health, and alcohol or substance use."
Population: Ages 18 and over.
Publication Date: 1989-2003.

Acronym: QLQ.

Scores, 17: Material Well-Being, Physical Well-Being, Personal Growth, Marital Relations, Parent-Child Relations, Extended Family Relations, Extramarital Relations, Altruistic Behavior, Political Behavior, Job Characteristics, Occupational Relations, Job Satisfiers, Creative/Aesthetic Behavior, Sports Activity, Vacation Behavior, Social Desirability, Total Quality of Life.

Administration: Individual or Group.

Price Data, 2015: $109 per complete kit including 25 QuikScore™ answer forms, 10 question booklets, and manual (38 pages); $35 per 10 reusable question booklets; $38 per 25 QuikScore™ answer forms; $44 per manual; $50 per QLQ Online Report Kit including manual and 3 QLQ reports; $6 per Online Report (min. purchase of 25).

Time: (30) minutes.

Comments: Self-report; Online version available.

Authors: David R. Evans and Wendy E. Cope.

Publisher: Multi-Health Systems, Inc.

Cross References: See T5:2132 (4 references) and T4:2172 (1 reference); for reviews by Gary B. Seltzer and Richard B. Stuart, see 11:318.

[1674]
Quality Potential Assessment.

Purpose: "Designed to provide information about an organization, such as data on its policies, practices, and logistics, and the degree to which the data contribute to encouraging staff to give their best to the organization."

Population: Adults.

Publication Dates: 1992–1995.

Acronym: QPA.

Scores: Actual and Desired ratings in 10 areas: Collaboration (Management Values, Support Structure, Managerial Credibility, Climate), Commitment (Impact, Relevance, Community), Creativity (Task Environment, Social Context, Problem Solving).

Administration: Group.

Price Data: Available from publisher.

Time: Administration time not reported.

Author: Jay Hall.

Publisher: Teleometrics International, Inc.

Cross References: For reviews by Theodore L. Hayes and Michael J. Zickar, see 14:305.

[1675]
Qualls Early Learning Inventory.

Purpose: Designed to provide a diagnostic review of six key developmental aras of learning that are important for success in school.

Population: Grades K–1.

Publication Date: 2003.

Acronym: QELI.

Scores, 6: General Knowledge, Oral Communication, Written Language, Math Concepts, Work Habits, Attentive Behavior.

Administration: Individual or group.

Price Data, 2015: $42.85 per 25 Inventories and 1 Teacher's Directions and Interpretive Guide; Score Reports (optional services): Student Profile Narrative is $1.06 per student and $.54 for additional copies; Class Diagnostic Report is $1.06 per student and $.54 for additional copies; Class, Building, and System Summaries is $.54 per student and $.54 for additional copies.

Time: (10) minutes per student.

Comments: Teacher-completed rating scale; observation of individual students; computer scoring and individual and group score reports available through Riverside Scoring Service; test was previously listed as Iowa Early Learning Inventory.

Authors: A. L. Qualls, H. D. Hoover, S. B. Dunbar, and D. A. Frisbie.

Publisher: Houghton Mifflin Harcourt.

Cross References: For reviews by Leslie Eastman Lukin and Carol M. McGregor, see 16:115.

[1676]
Quant Q.

Purpose: Designed to "target reasoning skills in relation to quantitative problems. The problems are designed to measure one's ability to think 'outside of the box' when solving quantitative problems."

Population: Undergraduates, students seeking advanced degrees, professionals, college prep students, adults of all ages.

Publication Date: 2005.

Scores: Total score only.

Administration: Group.

Manual: No manual.

Price Data: Available from publisher.

Time: (50) minutes.

Comments: This test can be administered online or via paper and pencil.

Author: Stephen W. Blohm.

Publisher: Insight Assessment-The California Academic Press LLC.

[1677]
QUIC Tests.

Purpose: Designed "to establish or verify the functional level of proficiency in the areas of either mathematics or the communicative arts."

Population: Grades 2–12.

Publication Dates: 1989–2006.

Scores, 8: Mathematics (Computation, Concepts, Problem Solving, Total), Communicative Arts (Reading, Reference Skills, Language Arts, Total).

Administration: Individual or group.

Forms, 2: G, H.

Price Data: 2015: $86.20 per self-scoring starter set including examiner's manual, 20 test booklets, and 20 response forms (specify mathematics or communicative arts and Form G or Form H); $38.80 per 20 response forms (specify mathematics or communicative arts and Form G or Form H); $47.40 per 20 test booklets (specify mathematics or communicative arts and Form G or Form H); $28 per self-scoring development and standardization manual; $20.95 per examiner's manual; $84.92 per machine-scorable starter set including examiner's manual, 20 test booklets, 20 answer sheets, and interpretative manual (specify mathematics or communicative arts and Form G or Form H); $23.75 per 20 machine-scorable answer sheets.

Time: (35) minutes or less.

Comments: Self-administered; competency-based interpretation.

Author: Scholastic Testing Service, Inc.

Publisher: Scholastic Testing Service, Inc.

Cross References: For a review by Delwyn L. Harnisch, see 11:320.

[1678]
Quick Language Assessment Inventory.

Purpose: Designed to provide information about student's English and Spanish language background.

Population: Grades K–6.

Publication Date: 1974.

Scores: Total score and grade level equivalents.

Administration: Individual.

Price Data: Available from publisher.

Time: (1–2) minutes.

Comments: Designed for children suspected of needing English as a second language; parents or guardians provide information about child's English and Spanish background.

Author: Steve Moreno.

Publisher: Moreno Educational Co.

Cross References: For reviews by Giuseppe Costantino and Beth L. Evard, see 9:1026.

[1679]
Quick Neurological Screening Test, 3rd Edition.

Purpose: Designed to assess "the development of motor coordination and sensory integration."

Population: Ages 5 and older.

Publication Dates: 1974-2012.

Acronym: QNST-3.

Scores, 16: Hand Skill, Figure Recognition and Production, Palm Form Recognition, Eye Tracking, Sound Patterns, Finger to Nose, Thumb and Finger Circle, Double Simultaneous Stimulation of Hand and Cheek, Rapidly Reversing Repetitive Hand Movements, Arm and Leg Extensions, Tandem Walk, Standing on One Leg, Skipping, Left-Right Discrimination, Behavioral Irregularities, Total.

Administration: Individual.

Price Data, 2015: $125 per test kit, including manual (2012, 124 pages), 25 record forms, and 25 remedial guidelines (developmental activities) forms in vinyl folder; $40 per 25 record forms; $20 per 25 remedial guidelines forms; $65 per manual.

Time: (20-30) minutes.

Authors: Margaret C. Mutti, Nancy A. Martin, Norma V. Spalding, and Harold M. Sterling.

Publisher: Academic Therapy Publications.

Cross References: For reviews by Bradley Merker and Shawn Powell, see 19:139; for a review by Edward E. Gotts of the second revised edition, see 14:306; see also T5:2141 (1 reference) and T4:2183 (3 references); for a review by Russell L. Adams of an earlier edition, see 9:1027.

[1680]
Quick Picture Reading Test.

Purpose: Designed "to quickly characterize an individual's general reading ability" through a picture-matching task.

Publication Date: 2010.

Acronym: QPRT.

Scores: Total score only.

Administration: Group.

Price Data, 2016: $78 per complete kit including 10 Adult AutoScore forms, 10 Child AutoScore forms, and manual (56 pages); $39 per 25 AutoScore forms (specify Adult or Child); $59.50 per manual.

Time: (10) minutes.

Authors: Amber M. Klein and David S. Herzberg.

Publisher: Western Psychological Services.
  a) CHILD FORM.
  Population: Ages 8-19.
  b) ADULT FORM.
  Population: Ages 17-89.

Cross References: For reviews by Kathleen Quinn and Timothy Shanahan, see 19:140.

[1681]
Quick Style Indicator.

Purpose: Designed to help identify "personal style as it relates to people, tasks, time and situations."

Population: Adults and teenagers.

Publication Dates: 1996-2006.

Acronym: QSI.

Scores, 4: Behavioral/Action, Cognitive/Analysis, Interpersonal/Harmony, Affective/Expression.

Administration: Individual or group.

Price Data, 2016: $20 per test booklet (2006, 12 pages); $20 per In-Depth Interpretations booklet (2006, 48 pages).

Foreign Language Edition: Available in Arabic and Swedish.

Time: (30) minutes; (90-180 minutes program options).

Comments: Shorter version of Personal Style Indicator (1516); self-administered and self-scored.

Authors: Ken Keis, Terry D. Anderson, Marilyn Hamilton, and Everett T. Robinson.
Publisher: Consulting Resource Group International, Inc.

[1682]
A Quick Test of Cognitive Speed.

Purpose: Designed to "screen adolescents and adults for parietal lobe dysfunctions indicative of mild cognitive impairments, acquired neurogenic disorders of language and communication … or degenerative neurological disorders such as Alzheimer's or Parkinson's disease."
Population: Adolescents and adults.
Publication Date: 2002.
Acronym: AQT.
Scores, 5: Color-Form, Color-Number, Color-Letter, Color-Animal, Color-Object.
Administration: Individual.
Price Data, 2015: $76 per examiner's manual; $63 per stimulus manual.
Foreign Language Edition: Spanish and French-Canadian directions included in examiner's manual.
Time: [3–5] minutes.
Comments: "Criterion-referenced"; previously titled Alzheimer's Quick Test: Assessment of Parietal Function.
Authors: Elisabeth H. Wiig, Niels Peter Nielsen, Lennart Minthon, and Siegbert Warkentin.
Publisher: Pearson.
Cross References: For reviews by Shawn K. Acheson and Joan C. Ballard of this test when it was titled Alzheimer's Quick Test: Assessment of Parietal Function, see 16:11.

[1683]
Quickview Social History.

Purpose: Psychosocial inventory designed to help standardize the collection of client information.
Population: Individuals 16 years and older.
Publication Dates: 1983–1992.
Administration: Group.
Price Data, 2015: $58.45 per Q Local starter kit; $64.60 per mail-in scoring starter kit; $7 per user's guide (1992, 33 pages); $55.85 per 10 social history test booklets; $72.25 per 1 hardcover social history test booklet; $23 per Q Local social history answer sheets; $16.50 per Q Local report.
Time: (30–45) minutes.
Author: Ronald A. Giannetti.
Publisher: Pearson.
   a) BASIC REPORT.
   Scores: 9 areas of inquiry: Demographic Data, Developmental History, Family of Origin, Educational History, Marital History, Occupational History/Financial Status, Legal History, Military History, Symptom Screen.
   Comments: The report also has a follow-up summary that includes contradictory responses, indeterminate responses, and client-requested follow-up sections.

   b) CLINICAL SUPPLEMENT.
   Scores: Includes 8 areas of inquiry listed in Basic Report, plus Physical and Psychological Symptom Screens including: Adult Problems (Substance Use, Psychotic Symptoms, Mood Symptoms, Anxiety Disorders, Somatoform Symptoms, Psychosexual Disorders, Sleep and Arousal, Antisocial Personality, Other Current or Past Potential Adult Problems/Stressors), Developmental Problems (Activity Level/Lability, Conduct Problems, Anxious/Avoidant, Eating/Weight, Tic/Elimination/Sleep, Other Disorders/Delays, Other Potential Developmental Problems/Stressors).
Cross References: For reviews by David N. Dixon and Edward R. Starr, see 13:251.

[1684]
Racial Attitude Survey.

Purpose: Measures attitudes toward an examiner-selected group of people using a generic semantic differential method.
Population: Teenagers through adults.
Publication Dates: 1989-2008.
Scores, 9: Physical, Ego Strength (Dominance, Control, Anxiety, Ethics, General Social, On-the-Job), Social Distance, Casual Contact.
Administration: Individual or group.
Manual: No manual.
Price Data: Price information for online testing for theses and other research is available from publisher.
Time: [20] minutes.
Comments: Previously titled Racial Attitude Test; technical information provided is from a thesis by Cynthia Lewis.
Author: Thomas J. Rundquist.
Publisher: Nova Media, Inc.
Cross References: For a review by Deborah L. Bandalos, see 16:206.

[1685]
Rahim Leader Power Inventory.

Purpose: Measures employees' perception of, and relationship with, immediate supervisors, in order to assess supervisors' power bases.
Population: Employees.
Publication Date: 1988.
Acronym: RLPI.
Scores, 5: Coercive, Reward, Legitimate, Expert, Referent.
Administration: Group.
Manual: No manual.
Price Data: Available from publisher.
Time: Administration time not reported.
Author: M. Afzal Rahim.
Publisher: Center for Advanced Studies in Management.

[1686]

Rahim Organizational Conflict Inventories.

Purpose: "Designed to measure three independent dimensions of organizational conflict: Intrapersonal, Intragroup, Intergroup" (ROCI-I) and "designed to measure five independent dimensions that represent styles of handling interpersonal conflict: Integrating, Obliging, Dominating, Avoiding, and Compromising" (ROCI-II).

Population: Managers, employees, supervisors.

Publication Date: 1983.

Acronym: ROCI.

Administration: Group.

Price Data: Available from publisher.

Comments: Self-administering; separate answer sheets must be used.

Author: M. Afzalur Rahim.

Publisher: Center for Advanced Studies in Management.
a) RAHIM ORGANIZATIONAL CONFLICT INVENTORY I.
   Acronym: ROCI-I.
   Scores: 3 subscales: Intrapersonal, Intragroup, Intergroup.
   Price Data: Available from publisher.
   Time: (10–12) minutes.
b) RAHIM ORGANIZATIONAL CONFLICT INVENTORY II.
   Acronym: ROCI-II.
   Scores, 5: Integrating, Obliging, Dominating, Avoiding, Compromising.
   Price Data: Available from publisher.
   Time: (10–12) minutes.

Cross References: See T5:2149 (5 references) and T4:2195 (1 reference); for a review by George C. Thornton III, see 10:303 (3 references).

[1687]

Rapid Automatized Naming and Rapid Alternating Stimulus Tests.

Purpose: "Designed to estimate an individual's ability to see a visual symbol … and name it accurately and rapidly."

Population: Ages 5-0 to 18-11.

Publication Date: 2005.

Acronym: RAN/RAS.

Scores, 6: Rapid Automatized Naming (Objects, Colors, Numbers, Letters), Rapid Alternating Stimulus (2-Set Letters and Numbers, 3-Set Letters/Numbers and Colors).

Administration: Individual.

Price Data, 2015: $157 per complete kit including examiner's manual (112 pages), 50 record forms, and set of 6 card packs; $72 per examiner's manual; $62 per 50 record forms; $31 per set of 6 card packs.

Time: (5–10) minutes.

Authors: Maryanne Wolf and Martha Bridge Denckla.

Publisher: PRO-ED.

Cross References: For reviews by Russell N. Carney and by Rayne A. Sperling and Nicholas D. Warcholak, see 17:161.

[1688]

Raven's Progressive Matrices.

Purpose: Constructed as a nonverbal assessment of perception and thinking skills.

Population: Ages 6–65

Publication Dates: 1938–2000.

Acronym: RPM.

Scores: Total score only.

Price Data: Available from publisher.

Foreign Language Edition: Spanish edition available.

Comments: Formerly called Progressive Matrices; may be used with Crichton Vocabulary Scale (569) or Mill Hill Vocabulary Scale (1270).

Authors: J. C. Raven, J. H. Court (manual), and J. Raven (manual).

Publisher: Pearson Clinical Assessment [Australia and New Zealand].
a) STANDARD.
   Population: Ages 6–65.
   Acronym: SPM.
   Administration: Group.
   Time: (45) minutes.
   Comments: Includes Classic, Parallel, and Plus Versions.
b) COLOURED.
   Population: Ages 5–11 and people with mental defects and elderly people.
   Acronym: CPM.
   Administration: Individual.
   Forms, 2: Board, Book.
   Time: (15–30) minutes.
c) ADVANCED.
   Population: Ages 11 and over with average or high intellectual ability.
   Acronym: APM.
   Administration: Group.
      1) *Set I.*
      Time: (10) minutes.
      2) *Set II.*
      Time: 40(45) or 60(65) minutes.

Cross References: See T5:2163 (356 references), T4:2208 (260 references), 9:1007 (67 references), T3:1914 (200 references), 8:200 (190 references), T2:439 (122 references), and 7:376 (194 references); for a review by Morton Bortner, see 6:490 (78 references); see also 5:370 (62 references); for reviews by Charlotte Banks, W. D. Wall, and George Westby, see 4:314 (32 references); for reviews by Walter C. Shipley and David Wechsler of the 1938 edition, see 3:258 (13 references); for a review by T. J. Keating, see 2:1417 (8 references).

[1689]

Reading and Arithmetic Indexes.

Purpose: "Measures level of development in reading and math." "Assesses proficiency levels in reading and math."

Population: Age 14–adult applicants for entry level jobs and special training programs.

Publication Dates: 1968–1996.

Administration: Group.

Forms, 2: Reading Index, Arithmetic Index.

Price Data: Available from publisher.

Author: Science Research Associates.

Publisher: General Dynamics Information Technology.

> *a)* READING–ARITHMETIC INDEX.
> **Purpose:** "Measures level of development in reading and math."
> **Acronym:** RAI.
> **Scores, 11:** Reading Index (Picture-Word Association, Word Decoding, Comprehension of Phrases, Comprehension of Sentences, Comprehension of Paragraphs, Total), Arithmetic Index (Addition and Subtraction of Whole Numbers, Multiplication and Division of Whole Numbers, Basic Operations Involving Fractions, Basic Operations Involving Decimals and Percentages, Total).
> **Time:** (25) minutes per Index.
> *b)* READING AND ARITHMETIC INDEXES (12).
> **Purpose:** "Assesses proficiency levels in reading and math."
> **Acronym:** RAI-12.
> **Scores, 14:** Reading Index (Picture-Word Association, Word Decoding, Comprehension of Phrases, Comprehension of Sentences, Comprehension of Paragraphs I, Comprehension of Paragraphs II, Total), Arithmetic Index (Addition and Subtraction of Whole Numbers, Multiplication and Division of Whole Numbers, Basic Operations Involving Fractions, Basic Operations Involving Decimals and Percentages, Basic Operations Involving Square Roots and Powers, Basic Operations Involving Geometry and Word Problems, Total).
> **Time:** (35) minutes per Index.

Cross References: For reviews by D. Joe Olmi and Jay R. Stewart, see 15:202; for a review by Dorothy C. Adkins of an earlier edition, see 7:20. See T4:2538 (1 reference) and 8:813 (3 references) for information regarding the Reading Index. See T5:171 (2 references) and 8:307 (3 references) for information regarding the Arithmetic Index.

[1690]
Reading Comprehension Battery for Aphasia, Second Edition.

Purpose: "Designed to provide systematic evaluation of the nature and degree of reading impairment in adolescents and adults with aphasia."

Population: Pre-adolescent to geriatric aphasic people.

Publication Dates: 1979–1998.

Acronym: RCBA-2.

Scores, 19: Word–Visual, Word–Auditory, Word–Semantic, Functional Reading, Synonyms, Sentence–Picture, Paragraph–Picture, Paragraph–Factual, Paragraph–Inferential, Morpho–Syntax, Overall Score of Core Subtests, Letter Discrimination, Letter Naming, Letter Recognition, Lexical Decision, Semantic Categorization, Oral Reading: Words, Oral Reading: Sentences, Overall Score of Supplemental Subtests.

Administration: Individual.

Price Data, 2015: $215 per complete kit including examiner's manual (1998, 38 pages), picture book, supplementary picture book, and 25 profile/summary record forms; $37 per examiner's manual, $67 per picture book or supplementary picture book; $56 per 25 profile/summary record forms.

Time: (30) minutes.

Comments: Instrument is criterion-referenced.

Authors: Leonard L. LaPointe and Jennifer Horner.

Publisher: PRO-ED.

Cross References: For reviews by Candice Haas Hollingsead and Robert Wall, see 14:308; see also T5:2172 (1 reference), T4:2220 (5 references), and 9:1033 (1 reference).

[1691]
Reading Evaluation Adult Diagnosis, Fifth Edition.

Purpose: Designed for assessing existing reading competencies.

Population: Illiterate adult students.

Publication Dates: 1972–1999.

Acronym: READ.

Scores: 3 parts, 21 scores: Sight Words (List 1, List 2, List 3, List 4), Word Analysis Skills (Letter Sound Relationships, Letter Names [Upper-Case], Letter Names [Lower-Case], Reversals, CVC, CV[CC], Final Digraphs, Initial Digraphs, Final Blends, Initial Blends, Multi-Syllabic Words, Silent Letters, Soft C & G, Suffixes), Reading/Listening Inventory (Word Recognition, Reading Comprehension, Listening Comprehension).

Administration: Individual.

Price Data: Now available at no charge from test publisher.

Time: Administration time not reported.

Authors: Original test by Ruth J. Colvin and Jane H. Root; 1999 revision by Kathleen A. Hinchman and Rebecca Schoultz.

Publisher: ProLiteracy Worldwide.

Cross References: For reviews by Howard Margolis and Timothy Shanahan, see 14:309; for reviews by Mary E. Huba and Diane J. Sawyer of an earlier edition, see 11:326 (1 reference).

[1692]
Reading Fluency Indicator.

Purpose: A brief, individually administered test of oral reading fluency that measures rate, accuracy, comprehension, and prosody.

Population: Grades 1–12.

Publication Date: 2004.

Acronym: RFI.

Scores: Total Reading Time, Total Miscues, Total Comprehension Passage Level, Words Read per Minute, Miscue Descriptive Analysis (Addition, Omission,

Provided Word, Repetition, Reversal, Substitution), Prosody Rating System, Comprehension Descriptive Analysis (Literal Comprehension Questions, Inferential Comprehension Questions).
Administration: Individual.
Levels, 10: P, K, 1–6, M, H.
Price Data, 2016: $173 per starter set including manual (42 pages), passage book, and 30 progress record forms; $94 per passage book; $34 per 10 progress record forms; $94 per manual.
Time: (5–10) minutes.
Comments: May be used as supplement to the Group Reading Assessment and Diagnostic Evaluation (898); "criterion-referenced."
Author: Kathleen T. Williams.
Publisher: Pearson.
Cross References: For reviews by Alice Corkill and George Engelhard, Jr., see 17:162.

[1693]

Reading-Free Vocational Interest Inventory: 2.

Purpose: "To measure the vocational interest of the special needs student/adult and regular classroom students."
Population: Ages 12 to 69.
Publication Dates: 1975–2000.
Acronym: RFVII:2.
Scores: 11 scales: Automotive, Building Trades, Clerical, Animal Care, Food Service, Patient Care, Horticulture, Housekeeping, Personal Service, Laundry Service, Materials Handling, plus 5 cluster scores: Mechanical, Outdoor, Mechanical—Outdoor, Food Service—Handling Operations, Clerical—Social Service.
Administration: Individual.
Price Data: Available from publisher.
Time: 20(30) minutes.
Comments: Revision of Reading-Free Vocational Interest Inventory; earlier edition listed as AAMD-Becker Reading-Free Vocational Interest Inventory; self-administered; hand-scorable only.
Author: Ralph L. Becker.
Publisher: Elbern Publications.
Cross References: For reviews by Zandra S. Gratz and Mark Pope, see 15:203; for information on an earlier edition, see T4:2177; for a review by Robert J. Miller of an earlier edition, see 11:327; see also T3:1996 (2 references); for reviews by Esther E. Diamond and George Domino of an earlier edition, see 8:988 (6 references).

[1694]

Reading Index.

Purpose: Measures level of development in reading.
Population: Individuals in a variety of occupations and rehabilitation environments.

Publication Dates: 1968-1995.
Acronym: RI.
Scores, 3: Proficiency Level (Picture-Word Association, Word Decoding, Phrase Comprehension, Sentence Comprehension, Paragraph Comprehension), Total Score, Grade Equivalency.
Administration: Individual or group.
Price Data: Available from publisher.
Time: No limit (approximately 25 minutes).
Comments: Previously listed as SRA Reading Index.
Authors: Science Research Associates.
Publisher: General Dynamics Information Technology.
Cross References: See T4:2538 (1 reference) and 8:813 (3 references); for a review by Dorothy C. Adkins of this test and the SRA Arithmetic Index, see 7:20.

[1695]

Reading-Level Indicator.

Purpose: Designed "to identify individual reading at a second-to-sixth-grade level and functional nonreaders."
Population: Upper elementary to college students.
Publication Dates: 2000-2002.
Scores, 5: Sentence Comprehension Score, Vocabulary Score, Total Raw Score, Instructional Reading Level, Independent Reading Level.
Administration: Group or individual.
Forms, 2: Blue Form, Purple Form.
Price Data, 2016: $30 per 25 forms (specify Purple or Blue); $32 per manual.
Time: (4–20) minutes.
Comments: Designed to work with Group Reading Assessment and Diagnostic Evaluation (GRADE; 898), a diagnostic reading test.
Author: Kathleen T. Williams.
Publisher: Pearson.
Cross References: For reviews by Elizabeth Kelley Boyles and Robert E. Wall, see 15:204.

[1696]

Reading Progress Tests.

Purpose: Designed to "provide a continuous measure of individual and group progress in reading comprehension."
Population: Ages 5-0 to 12-2.
Publication Dates: 1996–1997.
Acronym: RPT.
Scores: Total score only.
Administration: Group.
Price Data, 2016: £28 per Stage One manual (1996, 48 pages); £28 per Stage Two manual (1997, 47 pages); £30.50 per Stage One specimen set; see publisher for additional price data.
Time: (20) minutes per test.
Authors: Denis Vincent, Mary Crumpler, and Mike de la Mare.
Publisher: Hodder Education [United Kingdom].

a) STAGE ONE.

   1) *Literacy Baseline.*

   Purpose: "To provide a 'baseline' from which to measure subsequent progress."

   Population: Children in first term of their first year of compulsory schooling (ages 5-0 to 6-4).

   2) *RPT Test 1.*

   Purpose: Constructed to "assess developing reading skills."

   Population: Year 1 (ages 5-8 to 7-2).

   Time: (45–50) minutes.

   3) *RPT Test 2.*

   Population: Year 2 (ages 6-8 to 8-1).

b) STAGE TWO.

   1) *RPT Test 3.*

   Population: Year 3 (ages 7-8 to 9-2).

   2) *RPT Test 4.*

   Population: Year 4 (ages 8-8 to 10-2).

   3) *RPT Test 5.*

   Population: Year 5 (ages 9-8 to 11-2).

   4) *RPT Test 6.*

   Population: Year 6 (ages 10-8 to 12-2).

Cross References: For a review by Sharon deFur, see 17:163.

[1697]

Reading Style Inventory 2000.

Purpose: Designed to identify "the way each student learns best then (match) those strengths to the most effective reading methods, materials and strategies."

Population: Grade 1 to adults.

Publication Dates: 1980–2000.

Acronym: RSI.

Scores: 52 elements: Global Tendencies, Analytical Tendencies, Perceptual Strengths (Auditory Strengths, Visual Strengths, Tactile Strengths, Kinesthetic Strengths), Reading Methods (Carbo Recorded-Book Method, Fernald Method, Individualized Method, Modeling Methods, Language-Experience Method, Orton-Gillingham Method, Phonics Method, Whole-Word Method, Recorded Books, Computers), Preferred Reading Environment (Quiet—No Talking, Quiet—No Music, Dim Light, Warm Temperatures, Informal Design, Highly Organized), Emotional Profile (Peer Motivated, Adult Motivated, Self-Motivated, Persistent, Responsible), These Students Prefer (Choices, Direction, Work Checked), Sociological Preferences (Read to a Teacher, Read with Peers, Read Alone, Read with Peers/Teacher, Read with One Peer), Physical Preferences (Intake While Reading, Read in the Morning, Read in Early Afternoon, Read in Late Afternoon, Read in Evening, Mobility), Reading Materials (Audio-Visuals, Basal Reader Phonics, Basal Reader Whole-Word, Computers, Fernald Materials, Reading Activities, Orton-Gillingham Materials, Reading Kits, Recorded-Books, Tradebooks, Newspapers, etc.; Workbooks and Worksheets).

Administration: Individual and group.

Forms, 3: Primary, Intermediate, Adult.

Price Data: Available from publisher.

Time: Administration time not reported.

Comments: Available online only.

Author: National Reading Styles Institute.

Publisher: National Reading Styles Institute, Inc.

Cross References: For reviews by Alice Corkill and by Thomas Emerson Hancock and Kathleen Allen, see 16:207; see also T5:218 (2 references); for reviews by Jeri Benson and Alice J. Corkill of a previous edition, see 11:328 (1 reference).

[1698]

Reality Check Survey.

Purpose: Assesses "how managerial actions serve employee needs."

Population: Adults.

Publication Dates: 1989–1995.

Acronym: RCS.

Scores: Total score only.

Administration: Group.

Price Data, 2016: $15.95 per instrument.

Time: Untimed.

Comments: Self-administered survey.

Author: Jay Hall.

Publisher: Teleometrics International, Inc.

Cross References: For reviews by S. Alvin Leung and Sheldon Zedeck, see 12:322.

[1699]

Receptive-Expressive Emergent Language Test, Third Edition.

Purpose: Designed to identify babies or young children with delayed language acquisition, to determine discrepancy between receptive and expressive processes of emergent language and to document intervention effects.

Population: Ages 0–36 months.

Publication Dates: 1971–2003.

Acronym: REEL-3.

Scores, 3: Receptive Language Ability, Expressive Language Ability, Language Ability.

Administration: Individual.

Price Data, 2015: $121 per complete kit including examiner's manual (2003, 98 pages) and 25 profile/examiner record booklets; $72 per examiner's manual; $56 per 25 profile/examiner record booklets.

Time: (20–30) minutes.

Comments: Informants knowledgeable about child's language behavior are interviewed; first edition titled The Bzoch-League Receptive Expressive Emergent Language Scale: For the Measurement of Language Skills in Infancy.

Authors: Kenneth R. Bzoch, Richard League, and Virginia L. Brown.

Publisher: PRO-ED.

Cross References: For reviews by David P. Hurford and Gabrielle Stutman, see 16:208; see also T5:2189 (7 references); for reviews by Lyle F. Bachman and Lynn S. Bliss of a previous edition, see 12:323 (2 references); see also T4:2238 (3 references) and T3:338 (5 references); for excerpted reviews by Alex Bannatyne, Dale L. Johnson, and Barton B. Proger of the first edition, see 8:956 (5 references); see also T2:2067 (2 references).

[1700]

Receptive One-Word Picture Vocabulary Test–4: Spanish-Bilingual Edition.

Purpose: Designed to assess "an individual's ability to match a spoken word–in either Spanish or English–to an image of an object, action, or concept shown in a color illustration."
Population: Ages 2–70+.
Publication Dates: 2001–2013.
Acronym: ROWPVT-4: SBE.
Scores: Total score only.
Administration: Individual.
Price Data, 2015: $185 per test kit including manual (2013, 97 pages), test plates, and 25 record forms; $65 per manual; $40 per 25 record forms; $80 per test plates.
Time: (20-25) minutes.
Comments: Co-normed with the Expressive One-Word Picture Vocabulary Test–4: Spanish-Bilingual Edition (785).
Author: Nancy A. Martin.
Publisher: Academic Therapy Publications.
Cross References: For a review by John Anderson, see 19:141; for reviews by S. Kathleen Krach and Maria del R. Medina-Diaz of an earlier edition, see 16:209.

[1701]

Receptive One-Word Picture Vocabulary Test, 4th Edition.

Purpose: Designed to assess an individual's English hearing vocabulary.
Population: Ages 2 to 80 years and older.
Publication Dates: 1985-2011.
Acronym: ROWPVT-4.
Scores: Total score only.
Administration: Individual.
Price Data, 2015: $185 per kit including manual (2011, 93 pages), 25 record forms, and test plates, in portfolio; $80 per set of test plates; $40 per 25 record forms; $65 per manual.
Foreign Language Edition: Spanish-Bilingual version available.
Time: (20) minutes.
Authors: 1985 edition by Morrison F. Gardner; 2000 edition prepared by Rick Brownell; 4th Edition by Nancy A. Martin and Rick Brownell.
Publisher: Academic Therapy Publications.
Cross References: For reviews by Ronald A. Madle and Jonathan Sandoval, see 19:142; for reviews by Doreen

W. Fairbank and Sheila Pratt of the 2000 Edition, see 15:205; see also T5:2190 (9 references) and T4:2239 (1 reference); for reviews by Janice A. Dole and Janice Santogrossi of an earlier edition, see 10:312; for reviews by Laurie Ford and William D. Schafer of an earlier ediiton of the upper level, see 11:329.

[1702]

Recognition Memory Test.

Purpose: Allows clinicians to quickly distinguish between right- and left-hemisphere brain damage.
Population: Adult patients referred for neuropsychological assessment.
Publication Date: 1984.
Acronym: RMT.
Scores, 2: Words, Faces.
Administration: Individual.
Price Data, 2016: $219.50 per kit including 1 reusable test booklet and word card, 25 record forms, and manual (16 pages); $39 per 100 record forms; $45.50 per manual.
Time: (15) minutes.
Author: Elizabeth K. Warrington.
Publisher: Western Psychological Services.
Cross References: See T5:2193 (59 references) and T4:2241 (12 references); for a review by Russell L. Adams, see 10:313 (1 reference).

[1703]

REHAB: Rehabiliation Evaluation Hall and Baker.

Purpose: "Designed to assess people with a major psychiatric handicap."
Population: Psychiatric patients in residential care.
Publication Dates: 1984–1994.
Acronym: REHAB.
Scores, 8: Deviant Behaviour, General Behaviour (Social Activity, Speech Disturbance, Self Care, Community Skills, Overall Rating), Speech Skills.
Administration: Individual.
Price Data: Available from publisher.
Time: (1) week.
Comments: A multipurpose behavior rating scale requiring observation of the target client over a period of one week; raters can include any direct care staff.
Authors: Roger Baker and John N. Hall.
Publisher: Dr. Baker Partnership [England]. [No reply from publisher; status unknown].
Cross References: For reviews by James P. Choca and Pamilla Morales, see 14:312; see also T5:2195 (2 references).

[1704]

Rehabilitation Checklist.

Purpose: Designed to help determine the needs of clients recovering from serious and soft-tissue physical injuries,

cognitive impairment (mild to moderate brain injury), and related psychological adjustment and/or trauma.
Population: Adults.
Publication Dates: 1998–1999.
Acronym: RCL.
Scores, 7: (Physical, Cognitive, Emotional, Psychosocial, Employability, Job), plus Total and Total Rehabilitation subscale.
Administration: Group.
Price Data, 2015: $150 per kit including 25 QuikScore™ forms and manual (1998, 54 pages); $87 per 25 QuikScore™ forms; $85 per manual.
Time: (15) minutes.
Comments: Self-report.
Author: J. Douglas Salmon, Jr.
Publisher: Multi-Health Systems, Inc.
Cross References: For reviews by Michael G. Kavan and Carolyn Mitchell Person, see 15:206.

[1705]
Rehabilitation Compliance Scale.
Purpose: Intended to provide a measurement of compliance to a rehabilitation program in the severely injured musculoskeletal patient.
Population: Severely injured patients ages 17–85 years.
Publication Date: 1994.
Administration: Group.
Price Data: Available from publisher.
Time: Administration time not reported.
Author: Neil W. Rheiner.
Publisher: Mind Garden, Inc.
 a) REHABILITATION COMPLIANCE SCALE.
 Acronym: RHAB.
 Scores, 3: Appointment Compliance, Participation in Therapy, Progress in Therapy.
 Forms, 2: A, B.
 b) PATIENT EXPERIENCE QUESTIONNAIRE.
 Score: Total score only.
Cross References: For reviews by Michael P. Gamache and Robert A. Leark, see 14:313.

[1706]
Rehabilitation Survey of Problems and Coping.
Purpose: Intended for use as a symptom rating and disability management tool.
Population: Age 14 and over
Publication Date: 2002.
Acronym: R-SOPAC.
Scores, 12: Overall Total, Problem Total, Coping Total, Emotional Overall, Emotional Problem, Emotional Coping, Physical Overall, Physical Problem, Physical Coping, Cognitive Overall, Cognitive Problem, Cognitive Coping.
Administration: Group or individual.
Parts, 2: Survey of Problems, Survey of Coping.

Price Data, 2015: $144 per complete kit including manual (112 pages) and 25 QuikScore forms™; $97 per technical manual; $55 per 25 QuikScore™ forms.
Time: (10–15) minutes.
Comments: One of several measures comprising a broad battery of rehabilitation-oriented instruments together entitled the Rehabilitation Assessment Series (RAS).
Authors: J. Douglas Salmon, Jr. and Marek Celinski.
Publisher: Multi-Health Systems, Inc.
Cross References: For reviews by Theodore L. Hayes and Nambury S. Raju, see 16:210.

[1707]
The Reid Report.
Purpose: "The Report consists of a customized set of scales and questionnaires which focus on key, business-related employee behaviors. Measures attitudes toward conscientiousness and counterproductivity in the workplace and predicts overall work performance and counterproductive acts (turnover, absenteeism, tardiness, theft and inappropriate substance use)."
Population: Job applicants.
Publication Dates: 1969–1992.
Scores: 1 of 4 possible evaluations (Recommended, Qualified, Not Recommended, No Opinion) in 4 parts (Integrity Attitude, Antisocial History, Recent Drug Use, Work History) and overall evaluation.
Administration: Group.
Price Data: Available from publisher.
Time: Approximately 15 minutes.
Comments: Overall evaluation established by client organization, based upon specific organizational requirements; newer editions of this assessment are available.
Author: General Dynamics Information Technology.
Publisher: General Dynamics Information Technology.
Cross References: For reviews by George Domino and Kevin R. Murphy, see 12:324 (2 references); see also T4:2243 (1 reference); for a review by Stanley L. Brodsky, see 8:658 (3 references); for integrated version of Reid Report/Reid Survey, see T2:1353 (1 reference) and 7:132 (1 reference).

[1708]
Reiss-Epstein-Gursky Anxiety Sensitivity Index.
Purpose: To measure the fear of anxiety in order to "identify patients with high anxiety sensitivity" and "to obtain information relevant to the diagnosis of panic disorder or posttraumatic stress disorder; to evaluate treatment outcomes; to assess soldiers at risk to panic under stress."
Population: Adults and adolescents.
Publication Date: 1987.
Acronym: ASI.

Scores: Total Anxiety Sensitivity.
Administration: Individual or group.
Price Data: Available from publisher.
Foreign Language Editions: Available in Catalan, Chinese, Dutch, Farsi, French, German, Greek, Icelandic, Italian, Japanese, Polish, Portuguese, Russian, Spanish, Swedish, Turkish.
Time: [5] minutes.
Authors: Steven Reiss and Rolf A. Peterson.
Publisher: IDS Publishing Inc.
Cross References: See T5:2199 (14 references) and T4:2244 (2 references); for a review by Harrison G. Gough, see 11:330.

[1709]

A Religion Scale.

Purpose: Measures attitudes toward religion.
Population: Adolescents and adults.
Publication Date: 1961.
Scores: Total score only.
Administration: Group.
Manual: No manual.
Price Data, 2015: $2 per scale.
Time: [10] minutes.
Comments: Supplementary article available.
Author: Panos D. Bardis.
Publisher: Donna Bardis.
Cross References: See 8:465 (2 references).

[1710]

The Renfrew Bus Story, North American Edition.

Purpose: Designed as a "test of narrative recall."
Population: Ages 3.6–6.11.
Publication Date: 1994.
Scores, 4: Information, Sentence Length, Complexity, Independence.
Administration: Individual.
Price Data, 2015: $75 per complete kit including manual (56 pages), 15 record forms, and story booklet; $15 per 15 record forms.
Time: Administration time approximately 5-10 minutes.
Comments: American adaptation of original British version.
Authors: Judy Cowley and Cheryl Glasgow.
Publisher: Learning Tools LLC.
Cross References: For reviews by Sherry K. Bain and Robert R. Haccoun, see 14:314.

[1711]

Repeatable Battery for the Assessment of Neuropsychological Status Update.

Purpose: Designed to measure "attention, language, visuospatial/constructional abilities, and immediate and delayed memory."

Population: Ages 12–89 years.
Publication Dates: 1998–2012.
Acronym: RBANS Update.
Scores, 6: Immediate Memory, Visuospatial/Constructional, Language, Attention, Delayed Memory, Total Scale.
Subtests, 12: List Learning, Story Memory, Figure Copy, Line Orientation, Picture Naming, Semantic Fluency, Digit Span, Coding, List Recall, List Recognition, Story Recall, Figure Recall.
Administration: Individual.
Forms: 4 parallel forms: A, B, C, D.
Price Data, 2015: $563 per RBANS Update combo kit, including stimulus books A, B, C, and D, scoring templates A, B, C, and D, and manual (2012, 196 pages); $316.75 per RBANS Update kit (Form A), including manual, stimulus book, 25 record forms, and scoring template; $265.50 per RBANS Update kit (Form B, C, or D), including stimulus book, 25 record forms, and scoring template; $204 per RBANS Update Form A upgrade kit, including new manual and stimulus book A with new norms (designed for current users; record forms and scoring templates remain the same).
Foreign Language Edition: Forms A and B available in Spanish.
Time: (20-30) minutes.
Author: Christopher Randolph.
Publisher: Pearson.
Cross References: For reviews by Brian F. French and John F. Linck, see 19: 143; for reviews by Stephen J. Freeman and Timothy J. Makatura of an earlier edition, see 14:315.

[1712]

Report Completion Exercise for Firefighter, Police Officer, and Correctional Officer.

Purpose: "Video-based test designed to assess observation and listening skills as well as written communication skills."
Population: Candidates for entry-level firefighter, police officer, and correctional officer positions.
Publication Date: 2005.
Scores: Total score only.
Administration: Individual or group.
Price Data: Available from publisher (administration fee is waived if ordered with another testing product).
Time: 30 minutes.
Comments: Departments choosing to administer one of the tests must develop their own scoring criteria; administered via videos; joint technical report available for all three tests.
Author: International Public Management Association for Human Resources.
Publisher: International Public Management Association for Human Resources (IPMA-HR).

a) FIREFIGHTER REPORT COMPLETION EX-
ERCISE.
Population: Entry-level firefighter candidates.
Publication Date: 2005.
Acronym: F-RCE.
b) POLICE OFFICER REPORT COMPLETION
EXERCISE.
Population: Entry-level police officer candidates.
Publication Date: 2005.
Acronym: P-RCE.
c) CORRECTIONAL OFFICER REPORT COMPLE-
TION EXERCISE.
Population: Entry-level correctional officer candidates.
Publication Date: 2005.
Acronym: C-RCE.
Cross References: For a review by Chockalingam
Viswesvaran, see 18:106.

[1713]

Resiliency Scales for Children & Adolescents.

Purpose: Designed to assess "core characteristics of
personal resiliency in children and adolescents."
Population: Ages 9-18.
Publication Dates: 2006-2007.
Scores, 13: Sense of Mastery (Optimism, Self-Efficacy,
Adaptability, Total), Sense of Relatedness (Trust, Sup-
port, Comfort, Tolerance, Total), Emotional Reactivity
(Sensitivity, Recovery, Impairment, Total).
Administration: Individual or group.
Price Data, 2015: $122.70 per complete kit includ-
ing manual (2007, 183 pages) and 25 combination scales
booklets; $76.50 per 25 combination scales booklets;
$77.65 per manual.
Time: (10-25) minutes.
Comments: A downward extension of the Resiliency
Scales for Adolescents.
Author: Sandra Prince-Embury.
Publisher: Pearson.
Cross References: For reviews by Christopher A.
Sink and Nyaradzo H. Mvududu and by John J. Venn,
see 18:107.

[1714]

Retail Management Applicant Inventory.

Purpose: Designed for "personnel selection and place-
ment and the identification of strengths and areas to
improve" in the field of retail management.
Population: Retail management applicants.
Publication Dates: 1994–1998.
Acronym: RMAI.
Scores, 13: Validity (Candidness, Accuracy), Man-
agement Focus (Background and Work Experience,
Management and Leadership Interest), Motivation and
Attitudes (Management Responsibility, Customer Service,
Energy Level, Management Orientation), Job Knowledge
(Managerial Arithmetic, Understanding Management
Procedures and Practices), Stability and Risk (Business
Ethics, Job Stability), Management Potential Index.

Administration: Individual or group.
Forms, 5: Quanta Touch Test, Quanta Software
for Windows—administration and scoring, Quanta
Software for Windows—scoring only, RLH Online,
Mail-in Scoring.
Price Data: Available from publisher.
Time: [40–60] minutes.
Author: General Dynamics Information Technology.
Publisher: General Dynamics Information Technology.

[1715]

Retail Sales Evaluation.

Purpose: Designed to "examine how well the test-taker
is suited for a career in the retail field."
Population: Potential retail sales workers.
Publication Date: 2011.
Acronym: RESALE.
Scores, 37: Attitude Towards Teamwork, Communica-
tion Skills, Self-Discipline, Time Management, Neatness,
Meticulousness, Honesty Attitude, Honesty Ownership,
Adaptability/Flexibility, Stress Reaction, Comfort with
Routine, Comfort with Authority, Conflict Resolution,
Optimism, Helpfulness, Hostility, Patience, Reaction
to Criticism, Salesmanship, Drive, Self-Monitoring,
Agreeableness, Assertiveness with Clients, Hardiness,
Friendliness/Approachability, Extroversion, Social Skills,
Comfort with Pressure Sales Tactics, Impression Manage-
ment, Acquiescence, Work Attitude, Interpersonal Skills,
Organizational Skills, Coping Skills, Self-Control Skills,
Integrity, Overall Score.
Administration: Individual.
Price Data: Available from publisher.
Time: (30) minutes.
Comments: Self-administered online assessment. The
test publisher provides clients with information about the
methods and theoretical basis used in the development
of the test as well as benchmarks for relevant industries
and racial/ethnic group comparison data.
Author: PsychTests AIM, Inc.
Publisher: PsychTests AIM, Inc. [Canada].
Cross References: For a review by Gypsy M. Den-
zine, see 19:144.

[1716]

Retail Sales Skills Test.

Purpose: To evaluate the knowledge necessary for suc-
cessful performance as a retail salesperson.
Population: Candidates for the position of retail
salesperson.
Publication Date: 1994.
Acronym: RETSALES.
Scores: Total Score, Narrative Evaluation, Ranking,
Recommendation.
Administration: Group.
Price Data: Available from publisher.
Time: (70) minutes.

Author: Walden Personnel Performance, Inc.
Publisher: Walden Personnel Testing & Consulting Inc. [Canada].

[1717]

Retail Store Manager Staff Selector.

Purpose: To evaluate the knowledge necessary for successful performance in retail store management.
Population: Candidates for the position of store manager or assistant manager.
Publication Date: 1996.
Acronym: RSALES.
Scores, 4: Total Score, Narrative Evaluation, Ranking, Recommendation.
Administration: Group.
Price Data: Available from publisher.
Time: (255) minutes.
Comments: Scored by publisher; must be proctored.
Author: Walden Personnel Performance, Inc.
Publisher: Walden Personnel Testing & Consulting Inc. [Canada].

[1718]

Retirement Descriptive Index.

Purpose: Designed to measure satisfaction with facets of retirement.
Population: Retirees
Publication Dates: 1969–1993.
Acronym: RDI.
Scores, 4: Present Work and Activities, Financial Situation, Present Health, People You Associate With.
Administration: Group or individual.
Price Data, 2015: There is no charge to use the copyrighted scales; ontact test publisher for permission.
Time: 5 minutes.
Comments: Previously listed with the Job Descriptive Index (1043).
Authors: Patricia C. Smith, Lorne M. Kendall, and Charles L. Hulin.
Publisher: Bowling Green State University.
Cross References: For reviews by Charles K. Parsons and Norman D. Sundberg of the Job Descriptive Index and Retirement Descriptive Index, see 12:199 (33 references); see also T4:1312 (63 references).

[1719]

Revised Behavior Problem Checklist [PAR Edition].

Purpose: Developed to "rate problem behaviors observed in adolescents and young children."
Population: Ages 5–18.
Publication Dates: 1979–1987.
Acronym: RBPC.
Scores, 6: Conduct Disorder, Socialized Aggression, Attention Problems-Immaturity, Anxiety-Withdrawal, Psychotic Behavior, Motor Tension-Excess.

Administration: Individual.
Price Data, 2015: $244 per introductory kit including professional manual, 50 test booklets, and 50 profiles.
Time: 20(30) minutes.
Comments: Ratings by teachers, parents, and child care staff.
Authors: Herbert C. Quay and Donald R. Peterson.
Publisher: Psychological Assessment Resources, Inc.
Cross References: See T5:2211 (52 references) and T4:2254 (45 references); for reviews by Denise M. Dezolt and by Edward S. Shapiro and Stewart M. Shear, see 11:332 (80 references); for a review by Anthony A. Cancelli, see 9:1043 (31 references); see also T3:2012 (6 references).

[1720]

Revised Children's Manifest Anxiety Scale: Second Edition.

Purpose: "Designed to assess the level and nature of anxiety in children and adolescents."
Population: Ages 6-19.
Publication Dates: 1985-2008.
Acronym: RCMAS-2.
Administration: Group.
Scores, 6: Inconsistent Responding Index, Defensiveness, Total Anxiety, Physiological Anxiety, Worry, Social Anxiety.
Price Data, 2016: $131.50 per kit including 25 autoscore forms, one audio CD, and one technical manual (2008, 83 pages); $52.50 per 25 autoscore forms; $76 per technical manual; $19.50 per audio CD.
Foreign Language Edition: Spanish version available.
Time: (10-15) minutes.
Comments: The revised edition includes the addition of an inconsistent responding index.
Authors: Cecil R. Reynolds and Bert O. Richmond.
Publisher: Western Psychological Services.
Cross References: For reviews by Gypsy M. Denzine and Margot B. Stein, see 18:108; see T5:2214 (140 references) and T4:2257 (47 references); for a review by Frank M. Gresham of an earlier edition, see 10:314.

[1721]

Revised Hamilton Rating Scale for Depression.

Purpose: Designed as a clinician-rated scale for evaluating individuals already diagnosed with depressive illness.
Population: Depressed adults.
Publication Date: 1994.
Acronym: RHRSD.
Scores, 22: General Screening, Depressed Mood, Feelings of Guilt, Suicide, Insomnia, Nocturnal Waking, Early Morning Waking, Work and Activities, Sexual Symptoms, Loss of Insight, Retardation,

Agitation, Worry, Somatic Anxiety, Gastrointestinal Somatic Symptoms, General Somatic Symptoms, Hypochondriasis, Loss of Weight, Diurnal Variation, Obsessive-Compulsive Symptoms, Paranoid Symptoms, Depersonalization/Derealization.

Administration: Individual.

Price Data, 2015: $136.50 per kit, including 20 AutoScore Clinician Forms, 20 AutoScore Self-Report Problem Inventories, and manual; $50 per 25 AutoScore Clinician Forms; $50 per 25 AutoScore Self-Report Problem Inventories; $68.50 per manual; $270.50 per 20-use administration, scoring and interpretation CD; $18.50 per 100 Clinician Form PC Answer Sheets, for use with the CD; $18.50 per 100 Self-Report Problem Inventory PC answer sheets, for use with the CD.

Time: (5–10) minutes.

Comments: A self-report scale is also provided; The RHRSD CD will administer, score, and interpret both the RHRSD Clinician Form and the Self-Report Problem Inventory.

Author: W. L. Warren.

Publisher: Western Psychological Services.

Cross References: For reviews by Paul C. Burnett and Barbara J. Kaplan, see 13:263 (382 references); see also T4:2261 (10 references).

[1722]

Revised IDEA Feedback for Administrators System.

Purpose: Designed to provide feedback "to academic administrators about their performance of relevant administrative responsibilities and their leadership style and interpersonal characteristics."

Population: Academic administrators.

Publication Dates: 2001-2011.

Scores, 27: Item scores in 4 parts: Administrative Roles (10 items), Leadership Style (7 items), Personal Characteristics (8 items), Overall Effectiveness (2 items).

Administration: Individual.

Forms, 2: Administrator Information Form, Impressions of Administrator.

Price Data, 2016: $350 per administrator including initial and reminder e-mails to respondents and e-mail delivery of reports plus $1.75 for each individual notified of survey via e-mail; $25 cancellation fee after e-mail addresses loaded into system; $50 fee assessed to correct undeliverable e-mails.

Time: Administration time not reported.

Comments: Online administration; ratings by faculty members and administrator; publisher scores and generates interpretive reports.

Authors: IDEA.

Publisher: IDEA.

Cross References: Reviews are scheduled for *The Twentieth Mental Measurements Yearbook.*

[1723]

Revised IDEA Feedback for Department Chairs System.

Purpose: Designed to provide "feedback to academic department heads/chairs about their performance of relevant administrative responsibilities" for formative and/or summative evaluation.

Population: Academic department chairs.

Publication Dates: 1977-2010.

Scores, 55: Item scores in 4 parts: Responsibilities (21 items), Personal Characteristics (11 items), Administrative Methods (21 items), Summary Judgment (2 items).

Administration: Individual.

Forms, 2: Chair Information Form-Revised, Faculty Survey-Revised.

Price Data, 2016: $295 per chair including initial and reminder e-mails to respondents and e-mail delivery of reports; $25 cancellation fee after e-mail addresses loaded into system; $50 fee assessed to correct undeliverable e-mails.

Time: Administration time not reported.

Comments: Online rating scales completed by both faculty members and department chair; publisher scores and generates interpretive reports; previous version titled Departmental Evaluation of Chairperson Activities for Development.

Authors: IDEA.

Publisher: IDEA.

Cross References: Reviews are scheduled for *The Twentieth Mental Measurements Yearbook.* For reviews by John W. Fleenor and M. David Miller of a previous (1998) edition, see 15:121; see T4:741 (1 reference).

[1724]

Revised Minnesota Paper Form Board Test, Second Edition.

Purpose: "Designed to measure aspects of mechanical ability requiring the capacity to visualize and manipulate objects in space."

Population: Grade 9 and over.

Publication Dates: 1934–1995.

Acronym: RMPFBT.

Scores: Total score only.

Administration: Group.

Forms, 4: Series AA, BB, MA, MB.

Price Data, 2015: $158 per 25 Form AA or BB test booklets for booklet scoring; $523 per 100 Form AA or BB test booklets; $150 per key for Forms AA and BB; $75 per manual.

Foreign Adaptations: Australian edition: 1981; revised edition prepared by J. Jenkinson; Australian Council for Education Research [Australia]; British norms supplement: 1978; Gil Nyfield, NFER-Nelson Publishing Co. [England].

Time: 20(40) minutes.

Authors: Rensis Likert and W. H. Quasha.
Publisher: Pearson.
Cross References: For reviews by L. Carolyn Pearson and Michael J. Roszkowski, see 14:316; see also T5:2217 (3 references) and T4:2262 (2 references); for a review by Paul W. Thayer of an earlier edition, see 9:1045 (2 references); see also T3:2015 (19 references), T2:2266 (37 references), 7:1056 (19 references), and 6:1092 (16 references); for a review by D. W. McElwain, see 5:885 (29 references); for reviews by Clifford E. Jurgensen and Raymond A. Katzell, see 4:763 (38 references); for a review by Dewey B. Stuit, see 3:677 (48 references); for a review by Alec Rodger, see 2:1673 (9 references).

[1725]

Revised Pre-Reading Screening Procedures [1997 Edition].

Purpose: Designed to "find among children of average to superior intelligence the ones who show difficulties in Auditory, Visual, and/or Kinesthetic modalities that often indicate Specific Language Disability (SLD)."
Population: First grade entrants.
Publication Dates: 1968–1997.
Scores: 7 areas: Visual, Visual-Kinesthetic-Motor, Auditory, Auditory-Visual, Auditory-Visual-Kinesthetic-Motor, Language, Letter Knowledge.
Administration: Group.
Price Data, 2015: $88.20 per 12 test booklets (32 pages) including 12 Teacher Observation/Summary sheets, 12 Practice Pages, and 12 cardboard markers; $29.40 per Teacher's Manual (1997, 94 pages) including instructions plus detachable key; $33 per Teacher's Cards and Chart (2 sets of 5 x 10 cards and 2 copies of a wall chart used in giving the tests); quantity discounts available.
Time: Administration time not reported.
Authors: Beth H. Slingerland and Marty Aho.
Publisher: Educators Publishing Service, Inc.
Cross References: For a review by Maurine A. Fry of an earlier edition, see 9:1046; see also T2:1721 (1 reference); for reviews by Colleen B. Jamison and Roy A. Kress of an earlier edition, see 7:732 (1 reference).

[1726]

The Revised Sheridan Gardiner Test of Visual Acuity.

Purpose: To measure visual acuity.
Population: Age 5 and over.
Publication Dates: 1970–c1993.
Scores, 2: Distance Vision, Near Vision.
Administration: Individual.
Manual: No manual.
Price Data, 2016: $69 per test.
Time: Administration time not reported.
Authors: Mary D. Sheridan and Peter A. Gardiner.
Publisher: Keeler Instruments Inc. (U.S. Distributor).
Cross References: See T2:1926 (1 reference).

[1727]

Revised Token Test.

Purpose: Designed as a quantitative and descriptive test for "auditory disorders associated with aphasia and brain damage."
Population: Ages 20-80; Preliminary normative data based on the following standardization samples: non-brain-damaged, left hemisphere brain-damaged, right hemisphere brain-damaged.
Publication Date: 1978.
Acronym: RTT.
Scores, 22: 10 Subtest mean scores, Overall mean score, 11 Linguistic Element mean scores.
Administration: Individual.
Price Data, 2015: $183 per complete kit including 25 scoring forms, 25 profile forms, administration manual, 24 tokens, and manual (118 pages); $43 per profile forms; $43 per administration manual and 25 scoring forms; $45 per tokens; $62 per examiner's manual.
Time: Administration time varies with condition.
Comments: Reconstruction of the Token Test.
Authors: Malcolm Ray McNeil and Thomas E. Prescott.
Publisher: PRO-ED.
Cross References: See T5:2225 (21 references) and T4:2270 (5 references); for reviews by Michael D. Franzen and Charles J. Golden and by Thomas Hammeke, see 9:1048; see also T3:2017 (5 references).

[1728]

Rey Auditory Verbal Learning Test: A Handbook.

Purpose: Designed to measure "verbal learning and memory."
Population: Ages 7–89.
Publication Date: 1996.
Acronym: RAVLT.
Scores, 3: Learning, Recall, Recognition.
Administration: Individual.
Price Data, 2016: $109 per complete kit including handbook (148 pages) and 25 record sheets and score summaries; $35 per 25 record sheets and score summaries; $80.50 per handbook.
Time: (15) minutes.
Author: Michael Schmidt.
Publisher: Western Psychological Services.
Cross References: For reviews by Karen Mackler and Steven R. Shaw, see 14:317; see also T5:2226 (42 references).

[1729]

Rey Complex Figure Test and Recognition Trial.

Purpose: Designed to assess "visuospatial constructional ability and visuospatial memory."
Population: Ages 6–89.

Publication Dates: 1995–1996.
Acronym: RCFT.
Scores, 9: Immediate Recall, Delayed Recall, Recognition Total Correct, Copy, Time to Copy, Recognition True Positives, Recognition False Positives, Recognition True Negatives, Recognition False Negatives.
Administration: Individual.
Price Data, 2015: $320 per introductory kit including manual (1995, 126 pages), 50 test booklets, stimulus card, and supplemental norms for children and adolescents (1996, 21 pages).
Time: (45) minutes, including a 30-minute delay interval.
Authors: John E. Meyers and Kelly R. Meyers.
Publisher: Psychological Assessment Resources, Inc.
Cross References: For reviews by D. Ashley Cohen and Deborah D. Roman, see 14:318; see also T5:2227 (62 references).

[1730]
Reynolds Adaptable Intelligence Test.

Purpose: Designed to assess "crystallized intelligence, fluid intelligence, and quantitative aptitude or intelligence."
Population: Ages 10 to 75.
Publication Date: 2014.
Acronym: RAIT.
Scores, 12: 7 subtest scores: General Knowledge, Nonverbal Analogies, Sequences, Quantitative Knowledge, Quantitative Reasoning, Odd Word Out, Word Opposites; 5 index scores: Crystallized Intelligence Index, Fluid Intelligence Index, Total Intelligence Index, Quantitative Intelligence Index, Total Battery Intelligence Index.
Administration: Individual or group.
Price Data, 2015: $225 per introductory kit including manual (175 pages), fast guide, 10 item booklets, 25 answer sheets, 2 scoring keys, and 25 score summary forms; $95 per manual, $75 per 10 reusable item booklets; $45 per 25 score summary forms; $25 per 25 answer sheets; $10 per 2 scoring keys.
Time: (3-10) minutes per subtest; (50) minutes for full battery.
Comments: Administered via computer or paper and pencil.
Author: Cecil R. Reynolds.
Publisher: Psychological Assessment Resources, Inc.
Cross References: Reviews are scheduled for *The Twentieth Mental Measurements Yearbook*.

[1731]
Reynolds Adolescent Adjustment Screening Inventory.

Purpose: Designed as "a screening measure of adolescent adjustment."
Population: Ages 12–19.
Publication Dates: 1998–2001.

Acronym: RAASI.
Scores, 5: Antisocial Behavior, Anger Control Problems, Emotional Distress, Positive Self, Adjustment Total Score.
Administration: Individual or group.
Price Data, 2015: $197 per introductory kit including 50 test booklets and professional manual (2001, 134 pages).
Time: (5) minutes.
Author: William M. Reynolds.
Publisher: Psychological Assessment Resources, Inc.
Cross References: For reviews by Lynn Lakota Brown and Kevin M. Jones, see 15:207.

[1732]
Reynolds Adolescent Depression Scale–2nd Edition.

Purpose: Designed "to assess the severity of depressive symptomatology in adolescents in school and clinical settings."
Population: Ages 11–20.
Publication Dates: 1986–2002.
Acronym: RADS-2.
Scores, 5: Dysphoric Mood, Anhedonia/Negative Affect, Negative Self-Evaluation, Somatic Complaints, Depression Total.
Administration: Individual or group.
Price Data, 2015: $166 per introductory kit including professional manual (2002, 172 pages), 25 hand-scorable test booklets, and 25 summary/profile forms.
Time: (5–10) minutes.
Comments: Self-report measure; hand scored; may be administered aloud; test booklet is titled "About Myself."
Author: William M. Reynolds.
Publisher: Psychological Assessment Resources, Inc.
Cross References: For reviews by Kimberly A. Blair and Janet F. Carlson, see 16:211; see also T5:2230 (21 references) and T4:2274 (11 references); for reviews by Barbara J. Kaplan and Deborah King Kundert of an earlier edition, see 11:333 (6 references).

[1733]
Reynolds Adolescent Depression Scale–2nd Edition: Short Form.

Purpose: "Designed as a brief screening measure for the assessment of depression in adolescents."
Population: Ages 11-20.
Publication Dates: 1987-2008.
Acronym: RADS-2:SF.
Scores: Total score only.
Administration: Group.
Price Data, 2015: $95 per introductory kit including professional manual (2008, 91 pages) and 25 test booklets; $47 per 25 test booklets; $55 per professional.
Time: (2-3) minutes.

Comments: Abbreviated version of Reynolds Adolescent Depression Scale-2nd Edition (16:211); self-report measure; may be administered aloud.
Author: William M. Reynolds.
Publisher: Psychological Assessment Resources, Inc.
Cross References: For reviews by Michael G. Kavan and Rama K. Mishra, see 18:109.

[1734]
Reynolds Bully-Victimization Scales for Schools.
Purpose: Designed to evaluate "school-related violence and its impact on students."
Publication Date: 2003.
Acronym: RBVSS.
Administration: Individual or group.
Levels, 3: Bully-Victimization Scale, Bully-Victimization Distress Scale, School Violence Anxiety Scale.
Price Data, 2015: $226.35 per complete kit including manual (181 pages), 30 Bully-Victimization Scale forms, 30 School Violence Anxiety Scale forms, 30 Bully-Victimization Distress forms, Bully-Victimization Scale scoring key—English/Spanish, and Bully-Victimization Distress Scale scoring key—English/Spanish; $96.70 per manual; $44.70 per 30 Bully-Victimization Scale; $44.70 per 30 School Violence Anxiety Scale; $44.70 per 30 Bully-Victimization Distress Scale; $13.70 per Bully-Victimization Scale scoring key; $13.70 per Bully-Victimization Distress Scale scoring key.
Foreign Language Edition: Spanish edition available.
Time: (5–10) minutes per scale.
Comments: Scales may be used individually or as a battery; automated group testing available.
Author: William Reynolds.
Publisher: Pearson.
 a) BULLY-VICTIMIZATION SCALE.
 Purpose: "Designed to measure bullying behavior and victimization among peers in or near school settings."
 Population: Grades 3–12.
 Acronym: BVS.
 Scores, 2: Bullying, Victimization.
 b) BULLY-VICTIMIZATION DISTRESS SCALE.
 Purpose: Designed to "evaluate the dimensions of students' psychological distress specific to being bullied."
 Population: Grades 3–12.
 Acronym: BVDS.
 Scores, 3: Total Distress (Externalizing, Internalizing, Total).
 c) SCHOOL VIOLENCE ANXIETY SCALE
 Purpose: Designed to "measure student anxiety about schools as unsafe or threatening environments."
 Population: Grades 5–12.
 Acronym: SVAS.
 Scores: Total score only.
Cross References: For reviews by Christopher A. Sink and Cher I. Edwards and by Susan M. Swearer and Kelly Brey Love, see 16:212.

[1735]
Reynolds Child Depression Scale–2nd Edition and Short Form.
Purpose: "Designed to screen for depression in children."
Population: Ages 7-13 years.
Publication Dates: 1981-2010.
Acronyms: RCDS-2; RCDS-2:SF.
Scores: Total score only.
Administration: Individual or group.
Forms, 2: Full length, Short.
Price Data, 2015: $160 per introductory kit including 25 full length test booklets, 25 short test forms, and manual (2010, 133 pages); $64 per 25 full length test booklets; $45 per 25 short forms; $66 per manual.
Time: (10-15) minutes for full length form; (2-3) minutes for short form.
Comments: Both forms should be administered orally to children in Grades 2 through 4; test items have not been revised since the original version, although Short Form has been added, which contains 11 of the 30 items on the full form.
Author: William M. Reynolds.
Publisher: Psychological Assessment Resources, Inc.
Cross References: For reviews by Eric S. Buhs and Robert Wright, see 19:145; see also T5:2231 (7 references) and T4:2275 (3 references); for reviews by Janet F. Carlson and Cynthia A. Rohrbeck of the first edition, see 11:334 (1 reference).

[1736]
Reynolds Depression Screening Inventory.
Purpose: Constructed as a "self-report measure of the severity of depressive symptoms."
Population: Ages 18–89.
Publication Date: 1998.
Acronym: RDSI.
Scores: Total score only.
Administration: Individual or group.
Price Data, 2015: $92 per introductory kit including manual (64 pages) and 25 booklets.
Time: (5–10) minutes.
Authors: William M. Reynolds and Kenneth A. Kobak.
Publisher: Psychological Assessment Resources, Inc.
Cross References: For reviews by Michael H. Campbell and Rosemary Flanagan, see 14:320.

[1737]
Reynolds Intellectual Assessment Scales, Second Edition and Reynolds Intellectual Screening Test, Second Edition.
Purpose: Designed to assess verbal and nonverbal intelligence and memory.
Population: Ages 3-94.
Publication Dates: 1998-2015.

Administration: Individual.
Price Data, 2016: $530 per RIAS-2/RIST-2 comprehensive kit including professional manual (2015, 341 pages) with fast guide, 25 RIAS-2 record forms, 25 RIAS-2 response forms, 25 RIST-2 record forms, RIAS-2/RIST-2 stimulus book 1, RIAS-2 stimulus book 2, RIAS-2 stimulus book 3, RIAS-2 stimulus book 4; 135 per manual; $95 per RIAS-2/RIST-2 stimulus book 1; $110 per RIAS-2 stimulus book 2; $110 per RIAS-2 stimulus book 3; $25 per RIAS-2 stimulus book 4; $75 per 25 RIAS-2 record forms; $25 per 25 RIAS-2 response forms; $50 per 25 RIST-2 record forms.
Authors: Cecil R. Reynolds and Randy W. Kamphaus.
Publisher: Psychological Assessment Resources, Inc.
a) REYNOLDS INTELLECTUAL SCREENING TEST, SECOND EDITION.
Purpose: Designed "to produce a single composite score that is an indicator of risk for intellectual impairment."
Acronym: RIST-2.
Scores, 3: Guess What, Odd-Item Out, RIST-2 Index.
Time: (10-15) minutes.
Comments: A "separate use for the RIST-2" is to obtain "an overall estimate of intelligence [when that is] all that is needed."
b) REYNOLDS INTELLECTUAL ASSESSMENT SCALES, SECOND EDITION.
Purpose: Designed as "an individually administered test of intelligence...with conormed, supplemental measures of memory and processing speed."
Acronym: RIAS-2.
Scores, 13:, Verbal Intelligence Index (Guess What, Verbal Reasoning), Nonverbal Intelligence Index (Odd-Item Out, What's Missing), Composite Intelligence Index, Composite Memory Index (Verbal Memory, Nonverbal Memory), Speeded Processing Index (Speeded Naming Task, Speeded Picture Search).
Time: (40-45) minutes for complete battery.
Cross References: For reviews by Bruce A. Bracken and Gregory Schraw of the original edition, see 16:213.

[1738]
Rhode Island Test of Language Structure.
Purpose: "Provides a measure of English language development—a profile of the child's understanding of language structure—and assessment data."
Population: Hearing-impaired children ages 3-20, hearing children ages 3-6.
Publication Date: 1983.
Acronym: RITLS.
Scores: Measures syntax response errors for 20 sentence types, both simple and complex, including Relative and Adverbial Clauses, Subject and Other Complements, Reversible and Nonreversible Passives, Datives, Deletions, Negations, Conjunctives, Embedded Imperatives.
Administration: Individual.
Price Data, 2015: $171 per complete kit including scoring forms, test booklet, and manual (114 pages); $37 per scoring forms; $81 per test booklet; $63 per manual.
Time: (25-35) minutes.

Authors: Elizabeth Engen and Trygg Engen.
Publisher: PRO-ED.
Cross References: See T5:2233 (4 references) and T4:2276 (1 reference); for reviews by Lynn S. Bliss and Joan I. Lynch, see 10:315.

[1739]
RIASEC Inventory.
Purpose: "Designed to help people identify their most dominant work interests and [to use the] information to explore career options."
Population: Individuals involved in career exploration.
Publication Date: 2009.
Scores: 6 interest areas: Realistic, Investigative, Artistic, Social, Enterprising, Conventional.
Administration: Group.
Price Data, 2016: $47.95 per package of 25 inventories; administrator's guide (7 pages) downloadable from publisher's website.
Time: (10-15) minutes.
Comments: Self-scoring and self-interpreted.
Author: JIST Publishing.
Publisher: JIST Publishing, Inc.

[1740]
Risk-Sophistication-Treatment Inventory.
Purpose: Designed to assess juvenile offenders' risk for dangerousness, sophistication-maturity, and amenability to treatment.
Population: Juvenile offenders ages 9–18.
Publication Dates: 1998–2004.
Acronym: RSTI.
Scores, 12: Risk for Dangerousness (Violent and Aggressive Tendencies, Planned and Extensive Criminality, Psychopathic Features, Total), Sophistication-Maturity (Autonomy, Cognitive Capacities, Emotional Maturity, Total), Treatment Amenability (Psychopathology-Degree and Type, Responsibility and Motivation to Change, Consideration and Tolerance of Others, Total).
Administration: Individual.
Price Data, 2015: $226 per introductory kit including professional manual (2004, 109 pages), 25 interview booklets, and 25 rating forms.
Time: (50–65) minutes for semistructured interview; [15–20] minutes for rating form.
Comments: Semistructured interview and rating scale.
Author: Randall T. Salekin.
Publisher: Psychological Assessment Resources, Inc.
Cross References: For reviews by John S. Geisler and Steven I. Pfeiffer, see 17:165.

[1741]
Risk Taking Inventory & Guide.
Purpose: Designed to "help respondents see the filters through which they assess risk" and "also guides them

in improving the likelihood of gains while reducing uncertainty and the likelihood of losses."
Population: Managers.
Publication Date: 1997.
Scores, 3: Risk-Preference Pattern, Risk-Avoidance Pattern, Risk-Neutral Pattern.
Administration: Group.
Manual: No manual.
Price Data, 2016: $10.95 per inventory and guide; minimum of 20 (volume discounts available).
Time: [15] minutes including self-scoring.
Author: Herbert S. Kindler.
Publisher: The Center for Management Effectiveness, Inc.

[1742]

The Rivermead Behavioural Memory Test–Third Edition.

Purpose: Designed to provide information about memory "for general clinical and neuropsychological evaluations, as well as for rehabilitation evaluations."
Population: Ages 16 to 89 years.
Publication Dates: 1985-2008.
Acronym: RMBT-3.
Scores, 15: First and Second Names-Delayed Recall, Belongings-Delayed Recall, Appointments-Delayed Recall, Picture Recognition-Delayed Recognition, Story-Immediate Recall, Story-Delayed Recall, Face Recognition-Delayed Recognition, Route-Immediate Recall, Route-Delayed Recall, Messages-Immediate Recall, Messages-Delayed Recall, Orientation and Date, Novel Task-Immediate Recall, Novel Task-Delayed Recall, General Memory Index.
Administration: Individual.
Forms, 2: Version 1, Version 2.
Price Data, 2016: $470 per complete kit including administration and scoring manual (2008, 129 pages), 25 record forms, 2 stimulus books (version 1 and version 2), novel task stimulus material, story card, message envelope, and alarm; $102 per manual; $104 per stimulus book (version 1 or version 2); $90 per 25 record forms; $67 per novel task stimulus material; $14 per story card; $13.50 per alarm.
Time: (30) minutes.
Authors: Barbara A. Wilson, Eve Greenfield, Linda Clare, Alan Baddeley, Janet Cockburn, Peter Watson, Robyn Tate, Sara Sopena, Rory Nannery, and John R. Crawford.
Publisher: Pearson.
Cross References: Reviews are scheduled for *The Twentieth Mental Measurements Yearbook*. For reviews by Anthony M. Paolo and by Goran Westergren and Ingela Westergren of the second edition, see 14:321; see also T5:2239 (35 references); for reviews by Andrew S. Davis and W. Holmes Finch and by Harrison Kane and Daniel Krenzer of the Extended Version, see 17:167.

[1743]

Roberts-2.

Purpose: Designed to provide an "assessment of a child's or adolescent's level of social cognitive understanding."
Population: Ages 6-18 years.
Publication Dates: 1982-2005.
Scores, 28: 2 Theme Overview scales (Popular Pull, Complete Meaning), 6 Available Resources scales (Support from Self-Feeling, Support from Self-Advocacy, Support from Other-Feeling, Support from Other-Help, Reliance on Other, Limit Setting), 5 Problem Identification scales (Recognition, Description, Clarification, Definition, Explanation), 5 Resolution scales (Simple Closure or Easy Outcome, Easy and Realistically Positive Outcome, Constructive Resolution, Constructive Resolution of Feeling and Situation, Elaborated Process with Possible Insight), 4 Emotion scales (Anxiety, Aggression, Depression, Rejection), 4 Outcome scales (Unresolved Outcome, Nonadaptive Outcome, Maladaptive Outcome, Unrealistic Outcome), 2 Unusual or Atypical Responses scales (Unusual-Refusal/No Score/Antisocial, Atypical Categories).
Administration: Individual.
Editions, 3: Set of Test Pictures Featuring White Children and Adolescents, Set of Test Pictures Featuring Black Children and Adolescents, Set of Test Pictures Featuring Hispanic Children and Adolescents.
Price Data, 2016: $255.50 per complete kit including manual (2005, 171 pages), Casebook, Quick Reference Guide, Set of Test Pictures (specify White children and adolescents, Black children and adolescents, or Hispanic children or adolescents), and 25 record forms; $69.95 per manual; $79 per set of test pictures featuring White, Black, or Hispanic children and adolescents; $46.50 per 25 record forms; $69.50 per Casebook (including 1 Quick Reference Guide); $249.50 per unlimited use scoring CD.
Time: (30-40) minutes.
Comments: Previous version titled Roberts Apperception Test for Children.
Authors: Glen E. Roberts (test and manual) and Chris Gruber (manual only).
Publisher: Western Psychological Services.
Cross References: For reviews by Frederic J. Medway and by Rachel J. Valleley and Brandy L. Clarke, see 18:110; for reviews by Merith Cosden and Niels G. Waller of an earlier version, see 14:322; see also T5:2242 (8 references) and T4:2285 (5 references); for a review by Jacob O. Sines of an earlier edition, see 9:1054.

[1744]

Rockford Infant Developmental Evaluation Scales.

Purpose: Developed as a developmental checklist offering an informal assessment of developmental function.
Population: Birth-4 years.

Publication Date: 1979.
Acronym: RIDES.
Scores, 5: Personal-Social/Self-Help, Fine Motor/Adaptive, Receptive Language, Expressive Language, Gross Motor.
Administration: Individual.
Price Data, 2015: $52 per starter set including manual and 20 checklists; $30.75 per manual; $23.90 per 20 checklists.
Time: Administration time varies; author recommends administration in several sessions in one week.
Comments: 3 ways of administering items: ask parents for information, observe spontaneous actions and informal play, present specific tasks or set up situation that will elicit a particular kind of response.
Author: Developed by PROJECT RHISE, Children's Development Center, Rockford, IL.
Publisher: Scholastic Testing Service, Inc.
Cross References: See T5:2243 (1 reference); for a review by Dennis C. Harper, see 9:1055.

[1745]

Roeder Manipulative Aptitude Test.

Purpose: Measures manual and finger dexterity and hand-eye coordination.
Population: Elementary school to adult.
Publication Date: 1967.
Scores, 1 to 3: Left Hand Dexterity (optional), Right Hand Dexterity (optional), Total.
Administration: Group.
Price Data, 2016: $225 per test.
Time: 5(10) minutes.
Author: Wesley S. Roeder.
Publisher: Lafayette Instrument.
Cross References: For reviews by Jean Powell Kirnan and Shauna Faltin and by Suzanne Lane, see 12:333.

[1746]

Rogers Criminal Responsibility Assessment Scales.

Purpose: "To quantify essential psychological and situational variables at the time of the crime and to implement criterion-based decision models for criminal responsibility."
Population: Adults.
Publication Date: 1984.
Acronym: R-CRAS.
Scores: 5 scales: Patient Reliability, Organicity, Psychopathology, Cognitive Control, Behavioral Control.
Administration: Individual.
Price Data, 2015: $154 per introductory kit including professional manual and 50 examination booklets.
Time: Administration time not reported.
Comments: "Criterion-referenced."
Author: Richard Rogers.

Publisher: Psychological Assessment Resources, Inc.
Cross References: See T4:2288 (1 reference); for a review by Robert J. Howell and R. Lynn Richards, see 10:316.

[1747]

The Roll Evaluation of Activities of Life.

Purpose: Designed to "assess children's ability to care for themselves at home, school, and in the community."
Population: Ages 2 through 18.
Publication Date: 2013.
Acronym: REAL.
Scores, 3: Activities of Daily Living, Instrumental Activities of Daily Living, Total Independent Living Skills Composite.
Administration: Individual.
Parts, 2: Activities of Daily Living Self-Care Domain, Instrumental Activities of Daily Living Home and Community Domain.
Price Data, 2016: $95 per kit including user's guide (134 pages) and 25 rating forms; $70 per user's guide; $32 per 25 rating forms.
Time: (15-20) minutes.
Comments: Ratings completed by parents or caregivers.
Authors: Kristin Roll and William Roll.
Publisher: Pearson.
Cross References: Reviews are scheduled for *The Twentieth Mental Measurements Yearbook*.

[1748]

Rorschach.

Purpose: A projective technique for clinical assessment and diagnosis.
Population: Ages 5 and over.
Publication Dates: 1921–1998.
Scores: Many variations of scoring and interpretation are in use with no single method generally accepted.
Administration: Individual.
Price Data, 2016: £183 per complete test kit, including manual, plates with 10 picture cards, recording blanks and location charts; £104 per set of 10 plates; £23 per 100 recording sheets; £57 per set of 5 location charts; £61 per manual (1998, 228 pages).
Time: (20–30) minutes.
Comments: Variously referred to by such titles as Rorschach Method, Rorschach Test, Rorschach Psychodiagnostics.
Author: Hermann Rorschach.
Publisher: Hogrefe Ltd [United Kingdom].
Cross References: For a review by Allen K. Hess, Peter Zachar, and Jeffrey Kramer, see 14:323; see also T5:2247 (136 references), T4:2292 (273 references), 9:1059 (79 references), and T3:2030 (155 references); for reviews by Richard H. Dana and Rolf A. Peterson, see 8:661 (360 references); see also T2:1499 (376 references); for reviews by Alvin G. Burstein, John F. Knutson, Charles

C. McArthur, Albert I. Rabin, and Marvin Resnikoff, see 7:175 (455 references); see also P:470 (719 references); for reviews by Richard H. Dana, Leonard D. Eron, and Arthur R. Jensen, see 6:237 (734 references); for reviews by Samuel J. Beck, H. J. Eysenck, Raymond J. McCall, and Laurance F. Shaffer, see 5:154 (1078 references); for a review by Helen Sargent, see 4:117 (621 references); for reviews by Morris Krugman and J. R. Wittenborn, see 3:73 (452 references); see also 2:1246 (147 references).

[1749]

Ross Information Processing Assessment–Geriatric: Second Edition.

Purpose: Designed to "identify, describe, and quantify cognitive-linguistic deficits in the geriatric population."
Population: Ages 55 and older.
Publication Dates: 1996-2012.
Acronym: RIPA-G:2.
Scores, 8: Immediate Memory, Temporal Orientation, Spatial Orientation, General Information, Situational Knowledge, Categorical Vocabulary, Listening Comprehension, Information Processing Index.
Administration: Individual.
Price Data, 2014: $142 per complete kit including examiner's manual (2012, 85 pages) and 25 examiner record booklets; $85 examiner's manual; $64 per 25 examiner record booklets.
Time: (25-35) minutes.
Authors: Deborah Ross-Swain and Paul T. Fogle.
Publisher: PRO-ED.
Cross References: Reviews are scheduled for *The Twentieth Mental Measurements Yearbook*. For reviews by Surendra P. Singh and Wilfred G. Van Gorp of the original edition, see 14:324.

[1750]

Ross Information Processing Assessment—Primary.

Purpose: Designed to "assess information processing skills in children ages 5-0 through 12-11 who have acquired or developmental problems involving the brain."
Population: 5-0 to 12-11.
Publication Date: 1999.
Acronym: RIPA-P.
Scores, 12: 8 subtests (Immediate Memory, Recent Memory, Recall of General Information, Spatial Orientation, Temporal Orientation, Organization, Problem Solving, Abstract Reasoning); 4 composite scores (Memory, Orientation, Thinking and Reasoning, Information Processing).
Administration: Individual.
Price Data, 2015: $157 per complete kit including manual (61 pages), 25 profile/summary forms, and 25 record forms; $71 per manual; $37 per 25 profile/summary forms; $56 per 25 record forms.

Time: (45) minutes for complete battery.
Comments: Certain subtests not administered to younger children.
Author: Deborah Ross-Swain.
Publisher: PRO-ED.
Cross References: For reviews by Dawn P. Flanagan and Leonard F. Caltabiano and by Matthew E. Lambert, see 15:208.

[1751]

Ross Information Processing Assessment, Second Edition.

Purpose: Designed to assess "cognitive-linguistic deficits following traumatic brain injury."
Population: Ages 15–90.
Publication Dates: 1986–1996.
Acronym: RIPA-2.
Scores, 20: 10 Subtest scores (Immediate Memory, Recent Memory, Temporal Orientation [Recent Memory, Remote Memory], Spatial Orientation, Orientation to Environment, Recall of General Information, Problem Solving and Abstract Reasoning, Organization, Auditory Processing and Retention); 10 Diacritical scores (Errors, Perseveration, Repeat Instructions/Stimulus, Denial/Refusal, Delayed Response, Confabulation, Partially Correct, Irrelevant, Tangential, Self-Corrected).
Administration: Individual.
Price Data, 2015: $179 per complete kit including examiner's manual (1996, 68 pages), 25 record forms, and 25 profile/summary forms in storage box; $67 per 25 record forms; $43 per 25 profile/summary forms; $79 per examiner's manual.
Time: (60) minutes.
Author: Deborah Ross-Swain.
Publisher: PRO-ED.
Cross References: For a review by Stephen R. Hooper, see 14:325; see also T4:2294; for a review by Jonathan Ehrlich of an earlier edition, see 11:337.

[1752]

Rothwell-Miller Interest Blank.

Purpose: Designed to assess vocational interests.
Population: Ages 12 and over.
Publication Date: 1986.
Acronym: RMIB.
Scores, 12: Outdoor, Mechanical, Computational, Scientific, Persuasive, Artistic, Literary, Musical, Social Service, Clerical, Practical, Medical.
Administration: Group.
Price Data: Available from publisher.
Foreign Language Edition: Test printed in English and Afrikaans.
Time: 30(40) minutes.
Authors: B. A. Hall, M. E. Halstead, and T. R. Taylor.
Publisher: Human Sciences Research Council [South Africa]. [Efforts to obtain updated information from

the test publisher were unsuccessful. This test could not be found on the test publisher's website; its status is unknown.]

[1753]
Rotter Incomplete Sentences Blank, Second Edition.

Purpose: Primarily used "as a screening instrument of overall adjustment."
Population: College students, adults, high-school students.
Publication Dates: 1950–1992.
Acronym: RISB.
Score: Index of Overall Adjustment.
Administration: Individual or group.
Forms, 3: College, Adult, High School.
Price Data, 2015: $73.80 per 25 response sheets (specify High School, College, or Adult); $168.10 per manual (1992, 256 pages).
Time: (20–40) minutes.
Authors: Julian B. Rotter, Michael I. Lah, and Janet E. Rafferty.
Publisher: Pearson.
Cross References: See T5:2258 (6 references); for reviews by Gregory J. Boyle and Mary J. McLellan, see 12:335 (3 references); see also T4:2300 (11 references), T3:2037 (11 references), 8:663 (21 references), T2:1501 (48 references), P:472 (35 references), 6:239 (17 references), and 5:156 (18 references); for reviews by Charles N. Cofer and William Schofield of an earlier edition and an excerpted review by Adolf G. Woltmann, see 4:130 (6 references).

[1754]
Ruff Figural Fluency Test.

Purpose: Developed with the "aim of providing clinical information regarding nonverbal capacity for fluid and divergent thinking, ability to flexibly shift cognitive set, planning strategies, and executive ability to coordinate this process."
Population: Ages 16–70.
Publication Dates: 1988–1996.
Acronym: RFFT.
Scores, 3: Unique Designs, Perseverative Errors, Index of Planning Efficiency (Error Ratio).
Administration: Individual.
Price Data, 2015: $155 per introductory kit including 25 test booklets and professional manual (1996, 43 pages).
Time: 5 minutes.
Comments: Especially useful in neuropsychological applications.
Author: Ronald M. Ruff.
Publisher: Psychological Assessment Resources, Inc.
Cross References: For reviews by Raymond S. Dean and John J. Brinkman, Jr. and by Vincent J. Samar, see 15:209.

[1755]
Ruff-Light Trail Learning Test.

Purpose: "To assess visuospatial learning and memory."
Population: Ages 16–70.
Publication Date: 1999.
Acronym: RULIT.
Scores, 7: Learning (Total Correct, Total Step Errors, Trials to Completion), Immediate Memory (Trial 2 Correct, Trial 2 Errors), Delayed Memory (Delayed Correct, Delayed Errors).
Administration: Individual.
Price Data, 2015: $60 per e-Manual; $19 per stimulus cards (set of 2); $60 per 25 test booklets.
Time: (5–15) minutes with a 60-minute delay.
Comments: Two alternate versions of a 15-step trail; long-term memory is evaluated by having the respondent retrace the trail after a 60-minute delay.
Authors: Ronald M. Ruff and C. Christopher Allen.
Publisher: Psychological Assessment Resources, Inc.
Cross References: For reviews by D. Ashley Cohen and Joseph G. Law, Jr., see 15:210.

[1756]
Ruff Neurobehavioral Inventory.

Purpose: Designed to measure cognitive, emotional, physical, and psychosocial problems both before and after a specified event—usually an injury or neuropsychiatric illness.
Population: Ages 18 and older.
Publication Date: 2003.
Acronym: RNBI.
Scores, 26: Inconsistency, Infrequency, Negative Impression, Positive Impression, Cognitive Composite, Emotional Composite, Physical Composite, Quality of Life Composite, Attention & Concentration, Executive Functions, Learning & Memory, Speech & Language, Anger & Aggression, Anxiety, Depression, Paranoia & Suspicion, Posttraumatic Stress Disorder, Substance Abuse, Neurological Status, Pain, Somatic Complaints, Abuse, Activities of Daily Living, Psychosocial Integration & Recreation, Vocation & Finance, Spirituality.
Administration: Individual or group.
Price Data, 2015: $286 per combination kit including RNBI software (CD-ROM) with on-screen help and quick start guide, 25 reusable item booklets, 25 answer booklets, 25 profile booklets, and professional manual (123 pages).
Time: [30–45] minutes.
Authors: Ronald M. Ruff and Kristin M. Hibbard.
Publisher: Psychological Assessment Resources, Inc.
Cross References: For reviews by Andrew S. Davis and W. Holmes Finch and by Wilfred G. Van Gorp and Jason Hassenstab, see 16:214.

[1757]

Ruff 2 & 7 Selective Attention Test.

Purpose: Developed to "measure two overlapping aspects of visual attention: sustained attention, and selective attention."

Population: Ages 16–70 years.

Publication Dates: 1995–1996.

Acronym: 2 & 7 Test.

Scores, 11: Automatic Detection Speed, Automatic Detection Errors, Automatic Detection Accuracy, Controlled Search Speed, Controlled Search Errors, Controlled Search Accuracy, Total Speed, Total Accuracy, Speed Difference, Accuracy Difference, Total Difference.

Administration: Individual.

Price Data, 2015: $200 per introductory kit including manual and 50 test booklets.

Time: (5) minutes.

Authors: Ronald M. Ruff and C. Christopher Allen.

Publisher: Psychological Assessment Resources, Inc.

Cross References: For a review by Daniel C. Miller, see 15:211.

[1758]

Rust Advanced Numerical Reasoning Appraisal.

Purpose: Measures the ability to recognize, understand, and apply mathematical and statistical reasoning abilities.

Population: Adults.

Publication Dates: 2001–2002.

Acronym: RANRA.

Scores: Total score only.

Administration: Group or individual.

Price Data, 2015: £319.80 per complete kit, including manual, 5 test booklets, scoring keys, and 25 record forms; £89.40 per 25 record forms; £31.80 per specimen set, including test booklet, practice test and record form; £49.20 per scoring key; £18.50 per test booklet; £39 per 10 practice tests.

Time: 20 minutes.

Author: John Rust.

Publisher: Pearson Assessment [England].

Cross References: For reviews by Cederick O. Lindskog and Eleanor E. Sanford, see 16:215.

[1759]

The Rutgers Drawing Test.

Purpose: A nonverbal "test of perception through motor response."

Population: Ages 4–6, 6–9.

Publication Dates: 1961–1973.

Scores: Total score only.

Administration: Group.

Price Data: Available from publisher.

Time: Administration time not reported.

Author: Anna Spiesman Starr.

Publisher: Institute of Psychological Research, Inc. [Canada].

   a) FORM A.

   Population: Ages 4–6.

   b) FORM B.

   Population: Ages 6–9.

Cross References: For a review by Melvyn I. Semmel, see 7:446 (6 references); see also 6:559 (2 references).

[1760]

Sales Achievement Predictor.

Purpose: Constructed to assess "characteristics that are critical for success in sales."

Population: Adults.

Publication Date: 1995.

Acronym: Sales AP.

Scores, 21: Validity Scores (Inconsistent Responding, Self-Enhancing, Self-Critical), Special Scores (Sales Disposition, Initiative-Cold Calling, Sales Closing), Basic Domain Scores (Achievement, Motivation, Competitiveness, Goal Orientation, Planning, Initiative-General, Team Player, Managerial, Assertiveness, Personal Diplomacy, Extroversion, Cooperativeness, Relaxed Style, Patience, Self-Confidence).

Administration: Group.

Price Data, 2016: $541 per kit including manual (73 pages), 100 PC answer sheets, and 10-use scoring CD; $69 per manual; $520 per 10-use scoring CD.

Time: 20 minutes.

Authors: Jotham G. Friedland, Sander I. Marcus, and Harvey P. Mandel.

Publisher: Multi-Health Systems, Inc.

Cross References: For reviews by Gordon C. Bruner II and Brent W. Roberts, see 14:329.

[1761]

Sales Aptitude Test.

Purpose: "To measure an individual's sales aptitude."

Population: Sales people and sales managers.

Publication Dates: 1993–1996.

Scores: Total score only.

Administration: Group.

Price Data: Available from publisher.

Time: (30) minutes.

Comments: Computer administration available.

Author: Science Research Associates.

Publisher: General Dynamics Information Technology.

Cross References: For reviews by Deniz S. Ones and Sheldon Zedeck, see 15:212.

[1762]

Sales Attitude Check List.

Purpose: To measure attitudes toward selling and habits in the sales situation.

Population: Applicants for sales positions.

Publication Dates: 1960–1992.

Acronym: SACL.
Scores: Total score only.
Administration: Individual or group.
Price Data: Available from publisher.
Time: No limit (approximately 10–15 minutes).
Author: Erwin K. Taylor.
Publisher: General Dynamics Information Technology.
Cross References: For reviews by Walter C. Borman and Stephan J. Motowidlo, see 9:1066 (1 reference); for a review by John P. Foley, Jr., see 6:1177.

[1763]
Sales Management Survey.

Purpose: Designed to assess skills essential for management development and to add thought leadership to the traditional sales manager role.
Population: First-line and middle sales managers.
Publication Dates: 1975-2011.
Acronym: SMS.
Scores, 20: Envisioning Opportunities, Communicating Effectively, Innovation & Risk Taking, Problem Solving & Decision Making, Planning and Collaboration, Customer Focus, Managing Conflict, Team Development, Coaching, Workforce Planning and Management, Providing Feedback, Awareness of Others, Self-Awareness, Standards of Performance, Personal Drive, Delegation, Goal Pressure, Recognition of Good Performance, Tension Level, Overall Effectiveness.
Administration: Individual.
Price Data: Available from publisher.
Comments: Publisher suggests allowing 2-3 weeks to collect feedback.
Time: 20-30 minutes.
Authors: Paul M. Connolly, Daniel Booth, and Clark L. Wilson.
Publisher: The Clark Wilson Group, Inc. (subsidiary of The Booth Company, Inc.).

[1764]
Sales Motivation Survey.

Purpose: Designed to assess the kinds of needs and values salespeople see as important considerations in making decisions about their work.
Population: Salespeople.
Publication Dates: 1972–1995.
Scores, 5: Basic Creative Comfort, Safety and Order, Belonging and Affiliation, Ego-Status, Actualization and Self-Expression.
Administration: Group.
Price Data, 2016: $8.95 per instrument.
Time: Administration time not reported.
Comments: Self-administered; self-scored.
Authors: Jay Hall and Norman J. Seim.
Publisher: Teleometrics International, Inc.
Cross References: For reviews by Leslie H. Krieger and Sheldon Zedeck, see 14:330.

[1765]
Sales Performance Assessment™.

Purpose: Designed to identify an individual's strengths and weaknesses in the area of sales.
Population: Salespeople.
Publication Dates: 1985-2005.
Acronym: SPA.
Scores, 25: Market Awareness, Technical, Strategic, Structure, Sales Focus, Prospecting, Entrepreneurship, Communication, Outgoing, Optimistic, Excitement, Persuasive Negotiation, Insight, Aggressiveness, Tactical, Empathy, Customer Identification, Team Player, Persistence, Production, Management Focus, Idealism, Ego Drive, Materialism, Exaggeration.
Administration: Group.
Price Data: Available from publisher.
Foreign Language Editions: Available in Chinese (simplified), English (American), English (British), Dutch, French, German, Japanese, Korean, Portuguese (Brazil), and Spanish.
Time: (45) minutes.
Comments: Purchase and use requires training by publisher; test previously listed as Sales Effectiveness Analysis.
Authors: James T. Mahoney (test) and Management Research Group Staff (manual).
Publisher: Management Research Group

[1766]
Sales Personality Questionnaire.

Purpose: Developed to assess personality characteristics necessary for sales success.
Population: Sales applicants.
Publication Dates: 1987–1990.
Acronym: SPQ.
Scores, 12: Interpersonal (Confidence, Empathy, Persuasive), Administration (Systematic, Conscientious, Forward Planning), Opportunities (Creative, Observant), Energies (Relaxed, Resilient, Results Oriented), Social Desirability.
Administration: Group.
Price Data: Available from publisher.
Time: (20-30) minutes.
Author: Saville & Holdsworth Ltd.
Publisher: CEB.
Cross References: For reviews by Wayne J. Camara and Michael J. Roszkowski, see 12:337.

[1767]
Sales Potential Inventory.

Purpose: "Designed to help select top sales performers and determine the sales ability levels of current employees in any external or internal sales position."
Population: Job applicants and employees in sales positions.
Publication Dates: 2000–2001.

Acronym: S.P.I.
Scores, 2: S.P.I. score, Deception Scale score.
Administration: Group.
Price Data: Available from publisher.
Time: (15-20) minutes.
Comments: The test publisher has indicated there is a newer edition of this test; description will be updated when complete test materials are received.
Comments: Online and paper-and-pencil versions of test are available; online version includes interpretive reports and follow-up interview questions.
Author: J. M. Llobet.
Publisher: HRdirect | G. Neil.
Cross References: For a review by Kathy E. Green, see 17:168.

[1768]

Sales Professional Assessment Inventory.

Purpose: Designed "to assess the individual's interest, motivation and skills needed for success in the sales profession."
Population: Salespeople.
Publication Dates: 1989–1992.
Acronym: SPAI.
Scores, 15: Validity (Candidness, Accuracy), Sales Motivation (Sales/Work Experience, Sales Interest, Sales Responsibility, Sales Orientation, Energy Level, Self Development), Sales Readiness (Sales Skills, Sales Understanding, Sales Arithmetic, Customer Service), Dependability (Business Ethics, Job Stability), Overall Index (Sales Potential).
Administration: Group or individual.
Price Data: Available from publisher.
Time: (45) minutes.
Author: London House.
Publisher: General Dynamics Information Technology.

[1769]

Sales Relations Survey.

Purpose: Designed to assess the interpersonal practices and customer orientation of salespeople.
Population: Salespeople.
Publication Dates: 1972–1995.
Scores, 2: Exposure, Feedback.
Administration: Group.
Price Data, 2016: $9.95 per instrument.
Time: Administration time not reported.
Comments: Self-administered; self-scored.
Author: Jay Hall.
Publisher: Teleometrics International, Inc.

[1770]

Sales Skills Test.

Purpose: Designed "to evaluate the knowledge, skills, and abilities for a sales position."
Population: Adult sales position applicants.

Publication Dates: 2001–2002.
Scores, 6: Sales Principles, Sales Terms, Vocabulary, Sales Comprehension, Sales Situations, Math/Logic & Attention to Detail.
Administration: Individual.
Price Data: Available from publisher.
Time: (65) minutes.
Author: Bruce Winrow.
Publisher: Walden Personnel Testing & Consulting Inc. [Canada].
Cross References: For reviews by JoEllen V. Carlson and Paul M. Muchinsky, see 16:216.

[1771]

Sales Staff Selector.

Purpose: "Evaluates the suitability of candidates of all levels of experience for the position of Sales Representative."
Population: Candidates for jobs as sales representatives.
Publication Date: 1984.
Scores, 4: Total score, Narrative Evaluation, Ranking, Recommendation.
Administration: Group.
Price Data: Available from publisher.
Foreign Language Edition: Available in French.
Time: (65) minutes.
Comments: Scored by publisher.
Author: Walden Personnel Performance, Inc.
Publisher: Walden Personnel Testing & Consulting Inc. [Canada].
Cross References: For reviews by Philip G. Benson and Richard W. Johnson, see 10:319.

[1772]

Sales Style Indicator [Revised].

Purpose: Designed to help an individual identify their preferred selling style and "assist individuals and teams to increase their sales and customer service performance."
Population: Sales personnel, sales managers, and customer service representatives.
Publication Dates: 1991-2006.
Acronym: SSI.
Scores, 4: Behavioral/Action, Cognitive/Analysis, Interpersonal/Harmony, Affective/Expression.
Administration: Individual or group.
Price Data, 2016: $25 per test booklet (2006, 20 pages); $20 per In-Depth Interpretations Booklet (2006, 48 pages); $45 per online version; $30 per Why Don't You Sell the Way That I Buy? participant workbook (2006, 80 pages); $40 per Trainer's Guidelines (1996, 24 pages).
Foreign Language Editions: Available in print in French and Swedish; available online in Chinese, German, and Spanish; the In-Depth interpretations booklet is available in French.
Time: 15 minutes to administer; 90-180 minutes for short program; up to 2 days for the full program.

Comments: Test can be self-administered, self-scored, and self-interpreted.
Authors: Ken Keis, Terry D. Anderson, and Bruce Wares.
Publisher: Consulting Resource Group International, Inc.
Cross References: For reviews by Wayne J. Camara and Gerald A. Rosen of an earlier edition, see 13:271.

[1773]

Sales Transaction Audit.
Purpose: Intended as an assessment of sales style and its impact on salesperson-customer transactions.
Population: Salespeople.
Publication Dates: 1972–1980.
Acronym: STA.
Scores, 3: Parent, Adult, Child.
Administration: Group.
Manual: No manual.
Price Data, 2016: $9.95 per instrument.
Time: Administration time not reported.
Authors: Jay Hall and C. Leo Griffith.
Publisher: Teleometrics International, Inc.
Cross References: For a review by Chantale Jeanrie, see 14:331; for a review by Stephen L. Cohen of an earlier edition, see 8:1127.

[1774]

SalesMax.
Purpose: A computerized testing system designed "to measure personality traits and sales knowledge that contribute to effectiveness in the sales role."
Population: Potential employees for consultative sales positions (selection) or current employees (development reports available).
Publication Dates: 1998-2010.
Scores, 25: Sales Personality (Energetic, Follows Through, Optimistic, Resilient, Assertive, Social, Expressive, Serious-Minded, Self-Reliant, Accommodating, Positive About People), Sales Knowledge (Prospecting/Pre-qualifying, First Meetings/First Impressions, Probing/Presenting, Overcoming Objections, Influencing/Convincing, Closing), Sales Motivations (Recognition/Attention, Control, Money, Freedom, Developing Expertise, Affiliation, Security/Stability, Achievement).
Administration: Group or individual.
Price Data, 2015: $150 one-time fee for account set-up and user training; reports are $128 to $170 each.
Foreign Language Editions: Spanish, Portuguese, Hungarian, Dutch, and Korean versions available.
Time: [90] minutes for all modules; [20] minutes for 1 or 2 modules.
Comments: Earlier version entitled SalesMax System Internet Version.
Author: Assess Systems.
Publisher: Assess Systems.

Cross References: For reviews by David J. Pittenger and Steven W. Schmidt, see 19:146; for reviews by Gerald R. Schneck and Michael Spangler of an earlier version called SalesMax System Internet Version, see 15:213.

[1775]

Salesperson Personality Profile.
Purpose: Designed to assess "whether a person has the skills, traits, and knowledge to make it in the field of sales."
Population: Under 25 through adult.
Publication Date: 2011.
Acronym: SPPP.
Scores, 45: Comfort with Public Speaking, Comfort with Risk-Taking, Comfort with Decision-Making, Comfort with Rejection/Criticism, Confidence, Adaptability, Assertiveness, Communication Skills, Persuasiveness, Networking Skills, Goal Orientation, Initiative, Energy, Research Skills, Problem-Solving, Competitiveness, Emotional Intelligence, Sales Techniques Knowledge, Neatness, Time Management, Meticulousness, Listening Skills, Integrity, Emotional Control, Helpfulness, Canned Presentation Style vs. Free-Flowing Presentation Style, Resourcefulness, Diplomacy, Memory for Names, Memory for Physical Details, Memory for Personal Details, Impression Management, Self-Efficacy, Sales Aptitude, Conscientiousness, Cooperativeness, Consultative Selling, Relationship Building, Resolving Objectives, Negotiating, Questioning Skills, Positioning, Getting Referrals, Memory Skills, Overall Score.
Administration: Individual.
Price Data: Available from publisher.
Time: (40) minutes.
Comments: Self-administered online assessment. The test publisher provides clients with information about the methods and theoretical basis used in the development of the test as well as benchmarks for relevant industries and racial/ethnic group comparison data.
Author: PsychTests AIM, Inc.
Publisher: PsychTests AIM, Inc. [Canada].
Cross References: For reviews by Warren Bobrow and Paul Muchinsky, see 19:147.

[1776]

Salford Sentence Reading Test (Revised).
Purpose: To assess level of oral reading achievement.
Population: Ages 6-0 to 10-6.
Publication Dates: 1976–2000.
Acronym: SSRT (R).
Scores: Reading Age.
Administration: Individual.
Forms, 2: X and Y.
Price Data: Available from publisher.
Time: [2–3] minutes.
Comments: The test publisher has indicated there is a newer edition of this test; description will be updated when complete test materials are received.

Authors: G. E. Bookbinder; revision by Denis Vincent and Mary Crumpler.
Publisher: Hodder Education [United Kingdom].
Cross References: See T4:2320 (1 reference); for a review by J. Douglas Ayers of an earlier edition, see 8:791.

[1777]

SAQ-Adult Probation III.

Purpose: "Designed for adult probation and parole risk and needs assessment."
Population: Adult probationers and parolees.
Publication Dates: 1985–1997.
Acronym: SAQ.
Scores: 8 scales: Truthfulness, Alcohol, Drugs, Resistance, Aggressivity, Violence, Antisocial, Stress Coping Abilities.
Administration: Group.
Price Data: Available from publisher.
Time: (30) minutes.
Author: Risk & Needs Assessment, Inc.
Publisher: Behavior Data Systems, Ltd.
Cross References: For reviews by John R. Hays and by Robert Spies and Mark Cooper, see 14:332; for a review by Tony Toneatto of an earlier edition, see 12:338.

[1778]

SASB [Structural Analysis of Social Behavior] Intrex Questionnaires.

Purpose: Designed to measure the patient's perceptions of self and others, based on trait x state x situational philosophy and Structural Analysis of Social Behavior.
Population: Psychiatric patients and normals.
Publication Dates: 1980–2000.
Acronym: SASB Intrex.
Scores: Pattern Coefficient Scores, cluster profiles, and weighted affiliation and autonomy scores for each of 3 areas: Interpersonal Transitive-Focus on Other, Interpersonal Intransitive-Focus on Self, Intrapsychic Introjection; 3 forms (short, medium, long), 6 subtests: Self (Best, Worst), He/I Present Tense (Best, Worst), She/I Present Tense (Best, Worst), Mother/I Past Tense, Father/I Past Tense, Mother with Father/Father with Mother Past Tense.
Administration: Individual or group.
Price Data: Available from publisher.
Time: (60) minutes for complete battery, short form.
Author: Lorna Smith Benjamin.
Publisher: Lorna Smith Benjamin, LLC.
Cross References: For reviews by Dennis Doverspike and Thomas P. Hogan, see 15:214; see T5:1298 (1 reference); for a review by Scott T. Meier of an earlier edition, see 12:192; see also T4:1258 (2 references).

[1779]

SAT.

Purpose: Designed to test the academic skills and knowledge that students acquired in high school and their ability to apply their knowledge for success in college.
Population: Candidates for college entrance.
Publication Dates: 1926–2016.
Acronym: SAT.
Scores, 18: 7 subscores (Words in Context, Heart of Algebra, Command of Evidence, Problem Solving and Data Analysis, Expression of Ideas, Passport to Advanced Mathematics, Standard English Conventions), 3 test scores (Reading, Writing and Language, Math), 2 cross-test scores (Analysis and Science, Analysis and History/Social Studies), 2 section scores (Evidence-based Reading and Writing, Math) plus Total Score; 3 optional essay scores not factored into Total Score.
Administration: Group.
Price Data: Available from publisher.
Time: (230) minutes total; (65) minutes for Reading, (35) minutes for Writing and Language, (80) minutes for Math, (50) minutes for SAT Essay.
Comments: The SAT is administered 7 times annually (January, March or April, May, June, October, November, and December) at centers established by the publisher.
Authors: The College Board and Educational Testing Service.
Publisher: The College Board.
Cross References: For information about the College Board SAT Program, see T5:615 (55 references), T3:500 (3 references), 8:472 (6 references), T2:1048 (9 references), and 7:663 (16 references); for information about the College Board SAT I Reasoning Test, see T5:592 (107 references) and T4:564 (167 references); for reviews by Sanford J. Cohn and Lee J. Cronbach of the College Board Scholastic Aptitude Test and Test of Standard Written English, see 9:244 (31 references); see T3:501 (152 references), 8:182 (217 references), and T2:357 (148 references); for reviews by Philip H. Dubois and Wimburn L. Wallace of an earlier form of the College Board Scholastic Aptitude Test, see 7:344 (298 references); for reviews by John E. Bowers and Wayne S. Zimmerman of the College Entrance Examination Board Scholastic Aptitude Test, see 6:449 (79 references); for a review by John T. Dailey, see 5:318 (20 references); for a review by Frederick B. Davis, see 4:285 (22 references). For reviews by Benno G. Fricke and Dean K. Whitla of the College Entrance Examination Board Admissions Testing Program, see 6:760 (2 reviews); see also 5:599 (3 references) and 4:526 (9 references).

[1780]

SAT On-Campus.

Purpose: Designed to allow colleges to administer SAT and SAT Subject Tests to incoming and continuing students for advisement and placement.

Population: Incoming and continuing college students.
Publication Dates: 1989–2016.
Scores: Total score only for each test.
Administration: Group.
Price Data: Available from publisher.
Time: (60) minutes per subject test.
Comments: In addition to the SAT (1779), all 20 SAT Subject Tests (1791) are available through SAT On-Campus testing; SAT On-Campus testing cannot be used to apply to other colleges, receive scores for college admission, or test younger students who may take the SAT for college admission in the future.
Author: Educational Testing Service.
Publisher: The College Board.
Cross References: See T5:1274 (2 references) and T3:507 (2 references); for a review by John R. Hills of the College Placement Tests, see 7:665.

[1781]

SAT Subject Tests.

Purpose: Designed as college admission exams that test students' knowledge of subjects on a high-school level.
Population: Candidates for college entrance.
Publication Dates: 1901–2016.
Scores: Total score only for 20 tests in 5 subject areas using the College Board's 200 to 800 scale. Some SAT Subject Tests also provide subscores.
Administration: Group.
Price Data: Available from publisher.
Time: (60) minutes per subject test.
Comments: Available for local administration and scoring by higher educational institutions through the SAT On-Campus program (1780); the SAT Subject Tests are administered 7 times annually (January, March, May, June, October, November, December) at centers established by the publisher, though not all tests are available at each administration.
Author: Educational Testing Service.
Publisher: The College Board.

a) MATHEMATICS.
  1) *Mathematics Level 1.*
  2) *Mathematics Level 2.*
b) HISTORY.
  1) *U.S. History.*
  2) *World History.*
c) SCIENCE.
  1) *Biology.*
  2) *Physics.*
  3) *Chemistry.*
d) LANGUAGES.
  1) *Spanish.*
  2) *Spanish with Listening.*
  3) *German.*
  4) *German with Listening.*
  5) *French.*
  6) *French Listening.*
  7) *Chinese Listening.*
  8) *Italian.*
  9) *Modern Hebrew.*
  10) *Latin.*
  11) *Japanese with Listening.*
  12) *Korean with Listening.*
e) ENGLISH.
  1) *Literature.*

Cross References: For reviews of earlier editions of individual tests, see 8:46 (2 reviews) for English Composition, 8:128 (1 review) for German Reading, 8:147 (1 review) for Russian Reading, 8:258 (2 reviews) for Mathematics Level 1, 6:287 (3 reviews) for English Composition, 6:289 (1 review) for Writing Sample, 6:383 (1 review) for German, 6:384 (2 reviews) for German Listening Comprehension, , 6:568 (1 review) for Advanced Mathematics, 6:569 (1 review) for Intermediate Mathematics, 6:914 (1 review) for Chemistry, 6:966 (1 review) for American History and Social Studies, 6:967 (1 review) for European History and World Cultures, 5:272 (1 review) for German, 5:277 (1 review) for Greek, 5:280 (1 review) for Latin, 5:723 (1 review) for Biology, 5:742 (1 review) for Chemistry, 5:749 (1 review) for Physics, 5:786 (1 review) for Social Studies, 4:178 (1 review) for English Composition, 4:237 (1 review) for French Reading, 4:244 (1 review) for German Reading, 4:250 (1 review) for Latin Reading, 4:367 (1 review) for Advanced Mathematics, 4:368 (1 review) for Intermediate Mathematics, 4:600 (1 review) for Biology, 4:617 (1 review) for Chemistry, 4:633 (1 review) for Physics, and 4:662 (1 review) for Social Studies.

[1782]

Scale for the Assessment of Negative Symptoms.

Purpose: To assess negative symptoms of schizophrenia.
Population: Psychiatric inpatients and outpatients of all ages.
Publication Dates: 1981-1984.
Acronym: SANS.
Scores: 25 behavioral rating scores within 5 areas: Affective Flattening or Blunting, Alogia, Avolition-Apathy, Anhedonia-Asociality, Attention.
Administration: Individual.
Price Data: Available free of charge from test publisher.
Foreign Language Editions: Available in Spanish, French, Italian, German, Portuguese, Japanese, Chinese, Greek, and Korean.
Time: [15-30] minutes.
Comments: May be used in conjunction with the Scale for the Assessment of Positive Symptoms (SAPS; 1783).
Author: Nancy C. Andreasen.
Publisher: Nancy C. Andreasen.
Cross References: See T5:2288 (85 references); for reviews by Suzanne King and Niels G. Waller, see 12:339 (75 references); see also T4:2325 (37 references); for information on an earlier edition, see 9:1069 (2 references).

[1783]

Scale for the Assessment of Positive Symptoms.

Purpose: "Designed to assess positive symptoms, principally those that occur in schizophrenia."
Population: Psychiatric inpatients and outpatients of all ages.
Publication Date: 1984.
Acronym: SAPS.
Scores: 35 behavior ratings within 5 areas: Hallucinations, Delusions, Bizarre Behavior, Positive Formal Thought Disorder, Inappropriate Affect.
Administration: Individual.
Price Data: Available free of charge from test publisher.
Time: [15-30] minutes.
Comments: Intended to serve as a complementary instrument to the Scale for the Assessment of Negative Symptoms (SANS; 1782).
Author: Nancy C. Andreasen.
Publisher: Nancy C. Andreasen.
Cross References: See T5:2289 (69 references); for reviews by John D. King and Suzanne King, see 12:340 (44 references); see also T4:2326 (24 references).

[1784]

Scale for the Assessment of Thought, Language, and Communication.

Purpose: Designed to assess clinical and pathological characteristics of language behavior.
Population: Manics, depressives, and schizophrenics.
Publication Date: 1980.
Acronym: TLC.
Scores: 19 ratings: Poverty of Speech, Poverty of Content of Speech, Pressure of Speech, Distractible Speech, Tangentiality, Derailment, Incoherence, Illogicality, Clanging, Neologisms, Word Approximations, Circumstantiality, Loss of Goal, Perseveration, Echolalia, Blocking, Stilted Speech, Self-Reference, Global Rating.
Administration: Individual.
Price Data: Available free of charge from test publisher.
Time: [45-60] minutes.
Author: Nancy C. Andreasen.
Publisher: Nancy C. Andreasen.
Cross References: See T5:2290 (2 references) and T4:2327 (4 references).

[1785]

Scale of Feelings and Behavior of Love: Revised.

Purpose: Designed to "identify the patterns of behavior and feelings people exhibit and experience in their love relationships."
Population: College and adults.
Publication Dates: 1973-1992.

Scores, 8: Verbal Expression of Affection, Self-Disclosure, Toleration of Loved Ones' Bothersome Aspects, Moral Support/Encouragement and Interest, Feelings Not Expressed, Material Evidence of Affection, Total Love Scale, Love Scale Index.
Administration: Group.
Price Data: Available from publisher.
Time: (30) minutes.
Comments: Separate answer sheets may be used; current edition now included in Innovations in Clinical Practice: A Source Book (Vol. II).
Authors: Clifford H. Swensen, Michele Killough Nelson, Jan Warner, and David Dunlap.
Publisher: Clifford H. Swensen.
Cross References: See T4:2328 (1 reference); for a review by H. Thompson Prout of an earlier edition, see 9:1072.

[1786]

Scale of Job-Related Social Skill Performance.

Purpose: Designed to assess the strengths and weaknesses of a student's social skill performance in work settings.
Publication Date: [Undated].
Administration: Individual.
Price Data: Price data available from publisher for complete kit including teaching guide and script, response form, and interpretation/scoring guide.
Authors: Michael Bullis, Vicki Nishioka-Evans, H. D. Bud Fredericks, and Cheryl D. Davis.
Publisher: James Stanfield Co., Inc.
 a) SCALE OF JOB-RELATED SOCIAL SKILLS KNOWLEDGE.
 Population: Ages 15–25.
 Acronym: SSSK.
 Scores: Total score only.
 Time: (45) minutes.
 Comments: Administered using a verbal role playing method.
 b) SCALE OF JOB-RELATED SOCIAL SKILL PERFORMANCE.
 Population: Ages 14–21.
 Acronym: SSSP.
 Scores: 6 scales: Positive Social Behaviors, Self Control, Personal Issues, Body Movements, Personal Appearance, Negative Social Behaviors.
 Time: Administration time not reported.

[1787]

Scale of Marriage Problems: Revised.

Purpose: Designed to measure marital conflicts.
Population: Couples.
Publication Dates: 1975–1992.
Scores, 7: Problem-Solving, Childrearing, Relatives, Personal Care, Money, Outside Relationships, Total.
Administration: Group.
Price Data: Available from publisher.

Time: Administration time not reported.

Comments: Current edition now included in Innovations in Clinical Practice: A Source Book (Vol. II).

Authors: Clifford H. Swensen, Michele Killough Nelson, Jan Warner, and David Dunlap.

Publisher: Clifford H. Swensen.

Cross References: For reviews by Cindy Carlson and Delores D. Walcott, see 14:334.

[1788]

Scales for Assessing Emotional Disturbance–Second Edition.

Purpose: Designed to identify students who qualify for the federal special education category of emotional disturbance.

Population: Students in Grades K-12.

Publication Dates: 1998-2010.

Acronym: SAED-2.

Administration: Individual.

Price Data, 2014: $215 per complete kit including examiner's manual (2010, 112 pages), 25 rating scales, 25 developmental/educational questionnaire, and 25 observation forms; $65 per examiner's manual; $50 per 25 forms (rating scales, developmental/educational questionnaires, or observation forms).

Comments: Components may be used alone or in various combinations.

Authors: Michael H. Epstein and Douglas Cullinan.

Publisher: PRO-ED.

a) RATING SCALE.

Purpose: Designed to "evaluate the emotional and behavioral problems of students in educational settings."

Scores, 7: Inability to Learn, Relationship Problems, Inappropriate Behavior, Unhappiness or Depression, Physical Symptoms or Fears, Rating Scale Index, Socially Maladjusted.

Time: [10] minutes.

Comments: Ratings completed by teachers or other school personnel.

b) OBSERVATION FORM.

Purpose: Designed for use in "observing, recording, and summarizing the classroom behavior of the target student."

Scores, 6: On-task Behavior, Inability to Learn, Relationship Problems, Inappropriate Behavior, Unhappiness or Depression, Physical Symptoms or Fears.

Time: [30-50] minutes.

Comments: Supplemental assessment.

c) DEVELOPMENTAL/EDUCATIONAL QUESTIONNAIRE.

Time: [25] minutes.

Comments: Supplemental assessment form for gathering information from parents or other primary caregivers.

Cross References: Reviews are scheduled for *The Twentieth Mental Measurements Yearbook.* For reviews by Sandra J. Carr and Gretchen Owens of the original version, see 14:333.

[1789]

Scales for Diagnosing Attention-Deficit/Hyperactivity Disorder.

Purpose: "To help identify children and adolescents who have attention-deficit/hyperactivity disorder (ADHD)."

Population: Ages 5-0 through 18-11.

Publication Date: 2002.

Acronym: SCALES.

Scores, 4: Inattention, Hyperactivity, Impulsivity, Total.

Administration: Individual.

Forms, 2: Summary/School Rating Scale Form (SRS), Home Rating Scale Form (HRS).

Price Data, 2015: $115 per complete kit including examiner's manual (78 pages), 25 summary/school rating forms, and 25 home rating scale forms; $63 per examiner's manual; $37 per 25 summary/school rating forms; $25 per 25 home rating scale forms.

Time: 15–20 minutes.

Comments: Completed by parents and teachers of target child; designed as part of a comprehensive ADHD assessment; identifies specific behavioral targets for intervention; allows for ratings on DSM-IV-TR criterion for ADHD.

Authors: Gail Ryser and Kathleen McConnell.

Publisher: PRO-ED.

Cross References: For a review by Joseph G. Law, Jr., see 15:215.

[1790]

Scales for Identifying Gifted Students.

Purpose: "Designed to assist school districts in the identification of students as gifted."

Population: Ages 5-18 years.

Publication Date: 2004.

Acronym: SIGS.

Scores: 7 areas: General Intellectual Ability, Language Arts, Mathematics, Science, Social Studies, Creativity, Leadership.

Administration: Individual.

Forms, 2: Home Rating Scale, School Rating Scale.

Price Data, 2015: $175 per complete kit including manual (57 pages), 25 Home Rating Scale forms, 25 School Rating Scale forms, and 25 Summary forms; $75 per manual; $50 per 25 Home Rating Scale forms; $50 per 25 School Rating Scale forms; $30 per 25 Summary forms; $200 per 100 seats (online version).

Foreign Language Edition: Spanish version available.

Time: (10-15) minutes.

Comments: This test "is designed to be completed by a teacher, counselor, or other professional who has an opportunity to observe the student for an extended period of time."

Authors: Gail R. Ryser and Kathleen McConnell.

Publisher: Prufrock Press Inc.

Cross References: For reviews by Michael S. Matthews and Sandra Ward, see 17:169.

[1791]

Scales for Rating the Behavioral Characteristics of Superior Students–Third Edition.

Purpose: Designed to use teacher ratings to "identify gifted and talented students" for educational programs and services.

Population: Students in kindergarten through Grade 12.

Publication Dates: 1976-2013.

Acronym: SRBCSS–III.

Scores, 14: Learning Characteristics, Creativity Characteristics, Motivation Characteristics, Leadership Characteristics, Artistic Characteristics, Musical Characteristics, Dramatics Characteristics, Communication Characteristics (Precision), Communication Characteristics (Expressiveness), Planning Characteristics, Mathematics Characteristics, Reading Characteristics, Technology Characteristics, Science Characteristics.

Administration: Individual.

Price Data, 2015: $29.95 per technical and administration manual (2013, 88 pages), $75 per 50 rating forms (print); $75 per 50 seats (online).

Time: Administration time not reported.

Comments: "The Scales for Rating the Behavioral Characteristics of Superior Students are commonly referred to as the Renzulli Scales or Renzulli-Hartman Scales."

Authors: Joseph S. Renzulli, Linda H. Smith, Alan J. White, Carolyn M. Callahan, Robert K. Hartman, Karen L. Westberg, M. Katherine Gavin, Sally M. Reis, Del Siegle, Rachael E. Sytsma Reed.

Publisher: Prufrock Press Inc.

Cross References: Reviews are scheduled for *The Twentieth Mental Measurements Yearbook*. See T5:2295 (9 references); for reviews by Edward N. Argulewicz and James O. Rust of the original edition, see 9:1073 (1 reference).

[1792]

Scales of Cognitive Ability for Traumatic Brain Injury.

Purpose: To "provide a systematic method of assessing cognitive deficits associated with traumatic brain injury."

Population: Patients with acquired brain damage; adolescents and adults.

Publication Date: 1992.

Acronym: SCATBI.

Scores, 46: Perception and Discrimination (Sound Recognition, Shape Recognition, Word Recognition [no distraction], Word Recognition [with distraction], Color Discrimination, Shape Discrimination, Size Discrimination, Discrimination of Color/Shape/ Size, Discrimination of Pictured Objects, Auditory Discrimination [real words], Auditory Discrimination [nonsense], Total); Orientation (Premorbid Questions, Postmorbid Questions, Total); Organization (Identifying Pictured Categories, Identifying Pictured Category Members, Word Associations, Sequencing Objects [size], Sequencing Words [alphabetical], Sequencing Events [time of year], Sequencing Events [pictured task steps], Sequencing Events [recall task steps], Total); Recall (Memory for Graphic Elements, Naming Pictures, Immediate Recall of Word Strings, Delayed Recall of Word Strings, Cued Recall of Words, Cued Recall of Words in Discourse, Word Generation, Immediate Recall of Oral Directions, Recall of Oral Paragraphs, Total); Reasoning (Figural Reasoning: Matrix Analogies, Convergent Thinking: Central Theme, Deductive Reasoning: Elimination, Inductive Reasoning: Opposites, Inductive Reasoning: Analogies, Divergent Thinking: Homographs, Divergent Thinking: Idioms, Divergent Thinking: Proverbs, Divergent Thinking: Verbal Absurdities, Multiprocess Reasoning: Task Insight, Multiprocess Reasoning: Analysis, Total).

Administration: Individual.

Price Data, 2015: $331 per complete kit; $68 per 25 record forms; $69 per stimulus card set; $86 per stimulus manual; $86 per examiner's manual; $37 per audio CD.

Time: 30 to 120 minutes.

Authors: Brenda Adamovich and Jennifer Henderson.

Publisher: PRO-ED.

Cross References: For reviews by Charles J. Long and Faith Gunning and by Deborah D. Roman, see 13:273.

[1793]

Scales of Cognitive and Communicative Ability for Neurorehabilitation.

Purpose: Designed "to identify cognitive and communicative impairments in English-speaking adults with known or suspected neuropathology."

Population: Adults ages 18 to 95 years who speak English fluently.

Publication Date: 2012.

Acronym: SCCAN.

Scores, 9: Oral Expression, Orientation, Memory, Speech Comprehension, Reading Comprehension, Writing, Attention, Problem Solving, Total.

Administration: Individual.

Price Data, 2014: $263 per complete kit including examiner's manual (54 pages), stimulus book, 25 examiner record booklets, 25 written response booklets, and 25 report summary forms; $65 per manual; $93 per stimulus book; $43 per 25 examiner record booklets; $33 per 25 written response booklets; $29 per 25 report summary forms.

Time: (35) minutes.

Authors: Lisa H. Milman and Audrey L. Holland.

Publisher: PRO-ED.

Cross References: Reviews are scheduled for *The Twentieth Mental Measurements Yearbook.*

[1794]

Scales of Independent Behavior—Revised.

Purpose: "Designed to measure functional independence and adaptive functioning in school, home, employment, and community settings."

Population: Infants to adults, with or without developmental disabilities.

Publication Dates: 1984–1996.

Acronym: SIB-R.

Scores, 24: Full Scale (Gross-Motor Skills, Fine Motor Skills, Social Interaction, Language Comprehension, Language Expression, Eating and Meal Preparation, Toileting, Dressing, Personal Self-Care, Domestic Skills, Time and Punctuality, Money and Value, Work Skills, Home/Community Orientation), Maladaptive Behavior Scale [optional] (Hurtful to Self, Unusual or Repetitive Habits, Withdrawal or Inattentive Behavior, Socially Offensive Behavior, Uncooperative Behavior, Hurtful to Others, Destructive to Property, Disruptive Behavior).

Administration: Individual.

Forms, 3: Full Scale, Short Form, Early Development.

Price Data, 2015: $339.60 per complete kit including interview book, comprehensive manual (1996, 306 pages), 15 full scale response booklets (IPR included), 5 short form response booklets and IPRs, and 5 early development form response booklets and IPRs; $127.75 per comprehensive manual; $92.30 per 25 full scale response booklets (IPR part of response booklet); $57.90 per 25 short form response booklets and pad of 25 IPRs; $57.90 per 25 early development form response booklets and pad of 25 IPRs; $79.20 per 25 short form for the visually impaired response booklets.

Time: (45–60) minutes for Full Scale; (15–20) minutes for Short Form; (15–20) minutes for Early Development.

Comments: SIB-R in conjunction with the Woodcock-Johnson® Psychoeducational Battery–Revised can be used as a comprehensive diagnostic system for measuring adaptive behavior, problem behavior, cognitive ability, language proficiency, and achievement; can be administered either via interview or checklist; short and early development forms available as part of test kit; computerized scoring system available in Windows or Macintosh; visually impaired short form also available.

Authors: Robert H. Bruininks, Richard W. Woodcock, Richard F. Weatherman, and Bradley K. Hill.

Publisher: Houghton Mifflin Harcourt.

Cross References: For reviews by Gloria Maccow and Leland C. Zlomke, see 14:337; see also T5:2299 (7 references) and T4:2335 (6 references); for reviews by Bonnie W. Camp and Louis J. Heifetz of the earlier version, see 10:321.

[1795]

SCAN-3 for Adolescents and Adults: Tests for Auditory Processing Disorders.

Purpose: "Designed to identify auditory processing disorders in adolescents and adults."

Population: Ages 13-50.

Publication Dates: 1986-2009.

Acronym: SCAN-3:A.

Scores, 21: 4 screening test scores: Gap Detection, Auditory Figure-Ground 0 dB, Competing Words-Free Recall, Total (P/F); 5 diagnostic test scores: Auditory Processing Composite (Filtered Words, Auditory Figure-Ground 0 dB, Competing Words-Directed Ear, Competing Sentences, Total); 3 supplementary test scores: Auditory Figure-Ground +8 dB, Auditory Figure-Ground +12 dB, Time Compressed Sentences; ear advantage summary score for each of the following: Auditory Figure-Ground 0 dB, Competing Words-Free Recall, Filtered Words, Competing Words-Directed Ear-Directed Right Ear, Competing Words-Directed Ear-Directed Left Ear, Competing Sentences, Auditory Figure-Ground +8 dB, Auditory Figure-Ground +12 dB, Time Compressed Sentences.

Administration: Individual.

Price Data, 2015: $282.30 per complete kit including 25 record forms, manual (2009, 120 pages), and Audio CD; $63.55 per 25 record forms; $160.10 per manual; $120.75 per Audio CD.

Time: (10-15) minutes for the screening tests; (20-30) minutes for the diagnostic and supplementary tests.

Comments: Screening test scores are "criterion-referenced"; Auditory Figure-Ground 0 dB test is identical across the screening and diagnostic levels; all scores (except for Gap Detection) are calculated as a composite of the participant's right ear score and left ear score, and the ear-advantage score is the difference between the right and left ear scores; additional materials required: "CD player with a track display or a two-channel audiometer" or access to a computer, two sets of stereo headphones, and a stereo Y-adapter if necessary; revision of SCAN-A: A Test for Auditory Processing Disorders in Adolescents and Adults.

Author: Robert W. Keith.

Publisher: Pearson.

Cross References: For reviews by Jerrell Cassady and Catherine Wagner and by Rick Eigenbrood, see 18:111; for reviews by William R. Merz, Sr. and Jaclyn B. Spitzer of the earlier edition titled SCAN-A: A Test for Auditory Processing Disorders in Adolescents and Adults, see 13:275.

[1796]

SCAN-3 for Children: Tests for Auditory Processing Disorders.

Purpose: "Designed to identify auditory processing disorders in children."

Population: Ages 5-12.

Publication Dates: 1986-2009.

Acronym: SCAN-3:C.

Scores, 21: 4 screening test scores: Gap Detection (ages 8-12 only), Auditory Figure-Ground +8 dB, Competing Words-Free Recall, Total (P/F); 5 diagnostic test scores: Auditory Processing Composite (Filtered Words, Auditory Figure-Ground +8 dB, Competing Words-Directed Ear, Competing Sentences, Total); 3 supplementary test scores: Auditory Figure-Ground +12 dB, Auditory Figure-Ground 0 dB, Time Compressed Sentences; ear advantage summary score for each of the following: Auditory Figure-Ground +8 dB, Competing Words-Free Recall, Filtered Words, Competing Words-Directed Ear-Directed Right Ear, Competing Words-Directed Ear-Directed Left Ear, Competing Sentences, Auditory Figure-Ground +12 dB, Auditory Figure-Ground +0 dB, Time Compressed Sentences.

Administration: Individual.

Price Data, 2015: $282.30 per kit including 25 record forms, manual (2009, 124 pages), and Audio CD; $65.35 per 25 record forms; $160.10 per manual; $120.25 per CD.

Time: (10-15) minutes for the screening tests; (20-30) minutes for the diagnostic and supplementary tests.

Comments: Screening test scores are "criterion-referenced"; Auditory Figure-Ground +8 dB test is identical across the screening and diagnostic levels; all scores (except for Gap Detection) are calculated as a composite of the participant's right ear score and left ear score, and the ear-advantage score is the difference between the right and left ear scores; additional materials required: "CD player with a track display or a two-channel audiometer" or access to a computer, two sets of stereo headphones, and a stereo Y-adapter if necessary; revision of SCAN-C Test for Auditory Processing Disorders in Children-Revised.

Author: Robert W. Keith.

Publisher: Pearson.

Cross References: For reviews by Gary L. Canivez and Connie Theriot England, see 18:112; for reviews by Annabel J. Cohen and Jaclyn B. Spitzer and Abbey L. Berg of an earlier edition titled SCAN-C Test for Auditory Processing Disorders in Children-Revised, see 16:217; for an earlier edition see also T5:2300 (1 reference); for a review by Sami Gulgoz of the original edition, see 11:341 (2 references).

[1797]

The Scenotest: A Practical Technique for Understanding Unconscious Problems and Personality Structure.

Purpose: A projective instrument intended "to help very quickly assess emotional problems in children."

Population: Children and adolescents.

Publication Dates: 1971–1998.

Scores: Score information available from publisher.

Administration: Individual.

Price Data, 2016: £1,361 per complete test kit excluding manual (von Staabs, 1998, 110 pages, £46).

Time: Administration time not reported.

Comments: Material in the test kit consists of flexible human figures and accessories including animals, trees, symbolic figures, and items from everyday life.

Authors: G. von Staabs (original edition) and Joseph A. Smith (manual translated from the German edition).

Publisher: Hogrefe Ltd [United Kingdom].

Cross References: For reviews by Joseph C. Kush and Paul Retzlaff, see 15:216.

[1798]

The SCERTS Model: A Comprehensive Educational Approach for Children with Autism Spectrum Disorders.

Purpose: "Criterion-referenced" assessment designed as a "multidisciplinary approach to enhancing communication and social-emotional abilities" of people with Autism Spectrum Disorders and related disabilities.

Population: People of all ages with Autism Spectrum Disorders and related disabilities.

Publication Date: 2006.

Acronym: SCERTS.

Scores: 3 Communication Stages: Social Partner, Language Partner, Conversational Partner; 3 domains: Social Communication (Joint Attention, Symbol Use), Emotional Regulation (Mutual Regulation, Self-Regulation), Transactional Support (Interpersonal Support, Learning Support).

Administration: Individual.

Price Data, 2016: $124.95 per two-volume manual (344 pages, 400 pages) set.

Time: (120-240) minutes.

Comments: An ongoing curriculum-based assessment, planning, and implementation model.

Authors: Barry M. Prizant, Amy M. Wetherby, Emily Rubin, Amy C. Laurent, and Patrick J. Rydell.

Publisher: Paul H. Brookes Publishing Co., Inc.

[1799]

Schaie-Thurstone Adult Mental Abilities Test.

Purpose: Designed to "measure the mental abilities of adults."

Population: Ages 22-95.

Publication Dates: 1985-2013.

Acronym: STAMAT.

Scores: 7 scale scores: Recognition Vocabulary (V), Figure Rotation (FR), Object Rotation (OR, Form OA only), Letter Series (LS), Word Series (WS, Form OA only), Number Addition (N), Word Fluency (W).

Administration: Group.

Forms, 2: Form A (for "Adult," essentially the Thurstone Primary Mental Abilities Test Form II-17 (PMA) with new adult norms), Form OA (for "Older Adult," large-type version of the original plus two additional scales for adults over age 55).

Price Data: Price information available from publisher for Form OA expendable test booklets, Form A booklets, Form A answer sheets, Form A scoring key, profiles for both OA and A, and manual (86 pages).

Time: (50–60) minutes.

Comments: Norms updated in 2013.

Author: K. Warner Schaie.

Publisher: K. Warner Schaie (the author).

Cross References: See T5:2304 (4 references) and T4:2339 (3 references); for a review by Eric F. Gardner, see 10:322.

[1800]

Schedule for Affective Disorders and Schizophrenia, Third Edition.

Purpose: "To record information regarding a subject's functioning and psychopathology."

Population: Adults.

Publication Dates: 1977-1988.

Acronym: SADS.

Administration: Individual.

Price Data: Available from publisher.

Time: [30–120] minutes.

Authors: Robert L. Spitzer, Jean Endicott, Jo Ellen Loth (SADS-LB, SADS-LI), Patricia McDonald-Scott (SADS-LI), and Patricia Wasek (SADS-LI).

Publisher: Department of Research Assessment and Training.

a) SCHEDULE FOR AFFECTIVE DISORDERS AND SCHIZOPHRENIA.

Scores, 24: Current Syndromes (Depressive Mood/Ideation, Endogenous Features, Depressive-Associated Features, Suicidal Ideation/Behavior, Anxiety, Manic Syndrome, Delusions-Hallucinations, Formal Thought Disorder, Impaired Functioning, Alcohol or Drug Abuse, Behavioral Disorganization, Miscellaneous Psychopathology, GAS [worst period], Extracted Hamilton); Past Week Functioning (Depressive Syndrome, Endogenous Features, Manic Syndrome, Anxiety, Delusions-Hall-Disorganization, GAS rating, Extracted Hamilton, Miscellaneous Psychopathology); Past Other than Diagnosis (Social Functioning, Suicidal Behavior).

b) SCHEDULE FOR AFFECTIVE DISORDERS AND SCHIZOPHRENIA LIFETIME (VARIOUS VERSIONS).

1) *SADS-L.*
Purpose: To record information regarding a subject's functioning and psychopathology; includes current disturbance.

2) *SADS-LB.*
Purpose: To record information regarding a subject's functioning and psychopathology; includes current disturbance and additional items related to bipolar affective disorder.

3) *SADS-LI.*
Purpose: To record information regarding a subject's functioning and psychopathology; specifies follow-up interval.

Cross References: See T5:2305 (248 references); for reviews by Paul A. Arbisi and James C. Carmer, see 12:343 (414 references); see also T4:2340 (152 references).

[1801]

Schedule for Nonadaptive and Adaptive Personality–2nd Edition.

Purpose: "Designed to assess trait dimensions in the domain of personality disorders."

Population: Ages 18 and older.

Publication Dates: 1993-2015.

Acronyms: SNAP-2.

Scores, 36 scales: Trait (Negative Temperament, Mistrust, Manipulativeness, Aggression, Self-harm, Eccentric Perceptions, Dependency, Positive Temperament, Exhibitionism, Entitlement, Detachment, Disinhibition, Impulsivity, Propriety, Workaholism), Diagnostic (Paranoid, Schizoid, Schizotypal, Antisocial, Borderline, Histrionic, Narcissistic, Avoidant, Dependent, Obsessive-Compulsive, Negativistic [Passive-Aggressive], Depressive, Sadistic, Self-Defeating), Validity (Variable Response Inconsistency, True Response Inconsistency, Desirable Response Inconsistency, Deviance, Rare Virtues, Invalidity Index, Back Deviance).

Administration: Individual or group.

Forms, 4: Self (SRF), Other (ORF), Brief (Brief SRF and ORF).

Price Data: License is required; test is available at no cost from publisher for unfunded, non-commercial research; price available from publisher for funded or commercial research.

Time: (45) minutes.

Author: Lee Anna Clark.

Publisher: Dr. Lee Anna Clark (University of Notre Dame).

a) SCHEDULE FOR NONADAPTIVE AND ADAPTIVE PERSONALITY-YOUTH.

Population: Ages 11-17.

Acronym: SNAP-Y.

Cross References: For reviews by Lizanne DeStefano and Niels G. Waller of the original edition, see 14:338; see also T5:2306 (1 reference) and T4:2341 (1 reference).

[1802]

A Schedule of Adaptive Mechanisms in CAT Response.

Purpose: "Designed to aid in qualitative evaluation of C.A.T. stories."

Population: Children.

Publication Date: [ca. 1963].

Scores: 12 categories: Defense Mechanisms (Reaction-Formation, Undoing and Ambivalence, Isolation, Repres-

sion and Denial, Deception, Symbolization, Projection and Introjection, Fear and Anxiety, Regression, Controls Weak or Absent), Identification (Adequate/Same-Sex, Confused/or Opposite Sex).
Administration: Individual.
Manual: No manual.
Price Data, 2015: $22.50 per 30 forms.
Time: Administration time not reported.
Comments: See Children's Apperception Test (13:58).
Author: Mary Haworth.
Publisher: C.P.S. Publishing, LLC

[1803]

The Schedule of Growing Skills: Second Edition.

Purpose: Designed as an assessment of child development.
Population: Ages 0–5 years.
Publication Dates: 1987–1996.
Acronym: SGS II.
Scores, 9: Passive Postural, Active Postural, Locomotor, Manipulative, Visual, Hearing and Language, Speech and Language, Interactive Social, Self-Care Social.
Administration: Individual.
Price Data, 2016: £220 per starter set including 10 child records, 50 profiles, user's guide (1996, 109 pages), and all stimulus materials; £130 per 50 record forms; £80 per 50 profiles; £60 per user's guide.
Time: (20) minutes.
Authors: Martin Bellman, Sundara Lingam, and Anne Aukett.
Publisher: GL Assessment [England].
Cross References: For reviews by Carol M. McGregor and Leah M. Nellis, see 15:217; see T5:2308 (1 reference); for reviews by Michelle M. Creighton and Scott R. McConnell and by Donna Spiker of an earlier edition, see 11:342.

[1804]

Schedules for Clinical Assessment in Neuropsychiatry, Version 2.0.

Purpose: "Aimed at assessing, measuring and classifying the psychopathology and behavior associated with the major psychiatric syndromes of adult life."
Population: Adults.
Publication Dates: 1982-1995.
Acronym: SCAN.
Scores: Item scores only.
Administration: Individual.
Parts, 3: Present State Examination, Item Group Checklist, Clinical History Schedule.
Price Data, 2016: $62 per manual; $56 per Glossary; $38.95 per recording booklets.
Time: Administration time not reported.
Author: World Health Organization.
Publisher: American Psychiatric Publishing, Inc.

a) PRESENT STATE EXAMINATION.
Acronym: PSE10.
Subtests, 2: Part One, Part Two.
Comments: Part One covers somatoform, dissociative, anxiety, depressive, and bipolar disorders and problems associated with basic bodily functions and use of alcohol and other substance use. Part Two covers psychotic and cognitive disorders and observed abnormalities of speech, affect, and behavior.
b) ITEM GROUP CHECKLIST.
Acronym: IGC.
Comments: 40 Item Groups cover disorders in subchapters F2 (psychotic disorders), F3 (affective disorders), and F40-42 (neurotic disorders) of ICD10.
c) CLINICAL HISTORY SCHEDULE.
Acronym: CHS.
Comments: Includes broader clinical and social history data.

[1805]

Scholastic Abilities Test for Adults.

Purpose: "Designed to be a general measure of scholastic accomplishment."
Population: Ages 16 through 70.
Publication Date: 1991.
Acronym: SATA.
Scores: 9 subtest scores: Verbal Reasoning, Nonverbal Reasoning, Quantitative Reasoning, Reading Vocabulary, Reading Comprehension, Math Calculation, Math Application, Writing Mechanics, Writing Composition, and 9 composite scores: Scholastic Abilities, General Aptitude, Total Achievement, Verbal, Quantitative, Reading, Mathematics, Writing, Achievement Screener.
Administration: Group.
Price Data, 2015: $215 per complete kit including 10 test books, 25 response booklets, 25 profile/examiner record forms, and examiner's manual (102 pages); $67 per 10 test books; $56 per 25 response booklets; $37 per 25 profile/examiner record forms; $67 per examiner's manual.
Time: (60-120) minutes.
Authors: Brian R. Bryant, James R. Patton, and Caroline Dunn.
Publisher: PRO-ED.
Cross References: See T5:2309 (2 references); for reviews by Nambury S. Raju and Douglas K. Smith, see 12:344.

[1806]

School-Age Care Environment Rating Scale, Updated Edition.

Purpose: Designed to assess the quality of center-based child care for school-aged children.
Population: Child care programs for children ages 5-12.
Publication Dates: 1980-2014.
Acronym: SACERS Updated.
Scores, 7-8: Space and Furnishings, Health and Safety, Activities, Interactions, Program Structure, Staff Development, Exceptional Children (supplemental), Total.

Administration: Individual programs.
Price Data, 2016: $23.95 per manual with form and scoresheet (2014, 69 pages).
Time: (120) minutes.
Comments: The test publisher advises that this edition is "not a revision but rather an updated version of the original ... with relatively minor changes."
Authors: Thelma Harms, Ellen Vineberg Jacobs, and Donna Romano White.
Publisher: Teachers College Press.
Cross References: For reviews by Patricia B. Keith and Hillary Michaels of an earlier edition, see 14:339.

[1807]
School-Age Program Quality Assessment.
Purpose: Designed as "a set of scoreable standards for best practices" in afterschool programs, community organizations, schools, [and] summer programs" to evaluate program quality and identity staff training needs.
Population: Programs for school-age children.
Publication Date: 2012.
Acronym: School-Age PQA.
Administration: Individual programs.
Forms, 2: Program Offerings Items, Organization Items.
Price Data, 2016: $12 per hardcopy handbook; $30 per 10 instruments; also available for download from test publisher's website.
Foreign Language Edition: Spanish version available.
Time: (45-90) minutes for observations.
Comments: Based on observations and interviews by independent raters or for use as a self-assessment; based on the Youth Program Quality Assessment (2311).
Authors: High/Scope Educational Research Foundation.
Publisher: David P. Weikart Center for Youth Program Quality.
  a) FORM A – PROGRAM OFFERINGS ITEMS.
  Population: Grades K-6.
  Scores, 23: 19 scales in 4 domains: Safe Environment (Emotional Safety, Healthy Environment, Emergency Preparedness, Accommodating Environment, Nourishment), Supportive Environment (Warm Welcome, Session Flow, Active Engagement, Skill-Building, Encouragement, Child-Centered Space), Interaction (Managing Feelings, Belonging, School-Age Leadership, Interaction with Adults), Engagement (School-Aged Planning, School-Aged Choice, Reflection, Responsibility), plus item scores.
  b) FORM B – ORGANIZATION ITEMS.
  Population: Grades 4-12.
  Scores, 3: Youth Centered Policies and Practices, High Expectations for Youth and Staff, Access, plus item scores.

[1808]
School Behaviours Rating Scale.
Purpose: Designed for assessing behavior in the primary school years and for developing supportive interventions.

Population: Students ages 5 to 12.
Publication Date: 2009.
Acronym: SBRS.
Scores, 6: General Classroom Behaviour, General Playground Behaviour, Getting Along With Other Students, Development of Social Skills, Attempting Tasks Presented, Aggressive Behaviours.
Administration: Individual.
Price Data, 2015: A$279.95 per kit including manual, 25 questionnaires, 25 profiles for boys, and 25 profiles for girls; $159.95 per manual (100 pages); $49.95 per 25 questionnaires; $39.95 per 25 profiles (boys or girls).
Foreign Language Edition: Chinese version available.
Time: (30) minutes or less.
Comments: Teacher rating scale developed in Australia.
Authors: Lyn Gardon.
Publisher: School Behaviour Solutions [Australia].
Cross References: Reviews are scheduled for *The Twentieth Mental Measurements Yearbook.*

[1809]
School Environment Preference Survey.
Purpose: "Designed to measure the student's commitment to the set of attitudes, values and behaviors that have been characteristically fostered and rewarded in traditional school environments."
Population: Grades 4–12.
Publication Date: 1978.
Acronym: SEPS.
Scores, 5: Self-Subordination, Traditionalism, Rule Conformity, Uncriticalness, Structured Role Orientation.
Administration: Group.
Price Data, 2016: $14.75 per 25 SEPS booklet and answer sheet combined [$53 per 100, $211 per 500]; $21.25 per hand-scoring keys; $6.50 per manual; $12 per specimen set including a manual and one copy of all forms.
Time: (10–15) minutes.
Author: Leonard V. Gordon.
Publisher: EdITS/Educational and Industrial Testing Service.
Cross References: See T5:2315 (1 reference) and T4:2360 (1 reference); for a review by Joan Silverstein, see 10:324.

[1810]
School Function Assessment.
Purpose: Designed to "measure a student's performance of functional tasks that support his or her participation in the academic and social aspects of an elementary school program."
Population: Grades K–6.
Publication Date: 1998.
Acronym: SFA.

Scores, 26: Participation, Task Supports (Physical Tasks Assistance, Physical Tasks Adaptations, Cognitive/Behavioral Tasks Assistance, Cognitive/Behavioral Tasks Adaptations), Activity Performance (Travel, Maintaining and Changing Positions, Recreational Movement, Manipulation with Movement, Using Materials, Setup and Cleanup, Eating and Drinking, Hygiene, Clothing Management, Up/Down Stairs, Written Work, Computer and Equipment Use, Functional Communication, Memory and Understanding, Following Social Conventions, Compliance with Adult Directives and School Rules, Task Behavior/Completion, Positive Interaction, Behavior Regulation, Personal Care Awareness, Safety).
Administration: Individual.
Price Data, 2015: $230.65 per kit including 25 record forms with 3 rating scale guides and user's manual (136 pages); $96.85 per 25 record forms with 3 rating scale guides; $143.50 per manual; $23.60 per rating scale guides.
Time: Untimed; (5–10) minutes per scale.
Comments: Ratings to be completed by an educational and therapeutic professional who is familiar with the child's typical performance.
Authors: Wendy Coster, Theresa Deeney, Jane Haltiwanger, and Stephen Haley.
Publisher: Pearson.
Cross References: For reviews by Wayne C. Piersel and William D. Schafer, see 14:340.

[1811]

The School Leadership Series.

Purpose: Consists of three assessments developed to provide states with assessments to use as part of the licensure process for principals, superintendents, and school leaders.
Population: Prospective school principals, superintendents, and school leaders.
Publication Date: 1998-2016.
Scores: Total score only.
Administration: Group.
Restricted Distribution: Secure instruments administered 3 times annually at testing centers.
Price Data: Available from publisher.
Time: 360 minutes in three 120-minute modules.
Comments: State department of education for a particular state should be consulted to determine whether the School Leaders Licensure Assessment, the School Superintendent Assessment, or the Kentucky Specialty Test of Instructional and Administrative Practices is required.
Author: Educational Testing Service.
Publisher: Educational Testing Service.

[1812]

School Life Questionnaire.

Purpose: Designed to provide "data on students' ratings of their school connectedness, engagement and motivation to learn."

Population: Upper Primary and Secondary students.
Publication Dates: 1984-2009.
Acronym: SLQ.
Scores: 8 scales: General Satisfaction, Interaction with Teachers, Relevance/Opportunity, Success/Achievement, Social Integration, Negative Feelings, Status [Secondary version], Adventure [Primary version].
Administration: Group.
Forms, 2: Primary School, Secondary School.
Price Data, 2016: A$6.50 per respondent for paper questionnaire; A$5.95 per respondent for online questionnaire; contact publisher for cost of scoring and report service; manual (2009, 11 pages) is free to print from publisher's website.
Time: (40) minutes.
Comments: Available online or in paper-and-pencil format; publisher provides scoring and summary report; summary report does not provide data for individual students.
Author: Australian Council for Educational Research Ltd.
Publisher: Australian Council for Educational Research Ltd. [Australia].

[1813]

School Motivation and Learning Strategies Inventory.

Purpose: Designed to measure "strategies students actively employ in learning and test taking."
Population: Ages 8-12, 13-18.
Publication Date: 2006.
Acronym: SMALSI.
Scores, 11: Study Strategies, Note-Taking and Listening Skills, Reading and Comprehension Strategies, Writing and Research Skills, Test-Taking Strategies, Time Management (teen only), Organizational Techniques (teen only), Time Management/Organizational Techniques (child only), Academic Motivation, Test Anxiety, Attention and Concentration.
Administration: Group.
Levels, 2: Child, Teen.
Forms, 2: Child, Teen.
Price Data, 2016: $295 per combined child and teen kit including manual (108 pages), 25 child test forms, 25 child profile sheets, child scoring template, 25 teen test forms, 25 teen profile sheets, teen scoring template, and audio CD; $211 per child or teen kit including manual, 25 test forms and 25 profile sheets, scoring template, and audio CD; $57.50 per 25 test forms, $44 per scoring template, $38 per 100 profile sheets; $21.50 per audio CD; $69.50 per manual; $499.50 per unlimited-use scoring CD.
Foreign Language Edition: Availale in Spanish.
Time: (20-30) minutes.
Comments: The same manual is used for both Child and Teen forms. The test publisher advises that a form for college students is now available; description will be updated when materials are received.

Authors: Kathy Chatham Stroud and Cecil R. Reynolds.
Publisher: Western Psychological Services.
Cross References: For reviews by Christine Novak and Claudia R. Wright, see 18:113.

[1814]
School-Readiness Evaluation by Trained Teachers.

Purpose: To screen all school entrants to identify different levels of school-readiness.
Population: South African school beginners.
Publication Date: 1984.
Acronym: SETT.
Scores, 9: Language and General Development (Basic Level, Potential Level, Total), Physical Motor Development (Motor Ability, Integration, Total), Emotional Social Development (Sociability, Emotionality, Total).
Administration: Individual.
Price Data: Available from publisher.
Time: (30) minutes.
Comments: Parent Questionnaire for the Evaluation of School-Readiness and Nursery-School Questionnaire for the Evaluation of School-Readiness may be used in conjunction with this test.
Author: Marianne Joubert.
Publisher: Human Sciences Research Council [South Africa].

[1815]
School Readiness Test, Fourth Edition.

Purpose: Designed to assist in determining student readiness for first grade.
Population: Students at the end of kindergarten or before their third full week of first grade.
Publication Dates: 1974-2015.
Acronym: SRT.
Scores, 11-12: Letter/Word Recognition, Phonemic Awareness, Phonics, Listening Comprehension, Vocabulary, Reading Comprehension, Developmental Spelling Ability, Handwriting (optional), Numbers and Operations, Measurement, Geometric Concepts, Overall Readiness.
Administration: Group.
Restricted Distribution: Sold only to schools and school districts.
Price Data, 2016: $69 per starter set including user's manual (2014, 38 pages), answer key, and 20 test booklets; $56.75 per 20 test booklets; $15.50 per user's manual; $4.35 per answer key, $26 per 20 parent/teacher report forms.
Time: (95) minutes total in 3 sessions.
Author: Scholastic Testing Service, Inc.
Publisher: Scholastic Testing Service, Inc.
Cross References: Reviews are scheduled for *The Twentieth Mental Measurements Yearbook*. For reviews by

Esther Stavrou Toubanos and Larry Weber of an earlier (1990) edition, see 12:346; for a review by Thorsten R. Carlson of an earlier (1974-77) edition see 8:808.

[1816]
School Situation Survey.

Purpose: Designed to measure "school-related student stress."
Population: Grades 4-12.
Publication Date: 1989.
Acronym: SSS.
Scores, 7: Sources of Stress (Teacher Interactions, Academic Stress, Peer Interactions, Academic Self-Concept), Manifestations of Stress (Emotional, Behavioral, Physiological).
Administration: Individual or group.
Price Data, 2015: $50 for manual, including review-only copy of SSS form; $2 per Remote Online Survey License (minimum 50); $2 per License to Reproduce (minimum 50).
Time: (10-15) minutes.
Authors: Barbara J. Helms and Robert K. Gable.
Publisher: Mind Garden, Inc.
Cross References: For reviews by Theodore Coladarci and LeAdelle Phelps, see 12:347; see also T4:2368 (1 reference).

[1817]
School Social Behavior Scales, Second Edition.

Purpose: Designed to evaluate social competence and antisocial behavior of children and youth in Grades K-12 (ages 5-18).
Population: Grades K–12.
Publication Dates: 1993–2002.
Acronym: SBSS-2.
Scores, 8: Social Competence Scale (Peer Relations, Self-Management/Compliance, Academic Behavior, Social Competence Total), Antisocial Behavior Scale (Hostile/Irritable, Antisocial/Aggressive, Defiant/Disruptive, Antisocial Behavior Total).
Administration: Individual.
Price Data, 2016: $39.95 per 25 rating forms; $49.95 per user's guide (2002, 114 pages).
Time: (8–10) minutes.
Comments: Companion to Home & Community Social Behavior Scales (942); rated by teachers or other school personnel.
Author: Kenneth W. Merrell.
Publisher: Paul H. Brookes Publishing Co., Inc.
Cross References: For reviews by Rosemary Flanagan and by Michael J. Furlong and Alicia Soliz, see 16:218; for reviews by Stephen R. Hooper and Lesley A. Welsh of a previous edition, see 13:277 (2 references); see also T4:2369 (1 reference).

[1818]

School Social Skills.

Purpose: Developed to assess social skills exhibited in a school setting.

Population: Elementary school and junior high school and high school.

Publication Date: 1984.

Acronym: S3.

Scores: Ratings in 4 categories: Adult Relations, Peer Relations, School Rules, Classroom Behaviors.

Administration: Individual.

Price Data, 2016: $41 per complete kit including manual (25 pages); $26.25 per 25 rating scales; $21 per manual.

Time: (10) minutes.

Comments: Ratings by teachers.

Authors: Laura J. Brown, Donald D. Black, and John C. Downs.

Publisher: Slosson Educational Publications, Inc.

Cross References: For reviews by Beth D. Bader and William K. Wilkinson, see 12:348; see also T4:2370 (1 reference).

[1819]

Schubert General Ability Battery.

Purpose: Developed as a test of an individual's ability to understand and think in terms of words, numbers, and ideas.

Population: Grades 12–16 and adults.

Publication Dates: 1946–1965.

Acronym: SGAB.

Scores, 5: Vocabulary, Analogies, Arithmetic Problems, Syllogisms, Total.

Administration: Group.

Price Data, 2016: $102.25 per complete kit including 25 tests and manual (1965, 24 pages); $68.50 per 25 tests.

Time: 16(25) or 32(40) minutes.

Authors: Herman J. P. Schubert and Daniel S. P. Schubert (test).

Publisher: Slosson Educational Publications, Inc.

Cross References: See 7:386 (1 reference); for a review by William B. Schrader, see 5:382.

[1820]

Science: Thinking with Evidence.

Purpose: "Designed to assess how well students use evidence to think about scientific contexts and issues."

Population: Years 7-10 in New Zealand schools.

Publication Date: 2010.

Score: Total score only.

Administration: Group.

Levels, 4: 1, 2, 3, 4.

Price Data, 2016: NZ$60 per full starter kit for Tests 1-4 including teacher's manual (60 pages), one of each test booklet, answer sheet, and marking key; NZ$29 per teacher's manual; NZ$4.20 per marking key; NZ$2.35 per 10 answer sheets; NZ$6.80 per test booklet.

Time: (55) minutes.

Authors: Ally Bull, Hilary Ferral, Rosemary Hipkins, Chris Joyce, and Lorraine Spiller.

Publisher: New Zealand Council for Educational Research.

Cross References: Reviews are scheduled for *The Twentieth Mental Measurements Yearbook.*

[1821]

Screening Assessment for Gifted Elementary and Middle School Students, Second Edition.

Purpose: "Used to identify students who are gifted in academics and reasoning."

Population: Ages 5–14.

Publication Dates: 1987–2001.

Acronym: SAGES-2.

Scores, 3: Mathematics/Science, Language Arts/Social Studies, Reasoning.

Administration: Group.

Price Data, 2015: $257 per kit including 10 K–3 mathematics/science student response booklets, 10 K–3 language arts/social studies student response booklets, 10 K–3 reasoning student response booklets, 10 4–8 mathematics/science student response booklets, 10 4–8 language arts/social studies student response booklets, 10 4–8 reasoning response booklets, manual (2001, 128 pages), 50 K–3 profile/scoring sheets, 50 4–8 profile/response sheets, and a 4–8 scoring transparency; $25 per 10 K–3 mathematics/science student response booklets; $25 per 10 K–3 language arts/social studies student response booklets; $25 per 10 K–3 reasoning student response booklets; $20 per 10 4–8 mathematics/science student response booklets; $20 per 10 4–8 language arts/social studies student response booklets; $20 per 10 4–8 reasoning student response booklets; $63 per manual; $37 per 50 K–3 profile/scoring sheets; $37 per 50 4–8 profile/response sheets; $14 per 4–8 scoring transparency.

Time: (30–45) minutes.

Comments: This edition replaces both the earlier Screening Assessment for Gifted Elementary Students (T5:2328) and the Screening Assessment for Gifted Elementary Students—Primary (T5:2329).

Authors: Susan K. Johnsen and Anne L. Corn.

Publisher: PRO-ED.

Cross References: For reviews by Carolyn M. Callahan and Howard M. Knoff, see 15:219; see T5:2328 (1 reference); for reviews by Lewis R. Aiken and Susana Urbina of an earlier edition, see 12:349; for a review by E. Scott Huebner of an earlier edition, see 10:327.

[1822]

Screening Kit of Language Development.

Purpose: Assesses preschool language development in order to identify language disorders/delays.

Population: Ages 2–5.
Publication Dates: 1983–2002.
Acronym: SKOLD.
Scores, 6: Vocabulary, Comprehension, Story Completion, Individual and Paired Sentence Repetition with Pictures, Individual Sentence Repetition without Pictures, Comprehension of Commands.
Administration: Individual.
Editions, 2: Standard English, Black English.
Price Data, 2016: $150.25 per complete kit including manual (37 pages), stimulus book, and 1 set of standard English scoring forms or 1 set of Black English scoring forms; $70.25 per 25 standard English scoring forms; $70.25 per 25 Black English scoring forms; $51.25 per stimulus materials and scoring guidelines; $43 per examiner's manual.
Time: (15) minutes.
Authors: Lynn S. Bliss and Doris V. Allen.
Publisher: Slosson Educational Publications, Inc.
Cross References: See T4:2381 (1 reference).

[1823]

Screening Test for Developmental Apraxia of Speech—Second Edition.

Purpose: Developed "to screen for the potential presence of developmental apraxia of speech in children."
Population: Ages 4-0 to 12-11.
Publication Dates: 1980–2001.
Acronym: STDAS-2.
Scores, 3: Prosody, Verbal Sequencing, Articulation.
Administration: Individual.
Price Data, 2015: $115 per complete kit including examiner's manual (2001, 37 pages) and 50 profile/examiner record forms; $56 per 50 profile/examiner record forms; $67 per examiner's manual.
Time: (10–15) minutes.
Author: Robert W. Blakeley.
Publisher: PRO-ED.
Cross References: For reviews by Rebecca McCauley and Janet Norris, see 15:220; see T5:2332 (2 references) and T4:2383 (3 references); for a review by Ronald K. Sommers of an earlier edition, see 11:347.

[1824]

Screening Test for Educational Prerequisite Skills.

Purpose: Developed to screen for skills needed for beginning kindergarten.
Population: Ages 4–5 years.
Publication Dates: 1976–1990.
Acronym: STEPS.
Scores: 5 areas: Motor Skills, Intellectual Skills, Verbal Information Skills, Cognitive Strategies, Attitudes.
Administration: Individual.

Price Data, 2016: $209 per complete kit including test materials (pictures, bears, pencil), 25 AutoScore™ forms, 25 AutoScore™ home questionnaires, and manual (1990, 68 pages); $54 per set of test materials; $69 per 25 AutoScore™ forms; $44.50 per 25 AutoScore™ home questionnaires; $62.50 per manual.
Time: (8–10) minutes.
Author: Frances Smith.
Publisher: Western Psychological Services.
Cross References: For reviews by John Christian Busch, M. Elizabeth Graue, and Jeffrey K. Smith, see 12:351.

[1825]

Screening Test of Adolescent Language.

Purpose: Designed to identify adolescents at risk of having language disorders.
Population: Ages 11-18.
Publication Date: 1980.
Acronym: STAL.
Scores, 5: 4 subtests (Vocabulary, Auditory Memory Span, Language Processing, Proverb Explanation), Total.
Administration: Individual.
Price Data, 2016: $86.50 per kit, including manual (24 pages) with mini-screen, 50 tests, administration and scoring card, and scoring instructions; $35 per 50 test forms; $54 per manual.
Time: (7) minutes.
Authors: Elizabeth M. Prather, Sheila Van Ausdal Breecher, Marimyn Lee Stafford, and Elizabeth Matthews Wallace.
Publisher: Western Psychological Services.
Cross References: See T4:2387 (1 reference); for a review by Ronald K. Sommers, see 9:1086 (1 reference).

[1826]

Search Institute Profiles of Student Life: Attitudes and Behaviors.

Purpose: Designed to "assist … communities in measuring 40 developmental assets related to youth well-being."
Population: Grades 6–12.
Publication Dates: 1989–2012.
Scores: Total score only.
Administration: Group.
Price Data, 2015: $150 for the set up of an account plus $2 per survey. This cost includes the analysis and report.
Time: (30) minutes.
Author: Search Institute.
Publisher: Search Institute.
Cross References: For reviews by George Engelhard, Jr. and Carol M. McGregor, see 15:221; for reviews by Ernest A. Bauer and Sharon Johnson-Lewis of an earlier edition, see 11:350.

[1827]

SELECT Associate Screening System.

Purpose: Designed to assist organizations in making employee selection decisions for associate and entry-level positions.

Publication Dates: 1995-2010.

Acronym: SELECT.

Price Data, 2015: $150 one-time fee for account set-up and user training. Report costs are $15 to $40 each (depending on quantity of order and complexity of report). Annual licenses for larger volume usage are also available.

Foreign Language Editions: Spanish, French, Portuguese, Hungarian, Dutch, Bahasa Indonesia, Chinese, and Korean versions available.

Time: (15-40) minutes depending on survey.

Authors: Assess Systems.

Publisher: Assess Systems.

a) SELECT FOR ADMINISTRATIVE SUPPORT.

Purpose: "A personality-based survey designed to measure characteristics that have been found to predict job effectiveness in administrative or clerical positions."

Population: Applicants for administrative support positions.

Scores, 2: Provides Overall Performance and Integrity indices with recommended ranges; subscale results for Energy, Multi-Tasking, Attention to Detail, Self-Reliance, Task Focus, Interpersonal Insight, Criticism Tolerance, Acceptance of Diversity, Self-Control, Productive Attitude; optional modules available for willingness to perform job tasks and Counterproductive Behaviors.

b) SELECT FOR ENTRY LEVEL RETAIL MANAGERS.

Purpose: Designed to measure "personality characteristics related to effective job performance in managerial jobs that require individuals to produce sales, lead associates, and build customer loyalty."

Population: Applicants for entry level retail management positions.

Scores, 2: Provides Overall Performance and Integrity indices with recommended ranges; subscale results for Energy, Frustration Tolerance, Persuasiveness, Positive Sales Attitude, Leadership, Good Judgment, Organization and Attention to Detail; optional modules available for Retail Manager Math and Counterproductive Behaviors.

c) SELECT FOR RETAIL SALES ASSOCIATES.

Purpose: Designed to measure "personality characteristics related to effective job performance in sales-oriented jobs that require associates to sell and build customer loyalty."

Population: Applicants for retail sales associate positions.

Scores, 2: Provides Overall Performance and Integrity indices with recommended ranges; subscale results for Energy, Frustration Tolerance, Initiative, Positive Sales Attitude, Leadership, Persuasiveness, Good Judgment; optional modules available for Retail Math, willingness to perform job tasks, and Counterproductive Behaviors.

d) SELECT FOR RETAIL CLERK/CASHIER.

Purpose: Designed to measure "personality characteristics related to effective job performance in retail jobs that require employees to enjoy serving the customer."

Population: Applicants for clerk or cashier positions in a retail store.

Scores, 2: Provides Overall Performance and Integrity indices with recommended ranges; subscale results for Positive Service Attitude, Energy, Accommodation to Others, Frustration Tolerance, Acceptance of Diversity; optional modules available for Retail Math, willingness to perform job tasks, and Counterproductive Behaviors.

e) SELECT FOR PRODUCTION AND DISTRIBUTION.

Purpose: "A personality-based survey designed to measure characteristics important to team-oriented manufacturing and distribution jobs."

Population: Applicants for production, manufacturing, and distribution positions.

Scores, 2: Provides Overall Performance and Integrity indices with recommended ranges; subscale results for Energy, Frustration Tolerance, Acceptance of Diversity, Self-Control, Productive Attitude, Acceptance of Structure; optional modules available for willingness to perform job tasks and Counterproductive Behaviors

f) SELECT FOR LEASING AGENTS.

Purpose: Designed to measure "personality characteristics related to effective job performance in rental property sales positions."

Population: Applicants for leasing agent positions.

Scores, 2: Provides Overall Performance and Integrity indices with recommended ranges; subscale results for Energy, Assertiveness, Positive Sales Attitude, Social Comfort, Accommodation to Others, Frustration Tolerance, Criticism Tolerance, Self-Reliance, Acceptance of Diversity; optional modules available for Leasing Agent Math, willingness to perform job tasks, and Counterproductive Behaviors.

g) SELECT FOR HEALTH CARE.

Purpose: "A work-personality survey designed to measure characteristics important in most health care jobs."

Population: Applicants for jobs in hospitals or caregiving environments that have high patient (or patient family) contact.

Scores, 2: Provides Overall Performance and Integrity indices with recommended ranges; subscale results for Positive Service Attitude, Energy, Accommodation to Others, Frustration Tolerance, Accountability, Rapport, Empathy, Acceptance of Diversity, Multi-Tasking; optional modules available for willingness to perform job tasks and Counterproductive Behaviors.

h) SELECT FOR CUSTOMER SERVICE.

Purpose: Designed to measure personality characteristics that contribute to success in customer service jobs.

Population: Applicants for general customer service representative positions.

Scores, 2: Provides Overall Performance and Integrity indices with recommended ranges; subscale results for Energy, Frustration Tolerance, Accommodation to Others, Acceptance of Diversity, Positive Service Attitude; optional modules available for Retail Math, willingness to perform job tasks, and Counterproductive Behaviors.

i) SELECT FOR PERSONAL SERVICE.

Purpose: Designed to measure personality characteristics that contribute to success in customer service jobs.

Population: Applicants for positions that require providing high quality customer service as well as developing and maintaining a client base.

Scores, 2: Provides Overall Performance and Integrity indices with recommended ranges; subscale results for Energy, Frustration Tolerance, Accommodation to Others, Acceptance of Diversity, Positive Service Attitude, Social Comfort; optional modules available for willingness to perform job tasks and Counterproductive Behaviors.

j) SELECT FOR RECEPTIONISTS.

Purpose: Designed to measure personality characteristics that contribute to success in customer service jobs.

Population: Applicants for receptionist or information clerk positions.

Scores, 2: Provides Overall Performance and Integrity indices with recommended ranges; subscale results for Energy, Frustration Tolerance, Accommodation to Others, Acceptance of Diversity, Positive Service Attitude, Social Comfort; optional modules available for willingness to perform job tasks and Counterproductive Behaviors.

k) SELECT FOR CALL CENTERS-INBOUND SERVICE.

Purpose: Designed to "measure personality characteristics related to effective job performance in call center positions."

Population: Applicants for service-oriented jobs in call centers.

Scores, 2: Provides Overall Performance and Integrity indices with recommended ranges; subscale results for Energy, Frustration Tolerance, Accommodation to Others, Acceptance of Diversity, Positive Service Attitude; optional modules available for willingness to perform job tasks and Counterproductive Behaviors.

l) SELECT FOR CALL CENTERS-INBOUND SALES.

Purpose: Designed to "measure personality characteristics related to effective job performance in call center positions."

Population: Applicants for jobs that require representatives to answer customer calls and use effective selling and persuasion techniques.

Scores, 2: Provides Overall Performance and Integrity indices with recommended ranges; subscale results for Energy, Accountability, Positive Sales Attitude, Preference for Structure, Influence, Social Comfort, Frustration Tolerance; optional modules available for willingness to perform job tasks and Counterproductive Behaviors.

m) SELECT FOR CALL CENTERS-OUTBOUND SALES.

Purpose: Designed to "measure personality characteristics related to effective job performance in call center positions."

Population: Applicants for jobs that require representatives to actively solicit and sell to potential customers.

Scores, 2: Provides Overall Performance and Integrity indices with recommended ranges; subscale results for Energy, Multi-Tasking Ability, Accountability, Positive Sales Attitude, Assertiveness, Social Comfort, Diplomacy, Acceptance of Diversity, Frustration Tolerance, Criticism Tolerance; optional modules available for willingness to perform job tasks and Counterproductive Behaviors.

n) SELECT FOR CALL CENTERS-HELP DESK.

Purpose: Designed to "measure personality characteristics related to effective job performance in call center positions."

Population: Applicants for help desk and technical phone support positions.

Scores, 2: Provides Overall Performance and Integrity indices with recommended ranges; subscale results for Energy, Frustration Tolerance, Accountability, Criticism Tolerance, Assertiveness, Collaboration, Problem Solving, Multi-Tasking, Acceptance of Diversity; optional modules available for willingness to perform job tasks and Counterproductive Behaviors.

o) SELECT FOR CONVENIENCE STORE MANAGERS.

Purpose: "Work-personality survey designed to measure characteristics important in convenience store jobs."

Population: Applicants for convenience store manager positions.

Scores, 2: Provides Overall Performance and Integrity indices with recommended ranges; subscale results for Energy, Frustration Tolerance, Persuasiveness, Positive Sales Attitude, Leadership, Good Judgment, Organization and Attention to Detail; optional modules available for math and Counterproductive Behaviors.

p) SELECT FOR CONVENIENCE STORE ASSOCIATES.

Purpose: "Work-personality survey designed to measure characteristics important in convenience store jobs."

Population: Applicants for convenience store associate positions.

Scores, 3: Provides Overall Performance, Integrity, and Math Ability indices with recommended ranges; subscale results for Positive Service Attitude, Accommodation to Others, Frustration Tolerance, Acceptance of Diversity, Self-Control, Energy; optional modules available for willingness to perform job tasks and Counterproductive Behaviors.

q) SELECT FOR BANKING SALES ASSOCIATES.

Purpose: "Personality-based survey designed to measure characteristics that have been found to predict job effectiveness for positions in retail banking work environments."

Population: Applicants for positions that are responsible for handling daily customer transactions as well as selling retail banking services.

Scores, 2: Provides Overall Performance and Integrity indices with recommended ranges; subscale results for Positive Service Attitude, Acceptance of Diversity, Accommodation to Others, Energy, Resilience/Frustration Tolerance, Interpersonal Influence, Social Comfort, Preference for Objective Measures, Dependability, Process Focused, Multi-Tasking, Self-Reliance, Leadership, Responsibility, Flexible Thinking; optional modules available for Retail Banking Associate Math, willingness to perform job tasks, and Counterproductive Behaviors.

r) SELECT FOR IN-STORE SALES ASSOCIATES.

Purpose: "Personality-based survey designed to measure characteristics that have been found to predict job effectiveness for positions in retail banking work environments."

Population: Applicants for sales associate positions within an in-store banking environment.

Scores, 2: Provides Overall Performance and Integrity indices with recommended ranges; subscale results for Positive Service Attitude, Acceptance of Diversity, Accommodation to Others, Energy, Resilience/Frustration Tolerance, Interpersonal Influence, Social Comfort, Preference for Objective Measures, Dependability, Process Focused, Multi-Tasking, Self-Reliance, Leadership, Responsibility, Flexible Thinking; optional modules available for Retail Banking Associate Math, willingness to perform job tasks, and Counterproductive Behaviors.

s) SELECT FOR BRANCH MANAGERS.

Purpose: "Personality-based survey designed to measure characteristics that have been found to predict job effectiveness for positions in retail banking work environments."

Population: Applicants for positions that require managing daily operations of a bank branch and promoting customer service.

Scores, 2: Provides Overall Performance and Integrity indices with recommended ranges; subscale results for Positive Service Attitude, Acceptance of Diversity, Accommodation to Others, Energy, Resilience/Frustration Tolerance, Interpersonal Influence, Social Comfort, Preference for Objective Measures, Dependability, Process Focused, Multi-Tasking, Self-Reliance, Leadership, Responsibility, Flexible Thinking; optional modules available for Retail Banking Manager Math, Job Experience Checklist, and Counterproductive Behaviors.

t) SELECT FOR BANKING SERVICE ASSOCIATES.

Purpose: "Personality-based survey designed to measure characteristics that have been found to predict job effectiveness for positions in retail banking work environments."

Population: Applicants for service-only positions, including bank tellers.

Scores, 2: Provides Overall Performance and Integrity indices with recommended ranges; subscale results for Positive Service Attitude, Acceptance of Diversity, Accommodation to Others, Energy, Resilience/Frustration Tolerance, Interpersonal Influence, Social Comfort, Preference for Objective Measures, Dependability, Process Focused, Multi-Tasking, Self-Reliance, Leadership, Responsibility, Flexible Thinking; optional modules available for Retail Banking Associate Math, willingness to perform job tasks, and Counterproductive Behaviors.

Cross References: For a review by Alvin Leung, see 19:148; for reviews by James T. Austin and Vicki S. Packman of an earlier version, see 14:344.

[1828]

Self-Appraisal Questionnaire.

Purpose: "Multi-dimensional self-administered questionnaire designed to predict violent and non-violent offender recidivism among correctional/forensic populations and to assist with the assignment of these populations to appropriate treatment/correctional programs and different institutional security levels."

Population: Offenders, age 18 and older.

Publication Date: 2005.

Acronym: SAQ.

Scores, 8: Criminal Tendencies, Antisocial Personality Problems, Conduct Problems, Criminal History, Alcohol/Drug Abuse, Antisocial Associates, Anger, Total.

Administration: Individual or group.

Price Data, 2015: $121 per complete kit including manual (80 pages) and 25 QuikScore forms; $74 per technical manual; $54 per 25 QuikScore forms.

Time: (10–15) minutes.

Comments: Can be administered verbally.

Author: Wagdy Loza.

Publisher: Multi-Health Systems, Inc.

Cross References: For reviews by Phillip L. Ackerman and and Rita Budrionis, see 17:170.

[1829]

Self-Assessment in Writing Skills.

Purpose: Developed as a self-assessment tool to assess writing skills.

Population: Clerical, managerial, and sales employees.

Publication Date: 1990.

Scores, 3: Content and Style, Organization and Format, Total.

Administration: Group or individual.

Price Data, 2016: $195; quantity discounts available.

Time: [90–120] minutes.

Comments: Self-administered, self-scored; now sold as part of the Training House Asessment Kit.

Author: Training House, Inc.

Publisher: HRD Press, Inc.

Cross References: For reviews by Gabriel M. Della-Piana and Stephen Jurs, see 12:352.

[1830]

Self-Audit.

Purpose: Designed as an "assessment instrument ... for use at intake (pre-treatment) and post-treatment intervals."

Population: Ages 16 to 76.

Publication Date: 2001.

Acronym: SA.

Scores, 9: Truthfulness, Distress, Resistance, Morale, Violence, Alcohol, Drugs, Self-Esteem, Stress Coping Abilities.

Administration: Group.

Price Data, 2016: $9.95 per test; volume discounts available.

Foreign Language Edition: Spanish version available.

Time: (30-35) minutes.

Comments: May be administered via paper and pencil, computer, or human voice audio.

Author: Behavior Data Systems, Ltd.

Publisher: Behavior Data Systems, Ltd.

[1831]

Self-Awareness Profile.

Purpose: "This self-assessment provides insight into the basic personality attributes that influence the way we behave."

Population: Industry.
Publication Dates: 1980–1987.
Scores, 4: Dominance, Influence, Conformity, Evenness.
Administration: Individual or group.
Price Data, 2016: $195; quantity discounts available.
Time: (80–100) minutes.
Comments: Now sold as part of the Training House Assessment Kit.
Author: Scott B. Parry.
Publisher: HRD Press, Inc.
Cross References: For a review by Timothy M. Osberg, see 11:353.

[1832]

Self-Determination Assessment Internet.

Purpose: Designed to measure "cognitive, affective, and behavioral factors related to self-determination."
Population: Middle school to college-age students.
Publication Date: 2015.
Acronym: SDAi.
Administration: Individual.
Forms: 4 forms.
Price Data, 2016: $3.25 per assessment for quantities 10-99, volume discounts available.
Comments: Online administration and scoring; student, parent, and advisor scales originally developed as part of a battery titled Self-Determination Assessment Battery.
Authors: Alan Hoffman, Sharon Field Hoffman, and Shlomo Sawilowsky.
Publisher: Ealy Education Group, Inc.
  a) SELF-DETERMINATION STUDENT SCALE.
  Population: Middle and high school students.
  Acronym: SDSS.
  Scores, 6: Know Yourself and Your Context, Value Yourself, Plan, Act, Experience Outcomes and Learn, Total.
  Time: (30-50) minutes.
  b) SELF-DETERMINATION STUDENT SCALE-SHORT FORM.
  Population: College and college-bound students.
  Acronym: SDSS-SF.
  Scores, 6: Know Yourself and Your Context, Value Yourself, Plan, Act, Experience Outcomes and Learn, Total.
  Time: (30-40) minutes.
  c) SELF-DETERMINATION PARENT PERCEPTION SCALE.
  Population: Parents of students.
  Acronym: SDPPS.
  Score: Total score only.
  Time: (5-10) minutes.
  d) SELF-DETERMINATION ADVISOR PERCEPTION SCALE.
  Population: Advisors of students.
  Acronym: SDAPS.
  Score: Total score only.
  Time: (5-10) minutes.
Cross References: Reviews are scheduled for *The Twentieth Mental Measurements Yearbook.*

[1833]

Self-Directed Learning Readiness Scale/ Learning Preference Assessment.

Purpose: Designed to measure attitudes, abilities, and characteristics that comprise readiness to engage in self-directed learning.
Population: Ages 7 and above.
Publication Dates: 1977-2005.
Acronym: SDLRS/LPA.
Scores: Total score only.
Administration: Individual or group.
Price Data, 2016: $6.95 per single copy of test; quantity discounts available.
Foreign Language Editions: Afrikaans, Arabic, Chinese, Dutch (ABE form only), Finnish, German, Greek, Hungarian, Indonesian, Italian, Japanese, Korean, Latvian, Lithuanian, Malay, Nepali, Persian (Farsi—ABE and E forms) Polish, Portuguese, Russian, Spanish, Thai, and Turkish.
Time: [25] minutes.
Comments: Publisher recommends online administration; paper-and-pencil versions are also available.
Authors: Lucy M. Guglielmino (all forms) and Paul J. Guglielmino (self-scoring form).
Publisher: Guglielmino & Associates, LLC.
Cross References: See T5:2359 (2 references).

[1834]

Self-Directed Search, 5th Edition [Form R].

Purpose: Designed as a "career decision-making" tool.
Population: Ages 11 years and older.
Publication Dates: 1970-2013.
Acronym: SDS.
Scores, 6: Realistic, Investigative, Artistic, Social, Enterprising, Conventional.
Administration: Individual or group.
Price Data, 2015: $199 per kit including manual (2013, 95 pages), fast guide, 25 assessment booklets, 25 Occupations Finders, 25 You and Your Career Booklets, Leisure Activities Finder (revised for 5th edition), and Educational Opportunities Finder (revised for 5th edition); $70 per manual; $50 per 25 assessment booklets.
Foreign Language Edition: Spanish version available.
Time: (25-35) minutes.
Comments: Self-administered, scored, and interpreted; can be administered online or via paper and pencil.
Authors: John L. Holland (test and manuals), Melissa A. Messer (test and manuals), Jennifer A. Greene (Leisure Activities Finder), and Amy M. Kovacs (Leisure Activities Finder).
Publisher: Psychological Assessment Resources, Inc.
  a) SELF-DIRECTED SEARCH VETERANS AND MILITARY OCCUPATIONS FINDER.
  Purpose: Designed to work "in conjunction with the SDS Form R 5th Edition Assessment Booklet" to "help

veterans and military clients explore career options and transition to civilian life."
Population: Veterans and those enlisted in the military.
Acronym: VMOF.
Price Data, 2015: $80 per combination package including 10 assessment booklets (SDS Form R 5th Edition), 10 Occupations Finders, and 10 Veterans and Military Occupations Finders; $35 per 10 Veterans and Military Occupations Finders.
Comments: The Veterans and Military Occupations Finder may be used after an individual obtains his/her summary code from Form R.
Authors: Melissa A. Messer, Jennifer A. Greene, and John L. Holland.

Cross References: Reviews are scheduled for *The Twentieth Mental Measurements Yearbook*. For a review by Michael B. Brown of the fourth edition, see 14:345; see also T5:2360 (13 references); for reviews by Joseph C. Ciechalski and Esther E. Diamond of the 1990 revision, see 13:281 (48 references); see also T4:2414 (23 references); for reviews by M. Harry Daniels and Caroline Manuele-Adkins of the 1985 revision, see 10:330 (19 references); for a review by Robert H. Dolliver of an earlier edition, see 9:1098 (12 references); see also T3:2134 (55 references); for a review by John O. Crites and excerpted reviews by Fred Brown, Richard Seligman, Catherine C. Cutts, Robert H. Dolliver, and Robert N. Hanson, see 8:1022 (88 references); see also T2:2211 (1 reference).

[1835]

Self-Directed Search—Revised 2001 Australian Edition.

Purpose: Designed as an instrument "for students and adults wishing to explore their career options."
Population: Ages 15 and over.
Publication Dates: 1970–2006.
Acronym: SDS.
Scores: 4 scales: Activities, Competencies, Occupations, Summary.
Administration: Group or individual.
Price Data, 2006: A$30.80 per 10 assessment booklets; $39.95 per 10 Occupations finder; $16.50 per 10 "You and Your Career"; $5.95 per Alphabetical Occupations Finder; $60.50 per manual; $70.40 per specimen set.
Foreign Language and Special Editions: Spanish, Vietnamese, French, and Braille editions available.
Time: (50) minutes.
Authors: John L. Holland, Meredith Shears (Australian Manual), and Adrian Harvey-Beavis (Australian Manual).
Publisher: Australian Council for Educational Research Ltd. [Australia; Efforts to obtain updated information from the test publisher were unsuccessful. An updated edition of this test appears on the test publisher's website].
Cross References: For a review by Nancy L. Crumpton, see 15:223.

[1836]

Self-Esteem Assessment.

Purpose: "Designed to evaluate an individual's general level of self-esteem."
Population: Under age 17 through adult.
Publication Date: 2011.
Acronym: SEA.
Scores, 9: Feelings of Inadequacy, Sense of Self-Worth, Need for Approval, Unrealistic Self-Expectations, Sense of Social Acceptance, Narcissism, Defensiveness, Self-Deception, Overall Score.
Administration: Individual.
Price Data: Available from publisher.
Time: (30) minutes.
Comments: Self-administered online assessment. The test publisher provides clients with information about the methods and theoretical basis used in the development of the test as well as benchmarks for relevant industries and racial/ethnic group comparison data.
Author: PsychTests AIM, Inc.
Publisher: PsychTests AIM, Inc. [Canada].
Cross References: For reviews by Eric S. Buhs and Amy Scott, see 19:149.

[1837]

Self-Esteem Index.

Purpose: "Designed to measure the way individuals perceive themselves."
Population: Ages 7-0 to 18-11.
Publication Date: 1991.
Acronym: SEI.
Scores, 5: Familial Acceptance, Academic Competence, Peer Popularity, Personal Security, Self-Esteem Quotient.
Administration: Group.
Price Data, 2015: $153 per complete kit including 50 student response booklets, 50 profile/record forms, and manual (1991, 51 pages); $48 per 50 student response booklets; $48 per 50 profile/record forms; $63 per examiner's manual.
Time: (30-35) minutes.
Authors: Linda Brown and Jacquelyn Alexander.
Publisher: PRO-ED.
Cross References: See T5:2361 (4 references); for reviews by E. Scott Huebner and by Ralph O. Mueller and Paula J. Dupuy, see 11:354.

[1838]

The Self Image Profiles.

Purpose: To quickly assess self image and self esteem in children and adolescents.
Publication Date: 2001.
Acronym: SIP.
Administration: Group or individual.
Price Data, 2015: £106.50 per complete kit including Adolescent Profiles, Child Profiles, 25 SIP-C record

forms, 25 SIP-A record forms, and manual (43) pages; £54 per 25 record forms (adolescent or child); £47.50 per manual.

Author: Richard J. Butler.
Publisher: Pearson Assessment [England].
   a) THE SELF IMAGE PROFILE FOR CHILDREN.
   Population: Ages 7–11.
   Acronym: SIP-C.
   Scores, 11: Positive Self Image, Negative Self Image, Sense of Difference, Self Esteem, Aspects of Self (Behaviour, Social, Emotional, Outgoing, Academic, Resourceful, Appearance).
   Time: (12–25) minutes.
   b) THE SELF IMAGE PROFILE FOR ADOLES-CENTS.
   Population: Ages 12–16.
   Acronym: SIP-A.
   Scores, 14: Positive Self Image, Negative Self Image, Sense of Difference, Self Esteem, Aspects of Self (Expressive, Caring, Outgoing, Academic, Emotional, Hesitant, Feel Different, Inactive, Unease, Resourceful).
   Time: (9–17) minutes.
Cross References: For a review by Jayne E. Stake, see 15:224.

[1839]

Self-Perception Profile for College Students.
Purpose: To measure college students' self-concept.
Population: College students.
Publication Date: 1986.
Scores: 13 domains: Creativity, Intellectual Ability, Scholastic Competence, Job Competence, Athletic Competence, Appearance, Romantic Relationships, Social Acceptance, Close Friendships, Parent Relationships, Finding Humor in One's Life, Morality, Global Self-Worth.
Administration: Group.
Price Data: Available at no charge from test publisher.
Time: 30(40) minutes.
Authors: Jennifer Neemann and Susan Harter.
Publisher: Susan Harter, University of Denver.
Cross References: See T5:2369 (12 references); for reviews by Robert D. Brown and Stephen F. Davis, see 11:357 (1 reference).

[1840]

Self-Perceptions of Adolescents.
Purpose: Designed to measure an adolescent's concept of self.
Population: Adolescents.
Publication Dates: 1965-2007.
Scores: 8 scales: Self as a Person (Self Concept, Ideal Concept, Reflected Self, Perceptions of Others), Self as a Student (Self Concept, Ideal Concept, Reflected Self, Perceptions of Others).
Administration: Group.
Forms, 8: Self as a Person Scales (Self Concept, Ideal Concept, Reflected Self/Other, Perceptions of Others), Self as a Student (Student Self, Ideal Concept as a

Student, Reflected Self as a Student/Other, Perceptions of Others/Student Self).
Price Data: Available from publisher.
Time: (5-20) minutes.
Comments: Developed from the original Self-Perceptions Inventory (T8:2414) and is part of the SPI series that includes: Self-Perceptions of Adults (1841), Self-Perceptions of Children (1842), Self-Perceptions of College Students, Self-Perceptions of School Administrators (1843), Self-Perceptions of University Instructors (1844), Self-Perceptions of Teachers, and Self-Perceptions of Nurses.
Author: Louise M. Soares.
Publisher: Soares Institute of Neuroscience and Education.
Cross References: For reviews by Stephen Axford and Eric S. Buhs, see 18:114; for reviews by Mary M. Clare and Aimin Wang of the 1999 Revision of the Self-Perceptions Inventory, see 15:226; see also T4:2421 (1 reference); for a review by Janet Morgan Riggs of an earlier edition, see 9:1101; for a review by Lorrie Shepard of an earlier edition, see 8:673 (2 references).

[1841]

Self-Perceptions of Adults.
Purpose: Designed to measure an adult's concept of self.
Population: Adults.
Publication Dates: 1965-2006.
Scores: 8 scales: Self as a Person (Self Concept, Ideal Concept, Reflected Self, Perceptions of Others), Self as a Working Adult (Self Concept, Ideal Concept, Reflected Self, Perceptions of Others).
Administration: Group.
Forms, 16: Self as Person Scales (Self Concept/Adjectives, Self Concept/Sentences, Ideal Concept/Adjectives, Ideal Concept/Sentences, Reflected Self/Adjectives, Reflected Self/Sentences, Perceptions of Others/Adjectives, Perceptions of Others/Sentences), Self as a Working Adult (Self Concept/Adjectives, Self Concept/Sentences, Ideal Concept/Adjectives, Ideal Concept/Sentences, Reflected Self/Adjectives, Reflected Self/Sentences, Perceptions of Others/Adjectives, Perceptions of Others/Sentences).
Price Data, 2008: $40 per 25 scales (specify form); $40 per 50 answer sheets; $.25 per customized booklet; $.40 per profile chart; $40 per test manual (2006, 44 pages); $.40 per scale for scoring.
Time: (5-20) minutes.
Comments: Developed from the original Self-Perceptions Inventory (T8:2414) and is part of the SPI series that includes: Self-Perceptions of Adolescents (1840), Self-Perceptions of Children (1842), Self-Perceptions of College Students, Self-Perceptions of School Administrators (1843), Self-Perceptions of University Instructors (1844), Self-Perceptions of Teachers, and Self-Perceptions of Nurses.
Author: Louise M. Soares.

Publisher: Soares Institute of Neuroscience and Education.
Cross References: For reviews by Nancy L. Crumpton and Richard F. Farmer, see 18:115; for reviews by Mary M. Clare and Aimin Wang of the 1999 Revision of the Self-Perceptions Inventory, see 15:226; see also T4:2421 (1 reference); for a review by Janet Morgan Riggs of an earlier edition, see 9:1101; for a review by Lorrie Shepard of an earlier edition, see 8:673 (2 references).

[1842]
Self-Perceptions of Children.
Purpose: Designed to assess children's self-concepts and "determine developmental differences in the self during the typical growth periods of childhood."
Publication Dates: 1965-2008.
Acronym: SPI/Children.
Administration: Group.
Price Data, 2009: $40 per 25 scales (specify form); $40 per test manual (2008, 38 pages); $.40 per scoring per scale; $40 per analysis report.
Time: (10) minutes per scale.
Authors: Louise M. Soares and Anthony T. Soares (test).
Publisher: Soares Institute of Neuroscience and Education.
Comments: Revision of the Student Forms of the Self-Perceptions Inventory (T8:2414).
  a) SELF AS PERSON.
  Population: Ages 6-8.
  Scores, 4: Self Concept, Student Self, Perceptions of Others (Self), Perceptions of Others (Student).
  b) SELF AS STUDENT.
  Population: Ages 9-11.
  Scores, 4: Self Concept, Student Self, Perceptions of Others (Self), Perceptions of Others (Student).
Cross References: For reviews by Kathleen D. Allen and Cher Edwards, see 18:116; for reviews by Mary M. Clare and Aimin Wang of the entire Self-Perceptions Inventory [1999 Revision], see 15:226; see also T4:2421 (1 reference); for a review by Janet Morgan Riggs of an earlier edition, see 9:1101; for a review by Lorrie Shepard of an earlier edition, see 8:673 (2 references). For reviews by Gerald E. DeMauro and Michael R. Harwell of an earlier edition of the Nursing forms, see 11:356.

[1843]
Self-Perceptions of School Administrators.
Purpose: Designed to measure a school administrator's concept of self.
Population: Adults.
Publication Dates: 1965-2005.
Scores: 8 scales: Self as a Person (Self Concept, Ideal Concept, Reflected Self, Perceptions of Others), Self as a School Administrator (Self Concept, Ideal Concept, Reflected Self, Perceptions of Others).
Administration: Group.

Forms, 8: Self as Person Scales (Self Concept, Ideal Concept, Reflected Self, Perceptions of Others), Self as a School Administrator (Self Concept, Ideal Concept, Reflected Self, Perceptions of Others).
Price Data: Available from publisher.
Time: (5-20) minutes.
Comments: Developed from the original Self-Perceptions Inventory (T8:2414) and is part of the SPI series that includes: Self-Perceptions of Adolescents (1840), Self-Perceptions of Children (1842), Self-Perceptions of College Students, Self-Perceptions of Adults (1841), Self-Perceptions of University Instructors (1844), Self-Perceptions of Teachers, and Self-Perceptions of Nurses.
Author: Louise M. Soares.
Publisher: Soares Institute of Neuroscience and Education.
Cross References: For reviews by Marta Coleman and Suzanne Young, see 18:117; for reviews by Mary M. Clare and Aimin Wang of the 1999 Revision of the Self-Perceptions Inventory, see 15:226; see also T4:2421 (1 reference); for a review by Janet Morgan Riggs of an earlier edition, see 9:1101; for a review by Lorrie Shepard of an earlier edition, see 8:673 (2 references).

[1844]
Self-Perceptions of University Instructors.
Purpose: Designed to measure an adult's concept of self.
Population: University instructors.
Publication Dates: 1965-2008.
Scores: 16 scales: Self as a Person [College Professors] (Self Concept, Ideal Concept, Reflected Self, Perceptions of Others), Self as a Person [Adjunct Faculty] (Self Concept, Ideal Concept, Reflected Self, Perceptions of Others), Self as a College Professor (Self Concept, Ideal Concept, Reflected Self, Perceptions of Others), Self as an Adjunct Faculty Member (Self Concept, Ideal Concept, Reflected Self, Perceptions of Others).
Administration: Group.
Forms, 16: Self as a Person [College Professors] (Self Concept, Ideal Concept, Reflected Self, Perceptions of Others), Self as a Person [Adjunct Faculty] (Self Concept, Ideal Concept, Reflected Self, Perceptions of Others), Self as a College Professor (Self Concept, Ideal Concept, Reflected Self, Perceptions of Others), Self as an Adjunct Faculty Member (Self Concept, Ideal Concept, Reflected Self, Perceptions of Others).
Price Data: Available from publisher.
Time: (5-20) minutes.
Comments: Developed from the original Self-Perceptions Inventory (T8:2414) and is part of the SPI series that includes: Self-Perceptions of Adolescents (1840), Self-Perceptions of Children (1842), Self-Perceptions of College Students, Self-Perceptions of Adults (1841), Self-Perceptions of School Administrators (1843), Self-Perceptions of Teachers, and Self-Perceptions of Nurses.

Author: Louise M. Soares.
Publisher: Soares Institute of Neuroscience and Education.
Cross References: For reviews by Theodore Coladarci and Sandra M. Harris, see 18:118; for reviews by Mary M. Clare and Aimin Wang of the 1999 Revision of the Self-Perceptions Inventory, see 15:226; see also T4:2421 (1 reference); for a review by Janet Morgan Riggs of an earlier edition, see 9:1101; for a review by Lorrie Shepard of an earlier edition, see 8:673 (2 references).

[1845]

Self Worth Inventory.

Purpose: "Helps respondents increase their understanding of self-worth and how it is developed."
Population: Adults and teenagers.
Publication Dates: 1990-2006.
Acronym: SWI.
Scores, 8: Self, Family, Peers, Work, Projected Self, Self-Concept, Self-Esteem, Self-Worth.
Administration: Individual and group.
Price Data, 2016: $25 per inventory (1990, 8 pages); $35 per online version; $40 per Trainer's Guidelines (1996, 24 pages).
Foreign Language Edition: Arabic version available.
Time: 60 minutes (short program); 120-180 minutes (longer program).
Comments: May be self-administered.
Author: Everett Robinson.
Publisher: Consulting Resource Group International, Inc.
Cross References: For reviews by Jayne E. Stake and Norman D. Sundberg, see 13:282.

[1846]

The Senior Apperception Technique [1985 Revision].

Purpose: A projective instrument to gather information on forms of depression, loneliness, or rage in the elderly.
Population: Ages 65 and over.
Publication Dates: 1973–1985.
Acronym: S.A.T.
Scores: No scores.
Administration: Individual.
Price Data, 2015: $43 per manual (1985, 12 pages) and set of picture cards.
Time: Administration time not reported.
Author: Leopold Bellak.
Publisher: C.P.S. Publishing, LLC
Cross References: For reviews by Paul A. Arbisi and Michael G. Kavan, see 13:283; see also T3:2148 (2 references); for a review by K. Warner Schaie of an earlier edition, see 8:676 (1 reference).

[1847]

Senior Aptitude Tests.

Purpose: Constructed "to measure a number of aptitudes of pupils … for the purpose of guidance and selection."
Population: Standards 8–10 in South African schools, college, and adults.
Publication Dates: 1969–1970.
Acronym: SAT.
Scores, 12: Verbal Comprehension, Numerical Fluency, Word Fluency, Visual Perception Speed, Reasoning (Deductive, Inductive), Spatial Visualization (2 Dimensional, 3 Dimensional), Memory (Paragraphs, Symbols), Psychomotor Coordination, Writing Speed.
Administration: Group.
Price Data: Available from publisher.
Time: 88(120) minutes.
Comments: Test materials in English and Afrikaans.
Authors: F. A. Fouche and N. F. Alberts.
Publisher: Human Sciences Research Council [South Africa].
Cross References: See T5:2373 (1 reference) and T4:2430 (1 reference).

[1848]

Senior South African Individual Scale—Revised.

Purpose: Measures general intelligence.
Population: Ages 7-0 to 16-11.
Publication Dates: 1964–1991.
Acronym: SSAIS-R.
Scores: 11 tests: Verbal (Vocabulary, Comprehension, Similarities, Number Problems, Story Memory, Memory for Digits), Nonverbal (Pattern Completion, Block Designs, Missing Parts, Form Board, Coding).
Administration: Individual.
Price Data: Available from publisher.
Time: Tests 1–9: (75) minutes; Tests 10–11: (10) minutes; Tests 3, 4, 7, and 8 (Abbreviated Scale): (45) minutes.
Comments: Developed for Afrikaans-speaking and English-speaking South African students.
Author: Human Sciences Research Council.
Publisher: Human Sciences Research Council [South Africa].
Cross References: For information regarding an earlier edition, see T3:2153 (1 reference) and 7:413 (1 reference).

[1849]

Sensory Integration and Praxis Tests.

Purpose: Designed to assess several practic abilities, various aspects of sensory processing status, and behavioral manifestations of deficits in integration of sensory inputs from these systems.
Population: Ages 4–8.11.

Publication Date: 1989.

Acronym: SIPT.

Scores: 17 tests: Space Visualization, Figure-Ground Perception, Standing and Walking Balance, Design Copying, Postural Praxis, Bilateral Motor Coordination, Praxis Verbal Command, Constructional Praxis, Postrotary Nystagmus, Motor Accuracy, Sequencing Praxis, Oral Praxis, Manual Form Perception, Kinesthesia, Finger Identification, Graphesthesia, Localization of Tactile Stimuli.

Administration: Individual.

Price Data, 2015: $1,095 per kit including all test materials, 10 design copying booklets, 10 motor accuracy booklets, 10 kinesthesia test sheets, manual, and carrying case with wheels; $295 per 10-use CD (PC with Microsoft Windows; 10 complete test batteries or individual tests); $24.50 per 25 test booklets (specify Design Copying, Motor Accuracy, or Kinesthesia); $93.50 per manual; $235 per administration DVD; $50 per 10 PC answer booklets; $588 per 25-use scoring CD package (25 complete test batteries or 375 individual tests).

Time: (10) minutes or less per individual test.

Comments: Extension and revision of the Southern California Sensory Integration Tests (SCSIT) and the Southern California Postrotary Nystagmus Test (SCPNT); computer-scoring only; stopwatch capable of recording 1/10 seconds needed (available from publisher).

Author: A. Jean Ayres.

Publisher: Western Psychological Services.

Cross References: See T5:2377 (4 references); for a review by James E. Ysseldyke, see 12:353 (18 references); see also T4:2433 (9 references). For a review by Byron P. Rourke of the SCPNT, see 9:1157 (20 references); for information on the SCSIT, see 9:1158 (5 references) and T3:2244 (21 references); for reviews by Homer B. C. Reed, Jr. and Alida S. Westman of the SCSIT, see 8:875 (5 references); see also T2:1887 (18 references).

[1850]

Sensory Integration Inventory—Revised for Individuals with Developmental Disabilities.

Purpose: "Designed to screen for [occupational therapy] clients who might benefit from a sensory integration treatment approach."

Population: Developmentally disabled occupational therapy clients school aged to adults, including autism spectrum and PDD.

Publication Dates: 1990–1992.

Acronym: SI Inventory.

Scores: Item scores in each of 4 sections interpreted individually: Tactile, Vestibular, Proprioception, General Reactions.

Administration: Individual.

Price Data, 2016: $20 per user's guide; $15 per 20 test forms.

Time: Administration time not reported.

Comments: A semistructured interview of a person who works/lives closely with the client (e.g., parent or therapeutic staff member); space also provided for qualitative comments.

Authors: Judith E. Reisman and Bonnie Hanschu.

Publisher: P.D.P. Press, Inc.

Cross References: For a review by William Verdi, see 14:346.

[1851]

Sensory Processing Measure.

Purpose: "Enables assessment of sensory processing issues, praxis, and social participation in elementary school-aged children."

Population: Ages 5-12.

Publication Date: 2007.

Acronym: SPM.

Scores, 15: Social Participation, Vision, Hearing, Touch, Body Awareness, Balance and Motion, Planning and Ideas, Total Sensory Systems, Environment Difference, Art Class Total, Music Class Total, Physical Education Class Total, Recess/Playground Total, Cafeteria Total, School Bus Total.

Administration: Group.

Price Data, 2016: $199.50 per comprehensive kit including 25 Home AutoScore Forms, 25 Main Classroom AutoScore Forms, School Environments Form CD, and manual (102 pages); $156.50 per School kit including 25 Main Classroom AutoScore Forms, School Environments Form CD, and manual; $124.50 per Home kit including 25 Home AutoScore Forms and manual; $52.50 per 25 AutoScore Forms; $41 per School Environments Form CD (unlimited use); $83 per manual.

Time: (15-20) minutes each for the Home and Main Classroom Forms; (5) minutes for each School Environment Form.

Comments: The Home and Main Classroom Forms may be used individually or together, but the School Environments Forms may only be used in conjunction with the Main Classroom Form.

Authors: L. Diane Parham and Cheryl Ecker (Home Form); Heather Miller Kuhaneck, Diana A. Henry, and Tara J. Glennon (Main Classroom and School Environments Forms).

Publisher: Western Psychological Services.

Cross References: For reviews by Michael K. Cruce and by T. Steuart Watson and Michael F. Woodin, see 18:119.

[1852]

Sensory Processing Measure-Preschool.

Purpose: "Enables assessment of sensory processing issues, praxis, and social participation in children of preschool age."

Population: Children ages 2-5 who have not started kindergarten.

Publication Date: 2010.
Acronym: SPM-P.
Scores: 8 for each form: Social Participation, Vision, Hearing, Touch, Body Awareness, Balance and Motion, Planning and Ideas, Total Sensory Systems.
Administration: Individual.
Forms, 2: Home, School.
Price Data, 2016: $160 per complete kit including 25 Home AutoScore forms, 25 School AutoScore forms, and manual (94 pages); $52.50 per 25 AutoScore forms (Home or School); $83 per manual.
Time: (15-20) minutes.
Comments: The Home and School forms are intended for use together, but each form may also be used separately; the SPM-P is "the companion instrument to the Sensory Processing Measure [1851], which facilitates assessment of sensory processing issues for elementary school-aged children."
Authors: Cheryl Ecker and L. Diane Parham (Home Form); Heather Miller Kuhaneck, Diana A. Henry, and Tara J. Glennon (School Form).
Publisher: Western Psychological Services.
Cross References: For reviews by Sherry K. Bain and Allison Hunt and by Rebecca Gokiert and Rebecca Georgis, see 19:150.

[1853]

Sensory Profile, Second Edition.

Purpose: Designed as "a set of standardized tools for evaluating a child's sensory processing patterns in the context of everyday life."
Population: Birth through 14 years.
Publication Dates: 1999-2014.
Acronym: Sensory Profile 2.
Administration: Individual.
Levels, 3: Infant, Toddler, Child.
Price Data, 2015: $260 per starter kit including user's manual (2014, 294 pages) and 25 of each record form (Infant, Toddler, Child, Short, and School Companion); $70 per manual; $50 per 25 forms (Infant, Toddler, Child, or School Companion); $35 per 25 Short forms, $2 per Q-global summary report, including administration, scoring, and reporting.
Comments: All forms are available in both paper and digital formats; forms are completed by caregivers except School Companion form, which is completed by teachers.
Author: Winnie Dunn.
Publisher: Pearson.
a) INFANT SENSORY PROFILE 2.
Population: Birth to 6 months.
Scores, 7: General Processing, Auditory Processing, Visual Processing, Touch Processing, Movement Processing, Oral Sensory Processing, Total.
Foreign Language Edition: Available in Spanish.
Time: (5-10) minutes.
b) TODDLER SENSORY PROFILE 2.
Population: Ages 7 to 35 months.

Scores, 11: 4 Quadrant scores (Seeking/Seeker, Avoiding/Avoider, Sensitivity/Sensor, Registration/Bystander), 6 Sensory Section scores (General Processing, Auditory Processing, Visual Processing, Touch Processing, Movement Processing, Oral Sensory Processing), Behavioral Responses.
Foreign Language Edition: Available in Spanish.
Time: (10-15) minutes.
c) CHILD SENSORY PROFILE 2.
Population: Ages 3 through 14 years.
Scores, 13: 4 Quadrant scores (Seeking/Seeker, Avoiding/Avoider, Sensitivity/Sensor, Registration/Bystander), 6 Sensory Section scores (Auditory Processing, Visual Processing, Touch Processing, Movement Processing, Body Position Processing, Oral Sensory Processing), 3 Behavioral Section scores (Conduct, Social Emotional Responses, Attentional Responses).
Foreign Language Edition: Available in Spanish.
Time: (15-20) minutes.
d) SHORT SENSORY PROFILE 2.
Population: Ages 3 through 14 years.
Scores, 6: 4 Quadrant scores (Seeking/Seeker, Avoiding/Avoider, Sensitivity/Sensor, Registration/Bystander), Sensory Processing, Behavioral Responses.
Foreign Language Edition: Available in Spanish.
Time: (5-10) minutes.
e) SCHOOL COMPANION SENSORY PROFILE 2.
Population: Ages 3 through 14 years.
Scores, 13: 4 Quadrant scores (Seeking/Seeker, Avoiding/Avoider, Sensitivity/Sensor, Registration/Bystander), 4 Sensory Section scores (Auditory Processing, Visual Processing, Touch Processing, Movement Processing), Behavioral Responses, 4 School Factor scores (School Factors 1, 2, 3, 4).
Time: (15) minutes.
Cross References: Reviews are scheduled for *The Twentieth Mental Measurements Yearbook*. For reviews by Doreen W. Fairbank and John J. Vacca of the Sensory Profile, which includes Infant/Toddler Sensory Profile—Clinical Edition, Sensory Profile, and Short Sensory Profile, see 16:220; for reviews by Elizabeth Bigham and Shawn Powell of the Sensory Profile School Companion, see 18:120.

[1854]

Sentence Completion Series.

Purpose: Designed to "identify underlying concerns and specific areas of distress."
Population: Adolescents and adults.
Publication Dates: 1991–1992.
Acronym: SCS.
Scores: No scores.
Administration: Individual or group.
Forms, 8: Adult, Adolescent, Family, Marriage, Parenting, Work, Illness, Aging.
Price Data, 2015: $112 per introductory kit including manual and 15 of each of 8 forms.
Time: [10–45] minutes.
Comments: Forms may be administered alone or in any combination; clinicians evaluates responses.

Authors: Larry H. Brown and Michael A. Unger.
Publisher: Psychological Assessment Resources, Inc.
Cross References: For reviews by Kevin L. Moreland and Paul D. Werner, see 14:347.

[1855]

Sequenced Inventory of Communication Development, Revised Edition.

Purpose: Designed as a diagnostic assessment to evaluate the communication abilities of normally developing and developmentally delayed children.
Population: Ages 4 months through 4 years.
Publication Dates: 1975–1984.
Acronym: SICD-R.
Administration: Individual.
Price Data, 2015: $511 per complete kit (includes all test materials in a sturdy carrying case, 50 record/booklet/ profiles, 1 instruction manual, and 1 test manual); $65 per 25 record booklet/profile forms; $42 per instruction manual; $42 per test manual.
Foreign Language Editions: Cuban-Spanish edition available; Spanish translation included in test manual and separate Spanish-language forms with pictures are available.
Time: (30–75) minutes.
Comments: Some test accessories (e.g., paper, coins, and picture book) must be assembled locally.
Authors: Dona Lea Hedrick, Elizabeth M. Prather, and Annette R. Tobin, with contributions by Doris V. Allen, Lynn S. Bliss, and Lillian R. Rosenberg.
Publisher: Western Psychological Services.
   a) RECEPTIVE SCALE.
     Scores, 3: Awareness, Discrimination, Understanding.
   b) EXPRESSIVE SCALE.
     Scores, 4: Imitating, Initiating, Responding, Verbal Output.
Cross References: See T5:2382 (40 references) and T4:2438 (21 references); for reviews by Carol Mardell-Czudnowski and Mary Ellen Pearson, see 10:331 (6 references); for reviews by Barbara W. Hodson and Joan I. Lynch of the earlier edition, see 9:1109 (4 references); see also T3:2159 (4 references).

[1856]

Service Ability Inventory.

Purpose: Designed "to select job applicants who have a service orientation ... to determine the service skill levels of current employees."
Population: Current and prospective employees.
Publication Dates: 1999–2004.
Acronym: S.A.I.
Scores, 7: Service Orientation, Interpersonal Skills, Tolerance for Stress, Team Skills, Patience, Coping Skills, Deception Scale.
Administration: Individual or group.
Price Data: Available from publisher.

Time: (20–25) minutes.
Comments: Online and paper-and-pencil versions of test are available; online version includes interpretive reports and follow-up interview questions. The test publisher has indicated there is a newer edition of this test; description will be updated when complete test materials are received.
Author: J. M. Llobet.
Publisher: HRdirect | G. Neil.
Cross References: For reviews by Michael B. Bunch and Denice Ward Hood, see 17:171.

[1857]

Service Animal Adaptive Intervention Assessment.

Purpose: Constructed for "evaluating predispositions to and outcomes of service animal use."
Population: Occupational, physical, and recreational therapists, assistive technology professionals, and animal assisted therapy specialists.
Publication Date: 1998.
Acronym: SAAIA.
Scores, 5: Knowledge and Experience of Animals, Typical Activities/Skills, Personal/Social Characteristics, Requirements of Service Animal Compared to Resources of Person, Total Predisposition Score.
Administration: Group or individual.
Price Data, 2016: $29.95 per complete kit including all assessments as masters for photocopying and manual (10 pages).
Time: (90–120) minutes.
Comments: Ratings by professionals; also includes qualitative information.
Author: Susan A. Zapf.
Publisher: Institute for Matching Person & Technology, Inc.
Cross References: For reviews by Ronald A. Berk and Judith A. Rein, see 15:227.

[1858]

ServiceFirst.

Purpose: Constructed to measure "customer service orientation or potential."
Population: Employees in service-oriented positions.
Publication Dates: 1990–2001.
Scores, 5: Active Customer Relations, Polite Customer Relations, Helpful Customer Relations, Personalized Customer Relations, Total.
Administration: Group.
Price Data: Available from publisher.
Time: (20) minutes.
Author: Larry Fogli.
Publisher: Assessio.
Cross References: For reviews by Michael B. Bunch and Mary A. Lewis, see 14:348.

[1859]

Severe Cognitive Impairment Profile.

Purpose: Designed to "measure and track impairment of cognitive abilities in adults with primary progressive dementia."
Population: Ages 42–90 and older.
Publication Dates: 1995–1998.
Acronym: SCIP.
Scores, 9: Comportment, Attention, Language, Memory, Motor, Conceptualization, Arithmetic, Visuospatial, Total.
Administration: Individual.
Price Data: Available for free from publisher.
Time: (30–45) minutes.
Author: Guerry M. Peavy.
Publisher: Guerry M. Peavy.
Cross References: For reviews by Joan C. Ballard and Lawrence J. Ryan, see 14:349.

[1860]

The Severe Impairment Battery.

Purpose: Designed "to assess severe dementia in the elderly."
Population: Ages 51-91.
Publication Date: 1993.
Acronym: SIB.
Scores, 7: Attention, Orientation, Language, Memory, Visual-Spatial Ability, Construction, Total.
Administration: Individual.
Price Data, 2015: £283 per complete kit including manual (16 pages), 25 scoring sheets, stimulus cards, plastic shapes, spoon, cup, and full distractor pack in bag; £69.50 per 25 score sheets; £36.50 per manual.
Time: 20 minutes.
Comments: Test takes into account specific behavioral and cognitive deficits associated with severe dementia; provides an assessment of social interaction skills abstracted from the Communicative Activities in Daily Living Scale.
Authors: J. Saxton, K. L. McGonigle, A. A. Swihart, and F. Boller.
Publisher: Pearson Assessment [England].
Cross References: For a review by Brad M. Merker and John Linck, see 17:172.

[1861]

Sex-Role Egalitarianism Scale.

Purpose: "Developed to measure attitudes toward the equality of men and women."
Population: High school to adult.
Publication Date: 1993.
Acronym: SRES.
Scores, 6: Marital Roles, Parental Roles, Employment Roles, Social-Interpersonal-Heterosexual Roles, Educational Roles, Total.

Administration: Group or individual.
Price Data, 2015: $70 per examination kit including manual on CD (1993, 58 pages), 5 Form B question-and-answer documents, and 5 profile sheets; $25 per test manual on CD; $66 per 25 Form B question-and-answer documents; $50 per 25 Form K Research Forms; $55 per 25 profile sheets; $55 per 25 Short Form BB or KK question-and-answer sheets; $65 per researcher's kit including manual on CD, one Form K question-and-answer document, and one each of Form BB and KK Short Forms.
Time: 25 minutes.
Comments: Two full forms, B and K; two abbreviated forms, BB and KK.
Authors: Lynda A. King and Daniel W. King.
Publisher: SIGMA Assessment Systems, Inc.
Cross References: See T5:2389 (1 reference); for a review by Carol Collins, see 13:285.

[1862]

Sexometer.

Purpose: Designed to measure one's sex information.
Population: Adolescents and adults.
Publication Dates: 1974–1988.
Scores: Total score only.
Administration: Group.
Manual: No manual.
Price Data, 2015: $2 per scale.
Time: [20] minutes.
Comments: Supplementary article available.
Author: Panos D. Bardis.
Publisher: Donna Bardis.
Cross References: See 8:353 (1 reference).

[1863]

Sexual Adjustment Inventory.

Purpose: "Designed to identify sexually deviate and paraphiliac behavior."
Population: People accused or convicted of sexual offenses.
Publication Date: 1991.
Acronym: SAI.
Scores: 13 scales: Test Item Truthfulness, Sex Item Truthfulness, Sexual Adjustment, Child Molest, Sexual Assault, Exhibitionism, Incest, Alcohol, Drugs, Violence, Antisocial, Distress, Judgment.
Administration: Group.
Forms, 2: Adult, Juvenile.
Price Data, 2016: $9.95 per test; volume discounts available.
Time: (35–40) minutes.
Author: Risk & Needs Assessment, Inc.
Publisher: Behavior Data Systems, Ltd.
Cross References: For reviews by Richard F. Farmer and Sheila Mehta, see 14:351.

[1864]
Sexual Violence Risk-20.
Purpose: Designed as a "method" (not a test or scale) of assessing an individual's risk for committing sexual violence.
Population: Individuals suspected to be at-risk for committing sexual violence.
Publication Dates: 1997–1998.
Acronym: SVR-20.
Scores: Not scored; ratings in five areas: Psychosocial Adjustment, Sexual Offenses, Future Plans, Other Considerations, Summary Risk Rating.
Administration: Individual.
Price Data: Available from publisher.
Time: Administration time not reported.
Comments: "Designed to assist evaluations of risk for sexual violence"; administration and coding by trained professionals only; rating done by the professional about a client/offender.
Authors: Douglas P. Boer, Stephen D. Hart, P. Randall Kropp, and Christopher D. Webster.
Publisher: Mental Health, Law, and Policy Institute.
Cross References: For reviews by Rita M. Budrionis and Paul Retzlaff, see 15:228.

[1865]
SF-36v2 Health Survey.
Purpose: Designed as a "survey of general health concepts."
Population: Ages 14 and older.
Publication Dates: 1989–2007.
Acronym: SF-36v2.
Scores: 8 scales: Physical Functioning, Role-Physical, Bodily Pain, General Health, Vitality, Social Functioning, Role-Emotional, Mental Health, plus 2 summary component scores.
Administration: Group.
Price Data: Available from publisher.
Foreign Language Editions: Translated into more than 160 languages.
Time: [5-10] minutes.
Author: John E. Ware, Jr.
Publisher: Quality Metric.
Cross References: For reviews by Ashraf Kagee and Nathaniel J. Pallone of the first version of this test, see 14:352; see also T5:2397 (1 reference).

[1866]
Shapiro Control Inventory.
Purpose: Designed to "categorize, refine, and articulate a person's state of consciousness regarding control."
Population: Ages 14–88.
Publication Date: 1994.
Acronym: SCI.
Scores, 9: General Domain (Overall Sense of Control, Positive Sense of Control, Negative Sense of Control), Modes of Control (Positive Assertive, Positive Yielding, Negative Assertive, Negative Yielding), Domain-Specific Sense of Control, Overall Desire for Control.
Administration: Group or individual.
Price Data: Available at no charge.
Time: (20–30) minutes.
Author: Deane H. Shapiro, Jr.
Publisher: Behaviordata, Inc.
Cross References: See T5:2399 (1 reference); for reviews by Wesley E. Sime and Claudia R. Wright, see 13:286.

[1867]
Shipley-2.
Purpose: Measures cognitive functioning and impairment in children and adults, including crystallized knowledge and fluid reasoning.
Population: Ages 7-89.
Publication Dates: 1939-2009.
Scores: 7 scores possible, 4 scores per profile form: Vocabulary, Abstraction, Composite A, and Impairment Index (AQ) for Composite A Form, or Vocabulary, Block Patterns, Composite B, and Impairment Index (BQ) for Composite B Form.
Administration: Group.
Price Data, 2016: $151 per kit including 20 Vocabulary AutoScore forms, 10 Abstraction AutoScore forms, 10 Block Patterns forms, and manual (1009, 148 pages); $44 per 25 AutoScore forms; $100.50 per manual; $249.50 per unlimited-use scoring CD.
Time: (20-25) minutes.
Comments: Previous edition titled Shipley Institute of Living Scale; earlier versions titled Shipley-Institute of Living Scale for Measuring Intellectual Impairment and Shipley-Hartford Retreat Scale for Measuring Intellectual Impairment.
Authors: Walter C. Shipley (all forms and manual), Christian P. Gruber (manual, Abstraction form, Vocabulary form, Composite A profile sheet, Composite B profile sheet), Thomas A. Martin (manual, Block Patterns form, Composite B profile sheet), and Amber M. Klein (manual).
Publisher: Western Psychological Services.
Cross References: For reviews by Theodore L. Hayes and Tracy Thorndike-Christ, see 18:121; for information for previous edition see T5:2402 (71 references) and T4:2453 (63 references); for a review by William L. Deaton of the Shipley Institute of Living Scale, see 11:360 (56 references); see also 9:1122 (13 references), T3:2179 (64 references), 8:677 (39 references), and T2:1380 (34 references); for a review by Aubrey J. Yates, see 7:138 (21 references); see also P:244 (38 references), 6:173 (13 references), and 5:111 (23 references); for reviews by E. J. G. Bradford, William A. Hunt, and Margaret Ives, see 3:39 (25 references).

[1868]

Shoplifting Inventory.

Purpose: "Designed to evaluate people charged or convicted of shoplifting."
Population: Shoplifting offenders.
Publication Date: 1995.
Acronym: SI.
Scores: 9 scales: Truthfulness, Entitlement, Shoplifting, Antisocial, Peer Pressure, Self-Esteem, Impulsiveness, Alcohol, Drugs.
Administration: Group.
Price Data: Available from publisher.
Time: (35) minutes.
Author: Risk & Needs Assessment, Inc.
Publisher: Behavior Data Systems, Ltd.
Cross References: For reviews by G. Gage Kingsbury and Kwong-Liem Karl Kwan, see 14:353.

[1869]

Shorr Imagery Test.

Purpose: "Designed to elicit and score the degree of conflict in the visual images projected by the subject."
Population: College students and adults.
Publication Dates: 1974–1977.
Acronym: SIT.
Scores, 6: Item scores in 5 areas (Human, Animal, Inanimate, Botanical, Others) plus Total score for Conflict.
Administration: Individual.
Price Data: Available from publisher.
Time: (15-40) minutes.
Comments: For information for Group Shorr Imagery Test, see 901.
Author: Joseph E. Shorr.
Publisher: Institute for Psycho-Imagination Therapy.

[1870]

Short Category Test, Booklet Format.

Purpose: A sensitive indicator of brain damage measuring an individual's ability to solve problems requiring careful observation, development of organizing principles, and responsiveness to feedback.
Population: Ages 20 and over.
Publication Dates: 1986–1987.
Scores: Total score only.
Subtests, 5: 1, 2, 3, 4, 5.
Administration: Individual.
Price Data, 2015: $226.50 per complete kit including 100 answer sheets, set of stimulus cards, and manual (1987, 40 pages); $147.50 per set of stimulus cards, 5 booklets (1986, 20 cards per booklet); $33.50 per 100 answer sheets; $59.50 per manual.
Time: (15–30) minutes.
Comments: Revision of the Halstead-Reitan Category Test.
Authors: Linda Wetzel and Thomas J. Boll.

Publisher: Western Psychological Services.
Cross References: See T5:2405 (1 reference); for reviews by Scott W. Brown and Hope J. Hartman, see 11:361.

[1871]

Short Employment Tests, Second Edition.

Purpose: "Measures verbal, numerical, and clerical skills."
Population: Adults.
Publication Dates: 1951–1993.
Acronym: SET.
Scores, 4: Verbal, Numerical, Clerical, Total.
Administration: Group or individual.
Forms: 2 forms of each subtest (Verbal, Numerical, Clerical Aptitude).
Price Data, 2016: $436 per starter kit, including 25 each of the Verbal, Numerical, and Clerical Aptitude test booklets, scoring key, and manual; $150 per 25 test booklets (specify version and form 1 or 2); $511 per 100 test booklets (specify version and Form 1 or 2); $150 per combination scoring key; $75 per manual.
Time: 5(10) minutes.
Comments: Distribution of Form 1 restricted to banks that are members of the American Banking Association.
Authors: George K. Bennett and Marjorie Gelink.
Publisher: Pearson.
Cross References: For reviews by Caroline Manuele-Adkins and by Bert W. Westbrook and Michael C. Hansen, see 13:287; see also T4:2456 (3 references); for reviews by Samuel Juni and Ronald Baumanis and by Leonard J. West of an earlier edition, see 9:1124 (1 reference); see also T3:2180 (1 reference); for reviews by Ronald N. Taylor and Paul W. Thayer, see 8:1037 (4 references); see also T2:2151 (6 references); for a review by Leonard W. Ferguson, see 6:1045 (9 references); for a review by P. L. Mellenbruch, see 5:854 (16 references).

[1872]

Short Parallel Assessments of Neuropsychological Status.

Purpose: Designed to assess "cognitive, perceptual and language abilities of acute/post-acute inpatients following acquired brain injury (ABI), but may also be used as a brief comprehensive assessment in outpatient clinics."
Population: Ages 18 to 74.
Publication Date: 2014.
Acronym: SPANS.
Scores, 40: 7 indices and 30 subtests: Orientation Index (Orientation, Time Estimation), Attention/Concentration Index (Digit Span Forward, Digit Span Backward, Sustained and Divided Listening–Round 1, Sustained and Divided Listening–Round 2, Counting Backwards, Monetary Calculations), Language Index (Repetition, Naming, Yes/No Questions, Following Directions, Reading, Writing Sentences, Similarities), Memory/Learning Index (Object

Recall, Figures Recall, List Learning, List Recall, List Recognition, Symbol-Word Paired-Associates), Visuo-Motor Performance Index (Object Recognition, Spatial Decision, Unusual Views, Figures Copy, Letter-Number Coding, Figures Recognition, Facial Expressions, 3-and-1 Concept Test), Efficacy Index (Sustained and Divided Listening–Round 2, Spatial Decision, Letter-Number Coding, Counting Backwards, Monetary Calculations), Conceptual Flexibility Index (Similarities, 3-and-1 Concept Test); 3 error scores: Sustained Attention Commissions, Perceptual Naming Errors, Memory Intrusions.
Administration: Individual.
Forms, 2: A, B.
Price Data, 2015: £325 per kit including manual (167 pages), 2 stimulus books (A, B), 25 of each scoring booklet (A, B), clipboard, stopwatch, and Letter-Number Coding scoring card; £85 per manual; £50 per 25 scoring booklets (A or B); £65 per stimulus book (A or B).
Time: (30-70) minutes.
Authors: Gerald Burgess.
Publisher: Hogrefe Ltd [United Kingdom].
Cross References: Reviews are scheduled for *The Twentieth Mental Measurements Yearbook*.

[1873]

Short Tests of Clerical Ability.

Purpose: Designed to measure aptitudes and abilities in tasks common to various office jobs.
Population: Applicants for office positions.
Publication Dates: 1959–1997.
Acronym: STCA.
Administration: Individual or group.
Price Data: Available from publisher.
Author: Science Research Associates.
Publisher: General Dynamics Information Technology.
  a) ARITHMETIC.
  Scores, 3: Computation, Business Arithmetic, Total.
  Time: 6 minutes.
  b) BUSINESS VOCABULARY.
  Time: 5 minutes.
  c) CHECKING.
  Time: 5 minutes.
  d) CODING.
  Time: 5 minutes.
  e) DIRECTIONS—ORAL AND WRITTEN.
  Time: 5 minutes.
  f) FILING.
  Time: 5 minutes.
  g) LANGUAGE.
  Time: 5 minutes.
Cross References: For reviews by Lorraine D. Eyde and Dean R. Malsbary, see 8:1039 (1 reference); for reviews by Philip H. Kriedt and Paul W. Thayer, see 6:1046.

[1874]

SIGMA Survey for Police Officers.

Purpose: "Designed to identify job applicants possessing the cognitive skills necessary to use sound practical judgement in police situations, and to write meaningful and credible police incident reports."
Population: Ages 18 and over.
Publication Dates: 2001–2002.
Acronym: SSPO.
Scores, 6: Incident Report Writing (Spelling, Grammar, Vocabulary, Total), Police Problem Solving, Total.
Administration: Individual or group.
Forms, 4: A, B, C, and D.
Price Data, 2015: $25 per test manual; $9 per booklet; $16-$21 (depending on volume) per report.
Time: 35 minutes.
Comments: Fax-in scoring service available through publisher; available in Canadian format and American format; publisher recommends using in conjunction with the Employee Screening Questionnaire (756).
Author: Douglas N. Jackson.
Publisher: SIGMA Assessment Systems, Inc.
Cross References: For reviews by Thomas M. Dunn and Chockalingam Viswesvaran, see 16:221.

[1875]

SIGMA Survey for Sales Professionals.

Purpose: Designed to analyze "the strengths and weaknesses of sales and sales manager job candidates on 28 dimensions of expected job performance."
Population: 18 and over.
Publication Dates: 2002–2003.
Acronym: 3SP.
Scores, 28: Technical Orientation, Creativity, Thoroughness, Risk Taking, Open Mindedness, First Impression, Interpersonal Relations, Sensitivity, Social Astuteness, Communication, Formal Presentation, Persuasiveness, Negotiation, Listening Skill, Achievement and Motivation, Self-Discipline, Flexibility, Independence, Self Esteem, Emotional Control, Dependability, Ambition, Organizational Spokesperson, Assuming Responsibility, Vision, Short-Term Planning, Strategic Planning, Productivity.
Administration: Group and individual.
Price Data, 2015: $25 per test manual; $6 per test booklet; $40-$58 (depending on volume) per report for online administration.
Time: 40 minutes.
Comments: Publisher scoring services available via fax-in scoring or online administration.
Author: Douglas N. Jackson.
Publisher: SIGMA Assessment Systems, Inc.
Cross References: For reviews by Martha E. Hennen and Stephen B. Johnson, see 16:222.

[1876]

SIGMA Survey for Security Officers.

Purpose: Designed as a "test for screening job applicants for the position of security officer."
Population: Ages 18 and over.

Publication Dates: 1996–2003.
Acronym: SSSO.
Scores, 5: Security Officer Problem Solving, Incident Report Writing Aptitude (Spelling, Grammar and Punctuation, Total), Overall Score.
Administration: Individual or group.
Parts, 2: Security Problem Solving, Incident Report Writing.
Price Data, 2015: $25 per test manual; $9 per test booklet; $16-$18 (depending on volume) per report.
Time: 30 minutes.
Comments: Fax-in scoring services available through publisher; recommended by publisher for use in conjunction with the Employee Screening Questionnaire (756). Canadian and American version available.
Author: Douglas N. Jackson.
Publisher: SIGMA Assessment Systems, Inc.
Cross References: For reviews by James T. Austin and Erich C. Fein and by David J. Pittenger, see 16:223.

[1877]
Signposts Early Assessment System.

Purpose: Designed to provide an integrated set of measures with an emphasis on literacy development focusing on prereading and reading skills.
Population: Grades K–3.5.
Publication Dates: 2000–2001.
Scores: Total score only.
Subtests: 4 components: Early Literacy Battery, Pre-DRP Tests, Performance Tasks, Informal Assessments.
Administration: Group (individual for some components).
Levels, 5: SA-1 (Grades K–K.5), SA-2 (Grades K.5–1.4), SA-3 (Grades 1.0–1.9), SA-4 (Grades 1.7–2.7), SA-5 (Grades 2.5–3.5).
Price Data, 2016: $56 per examination set including 1 test booklet of each level, administration procedures, handbook (2001, 68 pages), and norms book (2001, 31 pages); $116 per Early Literacy Battery classroom set including 25 test booklets (specify level) including administration procedures, a class record, handbook, and norms book; $91 per Pre-DRP Test classroom set including 25 test booklets (specify level) including administration procedures, a class record, handbook, and norms book; $80 per 25 Early Literacy Battery test booklets (specify level) including administration procedures and a class record sheet; $53 per 25 Pre-DRP Test booklets (specify level) including administration procedures and a class record sheet; $12 per scoring key (specify level); $26 per handbook; $22 per norms book.
Time: (110–165) minutes.
Comments: Scoring keys must be purchased separately.
Author: Touchstone Applied Science Associates, Inc.
Publisher: Questar Assessment, Inc.
Cross References: For reviews by Thomas P. Hogan and Judith A. Monsaas, see 16:224.

[1878]
Singer-Loomis Type Deployment Inventory.

Purpose: Designed to assess "personality factors that may help an individual in self-understanding and in utilizing skills, talents, and abilities, so as to better deal with interactions between oneself and the environment."
Population: High school and college and adults.
Publication Dates: 1984–1997.
Acronym: SL-TDI.
Scores: Profile of 8 scores: Introverted, Extroverted for each of 4 functions (Thinking, Feeling, Sensing, Intuition), plus Extraversion, Introversion, Judging, Perceiving.
Administration: Group.
Price Data: Available from publisher.
Time: (30–40) minutes.
Comments: Self-report type profile based on Jung's typology; available online.
Authors: June Singer, Mary Loomis, Elizabeth Kirkhart (revision), and Larry Kirkhart (revision).
Publisher: Moving Boundaries, Inc.
Cross References: For reviews by Joni R. Hays and Kevin Lanning, see 14:356; for a review by Richard B. Stuart of the earlier edition, see 10:334 (1 reference).

[1879]
Situational Attitude Scale.

Purpose: "Measures the attitudes of whites toward blacks."
Population: College and adults.
Publication Dates: c1969–1972.
Acronym: SAS.
Scores, 11: 10 situation scores, Total.
Administration: Group.
Forms, 2: A, B.
Price Data: This test is now available at no charge from the test publisher.
Time: Untimed.
Authors: William E. Sedlacek and Glenwood C. Brooks, Jr.
Publisher: William E. Sedlacek.
Cross References: See T5:2413 (1 reference) and T4:2466 (2 references); for reviews by Ralph Mason Dreger and Marvin E. Shaw, see 8:678 (1 reference); see also T2:1381 (3 references).

[1880]
Situational Leadership®.

Purpose: Designed to identify successful leaders as "those who can adapt their behavior to meet the demands of their own unique situation."
Population: Managers, leaders, administrators, supervisors, and staff.
Publication Dates: 1973–1998.
Acronym: SL.
Administration: Group.

Manual: No manual.
Price Data: Available from publisher.
Time: Administration time not reported.
Comments: Related programs Situational Leadership Simulator, Situational Leadership: Leveraging Human Performance, and Situational Leadership One-Day, also available.
Authors: Paul Hersey and Ron Campbell.
Publisher: The Center for Leadership Studies, Inc.
    a) LEADER EFFECTIVENESS AND ADAPT-ABILITY.
    Publication Dates: 1973–1998.
    Acronym: LEAD.
    Comments: Ratings of self and others.
    Forms, 2: LEAD Self, LEAD Other.
    b) READINESS STYLE MATCH.
    Publication Date: 1979.
    Acronym: RSM.
    Scores: Ratings in 4 areas: Major Objectives, Readiness, Integration of Style and Readiness, Readiness Style Match Matrix.
    Forms, 2: Staff Member Rating Form, Manager Rating Form.
    c) READINESS SCALE.
    Publication Date: 1977.
    Acronym: MS.
    Scores: 2 scores (Task Readiness, Psychological Readiness) for each of 5 major objectives or responsibilities.
    Forms, 2: Self Rating Form, Manager Rating Form.
    d) POWER PERCEPTION PROFILE.
    Publication Date: 1979–1998.
    Acronym: PPP.
    Scores, 7: Coercive, Connection, Expert, Information, Legitimate, Referent, Reward.
    Forms, 2: Perception of Self, Perception of Other.
    e) LEADERSHIP SCALE.
    Publication Date: 1980–1997.
    Acronym: LS.
    Scores: 2 scores (Total Task-Behavior, Total Relationship-Behavior) for each of 5 major objectives or responsibilities.
    Forms, 2: Staff Member Form, Manager Form.
Cross References: For reviews by Bruce J. Eberhardt and Sheldon Zedeck, see 9:1133.

[1881]
Situational Outlook Questionnaire®.

Purpose: Designed to assess "the work environment for creativity, innovation, and change within organizations and teams, and can be used for leadership development."
Population: Adult employees or members of a company, organization, or team.
Publication Dates: 1995-2007.
Acronym: SOQ.
Scores, 9: Challenge/Involvement, Freedom, Trust/Openness, Idea-Time, Playfulness/Humor, Conflict, Idea-Support, Debate, Risk-Taking.
Administration: Group.
Restricted Distribution: Qualification program required for test administrators.

Price Data: Available from publisher.
Foreign Language Editions: Research editions available in German and Portuguese.
Time: (25) minutes.
Comments: Includes analysis of narrative comments from open-ended questions; web-based assessment; in addition to computing scores for individual participants, averages for the organization are also computed for comparison purposes.
Authors: Scott G. Isaksen and Göran Ekvall, with contributions from Hans Akkermans, Glenn V. Wilson, and John P. Gaulin.
Publisher: The Creative Problem Solving Group, Inc.
Cross References: For reviews by Julia Y. Porter and John Sample, see 18:122.

[1882]
Situational Preference Inventory.

Purpose: "Designed to assess individual styles of social interaction."
Population: Grades 9-16 and adults.
Publication Dates: 1968-1973.
Acronym: SPI.
Scores, 3: Cooperational, Instrumental, Analytic.
Administration: Group.
Price Data: Available from publisher.
Time: (10-15) minutes.
Comments: Self-administered.
Author: Carl N. Edwards.
Publisher: Carl N. Edwards.
Cross References: See T2:1382 (2 references).

[1883]
Six Factor Personality Questionnaire.

Purpose: Designed as a measure of six personality dimensions or broad factors.
Population: Adults.
Publication Date: 2000.
Acronym: SFPQ.
Scores, 6: Extraversion, Agreeableness, Independence, Openness to Experience, Methodicalness, Industriousness.
Administration: Individual or group.
Price Data, 2015: $90 per examination kit including manual on CD (2000, 68 pages), 5 quick score answer sheets, 5 profile sheets, and one machine-scorable answer sheet for a Mail-in Basic Report; $25 per test manual on CD; $65 per 25 test booklets; $70 per Quick Answer Score sheets; $55 per 25 profile forms; $67–$77 (depending on volume) per 10 machine-scorable answer sheets and coupons for Mail-in Basic Report; $155 per SigmaSoft SFPQ for Windows Software installation package, includes 10 scoring coupons; $12-$20 (depending on volume) per online password.
Time: 20 minutes.
Foreign Language Edition: French booklet and online administration available.

Comments: Online administration available.
Authors: Douglas N. Jackson, Sampo V. Paunonen, and Paul F. Tremblay.
Publisher: SIGMA Assessment Systems, Inc.
Cross References: For a review by Jeffrey A. Jenkins, see 15:229.

[1884]

Sixteen Personality Factor Questionnaire, Fifth Edition.

Purpose: Designed to measure 16 personality traits that describe and predict a person's behavior in a variety of contexts.
Population: Ages 16 and over.
Publication Dates: 1949–2002.
Acronym: 16PF, 16PFQ.
Scores, 24: 16 Primary Factor Scores (Warmth, Reasoning, Emotional Stability, Dominance, Liveliness, Rule-Consciousness, Social Boldness, Sensitivity, Vigilance, Abstractedness, Privateness, Apprehension, Openness to Change, Self-Reliance, Perfectionism, Tension); 5 Global Factors (Extraversion, Anxiety, Tough-Mindedness, Independence, Self-Control); 3 Response Style Indices (Impression Management, Infrequency, Acquiescence).
Administration: Group or individual.
Price Data: Available from publisher.
Time: (35–50) minutes.
Foreign Language Editions: The 16PF Questionnaire is available in the following languages: Chinese (traditional), Czech, Danish, Dutch, English (Canada, India, U.S., U.K.), French, German, Greek, Italian, Japanese, Norwegian, Portuguese (Brazilian), Portuguese (European), Slovak, Spanish-American, Spanish (European), Swedish, Tagalog (Philippines), Turkish. Contact the publisher regarding the availability of other languages.
Comments: Computer (software and Internet) and paper-and-pencil administration, scoring, and interpretive reports available. Reports include: 16PF Interpretive Report, 16PF Profile Report, 16PF Competency Report, 16PF Comprehensive Insights Report, 16PF Profile and Manager Feedback Report, 16PF Career Development Report, 16PF Leadership Coaching Report, 16PF Management Potential Report, 16PF Teamwork Development Report, 16PF Career Success Report, 16PF Protective Services Report, 16PF Security Selection Report, 16PF Cattell Comprehensive Personality Interpretation, 16PF Karson Clinical Report.
Authors: Raymond B. Cattell, A. Karen S. Cattell, and Heather E. P. Cattell.
Publisher: Institute for Personality and Ability Testing, Inc. (IPAT).
Cross References: See T5:2417 (43 references); for reviews by Mary J. McLellan and Pamela Carrington Rotto, see 12:354 (38 references); see also T4:2470 (140

references); for reviews of an earlier edition by James N. Butcher and Marvin Zuckerman, see 9:1136 (67 references); see also T3:2208 (182 references); for reviews by Bruce M. Bloxom, Brian F. Bolton, and James A. Walsh, see 8:679 (619 references); see also T2:1383 (244 references); for reviews by Thomas J. Bouchard, Jr. and Leonard G. Rorer, see 7:139 (295 references); see also P:245 (249 references); for a review by Maurice Lorr, see 6:174 (81 references); for a review by C. J. Adcock, see 5:112 (21 references); for reviews by Charles M. Harsh, Ardie Lubin, and J. Richard Wittenborn, see 4:87 (8 references).

[1885]

16PF Adolescent Personality Questionnaire.

Purpose: Designed to "measure normal personality of adolescents, problem-solving abilities, and preferred work activities," and to identify problems in areas known to be problematic to adolescents.
Population: Ages 11–22.
Publication Date: 2001.
Acronym: APQ.
Scores, 21: 21 normal personality scales: Primary Personality Factor Scales (Warmth, Reasoning, Emotional Stability, Dominance, Liveliness, Rule-Consciousness, Social Boldness, Sensitivity, Vigilance, Abstractedness, Privateness, Apprehension, Openness to Change, Self-Reliance, Perfectionism, Tension), Global Factor Scales (Extraversion, Anxiety, Tough-Mindedness, Independence, Self-Control); plus a ranking of Work Activity Preferences (Manual, Scientific, Artistic, Helping, Sales/Management, and Procedural), Personal Discomfort (Discouragement, Worry, Poor Body Image, Overall Discomfort), "Getting in Trouble" (Anger or Aggression, Problems with Authority, Alcohol or Drugs, Overall Trouble), Context (Home or School), Coping/Managing Difficulty, Impression Management, Missing Responses, Central Responses, Predicted Grade Point Average.
Administration: Group or individual.
Price Data: Available from publisher.
Time: (54–65) minutes (untimed).
Comments: Computerized scoring and interpretive reports available (APQ Guidance Report and APQ Psychological Report); optional Life's Difficulties section provides an opportunity for the youth to indicate particular problems in areas known to be problematic for adolescents, making the APQ appropriate for screening and for introducing sensitive topics in a counseling setting.
Author: J. M. Schuerger.
Publisher: Institute for Personality and Ability Testing, Inc. (IPAT).
Cross References: For reviews by William M. Reynolds and by Susan C. Whiston and Jennifer C. Bouwkamp, see 15:230.

[1886]
16PF® Human Resource Development Report.

Purpose: Assesses an individual's management potential and style, provides insights into the individual's personality, and focuses on five management dimensions frequently identified in research on successful managers.
Population: Managerial candidates.
Publication Dates: 1982–1997.
Acronym: HRDR.
Scores, 26: 5 management dimensions: Leadership, Interaction with Others, Decision-Making Abilities, Initiative, Personal Adjustment; 16 primary factor scores; 5 global factor scores.
Administration: Group or individual.
Price Data: Available from publisher.
Time: 35–50 minutes.
Comments: Based on the Sixteen Personality Factor Questionnaire. The test publisher has indicated there is a newer edition of this test titled 16PF® Management Potential Report; description will be updated when complete materials are received.
Author: IPAT staff.
Publisher: Institute for Personality and Ability Testing, Inc. (IPAT).
Cross References: For reviews by S. Alvin Leung and Mary A. Lewis, see 11:169.

[1887]
Skills and Attributes Inventory.

Purpose: Assesses the relative importance of job-related skills and attributes for a position as well as the degree to which an individual possesses thos skills and attributes.
Population: Non-management positions.
Publication Dates: 1976–1979.
Acronym: SAI.
Scores, 13: General Functioning Intelligence, Visual Acuity, Visual and Coordination Skills, Physical Coordination, Mechanical Skills, Graphic and Clerical Skills, General Clerical Skills, Leadership Ability, Tolerance in Interpersonal Relations, Organization Identification, Conscientiousness and Reliability, Efficiency Under Stress, Solitary Work.
Administration: Individual or group.
Price Data: Available from publisher.
Time: No limit (approximately 30–45 minutes).
Author: Melany E. Baehr.
Publisher: General Dynamics Information Technology.
Cross References: For a review by Lenore W. Harmon, see 9:1137.

[1888]
Skills Assessment Module.

Purpose: To assess a student's affective, cognitive, and manipulative strengths and weaknesses in relation to vocational skills required in various training programs within a school system.
Population: Average, handicapped, and disadvantaged vocational training school students ages 14-18.
Publication Dates: 1985–2000.
Acronym: SAM.
Scores, 13: Digital Discrimination, Clerical Verbal, Motor Coordination, Clerical Numerical, Following Written Directions, Finger Dexterity, Aiming, Reading a Ruler (Measurement), Manual Dexterity, Form Perception, Spatial Perception, Color Discrimination, Following Diagrammed Instructions.
Administration: Individual in part.
Price Data, 2016: $3,195 for complete test including all subtests.
Time: (90-150) minutes.
Comments: Module includes Career Development ITEP software, Basic Skills Locater Test (198), Learning Styles Inventory (1137), Auditory Directions Screen, Voc-Ties Interest Survey, and 13 hands on performance work samples; web-based version available.
Author: Michele Rosinek.
Publisher: Piney Mountain Press.
Cross References: For reviews by Jean Powell Kirnan and Wilbur L. Layton, see 11:364.

[1889]
Skills Confidence Inventory, Revised Edition.

Purpose: Designed as part of the process of educational or career exploration to measure the confidence of career professionals in their abilities to successfully perform various work-related tasks and activities.
Population: Ages 15 and up.
Publication Dates: 1996-2004.
Scores, 6: Realistic, Investigative, Artistic, Social, Enterprising, Conventional.
Administration: Individual or group.
Price Data, 2016: $12.95 each for Strong Interest Inventory® And Skills Confidence Inventory online administration; $39 per Skills Confidence Inventory manual.
Time: (45-55) minutes.
Comments: This instrument can only be taken with the Strong Interest Inventory (1976).
Authors: Nancy E. Betz, Fred H. Borgen, and Lenore W. Harmon.
Publisher: CPP, Inc.
Cross References: For reviews by Joseph C. Ciechalski and Gypsy M. Denzine, see 18:123.

[1890]
Skills Inventory for Teams.

Purpose: To aid early intervention practitioners to "evaluate their ability to work as part of a team."
Population: Early intervention practitioners.
Publication Dates: 1978–1992.

Acronym: SIFT.

Scores, 12: Clarity of Purpose, Cohesion, Clarity of Roles, Communication, Use of Resources, Decision Making/Problem Solving, Responsibility Implementation, Conflict Resolution, View of Family Role, Evaluation, External Support, Internal Support.

Administration: Group.

Price Data, 2016: $24.95 per administration guide (1992, 66 pages) and inventory.

Time: Administration time not reported.

Comments: Previously called Skills Inventory for Teachers; self-administered inventory.

Authors: Corinne Garland, Adrienne Frank, Deana Buck, and Patti Seklemian.

Publisher: Child Development Resources.

Cross References: For reviews by Robert Johnson and E. Lea Witta, see 13:289.

[1891]

Skillscope®.

Purpose: Designed to assess managerial strengths and developmental needs from managers' and coworkers' perspectives.

Population: Supervisors and managers.

Publication Dates: 1988-2016.

Scores: 15 Skill Areas: Solves Problems, Communicates Information, Takes Action, Takes Risks/Innovates, Manages Conflict, Manages Teams, Develops Relationships, Influences Others, Open to Influence, Develops People, Knows the Job/Business, Drives for Results, Manages Time, Copes with Pressure/Demonstrates Integrity, Manages and Develops Self.

Administration: Group.

Price Data, 2016: $160 per 1-10 participants including all surveys, online status for administrators and participants, feedback report, Development Planning Guide, and access to online user's guide (2016, 48 pages) and other facilitator materials; $195 per Group Profile.

Foreign Language Editions: Available in Portuguese (Brazilian), Dutch, French, German, Italian, Latin American Spanish, Russian, Simplified Chinese, and Spanish.

Time: (20-30) minutes.

Comments: Previously titled SKILLSCOPE for Managers® and SKILLSCOPE®; new edition of manual; assessment content has not changed.

Authors: Robert E. Kaplan, John Fleenor (user's guide), Dawn Barts (user's guide), Sylvester Taylor (user's guide), and Craig Chappelow (user's guide).

Publisher: Center for Creative Leadership.

Cross References: For a review by Linda F. Wightman of SKILLSCOPE for Managers, see 12:355.

[1892]

Sleep Disorders Inventory for Students.

Purpose: Designed to "determine risk level for sleeping disorders, including bedwetting and sleepwalking."

Publication Date: 2004.

Acronym: SDIS.

Administration: Individual.

Forms: 2 forms.

Price Data, 2015: $435.65 per kit including 25 child record forms, 25 adolescent record forms, and technical manual (93 pages) with scoring and reporting on CD-ROM; $46.15 per 25 record forms (child or adolescent).

Foreign Language Edition: Record forms available in Spanish.

Time: (8-10) minutes.

Author: Marsha Luginbuehl.

Publisher: Pearson.

   a) SLEEP DISORDERS INVENTORY FOR STUDENTS—CHILDREN'S FORM.

   Population: Ages 2–10.

   Acronym: SDIS-C.

   Scores, 5: 4 Sleep Scales (Obstructive Sleep Apnea Syndrome, Periodic Limb Movement Disorder, Delayed Sleep Phase Syndrome, Excessive Daytime Sleepiness); Total Sleep Disturbance Index.

   b) SLEEP DISORDERS INVENTORY FOR STUDENTS—ADOLESCENT FORM.

   Population: Ages 11–18.

   Acronym: SDIS-A.

   Scores, 6: 5 Sleep Scales (Obstructive Sleep Apnea Syndrome, Periodic Limb Movement Disorder/Restless Legs Syndrome, Delayed Sleep Phase Syndrome, Excessive Daytime Sleepiness, Narcolepsy); Total Sleep Disturbance Index.

Cross References: For reviews by Michael Sachs and Marc A. Silva, see 19:151.

[1893]

Slingerland Screening Tests for Identifying Children with Specific Language Disability.

Purpose: "To screen from among a group of children those with potential language difficulties and those with already present specific language disabilities who are in need of special attention."

Population: Grades 1–2.5, 2.5–3.5, 3.5–4, 5–6.

Publication Dates: 1962–2005.

Subtests, 8 or 9: Copying-Chart, Copying-Page, Visual Perception-Memory, Visual Discrimination, Visual Perception-Memory with Kinesthetic Memory, Auditory Recall, Auditory Sounds, Auditory Association, Orientation (Form D only); plus individual Echolalia test.

Administration: Group (Echolalia test individually administered).

Author: Beth H. Slingerland.

Publisher: Educators Publishing Service, Inc.

   a) FORMS A, B, C, REVISED EDITION.

   Population: Grades 1–2.5, 2.5–3.5, 3.5–4.

   Publication Dates: 1962-2005.

   Scores, 13 (8 tests): Visual Copying Far Point, Visual Copying Near Point, Total, Visual Perception-Memory, Visual Discrimination, Visual Perception-Memory with Kinesthetic Memory, Auditory Recall (Letters, Numbers, Spelling), Auditory Discrimination of Sounds,

Auditory-Visual Association, Total Errors (excluding Visual Copying), Total Errors plus Self-Corrections and Poor Formations.

Price Data, 2015: $44.45 per 12 tests (A, B, or C); $26.95 per cards and charts (A, B, or C); $24.10 per teacher's manual (2005, 172 pages); quantity discounts available.

Time: 56(66) minutes in 2 or 3 sessions.

Authors: Revisions by Beth H. Slingerland and Alice S. Ansara.

1) *Form A.*
Population: Grades 1–2.5.
2) *Form B.*
Population: Grades 2.5–3.5.
3) *Form C.*
Population: Grades 3.5–4.

b) FORM D.

Population: Grades 5–6.

Publication Date: 1974.

Scores, 14 (9 tests): Visual Copying Far Point, Visual Copying Near Point, Total, Visual Perception-Memory, Visual Discrimination, Visual Perception-Memory with Kinesthetic Memory, Auditory Recall (Letters, Numbers, Spelling), Auditory Discrimination of Sounds, Auditory-Visual Association, Auditory Perception and Individual Orientation, Total Errors (excluding Visual Copying), Total Errors and Confusions.

Price Data: $33.40 per 12 tests and 12 summary sheets; $30.70 per cards and charts including directions for administration and scoring; $19.30 per teacher's manual; quantity discounts available.

Time: (110-125) minutes in 2 sessions.

Cross References: See T4:2478 (2 references); for reviews by Martin Fujiki and Elisabeth H. Wiig, see 9:1141 (4 references); see also T3:2214 (2 references); for an excerpted review by Barton B. Proger, see 8:446 (3 references); see also T2:989 (4 references); for reviews by Evelyn Deno and Joseph M. Wepman of *a*, see 7:969 (3 references).

[1894]

Slosson Articulation, Language Test with Phonology.

Purpose: Measures the communicative competence of a child by combining into a single score the assessment of articulation, phonology and language.

Population: Ages 3-0 to 5-11.

Publication Date: 1986.

Acronym: SALT-P.

Scores, 4: Consonants + Vowels/Diphthongs, Phonological Processes, Language Errors, Composite Score.

Administration: Individual.

Price Data, 2016: $126 per complete kit; $60.75 per examiner's manual (12 pages); $43 per 50 scoring forms; $51.25 per test book/picture plates.

Time: (7-10) minutes.

Author: Wilma Jean Tade.

Publisher: Slosson Educational Publications, Inc.

Cross References: For reviews by Clinton W. Bennett and Robert A. Reineke, see 12:357.

[1895]

Slosson Full-Range Intelligence Test.

Purpose: Constructed as a "quick estimate of general cognitive ability."

Population: Ages 5–21.

Publication Dates: 1988–2002.

Acronym: S-FRIT.

Scores, 8: General Cognition (Full-Range Intelligence Quotient, Rapid Cognitive Index, Best g Index), Cognitive Subdomains (Verbal Index, Abstract Index, Quantitative Index, Memory Index, Performance Index).

Administration: Individual.

Forms, 2: Item Profiles/Score Summaries Form, Brief Score Form.

Price Data, 2015: $191 per complete kit including examiner's manual (1994, 80 pages), normative/technical manual (1994, 93 pages), picture book, 50 motor response forms, 50 brief score forms, and 50 item profiles/score summaries: $35.25 per 25 forms (specify Motor response, brief score, or item profiles/score summaries); $75 per examiner's manual; $75 per normative/technical manual; $51.25 per picture book.

Time: (20–35) minutes.

Authors: Bob Algozzine, Ronald C. Eaves, Lester Mann, H. Robert Vance, and Steven W. Slosson (Brief Score Form).

Publisher: Slosson Educational Publications, Inc.

Cross References: For reviews by Gerald S. Hanna and Gerald Tindal, see 14:359.

[1896]

Slosson Intelligence Test 3rd [2002 Edition].

Purpose: Designed for use as a "quick estimate of general verbal cognitive ability."

Population: Ages 4-65 and over.

Publication Dates: 1961–2002.

Acronym: SIT-R3.

Scores: Total score only.

Administration: Individual.

Price Data, 2015: $165 per complete kit including 50 test forms, manual (1991, 45 pages), and norms tables/technical manual (1991, 39 pages); $56.50 per 50 test forms; $75 per norms tables/technical manual; $75 per manual.

Time: (10-20) minutes.

Authors: Richard L. Slosson, Charles L. Nicholson (revision), and Terry H. Hibpshman (revision).

Publisher: Slosson Educational Publications, Inc.

Cross References: See T5:2432 (33 references); for reviews by Randy W. Kamphaus and T. Steuart Watson, see 12:358 (16 references); see also T4:2482 (43 references); for reviews by Thomas Oakland and William M. Reynolds of an earlier edition , see 9:1142 (11 references); see also T3:2217 (82 references), 8:227 (62 references), and T2:524 (12 references); for reviews by Philip Himelstein and Jane V. Hunt, see 7:424 (31 references).

[1897]
Slosson Oral Reading Test—Revised.
Purpose: Designed as a "quick estimate to target word recognition levels for children and adults."
Population: Preschool–adult.
Publication Dates: 1963–2002.
Acronym: SORT-R.
Scores: Total score only.
Administration: Individual.
Price Data, 2015: $115.50 per complete kit; $75.50 per manual (1990, 38 pages); $56.50 per 50 score sheets; $27 per spiral-bound word lists; $15 per large print word lists.
Special Editions: Large print edition available for individuals with visual handicaps.
Time: (3-5) minutes.
Comments: Grade equivalent (GE) and age equivalent (AE) scores are also available.
Authors: Richard L. Slosson and Charles L. Nicholson.
Publisher: Slosson Educational Publications, Inc.
Cross References: See T5:2433 (4 references); for reviews by Steven R. Shaw and Carol E. Westby, see 12:359 (4 references); see T4:2483 (16 references), T3:2218 (15 references), T2:1688 (5 references), and 6:844.

[1898]
Slosson Test of Reading Readiness.
Purpose: "Designed to identify children who are at risk of failure in programs of formal reading instruction."
Population: Latter kindergarten-grade 1.
Publication Date: 1991.
Acronym: STRR.
Scores, 12: Visual Skills (Recognition of Capital Letters, Recognition of Lower Case Letters, Matching Capital and Lower Case Letters, Visual Discrimination-Matching Word Forms, Total), Auditory Skills (Auditory Discrimination-Rhyming Words, Auditory Discrimination and Memory—Recognition of Beginning Sounds, Total), Cognitive Skills (Sequencing, Opposites, Total), Total Inventory.
Administration: Individual.
Price Data, 2016: $121 per complete kit; $44.50 per manual (24 pages); $32 per test stimulus booklet; $47.50 per 50 scoring booklets; $14.25 per 50 letter to parent.
Time: (15) minutes.
Authors: Leslie Anne Perry and Gary J. Vitali.
Publisher: Slosson Educational Publications, Inc.
Cross References: For reviews by Gerald S. Hanna and Diane J. Sawyer, see 12:360.

[1899]
Smedley Hand Dynamometer.
Purpose: Developed to "measure the muscular torque (grip) of the hand and forearm."
Population: Ages 6–18.
Publication Dates: [1920–1953].
Scores: Total score only.
Administration: Individual.
Price Data, 2015: $395 per hand dynamometer.
Time: Administration time not reported.
Author: F. Smedley.
Publisher: Stoelting Co.
Cross References: See T2:1901 (10 references).

[1900]
Smell Identification Test™ [Revised].
Purpose: Designed to measure an individual's ability to "identify a number of odorants at the suprathreshold level."
Population: People 5 years and up with suspected olfactory dysfunction.
Publication Dates: 1981–1995.
Acronym: SIT; UPSIT.
Scores: Total score only.
Administration: Individual.
Price Data: Available from publisher.
Time: [10–15] minutes.
Comments: A 40-item forced-choice questionnaire; also known as University of Pennsylvania Smell Identification Test; for use only by individuals "professionally engaged in the scientific or medical evaluation of smell function"; related versions include the Pocket Smell Test, the Cross-Cultural Smell Identification Test, and the Picture Identification Test (equivalent to the SIT except stimuli are pictures rather than odors).
Author: Richard L. Doty.
Publisher: Sensonics, Inc.
Cross References: For a review by Ralph G. Leverett, see 14:360; see also T5:2437 (4 references).

[1901]
Smoker Complaint Scale.
Purpose: Designed to measure changes in physiological/emotional/craving states as a function of smoking cessation.
Population: Persons quitting smoking.
Publication Date: 1984.
Acronym: SCS.
Scores: Total score and item scores only.
Administration: Individual or group.
Manual: No manual.
Price Data: Instrument now available without charge from publisher.
Foreign Language Editions: Translations available in Danish, Dutch, English for Australia, German, Italian, and Norwegian.
Time: (1-5) minutes.
Comments: Self-administered; also available at www.proqolid.org.
Author: Nina G. Schneider.
Publisher: Nina G. Schneider, Ph.D.
Cross References: See T5:2440 (1 reference).

[1902]

Social Adjustment Scale—Self Report.

Purpose: Designed to assess "the ability of an individual to adapt to, and derive satisfaction from, their social roles."

Population: Age 17 and older

Publication Date: 1999.

Acronym: SAS-SR.

Scores, 7: Work, Social and Leisure Activities, Relations with Extended Family, Primary Relationship, Parenthood, Family Life, Overall Mean.

Administration: Individual or group.

Price Data, 2015: $199 per complete kit including 10 question booklets, 25 QuikScore™ forms, and user's manual; $55 per 10 question booklets; $55 per 25 Quik-Score™ forms; $104 per technical manual.

Foreign Language Editions: Available in Afrikaans, Cantonese, Czech, Danish, Dutch, Finnish, Flemish, French (European), French-Canadian, German, Greek, Hebrew, Hungarian, Italian, Japanese, Korean, Mandarin, Norwegian, Portuguese, Russian, Spanish (European), Spanish (South American), and Swedish.

Time: (15–20) minutes.

Author: Myrna Weissmann.

Publisher: Multi-Health Systems, Inc.

Cross References: For reviews by Julie A. Allison and Romeo Vitelli, see 15:232.

[1903]

Social Behavior Assessment Inventory.

Purpose: Assesses social skill levels in students.

Population: Grades K–9.

Publication Dates: 1978–1992.

Acronym: SBAI.

Scores, 30: Environmental Behaviors (Care for the Environment, Dealing with Emergencies, Lunchroom Behavior, Movement Around Environment), Interpersonal Behaviors (Accepting Authority, Coping with Conflict, Gaining Attention, Greeting Others, Helping Others, Making Conversation, Organized Play, Positive Attitude Toward Others, Playing Informally, Property: Own and Others), Self-Related Behaviors (Accepting Consequences, Ethical Behavior, Expressing Feelings, Positive Attitude Toward Self, Responsible Behavior, Self-Care), Task-Related Behaviors (Asking and Answering Questions, Attending Behavior, Classroom Discussion, Completing Tasks, Following Directions, Group Activities, Independent Work, On-Task Behavior, Performing Before Others, Quality of Work).

Administration: Individual or group.

Price Data: Available from publisher.

Time: (30–45) minutes.

Comments: Observations made by teacher or trained paraprofessional.

Authors: Thomas M. Stephens and Kevin D. Arnold.

Publisher: Universal Publishing.

Cross References: See T5:2444 (1 reference); for reviews by Kathryn A. Hess and David MacPhee, see 12:361; see also T4:2493 (1 reference); for a review by Ronald S. Drabman of an earlier edition, see 9:1148; see also T3:2226 (1 reference).

[1904]

Social Competence and Behavior Evaluation, Preschool Edition.

Purpose: "Designed to assess patterns of social competence, affective expression, and adjustment difficulties."

Population: Children aged 30 months to 76 months (2 1/2 to 6 years).

Publication Date: 1995.

Acronym: SCBE.

Scores: 8 Basic scales (Depressive-Joyful, Anxious-Secure, Angry-Tolerant, Isolated-Integrated, Aggressive-Calm, Egotistical-Prosocial, Oppositional-Cooperative, Dependent-Autonomous); 4 Summary scales (Social Competence, Internalizing Problems, Externalizing Problems, General Adaptation).

Administration: Group.

Price Data, 2016: $118 per complete kit including 25 AutoScore™ forms and manual (67 pages); $52.50 per 25 AutoScore™ forms; $68.50 per manual.

Time: (15) minutes.

Comments: Ratings by teachers or other child care professionals.

Authors: Peter J. LaFreniere and Jean E. Dumas.

Publisher: Western Psychological Services.

Cross References: For reviews by Ronald A. Madle and G. Michael Poteat, see 14:362.

[1905]

Social-Emotional Assessment/Evaluation Measure (SEAM™), Research Edition.

Purpose: Designed "for assessing and monitoring social-emotional and behavioral development in [persons] at risk for social-emotional delays or problems."

Population: Ages 2 months to 66 months.

Publication Date: 2014.

Acronym: SEAM.

Scores: 10 benchmarks: Participates in Healthy Interactions, Expresses a Range of Emotions, Regulates Social-Emotional Responses, Begins to Show Empathy for Others, Attends to and Engages with Others, Explores Hands and Feet and Surroundings (infants), Demonstrates Independence (toddlers/preschoolers), Displays a Positive Self-Image, Regulates Activity Level (infants), Regulates Attention and Activity Level (toddlers/preschoolers), Cooperates with Daily Routines and Requests, Shows a Range of Adaptive Skills.

Administration: Individual.

Levels, 3: Infant, Toddler, Preschool.

Forms, 2: SEAM, SEAM with Ages.

Price Data, 2015: $49.95 per complete kit including manual (62 pages) and CD-ROM with printable forms in English and Spanish (forms may be reproduced for clinical or educational purposes).
Foreign Language Edition: Spanish forms available.
Time: (15-30) minutes.
Comments: SEAM and SEAM with Ages have identical items; SEAM with Ages includes corresponding age ranges for the examples provided with each item.
Authors: Jane Squires, Diane Bricker, Misti Waddell, Kristin Funk, Jantina Clifford, and Robert Hoselton.
Publisher: Paul H. Brookes Publishing Co., Inc.

a) SEAM FAMILY PROFILE
Purpose: "Designed to assess caregiver strengths, concerns, and needs for additional support and resources."
Scores: 4 benchmarks: Responding to Baby's/Child's Needs, providing activities that match Baby's/Child's Developmental Level, Providing Predictable Schedules/Routines and an Appropriate Environment, Providing a Safe Home and Play Environment.
Time: (10-15) minutes.

Cross References: Reviews are scheduled for *The Twentieth Mental Measurements Yearbook*.

[1906]

Social Emotional Assets and Resilience Scales.

Purpose: Designed as "a cross-informant system for measuring the social-emotional competencies and assets of children and adolescents."
Publication Date: 2011.
Administration: Individual.
Price Data, 2015: $310 per long form/short form introductory kit, including professional manual (118 pages), 25 of each rating booklet (SEARS-C, SEARS-A, SEARS-P, and SEARS-T), 25 of each summary/profile form (SEARS-C, SEARS-A, SEARS-P English & Spanish, and SEARS-T) 25 of each short form (SEARS-C, SEARS-A, SEARS-P, and SEARS-T); $240 per long form introductory kit, including professional manual, 25 of each rating booklets (SEARS-C, SEARS-A, SEARS-P, and SEARS-T), 25 of each summary/profile form (SEARS-C, SEARS-A, SEARS-P English & Spanish, and SEARS-T); $120 per short form introductory kit, including professional manual and 25 of each short form (SEARS-C, SEARS-A, SEARS-P, and SEARS-T short forms); $130 per score reporting CD-ROM; $58 per professional manual; $40 per 25 rating booklets (SEARS-C, SEARS-A, SEARS-P, SEARS-P Spanish, or SEARS-T); $16 per 25 summary/profile forms (SEARS-C, SEARS-A, SEARS-P English & Spanish, or SEARS-T); $22 per 25 short forms (SEARS-C, SEARS-A, SEARS-P, SEARS-P Spanish, or SEARS-T short forms).
Time: (10-12) minutes.
Author: Kenneth W. Merrell.
Publisher: Psychological Assessment Resources, Inc.

a) SEARS-CHILD.
Purpose: Designed "to obtain a global assessment of a child's social-emotional assets and resilience."
Population: Ages 8-12 years.
Acronym: SEARS-C.
Scores: Total score only.
Comments: Child self-report.

b) SEARS-ADOLESCENT.
Purpose: "Designed to measure an adolescent's perception of his or her self-awareness, metacognition, intrapersonal insight, self-management, and self-direction."
Population: Ages 13-18 years.
Acronym: SEARS-A.
Scores, 5: Self-Regulation, Social Competence, Empathy, Responsibility, Total.
Comments: Adolescent self-report.

c) SEARS-TEACHER.
Population: Teachers of students ages 5-18 years.
Acronym: SEARS-T.
Scores, 4: Self-Regulation, Social Competence, Empathy, Responsibility.
Comments: Focused on school context and designed to be completed by classroom teachers or other educators who know the student well.

d) SEARS-PARENT.
Population: Parents or guardians of children ages 5-18 years.
Acronym: SEARS-P.
Scores, 3: Self-Regulation/Responsibility, Social Competence, Empathy.
Foreign Language Edition: Spanish version available.
Comments: Focused on home and community context and designed to be completed by home-based caregivers.

e) SHORT FORMS.
Acronyms: SEARS-C-SF, SEARS-A-SF, SEARS-T-SF, SEARS-P-SF.
Scores: Total score only.
Time: (2) minutes.
Comments: "Developed primarily for use in intervention outcome measurement and progress monitoring."

Cross References: For reviews by Elizabeth Bigham and Kathy J. Bohan, see 19:152.

[1907]

Social-Emotional Developmental Age Level.

Purpose: Designed as "a behavioural assessment scale that aims to establish an individual's level of social-emotional development."
Population: Children and adults with a developmental age between birth and 14 years.
Publication Date: 2015.
Acronym: SEDAL.
Scores, 19: Social Development (Social Independence, Moral Development, Impulse Control, Initiating Contact, Self-Awareness in Social Contexts, Social Assessment Skills, Social Skills, Relating to Authority, Social Aspects of Sexual Development), Emotional Development (Emotional Independence, Moral Development, Impulse Control, Self Image, Sense of Reality, Fears, Regulation of Emotions), Developmental Age.

Administration: Individual.
Price Data, 2016: £257 per kit including manual (2015, 74 pages), 25 scoring booklets, and scoring program; £47 per manual; £87 per 25 scoring booklets; £137 per scoring program.
Foreign Language Editions: Dutch and German versions available.
Time: Administration time not reported.
Authors: Joop Hoekman, Aly Miedema, Bernard Otten, and Jan Gielen.
Publisher: Hogrefe Ltd [United Kingdom].

[1908]

Social-Emotional Dimension Scale—Second Edition.

Purpose: "Designed to provide school personnel ... with a means for rating student behavior problems that may interfere with academic functioning."
Population: Ages 6.0-18.11.
Publication Dates: 1986–2004.
Acronym: SEDS-2.
Administration: Individual.
Price Data, 2015: $178 per complete kit; $56 per examiner's manual; $48 per 25 comprehensive forms; $49 per 50 screener forms; $49 per 50 screener summary forms.
Comments: Norm-referenced behavior rating scale.
Authors: Jerry B. Hutton and Timothy G. Roberts.
Publisher: PRO-ED.
  a) SCREENER FORM.
  Scores: Total score only.
  Time: (5–8) minutes.
  b) COMPREHENSIVE FORM.
  Scores, 8: Externalizing Behavior (Interpersonal Relationships, Conduct Problems, Total), Internalizing Behavior (Inappropriate Behavior, Depression, Anxiety/Inattention, Total), Overall Social-Emotional Disturbance.
  Time: (15–20) minutes.
  c) FUNCTIONAL ASSESSMENT INTERVIEW.
  Scores: Not scored.
  Time: (30) minutes.
Cross References: For a review by Mark D. Shriver, see 16:226; for a review by Jean Powell Kirnan of the earlier edition, see 11:368.

[1909]

Social-Emotional Wellbeing Survey.

Purpose: Allows "schools...to survey their students and receive a report on a wide variety of social, emotional and, behavioural outcomes of their student population."
Population: Ages 3-18.
Publication Dates: 2003-2009.
Acronym: SEWB.
Scores: Item summaries only.
Administration: Group.
Forms, 4: Teacher-Early Years (Kinder-Grade 2), 'Student-Primary (Grades 2-6), Student-Secondary (Grades 5-12), Teacher Perceptions (Grades 2-12).

Price Data, 2016: A$8.50 per paper survey form (quantity discounts available); A$550 per single ACER report service; A$800 for ACER report service on two or more forms; online survey price information available from publisher; manual (2009, 18 pages) is free to print from publisher's website.
Time: (30) minutes.
Comments: Based on surveys developed by Michael E. Bernard and published by ACER in 2003: Social and Emotional Wellbeing Survey (Student Form, Grades 2-4; Student Form, Grades 5-12; Teacher Form, Grades 2-12) and Survey of Young Children's Social and Emotional Wellbeing (Teacher Form, pre-Grade 2); publisher provides scoring and summary report; Teacher Form-Early Years completed by teacher "on behalf of student"; Student Form-Primary may be read aloud to student; Student Form-Secondary also includes "perceptions of home, school and community"; Teacher Perceptions Form (optional) completed by teacher and reflects teacher perceptions of particular student; item summaries only; data are aggregated across like subjects; 50 items per Teacher Form-Early Years, 53 items per Student Form-Primary, 94 items per Student Form-Secondary, 60 items per Teacher Perceptions Form; the client school's scores are separated by gender and year level, and are compared "against 'All Schools' results"; summary report does not provide data for individual students; "to protect student anonymity, at least five students of each gender, at each year level [per form used], must complete a survey."
Author: Australian Council for Educational Research Ltd.
Publisher: Australian Council for Educational Research Ltd. [Australia].

[1910]

Social Intelligence Profile.

Purpose: Designed to provide an "understanding of one's strengths and developmental needs" regarding social intelligence.
Population: Clients of trainers, consultants, coaches, counselors, or other human resource professionals.
Publication Date: Not dated.
Acronym: SI Profile.
Scores, 6: Situational Radar, Presence, Authenticity, Clarity, Empathy, Interaction Style.
Administration: Individual or group.
Manual: No manual.
Price Data, 2016: $495 per online certification course including lifetime license and set of user materials; $20 per 1-50 profile booklets (paper-and-pencil or online administration).
Time: (20-25) minutes.
Author: Karl Albrecht.
Publisher: Karl Albrecht International.

[1911]

Social Personality and Skills Assessment.

Purpose: Designed "to measure how well developed" a test-taker's social skills are in areas including "social awareness, communication, and conflict management."
Population: Under 17 through adult.
Publication Date: 2011.
Acronym: SPSA.
Scores, 8: Communication Skills, Body Language, Conflict Resolution Skills, Relationship Skills, Social Insight, Social Behavior, Social Comfort, Overall Score.
Administration: Individual.
Price Data: Available from publisher.
Time: (30) minutes.
Comments: Self-administered online assessment. The test publisher provides clients with information about the methods and theoretical basis used in the development of the test as well as benchmarks for relevant industries and racial/ethnic group comparison data.
Author: PsychTests AIM, Inc.
Publisher: PsychTests AIM, Inc. [Canada].
Cross References: For a review by Kenneth S. Shultz, see 19:153.

[1912]

Social Phobia and Anxiety Inventory.

Purpose: Constructed for assessment of the "somatic, cognitive and behavioral aspects of social phobia."
Population: Ages 14 and older.
Publication Date: 1996.
Acronym: SPAI.
Scores, 3: Social Phobia, Agoraphobia, Difference.
Administration: Individual or group.
Price Data, 2015: $120 per complete kit including manual (42 pages) and 25 QuikScore™ forms; $55 per 25 QuikScore™ forms; $81 per manual.
Time: (15) minutes.
Comments: Self-report.
Authors: Samuel M. Turner, Deborah C. Beidel, and Constance V. Dancu.
Publisher: Multi-Health Systems, Inc.
Cross References: For reviews by George Engelhard, Jr. and Delores D. Walcott, see 14:363.

[1913]

Social Phobia & Anxiety Inventory for Children.

Purpose: "Assesses the frequency and range of social fears and anxiety in children and adolescents."
Population: Ages 8–14.
Publication Date: 1998.
Acronym: SPAI-C.
Scores: Total score only.
Administration: Group or individual.

Price Data, 2015: $116 per complete kit including manual and 25 QuikScore™ forms; $55 per 25 QuikScore™ forms; $55 per 25 Spanish QuikScore™ forms.
Time: (20–30) minutes.
Comments: Self-report; "has been translated into several languages."
Authors: Deborah C. Beidel, Samuel M. Turner, and Tracy L. Morris.
Publisher: Multi-Health Systems, Inc.
Cross References: For reviews by Sarah J. Allen and Loraine J. Spenciner, see 15:233.

[1914]

The Social Problem-Solving Inventory for Adolescents.

Purpose: Designed to "measure self-reported covert and overt social problem solving behaviors in personal as well as social contexts."
Population: Grades 6-12, college.
Publication Date: 2003.
Acronym: SPSI-A.
Scores, 13: Automatic Process, Problem Orientation (Cognition, Emotion, Behavior), Problem-Solving Skills (Problem Identification, Alternative Generation, Consequence Prediction, Implementation, Evaluation, Reorganization), Total Score.
Administration: Group.
Forms, 2: Long, Short.
Price Data, 2015: $6 per reproducible Long & Short versions; $50 per manual (2003, 114 pages, includes English Long & Short versions); contact publisher for electronic scoring and interpretation pricing.
Foreign Language Editions: Long and Short versions available in Spanish, French, Romanian, Hungarian, Chinese Republic, Portuguese, Thai, Pakistani, and Persian.
Time: Administration time not reported.
Authors: Marianne Frauenknecht and David R. Black.
Publisher: Creative Solutions Press LLC.
Cross References: For reviews by Stephanie Stein and Claudia R. Wright, see 18:124.

[1915]

Social Problem-Solving Inventory—Revised.

Purpose: Designed to measure people's "ability to resolve problems of everyday living."
Population: Ages 13 and over.
Publication Dates: 1990–2002.
Acronym: SPSI-R.
Administration: Individual or group.
Price Data, 2015: $179 per complete kit including manual (2002, 100 pages), 25 SPSI-R:L (long) forms, and 25 SPSI-R:S (short) forms; $81 per technical manual; $55 per 25 QuikScore™ forms (specify long or short forms).

Foreign Language Editions: Also available in French-Canadian, German, Russian, Spanish, and Turkish upon special request.

Authors: Thomas J. D'Zurilla, Arthur M. Nezu, and Albert Maydeu-Olivares.

Publisher: Multi-Health Systems, Inc.

a) LONG VERSION.

Acronym: SPSI-R: L.

Scores, 10: Positive Problem Orientation, Negative Problem Orientation, Rational Problem Solving (Problem Definition and Formulation, Generation of Alternative Solutions, Decision Making, Solution Implementation and Verification), Impulsivity/Carelessness Style, Avoidance Style and Total.

Time: (15–20) minutes.

b) SHORT VERSION.

Acronym: SPSI-R: S.

Scores, 5: Positive Problem Orientation, Negative Problem Orientation, Rational Problem Solving, Impulsivity/Carelessness Style, Avoidance Style.

Time: (10) minutes.

Cross References: For reviews by Pam Lindsey and Gretchen Owens, see 16:227.

[1916]

Social Responsiveness Scale, Second Edition.

Purpose: Designed as a "measure of symptoms associated with autism."

Population: Ages 2-6 to adult.

Publication Dates: 2005-2012.

Acronym: SRS-2.

Scores, 7: Social Communication and Interaction, Restricted Interests and Repetitive Behavior, Social Awareness, Social Cognition, Social Communication, Social Motivation, Total.

Administration: Individual.

Forms, 4: Preschool, School-Age, Adult, Adult Self-Report.

Price Data, 2016: $272.50 per hand-scored kit, including 25 School-Age AutoScore forms, 25 Preschool AutoScore forms, 25 Adult AutoScore forms, 25 Adult Self-Report AutoScore forms, and manual (2012, 117 pages); $386 per software kit, including all of the above plus unlimited-use scoring CD; $52.50 per 25 AutoScore forms (Preschool, School-Age, Adult, or Adult Self-Report); $147.50 per unlimited-use scoring CD; $93 per manual.

Time: (15-20) minutes.

Authors: John N. Constantino and Christian P. Gruber.

Publisher: Western Psychological Services.

Cross References: For reviews by Kathryn E. Hoff and Karla J. Doepke and by Georgette Yetter, see 19:154; for reviews by Francine Conway and John J. Venn of an earlier edition, see 17:173.

[1917]

Social Reticence Scale.

Purpose: To assess an individual's shyness.

Population: High school and college and adults.

Publication Date: 1986.

Acronym: SRTS.

Scores: Total score only.

Administration: Individual or group.

Price Data: Available from publisher.

Time: (5-10) minutes.

Authors: Warren H. Jones and Stephen Briggs.

Publisher: Mind Garden, Inc.

Cross References: See T4:2499 (1 reference); for reviews by Owen Scott, III and William K. Wilkinson, see 11:370 (1 reference).

[1918]

Social Skills Improvement System Rating Scales.

Purpose: "Assists professionals in screening and classifying students suspected of having significant social skills deficits."

Population: Ages 3-18 years.

Publication Dates: 1990-2008.

Acronym: SSIS Rating Scales.

Scores, 51: 2 scale scores with 7 and 5 subscales, respectively, per teacher, parent, and student rater: Social Skills (Communication, Cooperation, Assertion, Responsibility, Empathy, Engagement, Self-Control) and Problem Behaviors (Externalizing, Bullying, Hyperactivity/Inattention, Internalizing, Autism Spectrum [not included on Student forms]), 1 Academic Competence Scale score [Teacher form only], and 3 Validity Indexes per rater (F Index, Response Pattern Index, Response Consistency Index).

Administration: Group.

Forms, 4: Teacher, Parent, Student (ages 8-12), Student (ages 13-18).

Price Data, 2015: $271.50 per English Hand-Scored Starter Set including manual (2008, 227 pages) and 25 of each rating form; $356.25 per English/Spanish Hand-Scored Starter Set including manual and 25 of each rating form.

Foreign Language Edition: Parent and student forms available in Spanish.

Time: (15-20) minutes.

Comments: Student form not administered for children age 7 and younger; revision of Social Skills Rating System (T7:2375); SSIS Rating Scales are part of larger Social Skills Improvement System, which includes SSIS Performance Screening Guide, SSIS Classwide Intervention Program, and SSIS Intervention Guide; hand-scored or computer-entry forms available for all Rating Scales; Parent and Student forms available as audio recordings; optional ASSIST Scoring and Reporting System Software available (computer-entry or scanning version).

Authors: Frank M. Gresham and Stephen N. Elliott.

Publisher: Pearson.

Cross References: For reviews by Beth Doll and Kristin Jones and by Jeanette Lee-Farmer and Joyce

Meikamp, see 18:125; for information regarding the Social Skills Rating System, see T5:2452 (24 references); for reviews by Kathryn M. Benes and Michael Furlong and by Mitchell Karno of the Social Skills Rating System, see 12:362 (10 references); see also T4:2502 (4 references).

[1919]
Social Skills Inventory [Second Edition Manual].

Purpose: "Designed to measure the possession of basic emotional and social communication skills."
Population: Ages 14 and over reading at or above the eighth grade level.
Publication Dates: 1989-2003.
Acronym: SSI.
Scores, 7: Emotional Expressivity, Emotional Sensitivity, Emotional Control, Social Expressivity, Social Sensitivity, Social Control, Total.
Administration: Individual or group.
Forms, 2: Full-length, Brief SSI.
Price Data, 2016: $50 per PDF manual (2003, 44 pages) including review-only copy of form; $2 per Remote Online Survey License or License to Reproduce (minimum 50).
Time: (30–45) minutes.
Comments: Test booklet title is Self-Description Inventory; self-administered.
Authors: Ronald E. Riggio (test and manual) and Dana R. Carney (manual).
Publisher: Mind Garden, Inc.
Cross References: See T5:2451 (4 references) and T4:2501 (4 references); for reviews by Judith C. Conger and Susan M. Sheridan of an earlier version titled Social Skills Inventory, Research Edition, see 11:371 (3 references).

[1920]
Social Styles Analysis.

Purpose: Constructed to identify a person's social style of presentation and interaction.
Population: Adults.
Publication Date: 1989.
Scores: 4 style categories: Analytical, Driver, Amiable, Expressive, 1 Versatility score.
Administration: Group.
Forms, 2: Self, Other.
Price Data: Available from publisher.
Foreign Language Editions: Test is available in over 40 languages. Contact publisher for a detailed list.
Time: Administration time not reported.
Comments: No manual; includes User Feedback booklet.
Author: Wilson Learning Corporation.
Publisher: Wilson Learning Worldwide, Inc.
Cross References: For a review by C. Dale Carpenter, see 11:372.

[1921]
Socio-Sexual Knowledge and Attitudes Assessment Tool—Revised.

Purpose: Designed to assess sexual knowledge and attitudes of individuals with developmental disabilities.
Population: Developmentally disabled adults (ages 16-71), can be used with other adults.
Publication Dates: 1976–2003.
Acronym: SSKAAT-R.
Scores, 8: Anatomy, Women's Bodies and Women's Knowledge of Men, Men's Bodies and Men's Knowledge of Women, Intimacy, Pregnancy/Childbirth and Child Rearing, Birth Control and STDs, Sexual Boundaries, Total.
Administration: Individual.
Price Data, 2015: $295 per complete kit including easel, stimulus cards, 20 record forms, and manual (2003, 47 pages); $55 per 20 record forms; $75 per training video (DVD format); $40 per manual.
Time: Untimed.
Authors: Dorothy Griffiths and Yona Lunsky.
Publisher: Stoelting Co.
Cross References: For a review by Mary M. Clare, see 16:229; for a review by Edward S. Herold of an earlier edition, see 9:1152; see also T3:2237 (1 reference).

[1922]
SON-R 6-40 Non-Verbal Intelligence Test.

Purpose: Designed as a measure of intelligence that can be administered without the use of written or spoken language.
Population: Ages 6 to 40 years.
Publication Dates: 1939-2014.
Acronym: SON-R 6-40.
Scores, 5: Analogies, Mosaics, Categories, Patterns, IQ.
Administration: Individual.
Price Data, 2016: £1,024 per kit including 3 manuals (Research Report, Administration Guidelines, and Norm Tables), booklets for Patterns subtest, scoring forms, and CD with scoring program; £77 per manual set including Research Report (2014, 182 pages), Administration Guidelines (2014, 36 pages), and Norm Tables (2014, 51 pages); £47 per 40 record forms; £110 per 40 Patterns booklets; £68 per Research Report manual; £53 per Administration Guidelines manual; £53 per Norm Tables manual; £227 per scoring program CD.
Foreign Language Editions: Available in German, French, Spanish, Dutch, Czech, Danish/Norwegian, and Italian.
Time: (60) minutes.
Comments: Revised version of the SON-R 51/2-17; "fourth revision of the SON test for older children ... [and] the first SON test that is standardized for adults"; normative data collected in the Netherlands and Germany.
Authors: Jan T. Snijders and Nan Snijders-Oomen (original test); Peter Tellegen and Jacob A. Laros.

Publisher: Hogrefe Ltd [United Kingdom].

Cross References: See T5:2441 (2 references) and T4:2491 (2 references); see also T3:2221 (1 reference) and T2:512 (5 references); for a review by J. S. Lawes of the 1958 edition titled S.O.N. Snijders-Oomen Non-Verbal Intelligence Scale, see 6:529 (2 references).

[1923]

SON-R 2.5-7 Non-Verbal Intelligence Test.

Purpose: Developed as an untimed, nonverbal test of intelligence in children.

Population: Dutch, German, French, Czech, Slovak children ages 2-6 to 7-0.

Publication Dates: 1939–2009.

Acronym: SON-R 2.5-7.

Scores, 6: Sorting, Mosaic, Combination, Memory, Copying, Total.

Administration: Individual.

Price Data: Available from publisher.

Time: (45–50) minutes.

Authors: J. T. Snijders and N. Snijders-Oomen (original test); P. J. Tellegen, M. Winkel, and J. A. Laros.

Publisher: Hogrefe Ltd [United Kingdom].

Cross References: See T5:2441 (2 references) and T4:2491 (2 references); for reviews by Douglas K. Detterman and Timothy Z. Keith of an earlier edition titled Snijders-Oomen Non-Verbal Intelligence Scale For Young Children, see 9:1146; see also T3:2221 (1 reference) and T2:512 (5 references); for a review by J. S. Lawes of the 1958 edition, see 6:529 (2 references).

[1924]

Sources of Stress Scale [2006 Revision].

Purpose: Designed as "an instrument to identify origins of perceived and current anxiety, to quantify the intensity of such stresses, and to determine the pattern of such perceptions for predictions and subsequent interventions."

Population: High school and adults.

Publication Dates: 1986-2006.

Acronym: SOSS.

Administration: Group.

Price Data: Available from publisher.

Time: [5-15] minutes per scale.

Comments: Self-rating scale.

Authors: Louise M. Soares and Anthony T. Soares.

Publisher: Soares Institute of Neuroscience and Education.

a) CORPORATE EXECUTIVE FORM.
Scores: 12 categories: Daily Issues, Professional Issues, Internal Personnel, Outside Influence, Changes, Finances/Money, The Future, Health, My Personal Life, Myself, Personal Relationships, Time Management.
b) GRADUATE STUDENT FORM.
Scores: 12 categories: Campus Life, Academic Activities, Field Experiences, College Personnel, plus last 8 categories from *a* above.

c) CORPORATE EXECUTIVE FORM.
Scores: 12 categories: Daily Issues, Professional Issues, Internal Personnel, Outside Influence, Changes, Finances/Money, The Future, Health, My Personal Life, Myself, Personal Relationships, Time Management.
d) HIGH SCHOOL FORM.
Scores: 12 categories: Extracurricular Activities, Academic Activities, Life at School, High School, plus last 8 categories from *a* above.
e) NURSING FORM.
Scores: 12 categories: Same as *a* above.
f) PARENT FORM.
Scores: 12 categories: Children, Family Issues, Spouse/Partner, Work/Job/Occupation, plus last 8 categories from *a* above.
g) POLITICIAN FORM.
Scores: 12 categories: Same as *a* above.
h) SCHOOL ADMINISTRATOR FORM.
Scores: 12 categories: Instructional Leadership, Organizational Issues, Legal & Political Issues, Resource Allocation, plus last 8 categories from *a* above.
i) SENIOR CITIZEN FORM.
Scores: 12 categories: Same as *f* above but including Quality of Life Issues and excluding Work/Job/Occupation.
j) TEACHER FORM.
Scores: 12 categories: Classroom Issues, Professional Issues, School Issues, plus last 9 categories from *a* above.
k) YOUNG ADULTS FORM.
Scores: 12 categories: Same as *f* above.

Cross References: For reviews by Deborah Bandalos and by Jerrell C. Cassady and Molly M. Jameson, see 17:174; for reviews by JoAnn Murphey and Wesley E. Sime of an earlier edition, see 15:235.

[1925]

The Southern California Ordinal Scales of Development.

Purpose: To provide "differential assessment of educational needs and abilities."

Population: Multihandicapped, developmentally delayed, and learning disabled children.

Publication Dates: 1977–1985.

Acronym: SCOSD.

Scores: 6 scales: Cognition, Communication, Social-Affective Behavior, Practical Abilities, Fine Motor Abilities, Gross Motor Abilities.

Administration: Individual.

Price Data, 2016: $250 per complete instrument.

Time: (60–120) minutes per scale.

Comments: A Piagetian-based assessment system.

Authors: Donald I. Ashurst, Elaine Bamberg, Julika Barrett, Ann Bisno, Artice Burke, David C. Chambers, Jean Fentiman, Ronald Kadish, Mary Lou Mitchell, Lambert Neeley, Todd Thorne, and Doris Wents.

Publisher: Zilprint.

Cross References: See T5:2459 (1 reference); for reviews by Cameron J. Camp and Arlene C. Rosenthal, see 10:338.

[1926]

Space Relations (Paper Puzzles).

Purpose: Developed as an assessment of mechanical aptitude.
Population: Ages 17 and over.
Publication Dates: 1984–1996.
Scores: Total score only.
Administration: Group.
Price Data: Available from publisher.
Time: (9) minutes.
Authors: L. L. Thurstone and T. E. Jeffrey.
Publisher: General Dynamics Information Technology.
Cross References: For reviews by Phillip L. Ackerman and Mark A. Albanese, see 15:236.

[1927]

Space Thinking (Flags).

Purpose: To measure the ability to visualize a stable figure, drawing or diagram when it is moved into different positions.
Population: Industrial employees.
Publication Dates: 1959–1984.
Scores: Total score only.
Administration: Individual or group.
Price Data: Available from publisher.
Time: 5 minutes.
Authors: L. L. Thurstone and T. E. Jeffrey.
Publisher: General Dynamics Information Technology.
Cross References: See T4:2515 (1 reference), T3:898 (1 reference), and T2:2245 (1 reference); for a review by I. MacFarlane Smith, see 6:1086.

[1928]

Spanish Assessment of Basic Education, Second Edition.

Purpose: "Designed to measure achievement in the basic skills ... with students for whom Spanish is the language of instruction."
Population: Grades 1.0–1.9, 1.6–2.9, 2.6–3.9, 3.6–4.9, 4.6–6.9, 6.6–8.9.
Publication Dates: 1991–1994.
Acronym: SABE/2.
Administration: Group.
Price Data, 2015: $28.25 per 35 practice tests (select level); $69.30 or $74.15 per 100 student diagnostic profiles (depending on level); $28.25 per 35 parent reports (select level); $3.15 per class record sheet; $27.10 per examiner's manual (1991, 41–57 pages) (select level); $31.80 per user's guide (1991, 64 pages); $36.50 per technical report (1994, 43 pages); $27.10 per norms book (1994, 159 pages); scoring service available from publisher.
Author: CTB Macmillan/McGraw-Hill.
Publisher: DRC.

a) LEVEL 1.
Population: Grades 1.0–1.9.
Scores, 11: Word Attack, Vocabulary, Reading Comprehension, Mechanics, Expression, Mathematics Computation, Mathematics Concepts and Applications, Total Reading, Total Mathematics, Total Language, Total Battery.
Price Data: $250.75 per 35 scannable test books.
Time: (211) minutes.
b) LEVEL 2.
Population: Grades 1.6–2.9.
Scores, 12: Word Attack, Vocabulary, Reading Comprehension, Mechanics, Expression, Mathematics Computation, Mathematics Concepts and Applications, Spelling, Total Reading, Total Mathematics, Total Language, Total Battery.
Price Data: $268.25 per 35 scannable test books.
Time: (219) minutes.
c) LEVEL 3.
Population: Grades 2.6–3.9.
Scores: Same as *b* above.
Price Data: Same as *b* above.
Time: (255) minutes.
d) LEVEL 4.
Population: Grades 3.6–4.9.
Scores, 12: Vocabulary, Reading Comprehension, Spelling, Mechanics, Expression, Mathematics Computation, Mathematics Concepts and Applications, Study Skills, Total Reading, Total Mathematics, Total Language, Total Battery.
Price Data: $210.75 per 35 reusable test books; $80.05 per 50 answer sheets (for CompuScan® or handscoring); $84.75 per set of 3 handscoring stencils.
Time: (249) minutes.
e) LEVEL 5.
Population: Grades 4.6–6.9.
Scores: Same as *d* above.
Price Data: Same as *d* above.
Time: (260) minutes.
f) LEVEL 6.
Population: Grades 6.6–8.9.
Scores: Same as *d* above.
Price Data: Same as *d* above.
Time: (259) minutes.
Cross References: For reviews by Maria Prendes Lintel and Emelia C. Lopez, see 13:291.

[1929]

Spanish/English Reading Comprehension Test [Revised].

Purpose: Designed to "determine the degrees of bilingualism."
Population: Grades 1–6.
Publication Dates: 1974–1993.
Scores: Total score and grade level equivalents.
Administration: Group or individual.
Forms, 2: English, Spanish.
Price Data, 2015: $20 per packet including manual (1993, 42 pages) and 1 English and 1 Spanish rating/answer sheet (permission to copy answer sheets is included).
Time: (30) minutes.

Comments: Spanish Reading based on Mexican curriculum materials; English Reading based on U.S.A. curriculum materials; English Reading Comprehension Test is translated from the Spanish version; pretesting and posttesting used.

Author: Steve Moreno.

Publisher: Moreno Educational Co.

Cross References: For reviews by Jorge E. Gonzalez and Craig S. Shwery and by Salvador Hector Ochoa, see 15:237; for reviews by Esteban L. Olmedo and David T. Sanchez, see 9:1161.

[1930]

Spanish Reading Inventory, Second Edition.

Purpose: Designed "to help teachers and other professionals determine a student's reading proficiency in Spanish."

Population: Beginning readers through students in Grade 8.

Publication Dates: 1997-2010.

Scores, 5: Word Recognition in Isolation, Word Recognition in Context, Comprehension, Listening Level, Oral Reading Rate.

Administration: Individual.

Forms, 2: A, B.

Price Data, 2015: $54.55 per printed manual (2010, 164 pages) including forms; $45.64 per digital manual.

Time: Administration time not reported.

Comments: Test administrator "must be biliterate Spanish-English"; "A major function of the Spanish Reading Inventory is to identify a student's three reading levels: independent, instructional, and frustration."

Authors: Jerry L. Johns and Mayra C. Daniel.

Publisher: Kendall/Hunt Publishing Company.

Cross References: Reviews are scheduled for *The Twentieth Mental Measurements Yearbook*. For a review by Salvador Hector Ochoa of the original edition, see 16:230.

[1931]

Spanish Substance Abuse Subtle Screening Inventory (The).

Purpose: Designed as a screening tool to help "identify individuals who have a high probability of having a substance use disorder, i.e., substance abuse and substance dependence."

Population: Spanish-speaking adults ages 18 and older.

Publication Date: 2002.

Acronym: Spanish SASSI.

Scores: 10 scales: Face Valid Alcohol, Face Valid Other Drugs, Symptoms, Obvious Attributes, Subtle Attributes, Defensiveness, Supplemental Addiction Measure, False Positive Check, False Negative Check, Secondary Classification Scale.

Administration: Individual or group.

Price Data, 2015: $60 per small starter kit including 25 paper tests and profiles, scoring key, sample scored

test, administration and scoring instructions (21 pages), development and validation of the Spanish SASSI booklet (12 pages), and an English translation of the test; $10 per scoring key; $20 per audio CD; $55 per 25 paper tests.

Time: [15] minutes.

Comments: Information in administration and scoring instructions and development/validation booklet is presented in both English and Spanish.

Authors: Linda E. Lazowski, Michael W. Boye, Glenn A. Miller, and Franklin G. Miller.

Publisher: The SASSI Institute.

Cross References: Reviews are scheduled for *The Twentieth Mental Measurements Yearbook*.

[1932]

SPAR Spelling and Reading Tests, Third Edition.

Purpose: Designed as a "group test of literacy."

Population: Ages 7-0 to 12-11 years.

Publication Dates: 1976–1998.

Acronym: SPAR.

Scores, 2: Reading Total Score, Spelling Total Score.

Administration: Group.

Parts, 2: Reading Test, Spelling Test.

Price Data, 2016: £16.50 per 20 Form A or Form B; £28 per manual (1976, 32 pages) including photocopiable version of spelling test.

Time: 13 minutes for Spelling Test; (20–25) minutes for Reading Test.

Comments: Reading Test is available in parallel Forms (A and B); Spelling Test is created from three parallel banks of items found in the manual.

Author: Dennis Young.

Publisher: Hodder Education [United Kingdom].

Cross References: For reviews by Timothy Z. Keith and Brenda A. Stevens, see 14:365; see also T5:2467 (1 reference); for reviews by Cleborne D. Maddux and William R. Merz, Sr. of the second edition, see 12:365 (2 references); see also T4:2520 (3 references); for reviews by J. Douglas Ayers of earlier editions of the Spelling Test and the Reading Test, see 8:76 and 8:742.

[1933]

Spatial Reasoning.

Purpose: Designed to assess "a pupil's ability to manipulate shapes and patterns."

Population: Ages 5.4–15.5.

Publication Date: 2002.

Scores: Total score only.

Administration: Group.

Levels, 4: Age 6 and 7; Age 8 and 9; Age 10 and 11; Ages 12–14.

Price Data: Available from publisher.

Time: 20(35–40) minutes for Age 6 and 7; 27(40–45) minutes for Age 8 and 9; 28(45) minutes for Age 10 and 11; 33(45–50) minutes for Ages 12–14.

Comments: Designed to complement the publisher's Verbal (2196) and Non-Verbal (1384) Reasoning tests.
Authors: Pauline Smith and Thomas R. Lord.
Publisher: GL Assessment [England].
Cross References: For reviews by Kathy Bohan and Beth Doll, see 16:231.

[1934]

Speaking Proficiency English Assessment Kit.

Purpose: "To assess the English speaking proficiency of people who are not native speakers of English."
Population: Nonnative speakers of English.
Publication Date: 1996.
Acronym: SPEAK.
Scores: Total score only.
Administration: Individual or group.
Price Data: Available from publisher.
Time: (20) minutes.
Comments: Produced by the Test of English as a Foreign Language Program; provides a measure of an individual's speaking ability at the intermediate to advanced levels for English language programs, international teaching assistant training programs, and businesses.
Author: Educational Testing Service.
Publisher: Educational Testing Service.

[1935]

Speech and Language Evaluation Scale.

Purpose: "Designed for in-school screening and referral of students with speech and language problems."
Population: Ages 4.5-18.
Publication Dates: 1989-1990.
Acronym: SLES.
Scores, 6: Speech (Articulation, Voice, Fluency), Language (Form, Content, Pragmatics).
Administration: Individual.
Price Data: Available from publisher.
Time: (15-20) minutes.
Comments: Ratings by teachers. The test publisher has indicated there is a newer edition of this test; description will be updated when complete test materials are received.
Authors: Diane R. Fressola, Sandra Cipponeri-Hoerchler, Jacquelyn S. Hagan, Steven B. McDannold, Jacqueline Meyer (manual), and Stephen B. McCarney (technical manual).
Publisher: Hawthorne Educational Services, Inc.
Cross References: For reviews by Katharine G. Butler and Penelope K. Hall, see 12:367.

[1936]

Speech-Ease Screening Inventory (K–1).

Purpose: "Designed to screen the articulation, language development," and auditory comprehension of kindergartners and first-graders.
Population: Grades K–1.

Publication Date: 1985.
Scores: Item scores only in 5 areas (Articulation, Language Association, Auditory Recall, Vocabulary, Basic Concepts) and in 4 optional areas (Auditory, Similarities and Differences, Language Sample, Linguistic Relationships) plus 5 observational ratings (Voice Quality, Fluency, Syntax, Oral-Peripheral, Hearing).
Administration: Individual.
Price Data, 2015: $138 per complete kit; $40 per 100 screening forms; $33 per 50 summary sheets (specify kindergarten or first grade); $49 per manual (32 pages).
Time: (7-10) minutes.
Authors: Teryl Pigott, Jane Barry, Barbara Hughes, Debra Eastin, Patricia Titus, Harriett Stensel, Kathleen Metcalf, and Belinda Porter.
Publisher: PRO-ED.
Cross References: For reviews by Kris L. Baack and Eleanor E. Sanford, see 12:368.

[1937]

Speech Perception Instructional Curriculum and Evaluation.

Purpose: "Designed to provide a guide for developing listening skills in severely and profoundly deaf children."
Population: Hearing-impaired individuals ages 3–12.
Publication Date: 1995.
Acronym: SPICE.
Scores: Rates total of 16 goals within 4 categories: Detection (Detects Speech, Indicates Onset and Termination of Speech), Suprasegmental Perception (Discriminates between 2 Stimuli Differing in Duration/Stress/and/or Intonation, Identifies Among 3 Stimuli Differing in Duration/Stress/and/or Intonation, Identifies Among 4 Stimuli Differing in Duration/Stress/and/or Intonation, Differentiates Stimuli With Similar Duration but Differing in Stress and/or Intonation; Identifies Among Sentences Differing Only in Duration of Key Words, Vowels and Consonants (Identifies Among Six Sounds, Identifies Words of Similar Duration and Differing in Vowels and/or Consonants, Identifies Monosyllables With the Same Consonants and Differing Vowels; Engages in Discussion About a Familiar Topic, Engages in Connected Discourse Tracking), Connected Speech (Identifies Key Words in the Context of Sentences, Practiced Sentences, Converses Using Picture Context, Engaged in Discussion About a Familiar Topic, Engages in Connected Discourse Tracking.
Administration: Individual.
Price Data, 2015: $375 per complete kit including manual (221 pages), rating forms, box of 16 toys for listening activities, 374 illustrated word and sentence cards, auditory training screen; $20 additional auditory training screen.
Time: Administration time not reported.
Comments: Informally documents present auditory skill level, helps identify instructional objectives; instruc-

tional videotape contains 18 teaching segments; can be adapted for individuals over age 12 through adult.
Authors: Jean S. Moog, Julia J. Biedenstein, and Lisa S. Davidson.
Publisher: CID – Central Institute for the Deaf.

[1938]

The Speed and Capacity of Language Processing Test.

Purpose: "Designed to provide a wholistic measure of the efficacy of language comprehension."
Population: Ages 16–65.
Publication Date: 1992.
Acronym: SCOLP.
Scores, 2: The Speed of Comprehension Test, The Spot-the-Word Test.
Administration: Individual.
Price Data, 2015: £135.50 per complete kit including manual (16 pages), 3 acetates, and 6 packs of 25 scoring sheets; £26.50 per 25 scoring sheets (specify Speed of Comprehension Test A, Speed of Comprehension Test B, Speed of Comprehension Test C, Speed of Comprehension Test D, Spot-the-Word Vocabulary Test A, or Spot-the-Word Vocabulary Test B).
Time: Untimed.
Comments: Each subtest comes with different versions for the purpose of retesting.
Authors: Alan Baddeley, Hazel Emslie, and Ian Nimmo-Smith.
Publisher: Pearson Assessment [England].
Cross References: For a review by Kay B. Stevens and J. Randall Price, see 17:175.

[1939]

Spelling Performance Evaluation for Language and Literacy, Second Edition.

Purpose: Designed to identify language knowledge deficits based on analysis of "a student's patterns of misspelling."
Population: Grades 2-12 and adults.
Publication Dates: 2002-2006.
Acronym: SPELL-2.
Scores, 5: Phonological Awareness, Orthographic Knowledge, Morphological Knowledge, Semantic Relationships, Mental Orthographic Images.
Administration: Individual.
Price Data, 2015: $445 per complete kit including examiner's manual (2006, 138 pages), CD-ROM for single computer use, unlimited administrations; $150 for pay-per-student kit including examiner's manual, CD-ROM for single computer use, two administrations credit ($75 per additional test session); volume discounts available.
Time: (30-90) minutes.
Comments: Computer-adaptive test; performance determines which of 11 test modules are to be administered.

Authors: Julie J. Masterson, Kenn Apel, and Jan Wasowicz.
Publisher: Learning by Design, Inc.
Cross References: For reviews by Sharon deFur and Kay Stevens, see 18:126.

[1940]

Spiritual Well-Being Scale.

Purpose: "Developed as a general indicator of the subjective state of religious and existential well-being."
Population: Adults.
Publication Dates: 1982-1991.
Acronym: SWBS.
Scores, 3: Religious Well-Being, Existential Well-Being, Total Spiritual Well-Being.
Administration: Individual or group.
Price Data, 2015: $20 per specimen set including scale, manual (1991, 6 pages), bibliography, and scoring and research information; $2.25 or less per scale; volume discounts and student discounts available.
Foreign Language and Other Editions: Available in Arabic, Cebuano, Chinese, Korean, Norwegian, Malaysian, Portuguese, Spanish, and Tagalog; also available in English Childhood Retrospective edition.
Time: (10-15) minutes.
Comments: Even-numbered items produce Existential Well-Being Scale (EWB); odd-numbered items produce Religious Well-Being Scale (RWB).
Authors: Craig W. Ellison and Raymond F. Paloutzian.
Publisher: Life Advance, Inc.
Cross References: See T5:2474 (1 reference); for reviews by Ayres D'Costa and Patricia Schoenrade, see 12:369 (1 reference); see also T4:2529 (1 reference).

[1941]

Sport Personality Questionnaire.

Purpose: "Designed to provide information about the personality and mental factors that contribute to elite performance in sport. It is intended to be used by sport psychologists and coaches to help athletes understand and develop the mental skills needed to perform successfully in competition."
Population: Athletes ages 16 to 65.
Publication Date: 2011.
Acronym: SPQ20.
Scores, 27: 20 Scale scores (Competitiveness, Aggressiveness, Self-Efficacy, Flow, Achievement, Power, Conscientiousness, Ethics, Adaptability, Self-Awareness, Intuition, Relationships, Empathy, Emotions, Managing Pressure, Fear of Failure, Burnout, Self-Talk, Visualization, Goal Setting); 7 Summary scores (Overall Mental Skills, Leadership Potential, Achievement and Competitiveness, Confidence and Resilience, Interaction and Sportsmanship, Power and Aggressiveness, Response Style).
Administration: Group.
Price Data, 2016: $19.95 per test.

Time: [15-20] minutes.
Comments: Assessment, scoring, and feedback conducted online.
Author: MySkillsProfile.
Publisher: MySkillsProfile [United Kingdom].
Cross References: For reviews by Stephen Axford and Claudia R. Wright, see 19:155.

[1942]

Spousal Assault Risk Assessment Guide.

Purpose: "Helps criminal justice professionals predict the likelihood of domestic violence."
Population: Individuals suspected of or being treated for spousal or family-related assault.
Publication Date: 1999.
Acronym: SARA.
Scores: Total score only.
Administration: Individual.
Price Data, 2015: $119 per complete kit including 25 checklist forms, 25 QuikScore forms, and manual; $44 per 25 QuikScore forms; $31 per 25 checklist forms; $55 per manual.
Time: Administration time not reported.
Comments: Completed by clinician/rater (criminal justice professional) after all available sources of information from suspect/offender, victim, etc. are gathered.
Authors: P. Randall Kropp, Stephen D. Hart, Christopher D. Webster, and Derek Eaves.
Publisher: Multi-Health Systems, Inc.
Cross References: For reviews by Ira S. Katz and Michael J. Scheel, see 15:239.

[1943]

The Standard Timing Model.

Purpose: "Designed to simulate the motions, functions and operations of automatic production machines" for use in selection, evaluation, and training of employees.
Population: Mechanics, electricians, and operators.
Publication Date: 1971.
Scores: 4 tasks.
Administration: Individual.
Price Data: Available from publisher.
Time: [60] minutes.
Author: Scientific Management Techniques, Inc.
Publisher: Scientific Management Techniques, Inc.
Cross References: For reviews by Sami Gulgoz and Gary L. Marco, see 12:370.

[1944]

Standardized Assessment of Miranda Abilities.

Purpose: Designed to provide "a structure to address key elements of Miranda knowledge, misconceptions, and decision-making."
Population: Criminal defendants ages 18 and older who can communicate effectively in English.

Publication Date: 2012.
Acronym: SAMA.
Parts, 5: Miranda Quiz, Miranda Reasoning Measure, Miranda Comprehension Template, Miranda Acquiescence Questionnaire, Miranda Vocabulary Scale.
Administration: Individual.
Price Data, 2016: $174 per introductory kit including Professional Manual (175 pages), 10 MVS Record Forms, 10 MQ Test Forms, MQ Evaluator Template, 10 MRM Interview Forms, 10 MAQ Test Forms, 10 MAQ Scoring Forms, MAQ Evaluator Template, 10 MCT Record Forms, and 10 MCT Scoring Forms; $68 per manual.
Time: (60-90) minutes.
Comments: The test publisher advises this measure "should only be used and interpreted by forensic evaluators."
Authors: Richard Rogers, Kenneth W. Sewell, Eric Y. Drogin, and Chelsea E. Fiduccia.
Publisher: Psychological Assessment Resources, Inc.
  a) MIRANDA QUIZ.
  Purpose: Designed to assess "common misconceptions about Miranda rights and their potential effect on Miranda decision making."
  Acronym: MQ.
  Score: Total score only.
  b) MIRANDA REASONING MEASURE.
  Purpose: Semistructured interview designed to provide "a foundation for understanding the examinee's thoughts and basic reasoning at the time of the Miranda warning and subsequent relinquishment of Constitutional rights."
  Acronym: MRM.
  Scores: Each item scored separately.
  c) MIRANDA COMPREHENSION TEMPLATE.
  Purpose: Designed "to evaluate the examinee's ability to paraphrase the particular Miranda warning used in his or her case."
  Acronym: MCT.
  Scores: Tabulates "the 21 basic subcomponents found in many Miranda warnings."
  Comments: The MCT "is conceptualized as a tool rather than a psychological measure."
  d) MIRANDA ACQUIESCENCE QUESTIONNAIRE.
  Purpose: Designed "to assess the examinee's level of yea-saying (acquiescence) and nay-saying."
  Acronym: MAQ.
  Scores: Congruent Content, Acquiescence, Nay-Saying.
  e) MIRANDA VOCABULARY SCALE.
  Purpose: Designed "to ascertain an examinee's knowledge of Miranda-relevant words."
  Acronym: MVS.
  Scores: Easy Words, Midrange Words, Difficult Words, Total Score.
Cross References: Reviews are scheduled for *The Twentieth Mental Measurements Yearbook*.

[1945]

Standardized Bible Content Tests, Forms I and J.

Purpose: Intended for "assessment of biblical knowledge (Bible/Theology/World View)."

Population: College freshman and seniors.
Publication Dates: 1956-1996.
Acronym: SBCT
Scores: Total score only.
Administration: Group or individual.
Restricted Distribution: Open to any Bible college.
Price Data, 2016: $4 per exam (quantity discounts available).
Time: (45) minutes.
Author: Commission on Professional Development of the Accrediting Association of Bible Colleges.
Publisher: Association for Biblical Higher Education.
Cross References: See 7:651 (1 reference).

[1946]

Standardized Reading Inventory, Second Edition.

Purpose: "Designed primarily to assess children's independent, instructional, and frustration reading levels in word recognition and comprehension skills."
Population: Ages 6-0 to 14-6.
Publication Dates: 1986–1999.
Acronym: SRI-2.
Scores, 4: Passage, Comprehension, Word Accuracy, Vocabulary in Context, Reading Quotient.
Administration: Individual.
Forms, 2: A, B.
Price Data, 2015: $319 per complete kit including manual (1999, 134 pages), story book, 25 each Forms A and B vocabulary sheets, 25 each Forms A and B record booklets, and 50 profile scoring forms; $25 per 25 vocabulary sheets (specify form); $67 per 25 examiner record booklets (specify form); $31 per 50 profile scoring forms; $62 per story book; $62 per examiner's manual.
Time: (30–90) minutes.
Comments: Second Edition is norm-referenced.
Author: Phyllis L. Newcomer.
Publisher: PRO-ED.
Cross References: For reviews by Alan Solomon and Brenda A. Stevens, see 14:366; for reviews by Kenneth W. Howell and Cleborne D. Maddux of the original edition, see 10:340.

[1947]

Stanford Achievement Test, Tenth Edition.

Purpose: Measures student achievement in reading, language, spelling, study skills, listening, mathematics, science and social science.
Population: Grades K–12.
Publication Dates: 1923–2003.
Acronym: Stanford 10.
Administration: Group.
Forms, 4: A, B, D, E.
Levels, 13: Stanford Early School Achievement Test 1, Stanford Early School Achievement Test 2, Primary 1, Primary 2, Primary 3, Intermediate 1, Intermediate 2, Intermediate 3, Advanced 1, Advanced 2, Stanford Test of Academic Skills 1, Stanford Test of Academic Skills 2, Stanford Test of Academic Skills 3.
Price Data: Available from publisher.
Comments: A variety of assessment options are available including full-length and abbreviated multiple-choice batteries; large-print and Braille editions are available.
Author: Harcourt Assessment, Inc.
Publisher: Pearson.
a) STANFORD EARLY SCHOOL ACHIEVEMENT TEST 1.
Population: Grades K.0–K.5.
Acronym: SESAT 1.
Forms, 2: Basic Battery, Complete Battery.
Scores, 6: Reading (Sounds and Letters, Word Reading, Total), Mathematics, Listening to Words and Stories, Environment.
Time: (105) minutes for Basic Battery; (135) minutes for Complete Battery.
b) STANFORD EARLY SCHOOL ACHIEVEMENT TEST 2.
Population: Grades K.5–1.5.
Acronym: SESAT 2.
Forms, 2: Basic Battery, Complete Battery.
Scores, 7: Reading (Sounds and Letters, Word Reading, Sentence Reading, Total), Mathematics, Listening to Words and Stories, Environment.
Time: (140) minutes for Basic Battery; (170) minutes for Complete Battery.
c) PRIMARY 1.
Population: Grades 1.5–2.5.
Forms, 4: Basic Battery, Complete Battery, Abbreviated Battery, Language.
Scores, 11-12: Reading (Word Study Skills, Word Reading, Sentence Reading, Reading Comprehension, Total), Mathematics (Mathematics Problem Solving, Mathematics Procedures, Total), Language, Spelling, Listening (not available in Abbreviated Battery), Environment.
Time: (295) minutes for Basic Battery; (325) minutes for Complete Battery; (212) minutes for Abbreviated Battery.
d) PRIMARY 2.
Population: Grades 2.5–3.5.
Forms, 4: Same as *c* above.
Scores, 10-11: Reading (Word Study Skills, Reading Vocabulary, Reading Comprehension, Total), Mathematics (Mathematics Problem Solving, Mathematics Procedures, Total), Language, Spelling, Listening (not available in Abbreviated Battery), Environment.
Time: (265) minutes for Basic Battery; (295) minutes for Complete Battery; (189) minutes for Abbreviated Battery.
e) PRIMARY 3.
Population: Grades 3.5–4.5.
Forms, 4: Same as *c* above.
Scores, 11-12: Reading (Word Study Skills, Reading Vocabulary, Reading Comprehension, Total), Mathematics (Mathematics Problem Solving, Mathematics Procedures, Total), Language, Spelling, Listening (not available in Abbreviated Battery), Science, Social Science.
Time: (280) minutes for Basic Battery; (330) minutes for Complete Battery; (203) minutes for Abbreviated Battery.

f) INTERMEDIATE 1.
Population: Grades 4.5–5.5.
Forms, 4: Same as *c* above.
Scores, 11-12: Same as *c* above.
Time: (280) minutes for Basic Battery; (330) minutes for Complete Battery; (201) minutes for Abbreviated Battery.
g) INTERMEDIATE 2.
Population: Grades 5.5–6.5.
Forms, 4: Same as *c* above.
Scores, 10-11: Reading (Reading Vocabulary, Reading Comprehension, Total), Mathematics (Mathematics Problem Solving, Mathematics Procedures, Total), Language, Spelling, Listening (not available in Abbreviated Battery), Science, Social Science.
Time: (260) minutes for Basic Battery; (310) minutes for Complete Battery; (187) minutes for Abbreviated Battery.
h) INTERMEDIATE 3.
Population: Grades 6.5–7.5.
Forms, 4: Same as *c* above.
Scores, 10-11: Same as *g* above.
Time: (260) minutes for Basic Battery; (310) minutes for Complete Battery; (187) minutes for Abbreviated Battery.
i) ADVANCED 1.
Population: Grades 7.5–8.5.
Forms, 4: Same as *c* above.
Scores, 10-11: Same as *g* above.
Time: (260) minutes for Basic Battery; (310) minutes for Complete Battery; (186) minutes for Abbreviated Battery.
j) ADVANCED 2.
Population: Grades 8.5–9.9.
Forms, 4: Same as *c* above.
Scores, 10-11: Same as *g* above.
Time: (260) minutes for Basic Battery; (310) minutes for Complete Battery; (185) minutes for Abbreviated Battery.
k) STANFORD TEST OF ACADEMIC SKILLS 1.
Population: Grades 9.0–9.9.
Acronym: TASK 1.
Forms, 4: Same as *c* above.
Scores, 8: Reading (Reading Vocabulary, Reading Comprehension, Total), Mathematics, Language, Spelling, Science, Social Science.
Time: (180) minutes for Basic Battery; (230) minutes for Complete Battery; (160) minutes for Abbreviated Battery.
l) STANFORD TEST OF ACADEMIC SKILLS 2.
Population: Grades 10.0–10.9.
Acronym: TASK 2.
Forms, 4: Same as *c* above.
Scores, 8: Same as *k* above.
Time: Same as *k* above.
m) STANFORD TEST OF ACADEMIC SKILLS 3.
Population: Grades 11.0–12.9.
Acronym: TASK 3.
Forms, 4: Same as *c* above.
Scores, 8: Same as *k* above.
Time: Same as *k* above.

Cross References: For reviews by Russell N. Carney and David T. Morse, see 16:232; see T5:2484 (15 references); for reviews by Ronald A. Berk and Thomas M. Haladyna of an earlier edition, see 13:292 (80 references); for reviews of the Stanford Achievement Test-Abbreviated-8th Edition by Stephen N. Elliott and James A. Wollack and by Kevin L. Moreland, see 12:371; for information on an earlier edition of the Stanford Achievement Test, see T4:2551 (44 references); for reviews by Frederick G. Brown and Howard Stoker, see 11:377 (78 references); for reviews by Mark L. Davison and by Michael J. Subkoviak and Frank H. Farley of the 1982 Edition, see 9:1172 (19 references); see also T3:2286 (80 references); for reviews by Robert L. Ebel and A. Harry Passow and an excerpted review by Irvin J. Lehmann of the 1973 edition, see 8:29 (51 references); see also T2:36 (87 references); for an excerpted review by Peter F. Merenda of the 1964 edition, see 7:25 (44 references); for a review by Miriam M. Bryan and an excerpted review by Robert E. Stake (with J. Thomas Hastings), see 6:26 (13 references); for a review by N. L. Gage of an earlier edition, see 5:25 (19 references); for reviews by Paul R. Hanna (with Claude E. Norcross) and by Virgil E. Herrick, see 4:25 (20 references); for reviews by Walter W. Cook and Ralph C. Preston, see 3:18 (33 references). For reviews of subtests, see 9:1173 (1 review), 9:1174 (1 review), 9:1175 (1 review), 8:291 (2 reviews), 8:745 (2 reviews), 7:209 (2 reviews), 7:537 (1 review), 7:708 (1 review), 7:802 (1 review), 7:895 (1 review), 6:637 (1 review), 5:656 (2 reviews), 5:698 (2 reviews), 5:799 (1 review), 4:419 (1 review), 4:555 (1 review), 4:593 (2 reviews), 3:503 (1 review), and 3:595 (1 review); for a review of the Stanford Test of Academic Skills [1982 Edition] by John C. Ory, see 9:1182; see also T3:2298 (3 references); for reviews by Clinton I. Chase and Robert L. Thorndike of an earlier edition, see 8:31.

[1948]

Stanford-Binet Intelligence Scales, Fifth Edition.

Purpose: Designed to assess "intelligence and cognitive abilities."
Population: Ages 2-0 to 89-9.
Publication Dates: 1916–2003.
Acronym: SB5.
Scores, 13: Nonverbal Fluid Reasoning, Verbal Fluid Reasoning, Nonverbal Knowledge, Verbal Knowledge, Nonverbal Quantitative Reasoning, Verbal Quantitative Reasoning, Nonverbal Visual-Spatial Processing, Verbal Visual-Spatial Processing, Nonverbal Working Memory, Verbal Working Memory, Nonverbal IQ, Verbal IQ, Full Scale IQ.
Subtests: Subtests and Partial Batteries: Abbreviated Battery (Nonverbal Fluid Reasoning and Verbal Knowledge).
Administration: Individual.
Price Data, 2015: $1,087 per complete kit including examiner's manual (336 pages), 3 item books (Routing, Nonverbal, and Verbal subtests), technical manual, 25 record forms, and manipulatives; $142 per examiner's manual; $142 per technical manual; $94 per 25 record forms.
Time: (45–75) minutes; (15–20) minutes for Abbreviated Battery.
Author: Gale H. Roid.
Publisher: PRO-ED.

Cross References: For reviews by Judy A. Johnson and Rik Carl D'Amato and by Joseph C. Kush, see 16:233; for information on an earlier edition, see T5:2485 (245 references) and T4:2553 (120 references); for reviews by Anne Anastasi and Lee J. Cronbach, see 10:342 (89 references); see also 9:1176 (41 references), T3:2289 (203 references), 8:229 (176 references), and T2:525 (428 references); for a review by David Freides, see 7:425 (258 references); for a review by Elizabeth D. Fraser and excerpted reviews by Benjamin Balinski, L. B. Birch, James Maxwell, Marie D. Neale, and Julian C. Stanley, see 6:536 (110 references); for reviews by Mary R. Haworth and Norman D. Sundberg of the second revision, see 5:413 (121 references); for a review by Boyd R. McCandless, see 4:358 (142 references); see also 3:292 (217 references); for excerpted reviews by Cyril Burt, Grace H. Kent, and M. Krugman, see 2:1420 (132 references); for reviews by Francis W. Maxfield, J. W. M. Rothney, and F. L. Wells, see 1:1062.

[1949]

Stanford-Binet Intelligence Scales for Early Childhood, Fifth Edition.

Purpose: Designed to assess intelligence and cognitive abilities.

Population: Ages 2 years to 7 years, 3 months.

Publication Date: 2005.

Acronym: Early SB5.

Scores, 14: Full Scale IQ (Nonverbal IQ, Verbal IQ), Nonverbal IQ (Nonverbal Fluid Reasoning, Nonverbal Knowledge, Nonverbal Quantitative Reasoning, Nonverbal Visual-Spatial Processing, Nonverbal Working Memory); Verbal IQ (Verbal Fluid Reasoning, Verbal Knowledge, Verbal Quantitative Reasoning, Verbal Visual-Spatial Processing, Verbal Working Memory); Abbreviated Battery IQ (Nonverbal Fluid Reasoning, Verbal Knowledge).

Administration: Individual.

Price Data, 2015: $405 per complete package including examiner's manual (282 pages), Item Book 1, Item Book 2, 25 record forms, and manipulatives; $75 per 25 record forms; $68 per examiner's manual.

Time: (15–50) minutes.

Comments: Adaptation of Stanford-Binet Intelligence Scales, Fifth Edition (1948).

Author: Gale H. Roid.

Publisher: PRO-ED.

Cross References: For reviews by Christopher A. Sink and Christie Eppler and by John J. Vacca, see 17:176.

[1950]

Stanford Writing Assessment Program, Third Edition.

Purpose: Provides for the direct assessment of written expression in four modes: Descriptive, Narrative, Expository, and Persuasive.

Population: Grades 3–12.

Publication Dates: 1982–1997.

Scores: 4 writing modes: Descriptive, Narrative, Expository, Persuasive.

Administration: Group.

Levels, 9: Primary 3, Intermediate 1, Intermediate 2, Intermediate 3, Advanced 1, Advanced 2, TASK 1, TASK 2, TASK 3.

Forms, 2: S, T (Form T is a secure form).

Price Data, 2015: $44.75 per 25 writing prompts, 25 response forms, and Directions for Administering (specify Descriptive, Narrative, Expository, or Persuasive); $17 per Directions for Administering (specify Descriptive, Narrative, Expository, or Persuasive); $31 per writing exam kit including 1 prompt each of Descriptive, Narrative, Expository and Persuasive, 1 Directions for Administering, 1 response form, and Reviewer's Edition; $35 per manual for interpreting (1997, 70 pages) (all forms and levels); scoring prices available from publisher.

Time: (50) minutes.

Comments: Holistic and analytic scoring available; computer scoring available; Form T is a secure form; Third edition provides information about student strengths and weaknesses, which can assist in instructional planning.

Authors: Harcourt Brace Educational Measurement.

Publisher: Pearson.

Cross References: For reviews by Linda Crocker and Sharon H. deFur, see 14:367; for reviews by Philip Nagy and Wayne H. Slater of an earlier editions, see 13:295.

[1951]

The Stanton Survey and the Stanton Survey Phase II.

Purpose: Provides indications of previous counterproductive work behavior and attitudes toward honesty.

Population: Applicants for employment.

Publication Dates: 1964–1995.

Scores: Total score only.

Administration: Individual or group.

Price Data: Available from publisher.

Time: Untimed.

Authors: Carl S. Klump, Homer B. C. Reed, Jr., and Sherwood Perman.

Publisher: The Plotkin Group.

Cross References: For reviews by H. C. Ganguli and Kenneth G. Wheeler, see 9:1185. (An additional review by William G. Harris is available electronically from the Buros Institute national database: available from EBSCO and Ovid and from Tests Reviews Online via the Buros webpage.)

[1952]

STAR Early Literacy®.

Purpose: Designed as a computer-adaptive, progress-monitoring tool for assessing the early literacy skills of beginning readers.

Population: Students in prekindergarten through Grade 3.

Publication Dates: 2001-2016.

Scores, 52: Proficiency ratings in 10 subdomains: Alphabetic Principle, Concept of Word, Visual Discrimination, Phonemic Awareness, Phonics, Structural Analysis, Vocabulary, Sentence-Level Comprehension, Paragraph-Level Comprehension, Early Numeracy; proficiency ratings for 41 skill sets; Overall Score.

Administration: Group.

Price Data: Price information available from publisher for a one-time school fee (based on each school/district's specific needs) plus an annual subscription cost per student.

Time: (10) minutes.

Comments: Administered aurally by computer; reports norm-referenced scores and criterion-referenced scores; software includes report capabilities (e.g., diagnostic reports); capable of sharing databases with other Renaissance Learning software; data may be maintained on-site or hosted by the test publisher; may be administered as often as weekly for progress monitoring. Information regarding complete system requirements available from test publisher.

Author: Renaissance Learning, Inc.

Publisher: Renaissance Learning, Inc.

Cross References: For reviews by Theresa Graham and Sandra B. Ward of the original edition, see 15:240.

[1953]
STAR Math®.

Purpose: A computer-adaptive, progress-monitoring assessment designed to measure students' mathematical abilities and overall mathematics achievement.

Population: Students in Grades 1–12.

Publication Dates: 1998–2016.

Scores: Assesses 210 skills in 8 strands: Numeration, Computation, Word Problems, Geometry, Measurement, Algebra, Estimation, Data Analysis and Statistics.

Administration: Group.

Price Data: Price information available from publisher for a one-time school fee (based on each school/district's specific needs) plus an annual subscription cost per student.

Time: (10-15) minutes.

Comments: Software includes report capabilities (e.g., diagnostic reports); capable of sharing databases with other Renaissance Learning software; information regarding complete system requirements available from test publisher.

Author: Renaissance Learning, Inc.

Publisher: Renaissance Learning, Inc.

a) STAR MATH ENTERPRISE.
Purpose: Designed as a standards-based version of STAR Math to measure "standards appropriate to a student's grade, or standards the student should have mastered at lower grades."

Scores: Assesses 550 skills in 4 standards-based domains: Numbers and Operations, Algebra, Geometry and Measurements, Data Analysis/Statistics/Probability.
Time: (20) minutes.

Cross References: For reviews by Mary L. Garner and G. Michael Poteat of an earlier version titled STAR Math, Version 2.0, see 16:234; for reviews by Joseph C. Ciechalski and Cindy M. Walker of the original version, see 15:241.

[1954]
STAR Reading®.

Purpose: A computer-adaptive, progress-monitoring assessment designed to assess students' reading comprehension and overall reading achievement.

Population: Grades 1–12.

Publication Dates: 1996–2016.

Scores: Skills assessed in 11 domains: Foundational Skills (Phonics and Word Recognition, Fluency), Reading: Literature (Key Ideas and Details, Craft and Structure Integration of Knowledge and Ideas, Range of Reading and Level of Text Complexity), Reading Informational Text (Key Ideas and Details, Craft and Structure Integration of Knowledge and Ideas, Range of Reading and Level of Text Complexity), Language (Vocabulary Acquisition and Use).

Administration: Group.

Price Data: Price information available from publisher for a one-time school fee (based on each school/district's specific needs) plus an annual subscription cost per student.

Time: (5-15) minutes.

Comments: Reports norm-referenced (percentile ranks, normal curve equivalents, grade equivalents) and criterion-referenced (instructional reading levels) scores; software includes report capabilities (e.g., diagnostic reports); capable of sharing databases with other Renaissance Learning software; data may be maintained on-site or hosted by the test publisher; information regarding system requirements available from test publisher.

Author: Renaissance Learning, Inc.

Publisher: Renaissance Learning, Inc.

a) STAR READING ENTERPRISE.
Purpose: Designed as a standards-based version of STAR Reading.
Scores: Assesses skills in 5 domains: Word Knowledge and Skills, Comprehension Strategies and Constructing Meaning, Understanding Author's Craft, Analyzing Literary Text, Analyzing Argument and Evaluating Text.
Time: Varies by grade.

Cross References: For reviews by Lori Nebelsick-Gullett and by Betsy B. Waterman and David M. Sargent of a previous version titled STAR Reading Version 2.2, see 15:242; for reviews by Theresa Volpe-Johnstone and Sandra Ward of the original edition, see 14:368.

[1955]

STAR Reading Test, 2nd Edition, 2014 Update.

Purpose: Designed to "supplement the assessments that teachers make about their students' progress and achievement in reading."

Population: Students in Years 3-9 in New Zealand schools.

Publication Dates: 2000-2013.

Acronym: STAR.

Administration: Group.

Levels, 4: Years 3-4, Years 5-6, Years 7-8, Year 9.

Price Data, 2015: NZ$60 per starter kit for Years 3-4 including teacher's manual, one of each test booklet, and marking keys; NZ$88 per starter kit for Years 3-8 including teacher's manual, one of each test booklet, and marking keys; NZ$50 per starter kit for Years 7-9 including teacher's manual, one of each test booklet, and marking keys; NZ$22 per teacher's manual; NZ$17 per marking keys for Years 3-6; NZ$22 per marking keys for Years 7-9; NZ$13 per 10 test booklets.

Comments: "Each STAR test has been designed with a particular year level in mind. However, each of the new STAR tests can be used productively with students at two or more year levels." Years 3-4, 5-6, and 7-8 each have 3 tests of increasing difficulty (i.e., A, B, C); 2nd edition tests published in 2011, update applies only to manual.

Authors: Warwick Elley, Hilary Ferral, and Verena Watson.

Publisher: New Zealand Council for Educational Research [New Zealand].

a) YEARS 3-4.

Population: Students in Years 3-4 in New Zealand schools.

Scores, 5: Word Recognition, Sentence Comprehension, Paragraph Comprehension, Vocabulary, Total.

Levels, 3: A, B, C.

Time: (30) minutes.

b) YEARS 5-6.

Population: Students in Years 5-6 in New Zealand schools.

Scores, 5: Word Recognition, Sentence Comprehension, Paragraph Comprehension, Vocabulary, Total.

Levels, 3: A, B, C.

Time: (30) minutes.

c) YEARS 7-8.

Population: Students in Years 7-8 in New Zealand schools.

Scores, 7: Word Recognition, Sentence Comprehension, Paragraph Comprehension, Vocabulary, Language of Advertising, Reading of Different Text Types, Total.

Levels, 3: A, B, C.

Time: (40) minutes.

d) YEAR 9.

Population: Students in Year 9 in New Zealand schools.

Scores, 7: Word Recognition, Sentence Comprehension, Paragraph Comprehension, Vocabulary, Language of Advertising, Reading of Different Text Types, Total.

Time: (40) minutes.

Cross References: For a review by John W. Young of an earlier edition titled STAR Supplementary Tests of Achievement in Reading, see 15:243.

[1956]

START—Strategic Assessment of Readiness for Training.

Purpose: Designed to diagnose adults' learning strengths and weaknesses for workplace application.

Population: Adults.

Publication Date: 1994.

Acronym: START.

Scores, 8: Anxiety, Attitude, Motivation, Concentration, Identifying Important Information, Knowledge Acquisition Strategies, Monitoring Learning, Time Management.

Administration: Group or individual.

Price Data, 2015: $5.95 per assessment for 1-99 assessments; $4.95 per assessment for 100 or more; free training manual.

Time: (15) minutes.

Authors: Claire E. Weinstein and David R. Palmer.

Publisher: H & H Publishing Co., Inc.

Cross References: For reviews by Phillip L. Ackerman and Patricia A. Bachelor, see 14:369.

[1957]

State-Trait Anger Expression Inventory-2.

Purpose: "Designed to measure the experience, expression, and control of anger for adolescents and adults."

Population: Ages 16 and over.

Publication Dates: 1988–1999.

Acronym: STAXI-2.

Scores, 12: State Anger Scale (Feeling Angry, Feel like Expressing Anger Verbally, Feel like Expressing Anger Physically, Total), Trait Anger Scale (Angry Temperament, Angry Reaction, Total), Angry Expression and Anger Control Scales (Anger Expression—Out, Anger Expression—In, Anger Control—Out, Anger Control—In), Anger Expression Index.

Administration: Group or individual.

Price Data, 2015: $290 per introductory kit including professional manual, 25 reusable item booklets, 50 rating sheets, and 50 profile forms; $515 per software (CD-ROM) with on-screen help and quick start guide.

Foreign Language Edition: Available in Spanish.

Time: (12–15) minutes.

Author: Charles D. Spielberger.

Publisher: Psychological Assessment Resources, Inc.

Cross References: For reviews by Stephen J. Freeman and Beverly M. Klecker, see 15:244; see T5:2496 (6 references); for reviews by David J. Pittenger and Alan J. Raphael of the Revised Research Edition, see 13:296 (52 references); see also T4:2562 (12 references); for reviews by Bruce H. Biskin and Paul Retzlaff of the STAXI-Research Edition, see 11:379 (8 references).

[1958]

State-Trait Anger Expression Inventory-2: Child and Adolescent.

Purpose: Designed to "assess state and trait anger with anger expression and control."
Population: Ages 9 to 18 years.
Publication Date: 2009.
Acronym: STAXI-2 C/A.
Scores, 9: State Anger, State Anger-Feelings, State Anger-Expression, Trait Anger, Trait Anger-Temperament, Trait Anger-Reaction, Anger Expression-Out, Anger Expression-In, Anger Control.
Administration: Group.
Price Data, 2015: $170 per introductory kit including professional manual (87 pages), 25 rating booklets, and 25 profile forms; $58 per professional manual; $90 per 25 rating booklets; $39 per 25 profile forms.
Foreign Language Edition: Available in Spanish.
Time: (10-15) minutes.
Authors: Thomas M. Brunner and Charles D. Spielberger.
Publisher: Psychological Assessment Resources, Inc.
Cross References: For reviews by Stephanie Stein and Jeremy R. Sullivan, see 19:156.

[1959]

State-Trait Anxiety Inventory.

Purpose: Designed to assess anxiety as an emotional state (S-Anxiety) and individual differences in anxiety proneness as a personality trait (T-Anxiety).
Population: Grades 9-16 and adults.
Publication Dates: 1968-1984.
Acronym: STAI.
Scores, 2: State Anxiety, Trait Anxiety.
Administration: Group.
Forms, 2: X, Y.
Parts, 2: 2 parts for each form labeled Form 1 (State), Form 2 (Trait).
Price Data, 2015: $50 for manual, including review-only copy of form; $2.40 per Transform Survey Hosting license (minimum 50); $250 Group Report; $2 per Remote Online Survey License or License to Reproduce (minimum 50); $15 per Individual Report; $15 per Report About Me.
Foreign Language Editions: Arabic, Bengali, Cambodian, Chinese (Mandarin and Traditional), Croatian, Czech, Danish, Dutch (both non-specific and Belgium), English (New Zealand and UK dialects), Finnish, French (France, Belgium, and Canada), German, Greek, Hebrew, Hungarian, Icelandic, Indonesian (Y-1 S-Anxiety Form only), Italian, Kannada, Korean, Lithuanian, Malay, Malayam, Maltese, Marathi, Nepali, Norwegian, Polish, Portuguese (Portugal and Brazil), Romanian, Russian, Serbian, Slovak, Slovene, Spanish (Spain and Columbia), Swedish (Sweden and Finland), Tagalog, Thai, and Urdu.

Time: (10-20) minutes.
Comments: Title on test is Self-Evaluation Questionnaire.
Authors: Charles D. Spielberger; Form Y and manual prepared in collaboration with R. L. Gorsuch, R. Lushene, P. R. Vagg, and G. A. Jacobs.
Publisher: Mind Garden, Inc.
Cross References: See T5:2497 (680 references), T4:2563 (646 references), 9:1186 (158 references), and T3:2300 (277 references); for reviews by Ralph Mason Dreger and Edward S. Katkin, see 8:683 (268 references); see also T2:1391 (45 references) and 7:141 (20 references).

[1960]

State-Trait Anxiety Inventory for Children.

Purpose: Designed to measure anxiety in children; distinguishes between a general proneness to anxious behavior rooted in the personality and anxiety as a fleeting emotional state.
Population: Upper elementary through junior high school children.
Publication Dates: 1970-1973.
Acronym: STAIC.
Scores, 2: State Anxiety, Trait Anxiety.
Administration: Group.
Price Data, 2015: $50 per manual, including review-only copy of STAIC form; $2 per Remote Online Survey License; $2 per License to Reproduce.
Foreign Language Editions: Translated materials available in Arabic, Cambodian (Khmer), Chinese (Simplified Mandarin), Croatian, Danish, Filipino, Finnish, French (Canadian), German, Greek, Hungarian, Italian, Korean, Malay, Norwegian, Persian, Polish, Portuguese (Portugal and Brazil), Romanian, Russian, Slovak, Spanish, Swedish, Thai, and Turkish.
Time: (20) minutes.
Comments: Downward extension of State-Trait Anxiety Inventory (1959); title on test is "How-I-Feel Questionnaire"; self-administering; can be administered verbally to younger children.
Authors: Charles D. Spielberger, C. Drew Edwards, R. L. Gorsuch, G. A. Jacobs, Robert E. Lushene, Joseph Montuori, Denna Platzek, P. R. Vagg.
Publisher: Mind Garden, Inc.
Cross References: See T5:2498 (78 references), T4:2564 (58 references), and T3:2301 (15 references); for a review by Norman S. Endler, see 8:684 (19 references); see also T2:1392 (2 references).

[1961]

State Trait-Depression Adjective Check Lists.

Purpose: "To measure both state and trait depression mood and feelings."
Population: Ages 14 and over.
Publication Dates: 1967–2002.
Acronym: ST-DACL.

Scores, 6: State-Positive Mood, State-Negative Mood, State Mood-Total, Trait-Positive Mood, Trait-Negative Mood, Trait Mood-Total.
Administration: Group.
Forms, 4: 1, 2, A-B, C-D.
Price Data, 2016: $14.50 per 25 forms (specify State Form A-B, State Form C-D, or Form 1 and Form 2 check lists); $10.50 per 25 profile sheet with scoring instructions; $36.50 per technical manual (2002, 83 pages); $39.25 per specimen set including manual and one copy of all forms; volume discounts available.
Time: (4–8) minutes per list.
Comments: Developed from the Depression Adjective Check List.
Author: Bernard Lubin.
Publisher: EdITS/Educational and Industrial Testing Service.
Cross References: See T5:2499 (1 reference); for reviews by Andres Barona and by Janet F. Carlson and Betsy Waterman of an earlier edition, see 13:297 (21 references); see also T4:742 (79 references), 9:315 (21 references), T3:681 (46 references), 8:536 (20 references), and T2:1154 (2 references); for reviews of the earlier edition by Leonard D. Goodstein and Douglas M. McNair, see 7:65 (3 references); see also P:57 (4 references).

[1962]

State-Trait Personality Inventory.

Purpose: Self-administered questionnaire designed to "measure transitory and dispositional anger, anxiety, curiosity, and depression in adults."
Population: Ages 18 and older.
Publication Date: 1995.
Acronym: STPI.
Scores, 8: Trait Anxiety, State Anxiety, Trait Curiosity, State Curiosity, Trait Anger, State Anger, Trait Depression, State Depression.
Administration: Individual or group.
Price Data, 2016: $50 per PDF manual (35 pages; research manual contains only tables, with no explanatory text); $2 per Remote Online Survey License or License to Reproduce (minimum 50).
Time: [20] minutes.
Author: Charles D. Spielberger.
Publisher: Mind Garden, Inc.

[1963]

Station Employee Applicant Inventory.

Purpose: Designed to help "assess a potential employee's willingness to contribute to team efforts, practice safe work habits, handle cash and merchandise with complete trustworthiness, stay on the job once hired" and "follow company policies."
Population: Service station applicants.
Publication Date: 1997.
Acronym: SEAI.

Scores, 9: Validity/Candidness, Honesty, Interpersonal Cooperation, Drug Avoidance, Applied Arithmetic, Skills and Abilities, Safety, Tenure, Employability Index.
Administration: Individual or group.
Price Data: Available from publisher.
Foreign Language Edition: Available in Spanish.
Time: (45–60) minutes.
Author: General Dynamics Information Technology.
Publisher: General Dynamics Information Technology.

[1964]

STEM Careers Inventory.

Purpose: Designed to help people "discover their personality types and match them to STEM and green careers."
Population: Individuals involved in career exploration.
Publication Date: 2011.
Scores: 6 personality types: Realistic, Investigative, Artistic, Social, Enterprising, Conventional.
Administration: Group.
Price Data, 2016: $42.95 per 25 inventories; administrator's guide (12 pages) downloadable from publisher's website.
Time: (15) minutes.
Comments: Self-scoring and self-interpreted.
Authors: Laurence Shatkin.
Publisher: JIST Publishing, Inc.

[1965]

Stoelting Brief Nonverbal Intelligence Test.

Purpose: Designed as a nonverbal, nonlanguage measure of cognitive functions.
Population: Ages 6-0 to 20-11.
Publication Date: 1999.
Acronym: S-BIT.
Scores, 7: Figure Ground, Form Completion, Sequential Order, Repeated Patterns, S-BIT IQ, Visualization, Fluid Reasoning.
Administration: Individual.
Price Data, 2015: $295 per complete kit including 20 record forms, examiner's manual (1999, 191 pages), easel book, and response cards; $20 per 20 record forms; $50 per examiner's manual; $170 per easel book; $35 per carrying case; $70 per response cards.
Time: (25) minutes.
Authors: Gale H. Roid and Lucy J. Miller.
Publisher: Stoelting Co.
Cross References: For reviews by Russell N. Carney and Susana Urbina, see 15:245.

[1966]

Store Manager Aptitude Personality & Attitude Profile.

Purpose: Designed "to assess whether a test-taker's preferences and personality traits match those required to work as a store manager."

Population: Potential store managers.
Publication Date: 2011.
Acronym: SMAPAP.
Scores, 15: Adherence to Rules, Approachability, Communication, Conscientiousness, Cultural Sensitivity, Goal-Orientation, Go-Getting, Innovation, Leading, Logical Thinking, Organizing, Salesmanship, Self-Efficacy, Staffing, Overall Score.
Administration: Individual.
Price Data: Available from publisher.
Time: (25) minutes.
Comments: Self-administered online assessment. The test publisher provides clients with information about the methods and theoretical basis used in the development of the test as well as benchmarks for relevant industries and racial/ethnic group comparison data.
Author: PsychTests AIM, Inc.
Publisher: PsychTests AIM, Inc. [Canada].
Cross References: For reviews by Phillip L. Ackerman and Michael J. Scheel, see 19:157.

[1967]

Stress Assessment Questionnaire.

Purpose: Designed to "provide an integrated multi-factor stress assessment measure for counseling and self-development."
Population: Ages 16-65.
Publication Date: 2010.
Acronym: SAQ.
Scores, 16: Work, Relationship, Parenting, Emotional Symptoms, Behavioral Symptoms, Physical Symptoms, Social Support, Self-Regulation, Problem Solving, Distraction, Health, Procrastination, Perfectionism, Self-Esteem, Depression, Anxiety.
Administration: Group.
Price Data, 2016: $19.95 per assessment.
Time: (10-15) minutes.
Comments: Assessment, scoring, and feedback conducted online.
Author: MySkillsProfile.
Publisher: MySkillsProfile [United Kingdom].
Cross References: For reviews by James A. Athanasou and Jean Powell Kirnan, see 19:158.

[1968]

Stress in General Scale.

Purpose: To measure job stress.
Population: Employees.
Publication Dates: 1992–2002.
Acronym: SIG.
Scores, 2: Pressure, Threat.
Administration: Individual or group.
Price Data, 2015: There is no charge to use the copyrighted scales. For permission, please contact the test publisher.
Time: 3-5 minutes.

Comments: Previously listed with the Job Descriptive Index (1043).
Authors: Jeffrey M. Stanton, William K. Balzer, Patricia C. Smith, Luis Fernando Parra, and Gail H. Ironson.
Publisher: Bowling Green State University.
Cross References: For reviews by Christopher G. Bellah and by Leonard Handler and Amanda Jill Clemence, see 15:246.

[1969]

Stress Index for Parents of Adolescents.

Purpose: Designed to "identify stressful areas in parent-adolescent interactions."
Population: Parents of adolescents ages 11–19 years.
Publication Date: 1998.
Scores, 11: Adolescent Domain (Moodiness/Emotional Lability, Social Isolation/Withdrawal, Delinquency/Antisocial, Failure to Achieve or Persevere), Parent Domain (Life Restrictions, Relationship with Spouse/Partner, Social Alienation, Incompetence/Guilt), Adolescent-Parent Relationship Domain, Life Stressors, Total Parenting Stress.
Administration: Individual.
Price Data, 2015: $158 per introductory kit including 25 reusable item booklets, 25 hand-scorable answer sheet/profile forms, and professional manual (70 pages).
Time: (20) minutes.
Authors: Peter L. Sheras and Richard R. Abidin.
Publisher: Psychological Assessment Resources, Inc.
Cross References: For reviews by Elizabeth L. Jones and Susan M. Swearer, see 14:372.

[1970]

Stress Indicator & Health Planner [Revised].

Purpose: Designed to help an individual assess their current levels of stress, health, and wellness.
Population: Adults.
Publication Dates: 1990-2006.
Acronym: SIHP.
Scores, 10: Physical Distress, Psychological Distress, Behavioral Distress, Total Distress, Interpersonal Stress Assessment, Nutritional, Health Assessment, Total Wellness Assessment, Time-Stress Assessment, Occupational Stress Assessment.
Administration: Individual or group.
Parts, 5: Personal Distress Assessment, Interpersonal Stress Assessment, Wellness Assessment, Time-Stress Assessment, Occupational Stress Assessment.
Price Data, 2016: $30 per test booklet (2006, 24 pages); $40 per Professional/Trainer's Guidelines (1993, 15 pages); $35 per online version.
Time: [30-60] minutes for basic; [180-360] minutes for facilitated/advanced.
Comments: Test can be self-administered and self-scored and includes a health planner.

Authors: Ken Keis, Terry D. Anderson, and Gwen Faulkner.
Publisher: Consulting Resource Group International, Inc.
Cross References: For reviews by Dennis C. Harper and Barbara L. Lachar of an earlier edition, see 13:300.

[1971]

Stress Management Questionnaire [Revised].
Purpose: Designed to identify stress warning signs and how one responds to life stressors.
Population: Adults and adolescents.
Publication Dates: 1980–2016.
Acronym: SMQ.
Scores, 11: Warning Signs (Hostility/Anger, Perfectionism, Time Orientation, Disappointment, Negative Mood, Underachievement, Tension), Stress Effects (Physical, Live Work Satisfaction), Stressors (Life Events, Hassles).
Administration: Group or individual.
Forms, 2: Participant, Companion.
Price Data: Available from publisher.
Foreign Language Editions: Available in French, Spanish, Slovenian, and Norwegian.
Time: (20–25) minutes.
Comments: Administered via paper and pencil or online; Companion form is paper and pencil only.
Author: James C. Petersen.
Publisher: Stressmaster International.
Cross References: For a review by Jayne E. Stake of an earlier version (1987), see 10:348.

[1972]

Stress Processing Report.
Purpose: Enables individuals to identify, understand and change their reactions to stress, thereby improving their receptivity to organizational change.
Population: Adults.
Publication Date: 1994.
Acronym: SPR.
Scores: 19 domains: Self (Self-Image, Past View, Control, Approval, Growth, Effectiveness), Others (Inclusion, Interpersonal, Intimacy, Trust), Process (Receptiveness, Synergy, Cooperation, Time Orientation, Time Utilization), Goals (Satisfaction, Directedness, Expectations, Future View).
Administration: Individual or group.
Price Data: Price data for test materials including Self-Development Guide and Leader's Guide available from publisher.
Foreign Language Editions: Available in Finnish, French (Canadian), and Spanish (Latin American).
Time: Administration time not reported.
Author: Human Synergistics International.
Publisher: Human Synergistics International.

[1973]

Stress Profile.
Purpose: "Developed to provide a brief yet comprehensive stress and health risk assessment."
Population: Adults.
Publication Date: 1999.
Scores, 16: Stress, Health Habits, Exercise, Rest/Sleep, Eating/Nutrition, Prevention, ARC Item Cluster, Social Support Network, Type A Behavior, Cognitive Hardiness, Coping Style, Positive Appraisal, Negative Appraisal, Threat Minimization, Problem Focus, Psychological Well-Being.
Administration: Group.
Price Data, 2016: $137 per kit including 25 AutoScore™ forms, manual (63 pages), and 1 reusable administration booklet; $57 per 25 AutoScore™ forms to be used with administration booklet; $72 per manual; $35.50 per 25 disposable administration booklets; $73 per 5 reusable administration booklets (quantity discounts available); $358.50 per 25-use scoring and interpretation CD.
Foreign Language Edition: Spanish version available.
Time: (20–30) minutes.
Comments: Can be administered and scored by hand or by computer.
Author: Kenneth M. Nowack.
Publisher: Western Psychological Services.
Cross References: For reviews by Carl Isenhart and Kevin J. McCarthy, see 15:247.

[1974]

Stress Resiliency Profile.
Purpose: Designed to identify some ways individuals unintentionally contribute to their own stress levels.
Population: Employees.
Publication Dates: 1974-1992.
Acronym: SRP.
Scores, 3: Deficiency Focusing, Necessitating, Skill Recognition.
Administration: Group or individual.
Price Data, 2016: $18.50 per test booklet/manual; $144.50 per 10 test booklet/manual.
Time: (15) minutes.
Comments: Self-administered and self-scored.
Authors: Kenneth W. Thomas and Walter G. Tymon, Jr.
Publisher: CPP, Inc.
Cross References: For reviews by John A. Mills and William R. Merz, Sr., see 13:301.

[1975]

Strong Interest Explorer.
Purpose: Self-scorable assessment intended to help individuals learn more about their interests to help them "define a career direction, select classes or activities," and/

or "choose a major or technical program."

Population: High school and community college students, or early career populations.

Publication Dates: 1933-2001.

Acronym: SIE.

Scores, 14: Working with Numbers, Health and Science, Music and Arts, Writing and Mass Communications, Cultural Relations, Helping Others, Teaching and Training, Law and Politics, Office and Project Management, Business/Sales/and Marketing, Working with Computers, Outdoor Environment/Plants & Animals, Construction and Engineering, Protective Services.

Administration: Individual or group.

Price Data, 2016: $9.95 each for Strong Interest Explorer Self-Scorable.

Time: (8-10) minutes.

Comments: It is suggested the SIE be given in a classroom or group setting and led by a teacher or counselor; developed as a simplified alternative to the Strong Interest Inventory (1976).

Author: Judy Chartrand.

Publisher: CPP, Inc.

Cross References: For reviews by Bert A. Goldman and Eugene P. Sheehan, see 18:128.

[1976]

Strong Interest Inventory® [2012 Revision].

Purpose: Intended to generate an in-depth assessment of "interests among a broad range of occupations, work and leisure activities, and educational subjects"... "to help individuals match their interests with occupational, educational, and leisure pursuits that are compatible with those interests."

Population: Ages 16 and over.

Publication Dates: 1927-2012.

Acronym: Strong.

Scores, 306: 6 General Occupational Themes: Realistic, Investigative, Artistic, Social, Enterprising, Conventional; 30 Basic Interest Scales: Realistic (Mechanics & Construction, Computer Hardware & Electronics, Military, Protective Services, Nature & Agriculture, Athletics), Investigative (Science, Research, Medical Science, Mathematics), Artistic (Visual Arts & Design, Performing Arts, Writing & Mass Communication, Culinary Arts), Social (Counseling & Helping, Teaching & Education, Human Resources & Training, Social Sciences, Religion & Spirituality, Healthcare Services), Enterprising (Marketing & Advertising, Sales, Entrepreneurship, Politics & Public Speaking, Law), Conventional (Office Management, Taxes & Accounting, Programming & Information Systems, Finance & Investing); 244 Occupational Scales: Accountant (f, m), Actuary (f, m), Administrative Assistant (f, m), Advertising Account Manager (f, m), Architect (f, m), Art Teacher (f, m), Artist (f, m), Athletic Trainer (f, m), Attorney (f, m), Automobile Mechanic (f, m), Banker (f, m), Biologist (f, m), Bookkeeper (f, m),

Broadcast Journalist (f, m), Business Education Teacher (f, m), Buyer (f, m), Carpenter (f, m), Chef (f, m), Chemist (f, m), Chiropractor (f, m), College Instructor (f, m), Community Service Director (f, m), Computer & IS Manager (f, m), Computer Scientist (f, m), Computer Systems Analyst (f, m), Corporate Trainer (f, m), Cosmetologist (f, m), Credit Manager (f, m), Dentist (f, m), Dietitian (f, m), Editor (f, m), Elected Public Official (f, m), Electrician (f, m), Elementary School Teacher (f, m), Emergency Medical Technician (f, m), Engineer (f, m), Engineering Technician (f, m), English Teacher (f, m), ESL Instructor (f, m), Farmer/Rancher (f, m), Financial Analyst (f, m), Financial Manager (f, m), Firefighter (f, m), Flight Attendant (f, m), Florist (f, m), Food Service Manager (f, m), Foreign Language Teacher (f, m), Forester (f, m), Geographer (f, m), Geologist (f, m), Graphic Designer (f, m), Health Information Specialist (f, m), Horticulturist (f, m), Housekeeping/Maintenance Manager (f, m), Human Resources Manager (f, m), Interior Designer (f, m), Investments Manager (f, m), Landscape/Grounds Manager (f, m), Law Enforcement Officer (f, m), Librarian (f, m), Licensed Practical Nurse (f, m), Life Insurance Agent (f, m), Marketing Manager (f, m), Mathematician (f, m), Mathematics Teacher (f, m), Medical Illustrator (f, m), Medical Technician (f, m), Medical Technologist (f, m), Military Enlisted (f, m), Military Officer (f, m), Minister (f, m), Musician (f, m), Network Administrator (f, m), Nursing Home Administrator (f, m), Occupational Therapist (f, m), Operations Manager (f, m), Optician (f, m), Optometrist (f, m), Paralegal (f, m), Parks & Recreation Manager (f, m), Pharmacist (f, m), Photographer (f, m), Physical Education Teacher (f, m), Physical Therapist (f, m), Physician (f, m), Physicist (f, m), Production Worker (f, m), Psychologist (f, m), Public Administrator (f, m), Public Relations Director (f, m), Purchasing Agent (f, m), R&D Manager (f, m), Radiologic Technologist (f, m), Realtor (f, m), Recreation Therapist (f, m), Registered Nurse (f, m), Rehabilitation Counselor (f, m), Reporter (f, m), Respiratory Therapist (f, m), Restaurant Manager (f, m), Retail Sales Manager (f, m), Retail Sales Representative (f, m), Sales Manager (f, m), School Administrator (f, m), School Counselor (f, m), Science Teacher (f, m), Social Science Teacher (f, m), Social Worker (f, m), Sociologist (f, m), Software Developer (f, m), Special Education Teacher (f, m), Speech Pathologist (f, m), Technical Sales Representative (f, m), Technical Support Specialist (f, m), Technical Writer (f, m), Top Executive (f, m), Translator (f, m), Travel Consultant (f, m), University Professor (f, m), Urban & Regional Planner (f, m), Veterinarian (f, m), Vocational Agriculture Teacher (f, m); 5 Personal Style Scales: Work Style, Learning Environment, Leadership Style, Risk Taking, Team Orientation; 9 Administrative Indexes: Total Percentage, Occupations, Subject Areas, Activities, Leisure Activities, People, Your Characteristics, Total Response Index, Typicality Index.

Administration: Individual or group.

Price Data, 2016: $9.25 each for Strong Profile online administration; $9.95 each for Strong Profile plus College Edition online administration; $8.95 each for Strong Profile plus High School Edition online administration; $15.95 each for Strong Interpretive Report online administration; $12.95 each for Strong Interest Inventory and Skills Confidence Inventory online administration; $12.95 each for Strong and MBTI® Career Report (NOTE: this report requires simultaneous or previous purchase of an MBTI® administration); $75 each for Strong Interest Inventory manual (2005, 286 pages) with 2012 supplement; $33 each for Strong Interest Inventory User's Guide; $39 each for Strong Interest Inventory College Profile User's Guide; $11.25 each for Where Do I Go Next (Using Your Strong Results to Manage Your Career) booklet; $11.25 each for Career Exploration for College Students (Using the Strong and MBTI® Tools To Chart Your Course); $9.95 each for iStartStrong® Report.

Time: (35-40) minutes.

Comments: Occupational Scales updated in 2012; instrument itself did not change.

Authors: David A. C. Donnay, Michael L. Morris, Nancy A. Schaubhut, and Richard C. Thompson; Judith Grutter and Allen L. Hammer (user's guide); Nicole A. Herk and Richard C. Thompson (2012 manual supplement).

Publisher: CPP, Inc.

Cross References: For reviews by Kevin R. Kelly and by Neeta Kantamneni and Michael J. Scheel of the 2005 Edition, see 18:129; for reviews by Kevin R. Kelly and Eugene P. Sheehan of the 1994 Edition, see 15:248; see also T5:1790 (19 references); for reviews by John Christian Busch and by Blaine R. Worthen and Perry Sailor of the Fourth Edition, see 12:374 (43 references); see also T4:2581 (64 references); for reviews by Wilbur L. Layton and Bert W. Westbrook, see 9:1195 (17 references); see also T3:2318 (99 references); for reviews by John O. Crites, Robert H. Dolliver, Patricia W. Lunneborg, and excerpted reviews by Richard W. Johnson, David P. Campbell, and Jean C. Steinhauer, see 8:1023 (289 references, these references are for SVIB-M, SBIV-W, and SCII). For references on the Strong Vocational Interest Blank For Men, see T2:2212 (133 references); for reviews by Martin R. Katz and Charles J. Krauskopf and excerpted reviews by David P. Campbell and John W. M. Rothney, see 7:1036 (485 references); for reviews by Alexander W. Astin and Edward J. Furst, see 6:1070 (189 references); see also 5:868 (153 references); for reviews by Edward S. Bordin and Elmer D. Hinckley, see 4:747 (98 references); see also 3:647 (102 references); for reviews by Harold D. Carter, John G. Darley, and N. W. Morton, see 2:1680 (71 references); for a review by John G. Darley, see 1:1178. For references on the Strong Vocational Interest Blank For Women, see T2:2213 (30 references); for reviews by Dorothy M. Clendenen and

Barbara A. Kirk, see 7:1037 (92 references); see also 6:1071 (12 references) and 5:869 (19 references); for a review by Gwendolen Schneidler Dickson, see 3:649 (38 references); for a review by Ruth Strang, see 2:1681 (10 references); for a review by John G. Darley, see 1:1179.

[1977]

Stroop Color and Word Test [Adult and Children's Versions, Revised].

Purpose: Designed to test "the ability of the individual to separate the word and color naming stimuli."

Publication Dates: 1978-2003.

Scores, 4: Word, Color, Color-Word, Interference.

Administration: Individual or group.

Forms, 2: Children's Version, Adult Version.

Price Data, 2015: $98 per complete kit including manual and 25 test booklets (specify Children's or Adult Version); $39 per manual (specify Children's [2003, 35 pages] or Adult Version [2002, 72 pages]); $62 per 25 test booklets (specify Children's or Adult Version); $30 per computerized scoring.

Foreign Language Edition: Spanish version available.

Time: (5-15) minutes.

Publisher: Stoelting Co.

a) CHILDREN'S VERSION.

Population: Ages 5-14 years.

Authors: Charles J. Golden, Shawna M. Freshwater, and Zarabeth Golden.

b) ADULT VERSION.

Population: Ages 15 years and older.

Authors: Charles J. Golden and Shawna M. Freshwater.

Cross References: For reviews by Mark Roybal and Louise M. Soares, see 17:179; see also T5:2516 (122 references) and T4:2582 (40 references); for reviews by James R. Evans and George W. Hynd of an earlier edition of the adult version, see 9:1196 (15 references); see also T3:2319 (1 reference).

[1978]

Stroop Neuropsychological Screening Test.

Purpose: Provides "an efficient and sensitive neuropsychological screening measure based on the Stroop procedure."

Population: Ages 18 and over.

Publication Date: 1989.

Acronym: SNST.

Scores, 2: Color, Color-Word.

Administration: Individual.

Price Data, 2015: $164 per introductory kit including manual, 25 Form C stimulus sheets, 25 Form C-W stimulus sheets, and 50 record forms.

Time: 4 minutes (timed).

Authors: Max R. Trenerry, Bruce Crosson, James DeBoe, and William R. Leber.

Publisher: Psychological Assessment Resources, Inc.

Cross References: See T5:2517 (8 references) and T4:2583 (3 references); for reviews by Manfred J. Meier and Cecil R. Reynolds, see 11:382 (1 reference).

[1979]

Structure of Intellect Learning Abilities Test.

Purpose: "Designed to assess a wide variety of cognitive abilities or factors of intelligence in children and adults."

Population: Preschool–adult.

Publication Dates: 1975–1985.

Acronym: SOI-LA.

Administration: Group or individual.

Price Data, 2015: $284 per complete kit including 10 standard test booklets (5 Form A and 5 Form B), set of scoring keys, set of stimulus cards, 10 worksheets/profiles, and manual (1985, 165 pages); $34 per 5 standard test booklets (specify Form A or B); $51.50 per scoring keys for Forms A, B, and G; $102.50 per manual; $82.50 per stimulus cards; $32 per 100 worksheet and profile forms.

Authors: Mary Meeker, Robert Meeker, and Gale H. Roid (manual).

Publisher: Western Psychological Services.

a) FORM A.

Population: Grade 2–adult.

Scores: 26 subtests in 5 test areas: Cognition (Cognition of Figural Units, Cognition of Figural Classes, Cognition of Figural Systems, Cognition of Figural Transformations, Cognition of Symbolic Relations, Cognition of Symbolic Systems, Cognition of Semantic Units, Cognition of Semantic Relations, Cognition of Semantic Systems), Memory (Memory of Figural Units, Memory of Symbolic Units—Visual, Memory of Symbolic Systems—Visual, Memory of Symbolic Units—Auditory, Memory of Symbolic Systems—Auditory, Memory of Symbolic Implications), Evaluation (Evaluation of Figural Units, Evaluation of Figural Classes, Evaluation of Symbolic Classes, Evaluation of Symbolic Systems), Convergent Production (Convergent Production of Figural Units, Convergent Production of Symbolic Systems, Convergent Production of Symbolic Transformations, Convergent Production of Symbolic Implications), and Divergent Production (Divergent Production of Figural Units, Divergent Production of Semantic Units, Divergent Production of Symbolic Relations) yielding 14 general ability scores: Cognition, Memory, Evaluation, Convergent Production, Divergent Production, Figural, Symbolic, Semantic, Units, Classes, Relations, Systems, Transformations, Implications.

Time: (150–180) minutes.

b) FORM B.

Purpose: Alternative to Form A.

c) GIFTED SCREENING FORM (FORM G).

Population: Grade 2–adult.

Subtests, 12: From Form A that best predict gifted status.

Price Data: $34 per 5 test booklets.

Time: (60–90) minutes.

d) PRIMARY FORM (FORM P).

Population: Grades K–3.

Subtests, 11: Similar to Form A, 5 measuring figural abilities, 3 measuring symbolic abilities, and 3 measuring semantic abilities.

Price Data: $36 per 5 test booklets; $56 per scoring key.

Time: (60–90) minutes.

Comments: Formerly called Process and Diagnostic Screening Test.

Cross References: See T5:2518 (4 references); for reviews by Jack A. Cummings and Dianna L. Newman, see 10:349 (5 references); for reviews by William E. Coffman and Donald A. Leton of an earlier form, see 9:1197 (2 references); see also T3:2320 (2 references).

[1980]

Structure of Temperament Questionnaire.

Purpose: Designed to "measure the traits which appear as consistent patterns and dynamics of behavior, more or less independently of the content of the situation."

Population: Ages 15-75.

Publication Date: 2007.

Administration: Individual or group.

Price Data, 2016: The test is free for research/academic purposes; contact publisher for additional information; prices follow for clinical/organizational settings: $147 per complete Extended STQ or Compact STQ test kits including professional manual, 50 response forms, and 50 scoring summary/profile forms; $77 per manual; $77 per 50 Extended STQ or Compact STQ carbonless response forms; $20 per 50 scoring summary/profile forms.

Foreign Language Editions: Available in Chinese, Polish, Russian and Urdu.

Authors: Vladimir Rusalov and Irina Trofimova.

Publisher: Psychological Services Press.

a) EXTENDED STQ.

Acronym: STQ-E.

Scores, 13: Motor Ergonicity, Social Ergonicity, Intellectual Ergonicity, Motor Plasticity, Social Plasticity, Intellectual Plasticity, Motor Tempo, Social Tempo, Intellectual Tempo, Object-Related Emotionality, Social Emotionality, Intellectual Emotionality, Validity Scale.

Time: (30) minutes.

b) COMPACT STQ.

Acronym: STQ-77.

Scores, 13: Motor Ergonicity, Social Ergonicity, Motor Tempo, Social Tempo, Sensitivity to Physical Sensations, Empathy, Intellectual Ergonicity, Plasticity, Sensitivity to Probabilities, Self-Confidence, Impulsivity, Neuroticism, Validity Scale.

Time: (15) minutes.

c) SHORT STQ.

Acronym: STQ-26.

Scores, 13: Motor Ergonicity, Social Ergonicity, Intellectual Ergonicity, Motor Plasticity, Social Plasticity, Intellectual Plasticity, Motor Tempo, Social Tempo, Intellectual Tempo, Object-Related Emotionality, Social Emotionality, Intellectual Emotionality, Validity Scale.

Time: (10) minutes.

Cross References: For reviews by Gerald E. De-Mauro and Steven V. Rouse, see 18:130.

[1981]

Structured Assessment of Violence Risk in Youth.

Purpose: Designed to "assist professional evaluators in assessing and making judgments about a juvenile's risk for violence."

Population: Ages 12-18.

Publication Dates: 2002-2006.

Acronym: SAVRY.

Scores: Total rating only.

Administration: Individual.

Price Data, 2015: $116 per complete kit including professional manual (2006, 97 pages) and 50 rating forms; $68 per 50 rating forms; $52 per professional manual.

Time: [10-15] minutes.

Comments: Completed by a mental health professional utilizing multiple sources to provide accurate estimates of behavior; structured interview questions also included.

Authors: Randy Borum, Patrick Bartel, and Adelle Forth.

Publisher: Psychological Assessment Resources, Inc.

Cross References: For reviews by Cynthia Hazel and Shawn Powell, see 18:131.

[1982]

Structured Clinical Interview for DSM-5 Disorders–Clinician Version.

Purpose: Designed as a semistructured diagnostic interview covering "the DSM-5 diagnoses most commonly seen in clinical settings."

Population: Psychiatric or general medical patients ages 18 or older.

Publication Dates: 1997-2016.

Acronym: SCID-5-CV.

Scores: Screens for Depressive and Bipolar Disorders, Schizophrenia Spectrum and Other Psychotic Disorders, Substance Use Disorders, Anxiety Disorders, Obsessive-Compulsive Disorder, Posttraumatic Stress Disorder, Attention-Deficit/Hyperactivity Disorder, Adjustment Disorder, and 17 additional DSM-5 disorders.

Administration: Individual.

Price Data, 2016: $82 per user's guide; $81 per 5 interviews.

Time: Administration time not reported..

Comments: Abridged and reformatted version of the Structured Clinical Interview for DSM-5–Research Version.

Authors: Michael B. First, Janet B. W. Williams, Rhonda S. Karg, and Robert L. Spitzer.

Publisher: American Psychiatric Publishing, Inc.

Cross References: For reviews by Paul D. Werner and Thomas A. Widiger of the Structured Clinical Interview for DSM-IV Axis I Disorders: Clinician Version, see 14:373; see also T5:2519 (56 references).

[1983]

Structured Clinical Interview for DSM-5 Personality Disorders.

Purpose: Designed as a semistructured diagnostic interview for assessing the 10 DSM-5 personality disorders.

Population: Adults receiving psychiatric or general medical care.

Publication Dates: 1997-2016.

Acronym: SCID-5-PD.

Scores, 10: Avoidant, Dependent, Obsessive-Compulsive, Paranoid, Schizotypal, Schizoid, Histrionic, Narcissistic, Antisocial, Other Specified.

Administration: Individual.

Price Data, 2016: $79 per user's guide; $74 per 5 interviews.

Time: Administration time not reported.

Comments: Also includes optional, self-report SCI-5-SPQ self-report screening tool.

Authors: Michael B. First, Janet B. W. Williams, Lorna Smith Benjamin, and Robert L. Spitzer.

Publisher: American Psychiatric Publishing, Inc.

Cross References: For reviews by Paul A. Arbisi and Suzanne G. Martin of the Structured Clinical Interview for DSM-IV Axis II Personality Disorders, see 14:374; see also T5:2520 (25 references).

[1984]

Structured Interview for the Five-Factor Model of Personality.

Purpose: Designed to "assess both normal and abnormal personality functioning" using the Five-Factor Model.

Population: Ages 18 and above.

Publication Date: 1997.

Acronym: SIFFM.

Scores, 35: Neuroticism (Anxiety, Hostility, Depression, Self-Consciousness, Impulsiveness, Vulnerability, Total), Extraversion (Warmth, Gregariousness, Assertiveness, Activity, Excitement-Seeking, Positive Emotions, Total), Openness to Experience (Fantasy, Aesthetics, Feelings, Actions, Ideas, Values, Total), Agreeableness (Trust, Straightforwardness, Altruism, Compliance, Modesty, Tender-Mindedness, Total), Conscientiousness (Competence, Order, Dutifulness, Achievement-Striving, Self-Discipline, Deliberation, Total).

Administration: Individual.

Price Data, 2015: $56 per e-Manual; $120 per 25 interview booklets.

Time: (60) minutes.

Authors: Timothy J. Trull and Thomas A. Widiger.

Publisher: Psychological Assessment Resources, Inc.

Cross References: For reviews by Paul M. Mastrangelo and Susana Urbina, see 15:249.

[1985]

Structured Interview of Reported Symptoms, 2nd Edition.

Purpose: Designed to "evaluate feigning of psychiatric symptoms" and "the manner in which it is likely to occur."
Population: Ages 18 and over.
Publication Dates: 1986-2010.
Acronym: SIRS-2.
Scores, 14: Primary Scales (Rare Symptoms, Symptom Combinations, Improbable or Absurd Symptoms, Blatant Symptoms, Subtle Symptoms, Selectivity of Symptoms, Severity of Symptoms, Reported vs. Observed Symptoms), Classification Scale (Rare Symptoms-Total), Supplementary Scales (Direct Appraisal of Honesty, Defensive Symptoms, Improbable Failure, Overly Specified Symptoms, Inconsistency of Symptoms); plus 2 indexes (Modified Total Index, Supplementary Scale Index).
Administration: Individual.
Price Data, 2015: $315 per complete kit including 25 interview booklets, 2 security templates, and manual (2010, 130 pages); $245 per 25 interview booklets; $12 per set of 2 security templates; $86 per manual.
Foreign Language Edition: Interview booklet available in Spanish.
Time: (30-45) minutes.
Authors: Richard Rogers (interview booklet and manual), Kenneth W. Sewell (manual), and Nathan D. Gillard (manual).
Publisher: Psychological Assessment Resources.
Cross References: For reviews by Jeffrey A. Jenkins and Geoffrey L. Thorpe, see 19:159; for reviews by David N. Dixon and Ronald J. Ganellen of an earlier edition, see 12:375.

[1986]

Structured Inventory of Malingered Symptomatology.

Purpose: Designed as a screening measure of malingering to assess symptoms of both feigned psychopathology and cognitive function.
Population: Ages 18 and over.
Publication Date: 2005.
Acronym: SIMS.
Scores, 6: Neurologic Impairment, Affective Disorders, Psychosis, Low Intelligence, Amnestic Disorders, Total.
Administration: Individual.
Price Data, 2015: $156 per complete kit including professional manual (46 pages) and 25 response forms; $82 per professional manual; $80 per 25 response forms.
Time: (10-15) minutes.
Comments: This test can be self-administered.
Authors: Glenn P. Smith and Michelle R. Widows.
Publisher: Psychological Assessment Resources, Inc.
Cross References: For reviews by Thomas M. Dunn and Ronald J. Ganellen, see 17:180.

[1987]

Structured Photographic Articulation Test II Featuring Dudsberry.

Purpose: Designed to assess children's articulation and phonological skills.
Population: Ages 3-0 through 9-11 years.
Publication Dates: 1989–2001.
Acronym: SPAT-D II.
Scores: Total score only.
Administration: Individual.
Price Data, 2016: $199 per kit including manual, 48 color photographs in album, and 30 response forms.
Time: Administration time not reported.
Comments: Forty photographs are used to assess 59 singleton consonants and 10 consonant blends; revision of the Structured Photographic Articulation Test Featuring Dudsberry (SPAT-D).
Authors: Janet I. Dawson and Patricia J. Tattersall.
Publisher: Janelle Publications, Inc.
Cross References: For reviews by Mildred Murray-Ward and Roger L. Towne, see 16:236; for reviews by Clinton W. Bennett and Susan Felsenfeld of the earlier edition, see 12:376.

[1988]

Structured Photographic Expressive Language Test-Preschool 2.

Purpose: Designed to "probe a child's ability to generate early developing morphological and syntactic forms."
Population: Ages 3 to 5-11.
Publication Dates: 1983-2004.
Acronym: SPELT-P 2.
Scores: Total score only.
Administration: Individual.
Price Data, 2016: $199 per manual (2005, 79 pages), 37 color photographs, and 50 response forms.
Time: (20) minutes.
Comments: Includes a system of alternative response structures for assessment of the African American population.
Authors: Janet Dawson, Connie Stout, Julia Eyer, Patricia Tattersall, Janice Fonkalsrud, and Karen Croley.
Publisher: Janelle Publications, Inc.
Cross References: For reviews by Tiffany L. Hutchins and Roger L. Towne, see 18:132; see T5:2524 (13 references) and T4:2588 (1 reference); for a review by Joan D. Berryman of an earlier edition, see 9:1198 (2 references).

[1989]

Structured Photographic Expressive Language Test-Third Edition.

Purpose: Designed to "examine expressive use of morphology and syntax."
Population: Ages 4 to 9-11.
Publication Dates: 1983-2003.

Acronym: SPELT-3.
Score: Total score only.
Administration: Individual.
Price Data, 2016: $199 per manual (2003, 97 pages), 54 color photographs, 30 response forms, and storage box.
Time: (20) minutes.
Comments: Includes a system of alternative response structures for assessment of the African American population.
Authors: Janet I. Dawson, Connie E. Stout, and Julia A. Eyer.
Publisher: Janelle Publications.
Cross References: For reviews by Jorge E. Gonzalez and Craig S. Shwery and by Darrell L. Sabers and Hua-ping Sun, see 18:133; see T5:2524 (13 references) and T4:2588 (1 reference); for a review by Joan D. Berryman of an earlier edition, see 9:1198 (2 references).

[1990]
Student Adaptation to College Question-naire.

Purpose: "Designed to assess how well a student is adapting to the demands of the college experience."
Population: College students.
Publication Date: 1989.
Acronym: SACQ.
Scores, 5: Academic Adjustment, Social Adjustment, Personal Emotional Adjustment, Attachment, Full Scale.
Administration: Group or individual.
Price Data, 2016: $118 per complete kit including 25 hand-scorable questionnaires and manual (76 pages) $59 per 25 hand-scorable questionnaires; $72 per manual.
Time: 15 to 20 minutes.
Authors: Robert W. Baker and Bohdan Siryk.
Publisher: Western Psychological Services.
Cross References: See T5:2525 (13 references) and T4:2590 (9 references); for a review by E. Jack Asher, Jr., see 11:383 (4 references).

[1991]
Student Behavior Survey.

Purpose: A multidimensional assessment to rate behavior and classroom performance to reflect the presence of problems in emotional and behavioral adjustment.
Population: Ages 5–18.
Publication Date: 2000.
Acronym: SBS.
Scores: 14 scales: Academic Performance, Academic Habits, Social Skills, Parent Participation, Health Concerns, Emotional Distress, Unusual Behavior, Social Problems, Verbal Aggression, Physical Aggression, Behavior Problems, Attention-Deficit/Hyperactivity, Oppositional Defiant, Conduct Problems.
Administration: Individual.
Price Data, 2016: $124 per kit including 25 AutoScore™ answer/profile forms and manual (72 pages);

$52.50 per 25 AutoScore™ answer/profile forms; $81 per manual; 21.50 per 100 PC answer sheet.
Time: Untimed.
Comments: Ratings by teachers.
Authors: David Lachar, Sabine A. Wingenfeld, Rex B. Kline, and Christian P. Gruber.
Publisher: Western Psychological Services.
Cross References: For reviews by Stephen N. Axford and by Michael J. Furlong and Renee Pavelski, see 15:250.

[1992]
Student Developmental Task and Lifestyle Assessment.

Purpose: "Assisting students in understanding their own development and establishing goals and plans to shape their own futures."
Population: College students ages 17-24.
Publication Date: 1987.
Acronym: SDTLA.
Scores, 12: Establishing and Clarifying Purpose Task (Educational Involvement Subtask, Career Planning Subtask, Life Management Subtask, Lifestyle Planning Subtask, Cultural Participation Subtask), Developing Mature Interpersonal Relationships Task (Peer Relationships Subtask, Tolerance Subtask, Emotional Autonomy Subtask), Academic Autonomy Task, Salubrious Lifestyle Scale, Intimacy Scale, Response Bias Scale.
Administration: Group.
Price Data: Instrument, manual, and answer key now available free of charge at test publisher's website.
Time: (30-40) minutes.
Comments: Revision of the Student Developmental Task Inventory, Revised, Second Edition.
Authors: Roger B. Winston, Jr., Theodore K. Miller, and Diane L. Cooper.
Publisher: Appalachian State University.
Cross References: See T5:2527 (17 references) and T4:2592 (9 references); for reviews by Mary Henning-Stout and Willam D. Porterfield, see 11:384 (13 references); for reviews by Fred H. Borgen and Steven D. Brown of the Second Edition, see 9:1199 (5 references).

[1993]
Student Instructional Report II.

Purpose: Designed to objectively capture students' evaluations of faculty performance.
Population: College faculty and administrators.
Publication Dates: 1971–2006.
Acronym: SIR II.
Scores: 8 dimensions of college instruction: Course Organization and Planning; Faculty Communication; Faculty-Student Interaction; Assignments, Exams and Grading; Instructional Methods and Materials; Course Outcomes; Student Effort and Involvement; Course Difficulty, Workload and Pace.
Administration: Group.

Price Data: Available from publisher.

Time: (10–15) minutes.

Comments: May be taken online, via e-SIR online or paper and pencil.

Author: Educational Testing Service.

Publisher: Educational Testing Service.

Cross References: See T5:2531 (3 references), T4:2597 (1 reference), and T3:2334 (3 references); for reviews by Frank Costin and William C. McGaghie of the earlier edition, see 8:398 (16 references); see also T2:894 (1 reference).

[1994]

Student Styles Questionnaire™.

Purpose: "Designed to detect individual differences students display in their preferences, temperaments, and personal styles."

Population: Ages 8–13.

Publication Date: 1996.

Acronym: SSQ.

Scores, 8: Extroverted, Introverted, Practical, Imaginative, Thinking, Feeling, Organized, Flexible.

Administration: Group or individual.

Price Data, 2015: $85.25 per starter kit including manual (241 pages), classroom applications booklet, 5 Ready Score™ answer documents, and question booklet; $100.10 per 25 question booklets; $35 per 25 Ready Score™ answer documents; $27.60 per 25 record forms; $117.10 per manual; $35.50 per classroom applications booklet.

Time: (30) minutes.

Authors: Thomas Oakland, Joseph Glutting, and Connie Horton.

Publisher: Pearson.

Cross References: For reviews by Gregory Schraw and Jay R. Stewart, see 14:375.

[1995]

Student-Teacher Relationship Scale.

Purpose: "Provides a quantitative self-report assessment of the relationship between a teacher and a specific student."

Population: Teachers of preschool through Grade 3 students.

Publication Date: 2001.

Acronym: STRS.

Scores, 4: Conflict, Closeness, Dependency, Total.

Administration: Group or individual.

Price Data: This measure is now available for free from the publisher.

Comments: Intended to inform consultation and intervention efforts as part of the Student, Teachers, and Relationship Support (STARS) program.

Author: Robert C. Pianta.

Publisher: Robert C. Pianta.

Cross References: For reviews by Gerald Giraud and by Jorge E. Gonzalez and Chris Gonzalez, see 15:251.

[1996]

Study Attitudes and Methods Survey [Revised Short Form].

Purpose: "Developed to measure non-cognitive factors associated with success in school."

Population: Students in junior high, high school, and college.

Publication Dates: 1972–1985.

Acronym: SAMS.

Scores, 6: Academic Interest-Love of Learning, Academic Drive-Conformity, Study Methods, Study Anxiety, Manipulation, Alienation Toward Authority.

Administration: Group.

Price Data, 2016: $20 per 25 SAMS booklet & answer sheet combined; $7.25 per profile & interpretation guides; $22.25 per hand-scoring keys; $13 per manual; $14.25 per specimen set including one copy of all forms and manual; quantity discounts provided.

Time: (20–25) minutes.

Comments: Test publisher indicates materials have been updated; description will be updated when those test materials are received.

Authors: William B. Michael, Joan J. Michael, and Wayne S. Zimmerman.

Publisher: EdITS/Educational and Industrial Testing Service.

Cross References: For reviews by Robert G. Harrington and Kenneth A. Kiewra, see 14:376; see also T5:2538 (1 reference), T4:2604 (6 references), and T3:2340 (2 references); for reviews by Allen Berger and John W. Lombard of an earlier edition, see 8:818 (6 references); see also T2:1766 (4 references).

[1997]

Stuttering Prediction Instrument for Young Children.

Purpose: Designed to "measure severity and predict chronicity."

Population: Ages 3-8.

Publication Date: 1981.

Acronym: SPI.

Scores, 5: Reactions, Part-Word Repetitions, Prolongations, Frequency, Total.

Administration: Individual.

Price Data, 2015: $126 per complete kit including 50 tests, picture plates, and manual (45 pages); $62 per 50 test forms; $72 per manual with picture plates.

Time: Administration time not reported.

Comments: Information taken from parent interview, observation and tape recording of the child's speech, and analysis of the tape recording.

Author: Glyndon D. Riley.

Publisher: PRO-ED.

Cross References: See T5:2542 (2 references) and T4:2612 (1 reference).

[1998]

Stuttering Severity Instrument–Fourth Edition.

Purpose: Designed to measure the frequency, duration, and physical concomitants of stuttering as well as the naturalness of an individual's speech.
Population: Ages 2-10 to adult.
Publication Dates: 1980-2009.
Acronym: SSI-4.
Scores, 5: Frequency, Duration, Physical Concomitants, Total, Naturalness.
Administration: Individual.
Price Data, 2015: $161 per complete kit including examiner's manual (2009, 68 pages), picture plates, 50 test record and frequency computation forms, and computerized scoring software (CSSS 2.0); $80 per manual and picture plates; $29 per computerized scoring software; $62 per 50 test record and fluency computation forms.
Time: [15-20] minutes.
Comments: Recorded speech sample necessary; includes Clinical Use of Self-Reports form, an oral interview designed to "help clients communicate their feelings about their stuttering to the clinician."
Authors: Glyndon D. Riley.
Publisher: PRO-ED.
Cross References: Reviews are scheduled for *The Twentieth Mental Measurements Yearbook*. See T5:2543 (3 references); for reviews by Ronald B. Gillam and Rebecca McCauley of the third edition, see 13:304 (21 references); see also T4:2613 (5 references).

[1999]

Style of Learning and Thinking.

Purpose: To indicate a student's learning stategy and brain hemisphere preference in problem solving.
Population: Grades K–5, 6–12.
Publication Date: 1988.
Acronym: SOLAT.
Scores, 3: Whole Brain, Left Brain, Right Brain.
Administration: Group.
Forms, 2: Elementary, Youth.
Price Data, 2015: $48 per starter set (specify elementary or youth) including administrator's manual and 35 questionnaires; $12 per administrator's manual; $32 per 35 questionnaires (specify elementary or youth).
Time: [30-40] minutes.
Comments: Self-scored.
Authors: E. Paul Torrance, Bernice McCarthy, Mary Kolesinski, and Jamie Smith.
Publisher: Scholastic Testing Service, Inc.
Cross References: See T5:2545 (6 references); for reviews by Kenneth A. Kiewra and Damian McShane and by Donald U. Robertson and Virginia L. Brown, see 11:390 (2 references).

[2000]

Styles of Leadership Survey.

Purpose: Assesses individual leadership skills under a variety of conditions.
Population: Adults.
Publication Dates: 1968-1995.
Scores, 5: Philosophy, Planning and Goal Setting, Implementation, Performance and Evaluation, Total.
Administration: Group.
Price Data, 2016: $12.95 per instrument.
Time: Untimed.
Comments: Self-administered survey.
Authors: Jay Hall, Jerry B. Harvey, and Martha S. Williams.
Publisher: Teleometrics International, Inc.
Cross References: See T5:2547 (1 reference); for reviews by Kenneth N. Anchor and Norman D. Sundberg, see 12:379 (1 reference); see T3:2351 (1 reference); for a review by Abraham K. Korman of [Styles of Leadership and Management], see 8:1185 (8 references).

[2001]

Styles of Management Inventory.

Purpose: Assesses individual management style under a variety of conditions.
Population: Adults.
Publication Dates: 1964-2000.
Scores, 5: Philosophy, Planning and Goal Setting, Implementation, Performance Evaluation, Total.
Administration: Group.
Price Data, 2016: $12.95 per instrument.
Time: Untimed.
Comments: Self-administered survey.
Authors: Jay Hall, Jerry B. Harvey, and Martha S. Williams.
Publisher: Teleometrics International, Inc.
Cross References: For reviews by Richard W. Faunce and Linda F. Wightman, see 12:380; see T3:2351 (1 reference); for a review by Abraham K. Korman of [Styles of Leadership and Management], see 8:1185 (8 references).

[2002]

Styles of Teamwork Inventory.

Purpose: Assess individual feelings about working in teams and the behaviors one typically employs in work-team situations.
Population: Individuals whose work responsibilities require work-team cooperation.
Publication Dates: 1963-1995.
Acronym: STI.
Scores, 5: Synergistic, Compromise, Win-Lose, Yield-Lose, Lose-Leave.
Administration: Group.
Price Data, 2016: $12.95 per instrument.
Time: Administration time not reported.

Comments: Based on Team Behaviors Model of analysis of individual behaviors in a team setting; self ratings; self scored; formerly called Group Encounter Survey (T3:1014).
Author: Jay Hall.
Publisher: Teleometrics International, Inc.
Cross References: See 8:1048 (2 references).

[2003]

Substance Abuse in Vocational Rehabilitation–Screener2.

Purpose: Designed to screen for high or low probability of substance use disorders, including misuse of prescription medication.
Population: Disability clients ages 18 and older.
Publication Date: 2013.
Acronym: SAVR-S2.
Scores, 3: Probability of having a substance use disorder (high or low), Defensiveness, Random Answering Pattern (validity score).
Administration: Individual.
Price Data, 2015: $11.50 per 1 to 9 Auto-Score reports including user's guide (34 pages) and support materials; volume discounts available.
Time: (10-15) minutes.
Comments: Paper questionnaire; scoring and reporting completed by test publisher.
Authors: Glenn A. Miller (screener), Nancy Winningham (user's guide), and Linda E. Lazowski (user's guide).
Publisher: The SASSI Institute.
Cross References: Reviews are scheduled for *The Twentieth Mental Measurements Yearbook*.

[2004]

Substance Abuse Life Circumstance Evaluation.

Purpose: "Designed to assess alcohol and drug use/abuse behavior, as well as the role that attitude and stress may play in this use/abuse."
Population: Adults.
Publication Date: 1988.
Acronym: SALCE.
Scores, 6: Test-Taking Attitude, Life Circumstance Evaluation, Drinking Evaluation Category, Alcohol Addiction Evaluation, Drug Use Evaluation, Summary Score.
Administration: Individual or group.
Foreign Language Edition: Available in Spanish.
Price Data: Available from publisher.
Time: (20) minutes.
Comments: Self-administered; computer scored; provides both DSM-5 classification and ASAM patient placement criteria.
Author: ADE Incorporated.
Publisher: ADE Incorporated.
Cross References: For a review by Anita M. Hubley, see 14:377.

[2005]

Substance Abuse Screener in American Sign Language.

Purpose: Designed to "to help identify substance abuse issues and determine the appropriate steps to take in order to improve clients' chances of success in employment, optimal health, and increased self-sufficiency."
Population: Deaf and hard-of-hearing individuals ages 18 and older.
Publication Date: 2013.
Acronym: SAS-ASL.
Scores: Probability of having a substance use disorder (high or low).
Administration: Individual.
Price Data, 2016: Access to questionnaire and video is free to registered users; $11.50 per 1 to 9 auto-score reports (quantity discounts available).
Time: (10-15) minutes.
Comments: Computer administered via video.
Authors: Nancy Winningham and Linda E. Lazowski.
Publisher: The SASSI Institute.
Cross References: Reviews are scheduled for *The Twentieth Mental Measurements Yearbook*.

[2006]

Substance Abuse Screening Test.

Purpose: "Designed to screen-out those students who are unlikely to have a substance abuse problem."
Population: Ages 13–adult.
Publication Date: 1993.
Acronym: SAST.
Scores: Total Level of Risk.
Administration: Group.
Forms, 2: Response Form, Observation Report.
Price Data, 2016: $79 per complete kit including 50 Response Forms, 50 Observation Reports, and manual (34 pages); $25.75 per 50 Response Forms; $25.75 per 50 Observation Reports; $34.75 per manual.
Time: (5) minutes.
Authors: Terry Hibpshman and Sue Larson.
Publisher: Slosson Educational Publications, Inc.
Cross References: For reviews by Mary Lou Kelley and Mariela C. Shirley, see 13:307.

[2007]

The Substance Abuse Subtle Screening Inventory—3.

Purpose: Designed to identify individuals who have a high probability or low probability of having a substance use disorder.
Population: Ages 18 and older.
Publication Dates: 1983–1997.
Acronym: SASSI-3.
Scores: 10 subscales: Face Valid Alcohol, Face Valid Other Drugs, Symptoms, Obvious Attributes, Subtle

Attributes, Defensiveness, Supplemental Addiction Measure, Family vs. Controls, Correctional, Random Answering Pattern.
Administration: Individual or group.
Price Data: Available from publisher.
Foreign Language Edition: Spanish version available.
Time: [15] minutes.
Comments: May be administered via paper and pencil with hand scoring or scoring by optical scanning; computer software (for PC) or online administration available; audio CD available for people with special needs regarding vision or literacy.
Author: Glenn A. Miller.
Publisher: The SASSI Institute.
Cross References: For reviews by Ephrem Fernandez and David J. Pittenger, see 15:252; see T5:2553 (6 references); for reviews by Barbara Kerr and Nicholas A. Vacc of an earlier edition, see 12:381 (1 reference); see also T4:2623 (1 reference).

[2008]
Substance Use Disorder Diagnostic Schedule–5.

Purpose: A structured interview designed to provide "a detailed assessment of substance use disorders in accordance with the DSM-5."
Population: Adults.
Publication Dates: 1995-2013.
Acronym: SUDDS-5.
Scores: 4 diagnostic conclusions (No Diagnosis, Mild Substance Use Disorder, Moderate Substance Use Disorder, Severe Substance Use Disorder) for 9 substance categories (Alcohol, Cannabis, Cocaine, Stimulants-amphetamine or other, Inhalants, Opiods, Sedatives/hynotics/anxiolytic, Hallucinogens: Phencyclinidine/other, Other/unknown) plus screening information for Stress, Anxiety, PTSD, and Depression.
Administration: Individual.
Price Data, 2015: $67.50 per 25 assessments; $20 per manual (2013, 35 pages).
Time: (35-45) minutes.
Authors: Norman G. Hoffmann and Patricia A. Harrison.
Publisher: The Change Companies.
Cross References: Reviews are scheduled for *The Twentieth Mental Measurements Yearbook*. For reviews by Tony Cellucci and Mark H. Stone of the previous edition (DSM-IV), see 15:253; for reviews by Andres Barona and Steven I. Pfeiffer of an earlier edition (DSM-III), see 13:308 (2 references).

[2009]
Suffolk Reading Scale 2.

Purpose: Designed to assess "reading ability."
Population: Ages 6.0 to 14.11.

Publication Dates: 1986–2002.
Acronym: SRS2.
Scores: Total score only.
Administration: Individual or group.
Levels, 3: 1 (Ages 6.0 to 8.11), 2 (Ages 8.0 to 11.11), 3 (Ages 10.0 to 14.11).
Forms, 2: A, B.
Price Data: Available from publisher.
Time: (50) minutes.
Author: Fred Hagley.
Publisher: GL Assessment [England].
Cross References: For reviews by Jennifer N. Mahdavi and Howard Margolis, see 16:237; see also T5:2556 (3 references); for reviews by Robert B. Cooter, Jr. and Richard Lehrer of an earlier edition, see 11:392.

[2010]
Suicidal Ideation Questionnaire.

Purpose: Designed to "screen for suicidal ideation in adolescents."
Population: Grades 7–9 (SIQ), 10–12 (SIQ-JR).
Publication Dates: 1987–1988.
Acronym: SIQ.
Scores: Total Suicidal Ideation.
Administration: Individual or small group.
Levels, 2: SIQ (senior high school), SIQ-JR (junior high school).
Price Data, 2015: $196 per introductory kit including manual (1988, 47 pages), 25 each SIQ and SIQ-JR hand-scorable answer sheets, and scoring keys for SIQ and SIQ-JR.
Time: (5–10) minutes.
Author: William M. Reynolds.
Publisher: Psychological Assessment Resources, Inc.
Cross References: See T5:2556 (11 references) and T4:2627 (1 reference); for reviews by James C. Carmer and Collie W. Conoley, see 11:393 (2 references).

[2011]
Suicide Intervention Response Inventory [Revised].

Purpose: Designed to assess "the paraprofessional's ability to select an appropriate response to the self-destructive client."
Population: Mental health paraprofessionals.
Publication Dates: 1980–1997.
Acronym: SIRI.
Scores: Total score only.
Administration: Group.
Price Data: Available from publisher.
Time: (15) minutes.
Author: Robert A. Neimeyer.
Publisher: Robert A. Neimeyer, Ph.D.
Cross References: See T5:2558 (3 references).

[2012]

Suicide Probability Scale.

Purpose: Designed to "measure an individual's self-reported attitudes and behaviors which have a bearing on suicide risk."
Population: Ages 14 and over.
Publication Date: 1982-1988.
Acronym: SPS.
Scores, 5: Hopelessness, Suicide Ideation, Negative Self-Evaluations, Hostility, Total.
Administration: Group or individual.
Price Data, 2016: $118 per kit including 25 tests, 25 profiles, and manual (73 pages plus test and profile); $52.50 per 25 tests; $52.50 per 100 profiles; $65.50 per manual.
Time: (5–10) minutes.
Authors: John G. Cull and Wayne S. Gill.
Publisher: Western Psychological Services.
Cross References: See T5:2559 (13 references) and T4:2629 (6 references); for a review by Stephen L. Golding, see 9:1210.

[2013]

Super's Work Values Inventory—Revised.

Purpose: Assesses relative importance of selected attributes of occupations and jobs.
Population: Middle school students through adults.
Publication Date: 2001-2015.
Acronym: SWVI-R.
Scores, 12: Achievement, Co-Workers, Creativity, Income, Independence, Lifestyle, Challenge, Prestige, Security, Supervision, Variety, Workplace.
Administration: Individual or group.
Price Data: Available from publisher.
Foreign Language and Other Editions: The test is available in U.S. Spanish and has been localized for English use in the Middle East (Abu Dhabi, Qatar) and central Africa (Rwanda).
Time: (15–20) minutes.
Authors: Donald E. Super (original inventory); Donald G. Zytowski (revised version).
Publisher: Kuder, Inc.
Cross References: See T4:2998 (9 references) and T3:2567 (17 references); for an excerpted review by Frederick Brown of an earlier edition, see 8:1030 (52 references); see also T2:2221 (12 references); for reviews by Ralph F. Berdie and David V. Tiedeman, and an excerpted review by John W. French, see 7:1042 (33 references).

[2014]

Supervisory Simulator.

Purpose: "Designed to assess supervisory skills of first-level supervisors, forepersons and/or team leaders independent of any particular job title or organization; may be used for selection and/or career development."
Population: First-level supervisors, forepersons, or team leaders.
Publication Dates: 1991–2011.
Acronym: SupSim.
Scores, 3: Leadership/Decision Making, Team Relations, Total .
Administration: Group or individual.
Forms, 5: Public and private sector forms include Blue-Collar Teams, Office/Clerical Teams, Police, Fire, Transportation.
Restricted Distribution: Clients may be required to pay a nominal one-time overhead/sign-up fee.
Price Data, 2015: $320-$360 per candidate (depending on the version) for rental/scoring and a detailed Career Development Report that identifies strengths, weaknesses, and developmental needs with specific learning objectives for each of the two factors measured by the test.
Time: (75) minutes.
Comments: All versions are available for online administration.
Author: Richard C. Joines.
Publisher: Management & Personnel Systems, Inc.

[2015]

Supplementary Spelling Assessments.

Purpose: Designed to "augment the assessments of spelling teachers make on the basis of how, and how well, children spell in their writing."
Population: Years 4-8.
Publication Date: 2007–2010.
Acronym: SSpA.
Administration: Group.
Price Data, 2015: A$52.50 per starter set including teacher manual (2010, 47 pages), administration and scoring guide (2010, 35 pages), plus one of each test booklet and diagnostic assessment; $11.50 per 10 test booklets (specify Year 4, 5, 6, 7, or 8; $29 per 10 Diagnostic Assessments (specify 1 or 2); $26 per teacher manual; $21 per administration and scoring guide.
Author: Cedric Croft.
Publisher: New Zealand Council for Educational Research [New Zealand].
    a) PART 1: ACHIEVEMENT AND PROGRESS.
    Time: (35) minutes.
    Population: Years 4-8.
      1) *Test 1.*
      Scores, 4: Dictated Words, Beginning Sounds, Recognising Errors in Words, Recognising Errors in Sentences.
      2) *Test 2.*
      Scores, 5: Dictated Words, Dictated Paragraph, Recognising Errors in Words, Recognising Errors in Sentences, Recognising Correct Words.
      3) *Test 3.*
      Scores, 5: Dictated Words, Dictated Paragraph, Recognising Errors in Words, Recognising Errors in Sentences, Recognising Correct Words.

4) *Test 4.*

Scores, 4: Dictated Words, Correcting Errors in Paragraph, Recognising and Classifying Errors in Sentences, Correcting Errors in Words.

5) *Test 5.*

Scores, 4: Dictated Words, Correcting Errors in Paragraph, Recognising and Classifying Errors in Sentences, Correcting Errors in Words.

b) PART 2: DIAGNOSTIC ASSESSMENTS.
Time: Untimed.
Population: Years 5-6.
Scores, 6: Beginning Sounds/Initial Consonants, Beginning Sounds/Prefixes, Ending Sounds/Suffixes, Short and Long Vowel Sounds, Silent Letters, Shortened Words/Contractions.
Cross References: For reviews by Kathleen D. Allen and Maureen Siera and by Jeffrey K. Smith, see 19:160.

[2016]
Supports Intensity Scale–Adult Version.

Purpose: Designed to "measure the relative intensity of support that each person with intellectual disability or related developmental disabilities needs to fully participate in community life."
Population: Individuals ages 16-64 with intellectual or closely related developmental disabilities.
Publication Dates: 2004-2015.
Acronym: SIS-A.
Scores, 9: Home Living, Community Living, Lifelong Learning, Employment, Health and Safety, Social, Support Needs Index, Exceptional Medical Needs, Exceptional Behavioral Needs.
Administration: Individual.
Price Data, 2016: $155 per user's manual (2015, 136 pages) and 25 interview forms; $50 per 25 interview forms; $190 per 100 interview forms.
Time: (120-150) minutes.
Comments: Structured interview format.
Authors: James R. Thompson, Brian R. Bryant, Robert L. Schalock, Karrie A. Shogren, Marc J. Tassé, Michael L. Wehmeyer, Edward M. Campbell, Ellis M. (Pat) Craig, Carolyn Hughes, and David A. Rotholz.
Publisher: American Association on Intellectual and Developmental Disabilities.
Cross References: For reviews by Sandra A. Loew and David J. Pittenger of an earlier edition, see 16:238.

[2017]
Supports Intensity Scale–Children's Version.

Purpose: Designed as a standardized measure to assess the intensity of support needs of children with intellectual or developmental disabilities.
Population: Individuals ages 5-16 with intellectual or closely related developmental disabilities.
Publication Date: 2016.
Acronym: SIS-C.
Scores, 10: Exceptional Medical Needs, Exceptional Behavioral Needs, Home Life, Community & Neighbor-

hood, School Participation, School Learning, Health & Safety, Social, Advocacy, Support Needs Index.
Administration: Individual.
Price Data: Available from publisher.
Time: Administration time not reported.
Comments: Structured interview format; information must be collected from at least 2 respondents.
Authors: James R. Thompson, Michael L. Wehmeyer, Carolyn Hughes, Karrie A. Shogren, Hyojeong Seo, Todd D. Little, Robert L. Schalock, Rodney E. Realon, Susan R. Copeland, James R. Patton, Edward A. Polloway, Debbie Shelden, Shea Tanis, and Marc J. Tassé.
Publisher: American Association on Intellectual and Developmental Disabilities.

[2018]
Surgical Weight Loss Psychological Screening.

Purpose: Designed to identify "suitable candidate[s] for Bariatric Surgery."
Population: Potential candidates for bariatric surgery.
Publication Date: 2011.
Acronym: SWLPS.
Scores, 34: Overall Results, Compliance [Sense of Control Over Health, Adherence History, Self-Discipline, Procrastination], Self-Motivation [Reward Dependence, Proactive Attitude, Self-Efficacy], Emotional Strength [Resilience, Anger Control, Tolerance for Frustration, Emotional Eating], Coping Skills [Problem Solving, Information Seeking, Negotiation, Support Seeking, Positive Cognitive Restructuring, Emotional Regulation, Distraction, Rumination, Avoidance, Helplessness, Opposition, Social Withdrawal], Current Mental Health Issues, Suicide Concern, Mental Disorder History, Drug History, Substance Use History, Impression Management.
Administration: Individual.
Price Data: Available from publisher.
Time: (45) minutes.
Comments: Self-administered online assessment. The test publisher provides clients with information about the methods and theoretical basis used in the development of the test as well as benchmarks for relevant industries and racial/ethnic group comparison data.
Author: PsychTests AIM, Inc.
Publisher: PsychTests AIM, Inc.
Cross References: For reviews by Stephen J. Freeman and Michael G. Kavan, see 19:161.

[2019]
Survey of Client Relations.

Purpose: Designed to measure the skills necessary to build strong client relationships.
Population: Consultants, sales persons, and service and client representatives.
Publication Dates: 1996-2010.

Acronym: SCR.

Scores, 13: Understanding Clients, Communicating Effectively, Account Service, Analyzing Needs, Presenting Benefits, Making Recommendations, Answering Objections, Personal Enthusiasm, Personal Pressure, Acknowledging Client Responses, Professionalism, Approachability, Overall Satisfaction.

Administration: Individual.

Price Data: Available from publisher.

Comments: Publisher suggests allowing 2-3 weeks to collect feedback.

Time: 20-30 minutes.

Authors: Clark L Wilson.

Publisher: The Clark Wilson Group, Inc. (subsidiary of The Booth Company, Inc.).

[2020]
Survey of Coaching Practices.

Purpose: Designed to assess the coaching skills of a manager.

Population: Managers and supervisors.

Publication Dates: 1993-2004.

Acronym: SCP.

Scores, 12: Commitment to Coaching, Goal Setting, Technical/Functional Expertise, Coaching Skills, Coaching for Teamwork, Assessment Skills, Defensiveness, Control of Performance, Recognizing Good Performance, Approachability, Trust, Overall Effectiveness.

Administration: Individual.

Price Data: Available from publisher.

Comments: Publisher suggests allowing 2-3 weeks to collect feedback.

Time: 20-30 minutes.

Authors: Richard L. Dowall and Clark L. Wilson.

Publisher: The Clark Wilson Group, Inc. (subsidiary of The Booth Company, Inc.).

[2021]
Survey of Employee Access.

Purpose: Measures effective managerial behavior.

Population: Adults.

Publication Dates: 1989–2000.

Acronym: SEA.

Scores, 5: Access to the Problem, Access to People, Access to Information and Resources, Access to Emotional/Procedural Supports, Access to Solution.

Administration: Group.

Price Data, 2016: $12.95 per instrument.

Time: Untimed.

Comments: Self-administered survey.

Author: Jay Hall.

Publisher: Teleometrics International, Inc.

Cross References: For reviews by Marcia J. Belcher and Robert Fitzpatrick, see 12:382.

[2022]
Survey of Functional Adaptive Behaviors.

Purpose: To assess an individual's skill level of adaptive behavior.

Population: Ages 16 and over.

Publication Date: 1986.

Acronym: SFAB.

Scores, 5: Residential Living Skills, Daily Living Skills, Academic Skills, Vocational Skills, SFAB Total Score.

Administration: Individual.

Manual: No manual.

Price Data, 2016: $93.50 per 25 surveys.

Authors: Jack G. Dial, Carolyn Mezger, Theresa Massey, Steve Carter, and Lawrence T. McCarron.

Publisher: McCarron-Dial Systems, Inc.

Cross References: For reviews by Steven W. Lee and Steven I. Pfeiffer, see 11:404.

[2023]
Survey of Interpersonal Values.

Purpose: Designed to measure certain values involving an individual's relationships with others.

Population: Individuals in a variety of occupations and job levels.

Publication Dates: 1960–1993.

Acronym: SIV.

Scores, 6: Support, Conformity, Recognition, Independence, Benevolence, Leadership.

Administration: Individual or group.

Price Data: Available from publisher.

Time: No limit (approximately 15 minutes).

Author: Leonard V. Gordon.

Publisher: General Dynamics Information Technology.

Cross References: See T5:2581 (3 references), T4:2653 (3 references), and T3:2366 (14 references); for reviews by John D. Black and Allan L. LaVoie, see 8:688 (51 references); see also T2:1407 (78 references) and P:261 (48 references); for reviews by Lee J. Cronbach, Leonard D. Goodstein, and John K. Hemphill and an excerpted review by Laurence Siegel, see 6:184 (12 references).

[2024]
Survey of Management Practices [Teleometrics International, Inc.].

Purpose: To assess a manager's organizational practices, and whether they enhance employee productivity.

Population: Subordinates of managers.

Publication Dates: 1987–1995.

Acronym: SMP.

Scores, 12: Dimension I (Management Values, Support Structure, Managerial Credibility, Total), Dimension II (Impact, Relevance, Community, Total), Dimension III (Task Environment, Social Context, Problem Solving, Total).

Administration: Group.

Price Data, 2016: $12.95 per instrument.

Time: Administration time not reported.
Comments: Manager behavior rated by subordinates.
Author: Jay Hall.
Publisher: Teleometrics International, Inc.

[2025]

Survey of Management Practices [The Clark Wilson Group, Inc.].

Purpose: Designed to assess supervisory development and basic managerial practices.
Population: Managers and supervisors at all levels.
Publication Dates: 1973-1997.
Acronym: SMP.
Scores, 17: Clarification of Goals and Objectives, Upward Communication/Participation, Orderly Work Planning, Expertise, Stakeholder Management, Work Facilitation, Teambuilding, Feedback, Time Emphasis, Control of Details, Goal Pressure, Delegation (Permissiveness), Recognizing Good Performance, Work Group Effectiveness, Tension Level, General Morale, Commitment.
Administration: Individual.
Price Data: Available from publisher.
Time: 20-30 minutes.
Comments: Publisher suggests allowing 2-3 weeks to collect feedback.
Author: Clark L. Wilson.
Publisher: The Clark Wilson Group, Inc. (subsidiary of The Booth Company, Inc.).

[2026]

Survey of Organizational Climate.

Purpose: To assess an individual's opinion of his/her organizational climate.
Population: Employees.
Publication Dates: 1977–1985.
Scores, 12: Clarity of Goals, Job Interest and Challenge, Rewards and Satisfactions, Standards of Excellence, Degree of Responsibility, Personal Development, Working Relationships, Advancement/Mobility, Job Security, Management's Credibility, Personnel Policies and Procedures, Self-Confidence.
Administration: Group or individual.
Manual: No manual.
Price Data, 2016: $59.95; volume discounts available.
Time: (20) minutes.
Comments: Self-scored.
Author: Training House, Inc.
Publisher: HRD Press, Inc.
Cross References: For a review by Charles K. Parsons, see 11:406.

[2027]

Survey of Pain Attitudes.

Purpose: "Developed to assess a patient's attitudes and beliefs about pain."

Population: Individuals ages 21-80 who are suffering from chronic pain.
Publication Dates: 1987-2007.
Acronym: SOPA.
Administration: Group.
Scores, 7: Adaptive Beliefs (Control Scale, Emotion Scale), Maladaptive Beliefs (Disability Scale, Harm Scale, Medication Scale, Solicitude Scale, Medical Cure Scale).
Price Data, 2015: $202 per kit including technical manual (2007, 52 pages), 25 rating forms, 25 score summary/profile sheets, and 25 pain worksheets; $66 per technical manual; $80 per 25 rating forms; $39 per 25 score summary/profile sheets; $29 per 25 pain worksheets.
Time: (10-15) minutes.
Authors: Mark P. Jensen and Paul Karoly.
Publisher: Psychological Assessment Resources, Inc.
Cross References: For reviews by Jennifer G. Fillingim and Conn Thomas and by Stephen J. Freeman, see 18:134.

[2028]

Survey of Personal Values.

Purpose: To "measure certain critical values that help to determine the manner in which individuals cope with the problems of everyday living."
Population: Individuals in a variety of occupations, high school and college students.
Publication Dates: 1964–1992.
Acronym: SPV.
Scores, 6: Practical Mindedness, Achievement, Variety, Decisiveness, Orderliness, Goal Orientation.
Administration: Individual or group.
Price Data: Available from publisher.
Time: No limit (approximately 15 minutes).
Author: Leonard V. Gordon.
Publisher: General Dynamics Information Technology.
Cross References: For reviews by William P. Erchul and Rodney L. Lowman, see 10:354; see also T3:2370 (5 references) and T2:1409 (5 references); for a review by Gene V Glass, see 7:148 (6 references); see also P:263 (3 references).

[2029]

Survey of Student Assessment of Study Behaviors.

Purpose: Designed to help students understand their current study behaviors.
Population: Grades 6–13.
Publication Date: 1991.
Scores, 6: Positive Attitudes, Useful Work Habits, Efficient Learning Tools, Good Comprehension, High Performance Writing, Effective Test Taking.
Administration: Individual.
Price Data, 2016: $3 per survey.
Time: Administration time not reported.
Comments: Self-report survey.

Author: The Cambridge Stratford Study Skills Institute.
Publisher: The Cambridge Stratford Study Skills Institute.

[2030]
Survey of Work Styles.
Purpose: A "measure of six components of the Type A behavior pattern."
Population: Adults.
Publication Dates: 1987–1998.
Acronym: SWS.
Scores, 8: Impatience, Anger, Time Urgency, Work Involvement, Job Dissatisfaction, Competitiveness, Scale A, Total.
Administration: Group or individual.
Price Data, 2015: $25 per test manual on CD; $155 per software installation package, includes 10 coupons for computer reports; $12-$20 (depending on volume) per online password.
Time: 15 minutes.
Comments: Available for online scoring at www.sigmatesting.com.
Authors: Douglas N. Jackson and Anna Mavrogiannis Gray.
Publisher: SIGMA Assessment Systems, Inc.
Cross References: See T5:2592 (1 reference); for a review by Peggy A. Hicks, see 13:311 (1 reference); see also T4:2664 (1 reference).

[2031]
Survey of Work Values, Revised, Form U.
Purpose: To measure work values.
Population: Employees.
Publication Dates: 1975-1976.
Scores, 6: Social Status, Activity Preference, Upward Striving, Attitude Toward Earnings, Pride in Work, Job Involvement.
Administration: Group or individual.
Manual: No manual.
Price Data: Available at no charge from test publisher.
Time: 15 minutes.
Authors: Bowling Green State University.
Publisher: Bowling Green State University.
Cross References: For reviews by Julie A. Allison and by H. John Bernardin and Donna K. Cooke, see 12:383 (1 reference); see also T4:2665 (1 reference).

[2032]
Swallowing Ability and Function Evaluation.
Purpose: "Designed for evaluating and treating dysphagia."
Population: Adolescents and adults.
Publication Date: 2003.
Acronym: SAFE.
Scores, 3: Physical Examination, Oral Phase, Pharyngeal Phase.

Administration: Individual.
Price Data, 2015: $157 per complete kit including examiner's manual (37 pages), Treatment and Resource Manual (235 pages), and 50 profile/examiner record forms; $63 per examiner's manual; $72 per Treatment Manual; $34 per 50 profile/examiner record forms.
Time: (20–25) minutes.
Authors: Peggy Kipping, Deborah Ross-Swain and Patricia Yee.
Publisher: PRO-ED.
Cross References: For a review by Carolyn Mitchell Person, see 16:240.

[2033]
Symbol Digit Modalities Test.
Purpose: Designed as an early screening of cerebral dysfunction.
Population: Ages 8 and over.
Publication Date: 1973.
Acronym: SDMT.
Scores: Total score only.
Administration: Group or individual.
Forms, 2: Written, Oral.
Price Data, 2016: $124 per complete kit including 25 WPS AutoScore™ test forms and manual (10 pages plus test); $62.50 per 25 AutoScore™ test forms; $69.50 per manual.
Time: 1.5(10) minutes.
Author: Aaron Smith.
Publisher: Western Psychological Services.
Cross References: See T5:2599 (43 references), T4:2671 (20 references), and T3:2380 (2 references); for reviews by Brad S. Chissom and James C. Reed, see 8:878; see also T2:1889 (4 references).

[2034]
Symbol Imagery Test.
Purpose: "Designed to measure a student's symbol imagery for letters in both random and orthographically regular combinations."
Population: Ages 6-0 to 17-11.
Publication Date: 2010.
Acronym: SI Test.
Scores: Total score only.
Administration: Individual.
Price Data, 2015: $179.95 per complete kit, including letters and words cards, 25 examiner's record booklets, and examiner's manual (128 pages); $114.95 per examiner's manual; $69.95 per 25 record booklets; $34.95 per set of letter and word cards.
Time: (10-20) minutes.
Author: Nanci Bell.
Publisher: Gander Publishing.
Cross References: For reviews by C. Dale Carpenter and Thomas McKnight, see 19:162.

[2035]

Symbolic Play Test, Second Edition.

Purpose: Developed to assess early concept formation and symbolization based on a child's spontaneous non-verbal play.
Population: Ages 1–3.
Publication Dates: 1976–1988.
Scores: Total score only.
Administration: Individual.
Price Data, 2016: £310 per complete set including toys, 25 record forms, and manual (1988, 39 pages); £40 per 25 record forms.
Time: (10–15) minutes.
Authors: Marianne Lowe and Anthony J. Costello.
Publisher: GL Assessment [England].
Cross References: See T5:2601 (3 references); for reviews by Anthony W. Paolitto and Harvey N. Switzky, see 12:384; see also T4:2673 (2 references) and T3:2383 (1 reference).

[2036]

Symptom Assessment—45 Questionnaire.

Purpose: "Designed as a brief yet comprehensive general assessment of psychiatric symptomalogy."
Population: Ages 13 and over, reading at the 6th grade level or higher.
Publication Dates: 1996–1998.
Acronym: SA-45.
Scores, 11: 9 subscales (Anxiety, Depression, Hostility, Interpersonal Sensitivity, Obsessive-Compulsive, Paranoid Ideation, Phobic Anxiety, Psychoticism, Somatization), 2 composite scores (Global Severity Index, Positive Symptom Total).
Administration: Individual or Group.
Price Data, 2015: $117 per kit including manual (113 pages) and 25 Quikscore forms; $55 per 25 Quikscore forms; $69 per technical manual.
Time: (10–15) minutes.
Comments: Derived from the original Symptom Checklist—90 (SCL-90; 2037); self-report inventory.
Authors: Strategic Advantage, Inc. and Mark Marush.
Publisher: Multi-Health Systems, Inc.
Cross References: For reviews by William M. Reynolds and Chockalingam Viswesvaran, see 14:378.

[2037]

Symptom Checklist-90-Revised.

Purpose: "Designed primarily to reflect the psychological symptom patterns of psychiatric and medical patients," as well as nonpatients.
Population: Adults and adolescents age 13 and older.
Publication Date: 1975.
Acronym: SCL-90-R®.
Scores: 9 primary symptom dimensions: Somatization, Obsessive-Compulsive, Interpersonal Sensitivity, Depression, Anxiety, Hostility, Phobic Anxiety, Paranoid

Ideation, Psychoticism; plus 3 indices of distress: Global Severity Index, Positive Symptom Distress Index, Positive Symptom Total.
Administration: Group or individual.
Price Data, 2015: $78.50 per web-based starter kit including manual, 3 answer sheets, 1 test booklet, and 3 administrations; $124 per hand-scoring starter kit including manual, 50 answer sheets, 50 profile forms, 2 worksheets, and answer keys (specify Nonpatient Adult, Nonpatient Adolescent, Outpatient Psychiatric, Inpatient Psychiatric); $80.45 per mail-in scoring service starter kit with interpretive reports including manual, softcover test booklet, and answer sheets for 3 administrations.
Foreign Language Edition: Spanish materials available.
Time: (12–15) minutes.
Comments: Self-report test; companion clinician and observer rating forms also available.
Author: Leonard R. Derogatis.
Publisher: Pearson.
Cross References: See T5:2603 (593 references) and T4:2674 (318 references); for reviews by Jerome D. Pauker and Robert W. Payne, see 9:1082 (61 references); see also T3:2100 (13 references).

[2038]

System for Testing and Evaluation of Potential.

Purpose: "To evaluate managerial and professional personnel."
Population: Managerial and professional personnel.
Publication Dates: 1986–1995.
Acronym: LH-STEP.
Administration: Group or individual.
Price Data: Available from publisher.
Author: Human Resources Center, The University of Chicago.
Publisher: General Dynamics Information Technology.
a) LH-STEP (STANDARD REPORT).
Scores: 6 ratings: Potential Estimates (Executive, Middle Manager, Supervisors and Nonsupervisory Professionals), Job Skills (Executive, Middle Manager, Supervisors and Nonsupervisory Professionals); 39 scores: Predictor Profile: (School Achievement, Drive, Vocational Satisfaction, Financial Responsibility, General Family Responsibility, Leadership, Relaxation Pursuits, Non-Verbal Reasoning, Word Fluency, Vocabulary, Closure Flexibility, Creative Potential, Sales Aptitude, Personal Insight, Extroversion, Emotional Responsiveness, Self-Reliance, Ability to Work Under Pressure, Level of Stress Response, Internal Adjustment, External Adjustment, Social Adjustment, General Adjustment), Job Skills: Organization (Setting Organizational Objectives, Financial Planning and Review, Improving Work Procedures and Practices, Interdepartmental Coordination), Leadership (Developing and Implementing Technical Ideas, Judgment and Decision Making, Developing Group Cooperation and Teamwork, Coping With Difficulties and Emergencies, Promoting

Safety Attitudes and Practices, Communications), Human Resources (Developing Employee Potential, Supervisory Practices, Self-Development and Improvement, Personnel Practices), Community (Promoting Community/Organization Relations, Handling Outside Contacts).

Price Data: $230 or less per battery.

Time: (190–210) minutes.

b) LH-STEP (EXTENDED REPORT).

Scores: 6 ratings: same as LH-STEP Standard Report; 63 scores: same as LH-STEP Standard Report, plus Calm, Cautious, Composed, Decisive, Demonstrative, Even-Tempered, Persevering, Seeks Company, Self-Confident, Serious, Steady Worker, Talkative, Reaction Time to Verbal Stimuli, Reaction Time to Color Stimuli, Dominance, Independence, Autonomous Work Environment, Pressure Performance, Energy Level, Speed of Reaction, Ideational Spontaneity, Theoretical Interests, Artistic Interests, Mechanical Interests; 12 tests: Managerial and Professional Job Functions Inventory for Ability, Experience and Background Inventory, Word Fluency, Temperament Comparator, Vocabulary Inventory, Non-Verbal Reasoning, Sales Inventory, Cree Questionnaire, The Press Test, Closure Flexibility, EMO Questionnaire, Management Style Questionnaire.

Price Data: $230 or less per battery.

Time: (190–210) minutes.

[2039]

Systematic Analysis of Language Transcripts 16 (SALT 16).

Purpose: Clinical software designed to assess language acquisition and disorders through the use of language samples.

Population: Students in prekindergarten through Grade 12.

Publication Dates: 2009-2016.

Acronym: SALT 16.

Scores: 8 variables in Standard Measures Report: Transcript Length, Intelligibility, Narrative/Expositor/Persuasion Structure, Syntax/Morphology, Semantics, Discourse, Verbal Facility, Errors.

Administration: Individual.

Price Data, 2016: $189 per clinical version of software and textbook (2nd edition clinician's guide); $69 per student version with textbook; $599 per instructional version site license; $549 per research version; $30 per textbook.

Foreign Language & Other Editions: Bilingual Spanish/English and Australian databases available.

Time: Unlimited.

Author: Jon F. Miller and Aquiles Iglesias (software); Jon F. Miller, Karen Andriacchi, and Ann Nockerts (clinician's guide).

Publisher: SALT Software, LLC.

Cross References: For reviews by Abigail Baxter and Kathy L. Shapley of the 2010 English Version, see 19:164; for reviews by Jeanette W. Farmer and by Tiffany L. Hutchins and Michael S. Cannizzaro of the 2010 Bilingual SE Version, see 19:163.

[2040]

Systematic Screening for Behavior Disorders, Second Edition.

Purpose: Designed as a universal screener for identifying students with either externalizing or internalizing behavior problems and disorders.

Population: Students in preschool through Grade 9.

Publication Dates: 1990-2014.

Acronym: SSBD.

Administration: Group.

Price Data, 2016: $225 per portfolio, including administrator's guide (2014, 210 pages), 1 CD with technical manual, 10 classroom screening packets Grades 1-9, and 2 classroom screening packets PreK-K; $10 per screening packet, including 1 copy Stage 1 screening form, 3 copies Stage 2 Screening for Externalizing Students form, and 3 copies Stage 2 Screening for Internalizing Students form.

Time: (45) minutes for each stage.

Comments: Completed via pencil and paper or online; rankings completed by teacher at each stage.

Authors: Hill M. Walker, Herbert H. Severson, and Edward G. Feil.

Publisher: Pacific Northwest Publishing.

a) STAGE 1.

Scores: 2 rankings: Internalizing, Externalizing.

b) STAGE 2.

1) *PreK-K.*

Scores, 4: Critical Events Index, Aggressive Behavior Scale (for externalizers), Social Interaction Scale (for internalizers), Combined Frequency Index for Adaptive and Maladaptive Behavior.

2) *Grades 1-9.*

Scores, 2: Critical Events Index, Combined Frequency Index for Adaptive and Maladaptive Behavior.

Cross References: See T5:2607 (1 reference); for reviews by Mary Lou Kelley and by Leland C. Zlomke and Robert Spies of an earlier edition, see 13:313.

[2041]

Tapping Students' Science Beliefs: A Resource for Teaching and Learning.

Purpose: Designed to "assess the belief students have about certain natural phenomena and permits appropriate learning experiences to be planned."

Population: Primary grade level students.

Publication Date: 1993.

Acronym: TSSB.

Scores, 5: Skateboard News, What Happened Last Night, The Day We Cooked Pancakes in School, Children's Week, Our School Garden.

Administration: Group.

Price Data, 2016: A$46.95 per kit including manual (77 pages), test booklets, score sheet, and profile.

Time: (30) minutes per unit.

Authors: Brian Doig and Ray Adams.

Publisher: Australian Council for Educational Research Ltd. [Australia].
Cross References: For reviews by Jerrilyn V. Andrews and James P. Van Haneghan, see 13:314.

[2042]

Tasks of Emotional Development Test.

Purpose: Assesses "the emotional and social adjustment of children" by means of projective techniques.
Population: Ages 6-11, 12-18.
Publication Dates: 1960-1971.
Acronym: TED
Scores: LATENCY: 5 scores: (Perception, Outcome, Affect, Motivation, Spontaneity) in each of 12 areas (Peer Socialization, Trust, Aggression Toward Peers, Attitudes For Learning, Respect For Property of Others, Separation From Mother Figure, Identification With Same-Sex Parent, Acceptance of Siblings, Acceptance of Need-Frustration, Acceptance of Parents' Affection to One Another, Orderliness and Responsibility, Self-Image); ADOLESCENCE: 5 scores in each of 13 areas: Same as for Latency plus Heterosexual Socialization.
Administration: Individual.
Levels, 2: Latency (Ages 6-11); Adolescence (Ages 12-18).
Price Data, 2015: $100 per kit, including shipping.
Time: [30-40] minutes.
Authors: Haskel Cohen and Geraldine Rickard Weil.
Publisher: TED Publishing.
Cross References: See T5:2614 (2 references) and T4:2686 (1 reference); for excerpted reviews by Edward Earl Gotts and by C. H. Ammons and R. B. Ammons, see 8:691 (7 references); see also T2:1517 (2 references) and P:481 (1 reference).

[2043]

Tasks of Executive Control.

Purpose: Designed to "assess attention, working memory, and inhibitory control."
Population: Ages 5 to 18.
Publication Dates: 2006-2010.
Acronym: TEC.
Administration: Individual.
Forms, 5: Forms 1, 2, and 3 are statistically equivalent; Forms 4 and 5 are to be used in research.
Price Data, 2015: $495 per introductory kit including TEC software with on-screen help and quick start guide, professional manual (2010, 188 pages), 1 set of keytops, and software guide; $84 per professional manual.
Time: (20-30) minutes.
Comments: The TEC is a computer-administered test; information regarding technical requirements available from test publisher.
Authors: Peter K. Isquith, Robert M. Roth, and Gerard A. Gioia.
Publisher: Psychological Assessment Resources, Inc.

a) AGES 5 TO 7 YEARS.
Scores, 23: 3 Factor Scores: Response Control, Selective Attention, Response Speed; 10 Summary Scores: Accuracy, Target Correct, Standard Correct, Target Omissions, Standard Omissions, Incorrect, Commissions, Target RT, Standard RT, Standard RTSD, Standard ICV; 10 Task Scores: Target Correct, Standard Correct, Target Omissions, Standard Omissions, Incorrect, Commissions, Target RT, Standard RT, Standard RTSD, Standard ICV.
b) AGES 8 TO 18 YEARS.
Scores, 24: 4 Factor Scores: Sustained Accuracy, Selective Attention, Response Speed, Response Variability; 10 Summary Scores: Accuracy, Target Correct, Standard Correct, Target Omissions, Standard Omissions, Incorrect, Commissions, Target RT, Standard RT, Standard RTSD, Standard ICV; 10 Task Scores: Target Correct, Standard Correct, Target Omissions, Standard Omissions, Incorrect, Commissions, Target RT, Standard RT, Standard RTSD, Standard ICV.
Cross References: For reviews by Rama K. Mishra and Gabrielle Stutman, see 19:165.

[2044]

Taylor-Johnson Temperament Analysis® [2012 Edition].

Purpose: Designed to "measure a number of … personality variables or attitudes and behavioral tendencies that influence personal, social, marital, parental, family, scholastic, and vocational adjustment."
Population: Ages 11 and older.
Publication Dates: 1941–2014.
Acronym: T-JTA®.
Scores, 11: Nervous vs. Composed, Depressive vs. Light-Hearted, Active-Social vs. Quiet, Expressive-Responsive vs. Inhibited, Sympathetic vs. Indifferent, Subjective vs. Objective, Dominant vs. Submissive, Hostile vs. Tolerant, Self-Disciplined vs. Impulsive, Test-Taking Attitude, Total Mids; computer scoring includes 10 supplemental scales: Overall Adjustment, Emotional Stability, Alienating, Self-Esteem, Outgoing/Gregarious, Interpersonal Effectiveness, Industrious/Persevering, Persuasive/Influential, Consistency (validity scale), Stress Syndrome.
Administration: Individual or group.
Editions, 3: Regular Edition (criss-cross and self-report forms); Secondary Edition (self-report); Regular Edition Non-Criss-Cross (self-report).
Price Data, 2016: $212 per manual (2014, 75 pages) and handbook (2014, 107 pages); $143.50 per manual; $79 per handbook; $519 per computer scoring counselor's kit (manual, software, 15 scoring coupons); $242 per mail-in/fax-in scoring counselor's kit (manual, 10 question booklets, 25 answer sheets, 10 report booklets); $393.50 per online scoring counselor's kit (manual, online registration fee, $250 scoring credit); $41 per 10 question booklets; $51 per 100 hand scoring answer sheets; $21 per 25 computer scoring answer sheets; $51 per 100 shaded profiles.

Foreign Language Editions: Available in Spanish, German, French, Portuguese, Chinese, Korean, Danish, and Indonesian.

Time: Untimed.

Comments: Can be used as a self-report questionnaire or as a tool for obtaining perceptions of another person (criss-cross form); Secondary Edition generally used with adolescents or adults with low reading skills.

Authors: Original edition by Roswell H. Johnson, revision by Robert M. Taylor and Lucile P. Morrison with W. Lee Morrison (statistical consultant) and Richard C. Romoser (statistical consultant).

Publisher: Psychological Publications, Inc.

Cross References: Reviews are scheduled for *The Twentieth Mental Measurements Yearbook*. For reviews by Stephen N. Axford and Gregory J. Boyle of the 2002 Edition, see 16:241; for reviews by Michael J. Sporakowski and Stephen E. Trotter of the 1996 Edition, see 14:381; for reviews by Jeffrey A. Jenkins and Barbara J. Kaplan of the 1992 Edition, see 13:315; see also T4:2690 (3 references); for reviews by Cathy W. Hall and Paul McReynolds of the 1984 Edition, see 10:357; see also T3:2396 (1 reference) and T2:840 (3 references); for a review by Robert F. Stahmann of an earlier edition, see 8:692 (18 references); for a review by Donald L. Mosher of an earlier edition, see 7:572 (1 reference); see also P:264 (3 references) and 6:130 (10 references); for a review by Albert Ellis of the original edition, see 4:62 (6 references); for a review by H. Meltzer of the original edition, see 3:57.

[2045]

TEACCH Transition Assessment Profile, Second Edition.

Purpose: Designed to "assess and develop goals for [adolescents and older children] in the autism spectrum [or who have] related developmental disorders."

Population: Children and adolescents grades 3-12 and adults "with mild to severe mental disabilities."

Publication Dates: 1988-2007.

Acronym: TTAP.

Scores, 18: 6 scores per scale: Vocational Skills, Vocational Behaviors, Independent Functioning, Leisure Skills, Functional Communication, Interpersonal Behavior.

Administration: Individual.

Parts, 3: Direct Observation Scale, Home Scale, School/Work Scale.

Price Data, 2015: $88 per complete kit including 10 profile/scoring forms and examiner's manual (2007, 221 pages); $23 per 10 profile/scoring forms; an assembled materials kit is available from OC Enterprises, Inc.

Time: (1.5-2) hours to complete the Direct Observation Scale; (1) hour each to complete the Home and School/Work Scales.

Comments: Revision of The Adolescent and Adult Psychoeducational Profile: Volume IV (AAPEP; 11:8);

"Direct Observation Scale is administered by a teacher, psychologist, job coach, or other trained professional"; Home and School/Work Scales are behavior checklists completed through interviews with parents and with teachers and supervisors, respectively; other test materials for the Direct Observation Scale (e.g., washers, bolts, pill bottles) may be supplied by examiner or purchased from OE Enterprises, Inc.; set of reproducible forms included in the manual act as supplements to the TTAP by providing an ongoing, informal assessment: Cumulative Record of Skills (CRS), Community Site Assessment Worksheet (CSAW), Community Skills Checklist (CSC), Community Behaviors Checklist (CBC), and Daily Accomplishment Chart (DAC).

Authors: Gary Mesibov, John B. Thomas, S. Michael Chapman, and Eric Schopler.

Publisher: PRO-ED.

Cross References: For reviews by Lena R. Gaddis and J. Jeffrey Grill of an earlier edition entitled Adolescent and Adult Psychoeducational Profile: Volume IV, see 11:8; see also T5:70 (1 reference).

[2046]

Teacher Assessment of Grammatical Structures [2014 Revision].

Purpose: Designed to evaluate a child's understanding and use of the grammatical structures of English in order to determine present levels of syntax skills, determine goals for IEPs and lessons, track development over time, and report progress to parents and other professionals.

Population: Children with hearing loss who use spoken and/or signed English and children with typical hearing who show delays in spoken English development.

Publication Dates: 1983-2014.

Acronym: TAGS.

Scores: 4 levels of competence: Receptive: Comprehension; Expressive: Imitated, Prompted, Spontaneous.

Administration: Individual.

Price Data, 2016: $40 per starter kit including manual (2014, 98 pages) and 5 each of 3 rating forms; $15 per 25 forms (specify TAGS-1, TAGS-2, or TAGS-3).

Time: Administration time not reported.

Comments: Ratings are based on informal administration in classroom or therapy setting; test publisher advises that teacher usually needs 4-6 weeks of extensive daily language sampling in a variety of natural settings to collect enough information to complete the assessment.

Authors: Jean S. Moog and Victoria J. Kozak-Robinson (original TAGS); Ellie White (revision).

Publisher: CID - Central Institute for the Deaf.

a) TAGS-1.

    Population: Children who are learning to understand and use single words or combinations of up to 3 words.

    Comments: Includes ratings in 6 grammatical categories: Single Words, Two-Word Combinations, Three-Word Combinations, Tense Markers, Pronouns, Wh-questions.

b) TAGS-2.

Population: Children who are learning to understand and use simple sentences of at least 4 words that contain a subject and a verb and express a complete thought or idea.

Comments: Includes ratings in 6 grammatical categories: Noun Modifiers, Pronouns, Prepositions, Adverbs, Verbs, Questions.

c) TAGS-3.

Population: Children who are learning to understand and use simple sentences with later-developing grammatical structures, compound sentences, and complex sentences.

Comments: Includes ratings in 7 grammatical categories: Nouns, Pronouns, Verbs, Secondary Verbs, Simple Questions, Compound Sentences, Complex Sentences.

Cross References: See T5:2620 (1 reference) and T4:2691 (1 reference); for reviews by Elizabeth M. Prather and Kenneth G. Shipley of the original version, see 10:358 (1 reference).

[2047]
Teacher Observation Scales.

Purpose: Designed as an assessment instrument for identifying gifted children, tailored to be culturally appropriate for use in New Zealand.

Population: Ages 6-12.

Publication Date: 1996.

Acronym: TOS.

Scores, 5: Learning Characteristics, Social Leadership Characteristics, Creative Thinking Characteristics, Self-Determination Characteristics, Motivational Characteristics.

Administration: Individual.

Price Data, 2015: NZ$8.10 per 10 observation scales record sheets; $15.50 per manual (9 pages).

Time: Untimed.

Authors: Don McAlpine and Neil Reid.

Publisher: New Zealand Council for Educational Research [New Zealand].

Cross References: For reviews by Ira Stuart Katz and Kenneth A. Kiewra, see 14:382.

[2048]
Teacher Performance Assessment.

Purpose: "Developed to provide both an objective assessment and a self-assessment of classroom instructional activities from individuals who work in different roles and who make different contributions to the schools."

Population: Teachers; student teachers; classroom assistants.

Publication Dates: 1991–2000.

Acronym: TPA.

Scores, 3: Performance Assessment, Self-Assessment, Reflected Self-Assessment.

Administration: Group.

Forms, 8: Classroom Teachers, Substitute Teachers, Field Associates, Internship I, Internship II, Student Teachers, Classroom Aides, Residents; plus supervisor forms for each.

Price Data: Available from publisher.

Time: (15) minutes.

Authors: Louise M. Soares and Anthony T. Soares.

Publisher: Soares Institute of Neuroscience and Education.

Cross References: For reviews by Raoul A. Arreola and Samuel Hinton, see 15:256.

[2049]
Teacher Values Inventory.

Purpose: Measures "teacher's preferences and opinions."

Population: Teachers.

Publication Dates: 1980–1981.

Acronym: TVI.

Scores, 6: Theoretical, Economic, Aesthetic, Social, Political, Religious.

Administration: Group.

Price Data: Available from publisher.

Foreign Language Edition: Hindi version available.

Time: Administration time not reported.

Authors: Harbhajan L. Singh and S. P. Ahluwalia.

Publisher: National Psychological Corporation [India].

[2050]
Teaching Pyramid Observation Tool for Preschool Classrooms, Research Edition.

Purpose: Designed "to measure practitioners' implementation of teaching and behavior support practices associated with the Pyramid Model for Promoting Social Emotional Competence in Infants and Young Children."

Population: Preschool classroom teachers.

Publication Date: 2014.

Acronym: TPOT.

Scores, 17: Key Practices (Schedules/Routines/Activities, Transitions Between Activities Are Appropriate, Teachers Engage in Supportive Conversations with Children, Promoting Children's Engagement, Providing Directions, Collaborative Teaming, Teaching Behavior Expectations, Teaching Social Skills and Emotional Competencies, Teaching Friendship Skills, Teaching Children to Express Emotions, Teaching Problem Solving, Interventions for Children with Persistent Challenging Behavior, Connecting with Families, Supporting Family Use of the Pyramid Model Practices), Red Flags, Responses to Challenging Behavior.

Administration: Individual.

Price Data, 2015: $80 per complete set including manual (135 pages) and 5 forms; $50 per manual; $30 per 5 forms.

Time: (120) minutes for observation; (15-20) minutes for interview.

Authors: Mary Louise Hemmeter, Lise Fox, and Patricia Snyder.

Publisher: Paul H. Brookes Publishing Co., Inc.

Cross References: Reviews are scheduled for *The Twentieth Mental Measurements Yearbook*.

[2051]

Team Competency Assessment.

Purpose: Designed to "evaluate the level at which a team is performing on ten team competencies."
Population: Team members.
Publication Date: Not dated.
Scores, 11: Committing to a Team Approach, Communicating Effectively Within Teams, Utilizing Team Member Abilities, Resolving Team Conflicts, Creating a Shared Team Purpose, Planning for Results, Making Meetings Work, Evaluating Team Process and Performance, Making Team Decisions by Consensus, Solving Team Problems, Climate.
Administration: Group.
Price Data, 2016: $195; quantity discounts available.
Time: Administration time not reported.
Comments: A 65-item questionnaire; can be computer administered, scored, and interpreted or available in pencil-paper format; can be used separately or as one component of a team skills workshop; now sold as part of the Training House Assessment Kit.
Author: Human Technology, Inc.
Publisher: HRD Press, Inc.

[2052]

Team Effectiveness Survey.

Purpose: Designed to assess process issues associated with team dynamics.
Population: Team members.
Publication Dates: 1968-1996.
Acronym: TES.
Scores: 4 scores for each team member: Exposure, Feedback, Defensive, Supportive, plus Total Team Effectiveness score.
Administration: Group.
Price Data, 2016: $12.95 per instrument.
Time: Administration time not reported.
Author: Jay Hall.
Publisher: Teleometrics International, Inc.
Cross References: For reviews by Gregory H. Dobbins and Harrison G. Gough, see 12:388; for a review by William G. Mollenkopf of an earlier version, see 8:1055.

[2053]

Team Process Diagnostic.

Purpose: To analyze and classify group processes according to their implications for member and team effectiveness.
Population: Individuals whose work responsibilities require work-team cooperation.
Publication Dates: 1974–1989.
Scores: 9 clusters in 3 modes: Problem Solving (Integrative, Content-Bound, Process-Bound), Fight (Perceptual Difference, Status-Striving, Frustration), Flight (Fear, Indifference, Powerlessness).

Administration: Group.
Price Data, 2016: $12.95 per instrument (1989, 21 pages).
Time: Administration time not reported.
Comment: Team associate ratings, self ratings, self scored.
Author: Jay Hall.
Publisher: Teleometrics International, Inc.
Cross References: For a review by Lawrence M. Aleamoni, see 11:416.

[2054]

Team Skills.

Purpose: Designed to evaluate a candidate's ability to work as a member or leader of a team.
Population: Applicants and incumbents for jobs requiring knowledge of team principles.
Publication Dates: 1998-2013.
Scores: Total score only covering 7 areas: Conflict Resolution, Group Dynamics, Team Decision Making, Productivity and Motivation, Communication Skills, Leader & Member Skills, Interpersonal Skills.
Administration: Group.
Price Data, 2015: $16 per consumable self-scoring test booklet or $17 per online test administration (minimum order of 20); $24.95 per manual (15 pages).
Foreign Language Edition: Available in Spanish and French.
Time: (30-50) minutes.
Comments: Self-scoring instrument; test publisher advises changes in form names indicate minor revisions and updating.
Author: Roland T. Ramsay.
Publisher: Ramsay Corporation.
Cross References: For reviews by Neeta Kantamneni and Tracy Kantrowitz of Form AR-C (2009), see 19:166; for a review by Gerald Tindal of an earlier edition, see 17:181.

[2055]

Team vs. Individual Orientation Test.

Purpose: Designed to evaluate "work style."
Population: Under age 18 through adult.
Publication Date: 2011.
Acronym: TIOT.
Scores, 21: Overall Results, Self-Confidence, Interpersonal Discomfort, Feeling Inferior, Fear of Accountability, Peer Confidence, Unwillingness to Depend on Others, Issues with Consulting Others, Need to Compromise, Fear of Criticism, Having to Adjust for the Group, Loss of Control, Unfairness, Concern About Being Held Back, Not Getting Due Credit, Unfair Workload, Communication Issues, Meeting the Need to Communicate, Issues with Listening to Team Members, Fear of Speaking up in Front of Group, Worry About Unclear Roles.
Administration: Individual.

Price Data: Available from publisher.
Time: (20) minutes.
Comments: Self-administered online assessment. The test publisher provides clients with information about the methods and theoretical basis used in the development of the test as well as benchmarks for relevant industries and racial/ethnic group comparison data.
Author: PsychTests AIM, Inc.
Publisher: PsychTests AIM, Inc.
Cross References: For reviews by Theodore L. Hayes and Jean Powell Kirnan, see 19:167.

[2056]

Teamness Index.
Purpose: To "survey … conditions of work and the array of feelings that might exist among two or more people as they seek to work together."
Population: Individuals whose work responsibilities require work-team cooperation.
Publication Dates: 1988–1995.
Scores: Item scores only.
Administration: Group.
Price Data, 2016: $12.95 per instrument.
Time: Administration time not reported.
Comments: Self-ratings; self-scored.
Author: Jay Hall.
Publisher: Teleometrics International, Inc.
Cross References: For reviews by Barbara Lachar and Frederick T. L. Leong, see 11:417.

[2057]

Teamwork Appraisal Survey.
Purpose: To assess "an associate's feelings about working in teams and the behaviors he or she employs in work-team situations."
Population: Individuals whose work responsibilities require work-team cooperation.
Publication Date: 1987.
Acronym: TAS.
Scores, 5: Synergistic, Compromise, Win-Lose, Yield-Lose, Lose-Leave.
Administration: Group.
Price Data: 2016: $12.95 per instrument (24 pages).
Time: Administration time not reported.
Comment: Based on Team Behaviors Model of analysis of individual behaviors in a team setting; work associates rate each other's behavior.
Author: Jay Hall.
Publisher: Teleometrics International, Inc.

[2058]

Teamwork-KSA Test.
Purpose: Designed to "measure the essential knowledge, skills, and abilities that are predictive of working effectively in teams."

Population: Adults (industry),
Publication Date: 1994.
Scores: 7 subscales: Conflict Resolution, Collaborative Problem Solving, Communication, Interpersonal Skills, Goal Setting and Performance Management, Planning and Task Coordination, Self-Management Skills, plus Overall Score.
Administration: Group or individual.
Price Data: Available from publisher.
Time: [30–40] minutes.
Comments: Administered via paper and pencil or computer.
Authors: Michael J. Stevens and Michael A. Campion.
Publisher: General Dynamics Information Technology.
Cross References: For reviews by Patricia A. Bachelor and Patricia H. Wheeler, see 15:257.

[2059]

Teamwork Skills Inventory.
Purpose: Designed as a self and peer evaluation system for assessing teamwork skills in the classroom.
Population: Students in Grades 6-12 as well as undergraduate and graduate students.
Publication Date: 2014.
Acronym: TSI.
Scores: Ratings in 5 clusters: Attends to Teamwork, Seeks and Shares Information, Communicates with Teammates, Thinks Critically and Creatively, Gets Along in the Team.
Administration: Group.
Price Data, 2015: $50 per semester, contingent on agreement to submit data for normative study.
Time: (15-20) minutes.
Authors: Paris S. Strom and Robert D. Strom.
Publisher: Paris Strom and Robert Strom (the authors).
Cross References: Reviews are scheduled for *The Twentieth Mental Measurements Yearbook*. For reviews by Bruce Biskin and Arthur S. Ellen of a previous edition titled Interpersonal Intelligence Inventory, see 17:91.

[2060]

Technical Professional Survey.
Purpose: Designed to assess skills essential for success as a technical/professional contributor.
Population: Non-supervisory staff or the technical or professional leader.
Publication Date: 2007.
Acronym: TPS.
Scores, 14: Clarity of Personal Goals, Innovativeness, Work Planning, Problem Solving, Technical and Functional Expertise, Teamwork, Leadership for Consensus/Negotiating, Using Feedback, Personal Drive, Coping with Stress and Ambiguity, Pressure on Others, Acknowledging Others' Efforts, Personal Values, Personal Effectiveness.
Administration: Individual.

Price Data: Available from publisher.
Comments: Publisher suggests allowing 2-3 weeks to collect feedback.
Time: 20-30 minutes.
Authors: Daniel Booth and Paul M. Connolly.
Publisher: The Clark Wilson Group, Inc. (subsidiary of The Booth Company, Inc.).

[2061]

Technical Test Battery.

Purpose: "Designed for occupational selection and placement."
Population: Technical job applicants and incumbents entry level to professional.
Publication Date: 1990.
Acronym: TTB.
Scores: Total score only for each of 9 tests.
Administration: Individual or group.
Price Data: Available from publisher.
Comments: Subtests available as separates.
Author: Saville & Holdsworth Ltd.
Publisher: CEB.
  a) FOLLOWING INSTRUCTIONS (VTS1).
  Time: 20(25) minutes.
  b) NUMERICAL COMPUTATION (NT2).
  Time: 10(15) minutes.
  c) MECHANICAL COMPREHENSION (MT4).
  Time: 15(20) minutes.
  d) NUMERICAL ESTIMATION (NTS2).
  Time: 10(15) minutes.
  e) MECHANICAL COMPREHENSION (MTS3).
  Time: 15(20) minutes.
  f) FAULT FINDING (FTS4).
  Time: 20(25) minutes.
  g) DIAGRAMMATIC THINKING (DTS6).
  Time: 20(25) minutes.
  h) SPATIAL REASONING (ST7).
  Time: 20(25) minutes.
  i) DIAGRAMMATIC REASONING (DT8).
  Time: 15(20) minutes.
Cross References: For a review by Sami Gulgoz, see 11:419.

[2062]

Technical Test Battery [British Edition].

Purpose: Assess vocational skills and abilities.
Population: Apprentice and technical personnel.
Publication Dates: 1979–1982.
Acronym: TTB.
Administration: Group.
Restricted Distribution: Individuals who have completed the test publisher's training course or who are members of the Division of Occupational Psychology of the British Psychological Society.
Price Data: Available from publisher.
Comments: Subtests available as separates.

Authors: David Hawkey, Peter Saville, Robert Page (MT4), and Gill Nyfield (manual).
Publisher: CEB.
  a) LEVEL 1.
  Purpose: "Basic skills and comprehension."
  Publication Dates: 1979–1981.
    1) *Verbal Comprehension.*
    Acronym: VT 1.
    Time: 10(15) minutes.
    2) *Numerical Computation.*
    Acronym: NT 2.
    Time: 10(15) minutes.
    3) *Visual Estimation.*
    Acronym: ET 3.
    Time: 10(15) minutes.
    4) *Mechanical Comprehension.*
    Acronym: MT 4.
    Time: 15(20) minutes.
  b) LEVEL 2.
  Purpose: "Higher older reasoning and analytical skills."
  Publication Dates: 1979-1981.
    1) *Verbal Reasoning.*
    Acronym: VT 5.
    Time: 10(15) minutes.
    2) *Numerical Reasoning.*
    Acronym: NT 6.
    Time: 10(15) minutes.
    3) *Spatial Reasoning.*
    Acronym: ST 7.
    Time: 20(25) minutes.
    4) *Diagrammatic Reasoning.*
    Acronym: DT 8.
    Time: 15(20) minutes.
    5) *Spatial Recognition (optional test for Levels 1 and 2).*
    Acronym: ST 9.
    Time: 15(20) minutes.

[2063]

Technology and Internet Assessment.

Purpose: Designed to determine strengths and weaknesses in eight areas related to computer, Internet, and information skills.
Population: Middle school, high school, and college students, potential and existing employees.
Publication Date: 1999.
Acronym: TIA.
Scores, 8: Use of Technology, Specific Computer Skills, Acquisition of Technology Knowledge, Basic Internet Knowledge, Internet Information Skills, Adapting to Technological Change, Impact of Technology, Ethics of Technology.
Administration: Individual or group.
Price Data, 2015: $3.75 per test (100 copies or fewer); $3.50 per test (more than 100 copies); user's manual free.
Time: (20–30) minutes.
Comments: Administered online.
Author: Michael Ealy.
Publisher: H & H Publishing Co., Inc.

[2064]

Teele Inventory for Multiple Intelligences.

Purpose: Designed to examine the dominant intelligences of individuals from the age of 3 to adults to identify the dominant ways individuals learn and process information.
Population: Age 3 to adult.
Publication Dates: 1992–1997.
Acronym: TIMI.
Scores, 7: Linguistic, Logical-Mathematical, Musical, Spatial, Bodily-Kinesthetic, Intrapersonal, Interpersonal.
Administration: Individual or group.
Price Data, 2015: $275 per complete kit including 35 pictorial inventories, 35 answer sheets, 1 scoring transparency and a teacher's manual (1997) plus postage; $25 per single set, includes one inventory, 35 answer sheets, and 1 scoring transparency; $10 per 35 scoring sheets plus transparency; $325 per test kit, includes 35 pictorial inventories, 35 answer sheets, 1 scoring transparency plus set of 25 rigid polished vinyl overhead transparencies for presentations.
Time: (15-20) minutes.
Comments: A spatial, forced-choice pictorial inventory that does not require the English language to complete.
Author: Sue Teele.
Publisher: Sue Teele & Associates.
Cross References: For reviews by Allen K. Hess and Sally Kuhlenschmidt, see 16:242.

[2065]

Telemarketing Applicant Inventory.

Purpose: "Provides a standardized measure of telemarketing potential and is an ideal instrument for selecting inbound and outbound telemarketing professionals" and is "ideal for personnel selection and placement, as well as identification of basic training needs."
Population: Applicants for telephone sales and service positions.
Publication Dates: 1992–2003.
Acronym: TMAI.
Scores, 13: Candidness, Accuracy, Sales Interest/Skill, Sales Responsibility, Productivity, Confidence/Influence, Interpersonal Orientation, Stress Tolerance, Job Stability, Job Stimulation Rating, Communicator Competence, Applied Verbal Reasoning, Readiness Index.
Administration: Individual.
Price Data: Available from publisher.
Time: (40–50) minutes.
Author: General Dynamics Information Technology.
Publisher: General Dynamics Information Technology.

[2066]

Telemarketing Staff Selector.

Purpose: To evaluate the necessary knowledge and skills needed for the position of telemarketing representative.

Population: Candidates for the position of telemarketing representative.
Publication Date: 1997.
Scores: Total Score, Narrative Evaluation, Ranking, Recommendation.
Administration: Group.
Price Data: Available from publisher.
Time: (81) minutes.
Comments: Scored by publisher; must be proctored.
Author: Walden Personnel Performance, Inc.
Publisher: Walden Personnel Testing & Consulting Inc. [Canada].

[2067]

Telephone Interview for Cognitive Status.

Purpose: Designed to serve as a "brief test of global cognitive functioning" for administration over the telephone.
Population: Ages 60–98.
Publication Dates: 1987–2003.
Acronym: TICS.
Scores: Total score only.
Administration: Individual.
Price Data, 2015: $98 per introductory kit including manual (2003, 31 pages) and 50 record forms.
Time: (10) minutes.
Authors: Jason Brandt and Marshal F. Folstein.
Publisher: Psychological Assessment Resources, Inc.
Cross References: For reviews by Ronald J. Ganellen and Robert M. Thorndike, see 16:243.

[2068]

TEMAS (Tell-Me-A-Story).

Purpose: A culturally revelant apperception test for children.
Population: Ages 5–18.
Publication Dates: 1986–1988.
Acronym: TEMAS.
Scores, 34: Quantitative Scales (Cognitive Functions [Reaction Time, Total Time, Fluency, Total Omissions], Personality Functions [Interpersonal Relations, Aggression, Anxiety/Depression, Achievement Motivation, Delay of Gratification, Self-Concept, Sexual Identity, Moral Judgment, Reality Testing], Affective Functions [Happy, Sad, Angry, Fearful]), Qualitative Indicators (Affective Functions [Neutral, Ambivalent, Inappropriate Affect], Cognitive Functions [Conflict, Sequencing, Imagination, Relationships, Total Transformations, Inquiries, Omissions and Transformations scores for each of the following: Main Character, Secondary Character, Event, Setting]).
Administration: Individual.
Forms, 2: Short, Long.
Versions, 2: Minority, Nonminority.
Price Data, 2016: $299 per complete kit including nonminority stimulus cards (1986, 36 cards), minority stimulus cards (1986, 36 cards), 25 record booklets,

administration instruction card, and manual (1988, 166 pages); $99 per set of stimulus cards; $27 per 25 record booklets; $15 per administration instruction card; $72 per manual.

Time: (45) minutes (short form); (120) minutes (long form).

Authors: Giuseppe Costantino, Robert G. Malgady (manual and record booklet), and Lloyd H. Rogler (manual).

Publisher: TEMAS (Tell-Me-A-Story) Test Publishing.

Cross References: See T5:2647 (2 references) and T4:2716 (1 reference); for a review by William Steve Lang, see 11:422.

[2069]

Temperament and Atypical Behavior Scale.

Purpose: Designed to measure temperament and dysfunctional behavior.

Population: 11–71 months.

Publication Date: 1999.

Acronym: TABS.

Scores, 5: Detached, Hyper-Sensitive/Active, Underreactive, Dysregulated, Temperament and Regulatory Index.

Administration: Individual.

Price Data, 2015: $105 per complete set including manual (122 pages), screener with 50 forms, and 30 assessment tools; $30 per 50 screener forms; $35 per 30 assessment tool forms; $50 per manual.

Time: (5) minutes for screener; (15) minutes for assessment tool.

Comments: Ratings by parents, surrogates, or other professionals.

Authors: Stephen J. Bagnato, John T. Neisworth, John Salvia, and Frances M. Hunt.

Publisher: Paul H. Brookes Publishing Co., Inc.

Cross References: For reviews by Harold R. Keller and Loraine J. Spenciner, see 16:244.

[2070]

Temperament Comparator.

Purpose: "Designed to assess the relatively permanent temperament traits which are characteristic of an individual's behavior."

Population: Managers, supervisors, salespeople, and other higher-level professionals.

Publication Dates: 1958–1996.

Acronym: TC.

Scores, 15: Trait Scores (Calm, Cautious, Decisive, Demonstrative, Composed, Even-Tempered, Persevering, Seeks Company, Self-Confident, Serious, Steady Worker, Talkative), Factor Scores (Extroversive/Impulsive vs. Introvertive/Cautious, Emotionally Responsive vs. Non-Emotionally Controlled, Self-Reliant/Self-Oriented vs. Dependent/Group Oriented).

Administration: Individual or group.

Price Data: Available from publisher.

Time: No limit (approximately 15 minutes).

Author: Melany E. Baehr.

Publisher: General Dynamics Information Technology.

Cross References: See T5:2648 (1 reference); for reviews by Paul M. Muchinsky and Aharon Tziner, see 9:1234; see also T2:1413 (1 reference); for reviews by Lawrence J. Stricker and Robert L. Thorndike, see 6:187 (1 reference).

[2071]

Tennessee Self-Concept Scale, Second Edition.

Purpose: Designed as a multidimensional self-concept assessment instrument.

Population: Ages 7 to 90.

Publication Dates: 1964–1996.

Acronym: TSCS: 2.

Scores, 15: Validity scores (Inconsistent Responding, Self-Criticism, Faking Good, Response Distribution); Summary scores (Total Self-Concept, Conflict); Self-Concept scales (Physical, Moral, Personal, Family, Social, Academic/Work); Supplementary scores (Identity, Satisfaction, Behavior).

Administration: Group.

Price Data, 2016: $150.50 per complete kit including 24 AutoScore™ answer forms (12 for adults and 12 for children) and manual (1996, 141 pages); $62 per 25 AutoScore™ forms (specify Adult of Child); $426.50 per 25-use CD-ROM (PC with Windows; specify Adult or Child form); $21.50 per 100 answer sheets for use with CD-ROM; $87.50 per manual.

Foreign Language Edition: Answer sheets available in Spanish.

Time: (10–20) minutes.

Comments: Self-administered.

Authors: William H. Fitts and W. L. Warren.

Publisher: Western Psychological Services.

    a) TSCS:2 ADULT FORM.

    Population: Ages 13 and older.

    b) TSCS:2 CHILD FORM.

    Population: Ages 7–14.

    c) TSCS:2 SHORT FORM.

    Population: Adults (13 and older); child (7–14).

    Comments: The Short Form consists of the first 20 items on the adult and child forms.

Cross References: See T5:2652 (12 references); for reviews by Ric Brown and John Hattie, see 13:320 (41 references); see also T4:2723 (32 references); for reviews by Francis X. Archambault, Jr. and E. Thomas Dowd, see 11:424 (89 references); see also 9:1236 (60 references), T3:2413 (120 references), 8:693 (384 references), and T2:1415 (80 references); for reviews by Peter M. Bentler and Richard M. Suinn and an excerpted review by John O. Crites of an earlier edition, see 7:151 (88 references); see also P:266 (30 references).

[2072]

TerraNova, Third Edition.

Purpose: "An assessment system designed to measure concepts, processes, and skills taught throughout the (U.S.) nation."

Population: Grades K-12.

Publication Dates: 1997-2009.

Acronym: TerraNova 3.

Administration: Group.

Levels, 12: 10 (Grades K-6 to 1-6), 11 (Grades 1-6 to 2-6), 12 (Grades 2-0 to 3-2), 13 (Grades 2-6 to 4-2), 14 (Grades 3-6 to 5-2), 15 (Grades 4-6 to 6-2), 16 (Grades 5-6 to 7-2), 17 (Grades 6-6 to 8-2), 18 (Grades 7-6 to 9-2), 19 (Grades 8-6 to 10-2), 20 (Grades 9-6 to 11-2), 21/22 (Grades 10-6 to 12-9).

Price Data, 2016: Price data for Teacher's Guide (2009, 353 pages) and Technical Report (on CD only, 2008, 384 pages) available from publisher; $73 per norms book (specify year and season).

Time: Administration time varies by test and level.

Comments: Earlier versions were called California Achievement Test and Comprehensive Test of Basic Skills.

Author: CTB/McGraw-Hill.

Publisher: DRC.

a) TERRANOVA, THIRD EDITION SURVEY EDITION.

Purpose: Designed to "yield norm-referenced information and some curriculum-referenced information in a minimum of testing time."

Price Data: $186.50 per 25 consumable Survey test books (Levels 12-13, specify level); $168 per 25 reusable Survey test books (Levels 14-21/22, specify level); $30.60 per Survey Test Directions for Teachers (Levels 12 and 14-21/22, specify level); $31.75 per Survey Test Directions for Teachers (Levels 13, specify level); $7.80 per Survey Directions for Practice Activities (Levels 12-18, specify level).

Comments: All items are selected-response items.

1) *Level 12.*

Population: Grades 2-0 to 3-2.

Scores: 4 Survey scores (Reading, Mathematics, Science, Social Studies).

Time: (135) minutes.

2) *Level 13-21/22.*

Population: Grades 2-6 to 12-9.

Scores: 5 Survey scores (Reading, Language, Mathematics, Science, Social Studies).

Time: (170) minutes.

b) TERRANOVA, THIRD EDITION COMPLETE BATTERY.

Purpose: Designed to be "capable of generating precise norm-referenced achievement scores and a full complement of objective mastery scores."

Price Data: $239.50 per 25 consumable Complete Battery test books (Levels 10-13, specify level); $186.50 per 25 reusable Complete Battery test books (Levels 14-21/22, specify level)

Comments: A combination of the Survey items and additional selected-response items.

1) *Level 10.*

Population: Grades K-6 to 1-6.

Scores: 2 Complete Battery scores (Reading, Mathematics).

Time: (95) minutes.

2) *Levels 11-12.*

Population: Grades 1-6 to 3-2.

Scores: 4 Complete Battery scores (Reading, Mathematics, Science, Social Studies).

Time: (160-180) minutes.

3) *Levels 13-21/22.*

Population: Grades 2-6 to 12-9.

Scores: 5 Complete Battery scores (Reading, Language, Mathematics, Science, Social Studies).

Time: (245) minutes.

c) TERRANOVA, THIRD EDITION MULTIPLE ASSESSMENTS.

Purpose: This edition "combines selected-response items of the Survey edition with sections of constructed-response items that allow students to produce their own short and extended responses."

Price Data: $250 per 25 consumable Multiple Assessments test books (Levels 11-21/22, specify level); $30.60 per Multiple Assessments Directions for Teachers (Levels 11-21/22, specify level); $30.60 per 25 Multiple Assessments Practice Activities (Levels 11-21/22, specify level); $7.80 per Multiple Assessments Teacher Directions for Practice Activities (Levels 11-21/22, specify level).

1) *Levels 11-12.*

Population: Grades 1-6 to 3-2.

Scores: 4 Multiple Assessments scores (Reading, Mathematics, Science, Social Studies).

Time: (260-270) minutes.

2) *Levels 13-21/22.*

Population: Grades 2-6 to 12-9.

Scores: 5 Multiple Assessments scores (Reading, Language, Mathematics, Science, Social Studies).

Time: (335) minutes.

d) TERRANOVA, THIRD EDITION PLUS TESTS.

Purpose: Designed to "provide additional in-depth information about students' basic skills."

Price Data: $82.10 per 25 Form C Plus test booklets (Levels 11-13, specify level).

Time: Administration time not reported.

Comments: "Used in conjunction with the Survey, Complete Battery, and Multiple Assessments components."

1) *Level 11.*

Population: Grades 1-6 to 2-6.

Scores, 3: Word Analysis, Vocabulary, Mathematics Computation.

2) *Levels 12-13.*

Population: Grades 2-0 to 4-2.

Scores, 5: Word Analysis, Vocabulary, Language Mechanics, Spelling, Mathematics Computation.

3) *Levels 14-21/22.*

Population: Grades 3-6 to 12-9.

Scores, 4: Vocabulary, Language Mechanics, Spelling, Mathematics Computation.

Cross References: For reviews by John O. Anderson and Michael Harwell, see 18:135; for reviews by Gregory J. Cizek and Robert L. Johnson of the Second edition, see 16:245; for reviews by Judith A. Monsaas and Anthony J. Nitko of an earlier edition, see 14:383; for information on the Comprehensive Tests of Basic Skills, see T5:665 (95 references); see also T4:623 (23 references); for reviews by Kenneth D. Hopkins and M. David Miller of the CTBS, see 11:81 (70 references); for reviews by Robert L. Linn and Lorrie A. Shepard of an earlier form, see 9:258 (29 references); see also T3:551 (59 references); for reviews by Warren G. Findley and Anthony J. Nitko of an earlier edition, see 8:12 (13 references); see also T2:11 (1 references); for reviews by J. Stanley Ahmann and Frederick G. Brown and excerpted reviews by Brooke B. Collison and Peter A. Taylor (rejoinder by Verna White) of Forms Q and R, see 7:9. For reviews of subtests of earlier editions, see 8:721 (1 review), 8:825 (1 review), 7:685 (1 review), 7:514 (2 reviews), and 7:778 (1 review).

[2073]
Test Attitude Inventory [Test Anxiety Inventory].

Purpose: "Developed to measure individual differences in test anxiety as a situation-specific personality trait."
Population: High school and college students.
Publication Dates: 1977–1980.
Acronym: TAI.
Scores, 3: Worry, Emotionality, Total.
Administration: Individual and group.
Price Data, 2015: $50 for manual, including review-only copy of TAI form; $2.40 per Transform Survey Hosting license (minimum 50); $2 per Remote Online Survey License (minimum 50); $2 per License to Reproduce; $15 Individual Report; $15 Report About Me.
Foreign Language Editions: Chinese, Dutch, Greek, Romanian, and Urdu.
Time: (5–10) minutes.
Comments: Self-report inventory of test anxiety; title of manual is Test Anxiety Inventory.
Author: Charles D. Spielberger.
Publisher: Mind Garden, Inc.
Cross References: See T5:2656 (25 references) and T4:2726 (16 references); for reviews by John P. Galassi and Thomas R. Knapp, see 9:1238 (3 references); see also T3:2417 (2 references).

[2074]
Test de Vocabulario en Imágenes Peabody: Adaptación Hispanoamericana.

Purpose: Designed to measure "an individual's receptive or hearing vocabulary of single Spanish words spoken by the examiner"; described as an "achievement test, since it shows the extent of Spanish vocabulary acquisition of the subject" as well as a "screening test of scholastic aptitude."
Population: Ages 2-6 to 17-11.
Publication Date: 1986.
Acronym: TVIP.
Scores: Total score only.
Administration: Individual.

Price Data, 2015: $197.60 per test kit (specify English or Spanish) including test easel, manual (172 pages), 25 record forms, and carrying case.
Time: (15) minutes.
Comments: A Spanish language adaptation of the 1981 Peabody Picture Vocabulary Test-Revised, with manuals in Spanish and English.
Authors: Lloyd M. Dunn, Eligio R. Padilla, Delia E. Lugo, and Leota M. Dunn.
Publisher: Pearson.

[2075]
Test for Auditory Comprehension of Language–Fourth Edition.

Purpose: Designed "to evaluate the receptive language proficiency of children who are having difficulty communicating orally."
Population: Ages 3 through 12.
Publication Dates: 1973-2014.
Acronym: TACL-4.
Scores, 4: Vocabulary, Grammatical Morphemes, Elaborated Phrases and Sentences, Receptive Language Index.
Administration: Individual.
Price Data, 2015: $355 per kit including examiner's manual (2014, 103 pages), picture book, 25 examiner record booklets, Critical Reviews and Research Findings for TACL: 1965-2013, and TACL-4/TEXL comprehensive scoring supplement; $197 per picture book; $101 per manual; $57 per 25 examiner record booklets.
Time: (15-20) minutes.
Comments: Co-normed with the Test of Expressive Language.
Author: Elizabeth Carrow-Woolfolk.
Publisher: PRO-ED.
Cross References: Reviews are scheduled for *The Twentieth Mental Measurements Yearbook*. For reviews by Ramasamy Manikam and Christine Novak of the third edition, see 14:384; see also T5:2657 (37 references) and T4:2727 (20 references); for reviews by Nicholas W. Bankson and William O. Haynes of the revised edition, see 10:363; see also T3:2472 (25 references); for reviews by John T. Hatten and Huberto Molina of the original edition, see 8:454 (6 references); see also T2:997A (2 references).

[2076]
Test for Creative Thinking—Drawing Production.

Purpose: "Meant to be a screening instrument which allows for a first rough, simple, and economic assessment of a person's creative potential."
Population: Age 5-95.
Publication Date: 1996.
Acronym: TCT-DP.

Scores, 15: Continuations, Completions, New Elements, Connections Made with Lines, Connections that Contribute to a Theme, Boundary-Breaking Being Fragment—Dependent, Perspective, Humour/Affectivity/Emotionality/Expressive Power of the Drawing, Unconventionality A—Uncoventional Manipulation, Unconventionality B—Symbolic/Abstract/Fictional, Unconventionality C—Symbol-Figure-Combinations, Unconventionality D—Nonstereotypical Utilization of Given Fragments/Figures, Speed, Total.
Administration: Individual or group.
Forms, 2: A, B.
Price Data, 2015: €52,00 per manual; €27,00 per test forms B; €27,00 per test forms A.
Time: (30) minutes.
Authors: Klaus K. Urban and Hans G. Jellen.
Publisher: Pearson Assessment [England].
Cross References: For reviews by Alice J. Corkill and William Steve Lang, see 14:385.

[2077]

Test for Reception of Grammar Version 2.

Purpose: A receptive language test that "assesses understanding of English grammatical contrasts marked by inflections, function words and word order."
Population: Ages 4 through 86.
Publication Dates: 1983-2003.
Acronym: TROG-2.
Score: Total score only.
Administration: Individual.
Price Data, 2015: £212 per kit including manual (2003, 69 pages), stimulus book, and 25 record forms; £84 per manual; £49.50 per 25 record forms.
Time: (10-20) minutes.
Comments: Standardized in the United Kingdom.
Authors: D. V. M. Bishop.
Publisher: Pearson Clinical Assessment, a division of Pearson Education Ltd. [England].
Cross References: Reviews are scheduled for *The Twentieth Mental Measurements Yearbook*. For a review by Roger L. Towne of an earlier edition, see 15:258; see also T5:2662 (8 references).

[2078]

Test Lessons in Primary Reading, Second Enlarged and Revised Edition.

Purpose: "Designed to evaluate students' reading progress and thinking skills."
Population: Children.
Publication Date: 1980.
Scores: Item scores only.
Administration: Group.
Price Data, 2016: $12 per lesson booklet; $3.95 per teacher's manual/answer key (17 pages).
Time: Administration time not reported.

Authors: William A. McCall and Mary Lourita Harby.
Publisher: Teachers College Press.

[2079]

Test of Academic Achievement Skills—Reading, Arithmetic, Spelling, and Listening Comprehension.

Purpose: Measures a child's reading, arithmetic, spelling, and listening comprehension skills.
Population: Ages 4-0 to 12-0.
Publication Date: 1989.
Scores, 6: Spelling, Total Reading (Letter/Word Identification, Listening Comprehension, Total), Arithmetic, Total.
Administration: Individual.
Price Data: Not available.
Time: (15–25) minutes.
Author: Morrison F. Gardner.
Publisher: Academic Therapy Publications.
Cross References: For reviews by C. Dale Carpenter and Steve Graham, see 13:321.

[2080]

Test of Adolescent/Adult Word Finding–Second Edition.

Purpose: Designed as a "diagnostic tool for assessing word finding skills."
Population: Ages 12-80.
Publication Dates: 1989-2016.
Acronym: TAWF-2.
Score: Total score only.
Administration: Individual.
Forms, 2: Complete, Brief.
Price Data, 2016: $385 per complete kit including examiner's manual (2016, 157 pages), Word Finding Assessment Picture Book, Comprehension Check Picture Book, and 25 record forms; $80 per manual; $131 per Word Finding Assessment Picture Book; $115 per Comprehension Check Picture Book; $59 per 25 record booklets.
Time: (20-30) minutes for Complete Test, (10-15) minutes for Brief Test.
Comments: "Both the Complete Test and the Brief Test consist of two assessment components: the standardized assessment and the informal assessment."
Author: Diane J. German.
Publisher: PRO-ED.
Cross References: See T5:2667 (1 reference); for reviews by Ronald B. Gillam and Richard E. Harding of the original edition, see 12:391.

[2081]

Test of Adolescent and Adult Language, Fourth Edition.

Purpose: Designed "(a) to identify adolescents and adults who score significantly below their peers and therefore might need help improving their language proficiency, (b) to determine areas of relative strength and weakness among language abilities, and (c) to serve as a research tool in studies investigating language problems in adolescents and adults."

Population: Ages 12-0 to 24-11.
Publication Dates: 1980-2007.
Acronym: TOAL-4.
Scores, 7: Spoken Language (Word Opposites, Word Derivations, Spoken Analogies), Written Language (Word Similarities, Sentence Combining, Orthographic Usage), General Language.
Administration: Individual or group.
Price Data, 2015: $233 per complete kit including 25 examiner record booklets, 25 written language forms, and examiner's manual (2007, 109 pages); $67 per 25 examiner record booklets; $91 per 25 written language forms; $91 per manual.
Time: (60) minutes.
Authors: Donald D. Hammill, Virginia L. Brown, Stephen C. Larsen, and J. Lee Wiederholt.
Publisher: PRO-ED.
Cross References: For reviews by Aimee Langlois and Dolores Kluppel Vetter, see 18:136; see T5:2668 (7 references); for reviews by John MacDonald and Roger A. Richards of an earlier edition, see 13:323 (6 references); see also T4:2738 (9 references); for reviews by Allen Jack Edwards and David A. Shapiro of an earlier edition, see 10:365; for a review by Robert T. Williams of an earlier edition, see 9:1243.

[2082]

Test of Auditory Processing Skills—Third Edition.

Purpose: "To measure a child's functioning in various areas of auditory perception."
Population: Ages 4–0 through 18-11.
Publication Dates: 1985-2005.
Acronym: TAPS-3.
Scores, 9: Word Discrimination, Phonological Segmentation, Phonological Blending, Number Memory Forward, Number Memory Reversed, Word Memory, Sentence Memory, Auditory Comprehension, Auditory Reasoning.
Administration: Individual.
Price Data, 2015: $175 per test kit including 25 test booklets, Auditory Figure-Ground CD, and manual (2005, 102 pages); $80 per 25 test booklets; $25 per Auditory Figure-Ground CD; $70 per manual.
Foreign Language Edition: Spanish version is available.
Time: (60) minutes (untimed).
Authors: Nancy A. Martin and Rick Brownell (TAPS-3); earlier editions by Morrison F. Gardner.
Comments: Represents a complete reshaping of the Test of Auditory-Perceptual Skills, Revised.

Publisher: Academic Therapy Publications.
Cross References: For reviews by Timothy R. Konold and Rebecca Blanchard and by Dolores Kluppel Vetter, see 18:137; for reviews by Annabel J. Cohen and by Anne R. Kessler and Jaclyn B. Spitzer of the Test of Auditory-Perceptual Skills, see 13:324 (2 references).

[2083]

Test of Auditory Processing Skills 3: Spanish-Bilingual Edition.

Purpose: Designed to assess "auditory skills commonly utilized in academic and everyday activities."
Population: Spanish-bilingual children ages 5-0 to 18-11.
Publication Dates: 1985-2009.
Acronym: TAPS-3:SBE.
Scores, 13: Word Discrimination, Phonological Segmentation, Phonological Blending, Number Memory Forward, Number Memory Reversed, Word Memory, Sentence Memory, Auditory Comprehension, Auditory Reasoning, Phonologic Index, Memory Index, Cohesion Index, Overall Score.
Subtests, 9: Word Discrimination, Phonological Segmentation, Phonological Blending, Number Memory Forward, Number Memory Reversed, Word Memory, Sentence Memory, Auditory Comprehension, Auditory Reasoning.
Administration: Individual.
Price Data, 2015: $160 per complete kit including manual (2009, 104 pages), 25 test booklets, and Auditory Figure-ground CD; $60 per manual.
Foreign Language Edition: English edition available.
Time: 60(10) minutes.
Comments: Spanish edition, based on but not a translation of the English-language Test of Auditory Processing Skills—Third Edition (2082).
Author: Nancy A. Martin.
Publisher: Academic Therapy Publications.
Cross References: For reviews by Victoria A. Comerchero and S. Kathleen Krach, see 19:168; for reviews by Timothy R. Konold and Rebecca Blanchard and by Dolores Kluppel Vetter of the Test of Auditory Processing Skills-Third Edition, see 18:137; for reviews by Annabel J. Cohen and by Anne R. Kessler and Jaclyn B. Spitzer of the Test of Auditory-Perceptual Skills, Revised, see 13:324 (2 references).

[2084]

Test of Childhood Stuttering.

Purpose: Assesses "speech fluency skills and stuttering-related behaviors."
Population: Ages 4 through 12.
Publication Date: 2010.
Acronym: TOCS.

Scores, 9: 5 Speech Fluency Scores (Rapid Picture Naming, Modeled Sentences, Structured Conversation, Narration, Speech Fluency Index), 4 Observation Rating Scale Scores (Speech Fluency Rating Scale Score, Speech Fluency Rating Scale Index, Disfluency-Related Consequences Rating Scale Score, Disfluency-Related Consequences Rating Scale Index).
Administration: Individual.
Price Data, 2015: $191 per complete kit including examiner's manual (134 pages), picture book, 25 examiner record booklets, and 25 Observational Rating scales; $46 per 25 examiner record booklets; $70 per examiner's manual; $31 per 25 Observational Rating scales; $48 per picture book.
Time: 20 to 30 minutes.
Authors: Ronald B. Gillam, Kenneth J. Logan, and Nils A. Pearson.
Publisher: PRO-ED.
Cross References: For a review by Kathy Shapley and Thomas Guyette, see 18:138.

[2085]
Test of Creativity.
Purpose: To gain a quick measure of a person's creativity.
Population: Adolescents and adults.
Publication Date: 1994.
Scores: Total score only.
Administration: Group.
Manual: No manual.
Price Data, 2016: $195; quantity discounts available.
Time: 35(40) minutes.
Comments: Self-administered, self-scored; now sold as part of the Training House Assessment Kit.
Author: Training House, Inc.
Publisher: HRD Press, Inc.

[2086]
Test of Early Communication and Emerging Language.
Purpose: Designed to "identify [individuals] who have communication and/or language impairments or to rule out such impairments."
Population: Ages 2 weeks through 24 months.
Publication Date: 2011.
Acronym: TECEL.
Score: Communicative Ability Index.
Administration: Individual.
Price Data, 2014: $276 per complete kit including examiner's manual (76 pages), picture plates, 25 examiner record booklets, 25 informal assessment and intervention plans, and object kit; $68 per manual; $66 per 25 examiner record booklets; $66 per object kit; $41 per picture plates; $37 per 25 informal assessment and intervention plans.
Time: (15-45) minutes.
Comments: Revision of the Nonspeech Test for Receptive/Expressive Language.

Authors: Mary Blake Huer and Lynda Miller.
Publisher: PRO-ED.
Cross References: Reviews are scheduled for *The Twentieth Mental Measurements Yearbook.*

[2087]
Test of Early Language Development, Third Edition.
Purpose: Designed to measure the early development of spoken language in the areas of receptive and expressive language, syntax, and semantics.
Population: Ages 2-0 to 7-11.
Publication Date: 1981–1999.
Acronym: TELD-3.
Scores, 3: Receptive Language, Expressive Language, Spoken Language Quotient.
Administration: Individual.
Forms, 2: A, B.
Price Data, 2015: $341 per complete kit; $92 per manual (1999, 159 pages); $85 per Picture Book; $56 each per profile/Examiner Record booklet; $68 per manipulatives.
Time: (15–40) minutes.
Authors: Wayne P. Hresko, D. Kim Reid, and Donald D. Hammill.
Publisher: PRO-ED.
Cross References: For reviews by Sherwyn P. Morreale and Hoi K. Suen, see 14:388; see also T5:2680 (19 references) and T4:2749 (6 references); for reviews by Javaid Kaiser and David A. Shapiro of an earlier edition, see 12:393 (4 references); for reviews by Janice Arnold Dale and Elizabeth M. Prather of an earlier edition, see 9:1250 (1 reference).

[2088]
Test of Early Language Development–Third Edition: Spanish Version.
Purpose: Designed to identify children in need of intervention in the area of language development and gather information on their strengths and weaknesses in different skill areas involved in language development; the test may also be used "as a measure in research studying language development in young children and to accompany other assessment techniques."
Population: Ages 2-0 to 7-11.
Publication Date: 2007.
Acronym: TELD-3:S.
Scores, 3: Receptive Language, Expressive Language, Spoken Language Ability.
Administration: Individual.
Price Data, 2015: $174 per complete kit including 25 examiner record booklets, picture book, manipulatives, and examiner's manual (79 pages); $37 per 25 examiner's record booklets; $37 per examiner's manual; $75 per picture book.

Time: (15-40) minutes.

Comments: The test must be administered and interpreted by "fluent Spanish speakers with knowledge of and speaking ability in the appropriate Spanish dialect"; authors also advise that although "results may contribute to the selection of long-term educational goals, they should not be used as the basis for planning day-to-day instructional programs for individual children."

Authors: Margarita Ramos and Jorge Ramos with Wayne P. Hresko, D. Kim Reid, and Donald D. Hammill.

Publisher: PRO-ED.

Cross References: For reviews by Sandra T. Acosta and Arturo Olivarez, Jr., see 18:139.

[2089]

Test of Early Mathematics Ability, Third Edition.

Purpose: Designed as a test of early mathematical ability.

Population: Ages 3-0 to 8-11.

Publication Dates: 1983–2003.

Acronym: TEMA-3.

Scores: Math Ability Score.

Administration: Individual.

Forms, 2: A, B.

Price Data, 2015: $321 per complete kit including examiner's manual (2003, 71 pages), picture book Form A, picture book Form B, 25 examiner record booklets Form A, 25 examiner record booklets Form B, 25 worksheets Form A, 25 worksheets Form B, assessment probes, 5"x8" cards, 25 blocks, 25 tokens, and a mesh bag; $63 per picture book A; $60 per picture book B; $31 per 25 Form A or Form B examiner record booklets; $24 per 25 Form A or Form B worksheets; $43 per Assessment Probes manual (2003, 82 pages); $60 per examiner's manual; $30 per objects kit.

Time: Untimed.

Authors: Herbert P. Ginsburg and Arthur J. Baroody.

Publisher: PRO-ED.

Cross References: For reviews by Kevin D. Crehan and Judith A. Monsaas, see 16:246; see also T5:2681 (2 references); for a review by Jerry Johnson and Joyce R. McLarty of an earlier edition, see 11:428 (1 reference); for a review by David P. Lindeman, see 9:1252.

[2090]

Test of Early Reading Ability—Deaf or Hard of Hearing.

Purpose: Designed to measure "children's ability to attribute meaning to printed symbols, their knowledge of the alphabet and its functions, and their knowledge of the conventions of print."

Population: Deaf and hard of hearing children ages 3-0 to 13-11.

Publication Date: 1991.

Acronym: TERA-D/HH.

Scores: Total score only.

Administration: Individual.

Forms, 2: A, B.

Price Data, 2015: $228 per complete kit including picture book, 25 Form A and 25 Form B profile/examiner record forms, and manual (49 pages); $79 per picture book; $48 per 25 profile/examiner record forms (Form A); $26 per 25 profile/examiner record forms (Form B); $62 per manual.

Time: (20–30) minutes.

Comments: Adaptation of the Test of Early Reading Ability-2 (2091).

Authors: D. Kim Reid, Wayne P. Hresko, Donald D. Hammill, and Susan Wiltshire.

Publisher: PRO-ED.

Cross References: For reviews by Barbara A. Rothlisberg and Esther Stavrou Toubanos, see 12:394.

[2091]

Test of Early Reading Ability, Third Edition.

Purpose: Designed to "assess children's mastery of early developing reading skills."

Population: Ages 3-6 to 8-6.

Publication Dates: 1981–2001.

Acronym: TERA-3.

Scores, 3: Alphabet, Conventions, Meaning.

Administration: Individual.

Forms, 2: A, B.

Price Data, 2015: $316 per complete kit including examiner's manual (2001, 127 pages), 2 picture books (Form A and Form B), and 2 packets of 25 profile/examiner record forms (Form A and Form B); $97 per examiner's manual; $79 per picture book (specify Form A or Form B); $37 per 25 profile/examiner record forms (specify Form A or Form B).

Time: (30) minutes.

Authors: D. Kim Reid, Wayne P. Hresko, and Donald D. Hammill.

Publisher: PRO-ED.

Cross References: For reviews by Sharon H. deFur and Lisa F. Smith, see 15:259; see T5:2682 (13 references) and T4:2751 (2 references); for reviews by Michael D. Beck and Robert W. Hiltonsmith of an earlier edition, see 11:429 (1 reference); for reviews by Isabel L. Beck and Janet A. Norris of the original edition, see 9:1253.

[2092]

Test of Early Written Language–Third Edition.

Purpose: Designed to measure the writing ability of children.

Population: Ages 4 through 11.

Publication Dates: 1988-2012.

Acronym: TEWL-3.

Scores, 3: Basic Writing, Contextual Writing, Overall Writing.
Administration: Individual.
Forms, 2: A, B.
Price Data, 2014: $275 per complete kit including examiner's manual (2012, 121 pages), 10 administration/record booklets (Form A), 10 administration/record booklets (Form B), 10 student workbooks (Form A), 10 student workbooks (Form B), and 3 Picture Cards; $75 per Examiner's manual; $65 per 10 student workbooks (Form A or Form B); $35 per 10 administration/record booklets (Form A or Form B); $24 per set of 3 picture cards.
Time: (30-50) minutes.
Comments: Overall Writing index score can be completed only if examinee completes both subtests and is at least 5 years old.
Authors: Wayne P. Hresko, Shelley R. Herron, Pamela K. Peak, and Deanna L. Hicks.
Publisher: PRO-ED.
Cross References: Reviews are scheduled for *The Twentieth Mental Measurements Yearbook*. For reviews by David P. Hurford and Michael S. Trevisan of the second edition, see 13:326; for a review by Patricia Wheeler of the original edition, see 11:430.

[2093]

Test of Economic Knowledge, Second Edition.

Purpose: Measures knowledge of economic concepts.
Population: Grades 7–9.
Publication Date: 1987.
Acronym: TEK.
Scores: Total score only.
Administration: Group.
Forms, 2: A, B.
Price Data: Available at no cost from test publisher.
Time: (40) minutes.
Comments: "Designed to replace the Junior High School Test of Economics."
Authors: William B. Walstad and John C. Soper.
Publisher: Council for Economic Education.
Cross References: For reviews by William A. Mehrens and Anthony J. Nitko, see 11:431.

[2094]

Test of Economic Literacy, Fourth Edition.

Purpose: Designed to "evaluate a student's performance and make decisions about economics instruction at the senior high school level."
Population: Grades 11–12.
Publication Dates: 1978–2013.
Acronym: TEL.
Scores: Total score only.
Administration: Group.
Forms, 2: A, B.
Price Data: Available at no cost from test publisher.

Time: (40-50) minutes.
Authors: William B. Walstad, Ken Rebeck, and Roger B. Butters.
Publisher: Council for Economic Education.
Cross References: For a review by John W. Young of the third edition, see 15:260; see T5:2686 (2 references); for reviews by Jennifer J. Fager and Dan Wright of the second edition, see 12:395; for a review by Anna S. Ochoa of an earlier (1978-79) edition, see 9:1256; see also T2:1968 (19 references); for reviews by Edward J. Furst and Christine H. McGuire, and an excerpted review by Robert L. Ebel of an earlier edition titled Test of Economic Understanding, see 7:901 (10 references).

[2095]

Test of English for International Communication (TOEIC).

Purpose: To evaluate the English proficiency of those whose native language is not English.
Population: Adult nonnative speakers of English.
Publication Dates: 1980–1999.
Acronym: TOEIC.
Scores, 3: Listening Comprehension, Reading Comprehension, Total.
Administration: Group.
Price Data: Available from publisher.
Time: (120) minutes.
Author: Educational Testing Service.
Publisher: Educational Testing Service.
Cross References: For reviews by Dan Douglas and Roger A. Richards, see 11:432.

[2096]

The Test of Everyday Attention.

Purpose: To measure "selective attention, sustained attention and attentional switching."
Population: Ages 18–80.
Publication Date: 1994.
Acronym: TEA.
Scores, 9: Map Search, Elevator Counting, Elevator Counting with Distraction, Visual Elevator, Elevator Counting with Reversal, Telephone Search, Telephone Search While Counting, Lottery, Total.
Administration: Individual.
Forms, 3: A, B, C.
Price Data, 2015: £382 per complete kit including manual (32 pages), 25 scoring sheets, cue book, stimulus cards and maps, 3 CDs, and 1 DVD; £30 per 25 scoring sheets; £41 per manual.
Time: (45–60) minutes.
Authors: Ian H. Robertson, Tony Ward, Valerie Ridgeway, and Ian Nimmo-Smith.
Publisher: Pearson Assessment [England].
Cross References: For reviews by William D. Schafer and Terry A. Stinnett, see 17:183.

[2097]

The Test of Everyday Attention for Children.

Purpose: To measure "selective attention, sustained attention and attentional switching."

Population: Ages 6–16.

Publication Date: 1998.

Acronym: TEA-ch.

Scores: 9 subtests: Sky Search, Score!, Creature Counting, Sky Search DT, Map Mission, Score DT, Walk/Don't Walk, Opposite Worlds, Code Transmission.

Administration: Individual.

Forms, 2: A, B.

Price Data, 2015: £503.50 per complete kit including manual, 25 scoring sheets, cue book, stimulus cards and maps, and 2 CDs; £53 per 25 scoring sheets; £51 per manual; £16 per audio CD A or B.

Time: (55–60) minutes.

Authors: Tom Manly, Ian H. Robertson, Vicky Anderson, and Ian Nimmo-Smith.

Publisher: Pearson Assessment [England].

Cross References: For reviews by Merilee McCurdy and Amanda Albertson and by Martin J. Wiese, see 17:182.

[2098]

The Test of Everyday Reasoning.

Purpose: Designed to supplement information on applications for employment, educational assessments, and program evaluations by assessing basic reasoning skills.

Population: Middle school students, high school students, and adults.

Publication Dates: 2000-2007.

Acronym: TER.

Scores, 6: Analysis, Evaluation, Inference, Deductive Reasoning, Inductive Reasoning, Total.

Administration: Group.

Price Data: Available from publisher.

Time: (50) minutes.

Authors: Peter A. Facione and Stephen W. Blohm.

Publisher: Insight Assessment-The California Academic Press LLC.

Cross References: For reviews by Timothy J. Makatura and by Renee M. Tobin and Corinne Zimmerman, see 18:140.

[2099]

Test of Expressive Language.

Purpose: Designed "to evaluate the expressive language proficiency of children who are having difficulty communicating orally."

Population: Ages 3 through 12.

Publication Date: 2014.

Acronym: TEXL.

Scores, 4: Vocabulary, Grammatical Morphemes, Elaborated Phrases and Sentences, Expressive Language Index.

Administration: Individual.

Price Data, 2015: $349 per kit including examiner's manual (2014, 105 pages), picture book, 25 examiner record booklets, and TACL-4/TEXL comprehensive scoring supplement; $179 per picture book; $101 per manual; $69 per 25 examiner record booklets.

Time: (15-20) minutes.

Comments: "Designed to be the expressive language companion to the Test for Auditory Comprehension of Language, Fourth Edition."

Authors: Elizabeth Carrow-Woolfolk and Elizabeth A. Allen.

Publisher: PRO-ED.

Cross References: Reviews are scheduled for *The Twentieth Mental Measurements Yearbook*.

[2100]

Test of General Reasoning Ability.

Purpose: Designed as "a speeded measure of reasoning ability and problem-solving skills."

Population: Ages 10 to 75.

Publication Date: 2014.

Acronym: TOGRA.

Score: General Reasoning Index.

Administration: Individual or group.

Forms: 2 equivalent forms: Blue, Green.

Price Data, 2015: $165 per introductory kit including manual (92 pages), fast guide, 10 Blue item booklets, 10 Green item booklets, 25 answer sheets, 2 scoring keys, and 25 score summary forms; $75 per manual; $40 per 25 score summary forms; $25 per 10 reusable item booklets (Blue or Green); $20 per 25 answer sheets; $10 per set of 2 scoring keys.

Time: 16 minutes.

Comments: Administered via computer or paper and pencil.

Author: Cecil R. Reynolds.

Publisher: Psychological Assessment Resources, Inc.

Cross References: Reviews are scheduled for *The Twentieth Mental Measurements Yearbook*.

[2101]

Test of Gross Motor Development—Second Edition.

Purpose: To "measure gross motor abilities that develop early in life."

Population: Ages 3-10.

Publication Dates: 1985–2000.

Acronym: TGMD-2.

Scores, 2: Locomotor, Object Control.

Administration: Individual.

Price Data, 2015: $126 per kit including 50 profile/ examiner record booklets, and examiner's manual (2000, 69 pages) in a sturdy storage box; $67 per 50 profile/ examiner record booklets; $67 per manual.

Time: (15–20) minutes.
Author: Dale A. Ulrich.
Publisher: PRO-ED.
Cross References: For reviews by Libby G. Cohen and G. Michael Poteat, see 15:261; see T5:2689 (2 references) and T4:2762 (2 references); for reviews by Linda K. Bunker and Ron Edwards of an earlier edition, see 10:370.

[2102]

Test of Handwriting Skills-Revised.

Purpose: Designed to assess "neurosensory integration ability as evidenced by manuscript or cursive writing."
Population: Ages 6 to 18.
Publication Date: 2007.
Acronym: THS-R.
Scores: Total score only.
Administration: Group.
Forms, 2: Manuscript, Cursive.
Price Data, 2015: $160 per test kit including 15 manuscript test booklets, 15 cursive test booklets, 30 record forms, manual (190 pages), and training video; $40 per 15 test booklets and record forms (specify manuscript or cursive); $60 per manual; $20 per training video.
Time: (15-20) minutes.
Comments: Examiner's manual contains scoring directions for both manuscript and cursive formats.
Author: Michael Milone.
Publisher: Academic Therapy Publications.
Cross References: For reviews by Phillip L. Ackerman and Gene Schwarting, see 18:141.

[2103]

Test of Infant Motor Performance.

Purpose: Designed to test "postural and selective motor control needed for functional performance in daily life during infancy."
Population: Ages birth to 17 weeks (term-born infants); 34 weeks postmenstrual age through 4 months post-term (premature infants).
Publication Dates: 2001-2012.
Acronym: TIMP; TIMPSI.
Score: Total score only.
Administration: Individual.
Forms, 2: Test of Infant Motor Performance, Version 5.1; TIMP Screening Items, Version 1.0.
Price Data, 2015: $38 per manual (2012, 65 pages); $68 per 25 TIMP test forms; $10 per 100 Percentile Rank score sheets; $85 per self-instructional DVD V4.1; $15 per age calculator; $65 per 50 TIMPSI test forms.
Foreign Language Editions: French and Portuguese editions available for the TIMP.
Time: (21-45) minutes.
Comments: Additional materials required for administration but not included: rattle, squeaky object, shiny red ball, age calculation wheel; after getting a total raw

score, it is possible to obtain standard scores based on age norms as well as percentile rank scores; electronic version of the TIMP available (the TIMP Online).
Authors: Suzann K. Campbell, Gay L. Girolami, Thubi H.A. Kolobe, Elizabeth T. Osten, and Maureen C. Lenke.
Publisher: Infant Motor Performance Scales, LLC.
Cross References: For reviews by Koressa Kutsick Malcolm and Catherine Ruth Solomon Scherzer, see 19:169.

[2104]

Test of Inference Ability in Reading Comprehension.

Purpose: "Designed to provide diagnostic information about the inference ability of students."
Population: Grades 6–8.
Publication Dates: 1987–1989.
Scores: Total score only.
Administration: Individual or group.
Forms, 2: Multiple-choice, Constructed-response.
Price Data, 2015: $159 per 30 tests (multiple-choice format or constructed-response format); $49 per manual (1989, 24 pages); $49 per technical report (1989, 58 pages).
Time: (40–45) minutes per form.
Authors: Linda M. Phillips (constructed-response format and multiple-choice format) and Cynthia C. Patterson (multiple-choice format).
Publisher: Linda Phillips (the author).
Cross References: For reviews by Douglas K. Smith and Robert Wall, see 13:327.

[2105]

Test of Information Processing Skills.

Purpose: Designed to assess "how well a person learns and retains new information and the effects of interference on those processes."
Population: Ages 5-0 and over.
Publication Dates: 1981-2009.
Acronym: TIPS.
Scores, 6: Visual Modality, Auditory Modality, Delayed Recall, Word Fluency, Modality, Process.
Administration: Individual.
Parts, 4: Part 1: Visual Modality, Part 2: Auditory Modality, Part 3: Delayed Recall, Part 4: Word Fluency.
Price Data, 2015: $160 per test kit including manual (2009, 224 pages), stimulus card booklet, and 25 protocols; $60 per manual.
Time: 30(15) minutes.
Comments: Based on the Learning Efficiency Test.
Author: Raymond E. Webster.
Publisher: Academic Therapy Publications.
Cross References: For reviews by Mary (Rina) M. Chittooran and Amanda Nolen, see 19:170; for information on the Learning Efficiency Test, see T5:1462 (3 references); for reviews by Alice J. Corkill and Gregory

Schraw of the 1992 Revision of the Learning Efficiency Test, see 12:215; see also T4:1423 (1 reference); for a review by Robert G. Harrington of an earlier form of the Learning Efficiency Test, see 9:601.

[2106]

Test of Integrated Language and Literacy Skills.

Purpose: Designed as a "test of curriculum-relevant oral and written language skills that can be used for diagnosing disorders of language and literacy in school-age children."

Population: Ages 6-18.

Publication Date: 2016.

Acronym: TILLS.

Scores, 21: 15 subtest scores (Vocabulary Awareness, Phonemic Awareness, Story Retelling, Nonword Repetition, Nonword Spelling, Listening Comprehension, Reading Comprehension, Following Directions, Delayed Story Retelling, Nonword Reading, Reading Fluency, Written Expression, Social Communication, Digit Span Forward, Digit Span Backward), 4 composite scores (Sound/Word, Sentence/Discourse, Oral, Written), Identification Core, Total.

Administration: Individual.

Price Data, 2016: $499.95 per complete kit including examiner's manual (249 pages), stimulus book, technical manual (54 pages), quick start guide, examiner's practice workbook, 25 examiner record forms, 25 student response forms, 50 student language scales, digital audio files (on USB drive), and tote bag; $24.95 per examiner's practice workbook; $99.95 per 50 record forms; $99.95 per 50 student response forms; $30 per 50 student language scale forms; $79.95 per examiner's manual; $134.95 per stimulus book; $79.95 per technical manual; $29.95 per quick start guide.

Time: (70-90) minutes for total battery.

Comments: May be administered in more than one session as long as testing is completed within 4 weeks; test publisher recommends audio recording oral responses; digital audio player needed to administer Nonword Reading and Nonword Spelling subtests.

Authors: Nickola Wolf Nelson, Elena Plante, Nancy Helm-Estabrooks, and Gillian Hotz.

Publisher: Paul H. Brookes Publishing Co., Inc.

a) VOCABULARY AWARENESS.
Purpose: "Designed to assess students' lexical knowledge, awareness of semantic relationships, and cognitive-linguistic flexibility."
Time: (15) minutes.
Comments: Can be used as a stand-alone measure.

b) PHONEMIC AWARENESS.
Purpose: "Designed to assess students' awareness of the individual speech sounds of language (phonemes)."
Time: (3) minutes.
Comments: Can be used as a stand-alone measure.

c) STORY RETELLING.
Purpose: "Designed to assess students' abilities to listen to, comprehend, and retell a story."

Time: (4) minutes.
Comments: Can be used as a stand-alone measure.

d) NONWORD REPETITION.
Purpose: Designed to assess "student's speech perception, the ability to hold a sequence of speech sounds in immediate memory, and the ability to reproduce those speech-sound (phonological) sequences accurately."
Time: (4) minutes.
Comments: Can be used as a stand-alone measure.

e) NONWORD SPELLING.
Purpose: "Designed to assess students' ability to represent phonemic and morphemic components of novel spoken words by spelling them with conventional orthographic (letter sequence) patterns."
Time: (6) minutes.
Comments: Cannot be used as a stand-alone measure.

f) LISTENING COMPREHENSION.
Purpose: "Designed to assess students' ability to comprehend the complex syntax of academic language and to draw inferences allowed by the text."
Time: (7) minutes.
Comments: Can be used as a stand-alone measure.

g) READING COMPREHENSION.
Purpose: Designed to parallel the Listening Comprehension subtest so "language comprehension skills in the oral and written modalities can be compared directly."
Time: (8) minutes.
Comments: Cannot be used as a stand-alone measure.

h) FOLLOWING DIRECTIONS.
Purpose: "Designed to measure students' ability to listen to a sequence of directions, to understand them, and to hold them in short-term memory long enough to carry them out."
Time: (8) minutes.
Comments: Can be used as a stand-alone measure.

i) DELAYED STORY RETELLING.
Purpose: Designed "to measure retention of narrative information over a period of 20-30 minutes."
Time: (2) minutes.
Comments: Cannot be used as a stand-alone measure.

j) NONWORD READING.
Purpose: Designed "as a measure of reading decoding."
Time: (4) minutes.
Comments: Can be used as a stand-alone measure.

k) READING FLUENCY.
Purpose: "Designed to assess automatic word recognition."
Time: (2) minutes.
Comments: Can be used as a stand-alone measure.

l) WRITTEN EXPRESSION.
Purpose: Designed to allow for observations of "students' written expression skills at the sound/word level and the sentence/discourse level."
Time: (10) minutes.
Comments: Cannot be used as a stand-alone measure.

m) SOCIAL COMMUNICATION.
Purpose: "Designed to assess students' pragmatic ability to formulate responses to fit a social context, including in their tone of voice."
Time: (9) minutes.
Comments: Can be used as a stand-alone measure.

n) DIGIT SPAN FORWARD.
Purpose: Designed as "a test of short-term auditory verbal memory and attention."

Time: (3) minutes.
Comments: Can be used as a stand-alone measure.
o) DIGIT SPAN BACKWARD.
Purpose: Designed to stress "verbal working memory to manipulate the stimuli and respond."
Time: (3) minutes.
Comments: Cannot be used as a stand-alone measure.
Cross References: Reviews are scheduled for *The Twentieth Mental Measurements Yearbook.*

[2107]
Test of Interpersonal Competence for Employment.

Purpose: Designed to assess social interaction skills necessary for job tenure for mentally retarded adults.
Population: Mildly retarded adolescents and adults.
Publication Date: 1986.
Acronym: TICE.
Scores, 6: Handling Criticism and Correction, Requesting Assistance, Following Instructions, Cooperative Work Behavior, Handling of Teasing and Provocation, Resolving Personal Concerns.
Administration: Group.
Price Data: Available from publisher.
Time: (60) minutes.
Authors: Gilbert Foss, Doug Cheney, and Michael Bullis.
Publisher: James Stanfield Co., Inc.
Cross References: For reviews by Sharon H. deFur and Lawrence J. Ryan, see 15:262.

[2108]
Test of Irregular Word Reading Efficiency.

Purpose: Designed to use "the pronunciation of phonetically irregular words to measure reading comprehension."
Population: Ages 3-94.
Publication Date: 2007.
Acronym: TIWRE.
Score: Reading Efficiency Index.
Administration: Individual.
Forms, 3: Form 1, Form 2, Form 3.
Price Data, 2015: $186 per kit including manual, 25 record forms, 25 profile forms, and 3 stimulus cards.
Time: (2) minutes.
Comments: Three equivalent forms are to be used to monitor progress over time; a profile form is included with a score log and a table for comparing scores.
Authors: Cecil R. Reynolds and Randy W. Kamphaus.
Publisher: Psychological Assessment Resources, Inc.
Cross References: For reviews by Mildred Murray-Ward and Michael S. Trevisan, see 18:142.

[2109]
Test of Language Development–Intermediate: Fourth Edition.

Purpose: Designed to identify "strengths and weaknesses in oral language skills."

Population: Ages 8 through 17.
Publication Dates: 1977-2008.
Acronym: TOLD-I:4.
Scores, 12: 6 subtest scores: Picture Vocabulary, Morphological Comprehension, Word Ordering, Relational Vocabulary, Sentence Combining, Multiple Meanings; 6 composite scores: Listening, Organizing, Speaking, Grammar, Semantics, Spoken Language.
Administration: Individual.
Price Data, 2016: $239 per complete kit including examiner's manual (2008, 113 pages), picture book, and 25 examiner/record forms; $94 per manual; $93 per picture book; $61 per 25 examiner/record forms; $134 per scoring software and reporting system version 1.0; $309 per print/software combination kit.
Time: (30-50) minutes.
Authors: Donald D. Hammill and Phyllis L. Newcomer.
Publisher: PRO-ED.
Cross References: Reviews are scheduled for *The Twentieth Mental Measurements Yearbook.* For reviews by David P. Hurford and Pat Mirenda of the third edition, see 14:389; see also T5:2694 (27 references) and T4:2767 (7 references); for reviews by Rebecca McCauley and Kenneth G. Shipley of the second edition, see 11:436 (5 references). For a review by Doris V. Allen of an earlier version of the entire Test of Language Development, see 9:1261 (5 references).

[2110]
Test of Language Development–Primary: Fourth Edition.

Purpose: Designed to identify "strengths and weaknesses in language skills."
Population: Ages 4 through 8.
Publication Dates: 1977-2008.
Acronym: TOLD-P:4.
Scores, 15: 9 subtest scores: Picture Vocabulary, Syntactic Understanding, Relational Vocabulary, Sentence Imitation, Oral Vocabulary, Morphological Completion, Word Discrimination (Supplemental), Phonemic Analysis (Supplemental), Word Articulation (Supplemental); 6 composite scores: Language, Organizing, Speaking, Grammar, Semantics, Spoken Language.
Administration: Individual.
Price Data, 2014: $345 per complete kit including examiner's manual (2008, 103 pages), picture book, 25 examiner/record forms, and Critical Reviews and Research Findings monograph (2008, 36 pages); $30 per Critical Reviews and Research Findings monograph; $83 per 25 examiner/record forms; $105 per manual; $139 per picture book; $134 per scoring software and reporting system version 1.0; $399 per print/software combination kit.
Time: (35-50) minutes for core subtests; (30) minutes for supplemental subtests.

Comments: Test publisher recommends core subtests and supplemental subtests be administered in separate sessions.
Authors: Phyllis L. Newcomer and Donald D. Hammill.
Publisher: PRO-ED.
Cross References: Reviews are scheduled for *The Twentieth Mental Measurements Yearbook*. For reviews by Ronald A. Madle and Gabrielle Stutman of the third edition, see 14:390; see also T5:2695 (72 references) and T4:2768 (21 references); for reviews by Linda Crocker and Carol E. Westby of the second edition, see 11:437 (20 references).

[2111]

Test of Mathematical Abilities for Gifted Students.

Purpose: "Designed to identify students who have talent or giftedness in mathematics."
Population: Ages 6–12.
Publication Date: 1998.
Acronym: TOMAGS.
Scores: Total score only.
Administration: Group or individual.
Levels, 2: Primary, Intermediate.
Price Data, 2015: $209 per complete kit including manual (53 pages), 25 each Primary Level and Intermediate Level student booklets, and 25 each Primary Level and Intermediate Level profile/scoring sheets; $56 per 25 student booklets (specify level); $25 per 25 profile/scoring sheets (specify level); $68 per manual.
Time: (30–60) minutes.
Authors: Gail R. Ryser and Susan K. Johnsen.
Publisher: PRO-ED.
Cross References: For reviews by Robert B. Frary and Delwyn L. Harnisch, see 14:391.

[2112]

Test of Mathematical Abilities–Third Edition.

Purpose: Designed "to identify, describe, and quantify mathematical deficits in school age children."
Population: Ages 8 through 18.
Publication Dates: 1984-2013.
Acronym: TOMA-3.
Scores, 6: Mathematical Symbols and Concepts, Computation, Mathematics in Everyday Life, Word Problems, Mathematical Ability Index, Attitude Toward Math (supplemental).
Administration: Individual or group.
Price Data, 2014: $181 per complete kit including examiner's manual (2013, 87 pages), 25 examiner record forms, and 25 student response booklets; $67 per manual; $49 per 25 examiner record forms; $65 per 25 student response booklets.
Time: (90) minutes.
Authors: Virginia L. Brown, Mary E. Cronin, and Diane P. Bryant.

Publisher: PRO-ED.
Cross References: Reviews are scheduled for *The Twentieth Mental Measurements Yearbook*. For reviews by Delwyn L. Harnisch and Rosemary Sutton of the second edition, see 13:329 (1 reference); for a review by Mark L. Davison of the original edition, see 9:1263.

[2113]

Test of Mechanical Concepts.

Purpose: "Designed to measure an individual's ability to visualize and understand basic mechanical relationships."
Population: Applicants for industrial positions.
Publication Dates: 1976–1995.
Scores, 4: Mechanical Interrelationships, Mechanical Tools and Devices, Spatial Relations, Total.
Administration: Individual or group.
Forms, 2: A, B.
Price Data: Available from publisher.
Time: No limit (approximately 35–45 minutes).
Author: Science Research Associates.
Publisher: General Dynamics Information Technology.
Cross References: See T5:2700 (1 reference); for reviews by Lorraine D. Eyde and Lyle F. Schoenfeldt, see 8:1045.

[2114]

Test of Memory and Learning, Second Edition.

Purpose: Designed to assess the "key features of memory" and to "evaluate learning as reflected in changes in recall and recognition over multiple trials of various stimuli."
Population: Ages 5-0 to 59-11.
Publication Dates: 1994-2007.
Acronym: TOMAL-2.
Scores, 25: 10 Verbal subtest scores (Memory for Stories, Word Selective Reminding, Object Recall, Paired Recall, Digits Forward, Letters Forward, Digits Backward, Letters Backward, Memory for Stories Delayed, Word Selective Reminding Delayed); 6 Nonverbal subtest scores (Facial Memory, Abstract Visual Memory, Visual Sequence Memory, Memory for Location, Visual Selective Reminding, Manual Imitation); 3 core composite scores (Verbal Memory Index, Nonverbal Memory Index, Composite Memory Index); 6 supplemental composite scores (Verbal Delayed Recall Index, Attention/Concentration Index, Sequential Recall Index, Free Recall Index, Associative Recall Index, Learning Index).
Administration: Individual.
Price Data, 2015: $433 per complete kit including Picture Book A, Picture Book B, 25 profile forms, 25 examiner record booklets, Delayed Recall Cue Cards, Visual Selective Reminding Test Board, 15 vinyl chips, and examiner's manual (2007, 165 pages); $85 per Picture Book A; $96 per Picture Book B; $49 per 25 profile forms; $72 per 25 examiner record booklets; $37 per set

of Delayed Recall Cue Cards; $20 per Visual Selective Reminding Test Board; $11 per 15 vinyl chips; $86 per examiner's manual (2007, 159 pages).
Time: Core battery (30-35) minutes; Supplemental subtests (25-35) minutes.
Authors: Cecil R. Reynolds and Judith K. Voress.
Publisher: PRO-ED.
Cross References: For reviews by R. Anthony Doggett and Steven R. Shaw, see 18:143; for reviews by Karen Geller and Susan J. Maller of an earlier edition, see 13:330 (1 reference).

[2115]
Test of Memory Malingering.
Purpose: "To assist neuropsychologists in discriminating between true memory-impaired patients and malingerers."
Population: Ages 16 to 84.
Publication Date: 1996.
Acronym: TOMM.
Scores: Total score only.
Administration: Individual.
Price Data, 2015: $234 per complete kit including manual (45 pages), TOMM Research Monograph, 25 record forms, and 1 set of stimulus booklets; $50 per 25 record forms; $113 per set of 3 stimulus booklets; $83 per user's manual; $29 per Research Monograph; $93 per TOMM for Windows preview kit including user's manual, software manual, and 3 reports; $10 per TOMM for Windows Report.
Time: (15–20) minutes.
Comments: Self-completed; computer software available to administer, score, and report results of TOMM.
Author: Tom N. Tombaugh.
Publisher: Multi-Health Systems, Inc.
Cross References: For reviews by M. Allan Cooperstein and Romeo Vitelli, see 14:392.

[2116]
Test of Narrative Language.
Purpose: Designed to measure "children's ability to understand and tell stories."
Population: Ages 5-0 to 11-11.
Publication Date: 2004.
Acronym: TNL.
Scores, 3: 2 subtests: Narrative Comprehension, Oral Narration, plus Narrative Language Ability Index.
Administration: Individual.
Price Data, 2015: $192 per complete kit including examiner's manual (119 pages), picture book, and 25 examiner record booklets; $72 per examiner's manual; $79 per picture book; $56 per 25 examiner record booklets.
Time: (15–20) minutes.
Authors: Ronald B. Gillam and Nils A. Pearson.
Publisher: PRO-ED.
Cross References: For reviews by Abigail Baxter and Gabriele van Lingen, see 16:247.

[2117]
Test of Nonverbal Intelligence, Fourth Edition.
Purpose: "Developed to assess aptitude, intelligence, abstract reasoning, and problem solving in a completely language-free format."
Population: Ages 6-0 to 89-11.
Publication Dates: 1982-2010.
Acronym: TONI-4.
Scores: Total score only.
Administration: Individual.
Forms, 2: Form A, Form B.
Price Data, 2015: $376 per kit including examiner's manual (2010, 107 pages), picture book, Critical Reviews and Research Findings (1982-2009), 50 Form A answer booklets and record forms, and 50 Form B answer booklets and record forms.
Foreign Language Editions: Spanish, French, German, Chinese, Vietnamese, Korean, Tagalog instructions available.
Time: (15-20) minutes.
Author: Linda Brown, Rita J. Sherbenou, and Susan K. Johnsen.
Publisher: PRO-ED.
Cross References: For reviews by Tawny N. Evans-McCleon and Cleoborne D. Maddux, see 19:171; for reviews by Jeffrey A. Atlas and Gerald E. DeMauro of the third edition, see 14:393; see also T5:2704 (47 references) and T4:2775 (10 references); for reviews by Kevin K. Murphy and T. Steuart Watson of the second edition, see 11:439 (9 references); for reviews by Philip M. Clark and Samuel T. Mayo of the original edition, see 9:1266.

[2118]
Test of Oral Structures and Functions.
Purpose: "Assesses oral structures and motor integrity during verbal and nonverbal oral functioning."
Population: Ages 7–Adults.
Publication Dates: 1986–2002.
Acronym: TOSF.
Scores, 16: Speech Survey (Articulation, Rate/Prosody, Fluency, Voice, Total); Verbal Oral Functioning (Resonance, Balance, Sequenced Syllables, Mixed Syllable Sequence, Sequenced Vowels, Sequenced Syllable Rates, Total); Nonverbal Oral Functions (Isolated Functioning, Sequenced Functioning); Survey of Orofacial Structures; History-Behavioral Survey.
Administration: Individual.
Price Data, 2016: $132.50 per complete kit including manual (36 pages), 25 test booklets, finger cots, tongue blades, penlight, and balloons; $56.75 per examiner's manual; $63.75 per 25 test booklets; $13.75 per oroscope penlight.
Time: (20) minutes.
Author: Gary J. Vitali.

Publisher: Slosson Educational Publications, Inc.
Cross References: See T5:2706 (2 references); for reviews by Ronald B. Gillam and Roger L. Towne, see 12:397.

[2119]
Test of Orthographic Competence.

Purpose: Designed to assess "aspects of the English writing system that are integral to proficient reading and writing. These aspects include letters, spelling, punctuation, abbreviations, and special symbols."
Population: Ages 6 through 17.
Publication Date: 2008.
Acronym: TOC.
Price Data, 2014: $305 per complete kit including examiner's manual (130 pages), picture book, 25 examiner record forms (ages 6-7), and 25 student response booklets for each age group (ages 6-7, 8-12, 13-17); $60 per picture book; $60 per 25 student response booklets (ages 8-12 or ages 13-17); $53 per 25 student response booklets (ages 6-7); $53 per manual; $30 per 25 examiner record forms (ages 6-7).
Time: (20-60) minutes.
Authors: Nancy Mather, Rhia Roberts, Donald D. Hammill, and Elizabeth A. Allen.
Publisher: PRO-ED.
a) AGES 6-7.
Population: Ages 6-0 through 7-11.
Scores, 5: Signs and Symbols, Grapheme Matching, Homophone Choice, Punctuation, Orthographic Ability.
Administration: Individual.
b) AGES 8-12.
Population: Ages 8-0 through 12-11.
Scores, 10: Homophone Choice, Punctuation, Abbreviations, Letter Choice, Word Scramble, Sight Spelling, Conventions, Spelling Accuracy, Spelling Speed, Orthographic Ability.
Administration: Individual or group.
c) AGES 13-17.
Population: Ages 13-0 through 17-11.
Scores, 10: Punctuation, Abbreviations, Letter Choice, Word Scramble, Sight Spelling, Word Choice, Conventions, Spelling Accuracy, Spelling Speed, Orthographic Ability.
Administration: Individual or group.
Cross References: Reviews are scheduled for *The Twentieth Mental Measurements Yearbook.*

[2120]
Test of Phonological Awareness in Spanish.

Purpose: To assess phonological awareness in children whose first language is Spanish.
Population: Ages 4-0 to 10-11.
Publication Date: 2004.
Acronym: TPAS.
Scores, 5: Phonological Awareness Ability, Initial Sounds, Final Sounds, Rhyming Words, Deletion.
Administration: Individual.

Price Data, 2015: $100 per complete kit; $61 per examiner's manual; $47 per examiner record booklets.
Time: (10–15) minutes.
Authors: Cynthia A. Riccio, Brian Imhoff, Jan E. Hasbrouck, and G. Nicole Davis.
Publisher: PRO-ED.
Cross References: For reviews by Carlos Inchaurralde and Vincent J. Samar, see 16:248.

[2121]
Test of Phonological Awareness—Second Edition: PLUS.

Purpose: Designed to measure "young children's ability to isolate individual phonemes in spoken words and their knowledge of relationships between letters and phonemes in English."
Population: Ages 5–8.
Publication Dates: 1994–2004.
Acronym: TOPA-2+.
Scores: 2 subtests: Phonological Awareness, Letter Sounds.
Administration: Individual or group.
Levels, 2: Kindergarten, Early Elementary.
Price Data, 2015: $250 per kit including examiner's manual (2004, 78 pages), 50 Kindergarten summary forms, 50 Early Elementary summary forms, 25 student booklets for Kindergarten, and 25 student booklets for Early Elementary; $88 per examiner's manual; $37 per 50 Kindergarten summary forms; $37 per 50 Early Elementary summary forms; $58 per 25 Kindergarten student booklets; $58 per 25 Early Elementary student booklets.
Time: (15–30) minutes for Early Elementary version; (30-45) minutes for Kindergarten version.
Authors: Joseph K. Torgesen and Brian R. Bryant.
Publisher: PRO-ED.
Cross References: For a review by Ray Fenton, see 16:249; for reviews by Steven H. Long and by Rebecca McCauley of a previous edition, see 13:333 (3 references).

[2122]
Test of Pragmatic Language–Second Edition.

Purpose: Designed to "assess a student's ability to effectively use pragmatic, or social, language."
Population: Ages 6 through 18.
Publication Dates: 1992-2007.
Acronym: TOPL-2.
Score: Pragmatic Language Usage Index.
Administration: Individual.
Forms, 2: Ages 6-7, ages 8-18.
Price Data, 2016: $257 per complete kit including examiner's manual (2007, 146 pages), picture book, 25 examiner record booklets for ages 6-7, and 25 examiner record booklets for ages 8-18; $56 per 25 examiner record booklets for ages 6-7; $62 per 25 examiner record booklets for ages 8-18; $72 per manual; $80 per picture book.
Time: (60-90) minutes.

Authors: Diana Phelps-Terasaki and Trisha Phelps-Gunn.
Publisher: PRO-ED.
Cross References: Reviews are scheduled for *The Twentieth Mental Measurements Yearbook*. For reviews by Salvador Hector Ochoa and William K. Wilkinson of the original edition, see 12:398.

[2123]

Test of Preschool Early Literacy.
Purpose: Designed to "identify children at risk of having or developing problems in literacy."
Population: Ages 3-0 to 5-11.
Publication Date: 2007.
Acronym: TOPEL.
Scores, 4: Print Knowledge, Definitional Vocabulary, Phonological Awareness, Early Literacy Index.
Administration: Individual.
Price Data, 2015: $247 per complete kit including examiner's manual (72 pages), picture book, and 25 record booklets; $101 per picture book; $62 per 25 record booklets; $97 per examiner's manual.
Time: (30) minutes.
Authors: Christopher J. Lonigan, Richard K. Wagner, Joseph K. Torgesen, and Carol A. Rashotte.
Publisher: PRO-ED.
Cross References: For reviews by Ronald A. Madle and by Gretchen Owens and Claire Lenz, see 18:144.

[2124]

Test of Preschool Vocabulary.
Purpose: Designed to assess receptive and expressive oral vocabulary abilities of preschool children.
Population: Ages 2 through 5.
Publication Date: 2015.
Acronym: TOPV.
Scores, 3: Expressive Vocabulary, Receptive Vocabulary, General Vocabulary.
Administration: Individual.
Price Data, 2015: $279 per kit including examiner's manual (68 pages), 25 Examiner Record Booklets, picture plate, and object kit; $63 per manual; $59 per 25 record booklets; $111 per object kit; $27 per picture card.
Time: (15-30) minutes.
Comments: Subtests may be administered in two sessions, but Expressive Vocabulary subtest must be administered first.
Authors: Steven C. Mathews and Lynda Miller.
Publisher: PRO-ED.
Cross References: Reviews are scheduled for *The Twentieth Mental Measurements Yearbook*.

[2125]

Test of Problem Solving 3: Elementary.
Purpose: Designed to assess children's critical thinking and problem solving skills.

Population: Ages 6.0-12.11.
Publication Dates: 1984-2005.
Acronym: TOPS-3:E.
Scores, 7: Making Inferences, Sequencing, Negative Questions, Problem Solving, Predicting, Determining Causes, Total.
Administration: Individual.
Price Data, 2016: $169.95 per kit including manual, picture stimulus book, and 20 test forms.
Time: (35) minutes.
Authors: Linda Bowers, Rosemary Huisingh, and Carolyn LoGiudice.
Publisher: PRO-ED.
Cross References: For a review by Patti L. Harrison, see 17:184; see also T5:2710 (8 references).

[2126]

Test of Reading Comprehension–Fourth Edition.
Purpose: Designed "(a) to identify children and adolescents who score significantly below their peers and who therefore might need help in improving their reading proficiency and comprehension; (b) to document student progress; and (c) to serve as a research tool in studies investigating reading problems in children and adolescents."
Population: Ages 7 through 17.
Publication Dates: 1978-2009.
Acronym: TORC-4.
Scores, 6: Relational Vocabulary, Sentence Completion, Paragraph Construction, Text Comprehension, Contextual Fluency, Reading Comprehension.
Administration: Individual or group.
Price Data, 2016: $263 per complete kit including examiner's manual (2009, 120 pages), 50 examiner/record forms, 25 student question booklets, and 50 student answer booklets; $84 per 25 student question booklets; $72 per manual; $59 per 50 examiner/record forms, $59 per 50 student answer booklets.
Time: (45) minutes.
Comments: Group administration may be used for research purposes or for classroom screening; individual administration must be used when testing for special services or placement.
Authors: Virginia L. Brown, J. Lee Wiederholt, and Donald D. Hammill.
Publisher: PRO-ED.
Cross References: Reviews are scheduled for *The Twentieth Mental Measurements Yearbook*. See T5:2712 (1 reference); for reviews by Felice J. Green and Carole Perlman of the third edition, see 13:334 (3 references); see also T4:2785 (3 references); for reviews by James A. Poteet and Robert J. Tierney of the revised edition, see 10:372 (4 references); for reviews by Brendon John Bartlett and Joyce Hood of the original edition, see 9:1270; see also T3:2456 (1 reference).

[2127]

Test of Sensory Functions in Infants.

Purpose: Developed to measure "sensory processing and reactivity in infants."
Population: Infants ages 4-18 months.
Publication Date: 1989.
Acronym: TSFI.
Scores, 6: Reactivity to Tactile Deep Pressure, Adaptive Motor Functions, Visual-Tactile Integration, Ocular-Motor Control, Reactivity to Vestibular Stimulation, Total.
Administration: Individual.
Price Data, 2015: $226.50 per complete kit including set of test materials, 100 administration and scoring forms, and manual (45 pages) in carrying case; $34 per 100 administration and scoring forms; $51.50 per manual.
Time: (20) minutes.
Authors: Georgia A. DeGangi and Stanley I. Greenspan.
Publisher: Western Psychological Services.
Cross References: See T5:2715 (1 reference); for a review by Mark Albanese, see 11:441.

[2128]

Test of Silent Contextual Reading Fluency–Second Edition.

Purpose: Designed to measure "the speed with which students can recognize the individual words in a series of printed passages that become progressively more difficult in their content, vocabulary, and grammar."
Population: Ages 7 through 24.
Publication Dates: 2006-2014.
Acronym: TOSCRF-2.
Score: Total score only.
Administration: Individual or group.
Forms, 4: A, B, C, D.
Price Data, 2014: $297 per complete kit including examiner's manual (2014, 137 pages), and student record forms (25 of each form: A, B, C, D); $69 per manual; $57 per 25 student record forms (A, B, C, or D), volume discounts available.
Time: 3(6) minutes.
Authors: Donald D. Hammill, J. Lee Wiederholt, and Elizabeth A. Allen.
Publisher: PRO-ED.
Cross References: Reviews are scheduled for *The Twentieth Mental Measurements Yearbook*. For reviews by Lisa F. Smith and Louise M. Soares of the original edition, see 17:185.

[2129]

Test of Silent Word Reading Fluency–Second Edition.

Purpose: Designed to measure "word identification, word comprehension, and reading speed."
Population: Ages 6-3 to 24-11.

Publication Dates: 2004-2014.
Acronym: TOSWRF-2.
Score: Silent Word Reading Fluency.
Administration: Individual or group.
Forms, 4: A, B, C, D.
Price Data, 2014: $297 per complete kit including examiner's manual (2014, 139 pages) and student record forms (25 each of A, B, C, and D); $69 per examiner's manual; $57 per 25 student record forms (A, B, C, or D).
Time: 3 minutes.
Authors: Nancy Mather, Donald D. Hammill, Elizabeth A. Allen, and Rhia Roberts.
Publisher: PRO-ED.
Cross References: Reviews are scheduled for *The Twentieth Mental Measurements Yearbook*. For reviews by Michael D. Beck and John W. Young of the original edition, see 16:251.

[2130]

Test of Supervisory Skills.

Purpose: Designed to measure an individual's understanding of "the roles and responsibilities of a first-line supervisor."
Population: Business supervisors and potential business supervisors.
Publication Date: 2004.
Acronym: TOSS.
Scores, 8: Management of Performance Quality, Staffing/Personnel Actions, Communications, Interpersonal Relations, Problem Analysis/Resolution, Project Planning, Direct Supervision, Total.
Administration: Individual or group.
Price Data, 2016: $39.95 per administrator manual; $75 per 25 answer sheets; $59.95 per 10 test booklets.
Time: (30–45) minutes.
Comments: Available in paper-and-pencil and online versions.
Authors: Erich P. Prien and Leonard D. Goodstein.
Publisher: HRD Press, Inc.
Cross References: For reviews by Ayres G. D'Costa and John W. Fleenor, see 17:186.

[2131]

Test of Understanding in College Economics-Fourth Edition.

Purpose: Intended "to provide norming data for a large national sample of students in [economics] principles classes, allowing instructors to compare performance in their classes on both pretests and posttests to the performance of the national sample of students and instructors."
Population: Introductory economics students.
Publication Dates: 1967-2007.
Acronym: TUCE-4.
Scores: 2 tests: Microeconomics, Macroeconomics.
Administration: Group.
Price Data: Available at no cost from test publisher.

Time: (45) minutes.
Authors: William B. Walstad, Michael Watts, and Ken Rebeck.
Publisher: Council for Economic Education.
Cross References: For reviews by George Engelhard, Jr. and Jean P. Kirnan, see 18:145; for reviews by Joseph C. Ciechalski and Jennifer J. Fager of the third edition, see 13:335; see also T2:1970 (10 references); for a review by Christine H. McGuire of an earlier edition, see 7:902.

[2132]
Test of Variables of Attention (Version 8).

Purpose: Developed to "assess attention and impulse control in normal and clinical populations."
Population: Ages 4-80+.
Publication Dates: 1988-2015.
Acronym: TOVA.
Scores, 7: Commission, Omission, Response Time, Response Time Variability, Signal Detection, Attention Performance Index, Symptom Exaggeration Index.
Administration: Individual.
Editions, 2: Clinical TOVA (for licensed clinicians), Screening TOVA (for professionals who do not have a clinical license).
Parts, 2: Auditory TOVA, Visual TOVA.
Price Data, 2016: $695 per TOVA 8 kit, including Visual and Auditory TOVA tests, TOVA USB hardware, user's manual (2015, 163 pages), installation CD, and 5 free test credits; $295 per upgrade from TOVA 7.
Time: (21.6) minutes for each part.
Comments: Computer administered via TOVA 8 software and the TOVA 8 hardware kit; professional manual (2015, 140 pages), screening manual (2008, 63 pages), and clinical manual (2015, 76 pages) available for download; test itself has not changed between versions; TOVA 8 includes new user interface, hardware, data storage, reports, credit system, and online help.
Authors: Lawrence M. Greenberg (computer software and manuals), Robert A. Leark (professional manual), Carol L. Kindschi (professional manual, clinical manual), Tammy R. Dupuy (professional manual, clinical manual), and Steven J. Hughes (professional manual, clinical manual).
Publisher: The TOVA Company.
Cross References: For reviews by Sandra Loew and by Susan C. Whiston and Harrison Kane of Version 7.03, see 14:394; see also T5:2720 (2 references); for reviews by Rosa A. Hagin and Peter Della Bella and by Margot B. Stein of an earlier version, see 13:336 (1 reference).

[2133]
Test of Visual-Motor Skills–3rd Edition.

Purpose: Designed to assess visual-motor skills.
Population: Ages 3 to 90.
Publication Dates: 1986–2010.
Acronym: TVMS–3.
Scores, 2: Accuracy, Errors.
Administration: Group.
Price Data, 2015: $145 per kit, including manual (2010, 96 pages), 15 test booklets, and 15 record forms; $70 per manual; $55 per 15 test booklets; $20 per 15 record forms.
Time: (20–30) minutes.
Comments: Third edition combines lower and upper levels and extends age range.
Authors: Nancy A. Martin (TVMS-3); earlier editions by Morrison F. Gardner.
Publisher: Academic Therapy Publications.
Cross References: For reviews by Ayres G. D'Costa and Kenneth M. Hanig, see 19:172; for reviews by Deborah Erickson and Janet E. Spector of an earlier edition, see 13:337 (2 references); see also T4:2791 (1 reference).

[2134]
Test of Visual Perceptual Skills, 3rd Edition.

Purpose: Constructed to "determine a child's visual-perceptual strengths and weaknesses."
Population: Ages 4-0 through 18-11.
Publication Dates: 1982-2006.
Acronym: TVPS-3.
Scores: 7 subtests: Visual Discrimination, Visual Memory, Spatial Relationships, Form Constancy, Sequential Memory, Visual Figure-Ground, Visual Closure, Total Score.
Administration: Individual.
Price Data, 2015: $175 per test kit including manual (2006, 88 pages), test plates, and 25 record forms; $55 per manual; $80 per test plates; $40 per 25 record forms.
Time: (30) minutes (untimed).
Authors: Nancy Martin (TVPS-3); earlier editions by Morrison F. Gardner.
Publisher: Academic Therapy Publications.
Cross References: For reviews by Phillip L. Ackerman and Brian F. French, see 18:146; see T5:2724 (13 references); for reviews by Nancy A. Busch-Rossnagel and Joseph W. Denison of an earlier edition entitled Test of Visual-Perceptual Skills (Non-Motor), see 9:1276.

[2135]
Test of Word Finding in Discourse.

Purpose: Designed to assess children's word-finding skills in discourse.
Population: Ages 6-6 to 12-11.
Publication Date: 1991.
Acronym: TWFD.
Scores, 2: Productivity Index, Word-Finding Behaviors Index.
Administration: Individual.
Price Data, 2015: $143 per complete test including manual (173 pages) and 25 test record forms; $48 per 25 test record forms; $97 per manual.
Time: (15-20) minutes.

Author: Diane J. German.
Publisher: PRO-ED.
Cross References: For reviews by James Dean Brown and Rebecca J. Kopriva, see 12:399; see also T4:2800 (1 reference).

[2136]
Test of Word Finding–Third Edition.

Purpose: Designed as a diagnostic tool for assessing children's word finding skills and providing a structure for describing their retrieval behavior.
Population: Ages 4-6 to 12-11.
Publication Dates: 1986-2015.
Acronym: TWF-3.
Scores, 8: 2 for the Standardized Assessment (Comprehension, Word Finding Index); 6 for the Informal Assessment (Comprehension Check, Delayed Response Procedure, Secondary Characteristics Tally, Phonemic Cueing Procedure, Imitation Procedure, Substitution Analysis).
Administration: Individual.
Levels, 3: Preprimary, Primary, Intermediate.
Forms, 2: Standardized Assessment, Informal Assessment.
Price Data, 2015: $471 per complete kit including examiner's manual (2015, 180 pages), Word Finding Assessment Picture Book, Comprehension Check Picture Book, 10 Preprimary Examiner Record Forms, 10 Primary Examiner Record Forms, and 10 Intermediate Examiner Record Forms; $197 per Word Finding Assessment Picture Book; $145 per Comprehension Check Picture Book; $101 per manual; $27 per 10 Examiner Record Booklets (Preprimary, Primary, or Intermediate).
Time: (20-30) minutes.
Comments: Informal Assessment analyses are designed as follow-up to the Standardized Assessment to clarify findings and to aid intervention planning.
Author: Diane J. German.
Publisher: PRO-ED.
Cross References: Reviews are scheduled for *The Twentieth Mental Measurements Yearbook*. For a review by D. Joe Olmi of the second edition, see 15:264; see T5:2725 (10 references); for reviews by Sharon L. Weinberg and Susan Ellis Weisman of an earlier edition, see 11:443 (1 reference); for reviews by Mavis Donahue and Priscilla A. Drum of the original edition, see 10:373.

[2137]
Test of Word Knowledge.

Purpose: Developed to "assess a student's skill in the reception and expression of ... semantics."
Population: Ages 5–17.
Publication Date: 1992.
Acronym: TOWK.
Scores, 11: Expressive Vocabulary, Receptive Vocabulary, Word Opposites, Word Definitions, Synonyms, Multiple Contexts, Figurative Usage, Conjunctions and Transition Words, Receptive Composite, Expressive Composite, Total.
Administration: Individual.
Levels, 2: Ages 5–8, Ages 8–17.
Price Data, 2015: $233.70 per complete kit including stimulus manual, examiner's manual (118 pages), and 12 record forms; $45.35 per 12 record forms; $98 per examiner's manual; $109.80 per stimulus manual.
Time: (25) minutes for Level 1; (65) minutes for Level 2.
Authors: Elisabeth H. Wiig and Wayne Secord.
Publisher: Pearson.
Cross References: See T5:2727 (1 reference); for a review by Rick Lindskog, see 13:338 (3 references).

[2138]
Test of Word Reading Efficiency–Second Edition.

Purpose: Designed to measure "an individual's ability to pronounce printed words accurately and fluently."
Population: Ages 6 through 24.
Publication Dates: 1999-2012.
Acronym: TOWRE-2.
Scores, 3: Sight Word Efficiency, Phonemic Decoding Efficiency, Total Word Reading Efficiency Index.
Administration: Individual.
Forms: 4 equivalent forms per subtest (A, B, C, D).
Price Data, 2014: $302 per complete kit including examiner's manual (2012, 140 pages), Form A word cards, Form B word cards, Form C word cards, Form D word cards, 25 Form A examiner record booklets, 25 Form B examiner record booklets, and 25 response to intervention booklets; $75 per examiner's manual; $41 per 25 examiner record booklets (Form A or Form B); $25 per word cards (Form A, B, C, or D); $43 per 25 response to intervention booklets.
Time: (5) minutes for one form of a subtest; (7-8) minutes for two forms of the same subtest.
Authors: Joseph K. Torgesen, Richard K. Wagner, and Carol A. Rashotte.
Publisher: PRO-ED.
Cross References: Reviews are scheduled for *The Twentieth Mental Measurements Yearbook*. For reviews by Gerald Tindal and John J. Vacca of the original edition, see 15:265.

[2139]
Test of Written Expression.

Purpose: Constructed as a "norm-referenced test of writing."
Population: Ages 6-6 to 14-11.
Publication Date: 1995.
Acronym: TOWE.
Scores, 2: Items, Essay.
Administration: Individual or group.

Price Data, 2015: $174 per complete kit including manual (58 pages), 25 profile/examiner record forms, and 25 student booklets in storage box; $56 per 25 student booklets; $62 per profile/examiner record forms; $69 per examiner's manual.
Time: (60) minutes.
Authors: Ron McGhee, Brian R. Bryant, Stephen C. Larsen, and Diane M. Rivera.
Publisher: PRO-ED
Cross References: For reviews by Mildred Murray-Ward and Carole Perlman, see 13:339 (1 reference).

[2140]

Test of Written Language–Fourth Edition.

Purpose: Designed to "(a) identify students who write poorly and, therefore, need special help; (b) determine students' particular strengths and weaknesses in various writing abilities; (c) document students' progress in special writing programs," and to be used in research on writing.
Population: Ages 9 through 17.
Publication Dates: 1978-2009.
Acronym: TOWL-4.
Scores, 10: Vocabulary, Spelling, Punctuation, Logical Sentences, Sentence Combining, Contextual Conventions, Story Composition, Overall Writing, Contrived Writing, Spontaneous Writing.
Administration: Individual or group.
Forms, 2: A, B.
Price Data, 2014: $274 per complete kit including examiner's manual (2009, 180 pages), 3 colored picture cards, 50 record/story scoring forms, 25 student response booklets (Form A), 25 student response booklets (Form B), and supplemental practice scoring booklet; $84 per examiner's manual; $60 per 25 student response booklets (Form A or Form B); $27 per set of picture cards.
Time: (60-90) minutes.
Authors: Donald D. Hammill and Stephen C. Larsen.
Publisher: PRO-ED.
Cross References: Reviews are scheduled for *The Twentieth Mental Measurements Yearbook*. See T5:2731 (8 references); for reviews by Joe B. Hansen and by Jayne E. Bucy and Mark E. Swerdlik of the third edition, see 13:340 (16 references); see also T4:2804 (2 references); for reviews by Stephen L. Benton and Joseph M. Ryan of the second edition, see 11:444 (6 references); for reviews by Edward A. Polloway and Robert T. Williams of the original edition, see 9:1278.

[2141]

Test of Written Spelling–Fifth Edition.

Purpose: Designed "to identify poor spellers and to establish the severity of their problem."
Population: Ages 6 through 18.
Publication Dates: 1976-2013.
Acronym: TWS-5.
Score: Total score only.

Administration: Individual or group.
Forms, 2: A, B.
Price Data, 2014: $125 per complete kit including examiner's manual (2013, 85 pages), 50 answer and record forms, and 1 laminated double-sided card with stimulus words; $63 per manual; $51 per 50 answer and record forms; $11 per stimulus words card.
Time: (15-20) minutes.
Authors: Stephen C. Larsen, Donald D. Hammill, and Louisa S. Moats.
Publisher: PRO-ED.
Cross References: Reviews are scheduled for *The Twentieth Mental Measurements Yearbook*. For a review by Gerald E. DeMauro of the fourth edition, see 15:266; see T5:2732 (2 references); for reviews by Alfred P. Longo and Hoi K. Suen of the third edition, see 13:341 (5 references); see also T4:2805 (4 references); for reviews by Deborah B. Erikson and Ruth M. Noyce of the second edition, see 10:374; for reviews by John M. Bradley and Deborah B. Erickson of the original edition, see 9:1279.

[2142]

Tests of Achievement in Basic Skills: Mathematics.

Purpose: To assess mathematics achievement.
Population: Preschool-kindergarten, Grades 1, 2, 3–4, 4–6, 7–9, 10–adult.
Publication Dates: 1970–1976.
Acronym: TABS-M.
Administration: Group.
Price Data: Available from publisher.
Time: (45–70) minutes.
Comments: May be used separately or as part of instructional Individualized Mathematics Program (IMP); "criterion-referenced tests"; 18-69 item scores, each item measuring a specific objective, and part and total scores; separate answer sheets must be used with Levels B-D.
Authors: James C. Young and Robert R. Knapp (Level C manuals).
Publisher: EdITS/Educational and Industrial Testing Service.
> *a)* LEVEL K.
> **Population:** Preschool-kindergarten.
> **Publication Date:** 1974.
> **Scores:** 18 item scores in 3 areas: Arithmetic Skills, Geometry-Measurement, Modern Concepts.
> *b)* LEVEL 1.
> **Population:** Grade 1.
> **Publication Date:** 1974.
> **Scores:** 36 item scores in 3 areas: same as *a* above.
> *c)* LEVEL 2.
> **Population:** Grade 2.
> **Publication Date:** 1974.
> **Scores:** 41 item scores in 3 areas: same as *a* above.
> *d)* LEVEL A.
> **Population:** Grades 3–4.
> **Publication Date:** 1973.
> **Scores:** 49 item scores in 3 areas: same as *a* above.

e) LEVEL B.
Population: Grades 4–6.
Publication Dates: 1972–1973.
Scores: 73 items and total scores in 3 areas: same as *a* above, plus Total.
f) LEVEL C.
Population: Grades 7–9.
Publication Dates: 1970–1971.
Scores: 68 items and total scores in 3 areas: same as *e* above.
g) LEVEL D.
Population: Grades 10-12.
Publication Dates: 1972–1976.
Scores: 47 items and total scores in 2 areas: Arithmetic Skills, Arithmetic Application, plus Total.
Cross References: For reviews by James Braswell and C. Alan Riedesel, and an excerpted review by Barton B. Proger, see 8:293 (2 references); see also 7:492 (1 reference).

[2143]

Tests of Adult Basic Education, Forms 9 & 10.

Purpose: "Designed and developed to provide achievement scores that are valid for most types of adult education decision-making."
Population: Adults.
Acronym: TABE.
Subtests, 4-11: Pre-Reading (Level L), Reading, Mathematics Computation, Applied Mathematics, Language, Language Mechanics (optional), Vocabulary (optional), Spelling (optional), Science/Social Studies (Level A), Algebra/Geometry (Level A), Writing (Level A).
Administration: Individual or group.
Editions, 2: Complete Battery, Survey.
Forms, 2: 9, 10.
Price Data: Available from publisher.
Special Editions: Form 9 is available in Large Print, Braille, and Audio.
Comments: Both forms available online.
Author: CTB/McGraw-Hill.
Publisher: DRC.
a) COMPLETE BATTERY.
Purpose: Designed to "assess skill levels and help determine appropriate career or training programs."
Publication Dates: 1957-2004.
Levels, 4-5: L (Limited Literacy), E (Easy), M (Medium), D (Difficult), A (Advanced).
Scores, 4: Total Mathematics (Mathematics Computation, Applied Mathematics), Total Battery (Pre-Reading/Reading, Total Mathematics, Language).
1) *Pre-Reading.*
Scores, 4: Match Letters, Recognize Letters, Recognize Beginning/Ending Sounds, Middle Sounds.
Levels: Level L only.
Time: 13(23) minutes.
2) *Reading.*
Scores, 4-5: Interpret Graphic Information, Words in Context, Recall Information, Construct Meaning, Evaluate/Extend Meaning [Levels E-A only].

Time: 32(42) minutes for Level L; 50(60) minutes for Levels E-A.
3) *Mathematics Computation.*
Scores, 2-6: Add Whole Numbers [Levels L-M], Subtract Whole Numbers [Levels L-M], Multiply Whole Numbers [Levels E-D], Divide Whole Numbers [Levels E-D], Decimals [Levels E-A], Fractions [Levels M-A], Integers [Levels D, A], Percents [Levels D, A], Order of Operations [Level A], Algebraic Operations [Level A].
Time: 15(25) minutes for Level L; 24(34) minutes for Levels E-A.
4) *Applied Mathematics.*
Scores, 6-9: Number & Number Operations, Computation in Context, Estimation [Levels E-A], Measurement, Geometry & Spatial Sense, Data Analysis, Statistics & Probability [Levels E-A], Patterns/Functions/Algebra, Problem Solving & Reasoning [Levels E-A].
Levels: Level L only.
Time: 45(55) minutes for Level L; 50(60) minutes for Levels E-A.
5) *Language.*
Scores, 6: Usage, Sentence Formation, Paragraph Development, Capitalization, Punctuation, Writing Conventions.
Levels: Levels E-A only.
Time: 55(65) minutes.
6) *Vocabulary.*
Scores, 3: Word Meaning, Multi-Meaning Words, Words in Context.
Levels: Levels E-A only.
Time: 14(24) minutes.
Comments: This subtest is optional.
7) *Language Mechanics.*
Scores, 2: Sentences/Phrases/Clauses, Writing Conventions.
Levels: Levels E-A only.
Time: 14(24) minutes.
Comments: This subtest is optional.
8) *Spelling.*
Scores, 3: Vowel, Consonant, Structural Unit.
Levels: Levels E-A only.
Time: 10(20) minutes.
Comments: This subtest is optional.
9) *Science/Social Studies.*
Scores: Scores not presented.
Level: Level A only.
Time: Administration time not reported.
Comments: This subtest is optional.
10) *Algebra/Geometry.*
Scores: Scores not presented.
Level: Level A only.
Time: Administration time not reported.
Comments: This subtest is optional.
11) *Writing.*
Scores: Scores not presented.
Level: Level A only.
Time: 45(55) minutes.
Comments: This subtest is optional.
b) SURVEY.
Purpose: Provides a skill snapshot for placement information.

Publication Dates: 1987-2004.
Levels, 4: Same as Complete Battery except for omission of Level L.
Scores, 2: Same as Complete Battery.

1) *Reading.*
Scores, 5: Same as Complete Battery.
Time: 25(35) minutes.

2) *Mathematics Computation.*
Scores, 5-6: Same as Complete Battery.
Time: 15(25) minutes.

3) *Applied Mathematics.*
Scores, 9: Same as Complete Battery.
Time: 25(35) minutes.

4) *Language.*
Scores, 6: Same as Complete Battery.
Time: 25(35) minutes.

5) *Language Mechanics.*
Scores, 3: Same as Complete Battery.
Time: 14(24) minutes.
Comments: This subtest is optional.

6) *Vocabulary.*
Scores, 3: Same as Complete Battery.
Time: 14(24) minutes.
Comments: This subtest is optional.

7) *Spelling.*
Scores, 3: Same as Complete Battery.
Time: 10(20) minutes.
Comments: This subtest is optional.

c) LOCATOR TEST.
Purpose: Designed to "help teachers in assigning the level of the TABE test to administer."
Subtests, 4: Reading, Mathematics Computation, Applied Mathematics, Language.
Scores: Total score only.

d) WORD LIST.
Scores: Total score only.
Time: 15(25) minutes.

e) PRACTICE EXERCISE.
Scores: Not scored.
Time: 20(30) minutes.

Cross References: For a review by Judith A. Monsaas, see 17:187; for reviews by Michael D. Beck and Bruce G. Rogers of an earlier edition, see 13:343; for reviews by Robert W. Lissitz and Steven J. Osterlind of an earlier edition, see 11:446 (2 references); for reviews by Thomas F. Donlon and Norman E. Gronlund of an earlier edition, see 8:33 (1 reference); for a review by A. N. Hieronymus and an excerpted review by S. Alan Cohen of an earlier edition, see 7:32.

[2144]

Tests of Reading Comprehension, Second Edition.

Purpose: "They aim at assessing the extent to which readers are able to obtain meaning from text."
Population: Grades 3–7, 6–10, and individuals with special needs.
Publication Dates: 1987–2003.
Acronym: TORCH.

Scores, 14: Grasshoppers, The Bear Who Liked Hugging People, Lizards Love Eggs, Getting Better, Feeding Puff, Shocking Things/Earthquakes!, The Swamp-creature, The Cats, A Horse of Her Own, Iceberg Towing, The Accident, The Killer Smog of London, I Want to be Andy, The Red Ace of Spades.
Administration: Individual or group.
Price Data, 2006: A$109.95 per complete kit including reading booklet, one of each answer sheet, and manual; A$89.95 per manual; A$8.95 per test booklet; A$11 per pack of 10 answer sheets for each of 12 levels.
Time: (30) minutes, untimed.
Comments: "Content-referenced" and/or "norm-referenced."
Authors: Leila Mossenson, Peter Hill, and Geoffrey Masters.
Publisher: Australian Council for Educational Research Ltd. [Australia; Efforts to obtain updated information from the test publisher were unsuccessful. An updated edition of this test appears on the test publisher's website].
Cross References: See T5:2743 (3 references) and T4:2817 (1 reference); for reviews by Robert B. Cooter, Jr. and Diane J. Sawyer of the earlier edition, see 11:448.

[2145]

TestWell: Health Risk Appraisal.

Purpose: "Designed to provide an awareness of how current behaviors and physical health measurements impact health risks."
Population: Adults ages 18–60 with a minimum of 10th grade education.
Publication Date: 1992.
Scores, 5: Appraised Age, Achievable Age, Positive Lifestyle Behaviors, Top 10 Risks of Death, Suggestions for Improvement.
Administration: Group.
Manual: No manual.
Price Data: Available from publisher.
Time: (20) minutes.
Comments: Scoring by National Wellness Institute; individual and group reports available.
Author: National Wellness Institute, Inc.
Publisher: National Wellness Institute, Inc.
Cross References: For reviews by Barbara L. Lachar and Steven G. LoBello, see 13:346.

[2146]

TestWell: Wellness Inventory for Windows.

Purpose: Designed to promote awareness of wellness.
Population: Adults with a minimum of 10th grade education.
Publication Date: 1992.
Scores, 11: Physical Fitness and Nutrition, Social Awareness, Medical Self-Care, Spirituality and Values, Emotional Management, Intellectual Wellness, En-

vironmental Wellness, Safety, Occupational Wellness, Sexuality and Emotional Awareness, Total.
Administration: Group.
Manual: No manual.
Price Data: Available from publisher.
Time: (20) minutes.
Author: National Wellness Institute, Inc.
Publisher: National Wellness Institute, Inc.
Cross References: For reviews by William W. Deardorff and Theodore L. Hayes, see 13:347; see also T4:2821 (1 reference).

[2147]

TestWell: Wellness Inventory for Windows— College Version.

Purpose: "Designed to address lifestyle choices facing today's college students."
Population: College students.
Publication Date: 1993.
Scores, 11: Physical Fitness, Nutrition, Social Awareness, Self-Care and Safety, Emotional and Sexuality, Intellectual Wellness, Environmental Wellness, Emotional Management, Occupational Wellness, Spirituality and Values, Total.
Administration: Group.
Price Data: Available from publisher.
Time: (20) minutes.
Author: National Wellness Institute, Inc.
Publisher: National Wellness Institute, Inc.
Cross References: For reviews by David L. Bolton and Richard E. Harding, see 13:348.

[2148]

Texas Functional Living Scale.

Purpose: Intended to be a "performance-based measure of instrumental activities of daily living."
Population: "Individuals ages 16-90 diagnosed with a variety of clinical disorders or requiring an assessment of functional abilities."
Publication Dates: 2006-2009.
Acronym: TFLS.
Scores, 5: Time, Money and Calculation, Communication, Memory, Total.
Administration: Individual.
Price Data, 2015: $163 per complete kit; $16.40 per 2 stimulus cards; $25.65 per 5 simulated phone books; $79.95 per examiner's manual.
Time: (10-20) minutes.
Comments: Initial version also referred to as the Test of Everyday Functional Abilities (TEFA); paper-and-pencil format; examiner must provide the following materials: stopwatch, timer, calendar for the current year, small edible objects/candies to mimic pills, 2 pencils, zip-top bag(s) for money, telephone, 1 $5 bill, 2 $1 bills, 7 quarters, 5 dimes, 5 nickels, and 5 pennies.

Authors: C. Munro Cullum, Myron F. Weiner, and Kathleen C. Saine.
Publisher: Pearson.
Cross References: For reviews by Pam Lindsey-Glenn and Jennifer M. Strang, see 18:147.

[2149]

Thanatometer.

Purpose: Measures attitudes concerning death.
Population: Adults.
Publication Date: 1986.
Scores: Total score only.
Administration: Group or individual.
Manual: No manual.
Price Data, 2015: $2 per scale.
Time: [5-10] minutes.
Comments: Supplementary article available.
Author: Panos D. Bardis.
Publisher: Donna Bardis.

[2150]

Thematic Apperception Test.

Purpose: "A method of revealing to the trained interpreter some of the dominant drives, emotions, sentiments, complexes and conflicts of a personality."
Population: Ages 4 and over.
Publication Dates: 1935–1943.
Acronym: TAT.
Scores: Total score only.
Administration: Individual.
Price Data, 2015: $81 per test.
Foreign Language Edition: Spanish edition available.
Time: 100(200) minutes in 2 sessions 1 day apart.
Author: Henry A. Murray.
Publisher: Harvard University Press.
Cross References: See T5:2749 (87 references), T4:2824 (107 references), 9:1287 (51 references), and T3:2491 (105 references); for a review by Jon D. Swartz, see 8:697 (241 references); see also T2:1519 (231 references); for a review by Richard H. Dana and Leonard D. Eron, see 7:181 (297 references); see also P:484 (339 references); for a review by C. J. Adcock, see 6:245 (287 references); for reviews by Leonard D. Eron and Arthur R. Jensen, see 5:164 (311 references); for a review by Arthur L. Benton, see 4:136 (198 references); for reviews by Arthur L. Benton, Julian Rotter, and J. R. Wittenborn and an excerpted review, see 3:103 (102 references).

[2151]

Therapy Attitude Inventory.

Purpose: Provides ratings of parental satisfaction with parent training interventions for child behavior problems.
Population: Parents.
Publication Date: 1974.

Scores: Total score only.
Administration: Individual.
Price Data: Available free of charge from test publisher.
Time: (5) minutes.
Author: Sheila M. Eyberg.
Publisher: Sheila M. Eyberg (the author).
Cross References: See T5:2752 (2 references) and T4:2827 (1 reference); for a review by Terry B. Gutkin, see 9:1289 (2 references); see also T3:2494 (1 reference).

[2152]

Thinking Creatively in Action and Movement.

Purpose: Designed to sample creative thinking abilities of preschool children with limited verbal and drawing skills.
Population: Ages 3–6.
Publication Date: 1981.
Acronym: TCAM.
Scores, 3: Fluency, Originality, Imagination.
Administration: Individual.
Price Data: 2015: $45.60 per starter set including 1 manual and 20 test booklets; $33.25 per 20 test booklets; $24.70 per manual.
Time: (10–30) minutes.
Author: E. Paul Torrance.
Publisher: Scholastic Testing Service, Inc.
Cross References: See T5:2754 (5 references) and T4:2829 (2 references); for reviews by Joseph S. Renzulli and James O. Rust, see 9:1290.

[2153]

Thinking Creatively With Sounds and Words.

Purpose: Developed to assess creative thinking through response to sound and words.
Population: Grades 3–12, adults.
Publication Dates: 1973-1990.
Acronym: TCSW.
Scores, 2: Sounds and Images, Onomatopoeia and Images.
Administration: Group.
Levels, 2: I (Grades 3-12), II (adult).
Forms, 2: A, B.
Price Data: 2015: $73.80 per starter set including directions manual and scoring guide, 20 tests booklets, 1 norms technical manual, 1 CD (specify level I or II and form A or B); $32.80 per 20 test booklets; $25 per audio CD; $16.40 per 1 directions manual and scoring guide.
Time: (30–35) minutes for each test.
Authors: E. Paul Torrance, Joe Khatena, and Bert F. Cunnington (except technical manual).
Publisher: Scholastic Testing Service, Inc.
Cross References: See T5:2755 (2 references) and T4:2830 (5 references); for a review by Lynn H. Fox, see 9:1291 (3 references); see also T3:2496 (5 references); for reviews by Philip M. Clark and Mary Lee Smith, see 8:248 (6 references); see also T2:587 (17 references).

[2154]

Thomas-Kilmann Conflict Mode Instrument [2007 Normative Update].

Purpose: Designed to assess "an individual's behavior in conflict situations" and to aid in the understanding of "how different conflict-handling styles affect interpersonal and group dynamics."
Population: Ages 13 and older.
Publication Dates: 1974-2007.
Acronym: TKI.
Scores: 5 conflict-handling modes: Competing, Collaborating, Compromising, Avoiding, Accommodating.
Administration: Individual or group.
Price Data, 2016: $379 per Conflict Resolution Starter Kit package, including 10 instrument booklets and Conflict Workshop Facilitator's Guide; $18.50 per instrument booklet; $18.50 per online administration with profile and interpretive report; $17.95 per Introduction to Conflict Management booklet; $17.95 per Introduction to Conflict and Teams booklet available in print and PDF formats; $250 per Conflict Workshop Facilitator's Guide; $19.95/$24.95 per ready-to-download activities available; volume discounts available; downloadable technical brief available from test publisher's website.
Foreign Language Editions: Chinese (Simplified and Traditional), Portuguese (Brazilian), and Spanish (Latin American) versions available.
Time: (15) minutes.
Comments: Administered via paper and pencil or online.
Authors: Kenneth W. Thomas (assessment), Ralph H. Kilmann (assessment), and Nancy A. Schaubhut (technical brief).
Publisher: CPP, Inc.
Cross References: Reviews are scheduled for *The Twentieth Mental Measurements Yearbook*. See T5:2756 (2 references); for reviews by Richard E. Harding and Ronn Johnson of the original 1974 edition, see 10:377 (4 references).

[2155]

3-Minute Reading Assessments.

Purpose: Designed to "assess reading performance throughout the year" and "identify students who need help."
Publication Date: 2005.
Scores, 4: Word Recognition Accuracy, Reading Fluency-Automaticity, Reading Fluency-Expression, Comprehension.
Administration: Individual.
Time: (3-5) minutes.
Comments: The authors suggest students be assessed at regular intervals throughout the year in order to track progress over time (the four equivalent forms for each grade are provided for this purpose).
Authors: Timothy V. Rasinski and Nancy Padak.
Publisher: Scholastic Inc.

a) 3-MINUTE READING ASSESSMENTS GRADES 1-4.
Population: Grades 1-4.
Levels, 4: Grade 1, Grade 2, Grade 3, Grade 4.
Forms, 4: Form A, Form B, Form C, Form D.
Parts, 2: Student, Teacher.
Price Data, 2016: $11.24 per complete set Grades 1-4.
b) 3-MINUTE READING ASSESSMENTS GRADES 5-8.
Population: Grades 5-8.
Levels, 4: Grade 5, Grade 6, Grade 7, Grade 8.
Forms, 4: Form A, Form B, Form C, Form D.
Parts, 2: Student, Teacher.
Price Data: $11.24 per complete set Grades 5-8.

[2156]
Thurstone Temperament Schedule.

Purpose: Measures personality traits related to job performance.
Population: Variety of occupations from entry-level to management.
Publication Dates: 1949–1991.
Acronym: TTS.
Scores, 6: Active, Impulsive, Dominant, Stable, Sociable, Reflective.
Administration: Individual or group.
Price Data: Available from publisher.
Time: No limit (approximately 15–20 minutes).
Comments: Administered via paper and pencil; hand-scored carbon format.
Author: L. L. Thurstone.
Publisher: General Dynamics Information Technology.
Cross References: See T5:2757 (1 reference), T4:2833 (6 references), T3:2499 (2 references), T2:1423 (32 references), P:277 (20 references), and 6:192 (17 references); for a review by Neil J. Van Steenberg, see 5:118 (12 references); for reviews by Hans J. Eysenck, Charles M. Harsh, and David G. Ryans, and an excerpted review by Laurance F. Shaffer, see 4:93.

[2157]
Thurstone Test of Mental Alertness.

Purpose: Measures general mental ability to learn and comprehend.
Population: Wide variety of occupations.
Publication Dates: 1943–1998.
Acronym: TMA.
Scores, 3: Quantitative, Linguistic, Total.
Administration: Individual or group.
Forms, 2: A, B.
Price Data: Available from publisher.
Time: 20 minutes.
Authors: Thelma Gwinn Thurstone and L. L. Thurstone.
Publisher: General Dynamics Information Technology.
Cross References: See T5:2758 (1 reference) and T2:469 (5 references); for a review by Robert D. North, see 7:392 (4 references); for a review by Joshua A. Fishman, see 5:391; see also 4:326 (3 references); for reviews by Anne Anastasi and Emily T. Burr of an earlier edition, see 3:265.

[2158]
Tiffany Control Scales.

Purpose: Designed to evaluate personality problems related to one's experience of control across different situations.
Population: Ages 12–60+.
Publication Dates: 1985–2007.
Acronym: TCS.
Scores, 16: Control from Self/Internal, Control over Self, Control over the Environment, Control from the Environment, Coping Index, Passive/Assertive/Aggressive Index, Extratensive/Intratensive Index, Repression, Expressive, Self-Directed, Non-Self-Directed, and 5 other measures.
Administration: Individual or group.
Editions, 2: Paper and pencil, computer administered.
Price Data: Available from distributor.
Foreign Language Edition: Spanish version available.
Time: (10-20) minutes.
Comments: For research or clinical use or in employment screening; may be customized to fit examiner's needs; self-rating; scoring and interpretation by computer.
Authors: Donald W. Tiffany and Phyllis G. Tiffany.
Publisher: Psychological Growth Associates, Inc. [Test distributed through the Test Collection at ETS].
Cross References: For a review by Brian F. Bolton, see 14:397.

[2159]
The Time of Your Life.

Purpose: Constructed as a self-assessment tool to provide "insight" into time management.
Population: Employees.
Publication Date: 1988.
Scores: Total score only.
Administration: Group or individual.
Price Data, 2016: $195; quantity discounts available.
Time: [30] minutes.
Comments: Self-administered, self-scored; now sold as part of the Training House Assessment Kit.
Author: Training House, Inc.
Publisher: HRD Press, Inc.
Cross References: For reviews by Ralph F. Darr, Jr. and Richard W. Faunce, see 12:400.

[2160]
TMJ Scale.

Purpose: "Designed to measure the [clinical significance of] symptom patterns of dental patients with temporomandibular joint disorders and orofacial pain."

Population: Dental and medical patients ages 13 and over.

Publication Dates: 1984–1987.

Scores: 10: Physical Domain (Pain Report, Palpation Pain, Perceived Malocclusion, Joint Dysfunction, Range of Motion Limitation, Non-TM Disorder), Psychosocial Domain (Psychological Factors, Stress, Chronicity), Global Scale.

Administration: Individual or group.

Price Data, 2016: $21 per online test scoring; quantity discounts available.

Time: (10–15) minutes.

Comments: Self-administered by paper-and-pencil or online on a secure testing website; scoring and report generation online on a secure testing website.

Authors: Stephen R. Levitt, Tom F. Lundeen, and Michael W. McKinney.

Publisher: Pain Resource Center, Inc.

Cross References: For a review by William W. Deardorff, see 12:402; see also T4:2842 (3 references).

[2161]
Toddler and Infant Motor Evaluation.

Purpose: Designed to be used for "diagnostic, comprehensive assessment of children who are suspected to have motor delays or deviations, the development of appropriate remediation programs, and treatment efficacy research."

Population: Ages 4 months to 3.5 years.

Publication Date: 1994.

Acronym: TIME.

Scores: 5 Primary Subtests: Mobility, Stability, Motor Organization, Social-Emotional, Functional Performance; 3 Clinical Subtests: Quality Rating, Component Analysis Rating, Atypical Positions.

Administration: Individual.

Price Data, 2015: $485 per complete kit including manual (324 pages), 10 record forms, timer, rattle, 2 balls, squeak toy, toy car, 3 containers, toy telephone, 2 shoelaces, 6 blocks, and nylon tote bag; $55 per 10 record booklets; $206 per manual; $12 per ball; $15 per 6 blocks and 2 shoelaces; $15 per car; $10.75 per large container; $5.55 per small container; $5.60 per 1-cup container; $30 per timer; $35 per telephone.

Time: (15–40) minutes.

Comments: Diagnostic assessment tool designed to be used by licensed/highly trained physical and occupational therapists, or appropriately trained adaptive physical educators, special education teachers, or others with expertise in the motor domain; administered utilizing a partnership between parent(s) or caretaker(s) and a trained examiner.

Authors: Lucy J. Miller and Gale H. Roid.

Publisher: Pearson.

Cross References: For reviews by Larry M. Bolen and William R. Merz, Sr., see 14:399.

[2162]
TOEFL (Test of English as a Foreign Language).

Population: Students planning to study at a higher education institution, English-language learners, and students and workers applying for visas.

Publication Dates: 1964-2016.

Acronym: TOEFL.

Administration: Group.

Price Data: Available from publisher.

Authors: Program sponsored jointly by The College Board and Educational Testing Service.

Publisher: Educational Testing Service.

a) TOEFL iBT TEST.

Purpose: Designed to measure a person's ability to use and understand English at the university level in order to make determinations about admissions.

Scores, 5: Reading, Listening, Speaking, Writing, Total.

Time: (270) minutes.

Comments: The TOEFL iBT is administered at testing centers on specified dates.

b) TOEFL ITP ASSESSMENT SERIES.

Purpose: Designed to allow university-level English-language learning programs to measure and evaluate students' skills.

Scores, 5: Listening Comprehension, Structure and Written Expression, Reading Comprehension (Level 1 only), Reading and Vocabulary (Level 2 only), Total.

Levels, 2: Level 1 (Intermediate to Advanced), Level 2 (High Beginning to Intermediate).

Time: (120) minutes for Level 1, (70) minutes for Level 2.

Comments: The TOEFL ITP is administered by institutions to help with placement and progress monitoring.

c) TOEFL YOUNG STUDENTS SERIES.

1) *TOEFL Primary.*

Purpose: Designed to allow foundational development of English-language skills.

Population: Ages 8 and older.

Scores, 3: Reading, Listening, Speaking.

Time: (80) minutes.

Comments: Reading and Listening tests administered via paper and pencil; Speaking test administered via computer.

2) *TOEFL Junior.*

Purpose: Designed to measure students' English communication skills.

Population: Ages 11 and older.

a) *Standard Test.*

Scores, 4: Reading Comprehension, Listening Comprehension, Language Form and Meaning, Total.

Time: (115) *minutes.*

Comments: Administered via paper and pencil.

b) *Comprehensive Test.*

Scores, 5: Reading Comprehension, Listening Comprehension, Speaking, Writing, Overall.

Time: (154) *minutes.*

Comments: Administered via computer.

Cross References: For reviews by Clinton I. Chase and George Domino of the 1970 edition, see 7:266.

[2163]
The Token Test for Children, Second Edition.

Purpose: Designed to identify "children who are significantly below their peers in early receptive language development."

Population: Children ages 3-0 to 12-11.

Publication Dates: 1978-2007.

Scores: Total score only.

Administration: Individual.

Parts, 4: I, II, III, IV.

Price Data, 2015: $163 per complete kit including 50 examiner record forms, tokens kit, and examiner's manual (2007, 69 pages); $56 per 50 examiner record forms; $36 per 20 tokens; $79 per manual.

Time: (10-15) minutes.

Authors: Ronnie L. McGhee, David J. Ehrler, and Frank DiSimoni.

Publisher: PRO-ED.

Cross References: For reviews by Christine Novak and Zarabeth Gerling and by Gene Schwarting, see 18:148; see T5:2768 (43 references) and T4:2846 (24 references); for reviews by William M. Reynolds and John Salvia of an earlier edition, see 9:1295 (9 references); see also T3:2509 (1 reference).

[2164]
Torrance Tests of Creative Thinking.

Purpose: To identify and evaluate creative potential through words (verbal forms) and pictures (figural forms).

Population: Grades K through adult.

Publication Dates: 1966–2006.

Acronym: TTCT.

Administration: Individual and group.

Price Data, 2015: $63.35 per starter set (Figural or Verbal) including 1 directions manual, 20 response booklets, 20 scoring worksheets, and 1 class record sheet (specify English or Spanish and Form A or B); $54.15 per package of response booklets (Figural or Verbal) including 20 response booklets, 20 scoring worksheets, and 1 class record sheet (specify English or Spanish and Form A or B); $45 per streamlined scoring guide; $44 per norms-technical manual (Figural or Verbal); $21 per directions manual (Figural).

Foreign Language Edition: Spanish edition available.

Author: E. Paul Torrance.

Publisher: Scholastic Testing Service, Inc.

a) VERBAL TEST.

Scores: 3 for equivalent Forms A and B: Fluency, Flexibility, Originality.

Administration: Individual for Grades K to 3.

Time: 45(60) minutes.

Comments: Test booklet is titled Thinking Creatively With Words.

b) FIGURAL TEST.

Scores: 4 for equivalent Forms A and B: Fluency, Flexibility, Originality, Elaboration.

Time: 30(45) minutes.

Comments: Test booklet is titled Thinking Creatively with Pictures.

Cross References: See T5:2771 (45 references) and T4:2849 (33 references); for reviews by Clinton I. Chase and Donald J. Treffinger, see 9:1296 (20 references); see also T3:2512 (107 references), 8:249 (229 references), and T2:589 (88 references); for reviews by Leonard L. Baird and Robert L. Thorndike, and excerpted reviews by Ralph Hoepfner, John L. Holland, and Michael A. Wallach, see 7:448 (243 references).

[2165]
TotalSDI (Strength Deployment Inventory).

Purpose: Designed as a set of tools "for understanding the motives and values that drive behaviors" to help in improving working relationships.

Population: Adults.

Publication Dates: 1973-2015.

Administration: Individual.

Price Data: Available from publisher.

Foreign Language Editions: Available in 26 languages.

Time: Administration time not reported.

Comments: Feedback Editions are completed by one person about another; Expectations Editions are completed about a specific role or relationship.

Authors: Elias Porter (Strength Deployment Inventory, Strengths Portrait, Overdone Strengths Portrait), Tim Scudder (Strength Deployment Inventory, Strengths Portrait, Overdone Strengths Portrait, Facilitator Manual), Simon Gallon (Strengths Portrait, Overdone Strengths Portrait, Facilitator Manual).

Publisher: Personal Strengths Publishing.

a) STRENGTH DEPLOYMENT INVENTORY.

Purpose: Designed to help people "understand themselves by helping them understand the motives that drive their behaviors in two different conditions—when things are going well and when they face conflict."

Acronym: SDI.

Scores: Motivation Value System, Conflict Sequence, SDI Results

Editions, 3: Self Edition, Feedback Edition, Expectations Edition.

b) STRENGTHS PORTRAIT.

Purpose: Designed to "tell a story of 28 strengths, or behaviors, that people value and commonly use when they interact with each other."

Acronym: SP.

Scores: Rankings for 28 strengths/behaviors: Adaptable, Ambitious, Analytical, Caring, Cautious, Competitive, Devoted, Fair, Flexible, Forceful, Helpful, Inclusive, Loyal, Methodical, Modest, Open-to-Change, Option-Oriented, Persevering, Persuasive, Principled, Quick-to-Act, Reserved, Risk-Taking, Self-Confident, Sociable, Supportive, Tolerant, Trusting.

Editions, 3: Self Edition, Feedback Edition, Expectations Edition.

c) OVERDONE STRENGTHS PORTRAIT.
Purpose: Designed to show how a person "may appear to others when ... strengths are overdone or misapplied."
Acronym: OSP.
Scores: Rankings for 28 overdone strengths: Abrasive, Aggressive, Arrogant, Blind, Cold, Compliant, Distant, Domineering, Gullible, Inconsistent, Indecisive, Indifferent, Indiscriminate, Intrusive, Obsessed, Rash, Reckless, Rigid, Ruthless, Self-Effacing, Self-Sacrificing, Smothering, Stubborn, Submissive, Subservient, Suspicious, Unbending, Unpredictable.
Editions, 2: Self Edition, Feedback Edition.
Cross References: Reviews are scheduled for *The Twentieth Mental Measurements Yearbook*. For a review by Frederick T. L. Leong of a previous version of the Strength Deployment Inventory, see 13:371; for a review by Richard E. Harding of an previous version of the Feedback Edition of the Strength Deployment Inventory, see 17:72; for reviews by Frederic Medway and James A. Penny of a previous version of the Feedback Portrait of Personal Strengths, see 17:73.

[2166]
Tower of London—Drexel University: 2nd Edition.

Purpose: A neuropsychological instrument "designed to assess higher-order problem solving—specifically, executive planning abilities—in children and adults."
Population: Ages 7 and above.
Publication Dates: 1999–2005.
Acronym: TOLDX 2nd Ed.
Scores, 8: Total Move Score, Total Correct Score, Total Time Violation, Total Rules Violation, Total Initiation Time, Total Execution Time, Total Problem-Solving Time, Total Stimulus-Bound.
Administration: Individual.
Forms, 2: Adult, Child.
Price Data, 2015: $399 per complete kit including manual (2005, 94 pages), 2 peg boards with beads, 25 child record forms, and 25 adult record forms; $349 per complete adult kit including manual, 2 peg boards with beads, and 25 adult record forms; $349 per complete child kit including manual, 2 peg boards with beads, and 25 child record forms; $116 per manual; $55 per 25 child or adult record forms.
Time: (10–15) minutes.
Comments: Administered individually by clinicians; special instructions for mentally challenged populations.
Authors: William C. Culbertson and Eric A. Zilmer.
Publisher: Multi-Health Systems, Inc.
a) CHILD.
Population: Ages 7–15.
b) ADULT.
Population: Ages 16 and older.
Cross References: For reviews by Brad M. Merker and John Linck and by Gregory Schraw, see 17:188; for reviews by Carolyn M. Callahan and James P. Van Haneghan of the previous edition, see 15:267.

[2167]
TPRI.

Purpose: Designed to "measure students' progress in the acquisition of important skills related to early reading."
Population: K-3.
Publication Date: 2010.
Acronym: TPRI.
Scores, 5: Phonemic Awareness, Graphophonemic Knowledge, Word Reading, Listening Comprehension, Reading Accuracy/ Fluency/ and Comprehension.
Administration: Group.
Levels, 2: Progress Monitoring for Beginning Readers, Progress Monitoring for Emergent Readers.
Price Data, 2016: $189.95 per Benchmarking kit including teacher's guide, reading comprehension story booklet, task cards, and stopwatch; $69.95 per Progress Monitoring for Emergent Readers kit including PMER Teacher's Guide and task card booklet; $69.95 per Progress Monitoring for Beginning Readers kit including PMBR Teacher's Guide and story comprehension booklet; $29.95 per 25 student record sheets and 3 class summary sheets for use with Benchmarking kit; $29.95 per 15 PMER student record sheets; $29.95 per 15 PMER student record sheets.
Time: Administration time not reported.
Comments: The assessment has an administration schedule that can assess progress at the beginning of the year, middle of the year, and end of the year.
Author: Texas Education Agency.
Publisher: Paul H. Brookes Publishing Co., Inc.
Cross References: For reviews by James Dean Brown and by Carlen Henington and Carmen D. Reisener, see 19:173.

[2168]
Trade Aptitude Test Battery.

Purpose: "To select prospective pupils for admission to technical institutes and colleges."
Population: First-year South African students in the technical fields.
Publication Dates: 1981–1983.
Acronym: TRAT.
Scores, 16: Dexterity, Co-ordination, Patterns, Components, Classification, Assembly, Computations, Inspection, Graphs, Mechanical Insight, Mathematics, Spatial Perception/2-D, Vocabulary, Figure Series, Woordeskat, Spatial Perception/3-D.
Administration: Group.
Price Data: Available from publisher.
Time: 288(293) minutes.
Comments: Test materials in both English and Afrikaans.
Authors: J. J. Taljaard and J. W. von Mollendorf (test).
Publisher: Human Sciences Research Council [South Africa].

[2169]
Transdisciplinary Play-Based Assessment, 2nd Edition.

Purpose: Designed as a multidimensional approach to identifying service needs, developing intervention plans, and evaluating progress in children.
Population: Birth to age 6.
Publication Dates: 1993-2008.
Acronym: TPBA2.
Scores: 4 domains: Sensorimotor, Emotional and Social, Communication, Cognitive Development.
Administration: Individual.
Price Data, 2015: $329.95 per 3-volume set with forms CD including Administration Guide for TPBA2 & TPBI2 (2008, 408 pages), Transdisciplinary Play-Based Intervention, 2nd Edition, Transdisciplinary Play-Based Assessment, 2nd Edition, and forms CD; $149.95 per 3-volume set including Administration Guide for TPBA2 & TPBI2, Transdisciplinary Play-Based Intervention, 2nd Edition, and Transdisciplinary Play-Based Assessment, 2nd Edition; $54.95 per Transdisciplinary Play-Based Assessment, 2nd Edition; $59.95 per Transdisciplinary Play-Based Intervention, 2nd Edition; $54.95 per Administration Guide for TPBA2 & TPBI2; $39.95 per 5 tablets of forms; $229.95 per forms CD.
Time: (60-90) minutes.
Comments: Ratings by transdisciplinary team; no domain scores; compares observations to Age Tables that outline appropriate skills for each age.
Author: Toni Linder.
Publisher: Paul H. Brookes Publishing Co., Inc.
Cross References: For reviews by David R. Holliway and Becky L. Spritz, see 18:149; for reviews by Terry Overton and Gary J. Stainback of the previous edition, see 13:352.

[2170]
Transferable Skills Scale, Second Edition.

Purpose: Designed to help individuals "identify their transferable skills to assist in career exploration and the job search."
Population: Individuals at or above 8th-grade level.
Publication Date: 2011.
Acronym: TSS.
Scores, 8: Analytical, Numerical, Interpersonal, Organizational, Physical, Informational, Communicative, Creative.
Administration: Individual or group.
Price Data, 2016: $59.95 per package of 25 consumable booklets; volume discount available. Administrator's guide (24 pages) available for download from publisher's website.
Time: (20-25) minutes.
Comments: Self-scored and interpreted.
Authors: John J. Liptak and Laurence Shatkin.

Publisher: JIST/EMC Publishing.
Cross References: Reviews are scheduled for *The Twentieth Mental Measurements Yearbook*.

[2171]
Transition Behavior Scale—Second Edition.

Purpose: "Developed to be an educational-relevant measure of predicted success in employment and independent living based upon school personnel's observation of a student's behavior or skills."
Population: Ages 12–18.
Publication Dates: 1989–2000.
Acronym: TBS-2.
Scores, 3: Work-Related, Interpersonal Relations, Social/Community Expectations.
Administration: Group or individual.
Price Data: Available from publisher.
Time: (15–20) minutes.
Comments: The test publisher has indicated there is a newer edition of this test; description will be updated when complete test materials are received.
Authors: Stephen B. McCarney and Paul D. Anderson.
Publisher: Hawthorne Educational Services, Inc.
Cross References: For reviews by Susan K. Green and Michael S. Trevisan, see 16:253; for reviews by Martha Blackwell and David O. Herman of the original edition, see 12:404.

[2172]
Transition Planning Inventory–Second Edition.

Purpose: Designed to assess "transition needs, strengths, preferences, and interests of students at the secondary level."
Population: Ages 14 to 22.
Publication Dates: 1997-2014.
Acronym: TPI-2.
Scores, 14: 3 general areas and 11 transition domains: Working (Career Choice and Planning, Employment Knowledge and Skills), Learning (Further Education/Training, Functional Communication, Self-Determination), Living (Independent Living, Personal Money Management, Community Involvement and Usage, Leisure Activities, Health, Interpersonal Relationships).
Administration: Individual or group.
Forms, 8: Student Preferences and Interests Form–Basic, Student Preferences and Interests Form–Advanced, School Rating Form, Student Rating Form, Home Rating Form, Profile and Further Assessment Recommendations Form, Home Preferences and Interests Form (on CD), Modified Form for Students with Significant Support Needs (on CD).
Price Data, 2014: $243 per complete kit including Administration and Resource Guide (2014, 148 pages), Informal Assessments for Transition Planning-Second

Edition (2013, 174 pages), 25 Student Preferences and Interests Forms–Basic, 25 Student Preferences and Interests Forms–Advanced, 25 School Rating Forms, 25 Student Rating Forms, 25 Home Rating Forms, 25 Profile and Further Assessment Recommendations Forms, resources CD, and reproducible forms CD; $29 to $33 per 25 forms; $33 per Administration and Resource Guide; $47 per Informal Assessments for Transition Planning–Second Edition.

Foreign Language Editions: Home Rating Form translations available in Spanish, Chinese, and Korean; Home Preferences and Interests Form translations available in Spanish and Korean.

Time: (10-30) minutes per form, depending on administration format.

Authors: James R. Patton and Gary M. Clark.

Publisher: PRO-ED.

Cross References: Reviews are scheduled for *The Twentieth Mental Measurements Yearbook*. For reviews by Pam Lindsey and Julia Y. Porter of the Updated Version, see 17:189; for reviews by Robert K. Gable and by Rosemary E. Sutton and Theresa A. Quigney of the original edition, see 14:400.

[2173]

Transition-to-Work Inventory, Third Edition.

Purpose: Designed to "measure a person's leisure interests in order to help him or her turn these interests into possible employment opportunities, a small-business enterprise, or a home-based business."

Population: Job seekers.

Publication Dates: 2004-2012.

Acronym: TWI.

Scores, 16: Agriculture and Natural Resources, Architecture and Construction, Arts and Communication, Business and Administration, Education and Training, Finance and Insurance, Government and Public Administration, Health Science, Hopsitality/Tourism/Recreation, Human Service, Information Technology, Law and Public Safety, Manufacturing, Retail and Wholesale Sales and Service; Scientific Research/Engineering/Mathematics, Transportation/Distribution/Logistics.

Administration: Group.

Price Data, 2016: $60.95 per 25 inventories; administrator's guide (2012, 14 pages) available as free download from publisher's website.

Time: (20-25) minutes.

Comments: Self-administered and self-scored.

Author: John J. Liptak.

Publisher: JIST/EMC Publishing.

[2174]

Trauma and Attachment Belief Scale.

Purpose: Measures beliefs related to five need areas that are sensitive to the effects of traumatic experiences.

Population: Ages 9–18, 17–78.

Publication Date: 2003.

Acronym: TABS.

Scores, 11: Self-Safety, Other-Safety, Self-Trust, Other-Trust, Self-Esteem, Other-Esteem, Self-Intimacy, Other-Intimacy, Self-Control, Other-Control, Total.

Administration: Group.

Forms, 2: Profile Sheet, Profile Sheet for Youth.

Price Data, 2016: $138 per kit including 25 Adult AutoScore™ test/profile forms, 25 Youth AutoScore™ test/profile forms, and manual (52 pages); $52.50 per 25 AutoScore™ test/profile forms (Adult); $52.50 per 25 AutoScore™ test/profile forms (Youth); $65.50 per manual.

Time: (10–15) minutes.

Comments: Previously known as Traumatic Stress Institute (TSI) Belief Scale.

Author: Laurie Anne Pearlman.

Publisher: Western Psychological Services.

Cross References: For reviews by Eugene V. Aidman and Adrienne Garro, see 16:254.

[2175]

Trauma Assessment Inventories.

Purpose: "Designed to screen for Posttraumatic Stress Disorder" and designed to assess "Cognitive and emotional aspects of guilt associated with a specific traumatic event."

Population: Ages 18 years and older.

Publication Date: 2004.

Administration: Individual.

Price Data, 2016: $238 per complete kit including Screening Kit and Treatment Kit; $118 per 20-use scoring CD-ROM; $52.50 per 25 AutoScore forms (specify screening or treatment); $20.50 per 100 computerized answer sheets (specify screening or treatment).

Author: Edward S. Kubany.

Publisher: Western Psychological Services.

a) SCREENING KIT.

Purpose: "Designed to screen for Posttraumatic Stress Disorder."

Price Data: $137 per complete screening kit including 25 AutoScore forms, 25 test forms, and screening manual (47 pages); $59.50 per screening manual.

Time: (10-20) minutes.

Comments: This test can be abbreviated if time constraints are an issue.

1) *Traumatic Life Events Questionnaire.*

Acronym: TLEQ.

Scores, 3: Count of Events, Count of Events Associated with Fear or Hopelessness, Occurrences.

Price Data: $39 per 25 test forms.

2) *PTSD Screening and Diagnostic Scale.*

Acronym: PSDS.

Scores, 7: Criterion A, Criterion B, Criterion C, Criterion D, PSDS Symptom Score, Criterion E, Criterion F.

b) TREATMENT KIT.

Purpose: Designed to assess "Cognitive and emotional aspects of guilt associated with a specific traumatic event."

Price Data: $113.50 per complete treatment kit including 25 AutoScore forms, 25 test forms, and treatment manual (59 pages); $72 per treatment manual.
Time: Administration time not reported.
    1) *The Trauma-Related Guilt Inventory.*
    Acronym: TRGI.
    Scores, 6: Global Guilt, Distress, Guilt Cognitions (Wrongdoing, Insufficient Justification, Hindsight-Bias/Responsibility).
    Comments: This test is written at a 5th-grade reading level.
Cross References: For reviews by James P. Donnelly and Kerry Donnelly and by Carl J. Sheperis and April K. Heiselt, see 17:190.

[2176]
Trauma Symptom Checklist for Children.
Purpose: Designed "to measure acute and chronic posttraumatic stress and related psychological symptomatology."
Population: Ages 8–16.
Publication Date: 1996.
Acronym: TSCC.
Scores: 8 scales: Underresponse, Hyperresponse, Anxiety, Depression, Anger, Posttraumatic Stress, Dissociation, Sexual Concerns.
Administration: Group or individual.
Price Data, 2015: $186 per introductory kit including professional manual, 25 test booklets, 25 male profile forms, and 25 female profile forms; $360 per software (CD-ROM) with on-screen help and quick start guide.
Time: (15–20) minutes.
Author: John Briere.
Publisher: Psychological Assessment Resources, Inc.
Cross References: For reviews by Gregory J. Boyle and Chockalingam Viswesvaran, see 15:269.

[2177]
Trauma Symptom Checklist for Young Children.
Purpose: Designed "to measure acute and chronic posttraumatic stress and related psychological symptomatology."
Population: Ages 3–12 years.
Publication Dates: 1999–2005.
Acronym: TSCYC.
Scores, 11: Validity scales (Response Level, Atypical Response), Clinical scales (Anxiety, Depression, Anger/Aggression, Posttraumatic Stress-Intrusion, Posttraumatic Stress-Avoidance, Posttraumatic Stress-Arousal, Posttraumatic Stress-Total, Dissociation, Sexual Concerns).
Administration: Group.
Price Data, 2015: $244 per introductory kit including professional manual (2005, 61 pages), 25 item booklets, 25 hand-scorable answer sheets, 25 profile forms (Male & Female Ages 3–4 Years), 25 profile forms (Male & Female Ages 5–9 Years), and 25 profile forms (Male &

Female Ages 10–12 Years; $360 per software (CD-ROM) with on-screen help and quick start guide.
Time: (15–20) minutes.
Comments: Instrument is answered by the child's parents and/or caretakers.
Author: John Briere.
Publisher: Psychological Assessment Resources, Inc.
Cross References: For reviews by Karen Mackler and Terry A. Stinnett, see 17:191.

[2178]
Trauma Symptom Inventory-2.
Purpose: Designed to evaluate "acute and chronic symptomatology ... associated with trauma at any point in the respondent's lifespan."
Population: Ages 18 years and older.
Publication Dates: 1995-2011.
Acronym: TSI-2.
Administration: Group.
Price Data, 2015: $218 per TSI-2 or TSI-2-A introductory kit including 10 reusable item booklets, 25 hand-scorable answer sheets, 25 profile forms, and manual (2011, 111 pages); $52 per 10 reusable item booklets; $66 per 25 hand-scorable answer sheets; $52 per 25 profile forms; $66 per manual; $375 per software (CD-ROM) with on-screen help and quick start guide.
Time: (20-30) minutes.
Comments: Revisions include new scales, subscales, and norms. Alternate form TSI-2-A contains no sexual symptom items.
Author: John Briere.
Publisher: Psychological Assessment Resources, Inc.
    a) TSI-2.
    Scores, 30: Validity Scales (Response Level, Atypical Response); Factors (Self-Disturbance, Posttraumatic Stress, Externalization, Somatization); Clinical Scales/Subscales [Anxious Arousal (Anxiety, Hyperarousal), Depression, Anger, Intrusive Experiences, Defensive Avoidance, Dissociation, Somatic Preoccupations (Pain, General), Sexual Disturbance (Sexual Concerns, Dysfunctional Sexual Behavior), Suicidality (Ideation, Behavior), Insecure Attachment (Relational Avoidance, Rejection Sensitivity), Impaired Self-Reference (Reduced Self Awareness, Other-Directedness), Tension Reduction Behavior].
    b) TSI-2-A.
    Scores, 27: Validity Scales (Response Level, Atypical Response); Factors (Self-Disturbance, Posttraumatic Stress, Externalization, Somatization); Clinical Scales/Subscales [Anxious Arousal (Anxiety, Hyperarousal), Depression, Anger, Intrusive Experiences, Defensive Avoidance, Dissociation, Somatic Preoccupations (Pain, General), Suicidality (Ideation, Behavior), Insecure Attachment (Relational Avoidance, Rejection Sensitivity), Impaired Self-Reference (Reduced Self Awareness, Other-Directedness), Tension Reduction Behavior].
Cross References: For a review by Jody L. Kulstad, see 19:174; for reviews by Ephrem Fernandez and Jack E. Gebart-Eaglemont of an earlier edition, see 14:402; see also T5:2782 (3 references).

[2179]

Treatment Intervention Inventory.
Purpose: Designed for intake, referral and post-treatment comparisons of adult counseling clients.
Population: Ages 12–18; Adult counseling clients.
Publication Dates: 1991–1997.
Acronym: TII; TII-J.
Scores, 9: Truthfulness, Anxiety, Depression, Self-Esteem, Distress, Family, Alcohol, Drug, Stress Coping Abilities.
Administration: Group.
Levels, 2: Adult, Juvenile.
Price Data, 2016: $9.95 per test; volume discounts available.
Time: (35) minutes Adult; (25–30) minutes Juvenile.
Author: Behavior Data Systems Ltd.
Publisher: Behavior Data Systems Ltd.
Cross References: For reviews by Janice G. Murdoch and Linda J. Zimmerman, see 14:403.

[2180]

Triage Assessment for Addictive Disorders–5.
Purpose: A structured interview "designed to provide an indication of current addiction problems in the context of a 10-minute interview."
Population: Adults.
Publication Dates: 1995-2013.
Acronym: TAAD-5.
Scores: 4 diagnostic indicators: No Diagnosis, Mild Substance Use Disorder, Moderate Substance Use Disorder, Severe Substance Use Disorder.
Administration: Individual.
Price Data, 2015: $52.50 per 25 assessments; $15 per manual (2013, 18 pages).
Time: (10) minutes.
Comments: Screens for DSM-5 diagnostic criteria for alcohol and drug use; structured interview not for use as a paper-and-pencil questionnaire.
Author: Norman G. Hoffmann.
Publisher: The Change Companies.
Cross References: Reviews are scheduled for *The Twentieth Mental Measurements Yearbook.* For reviews by JoAnn Murphey and by Wendy Naumann and Robin Rix of an earlier edition, see 15:270.

[2181]

Triage Assessment for Psychiatric Disorders.
Purpose: Designed as a semistructured interview to assist clinicians in screening for frequently diagnosed psychiatric disorders.
Population: Adults.
Publication Dates: 1991-1999.
Acronym: TAPD.
Scores: Item scores only.
Administration: Individual.

Price Data, 2016: $52.50 per 25 interview forms; $15 per administration guide (1999, 5 pages).
Time: 15-20 minutes.
Author: Norman G. Hoffmann.
Publisher: The Change Companies.

[2182]

Tutor Evaluation and Self-Assessment Tool.
Purpose: "A structured profile that evaluates tutors' effectiveness … to improve growth and development."
Population: Tutors of all subjects and grade levels.
Publication Date: 1996.
Acronym: TESAT.
Scores, 12: Greeting, Identification of Task, Breaking the Task into Parts, Identification of Thought Process, Setting Agenda, Addressing the Task, Tutee Summary of Content, Tutee Summary of Underlying Process, Confirmation, What Next?, Arranging and Planning Next Session, Closing.
Administration: Group.
Price Data, 2016: $198 per 100 TESATs, quantity discount available; $64.95 per Tutor Trainer's Manual (64 pages); $85 per transparency set, $23.95 per Master Tutor Guidebook (124 pages), quantity discounts available.
Time: Untimed.
Comments: Ranks tutors into one of four skill categories (outstanding, proficient, adequate, needs improvement) for each of 12 steps of the "Tutor Cycle," based on the author's tutoring model; can be completed by tutor for self-assessment or by other evaluator.
Author: Ross B. MacDonald.
Publisher: The Cambridge Stratford Study Skills Institute.

[2183]

The Uncritical Inference Test.
Purpose: "Helps students learn to distinguish between observations (or facts) and inferences, assumptions, beliefs, and judgments."
Population: Adolescents and adults.
Publication Dates: 1955–1982.
Scores: Total score only.
Administration: Group.
Manual: No manual.
Price Data, 2015: $1 per test (minimum order of 10 paper tests); electronic delivery via email attachment or download in PDF format; includes license for multiple usages at $.75 per use.
Time: Administration time not reported.
Author: William V. Haney.
Publisher: Institute of General Semantics.

[2184]

Understanding Communication.
Purpose: Developed "to measure comprehension of verbal material in the form of short sentences and phrases."

Population: Variety of occupations.
Publication Dates: 1959–1992.
Scores: Total score only.
Administration: Individual or group.
Price Data: Available from publisher.
Time: 15 minutes.
Author: Thelma Gwinn Thurstone.
Publisher: General Dynamics Information Technology.
Cross References: See T4:2864 (1 reference) and T2:1747 (1 reference); for reviews by C. E. Jurgensen and Donald E. P. Smith, see 6:840.

[2185]
Uniform Child Custody Evaluation System.

Purpose: Constructed as a "uniform child custody evaluation procedure."
Population: Professionals involved in custody evaluation.
Publication Date: 1994.
Acronym: UCCES.
Scores: No scores.
Administration: Individual.
Forms, 25: General Data and Administrative Forms (UCCES Checklist, Initial Referral Form, Chronological Record of all Case Contacts Form, Case Notes Form, Consent for Psychological Services to Child(ren) Form, Authorization to Release Information Form, Suitability for Joint Custody Checklist, Collateral Interview Form, Consent for Evaluation of Minor(s) Form, UCCES Summary Chart), Parent Forms (Parent's Family/Personal History Questionnaire, Parent Interview Form, Parenting Abilities Checklist, Suitability for Joint Custody Interview, Analysis of Response Validity Checklist, Behavioral Observations of Parent-Child Interaction Form, Home Visit Observation Form, Agreement Between Parent and Evaluator Form, Explanation of Custody Evaluation Procedures for Parents and Attorneys), Child Forms (Child History Questionnaire, Child Interview Form, Child Abuse Interview Form, Abuse/Neglect Checklist, Child's Adjustment to Home and Community Checklist, Parent-Child Goodness of Fit Observation Form and Checklist).
Price Data, 2015: $196 per introductory kit including manual (47 pages), 2 sets of Parent Forms, 2 sets of Child Forms, and 1 set of Administrative and Data Forms.
Time: Administration time varies.
Authors: Harry L. Munsinger and Kevin W. Karlson.
Publisher: Psychological Assessment Resources, Inc.
Cross References: For a review by Steven Zucker, see 13:353.

[2186]
Universal Multidimensional Abilities Scales.

Purpose: Teacher rating scale designed "to screen student behavior in six areas associated with successful school performance: cognition, creativity, leadership, literacy, math, and science."

Population: Ages 5 through 17.
Publication Date: 2012.
Acronym: UMAS.
Scores, 7: Cognition, Creativity, Leadership, Literacy, Math, Science, General Aptitude Index.
Administration: Individual.
Price Data, 2016: $135 per kit including examiner's manual (71 pages) and 25 record booklets; $82 per examiner's manual; $53 per 25 record booklets.
Time: (30-45) minutes.
Authors: R. Steve McCallum and Bruce A. Bracken.
Publisher: PRO-ED.
Cross References: Reviews are scheduled for *The Twentieth Mental Measurements Yearbook.*

[2187]
Universal Nonverbal Intelligence Test–Second Edition.

Purpose: Designed to "assess general intelligence and three foundational cognitive abilities."
Population: Ages 5 through 21.
Publication Dates: 1998-2016.
Acronym: UNIT2.
Scores, 13: 6 subtest scores (Symbolic Memory, Nonsymbolic Quantity, Analogic Reasoning, Spatial Memory, Numerical Series, Cube Design), 7 composite scores (Memory, Reasoning, Quantitative, Abbreviated Battery IQ, Standard Battery with Memory, Standard Battery Without Memory, Full Scale IQ).
Administration: Individual.
Price Data, 2016: $799 per complete kit with case including examiner's manual (2016, 260 pages), 3 stimulus books, 25 record forms, 16 response chips, 2 response grids, 9 cubes, response mat, 10 symbolic memory cards and Administration at a Glance card in canvas case; $691 per kit without case; $125 per examiner's manual; $69 per 25 record forms; $199 per Online Scoring and Reporting System (includes 1 year starter subscription with unlimited scoring and reports for up to 5 users); $69 per annual renewal.
Time: (10-15) minutes for Abbreviated Battery; (30) minutes for Standard Battery; (45) minutes for Full Scale Battery.
Authors: Bruce A. Bracken and R. Steve McCallum.
Publisher: PRO-ED.
Cross References: For a review by Deborah L. Bandalos of the original edition, see 14:404.

[2188]
University Residence Environment Scale [Second Edition Manual].

Purpose: Designed to "assess the social climate of university student living groups."
Population: University students and staff.
Publication Dates: 1974–1988.

Acronym: URES.
Scores: 10: Involvement, Emotional Support, Independence, Traditional Social Orientation, Competition, Academic Achievement, Intellectuality, Order and Organization, Student Influence, Innovation.
Administration: Individual or group.
Forms, 4: Real (R), Ideal (I), Expectations (E), Short (S).
Price Data, 2015: $50 per manual, including review-only copy of form; $2 per Remote Online Survey License or License to Reproduce (minimum 50); $10 user's guide.
Foreign Language Editions: Translated materials for Dutch and Japanese.
Time: [15-20] minutes.
Comments: Part of the Social Climate Scales; focuses on student-student and student-staff relationships and the organizational structure of a living group; for use in student living groups and in program evaluation and counseling; can also be completed by observers and other nonresidents, such as parents and student visitors; provides information about student living groups and encourages staff to become involved in program planning and design.
Author: Rudolf H. Moos.
Publisher: Mind Garden, Inc.
Cross References: For reviews by Barbara A. Rothlisberg and Theresa G. Siskind, see 14:405; see also T4:2865 (8 references) and T3:2534 (3 references); for reviews by Fred H. Borgen and James V. Mitchell, Jr. of an earlier edition, see 8:700 (12 references).

[2189]

Useful Field of View.

Purpose: Designed as a "computer-administered and computer-scored test of visual attention," which may be used to help predict the degree to which a person may perform some everyday activities, such as driving a motor vehicle, safely.
Population: Adults.
Publication Date: 1998.
Acronym: UFOV.
Scores, 3: Central Vision and Processing Speed, Divided Attention, Selective Attention.
Administration: Individual.
Price Data, 2015: $800 for first license; $100 each additional license; includes CD and user's manual.
Time: (15) minutes.
Authors: Karlene K. Ball and Daniel L. Roenker.
Publisher: Visual Awareness Research Group.
Cross References: For reviews by Gregory Schraw and James P. Van Haneghan, see 15:271.

[2190]

Validity Indicator Profile.

Purpose: Designed to assess response styles to help determine whether the results of cognitive, neuropsychological, or other types of testing should be considered representative of an individual's overall capacities.

Population: Individuals 18-69.
Publication Date: 1997.
Acronym: VIP.
Scores, 2: Nonverbal Subtest Response Style, Verbal Subtest Response Style.
Administration: Group.
Price Data, 2015: $197 per Q Local software starter kit; $200 per mail-in scoring starter kit; $158.88 per manual; $47.15 per 1 reusable test booklet; $23 per 25 Q Local answer sheets; $25.65 per Q Local interpretive report; $20 per Q Local profile report; $28.70 per mail-in interpretive report; $24.10 per mail-in profile report.
Time: (50) minutes for both subtests; (20) minutes for verbal subtest and (30) minutes for nonverbal subtest.
Comments: Scoring options are Q Local software or mail-in; report options are Interpretive or Profile.
Author: Richard I. Frederick.
Publisher: Pearson.
Cross References: For reviews by Jack E. Gebart-Eaglemont and Stephen H. Ivens, see 14:406.

[2191]

Values Preference Indicator [Revised].

Purpose: Provides respondents with the tools to examine their values and priorities for the purpose of self-learning, group discussion, team development, and gaining insight into corporate culture.
Population: Adults.
Publication Dates: 1990-2006.
Acronym: VPI.
Scores, 21: Accomplishment, Acknowledgment, Challenge, Cooperation, Creativity, Expertise, Friendship, Honesty, Independence, Instruction, Intimacy, Organization, Pleasure, Quality, Recognition, Responsibility, Security, Spirituality, Tranquility, Variety, Wealth.
Administration: Individual or group.
Price Data, 2016: $25 per test booklet (2006, 12 pages); $35 per online version; $40 per Trainer's Guidelines (1996, 22 pages).
Time: [30-45] minutes to administer; 90-180 for program.
Comments: Test can be self-administered and self-scored.
Authors: Ken Keis and Everett T. Robinson.
Publisher: Consulting Resource Group International, Inc.

[2192]

Vasectomy Scale: Attitudes.

Purpose: To measure attitudes toward vasectomy.
Population: Adults.
Publication Dates: 1974–1988.
Scores: Total score only.
Administration: Group.
Manual: No manual.
Price Data, 2015: $2 per scale.

Time: [10] minutes.
Comments: Supplementary article available.
Author: Panos D. Bardis.
Publisher: Donna Bardis.

[2193]
Verbal Behavior Milestones Assessment and Placement Program.

Purpose: Designed "to provide a behaviorally based language assessment program for all children with language delays."
Population: Individuals with language delays.
Publication Dates: 2007-2011.
Acronym: VB-MAPP.
Administration: Individual.
Parts, 5: Milestones Assessment, Barriers Assessment, Transition Assessment, Task Analysis and Skills Tracking, Placement and IEP Goals.
Price Data, 2016: $69.95 per full set including guide (2008, 247 pages) and protocol for 1 student; $49.95 per guide; $24.95 per protocol (volume discounts available); $42.95 per Teaching Language to Children with Autism or Other Developmental Disabilities (1998, 258 pages).
Foreign Language Editions: Available in print in Chinese, Italian, Polish, and Russian; available digitally in French and Spanish.
Time: Untimed; varies according to child's general level and cooperation.
Comments: "The VB-MAPP can be conducted with any language-delayed individual, regardless of age or specific diagnosis"; "criterion-referenced"; digital (app and web-based) versions available.
Author: Mark L. Sundberg.
Publisher: AVB Press.

a) MILESTONES ASSESSMENT.
Purpose: "Designed to provide a representative sample of a child's existing verbal and related skills."
Levels: 3 developmental levels.
  1) *Level 1 (Birth to 18 months).*
  Scores, 9: Mand, Tact, Listener Responding, Visual Perceptual Skills and Matching-to-Sample, Independent Play, Social Behavior and Social Play, Motor Imitation, Echoic, Spontaneous Vocal Behavior.
  2) *Level 2 (18 to 30 months).*
  Scores, 12: Mand, Tact, Listener Responding, Visual Perceptual Skills and Matching-to-Sample, Independent Play, Social Behavior and Social Play, Motor Imitation, Echoic, Listener Responding by Function/Feature/Class, Intraverbal, Classroom Routines and Group Skills, Linguistic Structure.
  3) *Level 3 (30 to 48 months).*
  Scores, 13: Same as Level 2 (see above), plus Math.
b) BARRIERS ASSESSMENT.
Purpose: Designed to provide "an assessment of 24 common learning and language acquistion barriers faced by children with autism or other developmental disabilities."
Scores, 24: Negative Behavior, Poor Instructional Control, Absent/Weak/Impaired Mand, Absent/Weak/Impaired Tact, Absent/Weak/Impaired Echoic, Absent/ Weak/Impaired Matching-to-Sample, Absent/Weak/ Impaired Listener Repertoires, Absent/Weak/Impaired Intraverbal, Absent/Weak/Impaired Social Behavior, Prompt Dependent, Scrolling Responses, Impaired Scanning Skills, Failure to Make Conditional Discriminations, Failure to Generalize, Weak or Atypical Motivators, Response Requirement Weakens Motivation, Reinforcement Dependent, Self-Stimulation, Articulation Problems, Obsessive-Compulsive Behavior, Hyperactivity, Failure to Make Eye Contact or Attend to People, Sensory Defensiveness.
c) TRANSITION ASSESSMENT.
Purpose: Designed "to provide an objective evaluation of a child's overall skills and existing learning capabilities."
Scores, 18: Overall VB-MAPP Milestores Assessment Score, Overall VB-MAPP Barriers Assessment Score, Barriers Assessment Score on Negative Behaviors and Instructional Control, Milestones Assessment Score on Classroom Routines and Group Skills, Milestones Assessment Score on Social Behavior and Social Play, Works Independently on Academic Tasks, Generalization of Skills Across Time/Settings/Behaviors/Materials/People, Range of Items and Events that Function as Reinforcers, Rate of Acquisition of New Skills, Retention of New Skills, Learning from the Natural Environment, Demonstrates Transfer Between the Verbal Operants Without Training, Adaptability to Change, Spontaneous Behaviors, Self-Directed Play and Leisure Skills, General Self-Help Skills, Toileting Skills, Eating Skills.
Comments: "Some of the areas assessed in the Transition Assessment are covered in other sections of the VB-MAPP, but they also fit within the context of transition (e.g., group skills, generalization)."
d) TASK ANALYSIS AND SKILLS TRACKING.
Purpose: Designed to "provide further information about the many additional skills that can be incorporated into a daily program."
Comments: "Although the task analysis is not designed to be a formal assessment tool because of its size (approximately 900 skills), it can be used to identify skills that contribute to the development of a more complete intervention program."
e) PLACEMENT AND IEP GOALS.
Purpose: Designed to provide "specific direction for each of the 170 milestones in the Milestones Assessment as well as suggestions for IEP goals."

Cross References: Reviews are scheduled for *The Twentieth Mental Measurements Yearbook.*

[2194]
Verbal Form.

Purpose: Designed to measure general ability to learn and comprehend.
Population: Employees in a wide variety of occupations.
Publication Dates: 1946–1984.
Scores, 3: Quantitative, Linguistic, Total.
Administration: Individual or group.
Forms, 2: A, B.
Price Data: Available from publisher.
Time: 15 minutes.
Comments: Previously listed as SRA Verbal Form.
Authors: Thelma Gwinn Thurstone and L. L. Thurstone.

Publisher: General Dynamics Information Technology.
Cross References: See T4:2542 (3 references), T3:2276 (3 references), T2:452 (1 reference), and 7:383 (2 references); for reviews by W. D. Commins and Willis C. Schaefer, see 4:319.

[2195]

Verbal Reasoning [General Dynamics Information Technology].

Purpose: To measure the capacity to reason logically based on verbal problems.
Population: Wide variety of occupations and vocational counseling.
Publication Dates: 1958–1961.
Scores: Total score only.
Administration: Individual or group.
Price Data: Available from publisher.
Time: 15 minutes.
Authors: Raymond J. Corsini and Richard Renck.
Publisher: General Dynamics Information Technology.
Cross References: See T3:2553 (1 reference); for reviews by James E. Kennedy and David G. Ryans, see 6:509.

[2196]

Verbal Reasoning [GL Assessment].

Purpose: Designed to "assess a pupil's verbal skills."
Population: Ages 7.3–10.3; Ages 9.3–12.3; 11.3–14.3.
Publication Date: 1993.
Scores, 5: Vocabulary, Relationships, Sentences, Reasoning, Symbol Manipulation.
Administration: Group.
Levels, 3: 8 and 9, 10 and 11, 12 and 13.
Price Data: Available from publisher.
Comments: Available in paper-and-pencil and digital format.
Authors: Neil Hagues and Denise Courtenay.
Publisher: GL Assessment [England].
  a) VERBAL REASONING 8 and 9.
  Population: Ages 7.3–10.3.
  Time: (40) minutes.
  b) VERBAL REASONING 10 and 11.
  Population: Ages 9.3–12.3.
  Time: (45) minutes.
  c) VERBAL REASONING 12 and 13.
  Population: Ages 11.3–14.3.
  Time: (50) minutes.
Cross References: For reviews by Hoi K. Suen and by Rosemary E. Sutton and Jeremy Genovese, see 16:258.

[2197]

Versant™ English Placement Test.

Purpose: Designed to measure "how well a person can understand spoken and written English and respond appropriately in speaking and writing on everyday topics."
Population: Adults and students (over age 16) whose native language is not English.

Publication Date: 2012.
Scores, 5: Overall Score, Speaking, Listening, Reading, Writing.
Administration: Individual.
Price Data, 2015: $39.95 per test including score report.
Time: (50) minutes.
Comments: Computer administered and scored; headset with microphone required.
Authors: Pearson.
Publisher: Pearson.
Cross References: Reviews are scheduled for *The Twentieth Mental Measurements Yearbook.*

[2198]

Versant™ English Test.

Purpose: Designed to measure "how well a person can understand spoken English on everyday topics and respond appropriately."
Population: Adults and students (over age 15) whose native language is not English.
Publication Dates: 2000-2012.
Scores, 5: Overall Score, Sentence Mastery, Vocabulary, Fluency, Pronunciation.
Administration: Individual.
Price Data, 2015: $39.95 per a test including score report.
Time: (15) minutes.
Comments: Administered via telephone or computer; computer scored.
Author: Pearson.
Publisher: Pearson.
Cross References: Reviews are scheduled for *The Twentieth Mental Measurements Yearbook.* For reviews by Dennis Doverspike and Alan Garfinkel of an earlier version titled Ordinate Spoken English Test, see 16:177.

[2199]

Victoria Symptom Validity Test.

Purpose: Designed to "assess possible exaggeration or feigning of cognitive impairments."
Population: Ages 18 and over.
Publication Date: 1997.
Acronym: VSVT.
Scores, 6: Total Items Correct, Easy Items Correct, Difficult Items Correct, Easy Items Response Latency, Difficult Items Response Latency, Right-Left Preference.
Administration: Individual.
Price Data, 2015: $600 per software (CD-ROM) with quick start guide, and professional manual (93 pages).
Time: 18-25 minutes.
Authors: Daniel Slick, Grace Hopp, Esther Strauss, and Garrie B. Thompson.
Publisher: Psychological Assessment Resources, Inc.
Cross References: For reviews by Stephen J. Freeman and Linda J. Zimmerman, see 14:407.

[2200]

VIEW: An Assessment of Problem Solving Style.

Purpose: Designed to assess "problem-solving styles."
Population: Ages 12 years and older.
Publication Dates: 2002-2004.
Scores, 3: Orientation to Change, Manner of Processing, Ways of Decoding.
Administration: Individual or group.
Price Data: Available from publisher.
Foreign Language Editions: Information regarding translated tests available from test publisher.
Time: (10-15) minutes.
Comments: Administered online.
Authors: Edwin C. Selby, Donald J. Treffinger, Scott G. Isaksen, and Kenneth J. Lauer (technical manual only).
Publisher: The Creative Problem Solving Group, Inc.
Cross References: For reviews by Gregory Schraw and Mark A. Staal, see 17:193.

[2201]

ViewPoint.

Purpose: An assessment of work attitudes designed for use in employee selection.
Population: Applicants for nonexempt or entry-level positions in industries.
Publication Dates: 1998–2003.
Scores: 10 scales: WorkView Total, ServiceView Total, Conscientiousness, Trustworthiness, Managing Work Pressure, Getting Along with Others, Drug/Alcohol Avoidance, Safety Orientation, Carelessness, Faking.
Administration: Group or individual.
Price Data: Available from publisher for test materials including Technical Manual (1999, 62 pages), Technical Report Addendum: A Meta-Analysis of the Validity of ViewPoint (2001, 13 pages), and User's Manual (2005, 56 pages).
Comments: Published in five different forms, each one covering a different combination of work and service attitudes; computerized versions are available.
Authors: W. M. Gibson, M. L. Holcom, S. W. Stang, and W. W. Ruch.
Publisher: Psychological Services, Inc.
  a) WORKVIEW 6.
  Acronym: W6.
  Time: (15–20) minutes.
  b) WORKVIEW 4.
  Acronym: W4.
  Time: (10–15) minutes.
  c) SERVICEVIEW.
  Acronym: SV.
  Time: (10–15) minutes.
  d) WORKVIEW 6 + SERVICE.
  Acronym: W6SV.
  Time: (20–30) minutes.

  e) WORKVIEW 4 + SERVICE.
  Acronym: W4SV.
  Time: (20–25) minutes.
Cross References: For a review by Robert Fitzpatrick, see 16:259.

[2202]

ViewPoint General Personality Survey.

Purpose: "A general-purpose measure of normal personality [based on the Big Five structure] designed for business settings."
Population: "[Job] candidates across a broad range of positions."
Publication Dates: 2001-2009.
Acronym: ViewPoint GPS.
Scores, 37: 5 Major Scales based on 22 Component Scales: Agreeableness (Caring, Helpful, Complying, Considerate, Trusting), Conscientiousness (Thoroughness, Achievement Focus, Diligence, Initiative, Organization), Stability (Even Tempered, Self-Confidence, Optimism, Composure), Extraversion (Influential, Likes Attention, Sociable, Lively), Openness (Inventiveness, Flexibility, Curiosity, Quick Thinking); 8 Occupational Scales grouped into 3 categories: Associate (Implementing, Providing Service), Leadership (Establishing, Managing), Specialist (Analyzing, Creating, Selling), no category (Loyalty); 2 Special Scales: Careful Responding, Impression Management.
Administration: Group.
Price Data, 2015: $32 per online test; quantity discounts available; contact distributor for pricing information regarding paper-and-pencil version; Technical Manual (Version 8, 2009, 104 pages), can be downloaded free of charge with authorization from distributor.
Foreign Language Editions: Spanish and Chinese editions available.
Time: Online administration: (20-25) minutes, (15) additional minutes for optional component of the Caregiver Profile; paper-and-pencil administration: (25-30) minutes, (20-25) additional minutes for optional component.
Comments: Test previously listed as Performance Perspectives Inventory. Distributed exclusively by PSI Services LLC under the title "ViewPoint General Personality Survey" (ViewPoint GPS); available online or in paper-and-pencil format; optional PPI Caregiver Profile is a special method of scoring the ViewPoint GPS and is distributed under the title "CareView."
Authors: Joseph D. Abraham and John D. Morrison, Jr. (PPI Technical Manual [Version 8] and PPI Caregiver Profile: Administrator's Guide [Version 8]).
Publisher: A & M Psychometrics, LLC; sole distributor: PSI Services LLC.
Cross References: For reviews by Michael D. Biderman and Chockalingam Viswesvaran of the Performance Perspectives Inventory, see 18:91.

[2203]

Vineland Adaptive Behavior Scales, Second Edition.

Purpose: Designed as an adaptive behavior assessment system that measures self-sufficiency across the life-span.
Population: Birth to age 90-11.
Publication Dates: 1935-2008.
Acronym: Vineland-II.
Scores, 16: 3 Communication scores: Receptive, Expressive, Written; 5 Daily Living Skills scores: Personal, Domestic, Community, Academic (Teacher Rating Form only), School Community (Teacher Rating Form only); 3 Socialization scores: Interpersonal Relationships, Play and Leisure Time, Coping Skills; 2 Motor Skills scores: Gross, Fine; Adaptive Behavior Composite, Maladaptive Behavior Index (optional), Maladaptive Behavior Critical Items (optional).
Administration: Individual.
Foreign Language Edition: Spanish forms available for Survey and Expanded Interview forms.
Comments: A revision of the Vineland Social Maturity Scale by Edgar A. Doll.
Authors: Sara S. Sparrow, Domenic V. Cicchetti, and David A. Balla.
Publisher: Pearson.

a) SURVEY INTERVIEW FORM, PARENT/CAREGIVER RATING FORM.
Purpose: Designed to assess adaptive behavior via parent/caregiver report.
Population: Birth to age 90-11.
Price Data, 2016: $182.70 per Survey Forms starter kit including 10 Survey Interview forms, 10 Parent/Caregiver Rating forms, 10 Survey Interview reports to parents, 10 Survey reports to caregivers, and Survey Forms manual (2005, 326 pages); $87.15 per 25 Survey Interview forms; $87.15 per 25 Parent/Caregiver Rating forms; $36.60 per 25 Survey Interview forms report to parents; $36.60 per 25 Survey Forms report to caregivers; $119.50 per Survey Forms manual; $321.50 per Survey Forms ASSIST™ scoring software.
Time: 45(65) minutes.
b) TEACHER RATING FORM.
Purpose: Assessment of adaptive behavior within classroom and school settings.
Population: Ages 3-0 to 18-11.
Price Data: $123 per Teacher Rating Forms starter kit including 10 Teacher Rating Forms, 10 Teacher Rating reports to parents/caregivers, and Teacher Rating Form manual (2006, 238 pages); $81.60 per 25 Teacher Rating Forms; $36.60 per 25 Teacher Rating Form reports to parents/caregivers; $99 per Teacher Rating Form manual; $321.50 per Teacher Rating Form ASSIST™ scoring software.
Time: 20(40) minutes.
c) EXPANDED INTERVIEW FORM.
Purpose: Designed to provide a comprehensive assessment of adaptive behavior via a semistructured interview.
Population: Birth to age 90.
Price Data: $208.50 per Expanded Interview Form starter kit including 10 Expanded Interview Forms, 10

Expanded Form report to parents, 10 Expanded Form report to caregivers, and Expanded Form manual (2008, 326 pages); $439.75 per Expanded Form starter kit with ASSIST™ software; $84.75 per 25 Expanded Interview Forms; $36.60 per 25 Expanded Form report to parents; $36.60 per 25 Expanded Form report to caregivers; $99 per Expanded Form manual.
Time: 25(90) minutes.
Cross References: For reviews by Stephanie Stein and Keith F. Widaman, see 18:150; see T5:2813 (156 references) and T4:2882 (62 references); for a review by Jerome M. Sattler of an earlier edition, see 10:381 (9 references); for a review by Iris Amos Campbell of an earlier Survey Form and Expanded Form, see 9:1327 (8 references); see also T3:2557 (38 references), 8:703 (23 references), T2:1428 (50 references), P:281 (21 references), 6:194 (20 references), and 5:120 (15 references); for reviews by William M. Cruickshank and Florence M. Teagarden of an earlier edition, see 4:94 (21 references); for reviews by C. M. Louttit and John W. M. Rothney and an excerpted review, see 3:107 (58 references); for reviews by Paul H. Furfey, Elaine F. Kinder, and Anna S. Starr, see 1:1143.

[2204]

Vineland Social-Emotional Early Childhood Scales.

Purpose: Designed to assess the social and emotional functioning of young children.
Population: Birth to age 5-11.
Publication Date: 1998.
Acronym: SEEC.
Scores, 4: Interpersonal Relationships, Play and Leisure Time, Coping Skills, Composite.
Administration: Individual.
Price Data, 2015: $105.60 per complete kit; $46 per 25 record forms; $303.20 for reporting software (Early Childhood Assessment ASSIST).
Time: (15–25) minutes.
Comments: Administered as a structured oral interview; interviewee should be the person with the most knowledge of the child's social and emotional functioning (e.g., parent, grandparent, legal guardian).
Authors: Sara S. Sparrow, David A. Balla, and Dominic V. Cicchetti.
Publisher: Pearson.
Cross References: For reviews by Joseph C. Kush and Donald Lee Stovall, see 14:408.

[2205]

A Violence Scale.

Purpose: Designed to measure attitudes toward violence.
Population: Adolescents and adults
Publication Date: 1973.
Scores: Total score only.
Administration: Group.

Manual: No manual.
Price Data, 2015: $2 per scale.
Time: [10] minutes.
Comments: Supplementary article available.
Author: Panos D. Bardis.
Publisher: Donna Bardis.
Cross References: See 8:704 (1 reference).

[2206]
Visual Analog Mood Scales.
Purpose: Designed to "assess internal mood states in neurologically impaired adults and in patients in medical and psychiatric settings."
Population: Ages 18 and over.
Publication Dates: 1996–1997.
Acronym: VAMS.
Scores: 8 scales: Afraid, Confused, Sad, Angry, Energetic, Tired, Happy, Tense.
Administration: Group or individual.
Price Data, 2015: $166 per introductory kit including 25 response booklets, professional manual (1997, 48 pages), and metric ruler.
Time: 5 minutes.
Comments: Self-administered or administered by examiner.
Author: Robert A. Stern.
Publisher: Psychological Assessment Resources, Inc.
Cross References: For reviews by S. Alvin Leung and William E. Martin, Jr., see 15:272.

[2207]
Visual Association Test [2015 Manual].
Purpose: Designed to "detect anterograde amnesia and certain brain disorders it is connect with."
Population: Ages 16-85.
Publication Dates: 2003-2015.
Acronym: VAT.
Score: Total score only.
Administration: Individual.
Forms, 4: A, B, C, D.
Price Data, 2016: £248 per complete kit including manual (2015, 39 pages), picture booklets (A/B and C/D), and scoring forms (A/B and C/D); £56 per manual; £57 per picture booklet (A/B or C/D); £39 per 50 scoring forms A/B or C/D).
Foreign Language Editions: Dutch and German versions available.
Time: Administration time not reported.
Comments: Forms may be combined for longer form administration (recommended for test takers younger than age 65).
Authors: Jaap Lindeboom, Ben Schmand, Sascha Meyer (Forms C/D), and Jos de Jonghe (Forms C/D).
Publisher: Hogrefe Ltd [United Kingdom].
Cross References: For a review by Stephen J. Freeman of an earlier (2003) edition, see 16:261.

[2208]
The Visual Aural Digit Span Test.
Purpose: Intended as a "standardized test of intersensory integration and short-term memory for school-age children."
Population: Ages 5-6 to 12.
Publication Date: 1977.
Acronym: VADS Test.
Scores, 11: Aural-Oral, Visual-Oral, Aural-Written, Visual-Written, Aural Input, Visual Input, Oral Expression, Written Expression, Intrasensory Integration, Intersensory Integration, Total.
Subtests, 4: Aural-Oral, Visual-Oral, Aural-Written, Visual-Written.
Administration: Individual.
Price Data, 2015: $210 per complete kit including stimulus cards, directions for administering, and 100 scoring sheets; $165 per 100 scoring sheets; $60 per manual (1977, 216 pages); $29 per administration directions; $36.72 per stimulus cards.
Time: [10–15] minutes.
Author: Elizabeth M. Koppitz.
Publisher: Pearson.
Cross References: See T5:2816 (1 reference) and T4:2884 (1 reference); for reviews by H. Lee Swanson and Robert H. Zabel, see 9:1329 (2 references); see also T3:2560 (2 references).

[2209]
Visual Functioning Assessment Tool.
Purpose: "Assessment of a student's visual functioning in the educational setting."
Population: Visually impaired in grades preschool and over.
Publication Date: 1980.
Acronym: VFAT.
Scores: No scores.
Administration: Individual.
Price Data, 2015: $95 per complete kit; $38 per reproducible recording booklet; $65 per manual (123 pages).
Time: Untimed.
Authors: Kathleen Byrnes Costello, Patricia Pinkney, and Wendy Scheffers.
Publisher: Stoelting Co.

[2210]
Visual Motor Assessment.
Purpose: "Designed to identify visual-motor problems in children and adults."
Population: Ages 6 and older
Publication Dates: 1962-2006.
Acronym: ViMo.
Scores, 5: Total Rotation Score, T-Score, Total SPCD (Separation of the Circle-Diamond Figure), Total DCD (Distortion of the Circle-Diamond Figure), Total DD (Distortion of the Dot Figure).

Administration: Individual.
Price Data, 2015: $139 per complete kit including manual (104 pages), 25 record forms, and 2 sets of test cards; $81 per technical manual; $55 per 25 record forms.
Time: (5-15) minutes.
Comments: Formerly known as the Minnesota Percepto-Diagnostic (MPD) Test.
Author: Gerald B. Fuller.
Publisher: Multi-Health Systems, Inc.
Cross References: For reviews by Mark Roybal and by Kay B. Stevens and J. Randall Price, see 17:194; for information on the Minnesota Percepto-Diagnostic Test, see T5:1699 (2 references), T4:1647 (6 references), 9:719 (3 references), 8:872 (22 references), T2:1485 (17 references), and P:475 (19 references); for reviews by Richard W. Coan and Eugene E. Levitt of the original edition of the Minnesota Percepto-Diagnostic Test, see 6:231 (2 references).

[2211]

The Visual Object and Space Perception Battery.

Purpose: Designed to assess visual object and space perception.
Population: Adults.
Publication Date: 1991.
Acronym: VOSP.
Scores: 9 tests: Shape Detection Screening Test, Incomplete Letters, Silhouettes, Object Decision, Progressive Silhouettes, Dot Counting, Position Discrimination, Number Location, Cube Analysis.
Administration: Individual or group.
Price Data, 2015: £229.50 per complete kit including manual (20 pages), 25 scoring sheets, and 3 stimulus books; £22 per 25 scoring sheets; £45.50 per manual; £64.50 per stimulus book 1; £55 per stimulus book 2; £50 per stimulus book 3.
Time: Untimed.
Comments: Tests may be administered separately, in groups, or as a complete battery.
Authors: Elizabeth K. Warrington and Merle James.
Publisher: Pearson Assessment [England].
Cross References: For a review by Ayres G. D'Costa, see 17:195.

[2212]

Visual Search and Attention Test.

Purpose: Constructed to "measure attentional processes commonly disrupted in acute and chronic brain damage or disease."
Population: Ages 18 and over.
Publication Dates: 1987–1990.
Acronym: VSAT.
Scores, 3: Left, Right, Total.
Administration: Individual.

Price Data, 2015: $196 per introductory kit including 50 test booklets and manual (1990, 18 pages).
Time: 6 minutes.
Authors: Max R. Trenerry, Bruce Crosson, James DeBoe, and William R. Leber.
Publisher: Psychological Assessment Resources, Inc.
Cross References: See T5:2820 (1 reference); for reviews by Stephen R. Hooper and Wilfred G. Van Gorp, see 12:407.

[2213]

Vocabulary Assessment Scales–Expressive/Vocabulary Assessment Scales–Receptive.

Purpose: Designed to "evaluate an individual's understanding of words and the breadth of an individual's vocabulary."
Population: Ages 2-6 to 95.
Publication Date: 2013.
Scores, 4: Expressive Total, Receptive Total, Vocabulary Composite, Expressive–Receptive Discrepancy.
Subtests: Available as separates.
Administration: Individual.
Price Data, 2015: $295 per Form A combo kit including manual (171 pages), Fast Guide (23 pages), 25 VAS-E record forms, 25 VAS-R record forms, VAS-E stimulus book, and VAS-R stimulus book; $79 per manual.
Comments: Materials available in print or digitally.
Author: Rebecca Gerhardstein Nader.
Publisher: Psychological Assessment Resources, Inc.
   a) VOCABULARY ASSESSMENT SCALES–EXPRESSIVE.
   Purpose: Designed to measure "the oral articulation of word meaning."
   Acronym: VAS-E.
   Score: Total score only.
   Forms, 2: A, B.
   Price Data, 2015: $189 per kit including manual, Fast Guide, 25 Form A record forms, and Form A stimulus book; $120 per stimulus book (Form A or Form B); $45 per 25 record forms (Form A or Form B).
   Time: (15-20) minutes.
   Comments: Conormed with Vocabulary Assessment Scales–Receptive.
   b) VOCABULARY ASSESSMENT SCALES–RECEPTIVE.
   Purpose: Designed to measure "auditory comprehension of word meaning."
   Acronym: VAS-R.
   Score: Total score only.
   Forms, 2: A, B.
   Price Data, 2015: $189 per kit including manual, Fast Guide, 25 Form A record forms, and Form A stimulus book; $120 per stimulus book (Form A or Form B); $45 per 25 record forms (Form A or Form B).
   Time: (15-20) minutes.
   Comments: Conormed with Vocabulary Assessment Scales–Expressive.
Cross References: Reviews are scheduled for *The Twentieth Mental Measurements Yearbook*.

[2214]

Vocational Assessment and Curriculum Guide.

Purpose: "Designed to assess and identify skill deficits in terms of competitive employment expectations; to prescribe training goals designed to reduce identified deficits; to evaluate program effectiveness by reassessing the worker after training."
Population: Mentally handicapped employees.
Publication Dates: 1982–2003.
Acronym: VACG.
Scores, 10: Attendance/Endurance, Independence, Production, Learning, Behavior, Communication Skills, Social Skills, Grooming/Eating, Reading/Writing, Math.
Administration: Group.
Price Data, 2016: $12 per complete kit including manual (5 pages), 10 test booklets, curriculum guides, and summary profile sheets; $8 per set of 10 extra forms.
Time: (15–20) minutes.
Authors: Frank R. Rusch, Richard P. Schutz, Dennis E. Mithaug, Jeffrey E. Stewart, and Deanna K. Mar.
Publisher: Exceptional Education — Jeff Stewart's Teaching Tools.
Cross References: For reviews by Hinsdale Bernard and Gerald R. Schneck, see 13:356; see also T4:2898 (1 reference).

[2215]

Vocational Interest Inventory and Exploration Survey (Voc-Ties).

Purpose: Designed to "assess a student's interest in school based training programs" and provide "information about the training area."
Population: Vocational education students.
Publication Dates: 1991–2000.
Scores: 15 vocational interest areas: Auto Mechanics, Business and Office, Construction, Cosmetology, Drafting, Electromechanics, Electronics, Family and Consumer Science, Food Service, Graphic Arts, Health Services, Horticulture/Agriculture, Marketing, Metals, Technology Education.
Administration: Individual or group.
Price Data, 2016: $595 per media kit including guide, video, and software; $195 per single station version; $495 per multistation or Internet version with 1-year site license.
Time: (15-20) minutes.
Authors: Nancy L. Scott and Charles Gilbreath.
Publisher: Piney Mountain Press.
Cross References: For reviews by Larry Cochran and Kevin R. Murphy of an earlier edition, see 12:408.

[2216]

Vocational Preference Inventory, 1985 Edition.

Purpose: Designed to "assess career interests."

Population: High school and college and adults.
Publication Dates: 1953–1985.
Acronym: VPI.
Scores: 11 scales: Realistic, Investigative, Social, Conventional, Enterprising, Artistic, Self-Control, Masculinity-Femininity, Status, Infrequency, Acquiescence.
Administration: Individual or group.
Price Data, 2015: $134 per introductory kit including 50 test booklet/answer sheet/profile combinations and manual (1985, 36 pages).
Time: (15–30) minutes.
Author: John L. Holland.
Publisher: Psychological Assessment Resources, Inc.
Cross References: See T5:2835 (28 references) and T4:2910 (9 references); for reviews by John W. Shepard and Nicholas A. Vacc, see 10:382 (17 references); for reviews by James B. Rounds and by Nicholas A. Vacc and James Pickering of an earlier edition, see 9:1342 (19 references); see also T3:2581 (45 references); for an excerpted review by W. Bruce Walsh of an earlier edition, see 8:1028 (175 references); see also T2:1430 (48 references); for reviews by Joseph A. Johnston and Paul R. Lohnes, see 7:157 (39 references); see also P:283 (31 references); for reviews by Robert L. French and H. Bradley Sagen of an earlier edition, see 6:115 (13 references).

[2217]

Vulpe Assessment Battery—Revised.

Purpose: Designed as "a comprehensive, process-oriented, criterion-referenced assessment that emphasizes children's functional abilities."
Population: Children functioning between full term birth to six years of age.
Publication Date: 1994.
Acronym: VAB-R.
Scores: 8 scales: Basic Senses and Functions, Gross Motor, Fine Motor, Language, Cognitive Processes and Specific Concepts, Adaptive Behaviors, Activities of Daily Living, Environmental Assessment.
Administration: Individual or group.
Price Data, 2016: $175.25 per complete kit including manual (1994, 480 pages) and 50 record sheets; $34.75 per 50 record sheets.
Time: Administration time not reported.
Comments: Ratings by person familiar with the child.
Author: Shirley German Vulpe.
Publisher: Slosson Educational Publications, Inc.
Cross References: For reviews by Theresa Graham and Diane J. Sawyer, see 14:411.

[2218]

Wagner Enneagram Personality Style Scales.

Purpose: Designed "to measure the nine personality styles described by Enneagram."
Population: Ages 18 years and over.
Publication Date: 1999.

Acronym: WEKPSS.

Scores, 9: The Good Person, The Loving Person, The Effective Person, The Original Person, The Wise Person, The Loyal Person, The Joyful Person, The Powerful Person, The Peaceful Person.

Administration: Group or individual.

Price Data, 2016: $190.50 per kit including 25 autoscore forms, manual (114 pages), 100 glossary sheets, 100 brief guides to WEPSS results; $69 per 25 answer forms; $74 per manual; $20.50 per 100 PC answer sheets; $25 per 100 brief guide to WEPSS results; $387.50 per 25-use PC scoring disk; $25 per 100 glossary sheets.

Time: (20–40) minutes.

Comments: Paper-and-pencil or computer administration available.

Author: Jerome P. Wagner.

Publisher: Western Psychological Services

Cross References: For reviews by Frank M. Bernt and Johnnie A. Brown, see 15:274.

[2219]
Waksman Social Skills Rating Scale.

Purpose: "Developed to assist psychologists, educators, and other clinicians to identify specific and clinically important social skill deficits in children and adolescents."

Population: Grades K-12.

Publication Dates: 1983-1992.

Acronym: WSSRS.

Scores, 3: Aggressive, Passive, Total.

Administration: Individual.

Price Data, 2015: $45 per complete kit including 25 each of male and female forms, and manual (1992, 10 pages); $20 per 25 male or female forms; $15 per manual.

Time: 10 minutes.

Author: Steven A. Waksman.

Publisher: Enrichment Press.

Cross References: See T5:2841 (1 reference) and T4:2915 (2 references); for reviews by Harold R. Keller and Ellen McGinnis, see 10:383.

[2220]
Ward Atmosphere Scale [Third Edition Manual].

Purpose: Designed to evaluate treatment program social climates in psychiatric settings.

Population: Psychiatric patients and staff members.

Publication Dates: 1974–1996.

Acronym: WASC.

Scores, 10: Involvement, Support, Spontaneity, Autonomy, Practical Orientation, Personal Problems Orientation, Anger and Aggression, Order and Organization, Program Clarity, Staff Control.

Administration: Individual or group.

Forms, 4: R (Real), I (Ideal), E (Expectations), and S (Short).

Price Data, 2015: $50 per manual, including review-only copy of form; $2 per Remote Online Survey License or License to Reproduce (minimum 50); $10 per user's guide.

Foreign Language Editions: Translated materials available in Afrikaans, Danish, Dutch, Finnish, French, German, Hebrew, Italian, Norwegian, Spanish, and Swedish.

Time: [25-30] minutes.

Comments: Used to describe, plan for, and monitor change or improvements in treatment programs by examining patient and staff social climate perceptions.

Author: Rudolph H. Moos.

Publisher: Mind Garden, Inc.

Cross References: For reviews by Ronald A. Berk and Mary Anne Bunda, see 14:413; see also T5:2850 (3 references), T4:2925 (17 references), and T3:2587 (16 references); for a review by Earl S. Taulbee of an earlier edition, see 8:706 (31 references). For a review of the Social Climate Scales, see 8:681.

[2221]
Washer Visual Acuity Screening Technique.

Purpose: To assess visual acuity for near and far vision in very young children and mentally challenged or low functioning individuals.

Population: Mental ages 2.5-adult.

Publication Date: 1984.

Acronym: WVAST.

Scores, 6: Farpoint (Both Eyes, Right Eye, Left Eye), Nearpoint (Both Eyes, Right Eye, Left Eye).

Administration: Individual.

Price Data, 2015: $87.85 per starter set including 1 manual, 1 set of screening materials, and 20 screening records; $76.90 per 1 set of screening materials; $21.70 per package of 50 at home conditioning materials; $14.70 per administrator's manual; $11.70 per 20 screening records.

Time: Administration time varies.

Comments: Criterion-referenced scores.

Author: Rhonda Wiczer Washer.

Publisher: Scholastic Testing Service, Inc.

[2222]
Watson-Barker Listening Test [Revised Video Version Form E and Form F].

Purpose: Designed to assess listening comprehension abilities.

Population: Ages 18 and older.

Publication Dates: 1984-2011.

Acronym: WBLT.

Scores, 6: Evaluating Message Content, Understanding Meaning in Conversations, Understanding and Remembering Lectures, Evaluating Emotional Meanings in Messages, Following Instructions and Directions, Total.

Administration: Group.

Forms, 2: E, F.

Price Data, 2016: $299.99 per kit, including facilitator guide (2011, 50 pages), DVD, and 20 self-scoring answer sheets; $37.95 per 50 answer sheets.
Time: (40) minutes.
Comments: Administered via DVD.
Authors: Kittie W. Watson, Larry L. Barker, Charles V. Roberts, Rick Bommelje, and John D. Roberts.
Publisher: Innolect, Inc.
Cross References: For reviews by James R. Clopton and Joseph P. Stokes of an earlier edition, see 10:384.

[2223]

Watson-Glaser Critical Thinking Appraisal.
Purpose: Constructed to assess critical thinking abilities related to reading comprehension.
Population: Grades 9-12 and college and adults.
Publication Dates: 1942-1980.
Acronym: WGCTA.
Scores, 6: Inference, Recognition of Assumptions, Deduction, Interpretation, Evaluation of Arguments, Total.
Administration: Group or individual.
Forms, 2: A, B.
Price Data, 2015: $511 per comprehensive kit including 25 test booklets (Form A), 25 answer documents (Forms A and B), scoring key (Form A), and manual (Forms A and B); $380 per 25 test booklets (Form A or B) and manual; $135 per 25 answer documents (Forms A and B); $151 per hand scoring key (Form A or Form B); $76 per manual.
Time: (40–60) minutes.
Comments: Revision of Form YM and ZM.
Authors: Goodwin Watson and Edward M. Glaser.
Publisher: Pearson.
Cross References: See T5:2856 (13 references) and T4:2933 (5 references); for reviews by Allen Berger and Gerald C. Helmstadter, see 9:1347 (4 references); see also T3:2594 (15 references), 8:822 (49 references), and T2:1775 (35 references); for excerpted reviews by John O. Crites and G. C. Helmstadtler, see 7:783 (74 references); see also 6:867 (24 references); for reviews by Walker H. Hill and Carl I. Hovland of an earlier edition, see 5:700 (8 references); for a review by Robert H. Thouless and an excerpted review by Harold P. Fawcett, see 3:544 (3 references).

[2224]

Watson-Glaser Critical Thinking Appraisal, Short Form.
Purpose: Designed to help "select employees for any job requiring careful, analytical thinking."
Population: Adults with at least a ninth grade education.
Publication Date: 1994.
Acronym: WGCTA-S.

Scores: Composite score derived from following content areas: Inference, Recognition of Assumptions, Deduction, Interpretation, Evaluation of Arguments.
Administration: Group or individual.
Price Data, 2015: $511 per starter kit including 25 test booklets, 25 answer documents, hand scoring key, directions for administration, and manual (87 pages); $305 per 25 test booklets; $135 per 25 answer documents; $151 per scoring key; $76 per manual.
Time: (30–45) minutes.
Comments: Developed as a shorter version of the WGCTA Form A; Form S norms are developed from norms of original WGCTA (2223).
Authors: Goodwin B. Watson and Edward M. Glaser.
Publisher: Pearson.
Cross References: See T5:2857 (1 reference); for reviews by Kurt F. Geisinger and Stephen H. Ivens, see 13:358. For information on the original edition of the WGCTA, see T4:2933; for reviews by Allen Berger and Gerald C. Helmstadter, see 9:1347 (4 references); see also T3:2594 (15 references), 8:822 (49 references), and T2:1775 (35 references); for excerpted reviews by John O. Crites and G. C. Helmstadter, see 7:783 (74 references); see also 6:867 (24 references); for reviews by Walker H. Hill and Carl I. Hovland of an earlier edition, see 5:700 (8 references); for a review by Robert H. Thouless and an excerpted review by Harold P. Fawcett, see 3:544 (3 references).

[2225]

Ways of Coping Questionnaire.
Purpose: "To identify the thoughts and actions an individual has used to cope with a specific stressful encounter."
Population: Adults.
Publication Date: 1988.
Scores: 8: Confrontive Coping, Distancing, Self-Controlling, Seeking Social Support, Accepting Responsibility, Escape-Avoidance, Planful Problem-Solving, Positive Reappraisal.
Administration: Individual and group.
Price Data, 2015: $50 for manual, including review-only copy of the WAYS form; $2.40 per Transform Survey Hosting license (minimum 50); $250 Group Report; $2 per Remote Online Survey License (minimum 50); $2 per License to Reproduce (minimum 50); $15 Individual Report; $15 Report About Me.
Foreign Language Editions: Estonian, Norwegian, Russian, Swedish, Arabic, German, Korean, Spanish.
Time: (10-15) minutes.
Comments: Self-administered.
Authors: Susan Folkman and Richard S. Lazarus.
Publisher: Mind Garden, Inc.
Cross References: See T5:2858 (129 references) and T4:2936 (25 references); for reviews by Judith C. Conger and Kathryn D. Hess, see 11:462 (16 references).

[2226]

WebCAPE Language Placement Exam.

Purpose: Designed to place students in beginning-level Spanish, French, German, Russian, Chinese and ESL courses.

Population: College students.

Publication Dates: 1986–2002.

Acronym: WebCAPE.

Scores: Total score only.

Administration: Individual.

Price Data: Available from publisher.

Time: (20–30) minutes.

Comments: Test is taken online; sales and marketing done by Perpetual Technology Group.

Authors: Jerry W. Larson, Kim L. Smith, Don Jensen, Randall L. Jones, Marshall Murray, and Diane Strong-Krause.

Publisher: Brigham Young University, Humanities Technology and Research Support Center.

Cross References: For reviews by G. Gage Kingsbury and Steven L. Wise of an earlier version titled A Spanish Computerized Adaptive Placement Exam, see 12:364.

[2227]

Wechsler Abbreviated Scale of Intelligence—Second Edition.

Purpose: Designed as "a short and reliable measure of intelligence in clinical, psychoeducational, and research settings."

Population: Ages 6-90.

Publication Dates: 1999-2011.

Acronym: WASI-II.

Administration: Individual.

Price Data, 2015: $335.20 per complete kit, including stimulus booklet, 25 record forms, set of nine blocks, and manual (2011, 257 pages) in canvas bag; $80.45 per 25 record forms, $172.20 per stimulus book, $188 per manual.

Author: David Wechsler.

Publisher: Pearson.

a) TWO SUBTEST FORM.

Scores, 3: Vocabulary, Matrix Reasoning, Full Scale IQ-2.

Time: (15) minutes.

b) FOUR SUBTEST FORM.

Scores, 7: Verbal Comprehension Index (Vocabulary, Similarities), Perceptual Reasoning Index (Block Design, Matrix Reasoning), Full Scale IQ-4.

Time: (30) minutes.

Cross References: For reviews by Kathleen M. Johnson and Jonathan Sandoval, see 19:175; for reviews by Timothy Z. Keith and by Cederick O. Lindskog and Janet V. Smith of the original edition, see 14:414.

[2228]

Wechsler Adult Intelligence Scale-Fourth Edition.

Purpose: "Designed to assess the cognitive ability of adolescents and adults"; "provides subtest and composite scores that represent intellectual functioning in specific cognitive domains, as well as a composite score that represents general intellectual ability."

Population: Ages 16-0 to 90-11.

Publication Dates: 1939-2008.

Acronym: WAIS-IV.

Scores, 6: Verbal Comprehension Index, Perceptual Reasoning Index, Processing Speed Index, General Ability Index, Full Scale.

Subtests, 15: Block Design, Similarities, Digit Span, Matrix Reasoning, Vocabulary, Arithmetic, Symbol Search, Visual Puzzles, Information, Coding, Letter-Number Sequencing, Figure Weights, Comprehension, Cancellation, Picture Completion.

Administration: Individual.

Price Data, 2015: $1,174 per basic kit including Symbol Search scoring key, Coding scoring key, Cancellation scoring templates, 25 record forms, 25 response booklet #1, 25 response booklet #2, administration and scoring manual (2008, 258 pages), technical manual (2008, 218 pages), 2 stimulus books, and Block Design block set in a box.

Foreign Language Edition: Spanish edition available.

Time: (59-100) minutes.

Comments: If there are significant differences between Index scores, the General Ability Index can be used to further inform interpretation; Letter-Number Sequencing, Figure Weights, and Cancellation are supplemental subtests for individuals 16-0 to 69-11 only.

Author: David Wechsler.

Publisher: Pearson.

Cross References: For reviews by Gary L. Canivez and Gregory Schraw, see 18:151; for reviews by Allen K. Hess and Bruce G. Rogers of the third edition, see 14:415; see also T5:2860 (1422 references) and T4:2937 (1131 references); for reviews by Alan S. Kaufman and Joseph D. Matarazzo of the revised edition, see 9:1348 (291 references); see also T3:2598 (576 references), 8:230 (351 references), and T2:529 (178 references); for reviews by Alvin G. Burstein and Howard B. Lyman of the original edition, see 7:429 (538 references); see also 6:538 (180 references); for reviews by Nancy Bayley and Wilson H. Guertin, see 5:414 (42 references).

[2229]

Wechsler Fundamentals: Academic Skills.

Purpose: Designed as "a brief achievement test that measures broad skills in the areas of reading, spelling, and math computation."

Population: Children Kindergarten-Grade 12, adults age 18-50.

Publication Date: 2008.

Scores, 5: Word Reading, Reading Comprehension, Reading Composite, Spelling, Numerical Operations.

Administration: Group and individual.

Forms, 2: A & B.

Price Data, 2015: $204.90 per examination kit Form A including 25 Summary of Skills Inventory and Word Reading record forms, 25 Spelling and Numerical Operations response booklets, 25 Reading Comprehension response booklets (5 each of Grade K-3, Grade 4-5, Grade 6-8, Grade 9-12, and Adult), word card, and administration manual (268 pages); $106.40 per combination set (specify Form A or Form B) including 25 Summary of Skills Inventory and Word Reading record forms, 25 Spelling and Numerical Operations response booklets, and 25 Reading Comprehension response booklets (5 each of Grade K-3, Grade 4-5, Grade 6-8, Grade 9-12, and Adult); $51.75 per 25 Spelling and Numerical Operations response booklets (specify Form A or B); $11.70 per Word Card (specify Form A or Form B); $51.75 per 25 (Form A) Summary of Skills Inventory and Word Reading record forms; $50.75 per 25 (Form B) Summary of Skills Inventory and Word Reading record forms; $106.40 per manual.

Time: (45) minutes.

Author: Pearson.

Publisher: Pearson.

Cross References: For reviews by Susan M. Brookhart and Georgette Yetter, see 18:152.

[2230]

Wechsler Individual Achievement Test-Third Edition.

Purpose: "Designed to measure the achievement of students" in prekindergarten through Grade 12 in the areas of "listening, speaking, reading, writing and mathematics."

Population: Ages 4-0 to 19-11.

Publication Dates: 1992-2009.

Acronym: WIAT-III.

Scores, 24: 16 subtests (Listening Comprehension, Early Reading Skills, Reading Comprehension, Math Problem Solving, Alphabet Writing Fluency, Sentence Composition, Word Reading, Essay Composition, Pseudoword Decoding, Numerical Operations, Oral Expression, Oral Reading Fluency, Spelling, Math Fluency-Addition, Math Fluency-Subtraction, Math Fluency-Multiplication), 8 composite scores (Oral Language, Total Reading, Basic Reading, Reading Comprehension and Fluency, Written Expression, Mathematics, Math Fluency, Total Achievement).

Administration: Individual.

Price Data, 2016: $699 per Q-global kit including examiner's manual, technical manual CD, stimulus book, scoring workbook, oral reading fluency book, word card, pseudo word card, audio CD, 25 response booklets, 25 record forms, and 75 Q-global score reports; $88.25 per examiner's manual; $88.25 per technical manual CD.

Time: Administration time varies depending on the grade level of the student and the number of subtests administered.

Comments: Examiners may choose to administer one subtest, a subset of subtests, or all 16 subtests; not all subtests contribute to the Total Achievement composite; the Math Fluency subtests do not contribute to the Total Achievement composite; the Early Reading Skills subtest and the Alphabet Writing Fluency subtest are administered to students in prekindergarten through Grade 3 but only contribute to the Total Achievement composite for prekindergarten through Grade 1; the Oral Reading Fluency subtest is administered to students in Grades 1-12 but only contributes to the Total Achievement composite for Grades 2-12; the Spelling subtest is administered to students in kindergarten through Grade 12 but only contributes to the Total Achievement composite for kindergarten through Grade 2; the publisher advises that adult norms for ages 20-50 were published in 2010.

Author: Pearson.

Publisher: Pearson.

Cross References: For reviews by M. David Miller and John T. Willse, see 18:153; for reviews by Beth J. Doll and by Gerald Tindal and Michelle Nutter of the Second Edition, see 15:275; see also T5:2861 (4 references); for reviews by Terry Ackerman and Steven Ferrara of a previous edition, see 13:359 (17 references).

[2231]

Wechsler Intelligence Scale for Children—Fifth Edition.

Purpose: Designed as a "clinical instrument for assessing the intelligence of children."

Population: Ages 6 through 16.

Publication Dates: 1971-2014.

Acronym: WISC-V.

Scores, 35: 5 Primary Index Scales: Verbal Comprehension Index (Similarities, Vocabulary), Visual Spatial Index (Block Design, Visual Puzzles), Fluid Reasoning Index (Matrix Reasoning, Figure Weights), Working Memory Index (Digit Span, Picture Span), Processing Speed Index (Coding, Symbol Search); 5 Ancillary Index Scales: Quantitative Reasoning Index (Figure Weights, Arithmetic), Auditory Working Memory Index (Digit Span, Letter-Number Sequencing), Nonverbal Index (Block Design, Visual Puzzles, Matrix Reasoning, Figure Weights, Picture Span, Coding), General Ability Index (Similarities, Vocabulary, Block Design, Matrix Reasoning, Figure Weights), Cognitive Proficiency Index (Digit Span, Picture Span, Coding, Symbol Search); 3 Complementary Index Scales: Naming Speed Index (Naming Speed Literacy, Naming Speed Quantity), Symbol Translation Index (Immediate Symbol Translation, Delayed Symbol Translation, Recognition Symbol Translation), Storage and Retrieval Index (Naming Speed Index, Symbol Translation Index); Full Scale IQ: Verbal Comprehension (Similarities, Vocabulary, [allowable substitutions: Information, Comprehension]), Visual Spatial (Block Design [allowable substitution: Visual Puzzles],

Fluid Reasoning (Matrix Reasoning, Figure Weights [allowable substitutions: Picture Concepts, Arithmetic]), Working Memory (Digit Span [allowable substitutions: Picture Span, Letter-Number Sequencing]), Processing Speed (Coding [allowable substitutions: Symbol Search, Cancellation]).

Administration: Individual.

Price Data, 2016: $1,145 per complete kit including administration and scoring manual (2014, 380 pages), technical and interpretive manual (2014, 288 pages), stimulus books 1-3, 25 record forms, 25 response booklets #1, 25 response booklets #2, Symbol Search scoring key, Coding scoring template, Cancellation scoring template, and Wechsler Standard Block Design Set; $220.35 per technical and interpretive manual; $220.35 per administration and scoring manual with supplement; $143.50 per stimulus book (1, 2, or 3); $128.10 per 25 record forms; $83 per 25 response booklets (#1–Coding and Symbol Search); $52.25 per 25 response booklets (#2–Cancellation). $2 per Q-global score report (subscription discounts available).

Time: (65) minutes to obtain 5 primary index scores; (48) minutes to obtain Full Scale IQ.

Comments: Full Scale IQ is the only composite score that allows subtest substitutions; only one substitution permitted. Computer administration and scoring available.

Authors: David Wechsler.

Publisher: Pearson.

Cross References: Reviews are scheduled for *The Twentieth Mental Measurements Yearbook*. For reviews by Susan J. Maller and Bruce Thompson of the fourth edition, see 16:262; see also T5:2862 (740 references); for reviews by Jeffrey P. Braden and Jonathan Sandoval of the third edition, see 12:412 (409 references); see also T4:2939 (911 references); for reviews by Morton Bortner, Douglas K. Detterman, and by Joseph C. Witt and Frank Gresham of the revised edition, see 9:1351 (299 references); see also T3:2602 (645 references); for reviews by David Freides and Randolph H. Whitworth, and excerpted reviews by Carol Kehr Tittle and Joseph Petrosko of the revised edition, see 8:232 (548 references); see also T2:533 (230 references); for reviews by David Freides and R. T. Osborne of the original edition, see 7:431 (518 references); for a review by Alvin G. Burnstein, see 6:540 (155 references); for reviews by Elizabeth D. Fraser, Gerald R. Patterson, and Albert I. Rabin, see 5:416 (111 references); for reviews by James M. Anderson, Harold A. Delp, and Boyd R. McCandless, and an excerpted review by Laurance F. Shaffer, see 4:363 (22 references).

[2232]

Wechsler Intelligence Scale for Children–Fifth Edition, Integrated.

Purpose: Designed to "extend the clinical information about the cognitive processes and test-taking behaviors that may affect performance on the Wechsler Intelligence Scale for Children–Fifth Edition."

Population: Ages 6 years, 0 months through 16 years, 11 months.

Publication Dates: 2004-2015.

Acronym: WISC-V Integrated.

Scores, 59: 18 subtest scores (Similarities Multiple Choice, Vocabulary Multiple Choice, Picture Vocabulary Multiple Choice, Information Multiple Choice, Comprehension Multiple Choice, Block Design Multiple Choice, Figure Weights Process Approach, Arithmetic Process Approach Part A, Arithmetic Process Approach Part B, Written Arithmetic, Spatial Span, Spatial Span Forward, Spatial Span Backward, Sentence Recall, Coding Copy, Cancellation Abstract, Cancellation Abstract Random, Cancellation Abstract Structured), 2 index scores (Multiple Choice Verbal Comprehension Index, Visual Working Memory Index), 7 Raw Score to Base Rate Conversions (Longest Spatial Span Forward, Longest Spatial Span Backward, Coding Recall Cued Symbol, Coding Recall Free Symbol, Coding Recall Cued Digit, Coding Recall Pairing, Sentence Recall Question Errors), 27 pairwise difference scores, 5 discrepancy comparison scores.

Administration: Individual.

Price Data, 2016: $305 per kit including Administration and Scoring Manual (2015, 224 pages), Technical and Interpretive Manual (2015, 170 pages), Stimulus Books 1 and 2, 25 Record Forms, 25 Response Booklet 1, 25 Response Booklet 2, Coding Recall Scoring Key, and Cancellation Abstract Scoring Template; $95 per Administration and Scoring Manual; $95 per Technical and Interpretive Manual; $81 per 25 Response Booklet 1; $51 per 25 Response Booklet 2; $125 per 25 Record Forms; $140 per Stimulus Book (1 or 2).

Time: (2-10) minutes per subtest.

Comments: The WISC-V (2231) is not reprinted in the WISC-V Integrated; computer scoring available.

Author: David Wechsler and Edith Kaplan.

Publisher: Pearson.

Cross References: Reviews are scheduled for *The Twentieth Mental Measurements Yearbook*. For reviews by Ronald A. Madle and by Joyce Meikamp and Carolyn H. Suppa of the previous edition, see 17:197.

[2233]

Wechsler Memory Scale-Fourth Edition.

Purpose: Developed to "assess various memory and working memory abilities" among "individuals with suspected memory deficits or diagnosed with a range of neurological, psychiatric, and developmental disorders."

Publication Dates: 1945-2009.

Acronym: WMS-IV.

Subtest: Brief Cognitive Status Exam (optional).

Administration: Individual.

Price Data, 2016: $779 per kit including administration and scoring manual, technical and interpretive manual, Stimulus Book #1, Stimulus Book #2, 25 Adult record forms, 25 Older Adult record forms, 25 response booklets, Design and Spatial Addition card set, scoring template, and memory grid.

Comments: Roman numerals I and II indicate a subtest's immediate and delayed conditions, respectively; Standard administration guidelines require that 20-30 minutes should elapse between the completion of a subtest's immediate condition and the beginning of the delayed condition.

Author: David Wechsler.

Publisher: Pearson.

    a) ADULT BATTERY.

    Population: Ages 16-0 to 69-11.

    Time: [80-115] minutes.

    Scores, 12: 7 subtests; 6 primary (Logical Memory I, Logical Memory II, Verbal Paired Associates I, Verbal Paired Associates II, Designs I, Designs II, Visual Reproduction I, Visual Reproduction II, Spatial Addition, Symbol Span); 1 option (Brief Cognitive Status Exam); 5 indices (Auditory Memory, Visual Memory, Visual Working Memory, Immediate Memory, Delayed Memory).

    b) OLDER ADULT BATTERY.

    Population: 65-0 to 90-11.

    Time: [50-70] minutes.

    Scores, 10: 6 subtests; 5 primary (Logical Memory I, Logical Memory II, Verbal Paired Associates I, Verbal Paired Associates II, Visual Reproduction I, Visual Reproduction II, Symbol Span); 1 optional (Brief Cognitive Status Exam); 4 indices (Auditory Memory, Visual Memory, Immediate Memory, Delayed Memory).

Cross References: For reviews by Jerrell Cassady and Athena Dacanay and by Mary (Rina) M. Chittooran, see 18:154; for reviews by Rik Carl D'Amato and Cecil R. Reynolds of the third edition, see 14:416; see also T5:2863 (431 references) and T4:2940 (117 references); for reviews by E. Scott Huebner and Robert C. Reinehr of an earlier edition, see 11:465 (166 references); see also 9:1355 (49 references), T3:2607 (96 references), 8:250 (36 references), T2:592 (70 references), and 6:561 (9 references); for reviews by Ivan Norma Mensh and Joseph Newman of the original version, see 4:364 (6 references); for a review by Kate Levine Kogan, see 3:302 (3 references).

[2234]

Wechsler Nonverbal Scale of Ability.

Purpose: Designed as a nonverbal measure of general cognitive ability.

Population: Ages 4-0 to 21-11.

Publication Date: 2006.

Acronym: WNV.

Scores, 7: Matrices, Coding, Object Assembly, Recognition, Spatial Span, Picture Arrangement, Full Scale Score.

Administration: Individual.

Levels, 2: Ages 4-0 to 7-11, 8-0 to 21-11.

Price Data, 2016: $739 per complete kit including administration and scoring manual (198 pages), technical and interpretive manual (125 pages), stimulus book, 25

record forms, 25 response booklets, spatial span board, object assembly puzzles, picture arrangement cards, 1 pencil, soft-side carrying case, and Wechsler Nonverbal scoring assistant; $53.05 per 25 record forms; $38.80 per 25 response booklets; $254.45 per object assembly puzzle set; $198.85 per picture arrangement card set; $155.50 per administration and scoring manual; $93.30 per technical and interpretive manual; $159.70 per stimulus book.

Time: 2-subtest battery: (15-20) minutes; 4-subtest battery: (45) minutes.

Comments: Examinee instructions are delivered via pictorial sequences.

Authors: David Wechsler and Jack A. Naglieri.

Publisher: Pearson.

    a) AGES 4-0 to 7-11.

    Scores: Matrices, Coding (4-subtest battery only), Object Assembly (4 subtest battery only), Recognition, Full Scale Score.

    b) AGES 8-0 to 21-11.

    Scores: Matrices, Coding (4 subtest battery only), Spatial Span, Picture Arrangement (4 subtest battery only), Full Scale Score.

Cross References: For reviews by Cleborne D. Maddux and Gerald Tindal, see 18:155.

[2235]

Wechsler Preschool and Primary Scale of Intelligence—Fourth Edition.

Purpose: Designed "for measuring the intelligence of children."

Publication Dates: 1949-2012.

Acronym: WPPSI-IV.

Administration: Individual.

Price Data, 2015: $1,174 per complete box kit, including administration and scoring manual (2012, 342 pages), technical and interpretive manual (2012, 272 pages), 3 stimulus books, 25 of each record form (ages 2-6 through 3-11 and ages 4-0 through 7-7), 25 of each response booklet (1, 2, and 3), scoring keys, block set, puzzle set, zoo location set, and 2 ink daubers; $1,225 per complete box kit with 25 Q-global score reports; $217.30 per administration and scoring manual; $217.30 per technical and interpretive manual; $82.50 per 25 record forms (ages 2-6 through 3-11); $103 per 25 record forms (ages 4-0 through 7-7); $49.20 per 25 response booklets (3, Animal Coding); $82.50 per 25 response booklets (1 and 2, Bug Search and Cancellation); $130.70 per stimulus book (1, 2, or 3); $3.10 per ink dauber; $133.75 per 25 record forms with Q-global score report usages (ages 2-6 through 3-11); $154.25 per 25 record forms with Q-global score report usages (ages 4-0 through 7-7).

Author: David Wechsler.

Publisher: Pearson.

    a) 2-6 through 3-11 AGE BAND.

    Population: Ages 2-6 through 3-11.

Scores, 9 to 14: Primary Index Scales: Verbal Comprehension Index (Receptive Vocabulary, Information, Total), Visual Spatial Index (Block Design, Object Assembly, Total), Working Memory Index (Picture Memory, Zoo Locations, Total); Ancillary Index Scales: Vocabulary Acquisition Index (Receptive Vocabulary, Picture Naming, Total), Nonverbal Index (Block Design, Object Assembly, Picture Memory, Zoo Locations, Total), General Ability Index (Receptive Vocabulary, Information, Picture Naming [supplemental], Block Design, Object Assembly, Total); Full Scale IQ consists of Verbal Comprehension Index (with supplemental Picture Naming), Visual Spatial Index, and Working Memory Index (with supplemental Zoo Locations).
Time: [30-45] minutes
b) 4-0 through 7-7 AGE BAND.
Population: Ages 4-0 through 7-7.
Scores, 12 to 25: Primary Index Scales: Verbal Comprehension Index (Information, Similarities, Total), Visual Spatial Index (Block Design, Object Assembly, Total), Fluid Reasoning Index (Matrix Reasoning, Picture Concepts, Total), Working Memory Index (Picture Memory, Zoo Locations, Total), Processing Speed Index (Bug Search, Cancellation, Total); Ancillary Index Scales: Vocabulary Acquisition Index (Receptive Vocabulary, Picture Naming, Total), Nonverbal Index (Block Design, Object Assembly [supplemental], Matrix Reasoning, Picture Concepts, Picture Memory, Zoo Locations [supplemental] Bug Search, Cancellation [supplemental], Animal Coding [supplemental], Total), General Ability Index (Information, Similarities, Vocabulary [supplemental], Comprehension [supplemental], Block Design, Object Assembly [supplemental], Matrix Reasoning, Picture Concepts [supplemental], Total), Cognitive Proficiency Index (Picture Memory, Zoo Locations, Bug Search, Cancellation, Animal Coding [supplemental], Total); Full Scale IQ consists of Verbal Comprehension Index (with supplemental Vocabulary, Comprehension), Visual Spatial Index (with supplemental Object Assembly), Fluid Reasoning Index (with supplemental Picture Concepts), Working Memory Index (with supplemental Zoo Locations), and Processing Speed Index (with supplemental Cancellation and Animal Coding).
Time: [45-60] minutes.
Cross References: For reviews by Gary L. Canivez and Tracy Thorndike, see 19:176; for reviews by Ronald A. Madle and by Merilee McCurdy and Lynae A. Johnsen of the third edition, see 16:267; see also T5:2864 (146 references) and T4:2941 (38 references); for reviews by Bruce A. Bracken and Jeffery P. Braden of the revised edition, see 11:466 (118 references); for a review by B. J. Freeman, see 9:1356 (33 references); see also T3:2608 (280 references), 8:234 (84 references), and T2:538 (30 references); for reviews by Dorothy H. Eichorn and A. B. Silverstein, and excerpted reviews by C. H. Ammons and by O. A. Oldridge and E. E. Allison, see 7:434 (56 references).

[2236]
Wechsler Test of Adult Reading.

Purpose: Developed as an assessment tool for estimating premorbid (pre-injury) intellectual functioning and to predict a person's pre-injury IQ and memory abilities.
Population: Ages 16–89.

Publication Date: 2001.
Acronym: WTAR.
Scores: Total score only.
Administration: Individual.
Price Data, 2016: $250 per complete kit including manual, 25 record forms, word card, and audiotape; $100 per 25 record forms; $135 per manual; $30 per word card; $20 per audiotape.
Time: [5–10] minutes.
Comments: Co-normed with the Wechsler Adult Intelligence Scale—Third Edition (T7:2746) and the Wechsler Memory Scale—Third Edition (T7:2751); U.K. norms available.
Author: The Psychological Corporation.
Publisher: Pearson.
Cross References: For reviews by Nora M. Thompson and Sandra Ward, see 16:268.

[2237]
Weiss Comprehensive Articulation Test.

Purpose: "For making a thorough diagnosis of articulation and its associated parameters."
Population: All ages.
Publication Dates: 1978–1980.
Acronym: WCAT.
Scores, 5: Articulation, Articulation Age, Intelligibility, Stimulability, Number of Misarticulations.
Administration: Individual.
Forms, 2: Nonreading Subjects, Reading Subjects.
Price Data, 2015: $149 per complete kit including picture cards, sentence card, 50 picture response forms, 50 sentence response forms, and manual (1980, 32 pages); $48 per 100 picture response forms; $48 per 100 sentence response forms.
Time: [20] minutes.
Author: Curtis E. Weiss.
Publisher: PRO-ED.
Cross References: See T5:2866 (5 references) and T4:2942 (2 references); for a review by Richard J. Schissel, see 9:1357.

[2238]
Weld Test.

Purpose: Designed for selecting and evaluating journey-level, industrial welders.
Population: Welding job applicants.
Publication Dates: 1984-2013.
Scores: 7 areas: Print Reading, Welding/Cutting Torch and Arc Air Cutting, Welder Maintenance and Operation, Tools/Machines/Material and Equipment, Mobile Equipment and Rigging, Production Welding Practices, Total.
Administration: Group.
Price Data, 2015: $24 per consumable self-scoring test booklet; $26 per online test administration; $24.95 per manual (2013, 16 pages).
Time: (60-70) minutes.

Comments: Self-scoring instrument; available for online test administration; test publisher advises changes in form names indicate minor revisions and updating.
Author: Roland T. Ramsay.
Publisher: Ramsay Corporation.
Cross References: For a review by James Witte of Form AC, see 19:177; for reviews by John Peter Hudson, Jr. and David C. Roberts of an earlier edition, see 13:360.

[2239]
Wellness Evaluation of Lifestyle [2004 Update].

Purpose: Designed to help respondents make healthy lifestyle choices based on their responses to each of the five life tasks and subtasks defined in the Wheel of Wellness; the life tasks of spirituality, self-direction, work & leisure, friendship, and love interact with a variety of life forces and global events.
Population: Ages 18 and over.
Publication Dates: 1994–2004.
Acronym: WEL.
Scores, 20: Spirituality, Self-Direction (Sense of Worth, Sense of Control, Realistic Beliefs, Emotional Awareness and Coping, Intellectual Stimulation/Problem Solving/Creativity, Sense of Humor, Nutrition, Exercise, Self-Care, Stress Management, Gender Identity, Cultural Identity), Work, Leisure, Friendship, Love, Total Wellness, Perceived Wellness.
Administration: Group or individual.
Price Data, 2015: $50 per manual, including review-only copy of WEL form; $15 per Individual Report; $15 per Report About Me; $250 per Group Report; $10 Wellness Evaluation of Lifestyle Workbook; $2.40 per online administration license; $2 per Remote Online Survey License or License to Reproduce (minimum 50).
Foreign Language Editions: Translated materials available in German and Indonesian.
Time: (15–20) minutes.
Comments: Web-based administration and reporting available.
Authors: Jane E. Myers, Thomas J. Sweeney, and J. Melvin Witmer.
Publisher: Mind Garden, Inc.
Cross References: For reviews by Richard F. Farmer and Trenton R. Ferro, see 16:270; for reviews by Andrew A. Cox and Ashraf Kagee of a previous edition, see 15:277.

[2240]
Welsh Figure Preference Test.

Purpose: A nonverbal approach to personality measurement and research incorporating the Barron-Welsh Art Scale (185).
Population: Ages 6 and over.
Publication Dates: 1959-1980.
Acronym: WFPT.

Scores, 27: Like, Don't Like, Repeat, Conformance, Origence, Intellectence, Female Response, Movement, Figure Ground, Shading, Black, Anxiety, Repression, Conformity, Neuropsychiatric, Consensus Like, Female-Male, Children, Figure Ground Reversal, Sex Symbol (male and female).
Administration: Group or individual.
Price: Available from publisher.
Time: (50) minutes.
Comments: For research use only; self-administering.
Author: George S. Welsh.
Publisher: Mind Garden, Inc.
Cross References: See T5:2869 (1 reference) and T4:2945 (5 references); for a review by Julien Worland, see 9:1360 (1 reference); see also T3:2613 (4 references), T2:1437 (34 references), and P:287 (24 references); for a review by Harold Borko and an excerpted review by Gordon V. Anderson, see 6:197 (20 references); for information for Barron-Welsh Art Scale, see T3:243 (15 references).

[2241]
Wesman Personnel Classification Test.

Purpose: Developed to measure verbal reasoning and numerical ability.
Population: Grades 10-12 and applicants and employees.
Publication Dates: 1946-1965.
Acronym: PCT.
Scores, 3: Verbal, Numerical, Total.
Administration: Group or individual.
Forms, 3: A, B, C.
Price Data, 2016: $143, includes 25 test booklets, manual, and key for Form A.
Time: 28 minutes.
Author: Alexander G. Wesman.
Publisher: Pearson.
Cross References: See T5:2871 (4 references), T4:2947 (5 references), T3:2614 (4 references), and T2:480 (2 references); for a review by Arthur C. MacKinney, and an excerpted review by Jack C. Merwin, see 7:400 (7 references); see also 5:399 (8 references); for reviews by John C. Flanagan and Erwin K. Taylor, see 4:331 (3 references); for an excerpted review, see 3:253.

[2242]
The Wessex Head Injury Matrix.

Purpose: "Designed to assess and monitor recovery in patients after severe head injury."
Population: Ages 16 and over.
Publication Date: 2000.
Acronym: WHIM.
Scores: Not scored.
Administration: Individual.
Price Data, 2015: £97.50 per complete kit including manual and 25 scoring sheets; £43.50 per 25 scoring sheets; £55 per manual.

Time: Untimed.
Authors: Agnes Shiel, Barbara A. Wilson, Lindsay McLellan, Sandra Horn, and Martin Watson.
Publisher: Pearson Assessment [England].
Cross References: For reviews by Sandra D. Haynes and H. Dennis Kade, see 17:198.

[2243]

Western Aphasia Battery-Revised.

Purpose: "Designed to evaluate a patient's language function following stroke, dementia, or other acquired neurological disorder."
Population: Adults with acquired neurological disorders.
Publication Dates: 1980-2007.
Acronym: WAB-R.
Scores, 16: Spontaneous Speech (Information Content, Fluency/Grammatical Competence and Paraphasias, Total), Auditory Verbal Comprehension (Yes/No Questions, Auditory Word Recognition, Sequential Commands, Total), Repetition, Naming and Word Finding (Object Naming, Word Fluency, Sentence Completion, Responsive Speech, Total), Language Quotient, Cortical Quotient, Aphasia Quotient.
Administration: Individual.
Forms, 3: Part 1, Part 2, Bed-Side Administration.
Price Data, 2015: $352.35 per complete kit (with manipulatives) including examiner's manual (2007, 153 pages), stimulus book, 25 record forms, 25 bedside record forms, Raven's Progressive Matrices test booklet, and manipulatives; $49.40 per 20 record forms (Part 1); $36.80 per 10 record forms (Part 2); $31.15 per 25 bedside record forms; $136.95 per stimulus book; $71.90 per manipulative set; $89.70 per examiner's manual.
Time: (30-45) minutes for full battery; (15) minutes for bedside administration; (45-60) minutes for the Reading, Writing, Apraxia Constructional, Viuospatial, Calculation, and Supplemental Writing and Reading sections administration.
Comments: Utilizes criterion-referenced scores.
Author: Andrew Kertesz.
Publisher: Pearson.
Cross References: For reviews by Shawn K. Acheson and by Andrew S. Davis and W. Holmes Finch, see 18:156; see T5:2873 (74 references) and T4:2949 (33 references); for a review by Francis J. Pirozzolo of an earlier edition, see 9:1362 (1 reference).

[2244]

The Western Personality Inventory.

Purpose: Combines the Manson Evaluation and the Alcadd Test to predict the likelihood of alcoholic addiction or abuse.
Population: Adults.
Publication Dates: 1963–1988.
Acronym: WPI.

Scores, 14: Anxiety, Depressive Fluctuations, Emotional Sensitivity, Resentfulness, Incompleteness, Aloneness, Interpersonal Relations, Total, Regularity of Drinking, Preference for Drinking over Other Activities, Lack of Controlled Drinking, Rationalization of Drinking, Excessive Emotionality, Total.
Administration: Individual or group.
Manual: No manual; use manuals for The Manson Evaluation and The Alcadd Test.
Price Data, 2015: $125 per complete kit including 5 AutoScore test forms, Manson Evaluation Manual, and Alcadd Manual; $59.50 per Manson Evaluation Manual or Alcadd Manual; $50 per 25 AutoScore Forms.
Time: 10 to 20 minutes.
Comments: Combination of The Manson Evaluation (1200) and The Alcadd Test (93).
Author: Morse P. Manson.
Publisher: Western Psychological Services.

[2245]

The WH Question Comprehension Test: Exploring the World of WH Question Comprehension for Students With an Autism Spectrum Disorder.

Purpose: Designed to indicate a student's competence in WH question form comprehension through appropriate match of question form and response.
Population: Ages 3 and up with cognitive impairments.
Publication Dates: 2002-2004.
Scores: 6 areas: Who, What, Where, When, Why, How.
Administration: Individual.
Price Data, 2015: $10 per combination test booklet/manual (2004, 175 pages).
Time: (20-30) minutes.
Comments: Test can be administered in multiple sessions if necessary.
Author: Beverly Vicker.
Publisher: Indiana Resource Center for Autism.
Cross References: For reviews by Francine Conway and Doreen W. Fairbank, see 17:199.

[2246]

What Do You Say?

Purpose: Designed as a self-assessment tool to identify communication style and relate it to two basic types of human interactions: parent-child (McGregor's Theory X) and adult-adult (Theory Y).
Population: Employees.
Publication Dates: 1986–1991.
Scores, 4: Empathic, Critical, Searching, Advising.
Administration: Group or individual.
Price Data, 2016: $59.95; quantity discounts available.
Time: [20] minutes administration; [10] minutes scoring; [30-60] minutes interpretation.

Comments: Self-administered, self-scored.
Author: Training House, Inc.
Publisher: HRD Press, Inc.
Cross References: For reviews by William L. Deaton and Gerald L. Stone, see 12:413.

[2247]

The Whitener Group Industrial Assessments.

Purpose: "Designed to measure an individual's knowledge of competencies related specifically to industrial occupations. These assessments consist of only a written portion; intended for evaluating individuals with a combination of education, training, and work experience." Suggested uses include: selecting skilled workers (worry free); giving promotions based on objective, verifiable standards; providing blueprints for employee development; analyzing job requirements; and developing precise job descriptions, training curriculum, performance analysis charts, objective performance appraisals, valid interview protocol, and career paths.
Population: Industrial and potential industrial employees.
Publication Dates: 1996–2002.
Scores: Duty support scores and total scores are reported for 23 tests: Die Making, Electricity/Electronics, Electrical/Electronics Maintenance, General Industrial/Mechanical, General Maintenance, General Technical Skills, Industrial Maintenance Technician, Instrumentation and Control, Industrial Mechanic, Instrumentation and Electrician Technician, Lead Maintenance, Machine Repair, Maintenance, Maintenance Mechanic, Maintenance and Repair Mechanic, Maintenance Technician, Manufacturing Technician, Master Machine Repair, Mechanical Systems, Mechanical and Fluid Power Maintenance, Mechanical Maintenance, Pipefitter, Toolmaker.
Administration: Group.
Price Data, 2005: $75 per standardized industrial test, online or paper/pencil administration, including instructions for administration, scoring, and reporting services; contact publisher for pricing information on customized assessment services.
Time: (180) minutes per test.
Comments: Previously listed as NOCTI Industrial Assessments.
Authors: National Occupational Competency Testing Institute/The Whitener Group.
Publisher: National Occupational Competency Testing Institute/The Whitener Group.

[2248]

Who Am I?

Purpose: Assesses "a child's readiness for particular types of learning experiences and identifies the levels that children have reached in their understanding and use of conventional symbols and relevant early learning skills."

Population: Students in preschool–Year 2 in Australian school system.
Publication Date: 1999.
Scores, 4: Copying, Symbols, Drawing, Total.
Administration: Group or individual.
Price Data, 2006: 2016: A$62.95 per specimen set including task booklet, assessment manual (36 pages), and administration instructions; A$28.95 per 10 task booklets; A$47.95 per assessment manual; A$10.94 per administration instructions.
Time: (10–20) minutes.
Authors: Marion de Lemos and Brian Doig.
Publisher: Australian Council for Educational Research Ltd. [Australia].
Cross References: For reviews by G. Michael Poteat and Donald L. Stovall, see 15:278.

[2249]

Wide Range Achievement Test—Expanded Edition.

Purpose: An achievement test battery "designed to assess the core curricular domains of reading, mathematics, and oral and written language."
Population: Grades 2–12; Ages 5–24.
Publication Dates: 2001–2002.
Price Data: Available from publisher.
Comments: Designed to complement the WRAT-3.
Author: Gary J. Robertson.
Publisher: Pearson.
　　a) WRAT-EXPANDED GROUP ASSESSMENT (FORM G).
　　Population: Grades 2–12.
　　Scores, 5: Reading (Basic Reading, Reading Comprehension), Mathematics, Nonverbal Reasoning.
　　Administration: Group.
　　Levels, 5: G-1 (Grade 2), G-2 (Grades 3–4), G-3 (Grades 5–6), G-4 (Grades 7–9), G-5 (Grades 10–12).
　　Time: (125–135) minutes.
　　b) WRAT-EXPANDED INDIVIDUAL ASSESSMENT (FORM I).
　　Population: Ages 5–24.
　　Scores, 5: Reading, Mathemaics, Listening Comprehension, Oral Expression, Written Language.
　　Administration: Individual.
　　Time: [30] minutes.
Cross References: For reviews by George Engelhard, Jr., and by Bo Zhang and Cindy M. Walker, see 16:272.

[2250]

Wide Range Achievement Test 4.

Purpose: Designed to "measure the basic academic skills of reading, spelling, and math computation."
Population: Ages 5-94.
Publication Dates: 1940-2006.
Acronym: WRAT4.
Scores, 5: Word Reading, Sentence Comprehension, Spelling, Math Computation, Reading Composite.

Administration: Individual and group.

Levels, 2: Ages 5-7, Ages 8-94.

Forms, 3: Blue, Green, Combined.

Price Data, 2016: $335 per kit including professional manual (2006, 494 pages), 25 blue test/response forms, 25 green test/response forms, 25 blue sentence comprehension response booklets, 25 green sentence comprehension response booklets, set of 2 word reading/spelling cards, set of 3 sentence comprehension cards, and 1 place marker in canvas bag.

Time: (15-45) minutes.

Comments: "The Blue Form and the Green Form can be used interchangeably with comparable results, thus permitting retesting within short periods of time without the potential practice effects that may occur from repeating the same items."

Authors: Gary S. Wilkinson and Gary J. Robertson.

Publisher: Pearson.

Cross References: For reviews by Kathryn E. Hoff and Mark E. Swerdlik and by Darrell L. Sabers and Amy M. Olson, see 18:157; see T5:2879(237 references); for reviews by Linda Mabry and Annie W. Ward of the WRAT3, see 12:414 (111 references); see also T4:2956 (121 references); for reviews by Elaine Clark and Patti L. Harrison, see 10:389 (161 references); for reviews by Paula Matuszek and Philip A. Saigh of an earlier edition, see 9:1364 (103 references); see also T3:2621 (249 references), 8:37 (117 references), and T2:50 (35 references); for reviews by Jack C. Merwin and Robert L. Thorndike of an earlier edition, see 7:36 (49 references); see also 6:27 (15 references); for reviews by Paul Douglas Courtney, Verner M. Sims, and Louis P. Thorpe of the 1946 edition, see 3:21.

[2251]

Wide Range Assessment of Memory and Learning, Second Edition.

Purpose: Designed for use in "clinical assessments of memory including evaluation of immediate and/or delay recall as well as differentiating between verbal, visual or more global memory deficits."

Population: Ages 5–90.

Publication Dates: 1990–2003.

Acronym: WRAML2.

Scores, 25: Verbal Memory (Story Memory, Verbal Learning, Total), Visual Memory (Design Memory, Picture Memory, Total), Attention/Concentration (Finger Windows, Number Letter, Total), General Memory; Optional scores: Working Memory (Verbal Working Memory, Symbolic Working Memory, Total), Verbal Recognition (Story Recognition, Verbal Learning Recognition, Total), Visual Recognition (Design Recognition, Picture Memory Recognition, Total), General Recognition, Sound Symbol, Sentence Memory, Story Memory Recall, Verbal Learning Recall, Sound Symbol Recall.

Administration: Individual.

Price Data, 2016: $615 per introductory kit including administration and technical manual (2003, 245 pages), 25 examiner forms, 25 Picture Memory response forms, 25 Picture Memory Recognition forms, 25 Design Memory response forms, 25 Design Memory Recognition forms, 4 Picture Memory scenes, 5 Design Memory cards, 1 Finger Windows card, 1 Sound Symbol Booklet, and 2 Symbolic Working Memory cards.

Time: [60] minutes.

Authors: David Sheslow and Wayne Adams.

Publisher: Pearson.

Cross References: For reviews by Thomas M. Dunn and Sandra D. Haynes, see 16:273; see also T5:2880 (7 references); for reviews by Richard M. Clark and Frederic J. Medway of a previous edition, see 11:470.

[2252]

Wide Range Assessment of Visual Motor Abilities.

Purpose: A standardized assessment of visual-motor, visual-spatial, and fine motor skills.

Population: Ages 3–17 years.

Publication Date: 1995.

Acronym: WRAVMA.

Scores, 4: Fine Motor, Visual-Spatial, Visual-Motor, Visual-Motor Integration Composite.

Administration: Individual.

Price Data, 2016: $395 per introductory kit including manual (151 pages), 25 drawing forms, 25 visual matching forms, 25 examiner record forms, pegboard and pegs, pencils, markers, and sharpener in a canvas bag.

Time: (15–30) minutes; (5–10) minutes per subtest.

Comments: Best results when "integrated with data from other standardized tests and clinical observations"; test should be interpreted by "those with graduate or equivalent professional training in cognitive assessment."

Authors: Wayne Adams and David Sheslow.

Publisher: Pearson.

Cross References: For reviews by Linda K. Bunker and Keith F. Widaman, see 14:418.

[2253]

Wide Range Intelligence Test.

Purpose: "Designed to measure an individual's cognitive abilities."

Population: Ages 4–85.

Publication Date: 2000.

Acronym: WRIT.

Scores, 7: Verbal (Verbal Analogies, Vocabulary, Total), Visual (Matrices, Diamonds, Total), Total.

Administration: Individual.

Price Data, 2016: $379.25 per kit including test manual, Matrices and Diamonds easel stimulus book, 25 examiner forms, and set of 21 Diamond Chips in canvas bag.

Time: (20–30) minutes.
Authors: Joseph Glutting, Wayne Adams, and David Sheslow.
Publisher: Pearson.
Cross References: For reviews by Terry A. Stinnett and Keith F. Widaman, see 15:279.

[2254]

The Wiesen Test of Mechanical Aptitude.

Purpose: Designed to measure mechanical aptitude for purpose of personnel selection.
Population: Applicants (18 years and older) for jobs requiring mechanical aptitude.
Publication Dates: 1997–1999.
Acronym: WTMA.
Scores, 12: Total Score and 11 research scores: Basic Machines, Movement of Simple and Complex Objects, Center of Gravity and Gravity, Basic Electricity/Electronics, Transfer of Heat, Basic Physical Properties of Matter and Materials, Miscellaneous, Academic, Kitchen Objects, Non-Kitchen Objects, Other Everyday Objects.
Administration: Individual or group.
Price Data, 2015: $276 per introductory kit including manual, 10 reusable item booklets, 25 answer sheets, and 1 scoring key.
Time: 30 minutes.
Comments: A 60-item multiple-choice objective test.
Author: Joel P. Wiesen.
Publisher: Psychological Assessment Resources, Inc.
Cross References: For reviews by John M. Enger and Nambury S. Raju, see 14:419.

[2255]

Wife's or Husband's Marriage Questions.

Purpose: Designed to diagnose and treat marital problems.
Population: Husbands, wives.
Publication Date: 1994-2010.
Administration: Individual or group.
Forms, 2: Wife's Marriage Questions, Husband's Marriage Questions.
Manual: No manual.
Price Data: Available from publisher.
Time: [15-30] minutes.
Author: Allan Roe.
Publisher: Diagnostic Specialists, Inc.

[2256]

Wiig Assessment of Basic Concepts.

Purpose: "Designed to evaluate a child's understanding and use of basic word opposites and related concepts."
Publication Date: 2004.
Acronym: WABC.
Scores, 10: Scores in 7 areas (Color/Shape, Size/Weight/Volume, Distance/Speed/Time, Quantity/Completeness, Location/Direction, Condition/Quality,

Sensation/Emotion/Evaluation), Receptive raw score, Expressive raw score, Total raw score.
Administration: Individual.
Price Data, 2016: $229 per complete kit including manual, Level 1 and Level 2 Storybooks, 50 Level 1 record forms, 50 Level 2 record forms, clipboard with calculator, Puppy Bank reinforcer with 30 Doggy Dog tokens, and tote bag; $38 per 50 Level 1-A Day at the Zoo record forms; $38 per 50 Level 2-A Day at the Park record forms; $45 per manual.
Time: (10-15) minutes.
Author: Elisabeth H. Wiig.
Publisher: PRO-ED.
   a) LEVEL 1: A DAY AT THE ZOO.
   Population: Ages 2-6 to 5-11 years.
   b) LEVEL 2: A DAY AT THE PARK.
   Population: Ages 5-0 to 7-11 years.
Cross References: For reviews by Carol M. McGregor and Thomas McKnight, see 17:200.

[2257]

Winslow Profiles.

Purpose: Designed to measure personality characteristics to aid in applicant selection, employee development, personal coaching and individual self-improvement.
Publication Dates: 1968-2012.
Administration: Individual or group.
Foreign Language Editions: Available in Spanish, French, and German.
Time: (30-45) minutes.
Authors: John Stahl, Andria Brown, Richard Sudweeks, Joseph Olsen, and Scott Thayn (technical manuals).
Publisher: Winslow Research Institute.
   a) WINSLOW DYNAMICS PROFILE.
   Purpose: Measures 24 personality characteristics to aid in applicant selection, employee development, personal coaching, and self-improvement "to assist individuals in achieving career success and personal contentment."
   Population: Applicants for positions, current employees, coaching program participants.
   Scores: Assessment Validity (Objectivity, Accuracy), Interpersonal Traits (Sociability, Recognition, Conscientiousness, Exhibition, Trust, Nurturance); Organizational Traits (Alertness, Structure, Order, Flexibility, Creativity, Responsibility); Dedication Traits (Ambition, Endurance, Assertiveness, Boldness, Coachability, Leadership); Self-Control Traits (Self-Confidence, Composure, Tough-Mindedness, Autonomy, Contentment, Control).
   Administration: Individual or group.
   Price Data, 2016: Fees range from $195-$145 per report depending on quantity purchased. Fee includes the Assessment Profile, free re-takes (when the participant's answers to the Profile are invalid), Participant's Report, Manager's Report, Executive Report, Position Compatibility Summary Report, Group Profiles, and Sub-group Profiles.
   Time: (45) minutes or less.
   Comments: Previously listed as Personal Dynamics Profile; online administration and delivery or reports on confidential website provided free of charge to clients.

Authors: Denis Waitley, Lem Burnham, Charles C. Kaufman, J. Michael Priddy, Joan L. Francis, Thomas A. Tutko, Bruce C. Ogilvie, and Leland P. Lyon.

b) WINSLOW DISCOVERY PROFILE.

Purpose: Measures 16 personality characteristics to assist in hiring the best available applicants for many hourly positions in organizations and for personnel development.

Population: Applicants for hourly positions, current employees, coaching program participants.

Scores: Assessment Validity (Objectivity, Accuracy), Interpersonal Traits (Sociability, Recognition, Conscientiousness, Exhibition, Trust, Nurturance); Organizational Traits (Alertness, Structure, Order, Flexibility, Creativity, Responsibility); Dedication Traits (Ambition, Endurance, Assertiveness, Boldness, Coachability, Leadership); Self-Control Traits (Self-Confidence, Composure, Tough-Mindedness, Autonomy, Contentment, Control).

Administration: Individual or group.

Price Data, 2016: $75 to $95 per report depending on quantity purchased. Fee includes the Assessment Profile, free re-takes (when the participant's answers to the Profile are invalid), Participant's Report, Manager's Report, Executive Report, Position Compatibility Summary Report, Group Profiles, and Sub-group Profiles.

Time: (30) minutes.

Comments: Test is administered and results are immediately available online.

Author: Denis Waitley, Lem Burnham, Charles C. Kaufman, J. Michael Priddy, Linda G. Griggs, Joan L. Francis, Thomas A. Tutko, Leland P. Lyon, and Bruce C. Ogilvie.

c) WINSLOW SUCCESS PROFILE.

Purpose: A personality assessment instrument designed to measure 11 personality characteristics of individuals; can be utilized by organizations in hiring the best available applicants for minimum hourly positions and developing current employees in those positions to their potential.

Population: Current personnel and potential employees.

Scores: Assessment Validity (Objectivity, Accuracy), Competitiveness Traits (Drive, Assertiveness, Determination, Leadership), Self-Control Traits (Self-Confidence, Emotional Control, Mental Toughness), Dedication Traits (Coachability, Conscientiousness, Responsibility, Trust), Composite Traits (Competitiveness, Self-Control, Dedication).

Price Data, 2016: Fee per participant ranges from $25-49 depending on quantity of Profile Passwords purchased; fee includes assessment profile, free retakes (when participant's answers are invalid) Participant's Report, Manager's Report, Executive Report, PCS Summary Forms, Group Profiles, and Subgroup Profiles.

Time: (30) minutes or less.

Comments: Previously listed as Personal Success Profile; short version of comprehensive Winslow Dynamics Profile; derivation of Athletic Success Profile; online administration and delivery of reports.

Authors: Denis Waitley, Lem Burnham, Charles C. Kaufman, J. Michael Priddy, Linda G. Griggs, Joan L. Francis, Thomas A. Tutko, Leland P. Lyon, and Bruce C. Ogilvie.

Cross References: For reviews by Frederick T. L. Leong and Dzenana Husremovic and by Steven V. Rouse, see 19:178.

[2258]
Wisconsin Card Sorting Test.

Purpose: "Developed … as a measure of abstract reasoning among normal adult populations" and "has increasingly been employed as a clinical neuropsychological instrument."

Population: Ages 6.5–89.

Publication Dates: 1981–1993.

Acronym: WCST.

Scores, 11: Number of Trials Administered, Total Number Correct, Total Number of Errors, Perseverative Responses, Perseverative Errors, Nonperseverative Errors, Conceptual Level Responses, Number of Categories Completed, Trials to Complete First Category, Failure to Maintain Set, Learning to Learn.

Administration: Individual.

Price Data, 2015: $380 per introductory kit including manual (1993, 234 pages), 2 decks of cards, and 50 record booklets; $700 per WCST Computer Version 4 Research Edition software (CD-ROM) with on-screen help and quick start guide, 1 set of keytops, and 25 record forms; $515 per WCST Computer Version 4 Scoring Program software (CD-ROM) with on-screen help and quick start guide, and 25 record forms.

Time: (20–30) minutes.

Comments: Additional materials necessary for testing include a pen or pencil and a clipboard.

Authors: Robert K. Heaton, Gordon J. Chelune, Jack L. Talley, Gary G. Kay, and Glenn Curtiss.

Publisher: Psychological Assessment Resources, Inc.

Cross References: For reviews by Elaine Clark and Deborah D. Roman, see 14:420; see also T5:2892 (309 references) and T4:2967 (96 references); for reviews by Byron Egeland and Robert P. Markley of an earlier edition, see 9:1372 (11 references).

[2259]
Wisconsin Card Sorting Test—64 Card Version.

Purpose: "Developed … as a measure of abstract reasoning among normal adult populations" and "has increasingly been employed as a clinical neuropsychological instrument."

Population: Ages 6.5–89.

Publication Dates: 1981–2000.

Acronym: WCST-64.

Scores, 10: Total Number Correct, Total Number of Errors, Perseverative Responses, Perseverative Errors, Nonperseverative Errors, Conceptual Level Responses, Number of Categories Completed, Trials to Complete First Category, Failure to Maintain Set, Learning to Learn.

Administration: Individual.

Price Data, 2015: $296 per introductory kit including manual (1993, 234 pages), 50 record booklets, and 1 card deck; $595 per Computer Version 2 Research Edition software (CD-ROM) with on-screen help and quick start guide, 25 record forms, and 1 set of keytops; $375 per Computer Version 2 Scoring Program software (CD-ROM) with on-screen help and quick start guide, and 25 record forms.

Time: Untimed.

Comments: Abbreviated form of the standard 128-card version of the Wisconsin Card Sorting Test (2258).

Authors: Susan K. Kongs, Laetitia L. Thompson, Grant L. Iverson, and Robert K. Heaton.

Publisher: Psychological Assessment Resources, Inc.

Cross References: For a review by Michael S. Trevisan, see 15:280; for information on the Wisconsin Card Sorting Test, Revised and Expanded, see T5:2892 (309 references) and T4:2967 (96 references); for reviews by Byron Egeland and Robert P. Markley of an earlier edition, see 9:1372 (11 references).

[2260]

The Wolfe Computer Operator Aptitude Test.

Purpose: Used "to evaluate a candidate's potential for work as a computer operator."

Population: Applicants for computer training or employment.

Publication Dates: 1979–1982.

Acronym: WCOAT.

Scores: Total score only.

Administration: Group.

Price Data: Available from publisher.

Foreign Language Edition: Available in French.

Time: (90) minutes.

Comments: Report provided on each candidate.

Author: Jack M. Wolfe.

Publisher: Rose Wolfe Family Partnership LLP [Canada].

[2261]

Wolfe-Spence Programming Aptitude Test.

Purpose: Designed as a screening test to identify persons who should receive further consideration for hiring or training for programming.

Population: Applicants in computer programming.

Publication Date: 1970.

Scores: Total score and percentile.

Administration: Group.

Price Data: Available from publisher.

Time: (120) minutes.

Authors: Jack M. Wolfe and Richard J. Spence.

Publisher: Rose Wolfe Family Partnership LLP [Canada].

[2262]

Wonderlic Basic Skills Test.

Purpose: Designed to measure individual language and math skills; intended to serve in the selection and placement of individuals into suitable jobs that match identified skills, and the selection and placement of individuals into appropriate educational programs.

Population: High school students and adults.

Publication Dates: 1994–2003.

Acronym: WBST.

Scores, 24: Test of Verbal Skills (Word Knowledge, Sentence Construction, Information Retrieval, Verbal GED Level 1, Verbal GED Level 2, Verbal GED Level 3, Verbal GED Level Achieved, Verbal Grade Level Equivalent, Verbal Total), Test of Quantitative Skills (Explicit, Applied, Interpretive, Quantitative GED Level 1, Quantitative GED Level 2, Quantitative GED Level 3, Quantitative GED Level Achieved, Quantitative Grade Level Equivalent, Quantitative Total), Skills Composite (Skills Composite GED Level 1, Skills Composite GED Level 2, Skills Composite GED Level 3, Skills Composite GED Level Achieved, Skills Composite Grade Level Equivalent, Total Skills Composite).

Subtests, 2: Test of Verbal Skills, Test of Quantitative Skills.

Administration: Group or individual.

Forms: 2 equivalent forms for each subtest: VS-1, VS-2 for Test of Verbal Skills; QS-1, QS-2 for Test of Quantitative Skills.

Price Data: Available from publisher.

Time: (20) minutes for each subtest.

Comments: Designed for use in both education and business environments. The Verbal and Quantitative Skills subtests may be administered together or separately, and are available as separate booklets; an online version is available for administration in proctored settings. The WBST has been approved by the U.S. Department of Education for use in qualifying postsecondary students for Title IV Federal financial assistance. Schools using the WBST for this purpose must follow special procedures and guidelines published in the WBST User's Manual for Ability-to-Benefit Testing.

Authors: Eliot R. Long, Victor S. Artese, and Winifred L. Clonts.

Publisher: Wonderlic, Inc.

Cross References: For reviews by Thomas F. Donlon and Gerald S. Hanna, see 13:362.

[2263]

Wonderlic Personnel Test and Scholastic Level Exam.

Purpose: Designed for use by businesses and educational institutions to measure general cognitive ability; designed to determine whether an individual possesses the cognitive ability that is necessary to learn, be trained quickly, and solve problems at the level of complexity that is required.

Population: Ages 15 and up.

Publication Dates: 1937–2005.

Acronym: WPT and SLE.

Scores: Total score only.

Administration: Individual or group.

Forms: 6 alternate forms of the WPT, and 4 alternate forms of the SLE.

Price Data: Available from publisher.

Foreign Language and Special Editions: Chinese, French, Korean, Puerto Rican, Spanish, Swedish, U.K., Metric, large print, braille, and audio editions.

Time: 12 minutes.

Comments: Available online in proctored settings.

Author: Wonderlic, Inc.

Publisher: Wonderlic, Inc.

Cross References: For reviews by Kurt F. Geisinger and Gregory Schraw, see 14:421; see also T5:2899 (20 references) and T4:2972 (11 references); for a review by Marcia J. Belcher of an earlier edition, see 11:475 (10 references); for reviews by Frank L. Schmidt and Lyle F. Schoenfeldt, see 9:1385 (8 references); see also T3:2638 (24 references), and T2:482 (10 references); for reviews by Robert C. Droege and John P. Foley, Jr., see 7:401 (28 references); for reviews by N. M. Downie and Marvin D. Dunnette, see 6:513 (17 references); see also 5:400 (59 references); for reviews by H. E. Brogden, Charles D. Flory, and Irving Lorge, see 3:269 (7 references); see also 2:1415 (2 references).

[2264]
Woodcock-Johnson® IV.

Purpose: Designed as a set of "norm-referenced tests for measuring intellectual abilities, academic achievement, and oral language abilities."

Population: Ages 2-90+ years.

Publication Dates: 1977-2014.

Acronym: WJ IV®.

Administration: Individual.

Parts, 3: Tests of Achievement, Tests of Cognitive Abilities, Tests of Oral Language.

Price Data, 2015: $2,264 per Complete Battery Plus (Achievement Form A or Form B, Cognitive Abilities, Oral Language) with case; $1,912.40 per Complete Kit (Achievement Form A, Cognitive Abilities) with case; $1,911.90 per Complete Kit (Achievement Form B, Cognitive Abilities) with case; $2,046.60 per Complete Achievement Battery (Forms A, B, and C) with case; $943.65 per Achievement Battery (Form A, B, or C) with case; $1,315.60 per Cognitive Battery with case; $685.25 per Oral Language kit with case; $1,487.20 per Oral Language with Cognitive Battery with case; $1,292.70 per Oral Language with Achievement (Form A) with case; $158.85 per 25 Cognitive Abilities test records with individual score reports; $158.85 per 25 Achievement standard and extended test records and response books with individual score reports (Form A, B, or C); $82.15 per 25 Oral Language test records with individual score reports; $61.35 per 25 Cognitive Abilities response books; $61.35 per Achievement standard and extended response books (Form A, B, or C).

Comments: Cognitive, Achievement, and Oral Language batteries are co-normed and may be used separately or together; tests within each battery may be administered separately or in combinations. Online scoring and reporting available.

Authors: Frederick A. Schrank (tests, online scoring and reporting program), Kevin S. McGrew (tests), Nancy Mather (tests and examiner's manuals), Barbara J. Wendling (examiner's manuals), and David Dailey (online scoring and reporting program).

Publisher: Houghton Mifflin Harcourt.

a) TESTS OF ACHIEVEMENT.

Acronym: WJ IV ACH.

Scores, 42: 11 Standard Battery test scores: Letter Word Identification, Applied Problems, Spelling, Passage Comprehension, Calculation, Writing Samples, Word Attack, Oral Reading, Sentence Reading Fluency, Math Facts Fluency, Sentence Writing Fluency; 9 Extended Battery test scores: Reading Recall, Number Matrices, Editing, Word Reading Fluency, Spelling of Sounds, Reading Vocabulary, Science, Social Studies, Humanities; 22 cluster scores: Reading, Broad Reading, Basic Reading Skills, Reading Comprehension, Reading Comprehension–Extended, Reading Fluency, Reading Rate, Mathematics, Broad Mathematics, Math Calculation Skills, Math Problem Solving, Written Language, Broad Written Language, Basic Writing Skills, Written Expression, Brief Achievement, Broad Achievement, Academic Skills, Academic Fluency, Academic Applications, Academic Knowledge, Phoneme-Grapheme Knowledge.

Forms: Standard Battery has 3 parallel forms: A, B, C.

Time: (40) minutes for core set of 6 tests in Standard Battery; (15-20) minutes for Writing Samples test; (5-10) minutes each for remaining tests.

b) TESTS OF COGNITIVE ABILITIES:

Acronym: WJ IV COG.

Scores, 35: 10 Standard Battery test scores: Oral Vocabulary, Number Series, Verbal Attention, Letter-Pattern Matching, Phonological Processing, Story Recall, Visualization, General Information, Concept Formation, Numbers Reversed; 8 Extended Battery test scores: Number-Pattern Matching, Nonword Repetition, Visual-Auditory Learning, Picture Recognition, Analysis-Synthesis, Object-Number Sequencing, Pair Cancellation, Memory for Words; 4 ability scores: General Intellectual Ability, Gf-Gc Composite, Brief Intellectual Ability, Scholastic Aptitudes (Reading Aptitude, Math Aptitude, Writing Aptitude); 7 broad ability clusters: Comprehension-Knowledge, Fluid Reasoning, Short-Term Working Memory, Cognitive Processing Speed, Auditory Processing, Long-Term Retrieval, Visual Processing; 6 narrow ability clusters: Perceptual Speed, Quantitative Reasoning, Auditory Memory Span, Number Facility, Vocabulary, Cognitive Efficiency.

Time: (35) minutes for first 7 tests in Standard Battery; (5) minutes for each additional test.

c) TESTS OF ORAL LANGUAGE:

Acronym: WJ IV OL.

Scores, 24: 12 test scores: Picture Vocabulary, Oral Comprehension, Segmentation, Rapid Picture Naming, Sentence Repetition, Understanding Directions, Sound Blending, Retrieval Fluency, Sound Awareness, Vocabulario sobre dibujos, Comprensión oral, Comprensión de indicaciones; 9 cluster scores: Oral Language, Broad Oral Language, Oral Expression, Listening Comprehension,

Phonetic Coding, Speed of Lexical Access, Lenguaje oral, Amplio lenguaje oral, Comprensión auditiva; 3 additional cluster scores can be derived by combining Oral Language tests with certain tests from the Cognitive Abilities battery: Vocabulary, Comprehension-Knowledge—Extended, Auditory Memory Span.

Time: (40) minutes for first 8 tests.

Comments: The 3 Spanish clusters are parallel to 3 of the English clusters and can be used to compare the examinee's proficiency in English and Spanish.

Cross References: Reviews are scheduled for *The Twentieth Mental Measurements Yearbook*. For reviews by Gregory J. Cizek and Jonathan Sandoval of the third edition, see 15:281; see T5:2901 (140 references); for reviews by Jack A. Cummings and by Steven W. Lee and Elaine Flory Stefany of the 1991 edition, see 12:415 (56 references); see also T4:2973 (90 references); for reviews by Jack A. Cummings and Alan S. Kaufman of the 1977 edition, see 9:1387 (6 references); see also T3:2639 (3 references).

[2265]

Woodcock-Johnson® IV Tests of Early Cognitive and Academic Development.

Purpose: Designed to "identify emergent cognitive abilities and early academic skills ... for [use in] determining the presence and severity of cognitive delay and for identifying relative strengths and weaknesses ... that may be relevant to early interventions."

Population: Children ages 2-6 through 7-11; may be used with children ages 8 to 9 years who have a cognitive developmental delay.

Publication Date: 2015.

Acronym: ECAD.

Scores, 13: 10 test scores and 3 cluster scores: General Intellectual Ability–Early Development (Memory for Names, Sound Blending, Picture Vocabulary, Verbal Analogies, Visual Closure, Sentence Repetition, Rapid Picture Naming), Early Academic Skills (Letter-Word Identification, Number Sense, Writing), Expressive Language (Picture Vocabulary, Sentence Repetition).

Administration: Individual.

Price Data, 2015: $795 per test kit including test book, manual (164 pages), 25 test records and response worksheets with individual score reports, and audio CD; $82.15 per 25 test records and response worksheets with individual score reports.

Time: (50) minutes for entire battery.

Comments: Of the 10 tests in the battery, 4 are unique to the ECAD, and 6 are alternate forms of tests included in the Woodcock-Johnson® IV Tests of Oral Language (4) and Tests of Achievement (2); online scoring and reporting available.

Authors: Frederick A. Schrank (test, manual, online scoring and reporting program), Kevin S. McGrew (test, manual), Nancy Mather (test, manual), Barbara J. Wendling (manual), Erica M. LaForte (manual), and David Dailey (online scoring and reporting program).

Publisher: Houghton Mifflin Harcourt.

Cross References: Reviews are scheduled for *The Twentieth Mental Measurements Yearbook*.

[2266]

Woodcock-Johnson III® Diagnostic Reading Battery.

Purpose: "Measures important dimensions of phonological awareness, phonics knowledge, reading achievement, and related oral language abilities."

Population: Ages 2–80+.

Publication Date: 2004.

Acronym: WJ III DRB.

Scores, 8: Basic Reading Skills, Reading Comprehension, Phonics Knowledge, Phonemic Awareness, Oral Language Comprehension, Brief Reading, Broad Reading, Total Reading.

Subtests, 10: Letter-Word Identification, Passage Comprehension, Word Attack, Reading Vocabulary, Reading Fluency, Spelling of Sounds, Sound Awareness, Sound Blending, Oral Vocabulary, Oral Comprehension.

Administration: Individual.

Price Data, 2015: $441.85 per kit including carrying case, test book, comprehensive manual (197 pages), audio CD package, software package, and 25 test records and subject response booklets; $94.65 per 25 test records and subject response booklets; $97.35 per comprehensive manual; $211.45 per scoring and reporting program.

Time: (50-60) minutes.

Comments: Composed of 8 tests from the WJ III Tests of Achievement and 2 tests from the WJ III Tests of Cognitive Abilities (see Woodcock-Johnson III; T8:2952); includes software for scoring and printing reports.

Authors: Fredrick A. Schrank, Nancy Mather, and Richard W. Woodcock.

Publisher: Houghton Mifflin Harcourt.

Cross References: For reviews by Connie England and by Howard Margolis and Antonia D'Onofrio, see 17:201.

[2267]

Woodcock-Muñoz™ Language Survey–Revised Normative Update.

Purpose: Designed "to provide a broad sampling of proficiency in oral language, language comprehension, reading, and writing."

Population: Ages 2–90+.

Publication Dates: 1993-2010.

Acronym: WMLS-R NU.

Scores, 7: Picture Vocabulary, Verbal Analogies, Letter Word Identification, Dictation, Understanding Directions, Story Recall, Passage Comprehension.

Administration: Individual.

Forms, 3: English A, English B, Spanish.

Price Data, 2015: $516 per English complete kit including test book, 25 test records and 25 dictation worksheets, manual (174 pages), audio CD, and scoring and reporting software; $579.35 per English complete kit with instructional interventions program; $516 per Spanish complete kit including test book, 25 test records and 25 dictation worksheets, manual, audio CD, and scoring and reporting software; $601.90 per Spanish complete kit with instructional interventions program; $65 per 25 test records and 25 dictation worksheets (English or Spanish); $38.20 per audio CD; $250.55 per scoring and reporting software.

Foreign Language Edition: Available in Spanish.

Time: (45-55) minutes for complete; (25) minutes for screening.

Comments: Software available for scoring and generating narrative reports for any combination of tests.

Authors: Richard W. Woodcock, Ana F. Muñoz-Sandoval, Mary L. Ruef, and Criselda G. Alvarado; Fredrick A. Schrank, Criselda G. Alvarado, Barbara J. Wendling, and David E. H. Dailey (Normative Update interpretive supplement and technical supplement).

Publisher: Houghton Mifflin Harcourt.

Cross References: For reviews by James Dean Brown and Salvador Hector Ochoa of the 2005 revision, see 17:202; for reviews by Linda Crocker and Chi-Wen Kao of an earlier edition, see 13:364.

[2268]

Woodcock Reading Mastery Tests, Third Edition.

Purpose: Designed "to measure reading readiness and reading achievement."

Population: Pre-kindergarten through Grade 12; ages 4-6 through 79-11.

Publication Dates: 1973-2011.

Acronym: WRMT-III.

Scores: 9 individual test scores: Letter Identification, Phonological Awareness, Rapid Automatic Naming, Word Identification, Word Attack, Listening Comprehension, Word Comprehension, Passage Comprehension, Oral Reading Fluency; 4 cluster scores: Readiness, Basic Skills, Reading Comprehension, Total Reading.

Administration: Individual.

Forms, 2: A, B.

Price Data, 2016: $683.70 per Form A and B combined kit including administration manual (2011, 685 pages), 1 set Rapid Automatic Naming Cards, record forms (25 Form A and 25 Form B), Oral Reading Fluency forms (25 Form A and 25 Form B), Form A stimulus book with audio CD, and Form B Stimulus Book with audio CD in carrying case; $425.50 per Form A or Form B kit; $65.70 per 25 record forms (A or B); $33.15 per 25 Oral Reading Fluency forms (A or B); $165 per administration manual.

Time: (15-45) minutes for complete battery.

Comments: Tests may be administered individually or in combination.

Author: Richard W. Woodcock.

Publisher: Pearson.

    a) LETTER IDENTIFICATION.
    Population: Pre-kindergarten through Grade 1.
    Time: (1) minute.
    b) PHONOLOGICAL AWARENESS.
    Population: Pre-kindergarten through Grade 2.
    Time: (9) minutes.
    c) RAPID AUTOMATIC NAMING.
    Population: Pre-kindergarten through Grade 2.
    Time: (4) minutes.
    d) WORD IDENTIFICATION.
    Population: Grade 1 through age 79:11.
    Time: (2) minutes.
    e) WORD ATTACK.
    Population: Grade 1 through age 79:11.
    Time: (2) minutes.
    f) LISTENING COMPREHENSION.
    Population: Grade 1 through age 79:11.
    Time: (12) minutes.
    g) WORD COMPREHENSION.
    Population: Grade 1 through age 79:11.
    Time: (10) minutes.
    h) PASSAGE COMPREHENSION.
    Population: Grade 1 through age 79:11.
    Time: (7) minutes.
    i) ORAL READING FLUENCY.
    Population: Grade 1 through age 79:11.
    Time: (4) minutes.

Cross References: For reviews by Bethany Brunsman and Tawnya Meadows, see 19:179; for reviews by Linda Crocker and Mildred Murray-Ward of the 1998 normative update, see 14:423; see also T5:2905 (123 references) and T4:2976 (34 references); for reviews by Robert B. Cooter, Jr. and Richard M. Jaeger of an earlier edition, see 10:391 (38 references); see also T3:2641 (17 references); for reviews by Carol Anne Dwyer and J. Jaap Tuinman, and excerpted reviews by Alex Bannatyne, Richard L. Allington, Cherry Houck (with Larry A. Harris), and by Barton B. Proger of the 1973 edition, see 8:779 (7 references).

[2269]

Word Fluency.

Purpose: Measures ability to produce appropriate words rapidly for fluency in verbal expression.

Population: Positions requiring sharp verbal communication skills.

Publication Dates: 1959–1961.

Scores: Total score only.

Administration: Individual or group.

Price Data: Available from publisher.

Time: 10 minutes.

Author: Human Resources Center, The University of Chicago.

Publisher: General Dynamics Information Technology.

Cross References: See T5:2907 (9 references), T4:2979 (6 references), T3:2645 (1 reference), and T2:594 (2 references); for a review by James E. Kennedy, see 6:562.

[2270]

Word Identification and Spelling Test.

Purpose: Designed to "assess a student's fundamental literacy skills."
Population: Ages 7.0–18.11.
Publication Date: 2004.
Acronym: WIST.
Scores, 4: Word Identification, Spelling, Sound-Symbol Knowledge, Fundamental Literacy Ability Index.
Administration: Individual.
Levels, 2: Elementary, Secondary.
Price Data, 2015: $280 per complete kit including examiner's manual (142 pages), 25 Elementary examiner record booklets, 25 Secondary examiner record booklets, 50 Spelling response forms, word card-Regular Words, word card-Irregular Words, word card-Letter/Pseudo Words, Elementary Spelling card, Secondary Spelling card, and Irregular Spelling card; $79 per examiner's manual; $48 per 25 examiner's record booklets (Elementary or Secondary); $20 per 50 Spelling response forms; $20 per word card (Regular, Irregular, or Letter/Pseudo Words); $20 per Spelling card (Elementary or Secondary).
Time: (40) minutes.
Authors: Barbara A. Wilson and Rebecca H. Felton.
Publisher: PRO-ED.
Cross References: For reviews by W. Joel Schneider and Kathryn E. Hoff and by John T. Willse, see 16:276.

[2271]

Word Recognition and Phonic Skills.

Purpose: "Designed to give the teacher two assessments of a child's word recognition ability."
Population: Ages 5.0 to 8.6.
Publication Date: 1994.
Acronym: WRaPS.
Scores: Word Recognition.
Administration: Group.
Price Data: Available from publisher.
Time: (30) minutes.
Comments: The test publisher has indicated there is a newer edition of this test; description will be updated when complete test materials are received.
Authors: Clifford Carver and David Moseley.
Publisher: Hodder Education [United Kingdom].
Cross References: For reviews by Robert G. Harrington and Joyce R. McLarty, see 14:425; see also T5:2910 (1 reference).

[2272]

The WORD Test 3 Elementary.

Purpose: Designed to assess expressive vocabulary and semantics.
Population: Children ages 6 and older.
Publication Dates: 1981-2014.
Scores, 7: Associations, Synonyms, Semantic Absurdities, Antonyms, Definitions, Flexible Word Use, Total.

Administration: Individual.
Price Data, 2016: $159.95 per complete kit including examiner's manual (2014, 197 pages) and 20 test forms; $41.95 per 20 forms.
Time: (30) minutes.
Authors: Linda Bowers, Rosemary Huisingh, Carolyn LoGiudice, and Jane Orman.
Publisher: PRO-ED.
Cross References: For a review by Darrell L. Sabers and Huaping Sun of the second edition, see 17:203; see also T5:2911 (6 references) and T4:2983 (2 references); for reviews by Mavis Donahue and Nambury S. Raju of the original edition, see 9:1393.

[2273]

Wordchains: A Word Reading Test for All Ages.

Purpose: Designed to "screen for specific learning difficulties" and to help teachers "identify individual pupils with poor reading skills."
Population: Ages 7 and over.
Publication Date: 1999.
Scores, 2: Letterchains, Wordchains.
Administration: Individual or group.
Price Data, 2016: £50 per teacher's guide; £30 per 10 student booklets.
Time: (15) minutes.
Author: Louise Miller Guron.
Publisher: GL Assessment [England].
Cross References: For reviews by Colin Cooper and Steven R. Shaw, see 16:278.

[2274]

Work Accident Likelihood Assessment.

Purpose: Designed to assess "how risky the test-taker's decisions are, whether she/he takes unnecessary changes, and how likely she/he is to have an accident."
Population: Under age 17 through adult.
Publication Date: 2011.
Acronym: WALA.
Scores, 7: Overall Results, Sensation-Seeking, Harm-Avoidance, Conscientiousness, Attitudes Towards Safety, Attentiveness, Responsibility.
Administration: Individual.
Price Data: Available from publisher.
Time: (30) minutes.
Comments: Self-administered online assessment. The test publisher provides clients with information about the methods and theoretical basis used in the development of the test as well as benchmarks for relevant industries and racial/ethnic group comparison data.
Author: PsychTests AIM, Inc.
Publisher: PsychTests AIM, Inc. [Canada].
Cross References: For reviews by Bert A. Goldman and Ronald S. Landis, see 19:180.

[2275]

Work Aspect Preference Scale.

Purpose: "Constructed to assess the qualities of work that individuals consider important to them."
Population: Grades 10–12 and college and adults.
Publication Dates: 1983-1999.
Acronym: WAPS.
Scores: 13 scales: Independence, Co-Workers, Self-Development, Creativity, Money, Life Style, Prestige, Altruism, Security, Management, Detachment, Physical Activity, Surroundings, plus 3 second order dimensions: On-Work Orientation, Human/Personal Concern, Freedom.
Administration: Group.
Price Data, 2005: A$2.50 per question/answer booklet; $1.05 per profile; $75.60 per manual (41 pages).
Time: (10-20) minutes.
Author: Robert Pryor.
Publisher: Australian Council for Educational Research Ltd. [Australia; Efforts to obtain updated information from the test publisher were unsuccessful. An updated edition of this test appears on the test publisher's website].
Cross References: See T5:2915 (8 references) and T4:2987 (1 reference).

[2276]

Work Attitudes Questionnaire (Version for Research).

Purpose: "Designed to differentiate the 'workaholic' or the Type A personality from the highly committed worker."
Population: Managers.
Publication Dates: 1980–1981.
Acronym: WAQ.
Scores, 3: Work Commitment, Psychological Health, Total.
Administration: Group.
Price Data: Available at no charge from test publisher.
Time: Administration time not reported.
Authors: Maxene S. Doty and Nancy E. Betz.
Publisher: Nancy E. Betz, Ph.D.
Cross References: For a review by Mary L. Tenopyr, see 9:1395.

[2277]

Work Engagement Profile.

Purpose: Designed to measure "intrinsic rewards and… work engagement."
Population: Employees.
Publication Dates: 1993-2009.
Acronym: WEP.
Scores, 4: Sense of Meaningfulness, Sense of Choice, Sense of Competence, Sense of Progress.
Administration: Individual.
Price Data, 2016: $18.50 per Work Engagement Profile including self-scorable assessment and interpretive information booklet; $175 per 10 copies of Work Engagement Profile including self-scorable assessments and interpretive information booklets; $18.50 per Work Engagement Profile Interpretive Report; $29.00 Work Engagement Profile User's Guide.
Time: (12) minutes.
Comments: Earlier versions were entitled Empowerment Inventory and Profile of Intrinsic Motivation.
Authors: Kenneth W. Thomas and Walter G. Tymon, Jr.
Publisher: CPP, Inc.
Cross References: For reviews by Gary J. Dean and Julia Y. Porter, see 19:181; for reviews by Leslie Eastman Lukin and Patricia Schoenrade of the Empowerment Inventory, see 13:119.

[2278]

Work Environment Scale [Second Edition Manual].

Purpose: Developed to "measure the social environment of different types of work settings."
Population: Employees and supervisors.
Publication Dates: 1974-1986.
Acronym: WES.
Scores, 10 in 3 dimension: Relationship (Involvement, Peer Cohesion, Supervisor Support), Personal Growth (Autonomy, Task Orientation, Work Pressure), System Maintenance and System Change (Clarity, Control, Innovation, Physical Comfort).
Administration: Group.
Forms, 3: Real (R), Ideal (I), Expected (E).
Price Data, 2015: $50 per manual, including review-only copy of form; $15 per Individual Report; $15 per Report About Me; $250 per Group Report; $2 per Remote Online Survey License or License to Reproduce (minimum 50); $10 user's guide.
Foreign Language Edition: Translated materials available in Arabic, Chinese (Mandarin), Dutch, Estonian, French, German, Hindi, Indonesian, Italian, Japanese, Polish, Portuguese, and Spanish.
Time: [25-30] minutes.
Comments: A part of the Social Climate Scales.
Authors: Rudolf H. Moos and Paul N. Insel (tests).
Publisher: Mind Garden, Inc.
Cross References: See T5:2917 (5 references); for reviews by Ralph O. Mueller and Eugene P. Sheehan, see 12:417 (6 references); see also T4:2989 (19 references); for a review by Rabindra N. Kanungo, see 9:1398 (1 reference); see also T3:2652 (2 references) and 8:713 (3 references). For a review of the Social Climate Scales, see 8:681.

[2279]

The Work Experience Survey.

Purpose: Designed as a "structured interview protocol for identifying barriers (and possible solutions) to career maintenance" for a disabled person.

Population: "Individuals with disabilities who are either employed or about to begin employment."
Publication Date: 1995.
Acronym: WES.
Scores: Not scored.
Administration: Individual.
Price Data: Available as free download from Educational Resources Information Center (ERIC) database.
Time: (30–60) minutes.
Comments: Administered in a face-to-face or telephone interview.
Authors: Richard T. Roessler (survey and manual), Cheryl A. Reed (manual), and Phillip D. Rumrill (manual).
Publisher: The National Center on Employment & Disability.
Cross References: For reviews by Albert M. Bugaj and Lawrence H. Cross, see 14:426.

[2280]

Work Integrity Test.

Purpose: Designed to assess "potential for dishonest behavior in the work environment."
Population: Under age 17 through adult.
Publication Date: 2011.
Acronym: WINT.
Scores, 5: Overall Results, Lenient Attitude Towards Dishonest Behavior, Perceived Frequency of Dishonest Behavior, Rationalizing of Dishonest Behavior, Self-Reported Dishonesty.
Administration: Individual.
Price Data: Available from publisher.
Time: (30) minutes.
Comments: Self-administered online assessment. The test publisher provides clients with information about the methods and theoretical basis used in the development of the test as well as benchmarks for relevant industries and racial/ethnic group comparison data.
Author: PsychTests AIM, Inc.
Publisher: PsychTests AIM, Inc. [Canada]
Cross References: For reviews by Britton D. Miles and David J. Pittenger, see 19:182.

[2281]

Work Keys Assessments.

Purpose: A job skills assessment system that measures "real world" skills.
Population: Grades 9 to adult.
Publication Dates: 1992–1994.
Administration: Individual or group.
Price Data: Available from publisher.
Author: ACT, Inc.
Publisher: ACT, Inc.

   a) READING FOR INFORMATION ASSESSMENT.
   Purpose: "Measures the learner's skill in reading and understanding work-related instructions and policies."

Scores: Total score only.
Levels: 5 reading skill levels.
Time: (45) minutes.
   b) APPLIED MATHEMATICS ASSESSMENT.
   Purpose: "Measures the learner's skill in applying mathematical reasoning to work-related problems."
Scores: Total score only.
Levels: 5 mathematics skill levels.
Time: (45) minutes.
   c) LISTENING ASSESSMENT.
   Purpose: "Measures the learner's skill at listening to and understanding work-related messages."
Scores: Total score only.
Levels: 5 listening skill levels.
Time: [40] minutes.
Comments: Constructed-response; administered via audiotape; hand-scored by ACT.
   d) WRITING ASSESSMENT.
   Purpose: "Measures the learner's skill at writing work-related messages."
Scores: Total score only.
Levels: 5 writing skill levels.
Time: [40] minutes.
Comments: Constructed-response; administered via audiotape; hand-scored by ACT.
   e) LOCATING INFORMATION ASSESSMENT.
   Purpose: "Measures the learner's skill in using information taken from workplace graphics such as diagrams, floor plans, tables, forms, graphs, charts, and instrument gauges."
Scores: Total score only.
Levels: 4 information skill levels.
Time: (45) minutes.
   f) TEAMWORK ASSESSMENT.
   Purpose: "Measures the learner's skill in choosing behaviors and/or actions that simultaneously support team interrelationships and lead toward the accomplishment of work tasks."
Parts: 2
Scores: Total score only.
Levels: 4 teamwork skill levels.
Time: (62) minutes.
Comments: Administered via video.
   g) APPLIED TECHNOLOGY ASSESSMENT.
   Purpose: "Measures the learner's skill in solving problems of a technological nature."
Scores: Total score only.
Levels: 4 applied technology levels.
Time: (45) minutes.
   h) OBSERVATION ASSESSMENT.
   Purpose: "Measures the learner's skill in paying attention to instructions and demonstrations, and in noticing details."
Scores: Total score only.
Levels: 4 observation levels.
Time: (60) minutes.

[2282]

[Work Motivation].

Purpose: Assesses assumptions and practices characterizing attempts to motivate employees, and evaluate employee motivational needs and values.
Population: Managers, employees.
Publication Dates: 1967–2000.

Scores, 5: Basic-Creature Comfort, Safety and Order, Belonging and Affiliation, Ego-Status, Actualization and Self-Expression.
Administration: Group.
Manual: No manual.
Price Data, 2016: $13.95 per instrument.
Time: [15-30] minutes.
Comments: Self-administered inventory.
Authors: Jay Hall and Martha Williams.
Publisher: Teleometrics International, Inc.
   a) MANAGEMENT OF MOTIVES INDEX.
   Purpose: Assesses assumptions and practices characterizing attempts to motivate employees.
   Acronym: MMI.
   b) WORK MOTIVATION INVENTORY.
   Purpose: Evaluate employee motivational needs and values.
   Acronym: WMI.
Cross References: See T3:2655 (4 references) and 8:1189 (3 references).

[2283]
Work Motivation Scale.

Purpose: Designed to assist "individuals in career development and planning by helping them understand their work motives and values and apply that understanding to their career choices and preferred work environment."
Population: Ages 13-65.
Publication Dates: 2002-2008.
Acronym: WMS.
Scores, 12: Survival and Safety Motives (Earnings and Benefits, Working Conditions), Affiliation Motives (Co-worker Relations, Supervisor Relations), Self-Esteem Motives (Task Orientation, Managing Others), Fulfillment Motives (Mission Orientation, Success Orientation).
Administration: Individual or group.
Price Data, 2016: $52.95 per 25; administrator's guide (2008, 16 pages) may be downloaded at no charge.
Time: Administration time not reported.
Comments: Revision of the Work Orientation Values Survey.
Author: Robert P. Brady.
Publisher: JIST/EMC Publishing.
Cross References: For reviews by Alan C. Bugbee, Jr. and Bert A. Goldman of an earlier version, see 17:204.

[2284]
Work Performance Assessment.

Purpose: Designed to assess "work-related social/interpersonal skills."
Population: Job trainees.
Publication Dates: 1987–1988.
Acronym: WPA.
Scores: 19 supervisory demands: Greet Each Trainee, Direct Trainee to Work Station and Explain Nature of Work, Provide Vague Instructions, Explain Supervisory Error, Provide Detailed Instructions, Observe Trainees Working, Stand Next to Trainee, Create a Distraction, Show New Way to Work, Introduce Time Pressure, Criticize Trainee's Work, Compliment Trainee's Work, Ask Trainees to Switch Tasks, Ask Trainees to Socialize, Direct Trainees to Work Together, Ask Trainees to Criticize Each Other, Ask Trainees to Compliment Each Other, Observe Trainees Completing the Task Together, Socialize with Each Trainee, yielding a Total Score.
Administration: Group.
Price Data: Available as free download from Educational Resources Information Center (ERIC) database.
Time: (60–70) minutes.
Comments: Ratings by supervisor.
Authors: Richard Roessler, Suki Hinman, and Frank Lewis.
Publisher: The National Center on Employment & Disability.
Cross References: For reviews by Caroline Manuele-Adkins and Gerald R. Schneck, see 13:367.

[2285]
Work Personality Index (2nd Edition).

Purpose: Designed to "identify personality traits that directly relate to work performance" for use in "personnel selection, leadership development, personal development, and team building."
Population: Adults in the working population.
Publication Dates: 2001-2014.
Acronym: WPI.
Scores, 21: 21 primary scales organized in 5 global scales: Energy and Drive (Ambition, Intiative, Flexibility, Energy, Leadership, Multi-Tasking, Persuasion, Social Confidence), Work Style (Persistence, Attention to Detail, Rule-Following, Dependability, Planning), Working with Others (Teamwork, Concern for Others, Outgoing, Democratic), Problem Solving Style (Innovation, Analytical Thinking), Dealing with Pressure and Stress (Self-Control, Stress Tolerance).
Administration: Individual or group.
Price Data: Available from publisher.
Foreign Language Edition: Available in French.
Time: (20-30) minutes.
Comments: Scoring available online or by mail; manual (126 pages) may be downloaded from publisher's website.
Authors: Donald Macnab and Shawn Bakker.
Publisher: Psychometrics Canada Ltd. [Canada].
Cross References: Reviews are scheduled for *The Twentieth Mental Measurements Yearbook*. For reviews by Janet F. Carlson and Joseph G. Law, Jr., of the original edition, see 16:279.

[2286]
Work Personality Inventory [Edition 1.0].

Purpose: Designed to assess "drivers of behavior and competence at work."
Population: Adults.

Publication Dates: 2010-2014.
Acronym: WOPI.
Scores, 19: Achievement Motives (Focused Achievement, Competitive Achievement), Leadership Motives (Leadership, Inspiration), Interaction Motives (Sociability, Empathy, Reliance), Thinking (Orientation, Perception, Thinking, Decision Making), Attitudes (Ambiguity-Change, Optimism, Self-Reflection).
Administration: Individual or group.
Price Data: Available from publisher.
Foreign Language Editions: Available in 15 languages.
Time: (20-30) minutes.
Comments: Certification required to administer.
Author: Petteri Niitamo.
Publisher: Competence Dimensions Ltd.
Cross References: Reviews are scheduled for *The Twentieth Mental Measurements Yearbook.*

[2287]

Work Personality Profile.
Purpose: Designed to "assess fundamental work role requirements that are essential to achievement and maintenance of suitable employment."
Population: Vocational rehabilitation clients.
Publication Date: 1986.
Acronym: WPP.
Scores, 16: Acceptance of Work Role, Ability to Profit from Instruction or Correction, Work Persistence, Work Tolerance, Amount of Supervision Required, Extent Trainee Seeks Assistance from Supervisor, Degree of Comfort or Anxiety with Supervisor, Appropriateness of Personal Relations with Supervisor, Teamwork, Ability to Socialize with Co-Workers, Social Communication Skills, Task Orientation, Social Skills, Work Motivation, Work Conformance, Personal Presentation.
Administration: Individual.
Price Data: Available as free download from Educational Resources Information Center (ERIC) database. A newer version of this instrument, with reporting software on CD, is published and sold by PRO-ED.
Time: (5–10) minutes.
Comments: Observational ratings by vocational evaluators; to be administered after one week (20-30 hours) in evaluation setting.
Authors: Brian Bolton and Richard Roessler.
Publisher: The National Center on Employment & Disability.
Cross References: See T5:2924 (4 references) and T4:2994 (1 reference); for a review by Ralph O. Mueller and Paula J. Dupuy, see 11:476.

[2288]

Work Personality Survey.
Purpose: Designed to assess an individual's personality traits and how they are likely to affect his or her work.

Population: Ages 16 and older.
Publication Date: 2015.
Acronym: WPS.
Scores, 26: Extraversion (Friendly, Outgoing, Assertive, Energetic), Agreeableness (Trusting, Straightforward, Considerate, Modest), Openness (Imaginative, Innovative, Rule-Breaking, Adaptable), Conscientiousness (Competent, Organized, Achieving, Proactive), Emotional Stability (Relaxed, Contented, Self-Assured, Resilient), General Factor of Personality.
Administration: Individual.
Price Data, 2015: $19.95 per online administration; user's manual (53 pages) available for download from test publisher's website.
Time: [15-20] minutes.
Comments: Administered online.
Authors: MySkillsProfile.
Publisher: MySkillsProfile [United Kingdom].
Cross References: Reviews are scheduled for *The Twentieth Mental Measurements Yearbook.*

[2289]

Work Potential Profile.
Purpose: "Developed as a tool for the initial descriptive assessment of long-term unemployed individuals."
Population: Ages 16 and older.
Publication Date: 1997.
Scores, 25: Coping (General Satisfaction, Stress and Anxiety, Self-image, Self-Discipline, Time Sense/Use, Total), Freedom from Major Barriers (Preoccupation with Health, Agitation/Aggression, Depression/Resentment, Pervasive Distrust/Delusions, Total), Social Resources (Attitude Towards Others, Social Skills, Total), Abilities (Communication and Literacy, Technology Use, Numeracy, Problem Solving, Total), Motivation (Work Motivation, Intrinsic Motivation, Extrinsic Motivation, Need for Status, Total), Physical Abilities.
Administration: Group.
Price Data, 2016: A$229.94 per complete kit; $79.95 per manual; $49.95 per 10 questionnaire; $22 per 10 answer sheets; $22 per 10 group record forms; $22 per 10 individual record forms; $44.95 per set of 9 score keys.
Time: (10–30) minutes.
Author: Helga A. H. Rowe.
Publisher: Australian Council for Educational Research Ltd. [Australia].
Cross References: For reviews by JoEllen V. Carlson and Robert Fitzpatrick, see 15:282.

[2290]

Work Readiness Inventory.
Purpose: Designed "to help measure the readiness of the individual worker to recognize and address the expectations and demands" of the 21st Century workplace.
Population: Teenagers and adults.
Publication Date: 2010.

Acronym: WRI.
Scores, 6: Responsibility, Flexibility, Skills, Communication, Self-View, Heath & Safety.
Administration: Individual or group.
Price Data, 2016: $52.95 per package of 25 consumable booklets; volume discount available. Administrator's guide (16 pages) available for download from publisher's website.
Time: (15) minutes.
Comments: Self-scored and interpreted.
Authors: Robert P. Brady.
Publisher: JIST/EMC Publishing.
Cross References: Reviews are scheduled for *The Twentieth Mental Measurements Yearbook.*

[2291]

Work Readiness Profile.

Purpose: "Developed as a criterion-referenced tool for the initial descriptive assessment of individuals with disabilities."
Population: Older adolescents and adults with disabilities.
Publication Date: 1995.
Scores, 14: Physical Effectiveness (Health, Travel, Movement, Fine Motor Skills, Gross Motor Skills and Strength, Total Average), Personal Effectiveness (Social and Interpersonal, Work Adjustment, Communication Effectiveness, Abilities and Skills, Literacy and Numeracy, Total Average), Hearing, Vision.
Administration: Group.
Price Data, 2016: A$146.95 per complete kit including manual (64 pages), 10 answer booklets, 10 group record forms, and 10 individual record forms; A$39.95 per 10 answer booklets; A$24.20 per 10 group record forms; A$22 per 10 individual record forms; A$69.95 per manual.
Time: (10–15) minutes.
Comments: Self-administered or ratings by informant.
Author: Helga A. H. Rowe.
Publisher: Australian Council for Educational Research Ltd. [Australia].
Cross References: For reviews by Jean Powell Kirnan and S. Alvin Leung, see 14:427.

[2292]

The Work Sampling System, Fifth Edition.

Purpose: Designed as a "performance assessment ... to assist teachers in documenting and evaluating students' skills, knowledge, and behaviors using actual classroom-based experiences, activities, and products."
Population: Children in preschool through Grade 3.
Publication Date: 2013.
Acronym: WSS, 5th Edition.
Scores: Performance indicators organized into 27 components in 7 domains: Personal and Social Development (Self-Concept, Self-Control, Approaches to Learn-

ing, Interaction With Others), Language and Literacy (Listening, Speaking, Reading, Writing), Mathematical Thinking (Processes and Practices, Number, Operations and Algebraic Thinking, Measurement, Data Analysis [Grades K-3 only], Geometry), Scientific Thinking (Inquiry Skills and Practices, Physical Science, Life Science, Earth Science), Social Studies (People/Past and Present, Human Interdependence, Citizenship and Government, People and Where They Live), The Arts (Expression and Representation, Understanding and Appreciation), Physical Development/Health/Safety (Gross Motor Development, Fine Motor Development, Self-Care/Health/Safety); for English Language Learners, Language and Literacy domain components are Listening for English Language Learners, Phonological Awareness for English Language Learners, Speaking for English Language Learners.
Administration: Individual.
Forms, 6: Preschool-3, Preschool-4, Kindergarten, First Grade, Second Grade, Third Grade.
Price Data, 2015: $169 per classroom kit, including teacher's manual (136 pages), developmental guidelines, 30 checklists, wall charts, and reproducible masters flash drive (specify age/grade level); $42.80 per teacher's manual, $42.80 per omnibus guidelines; $32.80 per reproducible masters flash drive; $29.75 per developmental guidelines (specify age/grade level); $25.85 per 10 developmental checklists (specify age/grade level); $6.60 per wall chart.
Foreign Language Edition: Available in Spanish.
Time: Administration time not reported.
Comments: Can administer three times per year (fall, winter, spring); "criterion-referenced observational assessment."
Authors: Margo L. Dichtelmiller, Judy R. Jablon, Dorothea B. Marsden, and Samuel J. Meisels.
Publisher: Pearson.
Cross References: Reviews are scheduled for *The Twentieth Mental Measurements Yearbook.*

[2293]

Work Self-Efficacy Inventory (The).

Purpose: Designed to "measure job behaviors referring to beliefs in one's command of the social requirements necessary for success in the workplace."
Population: Working adults.
Publication Date: 2010.
Acronym: WS-Ei.
Scores, 8: Learning, Problem Solving, Pressure, Role Expectations, Teamwork, Sensitivity, Work Politics, Overall Work Self-Efficacy.
Administration: Individual or group.
Forms, 2: Form A (self version), Form B (performance version).
Price Data, 2016: $50 per PDF manual (48 pages); $60 per paper manual; $15 per Individual Report: Self Form; $15 per Report About Me: Self Form; $250 per

Group Report: Self Form; $1 per Transform Survey Hosting: Multi-rater Form ($20 set up fee); $2.40 per Transform Survey Hosting: Self Form (minimum purchase of 50); $2 per Remote Online Survey License (minimum purchase of 50).
Time: (10) minutes for Form A, (5) minutes for Form B.
Author: Joseph A. Raelin.
Publisher: Mind Garden, Inc.

[2294]

Work Skills Series Production.

Purpose: Designed to measure the ability to understand instructions, work with numbers, and accurately check machine settings visually.
Population: Manufacturing and production employees and prospective employees.
Publication Date: 1990.
Acronym: WSS.
Scores: Total score only for each of 3 tests: Understanding Instructions (VWP1), Working with Numbers (NWP2), Visual Checking (CWP3).
Administration: Individual or group.
Price Data: Available from publisher.
Time: 12 minutes for VWP1; 10 minutes for NWP2; 7 minutes for CWP3; 29(40) minutes for complete battery.
Author: Saville & Holdsworth Ltd.
Publisher: CEB.
Cross References: For reviews by Brian Bolton and Wayne J. Camara, see 12:418.

[2295]

Work Smarts.

Purpose: Designed to help individuals "identify their most-developed forms of intelligence ... [in order] to make more-informed career choices."
Population: Individuals at or above 8th-grade level.
Publication Date: 2009.
Scores, 8: People Smart, Self Smart, Logic Smart, Picture Smart, Body Smart, Word Smart, Music Smart, Nature Smart.
Administration: Individual or group.
Price Data, 2016: $59.95 per package of 25 consumable booklets; volume discount available. Administrator's guide (16 pages) available for download from publisher's website.
Time: (15-20) minutes.
Comments: Self-scored and interpreted.
Authors: John J. Liptak and Paul Allen.
Publisher: JIST/EMC Publishing.
Cross References: Reviews are scheduled for *The Twentieth Mental Measurements Yearbook*.

[2296]

Work Team Simulator.

Purpose: "Designed to identify individuals who have the attitude and skills needed to be an effective member of a work team; test requires candidates to respond in narrative fashion to a series of job-related situations in order to determine how they will relate to other team members and their supervisor."
Population: Team members.
Publication Date: 1991.
Acronym: WTS.
Scores, 3: Group Decision Making, Team Relations, Total.
Administration: Group.
Forms, 4: Private and public sector forms: Blue Collar, Clerical/Office, Fire Fighter, Transportation Agency Blue Collar.
Restricted Distribution: Clients may be required to pay a nominal one-time overhead/sign-up fee.
Price Data, 2015: $295 per candidate for rental/scoring and feedback report.
Time: 75 minutes.
Author: Richard C. Joines.
Publisher: Management & Personnel Systems, Inc.

[2297]

Work Temperament Inventory.

Purpose: Identifies "personal traits" of the worker that are then matched to suitable occupations.
Population: Workers.
Publication Date: 1993.
Acronym: WTI.
Scores: 12 scales: Directive, Repetitive, Influencing, Variety, Expressing, Judgments, Alone, Stress, Tolerances, Under, People, Measurable.
Administration: Group.
Price Data: Available as free download from Educational Resources Information Center (ERIC) database.
Time: (15–20) minutes.
Authors: Brian Bolton and Jeffrey Brookings.
Publisher: The National Center on Employment & Disability.
Cross References: For reviews by Peter F. Merenda and Alan J. Raphael, see 13:368.

[2298]

Working—Assessing Skills, Habits, and Style.

Purpose: "Designed to assess personal habits, skills, and styles that are associated with a positive work ethic."
Population: High school and college students and potential employees.
Publication Date: 1996.
Scores: 9 competencies: Taking Responsibility, Working in Teams, Persisting, Having A Sense of Quality, Life-Long Learning, Adapting to Change, Problem Solving, Information Processing, Systems Thinking.
Administration: Group or individual.
Price Data, 2015: $4 per assessment for 1-99 assessments; $3.50 per assessment for 100 or more; free user's manual and technical manual.

Time: (30–35) minutes.

Comments: Inventory for self-rating; can be self-administered and self-scored, or assessed online with automatic scoring.

Authors: Curtis Miles (test and user's manual), Phyllis Grummon (test, user's manual, and technical manual), and Karen M. Maduschke (technical manual).

Publisher: H & H Publishing Co., Inc.

Cross References: For reviews by Wayne Camara and Joyce Meikamp, see 14:429.

[2299]

Working Styles Assessment.

Purpose: Designed as a "self-administered, self-scored, and self-interpreted career exploration tool."

Population: Ages 17 and older.

Publication Date: 2014.

Acronym: WSA.

Scores, 20: Achievement, Initiative, Persistence, Confidence, Leadership, Cooperation, Concern for Others, Social Orientation, Self-Control, Stress Tolerance, Adaptability, Dependability, Attention to Detail, Integrity, Conscientiousness, Independence, Innovation, Analytical Thinking, Profile Elevation, Differentiation.

Administration: Individual or group.

Price Data, 2016: $145 per introductory kit including manual (64 pages), fast guide, 25 assessment booklets, 25 user's workbooks, and 25 score summary sheets; $60 per manual with fast guide; $55 per 25 assessment booklets; $35 per 25 user's workbooks; $20 per 25 score summary sheets.

Time: (20-25) minutes.

Comments: Computer administration and scoring available.

Authors: Melissa A. Messer and Heather Ureksoy.

Publisher: Psychological Assessment Resources, Inc.

Cross References: Reviews are scheduled for *The Twentieth Mental Measurements Yearbook*.

[2300]

Workplace Skills Survey.

Purpose: Designed to provide "information regarding basic work ethics and employment skills."

Population: Job applicants and employees.

Publication Date: 1998.

Acronym: WSS.

Scores, 7: Communication, Adapting to Change, Problem Solving, Work Ethics, Technological Literacy, Teamwork, Composite.

Administration: Individual or group.

Price Data, 2015: $47 per introductory kit including 5 reusable test booklets, 20 answer/score sheets, and technical manual (9 pages); $36 per 20 answer/score sheets; $22 per 10 reusable test booklets.

Time: 20 minutes.

Author: Industrial Psychology International Ltd.

Publisher: Industrial Psychology International Ltd.

Cross References: For reviews by Jean P. Kirnan and William I. Sauser, Jr., see 17:205.

[2301]

Workplace Skills Survey—Form E.

Purpose: Designed to assess students' work place readiness and employment skills.

Population: Students in school-to-work and vocational programs.

Publication Date: 2000.

Acronym: WSS-Form E.

Scores, 9: Career Planning, Job Attainment, Communication, Adapting and Coping with Change, Problem Solving, Work Ethics, Technological Literacy, Teamwork, Overall.

Administration: Individual or group.

Price Data, 2015: $4.50 per assessment per student includes manual, answer documents, shipment of test materials to the school, scoring, analysis reporting (individual student reports and data CD), and shipment of reports to the school; $25 per 25 reusable test booklets.

Time: 50 minutes.

Comments: Scoring and analysis provided by publisher.

Author: Industrial Psychology International Ltd.

Publisher: Industrial Psychology International Ltd.

[2302]

World Government Scale.

Purpose: Measures attitudes toward world government.

Population: Students.

Publication Date: 1985.

Scores: Total score only.

Administration: Group.

Manual: No manual.

Price Data, 2015: $2 per scale.

Time: [12] minutes.

Comments: Supplementary article available.

Author: Panos D. Bardis.

Publisher: Donna Bardis.

[2303]

World of Work Inventory.

Purpose: "Designed to assist clients in thinking about themselves in relation to their total environment" in relation to their personal career development.

Population: Ages 13–65+.

Publication Dates: 1970–2006.

Acronym: WOWI.

Scores, 35: Career Interest Activities (17 scores: Public Service, The Sciences, Engineering & Related, Business Relations, Managerial, The Arts, Clerical, Sales, Service, Primary Outdoor, Processing, Machine Work, Bench Work, Structural Work, Mechanical & Electrical Work, Graphic Arts, Mining); Job Satisfaction Indicators (12 scores: Versatile, Adaptable to Repetitive Work, Adaptable

to Performing Under Specific Instructions, Dominant, Gregarious, Isolative, Influencing, Self-Controlled, Valuative, Objective, Subjective, Rigorous); Aptitude/Achievement (6 scores: Verbal, Numerical, Abstractions, Spatial-Form, Mechanical/Electrical, Organizing Skill).
Administration: Individual or group.
Price Data, 2016: $189 site license fee (waived for purchases of 100 or more); $7 to $35 per assessment, depending on quantity purchased.
Time: (60) minutes.
Authors: Robert E. Ripley, Gregory P. M. Neidert, and Nancy L. Ortman.
Publisher: World of Work, Inc.
Cross References: For reviews by Jeffrey A. Jenkins and Eugene P. Sheehan, see 16:281.

[2304]
Worley's ID Profile.
Purpose: Designed to identify temperament.
Population: Ages 6 and over.
Publication Dates: 1995–2000.
Acronym: WIDP.
Scores, 8: 3 profile scores: Social, Leadership, Relationship; 5 behavior scores: Introverted Sanguine, Sanguine, Phlegmatic, Melancholy, Choleric.
Administration: Individual or group.
Forms, 2: Adult and Youth (Ages 6 to 16).
Price Data: Available from publisher.
Foreign Language Editions: Available in English, Spanish, and Portuguese.
Time: (10) minutes.
Comments: Certification training available for individuals and groups.
Author: John W. Worley.
Publisher: Worley's Identity Discovery Profile, Inc.
Cross References: For reviews by Eugene V. Aidman and Frederick T. L. Leong, see 15:284.

[2305]
Writing Process Test.
Purpose: "Measures the quality of students' written products."
Population: Grades 2–12.
Publication Dates: 1991–1992.
Acronym: WPT.
Scores, 14: Development [First Pass (Purpose/Focus, Audience, Vocabulary, Style/Tone, Total), Second Pass (Support/Development, Organization/Coherence, Total)], Fluency [Third Pass (Sentence Structure/Variety, Grammar/Usage, Capitalization/Punctuation, Spelling, Total)], Total.
Administration: Group.
Editions, 2: Individual, Classroom.
Price Data, 2015: $213 per complete kit including test manual (1992, 144 pages), technical manual (1992, 40 pages), 25 analytic scales, 25 Form A first draft booklets,

and 25 revision booklets; $69 per test manual; $24 per 25 analytic record forms; $27 per 25 Form A first draft booklet; $25 per 25 Form B first draft booklet; $18 per 25 revision booklets; $22 per score folder; $44 per technical manual; $24 per 25 Training and Calibration Record Forms; $69 per VHS; $44 per technical manual.
Time: [45] minutes (+30 minutes for revision).
Authors: Robin Warden and Thomas A. Hutchinson.
Publisher: PRO-ED.
Cross References: For reviews by Ernest W. Kimmel and Sandra Ward, see 13:369 (1 reference).

[2306]
Y-OQ-SR 2.0 [Youth Outcome Questionnaire-Self Report].
Purpose: Designed to "assess behavior change as the adolescent clients themselves perceive it."
Population: Ages 12-18 years.
Publication Dates: 1999-2005.
Acronym: Y-OQ-SR 2.0.
Scores, 7: Intrapersonal Distress, Somatic, Interpersonal Relations, Social Problems, Behavioral Dysfunction, Critical Items, Total.
Administration: Individual or group.
Restricted Distribution: Requires licensure from OQ Measures LLC.
Price Data, 2015: $250 per annual license fee per clinician includes unlimited administrations; $25 per manual (1999, 15 pages).
Foreign Language Editions: Software version available in Spanish; paper-and-pencil version available in Arabic, Armenian, Cambodian, Chilean, Chinese (Simplified and Traditional), Dutch, Farsi, Swedish, Tagalog, and Vietnamese.
Time: (7-15) minutes.
Authors: M. Gawain Wells, Gary M. Burlingame, Paul M. Rose (manual only), and Michael J. Lambert (test only).
Publisher: OQ Measures LLC.
Cross References: For reviews by John S. Geisler and Joseph C. Kush, see 17:207.

[2307]
Y-OQ-30.2 [Youth Outcome Questionnaire].
Purpose: Designed to measure "the treatment process for children and adolescents receiving any form of behavioral health treatment including psychoactive medications."
Population: Ages 12-18 years.
Publication Dates: 1998-2002.
Acronym: Y-OQ-30.2.
Scores: Total score only.
Administration: Individual or group.
Restricted Distribution: Requires licensure from OQ Measures LLC.

Price Data, 2016: License fee is $250 per clinician per year.

Foreign Language Editions: Software version available in Spanish; paper-and-pencil version available in Chinese (Simplified), Chinese (Traditional), Dutch, French, Spanish, Swedish, Tagalog, Turkish, and Vietnamese.

Time: (2-15) minutes.

Comments: Test can be parent-reported and self-reported.

Authors: Gary M. Burlingame, Bruce W. Jasper (manual only), Gary Peterson (manual only), M. Gawain Wells, Curtis W. Reisinger, G. S. (Jeb) Brown (manual only).

Publisher: OQ Measures LLC.

Cross References: For reviews by Sandra Loew and by W. Joel Schneider and Mark E. Swerdlik of the Y-OQ-30.1, see 17:206.

[2308]

Young Children's Achievement Test.

Purpose: Designed to help determine early academic abilities.

Population: Ages 4-0 to 7-11.

Publication Date: 2000.

Acronym: YCAT.

Scores, 6: General Information, Reading, Mathematics, Writing, Spoken Language, and Early Achievement Composite.

Administration: Individual.

Price Data, 2015: $250 per complete kit including examiner's manual (154 pages), picture book (48 pages), 25 student response forms, and 25 profile/examiner record booklets; $79 per examiner's manual; $85 per picture book; $37 per 25 student response forms; $62 per 25 profile/examiner record booklets; $32 per 15 profile booklets; $137 per Spanish translation of test; $15 per 15 Spanish version student response forms.

Foreign Language Edition: A Spanish translation of this test, Prueba de Habilidades Académicas Iniciales (PHAI) is available.

Time: (25–45) minutes.

Authors: Wayne P. Hresko, Pamela K. Peak, Shelley R. Herron, and Deanna L. Bridges.

Publisher: PRO-ED.

Cross References: For reviews by Russell N. Carney and Susan J. Maller, see 15:285.

[2309]

Youth Level of Service/Case Management Inventory 2.0.

Purpose: Designed for use in "assessing risk, need, and responsivity factors in youth and in the formulation of a case plan."

Population: Juvenile offenders, ages 12-18.

Publication Dates: 2002-2011.

Acronym: YLS/CMI 2.0.

Scores: 9 Risk Ratings: Prior and Current Offenses/Dispositions, Family Circumstances/Parenting, Education/Employment, Peer Relations, Substance Abuse, Leisure/Recreation, Personality/Behavior, Attitudes/Orientation, Total.

Administration: Individual.

Parts, 7: Assessment of Risks and Needs, Summary of Risks and Needs, Assessment of Other Needs and Special Considerations, Final Risk/Need Level and Professional Override, Program/Placement Decision, Case Management Plan, Case Management Review.

Price Data, 2015: $234 per complete kit including 25 interview guides, 25 Quikscore forms, 25 case management forms, and user's manual (2011, 92 pages); $89 per 25 interview guides; $54 per 25 Quikscore forms; $32 per 25 case management forms; $74 per user's manual.

Time: [30-40] minutes.

Comments: Reflects the theory and structure of the Level of Service Inventory-Revised (17:107).

Authors: Robert D. Hoge and D. A. Andrews.

Publisher: Multi-Health Systems, Inc.

Cross References: For reviews by Mark A. Albanese and Gene N. Berg, see 19:183; for reviews by Pam Lindsey and Stephen E. Trotter of an earlier edition, see 16:282.

[2310]

Youth Outcome Questionnaire (Y-OQ-2.01).

Purpose: Designed as a "measure of treatment progress for children and adolescents receiving psychological or psychiatric treatment."

Population: Ages 4–17.

Publication Dates: 1996-2005.

Acronym: Y-OQ-2.0.

Scores, 7: Intrapersonal Distress, Somatic, Interpersonal Relations, Critical Items, Social Problems, Behavioral Dysfunction, Total.

Administration: Individual.

Price Data, 2015: $250 per annual license fee per clinician includes unlimited administrations; $25 per manual (1996, 27 pages).

Foreign Language Editions: Software version available in Spanish; paper-and-pencil version available in Arabic, Armenian, Cambodian, Chinese (Simplified and Traditional), Dutch, Farsi, French, Japanese, Korean, Russian, Spanish, Swedish, Tagalog, and Vietnamese.

Time: (7–20) minutes.

Comments: Behavior rating scale completed by parent or "significant adult figure."

Authors: Gary M. Burlingame (test and manual), Michael J. Lambert (test and manual), M. Gawain Wells (manual), Matthew J. Hoag (manual), Carolen A. Hope (manual), R. Scott Nebeker (manual), Kimberly Konkel (manual), Pamela McCollam (manual), Gary Peterson (manual), Mark Latkowski (manual), and Curtis W. Reisinger (manual).

Publisher: OQ Measures LLC.
Cross References: For reviews by Susan K. Green and John Hattie, see 16:283.

[2311]
Youth Program Quality Assessment.

Purpose: "Designed to evaluate the quality of youth programs and identify staff training needs."
Population: Youth-serving programs.
Publication Date: 2005.
Acronyms: Youth PQA.
Administration: Individual or group.
Forms, 2: A, B.
Price Data, 2016: The tool is available for free download; hard copies and guidebooks can also be purchased for $40 per complete kit including administration manual (35 pages) and bundle of 10 Youth PQA instruments; $12 per administration manual; $30 per bundle of 10 Youth PQA instruments.
Foreign Language Edition: Spanish translation available.
Comments: This test is based on observations and interviews by either "independent raters or as a self-assessment."
Author: High/Scope Educational Research Foundation.
Publisher: Center for Youth Program Quality.
　a) FORM A-PROGRAM OFFERING ITEMS.
　Purpose: "Focuses on youth experiences during a program offering."
　Scores, 5: Safe Environment, Supportive Environment, Interaction, Engagement, Total.
　Time: (120) minutes.
　b) FORM B-ORGANIZATION ITEMS.
　Purpose: "Assesses the organization's infrastructure."
　Scores, 4: Youth Centered Policies/Practices, High Expectations for All Students/Staff, Access, Total.
　Time: (60) minutes.
Cross References: For a review by Georgette Yetter, see 17:208.

[2312]
Youth Risk and Resilience Inventory.

Purpose: Designed "to identify individual assets or resilience factors" and "screen for the presence of risk factors such as teasing, intimidation, bullying, physical abuse, violence, and victimization; to identify signs of emotional stress; and to assess their impact on the individual."
Population: Ages 10 to 17.
Publication Date: 2006.
Acronyms: YRRI.
Scores, 2: Risk Factor, Resilience Factor.
Administration: Individual or group.
Price Data, 2015: $36.95 per complete kit including 25 test booklets and administrator's guide (8 pages); bulk discounts are available.
Time: Administration time not reported.

Comments: Optional "My Journal" section at the end of the test does not affect the numeric scores.
Author: Robert P. Brady.
Publisher: JIST Publishing, Inc.
Cross References: For reviews by Merith Cosden and Timothy R. Konold, see 17:209.

[2313]
Youth's Inventory–4R.

Purpose: Designed to determine "the extent to which the adolescent patient is aware of his or her symptoms" [of adolescent psychopathology], as determined by self-report.
Population: Ages 12–18.
Publication Dates: 1999-2008.
Acronym: YI-4R.
Scores, 11: AD/HD Inattentive, Hyperactive–Impulsive, Combined, Oppositional Defiant Disorder, Conduct Disorder, Generalized Anxiety Disorder, Major Depressive Disorder, Dysthymic Disorder, Separation Anxiety Disorder, Eating Problems, Bipolar Disorder.
Administration: Individual.
Price Data, 2015: $92 per deluxe kit including 50 checklists, 50 symptom count score sheets, 50 symptom severity profile score sheets, and manual (1999, 170 pages); $63 per 50 checklists.
Foreign Language Edition: Available in Spanish.
Time: [15] minutes.
Comments: Update in 2008 added one impairment item for each disorder.
Authors: Kenneth D. Gadow and Joyce Sprafkin.
Publisher: Checkmate Plus, Ltd.
Cross References: For reviews by Harold R. Keller and John J. Vacca of the original version, see 15:286.

[2314]
Zarit Burden Interview.

Purpose: "Designed to assess the stresses experienced by family caregivers of elderly and disabled persons."
Population: Caregivers of elderly and disabled persons.
Publication Dates: 1983–1990.
Scores, 2: Personal Strain, Role Strain.
Administration: Individual.
Price Data: Available from distributor.
Time: Administration time not reported.
Comments: Administered by an interviewer or self-administered; previously titled Memory and Behavior Problems Checklist and The Burden Interview; a revised version of the Memory and Behavior Problems Checklist is available at no charge from the Alzheimer's Association.
Authors: Steven H. Zarit and Judy M. Zarit.
Publisher: Steven H. Zarit and Judy M. Zarit [Distributed by MAPI Research Trust].
Cross References: For reviews by Sally Kuhlenschmidt and Richard A. Wantz of Memory and Behavior Problems Checklist and The Burden Interview, see 14:229; see also T5:1643 (2 references).

INDEX OF
MMY TEST REVIEWERS

This record of Mental Measurements Yearbook *test reviewers lists all individuals reviewing in the 19 editions of the MMY series. The numbers after the names represent the* Mental Measurements Yearbooks *in which their reviews appeared.*

Based on the recommendation of our National Advisory Council, the Buros Center for Testing is now making special recognition of the long-term contributions of reviewers to the Mental Measurements Yearbook *series. To receive the "Distinguished Reviewer" designation, an individual must have contributed to six or more editions of this series beginning with* The Ninth Mental Measurements Yearbook. *By virtue of their long-term service, these reviewers exemplify an outstanding dedication in their professional lives to the principles of improving the science and practice of testing. Individuals receiving awards as Distinguished Reviewers as of the publication of* The Nineteenth Mental Measurements Yearbook *(2014) are indicated with an asterisk (*) below.*

Robert H. Bauernfeind, 5-8
Sheri Bauman, 15
Ronald Baumanis, 9
Deborah N. Bauserman, 9
Abigail Baxter, 16-19
Brent Baxter, 3-5
Ernest Edward Bayles, 1
Nancy Bayley, 2-3, 5
Kenneth L. Bean, 5-6
Robert M. Bear, 3-4
Harold P. Bechtoldt, 4-7
Isabel L. Beck, 9
Michael D. Beck, 11-13, 16
Roland L. Beck, 2-3
Samuel J. Beck, 2, 5
Wesley C. Becker, 6
Ralph C. Bedell, 3, 5
H. R. Beech, 6
Martha C. Beech, 9
Fred S. Beers, 1
Scott F. Beers, 17
Isaac I. Bejar, 8
Marcia J. Belcher, 11
John E. Bell, 4-6
Peter Della Bella, 13
C.G. Bellah, 15-16
Camilla Persson Benbow, 11
Kathryn M. Benes, 11-12
James K. Benish, 13-15
Albert A. Bennett, 2-3
Clinton W. Bennett, 12-13
George K. Bennett, 3-7
Jeri Benson, 11, 13
Mark J. Benson, 12-13
Nicholas Benson, 13, 19
*Philip G. Benson, 9-12, 16, 18
Marsha Bensoussan, 13, 16
Peter M. Bentler, 6-7
Arthur L. Benton, 3-4, 7
Sheryl Benton, 16
Stephen L. Benton, 11-12, 16
H. E. Benz, 2
Ralph F. Berdie, 3-7
Abbey L. Berg, 16
Gene N. Berg, 19
Harry D. Berg, 3-8
Paul Conrad Berg, 7
Allen Berger, 7-9
Michael Berger, 8
Peter Miles Berger, 14-15
Jennifer M. Bergeron, 16
Nancy Berglas, 19
Betty Bergstrom, 13
*Ronald A. Berk, 9, 12-16
Hinsdale Bernard, 12-13
H. John Bernardin, 9-12
Rita Sloan Berndt, 9-10
Jean-Jacques Bernier, 11-12
Robert G. Bernreuter, 1-4

Ira H. Bernstein, 19
*Frank M. Bernt, 12-16, 19
Jeff Berry, 18
Joan D. Berryman, 9
Frederick Bessai, 11-14
Emmett A. Betts, 6
William Betz, 1, 3
Charles L. Bickel, 2
Michael D. Biderman, 17-18
John Biggs, 9
Elizabeth Bigham, 18-19
Marion A. Bills, 3
Walter V. Bingham, 1
William C. Bingham, 6, 8
L. B. Birch, 6-7
Ricky Korey Birnbaum, 15
Herbert G. W. Bischoff, 9, 14
Lisa G. Bischoff, 11-15
Bruce H. Biskin, 11-12, 17, 19
Reign H. Bittner, 3-4
Harold H. Bixler, 3-4
Ake Bjerstedt, 5-6
Donald B. Black, 6-7
Hillel Black, 6
John D. Black, 5-6, 8-9
Michelle P. Black, 19
J. M. Blackbourn, 18
J. M. Blackburn, 2
James H. Blackhurst, 1
E. G. Blackstone, 3
Martha Blackwell, 11-12
Kimberly Ann Blair, 15-16
C. B. Blakemore, 6
Rebecca Blanchard, 18
Emery P. Bliesmer, 6
Lynn S. Bliss, 10-12
Sonya Blixt, 12
Jack Block, 8
Martin E. Block, 12
Paul J. Blommers, 3-6
Benjamin S. Bloom, 3-5, 7
Lisa A. Bloom, 12-13
Bruce M. Bloxom, 7-9
Milton L. Blum, 3-4
James A. Blumenthal, 9
Warren Bobrow, 19
Cynthia R. Bochna, 16
Jack L. Bodden, 7-9
Ann E. Boehm, 9
Kathy J. Bohan, 16, 19
Larry M. Bolen, 14
Carol A. Boliek, 11
Joan Bollenbacher, 5
Nancy B. Bologna, 12, 14
*Brian F. Bolton, 8-9, 11-15
David L. Bolton, 12-13
Guy L. Bond, 2
Stephen J. Boney, 12
Mike Bonner, 15-16

James N. Butcher, 8-9
John K. Butler, Jr., 9
Katharine G. Butler, 7-8, 10-12
Michelle A. Butler, 16
Dorcas Susan Butt, 8-9
Margaret C. Byrne, 7-9
Leonard S. Cahen, 7-8
G. P. Cahoon, 3-4
James R. Caldwell, 7
Kathryn Hoover Calfee, 8
Robert C. Calfee, 8-10
*Carolyn M. Callahan, 12-17
Leroy G. Callahan, 8
Leonard F. Caltabiano, 15
Wayne J. Camara, 12-14, 16
Bonnie W. Camp, 9-10
Cameron J. Camp, 10-11, 13
David P. Campbell, 6-8
Donald T. Campbell, 4-6
Dugal Campbell, 6
Hank Campbell, 10
Iris Amos Campbell, 9
J. Arthur Campbell, 6, 8-9
Joel T. Campbell, 6-7
Michael H. Campbell, 14-16
Thomas F. Campbell, 13
Vincent N. Campbell, 7
Anthony A. Cancelli, 9
Gary L. Canivez, 14, 16, 18-19
Michael S. Cannizzaro, 19
Joyce L. Carbonell, 9
*Karen T. Carey, 11-14, 16-18
Cindy I. Carlson, 11, 14-15
James E. Carlson, 12
*Janet F. Carlson, 11-17
*JoEllen V. Carlson, 11-16
Kenneth A. Carlson, 8
Roger D. Carlson, 11
Thorsten R. Carlson, 7-8
James C. Carmer, 11-12
Arlene E. Carney, 12
Russell N. Carney, 12-13, 15-17
*C. Dale Carpenter, 9-14, 16, 18-19
Sandra J. Carr, 14
W. L. Carr, 2
David J. Carroll, 8-9
James L. Carroll, 9
John B. Carroll, 4-8
L. Ray Carry, 7
Amber Carter, 18
Harold D. Carter, 1-4
Launor F. Carter, 4
W. H. Cartwright, 3
Heidi M. Carty, 15, 17
John C. Caruso, 14-15
J. Manuel Casas, 9-10
Michael W. Casby, 9
Thomas F. Cash, 9
Jerrell C. Cassady, 17-19

Frank P. Cassaretto, 5
Linda Castillo, 16
Burton M. Castner, 2
Felicia Castro-Villarreal, 19
Robert S. Cathcart, 5
Psyche Cattell, 1, 3
Raymond B. Cattell, 2
Darrell N. Caulley, 12
Courtney B. Cazden, 7-8
Stella Center, 1
Tony Cellucci, 14-16, 18-19
Edward J. Cervenka, 8
Robert W. Ceurvorst, 9
Hester Chadderdon, 1-2, 4
Robert C. Challman, 4, 6-7
E. G. Chambers, 3-5
Tiffany Chandler, 17
Carolyn Chaney, 11
Laura H. Chapman, 8
Clinton I. Chase, 7-10
Henry Chauncey, 3, 6
Maurice Chazan, 7
Henry M. Cherrick, 9
Kathleen Barrows Chesterfield, 9
Brad S. Chissom, 7-8
*Mary "Rina" Mathai Chittooran, 13-19
James P. Choca, 13-14
Andrew Christensen, 9
Sandra L. Christenson, 11
Robert Christopher, 14, 17
Edmund P. Churchill, 3
Ruth D. Churchill, 3, 5
David F. Ciampi, 17-19
*Joseph C. Ciechalski, 11-18
*Gregory J. Cizek, 11-18
Charles D. Claiborn, 9, 12
*Mary M. Clare, 15-16, 18-19
Cherry Ann Clark, 5
D. F. Clark, 7
Elaine Clark, 10, 12-15
Gale W. Clark, 5
J. F. Clark, 5
Jean N. Clark, 17-19
John L. D. Clark, 7-8
John R. Clark, 2
Kenneth E. Clark, 4
Philip M. Clark, 8-9
Richard M. Clark, 9, 11
Willis W. Clark, 6
Brandy L. Clarke, 17-18
H. Harrison Clarke, 4
Lora Claywell, 19
Glen U. Cleeton, 3
Lorraine Cleeton, 17
W. V. Clemans, 6
Amanda Jill Clemence, 15
Dorothy M. Clendenen, 5-7
Jeanette N. Cleveland, 9
Victor B. Cline, 7

John G. Darley, 1-2
Richard E. Darnell, 8-9
Ralph F. Darr, Jr., 11-13
J. P. Das, 9-10
Jane Dass, 8
John H. Daugherty, 3
James M. Daum, 9
Charles Davidshofer, 9
M. Meghan Davidson, 18-19
Andrew S. Davis, 15-17, 19
Brandon Davis, 11, 13
Charlotte Croon Davis, 3-6, 8
D. Russell Davis, 4-5
Edwin W. Davis, 3
Frederick B. Davis, 1-5, 7
Heather Davis, 19
Paul C. Davis, 6
R. Evan Davis, 19
Robert A. Davis, 3
Stanley E. Davis, 6
Steven F. Davis, 11-14
Parker Davis, Jr., 3
Mark L. Davison, 9
Helen C. Dawe, 3
Robyn M. Dawes, 8
Carolyn Dawson, 8
Linda S. Day, 11
*Ayres G. D'Costa, 11-15, 17-19
*Gary J. Dean, 12-15, 17-19
Raymond S. Dean, 9, 14-16
Sandra F. Dean, 17
Lester W. Dearborn, 6
William W. Deardorff, 12-13
William L. Deaton, 11-12
R. J. De Ayala, 14
David A. Decoster, 10
James Deese, 5
Sharon H. deFur, 14-15, 17-19
Frank P. DeLay, 2
Connie Kubo Della-Piana, 13-14
Gabriel M. Della-Piana, 6, 11-13
Vincent J. Dell'Orto, 8
Dennis J. Deloria, 7-9
Harold A. Delp, 4
Robert H. Deluty, 9
George J. Demakis, 16-17
Randy Demaline, 8
Robert G. Demaree, 4, 7-8
*Gerald E. DeMauro, 11-18
Marilyn E. Demorest, 10
George D. Demos, 6
Jennifer Denicolis, 12
Joseph W. Denison, 9
Evelyn Deno, 7
Gypsy M. Denzine, 15-19
Stephen J. DePaola, 15
Susan K. Deri, 3
Mayhew Derryberry, 3
Lawrence G. Derthick, 5

Harry R. DeSilva, 2
Lizanne Destefano, 11-12, 14
Douglas K. Detterman, 9
M. Vere DeVault, 7
Edward F. deVillafranca, 8
Anthony J. DeVito, 9
Joseph C. Dewey, 1-2
Michael L. Dey, 9
Robert E. Deysach, 10
Denise M. DeZolt, 11-13
Esther E. Diamond, 8-9, 11-13
Joseph O. Prewitt Diaz, 14
Phil Diaz, 16
Louis M. DiCarlo, 6
Charles F. Dicken, 6
Gwendolen S. Dickson, 1, 3
Paul B. Diederich, 1-2, 7
Allan O. Diefendorf, 11-12
John S. Diekhoff, 3-5
Stephen Dilchert, 16-19
Thomas E. Dinero, 12
Jonathan G. Dings, 12
Robert L. Dipboye, 8
James Clyde DiPerna, 14-16, 19
Jean Dirks, 9
David N. Dixon, 9-13
Joe W. Dixon, 18-19
Gregory H. Dobbins, 9-10, 12
Keith S. Dobson, 9
Richard F. Docter, 7
Leland K. Doebler, 9
Karla J. Doepke, 19
R. Anthony Doggett, 15-18
Janice A. Dole, 9-10
Kathleen A. Dolgos, 15
*Beth Doll, 10, 12-19
Robert H. Dolliver, 7-9
Stefan C. Dombrowski, 18-19
George Domino, 7-10, 12-14
Mavis L. Donahue, 9-10
Hei-Ki Dong, 9
Thomas F. Donlon, 8, 12-13
James Donnelly, 15, 17-18
Kerry Donnelly, 17
Antonia D'Onofrio, 17
Jerome E. Doppelt, 4-8
Dan Douglas, 11
Harl R. Douglass, 2-3
Dennis Doverspike, 15-16
E. Thomas Dowd, 9, 11-14
N. M. Downie, 6
John Downing, 8
Kenneth O. Doyle, Jr., 8
Vincent R. D'Oyley, 7
Ronald S. Drabman, 9
Raleigh M. Drake, 2-5
Richard M. Drake, 2-3
Penelope W. Dralle, 12
Ralph Mason Dreger, 8

Richard F. Farmer, 13-14, 16, 18
Paul R. Farnsworth, 1-3, 5-6
Roger Farr, 7-8
R. Joel Farrell II, 15
Wiltrud Fassbinder, 14
Ray N. Faulkner, 1-2
Richard W. Faunce, 11-12
James Fauth, 15
Harold P. Fawcett, 2-5
Jay W. Fay, 1
Karen Fay, 13
Ethel M. Feagley, 3
Howard F. Fehr, 4
Elizabeth Fehrer, 3
Erich C. Fein, 16
Henry Feinberg, 1
Candice Feiring, 9-10
Shirley C. Feldmann, 8
Leonard S. Feldt, 5-8
Susan Felsenfeld, 12
Ray Fenton, 12-13, 16, 19
George A. Ferguson, 3-6
Leonard W. Ferguson, 6
Ephrem Fernandez, 13-15
F. Felicia Ferrara, 14-15
Steven Ferrara, 11, 13
Robert H. Ferrell, 5
Trenton R. Ferro, 12-16
C. E. Ficken, 2
James A. Field, Jr., 5
Gordon Fifer, 5
Nikola N. Filby, 8
Jennifer G. Fillingim, 18
Maynard D. Filter, 11, 14
W. Holmes Finch, 16-19
Amy Finch-Williams, 10
Diane Billings Findley, 11
Warren G. Findley, 2-8
Stefan R. Fink, 8
Louis J. Finkle, 9
Carmen J. Finley, 11-12
Martin A. Fischer, 13
Seymour Fisher, 6
Wayne D. Fisher, 6
Joshua A. Fishman, 5
John L. Fisk, 9
Donald W. Fiske, 5
James A. Fitzgerald, 5
Colleen Fitzmaurice, 10
Anne R. Fitzpatrick, 11
Corine Fitzpatrick, 14-16
*Robert Fitzpatrick, 7-16
Dawn P. Flanagan, 12, 15
John C. Flanagan, 1, 3-4, 6
*Rosemary Flanagan, 14-19
Stephen G. Flanagan, 11
*John W. Fleenor, 11-17
Lisa Fleisher, 9
C. M. Fleming, 4

W. G. Fleming, 6
Charles D. Flory, 1, 3
Robert E. Floden, 9
Terri Flowerday, 16
Randy G. Floyd, 18
Joseph J. Foley, 8
John P. Foley, Jr., 5-7
Mary O. Folsom, 7
Janet H. Fontaine, 14
Marie C. Fontana, 8
Thomas G. Foran, 1
Donna Ford, 12
Laurie Ford, 11-12
Rex L. Forehand, 9
Bertram R. Forer, 6
Frank J. Fornoff, 6, 8-9
Elaine Forsyth, 3
Robert A. Forsyth, 7-8
Tomlinson Fort, 2
Jim C. Fortune, 11-14
Judson W. Foust, 2
Hanford M. Fowler, 4-5
Raymond D. Fowler, Jr., 7-8
Charles Fox, 2
Glen Fox, 13-14
Hazel M. Fox, 10
Lynn H. Fox, 8-9
Robert A. Fox, 9
Austin C. Frank, 8
Mary Lou Bryant Frank, 14
Thomas T. Frantz, 7-8
Michael D. Franzen, 9
Stephen L. Franzoi, 9
Robert B. Frary, 9, 12-14
Barry J. Fraser, 9
Elizabeth D. Fraser, 5-6
Richard I. Frederick, 14
Wayne A. Frederick, 5
Norman Frederiksen, 3-8
Norman Fredman, 12
B. J. Freeman, 9
Frank S. Freeman, 4-5
*Stephen J. Freeman, 14-19
David Freides, 7-8
J. Joseph Freilinger, 8
Patricia K. Freitag, 13-14
Brian F. French, 16, 18-19
John W. French, 3-8
Joseph L. French, 7
Robert L. French, 6
Sidney J. French, 3
Bruce R. Fretz, 9
Benno G. Fricke, 5-6
Marilyn Friend, 10
David A. Frisbie, 8-9
Clifford P. Froehlich, 4-5
Gustav J. Froehlich, 3-6
Benjamin Fruchter, 5
Bruce Frumkin, 17

Carol A. Gray, 9
William S. Gray, 1, 3-4
Felice J. Green, 13-14
Kathy E. Green, 12-13, 16-17
Malinda Hendricks Green, 17, 19
Russel F. Green, 6-7
Susan K. Green, 16
Edward B. Greene, 3-5
Harry A. Greene, 2-3
Jeffrey H. Greenhaus, 9
Noel Gregg, 10
Patrick Grehan, 16
Frank M. Gresham, 9-13
Konrad Gries, 4-5
Amy-Jane Griffith, 18
*J. Jeffrey Grill, 8-14
Arnold B. Grobman, 7
Hulda Grobman, 7-8
Martin G. Groff, 9
Patrick Groff, 9
Norman E. Gronlund, 8
Richard E. Gross, 5-8
Fred M. Grossman, 9-10
Foster E. Grossnickle, 1-4
William R. Grove, 3-4
Melissa M. Groves, 13
Wilson H. Guertin, 5-6
Richard E. Guest, 11
Walter S. Guiler, 4
J. P. Guilford, 1-5
Robert M. Guion, 8-10, 12-14
Sami Gulgoz, 11-12
Arlen R. Gullickson, 7-8, 12
R. Gulliford, 7
Harold Gulliksen, 1-2, 4
John Flagg Gummere, 2
Faith Gunning-Dixon, 13-14
John W. Gustad, 5
Rhonda L. Gutenberg, 9-10
George M. Guthrie, 8-9
John T. Guthrie, 7-8
Barbara Lapp Gutkin, 10
Terry B. Gutkin, 9, 14
*Thomas W. Guyette, 9-10, 12, 14, 17-18
Natasha Gwartney, 12
Malcolm D. Gynther, 7-8
Lyn R. Haber, 9-10
Manuella H. Habicht, 16
Robert R. Haccoun, 14
Laura B. Hadley, 2
Atiqa Hachimi, 16
John H. Haefner, 5-6
Edward H. Haertel, 9, 13
Geneva D. Haertel, 13-14
Elizabeth Hagen, 5-7
Rosa A. Hagin, 9, 11, 13
Michio P. Hagiwara, 7-8
Amos L. Hahn, 9
Milton E. Hahn, 3-4, 6

A. Ralph Hakstian, 7-8
Thomas M. Haladyna, 11-13
Robert Leslie Hale, 9
Alfred E. Hall, 8
Bruce W. Hall, 11
Cathy W. Hall, 9-11
Penelope K. Hall, 11-12
W. E. Hall, 3
Wallace B. Hall, 6
Raphael M. Haller, 7-8
Harvey Halpern, 8
Ronald K. Hambleton, 8-9, 11-12, 16
Wade L. Hamil, 11
Laura Hamilton, 18
Scott B. Hamilton, 9
Thomas A. Hammeke, 9
Nelson G. Hanawalt, 3-5
Thomas E. Hancock, 15-17
Leonard Handler, 15
C. H. Handschin, 2
Karl R. Hanes, 13, 16
Kenneth M. Hanig, 18-19
Gerald S. Hanna, 8-9, 11-14
Lavone A. Hanna, 2-3
Paul R. Hanna, 4
Michael J. Hannafin, 9
Mary Elizabeth Hannah, 9
Jane Hansen, 9
Joe B. Hansen, 13
Jo-Ida C. Hansen, 8-9
Michael C. Hansen, 13
Gary R. Hanson, 7
Gregory Hanson, 16
William E. Hanson, 14-16
*Richard E. Harding, 10, 12-17
David S. Hargrove, 10
Thomas G. Haring, 10-11
Marilyn J. Haring-Hidore, 9
Lenore W. Harmon, 8-10
Delwyn L. Harnisch, 11-15
Dennis C. Harper, 9-10, 13-14
Robert A. Harper, 6-7
Thomas H. Harrell, 11
Thomas W. Harrell, 3
Philip L. Harriman, 4-6
Robert G. Harrington, 9-10, 13-14
Albert J. Harris, 3, 6-7
Chester W. Harris, 3-4
Dale B. Harris, 4-8
David P. Harris, 7-8
Jerry D. Harris, 9
Jesse G. Harris, Jr., 6
Larry A. Harris, 7-8
Robert C. Harris, 7
Sandra M. Harris, 18-19
Theodore L. Harris, 6
Mary T. Harrison, 7
*Patti L. Harrison, 9-11, 13-15, 17
Charles M. Harsh, 3-4

Wayne H. Holtzman, 5, 7
Charles Holzwarth, 2
Susan P. Homan, 9
L. Michael Honaker, 11
Charles H. Honzik, 4
Marjorie P. Honzik, 6-7
Albert B. Hood, 8
Darlene Ward Hood, 17
Joyce E. Hood, 8-9
Stephen B. Hood, 8
Stephen R. Hooper, 10-14
Kenneth D. Hopkins, 6-9, 11
John L. Horn, 7
Thomas D. Horn, 7-8
John E. Horrocks, 5-6
William R. Horstman, 17
Clark W. Horton, 2-5
Daniel L. Householder, 8
Janet Houser, 17-19
Charles Houston, 12
Carl I. Hovland, 3-5
Robert W. Howard, 2
Edgar Howarth, 8
George W. Howe, 9
Kenneth W. Howell, 9-10
Robert J. Howell, 10
Duncan Howie, 5
Monica M. Hoye, 3
Cyril J. Hoyt, 4-7
Kenneth B. Hoyt, 6
Louis M. Hsu, 9
Te-Fang Hua, 13
Mary E. Huba, 11
Carl J. Huberty, 7-9
*Anita M. Hubley, 13-19
Edith M. Huddleston, 4
John Peter Hudson, Jr., 13
E. Scott Huebner, 10-11, 13-14
Mildred H. Huebner, 7-8
Allen Huffcutt, 19
David P. Huford, 17
Jan N. Hughes, 10-11
Selma Hughes, 11-12
Violet Hughes, 2
Doncaster G. Humm, 2
Lloyd G. Humphreys, 3-6, 9
Joel Hundert, 9
John D. Hundleby, 6
Stephen Hunka, 6
Albert L. Hunsicker, 4
Allison Hunt, 19
E. Patricia Hunt, 2
Jane V. Hunt, 7-8
Thelma Hunt, 3
William A. Hunt, 3
George W. Hunter, 1-2
Archer W. Hurd, 1
David P. Hurford, 13-16
Dzenana Husremovic, 19

Tiffany Hutchins, 18-19
Sylvia M. Hutchinson, 10
Robert R. Hutzell, 9
George W. Hynd, 9
Robert J. Illback, 9
Jason C. Immekus, 19
Ludwig Immergluck, 3
James C. Impara, 11
Henry A. Imus, 3
Carlos Inchaurralde, 14, 16
Mario Iona, 8
Carl Isenhart, 13-16
Steven Isonio, 13
Stephen H. Ivens, 12-14
Annette M. Iverson, 11-12
Margaret Ives, 3
Edward F. Iwanicki, 8-9
Douglas N. Jackson, 7-9
Joseph F. Jackson, 2-3
Robert W. B. Jackson, 5
Richard M. Jaeger, 8-10
Alice N. Jameson, 3
Molly M. Jameson, 17
Colleen B. Jamison, 7
Marc Janoson, 15, 17-18
Patsy Arnett Jaynes, 11
Frank C. Jean, 1
Chantale Jeanrie, 13-15
*Jeffrey A. Jenkins, 11-19
Jill Ann Jenkins, 14-16
John R. Jennings, 5
Karen E. Jennings, 15-16
Arthur R. Jensen, 5-7, 9
Joanne L. Jensen, 12
Patrick J. Jeske, 9
Carl F. Jesness, 7
Richard Jessor, 5
Frank B. Jex, 6
James E. Jirsa, 9
Lynae A. Johnsen, 16
A. Pemberton Johnson, 5
Cecil D. Johnson, 5
Christopher M. Johnson, 15-16, 19
Dale D. Johnson, 8
Jacqueline Johnson, 15
Jerry Johnson, 11, 16
Judy A. Johnson, 16
Kathleen M. Johnson, 15-19
Laura B. Johnson, 2
Leland P. Johnson, 4
Marjorie S. Johnson, 8
Palmer O. Johnson, 1-5
Richard T. Johnson, 6-8
Richard W. Johnson, 8-10, 12-14
Robert Johnson, 13
Robert L. Johnson, 15-16
Ronn Johnson, 10
Ruth Johnson, 12
Stephen B. Johnson, 16-17, 19

Sylvia T. Johnson, 11
Wade Johnson, 11
Kristin N. Johnson-Gros, 17
Sharon Johnson-Lewis, 11
Joseph A. Johnston, 7
Judith R. Johnston, 9, 13, 16
Barry W. Jones, 9-10
Carleton C. Jones, 1-2
Christina Finley Jones, 14
Clive Jones, 7
David Jones, 7
Dorothy L. Jones, 7
Edward S. Jones, 1-2
Elizabeth L. Jones, 12, 14
H. Gwynne Jones, 6
Harold E. Jones, 1-4
James A. Jones, 12
Katherine S. Jones, 12
Kenneth J. Jones, 6
Kevin M. Jones, 12-15
Kristin Jones, 18
Ll. Wynn Jones, 2
Randall L. Jones, 8
Randall M. Jones, 9
Robert A. Jones, 5
Worth R. Jones, 5-6
A. M. Jordan, 2
Richard H. Jordan, 3
Helen L. Jorstad, 8
Gerald A. Juhnke, 13
Lee N. June, 9
Ehud Jungwirth, 8
*Samuel Juni, 9-14
James J. Jupp, 9
Clifford E. Jurgensen, 3-6
Stephen Jurs, 11-12
Joseph Justman, 5
*Ashraf Kagee, 14-19
Javaid Kaiser, 11-13
Paul E. Kambly, 4
*Randy W. Kamphaus, 9-14
Harrison Kane, 14-17
Michael Kane, 13-14
Neeta Kantamneni, 18-19
Tracy Kantrowitz, 19
Rabindra N. Kanungo, 9-10
Chi-Wen Kao, 13
David E. Kapel, 11
Barbara J. Kaplan, 11-13
David M. Kaplan, 14
Robert M. Kaplan, 10
Stuart A. Karabenick, 9
Harry W. Karn, 4
M. Ray Karnes, 4
Mitchell Karno, 12
Lawrence M. Kasdon, 7-9
Walter Kass, 5
Edward S. Katkin, 8
Walter Katkovsky, 6, 11

Ira Stuart Katz, 14-15
Martin R. Katz, 5-8
Raymond A. Katzell, 3-8
Douglas, F. Kauffman, 16
James M. Kauffman, 9
Alan S. Kaufman, 8-10, 13-14
Nadeen L. Kaufman, 9, 13-14
Walter V. Kaulfers, 1-7
Kenneth A. Kavale, 10
*Michael G. Kavan, 11-19
Michael J. Kavanagh, 8
T. J. Keating, 2
J. A. Keats, 5-6
John M. Keene, Jr., 9
J. Ward Keesling, 9
Thomas J. Kehle, 9-10
Jerard F. Kehoe, 11
Gertrude Keir, 4
Patricia B. Keith, 12-14
*Timothy Z. Keith, 9-10, 12, 14-16
Thomas Kellaghan, 8
Harold R. Keller, 10, 14-16
Peggy Kellers, 15
Karl N. Kelley, 16-19
*Mary Lou Kelley, 9-16
Truman L. Kelley, 2
Donna J. Kelly, 17
Theodore E. Kellogg, 4-5
E. Lowell Kelly, 3-7
Kevin R. Kelly, 15-18
William E. Kendall, 6
Katherine G. Keneally, 4
James E. Kennedy, 6-7
Patricia H. Kennedy, 9
Kathryn W. Kenney, 10, 12
Douglas T. Kenny, 5
Leonard Kenowitz, 9
Grace H. Kent, 2-3
Barbara K. Keogh, 8-9
Robert E. Keohane, 2
Newell C. Kephart, 7
Barbara A. Kerr, 9-10, 12
Nancy Kerr, 9
Willard A. Kerr, 3-4, 6-7
Anne R. Kessler, 13
Carol E. Kessler, 14-15
Kathy S. Kessler, 11-12
Sandra M. Ketrow, 14
Gilbert C. Kettelkamp, 6
Thomas E. Kieren, 8
Kenneth A. Kiewra, 11-14
Edward Kifer, 9
Meghan Kiley, 19
Jeremy Kilpatrick, 7-8
Ernest W. Kimmel, 11, 13-14
Elaine F. Kinder, 1
Glen D. King, 8
John D. King, 12, 16
Joseph E. King, 3

Saunders MacLane, 6
David MacPhee, 11-13
George F. Madaus, 8-9
Faith Madden, 4
*Cleborne D. Maddux, 10-19
*Ronald A. Madle, 14-19
Thomas W. Mahan, Jr., 6
Jennifer N. Mahdavi, 16-19
Roderick K. Mahurin, 11-12
James Mainwaring, 5
Timothy J. Makatura, 14-18
*Koressa Kutsick Malcolm, 10-11, 13-19
Julius B. Maller, 1-2
Susan J. Maller, 13-16
George G. Mallinson, 6-8
Jacqueline V. Mallinson, 6-8
Berenice Mallory, 2
Margaret E. Malone, 13-14
Dean R. Malsbary, 8
Jay A. Mancini, 14
Milton M. Mandell, 4
Joseph R. Manduchi, 14
Kenneth J. Manges, 14
Ramasamy Manikam, 14
Lester Mann, 7-9
M. Jacinta Mann, 5
John Manning, 5, 7
Winton H. Manning, 6
Herschel T. Manuel, 2-5
*Caroline Manuele-Adkins, 9-10, 12-13, 16-19
Gregory J. Marchant, 12-14
Gary L. Marco, 11-14
Carol Mardell-Czudnowski, 10
Howard Margolis, 14, 17
Denise Maricle, 19
Suzanne Markel-Fox, 12
Robert P. Markley, 9-10
Howard J. Markman, 9
Melvin R. Marks, 6
Mary Beth Marr, 9
Marc Marschark, 12
Herbert W. Marsh, 9
David Marshall, 10
Brian K. Martens, 10-11
Charles Wm. Martin, 11
Roy P. Martin, 9
Suzanne G. Martin, 14
William E. Martin, Jr., 13-16, 18
Trey Martindale, 15
Norma Martinez, 19
Manuel Martinez-Pons, 16
Stanley S. Marzolf, 3
Bertram B. Masia, 6
Carolyn E. Massad, 8
M. Mastrangelo, 15
Paul Mastrangelo, 14
Joseph D. Matarazzo, 9-10
Johnny L. Matson, 9
Ross W. Matteson, 4

Michael S. Matthews, 17-19
Paula Matuszek, 9
Francis N. Maxfield, 1-2
James Maxwell, 3-5
Susanna Maxwell, 9
Helen Mayo, 19
Samuel T. Mayo, 6-9
Arthur B. Mays, 2
James J. Mazza, 10
Dawn Mazzie, 16
Charles C. McArthur, 7
Patrick P. McCabe, 16
John N. McCall, 7
Raymond J. McCall, 5
W. C. McCall, 2
William A. McCall, 2
James M. McCallister, 3
R. Steve McCallum, 9
Susan McCammon, 10
Boyd R. McCandless, 4, 6-7
James J. McCarthy, 7-9
Kevin J. McCarthy, 12, 14-15, 17
James Leslie McCary, 8
Robert L. McCaul, 2-3
Clara J. McCauley, 2
*Rebecca J. McCauley, 11-18
Erin McClure, 12
Daniel L. McCollum, 16
David McCone, 15
Scott R. McConnell, 11
Andrew J. McConney, 14
Richard J. McCowan, 14
Sheila C. McCowan, 14
Robert R. McCrae, 9
R. W. McCulloch, 5
Constance M. McCullough, 2-3, 5, 7
Merilee McCurdy, 14, 16-17, 19
S. P. McCutchen, 1-2
Hiram L. McDade, 9
Arthur S. McDonald, 6
Susan McDonald, 19
D. W. McElwain, 4-5
William C. McGaghie, 8
Ellen McGinnis, 10
Dixie McGinty, 16-17
Carol M. McGregor, 14-17
Kevin S. McGrew, 10
Christine H. McGuire, 5-8
Valentina McInerney, 15, 17
David E. McIntosh, 12
Robert M. McIntyre, 9
Michael G. McKee, 7
William T. McKee, 10
Margaret G. McKim, 3-4
Thomas McKnight, 14-17, 19
Joyce R. McLarty, 11, 14
Kenneth F. McLaughlin, 6
John McLeish, 4, 7
Mary J. McLellan, 12-14, 18-19

David T. Morse, 16-18
H. T. Morse, 3
N. W. Morton, 1-2, 4
P. L. Morton, 2
Robert G. Morwood, 14
Harold E. Moser, 5
Donald L. Mosher, 7-8
David Moshman, 10
Charles I. Mosier, 2-3
C. Scott Moss, 6
Pamela A. Moss, 9, 11
Kevin W. Mossholder, 9-10
Stephan J. Motowidlo, 8-9
Donald E. Mowrer, 10
Robert R. Mowrer, 10
*Paul M. Muchinsky, 9, 12-14, 16-17, 19
Daniel J. Mueller, 10
Kate Hevner Mueller, 5
Ralph O. Mueller, 11-13
Ann M. Muench, 11
Thomas D. Mulderink, 19
Ina V. S. Mullis, 8
Leo A. Munday, 7
Allyn M. Munger, 6
Janice W. Murdoch, 14
Joann Murphey, 15
Carolyn Colvin Murphy, 10
Joseph A. Murphy, 7-8
Kevin R. Murphy, 9-12
Wilbur F. Murra, 1-2
Elsie Murray, 4
*Mildred Murray-Ward, 13-14, 16-19
James L. Mursell, 1-3
Bernard I. Murstein, 6-8
Nyaradzo H. Mvududa, 18
Charles T. Myers, 5, 8
Roberta S. Myers, 9
Sheldon S. Myers, 6-7
Dean H. Nafziger, 8, 11-12
Jack A. Naglieri, 9, 11
Philip Nagy, 12-13
Louis C. Nanassy, 5
Scott A. Napolitano, 14, 16, 18
Doris E. Nason, 8
Diana S. Natalicio, 8-9
Theodor F. Naumann, 6-7
Wendy Naumann, 14-15
Lori Nebelsick-Gullett, 15
Leo Nedelsky, 5-6
Charles O. Neidt, 5-6
Leah M. Nellis, 14-17
Edward A. Nelsen, 9
Clarence H. Nelson, 3-8
Jack L. Nelson, 8
Rosemery O. Nelson-Gray, 11
Myrna K. Ness, 9
Debra Neubert, 11-12
Charles Neuringer, 8
Andrew F. Newcomb, 9

Theodore Newcomb, 2
Phyllis L. Newcomer, 8-9
Gwendolyn Newkirk, 10
T. Ernest Newland, 6-7
Bernard H. Newman, 7
Dianna L. Newman, 10-13
E. Jean Newman, 13-14
Isadore Newman, 12
Joseph Newman, 4
Kenneth R. Newton, 5
Arthur M. Nezu, 10
William H. Nibbelink, 8
Lois Nichols, 12
David S. Nichols, 9, 11
Robert C. Nichols, 6, 8-9
Nicole L. Nieset, 17-18
John Nisbet, 5-7
Stanley D. Nisbet, 4-7
Michael Nissenbaum, 12
*Anthony J. Nitko, 8-14
Amanda Nolen, 18-19
Victor H. Noll, 1-7
Patricia Noller, 9
Claude E. Norcross, 4
Warren T. Norman, 5-7
*Janet A. Norris, 9-15
Raymond C. Norris, 5
Robert D. North, 5-7
Paul A. Northrop, 1-2
Christine Novak, 12, 14, 18
Ruth M. Noyce, 9-10
Edward S. Noyes, 2-3
Jum C. Nunnally, 7
Michelle Nutter, 15
Thomas Oakland, 8-9
C. A. Oakley, 2-3
C. O. Oakley, 3
Lindsey O'Brennan, 18
Thomas C. O'Brien, 7-8
John E. Obrzut, 9, 11
Anna S. Ochoa, 8-9
*Salvador Hector Ochoa, 12-17
Charles W. Odell, 1-3
*Judy Oehler-Stinnett, 10-14, 16
Lynn R. Offermann, 13
Billy T. Ogletree, 13-14
Kevin E. O'Grady, 9-10
Stephen Olejnik, 11-12, 14
Arturo Olivarez, Jr., 16-19
Donald W. Oliver, 6
Mary Ellen Oliverio, 5, 7-8
Esteban L. Olmedo, 9
*D. Joe Olmi, 11-16
Amy M. Olson, 17-19
Carl J. Olson, 7
Thomas R. O'Neill, 16-18
Deniz S. Ones, 14-18
Albert C. Oosterhof, 12-13
Don B. Oppenheim, 9

Barbara S. Plake, 9
Gus P. Plessas, 6-9
Lynnette B. Plumlee, 3, 5-7
John Poggio, 14
Edward Polloway, 9-10
Joseph G. Ponterotto, 11
Marcel O. Ponton, 13
Robert C. Pooley, 2-7
Mark Pope, 11-12, 14-16
Donald B. Pope-Davis, 12
Mary S. Poplin, 9
Sameano F. Porchea, 19
Julia Y. Porter, 14, 16-19
Lyman W. Porter, 6
James M. Porter, Jr., 3
William D. Porterfield, 11
Stanley D. Porteus, 2
C. Dale Posey, 10
Winifred L. Post, 4-5
*G. Michael Poteat, 10-16, 19
James A. Poteet, 9-10
Kenneth E. Poucher, 8
Shawn Powell, 15-19
Thomas E. Powell, 11
Stephen Powers, 9
Elizabeth M. Prather, 9-11
Michael W. Pratt, 9
Sheila R. Pratt, 13-16
Norman T. Pratt, Jr., 1-2
Daniel A. Prescott, 1
Joan Preston, 7
Ralph C. Preston, 3-4
H. Vernon Price, 5
J. Randall Price, 17
Jack Price, 7
Ray G. Price, 3, 6-7
Roy A. Price, 2-3
Erich P. Prien, 13-14
Kristin O. Prien, 14
Hugh F. Priest, 7
George P. Prigatano, 9
M. L. Kellmer Pringle, 4-7
Barry M. Prizant, 11
Glen W. Probst, 7
Barton B. Proger, 8-9
H. Thompson Prout, 9
Richard C. Pugh, 12-13
Earl V. Pullias, 2
Alan C. Purves, 7-8
Joan E. Pynes, 10
Fred Pyrczak, 8
Edys S. Quellmalz, 9
M. Y. Quereshi, 7-8
Theresa A. Quigney, 14
Kathleen Quinn, 19
Michelle Quinn, 9
Albert I. Rabin, 4-5, 7
S. Rachman, 6
John A. Radcliffe, 5-6

Rudolf E. Radocy, 12-13
Jeffrey S. Rain, 12-13
*Nambury S. Raju, 9, 11-16
Pamilla Ramsden, 15-17
Bikkar S. Randhawa, 11-14
John F. Randolph, 3
Earl F. Rankin, 7-8
Alan J. Raphael, 13-14
Evelyn Raskin, 4
Leslie T. Raskind, 10
Natalie Rathvon, 16
Michael M. Ravitch, 9
Glen E. Ray, 12, 19
Alton L. Raygor, 6, 8
S. A. Rayner, 5
Mark D. Reckase, 9
Homer B. C. Reed, Jr., 8-9
James C. Reed, 7-9, 12-15
Janet S. Reed, 18-19
Michael L. Reed, 9
Edwin H. Reeder, 3-4
Amy M. Rees, 16
Jeff Reese, 14
Ronald E. Reeve, 9
William R. Reevy, 6
Laura W. Reid, 19
Sean P. Reilley, 16-17
Barbara A. Reilly, 11-12
David H. Reilly, 9
Nora P. Reilly, 19
Richard Reilly, 19
Judith A. Rein, 15-16
Robert C. Reinehr, 11-14
Robert A. Reineke, 11-12
Richard J. Reisboard, 8
Carmen D. Reisener, 19
Ralph M. Reitan, 6-7
Willard E. Reitz, 7
H. H. Remmers, 1, 3, 5
K. Ann Renninger, 9
Joseph S. Renzulli, 9
Harvey Resnick, 9
*Paul Retzlaff, 11-16
*Cecil R. Reynolds, 9, 11-15
Maynard C. Reynolds, 5
Sharon B. Reynolds, 10
William M. Reynolds, 9, 14-15
Marvin Reznikoff, 7
Elizabeth Kelley Rhoades, 16-17
James A. Rice, 8
Gilbert J. Rich, 3
David C. Richard, 14
R. Lynn Richards, 10
Roger A. Richards, 5-9, 11, 13-14
T. W. Richards, 4
James M. Richards, Jr., 7-8
J. A. Richardson, 5
M. W. Richardson, 1-2
S. C. Richardson, 5

Sharon Ann Richardson, 17
David M. Richman, 19
Bert O. Richmond, 9
James H. Ricks, Jr., 4-6, 8
T. Andrew Ridenour, 13
Paul R. Rider, 2
Stanley E. Ridley, 9
C. Alan Riedesel, 6-8
William Rieman, III, 3-4
Michelle L. Ries, 14
Edward G. Rietz, 5
Henry L. Rietz, 1
Janet Morgan Riggs, 9
Seymour Rigrodsky, 7
Alice R. Rines, 8
Henry D. Rinsland, 1-4
Charlene Rivera, 11
Harry N. Rivlin, 4-5
Robin Rix, 15
James P. Rizzo, 6
Brandy M. Roane, 18
Oscar H. Roberts, 7
Brent W. Roberts, 14
David C. Roberts, 13
Holland Roberts, 2-6
Mark W. Roberts, 9, 11, 14
Donald U. Robertson, 11
Gary J. Robertson, 9-10, 13
Elizabeth A. Robinson, 9
Eric Robinson, 12
G. Edith Robinson, 7
H. Alan Robinson, 6-8
Helen M. Robinson, 4-7
Richard D. Robinson, 8
Alec Rodger, 2-4
David A. Rodgers, 7
Ronald C. Rodgers, 9
*Bruce G. Rogers, 9-17
Carl R. Rogers, 2
Cyril A. Rogers, 5
Frederick R. Rogers, 2
Margaret R. Rogers, 12
Virginia M. Rogers, 7
W. Todd Rogers, 7
*Cynthia A. Rohrbeck, 11, 13-16, 19
Samuel Roll, 10
Deborah D. Roman, 12-14
Thomas A. Romberg, 7-8
Leonard G. Rorer, 7
Carl L. Rosen, 7-9
Ephraim Rosen, 4
Gerald A. Rosen, 13
Marvin Rosen, 8
John H. Rosenbach, 7-9
Robert L. Rosenbaum, 8
Jennifer A. Rosenblatt, 13
Sylvia Rosenfield, 9-10
Arlene Coopersmith Rosenthal, 9-11
Nancy L. Roser, 8-9

Benjamin Rosner, 5-7
Jerome Rosner, 7
Alan O. Ross, 6
C. C. Ross, 2-3
Charles S. Ross, 4-5
Paul F. Ross, 6
Myron F. Rosskopf, 5
*Michael J. Roszkowski, 9-10, 12-15
Rodney W. Roth, 11
Harold F. Rothe, 4
Robert D. Rothermel, 9
Barbara A. Rothlisberg, 11-14
John W. M. Rothney, 1, 3-7
Julian B. Rotter, 3
Pamela Carrington Rotto, 12
James B. Rounds, 9-10, 12
Byron P. Rourke, 9
Steven V. Rouse, 18-19
Denise M. Rousseau, 9-10
Mark C. Roybal, 17
Harold L. Royer, 6
Arthur B. Royse, 5-6
Thaddeus Rozecki, 13
Ronald H. Rozensky, 11
Mary Roznowski, 14
Donald L. Rubin, 11
Stanley I. Rubin, 6
Floyd L. Ruch, 3-4, 6
Giles M. Ruch, 2
Herbert C. Rudman, 9, 12-14
Lawrence M. Rudner, 11-12
Robert Rueda, 10
C. H. Ruedisili, 3
Mabel E. Rugen, 3
David L. Rule, 10
Edward A. Rundqust, 3
William H. Rupley, 9
David H. Russell, 2-4
Harry J. Russell, 2-3
Michael Lee Russell, 13-14
James O. Rust, 9-10
John Rust, 12
Leo P. Ruth, 8
Richard Ruth, 19
Roger A. Ruth, 7-8
Joseph M. Ryan, 11
Katherine Ryan, 18
Lawrence J. Ryan, 14-15
Michael Ryan, 9-10
David G. Ryans, 3-4, 6
Jane A. Rysberg, 9-10
Richard Rystrom, 7-8
David A. Sabatino, 9
*Darrell L. Sabers, 8-19
Donna S. Sabers, 13
Michael Sachs, 19
Everett B. Sackett, 1, 6
Paul R. Sackett, 9
Cyril J. Sadowski, 12-13

H. Bradley Sagen, 6-7
Philip A. Saigh, 9
Perry Sailor, 12
Kenneth Sakauye, 12
Rachel Salisbury, 2
John Salvia, 9
*Vincent J. Samar, 11-12, 14-17
John Sample, 18
David T. Sanchez, 9
Daryl Sander, 9
C. Sanders, 5
James R. Sanders, 9
Lia E Sandilos, 19
*Jonathan Sandoval, 9-10, 12-15, 17-19
Claude A. Sandy, 12
*Eleanor E. Sanford-Moore, 11-19
Dixie D. Sanger, 9
Toni E. Santmire, 9-10
Janice Santogrossi, 10
H. J. Sants, 6
Bert R. Sappenfield, 5-6
Irwin G. Sarason, 6
Theodore R. Sarbin, 4
Timothy Sares, 16
David M. Sargent, 15
Helen Sargent, 4
I. David Satlow, 5
George A. Satter, 3-4
Jerome M. Sattler, 8-10
Richard A. Saudargas, 10
Aulus W. Saunders, 2
David M. Saunders, 11
David R. Saunders, 5
*William I. Sauser, Jr., 9-17
Jean-Guy Savard, 7
*Diane J. Sawyer, 9-14, 17
Neroli Sawyer, 15
Gilbert Sax, 8
Peter Scales, 9
Dale P. Scannell, 9, 11-13
Douglas E. Scates, 1, 3, 5
William L. Schaaf, 4
Willis C. Schaefer, 4
*William D. Schafer, 11-14, 16-19
Joyce Parr Schaie, 8
K. Warner Schaie, 8-9
Michael J. Scheel, 15, 17-19
Susan J. Schenck, 9-10
Johann H. Schepers, 6
Charles A. Scherbaum, 19
Alvin W. Schindler, 1-2, 4
Steven P. Schinke, 10, 12
Richard J. Schissel, 9-10
Richard F. Schmid, 9
Frank L. Schmidt, 8-9, 13, 16
Steven W. Schmidt, 18-19
John F. Schmitt, 9
Neal Schmitt, 9, 12-13
Gerald R. Schneck, 13-15

Arnold E. Schneider, 3
W. Joel Schneider, 16-18
Leroy H. Schnell, 2-3
Lyle F. Schoenfeldt, 7-10
Patricia Schoenrade, 12-13, 19
Wiliiam Schofield, 4-6
Fred J. Schonell, 2, 4-5
Richard V. Schowengerdt, 14
William B. Schrader, 4-6
H. E. Schrammel, 1
Fredrick A. Schrank, 9-10
*Gregory Schraw, 12, 14-19
Robert L. Schreiner, 8
Stephen T. Schroth, 19
Herbert Schueler, 3-6
Douglas G. Schultz, 4, 6-7
Geoffrey F. Schultz, 11
Harold A. Schultz, 4, 6
Dale H. Schunk, 9
Richard Schupbach, 8
Donald H. Schuster, 6-7
Richard E. Schutz, 6-9
Joseph J. Schwab, 3
*Gene Schwarting, 9, 12-18
Neil H. Schwartz, 9-10
Mariette Schwarz, 6
Dean M. Schweickhard, 2
Gladys C. Schwesinger, 4
Amy Scott, 19
Craig S. Scott, 8
Louise B. Scott, 5
Owen Scott, III, 11
May V. Seagoe, 4
Carl E. Seashore, 2
Harold G. Seashore, 3-6
Virginia Seavey, 3
Don Sebolt, 12
Charles Secolsky, 9
William Seeman, 4
Stanley J. Segal, 6
David Segel, 1, 3-4
Esther F. Segner, 2
Natasha Segool, 18
S. B. Sells, 5-7
R. B. Selover, 3
Gary B. Seltzer, 11
Boris Semenonoff, 6
Melvin I. Semmel, 7
Trevor E. Sewell, 9
Nichole Shada, 19
Robert E. Shafer, 9
Laurance F. Shaffer, 3-6
Marcia B. Shaffer, 9-12
Timothy Shanahan, 9, 14, 16, 18-19
Spencer Shank, 1
Gregory A. Shannon, 11
David A. Shapiro, 10-12
Edward S. Shapiro, 10-11
Kathy Shapley, 18-19

Michael Spangler, 15-16
C. Spearman, 2
Donald Spearritt, 5
Janet E. Spector, 13-14
Robert K. Speer, 2
Daniel G. Spencer, 9
Douglas Spencer, 2-3
Loraine J. Spenciner, 14-18
Peter L. Spencer, 2
Rayne A. Sperling, 16, 18-19
Charles D. Spielberger, 8
Robert Spies, 13-14
Donna Spiker, 11-12, 17
Stephen A. Spillane, 14
Susan K. Spille, 12
Herbert F. Spitzer, 3-4
Jaclyn B. Spitzer, 9, 11, 13, 16
Gilbert M. Spivack, 9
Bernard Spolsky, 6
Michael J. Sporakowski, 12, 14
Scott Spreat, 12
Otfried Spreen, 6
Becky L. Spritz, 18
Mark A. Staal, 15, 17-18
Barrie G. Stacey, 9
Michael J. Stahl, 9-10
Steven A. Stahl, 11, 14
Robert F. Stahmann, 8
Gary J. Stainback, 11, 13-14
*Jayne E. Stake, 9-13, 15
Robert E. Stake, 6
John M. Stalnaker, 1-2, 4-6
Roy W. Stanhope, 5
Julian C. Stanley, 4-6
Charles W. Stansfield, 8-10, 14
Joel Stark, 7-8
Stephen Stark, 19
E. P. Starke, 4
Stanley Starkman, 9
Anna S. Starr, 1
Edward R. Starr, 13
F. Staskon, 19
Russell G. Stauffer, 5-6
John E. Stecklein, 6
Elaine Flory Stefany, 12
Leslie P. Steffe, 7-8
Harry L. Stein, 5-6
Jack M. Stein, 6-7
Margot B. Stein, 13-14, 18
*Stephanie Stein, 11-19
Wendy J. Steinberg, 10, 15-16
Hugh Stephenson, 15
William Stephenson, 4-6
F. E. Sterling, 9
Robert J. Sternberg, 9
Brenda A. Stevens, 14
Kay B. Stevens, 17-19
Jay R. Stewart, 13-15, 17-18
Krista J. Stewart, 9-10

Naomi Stewart, 4-6
Sheldon L. Stick, 9-10
Charles A. Stickland, 4
Harlan J. Stientjes, 11-12
*Terry A. Stinnett, 10-15, 17
William A. Stock, 11-12
Jill M. Stoefen-Fisher, 9
Howard Stoker, 11
Joseph P. Stokes, 9-10
Clarence R. Stone, 2
Gerald L. Stone, 9-13
L. Joseph Stone, 4-5
Mark Stone, 9, 15, 18
Gary Stoner, 11, 12
Janet M. Stoppard, 9
Donald Lee Stovall, 14-15
Phillip S. Strain, 9
David Strand, 10
Jennifer M. Strang, 18-19
Ruth M. Strang, 1-2, 5
Richard K. Stratton, 12
Christine F. Strauss, 12
Lois T. Strauss, 11
Lawrence J. Stricker, 6, 8
Ruth Strickland, 5
Douglas C. Strohmer, 9
Stanley R. Strong, 8-9
Charles R. Strother, 3-5
J. B. Stroud, 3
Hans H. Strupp, 7
*Richard B. Stuart, 9-13, 15
Dewey B. Stuit, 3-4
George W. Sturrock, 5
*Gabrielle Stutman, 12-19
Frederick H. Stutz, 3, 5
Michael J. Subkoviak, 9, 11-13
Richard R. Sudweeks, 13
*Hoi K. Suen, 11-16, 18-19
Alan R. Suess, 7-8, 10
Richard M. Suinn, 7
Gail M. Sullivan, 11
Jeremy R. Sullivan, 18-19
Patricia M. Sullivan, 9
W. L. Sumner, 4
Norman D. Sundberg, 5-9, 11-14
Donna L. Sundre, 12-13
Yong H. Sung, 9
Donald E. Super, 3-6, 8
Carolyn H. Suppa, 16-17, 19
J. P. Sutcliffe, 5
John Sutherland, 5-6
Rosemary E. Sutton, 11-14, 16
Marilyn N. Suydam, 7-9
John G. Svinicki, 10
Edward O. Swanson, 6
H. Lee Swanson, 9
Richard A. Swanson, 7-8
Robert M. Swanson, 8
Robert S. Swanson, 8

Kerri Turk, 12
Mary E. Turnbull, 4-6
Clarence E. Turner, 2-6
Mervyn L. Turner, 5
Austin H. Turney, 1-2
Lawrence J. Turton, 7-10, 12
F. T. Tyler, 3
Leona E. Tyler, 4-7
Ralph W. Tyler, 2-3, 5
Thomas A. Tyler, 8
Aharon Tziner, 9
Judy A. Ungerer, 9
C. C. Upshall, 3
Susana Urbina, 12-16
Marguerite Uttley, 3
Nicholas A. Vacc, 9-13
*John J. Vacca, 14-19
Curtis C. Vail, 1
Rebecca W. Valcarce, 9
Paolo Valesio, 7
Robert E. Valett, 7
Rachel J. Valleley, 17-18
William J. Valmont, 8
Forrest L. Vance, 6-7
Henry Van Engen, 4
*Wilfred G. Van Gorp, 11-16
*James P. Van Haneghan, 12-15, 18-19
Gerald R. Van Hecke, 8
Gabriele van Lingen, 13-14, 16
Byron H. Van Roekel, 5-9
Neil J. Van Steenberg, 4-5
Wendy Van Wyhe, 12
Molly L. Vanduser, 14
Jamie E. Vannice, 17
Stanley F. Vasa, 9-10
Elisa Vasquez, 19
Matt Vassar, 18
Robert P. Vecchio, 9
Donald J. Veldman, 6-7
Frank R. Vellutino, 8
John J. Venn, 16-18
William M. Verdi, 13-14
Magdalen D. Vernon, 5-6
Philip E. Vernon, 2, 4-9
Dolores Kluppel Vetter, 11, 13, 16-18
Verna L. Vickery, 5
Donald J. Viglione, Jr., 9
Peter Villanova, 11
Roland Vinette, 3
Jan Visser, 14
*Chockalingam Viswesvaran, 13-19
Morris S. Viteles, 2-3
Romeo Vitelli, 14-15, 17, 19
Daniel E. Vogler, 12
Metta Volker-Fry, 16
Robert J. Volpe, 15
Theresa Volpe-Johnstone, 14-15, 17
Alex Voogel, 11
Christine Calderon Vriesema, 19

David P. Wacker, 9-10
J. R. Jefferson Wadkins, 7-8
Catherine Wagner, 18
Edwin E. Wagner, 9
Elvis Wagner, 19
Guy W. Wagner, 1
John Wagner, 7
William W. Waite, 3-4
J. V. Waits, 3
John F. Wakefield, 11, 18
Delores D. Walcott, 14-16, 18
William J. Waldron, 12-14
Cindy M. Walker, 15-16
Helen M. Walker, 1
Justin M. Walker, 17
Robert Wall, 13-15
Shavaun M. Wall, 9
W. D. Wall, 4
S. Rains Wallace, 4-5
Wimburn L. Wallace, 5-8
Norman E. Wallen, 6
Niels G. Waller, 11-14
James A. Walsh, 7-8
W. Bruce Walsh, 7
Edwin Wandt, 4, 7
Aimin Wang, 15
Yuan Yuan Wang, 19
Sandra J. Wanner, 14
Morey J. Wantman, 4-6
Richard A. Wantz, 10, 12, 14
F. W. Warburton, 4-5
Annie W. Ward, 11-15
Annita Marie Ward, 15-17
Charles F. Ward, 7
*Sandra B. Ward, 13-19
William C. Ward, 7-8
George Wardlow, 10
James L. Wardrop, 8-10
E. M. Waring, 9
David M. Wark, 7
Charles F. Warnath, 6, 8
Neil D. Warren, 3, 5
Willard G. Warrington, 5-7
Ruth W. Washburn, 3
Christa E. Washington, 19
Orest E. Wasyliw, 12, 14
Alan T. Waterman, 2
Betsy Waterman, 13-15
Eugene A. Waters, 2
Everett Waters, 9
John G. Watkins, 6
Marley W. Watkins, 9
Ralph K. Watkins, 2
Richard W. Watkins, 7-8
Betty U. Watson, 9
Goodwin Watson, 1-3
Robert I. Watson, 3
*T. Steuart Watson, 11-18
Tonya S. Watson, 17

J. Richard Wittenborn, 3-4
Donna Wittmer, 12
Paul A. Witty, 3
Gregory C. Wochos, 16
David L. Wodrich, 9, 14
Kristen Wojcik, 13
Richard M. Wolf, 8-9, 11-14
Dael L. Wolfle, 1-2, 4
Leroy Wolins, 6
James A. Wollack, 12, 14
Myra N. Womble, 13, 17-18
E. F. Wonderlic, 3
Hugh B. Wood, 2
Jamie G. Wood, 17
Michelle Wood, 13
Ray G. Wood, 3
Michael F. Woodin, 18
Clifford Woody, 1, 3
D. A. Worcester, 2-4
Edward A. Workman, 9
Julien Worland, 9
Blaine R. Worthen, 7-9, 12-13
F. Lynwood Wren, 3
C. Gilbert Wrenn, 1-2, 5
Benjamin D. Wright, 9
*Claudia R. Wright, 11-19
Dan Wright, 9-12
Logan Wright, 11-12
Robert Wright, 18-19
Robert L. Wright, 7
William J. Wright, 8
J. Wayne Wrightstone, 1-3, 5
Jack Wrigley, 5
Thomas A. Wrobel, 11
Tony C. Wu, 18-19
Tracey Wyatt, 19

Michael K. Wynne, 12
Kaoru Yamamoto, 8
Alfred Yates, 5
Aubrey J. Yates, 7
Daniel L. Yazak, 14
Albert H. Yee, 7
Frank R. Yekovich, 9
Tamela Yelland, 12
Georgette Yetter, 16-19
Dale Yoder, 4
John W. Young, 12, 14-16
Suzanne Young, 16-19
*James E. Ysseldyke, 8-12, 14, 16
William Yule, 8
Robert H. Zabel, 9
Peter Zachar, 13-16, 19
Louis C. Zahner, 2-3, 5
Dan Zakay, 9
O. L. Zangwill, 3
John A. Zarske, 9-10
*Sheldon Zedeck, 8-9, 11-15, 19
Paul F. Zelhart, 10
Bo Zhang, 16
Yuanzhong Zhang, 19
Michael J. Zickar, 14, 17
Edwin Ziegfeld, 2-4
Corinne Zimmerman, 18
Linda J. Zimmerman, 14
Wayne S. Zimmerman, 6-7
Fred Zimring, 9
Joseph E. Zins, 9
Leland C. Zlomke, 10-14
Steven Zucker, 13
Marvin Zuckerman, 9
Donald G. Zytowski, 7-9, 12

INDEX OF TITLES

The titles index includes a comprehensive listing of tests currently in print and included in this volume as well as out-of-print (or status unknown) tests that were listed in Tests in Print VIII *and* The Nineteenth Mental Measurements Yearbook. *Numbers without colons refer to in-print tests included in this volume. Numbers with colons refer to out-of-print tests not listed in this volume; readers interested in these tests are referred to the last volume listing the tests. For example, T8:1826 refers to test 1826 in* Tests in Print VIII; *16:199 refers to test 199 in* The 16th MMY. *Superseded titles are listed with a cross reference to the present title. All numbers refer to test entries, not to page numbers.*

Skills Inventory for Teams, 1890

Skillscope®, 1891

SKILLSCOPE for Managers®, see Skillscope, 1891

Sleep Disorders Inventory for Students, 1892

Slingerland Screening Tests for Identifying Children with Specific Language Disability, 1893

Slosson Articulation, Language Test with Phonology, 1894

Slosson Full-Range Intelligence Test, 1895

Slosson Intelligence Test 3rd [2002 Edition], 1896

Slosson Oral Reading Test—Revised, 1897

Slosson Test of Reading Readiness, 1898

Smedley Hand Dynamometer, 1899

Smell Identification Test™ [Revised], 1900

Smoker Complaint Scale, 1901

Snijders-Oomen Non-Verbal Intelligence Scale, see SON-R 6-40 Non-Verbal Intelligence Test, 1922

Snijders-Oomen Non-Verbal Intelligence Scale For Young Children, see SON-R 2.5-7 Non-Verbal Intelligence Test, 1923

Social Adjustment Scale—Self Report, 1902

Social Behavior Assessment Inventory, 1903

Social Competence and Behavior Evaluation, Preschool Edition, 1904

Social-Emotional Assessment/Evaluation Measure (SEAM™), Research Edition, 1905

Social Emotional Assets and Resilience Scales, 1906

Social-Emotional Developmental Age Level, 1907

Social-Emotional Dimension Scale—Second Edition, 1908

Social-Emotional Wellbeing Survey, 1909

Social Intelligence Profile, 1910

Social Personality and Skills Assessment, 1911

Social Phobia and Anxiety Inventory, 1912

Social Phobia & Anxiety Inventory for Children, 1913

The Social Problem-Solving Inventory for Adolescents, 1914

Social Problem-Solving Inventory—Revised, 1915

Social Responsiveness Scale, Second Edition, 1916

Social Reticence Scale, 1917

Social Skills Improvement System Rating Scales, 1918

Social Skills Inventory [Second Edition Manual], 1919

Social Skills Training: Enhancing Social Competence with Children and Adolescents, T8:2505

Social Styles Analysis, 1920

Socio-Sexual Knowledge and Attitudes Assessment Tool—Revised, 1921

Softball Skills Test, T8:2505

Solid Geometry: National Achievement Tests, T8:2506

SON-R 51/2-17, see SON-R 6-40 Non-Verbal Intelligence Test, 1922

SON-R 6-40 Non-Verbal Intelligence Test, 1922

SON-R 2.5-7 Non-Verbal Intelligence Test, 1923

S.O.N. Snijders-Oomen Non-Verbal Intelligence Scale, see SON-R 6-40 Non-Verbal Intelligence Test, 1922

Sources of Stress Scale [2006 Revision], 1924

The Southern California Ordinal Scales of Development, 1925

Space Relations (Paper Puzzles), 1926

Space Thinking (Flags), 1927

Spadafore ADHD Rating Scale, T8:2511

Spadafore Diagnostic Reading Test, T8:2512

Spanish Assessment of Basic Education, Second Edition, 1928

Spanish/English Reading Comprehension Test [Revised], 1929

Spanish Reading Inventory, Second Edition, 1930

The Spanish Substance Abuse Subtle Screening Inventory, 1931

SPAR Spelling and Reading Tests, Third Edition, 1932

Spatial Awareness Skills Program, T8:2517

Spatial Reasoning, 1933

Speaking Proficiency English Assessment Kit, 1934

Speech and Language Evaluation Scale, 1935

Speech-Ease Screening Inventory (K–1), 1936

Speech Evaluation of the Patient with a Tracheostomy Tube, T8:2522

Speech Perception Instructional Curriculum and Evaluation, 1937

The Speed and Capacity of Language Processing Test, 1938

Spelling Performance Evaluation for Language and Literacy, Second Edition, 1939

Spelling Test: National Achievement Tests, T8:2526

Spiritual Well-Being Scale, 1940

Sport Personality Questionnaire, 1941

Sports Emotion Test, T8:2529

Spousal Assault Risk Assessment Guide, 1942

Stages of Concern Questionnaire, see Change Abilitator, 379

Standard Progressive Matrices, New Zealand Standardization, T8:2531

The Standard Timing Model, 1943

Standardized Assessment of Miranda Abilities, 1944

Standardized Bible Content Tests, Forms I and J, 1945

Standardized Reading Inventory, Second Edition, 1946

Standardized Test of Computer Literacy and Computer Anxiety Index (Version AZ), Revised, T8:2535

Stanford Achievement Test, Tenth Edition, 1947

Stanford-Binet Intelligence Scales, Fifth Edition, 1948

Stanford-Binet Intelligence Scales for Early Childhood, Fifth Edition, 1949

Stanford Diagnostic Mathematics Test, Fourth Edition, T8:2540

Stanford Diagnostic Reading Test, Fourth Edition, T8:2541

Stanford Early School Achievement Test, Third Edition, T8:2542

Stanford English Language Proficiency Test, T8:2543

Stanford Reading First, T8:2544

Stanford Writing Assessment Program, Third Edition, 1950

The Stanton Profile, T8:2546

The Stanton Survey and the Stanton Survey Phase II, 1951

STAR Early Literacy®, 1952

STAR Math®, 1953

INDEX OF OUT-OF-PRINT TESTS

The Index of Out-of-Print Tests is a cumulative listing of tests that appeared in Tests in Print III *through* The Nineteenth Mental Measurements Yearbook *but that do not appear in* Tests in Print IX. *The publishers of most of these tests have advised that the tests are now out of print. For some others, status has been unknown for many years or the last known publisher is no longer in business. In these cases, the tests are believed to be out of print; those assumed out of print since* Tests in Print VIII *are noted with an asterisk. Those tests in this index that appeared in* Tests in Print VIII *and/or* The Nineteenth Mental Measurements Yearbook *but that are not in* Tests in Print IX *are also integrated into the Index of Titles. All numbers refer to test entries, not page numbers. For example, T4:233 refers to test 233 in* Tests in Print IV, *12:121 refers to test 121 in* The 12th MMY, *and 15:301 refers to test 301 in* The 15th MMY.

INDEX OF ACRONYMS

This Index of Acronyms refers the reader to the appropriate test in Tests in Print IX. *In some cases tests are better known by their acronyms than by their full titles, and this index can be of substantial help to the person who knows the former but not the latter. Acronyms are only listed if the author or publisher has made substantial use of the acronym in referring to the test, or if the test is widely known by the acronym. A few acronyms are also registered trademarks (e.g., SAT); where this is known to us, only the test with the registered trademark is referenced. There is some danger in the overuse of acronyms, but this index, like all other indexes in this work, is provided to make the task of identifying a test as easy as possible. All numbers refer to test numbers, not page numbers.*

743

CLASSIFIED SUBJECT INDEX

The Classified Subject Index classifies all tests included in Tests in Print IX *into 18 major categories: Achievement, Behavior Assessment, Developmental, Education, English and Language, Fine Arts, Foreign Language, Intelligence and General Aptitude, Mathematics, Miscellaneous, Neuropsychological, Personality, Reading, Science, Sensory-Motor, Social Studies, Speech and Hearing, and Vocations. Each category appears in alphabetical order, and tests are ordered alphabetically within each category. The Miscellaneous category has 15 subcategories with tests ordered alphabetically within the subcategories. Each test entry includes test title, population for which the test is intended, and the test entry number in* Tests in Print IX. *All numbers refer to test entry numbers, not to page numbers. Brief suggestions for the use of this index are presented in the introduction. Revised definitions of the categories were effective with* The Fourteenth Mental Measurements Yearbook. *Most tests in TIP IX have been classified using the revised definitions, which are provided below.*

Achievement

Tests that measure acquired knowledge across school subject content areas. Included here are test batteries that measure multiple content areas and individual subject areas not having separate classification categories. (Note: Some batteries include both achievement and aptitude subtests. Such batteries may be classified under the categories of either Achievement or Intelligence and Aptitude depending upon the principal content area.)

See also Fine Arts, Intelligence and General Aptitude, Mathematics, Reading, Science, and Social Studies.

Behavior Assessment

Tests that measure general or specific behavior within educational, vocational, community, or home settings. Included here are checklists, rating scales, and surveys that measure observer's interpretations of behavior in relation to adaptive or social skills, functional skills, and appropriateness or dysfunction within settings/situations.

Developmental

Tests that are designed to assess skills or emerging skills (such as number concepts, conservation, memory, fine motor, gross motor, communication, letter recognition, social competence) of young children (0-7 years) or tests which are designed to assess such skills in severely or profoundly disabled school-aged individuals. Included here are early screeners, developmental surveys/profiles, kindergarten or school readiness tests, early learning profiles, infant development scales, tests of play behavior, social acceptance/social skills; and preschool psycho-educational batteries. Content specific screeners, such as those assessing readiness, are classified by content area (e.g., Reading).

See also Neuropsychological and Sensory-Motor.

Education

General education-related tests, including measures of instructional/school environment, effective schools/teaching, study skills and strategies, learning styles and strategies, school attitudes, educational programs/ curriculae, interest inventories, and educational leadership.

Specific content area tests (i.e., science, mathematics, social studies, etc.) are listed by their content area.

English and Language

Tests that measure skills in using or understanding the English language in spoken or written form. Included here are tests of language proficiency, applied literacy, language comprehension/development/proficiency, English skills/proficiency, communication skills, listening comprehension, linguistics, and receptive/expressive vocabulary. (Tests designed to measure the mechanics of speaking or communicating are classified under the category Speech and Hearing.)

Fine Arts

Tests that measure knowledge, skills, abilities, attitudes, and interests within the various areas of fine and performing arts. Included here are tests of aptitude, achievement, creativity/talent/giftedness specific to the Fine Arts area, and tests of aesthetic judgment.

Foreign Languages

Tests that measure competencies and readiness in reading, comprehending, and speaking a language other than English.

Intelligence and General Aptitude

Tests that measure general acquired knowledge, aptitudes, or cognitive ability and those that assess specific aspects of these general categories. Included here are tests of critical thinking skills, nonverbal/verbal reasoning, cognitive abilities/processing, learning potential/aptitude/efficiency, logical reasoning, abstract thinking, creative thinking/creativity, entrance exams and academic admissions tests.

Mathematics

Tests that measure competencies and attitudes in any of the various areas of mathematics (e.g., algebra, geometry, calculus) and those related to general mathematics achievement/proficiency. (Note: Included here are tests that assess personality or affective variables related to mathematics.)

Miscellaneous

Tests that cannot be sorted into any of the current MMY categories as listed and defined above. Included here are tests of handwriting, ethics and morality, religion, driving and safety, health and physical education, environment (e.g., classroom environment, family environment), custody decisions, substance abuse, and addictions. (See also Personality.)

Neuropsychological

Tests that measure neurological functioning or brain-behavior relationships either generally or in relation to specific areas of functioning. Included here are neuropsychological test batteries, questionnaires, and screening tests. Also included are tests that measure memory impairment, various disorders or decline associated with dementia, brain/head injury, visual attention, digit recognition, finger tapping, laterality, aphasia, and behavior (associated with organic brain dysfunction or brain injury).

See also Developmental, Intelligence and General Aptitude, Sensory-Motor, and Speech and Hearing.

Personality

Tests that measure individuals' ways of thinking, behaving, and functioning within family and society. Included here are projective and apperception tests, needs inventories, anxiety/depression scales; tests assessing substance use/abuse (or propensity for abuse), risk taking behavior, general mental health, emotional intelligence, self-image/-concept/-esteem, empathy, suicidal ideation, schizophrenia, depression/hopelessness, abuse, coping skills/stress, eating disorders, grief, decision-making, racial attitudes; general motivation, attributions, perceptions; adjustment, parenting styles, and marital issues/satisfaction.

For content-specific tests, see subject area categories (e.g., math efficacy instruments are located in Mathematics). Some areas, such as substance abuse, are cross-referenced with the Personality category.

Reading

Tests that measure competencies and attitudes within the broadly defined area of reading. Included here are reading inventories, tests of reading achievement and aptitude, reading readiness/early reading ability, reading comprehension, reading decoding, and oral reading. (Note: Included here are tests that assess personality or affective variables related to reading.)

Science

Tests that measure competencies and attitudes within any of the various areas of science (e.g., biology, chemistry, physics), and those related to general science achievement/proficiency. (Note: Included here are tests that assess personality or affective variables related to science.)

Sensory-Motor

Tests that are general or specific measures of any or all of the five senses and those that assess fine or gross motor skills. Included here are tests of manual dexterity, perceptual skills, visual-motor skills, perceptual-motor skills, movement and posture, laterality preference, sensory integration, motor development, color blindness/discrimination, visual perception/organization, and visual acuity. (Note: See also the categories Neuropsychological and Speech and Hearing.)

Social Studies

Tests that measure competencies and attitudes within the broadly defined area of social studies. Included here are tests related to economics, sociology, history, geography, and political science, and those related to general social studies achievement/proficiency. (Note: Also included here are tests that assess personality or affective variables related to social studies.)

Speech and Hearing

Tests that measure the mechanics of speaking or hearing the spoken word. Included here are tests of articulation, voice fluency, stuttering, speech sound perception/discrimination, auditory discrimination/comprehension, audiometry, deafness, and hearing loss/impairment. (Note: See Developmental, English and Language, Neuropsychological, and Sensory-Motor.)

Vocations

Tests that measure employee skills, behaviors, attitudes, values, and perceptions relative to jobs, employment, and the work place or organizational environment. Included here are tests of management skill/style/competence, leader behavior, careers (development, exploration, attitudes); job- or work-related selection/admission/entrance tests; tests of work adjustment, team or group processes/communication/effectiveness, employability, vocational/occupational interests, employee aptitudes/competencies, and organizational climate.

See also Intelligence and General Aptitude, and Personality and also specific content area categories (e.g., Mathematics, Reading).

ACHIEVEMENT

BEHAVIOR ASSESSMENT

DEVELOPMENTAL

EDUCATION

ENGLISH AND LANGUAGE

FINE ARTS

FOREIGN LANGUAGES

INTELLIGENCE AND GENERAL APTITUDE

MATHEMATICS

MISCELLANEOUS

BUSINESS EDUCATION AND RELATIONSHIPS

CRIMINAL JUSTICE AND FORENSIC

DRIVING AND SAFETY

FAMILY AND RELATIONSHIPS

NEUROPSYCHOLOGICAL

PERSONALITY

READING

SCIENCE

SENSORY-MOTOR

SOCIAL STUDIES

SPEECH AND HEARING

VOCATIONS

PUBLISHERS DIRECTORY
AND INDEX

This directory and index gives the names and test entry numbers of all publishers represented in Tests in Print IX. Current addresses are listed for all publishers for which this is known. This directory and index also provides telephone and FAX numbers and e-mail and Web page addresses for those publishers who responded to our request for this information. Please note that all test numbers refer to test entry numbers, not page numbers. Publishers are an important source of information about catalogs, specimen sets, price changes, test revisions, and other details.

A & M Psychometrics, LLC [distributed by PSI Services LLC]
2950 N. Hollywood Way, Suite 200
Burbank, CA 91505
Telephone: 818-847-6180
E-mail: taoperations@psionline.com
Web: www.psionline.com
Tests: 2202

ABackans DCP, Inc.
1700 West Market Street
Dept. RD301
Akron, OH 44313
Telephone: 330-745-4450
FAX: 330-745-4450
E-mail: banks@abackans.com
Web: abackans.com
Tests: 30, 1569

Academic Therapy Publications
20 Leveroni Court
Novato, CA 94949-5746
Telephone: 800-422-7249
FAX: 415-883-3720
E-mail: atp-jim@academictherapy.com
Web: www.academictherapy.com/
Tests: 166, 167, 186, 571, 593, 785, 786, 1051, 1081, 1153, 1156, 1312, 1542, 1590, 1679, 1700, 1701, 2079, 2082, 2083, 2102, 2105, 2133, 2134

Acanthus Publishing
180 Lincoln Street, Third Floor
Boston, MA 02111
Telephone: 617-230-2167
FAX: 617-995-0893
E-mail: info@achanthuspublishing.com
Web: www.AcanthusPublishing.com
Tests: 340

ACS DivCHED Examinations Institute
Iowa State University
0213 Gilman Hall
Ames, IA 50011
Telephone: 800-854-1672
FAX: 515-294-4492
E-mail: chmexams@iastate.edu
Web: chemexams.chem.iastate.edu
Tests: 32, 33, 34, 35, 36, 37, 38, 39, 40, 41, 42, 43, 44

ACT, Inc.
500 ACT Drive
P.O. Box 168
Iowa City, IA 52243-0168
Telephone: 319-337-1000
FAX: 319-341-2335
Web: www.act.org
Tests: 45, 46, 2281

ADE Incorporated
P.O. Box 660
Clarkston, MI 48347
Telephone: 800-334-1918
E-mail: support@adeincorp.com
Web: www.adeincorp.com
Tests: 1059, 1357, 2004

Adult Self Expression Scale
c/o John P. Galassi
105C Peabody Hall
CB 3500
University of North Carolina
Chapel Hill, NC 27599-3500
Telephone: 919-962-9196
E-mail: jgalassi@email.unc.edu
Tests: 79

American Association of Teachers of German, Inc.
112 Haddontowne Court, #104
Cherry Hill, NJ 08034-3668
Telephone: 856-795-5553
FAX: 856-795-9398
E-mail: info@aatg.org
Web: www.aatg.org
Tests: 1350

American Association on Intellectual and Developmental
   Disabilities
501 3rd Street, NW
Suite 200
Washington, DC 20001-1512
Telephone: 202-387-1968
FAX: 202-387-2193
E-mail: books@aaidd.org
Web: aaidd.org
Tests: 2016, 2017

American Dental Association
211 East Chicago Avenue, 6th Floor
Chicago, IL 60611-2678
Telephone: 312-440-2500
FAX: 312-587-4105
Web: www.ada.org
Tests: 336, 604

American Institutes for Research (formerly Southwest
   Educational Development Laboratory)
4700 Mueller Blvd.
Austin, TX 78723-3081
Telephone: 800-266-1832
FAX: 512-476-2286
E-mail: ktdrr@air.org
Web: www.ncddr.org/cgi-bin/selfinventory.cgi
Tests: 669

The American Occupational Therapy Association, Inc.
4720 Montgomery Lane, Suite 200
Bethesda, MD 20814-3449
Telephone: 800-729-2682
FAX: 240-762-5150
E-mail: praota@aota.org
Web: www.aota.org
Tests: 106, 1091

American Printing House for the Blind, Inc.
1839 Frankfort Avenue
P.O. Box 6085
Louisville, KY 40206-0085
Telephone: 800-223-1839
FAX: 502-899-2284
E-mail: info@aph.org
Web: www.aph.org
Tests: 839

American Psychiatric Publishing, Inc.
1000 Wilson Blvd., Suite #1825
Arlington, VA 22209
Telephone: 800-368-5777
FAX: 703-907-1091
E-mail: appi@psych.org
Web: www.appi.org
Tests: 407, 1804, 1982, 1983

Dr. Nancy C. Andreasen
Department of Psychiatry
200 Hawkins Drive
Room W278GH
Iowa City, IA 52242-1057
Telephone: 319-353-6601
FAX: 319-353-8300
E-mail: luann-godlove@uiowa.edu
Web: www.medicine.uiowa.edu/psychiatry/
Tests: 501, 1782, 1783, 1784

Appalachian State University
Office of Testing Services
287 Rivers St., Room 245
Boone, NC 28608
E-mail: sdtla@appstate.edu
Web: sdtla.appstate.edu/
Tests: 1992

Apperson, Inc.
13915 Cerritos Corporate Dr., Suite D
Cerritos, CA 90703
Telephone: 800-438-0162
Web: www.apperson.com
Tests: 637, 638

APR Testing Services
62 Candlewood Rd.
Scarsdale, NY 10583-6040
Telephone: 617-244-7405
E-mail: Info@APRTestingServices.com
Web: aprtestingservices.com
Tests: 655, 656

Arena Press
A Division of Academic Therapy Publications
20 Leveroni Court
Novato, CA 94949
Telephone: 800-422-7249
E-mail: customerservice@academictherapy.com
Web: www.arenapressbooks.com
Tests: 137

ASEBA Research Center for Children, Youth, and
    Families
1 South Prospect Street
St. Joseph's Wing (3rd Floor, Room 3207)
Burlington, VT 05401-3456
Telephone: 802-656-5130
FAX: 802-656-5131
E-mail: mail@ASEBA.org
Web: www.ASEBA.org
Tests: 24, 364

Assess Systems
12750 Merit Drive, Suite 300
Dallas, TX 75251
Telephone: 800-283-6055
FAX: 972-233-3154
E-mail: info@assess-systems.com
Web: www.assess-systems.com
Tests: 134, 1774, 1827

Assessio
P.O. Box 470 54
SE 100 74
Sweden
E-mail: info@assessio.se
Web: www.assessio.com
Tests: 1858

Assessment Enterprises
609 Stokely Management Center
College of Business Administration
University of Tennessee
Knoxville, TN 37996-0562
Telephone: 865-748-0991
E-mail: mstahl@utk.edu
Web: www.pemba.utk.edu
Tests: 1042

Assessment Resource Center
University of Missouri—Columbia
College of Education
2800 Maguire Blvd.
Columbia, MO 65201
Telephone: 800-366-8232
FAX: 573-882-8937
E-mail: umcarck-12@missouri.edu
Web: www.arc.missouri.edu
Tests: 475, 1298

Association for Biblical Higher Education
5850 T.G. Lee Blvd, Suite 130
Orlando, FL 32822-4408
Telephone: 407-207-0808
FAX: 407-207-0840
E-mail: info@abhe.org
Web: www.abhe.org
Tests: 1945

Association of American Medical Colleges
655 K Street NW, Suite 100
Washington, DC 20001-2399
Telephone: 202-828-0400
FAX: 202-828-1125
E-mail: mcat@aamc.org
Web: www.aamc.org
Tests: 1246

Athletic Success Institute
1933 Windward Point
Discovery Bay, CA 94505
Telephone: 925-516-8686
E-mail: winslow@winslowresearch.com
Web: www.athleticsuccess.org
Tests: 158

Australian Council for Educational Research Ltd.
19 Prospect Hill Road
Camberwell
Melbourne, Victoria 3124
Australia
Telephone: +61 3 9277 5411
FAX: +61 3 9277 5500
Web: www.acer.edu.au
Tests: 5, 19, 20, 21, 22, 23, 67, 124, 135, 164, 170, 382,
    547, 620, 621, 644, 763, 956, 957, 1205, 1206, 1218,
    1356, 1367, 1638, 1639, 1666, 1812, 1835, 1909,
    2041, 2144, 2248, 2275, 2289, 2291

AVB Press
4425-C Treat Blvd, Suite 210
Concord, CA 94521
Telephone: 925-705-9137
FAX: 925-682-5256
E-mail: admin@avbpress.com
Web: www.avbpress.com
Tests: 2193

AVIAT
8578 Cedar Hills Drive
Dexter, MI 48130
Telephone: 734-726-5404
Web: www.aviat.com
Tests: 897

Ballard & Tighe, Publishers
471 Atlas Street
Brea, CA 92821
Telephone: 800-321-4332
FAX: 714-255-9828
E-mail: info@ballard-tighe.com
Web: www.ballard-tighe.com
Tests: 1025, 1026, 1027

Donna Bardis
6512 Carrietowne Lane
Toledo, OH 43615
Telephone: 419-517-3279
E-mail: dbardis@bex.net
Tests: 4, 272, 472, 587, 772, 795, 805, 879, 982, 1029,
    1253, 1467, 1555, 1709, 1862, 2149, 2192, 2205, 2302

Bay State Psychological Associates
225 Friend Street
Boston, MA 02114
Telephone: 800-438-2772
FAX: 888-375-5636
E-mail: sales@eri.com
Web: www.eri.com
Tests: 754

James R. Beatty
San Diego State University
College of Business Administration
5500 Campanile Drive SSE 3443
San Diego, CA 92182-8230
Telephone: 619-594-6845
FAX: 619-594-3675
E-mail: jbeatty@mail.sdsu.edu
Web: www-rohan.sdsu.edu/~cba/facdev/beatty.html
Tests: 988

Lenore Behar
1821 Woodburn Road
Durham, NC 27705
Telephone: 919-489-1888
FAX: 919-489-1832
E-mail: lbehar@nc.rr.com
Web: www.lenorebehar.com
Tests: 1591

Behavior Analysts, Inc.
311 Lennon Lane, Suite A
Walnut Creek, CA 94598
Telephone: (925) 210-9378
FAX: (925) 210-0436
Web: www.partingtonbehavioranalysts.com
Tests: 140

Behavior Data Systems, Ltd.
P.O. Box 44256
Phoenix, AZ 85064-4256
Telephone: 602-234-3506
FAX: 602-266-8227
E-mail: info@bdsltd.com
Web: www.bdsltd.com/
Tests: 17, 66, 596, 673, 678, 840, 1060, 1407, 1611, 1777,
    1830, 1863, 1868, 2179

Behavioral-Developmental Initiatives
14636 North 55th Street
Scottsdale, AZ 85254
Telephone: 800-405-2313
FAX: 602-494-2688
E-mail: webmaster@temperament.com
Web: www.b-di.com
Tests: 366, 1373

Behavioral Institute for Children and Adolescents
203 Little Canada Road E., Suite 200
Roseville, MN 55117
Telephone: (651) 484-5510
E-mail: info@behavioralinstitute.org
Web: www.behavioralinstitute.org
Tests: 1099

Behaviordata, Inc.
20863 Stevens Creek Blvd., Suite 580
Cupertino, CA 95014-2154
Telephone: 800-627-2673
FAX: 408-342-0617
E-mail: BDI@behaviordat.com
Web: www.behaviordata.com/
Tests: 1866

Belbin
3-4 Bennell Court, West Street
Comberton, Cambridge CB23 7EN
England
Telephone: + 44 (0) 1223 264975
E-mail: info@belbin.com
Web: www.belbin.com
Tests: 242

BEST Instruments, LLC
P.O. Box 501
Niceville, FL 32588
Telephone: 800-748-9073
FAX: 850-678-4359
E-mail: sales@bestinstruments.net
Web: www.bestinstruments.net/
Tests: 255

Nancy E. Betz, Ph.D.
240b Lazenby Hall
1827 Neil Avenue Mall
The Ohio State University
Columbus, OH 43210
Telephone: 614-579-2453
E-mail: betz.3@osu.edu
Web: faculty.psy.ohio-state.edu/betz/
Tests: 2276

Biddle Consulting Group Inc.
195 Blue Ravine Rd., Suite 270
Folsom, CA 95630-4760
Telephone: 800-999-0438 x 242
FAX: 916-563-7557
E-mail: staff@opac.com
Web: www.opac.com
Tests: 1410

Laurence M. Binder, Ph.D.
4900 SW Griffith Dr., Suite 244
Beaverton, OR 97005
Telephone: 503-626-5246
FAX: 503-626-1686
E-mail: lmbinder4900@gmail.com
Tests: 1564

Biofeedback Certification Institute of America
5310 Ward Road, Suite 201
Arvada, CO 80002
Telephone: 720-502-5829
E-mail: info@bcia.org
Web: www.bcia.org
Tests: 261

Birkman International, Inc.
3040 Post Oak Blvd., Suite 1425
Houston, TX 77056
Telephone: 800-215-2760
FAX: 713-963-9142
E-mail: birkmanresearch@birkman.com
Web: www.birkman.com
Tests: 262

Sidney J. Blatt [c/o Dr. David C. Zuroff]
Department of Psychology
McGill University
1205 Dr. Penfield Ave.
Montreal, Quebec H2A 1B1
Canada
Telephone: 514-398-6126
FAX: 514-398-6126
E-mail: zuroff@ego.psych.mcgill.ca
Web: www.psych.mcgill.ca/perpg/fac/zuroff/dczhome.
   htm
Tests: 607

Sidney J. Blatt [c/o Dr. John S. Auerbach]
Psychosocial Rehabilitation and Recovery Center
North Florida/South Georgia Veterans Health System
852 NW 23rd Avenue, Building 3, Suite A
Gainesville, FL 32609
Telephone: 352-248-0252
FAX: 352-248-0268
E-mail: john.auerbach@va.gov
Tests: 155

Bowling Green State University
JDI Office
Department of Psychology
Bowling Green State University
Bowling Green, OH 43403
Telephone: 419-372-8247
FAX: 419-372-6013
E-mail: jdi_ra@bgnet.bgsu.edu
Web: www.bgsu.edu/arts-and-sciences/psychology/
   services/job-descriptive-index/jdi-products-and-
   services.html
Tests: 1043, 1718, 1968, 2031

Brain Injury Rehabilitation Trust
3 Westgate Court, Silkwood Park
Wakefield, West Sussex WF5 9TJ
England
Telephone: 01924 896100
FAX: 01924 899264
E-mail: director@birt.co.uk
Web: www.birt.co.uk
Tests: 279

Brain Technologies Corporation
P.O. Box 358655
Gainesville, FL 32635
Telephone: 352-792-1036
FAX: 888-639-2814
E-mail: info@braintechnologies.com
Web: www.braintechnologies.com
Tests: 280, 561, 1228, 1284

Brainmetric
52-13 Revere Rd.
Drexel Hill, PA 19026
Telephone: 856-503-7079
E-mail: jmicha5059@aol.com
Web: www.brainmetric.com
Tests: 467, 1249

BrainTrain
727 Twin Ridge Lane
North Chesterfield, VA 23235
Telephone: 804-320-0105
FAX: 804-320-2491
E-mail: virginia@braintrain.com
Web: www.braintrain.com
Tests: 1034

Branden Publishing Co.
P.O. Box 812094
Wellesley, MA 02482
Telephone: 781-235-3347
E-mail: branden@brandenbooks.com
Web: www.brandenbooks.com
Tests: 259

Brandon House, Inc. [Eidetic Image Psychology, distributor]
Telephone: 713-228-2457
E-mail: LJDag@aol.com
Web: eideticimagepsychology.com/
Tests: 88, 720

Dr. John Briere
Associate Professor of Psychiatry and Psychology
USC School of Medicine, Clinical Sciences Center
2250 Alcazar, Suite 2200
Los Angeles, CA 90089
E-mail: info@johnbriere.com
Web: www.johnbriere.com
Tests: 1336

Briggs Healthcare
P.O. Box 1355
Des Moines, IA 50305
Telephone: 800-247-2343
Web: www.briggscorp.com
Tests: 1268

Brigham Young University
Humanities Technology and Research Support Center
Foreign Language Testing
1163-E JFSB
Provo, UT 84602
Telephone: 801-422-5360
FAX: 801-422-0304
E-mail: info@perpetualworks.com
Web: htrsc.byu.edu/
Tests: 2226

Arnold R. Bruhn and Associates
4400 East West Highway, #24
Bethesda, MD 20814
Telephone: 301-654-2017
FAX: 301-654-4072
Web: www.arbruhn.com
Tests: 705

C. G. Jung Institute of San Francisco, Inc.
2040 Gough Street
Library
San Francisco, CA 94109
Telephone: 415-771-8055
FAX: 415-771-8926
E-mail: library@sfjung.org
Web: www.sfjung.org
Tests: 1055

C.P.S. Publishing, LLC
P.O. Box 345
Englewood, NJ 07631
Telephone: 201-248-2707
E-mail: CPSPSYCH2@aol.com
Web: www.CPSPublishingInc.com
Tests: 400, 719, 1802, 1846

Caliper Corporation
506 Carnegie Center, Suite 300
P.O. Box 2050
Princeton, NJ 08543-2050
Telephone: 609-524-1200
E-mail: info@calipercorp.com
Web: www.calipercorp.com/
Tests: 324

Callier Center for Communication Disorders
University of Texas at Dallas
1966 Inwood Road
Dallas, TX 75235
Telephone: 214-905-3000
FAX: 214-905-3022
E-mail: calliercenter@utdallas.edu
Web: www.utdallas.edu/calliercenter/
Tests: 326

Cambridge Center for Behavioral Studies
P.O. Box 7067
100 Cummings Center, Suite 338F
Beverly, MA 01915-0091
Telephone: 978-369-2227
FAX: 978-369-8584
E-mail: center@behavior.org
Web: www.behavior.org
Tests: 218, 1429

Cambridge Michigan Language Assessments
CaMLA
Argus 1 Building
535 West William Street, Suite 310
Ann Arbor, MI 48103-4978
Telephone: 734-615-9629
FAX: 734-763-0369
E-mail: info@cambridgemichigan.org
Web: www.cambridgemichigan.org
Tests: 762, 777, 778, 999, 1262, 1263

Cambridge Speech and Language Pathology, Inc.
2530 Cameo Drive
Cameron Park, CA 95682
Telephone: 530-306-7773
E-mail: PTAP@cambridgeSLP.com
Web: www.cambridgeslp.com
Tests: 1579

The Cambridge Stratford Study Skills Institute
8560 Main Street
Williamsville, NY 14221
Telephone: 800-747-5614
FAX: 716-626-9076
E-mail: cambridges@aol.com
Web: www.cambridgestratford.com
Tests: 1464, 2029, 2182

Cambridge University Press
100 Brook Hill Drive
West Nyack, NY 10994-2133
Telephone: 845-353-7500
E-mail: westnyack@cambridge.org
Web: cambridge.org/us
Tests: 1090, 1232, 1602

Canadian Test Centre
Educational Assessment Services
80 Citizen Court, Suite 10
Markham, Ontario L6G 1A7
Canada
Telephone: 905-513-6636
FAX: 800-668-1006
E-mail: info@canadiantestcentre.com
Web: www.canadiantestcentre.com
Tests: 333, 334, 337, 985

Career Cruising
1867 Yonge Street, Suite 1002
Toronto, Ontario M4S 1Y5
Canada
Telephone: 800-965-8541
FAX: 416-463-0938
Web: www.careercruising.com
Tests: 353

Career Kids
241 B Washington St
P.O. Box 1186
Weaverville, CA 96093
E-mail: help@bouldenpublishing.com
Web: www.careerkids.com/
Tests: 363

Career Research & Testing, Inc.
P.O. Box 611930
San Jose, CA 95161-1930
Telephone: 408-828-3858
E-mail: rknowdell@mac.com
Web: www.careernetwork.org
Tests: 362, 1143, 1308, 1405

CASAS
5151 Murphy Canyon Road, Suite 220
San Diego, CA 92123-4339
Telephone: 858-292-2900
FAX: 858-292-2910
E-mail: casas@casas.org
Web: www.casas.org
Tests: 372, 373, 374, 496

CEB
The Pavilion
1 Atwell Place
Thames Ditton, Surrey KT7 0NE
United Kingdom
Telephone: (678) 832-0569
E-mail: helpdeskUS@cebglobal.com
Web: www.cebglobal.com/
Tests: 85, 174, 573, 758, 769, 1174, 1182, 1404, 1419,
1535, 1633, 1766, 2061, 2062, 2294

Cengage Learning
10650 Toebben Drive
Independence, KY 41051
Telephone: 800-648-7450
FAX: 518-373-6306
E-mail: cengagebrain.support@cengage.com
Web: www.cengagebrain.com
Tests: 1469

Center for Advanced Studies in Management
1574 Mallory Court
Bowling Green, KY 42103
Tests: 494, 770, 1437, 1685, 1686

Center for Applications of Psychological Type, Inc.
2815 Northwest 13th Street, Suite 401
Gainesville, FL 32609
Telephone: (352) 375-0160
Web: www.capt.org
Tests: 1088, 1338, 1479

Center for Applied Linguistics
4646 40th Street, NW
Washington, DC 20016-1859
Telephone: 202-362-0700
FAX: 202-363-7204
E-mail: aea@cal.org
Web: www.cal.org
Tests: 256, 257, 516

Center for Architecture and Urban Planning Research
School of Architecture and Urban Planning
University of Wisconsin—Milwaukee
P.O. Box 413
Milwaukee, WI 53201-0413
Telephone: 414-229-6165
FAX: 414-229-6976
E-mail: susatrop@uwm.edu
Web: www4.uwm.edu/caupr/
Tests: 697

Center for Creative Leadership
One Leadership Place
Greensboro, NC 27410
Telephone: 336-545-2810
FAX: 336-282-3284
E-mail: info@ccl.org
Web: www.ccl.org
Tests: 248, 249, 250, 1041, 1074, 1139, 1891

The Center for Leadership Studies, Inc.
280 Towerview Court
Cary, NC 27513
Telephone: 919-335-8763
E-mail: info@situational.com
Web: www.situational.com
Tests: 1880

The Center for Management Effectiveness, Inc.
P.O. Box 1202
Pacific Palisades, CA 90272
Telephone: 310-459-6052
FAX: 310-459-9307
E-mail: info@cmeinc.org
Web: www.cmeinc.org
Tests: 592, 1183, 1512, 1741

Center for the Study of Aging and Human Development
Box 3003
Duke University Medical Center
Room 3502 Busse Building, Blue Zone, Duke South
Durham, NC 27710
Telephone: 919-660-7500
FAX: 919-668-0453
E-mail: jurgen.wanke@duke.edu
Web: www.geri.duke.edu
Tests: 1396

Center for the Study of Ethical Development
University of Alabama
307 Carmichael Hall
Box 870231
Tuscaloosa, AL 35487-0231
Telephone: 205-348-4571
E-mail: ethicalstudy@bamaed.ua.edu
Web: ethicaldevelopment.ua.edu/
Tests: 597

Center for the Study of Higher Education
304 Browning Hall
The University of Memphis
Memphis, TN 38152
Telephone: 901-678-4060
FAX: 901-678-4291
E-mail: mmisawa@memphis.edu
Web: www.memphis.edu/cshe
Tests: 490

Centre for Addiction and Mental Health
Marketing Services
33 Russell Street
Toronto, Ontario M5S 2S1
Canada
Telephone: 800-463-6273
FAX: 416-593-4694
E-mail: info@camh.ca
Web: www.camh.ca
Tests: 94, 679, 680, 1007, 1008

CERAD
Center for the Study of Aging and Human Development
Box 3003
Duke University Medical Center
Durham, NC 27710
Telephone: 919-660-7530
FAX: 919-668-0453
E-mail: gerda.fillenbaum@duke.edu
Web: cerad.mc.duke.edu
Tests: 376, 377

The Change Companies
5221 Sigstrom Drive
Carson City, NV 89706
Telephone: 888-889-8866
FAX: 775-885-0643
E-mail: contact@changecompanies.net
Web: www.changecompanies.net
Tests: 76, 238, 495, 663, 757, 1040, 1440, 1578, 2008,
    2180, 2181

Checkmate Plus, Ltd.
P.O. Box 696
Stony Brook, NY 11790-0696
Telephone: 800-779-4292
FAX: 631-360-3432
E-mail: info@checkmateplus.com
Web: www.checkmateplus.com
Tests: 56, 80, 390, 696, 2313

Child Development Resources
P.O. Box 280
Norge, VA 23127-0280
Telephone: 757-566-3300
FAX: 757-566-8977
Web: www.cdr.org
Tests: 950, 1890

Child Development Review -Behavior Science Systems, Inc.
P.O. Box 19512
5905 Elliot Avenue South
Minneapolis, MN 55419-9998
Telephone: 612-850-8700
FAX: 360-351-1374
E-mail: heidi@childdevrev.com
Web: www.childdevrev.com/
Tests: 392, 393, 976

Child Welfare League of America
1726 M St NW, Suite 500
Washington, DC 20036-4522
Telephone: 202-688-4200
FAX: 202-833-1689
E-mail: cwla@cwla.org
Web: www.cwla.org/publications
Tests: 575, 796

Children's Journey to Shine, Inc.
Friendswood, TX 77546
Telephone: 713-256-7097
FAX: 281-480-5648
E-mail: suezapf@me.com
Web: www.cjsi.net
Tests: 1212

CID - Central Institute for the Deaf
825 South Taylor Ave.
St. Louis, MO 63110
Telephone: 314-977-0133
FAX: 314-977-0025
E-mail: dgushleff@cid.edu
Web: cid.edu
Tests: 421, 422, 423, 424, 425, 426, 711, 1937, 2046

Dr. Lee Anna Clark
Department of Psychology
University of Notre Dame
124A Haggar Hall
Notre Dame, IN 46556
Telephone: 574-631-7482
E-mail: la.clark@nd.edu
Web: psychology.nd.edu/faculty/faculty-by-alpha/lee-anna-
    clark/
Tests: 1801

The Clark Wilson Group, Inc. (subsidiary of The Booth
    Company, Inc.)
4900 Nautilus Court N., Suite 220
Boulder, CO 80301-3242
Telephone: 800-332-6684
FAX: 303-581-9326
E-mail: info@boothco.com
Web: www.boothco.com
Tests: 82, 133, 781, 1112, 1115, 1763, 2019, 2020, 2025,
    2060

Clinical Psychometric Research, Inc.
1228 Wine Spring Lane
Towson, MD 21204
Telephone: 410-321-6165
E-mail: maureen@derogatis-tests.com
Web: www.derogatis-tests.com
Tests: 608, 609, 610, 611, 1663

CNS Vital Signs
598 Airport Blvd, Suite 1400
Morrisville, NC 27560
Telephone: 888-750-6941
FAX: 888-650-6795
E-mail: support@cnsvs.com
Web: www.cnsvs.com
Tests: 456, 470, 521

Cognistat, Inc.
P.O. Box 460
Fairfax, CA 94978
Telephone: 800-922-5840
FAX: 514-336-6537
E-mail: info@cognistat.com
Web: www.cognistat.com
Tests: 460

CogScreen, LLC
200 Central Avenue, Suite 1230
St. Petersburg, FL 33701
Telephone: 727-897-9000
FAX: 727-897-9009
Web: www.cogscreen.com
Tests: 471

The College Board
250 Vesey Street
New York, NY 10281
Telephone: 212-713-8000
E-mail: sat@info.collegeboard.org
Web: www.collegeboard.org
Tests: 16, 115, 436, 1643, 1779, 1780, 1781

Combined Program in Education and Psychology
University of Michigan
610 East University Avenue
Room 1406
Ann Arbor, MI 48109-1259
Telephone: 734-647-0626
E-mail: cpep@umich.edu
Web: www.soe.umich.edu/departments_services
    /academic_departments/combined_program_in_
    education_and_psychology/
Tests: 1309

Communi-Cog Publications
P.O. Box 27771
Tempe, AZ 85285
Telephone: 480-839-2733
E-mail: communicog@msn.com
Web: www.communi-cog.com
Tests: 141

Competence Dimensions Ltd.
Tekniikantie 14
Espoo 02150
Finland
Telephone: +358 40 836 4505
E-mail: info@wopi.net
Web: www.wopi.net
Tests: 2286

Consulting Resource Group International, Inc.
P.O. Box 8000, PMB 386
Sumas, WA 98295-8000
Telephone: 604-852-0566
FAX: 604-850-3003
E-mail: info@crgleader.com
Web: www.crgleader.com
Tests: 768, 987, 1049, 1122, 1133, 1516, 1681, 1772,
    1845, 1970, 2191

Corporate Mentoring Solutions® Inc.
Corporate Head Office
11316 Ravenscroft Place
North Saanichton
British Columbia V8L 5R4
Canada
Telephone: 250-652-0324
E-mail: wgray@mentoring-solutions.com
Web: www.mentoring-solutions.com
Tests: 1258

Council for Economic Education
122 East 42nd St., Suite 2600
New York, NY 10168
Telephone: 800-338-1192
FAX: 212-730-1793
E-mail: customerservice@councilforeconed.org
Web: www.CouncilforEconEd.org
Tests: 192, 2093, 2094, 2131

CPP, Inc.
185 N Wolfe Rd.
Sunnyvale, CA 94086
Telephone: 800-624-1765
FAX: 650-969-8608
E-mail: custserv@cpp.com
Web: www.cpp.com
Tests: 319, 564, 816, 817, 1344, 1345, 1346, 1432, 1465,
    1466, 1574, 1889, 1974, 1975, 1976, 2154, 2277

The Creative Problem Solving Group, Inc.
P.O. Box 648
6 Grand View Trail
Orchard Park, NY 14127
Telephone: 716-667-1324
E-mail: sgiaway@cpsb.com
Web: www.cpsb.com
Tests: 1881, 2200

Creative Solutions Press LLC
3724 Capilano Dr.
West Lafayette, IN 47906
Telephone: 765-807-2467
FAX: 765-746-2306
E-mail: mikejcpt@outlook.com
Web: bit.ly/SPSI-A
Tests: 1914

Creatrix
6709 Vernon Ave S.
Edina, MN 55436-1803
Telephone: 763-476-5815
E-mail: team@creatrix.com
Web: www.creatrix.com
Tests: 567

The Critical Thinking Co.
1991 Sherman Ave., Suite 200
North Bend, OR 97459
Telephone: 800-458-4195
FAX: 831-393-3277
E-mail: info@criticalthinking.com
Web: www.criticalthinking.com
Tests: 554, 1037

Curriculum Associates, LLC
Corporate Headquarters
P.O. Box 2001
153 Rangeway Road
North Billerica, MA 01862-0901
Telephone: 800-225-0248
FAX: 800-366-1158
E-mail: info@cainc.com
Web: www.curriculumassociates.com
Tests: 290, 291, 292, 293, 294, 498, 499, 958

David P. Weikart Center for Youth Program Quality
301 W. Michigan Ave., Suite 200
Ypsilanti, MI 48197
Telephone: 734-961-6900
E-mail: joe@cypq.org
Web: www.cypq.org
Tests: 1807, 2311

Department of Research Assessment and Training
1051 Riverside Drive, Unit 123
New York, NY 10032
Telephone: 646-774-7939
E-mail: je10@columbia.edu
Tests: 760, 860, 1671, 1800

Developmental Therapy Institute, Inc.
579 Milledge Circle
Athens, GA 30606
Telephone: 706-201-6399
E-mail: dti@developmentaltherapyinstitute.org
Web: www.developmentaltherapyinstitute.org
Tests: 628

The Devine Group, Inc.
7755 Montgomery Road, Suite 180
Cincinnati, OH 45236
Telephone: 513-792-7500
FAX: 513-793-8535
Web: www.devinegroup.com/
Tests: 639

Diagnostic Counseling Services, Inc.
P.O. Box 6178
Kokomo, IN 46904-6178
Tests: 1322

Diagnostic Specialists, Inc.
1170 North 660 West
Orem, UT 84057
Telephone: 801-221-7710
E-mail: allanroe@comcast.net
Tests: 87, 387, 2255

Dinosaurs, Trees, Religion and Galaxies
P.O. Box 61
Evanston, IL 60204
Telephone: 773-680-7024
E-mail: dinosaurs_galaxies@yahoo.com
Web: jamestimothystruck.page4.me
Tests: 1658

Directional Insight International, Inc.
1111 McKinley Street
Ft. Worth, TX 76126
Telephone: 817-249-6266
FAX: 817-249-6466
E-mail: test@nsightsuccess.com
Web: www.nsightsuccess.com
Tests: 1389

Dr. Baker Partnership
10 Elgin Rd.
Talbot Woods
Bournemouth, Dorset BH4 9NL
United Kingdom
Telephone: 01202 763836
E-mail: rbaker@bournemouth.ac.uk
Web: staffprofiles.bournemouth.ac.uk/display/rbaker
Tests: 1703

Rodney L. Doran, Ph.D.
Professor Emeritus
505 Baldy Hall
University of Buffalo
Buffalo, NY 14260
Telephone: 716-768-2508
E-mail: rdoran@buffalo.edu
Web: gse.buffalo.edu/node/2090
Tests: 1247

DRC
13490 Bass Lake Road
Maple Grove, MN 55311
Telephone: 763-268-2000
FAX: 763-268-3000
E-mail: SurveysInfo@datarecognitioncorp.com
Web: www.datarecognitioncorp.com
Tests: 1015, 1100, 1101, 1102, 1103, 1583, 1607, 1928,
2072, 2143

Ealy Education Group, Inc.
1043 Maravista Drive
Trinity, FL 34655
Telephone: 727-487-1890
E-mail: service@ealyeducation.com
Web: www.ealyeducation.com/
Tests: 1832

eCenter Research, Inc.
101 High St.
Sutton, Ontario L0E 1R0
Canada
Telephone: 866-856-2606
E-mail: steve@ecenterresearch.com
Web: www.einsight.net
Tests: 681

Ed & Psych Associates
Telephone: 814-235-9115
FAX: 814-235-9115
E-mail: EdPsychAssociates@gmail.com
Web: edpsychassociates.com/
Tests: 59

Edge Training Systems, Inc.
P.O. Box 326
Midlothian, VA 23113
Telephone: 800-305-2025
FAX: 804-272-1683
E-mail: paul.okeefe@edgetraining.com
Web: www.edgetrainingsystems.com
Tests: 1141

EdITS/Educational and Industrial Testing Service
P.O. Box 7234
San Diego, CA 92167
Telephone: 800-416-1666
FAX: 619-226-1666
E-mail: customerservice@edits.net
Web: www.edits.net
Tests: 341, 355, 356, 357, 358, 367, 518, 519, 520, 551,
666, 790, 791, 806, 1056, 1172, 1335, 1447, 1507,
1508, 1809, 1961, 1996, 2142

Educational & Psychological Consultants, LLC
1001 Cherry St., Suite102
Columbia, MO 65201-7931
Telephone: 573-446-1614
FAX: 573-446-8532
E-mail: info@personalstyles.org
Web: www.personalstyles.org
Tests: 1517

Educational Assessment Service, Inc.
W6050 Apple Road
Watertown, WI 53098-3937
Telephone: 800-795-7466
FAX: 920-261-6622
E-mail: srimm@sylviarimm.com
Web: www.sylviarimm.com
Tests: 25, 26, 891, 894, 895, 1588

Educational Records Bureau
470 Park Avenue South
Second Floor, South Tower
New York, NY 10016-6819
Telephone: 800-989-3721
E-mail: info@erblearn.org
Web: erblearn.org
Tests: 510, 771, 967

Educational Testing Service
Publication Order Services
ETS Corporate Headquarters
Rosedale Road
Princeton, NJ 08541
Telephone: 609-921-9000
FAX: 609-734-5410
E-mail: etsinfo@ets.org
Web: www.ets.org
Tests: 869, 870, 871, 872, 873, 874, 875, 876, 877, 1087,
1171, 1349, 1582, 1811, 1934, 1993, 2095, 2162

Educators Publishing Service, Inc.
P.O. Box 9031
Cambridge, MA 02139-9031
Telephone: 800-225-5750
FAX: 888-440-2665
E-mail: sales.eps@schoolspecialty.com
Web: eps.schoolspecialty.com
Tests: 246, 1725, 1893

Carl N. Edwards, Ph.D.
4113 Sunflower Lane
Temple, TX 76502-4803
Telephone: 774-200-0201
FAX: 866-210-0595
E-mail: cedwards@socialaw.com
Tests: 1882

Elbern Publications
P.O. Box 9497
Columbus, OH 43209
Telephone: 614-235-2643
FAX: 614-237-2637
E-mail: ebecker@wowway.com
Tests: 214, 1693

Patricia B. Elmore, Ph.D.
Professor Emerita
College of Education
115 Wham Education Building--SIU
Carbondale, IL 62901
Telephone: 618-453-2415
FAX: 618-453-1646
E-mail: pbelmore@siu.edu
Web: www.siu.edu/
Tests: 230, 381, 1111

eMed International Inc.
1956 Crown Pointe Blvd.
Pensacola, FL 32506
Telephone: 970-812-1790
E-mail: lori.schultz@emedcolorado.org
Web: www.emedcolorado.org
Tests: 63

Emergenetics International
2 Inverness Dr. East, Suite 189
Centennial, CO 80112
Telephone: 303-660-7920
E-mail: brains@emergenetics.com
Web: www.emergenetics.com
Tests: 727

Robert H. Ennis, Ph.D.
3904 Trentwood Place
Sarasota, FL 34243
Telephone: 941-358-0906
E-mail: rhennis@illinois.edu
Web: criticalthinking.net
Tests: 764

Enrichment Press
5441 SW Macadam Avenue, #206
Portland, OR 97239
Telephone: 503-222-4046
FAX: 503-222-9989
Web: stevewaksman.com
Tests: 1565, 2219

Enterprise Management Ltd.
4531 Roanoak Way
Palm Harbor, FL 34685
Telephone: 727-934-9810
E-mail: mlippitt@enterprisemgt.com
Web: www.enterprisemgt.com
Tests: 1124

Exceptional Education — Jeff Stewart's Teaching Tools
P.O. Box 5729
Vader, WA 98155
Telephone: 360-295-3038
FAX: 360-295-3038
E-mail: jeffs_ttools@hotmail.com
Tests: 1604, 2214

Sheila M. Eyberg, Ph.D.
6814 NW 81 Blvd.
Gainesville, FL 32653
Telephone: 352-373-4585
E-mail: pcit.international@gmail.com
Web: www.pcit.org
Tests: 684, 2151

The Focusing Institute
15 N. Mill Street
Nyack, NY 10960
Telephone: 845-480-5111
FAX: 845-704-0461
E-mail: info@focusing.org
Web: www.focusing.org
Tests: 783

Functional Resources
3905 Huntington Drive
Amarillo, TX 79109-4047
Telephone: 806-353-1114
E-mail: info@winfssi.com
Web: www.winfssi.com
Tests: 838

Gander Publishing
450 Front Street
P.O. Box 780
Avila Beach, CA 93424
Telephone: 800-554-1819
FAX: 805-782-0488
Web: ganderpublishing.com/
Tests: 2034

GB Software LLC
8718 Bonaventure Drive
Brighton, MI 48116
Telephone: 972-955-6765
E-mail: info@gb-software.com
Web: www.gb-software.com
Tests: 1652

GED Testing Service
1919 M Street N.W., Suite 600
Washington, DC 20036-1163
Telephone: 202-471-2200
E-mail: communications@gedtestingservice.com
Web: www.gedtestingservice.com
Tests: 844

Ruth M. Geiman, Ph.D.
8184 Crete Ln.
Blacklick, OH 43004
Tests: 849

General Dynamics Information Technology
30 North LaSalle, Suite 3110
Chicago, IL 60602
Telephone: (800) 922-7343
E-mail: hcrm@gdit.com
Web: hcrm.gdit.com
Tests: 47, 117, 118, 190, 329, 331, 332, 453, 454, 514,
515, 568, 578, 580, 583, 728, 753, 755, 782, 823, 824,
991, 1004, 1106, 1118, 1178, 1185, 1190, 1193, 1238,
1240, 1380, 1383, 1401, 1412, 1413, 1492, 1534, 1550,
1603, 1668, 1689, 1694, 1707, 1714, 1761, 1762, 1768,
1873, 1887, 1926, 1927, 1963, 2023, 2028, 2038, 2058,
2065, 2070, 2113, 2156, 2157, 2184, 2194, 2195, 2269

Gesell Institute of Child Development
310 Prospect Street, 2nd Floor
New Haven, CT 06511
Telephone: 800-369-7709
FAX: 203-776-5001
E-mail: mguddemi@gesellinstitute.org
Web: www.gesellinstitute.org
Tests: 851, 852

GIA Publications, Inc.
7404 South Mason Avenue
Chicago, IL 60638
Telephone: 800-442-1358
FAX: 708-496-3828
E-mail: custserv@giamusic.com
Web: www.giamusic.com
Tests: 83, 99, 917, 989, 996, 1023, 1301, 1340, 1341, 1606

Lucia A. Gilbert
Santa Clara University
Department of Psychology
500 El Camino Real
Santa Clara, CA 95053-0333
Telephone: 512-232-3310
FAX: 512-471-0577
E-mail: lgilbert@scu.edu
Web: www.scu.edu/cas/psychology/faculty-and-staff/
gilbert.html
Tests: 1490

GL Assessment
9th Floor East
389 Chiswick High Road
London W4 4AL
England
Telephone: +44 (0) 20 8996 3333
FAX: +44 (0) 20 8742 8767
E-mail: info@gl-assessment.co.uk
Web: www.gl-assessment.co.uk/
Tests: 144, 295, 296, 297, 687, 801, 900, 948, 1266,
1355, 1384, 1544, 1556, 1634, 1803, 1933, 2009,
2035, 2196, 2273

Golden Educational Center
857 Lake Blvd.
Redding, CA 96003
Telephone: 800-800-1791
FAX: 530-244-0101
E-mail: info@goldened.com
Web: www.goldened.com
Tests: 992

Gordon Systems, Inc.
P.O. Box 746
DeWitt, NY 13214
Telephone: 800-550-2343
FAX: 315-446-2012
E-mail: info@gsi-add.com
Web: www.gsi-add.com
Tests: 863

Robert S. Goyer
Department of Communication
Arizona State University
Tempe, AZ 85287
Test distributed by Test Collection at ETS
Tests: 865

Graham-Field Health Products, Inc.
2935 Northeast Parkway
Atlanta, GA 30360
Telephone: 800-347-5678
FAX: 800-726-0601
E-mail: cs@grahamfield.com
Web: www.grahamfield.com
Tests: 1031

Green Dragon Publishing
P.O. Box 1608
Lake Worth, FL 33460
Telephone: 800-874-8844
FAX: 888-874-8844
E-mail: info@greendragonbooks.com
Web: www.greendragonbooks.com
Tests: 391, 398, 955, 1161

Green's Publishing Inc.
18945 111 Avenue
Edmonton, Alberta T5S 2X4
Canada
Telephone: 780-484-5550
FAX: 780-484-5631
E-mail: greenspublishing@gmail.com
Web: www.wordmemorytest.com
Tests: 883, 884, 885, 886

Gregorc Associates, Inc.
15 Doubleday Road
P.O. Box 351
Columbia, CT 06237
Telephone: 860-228-0093
FAX: 860-228-0093
E-mail: agregorc@att.net
Web: www.gregorc.com
Tests: 888

Guglielmino & Associates, LLC
7339 Reserve Creek Drive
Port St. Lucie, FL 34986
Telephone: 772-429-2425
FAX: 772-429-2425
E-mail: guglielmino@rocketmail.com
Web: www.lpasdlrs.com
Tests: 1833

Guilford Publications, Inc.
370 Seventh Avenue, Suite 1200
New York, NY 10001-1020
Telephone: 800-365-7006
FAX: 212-966-6708
E-mail: info@guilford.com
Web: www.guilford.com
Tests: 55, 179, 180, 181, 182, 183

H&H Publishing Company, Inc.
1231 Kapp Drive
Clearwater, FL 33765-2116
Telephone: 800-366-4079
FAX: 727-442-7760
E-mail: hhservice@hhpublishing.com
Web: www.hhpublishing.com
Tests: 1128, 1129, 1485, 1956, 2063, 2298

Judith Hall
Social Interaction Lab
Dept. of Psychology, Northeastern University
360 Huntington Ave.
Boston, MA 02115
E-mail: j.hall@neu.edu
Web: repository.library.northeastern.edu/collections/
    neu:rx9144872
Tests: 1626

Hammill Institute on Disabilities
8700 Shoal Creek Blvd.
Austin, TX 78757-6897
Telephone: 512-451-3521
FAX: 512-451-3728
Web: hammill-institute.org/
Tests: 706, 1403, 1580

Susan Harter, Ph.D.
University of Denver
Department of Psychology
2155 South Race Street
Denver, CO 80208-0204
Telephone: 303-871-2478
FAX: 303-871-4747
E-mail: sharter@du.edu
Web: portfolio.du.edu/SusanHarter
Tests: 1551, 1839

Harvard University Press
79 Garden Street
Cambridge, MA 02138
Telephone: 617-495-2600
FAX: 617-495-5898
E-mail: contact_hup@harvard.edu
Web: www.hup.harvard.edu
Tests: 2150

Dr. Robert J. Harvey
Psychology Department
109 Williams Hall
Blacksburg, VA 24061
Telephone: 540-231-6581
FAX: 540-231-3652
E-mail: harveyrj@vt.edu
Web: cmqonline.com
Tests: 482

Hawthorne Educational Services, Inc.
800 Gray Oak Drive
Columbia, MO 65201
Telephone: 800-542-1673
FAX: 800-442-9509
E-mail: info@hes-inc.com
Web: www.hawthorne-ed.com/
Tests: 50, 75, 159, 221, 222, 223, 693, 694, 729, 738, 855,
    1131, 1586, 1593, 1935, 2171

Hay Group
Hay Resources Direct
399 Boylston Street
4th Floor, Suite 400
Boston, MA 02116
Web: www.haygroup.com
Tests: 458, 731, 980, 1125, 1132, 1135, 1433, 1518

Health and Disability Research Institute at Boston University
715 Albany St., 5th Floor West
Boston, MA 02118
Telephone: 617-638-1994
FAX: 612-638-1999
E-mail: aschmid8@bu.edu
Web: www.bu.edu/sph/research/research-landing-page/health-and-disability-research-institute/
Tests: 1482

Healthy Learning
P.O. Box 1828
Monterey, CA 93942
Telephone: 888-229-5745
FAX: 831-372-6075
E-mail: info@healthylearning.com
Web: www.healthylearning.com
Tests: 1549

Heinemann Publishing
P.O. Box 6926
Portsmouth, NH 03802-6926
Telephone: 800-225-5800
FAX: 877-231-6980
E-mail: custserv@heinemann.com
Web: www.heinemann.com
Tests: 1400

Mary J. Heppner, Ph.D.
Career Center
201 Student Success Center
University of Missouri
Columbia, MO 65211-6060
Telephone: 573-882-8574
FAX: 573-882-5440
E-mail: heppnerm@missouri.edu
Tests: 361

Puncky Paul Heppner
E-mail: Heppnerp@missouri.edu
Tests: 1614

Herrmann International
794 Buffalo Creek Road
Lake Lure, NC 28746
Telephone: 828-625-9153
FAX: 800-432-4234
E-mail: info@hbdi.com
Web: www.herrmannsolutions.com/
Tests: 931

Hewitt Research Foundation
P.O. Box 9
2103 Main Street
Washougal, WA 98671-0009
Telephone: 800-348-1750
FAX: 360-835-8697
E-mail: info@hewitthomeschooling.com
Web: www.hewitthomeschooling.com
Tests: 1529

Higher Education Research Institute
3005 Moore Hall
Box 951521
Los Angeles, CA 90095-1521
Telephone: 310-825-1925
E-mail: heri@ucla.edu
Web: www.heri.ucla.edu
Tests: 540

HighScope Educational Research Foundation
600 North River Street
Ypsilanti, MI 48198-2898
Telephone: 800-587-5639
FAX: 734-485-0704
E-mail: info@highscope.org
Web: www.highscope.org
Tests: 703, 1599

Hodder Education
Carmelite House
50 Victoria Embankment
London EC4Y 0DZ
England
Telephone: +44 203 122 6470
E-mail: education@bookpoint.co.uk
Web: www.hoddereducation.co.uk
Tests: 193, 194, 455, 717, 866, 899, 1379, 1451, 1473, 1557, 1696, 1776, 1932, 2271

Hogan Assessment Systems, Inc.
2622 East 21st Street
Tulsa, OK 74114
Telephone: 800-756-0632
FAX: 918-749-0635
Web: www.hoganassessments.com
Tests: 938, 939, 1311

Hogrefe Ltd
Hogrefe House
Albion Place
Oxford OX1 1QZ
United Kingdom
Telephone: +44 (0)1865 797920
FAX: +44 (0)1865 797949
E-mail: publishing@hogrefe.co.uk
Web: www.hogrefe.co.uk
Tests: 27, 107, 267, 309, 585, 590, 740, 794, 850, 889,
964, 993, 994, 1028, 1030, 1117, 1159, 1179, 1236,
1286, 1363, 1448, 1470, 1538, 1573, 1748, 1797,
1872, 1907, 1922, 1923, 2207

Hogrefe Psykologisk Forlag A/S [Denmark]
Kongevejen 155
2830 Virum
Denmark
Telephone: +45 35381655
E-mail: info@hogrefe.dk
Web: www.hogrefe.dk
Tests: 178

Home Inventory LLC
c/o Lorraine Coulson
2627 Winsor Drive
Eau Claire, WI 54703
Telephone: 715-835-4393
E-mail: lrcoulson@ualr.edu
Web: fhdri.clas.asu.edu/home/
Tests: 943

Houghton Mifflin Harcourt
One Pierce Place Suite 900
Itasca, IL 60143
Telephone: 800-323-9540
FAX: 630-467-7192
E-mail: RPC_Customer_Service@hmhpub.com
Web: www.hmhco.com/HMHAssessment
Tests: 201, 202, 251, 260, 385, 462, 589, 654, 714, 842,
1005, 1018, 1019, 1675, 1794, 2264, 2265, 2266, 2267

HRD Press, Inc.
22 Amherst Road
Amherst, MA 01002–9709
Telephone: 800-822-2801
FAX: 413-253-3490
E-mail: customerservice@hrdpress.com
Web: www.hrdpress.com
Tests: 111, 122, 143, 379, 486, 492, 525, 550, 826, 981,
1058, 1109, 1136, 1176, 1180, 1188, 1194, 1223,
1244, 1430, 1431, 1450, 1494, 1497, 1505, 1514,
1515, 1520, 1558, 1609, 1622, 1829, 1831, 2026,
2051, 2085, 2130, 2159, 2246

HRdirect | G. Neil
P.O. Box 668220
Pompano, FL 33066-8220
Telephone: 800-999-9111
E-mail: service@hrdirect.com
Web: www.hrdirect.com
Tests: 119, 438, 1767, 1856

HRDQ
827 Lincoln Ave., Suite B-10
West Chester, PA 19380
Telephone: 800-633-4533
FAX: 800-633-3683
Web: www.hrdqstore.com/
Tests: 574

Edwina E. Hubert, Ph.D.
313 Wellesley Dr., SE
Albuquerque, NM 87106-1421
Telephone: 505-256-1938
Tests: 1142

Human Sciences Research Council [South Africa]
Distributed by Mindmuzik Media
140 Gordon Road
Colbyn
Pretoria, Gauteng 0083
South Africa
Telephone: +27 (0)12-342-1606
FAX: +27 (0)12 3422728
E-mail: frikkie@mindmuzik.com
Web: www.mindmuzik.com
Tests: 125, 266, 808, 932, 933, 974, 1002, 1054, 1057,
1351, 1375, 1449, 1548, 1632, 1752, 1814, 1847,
1848, 2168

Human Synergistics International
39819 Plymouth Road
Plymouth, MI 48170
Telephone: 800-622-7584
FAX: 734-459-5557
E-mail: info@humansynergistics.com
Web: www.humansynergistics.com
Tests: 100, 902, 1116, 1152, 1162, 1181, 1434, 1436, 1972

IDEA
301 South Fourth Street, Suite 200
Manhattan, KS 66502
Telephone: 800-255-2757
FAX: 785-320-2400
E-mail: info@ideaedu.org
Web: www.ideaedu.org
Tests: 960, 1722, 1723

IDS Publishing Corporation
P.O. Box 389
Worthington, OH 43085
Telephone: 614-885-2323
FAX: 614-885-2323
E-mail: ids@idspublishing.com
Web: www.idspublishing.com
Tests: 1708

Illinois Critical Thinking Project; Department of Educational Policy Studies
University of Illinois at Urbana-Champaign
360 Education Bldg.
1310 South Sixth Street
Champaign, IL 61820
E-mail: rhennis@illinois.edu
Web: www.criticalthinking.net
Tests: 552, 553

Indiana Resource Center for Autism
Indiana Institute on Disability and Community
1905 North
Bloomington, IN 47408-2696
Telephone: 812-855-6508
FAX: 812-855-9630
E-mail: prattc@indiana.edu
Web: www.iidc.indiana.edu/irca
Tests: 2245

Indiana University Center for Postsecondary Research
1900 East Tenth Street
Eigenmann Hall, Suite 419
Bloomington, IN 47406-7512
Telephone: 812-856-5824
FAX: 812-856-5150
E-mail: cpr@indiana.edu
Web: cpr.iub.edu
Tests: 1354

Industrial Psychology International, Ltd.
4106 Fieldstone Road
P.O. Box 6479
Champaign, IL 61826-6479
Telephone: 800-747-1119
FAX: 217-398-5798
E-mail: mtinfo@metritech.com
Web: www.metritech.com
Tests: 563, 1024, 1388, 2300, 2301

Infant Motor Performance Scales, LLC
1301 W. Madison St., #526
Chicago, IL 60607
Telephone: 312-733-9604
FAX: 312-733-0565
E-mail: skc@thetimp.com
Web: www.thetimp.com
Tests: 919, 2103

Inflexxion, Inc.
320 Needham St., Suite 100
Newton, MA 02464
Telephone: 877-207-0645
FAX: 617-614-0400
E-mail: info@inflexxion.com
Web: www.inflexxion.com
Tests: 53

Innodyne, Inc.
734 Orchard Hill Drive
Pittsburgh, PA 15238
Telephone: 412-963-9691
FAX: 412-963-6751
E-mail: dpslevin@katz.pitt.edu
Tests: 1640

Innolect, Inc.
2764 Pleasant Rd, #11503
Fort Mill, SC 29708-7299
Telephone: 803-396-8500
E-mail: innolect@innolectinc.com
Web: www.innolectinc.com
Tests: 86, 485, 1155, 2222

INQ Educational Materials, Inc.
6933 Armour Drive
Oakland, CA 94611-1317
Telephone: 1-888-339-2323
FAX: 1-510-339-6729
E-mail: Paul@YourThinkingProfile.com
Web: www.YourThinkingProfile.com
Tests: 983, 984, 1198

Insight Assessment—The California Academic Press LLC
217 La Cruz Avenue
Millbrae, CA 94030
Telephone: 650-697-5628
FAX: 650-692-0141
E-mail: info@insightassessment.com
Web: www.insightassessment.com
Tests: 308, 315, 316, 317, 927, 1621, 1676, 2098

Insight Institute, Inc.
7205 NW Waukomis Drive
Kansas City, MO 64151
Telephone: 800-861-4769
FAX: 816-587-7198
E-mail: customerservice@insightinstitute.com
Web: www.insightinstitute.com
Tests: 986

Institute for Matching Person & Technology, Inc.
486 Lake Road
Webster, NY 14580
Telephone: 585-671-3461
FAX: 585-671-3461
E-mail: impt97@aol.com
Web: matchingpersonandtechnology.com
Tests: 1211, 1213, 1857

Institute for Personality and Ability Testing, Inc. (IPAT, Inc.)
1801 Woodfield Drive
Savoy, IL 61874
Telephone: 217-352-4739
FAX: 217-352-9674
E-mail: custserv@ipat.com
Web: www.ipat.com
Tests: 78, 412, 708, 935, 936, 1016, 1017, 1532, 1651, 1884, 1885, 1886

Institute for Psycho-Imagination Therapy
c/o Dr. Jack Connella
10811 Washington Blvd., Suite 280
Culver City, CA 90232
Telephone: 310-452-3000
Tests: 901, 1869

The Institute of Conflict Analysis and the Museum of the Creative Process
P.O. Box 287
3814 Main Street
Manchester, VT 05254
Telephone: 802-379-6350
FAX: 802-362-1107
E-mail: moralscience@hotmail.com
Web: www.ArtToScience.org
Tests: 523

Institute of General Semantics
72-11 Austin Street, #233
Forest Hills, NY 11375
Telephone: 212-729-7973
E-mail: igs@generalsemantics.org
Web: www.generalsemantics.org
Tests: 2183

Institute of Psychological Research
76 Mozart Avenue West
Montreal, Quebec H2S 1C4
Canada
Telephone: 514-382-3000
FAX: 514-382-3007
E-mail: info@irpcanada.com
Web: www.irpcanada.com
Tests: 1759

Integrated Assessment, LLC
1157 Cordoba Club Drive
Cordova, TN 38018
Telephone: 985-956-2121
E-mail: integratedassessment@gmail.com
Web: www.integrated-assessment.com
Tests: 739

International Assessment Network
7400 Metro Blvd., Suite #350
Edina, MN 55439
Telephone: 952-921-9368
E-mail: info@assessment.com
Web: www.assessment.com
Tests: 1202

International Public Management Association for Human Resources (IPMA-HR)
1617 Duke Street
Alexandria, VA 22314
Telephone: 800-381-8378
FAX: 703-684-0948
E-mail: assessment@ipma-hr.org
Web: testing.ipma-hr.org
Tests: 60, 311, 1444, 1642, 1712

Iowa State University Research Foundation, Inc.
Beardshear Hall
Iowa State University
Ames, IA 50011
Telephone: 515-294-4740
FAX: 515-294-0778
E-mail: sedahlia@iastate.edu
Tests: 1021, 1022

James Stanfield Co., Inc.
P.O. Box 41058
Santa Barbara, CA 93140
Telephone: 800-421-6534
FAX: 805-897-1187
E-mail: orderdesk@stanfield.com
Web: www.stanfield.com
Tests: 489, 1786, 2107

Janelle Publications, Inc.
P.O. Box 811
DeKalb, IL 60115
Telephone: 800-888-8834
FAX: 815-756-4799
E-mail: info@janellepublications.com
Web: www.janellepublications.com
Tests: 1987, 1988, 1989

JIST/EMC Publishing
875 Montreal Way
St. Paul, MN 55102-4245
Telephone: 800-648-5478
FAX: 800-547-8329
E-mail: educate@emcp.com
Web: jist.emcp.com/
Tests: 3, 184, 343, 351, 352, 477, 478, 748, 970, 1045, 1046, 1050, 1391, 1392, 1408, 1553, 1739, 1964, 2170, 2173, 2283, 2290, 2295, 2312

John Wiley & Sons, Inc.
111 River Street
Hoboken, NJ 07030
Web: www.wiley.com
Tests: 342, 457, 488, 591, 640, 672, 1003, 1364, 1488

Kaiser Leadership Solutions, LLC
1903 G Ashwood Ct.
Greensboro, NC 27455
Telephone: 336-217-2740
E-mail: info@kaiserleadership.com
Web: www.kaiserleadership.com
Tests: 1126

Kaplan Early Learning Company
1310 Lewisville-Clemmons Road
P.O. Box 67
Lewisville, NC 27023-0609
E-mail: info@kaplanco.com
Web: www.kaplanco.com
Tests: 633, 634, 635, 1127

Karl Albrecht International
3728 Old Cobble Road
San Diego, CA 92111-4050
Web: www.karlalbrecht.com
Tests: 1283, 1910

KBA, LLC
P.O. Box 3673
Carbondale, IL 62902
E-mail: info@benziger.org
Web: www.benziger.org
Tests: 254

Keegan & Company LLC
31 Purchase Street, Suites 3-4
Rye, NY 10580
Telephone: 914-967-9421
FAX: 914-967-8179
E-mail: info@keeganandco.com
Web: www.keeganandco.com
Tests: 1069

Keeler Instruments Inc.
456 Parkway
Broomall, PA 19008
Telephone: 610-353-4350
FAX: 610-353-7814
E-mail: keeler@keelerusa.com
Web: www.keelerusa.com
Tests: 428, 1726

Keirsey.com
6789 Quail Hill Parkway, Suite 401
Irvine, CA 92603
Telephone: 949-315-9000
FAX: 949-265-9056
E-mail: customer.relations@keirsey.com
Web: www.keirsey.com
Tests: 1070

The Ken Blanchard Companies
125 State Place
Escondido, CA 92029
Telephone: 760-489-5005
Web: www.kenblanchard.com
Tests: 1108

Kendall/Hunt Publishing Company
4050 Westmark Drive
P.O. Box 1840
Dubuque, IA 52004-1840
Telephone: 800-228-0810
FAX: 800-772-9165
E-mail: orders@kendallhunt.com
Web: www.kendallhunt.com
Tests: 196, 1930

Kilmann Diagnostics
One Suprema Drive
Newport Coast, CA 92657
Telephone: 949-497-8766
FAX: 949-230-8449
E-mail: chris@kilmanndiagnostics.com
Web: www.kilmanndiagnostics.com
Tests: 1078, 1079

Kolbe Corp
2355 E. Camelback Road, Suite 610
Phoenix, AZ 85016
Telephone: 602-840-9770
FAX: 602-952-2706
E-mail: info@kolbe.com
Web: www.kolbe.com
Tests: 1093

David S. Krantz
Department of Medical and Clinical Psychology
University of the Health Sciences
4301 Jones Bridge Road
Bethesda, MD 20814-4799
Telephone: 301-295-3273
E-mail: david.krantz@usuhs.edu
Web: www.usuhs.edu/content/david-s-krantz-phd
Tests: 1095

Kuder, Inc.
302 Visions Parkway
Adel, IA 50003-1632
Telephone: 800-314-8972
FAX: 515-993-5422
E-mail: info@kuder.com
Web: www.kuder.com
Tests: 1096, 1097, 2013

Lafayette Instrument
P.O. Box 5729
3700 Sagamore Parkway North
Lafayette, IN 47904-5729
Telephone: 765-423-1505
FAX: 765-423-4111
E-mail: info@lafayetteinstrument.com
Web: www.lafayetteinstrument.com
Tests: 890, 1292, 1745

Laurent Clerc National Deaf Education Center
KDES Suite 3600
Gallaudet University
800 Florida Avenue, NE
Washington, DC 20002-3695
Telephone: 202-651-5340
FAX: 202-651-5708
E-mail: clerc.center@gallaudet.edu
Web: clerccenter.gallaudet.edu
Tests: 1230

Law School Admission Council, Inc.
P.O. Box 40
Newtown, PA 18940-0040
Telephone: 215-968-1001
Web: www.lsac.org
Tests: 1107

The Leadership Challenge, A Wiley Brand
989 Market St.
San Francisco, CA 94103-1741
Telephone: 866 888 5159
E-mail: leadership@wiley.com
Web: www.leadershipchallenge.com
Tests: 759, 1121

Learning by Design, Inc.
1101 Davis Street #5448
Evanston, IL 60204-2235
Telephone: 847-328-8390
FAX: 847-328-2235
E-mail: customerservice@learningbydesign.com
Web: www.learningbydesign.com
Tests: 1939

Learning Tools LLC
P.O. Box 1066
Orchard Park, NY 14127-8066
Telephone: 413-588-8199
FAX: 440-425-9511
E-mail: info@busstoryus.com
Web: www.busstoryus.com
Tests: 1710

Lee Hecht Harrison
2301 Lucien Way, Suite 325
Maitland, FL 32751
Telephone: 407-618-2216
FAX: 407-618-2290
E-mail: bookstore@lhh.com
Web: www.lhh.com
Tests: 959

Life Advance
1250 Ferrelo Road
Santa Barbara, CA 93103
Telephone: 805-565-6233
E-mail: paloutz@westmont.edu
Web: www.lifeadvance.com
Tests: 1940

Life Innovations, Inc.
2660 Arthur St.
Roseville, MN 55113-1339
Telephone: 651-635-0511
FAX: 651-636-1668
E-mail: dolson@prepare-enrich.com
Web: www.prepare-enrich.com
Tests: 451, 792, 799, 803, 1584

LIMRA International
300 Day Hill Rd.
Windsor, CT 06095-1783
Telephone: 800-235-4672
FAX: 860-285-7792
E-mail: customer.service@limra.com
Web: www.limra.com
Tests: 359

Lorna Smith Benjamin Consulting, LLC
455 East, 200 South, Suite #110
Salt Lake City, UT 84111
Telephone: 801-558-9504
FAX: 435-649-4377
E-mail: intrex@psych.utah.edu
Web: lornasmithbenjamin.com/
Tests: 1778

MAA American Mathematics Competition
P.O. Box 471
Annapolis Junction, MD 20701
Telephone: 800-527-3690
E-mail: amcinfo@maa.org
Web: www.maa.org/
Tests: 102, 103, 104, 105, 1216

James B. Maas
Instrument distributed by Test Collection at ETS
Tests: 555

Maddak Inc.
661 Route 23 South
Wayne, NJ 07470
Telephone: 800-443-4926
FAX: 973-305-0841
E-mail: custservice@maddak.com
Web: www.maddak.com
Tests: 204, 1160

Madison Geriatric Research, Education, and Clinical
    Center
VA Medical Center
2500 Overlook Terrace
Madison, WI 53705
Telephone: 608-280-7000
FAX: 608-280-7248
E-mail: vhacogreccwm@va.gov
Web: www.va.gov/GRECC/Madison_GRECC.asp
Tests: 150

Madison Learning, LLC
#47337
P.O. Box 34628
Seattle, Washington 98124-1628
E-mail: mford@gmu.edu
Web: www.implicitself.com
Tests: 153

Management & Personnel Systems, Inc.
157 Twin Peaks Dr.
Walnut Creek, CA 94595-1728
Telephone: 800-576-7455
FAX: 925-977-8200
E-mail: mpscorp@value.net
Web: www.mps-corp.com
Tests: 582, 848, 2014, 2296

Management Research Group
14 York Street, #301
Portland, ME 04101-4556
Telephone: 207-775-2173
FAX: 207-775-6796
E-mail: info@mrg.com
Web: www.mrg.com
Tests: 120, 969, 1114, 1498, 1765

Management Research Institute, Inc.
11304 Spur Wheel Lane
Potomac, MD 20854
Telephone: 301-598-3985
FAX: 301-299-9227
E-mail: mrieaf@aol.com
Web: www.managementresearchinstitute.com/
Tests: 825

MATRICS Assessment, Inc.
11693 San Vicente Blvd. #322
Los Angeles, CA 90049
FAX: 310-312-1535
E-mail: matricsassessment@gmail.com
Web: www.matricsinc.org/
Tests: 1220

MAVEC Specialists Foundation, Inc.
13 Miller St., San Francisco Del Monte
Quezon City 1105
Philippines
Telephone: +632-441-0373
FAX: +632-373-3715
Web: www.mavec.com.ph
Tests: 809

McCann Associates
North American Business Office
444 Oxford Valley Road
3rd Floor
Langhorne, PA 19047
Telephone: 267-756-1163
FAX: 267-746-1440
E-mail: solutions@mccanntesting.com
Web: www.mccanntesting.com
Tests: 572, 613, 744, 745, 746, 810, 1399, 1560

McCarron-Dial Systems, Inc.
P.O. Box 35285
Dallas, TX 75235-0285
Telephone: 214-634-2863
FAX: 214-634-9970
E-mail: mds@mccarrondial.com
Web: mccarrondial.com
Tests: 29, 52, 146, 732, 1225, 1229, 1402, 1491, 2022

McGraw-Hill Higher Education
2 Penn Plaza, 20th Floor
New York, NY 10121
E-mail: HEP_Customer-Service@mheducation.com
Web: www.mheducation.com/
Tests: 435

MED-EL
Fürstenweg 77a
Innsbruck A-6020
Austria
Telephone: +43-512-28 88 89
FAX: +43-512-29 33 81
E-mail: office@medel.com
Web: www.medel.com
Tests: 713

Melamed & Melamed Psycho-Educational and Neuro-
    psychological Services
203 Frances Dr.
Kent, OH 44240
Telephone: 330-673-2986
E-mail: lmelamed@kent.edu
Tests: 1072

Mental Health, Law, and Policy Institute
Simon Fraser University
8888 University Drive
Burnaby, British Columbia V5A 1S6
Canada
Telephone: 877-585-9933
FAX: 604-669-0145
E-mail: info@proactive-resolutions.com
Web: members.psyc.sfu.ca/labs/mhlpi/publications
Tests: 923, 1864

Meta-Visions
2658 Bluestone Circle
Kalamazoo, MI 49009
Telephone: 269-267-0057
FAX: 269-353-9577
E-mail: jwalkermi@sbcglobal.net
Web: www.meta-visions.com/
Tests: 1260

MetriTech, Inc.
4106 Fieldstone Road
Champaign, IL 61822
Telephone: 800-747-4868
FAX: 217-398-5798
E-mail: mtinfo@metritech.com
Web: www.metritech.com
Tests: 54, 1105

Eric N. Miller
1775 E. Palm Canyon Drive, Suite 110-201
Palm Springs, CA 92264
Telephone: 323-386-8427
E-mail: emiller@calcaprt.com
Web: www.calcaprt.com
Tests: 314

Mind Garden, Inc.
855 Oak Grove Ave., Suite 215
Menlo Park, CA 94025
Telephone: 650-322-6300
FAX: 650-322-6398
E-mail: info@mindgarden.com
Web: www.mindgarden.com
Tests: 7, 58, 98, 126, 169, 185, 200, 245, 268, 318, 320,
    321, 347, 349, 380, 434, 491, 541, 544, 545, 558, 559,
    570, 616, 686, 765, 800, 804, 821, 827, 831, 892, 893,
    920, 924, 963, 1009, 1110, 1209, 1214, 1219, 1254,
    1269, 1305, 1331, 1371, 1414, 1435, 1519, 1524,
    1627, 1656, 1657, 1659, 1665, 1705, 1816, 1917,
    1919, 1959, 1960, 1962, 2073, 2188, 2220, 2225,
    2239, 2240, 2278, 2293

MKM Reading Systems
2311 E. Deacon Place
Sioux Falls, SD 57103
Telephone: 605-291-9854
E-mail: info@mkmreadingsystems.com
Web: mkmreadingsystems.com
Tests: 1299, 1300

Monaco & Associates Incorporated
4123 Gage Center Drive, Suite 130
Topeka, KS 66604
Telephone: 785-272-5501
FAX: 785-272-5152
E-mail: greg@monacoassociates.com
Web: www.monacoassociates.com
Tests: 1310

Kenneth R. Morel
6513 Pearcrest Rd.
Las Vegas, NV 89108-5918
Telephone: 304-240-1131
E-mail: mentptsd@gmail.com
Web: www.mentptsd.com
Tests: 1306

Moreno Educational Co.
P.O. Box 19329
San Diego, CA 92159-0329
Telephone: (619) 461-0565
FAX: (619) 469-1073
E-mail: sales@morenoed.com
Web: www.morenoed.com/tests.html
Tests: 1426, 1678, 1929

The Morrisby Organisation
Focus 31 North
Cleveland Road
Hemel Hempstead,
Hertfordshire HP2 7EY
England
Telephone: 44 (0)1442 215521
FAX: 44 (0)1442 240531
E-mail: support@morrisby.com
Web: www.morrisby.com
Tests: 562, 1201, 1307, 1486

Moving Boundaries, Inc.
1375 SW Blaine Court
Gresham, OR 97080
Telephone: 503-661-4126
Web: www.movingboundaries.com
Tests: 1878

Multi-Health Systems, Inc.
P.O. Box 950
North Tonawanda, NY 14120-0950
Telephone: 800-456-3003
FAX: 888-540-4484
E-mail: customerservice@mhs.com
Web: www.mhs.com
Tests: 28, 112, 113, 114, 172, 224, 247, 310, 371, 375,
    405, 411, 430, 459, 502, 517, 527, 528, 529, 530, 531,
    532, 533, 534, 543, 549, 579, 588, 683, 741, 742, 743,
    797, 807, 913, 914, 915, 916, 925, 940, 997, 1038,
    1039, 1145, 1146, 1147, 1148, 1149, 1221, 1222,
    1251, 1324, 1327, 1474, 1568, 1624, 1625, 1660,
    1673, 1704, 1706, 1760, 1828, 1902, 1912, 1913,
    1915, 1942, 2036, 2115, 2166, 2210, 2309

Multiple Intelligences Research and Consulting, Inc.
1316 South Lincoln Street
Kent, OH 44240
Telephone: 330-677-8534
E-mail: sbranton@kent.edu
Web: www.miresearch.org
Tests: 1265

MultiTED Publishing
217 Wildwood Drive
Madison, IN 47250-2939
Telephone: 812-265-2877
E-mail: edsh54@cinergymetro.net
Tests: 1321

MySkillsProfile
Suite 18803
145-157 St. John Street
London EC1V 4PW
United Kingdom
FAX: 44-114-238-5559
Web: MySkillsProfile.com
Tests: 736, 1120, 1175, 1941, 1967, 2288

The National Center on Employment & Disability
P.O. Box 1358
Hot Springs, AR 71902
Tests: 747, 1047, 2279, 2284, 2287, 2297

National Clearinghouse for Rehabilitation Training
    Materials
6524 Old Main Hill
Utah State University
Logan, UT 84322-6524
Web: ncrtm.ed.gov
Tests: 1417

National Communication Association
1765 N Street, NW
Washington, DC 20036
Telephone: 202-464-4622
FAX: 202-464-4600
Web: www.natcom.org
Tests: 136, 493, 538

National Occupational Competency Testing Institute/
    The Whitener Group [NOCTI]
500 N. Bronson Avenue
Big Rapids, MI 49307-2737
Telephone: 231-796-7890
FAX: 231-796-4699
E-mail: nocti@nocti.org
Web: www.nocti.org
Tests: 1376, 1377, 2247

National Psychological Corporation
Bhargava Bhawan, 4/230
Kacheri Ghat, Agra 282004
India
Telephone: +91 562 2464926
FAX: +91 562 2463929
E-mail: npc_agra@yahoo.com
Web: npcindia.com
Tests: 2049

National Reading Styles Institute, Inc.
P.O. Box 737
Syosset, NY 11791-0737
Telephone: 516-921-5500
FAX: 516-921-5591
E-mail: readingstyle@nrsi.com
Web: www.nrsi.com
Tests: 480, 1577, 1697

National Spanish Exams
2701 Beech Street, Suite P
Valparaiso, IN 46383
Telephone: 219-465-2100
FAX: 219-465-2116
E-mail: kcessna@nationalspanishexam.org
Web: www.nationalspanishexam.org
Tests: 1353

National Wellness Institute, Inc.
1300 College Court
P.O. Box 827
Stevens Point, WI 54481-2962
Telephone: 715-372-2969
FAX: 715-342-2979
E-mail: nwi@nationalwellness.org
Web: www.nationalwellness.org
Tests: 2145, 2146, 2147

Robert A. Neimeyer, Ph.D.
Memphis State University
Department of Psychology, Room 347
Memphis, TN 38152
Telephone: 901-678-4680
FAX: 901-678-2579
E-mail: neimeyer@memphis.edu
Web: www.memphis.edu/psychology/people/faculty/
    neimeyer.php
Tests: 2011

Nelson Education Ltd.
1120 Birchmount Road
Toronto, Ontario M1K 5G4
Canada
Telephone: 416-752-9448
FAX: 416-752-9646
E-mail: nelson.clinical@nelson.com
Web: www.nelson.com
Tests: 335, 338, 843

New Zealand Council for Educational Research
Education House West
178-182 Willis Street
Box 3237
Wellington 6011
New Zealand
Telephone: 00 64 4 384 7939
FAX: 00 64 4 384 7933
E-mail: sales@nzcer.org.nz
Web: www.nzcer.org.nz
Tests: 18, 304, 1471, 1635, 1636, 1637, 1820, 1955,
    2015, 2047

Nichols & Molinder Assessments
437 Bowes Drive
Fircrest, WA 98466-7047
Tests: 1334

C. W. Nichols
Telephone: 706-309-9155
Tests: 145

Noel-Levitz
2350 Oakdale Blvd
Coralville, IA 52241-9702
Telephone: 800-876-1117
FAX: 319-337-5274
E-mail: contactus@ruffaloNL.com
Web: www.noellevitz.com
Tests: 476

Northwest Evaluation Association
121 NW Everett St.
Portland, OR 97209-4049
Telephone: 503-624-1951
FAX: 866-654-3246
Web: www.nwea.org
Tests: 1233

Nova Media, Inc.
1724 N. State
Big Rapids, MI 49307-9073
Telephone: 231-796-4637
E-mail: trund@netonecom.net
Web: www.racialattitudesurvey.com
Tests: 1684

Dr. Thomas R. Oaster
Instrument distributed by Test Collection at ETS
Tests: 1397

The Occupational Research Centre
Cornerways
Cardigan Street
Newmarket, Suffolk CB8 8HZ
United Kingdom
Telephone: 01144 1638 662704
FAX: 01144 1638 662704
E-mail: ukinfo@kaicentre.com
Web: www.kaicentre.com
Tests: 1086

OPP Ltd.
15-17 Elsfield Way
Oxford OX2 8EP
United Kingdom
Telephone: +44 (0)1865 404500
FAX: +44 (0)
E-mail: enquiry@opp.com
Web: www.opp.com
Tests: 737

Opposite Strengths, Inc.
P.O. Box 160220
Austin, TX 78716-0220
E-mail: contact@oppositestrengths.com
Web: www.oppositestrengths.com
Tests: 1418

Optometric Extension Program Foundation
1921 E. Carnegie Ave.
Suite 3-L
Santa Ana, CA 92705-5510
Telephone: 949-250-8070
FAX: 949-250-8157
E-mail: kelin.kushin@oep.org
Web: www.oepf.org
Tests: 689

Optometry Admission Testing Program
211 East Chicago Avenue
Chicago, IL 60611-2637
Telephone: 800-232-1694
FAX: 312-587-4105
E-mail: oatexam@ada.org
Web: www.ada.org/en/oat
Tests: 1420

OQ Measures LLC
P.O. Box 521047
Salt Lake City, UT 84152-1047
Telephone: 1-888-647-2673
E-mail: Sales@OQMeasures.com
Web: www.oqmeasures.com
Tests: 1421, 1422, 1423, 2306, 2307, 2310

Organization Analysis and Design LLC
N 24 W30953 Fairway Court
Pewaukee, WI 53072
Telephone: 262-369-0987
E-mail: pchadwick@oadllc.com
Web: www.oadllc.com
Tests: 1395

Organizational Measurement Systems Press
34199 Country View Drive
Eugene, OR 97408
Telephone: 541-484-2715
E-mail: barb_john_miner@msn.com
Tests: 1285, 1415

P.D.P. Press, Inc.
1326 3rd Ave. South
Stillwater, MN 55082
Telephone: 877-439-8865
FAX: 877-259-5906
E-mail: orders@pdppro.com
Web: www.pdppro.com
Tests: 1850

Pacific Northwest Publishing
21 West 6th Avenue
Eugene, OR 97401
Telephone: 866-542-1490
FAX: 541-345-1507
Web: www.pacificnwpublish.com
Tests: 2040

Pain Assessment Resources
4790 Caughlin Parkway, Suite 173
Reno, NV 89519-0907
Telephone: 800-782-1501
FAX: 775-828-4275
E-mail: office@painassessmentresources.com
Web: www.painassessmentresources.com
Tests: 233

Pain Resource Center, Inc.
P.O. Box 763
Hillsborough, NC 27278
Telephone: 800-542-7246
E-mail: painres@tmjscale.com
Web: www.tmjscale.com
Tests: 419, 2160

PAQ Services, Inc.
11 Bellwether Way, Suite 107
Bellingham, WA 98225
Telephone: 800-292-2198
FAX: 877-395-0236
E-mail: paqinfo@paq.com
Web: www.paq.com
Tests: 1566

Paul Ekman Group
P.O. Box 26089
San Francisco, CA 94126
Web: www.paulekman.com/
Tests: 793

Paul H. Brookes Publishing Co., Inc.
P.O. Box 10624
Baltimore, MD 21285-0624
Telephone: 800-638-3775
FAX: 410-337-8539
Web: www.brookespublishing.com
Tests: 89, 90, 138, 339, 369, 418, 431, 432, 433, 484, 700, 701, 942, 977, 1164, 1390, 1460, 1483, 1601, 1798, 1817, 1905, 2050, 2069, 2106, 2167, 2169

Pearson
19500 Bulverde Road
San Antonio, TX 78259
Telephone: 800-627-7271 or 952-681-3232
FAX: 800-632-9011 or 952-681-3299
E-mail: pearsonassessments@pearson.com
Web: www.pearsonassessments.com
Tests: 11, 12, 57, 61, 96, 149, 168, 187, 188, 189, 203, 205, 206, 207, 208, 209, 210, 211, 212, 213, 217, 219, 220, 252, 253, 258, 269, 270, 276, 277, 278, 282, 283, 285, 286, 298, 299, 300, 301, 303, 322, 323, 330, 344, 345, 396, 402, 404, 410, 415, 429, 446, 447, 448, 449, 450, 469, 536, 600, 601, 623, 632, 636, 645, 646, 658, 659, 685, 691, 692, 704, 707, 709, 710, 716, 787, 818, 835, 846, 847, 853, 856, 862, 864, 887, 896, 898, 912, 918, 941, 961, 966, 973, 975, 1014, 1033, 1061, 1062, 1063, 1066, 1067, 1068, 1073, 1075, 1215, 1264, 1271, 1272, 1274, 1275, 1276, 1277, 1278, 1279, 1280, 1281, 1289, 1290, 1304, 1314, 1347, 1348, 1365, 1366, 1427, 1438, 1439, 1441, 1446, 1461, 1462, 1478, 1536, 1537, 1539, 1540, 1563, 1571, 1572, 1585, 1595, 1596, 1597, 1598, 1615, 1616, 1672, 1682, 1683, 1692, 1695, 1711, 1713, 1724, 1734, 1742, 1747, 1753, 1795, 1796, 1810, 1853, 1871, 1892, 1918, 1947, 1950, 1994, 2037, 2074, 2137, 2148, 2161, 2190, 2197, 2198, 2203, 2204, 2208, 2223, 2224, 2227, 2228, 2229, 2230, 2231, 2232, 2233, 2234, 2235, 2236, 2241, 2243, 2249, 2250, 2251, 2252, 2253, 2268, 2292

Pearson Assessment [England]
Halley Court
Jordan Hill
Oxford OX2 8EJ
United Kingdom
Telephone: 0845 630 88 88
FAX: 0845 630 55 55
E-mail: info@pearsonclinical.co.uk
Web: www.pearsonclinical.co.uk
Tests: 173, 175, 239, 240, 241, 327, 416, 560, 674, 688, 690, 859, 922, 1267, 1313, 1589, 1669, 1758, 1838, 1860, 1938, 2076, 2096, 2097, 2211, 2242

Pearson Clinical Assessment [Australia and New Zealand]
151 Castlereagh Street, Suite 1001, Level 10
Sydney, New South Wales 2000
Australia
Telephone: 1800 882 385
FAX: 61 2 9261 4975
E-mail: info@pearsonclinical.com.au
Web: www.pearsonclinical.com.au
Tests: 569, 1270, 1688

Pearson Clinical Assessment, a division of Pearson Education Ltd.
80 Strand
London WC2R 0RL
United Kingdom
E-mail: info@pearsonclinical.co.uk
Web: www.pearsonclinical.co.uk
Tests: 784, 2077

Pearson Education
501 Boylston St., Suite 900
Boston, MA 02116-3725
Web: www.pearsonhighered.com
Tests: 722

Pearson VUE
1 N Dearborn St., Suite 1050
Chicago, IL 60602-4322
Telephone: 952-681-3000
FAX: 952-681-3899
E-mail: PVAmericasChannelSales@pearson.com
Web: www.pearsonvue.com
Tests: 868

Guerry M. Peavy
Shiley-Marcos Alzheimer's Disease Research Center
University of California San Diego
8950 Villa La Jolla Drive, Suite C129
La Jolla, CA 92037
Telephone: 858-822-4800
FAX: 858-246-1287
E-mail: gpeavy@ucsd.edu
Web: adrc.ucsd.edu
Tests: 1859

PEDStest.com, LLC
1013 Austin Court
Nolensville, TN 37135
Telephone: 877-296-9972
FAX: 615-776-4119
E-mail: evpress@pedstest.com
Web: www.pedstest.com
Tests: 1484

Perfection Learning Corporation
1000 North Second Avenue
P.O. Box 500
Logan, IA 51546-0500
Telephone: 800-831-4190
FAX: 712-644-2831
E-mail: orders@perfectionlearning.com
Web: www.perfectionlearning.com
Tests: 1158

Personal Strengths Publishing
2647 Gateway Road #105360
Carlsbad, CA 92009
Telephone: 800-624-7347
FAX: 760-602-0087
E-mail: info@corestrengths.com
Web: www.personalstrengths.com
Tests: 2165

Personalysis Corporation
5847 San Felipe, Suite 650
Houston, TX 77057-3008
Telephone: 713-636-3473
FAX: 713-784-9909
E-mail: info@personalysis.com
Web: www2.personalysis.com
Tests: 1530

Dr. Linda M. Phillips
Canadian Centre for Research on Literacy
Room 653, Education Building South
University of Alberta
Edmonton, Alberta T6G 2G5
Canada
Telephone: 780-492-4250
E-mail: linda.phillips@ualberta.ca
Web: www.ualberta.ca/~lphillip/
Tests: 2104

Phonovisual Products, Inc.
119-A E. Chapline St., First Floor
P.O. Box 90
Sharpsburg, MD 21782
Telephone: 800-283-4888
FAX: 240-358-0228
E-mail: phonovisual@aol.com
Web: www.phonovisual.com
Tests: 1546

Dr. Robert C. Pianta
E-mail: pianta@virginia.edu
Web: curry.virginia.edu/about/directory/robert-c.-pianta/
   measures
Tests: 1995

Dr. Ralph L. Piedmont
Loyola University Maryland
Pastoral Counseling Department
8890 McGaw Road, Suite 380D
Columbia, MD 21045
Telephone: 410-617-7625
FAX: 410-617-7644
E-mail: rpiedmont@loyola.edu
Web: www.loyola.edu/academic/pastoralcounseling/
   faculty/piedmont
Tests: 157

Piney Mountain Press
P.O. Box 986
Dahlonega, GA 30533
Telephone: 800-255-3127
FAX: 800-905-3127
E-mail: cyberguy@windstream.net
Web: www.pineymountain.com
Tests: 198, 1137, 1140, 1605, 1888, 2215

The Plotkin Group
5650 El Camino Real, Suite 223
Carlsbad, CA 92008
Telephone: 800-877-5685
Web: www.plotkingroup.com
Tests: 1951

Predictive Surveys Corporation
5802 Howard Avenue
LaGrange, IL 60525
Telephone: 708-828-1369
E-mail: marklstrand@gmail.com
Tests: 1648, 1649

Preziosi Partners, Inc.
2269 South University Drive, Suite 244
Davie, FL 33324
Telephone: 954-915-0101
E-mail: kittyprez@aol.com
Web: www.preziosipartners.com/
Tests: 1618

Price Systems, Inc.
763 N 1750 Road
Lawrence, KS 66049-9016
Telephone: 785 843-7892
FAX: 785-843-0101
E-mail: gprice@ku.edu
Web: pricesys.com
Tests: 1134, 1619

PRO-ED
8700 Shoal Creek Blvd.
Austin, TX 78757-6897
Telephone: 800-897-3202
FAX: 800-397-7633
E-mail: info@proedinc.com
Web: www.proedinc.com
Tests: 49, 51, 71, 116, 121, 128, 132, 139, 147, 148, 160,
171, 176, 177, 191, 197, 215, 216, 229, 231, 265, 273,
274, 288, 370, 440, 461, 463, 464, 465, 466, 483, 504,
506, 507, 508, 511, 522, 566, 576, 586, 614, 615, 617,
618, 619, 624, 627, 629, 630, 631, 641, 642, 643, 660,
676, 677, 702, 730, 773, 779, 820, 828, 830, 834, 837,
854, 857, 858, 880, 881, 882, 910, 937, 962, 978, 1082,
1094, 1104, 1130, 1154, 1227, 1287, 1328, 1359, 1360,
1428, 1477, 1545, 1547, 1552, 1581, 1587, 1594, 1608,
1623, 1654, 1687, 1690, 1699, 1727, 1738, 1749, 1750,
1751, 1788, 1789, 1792, 1793, 1805, 1821, 1823, 1837,
1908, 1936, 1946, 1948, 1949, 1997, 1998, 2032, 2045,
2075, 2080, 2081, 2084, 2086, 2087, 2088, 2089,
2090, 2091, 2092, 2099, 2101, 2109, 2110, 2111,
2112, 2114, 2116, 2117, 2119, 2120, 2121, 2122,
2123, 2124, 2125, 2126, 2128, 2129, 2135, 2136,
2138, 2139, 2140, 2141, 2163, 2172, 2186, 2187,
2237, 2256, 2270, 2272, 2305, 2308

Professional Picture Framers Association
83 South St., Unit 303
Freehold, NJ 07728
Telephone: 732-536-5160
FAX: 732-536-5761
E-mail: info@ppfa.com
Web: www.ppfa.com
Tests: 378

Professional Resource Press
P.O. Box 3197
Sarasota, FL 34230-3197
Telephone: 800-443-3364
FAX: 866-804-4843
E-mail: cs.prpress@gmail.com
Web: www.prpress.com
Tests: 819, 1210, 1297, 1318

Profiles International, Inc.
Profiles Office Park
5205 Lake Shore Drive
Waco, TX 76710-1732
Telephone: 866-751-1644
Web: www.profilesinternational.com
Tests: 1628

ProLiteracy Worldwide
104 Marcellus St.
Syracuse, NY 13204
Telephone: 800-448-8878
FAX: 315-422-6369
E-mail: info@proliteracy.org
Web: www.newreaderspress.com
Tests: 761, 1691

Prometric
1501 South Clinton Street
Baltimore, MD 21224
Web: www.getcollegecredit.com
Tests: 682

Prufrock Press Inc.
P.O. Box 8813
Waco, TX 76714-8813
Telephone: 800-998-2208
FAX: 800-240-0333
E-mail: info@prufrock.com
Web: www.prufrock.com
Tests: 946, 995, 1790, 1791

PSI Services LLC
2950 N. Hollywood Way, Suite 200
Burbank, CA 91505-1072
Telephone: 818-847-6180
FAX: 818-847-8701
Web: corporate.psionline.com/contact/
Tests: 749, 811, 812, 1561, 1620, 1650, 2201

Psych Press
Level 6, 140 Queen Street
Melbourne, VIC 3000
Australia
Telephone: +61 3 9670 0590
FAX: +61 3 9642 3577
E-mail: info@psychpress.com.au
Web: www.psychpress.com/
Tests: 780

Psycho-Educational Services
5114 Balcones Woods Drive, Suite 307-163
Austin, TX 78759
Telephone: 512-699-9381
Web: www.psycho-educational.com
Tests: 836

Psychodiagnostics, Inc.
2360 Corporate Circle, Suite 400
Henderson, NV 89074-7739
Telephone: 702-997-2566
E-mail: psyinfo@psychodiagnostics.com
Web: www.psychodiagnostics.com
Tests: 1339

Psychological Assessment Resources, Inc.
16204 N. Florida Avenue
Lutz, FL 33549-8119
Telephone: 800-331-8378
FAX: 800-727-9329
E-mail: custsupp@parinc.com
Web: www4.parinc.com
Tests: 8, 9, 64, 70, 72, 73, 81, 226, 227, 228, 232, 271,
    275, 287, 289, 312, 313, 346, 348, 360, 384, 389, 394,
    397, 399, 401, 403, 413, 420, 441, 442, 443, 444, 445,
    468, 473, 474, 479, 535, 537, 546, 602, 603, 612, 622,
    626, 662, 712, 715, 733, 734, 750, 775, 789, 813, 814,
    815, 832, 926, 947, 949, 968, 998, 1000, 1006, 1011,
    1012, 1020, 1048, 1150, 1151, 1165, 1203, 1234,
    1250, 1252, 1255, 1256, 1257, 1273, 1282, 1288,
    1303, 1323, 1326, 1329, 1332, 1361, 1362, 1368,
    1370, 1406, 1416, 1452, 1459, 1463, 1475, 1476,
    1481, 1503, 1504, 1509, 1510, 1521, 1522, 1523,
    1562, 1567, 1662, 1664, 1667, 1719, 1729, 1730, 1731,
    1732, 1733, 1735, 1736, 1737, 1740, 1746, 1754, 1755,
    1756, 1757, 1834, 1854, 1906, 1944, 1957, 1958, 1969,
    1978, 1981, 1984, 1985, 1986, 2010, 2027, 2043, 2067,
    2100, 2108, 2176, 2177, 2178, 2185, 2199, 2206, 2212,
    2213, 2216, 2254, 2258, 2259, 2299

Psychological Growth Associates, Inc.
Instrument distributed by Test Collection at ETS
Tests: 2158

Psychological Publications, Inc.
2205 First St., Suite 110
Simi Valley, CA 93065
Telephone: 800-345-8378
FAX: 805-527-9266
E-mail: tjta@aol.com
Web: www.tjta.com
Tests: 802, 2044

Psychological Services Bureau, Inc.
977 Seminole Trail #317
Charlottesville, VA 22901-2894
Telephone: 434-293-5865
E-mail: support@psbtests.com
Web: www.psbtests.com
Tests: 1644, 1645, 1646, 1647

Psychological Services Press
92 Bowman St.
Hamilton, Ontario L8S 2T6
Canada
Telephone: 905-527-0129
FAX: 905-527-5726
E-mail: iratrofimov@gmail.com
Web: fhs.mcmaster.ca/cilab/PS/PS-STQ.htm
Tests: 1980

Psychology Press, Inc.
P.O. Box 328
Brandon, VT 05733-0328
Telephone: 800-639-4122
FAX: 802-247-8312
E-mail: info1@great-ideas.org
Web: www.great-ideas.org
Tests: 1541

Psychometric Research & Development Ltd.
P.O. Box 1143
St Albans, Hertfordshire AL1 9UT
United Kingdom
Telephone: +44 0 1727 841455
E-mail: enquiries@prd.co.uk
Web: www.prd.co.uk
Tests: 867, 1302, 1372

Psychometrics Canada Ltd.
7125 77 Avenue
Edmonton, Alberta T6B 0B5
Canada
Telephone: 800-661-5158
FAX: 780-469-2283
E-mail: info@psychometrics.com
Web: www.psychometrics.com
Tests: 971, 972, 2285

PsychTests AIM, Inc.
9001 Boulevard de l'Acadie, Suite 802
Montreal, Quebec H4N 3H5
Canada
Telephone: 514-745-3189
FAX: 514-745-6242
E-mail: ilona@psychtests.com
Web: corporate.psychtests.com/
Tests: 84, 151, 354, 365, 437, 487, 548, 565, 581, 735,
    751, 766, 767, 829, 905, 1032, 1119, 1157, 1187,
    1316, 1317, 1330, 1358, 1381, 1715, 1775, 1836,
    1911, 1966, 2018, 2055, 2274, 2280

Psytec Inc.
P.O. Box 564
DeKalb, IL 60115
Telephone: 815-758-1415
FAX: 815-758-1725
E-mail: psytecinc@comcast.net
Tests: 388

Donald K. Pumroy, Ph.D.
Instrument distributed by Test Collection at ETS
Tests: 1208

Quality Metric
24 Albion Road
Building 400
Lincoln, RI 02865
Telephone: 800-464-3649
E-mail: info@optum.com
Web: www.optum.com
Tests: 1865

Quantitative Methods in Education
University of Minnesota
250 Education Science Building
56 East River Road
Minneapolis, MN 55455
Telephone: 612-624-6083
FAX: 612-624-8241
E-mail: psyf-adm@umn.edu
Web: www.cehd.umn.edu/EdPsych/programs/QME
Tests: 1217

Questar Assessment, Inc.
5550 Upper 147th Street West
Minneapolis, MN 55124
Telephone: 877-997-0422
E-mail: customerservice@questarai.com
Web: www.questarai.com
Tests: 599, 1163, 1167, 1877

Ramsay Corporation
Boyce Station Offices
1050 Boyce Road
Pittsburgh, PA 15241-3907
Telephone: 412-257-0732
FAX: 412-257-9929
E-mail: sales@ramsaycorp.com
Web: www.ramsaycorp.com
Tests: 92, 386, 481, 675, 723, 724, 725, 726, 990, 1166,
1168, 1169, 1170, 1235, 1237, 1239, 1241, 1242, 1243,
1245, 1315, 1319, 1320, 1409, 1411, 1610, 2054, 2238

Reitan Neuropsychology Laboratory
2517 W. Monterey Ave.
Mesa, AZ 85202
Telephone: 520-954-6622
FAX: 520-829-3513
E-mail: REITANLABs@AOL.COM
Web: rn-lab.net/
Tests: 908

Renaissance Learning, Inc.
P.O. Box 8036
Wisconsin Rapids, WI 54495-8036
Telephone: 800-338-4204
FAX: 715-424-4242
E-mail: answers@renaissance.com
Web: www.renlearn.com
Tests: 1952, 1953, 1954

Research for Better Schools, Inc.
123 South Broad Street, Suite 1860
Philadelphia, PA 19109
Telephone: 215-568-6150
FAX: 215-568-7260
Web: www.rbs.org
Tests: 156, 665

Research Press
2612 N Mattis Ave.
Champaign, IL 61822
Telephone: 800-519-2707
FAX: 217-352-1221
E-mail: rp@researchpress.com
Web: www.researchpress.com
Tests: 235, 951, 952, 1333

Richmond Products, Inc.
4400 Silver Avenue, SE
Albuquerque, NM 87108
Telephone: 505-275-2406
FAX: 810-885-8319
E-mail: sales@richmondproducts.com
Web: www.RichmondProducts.com
Tests: 953

Rocky Mountain Behavioral Science Institute, Inc.
Publisher advised it dissolved in 2011.
Tests: 62, 101

Rose Wolfe Family Partnership LLP
c/o Walden Personnel Testing & Consulting, Inc.
1 Wood Avenue, Suite 1403
Montreal, Quebec H3Z 3C5
Canada
Telephone: 514-916-5908
E-mail: ssilver@waldentesting.com
Web: www.waldentesting.com
Tests: 123, 2260, 2261

Routledge Psychology
711 3rd Ave, 8th Floor
New York, NY 10017
Telephone: 212-216-7800
FAX: 212-564-7854
E-mail: psychology@routledge.com
Web: www.routledge.com/psychology
Tests: 161, 263, 264, 328, 497, 903, 1655

Kenneth H. Rubin, Ph.D., Professor
Center for Children, Relationships & Culture
Department of Human Development & Quantitative
    Methodology, 3304 Benjamin Building
University of Maryland
College Park, MD 20742-1131
E-mail: krubin@umd.edu
Web: www.umdrubinlab.com/
Tests: 1559

SALT Software, LLC
7006 Hubbard Avenue
Middleton, WI 53562
Telephone: 888-440-7258
FAX: 608-237-2220
E-mail: sales@saltsoftware.com
Web: www.saltsoftware.com
Tests: 2039

The SASSI Institute
201 Camelot Lane
Springville, IN 47462
Telephone: 800-726-0526
FAX: 800-546-7995
E-mail: sassi@sassi.com
Web: sassi.com
Tests: 74, 237, 1931, 2003, 2005, 2007

Scantron Corporation
1313 Lone Oak Road
Eagan, MN 55121
Telephone: 800-722-6876
FAX: 619-615-0522
E-mail: customer.service@scantron.com
Web: www.scantron.com
Tests: 1493

Dr. K. Warner Schaie
2500 6th Ave. N. Apt 1
Seattle, WA 98109
Telephone: 206-285-1764
FAX: 206-283-2460
E-mail: schaie@u.washington.edu
Web: slsuw.org
Tests: 1799

Ronald R. Schmeck, Ph.D.
Professor Emeritus
Department of Psychology, Life Science II 6502
Southern Illinois University at Carbondale
Carbondale, IL 62901-6502
E-mail: rae50@siu.edu
Tests: 1010

Nina G. Schneider, Ph.D.
Telephone: 310-268-3059
E-mail: ngs@ucla.edu
Tests: 1901

Scholastic Inc.
557 Broadway
New York, NY 10012
Telephone: 800-724-6527
Web: www.scholastic.com
Tests: 2155

Scholastic Testing Service, Inc.
480 Meyer Road
Bensenville, IL 60106-1617
Telephone: 800-642-6787
FAX: 866-766-8054
E-mail: sts@ststesting.com
Web: www.ststesting.com
Tests: 1, 452, 503, 542, 647, 648, 698, 718, 906, 934,
    954, 1076, 1077, 1084, 1098, 1231, 1677, 1744, 1815,
    1999, 2152, 2153, 2164, 2221

School Behaviour Solutions
E-mail: info@schoolbehavioursolutions.com
Web: www.schoolbehavioursolutions.com
Tests: 1808

Schoolhouse Educational Services, LLC
1052 Forest Oak Drive, Suite 200
Onalaska, WI 54650
Telephone: 608-787-5636
E-mail: cpps@psychprocesses.com
Web: www.schoolhouseeducationalservices.com
Tests: 414, 1080

Schuhfried
Hyrtlstrasse 45
Austria
Telephone: +43 2236 42315
FAX: +43 2236 46597
E-mail: info@schuhfried.com
Web: www.schuhfried.at
Tests: 907

Scientific Management Techniques, Inc.
19 Star Drive, Suite E
Merrimack, NH 03054
Telephone: 603-421-0222
FAX: 603-421-1881
E-mail: scibos@scientific-management.com
Web: www.scientific-management.com
Tests: 1943

Search Institute
The Banks Building
615 First Avenue NE, Suite 125
Minneapolis, MN 55413
Telephone: 800-888-7828
FAX: 612-692-5553
E-mail: si@search-institute.org
Web: www.search-institute.org
Tests: 1826

William E. Sedlacek
P.O. Box 539
Great Cacapon, WV 25422-0539
E-mail: wsed@umd.edu
Web: williamsedlacek.info
Tests: 1378, 1879

Melvin Selzer, M.D.
6967 Paseo Laredo
La Jolla, CA 92037
Telephone: 858-459-1035
FAX: 858-459-1021
Tests: 1261

SenseLabs
5850 El Camino Real
Atascadero, CA 93422
Telephone: 866-870-2982
E-mail: info@senselabs.com
Web: senselabs.com
Tests: 1480

Sensonics, Inc.
P.O. Box 112
Haddon Heights, NJ 08035
Telephone: 800-547-8838
FAX: 856-547-5665
E-mail: sales@sensonics.com
Web: www.sensonics.com
Tests: 1900

The Sidran Institute
P.O. Box 436
Brooklandville, MD 21022-0436
Telephone: 410-825-8888
FAX: 410-560-0134
E-mail: orders@sidran.org
Web: www.sidran.org
Tests: 69, 670, 671

SIGMA Assessment Systems, Inc.
P.O. Box 610757
Port Huron, MI 48061-0757
Telephone: 800-265-1285
FAX: 800-361-9411
E-mail: SIGMA@SigmaAssessmentSystems.com
Web: www.sigmaassessmentsystems.com
Tests: 131, 195, 350, 368, 539, 664, 756, 1035, 1036,
    1113, 1123, 1325, 1382, 1528, 1531, 1661, 1861,
    1874, 1875, 1876, 1883, 2030

Silverwood Enterprises, LLC
4627 Ridge Rd.
Wadsworth, OH 44281
Telephone: 330-239-1646
FAX: 330-239-0250
E-mail: dclarke@silverwoodassoc.com
Web: www.silverwoodassoc.com
Tests: 97, 928

Simpson Associates
World Trade Centre
999 Canada Place, Suite 404
Vancouver, British Columbia V6C 3E2
Canada
Telephone: 800-419-7473
E-mail: info@djsimpson.com
Web: www.djsimpson.com/homesimpsonassociates
Tests: 163

Slosson Educational Publications, Inc.
P.O. Box 280
East Aurora, NY 14052-0544
Telephone: 888-756-7766
FAX: 800-655-3840
E-mail: slossonprep@gmail.com
Web: www.slosson.com
Tests: 2, 108, 129, 417, 509, 649, 650, 651, 652, 653,
    661, 721, 1083, 1818, 1819, 1822, 1894, 1895, 1896,
    1897, 1898, 2006, 2118, 2217

Soares Institute of Neuroscience and Education
University of Bridgeport School of Education
Carlson Hall, Room 111
126 Park Avenue
Bridgeport, CT 06604
Telephone: 203-576-4213
Web: www.bridgeport.edu/academics/schools-colleges/
    school-education/
Tests: 13, 142, 1840, 1841, 1842, 1843, 1844, 1924, 2048

SOI Systems
39000 Bryant Lane
Springfield, OR 97478
Telephone: 541-746-5602
FAX: 541-746-5708
E-mail: soi@soisystems.com
Web: www.soisystems.com
Tests: 605, 606, 1248

Stanard & Associates, Inc.
309 West Washington Street, Suite 1000
Chicago, IL 60606
Telephone: 312-553-0213
FAX: 312-553-0218
E-mail: sales@stanard.com
Web: www.stanard.com
Tests: 1352

Jacqueline Stark
Krafftgasse 5/2/19
1020
Austria
Telephone: +43 1 3302830
E-mail: info@ela-photoseries.com
Web: www.ela-photoseries.com
Tests: 776

Stoelting Co.
620 Wheat Lane
Wood Dale, IL 60191-1164
Telephone: 800-860-9775
FAX: 630-860-9775
E-mail: psychtests@stoeltingco.com
Web: www.stoeltingco.com/psychologicaltesting.html
Tests: 6, 162, 225, 383, 556, 557, 833, 1013, 1044, 1053,
    1064, 1065, 1089, 1092, 1144, 1259, 1385, 1600, 1899,
    1921, 1965, 1977, 2209

Stress Directions, Inc.
P.O. Box 15712
Boston, MA 02215
Web: www.stressdirections.com
Tests: 1513

Stressmaster International
3219 E. Camelback Rd.
Phoenix, AZ 85018
Telephone: 480-444-6301
E-mail: info@stressmaster.com
Web: www.stressmaster.com
Tests: 1971

Professor Paris Strom
Dept. of Educational Foundations, Leadership & Technology
4036 Haley Center
Auburn University, AL 36849-5221
Telephone: 334-844-3077
E-mail: stromps@auburn.edu
Web: www.teamworkskillsinventory.org
Tests: 878, 1453, 1458, 2059

Student Development Associates, Inc.
Instrument distributed by National Academic Advising
    Association (NACADA)
Web: www.nacada.ksu.edu
Tests: 10

Stuttering Therapy Resources, Inc.
8005 Spectrum Drive
McKinney, TX 75070
Telephone: 412-366-4916
FAX: 412-366-4916
E-mail: info@stutteringtherapyresources.com
Web: www.stutteringtherapyresources.com
Tests: 1442

Clifford H. Swensen
Department of Psychological Sciences
Purdue University
703 3rd Street Psychological Sciences Building
West Lafayette, IN 47907
Telephone: 765-496-6977
FAX: 765-496-2670
E-mail: cswensen@psych.purdue.edu
Web: psych.purdue.edu
Tests: 1785, 1787

Talegent
Level 1, 18 Shortland Street
Auckland City 1010
New Zealand
E-mail: clientsupport@talegent.com
Web: www.talegent.com
Tests: 1472

Teachers College Press
1234 Amsterdam Avenue
New York, NY 10027
Telephone: 212-678-3929
FAX: 212-678-4149
E-mail: tcpress@tc.columbia.edu
Web: www.teacherscollegepress.com
Tests: 154, 305, 695, 798, 979, 1224, 1629, 1806, 2078

TED Publishing
c/o Haskel Cohen
59 Summit Street
Newton, MA 02458
Telephone: 812-265-2877
E-mail: edsh54@cinergymetro.net
Tests: 2042

Sue Teele & Associates
P.O. Box 7302
Redlands, CA 92375
Telephone: 909-793-1916
FAX: 909-793-4058
E-mail: scandsteele@verizon.net
Web: sueteele.net
Tests: 2064

Teleometrics International, Inc.
4567 Lake Shore Drive
Waco, TX 76710
Telephone: 800-876-2389
FAX: 254-772-9588
E-mail: teleocsrv@teleometrics.com
Web: www.teleometrics.com
Tests: 14, 524, 577, 752, 965, 1177, 1184, 1186, 1189,
    1191, 1192, 1195, 1196, 1197, 1468, 1495, 1506,
    1511, 1533, 1575, 1576, 1617, 1670, 1674, 1698,
    1764, 1769, 1773, 2000, 2001, 2002, 2021, 2024,
    2052, 2053, 2056, 2057, 2282

TEMAS (Tell-Me-A-Story) Test Publishing
492 3rd Street, Suite 1A
Brooklyn, New York 11215-2995
Telephone: 917-662-7150
E-mail: thetemastest@gmail.com
Web: temastest.com/
Tests: 2068

The PEOPLE Process
2620 Regatta Drive, Suite 102
Las Vegas, NV 89128
Telephone: 702-396-5126
FAX: 702-254-3069
E-mail: pamhollister@thepeopleprocess.com
Web: www.thepeopleprocess.com
Tests: 1487

The TOVA Company
3321 Cerritos Ave.
Los Alamitos, CA 90720-2105
Telephone: 800-729-2886
FAX: 800-452-6919
E-mail: info@tovatest.com
Web: www.tovatest.com
Tests: 2132

TRT Associates, Inc.
1579 Monroe Drive, Suite F510
Atlanta, GA 30324
Telephone: 404-406-8781
E-mail: trtbasis@hotmail.com
Web: www.basis-a.com
Tests: 199

Trust Tutoring
9525 Georgia Ave., Suite 200
Silver Spring, MD 20910-1416
Telephone: 800-301-3131
E-mail: havis@trusttutoring.com
Web: trusttutoring.com
Tests: 774

U.S. Department of Labor
Employment and Training Administration
200 Constitution Avenue, NW
Washington, DC 20210
Telephone: 877-872-5627
E-mail: ETAPagemaster@dol.gov
Web: www.mynextmove.org/explore/ip
Tests: 1393, 1394

United States Military Entrance Processing Command
ATTN: Operations Directorate
2500 Green Bay Road
North Chicago, IL 60064-3094
Telephone: 800-323-0513
E-mail: dmdc.official-asvab@mail.mil
Web: official-asvab.com/
Tests: 130

Universal Publishing
677 Roosevelt Highway
P.O Box 3900
Waymart, PA 18472
Telephone: 800-940-2270
FAX: 570-488-9750
E-mail: info@upub.net
Web: www.upub.net
Tests: 1903

University of Maryland
CHSE Department
3214 Benjamin Building
College Park, MD 20742
Telephone: 301-405-2858
FAX: 301-405-9995
E-mail: climate-assess@umd.edu
Web: www.education.umd.edu/CHSE/resources/Assessment/MVS.html
Tests: 1342

University of Michigan Press
839 Greene Street
Ann Arbor, MI 48104
Telephone: 800-621-2736
E-mail: um.press.bus@umich.edu
Web: www.press.umich.edu
Tests: 699, 1592

University of Minnesota Press
Test Division, University of Minnesota Press
111 Third Avenue South, Suite 290
Minneapolis, MN 55401-2520
Telephone: 612-627-1963
FAX: 612-627-1980
E-mail: kaemm002@umn.edu
Web: www.upress.umn.edu/test-division
Tests: 1293, 1294, 1295

Variety Child Learning Center
47 Humphrey Drive
Syosset, NY 11791-4098
Telephone: 516-921-7171
FAX: 516-921-8130
Web: www.vclc.org
Tests: 822

Village Publishing
73 Valley Drive
Furlong, PA 18925
Telephone: 800-553-7678
FAX: 215-794-3386
E-mail: villagepublishingstaff@gmail.com
Web: www.vp411.com
Tests: 152, 281, 668, 944, 1454, 1457, 1489

Visual Awareness Research Group
2580 Tarpon Cove, Suite 922
Punta Gorda, FL 33950
Telephone: 859-523-8007
FAX: 859-523-8007
E-mail: droenker@visualawareness.com
Web: www.visualawareness.com
Tests: 2189

Vocational Psychology Research
N612 Elliott Hall
University of Minnesota—Twin Cities
75 East River Road
Minneapolis, MN 55455-0344
Telephone: 612-625-1367
FAX: 612-625-1367
E-mail: vpr@umn.edu
Web: vpr.psych.umn.edu/
Tests: 1291, 1296

VORT Corporation
P.O. Box G
Menlo Park, CA 94026
Telephone: 888-757-8678
FAX: 650-327-0747
E-mail: sales@vort.com
Web: www.vort.com
Tests: 234, 929, 930

Voyager Sopris Learning
Cambium Learning Group
17855 Dallas Parkway, Suite 400
Dallas, TX 75287
Telephone: 800-547-6747
FAX: 888-819-7767
Web: www.voyagersopris.com
Tests: 657

Walden Personnel Testing & Consulting Inc.
1 Wood Avenue Suite 1403
Montreal, Quebec H3Z 3C5
Canada
Telephone: 514-916-5908
FAX: 514-221-3996
E-mail: ssilver@waldentesting.com
Web: www.waldentesting.com
Tests: 15, 109, 110, 306, 307, 325, 439, 512, 513, 584, 1398, 1445, 1630, 1631, 1641, 1716, 1717, 1770, 1771, 2066

Western Psychological Services
625 Alaska Ave.
Torrance, CA 90503-5124
Telephone: 424-201-8800
FAX: 424-201-6950
E-mail: customerservice@wpspublish.com
Web: www.wpspublish.com
Tests: 31, 48, 65, 77, 91, 93, 127, 165, 236, 243, 244, 284, 302, 395, 406, 408, 409, 427, 500, 526, 594, 595, 598, 625, 788, 841, 845, 861, 904, 909, 911, 945, 1001, 1052, 1071, 1085, 1138, 1173, 1199, 1200, 1204, 1207, 1226, 1337, 1343, 1369, 1386, 1387, 1424, 1425, 1443, 1456, 1499, 1500, 1501, 1502, 1526, 1527, 1543, 1554, 1570, 1612, 1613, 1653, 1680, 1702, 1720, 1721, 1728, 1743, 1813, 1824, 1825, 1849, 1851, 1852, 1855, 1867, 1870, 1904, 1916, 1973, 1979, 1990, 1991, 2012, 2033, 2071, 2127, 2174, 2175, 2218, 2244

Dr. Thomas Widiger
115 Kastle Hall
University of Kentucky
Lexington, KY 40506
Telephone: 859-257-6849
E-mail: widiger@email.uky.edu
Web: psychology.as.uky.edu/users/widiger
Tests: 1525

Wiley Publishing
6465 Wayzata Blvd., Suite 800
Minneapolis, MN 55426
Telephone: 800-653-3472
E-mail: partnercare@everythingdisc.com
Web: www.everythingdisc.com
Tests: 667

Wilson Learning Worldwide, Inc.
8000 W 78th Street, Suite 200
Minneapolis, MN 55439
Telephone: 800-328-7937
E-mail: info@wilsonlearning.com
Web: www.wilsonlearning.com
Tests: 1920

Winslow Research Institute
1933 Windward Point
Discovery Bay, CA 94513
Telephone: 925-516-8686
FAX: 925-516-7015
E-mail: winslow@winslowresearch.com
Web: www.winslowresearch.com
Tests: 2257

Ken C. Winters, Ph.D.
1575 Northrop St.
Falcon Heights, MN 55108
Telephone: 612-387-7691
E-mail: winte001@umn.edu
Tests: 68

Women & Infants Hospital
50 Holden St.
Providence, RI 02908
Telephone: 401-453-7640
Web: www.brown.edu/research/projects/children-at-risk/
   about
Tests: 1374

Wonderlic, Inc.
400 Lakeview Parkway, Suite 200
Vernon Hills, IL 60061
Telephone: 877-605-9496
FAX: 847-680-9492
E-mail: sales@wonderlic.com
Web: www.wonderlic.com
Tests: 505, 921, 1496, 2262, 2263

Judith Worell, Ph.D.
Instrument distributed by Test Collection at ETS
Tests: 1455

World Health Organization
Management of Substance Dependence
CH-1211
Geneva 27
Switzerland
Telephone: +41 22 791 3494
FAX: 41-22-791-4851
E-mail: msb@who.int
Web: www.who.int
Tests: 95

World of Work, Inc.
410 West 1st Street, Suite #103
Tempe, AZ 85281-2574
Telephone: 480-966-5100
FAX: 877-459-9694
E-mail: info@wowi.com
Web: www.wowi.com
Tests: 2303

Worley's Identity Discovery Profile (WIDP)
190 Bishop Road
Fitchburg, MA 01420-2993
Telephone: 978-400-5012
E-mail: jwworley@worleyid.com
Tests: 2304

Steven H. Zarit and Judy M. Zarit
Test distributed by Mapi Research Trust
27, rue de la Villette
69003 Lyon
France
Telephone: +33 (0) 472 13 65 75
E-mail: trust@mapi.fr
Web: eprovide.mapi-trust.org
Tests: 2314

Zilprint
1317 S. Diamond Bar Blvd. #5022
Diamond Bar, CA 91765
E-mail: contact@zilprint.com
Web: www.zilprint.com
Tests: 1925

INDEX OF NAMES

This index indicates whether a citation refers to authorship of a test or of a test review for a specific test in a previous Mental Measurements Yearbook. *Numbers refer to test entries in* Tests in Print IX, *not to pages. The abbreviations and numbers following the names may be interpreted as follows: "test, 73" indicates authorship of test 73; "rev, 86" is based on information listed in the cross references for a test and indicates authorship of a previous review of test 86.*

Boyce, B. A.: rev, 89, 1572
Boye, M. W.: test, 1931
Boyle, G. J.: rev, 203, 998, 1086, 1152, 1446, 1522, 1753, 2044, 2176
Boyles, E. K.: rev, 287, 1695
Braaten, S.: test, 235, 1099
Bracken, B. A.: rev, 1660, 1737, 2235; test, 276, 277, 278, 441, 442, 443, 444, 1328, 2186, 2187
Braddy, P.: test, 250
Braddy, P. W.: test, 248, 249
Braden, J. P.: rev, 167, 1062, 1417, 2231, 2235
Bradford, E. J. G.: rev, 1867
Bradley, J. M.: rev, 2141
Bradley, P.: test, 319, 564, 1532
Bradley, R. H.: rev, 851; test, 943
Bradley-Johnson, S.: test, 139, 461
Brady, J. P.: test, 700, 701
Brady, M.: test, 1044
Brady, R. P.: test, 1553, 2283, 2290, 2312
Bramson, R. M.: test, 984
Brandt, J.: test, 947, 2067
Brannigan, G. G.: test, 251
Braswell, J.: rev, 2142
Brazelton, T. B.: test, 1364
Brazier-Carter, P.: rev, 830
Breaux, K. C.: test, 1068
Breecher, S. V. A.: test, 1825
Brewer, J. H.: test, 255
Brickenkamp, R.: test, 585
Bricker, D.: test, 89, 90, 138, 1905
Bricklin, B.: rev, 720; test, 281, 668, 944, 1454, 1457, 1489
Bridges, D.: test, 2308
Bridges, W.: test, 1432
Briere, J.: test, 468, 612, 1006, 1336, 1667, 2176, 2177, 2178
Brigance, A. H.: test, 291
Briggs, K. C.: test, 1344, 1346
Briggs, S.: test, 1917
Briggs-Gowan, M. J.: test, 1033
Brighouse, A.: test, 1556
Brimer, M. A.: rev, 1355
Bringsjord, E. L.: rev, 1107
Brinkman, J. J.: rev, 317, 1282
Brinkman, J. J., Jr.: rev, 121, 1061, 1366, 1754
Britton, G.: test, 1343
Brocke, B.: test, 994
Brodsky, S. L.: rev, 1707
Brody, L. E.: rev, 327, 854, 1636
Brogden, H. E.: rev, 2263
Brookhart, S. M.: rev, 311, 523, 1019, 1166, 1496, 2229
Brookings, J.: test, 2297
Brookings, J. B.: rev, 1121
Brooks, B. L.: test, 389, 1252
Brooks, G. C., Jr.: test, 1879
Browder, D.: rev, 838
Brown, A. S.: rev, 42
Brown, C. E.: test, 61

Brown, C. M.: rev, 1546
Brown, D. T.: rev, 1036, 1275, 1276
Brown, F.: rev, 1834, 2013
Brown, F. G.: rev, 1947, 2072
Brown, G. K.: test, 208, 210
Brown, G. S.: test, 1423, 2307
Brown, J. A.: rev, 91, 2218
Brown, J. D.: rev, 450, 761, 762, 1026, 2135, 2167, 2267
Brown, J. I.: test, 1359, 1360
Brown, J. J. C.: test, 149
Brown, L.: test, 51, 229, 1837, 2117
Brown, L. H.: test, 1854
Brown, L. J.: test, 1818
Brown, L. L.: rev, 574, 1086, 1731
Brown, M. B.: rev, 346, 537, 1393, 1834
Brown, N. W.: rev, 1316
Brown, R.: rev, 136, 487, 488, 641, 743, 865, 958, 1086, 2071
Brown, R. D.: rev, 10, 1839
Brown, S. D.: rev, 1992
Brown, S. L.: test, 699, 1592
Brown, S. W.: rev, 1131, 1870
Brown, T. E.: test, 298, 299
Brown, V. L.: rev, 1999; test, 1699, 2081, 2112, 2126
Brown, W.: test, 571
Brownell, R.: test, 786, 1542, 1701, 2082
Browning, G.: test, 727
Brozovich, R.: rev, 661, 739
Bruce Davey Associates: test, 311, 1444
Bruhn, A. R.: test, 705
Bruininks, B. D.: test, 300, 301
Bruininks, R. H.: test, 300, 301, 385, 710, 1005, 1794
Brulles, D.: test, 1348
Bruner, G. C., II: rev, 758, 1760
Bruni, J. R., Jr.: test, 1127
Bruning, R.: rev, 599
Brunner, T. M.: test, 1958
Bruns, D.: test, 203, 282
Brunsman, B.: rev, 1424, 2268
Brunsman, B. A.: rev, 576, 615, 657, 685
Brush, J. A.: rev, 837
Bryan, M. M.: rev, 1947
Bryant, B. R.: test, 615, 836, 880, 881, 1130, 1805, 2016, 2121, 2139
Bryant, D. P.: test, 880, 2112
Bryden, D. A.: test, 1469
Buck, D.: test, 1890
Buck, J. N.: test, 904
Buckhalt, J. A.: test, 820
Buckheit, C.: test, 1250
Buckly, R.: test, 1620
Bucks, R. S.: test, 1159
Bucy, J. E.: rev, 2140
Budd, K. S.: rev, 683, 920
Budrionis, R.: rev, 819, 1828
Budrionis, R. M.: rev, 1864

Guy, S. C.: test, 228
Guyette, T.: rev, 645, 2084
Guyette, T. W.: rev, 1101, 1104, 1581
Guzzetta, J.: test, 553
Gwartney, N.: rev, 1013
Gynther, M. D.: rev, 319, 1294, 1295

Haber, L.: rev, 1100, 1104
Habicht, M. H.: rev, 688
Haccoun, R. R.: rev, 446, 1710
Hacker, B. J.: test, 369
Hackett, G.: test, 1219
Haertel, G. D.: rev, 458, 934, 1376
Hafner, H.: test, 1028
Hagan, J. S.: test, 1935
Hagen, E. P.: test, 335
Hagin, R. A.: rev, 13, 281, 412, 2132
Hagley, F.: test, 2009
Hagues, N.: test, 1384, 1634, 2196
Hahn, M. E.: rev, 845
Haladyna, T. M.: rev, 14, 1278, 1419, 1947
Haley, S.: test, 1810
Haley, S. M.: test, 1482
Hall, A. E.: rev, 892
Hall, B. A.: test, 1752
Hall, B. W.: rev, 1372
Hall, C. W.: rev, 1514, 2044
Hall, J.: test, 14, 524, 552, 577, 752, 965, 1177, 1184, 1186, 1189, 1191, 1192, 1195, 1196, 1302, 1468, 1495, 1506, 1511, 1533, 1575, 1576, 1617, 1626, 1674, 1698, 1764, 1769, 1773, 2000, 2001, 2002, 2021, 2024, 2052, 2053, 2056, 2057, 2282
Hall, J. N.: test, 1703
Hall, L. G.: test, 906
Hall, P. K.: rev, 127, 1935
Hall, V. C.: rev, 520
Hall, W. E.: rev, 844
Hallam, G.: test, 329
Haller, R. M.: rev, 127
Halligan, P.: test, 241
Halperin, J. M.: test, 399
Halpern, D. F.: test, 907
Halstead, M. E.: test, 1752
Haltiwanger, J.: test, 1810
Haltiwanger, J. T.: test, 1482
Hambleton, R.: test, 1108
Hambleton, R. K.: rev, 11, 252
Hamby, S. L.: test, 526
Hamil, W. L.: rev, 698
Hamilton, L.: rev, 1615
Hamilton, M.: test, 1681
Hamilton, S.: test, 1421
Hamlett, C.: test, 685
Hammeke, T.: rev, 1727
Hammeke, T. A.: rev, 271
Hammer, A. L.: test, 545, 817, 1344, 1345, 1346, 1976

Hammer, E.: test, 838
Hammer, E. F.: test, 904
Hammer, L. B.: test, 804
Hammill, D. D.: test, 197, 229, 506, 507, 614, 615, 631, 706, 834, 910, 962, 1130, 1312, 1580, 2081, 2087, 2088, 2090, 2091, 2109, 2110, 2119, 2126, 2128, 2129, 2140, 2141
Hamre, B. K.: test, 431, 432, 433
Hamsher, deS.: test, 1332
Hanawalt, N. G.: rev, 253
Hancock, T. E.: rev, 141, 1697
Handler, L.: rev, 549, 1968
Handley, P.: test, 986
Handley, R.: test, 743
Hanes, K. R.: rev, 212, 456, 705
Haney, W. V.: test, 2183
Hanig, K. M.: rev, 89, 300, 2133
Hanna, G. S.: rev, 599, 1654, 1895, 1898, 2262; test, 1359, 1360, 1438
Hanna, L. A.: rev, 1019
Hanna, P. R.: rev, 1947
Hannafin, M. J.: rev, 1153
Hannah, S. T.: test, 1110, 1305
Hannavy, S.: test, 1266
Hanner, M. A.: test, 1104
Hanschu, B.: test, 1850
Hansen, J. B.: rev, 2140
Hansen, M. C.: rev, 1871
Hansen, T. L.: test, 758
Hanson, G.: rev, 1572
Hanson, G. R.: rev, 868; test, 1485, 1490
Hanson, R. N.: rev, 1834
Hanson, W. E.: rev, 286, 310, 1421
Harby, M. L.: test, 2078
Harcourt Assessment, Inc.: test, 1271, 1947
Harcourt Brace Educational Measurement, a division of The Psychological Corporation: test, 1950
Harden, L.: test, 65
Harding, R.: rev, 119
Harding, R. E.: rev, 254, 1392, 1470, 2080, 2147, 2154, 2165
Hardy, E.: test, 215
Hardy, L. H.: test, 953
Hare, R. D.: test, 114, 913, 914, 915, 916
Hargrove, D. S.: rev, 1209
Haring, T. G.: rev, 52
Harman, H. H.: test, 1087
Harmon, C.: test, 1421
Harmon, L. W.: rev, 307, 348, 1887; test, 1889
Harms, T.: test, 695, 798, 979, 1806
Harnisch, D. L.: rev, 475, 1677, 2111, 2112
Harper, D. C.: rev, 617, 625, 1414, 1744, 1970
Harrell, A. V.: test, 70
Harrell, T. W.: rev, 1668
Harriman, P. L.: rev, 904
Harrington, J. C.: test, 3

Polk, M. J.: test, 691
Polloway, E. A.: rev, 2140; test, 2017
Polychroniou, P.: test, 770
Pomerleau, T. M.: test, 1601
Pomplun, M.: test, 1144
Pond, R. E.: test, 1595, 1597, 1598
Ponterotto, J. G.: rev, 1329, 1402
Ponton, M. O.: rev, 448
Pooley, R. C.: rev, 873
Pope, M.: rev, 17, 1059, 1391, 1693
Pope, M. L.: rev, 254, 918, 1496
Pope-Davis, D. B.: rev, 672
Poplin, M. S.: rev, 1051
Poppleton, S.: test, 1470
Porchea, S. F.: rev, 1419
Porter, B.: test, 1936
Porter, E.: test, 2165
Porter, G.: test, 497
Porter, J. Y.: rev, 493, 538, 907, 1384, 1553, 1881, 2172, 2277
Porter, R. B.: test, 412
Porterfield, W. D.: rev, 1141, 1992
Porteus, S. D.: rev, 258; test, 1563
Posey, C. D.: rev, 397
Posner, B. Z.: test, 759, 1121
Post, P. C.: test, 162
Poteat, G. M.: rev, 89, 217, 614, 623, 771, 838, 1218, 1355, 1390, 1904, 1953, 2101, 2248
Poteet, J. A.: rev, 764, 2126
Potter, G. B.: test, 951, 952
Potter, L.: test, 89
Poucher, K. E.: rev, 1376
Powell, D.: test, 1264
Powell, G.: test, 635
Powell, S.: rev, 293, 403, 615, 780, 1596, 1679, 1853, 1981
Powell, W. R.: rev, 842
Power, P. G.: test, 1342
Power, T. J.: test, 55
Powers, S.: rev, 1426
Poythress, N. G.: test, 1165
Poznanski, E. O.: test, 406
Prather, E. M.: rev, 2046, 2087; test, 1825, 1855
Pratt, C.: test, 1206
Pratt, S.: rev, 144, 646, 1583, 1701
Preminger, J. L.: test, 1127
Prescott, T. E.: test, 1727
Preston, R. C.: rev, 1947
Pretti-Frontczak, K.: test, 138
Preziosi, R. C.: test, 1618
Price, G. E.: test, 1134, 1619
Price, J. R.: rev, 1938, 2210
Priddy, J. M.: test, 2257
Prien, E. P.: rev, 242, 1433; test, 1176, 1244, 1558, 2130
Prien, K. O.: rev, 242; test, 1244
Prigitano, G. N.: rev, 1429
Prince, J. S.: test, 1992

Prince-Embury, S.: test, 1713
Prizant, B. M.: rev, 395; test, 484, 1798
Profiles International, Inc.: test, 1628
Proger, B. B.: rev, 127, 269, 1595, 1699, 1893, 2142, 2268
PROJECT RHISE, Children's Development Center: test, 1744
Prometric: test, 682
Proulx, G.-B.: test, 1061
Prout, H. T.: rev, 1785; test, 739, 1085
Provence, S.: test, 977, 978
Pryor, R.: test, 2275
Psenicka, C.: test, 770
Psychological Assessment Resources, Inc.: test, 1562
The Psychological Corporation: test, 482, 704, 707, 847, 973, 2236
Psychological Services Bureau, Inc.: test, 1644, 1646
Psychological Services Bureau, Inc. with consultant contributions: test, 1645
Psychological Services, Inc.: test, 811, 812, 1561
Psychometric Research & Development Ltd: test, 1372
Psychometric Research Unit, The Hatfield Polytechnic: test, 867
PsychTests AIM, Inc.: test, 84, 151, 354, 365, 437, 487, 548, 565, 581, 735, 751, 766, 767, 829, 905, 1032, 1119, 1157, 1187, 1316, 1317, 1330, 1358, 1381, 1715, 1775, 1836, 1911, 1966, 2018, 2055, 2274, 2280
Pugh, R. C.: rev, 330
Pumroy, D. K.: test, 1208
Purdue Research Foundation: test, 1668
Putnam, F.: test, 69
Putnam, F. W.: test, 670
Pynes, J. E.: rev, 1125
Pyrczak, F.: rev, 1019

Qualls, A. L.: test, 1675
Quasha, W. H.: test, 1724
Quay, H. C.: test, 1719
Quellmalz, E. S.: rev, 98, 1582
Quen, N.: test, 1346
Quenk, N. L.: test, 1344, 1345
Quereshi, M. Y.: rev, 518
Quesal, R. W.: test, 1442
Quigney, T. A.: rev, 2172
Quinby, S. S.: test, 910
Quinlan, D. M.: test, 155, 607
Quinn, K.: rev, 1330, 1680
Quirk, C. A.: test, 628

Rabbit, J.: test, 955
Rabin, A. I.: rev, 400, 1748, 2231
Radcliffe, J. A.: rev, 864
Radocy, R. E.: rev, 83, 1023
Raelin, J. A.: test, 2293
Rafferty, J. E.: test, 1753
Rahim, M. A.: test, 494, 770, 1437, 1685, 1686
Rahman, M. S.: test, 770

Saville, P.: test, 85, 573, 1535, 1633, 2062
Sawilowsky, S.: test, 1832
Sawyer, D. J.: rev, 899, 1071, 1691, 1898, 2144, 2217
Saxton, J.: test, 1860
Saxton, M. J.: test, 1078
Scannell, D. P.: rev, 1376; test, 338
Scantron Corporation: test, 1493
Schaefer, W. C.: rev, 2194
Schafer, D. S.: test, 699
Schafer, R. E.: rev, 653
Schafer, W.: rev, 1317
Schafer, W. D.: rev, 295, 317, 496, 510, 515, 1019, 1068, 1701, 1810, 2096
Schaffer, C. E.: test, 155, 607
Schaie, K. W.: rev, 1846; test, 1799
Schalock, R. L.: test, 2016, 2017
Schaubhut, N. A.: test, 817, 1976, 2154
Schaufeli, W. B.: test, 1209
Scheel, M. J.: rev, 1422, 1452, 1942, 1966, 1976
Scheffers, W.: test, 2209
Schein, E. H.: test, 342
Scherbaum, C. A.: rev, 1235
Scherer, M. J.: test, 1211, 1212, 1213
Schinka, J. A.: test, 413, 622, 926, 1255, 1256, 1257, 1370, 1503, 1504, 1509, 1510
Schinke, S.: rev, 101, 715
Schinke, S. P.: rev, 924
Schissel, R. J.: rev, 2237
Schlebusch, D.: test, 1002
Schlieve, P. L.: test, 504
Schmand, B.: test, 107, 2207
Schmeck, R. R.: test, 1010
Schmid, R. F.: rev, 1217
Schmidt, F.: rev, 255, 756
Schmidt, F. L.: rev, 2263
Schmidt, J. A.: test, 963
Schmidt, K. S.: test, 232, 603
Schmidt, M.: test, 1728
Schmidt, S. M.: test, 1627
Schmidt, S. W.: rev, 142, 766, 1774
Schmitt, N.: rev, 1049, 1622
Schmuckler, J.: rev, 38
Schneck, G. R.: rev, 20, 1000, 1774, 2214, 2284
Schneider, N. G.: test, 1901
Schneider, W. J.: rev, 223, 231, 390, 589, 1251, 1265, 1666, 2270, 2307
Schnell, E. R.: test, 817
Schneller, J.: test, 1664
Schoen, H. L.: test, 1018
Schoendorf, K.: test, 31
Schoenfeldt, L. F.: rev, 2113, 2263
Schoenrade, P.: rev, 157, 1152, 1940, 2277
Schofield, W.: rev, 253, 1753
Scholastic Testing Service, Inc.: test, 452, 934, 1084, 1677
Schopler, E.: test, 395, 1654, 2045
Schowengerdt, R. V.: rev, 59

Schrader, W. B.: rev, 1271, 1819
Schram, M.: test, 150
Schrank, F. A.: rev, 350; test, 201, 654, 2264, 2265, 2266, 2267
Schraw, G.: rev, 180, 228, 906, 1077, 1737, 1994, 2105, 2166, 2189, 2200, 2228, 2263
Schretlen, D.: test, 287
Schretlen, D. J.: test, 312, 313, 1303
Schroeder, L. C.: test, 1224
Schroth, S. T.: rev, 373
Schubert, D. S. P.: test, 1819
Schubert, H. J. P.: test, 1819
Schuerger, J. M.: test, 1885
Schuler, H.: test, 27
Schulte, A. C.: test, 1129
Schultz, D. G.: rev, 1238
Schultz, G. F.: rev, 26
Schur, S.: test, 838
Schuster, J. W.: test, 154
Schutz, R. P.: test, 2214
Schutz, W.: test, 544, 816, 1214
Schwab, R. L.: test, 1209
Schwarting, G.: rev, 278, 293, 449, 624, 643, 695, 1482, 1589, 1600, 2102, 2163
Schwesinger, G. C.: rev, 1563
Science Research Associates: test, 515, 1413, 1689, 1694, 1761, 1873, 2113
Scientific Management Techniques, Inc.: test, 1943
Scott, A.: rev, 1836
Scott, N. L.: test, 2215
Scott, O., III: rev, 1917
Scott, Vann B., Jr.: test, 1480
The Scottish Education Department: test, 717
Scudder, T.: test, 2165
Search Institute: test, 1826
Seashore, H.: rev, 876, 877
Seashore, H. G.: test, 659
Secolsky, C.: rev, 1438
Secord, W.: test, 449, 2137
Secord, W. A.: test, 440, 446, 447, 448, 450
Sedlacek, W. E.: test, 1378, 1879
Seel, R. T.: test, 1366
Segel, D.: rev, 1018, 1098
Segool, N.: rev, 1660
Seifert, K.: test, 340
Seim, N. J.: test, 965, 1764
Seklemian, P.: test, 1890
Selby, E. C.: test, 2200
Seligman, R.: rev, 1834
Selmar, J. W.: test, 1547
Selover, R. B.: rev, 1289
Seltzer, G. B.: rev, 1673
Selzer, M. L.: test, 1261
Semel, E.: test, 446, 448, 449, 450
Semeonoff, B.: rev, 1056
Semmel, M. I.: rev, 1759

Sutton, R.: rev, 2112
Sutton, R. E.: rev, 490, 597, 1083, 2172, 2196
Suydam, M. N.: rev, 194
Svinicki, J.: test, 202
Svinicki, J. G.: rev, 1565
Swain, C.: test, 504
Swanson, D.: test, 597
Swanson, H. L.: rev, 2208
Swanson, J. M.: test, 1480
Swart, D. J.: test, 125
Swartz, J. D.: rev, 1016, 2150
Swartz-Kulstad, J. L.: rev, 65, 1059
Swassing, C. S.: rev, 715, 1663
Swearer, S. M.: rev, 371, 997, 1734, 1969
Sweeney, T. J.: test, 821, 2239
Swensen, C. H.: rev, 155; test, 1785, 1787
Swerdlik, M. E.: rev, 223, 231, 290, 842, 1084, 1251, 1439, 1451, 1666, 2140, 2250, 2307; test, 1660
Swerdlik, P.: test, 1660
Swihart, A. A.: test, 1860
Swinburn, K.: test, 497
Swindle, F. L.: test, 628
Switzer, J.: test, 1386
Switzky, H. N.: rev, 50, 234, 618, 2035
Sykken, D. T.: rev, 320
Sytsma Reed, R. E.: test, 1791
Szczepanski, M.: test, 698

Tade, W. J.: test, 1894
Tafrate, R. C.: test, 112, 113
Taggart, B.: test, 954
Taggart, W.: test, 954
Tai, W. L.: rev, 971
Talan, T. N.: test, 305, 1629
Talegent: test, 1472
Taljaard, J. J.: test, 2168
Talley, J. L.: test, 401, 2258
Tan, X.: rev, 704
Tanguay, W.: rev, 339
Tanigawa, D.: rev, 173, 1664
Tanis, S.: test, 2017
Tarter, R. E.: test, 681
Tassé, M. J.: test, 2016, 2017
Tate, R.: test, 1742
Tattersall, P.: test, 1988
Tattersall, P. J.: test, 1987
Taulbee, E. S.: rev, 2220
Taylor, E. K.: rev, 749, 1289, 1536, 1537, 2241; test, 1762
Taylor, E. M.: rev, 851
Taylor, K. M.: test, 349
Taylor, P. A.: rev, 2072
Taylor, R. M.: test, 802, 2044
Taylor, R. N.: rev, 1191, 1871
Taylor, S.: test, 1891
Taylor, T. R.: test, 808, 933, 974, 1632, 1752

Teagarden, F. M.: rev, 2203
Tearnan, B. H.: test, 233
Teele, S.: test, 2064
Teeter, P. A.: rev, 58, 1065
Teitzel, T.: test, 1585, 1589
Teleometrics International: test, 1670
Tellegen, A.: rev, 790, 791; test, 1293, 1294, 1295
Tellegen, P.: test, 1922
Tellegen, P. J.: test, 1923
Telzrow, C.: rev, 710
Telzrow, C. F.: rev, 615, 695, 1053
Tenney-Blackwell, K.: test, 635
Tenopyr, M. L.: rev, 2276
Terborg, J. R.: test, 1197
Terwilliger, J. S.: rev, 46
Tesh, A.: rev, 1409, 1644
Test Development Committees, American Association of Teachers of Spanish and Portuguese: test, 1353
Testa, S. M.: test, 313
Testut, E. W.: rev, 1491
Texas Education Agency: test, 2167
Thal, D. J.: test, 1164
Thayer, P. W.: rev, 1413, 1724, 1871, 1873
Thetford, W. N.: rev, 941
Thoma, S.: test, 597
Thomas, A.: test, 1373
Thomas, C.: rev, 1221, 2027
Thomas, G. F.: test, 1574
Thomas, G. V.: test, 1525
Thomas, J. B.: test, 2045
Thomas, J. W.: test, 1418
Thomas, K. W.: test, 1574, 1974, 2154, 2277
Thomas, P.: test, 740
Thomas, R. G.: rev, 1036, 1289, 1403
Thomas, S.: test, 740
Thomas, T.: test, 1660
Thomas, T. J.: test, 1418
Thompson, B.: rev, 1015, 2231
Thompson, D.: rev, 464, 1405
Thompson, D. L.: rev, 654, 1325
Thompson, G. B.: test, 2199
Thompson, J. A.: test, 275
Thompson, J. R.: test, 2016, 2017
Thompson, L. L.: test, 2259
Thompson, L. W.: test, 318
Thompson, N. M.: rev, 449, 511, 832, 2236
Thompson, R. C.: test, 817, 1976
Thomson, L. K.: test, 1091
Thorndike, R. L.: rev, 319, 708, 1947, 2070, 2164, 2250; test, 335
Thorndike, R. M.: rev, 124, 241, 1062, 2067
Thorndike, T.: rev, 2235
Thorndike-Christ, T.: rev, 1867
Thorne, T.: test, 1925
Thornton, G. C., III: rev, 27, 1122, 1177, 1376, 1494, 1566, 1686

SCORE INDEX

This index lists all the scores, in alphabetical order, for all the tests included in Tests in Print IX. *Because test scores can be regarded as operational definitions of the variable measured, sometimes the scores provide better leads to what a test actually measures than the test title or other available information. The Score Index is very detailed, and the reader should keep in mind that a given variable (or concept) of interest may be defined in several different ways. Thus the reader should look up these several possible alternative definitions before drawing final conclusions about whether tests measuring a particular variable of interest can be located in* TIP IX. *If the kind of score sought is located in a particular test or tests, the reader should then read the test descriptive information carefully to determine whether the test(s) in which the score is found is (are) consistent with reader purpose. Used wisely, the Score Index can be another useful resource in locating the right score in the right test. As usual, all numbers in the index are test numbers, not page numbers.*

General Chemical Knowledge: 44
General Chemistry: 34, 35, 336, 604, 1420
General Classroom Behaviour: 1808
General Classroom Environment: 700, 701
General Clerical Skills: 1887
General Cognition: 1895
General Cognitive Abilities Tests: 659
General Cognitive Ability: 2263
General Cognitive Functioning: 1264
General Cognitive Proficiency: 1264
General Communication Composite: 404
General Conceptual Ability: 658
General Coping Ability: 476
General Development: 392
General Development Index: 619
General Development Score: 625
General Domain: 1866
General Drafting and Design: 1377
General Factor of Personality: 2288
General Family Responsibility: 2038
General Form: 142
General Functioning Intelligence: 1887
General Health: 926, 1865
General Impressions: 395
General Industrial/Mechanical: 2247
General Information: 1028, 1080, 1442, 1749, 2264, 2308
General Intellectual Ability: 854, 1790, 2264
General Intellectual Ability–Early Development: 2265
General Intelligence: 267
General Irritability: 1364
General Knowledge: 1582, 1675, 1730
General Knowledge and Language: 290
General Language: 828, 2081
General Leadership Effectiveness: 1123
General Learning Ability: 1380, 1550
General Logic: 1265
General Maintenance: 2247
General Maladjustment: 1343
General/Managerial Competence: 342
General Mathematics: 44, 475, 504, 1582
General Memory: 410, 2251
General Memory Index: 1742
General Memory Skills: 1475
General Mental Ability Composite: 614
General Mood: 743
General Mood Scale: 742
General Morale: 2025
General Occupational Themes: 350
General Pathology Composite: 310
General Playground Behaviour: 1808
General Processing: 1853
General Processing Ability: 414
General Psychological Maladjustment Composite: 715
General Psychopathology: 1568
General Questioning Following Recall: 536
General Reactions: 1850

General Reading: 880
General Reasoning: 1065, 1087
General Reasoning Index: 2100
General Recognition: 2251
General Responsibility: 782
General Risk/Need Factors: 1148
General Satisfaction: 1296, 1812, 2289
General Science: 130, 1233, 1315, 1582
General Screening: 1721
General Self: 541
General Self-Help Skills: 2193
General Self-Regulation: 590
General Service: 131
General Social: 1684
General Somatic Symptoms: 1721
General Technical Skills: 2247
General Themes: 345
General Tone: 1364
General Visual Perception: 631
General Visual Perception Index: 630
General Vocabulary: 506, 2124
Generalised Anxiety Disorder: 1666
Generalist: 751
Generalization of Skills Across Time/Settings/Behaviors/
    Materials/People: 2193
Generalized Anxiety: 1278
Generalized Anxiety Disorder: 73, 390, 407, 529, 696,
    1653, 2313
Generalized Anxiety Disorder (GAD) Index: 1324
Generalized Responding: 140
Generation of Alternative Solutions: 1915
Generativity: 1234
Genitourinary: 926
Geographer (f, m): 1976
Geographic Location: 906
Geographical Barriers: 346
Geography: 475, 825, 1349, 1582
Geologist (f, m): 1976
Geometric Analogies: 507
Geometric Categories: 507
Geometric Concepts: 571, 1084, 1815
Geometric Figure Copy Score: 1251
Geometric Figure Retention Score: 1251
Geometric Figure Total Score: 1251
Geometric Forms: 779
Geometric Puzzles: 1365
Geometric Scale: 507
Geometric Sequence: 1160
Geometric Sequences: 507
Geometrical Calculations: 475
Geometry: 475, 504, 655, 656, 958, 1073, 1233, 1349,
    1493, 1953, 2292
Geometry and Measurement: 958, 1529
Geometry & Spatial Sense: 2143
Geometry and Measurements: 1953
Geometry-Measurement: 2142
Geriatric Level of Dysfunction Scale: 1282

Total ADHD Score: 179
Total Adjustment: 1388
Total Affect: 765
Total Aggression Index: 399
Total Anger: 64
Total Animal: 1339
Total Anxiety: 1720, 1734
Total Anxiety Sensitivity: 1708
Total ASA: 168
Total Basic Academic Skills: 641
Total Battery: 334, 2143
Total Battery Intelligence Index: 1730
Total Behavior: 765
Total Bipolar Index: 1481
Total Change: 232
Total Cognition: 765
Total Competence: 24
Total Composite Severity Rating: 469
Total Comprehension Passage Level: 1692
Total Connection: 817
Total Correct Score: 2166
Total Critical Thinking Score: 907
Total Current: 232
Total Development Score: 292
Total Difference: 1757
Total Displacement: 1159
Total Distress: 1734
Total EF Summary: 180
Total EI: 741
Total Emotional Behavioral Checklist: 732
Total EQ: 742
Total Errors: 662
Total Execution Time: 2166
Total Expectation: 1138
Total Expressed Needs: 817
Total Extroversion: 563
Total Family Violence Score: 805
Total Gestures: 1164
Total Growth Chart Score: 887
Total Human: 1339
Total Independent Living Skills Composite: 1747
Total Index: 1061
Total Influence: 817
Total Initiation Time: 2166
Total Intelligence Index: 1730
Total Interaction: 204
Total Intrusions: 401, 1249
Total Involvement: 801, 817
Total Items Circled: 1369
Total Items Correct: 2199
Total Language: 650, 1595, 1597, 1928
Total Language Composite: 645
Total Left: 253
Total Level of Risk: 2006
Total Life Change Unit: 459
Total List Recognition: 279
Total Love Scale: 1785

Total Mathematics: 334, 1928, 1947, 2143
Total Mathematics Self-Efficacy Score: 1219
Total Memory: 1252
Total Memory Index: 389
Total Metalinguistics Index: 447
Total Mids: 2044
Total Miscues: 1692
Total Money: 1020
Total Mood Disturbance: 1625
Total Motor: 1477
Total Motor Composite: 300
Total Move Score: 2166
Total Negative: 1234
Total Negative Emotions: 175
Total Non-Story Reference: 1339
Total Number Correct: 2258, 2259
Total Number of Errors: 2258, 2259
Total Occurrences of Major Phonological Deviations: 937
Total Omissions: 2068
Total Other: 1339
Total Parenting Stress: 1969
Total Past: 232
Total Pathology: 739
Total Percent Implemented: 1601
Total Percentage: 1976
Total Percentile Rank: 75, 693, 694
Total Physical Child Abuse: 388
Total PMT: 146
Total Positive: 1234
Total Positive and Negative Emotions: 175
Total Positive Emotions: 175
Total Predisposition Score: 1857
Total Problem-Solving Time: 2166
Total Problems: 24
Total Protective Factors: 633, 635
Total Psychological Distress: 1326
Total Quality of Life: 850, 1673
Total Raw Score: 1695
Total Readiness: 1541
Total Reading: 334, 1025, 1928, 1947, 2079, 2230, 2266, 2268
Total Reading Standard Score: 1542
Total Reading Time: 1692
Total Recall: 289, 536, 833, 947
Total Recognition Discriminability: 323
Total Rehabilitation: 1704
Total Relationship-Behavior: 1880
Total Religious Sentiments: 157
Total Resolution: 1234
Total Response Index: 1976
Total Right: 253
Total Rules Violation: 2166
Total Scaled Score: 1
Total Science: 1420
Total Self-Concept: 2071
Total Self Score: 541
Total Sensory Systems: 1851, 1852

BUROS
CENTER FOR TESTING

HISPANICS ARE BOTH THE LARGEST AND FASTEST-GROWING MINORITY GROUP IN THE UNITED STATES.

ONE-THIRD OF HISPANICS LIVING IN THE U.S. ARE CHILDREN, LESS THAN 18 YEARS OF AGE.

SPANISH IS THE PRIMARY LANGUAGE SPOKEN IN 62% OF U.S. HISPANIC HOUSEHOLDS.

Surprisingly few resources exist to address the needs of Spanish-speaking individuals and families. When it comes to selecting tests to evaluate performance, aptitude, behavior, or needs of Spanish speakers, the Buros Center for Testing offers resources specifically designed to help test users identify appropriate tests.

"*Pruebas Publicadas en Español* provides a unique and exceptional resource for psychologists and others who work with Spanish-speaking populations" (Oakland, 2013).

Pruebas Publicadas en Español: An Index of Spanish Tests in Print (PPE) builds on the established traditions of the Buros Center for Testing and its long-standing publication series – *The Mental Measurements Yearbook* and *Tests in Print*.

PPE provides extensive information about tests published wholly or partly in Spanish. Its information is easily used by testing professionals—including students in training—in education, psychology, counseling, neuropsychology, speech/language pathology, audiology, and business who speak Spanish, English, or both. All content is presented side by side in both languages to serve as an all-in-one resource that acquaints test users with available measures and facilitates appropriate selection of tests.

PPE is available through our newest electronic database product, Mental Measurements Yearbook with Tests in Print Internacional, offered through EBSCO Information Services. A 30-day free trial is available from EBSCO. See https://www.ebscohost.com/academic/mental-measurements-yearbook-with-tests-in-print-internacional or contact your EBSCO representative today!

To order a print volume of PPE visit us at http://buros.org/pruebas-publicadas-en-espanol#eng.

Reference

Oakland, T. (2013, December). [Review of the book *Pruebas Publicadas en Español: An index of Spanish tests in print*, by J. E. Schlueter, J. F. Carlson, K. F. Geisinger, & L. L. Murphy (Eds.)]. *Testing International*, 30, 11.

BUROS.ORG